10-8-59

THE IRWIN SERIES IN ECONOMICS

BOOKS IN THE IRWIN SERIES IN ECONOMICS

Public Policies Toward Business
CLAIR WILCOX SWARTHMORE COLLEGE

Government Finance: An Economic Analysis
JOHN F. DUE UNIVERSITY OF ILLINOIS

Introduction to International Economics *Revised Edition*
DELBERT A. SNIDER MIAMI UNIVERSITY

Economics of Transportation *Fourth Edition*
D. PHILIP LOCKLIN UNIVERSITY OF ILLINOIS

International Economics *Revised Edition*
CHARLES P. KINDLEBERGER MASSACHUSETTS INSTITUTE OF TECHNOLOGY

The American Economy: Principles, Practices, and Policies *Revised Edition*
C. LOWELL HARRISS COLUMBIA UNIVERSITY

Economic Policy: Readings in Political Economy *Revised Edition*
WILLIAM D. GRAMPP UNIVERSITY OF ILLINOIS AND
EMANUEL T. WEILER PURDUE UNIVERSITY (EDITORS)

Intermediate Economic Analysis *Third Edition*
JOHN F. DUE UNIVERSITY OF ILLINOIS

Collective Bargaining: Principles and Cases *Revised Edition*
JOHN T. DUNLOP AND JAMES J. HEALY
HARVARD UNIVERSITY

Economics of Labor Relations
FREDERIC MEYERS UNIVERSITY OF TEXAS

Money, Income, and Monetary Policy
EDWARD S. SHAW STANFORD UNIVERSITY

Welfare and Competition: The Economics of a Fully Employed Economy
TIBOR SCITOVSKY UNIVERSITY OF CALIFORNIA

Economics
JOHN A. GUTHRIE STATE COLLEGE OF WASHINGTON

Principles of Money and Banking
HIRAM L. JOME DEPAUW UNIVERSITY

Economic Fluctuations
MAURICE W. LEE STATE COLLEGE OF WASHINGTON

Economics of Money and Banking
GEORGE N. HALM THE FLETCHER SCHOOL OF LAW AND DIPLOMACY TUFTS UNIVERSITY

Economics: An Analytical Approach
RALPH K. DAVIDSON, VERNON L. SMITH, AND JAY W. WILEY
ALL OF PURDUE UNIVERSITY

Introduction to Mathematical Economics
D. W. BUSHAW STATE COLLEGE OF WASHINGTON AND
R. W. CLOWER NORTHWESTERN UNIVERSITY

Readings in Current Economics
MORTON C. GROSSMAN, REED R. HANSEN, ELDON S. HENDRIKSEN, HARRY E. McALLISTER, KENJI OKUDA, AND WILLIAM WOLMAN ALL OF STATE COLLEGE OF WASHINGTON (EDITORS)

PUBLIC POLICIES TOWARD BUSINESS

PUBLIC POLICIES TOWARD BUSINESS

BY CLAIR WILCOX PH.D.

JOSEPH WHARTON PROFESSOR OF POLITICAL ECONOMY, SWARTHMORE COLLEGE

1955

RICHARD D. IRWIN, INC.

CHICAGO · HOMEWOOD, ILLINOIS

First Printing, April, 1955
Second Printing, July, 1956
Third Printing, June, 1957
Fourth Printing, December, 1958

PRINTED IN THE UNITED STATES OF AMERICA
Library of Congress Catalogue Card No. 55-8515

TO

ANDREA

AND

CAROLY

PREFACE

This book is designed to serve as a text for college and university courses in economics and political science dealing with public policy toward business enterprise. It differs in approach and in balance from most of the earlier volumes in the field. Many of these works have been concerned more largely with the constitutional and administrative aspects of the policies discussed than with their economic significance. Some of them have dealt at length with the problems encountered in the regulation of railroads and public utilities and only briefly with those arising in the enforcement of the antitrust laws. Others have gone into great detail concerning antitrust and devoted scant attention to regulation. Few of them have accorded much space to the problems of public enterprise. In its approach, the present volume seeks to give equal emphasis to the economic and the political aspects of the policies that it examines. In balance, it seeks to give equal attention to the major types of public policy toward business activity: maintaining competition, supplementing competition, moderating competition, substituting regulation for competition, and substituting public for private enterprise. Its general theme is an appraisal of the comparative merits and demerits of these policies, in the light of past experience, from the standpoint of their consequences for the general welfare.

The book is not intended as a comprehensive treatise on the relations between business and government. If it were, some of the matters that are here neglected would have been given greater space. Certain topics have been treated briefly or omitted altogether on the ground that they are normally covered elsewhere in the curriculum. The control of business by the Federal Reserve authorities, for instance, is usually covered in courses in Money and Banking; its control through public expenditures and taxation in courses in Public Finance. The regulation of the securities markets and corporate financial practices is considered in courses in Corporation Finance; that of labor relations in courses in Labor Economics; and that of international trade, finance, shipping, aviation, and telecommunications in courses in International Economics. As a result, despite their great importance, these subjects are not here given the attention they deserve. For comparative purposes, the volume includes a summary chapter on the policies pursued in other countries. But in the main, it confines itself to those that affect the allocation of resources among the producers of goods and services in the United States.

The analysis presented in these pages is an outgrowth of some twenty years, off and on, of reading, writing, and teaching in this field in courses and seminars at Swarthmore College. It is also a product of six or seven years of service as an adviser or an administrator with various agencies of the federal government. This experience, in particular, convinced me that business cannot always be expected so to govern itself as to serve the public interest, but must be subjected to external discipline; that competition affords a more effective discipline than public regulation; that the officers of regulatory agencies are often skillful, industrious, and consciencious; but that regulatory controls are bound to be cumbersome and costly; that such controls, in solving one problem, inevitably raise a host of others; that conflicts arising, in their application, between considerations of economics and those of politics are usually resolved by subordinating economics to politics; that the price system is one of the greatest achievements of civilization and that governmental action, however necessary, is at best a poor substitute.

I have made no attempt, in this text, to conceal my own judgments. The student will not have to be acutely perceptive to discover, for instance, that I am a believer in the antitrust laws and a critic of agricultural price supports; that I am not impressed by the performance of most public utility commissions but am an admirer of the Tennessee Valley Authority. I have felt that it would be at once more honest and more entertaining if I were to let my bias show. The reader, accordingly, is forewarned. But it may be well for me to make my point of view explicit, lest I be accused of seeking subtly to subvert the youth.

In my hierarchy of values, I put freedom first and plenty and progress above equality, stability, and security. I believe that these values are better served by the dispersion than by the concentration of power. I therefore prefer competition to monopoly, private enterprise to public enterprise, and free markets to administrative controls. In judging economic policies, my standard is that of consumer welfare, as measured by the quantity, quality, and variety of goods and services that are made available. But I recognize the need for compromise. I would not leave the worker or the farmer entirely at the mercy of the market. I see the wisdom of employing a rule of reason in the enforcement of the antitrust laws. I believe that government should take the initiative in conserving natural resources and in controlling the flow of water in river valleys. I admit the inevitability of comprehensive controls in time of war. If this be subversion, make the most of it.

My thinking in regard to the problems considered here has been influenced by the writings of many of those whom I have known among my predecessors in the field, particularly Walton H. Hamilton, F. A. Fetter, J. M. Clark, and Joseph A. Schumpeter. It has been influenced, too, by my association with other economists in working for the government, among them Corwin D. Edwards and Ben W. Lewis in the National Recovery Administration, J. K. Galbraith and Donald H. Wallace in the Office of Price Administration, and Edward S. Mason and Jacob Viner in the Department of State. My ideas have been subjected to a periodic check, moreover, by the economists who have come each year to examine my students at Swarthmore, among them several of those already mentioned and also Seymour E. Harris of Harvard, Paul A. Samuelson of M.I.T., Willard L. Thorp, Colston E. Warne, and James R. Nelson of Amherst, Emile Despres and Kermit Gordon of Williams, James Tobin and Charles E. Lindblom of Yale, Arthur R. Burns and George J. Stigler of Columbia, Lester V. Chandler of Princeton, Fritz Machlup of Johns Hopkins, Paul H. Douglas of Chicago, and Theodore J. Kreps of Stanford. Through these contacts and through my service, for some years, with the Executive Committee of the American Economic Association, I have come increasingly to be impressed with the essential qualities of my fellow members of the guild of economists: with their objectivity, their integrity, and their devotion to the common weal. I take pride in being one of them.

For the help they have given me in the preparation of this volume, I am indebted to many of my friends and to the members of my family. Several of the sections of the manuscript have been checked for errors by my colleagues at Swarthmore: the chapter on atomic energy by W. C. Elmore, a physicist who was formerly on the staff at Los Alamos, the chapter on radio and television by John D. McCrumm, an electrical engineer, that on the constitutional framework of public control by J. Roland Pennock and those on public enterprise by Paul Ylvisaker, both political scientists, the section on milk control by Edward K. Cratsley, an economist who was formerly a member of the New York Milkshed Price Committee, and those on labor by Frank C. Pierson, an economist and arbitrator of labor disputes. The chapter on agricultural policy has been read and criticized by J. K. Galbraith of Harvard and by D. Gale Johnson of the University of Chicago, both of whom are hereby absolved of all responsibility for the judgments that survived. I am indebted for help on recent antitrust decisions to Louis B. Schwartz of the Law School faculty at the University of Pennsylvania, and for suggestions regarding various sections of the manuscript to Thomas J. Anderson, Jr. of New York University, Francis M. Boddy of Minnesota, Richard B. Heflebower of Northwestern, and Lloyd G. Reynolds of Yale. The manuscript as a whole has been used with my students at Swarthmore, and large sections of it have been given a trial run by Joseph D. Coppock at Earlham, by Holland Hunter at Haverford, and by Kermit Gordon at Williams. Up to the time of her death, each chapter was edited, as it came from the typist, by my wife, Florence Chapman Wilcox. Thereafter, this task was assumed by my daughters, Andrea and Caroly. I am indebted most of all to Andrea Wilcox and to Mrs. Frédéric J. Grover for help in the work of reading proof and preparing the index.

To the teachers who will use this book as a text, let me say that I shall be grateful for advice concerning any errors that should be corrected and any material that should be added or omitted when it is revised. To the students who will be compelled to read it, let me express the hope that the issues here presented will seem as intriguing and provocative as they have seemed to me.

CLAIR WILCOX

SWARTHMORE, PA.
March, 1955

CONTENTS

PART I. BASES AND TYPES OF CONTROL

PART II. MAINTAINING COMPETITION

PART VII. ALTERNATIVES OF POLICY

INDEXES

PART I

Bases and Types of Control

Chapter 1 GOVERNMENT AND THE ECONOMY

Business, in the United States, is affected in many ways by the activities of government. The demand for its products and the nature of its costs are influenced by public regulations, by the character of public expenditures, and by the types of taxes that are used in raising public revenues. Its expectations—of stability or instability, of prosperity or depression, of profit or loss—depend upon the policies adopted by central banking authorities in controlling the volume of credit and on those pursued by government in balancing its budget, accumulating a surplus, or running a deficit. Its daily operations must be carried on within the limits that are fixed by a variety of public controls. The economic system within which business functions is shaped by government; the character of its performance depends, in large measure, upon decisions that are made by government.

It is the purpose of this book, not to examine all of the activities of government that have significance for business, but rather to analyze, in some detail, the nature and consequences of particular controls. In this introductory chapter, however, it is desirable to consider, in more general terms, the relation of business to government and the way in which government influences the character of the economy.

BUSINESS AND GOVERNMENT

In many instances activities of government affecting business are vigorously denounced by businessmen. When government imposes new controls, these critics frequently assert that it is interfering with business and meddling in private affairs. When government extends the scope of its activities, they are likely to contend that it is seeking to establish a planned economy, that industry is being regimented and economic freedom destroyed. Such complaints are not new: they have always been heard when public regulations have been imposed and the scope of public activities enlarged; they will always be heard in a society where speech is free. Have they any substance?

It is certainly true that government, in this country, goes a long way toward telling the businessman just what he can and cannot do. It tells him that he can neither misrepresent the securities that he sells to raise capital nor manipulate the markets in which they are subsequently bought and sold. It puts an upper limit on the hours that he can require of labor and a lower limit on the wages that he can pay. It compels him to bargain collectively with his workers and to insure them against accident, unemployment, and dependent old age. It forbids him either to take unfair advantage of his competitors or to agree with them upon the quantities that he will produce or the prices at which he will sell. It requires him to give full weight and measure and establishes standards to govern the quality of many of his products. It restrains him from misrepresenting the goods that he offers for sale and limits his freedom to discriminate among his customers. In some cases, it keeps him from producing goods by curtailing the quantity that he may sell, by taxing his output, or by imposing outright prohibitions. In others, it requires him to obtain permission before he may engage in production, specifies the character of the services that he must render, and fixes the rates that he may charge. In time of depression, it has forbidden him to sell below a minimum price and imposed widespread restrictions on his freedom to produce. In time of threatened inflation, it has forbidden him to sell above a maximum price and allocated his output among his customers. If this is what is meant by interference, it is clear that the government has interfered.

It is also true that many of the controls that have been imposed on business are open to serious criticism. Some of them have been designed to improve the position of one group at the expense of another. Some of them have tended to retard technical progress, to shelter inefficiency, to check the growth of output, to keep costs and prices high and standards of living low. Some of them have operated to freeze the economy into rigid patterns, impairing its ability to adapt itself to change. Some of them have been retained long after the need for them has passed. Many of them have been cumbersome, ineffective, and poorly enforced. Many of them have failed, in operation, to serve the interests of the community as a whole.

But those who voice complaints concerning the public regulation of business are not merely saying that controls are extensive and that some of them have been unwise. When they use such words as meddling and interference, they imply a great deal more than this. They imply, for instance, that the behavior of business is a private matter with which the public has no legitimate concern, that business can safely be left to its own devices, and that government need never intervene. They imply, further, that the control of business is not a normal function of government, that it represents a new departure in public policy, and that it is somehow alien to American tradition. And they imply, finally, that government is an entity that exists apart from the rest of the community, that it imposes controls of its own volition in pursuance of its own purposes, and that its activities as a regulator are neither invited nor desired by business itself. Each of these propositions merits some examination.

Private Enterprise and the Public Interest

The behavior of business is not a matter that affects business alone. A single enterprise may use the savings of thousands of investors, employ other thousands of workers, and serve still other thousands of customers. The opportunity that it affords and the security that it provides for investment and employment, the income that it distributes in the form of wages, salaries, interest, and dividends, the quantity and quality of the goods and services that it produces, and the prices at which it sells may influence the well-being of thousands on thousands of citizens. If it possesses a monopoly, suppliers may have no alternative but to sell to it and consumers no alternative but to buy from it. If it competes with other concerns, the methods it employs may affect everyone who invests in, works for, or buys from, its competitors. If it engages in the exploitation of exhaustible resources, the methods it uses may threaten the nation's security and do damage to generations yet to come. If the products that it supplies are not pure, if the working conditions that it provides are not safe, if its wastes go down the stream and up the flue, polluting the water and the air, it may impair the health of the whole community. The behavior of business inescapably affects the general welfare; it is properly a matter of public concern.

It is not always safe to leave business to its own devices; experience has shown that its freedom will sometimes be abused. Investors have been defrauded by promoters, corporate insiders, and market manipulators. Men, women, and children have been put to work under needless hazards, amid unhealthful surroundings, for long hours, at low pay, and without assurance of future security. Competitors have been harassed by malicious and predatory tactics, handicapped by discrimination, excluded from markets and sources of supply, and subjected to intimidation, coercion, and physical violence. Consumers have been victimized by short weights and measures, by adulteration, and by misrepresentation of quality and price; they have been forced to contribute to the profits of monopoly. Water and air have been polluted with the wastes of industry; the nation's resources have been dissipated through extravagant methods of exploitation. These abuses have not characterized all business at all times, but they have occurred with sufficient frequency to justify the imposition of controls. Regulation is clearly required, not only to protect the investor, the worker, the consumer, and the community at large against the unscrupulous businessman, but also to protect the honest businessman against his dishonest competitor.

The Normality of Public Controls

The regulation of business is a normal function of government. Indeed, it is government that provides the institutional foundation upon which business rests, the legal framework within which it functions, and many of the instruments through which its activities are carried on. Government establishes the status of the business unit, grants the privilege of incorporation, and makes the laws that control bankruptcy and reorganization. It defines and maintains the rights of ownership, enforces private contracts, and provides for the adjudication of disputes. It coins money, issues currency, controls credit, and regulates banking, thus freeing business from barter and providing it with a medium of exchange. It establishes standards of weight and measurement, sets up systems for grading commodities, inspects shipments, and regulates central markets, thus facilitating the processes of trade. It directs traffic on streets and highways, maintains police forces and fire departments, builds dams and dikes, inspects ships and aircraft, issues warnings of coming storms, operates lighthouses, and patrols the coasts, thus affording protection against the loss of life and property. All of these activities impinge upon the interests of business. But all of them are held, without question, to fall within the proper province of government.

The control of business is not a new departure in public policy. Government has always regulated business in the United States. Even before specific statutes were enacted, the practices of business were subject to decisions of the courts under the rules of common law: agreements to restrain trade were held to be unenforceable, unfair methods of competition were enjoined, enterprises affected with a public interest were required to serve all comers—adequately, speedily, continuously, and without discrimination—and persons who sustained injury at the hands of business were awarded damages. The enactment of state laws requiring safe and sanitary conditions of employment dates back to 1877, laws forbidding the misrepresentation of securities to 1911, laws insuring workers against industrial accidents and laws establishing maximum hours and minimum wages for women to 1911 and 1912. Commissions set up by the states have regulated banking since 1838, railroads since 1844, insurance companies since 1854, and public utilities since 1907. Intervention by the federal government, in the form of the restrictive tariff and the patent system, is as old as our national history. Federal regulation of the railroads goes back to the first administration of Grover Cleveland in 1887, the Sherman Antitrust Act to the administration of Benjamin Harrison in 1890. The Pure Food and Drug Law was enacted under Theodore Roosevelt in 1906, the Clayton and Federal Trade Commission Acts under Woodrow Wilson in 1914. The first conservation laws date from the seventies; the first law controlling the methods used in producing oil and gas was passed in Texas in 1919. A number of regulatory agencies, set up under Franklin D. Roosevelt in the early years of the New Deal, have now seen two decades of service. Regulation of business in the public interest is by no means alien to American tradition. It is an outgrowth of generations of experience.

Causes of Growing Controls

When government moves to extend its controls, it does not act of its own volition. Government, in the United States, is not an independent entity; it does not possess a will of its own; it is not animated by purposes that are alien to the desires of its citizens. The American government is a creature of the American people; it responds to the pressures that they bring to bear upon it; its policies and its programs, wise or unwise, find their origin in organized demand and depend for their survival upon popular sufferance. If government regulates the securities markets and the stock exchanges, it is because investors demand protection. If it establishes maximum hours and minimum wages, requires collective bargaining, and sets up a system of social insurance, it is because labor demands protection. If it outlaws unfair methods of competition and curbs discrimination in the prices that are quoted to competing firms, it is because competitors demand protection. If it prohibits the sale of impure foods and drugs, if it forbids falsehood in advertising, if it enforces competition in one industry and regulates monopoly in another, it is because consumers demand protection. If it seeks to conserve the nation's resources, it is because a substantial body of public opinion insists that it do so. Government does not willfully interfere with business. It intervenes only when it is forced to intervene. It acts reluctantly, deliberately, and tardily, in response to overwhelming pressures. Criticism of public intervention is criticism, not of dictatorship, but of the results of the democratic process.

The scope of public regulation has grown steadily with the passage of time. A century ago controls were few and simple. In the economy of that day they were all that seemed to be required. In relation to its great resources the population of the country was small. There were still free lands to be occupied, virgin forests to be cut, and deposits of minerals waiting to be tapped. Productive activity centered in agriculture, in the extractive industries, in handicrafts and small manufactures, and in petty trade. Enterprises were organized, in the main, as individual proprietorships or partnerships. They were managed by their owners; employers dealt directly with employees. The scale of industrial operations was small; the production of goods and services was scattered among many firms. Economic independence was the general rule.

Now all of these conditions have changed. The population has grown; the land has been settled, and its natural wealth exploited. Agriculture has declined in relative importance; manufacturing, transportation, and the public utilities have grown. The individual proprietorship and the partnership have given way, in many fields, to the modern corporation. Ownership has been divorced from management, and labor has been organized. Technology has advanced: new products, new materials, new machines, and new methods have been introduced. The scale of industrial operations has grown; production, in many industries, has come to be concentrated in the hands of a few large firms. Economic relationships have steadily grown in complexity. Interdependence, rather than independence, has come to be the rule.

These changes have brought with them a host of new problems, and as these problems have arisen solutions have been sought through the extension of public controls. New laws have been enacted, new agencies established, and new methods of regulation devised. But the process of adapting political institutions to economic change has not been a steady one. Public sentiment has swung from radicalism to conservatism and back again, and legislation has come in spurts as abuses have become so evident as to call for reforms. Controls have been extended most rapidly when deep depression has emphasized the need for individual security and in periods when preparation for the nation's defense has placed a heavy burden on the whole economy. These controls have generally been abandoned when the emergency has passed. But other controls, once adopted, have usually been retained. Regulation often advances; it seldom retreats.

Attitudes of Business

Business has prospered despite regulation—or even because of it. But businessmen, none the less, have tended to view their regulators with hostility. The reason for this attitude is to be found not so much in the economic costs of regulation as in its psychic costs. In a recent study of manufacturers in Connecticut, Robert E. Lane offers this explanation of their antagonism toward new controls: "First, the regulation challenged the businessman's belief system, profaned his idols, and depreciated his myths. . . . Second, it denegrated the businessman himself, lowered his status in the community, and allocated to him a role subordinate to the one he had enjoyed. . . ."[1] This resulted in frustration and gave rise to anxiety. In such a state of mind the businessman reacted aggressively. His hostility was directed, in the main, toward the bureaucrats who enforced the hated regulations. They were strangers to him. Their value systems, their group loyalties, their occupational traits, even their vocabularies differed from his. The consequence, at first, was violation of the law, litigation to hamper its enforcement, lobbying to change its terms, and pressure to influence its administration. In time, however, hostility was tempered by adaptation and adjustment. The regulations came to be accepted as a matter of course.

As controls have been extended, this process has been repeated again and again. It must be noted, however, that many of the laws that now regulate business have been enacted, not in the face of business opposition, but at the urgent solicitation of business itself. There are tariffs that prevent businessmen from buying goods abroad, statutes that prevent them from doing business across state lines, and ordinances that exclude them

[1] Robert E. Lane, *The Regulation of Businessmen* (New Haven: Yale University Press, 1954), p. 19.

from local markets. There are patents that keep businessmen from competing with the patentees, and licensing requirements that deny them entry into sheltered trades. There are regulations that prevent businessmen from reducing the costs of production, from introducing new methods, and from employing new materials. There are laws that handicap the efficient businessman and laws that subsidize the inefficient one. There are laws that prevent the businessman from increasing his output and laws that prevent him from reducing his price. None of these are measures which an aggressive government has forced upon a reluctant business community. All of them are measures which government has adopted at the behest of business itself. If government is interfering with business, it is largely because business has invited it to interfere.

It should be noted, too, that the relation of government to business is not exclusively that of the lawgiver, the policeman, and the judge. Government also renders valuable services to business, extends to it various forms of public assistance, and promotes its activities in many ways. It collects and disseminates data that provide businessmen with information on the availability of productive resources, credit, and investment funds, on methods and costs of production and distribution, on trends of business activity, on present market conditions and future market prospects. It engages in fundamental research relating to the problems of agriculture, industry, and public health, tests the properties of materials and the effectiveness of productive processes, contributes to the advancement of technology, and makes its discoveries available for general use. Through its system of public education, government trains the labor force and cultivates consumer demand. Through its consular service, it assists business in finding markets abroad. Through its diplomatic service, it seeks to protect investments made in other lands. Government offers technical advice to small business, makes loans to finance productive activities, and encourages expansion of investment, when it is needed, by remission of taxes. Railways were once the beneficiaries of grants of public lands. Highways, waterways, and airways are now maintained at public expense; transportation by water and by air are subsidized. Subsidies are also extended, in one way or another, to farmers, to silver producers, and to publishers of newspapers and magazines. In all of these matters, business leans heavily on government.

ECONOMIC SYSTEMS

It may safely be concluded that the relationship of government to business cannot, in general, be characterized by the use of such words as meddling and interference. But what is to be said of the further charge, heard with great frequency in the years that followed World War II, that the extension of public activities is converting the United States from a market economy to a planned economy, that industry is being regimented and economic freedom destroyed? Before this question can be answered, the essential characteristics of market and planned economies must be described and the meaning of freedom and regimentation defined.

The Market Economy

A market economy is one in which productive activity is governed by a multitude of individual decisions made by the consumers and producers of goods and services, each of these decisions being small in scope and all of them being co-ordinated through the processes of buying and selling. In such an economy the ultimate consumer exercises sovereign power. Each time he spends a dollar he casts a vote for the production of the thing he buys. His dollar votes, recorded in his purchases, express the character of his demands. Where his demand for a commodity declines, its price will tend to fall and the income received by its producers will be low. Where demand increases, price will tend to rise and the income of producers will be high. When these producers, in their turn, compete against each other to obtain the scarce resources needed in production—labor, capital, materials, fuel, and power—those with products where demand is weak will find themselves outbid by those with products where demand is strong. The resources of the community will be diverted from the one field to the other, away from producing goods that are wanted less and toward producing goods that are wanted more. Resources will thus tend to be allocated in accordance with the requirements of consumer sovereignty.

The votes that the consumer casts in the market differ from those that the citizen casts at the polling place. They are cast daily, not just once a year. The franchise, moreover, is universal, extending without discrimination to those of every race and every belief, to aliens as well as natives, to youngsters as well as oldsters—to everyone, in fact, who comes into possession of a coin. But the votes are unequal, some voters having many and others having few. In principle, however, the weight of each consumer's vote is determined by the value placed on his services to production through the impersonal forces of the market. Where the demand for these services is small and the supply large, the weight will be light. Where the demand is large and the supply small, it will be heavy. As a result, people will tend to move from the one field into the other. And as they do so, their voting power will be equalized.

In the market economy, economic freedom is the general rule. Consumers are free to determine by their choices what will be produced. Workers and investors are free to decide where their labor and their savings will be employed. Businessmen are free to enter the market, employ labor and capital, and produce goods and services in an effort to obtain profits by satisfying consumers' demands. This is economic freedom, but this is not all that the phrase implies. Freedom holds open the door to opportunity; it also requires the assumption of risks. It does not guarantee the businessman an income or assure him a permanent lease on life. It carries with it, not only freedom to make a profit, but also freedom to incur a loss; not only freedom to enter a market, but also freedom to leave it through bankruptcy. And these freedoms are as essential as the others to the successful operation of the market economy. For if losses and bankruptcy were not to be permitted, business would be under no compulsion to adapt its operations to changing conditions of demand and cost. The allocation of resources would not conform to the pattern of consumer preferences.

The Essentiality of Competition

Competition is implicit in the concept of the market economy. It is the regulator that compels producers to follow the guidance of consumer choice. Failure in business curtails the supply of unwanted goods. Freedom of entry into business enlarges the supply of wanted goods. Land, labor, and capital are withdrawn from one industry and added to another in response to the changing direction of demand. The mobility characteristic of competition thus tends to achieve the allocation of resources that consumers desire. Monopoly, by contrast, frustrates such an allocation. The monopolist is likely to increase his profit by raising his price. He will then limit his output to the quantity that the market will take at the price that he has fixed. Consumers who would be willing to purchase larger quantities of his product at a lower price are left, instead, to buy goods that are wanted less. Resources are thus diverted from those things which the community prefers to those which are, at best, a second choice. The resources that are excluded from the superior occupation compete with others for employment in inferior ones and their productivity declines.

Competition serves the consumer. It operates negatively to protect him against extortion. If the quality of the product offered by one producer is low, the quality of that offered by another may be high. If the price charged by one producer is high, that asked by another may be low. The consumer is not at the mercy of the one as long as he has the alternative of buying from the other. More than this, competition operates affirmatively to enhance quality and reduce price. The producer who wishes to enlarge his profits must increase his sales. To do so, he must offer the consumer more goods for less money. As he adds to quality and subtracts from price, his rivals are compelled to do the same. The changes which he initiates soon spread throughout the trade. Every consumer of its products gets more and pays less. Monopoly, on the other hand, affords the consumer no protection against extortion. The monopolist may persist in offering inferior quality at a high price, since the purchasers of his product lack the alternative of turning to other sources of supply. He may obtain his profit, not by serving the community, but by refusing to serve it.

Competition is conducive to continuous improvement of industrial efficiency. It leads some producers to eliminate wastes and cut costs so that they may undersell others. It compels others to adopt similar measures in order that they may survive. It weeds out those whose costs remain high and thus operates to concentrate production in the hands of those whose costs are low. As the former are superseded by the latter, the general level of industrial efficiency is accordingly enhanced. Monopoly, to the contrary, inflicts no penalty on inefficiency. The monopolist may eliminate wastes and cut costs, but he is under no compulsion to do so. Through inertia, he may cling to accustomed techniques. His hold upon the market is assured.

Competition is congenial to material progress. It keeps the door open to new blood and new ideas. It communicates to all producers the improvements made by any one of them. Monopoly, as such, is not conducive to progress. The large firm may engage in research and invent new products, materials, methods, and machines. But when it possesses a monopoly, it will be reluctant to make use of these inventions if they would compel it to scrap existing equipment or if it believes that their ultimate profitability is in doubt. The monopolist may introduce innovations and cut costs, but instead of moving goods by reducing prices he is prone to spend large sums on alternative methods of promoting sales. His refusal to cut prices deprives the community of any gain.

Competition is cumulative in its effects. When competitors cut their prices, consumers buy more goods, output increases, and unit costs may decline. The lower prices compel producers to seek still further means of cutting costs. The resulting gains in efficiency open the way to still lower prices. Goods are turned out in increasing volume, and the general plane of living is raised. Monopoly impedes this process. Because it does not compel the enhancement of quality or the reduction of price, because it fails to penalize inefficiency, because it is not conducive to progress, it makes the total output of goods and services smaller than it otherwise would be.

From the standpoint of the market economy, competition is the indispensable disciplinarian. Monopoly, by contrast, is a subversive force.

The Planned Economy

A planned economy is one in which productive activity is governed by decisions made by public officials, each of these decisions being broad in scope and all of them having the force of law. The ultimate seat of power in such an order will depend upon the nature of its political institutions. If it is a dictatorship, sovereignty will lie with the dictator. If it is a democracy, sovereignty will lie with the voter. In either case, the planners might conceivably attempt to allocate resources in accordance with consumer preferences. Whether they could succeed in doing so is still a matter of debate. This question, though interesting in theory, can be dismissed for present purposes as academic. For, as a matter of practical politics, it is virtually certain that the attempt would not be made.

In planning production, the officials of a planned economy will inevitably respond, not to the demands of the consumer but to those of the dictator or the electorate. And these demands will seldom be the same. The demands that are made by the consumer express his own judgment of his own needs. The decisions that are made by the planners will be influenced by considerations of politics: by the desire to strengthen and preserve the state, to perpetuate their own power, to promote the general welfare, or to confer special benefits on favored groups. The economy, in consequence, will produce more of some goods and less of others than consumers would freely choose. Where the payments that consumers are prepared to make for a particular good or service do not suffice to cover the costs that would be established by competition for the resources employed in its production, such production will be supported by measures that relieve producers of the necessity of meeting these costs, and the good or service will be provided in quantities greater than consumers would choose. And, on the other hand, where consumers stand ready to make payments that would more than cover the competitive costs of the resources employed in producing a good or service, these costs will be augmented by measures that impose a further burden on producers, the good or service will be provided in quantities smaller than consumers would choose, and its distribution will be limited through some form of rationing. The resulting pattern of production will be one that may be judged to be better or worse than the one that would have prevailed had the desires of consumers been satisfied. The point is that it will be different.

It is this impairment of the sovereignty of the consumer that is the essential characteristic of the planned economy. In such an economy, too, wages, interest, rents, and profits are not determined by impersonal market forces but depend upon political decisions. The distribution of income is influenced by the push and pull of organized group interests. Freedom of choice among occupations and freedom of entry into markets are necessarily limited. Monopoly is the general rule. Efficiency and progress are assured neither by the prospect of profit nor by the penalty of bankruptcy. They are obtained, if at all, by the establishment of legal standards and the enforcement of administrative rules. In the market economy, business is disciplined by competition. In the planned economy, it is regimented by the state.

The Mixed Economy

Both of these concepts are abstractions. All economies are a mixture of freedom and regimentation. There is none in which decisions are left entirely to the market. There is none in which decisions have been taken over completely by the state. The question, in each case, is one of relative emphasis. But it is clear that there are some economies that approach more closely to the pattern of guidance through the market and others to the pattern of guidance through official plans.

The economy of the United States is predominantly a market economy. Most of the decisions that guide production, in time of peace, are made by individuals and co-ordinated through the market place. To some extent, however, the allocation of resources is determined politically: through public expenditures, subsidies, taxes, and prohibitory laws. And in time of war, allocation is largely governed by direct controls. Most incomes are fixed by market forces. But distribution is influenced by political pressures. A considerable measure of redistribution is effected through taxation and public expenditures. And in wartime, again, some incomes are subject to direct controls. Most productive activity, finally, is disciplined by competition. But here, too, there are exceptions to the general rule.

In certain fields, notably the public utility industries, the nature of the service rendered is such as to require unified control. Here, the inevitability of monopoly is recognized, and the enterprise is either regulated or operated by an agency of government. In some cases, the methods employed in competition, if uncontrolled, would prove harmful to consumers or to workers or wasteful of natural resources, and government intervenes to raise competition to a plane where abuses will not occur. With certain groups, such as farmers and retailers, where producers are numerous and small, the impact of competition may be so severe that its full consequences are socially unacceptable, and here government may act to moderate its force. For the economy as a whole, finally, the extremes of inflation and depression, with their aftermath of loss of savings and unemployment, are productive of grave injustice and social unrest, and government is forced to assume responsibility for the maintenance of stability and the assurance of security. The resulting pattern, therefore, is an admixture of market direction and political direction of productive activity; of competitive controls and governmental controls.

GOVERNMENT AND THE ALLOCATION OF RESOURCES

If we are to determine whether the activities undertaken by government are tending, as is sometimes charged, to create a planned economy, to regiment industry, and to destroy economic freedom, there is a clear test that may be applied. Do these activities facilitate the operation of free markets, permit the prices established in these markets truly to reflect the demand for different products and the costs incurred in their production, support competition as a regulator of enterprise, and preserve the sovereignty of the consumer over the allocation of resources? Or, on the contrary, do they interfere with the operation of free markets, falsify price as an index of demand and cost, weaken the regulatory force of competition, and impair the sovereignty of the consumer by transferring authority over the allocation of resources from the market to the state?

When this test is applied to all of the activities of government, taken together, it is evident that no sweeping generalization can be made, for these activities differ from one another in purpose and in effect. But when particular measures are analyzed, one by one, it can be seen that many of them are consistent with the principle of consumer sovereignty and that many others are not. (1) Government acts, in general, to establish the foundations of the market economy. It provides a framework for private enterprise. It adds to the information available to buyers and sellers. It seeks to maintain competition and to prevent monopoly. (2) Government also undertakes to protect and strengthen the market economy. It checks the abuses of competition. It promotes industrial stability and individual security. (3) In certain cases, on the other hand, government replaces competition with other methods of control. It permits the creation of monopoly on one side of a market—as in the case of labor—to offset the monopsony inevitably found on the other. It brings monopolies under public regulation or takes them into public ownership. (4) At times, government intervenes deliberately to influence the allocation of resources. It does so whenever it collects taxes and spends money. It seeks to safeguard public safety, health, and morals by restricting certain types of activities. It serves the interests of particular groups by imposing discriminatory taxes and paying substantial subsidies; by curtailing competition and promoting monopoly. In order to check inflation, it applies comprehensive controls to the whole economy. Each of these activities will be described and analyzed in turn.

Providing the Basis for a Market Economy

Activities of government that are essential to the existence of a market economy include such functions as the provisions of legal status for the business unit, the definition and maintenance of rights of ownership, the enforcement of contracts, and the settlement of disputes. They include such services as the creation of a medium of exchange, the establishment of standards of weight, measure, quality, and value, and the provision of information and education. They include the construction and maintenance of avenues of transportation and communication, the regulation of traffic, the protection of property, and the preservation of order. Through such measures, government establishes the basic institutions of the market economy, supplies the media through which it functions, and provides the safeguards upon which it depends.

When purchases and sales are made in darkness, traders are seriously handicapped. To enable markets to function more effectively, government turns on the light. By forbidding sellers to misrepresent their wares and requiring them—in the case of foods, drugs, cosmetics, alcoholic beverages, insecticides, fabrics, stocks and bonds—to disclose essential facts, by itself reporting on the current prices and prospective supplies of agricultural commodities, and by assembling data through its employment offices concerning opportunities for work and the availability of workers, government adds to the quantity and improves the quality of information provided to the buyers and sellers of goods and services and thus contributes to the wisdom with which their choices can be made. By checking on the accuracy of scales and the capacity of containers, by inspecting shipments of goods that are sold in accordance with official grades, by enforcing regulations governing the quality of foodstuffs and the conditions under which they are produced, and by preventing manipulation of the exchanges where commodities and securities are bought and sold, it enables buyers to make their purchases without investigating the reliability of sellers and thus increases public confidence in the integrity of market processes. Proposals for the further extension of such activities—proposals, for instance, to establish official grades for consumers' goods and to require informative labeling—are frequently denounced as socialistic. But all of these activities are in accordance with the fundamental principle of the market economy: they operate to preserve and strengthen the institution of consumer sovereignty.

The whole philosophy of economic freedom is based on the assumption that competition will prevail. Monopoly, as we have seen, prevents the market from allocating resources in accordance with the pattern of consumer preferences. It is competition that compels it to do so. It is competition that leads producers to improve their products, reduce their prices, increase their efficiency, and cut their costs. It is competition that harnesses the profit motive and holds it to the paths marked out by free consumer choice. When government prohibits monopoly and forbids buyers or sellers to enter into agreements governing purchases, production, prices, or terms of sale, it seeks to strengthen the mechanism of the market and to promote its successful operation. By preserving the regulatory force of competition, it avoids the necessity of imposing alternative controls.

Protecting and Strengthening the Market Economy

While competition generally serves the public interest, it does not invariably do so. Where some of the members of a trade seek to hold down their costs by failing to provide for the health and safety of their employees, by paying inadequate wages, and by requiring excessive hours, others may be forced to follow suit and the well-being of labor may be impaired. Where some of them adulterate and misrepresent their products, it may be difficult for others to maintain quality and to tell the truth, and the consumer may be defrauded and deceived. Where competition manifests itself in malicious and predatory tactics, in discrimination, intimidation, and coercion, the dishonest competitor may prosper and his honest rival may disappear. Where the competitive exploitation of natural resources leads to the adoption of methods that entail serious waste, the nation's security may be imperiled and the cost of future supplies may be increased. Government acts, in all of these cases, to lay down the rules under which the game of competition may be played: it establishes standards of employment, forbids unfair competitive methods and deceptive practices, and makes provision for the conservation of natural resources. In doing so, it influences the allocation of resources, preventing the consumer from obtaining products made in sweatshops, from buying adulterated goods, from dealing with unscrupulous sellers, and from enjoying in the present that part of the supply of exhaustible materials that is reserved for future use. But, within these limits, government still leaves the guidance of production to free consumer choice. By checking the abuses of competition, it preserves the benefits.

The most serious shortcoming of the market economy, in the past, has been its instability and its consequent failure to provide assurance of individual security. In response to popular pressure, government has moved, since the great depression of the thirties, toward the adoption of policies through which industry may be stabilized and a measure of security assured. Its monetary policy requires it to tighten controls over bank credit during prosperity and to relax them during depression. Its fiscal policy, if consistently followed, would lead it to reduce its expenditures and increase taxes when times are good and to increase its expenditures and reduce taxes when times are bad. Its system of social insurance has a similar effect, collecting more money in premiums during booms and paying out more money in benefits during slumps. It is the purpose of all of these measures to moderate the swings of the business cycle and to protect the individual against the consequences of industrial instability. The adoption of such measures has frequently been cited as evidence in support of the assertion that government is creating a planned economy. It proves nothing of the sort. A planned economy is one in which the allocation of resources, instead of being governed by the choices of consumers, is determined by the state. These measures seek to influence the total volume of production, not to determine what will be produced. They are concerned with the size of the nation's income, not with its composition. They leave the allocation of resources to the market. Not only are they consistent with the principle of consumer sovereignty; they serve to strengthen it. For deep depression, protracted unemployment, and widespread insecurity must be prevented if the institutions of economic freedom are to be preserved.

Replacing Competition as a Regulator

The interests of traders are best protected when those on both sides of the market have equal bargaining power. But power to bargain may be unequal and, where it is, government may undertake to redress the balance by curbing the strong and strengthening the weak. The market for labor is a case in point. The worker who bargains for himself alone is seriously handicapped: he is dependent on his job, ignorant of other opportunities, and deficient in bargaining skill; his reserves are small—he cannot wait for long to strike a better deal. The employer, on the other hand, is better informed, has larger resources, and is more adept at bargaining; he can replace one worker with another, dispensing with those who will not accept his terms. Here, the balance cannot be redressed by depriving the employer of his advantages. Government has therefore attempted to equalize the strength of buyers and sellers by permitting workers to organize and forbidding employers to interfere, by insuring the independence of labor unions and requiring that they be recognized, and by promoting collective bargaining. In the case of agriculture, too, government has strengthened the weaker position of sellers by enabling them to deal collectively through agricultural co-operatives. There is danger, in such cases, that the balance may be tipped the other way. There is danger, too, that government may abandon its position of neutrality and throw its weight on one side of the scales. But the principle, at least, is clear: government, if it is neutral, does not undertake to determine the outcome of the bargaining process, but leaves this to the market, confining itself to the equalization of bargaining power.

In some industries, competition cannot be expected to obtain. In the postal system and in the telephone business, for instance, the nature of the service that is rendered is such as to demand co-ordinated operation under common control. In the case of other utility services, such as the operation of local transit systems and the distribution of water, gas, and electricity, though it might be possible for many firms to enter the market, efficiency requires that a single seller be permitted to provide the whole supply. Here, in the absence of competition, the interests of the consumer must be protected by other means. To this end, government has adopted one of two alternatives: in some cases, it has brought the industries under public regulation, specifying the services that they must render and fixing the rates that they may charge; in others, it has taken them into public ownership.

It is the purpose of public regulation to hold the rates charged by a monopolistic enterprise down to the level that is required to cover costs and to yield a profit comparable to that obtainable in competitive industries. If it does not succeed in doing so, the enterprise will not produce as much as the consumer would be willing to buy at a competitive price, and less of the community's resources will be devoted to its operations than he would have wished. If such regulation were to be extended to many industries, it is clear that the allocation of resources would be substantially modified. But the enterprises whose monopolistic character requires that they be so controlled are relatively few in number and account for but a minor fraction of industrial activity. Even though particular undertakings are regulated by the state, major responsibility for the direction of production in the economy as a whole can still be left to the consumer.

Where industries are taken into public ownership, government is under no compulsion to hold their costs within the limits fixed by their commercial revenues. Recurring deficits may be offset by contributions from the public treasury. Industries operated by government may thus be able to employ more of the community's resources than the consumer would freely choose. If all major industries were so operated, it is evident that the market economy would disappear. But public ownership, in the United States, is confined to a minor portion of the nation's industry. Federal ownership is significant, mainly, in such fields as the postal service, the development of atomic energy, and the generation of hydroelectric power; state ownership in the operation of turnpikes and liquor stores; municipal ownership in the operation of transit systems and the distribution of water and electricity. There is no significant pressure to force the extension of such activity into other fields. As long as public enterprise remains within such narrow boundaries, it still permits production as a whole to be guided by consumer choice.

Deliberately Influencing Allocation

The nature of productive activity is inevitably affected by the process of raising and spending money to finance the normal functions of government. The way in which the burden of taxation is distributed affects the allocation of resources by altering the character of consumers' demands and producers' costs. The expenditure of public funds—on roads and bridges, streets and sewers, police and fire departments, libraries and schools, hospitals and prisons, and on the military establishment—directs production into channels other than those that would have been established by free consumer choice. As government has taken on new functions, its expenditures have grown and the economy has responded, increasingly, to decisions that are arrived at, not through the processes of the market, but through those of politics.

In a few cases government has moved directly to curtail the consumption of particular goods and services. By imposing heavy taxes on luxury goods, it has sought to discourage their use. By forbidding the importation of obscene materials and refusing to admit them to the mails, by censoring plays and motion pictures, by prohibiting gambling and prostitution, and by limiting the sale of firearms, alcoholic beverages, and narcotic drugs, it has attempted to prevent consumers from obtaining things that some of them have desired. All of these measures are obviously inconsistent with the principle of consumer sovereignty. They have been adopted because people have believed it less important to preserve the principle, in these cases, than to check luxurious consumption and to safeguard public safety, health, and morals.

In certain other cases, acting in response to political pressure exerted by organized producing groups, government has adopted measures that clearly distort the pattern of allocation that consumers would desire. To aid producers of butter, it has imposed discriminatory taxes on oleomargarine; to aid independent retailers, it has imposed discriminatory taxes on chain stores. By thus moving to raise costs above the level established by competition, it has sought to prevent consumers from obtaining as much of a good or service as they stood ready to buy. To aid producers of agricultural commodities and operators of shipping companies and airlines, government has paid out subsidies from its treasury, thus maintaining the output of these goods and services at levels higher than the demands of consumers would have permitted. To aid producers of silver, it has purchased the metal and held it in storage, raising its price and thus not only causing more to be produced but also causing less to be consumed than market forces would have justified. In all of these cases, government has prevented price from truly reflecting demand and cost. It has altered the allocation of resources by subordinating the desires of the consumer to the purposes of politics.

Government has also sought, in many instances, to serve the interests of producers by preventing competition and promoting monopoly. It has imposed tariffs, granted patents, and required certificates or licenses for entry to the market, thus excluding outsiders from protected trades. It has encouraged producers of petroleum and agricultural products to restrict their output, thus undertaking to curtail supplies of these commodities. It has exempted certain groups, including shipping companies, exporters, retailers, and the producers, processors, and distributors of agricultural products, from the requirements of the antitrust laws, thus enabling them to agree upon the prices they will charge. In the case of trucking services and, at one time, in the case of bituminous coal, it has itself established a minimum price. In all of these ways, government has permitted or required prices to be fixed at levels higher than those that would have prevailed if sellers were free to compete. As a consequence, the consumer has purchased these goods and services in quantities smaller than he desired and spent his money, instead, on things he wanted less. His sovereignty has thus been violated, at the behest of business, by the action of the state.

Impairment of consumer sovereignty has been most serious when the nation has been at war. In the United States, in time of peace, government has demanded around one seventh of the national product. In time of war, it has demanded close to half. At such a time, moreover, the threat of runaway inflation has necessitated the imposition of detailed controls. Prices, under official ceilings, have ceased to perform their function of guiding production, allocating materials, and distributing finished goods. Wages, regulated by law, have no longer served to direct the flow of labor from job to job. Goods have therefore been rationed, materials allocated, and labor directed by public agencies. The state has largely superseded the market as the governor of productive activity. It is in circumstances such as these that the nation has approached most closely to the model of the planned economy.

The Effect of Public Activities

It is not intended, here, to suggest that it is always desirable that production respond to the guidance of the market and always undesirable that it respond to the guidance of the state. There would be general agreement, for instance, that public sale of narcotics should be forbidden and that parks and playgrounds should be provided at public expense. It would doubtless be conceded that, when inflation is not otherwise to be prevented, it is prudent to accept the lesser evil of direct controls. Opinions are likely to differ on the wisdom of policies that have been adopted in other cases where the state has intervened: on measures such as tariffs, subsidies, and the establishment of minimum prices for certain goods and services. But this is not the issue with which we are concerned. It is our present purpose, not to judge the wisdom of controls imposed by government, but to determine how they have affected the character of the economy.

Certain generalizations are justified. The measures adopted by government are not alike; each must be analyzed to determine its effects. Some measures serve to support and strengthen the principle of consumer sovereignty; others operate to impair it. Those in the latter group are a product of three major forces: popular demand for action to safeguard the general welfare, producer pressure for special privilege and for relief from competition, and—most important—the necessities of war. But, in the United States in peacetime, the market still governs the great bulk of industrial activity. In the guidance of production, private rather than public decisions predominate.

THE PLAN OF THIS BOOK

It will not be possible, within the scope of the present volume, to consider all of the activities of government that influence the allocation of resources and the stability of the economy. But many of the more important controls imposed by government on business will be examined, at some length, in the light of the foregoing analysis. Attention will be directed, successively, to measures that are designed (1) to maintain competition and prevent monopoly, (2) to check the possible abuses of competition, (3) to moderate the force of competition in particular fields, and (4) to substitute public authority as a regulator in fields where competition cannot exist. Consideration will also be given to the problems that are presented (5) by the imposition of comprehensive economic controls, and (6) by the public ownership and operation of industry. On the basis of this discussion, conclusions will be drawn, in the closing chapters, concerning the comparative merits of different methods of control and the means by which their shortcomings may be remedied.

SUGGESTIONS FOR FURTHER READING

A realization of the sharp contrast between the views held by liberal economists a century ago and at the present time with respect to the proper economic functions of government may be obtained by first reading the final chapter (Book V, chap. xi, "Of the Grounds and Limits of the Laissez-Faire or Non-Interference Principle") of John Stuart Mill's *Principles of Political Economy*, published in 1848, and then reading one or both of the following: J. M. Clark, *Social Control of Business* (2d ed.; New York: McGraw-Hill Book Co., 1939), chap. ix, "An Economic Constitution for the State"; and Henry C. Simons, *Economic Policy for a Free Society* (Chicago: University of Chicago Press, 1948), chap. ii, "A Positive Program for Laissez Faire." The causes of increasing public controls are discussed in George A. Steiner, *Government's Role in Economic Life* (New York: McGraw-Hill Book Co., 1953), chap. vi, vii, and viii. The reaction of businessmen to increasing controls is analyzed in Robert E. Lane, *The Regulation of Businessmen* (New Haven: Yale University Press, 1954). The theory of competition and monopoly is presented in Fritz Machlup, *The Economics of Sellers' Competition* (Baltimore: Johns Hopkins Press, 1952); and in Andreas G. Papandreou and John T. Wheeler, *Competition and Its Regulation* (New York: Prentice-Hall, Inc., 1954), Book I. An official pronouncement on the relations between government and business is contained in *Business and Government—Fourth Annual Report to the President by the Council of Economic Advisers, December 1949* (Washington: Government Printing Office, 1949), obtainable from the Superintendent of Documents for 15 cents.

Chapter 2 THE FRAMEWORK OF CONTROL

In a few cases, government itself undertakes the administration of business enterprises. In most cases, it subjects private enterprises to public controls. What is the meaning of this phrase "public control of business"?

By "business," of course, is meant that part of economic activity that has to do with the production, distribution, and sale of goods and services. By "public," in this connection, is meant some agency of government. The general public influences business, to be sure, through channels other than those of government: through buying or failing to buy its products, for instance, or through the force of public opinion. But it is only with control through government that we shall be concerned.

What, then, is "control"? Business is influenced, inevitably, by all of the activities of government. But many of them are not to be included in the concept of control. This is true, for instance, of such services as the provision of streets and highways, police and fire protection, public health and education, and national defense. It is true, too, of those activities that create the general environment within which business may be carried on: provision of legal status for the business unit, enforcement of contracts, standardization of weights and measures, establishment of a monetary system, stabilization of the level of prices through monetary and fiscal action, and maintenance of a large and growing volume of output and income in the whole economy. The meaning of "control," as the word is used here is confined to the deliberate adoption, by government, of measures designed to cause the policies of business managements to differ, in material respects, from those that they would voluntarily pursue. Control thus comprehends a great variety of measures that differ in purpose, method, and effect. Their common feature is modification of the behavior of business in response to pressures applied through government.

It is the purpose of the present chapter to provide a background for a more detailed description and analysis of many of these measures by outlining, in general terms, the methods of control employed by government, the structure through which they are developed and applied, and the limitations imposed by law upon their exercise.

THE METHODS OF CONTROL

The word "control" seems to imply coercion through the imposition of penalties. And, indeed, this is a major method of control. But the means employed by government are frequently more subtle and less harsh. Compliance may be obtained by mere persuasion, by offering inducements, or by threatening business with unfavorable publicity. And even where formal procedures are employed, they may lead to nothing more than an order directing an enterprise to obey the law. Business policy is influenced, in the vast majority of cases, without imposing fines on businessmen or putting them in jail.

The Common Law

Most of the regulations affecting business, at the present time, are based on statutes or ordinances enacted by the legislative bodies of federal, state, or local governments. But statutory law was long preceded by the common law, a body of decisions handed down by courts in cases brought by private litigants. The common law had its origin in England in the days before America was colonized. It embodied the customs and the concepts that grew out of an economy of agriculture, handicrafts, and petty trade. As conditions changed, however, new problems arose, and cases presenting novel issues were brought before the courts. And as decision followed decision, each of them built on old precedents, each of them creating a new precedent, the law developed, adapting its requirements to the changing circumstances of the times. It was through the English common law, transplanted and growing in America, that business in this country was first controlled.

Control by this method was incidental to protection of the rights of parties to private suits. When such suits were brought, the courts might refuse to enforce contracts on the ground that they were contrary to public policy. They might award damages in case of injury. They might enjoin defendants from doing certain things and punish for contempt those who disobeyed them. In this way, at common law, the courts refused to enforce contracts in restraint of trade and afforded redress to persons injured by unfair methods of competition and by the creation of monopolies. And, at the same time, the courts recognized certain occupations as common callings and required those who engaged in them to give adequate service to all comers, at reasonable rates, and without discrimination. They thus anticipated the antitrust laws and the regulation, by statute, of railways and public utilities.

This method of control, however, has its limitations. A person who has suffered injury may not know it. And if he does, he may lack the funds to sue. The prosecution of offenders is bound to be sporadic; offenses that harm the public may not give rise to suits. The procedures of litigation are cumbersome and time consuming. The courts are wanting in special competence to deal with issues of business policy. They decide the cases that are brought before them; whatever the urgency for action, they are granted no initiative. They can award damages to those who are injured; unless asked to do so, they cannot move to prevent infliction of an injury.

Statutes and Ordinances

A legislative body may leave enforcement of a statute to the initiative of private litigants. It may encourage the entry of suits by providing, as a punitive measure, for the assessment of multiple damages. But if it goes no farther than this, it advances little beyond the method of the common law. Provision is usually made, however, for the enforcement of statutory requirements by public prosecutors at public expense, for the imposition of penalties, and for the development and application of remedies. And here, the method of the statute is more effective than the method of the common law.

A legislature may enact a statute—or a city council pass an ordinance—that does no more than reaffirm the rulings of the common law. More often, however, these rulings will be modified and acts will be prohibited that formerly were allowed. The prohibitions of a statute may be set forth in general terms, their administration entrusted to an executive agency, and their ultimate interpretation to the courts. Or they may be spelled out at length and in considerable detail. In the former case, the law will be uncertain in content but flexible in its adjustment to changing needs. In the latter, it will be definite but rigid, and may soon go out of date. In 1907 West Virginia passed a law that fixed passenger fares on railroads at two cents per mile, and North Dakota a law that required the daily operation of at least one passenger train and one freight train on every line within the state. As conditions change, requirements of this sort must be adjusted, and this necessitates amendment of the law. But legislatures are not continually in session and their attention, when they meet, may well be claimed by many other things. Their action is certain to be tardy and likely to be clumsy and ill informed. If precise detail is modified by more precise detail, it, too, will soon go out of date. The statute is a good method for laying down general principles. It is a poor method of administering detailed controls.

Certificates, Franchises, Permits, and Licenses

Entry into businesses providing transportation and utility services is commonly restricted by laws requiring entrants to obtain certificates of public convenience and necessity from federal or state authorities and franchises from local governments. The requirement of certificates is deliberately designed to exclude competitors from fields where it is thought that better service is to be afforded by monopolies, and is usually accompanied by public regulation of services and rates. Certificates are issued as a privilege; they do not confer contractual rights. A franchise, on the other hand, is contractual in character; its terms can be enforced by suits brought in the courts. It gives to a private company the right (usually an exclusive right) to construct and operate facilities along a city's streets. Its provisions may be lax or rigorous, general or detailed. Its duration may be perpetual, for a long term or a short one, or indeterminate.

Franchises have been used, in the past, as means both of preventing and of exercising control over municipal utilities. Sweeping grants of monopoly power, obtained in perpetuity by bribing venal politicians, have stood, in certain cases, as contractual barriers to regulation in the public interest. But control of monopoly has been sought, on the other hand, by writing detailed requirements into franchises. Thus, in New York City, the franchise granted a subway corporation provided for a five cent fare, and, in Georgia, the one given a street railway company required it to run cars over its lines as often as once in thirty minutes, day and night. Here, as in the case of statutes, rigid requirements obstructed adjustment to change. But here, adjustment was made more difficult by the contractual character of the instrument in which they were contained. The franchise has been wisely used, in certain cases, to establish a general pattern of control. But it has proved to be a clumsy means of regulating in detail. Today this task is left, in the main, to administrative agencies; the franchise does little more than govern the use of city streets.

Entry to other occupations is frequently controlled by requiring permits or licenses. State and local governments make this requirement of doctors, dentists, pharmacists, barbers, brokers, plumbers, and those in other callings, of distributors of liquor, tobacco, milk, and other goods, and of operators of restaurants, hotels, theaters, pool rooms, dance halls, taxicabs, and those in other service trades. The federal government, in its regulations of trucking and shipping, requires certificates of common carriers, permits of contract carriers, and licenses of private carriers. It uses the licensing technique in controlling equipment and personnel in transportation and in allocating broadcasting channels among radio and television companies.

A licensing system may be used primarily as a source of revenue, as a method of obtaining registration for policing purposes, or as a means of protecting the public against unqualified practitioners of a profession or unsafe conditions in a trade. Licenses may be granted freely to all who make an application, or the system may be so designed or administered as to exclude competitors from a pre-empted field. Like the certificate, the license confers a privilege to which its holder has no legal right. It is usually temporary, renewable, and revocable. The government's power to refuse an application enables it—if it chooses—to impose conditions on its licensees. And its power to refuse renewal or to revoke a license affords a sanction whereby these conditions may be enforced. This penalty, however, is so harsh that it may seldom be applied.

The Regulatory Commissions

Where the policies of an industry are to be supervised in some detail, this task is now assigned, almost invariably, to a specialized administrative agency. The legislature typically enacts a statute, expressing its purposes in general terms, and establishes a commission to put them into effect. This body has its own identity, its own appropriation, and its own staff. Its members may be elected or appointed. They may be made subservient to the executive or given a measure of independence by requiring bipartisan representation, by fixing overlapping terms, and by forbidding removal until these terms expire. Such an agency may exercise wide discretion under a grant of legislative authority. The law may say that service must be adequate, rates just and reasonable, and discrimination not unreasonable or undue. The commission will go on to specify standards of service, to fix the general level of rates, and to pass upon complaints concerning differences in the charges paid by different customers. Its determinations will then be subject, on appeal, to confirmation or reversal by the courts.

The first commission in the United States was established by Massachusetts in 1838 to regulate the banking business. Railroad commissions with limited powers were set up by five New England states before the Civil War. Commissions were given mandatory powers over grain elevators and warehouses by Illinois in 1871 and over railroads by Illinois, Wisconsin, and Minnesota in 1874. The first such federal agency—the Interstate Commerce Commission—was established by Congress in 1887. State commissions, some of them formerly railroad commissions, were given authority over municipal utilities by Wisconsin, New York, and Georgia in 1907, by twenty-five other states by 1913, and by all the states but Delaware by 1927. Other federal commissions were established or re-established during the thirties, among them the Securities and Exchange Commission, the Federal Communications Commission, the Federal Power Commission, and the Civil Aeronautics Board.

The advantages of administrative regulation lie in its possible combination of expert knowledge, continuous oversight, informal procedure, and prompt action, and its emphasis on prevention rather than punishment. Its disadvantages are those inherent in democratic policies, bureaucratic administration, and division of authority. They will be discussed in greater detail later on.

Taxes and Subsidies

Taxation, though its primary function is that of obtaining revenue, may also be used as a method of control. Taxes have been imposed on liquor, tobacco, and various luxury goods for the purpose of discouraging consumption, on stock and commodity transfers to lessen speculation, and on narcotic drugs, white phosphorus matches, and the products of child labor at rates designed to prevent their production and sale. They have been levied on imported goods, on oleomargarine, and on chain stores to handicap them in their competition with domestic producers, dairymen, and independent retailers. Tax exemption, also, has been employed to induce the sorts of conduct that governments have desired. By granting exemptions from property taxes, local governments have encouraged the construction of new dwellings and the establishment of new industries. By taxing those who did not co-operate and exempting those who did, the federal government has forced the producers of bituminous coal and various agricultural commodities to adhere to programs fixing prices and restricting output and sales. Taxation of corporate income has been manipulated, too, in ways designed to foster the distribution of dividends, to stimulate the discovery and development of minerals, to speed the expansion of productive facilities, and to discourage the growth of profits in time of war.

Government also influences business through its expenditures. The federal government has promoted transportation by spending money on highways, waterways, and airways, fostered aviation by paying excessive sums for carrying the mails, and supported silver mining by buying the product to bury it again. It has instructed its procurement officers to "buy American," and attached to appropriations for foreign aid the instruction that the goods supplied be carried in American ships. It has required concerns accepting public contracts to maintain, at a specified level, the wages paid to laborers.

Government affects business by lending as well as by spending. In this way, it has promoted the ownership of homes and farms, the construction of low-rent housing in urban centers, and the extension of electrical power to rural areas. By making loans, through the Reconstruction Finance Corporation, to one industry rather than another, it has determined where expansion should occur. By denying Commodity Credit Corporation loans to farmers who do not co-operate in limiting production, it has induced adherence to its agricultural policies.

Subsidies may be concealed in purchases made at more than market prices or in loans made at rates of interest that fail to cover their costs. They may be hidden in sales made at less than market prices or in services rendered at a loss. This is the case when the government pays high prices for facilities and equipment in wartime and sells them at low prices as soon as the war is won. It is the case, too, when the Post Office delivers periodicals at a fraction of what the service costs. But subsidies may also be visible. Thus, in the nineteenth century, public lands were given to the railroads to open the country and to homesteaders to insure its settlement. And thus, at the present time, cash payments are made to builders and operators of merchant ships in order to keep the shipyards busy and the flag afloat upon the seas. In any of these cases, the payment of a subsidy may be accompanied by conditions laid down by the government. But here, compliance is voluntary. It is not commanded; it is bought.

Industry Codes and Marketing Agreements

Another method of control, inaugurated during the depression of the thirties, is called self-government in industry. Under this method, rules are adopted by agreement among the members of a trade, submitted for approval to a public agency, modified if rejected, given legal status when accepted, and then enforced, not only by industry itself, but also by the government. This was the method used in regulating business from 1933 to 1935, under the codes adopted and approved in accordance with the National Industrial Recovery Act. It is the method still employed in regulating the producers, processors, and distributors of milk and certain other agricultural commodities, under the terms of the Agricultural Marketing Agreements Act of 1938. The main advantage of the method is that it eases enforcement by enlisting the voluntary co-operation of industry. Its principal disadvantage—and a fatal one—is that it gives official endorsement to rules adopted in the interest of organized producers with little or no regard for the interests of consumers or the well-being of the whole community.

Investigations and Publicity

Government has sometimes called upon public opinion, employing no further sanctions, to influence the behavior of business. Congress set up a Bureau of Corporations in the Department of Commerce and Labor in 1903, and empowered it to investigate and report on business practices. This function was transferred to the Federal Trade Commission in 1914, the new agency being expected to keep business under control, in President Wilson's words, by "pitiless publicity." The first minimum wage law for women, enacted by Massachusetts in 1912, provided for the creation of joint boards to recommend wages, within the employers' ability to pay, that would cover the cost of living at a level of health and decency. But it carried no penalties, relying solely on public opinion to put these recommendations into effect. The same method has been employed repeatedly in an effort to prevent or settle strikes. Boards established by Congress or set up by the President have conducted investigations, issued factual reports, and presented recommendations which employers and workers were under no compulsion to accept. But it was hoped that the pressure of informed opinion would make for peaceful settlements.

Publicity, unaided by compulsion, has sometimes worked. Legislative investigations, reported in the press, have served, without new legislation, to bring about changes in business policy. The example set by the Tennessee Valley Authority in establishing promotional rates for electricity, and publication by the Federal Power Commission of rate comparisons for public and private companies in different cities, may have done more than commission regulation to modify the rate structures of privately owned utilities. In wartime, an appeal to patriotism might be more effective than the threat of fines and imprisonment in promoting general compliance with rationing and price controls.

But publicity, like other methods, has its limitations. Its use is violently resented by those against whom it is directed, and steps may be taken to limit the powers and to cut the appropriations of any agency employing it. Counterpropaganda may be issued, and the public, instead of being informed, will merely be confused. Popular disapproval alone may not deter offenders. If well enough entrenched, they may silently echo William H. Vanderbilt: "The public be damned!" It is not always possible to bring public opinion to bear. Its ultimate sanction is the boycott. But consumers may be unable to go without a product, even though convinced that its producers are at fault. And if they do refuse to buy, they may be unable to punish the guilty without injuring the innocent.

Emergency Controls

In time of war, or threat of war, the market has been largely superseded, as the governor of the economy, by authoritarian controls. Production has been diverted from civilian to military purposes. Prices and wages have been fixed, consumers' goods rationed, and materials and manpower allocated among competing demands. Laws have been piled upon laws, orders on orders. Administrative agencies have multiplied. All of the available methods of control have been put to use, all of the usual sanctions employed. And there have been two others: the conscription of labor—which has been little used, and the seizure of productive facilities—which has been used repeatedly.

Laws authorizing seizure have been enacted by Congress at least eighteen times, the first of them during the Civil War, and others during the two world wars and the war in Korea. These laws have authorized the President to take possession of factories, power plants, mines, and transportation and communications facilities, in the event of war or other national emergency, in order to insure production of essential goods and services and continued operation during wage disputes. The powers thus provided were exercised three times by President Lincoln, who seized the railroads and telegraph lines to obtain priority for the movement of troops and supplies and to guard the secrecy of communications. They were exercised eleven times by President Wilson, eight times to maintain production and three times to settle strikes. Seizure was resorted to on fifty-eight occasions during the second World War, eight times to assure capacity operation, the maintenance of quality, and the observance of delivery schedules in the production of military goods, and fifty times to enforce the decisions of labor boards in wage disputes. Seizure was used by President Truman in a dozen labor cases in the years that followed the war, the industries taken over including petroleum, meat packing, bituminous coal, the railroads, and iron and steel. The President's action, in all but the last of these cases, was based upon wartime statutes that had not expired. His seizure of the steel industry, on April 8, 1952, was without Congressional authority.[1]

Seizure has come to find its principal significance in the attempted settlement of industrial disputes. It does not involve the public ownership or operation of the properties that are seized. Public officials are placed in positions of nominal authority. But private managements are appointed to run their own concerns, and private owners continue to receive their dividends. The purpose of seizure is to maintain continued operation of essential services by preventing or ending a strike. The properties involved are returned to their owners as soon as this purpose has been served.

Government Ownership and Operation

Ownership and operation gives government the power directly to determine the policies of an industry. It thus affords a possible alternative to indirect controls. If extended to many fields, it makes for comprehensive economic planning. If limited to a few, it is consistent with the preservation of a free economy. This is the case, of course, in the United States. Water systems are owned and operated by most cities, liquor stores by many states, the postal service and the production of atomic energy by the federal government. Other activities are carried on by semiautonomous corporations, such as the Port of New York Authority and the TVA, whose directors are publicly appointed but whose managements are removed, to a degree, from the pressures of politics and the hampering rules of state and federal bureaucracies. The principal questions raised concerning public ownership, in such cases, are those of character of service and comparative efficiency.

THE STRUCTURE AND POWERS OF GOVERNMENT

In the government of the United States, four fundamental principles affect the application of controls. (1) Under the federal system, powers are distributed between the nation and the several states. The national government possesses the express powers that are delegated to it by the Constitution, the implied powers that may be inferred therefrom, the resulting powers—such as the power to issue paper money and make it legal tender —that are consequent upon a combination of express powers, and the inherent powers—relating primarily to international affairs—that are an attribute of national sovereignty. Under the Tenth Amendment, all other powers were reserved to the states. (2) Within both state and federal governments there is a separation of legislative, executive, and judicial powers. Protection against arbitrary action is thus afforded by a system of checks and balances. (3) These governments rest on written constitutions, containing guarantees of individual rights through which their powers are

[1] For a summary of the statutes giving seizure powers and the cases in which they have been used, see *Congressional Record,* June 2, 1952, pp. 6396–6404.

limited. (4) The acts of legislators and executives are subject to judicial review. The constitutions and the laws are interpreted, laws found to be unconstitutional are voided, and the acts of administrators are approved, modified, or reversed by the courts. This structure of government, and these limitations to its powers, determine whether a particular method of control may be employed and, if so, by whom, and how.

The Distribution of Powers

The economic powers delegated to the federal government by the states, as enumerated in Article I, Section 8 of the Constitution are these:

> To lay and collect Taxes, Duties, Imposts and Excises, to pay the Debts and provide for the common Defence and the general Welfare. . . .
>
> To borrow Money. . . .
>
> To regulate Commerce with foreign Nations and among the several States . . . and with the Indian tribes;
>
> To establish . . . uniform laws on the subject of Bankruptcies. . . .
>
> To coin Money, regulate the value thereof . . . and fix the Standard of Weights and Measures. . . .
>
> To establish Post Offices and post Roads;
>
> To promote the progress of Science and useful Arts, by securing for limited Times to Authors and Inventors the exclusive Right to their respective Writings and Discoveries. . . .

The most important of these clauses, for public control of business in time of peace, is the one—generally referred to as the interstate commerce clause—that gives the Congress power "To regulate Commerce . . . among the several States. . . ." Of even greater importance, however, are the extensive powers, conferred by subsequent clauses, to declare and wage war. And also significant, in some cases, is the fact that the states are forbidden to enter into treaties by Article I, Section 10 of the Constitution, while the President and the Senate are authorized to do so by Article II, Section 2.

The enumerated powers of the federal government are those expressly set forth in the Constitution. The implied powers are those inferred from the final clause of Article I, Section 8 of that document which authorized the Congress "To make all laws which shall be necessary and proper for carrying into Execution the foregoing Powers, and all other Powers vested by this Constitution in the Government of the United States. . . ." This may not have been intended as a grant of further powers, but it was so interpreted by the Supreme Court in the famous case of *McCulloch* v. *Maryland* in 1819.[2] The state of Maryland had imposed a tax on notes issued by a bank established by the federal government. When sued, it advanced the defense that nothing in the Constitution had empowered the Congress to set up a bank. The Court admitted that this power was not

[2] 4 Wheaton 316.

explicit, but held that it could reasonably be deduced from those that were. Said Chief Justice John Marshall, "Let the end be legitimate, let it be within the scope of the Constitution, and all means which are appropriate . . . which are not prohibited, but consist with the letter and spirit of the Constitution, are constitutional. . . ." This decision, as must be obvious, was of paramount importance in extending the scope of federal powers. From this time on, the national government was permitted, not only to do things that the Constitution said, but also to do things that the Court was willing to infer.

All governmental powers, save those denied them by the Constitution, are retained by the several states. Laws affecting business have thus been enacted, in the interest of public safety, health, and morals, and the general welfare, under what has been known as the police power of the states. This power, though not mentioned in the Constitution, has long been recognized by the courts.[3] Without definite limits, it has afforded a basis for such activities as the licensing of automobile drivers to insure public safety, the inspection of dairies to protect public health, the censorship of motion pictures to safeguard public morals, and the payment of mothers' pensions to promote the general welfare.

Where state and federal powers come into conflict, the latter must prevail. "This Constitution," says Article VI, "and the Laws of the United States which shall be made in Pursuance thereof . . . shall be the supreme Law of the Land." And this phrase was repeated by Justice Marshall in *McCulloch* v. *Maryland*, when he denied the states the right to tax a federal agency. "The government of the United States," he said, "though limited in its powers, is supreme; and its laws, when made in pursuance of the Constitution, form the supreme law of the land."

There has been a steady trend, over the years, toward increasing centralization of functions in the federal government. The reasons for this development are not hard to find. (1) Some regulatory activities require the establishment of uniform standards throughout the country if they are adequately to be performed. This is true, for instance, of the grading of commodities. (2) In other cases, the industries controlled extend beyond state borders, and controls must be given equal scope if they are to work at all. It was the failure of state regulation that led to the federal regulation of railway transportation and interstate sales of gas and electricity. (3) Elsewhere, a state may fail to act because its producers, if compelled to incur higher costs, would be placed at a disadvantage in competing with producers in surrounding states. Here, if competitors are to be put upon an equal footing, federal action is required. The establishment of a system of unemployment insurance is a case in point. (4) Sometimes, responsibility for a service is assumed by the federal government because it has not

[3] *Brown* v. *Maryland*, 12 Wheaton 419 (1827); *Charles River Bridge* v. *Warren Bridge*, 11 Peters 420 (1837); *Cooley* v. *Board of Wardens of Port of Philadelphia*, 12 Howard 299 (1852).

been met by the states. This is why Washington went into the business of conserving natural resources and providing social security. (5) The federal government can raise more money than the states. There is no constitutional limit on its power to borrow. And it can reach the larger incomes with progressive taxes, wherever their possessors may reside. As a result, it has been in a stronger position than the states to finance additional activities. (6) Each of these factors makes for centralization. But the great centralizers are war and depression. And war, depression, and war, since 1917, have contributed heavily to the growth of federal activities.

In some cases, common programs have been undertaken in regions larger than the separate states without concentrating their management in Washington. Three means of doing this have been devised. (1) The federal government has made grants, when matched by state appropriations, laying down certain conditions, but leaving detailed administration to the states. This method has been used in building roads, in providing low-rent housing, and in giving assistance to dependent children and the aged. (2) The federal government has imposed a tax, but granted exemptions where states have levied a comparable tax to finance a specified activity. It was through the tax offset device that unemployment insurance systems were set up in the several states. (3) The Constitution, in Article I, Section 10, forbids the states to enter into compacts with one another without the consent of Congress. In certain cases, this consent has been obtained. Interstate compacts have governed the sharing of water rights on lakes and rivers and provided for curtailment of the production of petroleum. They might well have been used with greater frequency had not interpretation allowed so broad a scope to federal powers.

The Separation of Powers

Within the state and federal governments, distinct responsibilities are traditionally assigned to three separate branches: the enactment of laws to the legislature, their enforcement to the executive, and their interpretation to the judiciary. Under the constitutions, these branches are equal. None has authority over the others, but each of them can check the others. The executive can veto a bill passed by the legislature. The legislature can pass it over his veto. The courts can change its meaning by interpretation. The legislature can revise the law, restating its former purpose, and pass it again. The executive may change the complexion of the courts when he appoints new judges. But these appointments must be confirmed by the upper house of the legislature. Through such checks and balances, protection is afforded against precipitate and ill-considered action and against the arbitrary exercise of power.

Though the three branches of government are equal, the courts have succeeded in establishing their own supremacy in one respect. The state courts can find a local ordinance or a state law to be in violation of the state or federal constitutions; in interpreting a state constitution, the highest court in the state is the final authority. The federal courts can find state or federal laws to be in violation of the federal constitution, and here the Supreme Court of the United States is the final authority. The power of the Supreme Court to invalidate state laws is clearly indicated in the provision of Article VI that the Constitution itself, and the enactments of the Congress, shall be the supreme law of the land. Its power to invalidate federal legislation was not mentioned in the Constitution but asserted by the Court in the historic case of *Marbury* v. *Madison* in 1803.[4] In the words of Justice Marshall, "an act of the legislature, repugnant to the Constitution, is void. . . ." The doctrine of judicial supremacy, thus established, now has behind it the prestige of tradition and the force of popular support.

The practice of government departs in another respect from the nominal pattern of three coequal branches each with a distinctive duty to perform. The legislature has been forced, by the increasing complexity of the problems with which it must deal, to delegate authority to the executive. It may assert the broad outlines of a policy, but must leave it to administration to fill in the details. In doing so, it confers the power to legislate. Executive agencies—departments and commissions—may issue rules and regulations that come to have the force of law. They may perform judicial functions, too, hearing complaints and rendering decisions, subject to appeal, in much the manner of a lower court. They thus combine, in varying degrees, the work of the administrator, the legislator, and the judge.

The blueprint of governmental organization is further complicated by the independent status usually accorded the regulatory commission. It is located within the executive branch. Its members are appointed by the governor or the President. But usually they may not be removed except for serious misconduct. And their terms of office may be so arranged as to make it difficult for him readily to obtain a majority committed to his policies. The independent commission is dependent on the executive to initiate its appointments, on the legislature to provide its powers and appropriations, on the judiciary to interpret its statute and enforce its rules. Sometimes described as a fourth branch of government, it is still a creature of the other three.

Constitutional Safeguards for Individual Rights

In both state and federal constitutions, the rights of citizens are protected against invasion by the acts of governments. State constitutions limit state action, some of them setting forth restrictions in elaborate detail, all of them safeguarding the rights of person and property in general terms. The federal constitution imposes limitations on both state and federal governments. The limitations on control of business by the federal government are found in the due process clause of the Fifth Amendment and in its protection against abuse of the right of eminent domain: "No person shall . . . be deprived of life, liberty, or property without due

[4] 1 Cranch 137.

process of law; nor shall private property be taken for public use, without just compensation." This Amendment was adopted when the Constitution was ratified, as a part of the Bill of Rights. The limitations on the power of the states to exercise controls over business are contained in the contracts clause in Article I, Section 10 of the Constitution itself, "No State shall . . . pass any . . . Law impairing the Obligation of Contracts. . . ," and in the clauses contained in the Fourteenth Amendment —adopted in connection with the abolition of slavery at the time of the Civil War—which relate (1) to the privileges and immunities of citizens, (2) to due process of law, and (3) to equal protection of the laws: "No State shall make or enforce any law which shall abridge the privileges or immunities of citizens of the United States; nor shall any State deprive any person of life, liberty, or property, without due process of law; nor deny to any person within its jurisdiction the equal protection of the laws." These provisions should be memorized, together with the enumeration of Congressional powers set forth above, for it is upon them that the system of law that governs the public control of business in the United States is based.

Judicial Review

The courts are at once powerful and impotent. They can invalidate or modify an act if it is brought before them. They cannot question it if it is not. They can veto legislation or, in effect, rewrite it. But they cannot initiate a law. They must wait for someone—a public prosecutor or a private plaintiff—to sue or to appeal a suit. It is only then they can speak.

The courts interpret the Constitution and the laws, determining whether laws shall stand, by giving the Constitution one meaning or another, and giving meanings to the laws themselves. In the process of interpretation, they follow precedents. But the precedents on both sides of an issue may be so numerous that judges are free to pick and choose. The Supreme Court of the United States, moreover, does not consider itself to be bound by earlier decisions. It may overrule them explicitly; it may do so silently; it may reverse them, in actuality, while arguing persuasively that it has made no change. The last word spoken by the last court, at any moment, is the law.

Interpretation has seemed to be narrow, ambiguous, and inconsistent, shifting and even reversing its direction from time to time. This may be true, in part, because judges are influenced by their background, training, and social outlook, because the Supreme Court, as Mr. Dooley once remarked, "follows th' illiction returns," and because the composition of the Court has changed. With the replacement (or conversion) of a single judge, the minority in a 5 to 4 division may form a majority in the next 5 to 4 vote. It is true, too, because decisions are handed down in specific cases, where issues may differ in detail, because differences in skill of presentation may lead to different judgments on similar facts, and because the courts confine themselves to narrow issues, leaving the way open to arrive at different decisions on the basis of somewhat different facts. It is true, finally, because the problems brought to judgment are complex and confusing, because lawyers and judges—and economists—fail to understand them, and because the answers, at best, are far from clear. It is easy to berate the judiciary, more difficult to fulfill the duties of a judge.

JUDICIAL LIMITATIONS ON CONTROL

When the validity of a law or an order regulating business is questioned, the courts may decide against it on any one of several grounds. They may find that the government enacting it has exceeded its powers: that a state has attempted to control an industry that is in interstate commerce, that the federal government has attempted to control one that is not, that it has made improper use of its taxing power, or gone beyond its power to make treaties or its power to wage war. They may hold that the separation of governmental functions has been disregarded: that the executive branch has acted without legislative authority, or that the legislature has made an undue delegation of powers. They may conclude that the safeguards of individual rights have been violated: that property has been taken without just compensation, that contracts have been impaired, that persons have been denied equality of treatment, or deprived of liberty or property without due process, whether by the procedures employed in a law's administration or by the substance of the law itself. The courts thus have wide latitude in passing judgment on controls established and administered by other branches of the government, and they have used it, from time to time, with varying effects.

Interstate Commerce

The Supreme Court first defined the word "commerce" in the case of *Gibbons* v. *Ogden*[5] in 1824. The scope it gave the term was broad. Commerce, said Justice Marshall, "is traffic, but it is something more. . . . It describes the commercial intercourse between nations and parts of nations, in all its branches. . . ." The concept was thus extended beyond the act of buying and selling across state lines to comprehend all of the processes through which trade is carried on. The Court applied it specifically to navigation in the Gibbons case, and to other forms of transportation and communications in cases decided in 1872 and 1877.[6] But it has gone much farther. In 1871 it upheld federal regulation of a steamer carrying goods between two ports in Michigan on the ground that the out-of-state origin and destination of these goods made the vessel "an instrument" of interstate commerce.[7] In 1914 it permitted the federal government to fix rail-

[5] 9 Wheaton 1.

[6] *Railway* v. *Van Husen*, 95 U.S. 465 (1872); *Pensacola Tel. Co.* v. *Western Union*, 96 U.S. 1 (1877).

[7] *Steamer Daniel Bell* v. *U.S.*, 10 Wallace 557.

way rates between points within the borders of a state because this traffic bore "such a close and substantial relation to interstate traffic that the control is essential or appropriate."[8] And in 1922 it approved the regulation of grain elevators and stockyards, saying that such enterprises, though tied to one location, were situated in the "stream" or "flow" of commerce.[9]

The trend of opinion, in these decisions, favored the federal government. But federal controls, in other cases, were limited in scope or completely outlawed, for many years, through narrow interpretations of the commerce clause. Thus, in 1887 and in 1895, the Court ruled that manufacturing was not commerce, excluding the entire area from the scope of federal power.[10] In 1918 it invalidated a law prohibiting interstate shipment of the products of child labor, on the ground that their production was not interstate.[11] In 1935 it found the National Industrial Recovery Act to be unconstitutional, for one reason, because the relation between industries covered by NRA codes, on the one hand, and interstate commerce, on the other, was remote.[12] And in 1936, invalidating a law providing for wage and price fixing in the coal industry, the Court asserted that the federal government could not control an intrastate activity unless its effect on interstate commerce was not merely "close and substantial," but "direct."[13]

The restrictive effect of these decisions was sharply reversed in 1937, when the Court upheld the constitutionality of the National Labor Relations Act. This law, requiring collective bargaining and giving a federal board the power to deal with unfair labor practices, was challenged by companies manufacturing steel, trailers, and men's clothing. In each case the Court held that the law applied.[14] Congress cannot be held powerless to regulate, said Chief Justice Hughes, "when industries organize themselves on a national scale, making their relation to interstate commerce the dominant factor in their activities. . . ." In later decisions the law was also held to cover a cannery that shipped only a third of its output to other states[15] and a power company that sold an insignificant fraction of its current across state lines.[16] In 1941 the Court went on to approve the Fair Labor Standards Act, a law forbidding interstate shipment of goods made by persons paid less than legally determined wages or required to work for more than legally determined hours, thus reversing the position it had taken in 1918, when the same method was used to eliminate child labor.[17] And

[8] *The Shreveport Rate Cases*, 234 U.S. 342.

[9] *Lemke* v. *Farmers Grain Co.*, 258 U.S. 50 (1922); *Stafford* v. *Wallace*, 258 U.S. 495 (1922).

[10] *Kidd* v. *Pearson*, 128 U.S. 1 (1887); *U.S.* v. *E. C. Knight Co.*, 156 U.S. 1 (1895).

[11] *Hammer* v. *Dagenhart*, 247 U.S. 251.

[12] *Schechter* v. *U.S.*, 295 U.S. 495.

[13] *Carter* v. *Carter Coal Co.*, 298 U.S. 238.

[14] *NLRB* v. *Jones & Laughlin Steel Corp.*, 301 U.S. 1; *NLRB* v. *Freuhauf Trailer Co.*, 301 U.S. 49; *NLRB* v. *Friedman–Harry Marks Clothing Co.*, 301 U.S. 58.

[15] *Santa Cruz Packing Co.* v. *NLRB*, 303 U.S. 453 (1938).

[16] *Consolidated Edison Co.* v. *NLRB*, 305 U.S. 197 (1938).

[17] *U.S.* v. *Darby Lumber Co.*, 312 U.S. 100.

in 1942, it upheld the Agricultural Adjustment Act of 1938, which enabled the federal government to control the quantity of a crop that a farmer could offer for sale.[18] In this decision, the Court explicitly rejected the rule it had laid down in the case of the coal industry in 1936: "Even if the appellee's activity be local and though it may not be regarded as commerce, it may still, whatever its nature, be reached by Congress if it exerts a substantial economic effect on interstate commerce, and this irrespective of whether such effect is what might at some earlier time have been defined as 'direct' or 'indirect.' "[19] In 1944 the Court upheld the application of a federal statute to the insurance business[20] and in 1945 to retail trade.[21] It thus appears that the interpretation of the commerce clause is no longer likely to impose significant limits on federal power.

The clause may still be used, however, to reject regulation by the states. Laws that incidentally affect interstate commerce are usually allowed to stand. But those that unduly burden or obstruct it may be found to trespass on federal authority. And where state and federal regulations overlap, those of the federal government are given precedence and those of the states must be made to conform.[22]

The General Welfare

The Supreme Court has shown no desire to restrict the activities of the federal government under its war or treaty powers. It has, however, rejected efforts by Congress, made under cover of its power to tax, to impose controls for which it had no other authority. The Constitution gives Congress the power "To lay and collect Taxes . . . and provide for the common Defence and general Welfare. . . ." But the Court long held that this reference to the general welfare conferred no power in itself, but merely described the purposes for which tax money would be used. It did not object to the imposition of taxes to check the sale of oleomargarine,[23] narcotics,[24] or firearms,[25] accepting the fiction that the levies were intended as a source of revenue. But in 1922 it branded as unconstitutional a second Congressional attempt to outlaw child labor, this time by taxing the profits of the children's employers.[26] In 1936 it nullified the Agricultural Adjustment Act of 1933 on the ground that collection of taxes from processors and payment of benefits to producers of agricultural commodities, in order to curtail their output, involved the use of taxation not for revenue but in the interest of a special group, in order to exercise control where power

[18] *Wickard* v. *Filburn,* 317 U.S. 111.

[19] *Ibid.,* p. 125.

[20] *U.S.* v. *South-Eastern Underwriters,* 322 U.S. 533.

[21] *U.S.* v. *Frankfort Distilleries,* 324 U.S. 293.

[22] *The Shreveport Rate Cases,* 234 U.S. 342.

[23] *McCray* v. *U.S.,* 195 U.S. 27 (1904).

[24] *U.S.* v. *Doremus,* 249 U.S. 87 (1919).

[25] *Sonzinsky* v. *U.S.,* 300 U.S. 506.

[26] *Bailey* v. *Drexel Furniture Co.,* 259 U.S. 20.

had not been delegated to Congress but reserved to the states.[27] And in the same year, in rejecting regulation of the coal industry, the Court denounced the effort to compel adherence to minimum wages and prices by taxing producers who did not co-operate in the program and exempting those who did.[28]

With the tax power, as with the commerce power, interpretation was reversed in 1937. In that year the Court was called upon to consider two programs of social insurance adopted under the Social Security Act of 1935. In the first, the federal government induced the states to enact unemployment insurance laws by taxing payrolls and allowing an offset where the states imposed such taxes to finance insurance benefits. In the second, it levied further taxes on wages and payrolls but obligated itself to pay annuities to wage earners upon their retirement from work. Each of these programs was held to be constitutional. Under the first, said Justice Cardozo, the tax was legitimate as a source of revenue, and the offset did not involve coercion of the states, in contravention of the Constitution, but merely afforded a temptation to co-operate.[29] Under the second, the taxes were again legitimate, and the decision of Congress to provide benefits for the aged lay within its power to spend for the general welfare. The concept of welfare, said Justice Cardozo, is not a static one; it changes with the times. Its content is for Congress to decide. The courts will not interfere "unless the choice is clearly wrong, a display of arbitrary power, not an exercise of judgment."[30] The power to control by taxing and spending, in consequence, is virtually unlimited.

The police power, as we have seen, was retained by the several states. Nowhere in the Constitution or in the decisions of the courts is this power given to the federal government. But Congress has none the less acted, under the authority of its other powers, to protect public safety, health, and morals, and to promote the general welfare. In addition to taxing oleo, narcotics, and firearms and providing insurance benefits, it has also excluded fradulent and obscene materials from the mails and prohibited the interstate movement of lottery tickets, stolen automobiles, and women for immoral purposes. It has used its powers, too, to insure the purity of foods and drugs, to enforce grain standards and plant quarantines, to improve conditions of labor, and to prevent misrepresentation in the distribution of securities. As a result, reference is sometimes made to the police powers of the federal government. Strictly speaking, no such powers exist. But their absence, today, presents no handicap.

Powers of the Executive

Action may be reversed not only because it exceeds the powers conferred upon the government, but also because it violates the separation of

[27] *U.S.* v. *Butler* (the Hoosac Mills case), 297 U.S. 1.

[28] *Carter* v. *Carter Coal Co.*, 298 U.S. 238.

[29] *Steward Machine Co.* v. *Davis*, 301 U.S. 548.

[30] *Helvering* v. *Davis*, 301 U.S. 619.

powers. It may be found that the executive branch has gone beyond its own authority, or that the legislative branch has gone too far in delegating authority to the executive.

On April 8, 1952, in order to prevent a strike, President Truman seized the steel mills. When a district court injunction staying this action was carried to the Supreme Court, the government did not contend that it was authorized by any legislation then in force, but argued that it fell within the inherent powers of the President. This argument was rejected by the Court. Said Justice Black,

> In the framework of our Constitution, the President's power to see that the laws are faithfully executed refutes the idea that he is to be a lawmaker. The Constitution limits his functions in the lawmaking process to the recommending of laws he thinks wise and the vetoing of laws he thinks bad. And the Constitution is neither silent nor equivocal about who shall make laws which the President is to execute. The first section of the first article says that "All legislative powers herein granted shall be vested in a Congress. . . ."
>
> The President's order does not direct that a Congressional policy be executed in a manner prescribed by Congress—it directs that a Presidential policy be executed in a manner prescribed by the President . . . The founders of this nation entrusted the lawmaking power to the Congress alone in both good times and bad . . . [T]his seizure order cannot stand.[31]

It does not appear, from the positions taken by the several justices, that executive action said to be justified by inherent powers will never be upheld. But it is clear that seizure is not permitted in time of peace unless authorized by Congress.

In 1935 the National Industrial Recovery Act was twice found to be unconstitutional, not only because it went beyond the authority conferred by the interstate commerce clause, but also because it involved an excessive delegation of legislative powers. In the first case, Section 9-c of the Act, permitting the President to prevent interstate shipment of oil produced in excess of state quotas, was rejected because Congress had neither set forth a statement of policy nor prescribed standards of behavior but had left unfettered discretion to the executive.[32] The second case was broader in scope, involving the NRA program as a whole. This program permitted the President to approve codes, prepared by trade associations, for the government of their respective industries. It was found to involve a virtual abdication of Congressional authority. The Act, said Justice Hughes, "does not undertake to prescribe rules of conduct to be applied to particular states of fact determined by appropriate administrative procedure. Instead of prescribing rules of conduct, it authorizes the making of codes to prescribe them." Under this procedure, said Justice Cardozo, "anything that Congress may do within the limits of the commerce clause for the betterment of business may be done by the President upon the recom-

[31] *Youngstown Sheet and Tube Co.* v. *Sawyer*, 343 U.S. 579 (1952).

[32] *Panama Refining Co.* v. *Ryan*, 293 U.S. 388.

mendation of a trade association by calling it a code. This is delegation running riot." The program was rejected by a unanimous court.[33]

In most cases where the delegation of power has been questioned, it has been upheld. Congress, in general, is permitted to delegate where it states its purposes and lays down rules to limit the exercise of delegated powers.[34]

The Obligation of Contracts

State laws impairing contracts may be invalidated under Article I, Section 10 of the Constitution. Federal laws having the same effect may be held to be in violation of the due process clause of the Fifth Amendment. The safeguards against impairment apply both to private contracts and to those to which a government is a party, such as charters and franchises. They do not apply to commitments that are lacking in consideration or to contracts involving commitments that are contrary to public policy. The safeguards are not absolute. Impairment is permitted when incidental to legislation enacted under the police powers of a state. The only condition laid down by the courts is that the end sought by a law must be legitimate and the means employed appropriate. This interpretation is inescapable, since, in its absence, a multitude of contracts would bar the enactment of legislation in the public interest.

One of the most serious issues that has arisen here relates to the constitutionality of laws giving relief to debtors in periods of business depression. Such laws do impair the obligation of contracts. But they may also preserve human values and social stability in times of stress and strain. Here the Supreme Court has applied the test of reasonableness, upholding laws that postponed payments for a limited period but compensated the creditor for his loss, and invalidating those that seemed to go too far in depriving the creditor of his rights.[35]

Any Person

The Fifth Amendment forbade the federal government to deprive any *person* of life, liberty, or property without due process of law, and the Fourteenth Amendment forbade the states (1) to abridge the privileges or immunities of *citizens*, (2) to deprive any *person* of life, liberty, or property without due process of law, and (3) to deny to any *person* the equal protection of the laws. The clause relating to privileges and immunities

[33] *Schechter* v. *U.S.*, 295 U.S. 495.

[34] See *U.S.* v. *Shreveport Grain & Elevator Co.*, 287 U.S. 77 (1932), upholding the Food and Drug Act; *U.S.* v. *Rock Royal Cooperative*, 307 U.S. 533 (1939), upholding the Agricultural Marketing Agreements Act; *Yakus* v. *U.S.*, 321 U.S. 414 (1944), upholding the Emergency Price Control Act; *American Power & Light Co.* v. *SEC*, 329 U.S. 90 (1946), upholding the Public Utility Holding Company Act; and *Lichter* v. *U.S.*, 332 U.S. 742 (1948), upholding the renegotiation of war contracts.

[35] *Home Building & Loan Assn.* v. *Blaisdell*, 290 U.S. 398 (1933), upholding the Minnesota moratorium law, and *Louisville Joint Stock Land Bank* v. *Radford*, 295 U.S. 955 (1935), invalidating the Frazier-Lemke Act.

has never been employed to limit regulation of business, since business units have not been held to qualify as *citizens*. But the other clauses have been so employed, ever since the Supreme Court decreed, in 1886, that a corporation is a *person*. In 1873, when a corporation challenged a Louisiana law zoning slaughter house locations, the Court had rejected this interpretation, and Justice Miller had expressed the view that the Fourteenth Amendment would never be used for any purpose other than its obvious one of protecting the Negro against discrimination.[36] But thirteen years later, in the case of *Santa Clara County* v. *Southern Pacific Railway*,[37] the Court extended the scope of the two amendments to cover corporate enterprise. This position was challenged, as recently as 1938, by Justice Black, who stated flatly, in a dissenting opinion, "I do not believe that the word 'person' in the Fourteenth Amendment includes corporations."[38] But this was not the view of the majority; the rule of 1886 still stands.

When applied to corporations, the clause assuring equal protection has been used to invalidate laws that discriminate against one business in favor of another. But this clause has not been so interpreted as to prevent distinctions based on principles of classification that are not arbitrary or capricious. The Supreme Court has thus upheld a minimum wage law for women, in Arizona, that exempted railway restaurants,[39] a tax on retail stores, in Indiana, that was graduated in accordance with the number of stores in a chain,[40] and a federal tax on payrolls that did not apply to employers with fewer than eight employees.[41] The equal protection clause, moreover, adds little to the safeguards of the law. For where a measure is rejected as discriminatory, it can also be found to violate due process. It is under the heading of due process that the most serious restrictions on public control have been imposed.

Liberty or Property

The liberty that is guaranteed by the due process clause has been held by the Supreme Court to include the freedom to enter into contracts. And the preservation of this freedom has been advanced by the Court, from time to time in the past, as its reason for rejecting laws that provided for the establishment of maximum hours and minimum wages. In 1905 the provisions of a New York law limiting the hours of bakers to ten per day or sixty per week were denounced as "mere meddlesome interferences with the rights of the individual."[42] But in 1908 an Oregon law limiting the hours of women was upheld on the ground that the state, under its police

[36] *The Slaughter House Cases*, 16 Wallace 36.

[37] 118 U.S. 394.

[38] *Connecticut General Life Insurance Co.* v. *Johnson*, 303 U.S. 77, 85.

[39] *Dominion Hotel* v. *Arizona*, 249 U.S. 265 (1919).

[40] *Indiana* v. *Jackson*, 283 U.S. 527 (1937).

[41] *Steward Machine Co.* v. *Davis*, 301 U.S. 548 (1937).

[42] *Lochner* v. *New York*, 198 U.S. 45.

powers, might safeguard the health of mothers in order to preserve the health of the community.[43] And in 1917 an Oregon law establishing a ten hour daily limit for men as well as women, in factories, was also upheld as falling within the police powers of the state.[44] In 1923, however, the Court invalidated a law fixing minimum wages for women in the District of Columbia. The differences between the sexes, said Justice Sutherland, "have now come almost if not quite to the vanishing point." Consequently, "we cannot accept the doctrine that women of mature age *sui juris* require or may be subjected to restrictions upon their liberty of contract. . . ."[45] And again in 1936, in the Tipaldo case,[46] a New York law fixing minimum wages for women was overthrown, by a 5 to 4 decision, on the same ground.

On this point, as on others, the Court reversed itself in 1937, its decision in the Parrish case[47] upholding a Washington law providing minimum wages for women. Said Justice Hughes, "The Constitution does not speak of freedom of contract. It speaks of liberty and prohibits the deprivation of liberty without due process of law. In prohibiting that deprivation, the Constitution does not recognize an absolute and uncontrollable liberty . . . The liberty safeguarded is liberty in a social organization which requires the protection of law against the evils which menace the health, safety, morals and welfare of the people." The Parrish decision, also rendered by a 5 to 4 vote, came but a few months after the decision in the Tipaldo case. There had been no change in the composition of the Court. There had been a change, however, in the mind of Mr. Justice Roberts.

To prevent persons (i.e. human beings) from being deprived of *liberty* without due process, it is no longer held that men and women must work for long hours at low pay. But to prevent persons (i.e. corporations) from being deprived of *property* without due process, it is still held that measures affecting the size of corporate incomes or the value of corporate assets, if questioned, must have the approval of the courts. And it is here that the due process clause has found its major use.

Affected with a Public Interest

Recognizing the necessity of approving regulation of the services rendered and the prices charged by natural monopolies, but unwilling to permit extension of such controls, under the due process clause, to industry in general, the Supreme Court, in 1877, hit upon the device of establishing a separate category of businesses affected with a public interest, and confining regulation to those that it might so define. In the famous case of *Munn* v. *Illinois*,[48] decided in that year, the Court approved a law, enacted

[43] *Muller* v. *Oregon*, 208 U.S. 412.

[44] *Bunting* v. *Oregon*, 243 U.S. 426.

[45] *Adkins* v. *Children's Hospital*, 261 U.S. 525.

[46] *Morehead* v. *New York ex rel Tipaldo*, 298 U.S. 587.

[47] *West Coast Hotel Co.* v. *Parrish*, 300 U.S. 379.

[48] 94 U.S. 113.

by the State of Illinois, controlling the charges made by grain elevators and warehouses. In the words of its opinion, "Property does become clothed with a public interest when used in a manner to make it of public consequence, and affect the community at large. When, therefore, one devotes his property to a use in which the public has an interest, he, in effect, grants to the public an interest in that use, and must submit to be controlled by the public for the common good. . . ." The elevators along the Chicago waterfront were found to stand "in the very gateway of commerce, and take toll from all who pass." It was permissible, therefore, that they be regulated, so that they might "take but reasonable toll."

This concept was subsequently employed in approving public regulation of such industries as the railroads, and water, gas, electric, and telephone companies. It was called upon in 1914 in upholding a Kansas law providing for the regulation of fire insurance rates.[49] But it was used for a decade to invalidate laws extending public controls to other fields. In 1923 the Court rejected a Kansas law providing for compulsory arbitration of labor disputes in basic industries;[50] in 1927, a New York law fixing the markup of theater ticket agencies,[51] in 1928, a New Jersey law regulating the fees of employment agencies;[52] in the same year, a Tennessee law controlling the price of gasoline;[53] and in 1932, an Oklahoma law restricting entry into the ice business.[54] In each of these cases, the Court, usually speaking through Justice Sutherland, held that the business concerned was not affected with a public interest. But no standards of judgment were consistently applied. Whether an industry could be regulated depended on no objective criteria, but upon the undisclosed predispositions of the members of the Court.

The concept of a peculiar category of industries affected with a public interest was abandoned in 1934 when the Court handed down its decision in the Nebbia case.[55] The State of New York had set up a milk control board and empowered it to fix the retail price of milk. The board had fixed the price at nine cents per quart. Nebbia, a grocer in Rochester, had sold two quarts for eighteen cents and thrown in a loaf of bread. When sued for violating the law, he argued that the milk business was competitive rather than monopolistic, having none of the characteristics of a public utility, and that the state was therefore powerless to regulate the prices that it charged. The Court, in a 5 to 4 decision, rejected this defense. Said Justice Roberts,

> It is clear that there is no closed class or category of businesses affected with a public interest. . . . The phrase "affected with a public interest" can,

[49] *German Alliance Insurance Co.* v. *Kansas*, 233 U.S. 389.

[50] *Wolff Packing Co.* v. *Court of Industrial Relations*, 262 U.S. 522.

[51] *Tyson* v. *Banton*, 273 U.S. 418.

[52] *Ribnik* v. *McBride*, 277 U.S. 350.

[53] *Williams* v. *Standard Oil Co.*, 278 U.S. 235.

[54] *New State Ice Co.* v. *Liebmann*, 282 U.S. 262.

[55] *Nebbia* v. *New York*, 291 U.S. 502.

in the nature of things, mean no more than that an industry, for adequate reason, is subject to control for the public good. . . . So far as the requirement of due process is concerned . . . a state is free to adopt whatever economic policy may reasonably be deemed to promote public welfare. . . . If the laws passed are seen to have a reasonable relation to a proper legislative purpose, and are neither arbitrary nor discriminatory, the requirements of due process are satisfied. . . .

Having thus broken with the past, the Court went on, in the next few years, to uphold a state law fixing the charges of tobacco warehouses,[56] federal laws requiring inspection of tobacco,[57] restricting the quantities of tobacco that could be marketed,[58] providing for the establishment of minimum prices for milk,[59] and providing—a second time—for minimum prices for bituminous coal,[60] and a state law curtailing the output of petroleum.[61] This legislation, arising largely from conditions of business depression, carried state and federal governments into new regions of control. Its approval by the Court removed a major barrier to the further extension of regulatory activity.

Due Process: Procedural and Substantive

The concept of due process originally had to do with the criminal law. Its extension to administration was a later development. In recent times, however, the courts have evolved a set of rules to govern the procedures of administrative agencies. Such agencies must have jurisdiction over the matters with which they deal. They must give fair hearings to all persons affected by their rulings. They must give adequate notice of such hearings well in advance of the dates when they are held. Their officers must be impartial, with no personal interest in the questions upon which they are called to pass. Their decisions must be based upon substantial evidence. In the orders they issue, specific findings of law and fact must be set forth. The persons affected by such orders must be given an opportunity to appeal. This is due process, in the procedural sense of the term.

Such safeguards against arbitrary administrative action are clearly in the public interest. There is danger, however, that administrative agencies might come to be so bound by procedural requirements that it would be impossible for them to operate efficiently. This danger is illustrated by two decisions handed down by the Supreme Court. In the first,[62] where the Secretary of Agriculture had issued an order on the advice of a trial ex-

[56] *Townsend* v. *Yeomans*, 301 U.S. 441 (1937).
[57] *Currin* v. *Wallace*, 306 U.S. 1 (1939).
[58] *Mulford* v. *Smith*, 307 U.S. 38 (1939).
[59] *U.S.* v. *Rock Royal Cooperative*, 307 U.S. 533 (1939).
[60] *Sunshine Anthracite Coal Co.* v. *Adkins*, 310 U.S. 381 (1940).
[61] *R.R. Commission* v. *Rowan & Nichols Oil Co.*, 310 U.S. 573 (1940).
[62] *Morgan* v. *U.S.*, 298 U.S. 468 (1936).

aminer, following extensive hearings, the Court complained that the Secretary had not himself read each of the 13,000 pages of testimony and 1,000 pages of exhibits in the transcript. In the second,[63] it invalidated one of the Secretary's orders on the grounds that the respondents had not received a copy of the trial examiner's intermediate report in time to use it in preparing their final brief. Whatever the merits of these two cases, it is clear that administration might well be put in a strait jacket if the courts were too meticulous in their insistence on form.

In the name of due process, the courts have gone on to interest themselves not only in form but also in substance. Instead of confining themselves to determining whether administrative orders were based upon sufficient evidence, they have arrived at independent judgments by going into the evidence themselves. From a review of questions of law they have slipped over into a review of questions of fact. When the Supreme Court upheld state regulation of public utility rates, in *Munn* v. *Illinois* in 1877, it did not attempt to pass upon the rates themselves. But in 1886 the Court issued a warning that the "power to regulate is not a power to destroy."[64] In 1890 it asserted that "the reasonableness of a rate . . . is eminently a question for judicial investigation."[65] And in 1898, in the historic case of *Smyth* v. *Ames*[66] (to be considered at length in Chapter 18), it enumerated the matters of substance that commissions would be required to take into consideration in fixing rates in order to give assurance that due process had been observed. From then on for nearly half a century the Court undertook to pass judgment, not only on the procedures employed in rate making, but also on the legitimacy of the rates themselves.

This position was substantially modified by the decisions handed down in the Natural Gas Pipeline and Hope Natural Gas cases[67] in 1942 and 1944. Said the Court, in the first of these cases, "The Constitution does not bind rate-making bodies to the service of any single formula or combination of formulas. . . . Once a fair hearing has been given, proper findings made, and other statutory requirements satisfied, the courts cannot intervene in the absence of a clear showing that the limits of due process have been overstepped. If the Commission's order, as applied to the facts before it and viewed in its entirety, produces no arbitrary result, our inquiry is at an end."[68] The boundaries of court review were thus narrowed by judicial self-restraint. Concern with the end result was not abandoned, but the presumption was made to run in favor of the substantive determinations of administrative agencies.

[63] *Morgan* v. *U.S.*, 304 U.S. 1 (1948).

[64] *Stone* v. *Farmers' Loan & Trust Co.*, 166 U.S. 307.

[65] *Chicago, Milwaukee & St. Paul Rwy.* v. *Minnesota,* 134 U.S. 418.

[66] 169 U.S. 466.

[67] *FPC* v. *Natural Gas Pipeline Co.*, 315 U.S. 575; *FPC* v. *Hope Natural Gas Co.*, 320 U.S. 591.

[68] 315 U.S. 586.

Ownership and Operation

Although the courts have handicapped the federal, state, and local governments in their efforts to preserve the system of private enterprise through the maintenance of competition and the regulation of monopoly, they have interposed no obstacles to public ownership. If a government seeks to socialize an existing private business whose owners do not wish to sell, it may do so by exercising the sovereign right of eminent domain. Under federal and state constitutions, the usual limitations are that the property must be taken for public use, and that just compensation must be paid. The courts have shown little disposition to question legislative judgment as to public use, or to check acquisition of property by supporting an unconscionable price. If a government goes into business by obtaining the assets of a private company through voluntary sale, or by itself constructing new facilities, the constitutional limits are those upon its power to spend. And these require only that expenditures be made for a public purpose or to promote the general welfare. The projects challenged on this basis have invariably been upheld.[69] The courts for many years strained at the gnat of public regulation and swallowed the camel of public ownership.

The Changing Constitution

For the better part of a century the Supreme Court raised no serious barriers to the expansion of public authority. From the founding of the republic to the end of the Civil War it declared only two acts of the Congress to be unconstitutional. It approved the granger legislation of the seventies, including the regulation of services and rates. But from the middle eighties until the middle thirties, a period of fifty years, the Court made of the Constitution an instrument with which to impose upon the country the philosophy of *laissez faire*. It restricted the regulatory powers of government, extended to corporate enterprise the guarantees of personal freedom, and transformed procedural safeguards into substantive restraints. The conservatism of the courts, during this period, led to repeated demands for judicial reform. It was Theodore Roosevelt who proposed, in 1912, that decisions declaring laws unconstitutional should be subject to reversal by popular vote.

In the middle thirties, as has been noted again and again in the preceding pages, interpretation of the Constitution was sharply changed. Between 1933 and 1937 a dozen federal laws and more than fifty state laws were invalidated by the Supreme Court, including some of the major legislation of the New Deal—the Railroad Retirement Act, providing the

[69] See *Jones* v. *City of Portland*, 246 U.S. 217 (1917); *Green* v. *Frazier*, 253 U.S. 233 (1920); *Standard Oil Co.* v. *City of Lincoln*, 275 U.S. 504 (1927); *Puget Sound Power & Light Co.* v. *Seattle*, 291 U.S. 619 (1934); *Ashwander* v. *TVA*, 297 U.S. 288 (1936); *Tennessee Electric Power Co.* v. *TVA*, 306 U.S. 118 (1939); *Oklahoma* v. *Atkinson Co.*, 313 U.S. 508 (1941).

first federal program of social insurance, the National Industrial Recovery Act, the Agricultural Adjustment Act of 1933, and the Bituminous Coal Conservation Act, and also the New York minimum wage law for women. In February, 1937, following his re-election, Franklin D. Roosevelt asked the Congress, in effect, to empower him to add as many as six new judges to the bench, thus turning its hostile majority into a powerless minority. This proposal evoked a violent storm of protest, and the power he asked was not obtained. Within the next two years, however, five vacancies occurred through death or retirement, and Mr. Roosevelt had appointed a majority of the justices. But the course of interpretation had been reversed before the first of these appointments was made. In March, 1937 the minimum wage law of the State of Washington was upheld, two weeks later the National Labor Relations Act, and two months later the Social Security Act. The President had lost—and won—his fight.

Since 1937 the courts have shown but little resistance to the application of controls. The institution of judicial review has been preserved by the exercise of moderation in its use.

SUGGESTIONS FOR FURTHER READING

One of the best statements of the institutional and legal background of public controls is contained in J. M. Clark, *Social Control of Business* (2d ed.; New York: McGraw-Hill Book Co., 1939), particularly chaps. v, vi, vii, x, and xiv. See also George A. Steiner, *Government's Role in Economic Life* (New York: McGraw-Hill Book Co., 1953), chaps. iv and v. A discussion of the structure of government as it relates to the exercise of controls will be found in any of the standard texts on American government. This matter is also treated in Melvin Anshen and Francis D. Wormuth, *Private Enterprise and Public Policy* (New York: Macmillan Co., 1954), chaps. ii and iii. In this volume, see also chap. vi on franchises, licenses, etc., and chap. ix on taxation as a regulatory device. A number of authors have dealt with constitutional limitations on public controls. A recent book, and a thorough one, is Franklin H. Cook, *Principles of Business and the Federal Law* (New York: Macmillan Co., 1951). Part I of this book deals with "Constitutional Principles," Part II with "Due Process of Law," and Part III with "The Commerce Clause."

PART II

Maintaining Competition

Chapter 3 THE ANTITRUST LAWS

Government, confronted by the problem of monopoly, may follow one of four courses. First, it may take no action, trusting the public interest to be served by the voluntary choice of the monopolist. Second, it may seek to break up existing monopolies and to prevent the formation of new monopolies, protecting the public interest by restoring and preserving the force of competition. Third, it may acquiesce in the existence of monopoly and seek to safeguard the public interest by regulating the services rendered and the prices charged by the monopolist. Fourth, it may take monopoly into public ownership.

There are dangers, for a society that values freedom, progress, and plenty, in a policy of *laissez faire*. Freedom demands ready access to markets; monopoly excludes newcomers from pre-empted fields. Progress requires hospitality to innovation—to new products and processes, new materials and methods, new blood and new ideas. Monopoly emphasizes the security of fixed investments; it protects existing ways of doing things; it resists change. Plenty depends upon continuous expansion of output; monopoly may augment its profits by restricting the production of goods and services. If freedom is to be preserved, progress encouraged, and plenty achieved, monopoly must be prevented or subjected to control. Government must make its choice between the maintenance of competition and the extension of public regulation or public ownership.

It is the stated policy of the government of the United States to prevent monopoly and to maintain a competitive economy. This policy, it must be admitted, has not been pursued consistently, continuously, or comprehensively. It has been accompanied by measures, such as the tariff and the patent system, that have operated to check competition and to promote monopoly. It has been abandoned temporarily in time of business depression and in time of war. In the case of public utilities it has given way to the administrative regulation of monopoly. In other cases it has been modified by excepting certain practices and by granting exemptions to particular industries. But despite these qualifications, the maintenance of competition has been and still remains a dominant goal of public policy.

America has stood almost alone in its official opposition to monopoly. It is only in Canada, among industrial nations, that a similar policy has been pursued. In Germany, France, Belgium, Holland, Italy, and elsewhere in Europe, before the second World War, public policy supported the organization of major industries into giant combines and the regulation of production and trade by powerful cartels. In Japan, where industrialism had been imposed upon a feudal society, control of business remained in the hands of a few great families. In Great Britain, where the growth of monopoly had long been impeded by competition from abroad, free trade was abandoned in 1932, and government subsequently acquiesced in the rapid cartelization of the domestic economy. International trade, among these nations and between them and the rest of the world, was controlled by supranational cartels.

In many of these countries industrial structure and public policy have undergone some modification since the war. In Germany and Japan the occupying powers have undertaken to break up the prewar cartels. In Great Britain and in some of the countries of Western Europe, tentative steps have been taken toward the suppression of monopoly. Consideration has also been given, through agencies of the United Nations, to means of eliminating the restrictive practices of international cartels. But these developments must be attributed, in large measure, to American influence in world affairs. Whether they will prove to have permanent significance remains to be seen. The policy of maintaining competition still finds its fullest expression in the antitrust laws of the United States.

HISTORICAL BACKGROUND OF THE ANTITRUST LAWS

Long before statutes condemning monopoly were enacted by state and federal legislatures, its legality was questioned in cases brought before the courts. In some of these cases the plaintiff sought to compel the defendant to adhere to the terms of a contract that limited his freedom to compete. In others, the plaintiff sued for damages, charging that he had been injured by the defendant's monopolistic practices. Judges, confronted by these issues, looked for precedents. They found them in decisions handed down by the courts of the several states, built on earlier decisions rendered by courts in the American colonies, and reaching back to still earlier decisions made by courts in England. It is through this chain of precedents, constituting the body of the common law, that rules defining the legality of monopolistic behavior first emerged.

The Common Law

In England, during the seventeenth century, the courts denounced as illegal grants of monopoly by the Crown. Their disapproval did not extend to grants conferred by Parliament, to monopolies acquired through individual effort, or to those resulting from private agreement. In the eighteenth century, however, monopolistic agreements were also condemned. Up to this time, the concept of conspiracy had been confined to cases in which the conspirators had attempted to obstruct the course of justice. But now the two concepts—monopoly and conspiracy—were brought together in the doctrine of conspiracy to monopolize. Under this doctrine a monopoly held by a single owner still remained undisturbed. But agreements to limit competition were denounced, persons injured by them were awarded damages, and the courts refused to enforce their terms.

The courts, since the fifteenth century, had also refused to enforce contracts in restraint of trade. This concept, however, had been given a narrow meaning: trade was held to be restrained when a person selling a business, a partner withdrawing from it, or an employee leaving it, agreed to refrain from competition with its purchaser, a remaining partner, or a former employer. In the eyes of the courts, such agreements were opposed to public policy because they deprived the community of the contracting party's services and restricted his freedom to follow his trade. In the eighteenth century, this rule was modified: the courts came to enforce such restrictions where they were needed to preserve the value of a business that had been sold and where they were so limited in extent and in duration as not to be unreasonable; but general restraints on former owners, partners, and employees were still held to be unenforceable.

These precedents in the common law were drawn upon, during the nineteenth century, as cases involving monopolistic agreements were brought before the courts. The doctrine of restraint of trade took on new meaning as it was extended to cover any arrangement whereby competitors sought to exclude outsiders from the market or otherwise to limit freedom to compete. From state to state decisions differed in detail. But in most jurisdictions the courts came to condemn all contracts that involved such practices as curtailment of output, division of territories, fixing of prices, and pooling of profits. And here no rule of reason was applied: these practices were held, by their very nature, to be prejudicial to the public interest, and contracts that required them were not enforced.

The maintenance of competition was thus supported by the common law. But as an instrument of public policy the common law was limited in its effectiveness. Initiative in taking action was left to plaintiffs in private suits. Where contracts were brought before the courts, refusal of enforcement weakened the position of monopoly. Where injury was proven, assessment of damages penalized monopoly. But where all of the participants in an agreement voluntarily adhered to its terms, and where no one had the courage or the means to sue for damages, no case was brought and here monopoly continued undisturbed. If competition were to be restored, in such cases, it was necessary to make provision, through legislative enactment, for public prosecution and the imposition of public penalties.

The Antitrust Movement

In the United States, during the years that followed the Civil War, the pattern of industrial organization was rapidly transformed. With the construction of a network of railways, local and regional markets gave way to markets that were national in scope. With the boundaries of markets thus extended, the scale of industrial operations was increased, production was mechanized, and small shops were displaced by large factories. As factories increased in size larger accumulations of capital were required, and the independent proprietor was supplanted by the corporation. The corporate form of organization, in turn, facilitated industrial consolidation and made for increasing concentration of control. In this situation the growth of monopoly was stimulated by a steady decline in the general level of prices, accompanied by recurring periods of business depression. Concerns with large investments, entailing heavy fixed charges, were impelled successively to slash their prices in an effort to cover some portion of their costs. Competition, on this basis, threatened to become mutually destructive, and business sought refuge in monopolistic agreements and in the combination of competing firms. This movement was stimulated, too, by the prospect of profits that were to be obtained in the process of promoting corporate reorganizations and those that were to be realized through the exercise of monopoly power. In consequence, during the 1880's, many of the country's major industries were brought under some form of concentrated control. In petroleum, cottonseed oil, linseed oil, meat packing, cordage, sugar, lead, coal, whisky, tobacco, matches, gunpowder, and elsewhere, power over markets was attained through the devices of monopoly.

As this process continued, many groups in the community—investors, small businessmen, producers of raw materials, workers, and consumers—suffered serious injury. Investors lost their savings when overcapitalization of corporate combinations prevented the payment of dividends and led, in many cases, to eventual bankruptcy. Independent businessmen, if they refused to be absorbed, were ruthlessly driven from the field. Producers of raw materials, where manufacturing was monopolized, found themselves selling to a single buyer who manipulated the market to depress the prices they received. Workers were crowded into growing cities, made dependent on industrial employment, and faced with increasing competition for uncertain jobs. Consumers, deprived of alternative sources of supply, saw prices boosted to cover the costs of overcapitalization and to provide the profits of monopoly.

All of these developments gave rise to widespread apprehension and alarm. With the growth of corporate concentration, it appeared that the welfare and the independence of the common man were threatened. With the disappearance of the frontier, it seemed that the door to opportunity was being closed. Out of these fears, there developed a strong political movement against monopoly. Finding its roots in farmers' organizations in the west and south, this movement drew support, as well, from labor unions, from consumers, and from independent businessmen. During the eighties, it brought about the formation of independent farmer-labor parties, ran an antimonopoly candidate for the presidency, elected a number of members to Congress, and came to control the legislatures of several states. As it grew in strength, the older parties sought to win the votes of its adherents by themselves professing opposition to monopoly. In this way, the movement soon achieved its purpose: antitrust laws were enacted, toward the end of the decade, by state and federal governments.

The antitrust laws owe their name to a method of business combination that has long been obsolete. In pursuit of this method, the owners of controlling shares of stock in competing corporations transferred legal title to these shares to a group of trustees, receiving trust certificates in return. The trustees then voted the stocks in all of the participating companies, electing their directors, controlling their policies, and running them, in effect, as a single enterprise. The holders of the trust certificates were entitled merely to participate in the profits of the combined concerns. This form of organization was first devised by the promoters of the Standard Oil combination in 1879; it was adopted by a number of other industries in the following decade. These combinations were properly designated as trusts. But the term was shortly generalized to cover all monopolistic combinations, whatever the devices through which they were achieved. The antimonopoly statutes were thus christened the antitrust laws. And when the trust, as a legal device, was abandoned, the word survived.

The State Antitrust Laws

Starting with Kansas in 1889, eighteen states had enacted antitrust laws by 1891. Such laws are now found on the statute books of more than forty states. These laws differ in detail: some of them forbid specific monopolistic practices, such as curtailment of output, division of markets, price fixing, and price discrimination; others condemn monopolization and agreement in restraint of trade in more general terms. The laws are enforced through suits brought by county or district attorneys under the direction of state attorneys general. They carry criminal penalties, with fines running up to $5,000 and imprisonment, typically, to one year. Provision is also made for private suits leading to the issuance of injunctions or to punitive awards of triple damages.

These laws have proved to be a feeble instrument for the prevention of monopoly. In most states, they have never really been enforced. Appropriations for enforcement have been meager. Officials have been deterred from bringing suits by the fear that such action might discourage the entry of new industries or drive existing industries to other states. State laws, at best, are limited in application; they are powerless to control agreements or combinations in major industries whose operations, extending beyond state borders, are not within their reach. There are some trades, to be sure, in which local markets may be confined within the boundaries of a single state: building construction, real estate operations, and the sale of sand and gravel, stone, and common brick; job printing, newspaper publishing, and the production of cut flowers, baked goods, beer, and ice; retailing, personal and professional services, and the operation of laundries, cleaning and dyeing establishments, garages, repair shops, theaters, restaurants, and hotels. But, even here, the laws are spasmodically enforced. The task of maintaining competition has been left, almost entirely, to the federal government.

SUBSTANTIVE PROVISIONS OF THE ANTITRUST LAWS

In the national campaign of 1888, the two major parties, while differing on the tariff, competed for the votes of farmers by professing opposition to monopoly. The Democrats, then in office, denounced the tariff as the mother of the trusts. The Republicans, proposing higher duties, replied that they could compel competition at home while preventing competition from abroad. Both party platforms promised enactment of legislation against monopoly. Following the Republican victory, President Harrison sent a message to Congress, in 1889, asking that this pledge be redeemed. A number of antimonopoly bills were introduced, one of them by Senator Sherman of Ohio. There was little active interest in the legislation; Congress was preoccupied with other matters, including the elevation of the tariff and the passage of the Silver Purchase Act. No hearings were held; the bill that finally emerged from the Congressional committees was enacted, following a brief debate that raised no fundamental issues, with only one dissenting vote in the Senate and without a record vote in the House. It was signed by the President on July 2, 1890. Bearing little or no resemblance to the bill originally introduced by Senator Sherman, it was given his name.

The Sherman Act

The Sherman Act, unlike most Acts of Congress, is short and simple. Its major provisions could easily be memorized:

> Sec. 1. Every contract, combination in the form of a trust or otherwise, or conspiracy, in restraint of trade or commerce among the several states, or with foreign nations, is hereby declared to be illegal. Every person who shall make any such contract or engage in any such combination or conspiracy, shall be deemed guilty of a misdemeanor. . . .
>
> Sec. 2. Every person who shall monopolize, or attempt to monopolize, or combine or conspire with any other person or persons, to monopolize any part of the trade or commerce among the several states, or with foreign nations, shall be deemed guilty of a misdemeanor. . . .

The Act thus took over the concepts of restraint of trade and monopolization from the common law, without attempting further to define their meaning. Its first section applies only to agreements in which two or more persons are involved. Its second section is broader, applying also to individual efforts to monopolize.

In substance, the legislation contained nothing that was new. Its real contribution was to turn restraint of trade and monopolization into offenses against the federal government, to require enforcement by federal officials, and to provide for the imposition of penalties. United States district attorneys, acting under the direction of the Attorney General, were instructed to institute proceedings in equity to compel observance of the law. It was also their duty to bring criminal suits against those who violated its terms. Such violations were made punishable by fines up to $5,000, imprisonment up to one year, or both. Persons injured by illegal restraints or monopolies were entitled to sue for triple damages.

The Sherman Act, with the continued support of both major parties, remained the only important antitrust law to be enacted for nearly a quarter of a century. In the Wilson Tariff Act of 1894, similar provisions were applied to persons importing goods into the United States. In legislation granting rights to certain lands, in 1908 and 1910, violation of the Sherman Act was made a basis for cancellation of these rights. In the Panama Canal Act of 1912, violators operating boats were denied the privilege of passing through the canal. But it was not until 1914 that major additions to the law were made.

The Clayton and Federal Trade Commission Acts

There was increasing dissatisfaction, in the years before 1914, with the operation of the Sherman Act. During the administrations of Cleveland and McKinley, the laws had scarcely been enforced. Powerful new combinations had been formed in steel, tin cans, corn products, farm machinery, and many other industries. During the administrations of Roosevelt and Taft, monopolistic abuses had been disclosed in hearings before committees of Congress, in the reports of public agencies, and in the evidence presented in cases brought before the courts. Though it was shown that competition had been eliminated by particular business practices, these practices had not been held to be in violation of the law. And in 1911 the Supreme Court had declared that combinations that were not unreasonable would be allowed to stand. Following these developments, the trusts again became an issue in the national campaign of 1912. Monopoly was denounced and further legislation promised by the Democrats, the Roosevelt Progressives, and the Republicans.

In 1913 the new Democratic Congress reduced the tariff, set up the Federal Reserve System, and inaugurated the income tax; in 1914 it turned to the problem of monopoly. Consideration of the problem was now more thorough than that accorded it a quarter-century before: the issues raised were subjected to exhaustive hearings and extended debate. President Wilson had recommended that uncertainty concerning the meaning of the Sherman Act be removed by prohibiting, item by item, each of the devices by which competition might be eliminated and monopoly obtained. He had also proposed that a specialized administrative agency be established to strengthen the observance and enforcement of the law. An Act setting up such a body—the Federal Trade Commission—was eventually forthcoming. But agreement on a comprehensive list of monopolistic practices was not to be obtained: opinions differed with respect to particular practices; it was difficult to define existing practices and impossible to frame definitions that would cover future practices; there was fear that such definitions would be so narrowly interpreted as to limit the scope of the law and seriously to impair its effectiveness. The attempt was finally abandoned; the list of devices to be specifically outlawed was reduced to four and provisions forbidding them were written into the Clayton Act; the other devices that had been debated were covered by a general prohibition of unfair methods of competition which was incorporated in the Federal Trade Commission Act. The two Acts, with Democratic and Progressive support, were passed by substantial majorities in both houses of Congress and signed by the President in the fall of 1914.

The particular devices that were outlawed by the Clayton Act were discrimination in prices, exclusive and tying contracts, intercorporate stockholdings, and interlocking directorates. Section 2 of the Act forbade sellers "to discriminate in price between different purchasers of commodities," but permitted such discrimination where there were "differences in the grade, quality, or quantity of the commodity sold," where the lower prices made "only due allowance for differences in the cost of selling or transportation," and where they were offered "in good faith to meet competition." Section 3 forbade sellers to "lease or make a sale or contract for sale of . . . commodities . . . on the condition that the lessee or purchaser thereof shall not use or deal in the . . . commodity . . . of a competitor. . . ." Section 7 forbade any corporation engaged in commerce to acquire the shares of a competing corporation or to purchase the stocks of two or more corporations that were competitors. It should be noted that none of these prohibitions was absolute; the three practices were forbidden only where their effect, in the words of the law, "may be to substantially lessen competition or tend to create a monopoly. . . ." Section 8 prohibited interlocking directorates between corporations engaged in commerce where one of them had a capital and surplus of more than $1 million and where "the elimination of competition . . . between them would constitute a violation of any of the provisions of the antitrust laws." The broader prohibition contained in Section 5 of the accompanying Federal Trade Commission Act provided, simply, "that unfair methods of competition in commerce are hereby declared unlawful."

In substance, these statutes added little to the content of the law. The specific practices that were prohibited might well have been attacked, as conspiracies in restraint of trade or as attempts to monopolize, under the provisions of the Sherman Act. Unfair methods of competition were already condemned, moreover, by the common law. There were, however, important differences. The Sherman Act was general in its terms; the Clayton Act was explicit. The older law dealt with monopoly as an accomplished fact; the new laws were concerned with the methods through which monopoly was attained. The one placed emphasis on punishment; the others were directed toward prevention. Practices that had not been held to violate the law unless pursued as part of a proved conspiracy were now forbidden in and of themselves. Even more important was the fact that enforcement was strengthened, as we shall see, by other provisions of the Clayton and Trade Commission Acts. Under the latter Act, moreover, attacks on unfair methods of competition, instead of being left to suits brought by private litigants on their own initiative and at their own expense, were to be made by public officials and financed by appropriations from the federal treasury. It is in these respects that the new legislation made its most significant contribution to the force of the law.

The Robinson-Patman Act

Section 2 of the Clayton Act, relating to price discrimination, was completely revised with the passage, in 1936, of the Robinson-Patman Act. The original section had been designed primarily to prevent large manufacturers from eliminating their smaller rivals by temporarily cutting prices on particular products and in particular markets while prices elsewhere were maintained, a notorious practice of certain of the early trusts. The new law was an outgrowth of a different situation. Independent wholesalers and retailers, in the years following World War I, found themselves faced with increasing competition from chain stores and other mass distributors. The lower prices that these organizations charged were to be attributed, in part at least, to the lower prices that they paid. Their bargaining power enabled them to obtain concessions from suppliers in many forms: brokers' commissions where no broker was employed, services provided by suppliers in addition to the delivery of goods, allowances for advertising the suppliers' products and rendering them other services, and discounts for purchasing in large quantities. The independents, contending that these concessions were larger than could be justified, demanded that the freedom of suppliers to discriminate be more strictly limited. The Robinson-Patman Act was passed in response to their demands.

Section 1 of the Act, amending Section 2 of the Clayton Act, flatly forbids the payment of a broker's commission in cases where an independent broker is not employed. It forbids sellers to provide supplementary services to buyers or to make allowances for services rendered them by buyers unless such concessions are available to all buyers "on proportionally equal terms." Other forms of discrimination, such as quantity discounts, are prohibited in cases where the effect (in the words of the Clayton Act, with the split infinitive corrected) "may be substantially to lessen competition or tend to create a monopoly in any line of commerce," either among sellers or among buyers. Persons accused of such discrimination may defend themselves by proving that their lower prices made only "due allowance" for differences in cost or were offered "in good faith to meet an equally low price of a competitor. . . ." But even where larger discounts can be justified by lower costs, the Federal Trade Commission is authorized to establish quantity limits beyond which discounts cannot be given, if such action is required to prevent large buyers from obtaining a monopoly. The section makes it unlawful, finally, for any person "knowingly to induce or receive" a prohibited discrimination in price.

Section 3 of the Act provides criminal penalties for three offenses. It flatly forbids giving or receiving a larger discount than that made available to competitors buying the same goods in the same quantity. It also forbids the establishment, in one locality, of prices lower than those charged elsewhere, and prohibits the sale of goods "at unreasonably low prices" where either of these practices is adopted "for the purpose of destroying competition or eliminating a competitor." Violation of any of these provisions is punishable by fines up to $5,000, or imprisonment up to one year, or both.

The Wheeler-Lea Act

The ability of the Federal Trade Commission to prevent the use of unfair methods in competition was seriously restricted by a decision handed down by the Supreme Court in 1931. In this case,[1] the Commission had ordered the Raladam Company, manufacturers of Marmola, to cease and desist from representing their product as a remedy for obesity. The court recognized that consumers had been deceived by Raladam's advertisements, but it vacated the order, finding that misrepresentation was common among the vendors of such nostrums and concluding, on this basis, that no injury had been done to Raladam's competitors. The Commission was thus denied authority to protect consumers in cases where injury to competitors could not be shown.

This loophole was closed when Section 5 of the Federal Trade Commission Act was amended by the passage of the Wheeler-Lea Act in 1938. The section, as thus amended, now outlaws not only "unfair methods of competition," but also "unfair or deceptive acts or practices."

The Celler Antimerger Act

The effectiveness of Section 7 of the Clayton Act—forbidding one corporation to acquire the shares of a competing corporation or to buy

[1] *FTC* v. *Raladam Co.*, 283 U.S. 643.

the stocks of two or more corporations that were competitors, where such action might substantially lessen competition or tend toward monopoly—was similarly impaired by subsequent decisions of the Supreme Court. In 1926 the court decided, in the Swift and Thatcher cases,[2] that the Federal Trade Commission could not order a company to divest itself of the assets of a competitor if it had effected a merger, while the proceeding was pending, by voting stock which it had unlawfully acquired. And again in 1934 the court decided, in the Arrow-Hart & Hegeman case,[3] that the Commission was powerless to act when a holding company, after acquiring the shares of two competing corporations, had distributed them to its stockholders who had thereupon voted to merge the two concerns. In the years that followed there was heavy traffic over the detour that the court had built around the law.

This situation was finally corrected, after repeated efforts, by the enactment of an amendment extending the prohibitions of Section 7 to cover not only the acquisition of stock, but also "the use of such stock by the voting or granting of proxies or otherwise" and the acquisition of "the whole or any part of the assets" of a competing corporation or those of two or more corporations in competition with one another. This amendment was passed over Republican opposition by Democratic votes and signed by President Truman on December 29, 1950.[4]

Summary

The prohibitions contained in the antitrust laws may now be summarized. It is illegal:

1. To enter into a contract, combination, or conspiracy in restraint of trade (Sherman Act, Sec. 1);
2. To monopolize, attempt to monopolize, or combine or conspire to monopolize trade (Sherman Act, Sec. 2).

In cases where the effect may be substantially to lessen competition or tend to create a monopoly, it is illegal:

3. To acquire the stock of competing corporations (Clayton Act, Sec. 7);
4. To acquire the assets of competing corporations (Clayton Act, Sec. 7 as amended in 1950);
5. To enter into exclusive and tying contracts (Clayton Act, Sec. 3);
6. To discriminate—to an extent that cannot be justified—among purchasers (Clayton Act, Sec. 2 as amended by Robinson-Patman Act, Sec. 1).

And, in general, it is also illegal:

7. To engage in particular forms of price discrimination (Robinson-Patman Act, Sec. 1 and 3);

[2] *Thatcher Manufacturing Co.* v. *FTC*, *Swift & Co.* v. *FTC*, 272 U.S. 554.

[3] *Arrow-Hart & Hegeman Electric Co.* v. *FTC*, 291 U.S. 587.

[4] 81st Cong., 2d Sess., Public Law No. 889.

8. To serve as a director of competing corporations (Clayton Act, Sec. 8);
9. To use unfair methods of competition (Federal Trade Commission Act, Sec. 5);
10. To employ unfair or deceptive acts or practices (Federal Trade Commission Act, Sec. 5 as amended by Wheeler-Lea Act, Sec. 3).

In the main these provisions are designed to prevent monopoly and to maintain a competitive economy. But some of them have other purposes. It is the purpose of the Robinson-Patman Act, for instance, less to maintain competition than to preserve the small competitor. In some cases the law may check the growth of monopoly by controlling discrimination; in others, it may merely moderate the force of competition by reducing the competitive advantage of the larger firm. It is the purpose of Section 5 of the Federal Trade Commission Act, not only to preclude the attainment of monopoly through unfair methods of competition, but also to prevent the employment of such methods where no danger of monopoly exists. And it is the purpose of the Wheeler-Lea amendment, not to maintain competition, but to protect the consumer against deceptive practices. These aspects of the antitrust laws will be discussed at greater length in Chapters 9 and 10. It should be noted, too, that Congress has acted, from time to time, to except certain practices and to exempt particular industries from the provisions of these laws, subjecting some of them to other methods of control. These matters are to be considered, in some detail, in Part IV. It is with the enforcement of the policy of maintaining competition that the present section is concerned.

METHODS OF ENFORCEMENT

The provisions of the antitrust laws are made effective through actions brought against violators, case by case. An order or decision resulting from such an action does not apply to industry in general, but only to those who are named as respondents or defendants in a particular case. The Sherman Act is enforced through criminal or civil suits brought in the federal courts by the Department of Justice and through suits initiated by private litigants. Section 5 of the Federal Trade Commission Act is enforced by orders issued by the Commission and, when these orders become final, through suits brought by the Department of Justice. The two agencies have been given concurrent jurisdiction in the enforcement of the Clayton Act. The procedures that they follow have been specified, in part, by statute and developed, in part, through administrative experience.

Under the Sherman and Clayton Acts

The prosecutor, in a criminal case, must first go before a grand jury and convince it that evidence pointing toward the guilt of the defendants is sufficient to justify a trial. If he succeeds in doing so, an indictment will be returned and the case will be set for trial before a jury in a district court. At this stage, if the defendants decide that they will not contest the suit, they may enter a plea of *nolo contendere*, involving no admission of their guilt. If the court accepts the plea, however, criminal penalties may be imposed. The government may drop a case, at any stage of the proceedings, by entering a nolle prosequi. In the absence of such actions, the case will go on trial. If the defendants are acquitted, the case is closed. If they are convicted, they may appeal. Again, if the Court of Appeals acquits them, the case is closed. If it upholds the lower court, they may petition the Supreme Court for review. This petition may be granted or denied. It is only when the final court to hear the case has spoken that criminal penalties may be imposed.

The penalties originally provided in the Sherman Act applied to individuals and to corporations found guilty of violating the law. But the directors and officers of guilty corporations could not be punished unless their personal guilt was proved. In Section 14 of the Clayton Act, however, Congress fixed responsibility for the conduct of a corporation on its directors and officers and extended to them the penalties of fine or imprisonment or both. The fine that may be imposed is limited by the Sherman Act to $5,000, but fines running into hundreds of thousands have been collected in a single case, since this penalty may be exacted under each of the counts in an indictment (monopolizing, attempting to monopolize, conspiring, and restraining trade) and imposed on each of the defendants in a suit, i.e. on a trade association, on every company that belongs to the association, and on each of their directors and officers. The Sherman Act also provided for seizure, in the course of transportation, of the goods involved in an illegal conspiracy and their forfeiture to the United States. This penalty, however, has rarely been imposed.

Further penalties have been provided in other acts. Denial of passage through the Panama Canal and forfeiture of certain land rights have already been mentioned. In 1920 Congress made further provision for the forfeiture of mineral rights. In the Federal Communications Act of 1934, it made antitrust violation a basis for the revocation of broadcasting licenses. Such violation was also penalized when Congress, in the Lanham Trademark Act of 1946, made it a defense available to persons against whom the violators might bring infringement suits. Violation of the antitrust laws by patentees has also been accepted by the courts as a defense when advanced by persons sued for infringing patent rights.[5]

Businessmen who wish to avoid the imposition of these penalties may enter into consultation with the Department of Justice, presenting their plans for proposed combinations or for the adoption of particular practices. If it appears, upon full disclosure, that nothing illegal is involved, the Department may commit itself not to bring criminal proceedings against

[5] *Mercoid Co.* v. *Mid-Continent Co.*, 320 U.S. 661.

such parties, at a later date, for participation in the activities described. But it will reserve the right to take civil action if competition should subsequently be restrained.

The government may normally proceed against offenders by bringing a criminal suit or a civil suit or both. In the latter case, the two actions may be brought either simultaneously or successively. It is the purpose of a civil suit, not to deter violation by inflicting punishment, but to restore competitive conditions by providing remedies. Such a suit is not initiated through an indictment or tried before a jury. Whatever the decision in a lower court, the government as well as the defendants may appeal. The provision of remedies, however, is the duty of the lower courts. When the government's contentions are sustained, upon appeal, the case will be remanded to a district court. Here, after hearings in which the remedies proposed by the government are debated by both parties, the court will issue a decree.

Under the wording of the Sherman Act, violations of the law may be "enjoined or otherwise prohibited." The latitude afforded by the phrase "or otherwise prohibited" is wide. The Supreme Court has held, however, that the provisions of decrees must be limited to parties brought before the courts, must be related to their past offenses, must not be punitive in character, must not impose new duties on defendants, and must be reasonably specific in their terms. But it has also held that the effects of illegal behavior may be corrected, that the pattern of industrial organization may be changed, and that doubts concerning the proper content of decrees may be resolved in favor of the government. The discretion accorded to the courts is, therefore, broad.

The provisions contained in decrees are of two main types: those that order dissolution, divorcement, or divestiture, and those that enjoin particular practices. Provisions of the first type may require defendants to dissolve a trade association or a corporate combination, to sell their stock in certain firms, or to dispose of ownership in other properties. They are designed to break up organizations that have eliminated competition and to increase the number of competitors. Injunctive provisions, on the other hand, concern themselves with business practices. In some cases they may be affirmative in character, seeking to restore competition by ordering defendants to take some action not otherwise required by law, such as permitting competitors to use their patents by granting unrestricted licenses. In other cases they may merely forbid the repetition of illegal acts, such as discriminating in prices or entering into exclusive or tying contracts. Since these practices are already outlawed, it may be asked whether anything is gained through the issuance of a decree. The answer is that here, as elsewhere, the violator of an injunction may be adjudged guilty of contempt of court and punished by fine or imprisonment or both.

A civil suit may also be concluded, before a court has rendered a decision, by the negotiation of an agreement between the defendants and the government. An accompanying criminal suit may then be dropped by entering a nolle prosequi. The defendants, in such an agreement, explicitly deny admission of their guilt. But they may accept provisions that go much farther than those that might otherwise have been imposed. These provisions, with the approval of the court, will be embodied in a consent decree. Such decrees are issued in the same way and with the same effect, as those that follow completed litigation. Their use had not been mentioned in the Sherman Act; it was recognized, by implication, in the Clayton Act. The consent decree is now one of the major instruments employed in the enforcement of these laws.

The laws are also enforced through private suits. Under the Sherman Act, persons injured by violations may sue for threefold damages. Such suits may be brought by individuals, by corporations, or by states, but not by the federal government. Under Section 16 of the Clayton Act, injunctive relief may also be granted to plaintiffs in private suits. In Section 5 of the Clayton Act, moreover, the position of such plaintiffs was greatly strengthened by permitting them to introduce, as prima facie evidence, decisions handed down by the courts in criminal and civil cases brought against the same defendants by the government. Defeat in public cases may thus lead to further penalties by inviting the initiation of private suits for triple damages. Where defendants in public suits have entered a plea of *nolo contendere*, however, and where they have accepted a consent decree, plaintiffs in private suits, lacking prima facie evidence of guilt, must sustain a heavier burden of proof.

Under the Federal Trade Commission Act

Most of the cases that come before the Federal Trade Commission relate to the use of unfair methods or deceptive practices in competitive industries. The Commission, however, was given concurrent jurisdiction with the Department of Justice in enforcing the prohibitions against monopolistic devices contained in the Clayton Act. It has also proceeded against agreements to curtail output, divide markets, and fix prices, condemning them as unfair methods of competition within the meaning of Section 5 of the Trade Commission Act. Such agreements, of course, instead of being methods of competition, give evidence of failure to compete. But the Commission's authority to move against them has long been upheld, by implication, by the courts;[6] it was recognized explicitly in the decision handed down by the Supreme Court in the Cement case in 1948.[7] "The Commission," said the court, "has jurisdiction to declare that conduct tending to restrain trade is an unfair method of competition even though the selfsame conduct may also violate the Sherman Act." The Commission has thus come to play an important part, not only in preventing the use of unfair methods, but also in maintaining competition itself.

[6] *FTC* v. *Pacific States Paper Trade Assn.*, 273 U.S. 52 (1927).

[7] *FTC* v. *Cement Institute*, 333 U.S. 683.

The procedures employed by the Commission, in promoting observance and effecting enforcement of the law, are informal as well as formal. Following one of these procedures, adopted in 1919, the members of an industry may be invited to attend a conference for the purpose of drawing up a code of fair trade practices. If such a code is agreed upon, after open hearings, the Commission will approve its terms. These will include provisions (called Group I rules) condemning certain practices that have been found to be illegal by the Commission and the courts, and further provisions (called Group II rules) denouncing other practices which, though not illegal, are felt by members of the industry to be unfair. The Commission will undertake to prosecute members who may subsequently violate the Group I rules. The codes evolved by these trade practice conferences add nothing to the content of the law. But they make its application explicit, call its provisions to attention, and thus, it is hoped, promote compliance by members of the industries concerned.

Another informal procedure, called the stipulation, was adopted in 1920 and has since been used in the settlement of cases involving minor infractions of the law. Under this procedure, a violator may sign a statement admitting the charges brought against him and promising to discontinue his illegal practices. If the promise is kept, no formal proceedings will ensue. If not, the Commission will issue an order requiring compliance with the law. This procedure is frequently used in handling unfair methods and deceptive practices in competitive industries. In cases of major importance, however, and in those involving monopoly and restraint of trade, more formal procedures are typically employed.

Whenever the Commission is of the opinion that a legal proceeding would be in the public interest, it is authorized by its basic statute to issue a document known as a complaint. This document names, as respondents, the parties accused of violation, presents the charges against them, and affords an opportunity for a reply. If the respondents do not file an answer, a formal order may then be issued in the case. If they are willing, at this stage, to promise compliance without admitting guilt, the terms of a consent order may be worked out with members of the Commission's staff and such an order issued, if approved by the Commission, in accordance with a procedure first adopted in 1951. If a complaint is contested, however, a public hearing is required. In such a hearing, the issues will be argued by Commission lawyers and by counsel for respondents, much as in a trial before a court. The case will be heard, in the first instance, by another employee of the Commission who is known as a trial examiner. This officer will then prepare an initial decision, supported by findings of fact and conclusions as to points of law. Until 1950 this decision took the form of a recommendation; the issuance of orders was reserved to the Commission itself. Under a new procedure adopted in that year, the trial examiner's decision achieves the status of an order unless reviewed by the Commission on its own motion or appealed within thirty days by either side to the dispute. A final hearing is held before the full Commission, sitting as a court. After considering the briefs and the arguments presented, the Commission will either dismiss the case or issue an order setting forth its findings and conclusions and directing the respondents to cease and desist from their illegal acts. The cease and desist order is the only mandatory action that the Commission is empowered to take.

The parties named in an order may carry it for review to a Circuit Court of Appeals. Until 1938, moreover, the Commission had to go before a Court of Appeals if it wished its orders to be enforced. This is still the case with orders issued under the Clayton Act. When an order is reviewed, the Commission's findings of fact, if supported by evidence, are conclusive. But the Commission may be reversed on points of law. The court may enter a decree affirming an order, requiring its modification, or setting it aside. Unless the Supreme Court grants a further review, an order becomes final when it has been affirmed by a Circuit Court. Violators of final orders can be prosecuted by the Department of Justice for contempt. But the law, as it was written in 1914, specified no penalty.

Under the Wheeler-Lea Act of 1938, orders issued under Section 5 of the Trade Commission Act become final if not appealed by respondents within sixty days or, if appealed, when affirmed by a Circuit Court. The law further provided that a fine, up to $5,000, might be imposed for each violation of a final order. In 1950, almost by inadvertance, this penalty was increased. In that year Congress repealed a federal tax on oleomargarine but sought to protect the dairy interests by requiring that margarine be plainly labeled, by compelling eating places that served the product to call this fact to the attention of their customers, and by making advertisement of margarine as a dairy product a deceptive practice within the meaning of the Trade Commission Act. To enforce these provisions, it further provided that each day of continuing violation of any Commission order, when final, should constitute a separate offense for which a fine of $5,000 might be imposed. The Commission's authority has thus been greatly strengthened. The parties named in an order cannot ignore it. They must appeal it, obey it, or face the imposition of substantial penalties.

ORGANIZATION FOR ENFORCEMENT

Responsibility for the administration of the antitrust laws is scattered among several departments and agencies of the federal government. In the case of particular industries, various bodies have been authorized by Congress to grant exemptions from the Sherman Act in favor of alternative controls, to enforce the provisions of the Clayton Act, and to administer similar statutes, such as the Packers and Stockyards Act of 1921, the Grain Futures Act of 1922, and the Commodity Exchange Act of 1936. Fragments of jurisdiction have thus been parceled out to the Interstate Commerce Commission, the Federal Communications Commission, the Federal

Power Commission, the Securities and Exchange Commission, the Civil Aeronautics Board, the Board of Governors of the Federal Reserve System, the Commodity Exchange Authority, and the Secretary of Agriculture. For business in general, however, responsibility for enforcement still lies with the Department of Justice and the Federal Trade Commission.

The Antitrust Division

Until 1903 no separate staff was set up in the Department of Justice to enforce the Sherman Act. In that year an Antitrust Division was established and an Assistant Attorney General was placed in charge. The Division is now required by Congress to enforce some forty laws and also to enforce the orders issued by a number of administrative agencies. Its principal function, however, is the enforcement of the Sherman Act.

The Division receives complaints, usually from customers or competitors, alleging violation of the law. On the basis of such complaints, or on its own initiative, it causes investigations to be made. From among the many cases that come to its attention, it selects the ones it will prosecute. The Division's lawyers appear before grand juries, present cases in the district courts, and argue them, upon appeal, in the circuit courts. Presentations before the Supreme Court are the responsibility of the Solicitor General. In negotiations with counsel for defendants, the Division agrees upon the substance of consent decrees. When civil suits are won, it prepares proposals for remedies. Its organization includes sections that specialize in each of these phases of its work.

The Federal Trade Commission

The Federal Trade Commission is an independent administrative agency composed of five commissioners who are appointed by the President, with the advice and consent of the Senate, for terms of seven years. No more than three of its members may belong to the same political party and continuity is afforded by provision for overlapping terms. Until 1950 the Commission's chairmanship rotated among its members, each of them serving, in turn, for a single year. Since that time, the Chairman has been designated by the President and has been made responsible for administration of the Commission's activities.

In addition to its duties under the Clayton and Trade Commission Acts, already mentioned, the Commission administers the antitrust exemption granted to export trade associations under the Webb-Pomerene Act of 1917, polices the advertising of foods, drugs, and cosmetics under the Wheeler-Lea Act of 1938, enforces the Wool Products Labeling Act of 1939, the Fur Products Labeling Act of 1951, and the Flammable Fabrics Act of 1953, and may ask the Patent Office, under the Lanham Act of 1946, to cancel a trade mark that has been used to create an illegal monopoly. The Commission's functions as envisaged by the framers of its original statute were also to include participation in the enforcement of the Sherman Act. The courts were authorized to refer civil suits to the Commission, acting as a master in chancery, for the recommendation of an appropriate decree. At the request of the Attorney General, the Commission was to prepare plans for the reorganization of corporations where a finding of illegal combination had been made. And, upon request or on its own initiative, the Commission was to investigate the manner in which decrees were being carried out and make reports to the Department of Justice with recommendations for further action where this might be required. These requests, however, have not been made and the contemplated duties have never been assumed.

The Commission's present functions include research and the publication of reports, promotion of compliance, investigation of unfair methods of competition, deceptive practices, monopolistic devices, and agreements in restraint of trade, and prosecution of those who violate the law. An internal reorganization, completed in 1954, established a separate bureau to handle each of these activities. A Bureau of Economics makes general studies and publishes reports. A Bureau of Consultation accepts stipulations and handles trade practice conferences. A Bureau of Investigation looks into charges of violation, and a Bureau of Litigation prepares formal complaints and presents arguments before the trial examiners and, upon appeal, before the Commission itself. Decisions are prepared by members of the staff of trial examiners. Formal hearings are held before the Commission, and cease and desist orders are issued in its name. Until orders become final, members of the Commission's counsel defend them in cases brought before the courts. When final, they are certified to the Department of Justice if further legal action is required.

SUGGESTIONS FOR FURTHER READING

The story of the early trusts, the antitrust movement, and the enactment of the antitrust laws is told, in some detail, in each of the following books: Eliot Jones, *The Trust Problem in the United States* (New York: Macmillan Co., 1921), Myron W. Watkins, *Industrial Combinations and Public Policy* (Boston: Houghton-Mifflin Co., 1927), and H. R. Seager and C. A. Gulick, *Trust and Corporation Problems* (New York: Harper & Bro., 1929). The complete texts of the *Antitrust Laws with Amendments 1890–1945*, compiled by Elmer A. Lewis, can be obtained from the Superintendent of Documents in Washington for 20 cents. The texts, together with an analytical summary and an outline of jurisdiction for enforcement, exemptions, and proposals for amendment were published in 1950, by the Select Committee on Small Business of the House of Representatives under the title "Congress and the Monopoly Problem—Fifty Years of Antitrust Development—1900–1950," and can be identified as House Doc. No. 599 of the 81st Cong., 2d Sess.

Chapter 4 THE TASK OF ANTITRUST

The problems that confront the administration of the antitrust laws are many and diverse. They are raised both by the elimination of competition among independent enterprises and by the attainment of monopoly by a single concern. They relate not only to forms of business organization, but also to the character of business practices. In some cases, violation is obvious and flagrant; in others, it is hidden and discreet. In the former evidence is readily available; in the latter it is difficult to obtain. There are activities, moreover, that may be either innocent or dangerous and others whose legality or illegality is still unclear. The line between competition and monopoly is sometimes hard to draw. The task of antitrust, in consequence, is one of great complexity. It is well, therefore, to examine the various types of cases to which the law must be applied.

Competition among independent enterprises may be eliminated in a variety of ways: (1) by simple conspiracy, (2) by formal organization, (3) by intercorporate relations, and (4) by habitual identity of behavior. Problems of quite a different nature are presented by concerns that stand alone or overtop their rivals in their respective fields. (1) Such a firm may have sought or may be seeking to obtain or to retain monopolistic powers by employing unfair methods to handicap or to eliminate its competitors. (2) It may have accomplished the same purpose by absorbing or merging with its competitors. (3) It may have achieved monopoly without employing unfair methods of competition or combining with other firms. (4) It may not even possess monopolistic powers but may so overshadow its rivals as to enjoy pronounced competitive advantages. More than one of these problems may be presented by a single case. But, for the purpose of analysis, they are logically separable. Each of them will be examined in turn.

SIMPLE CONSPIRACIES

Where several independent firms are present in a market, some or all of them may participate in overt arrangements that are designed to eliminate competition among themselves and to prevent competition by others.

They may establish the prices at which they will sell and fix the other terms and conditions that govern their sales. They may curtail their output as a means of raising the prices that may be charged. They may divide up territories or customers so that each of them will enjoy a monopoly within his allotted field. They may seek to coerce other firms, already in the market, and to exclude outsiders from entry. They may enforce these restrictions by methods that range from peaceful persuasion to the extremes of violence. Such arrangements have repeatedly been found in local, regional and national markets in the United States.

Rackets

The most spectacular and the most obviously objectionable of these arrangements are those whose provisions have been enforced by a resort to violence. At various times, in several local trades, thugs and gunmen, employed by racketeers, have damaged goods, destroyed them and interfered with their movement, broken windows, thrown bombs, demolished equipment, set fire to places of business, and assaulted, kidnapped, and even murdered tradesmen and their employees. Among the most notorious of these rackets was one which formerly controlled the market for live poultry in metropolitan New York:

> For many years a ring of 27 to 30 commission men fixed the price of chickens bought from producers in 40 states and the price of those sold to some 200 slaughter houses and several hundred retailers in New York City. In alliance with four trade unions, the ring was able to exclude other commission men from the market by denying them access to the supply of labor. It augmented its profits by granting one company a monopoly of the business of providing coops, another a monopoly of the business of selling chicken feed, and a third a monopoly of the trucking service. It compelled slaughter houses and distributors to deal with these concerns by calling strikes against those who turned elsewhere for supplies or services. It prevented poultry from reaching the market through other channels by having trucks overturned, chickens fed sand and gravel and plaster of paris or sprinkled with poison or kerosene. Ex-convicts and plug-uglies policed the trade; ten murders were committed within a period of five years. In this way, prices were maintained and profits realized by members of the ring.[1]

Violence was among the methods employed to enforce a succession of market-sharing and price-fixing plans adopted by members of an association of cleaners and dyers in Chicago:

> The association fixed prices and forbade cleaners to solicit accounts from retailers who were already being served by other plants. It imposed fines on violators, persuaded the truckers' union to instruct its drivers not to collect work from their customers and persuaded the inside workers' union to call

[1] Clair Wilcox, *Competition and Monopoly in American Industry*, Temporary National Economic Committee, Monograph 21 (Washington: Government Printing Office, 1940), pp. 294–95.

strikes in their plants. Cleaners maintaining retail outlets who failed to adhere to association prices might suffer the lighter penalty of having cut-rate "whip stores" opened nearby or the more severe punishment of bombing. Retail tailors were forbidden to open a shop within 100 street numbers of another shop, and were forced by refusal of cleaners to take their work, by fines, by "whip stores," by picketing under various pretexts, and by window smashing, to maintain the prices decreed by the tailors' union. Beatings were inflicted, trucks damaged, and clothing ruined; at least two persons connected with the trade were murdered, and the talents of such notorious gangsters as Al Capone and "Bugs" Moran were brought into play.[2]

This sort of terrorism has sometimes characterized the various branches of the construction industry. It has been employed in the coercion of fur dressers, laundrymen, barbers, undertakers, window washers, junkmen, truckers, operators of garages and filling stations, distributors of ice, milk, candy, and soft drinks, and dealers in fish, fresh fruits, and vegetables.[3] In method, such arrangements are universally condemned; in purpose and effect, they differ little from restraints enforced by measures that are more polite.

Bidding Rings

In buying supplies for public agencies and in purchasing construction services, it is customary to publish specifications, to invite sellers to submit bids, and to award the contract to the seller who submits the lowest bid. Where sellers act independently, their bids will reflect their varying estimates of cost. Where they are in collusion, however, all bids may be identical or differing bids may merely reflect agreement that one bidder is to get the job. The formalities of bidding may be preserved, though competition itself has been suppressed. Such collusion has been frequent among subcontractors in various branches of the building trades:

> In some cases, a group of subcontractors operates a central estimating bureau which either maintains a uniform costing system and circulates specifications for the material and labor to be included in each job, thus enabling all of its members to arrive at the same bid, or itself calculates the cost of jobs and tells its members what to charge. Since identical bids result, contract-letting authorities are forced to award contracts by lot and every member of the bidding group is ultimately afforded an equal share in the market, each of them accepting the particular jobs that come to him by chance. In other cases, the group determines in advance which of its members is to get a job and so arranges the bids that his is lower than the rest. In still others, it maintains a depository where copies of estimates and bids are filed. Here members may open, read, and revise their bids before submitting them to architects or general contractors. They may raise the level of these bids by making certain that they conform to prescribed prices for materials, labor, and overhead, or by requiring that an arbitrary sum be added to each. They may allocate contracts according to some general rule, making the lowest bidder withdraw his bid and

[2] *Ibid.*, pp. 296–97. [3] *Ibid.*, pp. 295–96.

submit a new one higher than the highest, averaging the bids and throwing out those that fall more than 10 per cent below the average, or assigning each job to the bidder whose bid comes closest to the average and requiring those whose bids fall below this figure to submit new bids to exceed it. Or they may merely decide which of their number is to receive each contract and rig the bids accordingly.[4]

Such activities have been found to exist among excavating, masonry, roofing, flooring, plumbing, heating, plastering, painting, glazing, tile, electrical, and other contractors in various cities. They have also been encountered among suppliers submitting bids on government contracts.

Other Restrictive Agreements

In local markets, where sellers have got together, competition has been eliminated in many other ways. Producers of ice have curtailed output, divided territories, and pooled profits. Bakers have entered into agreements limiting the sizes, regulating the weights, and fixing the prices of loaves of bread.[5] Automobile dealers have sought, through various devices, to control the allowances made on trade-ins. Druggists have informed one another concerning their charges by marking copies of prescriptions in accordance with a code in which the successive letters of the word "pharmocist" or "pharmecist" stand for the numerals 1 to 0. Operators of filling stations have disciplined price cutters by sending several trucks to blockade their driveways at the busiest time of day, each driver buying one gallon of gasoline, utilizing all of the free services of the station, proffering a $50 bill in payment, and waiting for his change.[6] Dealers in hardware and building materials have undertaken to confine the distribution of these products to "regular channels" by organizing boycotts against manufacturers who sell to mail order houses, to contractors, or directly to consumers. Groups of subcontractors have attempted to exclude competitors from the market by refusing to work on jobs where prefabricated products or materials produced by outsiders are employed.[7] Similar restraints have been experienced in other local trades.

In national markets, too, agreements among nominal competitors have frequently obtained. In complexity, these agreements range from one which formerly controlled the sale of typewriters to one which rigged the price of gasoline. In the former case, four companies, manufacturing 95–98 per cent of all the new standard typewriters sold in the United States, accepted a consent decree in 1940. It was charged that these concerns: "had agreed upon uniform prices, identical discounts, and a common schedule of trade-in allowances; that they had arranged to submit identical quotations whenever bids were requested; that they had cooperated in

[4] *Ibid.*, p. 289.

[5] *The Federal Antitrust Laws* (New York: Commerce Clearing House, 1949), Cases 572, 808.

[6] Wilcox, *op. cit.*, pp. 286–87.

[7] *Ibid.*, pp. 288, 291.

underbidding other manufacturers who sought to obtain a share of the business; that each of them had bought from the others machines of their own make that had been accepted in trade and that all of them had agreed to destroy machines that had been made by other firms."[8] In the second case, eight major companies and four smaller ones, producing about 85 per cent of the gasoline sold in ten midwestern states, raised and maintained prices during 1935 and 1936 by purchasing from independent refiners, producing the other 15 per cent, any portion of their output that would depress the market if it were freely sold:

Most of the output was distributed through filling stations owned by the major firms or sold under long-term contracts to independent jobbers who sold in turn to independent retailers. Daily exchanges at the independent refineries constituted no more than 5 to 7½ per cent of total sales. The price established in these transactions, however, was quoted as the spot market price and the contracts under which the jobbers obtained their supplies required them to pay this price. Retailers who bought from jobbers added their margins to this price. As a consequence, the major companies, by controlling the price at which the small volume of spot market gasoline changed hands, were in a position to fix the retail price. The firms participating in the program accordingly agreed to subject the spot quotation to control. Each of them selected an independent refiner as a "dancing partner" and assumed responsibility for his "surplus" output. Buying in the spot market, in small quantities, at progressively higher figures, they contrived to raise the price and to maintain it at an artificial level for the better part of two years. Independent refinery output no longer depressed the spot quotation. Independent jobbers, compelled to buy at this figure, advanced their own charges. Independent retailers were forced to follow suit. The integrated majors, protected thus from competition, augmented their profits by exacting higher prices from the consumers of gasoline.[9]

Agreements restricting competition in national markets have occurred in scores of cases, ranging from eyeglasses to explosives and including such important products as soap, cheese, watches, electric lamps, ball bearings, newsprint paper, stainless steel, fertilizers, viscose rayon yarn, and various drugs and chemicals.

Since understandings of the type described are clearly in violation of the law, their existence is usually shrouded in secrecy. But this fact presents no serious obstacle to enforcement. For, in the words of Corwin Edwards:

There is scarcely a collusive agreement of any size or duration which does not leave unmistakable traces. If there are many persons in the conspiracy, one of them is almost sure to develop a grievance and turn state's evidence. If the plan is complicated, it is almost certain to leave written records. If no letters or memoranda are written, there is evidence that meetings were held and evidence of the identity of action which followed the meetings. If files have been stripped, stray carbons and references to missing documents in other docu-

[8] *Ibid.*, pp. 140–41. [9] *Ibid.*, pp. 135–36.

ments make it possible to trace what happened. Once proved, a collusive agreement is relatively easy to terminate by law, since it operates through a system of joint action which may be stopped.[10]

If these were the only ways in which firms might conspire to restrain trade, the task of antitrust would be a fairly simple one. Unfortunately, they are not.

TRADE ASSOCIATIONS

Where traders are few in number, competition may be eliminated by simple agreement. Where they are numerous, it is more difficult to bring them together and to keep them in line. Some sort of contractual arrangement or formal organization is usually required. In Western Europe this need has long been satisfied by the activities of cartels. In the United States, it has frequently been met through the efforts of trade associations.

A trade association is an agency through which the sellers of a like commodity unite to promote their common interests. It exists solely to serve its members; it does not itself engage in the production or sale of goods. It is usually governed by a board of directors elected by its members and financed by dues which they contribute in proportion to their output, payrolls, capital, or sales. Its activities are typically administered by a salaried secretary and carried on by a paid staff. In some cases, however, administration may be delegated to one among the hundred or more firms of management engineers that specialize in this work. Association membership may number as few as a dozen or as many as several thousands; it may comprise a majority or a minority of the firms in an industry and cover a large or a small part of its sales. The members of such an association retain their legal independence; they are free to enter or withdraw from it at will; they cannot even be compelled to pay their dues. An association, therefore, may be strong or weak, according to the force of circumstances making for voluntary co-operation within the trade. The number of these organizations runs into the thousands; they are found in every market and in every industry in the United States.

Restrictive Activities

In more than 200 cases brought before the Federal Trade Commission and the courts, trade associations have been found to have eliminated competition in a variety of ways. They have established uniform prices. They have allocated markets and customers among their members. They have required their members to hold production to some fraction of past output or capacity. They have assigned to each of their members a quota in a permitted volume of sales. These activities are illustrated in the program developed by the firm of Stevenson, Jordan & Harrison when it was

[10] Corwin D. Edwards, "Can the Antitrust Laws Preserve Competition?" *American Economic Review,* Supplement (March 1940), pp. 164–80, esp. p. 175.

employed, in 1932, to manage the affairs of one national association and twelve regional associations comprising 165 manufacturers of fiber board shipping containers:

> The firm developed a "Basic Unit Plan" under which the numerous varieties of the industry's products were reduced to comparable elements. It prepared and circulated "Industry Estimating Manuals" containing "formulas, factors, and differentials" which were to be used by members in computing their prices. It urged members to ignore their actual costs and to employ the arbitrary estimates set forth in these manuals. It enforced compliance through a plan of "Invoice or Order Analysis" which required each member to submit copies of invoices or orders giving complete details on every sale. Association officials followed up members who failed to submit this information, checked the figures reported, and applied the "formulas, factors, and differentials" to members' sales in order to determine whether they were adhering to them in fixing their charges. They also prepared and circulated reports and charts which compared each member's basic unit price with the average for the industry. These materials were discussed at frequent meetings and members with prices below the average were urged to raise them. The program also involved the allocation of production under a plan which was variously designated as "Prorationing of Business," "Equitable Sharing of Available Business," and "Live and Let Live." The Stevenson firm divided the country into zones and made surveys of the volume of business transacted by each member in each zone during a "normal" or "base" period of three years. On the basis of these surveys, it assigned to members definite percentages of the business in their zones. Members agreed that they would adhere to their quotas and supplied copies of invoices in order to enable officials to determine whether they were doing so. Association employees prepared bi-weekly reports and charts showing each member's share in the sales made and comparing it with his quota. These materials were discussed at association meetings and members who had exceeded their quotas were urged to curtail production.[11]

Arrangements such as these have been enforced by campaigns of education and exhortation, by personal remonstrance and persuasion, by requiring members to make deposits against which the association may levy fines, and by the organization of boycotts. Associations have sought to confine the business of a trade to members, to force nonmember competitors to join the association or to withdraw from the field, and to compel members and nonmembers alike to adhere to association rules. To these ends, loyal association members have applied concerted pressure, directly by refusing to deal with recalcitrant members and nonmember competitors, and indirectly by refusing to buy from suppliers who have sold to them or to sell to purchasers who have bought from them.

Such arrangements, when they involve large numbers of participants, are readily attacked by antitrust. The detailed instructions and elaborate procedures required for their effectuation make them conspicuous and therefore highly vulnerable. Illegal activities, however, are by no means

[11] Wilcox, *op. cit.*, pp. 254–55.

characteristic of all associations; nine out of ten have never been charged with violation of the law. But there are other practices, more widely followed and not illegal in themselves, that may pass by almost imperceptible degrees from innocent co-operation to dangerous conspiracy. And it is here that trade associations present a problem of peculiar difficulty to the law.

Co-operative Activities

Many of the functions performed by trade associations do not appear to be inconsistent with the preservation of competition; many others may involve the imposition of restraints. Typical association activities include industrial research, market surveys, the development of new uses for products, the operation of employment bureaus, collective bargaining with organized labor, mutual insurance, commercial arbitration, the publication of trade journals, joint advertising and publicity, and joint representation before legislative and administration agencies—all of them undertakings that may serve a trade without disservice to its customers. But they also include the establishment of common cost accounting procedures, the operation of price reporting plans, the collection and dissemination of statistics, the standardization of products and terms of sale, the provision of credit information, the interchange of patent rights, the joint purchasing of supplies, and the promulgation of codes of business ethics—each of them a practice which may operate to restrain competition in quality, service, price, or terms of sale.

Conspicuous among association activities is the promotion of cost accounting or, in association parlance, cost education. As described by Arthur R. Burns,[12] this educational work is carried on through six grades:

> In the first, the association provides its members with standard forms for use in cost determination. This is expected to eliminate any price cutting that might arise from ignorance of costs. It may also carry the suggestion that no seller's price should fall below his costs as set forth on the standard forms. In the second grade, the association prescribes detailed procedures for computing costs, showing its members the proper way to figure charges for materials, the proper way to compute depreciation, and the proper way to distribute overhead. This is designed to reduce the price disparities that might result from the employment of diverse methods of calculation. In the third grade, the association suggests a uniform mark-up. Each of its members is encouraged to add the same per cent of profit to his costs to get his price. But one member may undersell another if he has lower costs. In the fourth grade, however, the association publishes some sort of an average of the costs of all the firms in the trade. Where this figure is adopted by members in place of their individual actual costs, it affords a basis for the establishment of a common price. But prices may still vary if members do not add a uniform mark-up to the uniform cost. In the fifth grade, therefore, some associations have taken the final step

[12] For a more complete description in his own words, see *The Decline of Competition* (New York: McGraw-Hill Book Co., 1936), pp. 47–55.

> and included an allowance for profit in the so-called average costs. Average costs then become merely a suggested selling price, uniform for all, and provide a means by which to define and detect price cutting and a stimulus to attempts to eliminate it.[13] In the sixth and final grade, the association undertakes to enforce adherence to the average "costs." Through editorials published in trade journals, through resolutions passed at association meetings, and through conferences, and correspondence between association officials and members of the trade, it endeavors to persuade all sellers that they should adopt the common estimate of "cost" and therefore charge a common price.[14]

It would scarcely be wise to prohibit the promotion of cost accounting as such; it certainly would not be safe to give this activity a free rein.

Price reporting systems are operated by some associations; they were found in 15 per cent of those covered in a survey made by Charles A. Pearce in 1939.[15] Through these systems, association members make available to one another, and sometimes to outsiders, information concerning the prices at which products have been, are being, or are to be sold. It is argued that such systems, by increasing the amount of knowledge available to traders, must lessen the imperfection of markets and make for more effective competition. Whether they do so, in fact, depends upon the characteristics of the industries which use them and upon the characteristics of the plans themselves:

> For a price reporting system to increase the effectiveness of competition in a trade, many conditions must be fulfilled. As for the characteristics of the trade: Sellers must be numerous, each of them relatively small, and no one of them dominant. Entrance to the field must not be obstructed by legal barriers or by large capital requirements. Otherwise a reporting system may implement a price agreement, or promote price leadership, and facilitate the application of pressure against price cutters. Moreover, the market for the trade must not be a declining one. Supply, demand, and price must not be subject to violent fluctuation. The product must consist of small units turned out in large volume and sales must be frequent. Otherwise sellers will have a stronger incentive than usual to restrict competition and, even though numerous, they may agree upon a common course of action. Under such circumstances, a price reporting plan may serve as a convenient instrument for the administration of a scheme of price control. And finally, the demand for the product of the trade must be elastic, falling as prices rise and rising as prices fall. Otherwise it is not to be expected that the provision of fuller information would force a seller to reduce his price.
>
> So, too, with the characteristics of the reporting plan itself: The price reports must not be falsified. If members do not return their lowest prices, if the association excludes such prices from the figures it reports, competitive reductions to meet the lowest figure actually charged will not occur. The

[13] Burns, *loc. cit.*, p. 52.

[14] Wilcox, *op. cit.*, pp. 226–27.

[15] Charles A. Pearce, *Trade Association Survey*, T.N.E.C. Monograph 18 (Washington: Government Printing Office, 1940), p. 374.

reports must be available to all sellers on equal terms. If they are not, the sellers who fail to see them will not be informed of lower prices that they otherwise might meet. The reports must also be available to buyers. If information is withheld from them, they cannot seek out the seller who has filed the lowest price or compel another seller to meet this price to make a sale. The reports must not identify individual traders. The reporting agency must be neutral, keeping each seller's returns in confidence and transmitting the collective information to all concerned. If price cutters are openly or secretly identified, those who desire to sell at higher prices may employ persuasion or even sterner methods to bring them into line. The prices reported must be limited to past transactions. If current or future prices are exchanged, sellers will hesitate to cut their charges to make a sale, since they will know that lower figures will instantly be met. Each seller must be free to change his price at any time. If a seller cannot cut a price until sometime after he has filed the lower figure, thus affording his rivals an opportunity to meet it instantly, the chances that he will do so are accordingly reduced. The plan must carry no recommendation as to price policy. If the publication of average "costs" suggests the figures to be filed, if uniform charges are voted at trade meetings, then the reporting system becomes a method of policing the observance of a common price. The system, finally, must make no provision for the supervision of prices charged or for the imposition of penalties on those who sell below the figures they have filed. If association officials supervise the filing and persuade sellers whose quotations are low to raise them, if penalties are imposed on those who quote figures below those recommended or sell at figures below those quoted, then the reporting plan becomes but an incident in the whole price-fixing scheme. When every one of these conditions is fulfilled, a price reporting system may promote effective competition. But where any one of them is unsatisfied, price reporting is likely to implement the non-competitive arrangements within the trade.[16]

Other association activities, not necessarily inconsistent with the maintenance of competition, may be carried to a point where they restrain the freedom of members to compete. Circulation of statistics on production, inventories, unfilled orders, idle capacity, sales, and shipments may serve merely to inform traders concerning the state of the market; it may also be used to facilitate a scheme for curtailment of output and sharing of sales. Standardization of products may contribute to convenience and lessen waste; it may also lessen competition in quality and restrict the consumer's range of choice. Standardization of terms of sale may benefit purchasers by saving time, preventing misunderstandings, and affording a common basis for price comparisons; it may also promote collusion by preventing indirect departures from an established price. Provision of information on credit risks may increase the safety with which credit may be granted; reporting on customers may also be employed as a means of boycotting those who deal with outsiders or fail to observe a recommended price. The pooling of patents may afford a readier access to technology;

[16] Wilcox, *op. cit.*, pp. 229–30.

it may be so administered that technology is monopolized. Joint purchasing may increase efficiency in buying; it may be used to establish prices that are unfair to suppliers and to exact concessions that are unfair to competitors. The promulgation of a code of ethics is avowedly designed to raise standards of conduct among the members of a trade, but such codes frequently contain provisions denouncing practices that are found to be offensive merely because they are competitive. Where an association lacks the power of enforcement, these prohibitions are merely persuasive. But where some measure of coercion is at hand, they may take on the force of law.

Co-operation or Conspiracy?

As Adam Smith remarked in 1776, "People of the same trade seldom meet together, even for merriment and diversion, but the conversation ends in a conspiracy against the public or in some contrivance to raise prices."[17] Does this observation apply to the modern trade association? How far do the members of these organizations engage in activities which enable them, without sacrificing their essential independence of action, to co-operate in increasing efficiency, reducing costs, and improving their service to the public? How far do they engage in activities which secure their adherence to common policies governing production and price? No one knows. There are thousands of trade association offices in the United States. In each of them a staff is working, presumably five days in every week and fifty-two weeks in every year, to administer activities in which competitors do not compete. Upon occasion the Federal Trade Commission or the Department of Justice makes an investigation and certain practices of an association are proscribed by the Commission or the courts. But no such sporadic action can be expected to disclose each of the cases in which competition is restrained. Nor can there ever be assurance that the merriment, diversion, and conversation, of which Adam Smith spoke, do not lead to the conspiracies or contrivances which he feared, unless an agent of the government is placed in every trade association office to read all correspondence, memoranda, and reports, attend all meetings, listen to all conversations, participate in all the merriment and diversion, and issue periodic reports on what transpires. No such systematic oversight is authorized by law.

INTERCORPORATE RELATIONS

Competition may also be impaired by bringing nominally independent corporations under some form of common control. Where such concerns are selling the same product, they can no longer be expected to compete. Where they stand at successive stages of the process of production, unified control may be employed to give them an advantage over their competi-

[17] *Wealth of Nations*, Book I, chap. x, Part II.

tors in obtaining raw materials or in marketing their goods. Such control may be achieved through common ownership of voting stock, through interlocking directorates, and through various ties of a less tangible sort.

Common Stockholdings

Purchase by one corporation of the shares of a competitor is a visible act that can be prevented under the present provisions of the law. But shares in competing companies may legally be owned by private individuals. Thus, on December 31, 1938, each of 58 among the 120 largest stockholders in 17 major oil companies owned shares in two to five of these concerns; 48 owned shares in 6 to 10 of them; 14 owned shares in 11 to 15 of them. Members of the Rockefeller family and foundations established by the Rockefellers were in a controlling minority position in 6 of the major firms.[18] Members of several other families identified with the former oil trust continued to hold stock in 2 or more of the successor companies. In view of the extent to which these concerns were owned by the same people, it seems unlikely that any one of them would pursue a course which was prejudicial to the interests of the others.

Intercorporate stockholdings may also operate to handicap competitors or even to exclude them from the field. The common ownership of anthracite mines and railroads once made it possible for the companies concerned to withhold cars and to collect high transportation rates from other mines. Ownership of pipe lines has afforded the major oil companies a similar advantage over independent refineries. Ownership of theater chains by major producers of motion pictures has made it difficult both for independent producers to obtain desirable outlets and for independent exhibitors to obtain desirable films. Ownership of General Motors and U.S. Rubber by the du Ponts is said to have given their company a preferred market for paints and fabrics and assured U.S. Rubber a preferred market for tires and tubes. Ownership of one subsidiary that operated sleeping cars and of another that manufactured them enabled the Pullman Company to exclude other manufacturers from the market for such equipment until recent years. Ownership of telephone operating companies and of the Western Electric Company by American Telephone and Telegraph has long excluded other manufacturers from markets for telephonic apparatus and materials. Such arrangements, however, have been held to fall within the purview of the law. Here, since they are open and above board, enforcement is not handicapped by lack of proof.

Interlocking Directorates

Unity of action may also be achieved through interlocking directorates. Six different types of interlocks, with varying effects on competition, were listed by the Federal Trade Commission in a report issued in 1950:

[18] *Hearings before the Temporary National Economic Committee*, Part 14-A, pp. 7776–78; National Resources Committee, *The Structure of the American Economy* (Washington: Government Printing Office, 1939), Part I, p. 311.

(1) Interlocking directorates between competitors, the tendency of which is to reduce or eliminate competition.

(2) Interlocking directorates between companies in closely related lines of production, which are capable of forestalling the competition that might develop from the normal expansion of these companies.

(3) Interlocking directorates between companies that face similar or closely related problems, the tendency of which is to consolidate communities of interest among these companies and to create a united front against enterprises that threaten the habitual relationships, ways of doing business, or established preeminence of members of the group.

(4) Interlocking directorates between companies and their suppliers or their customers, which may bring about preferential treatment in prices, in the distribution of materials that are in short supply, or in access to market outlets.

(5) Interlocking directorates between manufacturing corporations and financial institutions, which may give such manufacturers preferential access to credit or may constitute an obstacle to the access of competing enterprises to credit.

(6) Interlocking directorates which express a desire to protect an underlying ownership interest.[19]

The Commission's study covered interlocking relationships among the thousand largest manufacturing corporations and between these corporations and some 330 financial, railroad, public utility, wholesale, and retail companies. Its results are summarized in the following words:

(1) Among the largest companies there was in 1946 a substantial and significant variety of interlocking directorates, which, by virtue of the character of the businesses of the companies, involved reasonable probabilities that competition would be reduced thereby.

(2) Some of these interlocks appeared on their face to be violative of section 8 of the Clayton Act. The majority of them, however, did not fall within the prohibition contained in that Act.

(3) Many of the interlocks which were capable of reducing competition were lawful under the provisions of section 8 of the Clayton Act because the interlocked concerns, though potentially competitors, had not been competitors in the past, or because the interlocked concerns were related to each other as actual or potential suppliers and customers rather than as competitors, or because the individuals through whom the interlocking relationships were maintained were officers or stockholders rather than directors, or because the companies involved, instead of having common directors, had directors who were jointly members of the boards of third companies.

(4) In certain cases interlocking relationships involving several directors from the same company provided a broad base for the development of common policies and attitudes. In certain industries directors from various important companies sat together on particular boards which served as focal points of interlocking relationships. In certain other industries, though there were no

[19] Federal Trade Commission, *Annual Report, 1950*, p. 19; see also *Report of the Federal Trade Commission on Interlocking Directorates* (Washington: Government Printing Office, 1951).

focal points, there was such a multiplicity of interlocking relationships as to constitute a network in which it was evident that the effect of any one interlock was strengthened and supplemented by the existence of the others. The Clayton Act contains no recognition of the significance of multiple, focal, and network interlocks, as distinguished from single interlocks.

(5) The most common interlocks were those that linked a seller of goods or services with a buyer thereof. In a substantial number of cases the importance of the seller, the buyer, or both was such that establishment of preferential or exclusive-dealing relations between them might be expected to have adverse effects upon the opportunities of their competitors. This was particularly true in the case of interlocks between industrial companies and financial institutions. The problems raised by interlocks of the supplier-customer type appear to be similar to those which led the Congress to prohibit such interlocks in the case of common carriers except where steps are taken to assure arm's-length dealing. Nevertheless, there is no legal limitation upon this type of interlocking relationship among industrial and commercial companies.[20]

It thus appears that the prohibition contained in the Clayton Act applies to only one among the many means whereby competition may be impaired through the operation of interlocking directorates.

Interest Groupings

It has sometimes been noted that the security issues of competing corporations have been underwritten by the same investment banking houses, that their bonds have been held by the same banks and insurance companies, that their books have been audited by the same accountants, and that they have been served by the same law firms, engineering firms, advertising agencies, and public relations counsellors. Many writers have perceived, in these facts, influences that may discourage competition and make for uniformity of policy. The National Resources Committee went on, in 1939, to identify eight "corporate interest groupings" whose members were connected through stock ownership, interlocking directorates, common financial affiliations, and intangible personal ties. The Committee did not contend that the corporations in these groupings were subject to centralized control, but it did assert that they were not completely independent of one another, since their financing was carried on through the same channels, their policies were formulated or reviewed by many of the same people, and the climate of opinion within which these policies were developed was much the same.[21] Important as these influences may be, they are probably too tenuous to fall within the strictures of the law. The climate of opinion is beyond the reach of antitrust.

CONSCIOUS PARALLELISM OF ACTION

In markets characterized by oligopoly, where the entire output of a product is controlled by a few firms, or where the bulk of it is in the

[20] *Ibid.*, pp. 26–27. [21] National Resources Committee, *op. cit.*, p. 162.

hands of firms that are much larger than any of the rest, the decisions made by each large seller will have an appreciable effect upon supply and price. If any one of them increases his output or reduces his price, the others are likely to retaliate, and the profits of the trade may be impaired. The threat of this development has sometimes led to arrangements, of the sort described above, whereby independent action is forestalled. It may also lead, by force of circumstances or through long experience, to an identity of behavior that is achieved, without overt agreement or formal organization, through mutual forbearance by common consent. "Men may move in lockstep," as Walton Hamilton and Irene Till have put it, "not by agreement among themselves, but in automatic response to identical stimuli."[22] Such behavior has been described by the Federal Trade Commission as "conscious parallelism of action." It has manifested itself in the conventional sharing of markets, in price leadership and followership, and in the computation of delivered prices in accordance with a common formula.

Conventional Market Sharing

In certain industries competition is avoided by behavior which maintains a settled distribution of the business in the field. Here the dominant concerns amicably share supplies and markets, no one of them attempting to trespass on another's ground, each of them habitually abstaining from bidding against the others in making purchases and sales. In some cases they have acted in conformity with the terms of an explicit agreement; in others, they merely follow the conventions of the trade. Conventional market sharing is said to have existed for many years, before World War II, in the investment banking field. As the practice was described in testimony before the Temporary National Economic Committee in 1940:

> Bankers do not compete for corporate stocks and bonds. Each investment house has its territory where others do not intrude. Houses do not solicit business from a corporation that is dealing with another firm. They do not bid on securities that have been offered to others. Bankers speak of the "historical relationships" which exist between borrowing corporations and banking firms. The right to certain customers, the right to certain participations, and the right to share in the management of underwriting syndicates are regarded by the members of the trade, in a moral if not in a legal sense, as proprietary interests, are tenaciously defended by their owners, and are generally respected by others. The same groups of bankers, united in the same combinations in a long series of syndicates, continue to underwrite the issues of the same corporations over extended periods of time. Issuers of securities, in effect, are allocated among the members of the trade and bankers are assigned participations in their issues in proportions which are constantly maintained.[23]

[22] Walton Hamilton and Irene Till, *Antitrust in Action*, T.N.E.C., Monograph 16 (Washington: Government Printing Office, 1940), p. 14.

[23] Wilcox, *op. cit.*, pp. 177–78. Judge Harold R. Medina found no evidence of such a practice in an antitrust suit which he decided in 1953. For further comment on this decision see Chapter 5.

Market sharing, either by agreement or by convention, has also existed in the meat packing industry:

> In 1918, the Federal Trade Commission reported that the distribution of livestock purchases, slaughtering, and sales among the Swift, Armour, Morris, Wilson, and Cudahy companies, during the five years previous, had remained the same from week to week and month to month, regardless of the total quantity of sales. Again in 1925, the Commission reported that the percentage distribution of the slaughter in the five preceding years had shown little change. In 1940, William H. Nicholls published an analysis of the proportionate weekly purchases of hogs, cattle, and calves made by the "Big Four" companies in each of five terminal markets during the years from 1931 through 1937. Each packer's share of the "Big Four" purchases of each type of livestock in each of these markets was found to remain strikingly constant from week to week and from year to year. When the distribution of purchases in this period was compared with that which the Federal Trade Commission had published for 1913–1917, it was found that the situation had remained virtually unchanged for a quarter of a century.[24]

"As it weaves its way into the structure of an industry," say Hamilton and Till, "restraint shifts its home from collusion to the folkways."[25] And this, according to a Complaint issued by the Department of Justice in 1948, is what has happened in the meat industry. "During the first quarter of a century of the conspiracy, defendants engaged in joint enterprises and held numerous meetings to control their buying and selling activities. . . . During this period, each company adopted substantially identical policies and methods of doing business. . . . By about 1920, the executives of each concern had become so habituated to the use of these identical methods and policies that they were expert in conducting the operations of their respective companies along parallel non-competitive lines."[26] In such an arrangement, as in cases where market sharing is formally organized, no participant can increase his share of the market by paying higher prices or by charging lower ones. As a consequence, there is no incentive to do so. Nor is there pressure to improve the quality of products, to offer better service, to increase efficiency, or to reduce costs. As far as the consumer is concerned, the situation is much the same as if a single firm possessed a complete monopoly.

Price Leadership

Where a single firm overtops its rivals, it may invariably take the initiative in announcing changes in price. Where two or more concerns are dominant, one may habitually serve as leader or more than one may lead, each in a different territory or each in turn. The smaller firms in such a field will follow the changes that are announced and sell at the prices that

[24] *Ibid.*, pp. 183–85. [25] Hamilton and Till, *op. cit.*, p. 15.

[26] *U.S.* v. *Armour & Co., et al., Complaint,* September 15, 1948. The government dropped its suit against the industry in 1953.

are set. Not only will they follow the leader down, as competition would dictate; they will also follow him up, as it would not. They may do so because they fear annihilation in the warfare that might be provoked by an attempt to undercut the leader, because they hope to obtain larger profits by taking refuge under the price umbrella which he holds over the trade, or merely because they find it convenient to follow his lead. In any case, they abandon independence of judgment and adopt his prices as their own.

This procedure is illustrated by a passage from the *Hearings before the Temporary National Economic Committee* which deals with firms engaged in the fabrication of nonferrous alloys. The American Brass Company was doing 25 per cent of the business in this field; the Riverside Metal Company was doing 1½ per cent; the president of Riverside was on the stand:

> MR. COX: Mr. Randall, would it be correct to say that there is a well crystallized practice of price leadership in the industry in which you are engaged?
>
> MR. RANDALL: I would say so.
>
> MR. COX: And what company is the price leader?
>
> MR. RANDALL: I would say the American Brass Company holds that position.
>
> MR. COX: And your company follows the prices which are announced by the American Brass?
>
> MR. RANDALL: That is correct.
>
> MR. COX: So that when they reduce the price you have to reduce it too? Is that correct?
>
> MR. RANDALL: Well, we don't have to, but we do.
>
> MR. COX: And when they raise the price you raise the price?
>
> MR. RANDALL: That is correct . . .
>
> MR. ARNOLD: You exercise no individual judgment as to the price you charge for your product, then?
>
> MR. RANDALL: Well, I think that is about what it amounts to, yes sir.[27]

In the steel industry, United States Steel has been the leader. As a former president of the Corporation told a committee of the Senate in 1936, "We generally make the prices."[28] And the president of Bethlehem Steel subsequently testified that his company welcomed "the opportunity to follow the Corporation's lead in the publishing of new base prices,"[29] recalling no instance in which it had failed to follow these prices either up or down.[30] In the glass container industry, according to officials of the leading companies: "Thatcher sets a price on milk bottles. . . . Hazel-Atlas . . . initiates the prices covering wide-mouthed container ware . . . tumblers and table ware. As to prices on proprietary and prescription ware, we

[27] *Hearings before the T.N.E.C.*, Part V, pp. 2085–87.

[28] *Hearings before the Committee on Interstate Commerce, U.S. Senate, 74th Cong., 2d Sess. on S. 4055*, p. 595.

[29] *Hearings before the T.N.E.C.*, Part XIX, p. 10592. [30] *Ibid.*, p. 10603.

adopt the schedules of . . . Owens-Illinois . . . and make their prices ours. . . . We adopt the prices as published by . . . Ball Brothers . . . as our prices for fruit jars, jelly glasses, and fruit jar tops."[31] There has also been evidence of the leader-follower relationship among producers of agricultural implements, anthracite coal, bananas, biscuits and crackers, canned salmon, cement, cigarettes, copper, corn products, fertilizers, gasoline, industrial alcohol, lead, newsprint paper, sulphur, and tin cans.[32]

Prices established through leadership are not effectively competitive. The leader, controlling a substantial portion of the output of the trade, estimates the sales revenues and the production costs incident to the quantities salable at various prices and produces the amount, and sells at the figure, that is calculated to yield him the largest net return. In short, he behaves as a monopolist. When other sellers adopt the same figure, they offer buyers no real alternative. Leader and followers alike exact a monopoly price.

Prices resulting from market sharing and price leadership may be productive of high profits, but they are not invariably so. In some cases, they may temporarily afford a return so large that additional firms are encouraged to enter the field. The business obtainable at the established price is shared by an increasing number of participants. The leaders get a declining percentage of the trade. Idle capacity piles up, to be carried at heavy cost. Monopoly pricing persists, but monopoly profits are not secured. The restraints adopted serve but to forestall the competitive struggle that would otherwise obtain.

Delivered Pricing

In many industries where the cost of transporting the product is high, sellers located at different places have contrived to charge identical prices at any location where goods are delivered. This identity was once accomplished through the use of common basing points. Under such a system, each seller refuses to quote a price for the sale of goods at the door of his own mill and insists on making quotations that include a charge for their delivery to his customers. In computing this charge, all sellers employ the same city or cities as basing points, and each of them figures the freight on a particular sale from the same point. Goods may be shipped by water or by truck at rates that are lower than by rail, but every price is calculated on the basis of an all-rail haul. One railroad may quote a lower rate than another, but the freight included in the price is that recorded in a common rate book. As a result, all sellers, wherever located, charge the same amount for delivery.

In itself, this practice need not involve the quotation of identical prices.

[31] *Ibid.*, Part II, pp. 530, 547–48.

[32] Burns, *op. cit.*, pp. 77–140; Wilcox, *op. cit.*, pp. 121–32; George W. Stocking and Myron W. Watkins, *Monopoly and Free Enterprise* (New York: Twentieth Century Fund, 1951), pp. 132–84.

The delivered price includes two elements: the charge for freight and the price of the product at the basing point. The quotations made by different sellers will not be identical unless their base prices as well as their delivery charges are the same. This, however, is usually the case. Identity of base prices is achieved through agreement or through general acceptance of price leadership. Indeed, if this were not the case, there would be little reason for selling on a delivered basis, since the practice finds its significance in the enforcement of identity. Conversely, if prices were not quoted on this basis, identity through agreement or leadership would be less readily achieved. Each of these practices contributes to a common plan. Identical delivered prices at each delivery point are the result.

The operation of such a system may be illustrated by reference to the methods that were employed for many years in the steel industry:

> In conformity with the prevailing system, the producer of steel employs the following procedure in computing the price that he will quote: (1) He ascertains the base prices for a standard product that have been announced at a number of basing points. In doing this, he follows the announcements of United States Steel. (2) In the case of a non-standard product, he adds to or subtracts from these prices the extras or deductions which are charged or allowed for variations in size or quality. In doing this, he adopts the figures that have been agreed upon by members of the industry. (3) He adds to the base price—plus or minus the extras or deductions—freight charges from various basing points to the point of delivery. In doing this, he consults the same schedule of rates that is used by his competitors. (4) He selects the smallest total as his price. Since every seller employs the same formula and since every item in the formula is standardized, whether by price leadership, by agreement, or otherwise, the result must be the same in every case. As a consequence, when the system is working without interference, every seller of any steel product quotes to any buyer an identical delivered price.[33]

The character and the consequences of various delivered pricing systems will be analyzed in some detail in Chapter 8. It is sufficient, at this stage, to point out that such a system may enable sellers to eliminate competition without affording evidence of overt agreement or formal organization in restraint of trade. Faithful adherence to a common formula for computing prices is all that is required.

Constructive Conspiracy

Such patterns of behavior, once learned, continue of their own momentum. Compared with obvious conspiracy, they may be difficult to prosecute. The contrast is described by Hamilton and Till:

> Where units are many, heat has marked the struggle for markets, feelings have grown tense, suspicions have been quickened. As a result, the getting together has hard going. The meetings must be frequent, the talk frank, the understandings clean-cut, explicit, above board. The procedure generates evi-

[33] Wilcox, *op. cit.*, pp. 149–50.

dence as it goes forward; the industry virtually invites a suit through the very ease of getting proof. But where very few units are involved, where co-operation is a practice of long standing, where a large body of understandings is a matter of course, the situation is otherwise. The necessity for conference is infrequent, minutes of meetings are prepared in advance by skilled attorneys, the question direct is never put. Action is taken without fanfare of trumpets; conduct is clothed in accepted practice; records are barren of evidence to the overt act.[34]

In such a situation, the evidence available may be purely circumstantial. Statistics of purchases, sales, and prices may have to bear the burden of proof. Agreement may have to be inferred from identity of behavior. A case of conspiracy may have to be constructed on the basis of a probability that each of several firms adopting some common course of conduct has done so in the light of knowledge that all the others would do the same. Conscious parallelism of action thus presents a problem of particular difficulty to antitrust.

MONOPOLISTIC ABUSES

The unfair methods that may be used by a single firm are much the same as those employed by several independent enterprises in accordance with the terms of a restrictive agreement or in conformity with the provisions of a trade association plan. They include such practices as excluding competitors from access to supplies and markets, obtaining unduly discriminatory prices in buying and charging unduly discriminatory prices in selling, engaging in predatory price cutting, squeezing the margins of nonintegrated independents, and maliciously interfering with other firms.

Exclusive and Discriminatory Buying

Firms dominant in a field have sometimes prevented the emergence or survival of competitors by excluding them from access to productive facilities, credit, equipment, and materials. They have made pre-emptive purchases, buying in quantities greater than those required to satisfy their needs. They have forced suppliers to sign exclusive contracts, refusing to buy from those who sold to their competitors. They have also handicapped their rivals by demanding and obtaining from suppliers discriminatory concessions that could not be justified by differences in cost. Such practices were characteristic of the early trusts. The American Can Company prevented its competitors from obtaining up-to-date equipment by entering into exclusive contracts with the manufacturers of automatic can-making machinery; its connection with the American Tin Plate Company not only enabled it to obtain secret rebates on its raw material, but also threatened to interfere with the delivery of plate to other producers and even to cut them off completely from their source of supply.[35] Several of

[34] Hamilton and Till, *op. cit.*, p. 20.

[35] *U.S.* v. *American Can Co.*, 230 Fed. 859 (1916).

the trusts persuaded the railroads to grant them substantial rebates; Standard Oil not only recovered 40–50 per cent of the sums which it paid the roads for carrying its own products, but also collected a similar share of the rates paid by its rivals.[36] The Aluminum Company of America, enjoying a patent monopoly in its early years, made pre-emptive purchases of deposits of bauxite and sites for the generation of hydroelectric power, and bought power elsewhere under contracts which forbade suppliers to sell to other producers of aluminum; it eliminated one prospective competitor by purchasing the site he was arranging to develop and acquired the property of another when he could find no bankers to finance his enterprise.[37] To the same end, more recently, producers of the leading brands of cigarettes bought up the stocks of tobacco required for the production of ten-cent brands;[38] and exhibitors of motion pictures prevented other houses from obtaining films by renting more features than they had time to display in their own theaters.[39]

Exclusive Selling

Large concerns have frequently attempted to exclude their smaller rivals from the market by imposing upon distributors contracts forbidding them to handle goods produced by other firms. Contracts of this sort have been employed, in the past, in the sale of biscuits and crackers, cameras, dress patterns, canned sirups, petroleum products, and many other goods. Their use is now limited by Section 3 of the Clayton Act. Where products are small, simple, and relatively inexpensive, they are usually distributed by independent retailers who may be compelled by heavy advertising to carry the large firm's brand and may therefore find it necessary to accept exclusive contracts. When this occurs, smaller producers are seriously handicapped in reaching the market by exclusion from normal contacts with potential customers. Where goods are bulky, complicated, and expensive, they are usually distributed through exclusive agencies, and any firm that seeks to enter the market must establish an agency system of its own. The difficulties involved in doing so may operate to bar newcomers from the field.

Firms facing little or no competition in the sale of one product and substantial competition in the sale of another have employed restrictive contracts of another type, refusing to supply a purchaser with the first product unless he would agree to rely upon the same supplier for the second, thus closing the market to competitors in the latter field. Such a

[36] Eliot Jones, *The Trust Problem in the United States* (New York: Macmillan Co., 1921) pp. 49–52.

[37] *U.S.* v. *Aluminum Co. of America*, 148 F. 2d 416 (1945); Donald H. Wallace, *Market Control in the Aluminum Industry* (Cambridge: Harvard University Press, 1937), pp. 115–17; 132–37.

[38] *American Tobacco Co.* v. *U.S.*, 328 U.S. 781 (1946).

[39] Walter Adams, *The Structure of American Industry* (New York: Macmillan Co., 1950), p. 286.

practice was followed, for many years, by the United Shoe Machinery Corporation:

> Instead of selling its patented machines, the company adopted the policy of leasing them, charging shoe manufacturers a royalty for each pair of shoes on which they were used. It inserted in its leases a clause which forbade the manufacturer to use any other maker's machine for any process in which one of its own machines was employed. It denied him the right to use its own machines on shoes which were processed at any stage of their production on machines made by its rivals. By means of the latter device, the company extended its control from its exclusive fields to those in which it had formerly been faced by competition. The shoe manufacturer, who could obtain a lasting machine only by leasing it from the United Shoe Machinery Corporation, was compelled to turn to it also for his welter, stitcher, and metallic fastener, and the independent producers of these machines were robbed of their customers.[40]

In the same way, competitors were once excluded from the market for radio tubes by a provision in licenses granted by the Radio Corporation of America, under its patents, to manufacturers of radio sets, requiring them to buy their tubes from R.C.A.[41] Tying contracts of this sort have also been used in the sale of stencils and ink to purchasers of mimeograph machines, jute bagging to purchasers of steel ties for baling cotton, installment financing services to dealers in automobiles, motion picture films to lessees of projectors, tabulating cards to lessees of tabulating machines, and various materials to lessees of many other types of machinery, in each case giving the producer of the second good or service a marked advantage over his competitors in the production of the first.

Firms selling a large number of products have sometimes followed a similar practice, refusing to supply any of them to purchasers who would not agree to take several or all of them. Companies manufacturing a full line of agricultural implements once forced their distributors to carry every product in the line, forbidding them to handle equipment produced by other firms. This full-line forcing excluded the specialized manufacturer from thousands of retail outlets; in rural markets which were too small to support more than two or three dealers he may not have been represented at all.[42] The major producers of motion pictures have likewise imposed upon independent exhibitors, who must turn to them for the great majority of their feature attractions, contracts including a block-booking clause which compels these houses to take many pictures they do not want in order to obtain the ones they do. Independent producers have consequently been unable to rent their films to exhibitors whose programs were thus crowded with the products of the major firms.[43] Through such

[40] Wilcox, *op. cit.*, pp. 72–73.

[41] *Lord et al.* v. *Radio Corporation of America*, 24 F. 2d 565 (1928).

[42] Federal Trade Commission, *The Agricultural Implements and Machinery Industry* (Washington: Government Printing Office, 1938) pp. 276–83.

[43] *U.S.* v. *Paramount Pictures*, 334 U.S. 131 (1948).

devices, firms producing several different goods have contrived to handicap competitors whose operations were narrower in scope.

Discriminatory and Predatory Pricing

It is not unusual for sellers to fix different prices for different buyers. Nor is such differentiation necessarily unfair. For differences in price may reflect real differences in the cost at which particular sales are made. But there are cases in which differentiation cannot be so justified. Discriminatory reductions may carry particular prices far below real costs, and losses may be deliberately incurred for the purpose of driving weaker rivals from the field.

Discrimination of this sort is most likely to be practiced by a firm that operates in many different markets or produces many different goods. Such a seller enjoys a marked advantage over those whose operations are confined to a single market or a single line. He can cut a particular price to a point where he loses money and still preserve his solvency by maintaining prices elsewhere. But his smaller rivals, incurring losses on their entire output, may shortly be driven into bankruptcy. The diversified seller is thus in a position to select particular firms for destruction, picking them off at his pleasure, one at a time. He may discriminate among localities, temporarily cutting his price in one area and raising it again when he has eliminated his local competitors. He may discriminate among products, setting up bogus independents or producing fighting brands to sell at ruinous prices, and cutting them off when their purpose has been served. Such practices were employed by the early trusts to build up positions of monopoly in oil, sugar, tobacco, meat packing, and tin cans. They are now forbidden by the Clayton and Robinson-Patman Acts.

A firm possessing large financial resources, instead of engaging in discrimination, may reduce its prices uniformly, setting them below its costs at levels that make it impossible for its weaker rivals to survive, and accepting the resulting losses as an investment to be recovered in the later profits of monopoly. This was a common practice in the heyday of the trusts. Firms were combined, prices were raised, new competition was attracted, prices were slashed, the newcomers were bought up or driven out of business, and prices were raised again. Reduction of prices, under these circumstances, was monopolistic in purpose and effect.

Predatory price cutting may now be held to violate the law. But the practice is by no means easy to identify. The test of predation is intent, but the price cutter's purpose is known only to himself, is only to be inferred by others. In cases of flagrant discrimination, the inference may be plain; in cases of general price reduction, it is less so. The competitor who finds it difficult to meet another's price may well believe that his rival intends to eliminate him, but this conviction cannot be taken as sufficient proof of such intent. Every act of competition is designed to attract business to one competitor rather than another and, to that extent, to eliminate the latter from the field. The line beyond which such activity is properly to be attacked as predatory is not an easy one to draw.

The Squeeze

A large concern that is vertically integrated, controlling operations at each of the successive stages of production, may turn out at each stage the exact amounts that it requires for use at the next, entering the market only as a seller of finished goods. But integration may also be disproportionate; an integrated company may enter the market at earlier stages as a seller of materials; its nonintegrated competitors at later stages may depend upon it for supplies. To the integrated firm, the prices charged and the margins allowed at successive stages are a matter of convenience; to its nonintegrated competitors, they are a matter of life and death. Such a concern is thus in a position to squeeze its rivals by raising prices in the markets where they buy and reducing prices in the markets where they sell. Thus, the Aluminum Company of America, competing with independent companies in the fabrication of aluminum products, was for many years the only source from which these independents could obtain their supply of aluminum ingots and sheets; by raising the price of raw materials and lowering the price of finished products, the company has been said to have made it unprofitable for its rivals to remain in business.[44] A similar squeeze has been experienced by independent refiners of petroleum:

> The independent refiner must operate within the margin which exists between the price of crude and the price of gasoline. The majors take the lead in establishing each of these prices. The independent cannot buy crude for less than the price they pay. He cannot sell gasoline for more than the price they charge. The refinery margin, within which he must operate, is thus determined for him by his powerful competitors. The width of this margin is of crucial importance to him; it has little more than a book-keeping significance for them. If they should choose to reduce it, by raising the price of crude, by lowering the price of gasoline, or both, he might be driven from the field. This process is known to the industry as the "refinery squeeze." According to one witness who testified before the T.N.E.C., application of the squeeze closed 100 independent refineries in the East Texas field between 1937 and 1939.[45]

The squeeze, like the predatory reduction of prices, is difficult for antitrust authorities to attack, since here again price changes may be adjudged competitive or monopolistic according to their motivation, and motives are difficult to prove.

Malicious Interference

Large firms have sometimes undertaken to eliminate their smaller rivals by maliciously interfering with the production and sale of their goods.

[44] Burns, *op. cit.*, p. 441; Corwin D. Edwards, *Maintaining Competition* (New York: McGraw-Hill Book Co., 1949), p. 172.

[45] Wilcox, *op. cit.*, pp. 167–68.

The classic case of such behavior, dating back to the end of the last century, is that of the National Cash Register Company:

> The company set out deliberately to destroy its competitors. It hired their employees away from them. It bribed their employees and the employees of railroads and telephone and telegraph companies to spy on them and disclose their business secrets. It spread false rumors concerning their solvency. It instructed its agents to misrepresent the quality of their goods, interfere with their sales, and damage the mechanism of their machines in establishments where they were in use. It publicly displayed their cash registers under labels which read, "Junk." It made, and sold at less than cost, inferior machines called "knockers," which it represented to be just as good as theirs. It threatened to bring suit against them and their customers for alleged infringements of patent rights. It induced their customers to cancel their orders and repudiate their contracts. It intimidated prospective investors in competing plants by publishing lists of defunct competitors and by exhibiting in a "grave yard" at its factory samples of the machines which they had formerly made. Such practices, carried on over a period of twenty years, gave the company control of 95 percent of the nation's production of cash registers.[46]

Behavior of this sort clearly violates the law. Being conspicuous, it is easy to attack. While not unknown today, it has largely disappeared. The methods of monopolization that are currently employed are usually more circumspect.

COMBINATION WITHOUT ABUSE

A firm may acquire possession of the property of its competitors by employing methods of competition that are so oppressive as to leave them no choice but to sell out. And this, indeed, has frequently occurred. But business combinations may also be effected, without coercive pressure, through the voluntary choice of the participants. And where the firms combined produce the bulk of a product, monopoly may be painlessly achieved. In any case, combination is a process that should be examined apart from the unfair methods by which it has often been induced.

Forms of Combination

Two or more enterprises may be brought under common direction in a variety of ways: by the purchase of assets, by merger, by amalgamation, by intercorporate stockholding, and by the formation of a holding company. In the first case, Company A offers to purchase the assets of Company B, the stockholders of B consent to the sale, A pays cash to B and takes possession of its assets, B distributes the cash to its stockholders and goes out of business. In the case of a merger, A proposes to absorb B, the stockholders of B agree, they receive the stock in A in return for stock in B, and B disappears. In both cases, A retains its identity. In the case of

[46] *Ibid.*, p. 68.

amalgamation, it is proposed to establish a new Company C for the purpose of absorbing both A and B, the stockholders of A and B agree to the proposal, they surrender their stock and get stock in C, thereafter C survives and A and B both disappear. In all three cases, two companies are fused and one or both of them loses its identity. In the case of intercorporate stockholding, A goes into the market and purchases a majority or a controlling minority of the voting stock of B, the stockholders of B do not vote on the deal, B retains its corporate identity, but A now selects its directors and officers and determines its policies. In the holding company case, a new corporation H is established, H goes into the market and purchases controlling stock in A and B, the stockholders of A and B do not vote on the deal, A and B both retain their identity, but H now selects their directors and officers and determines their policies. The latter devices have two advantages: they do not necessitate the payment of cash or the issuance of securities to cover the full value of the companies brought under control, and they do not require the assent of their stockholders.

Before 1890 the principal form of combination, as explained in Chapter 3, was the voting trust. As a consequence of adverse judicial decisions and the adoption of the Sherman Act, this device was abandoned. But its place was shortly taken by the holding company. Up to this time, the laws of the several states had not permitted one corporation to hold stock in another. In 1889, however, New Jersey amended its statutes to permit corporations operating under its charters to do so. This lead was shortly followed by the other states. The way was thus opened to the formation of combinations that might not otherwise have been achieved. This deliberate relaxation of the law contributed heavily to the subsequent attainment of monopoly.

The types of activity that are brought under common direction by any of the methods described may differ fundamentally in character. Combinations may be classified as horizontal, chain, vertical, lateral, and conglomerate. The horizontal combination brings together firms at the same stage of production, turning out the same product, and selling it in the same market. This was the pattern adopted by the early trusts. The chain combination unites companies at the same stage of production that sell the same product in different local markets. It is typified by public utility and branch banking systems and by chains of restaurants, hotels, and retail stores. Vertical integration reaches forward or backward or both to combine firms at successive stages of production. It is seen in the ownership of iron mines by steel mills and movie theaters by producing companies. Lateral combination brings together companies engaged in the production of goods that are related but not competitive. International Business Machines, General Foods, and Standard Brands are examples of this type. Here a common trade mark or a common selling organization may be used for the various products in a corporate family. Conglomerate combination unites enterprises whose products may not be related in any way. The ownership by General Motors of subsidiaries manufacturing automobiles and refrigerators is a case in point. These types of combination do not always occur in isolation; a corporate complex will frequently encompass two or more of them.

The Merger Movement

The historical development of corporate combination, usually referred to as the merger movement, has been characterized by three widely separated periods of heightened activity, the first around the turn of the century, the second following World War I, and the last dating from World War II. The first of these periods opened with prosperity in 1897 and ended with depression in 1903. It was marked primarily by the use of the holding company device to effect horizontal combinations in mining and manufacturing. During this period more than 200 large combines were formed and many of the country's basic industries were monopolized. The second period began with prosperity in the twenties and ended with the stock market crash of 1929. It was marked by extension of the movement from mining and manufacturing to the public utilities, banking, and the distributive and personal service trades, by the emergence of many different patterns of combination—chain, vertical, lateral, and conglomerate as well as horizontal—and by the employment of each of the devices through which combination may be attained. In both of these periods, the movement was facilitated by the existence of a ready market for corporate securities and stimulated by the prospect of realizing quick profits through promotional and speculative activities.

The third period, following World War II, was characterized by numerous combinations in the food and beverage, textile and apparel, and chemical and drug industries. It was marked by vertical integration and diversification as much as by the merger of firms engaged in like activities. It did not involve the fusion of large enterprises or the establishment of new concerns to absorb existing companies, but manifested itself, rather, in the acquisition by larger units of the assets or the shares of smaller ones. Instead of being induced by speculative opportunities, these acquisitions were apparently encouraged by the existence of large wartime accumulations of working capital. From 1940 to 1947, according to the Federal Trade Commission, such combinations resulted in the disappearance of more than 2,450 corporations in mining and manufacturing, with assets exceeding 5 per cent of those invested in these fields, one third of them being absorbed by firms with assets of more than $50 million, and two thirds of them by smaller concerns.[47]

The significance of such figures is by no means clear since the effects of combination on competition will vary from case to case. Horizontal

[47] Federal Trade Commission, *The Merger Movement, A Summary Report* (Washington: Government Printing Office, 1948).

combination, where the companies involved control the whole supply of a product, will result in a complete monopoly. But where one small firm absorbs another, it may increase the vigor of competition by strengthening their ability to compete. In other forms of combination, where the units brought together do not sell the same product in the same market, the purpose may be something other than the attainment of monopoly; chain combination may be directed toward economies that are to be realized through mass buying, standardized operations, and unified management, vertical integration toward the assurance of raw material supplies and market outlets, lateral combination toward the employment of a common selling organization, and conglomerate combination toward the diversification of investment risks. In some cases, such a combination may contribute indirectly to the suppression of competition by giving the large concern an unfair advantage over its small competitors. In others, however, it may have no effect. And in still others, its results may be indeterminate. Combination must therefore be judged in accordance with its consequences, case by case. Over all, it appears to have contributed less to business size than has expansion through internal growth.[48]

The Control of Combination

Since combination is an overt act, its prosecution is not handicapped by lack of proof. It is a simple matter, moreover, to issue an order forbidding new acquisitions of stock or assets. But it is not so easy to break up a combination that has existed for many years. Combination is not outlawed as such; it is illegal only when it leads to monopoly. But no definition of monopoly is provided in the law, and no clear criteria of monopoly have been developed by the courts. And, in their absence, the courts are not compelled to find that a particular combination is in violation of the law. Where there is evidence of serious abuse, they are likely to do so. But where the position of a monopolistic combination is so secure that unfair methods are no longer needed, they may be reluctant to act. It is not easy to unscramble eggs that were scrambled many years ago. Where combination has been effected through intercorporate stockholdings or through the holding company device, divorcement can be accomplished by requiring the holders to sell their stock. But where firms have been merged or amalgamated, a complete reorganization is required. In either case, the task of reshuffling property interests, while not impossible, is difficult. The courts may also fear that dismemberment of a corporate giant would reduce efficiency and impede progress. They may doubt that competition would be restored or the public interest really served. In the face of difficulty, and in the light of uncertainty, it is easier to leave ill enough alone.

[48] See J. Fred Weston, *The Role of Mergers in the Growth of Large Firms* (Berkeley: University of California Press, 1953). See also John Lintner and J. Keith Butters, "Effect of Mergers on Industrial Concentration," in *Review of Economics and Statistics* for February, 1950.

MONOPOLY WITHOUT COMBINATION

Combination is the principal method by which a single firm is likely to attain a position of monopoly but is not the only one. Monopolistic powers are granted, in many cases, by local, state, and federal governments. There are franchises, certificates of public convenience and necessity, permits, and licenses which confer upon their holders exclusive privileges in the employment of limited facilities and the provision of important services. Such monopolies, being subject to other forms of regulation, are beyond the reach of antitrust. There are also patents, trademarks, and copyrights which give their owners the exclusive right to control the use of certain machines and processes and the manufacture and sale of certain goods, to employ certain names or symbols, or to publish certain materials. Trademark protection may be permanent; patents and copyrights are limited in time. The problems which they present to antitrust are to be considered in Chapter 6.

There are also fields in which the characteristics of the product, the scope of the market, or the location of resources are such that competition cannot be expected to obtain. A novelty is likely to be produced exclusively, for a time, by the company that was first in the field. The market for another product may be so small that a single firm can satisfy the whole demand. The supply of a mineral may be so concentrated as to give the owner of one deposit a monopoly. This was true, at one time, in the case of nickel, magnesium, and molybdenum. But such advantages will usually be temporary. Unless it is permanently protected by law, a monopoly is likely to be lost as markets expand, as substitutes are developed, as new resources are discovered, and as new competitors enter the field. In some cases, however, it is possible that a position of monopoly, once established, may be maintained, not through legal privilege, resort to unfair tactics, or combination with others, but simply by growing as the market grows.

Monopolies based on legal grants are excluded from the operation of antitrust laws. But other monopolies are covered by Section 2 of the Sherman Act which forbids any person to "monopolize or attempt to monopolize," and these words are separate from the ones which prohibit combination or conspiracy. Here again, however, enforcement is handicapped by the absence of clear criteria of monopoly, by the difficulties of dissolution, and by the uncertainty as to its consequences.

SIZE WITHOUT MONOPOLY

It would be a mistake to identify little business with competition, big business with monopoly. It is not the absolute size of a business unit that is significant, but its size in relation to the size of the market in which it operates. In a limited market a tiny firm may possess a complete monopoly. In a larger market a corporate giant may face severe competition. In many small towns there are only one or two bankers, butchers, plumbers, pharmacists, undertakers, hotels, garages, coal dealers, ice plants, and lumber yards. The largest corporations in the country, on the other hand, include such firms as Sears Roebuck, Macy's, and the A&P, all of them facing active competition in the markets where they buy and sell.

The large concern, however, possesses marked competitive advantages. Its vast resources and the scale of its operations give it a preferred position in buying and selling, in obtaining capital and credit, in conducting litigation, and in dealing with the government. It can obtain low prices from suppliers, not only by buying in quantity, but also by threatening to divert its purchases or to produce for itself. It can influence demand by spending huge sums on advertising and, in some cases, by providing assurance of trade-in values, continued supplies of parts, and servicing. It can obtain easy access to credit and find a ready market for its securities. It can afford to sue and be sued and can withstand the cost of repeated appeals. It can contribute heavily to campaign funds and make substantial investments in contacts with legislators and administrative agencies. Such a firm obtains still further advantages when its activities are diversified. As Edwards has observed:

> Its operations are spread across so many customers, so many geographical markets, and, in the case of the conglomerate enterprise, so many different types of commodities and services that its fortunes do not depend upon profit or loss in a particular transaction, a particular location, or a particular activity. This diversity of interests not only immunizes it from the effects of business fluctuations which would mean disaster to an enterprise operating more narrowly, but also gives it the power to lose money deliberately at any one point for the sake of disciplining or destroying its more specialized rivals.[49]

Even though the large concern lacks a monopoly in any of the fields in which it operates, the many advantages which it enjoys may thus threaten the survival of its smaller competitors.

If the corporate giant resorts to unfair methods of competition, it may be found to violate the law. But if it employs its powers with due restraint, it probably cannot be held to do so. It is sometimes asserted that the preservation, for its own sake, of an economy of numerous small units was the motivating purpose of the framers of the Sherman Act. But this is not what the law says. It is monopoly that is condemned, not size as such. And though antitrust has often been accused of attacking size alone, its proceedings against large firms have invariably been based on allegations of illegal behavior.

But the line between legality and illegality, in such a case, is not an easy one to draw. An integrated firm, in the words of Dirlam and Kahn,

> . . . must, if it is to compete vigorously, charge little more than incremental costs in some of its markets, relying on others to make up the larger portion

[49] Edwards, *op. cit.*, p. 101.

of the joint costs of integrated operations. Yet in so doing it cannot avoid "squeezing" non-integrated competitors in the more competitive markets, in the sense that it is accepting prices there which it could not long continue to accept but for the returns it obtains elsewhere. It is practically impossible, therefore, for a large, integrated firm to exploit its socially acceptable advantages, or even to meet competition, without at the same time exploiting those advantages which are purely strategic.[50]

The problem of size thus presents a serious dilemma to public policy. If differential advantages are not to be disturbed, the competitive struggle will go forward on unequal terms. But if they were, the law would be directed, not toward the maintenance of competition, but toward the preservation of small competitors. And this is quite a different thing. For it is often the large concern that sets the pace for competition in a trade. To break it up, in such a case, would be to sacrifice the force that makes for progress in efficiency. Protection of small business may be defended, however, on other than economic grounds. Personal independence and self reliance may have their social and political advantages. Their preservation might be taken, in itself, as an objective of public policy. But this is not the stated purpose of the law.

THE GOAL OF POLICY

In the face of this array of problems, it is the responsibility of antitrust to restore competition where it does not exist and to maintain it where it does. It may well be asked, however, whether such an undertaking is really feasible. The answer will depend upon the way in which competition is defined.

Perfect Competition

If the economist's ideal of perfect competition is accepted as the goal, five conditions must be satisfied:

1. The commodity dealt in must consist of innumerable units, each identical with the others, so that buyers can shift quickly from one seller to another in order to obtain a lower price; the advantages offered by different buyers must also be uniform, so that sellers can shift quickly from one buyer to another in order to obtain a higher price.
2. The market in which the commodity is bought and sold must be well organized, trading must be continuous, and traders must be so well informed that every unit sold at the same time will sell at the same price.
3. Sellers and buyers must be numerous, each of them must be small, and the quantity supplied or demanded by any one of them must be so insignificant a part of the total supply or demand that no increase or decrease in his sales or purchases can appreciably affect the price.
4. There must be no restraint upon the independence of any seller or buyer, whether by custom, contract, collusion, the fear of reprisals by

[50] Joel B. Dirlam and Alfred E. Kahn, *Fair Competition: the Law and Economics of Antitrust Policy* (Ithaca, N.Y.: Cornell University Press, 1954), p. 151.

competitors, or otherwise; each one must be free to act in his own interest without regard for the interests of any of the others.

5. There must be no friction to impede the movement of resources from industry to industry, from product to product, or from firm to firm; investment must be speedily withdrawn from unsuccessful undertakings and transferred to those that promise a profit. There must be no barrier to entrance into the market; access must be granted to all sellers and all buyers at home and abroad.

Perfect competition, thus defined, never has existed and never can exist. An attempt to realize it in practice would require an atomization of industry that is not within the bounds of possibility. The concept is useful merely as a standard by which to measure the varying degrees of imperfection that must always characterize the actual markets in which goods are bought and sold. It cannot be taken as a practical objective of public policy.

Workable Competition

Another concept, developed more recently by economists, defines competition in terms, not of perfection, but of workability, thus establishing a standard that is more nearly attainable. The workability of competition may be judged by market performance, i.e., by its consequences as measured in output, quality, and price. It may be judged by market structure alone.[51] In accordance with the latter approach, a market may be regarded as workably competitive when it is characterized by conditions that afford to buyers and sellers real opportunities to protect themselves, each against the other. Workable competition may be produced by conditions that are less exacting than those demanded for perfection:

1. It need not involve the standardization of commodities; it does require the availability of products so closely related that they may be readily substituted, one for another. It does not require that the advantages offered by all buyers be identical; it does require that they differ so little that sellers will not hesitate to shift from one to another.
2. It does not require that markets be formally organized, that trading be continuous, or that all buyers and sellers be intelligent, educated, and equally well informed; it does require that information be available and that no action be taken to grant it to some traders and withhold it from others.
3. It does not require that traders be present in such numbers and limited to such a size that none of them has an appreciable influence on supply, demand, or price; it does require that traders be sufficiently numerous to offer to buyers and to sellers, respectively, a considerable number of genuine alternatives in sources of supply and demand, so that, by shifting their purchases or sales, they can substantially influence quality, service, and price.
4. It does not require emancipation from custom or isolation from contacts with competitors; it does require substantial independence of action:

[51] The difference between these two approaches and the difficulties involved in using the concept of workable competition will be considered in Chapter 31.

each trader must be free to adopt his own policy governing output, purchases, and price; traders must not take part in formal agreements or tacit understandings; power must not be so distributed that lack of resources or fear of retaliation prevent one trader from encroaching on the sales or the purchases of another.

5. It does not require that transference of resources be frictionless or instantaneous or that entry to the market be unimpeded by such natural obstacles as the cost of facilities and sales promotion or the experience and contacts of existing firms; it does require that transference and entry be unobstructed by artificial barriers and that no preferences be accorded or handicaps imposed.

Workable competition cannot be expected to insure complete flexibility or optimum economy in the use of resources. In a rough way, however, it can contribute toward these ends. By subjecting traders to its discipline, it can prevent deliberate curtailment of output and the survival of extremes of inefficiency. By affording access to genuine alternatives, it can protect the weaker trader against the worst of the bargains that might otherwise be imposed upon him by the stronger one. By holding open the door to opportunity, it can encourage experimentation in products, processes, and prices, and forestall the suppression of innovation by established firms. This concept, admittedly, is less precise than that of perfect competition. It is more useful, however, as a goal for public policy.

SUGGESTIONS FOR FURTHER READING

Excellent analyses of the problems confronting antitrust are presented by Corwin D. Edwards in *Maintaining Competition* (New York: McGraw-Hill Book Co., 1949), chap. ii, iv, and v, and by Fritz Machlup in *The Political Economy of Monopoly* (Baltimore: Johns Hopkins Press, 1952), chaps. iv and v. Further illustrative material is contained in Clair Wilcox, *Competition and Monopoly in American Industry*, Temporary National Economic Committee, Monograph No. 21 (Washington: Government Printing Office, 1940), chaps. iii, iv, and v, and in George W. Stocking and Myron W. Watkins, *Monopoly and Free Enterprise* (New York: Twentieth Century Fund, 1951), chaps. v, vi, vii, viii, and x. A number of case studies, industry by industry, are to be found in Walter Adams (ed.), *The Structure of American Industry* (New York: Macmillan Co., 1950), and in H. L. Purdy, M. L. Lindahl, and W. A. Carter, *Corporate Concentration and Public Policy* (2d ed.; New York: Prentice-Hall, Inc., 1950), Parts II and IV.

On the objective of antitrust policy, see Edwards, chap. i, Andreas G. Papandreou and John T. Wheeler, *Competition and Its Regulation* (New York: Prentice-Hall, Inc., 1954), chap. xiii, and J. M. Clark, "Competition and the Objectives of Government Policy," in Edward H. Chamberlin (ed.), *Monopoly and Competition and Their Regulation* (London: Macmillan & Co., Ltd., 1954), pp. 317–37. On the concept of workable competition, see also J. M. Clark's article in the *American Economic Review*, Vol. XXX (1940), pp. 241–56, or in *Readings in the Social Control of Industry* (Philadelphia: Blakiston Co., 1942), pp. 452–75, and Stocking and Watkins, chap. iv.

Chapter 5 ANTITRUST AND THE COURTS

The Sherman Act forbade restraint of trade, monopolization, and attempts to monopolize. The Clayton Act outlawed certain practices when their effect might be substantially to lessen competition or to tend toward monopoly. The Trade Commission Act condemned unfair methods of competition. But Congress did not attempt, in any of these laws, to define the terms it used. What is restraint of trade, monopoly, and competition? When is the lessening of competition substantial? When are methods of competition unfair? The answers to these questions were left to the courts. The problems that Congress faced were so diverse, complex, and ever changing that precision of language was not to be obtained. As a result the laws have meant whatever the judges in particular cases have decided they should mean. Judicial interpretation has thus been crucial in determining their application and effect.

The number of cases brought before the courts, involving monopoly and restraint of trade, runs well beyond a thousand; the number carried to the Supreme Court reaches several score. In reviewing the history of interpretation, it will be possible only to consider the leading decisions and to indicate the major trends. The cases will be presented, not chronologically, but according to the issues which they raise.

THE SCOPE OF THE LAW

The first case to come before the Supreme Court under the Sherman Act, the E. C. Knight case,[1] decided in 1895, involved the sugar trust. The American Sugar Refining Company, already controlling 65 per cent of the sugar refined in the United States, had purchased the stock of the E. C. Knight Company and three other independent refiners, thus increasing its control to 98 per cent. The government sought, not to break up the American company, but merely to compel it to dispose of its stock in the Knight company and the three other concerns. The Court admitted that American had a monopoly, but it decided against the government on the ground that the Act applied only to commerce, that sugar refining was

[1] *U.S.* v. *E.C. Knight Co.*, 156 U.S. 1.

manufacturing, and that manufacturing was not commerce. This interpretation, had it stood, would have confined the law to firms engaged in moving goods from state to state. In decisions that shortly followed, however, though not overruled, it was consistently ignored. And in upholding the constitutionality of the National Labor Relations Act in 1937, the Court found explicitly that manufacturing involved commerce and thus fell within the scope of federal power.[2]

Groups Covered

Aside from its temporary aberration in the Knight case, the Court has given antitrust wide scope. In 1897, rejecting the contention that since common carriers were covered by the Interstate Commerce Act they were not included in the Sherman Act, it applied the law to railroads;[3] in 1917, extended it to ocean shipping companies.[4] In 1939, though association of farmers in agricultural co-operatives had been exempted by Congress in the Clayton Act and other measures, the Court held that an organization of milk producers was subject to the law when it joined with milk distributors, a milk wagon drivers union, and local health authorities to control the supply and fix the price of milk in Chicago.[5] In 1943, when a medical society in Washington, D.C., was charged with attempting to prevent the operation of a group health plan by expelling doctors from membership, denying them consultation privileges, and excluding them from hospitals, and the defendants argued that physicians, not being engaged in trade or commerce, were exempt, the Court ruled that restraint on the practice of medicine was restraint of trade.[6] In 1944, when fire insurance companies contended that insurance contracts were intrastate in character, that their business was regulated by state governments, and that decisions upholding such regulation exempted them from federal law, the Court found that documents, communications, and money were transmitted in interstate commerce and held that the Sherman Act applied.[7] In 1945, despite the exemption granted to export trade associations in the Webb-Pomerene Act of 1918, the Court held that it was illegal for such associations to participate in the restrictive activities of international cartels.[8] In the same year, rejecting the defense that transmission of news is not commerce, the Court applied the law to the Associated Press.[9] In 1950 it held the real estate brokerage business to be a trade within the meaning of the Sherman Act.[10] In 1951 it held that application of the law to a news-

[2] *NLRB* v. *Jones & Laughlin Steel Corp.*, 301 U.S. 1.

[3] *U.S.* v. *Trans-Missouri Freight Assn.*, 166 U.S. 290.

[4] *Thomsen* v. *Cayser*, 243 U.S. 66.

[5] *U.S.* v. *Borden Co.*, 308 U.S. 188.

[6] *U.S.* v. *American Medical Assn.*, 317 U.S. 519.

[7] *U.S.* v. *South-Eastern Underwriters Assn.*, 322 U.S. 533.

[8] *U.S. Alkali Export Assn.* v. *U.S.*, 325 U.S. 196.

[9] *U.S.* v. *Associated Press*, 326 U.S. 1.

[10] *U.S.* v. *National Assn. of Real Estate Boards*, 339 U.S. 485.

paper publisher did not violate the constitutional guarantee of freedom of the press.[11] And in 1954 it applied the law to the building construction industry.[12]

In 1953, in a suit brought by a baseball player against a club in one of the major leagues, the Court was asked to rule on the applicability of the Sherman Act to organized baseball. In view of the commercial nature of the business, and in light of the precedents just cited, it might well have held the law to apply. But it refused to do so, reaffirming a decision made in 1922 in which it was held that baseball was not a trade.[13] This precedent was ignored, however, in cases brought by the Department of Justice against the major professional boxing organizations and the Shubert theatrical interests. Despite the inconsistency of its position, the Court held, in 1955, that boxing and the theater were subject to the law.

It is principally in the case of labor, however, that interpretation now limits the boundaries of antitrust. The Sherman Act was originally directed toward restraints by industry. But unions were not exempted, and in the Danbury Hatters' case in 1908, the Court awarded damages to an employer who had been injured by a secondary boycott.[14] This led to the inclusion in the Clayton Act of a section providing that unions, as such, shall not "be held or construed to be illegal combinations or conspiracies in restraint of trade." In subsequent decisions, however, the Court continued to apply the law to union activities, permitting labor organization, strikes, and picketing, but forbidding secondary boycotts,[15] intentional interference with the movement of nonunion goods,[16] and agreement with other groups to control the supplies and the prices of goods and services.[17] But activities not including other groups, following decisions handed down in the Apex case of 1940 and the Hutcheson case in 1941, would now appear to be outside the law. In the Apex case, the Court held that a sit-down strike, involving the seizure of a hosiery plant, destruction of property, and interference with shipments, did not violate the Sherman Act because it did not monopolize the supply or control the price of hosiery.[18] And in the Hutcheson case, where a carpenters' union had gone on strike and conducted a boycott against Anheuser-Busch because the brewing company had employed the members of a machinists' union to install

[11] *Lorain Journal Co.,* v. *U.S.,* 342 U.S. 143.

[12] *U.S.* v. *Employing Plasterers' Assn.,* 347 U.S. 186.

[13] *Federal Baseball Club of Baltimore* v. *National League,* 259 U.S. 200 (1922); *Toolson* v. *New York Yankees,* 346 U.S. 356 (1953). On the economic and legal issues involved here, see "Monopsony in Manpower: Organized Baseball Meets the Antitrust Laws," *Yale Law Journal,* Vol. LXII (1953), pp. 576–639.

[14] *Loewe* v. *Lawlor,* 208 U.S. 274.

[15] *Duplex Printing Press Co.* v. *Deering,* 254 U.S. 443 (1921).

[16] *United Mine Workers* v. *Coronado Coal Co.,* 259 U.S. 344 (1922).

[17] *U.S.* v. *Brims,* 272 U.S. 549 (1926); *Local 167* v. *U.S.,* 291 U.S. 293 (1934); *U.S.* v. *Borden Co,* 308 U.S. 188 (1939).

[18] *Apex Hosiery Co.* v. *Leader,* 310 U.S. 469.

machinery, the Court found that the law did not apply "so long as a union acts in its self interest and does not combine with non-labor groups."[19] This position was reaffirmed in the Allen Bradley case in 1945.[20] Here, though the Court upheld the government in condemning a conspiracy involving an electrical workers' union, equipment manufacturers, and contractors, it went on to say that "the same labor union activities may or may not be in violation of the Sherman Act, dependent upon whether the union acts alone or in combination with business groups." The immunity now granted to labor by the law extends beyond the market for labor to the markets for other goods and services. Interference with competition in such markets, though forbidden to employers acting alone and to employers and organized workers acting together, is permitted to organized workers acting alone. Labor's immunity from prosecution for restrictive activities has been limited by the outlawry of certain unfair labor practices, such as secondary boycotts and jurisdictional strikes, under the Taft-Hartley Act of 1947. But unions are still given considerable freedom to restrain trade.

In many cases where judicial interpretation has brought particular groups within the scope of the law, Congress has subsequently exempted them. Rate agreements among shipping companies were legalized and brought under the authority of the United States Maritime Commission by the Shipping Act of 1916. Agreements among agricultural co-operatives, the processors, and the distributors of agricultural products, if approved by the Secretary of Agriculture, were authorized by the Agricultural Adjustment Act of 1933 and the Agricultural Marketing Agreements Act of 1937. Suits against insurance companies were suspended, under a Congressional moratorium, from 1945 to 1948, to give the states an opportunity to strengthen their regulation of insurance rates; following the enactment of more effective statutes, antitrust is now confined to the prosecution of boycotts and agreements preventing the filing of lower rates. Rate agreements among railroads were removed from the jurisdiction of the Antitrust Division and brought under the authority of the Interstate Commerce Commission by the Reed-Bulwinkle Act, passed over the veto of President Truman in 1948. The significance of such exemptions, legislative and judicial, will be considered in Chapter 13.

Activities Covered

Enforcement of the Sherman Act has not been handicapped by decisions preventing its application to particular forms of restrictive activity. In the second and third cases to come before the Supreme Court, the Act was applied to rate agreements,[21] and in the fourth to market sharing

[19] *U.S.* v. *Hutcheson*, 312 U.S. 219.

[20] *Allen Bradley Co.* v. *Local Union No. 3*, 325 U.S. 797.

[21] *U.S.* v. *Trans-Missouri Freight Assn.*, 166 U.S. 290 (1897); *U.S.* v. *Joint Traffic Assn.*, 171 U.S. 505 (1898).

through collusive bidding.[22] In the fifth, the Northern Securities Company, created in 1901 to control the Northern Pacific and Great Northern Railways, challenged its application to the holding company device, contending that the company had been authorized by its New Jersey charter to hold the stock of other concerns, and that denial of such authority, by federal action, would interfere with the internal commerce of a state. In a 5–4 decision, handed down in 1904, the Court rejected this defense, declaring that the power of a state to grant a corporate charter does not override the power of the federal government to eliminate combinations that restrain trade.[23] In subsequent decisions, the Court applied the Act to outright consolidation,[24] to control through minority stockholdings,[25] and to trade association activities,[26] saying, in the American Tobacco case, that the policy of the law could not be frustrated "by resorting to any disguise or subterfuge of form." With respect to the Sherman Act, this position has been consistently maintained. But under the Clayton Act, as previously noted, the Court refused to break up combinations, in the Thatcher, Swift, and Arrowhart & Hegeman cases, holding the acquisition of assets to be legal, even though effected through the illegal acquisition of stock.[27] This loophole has now been closed by law.

The Rule of Reason

The first word in the Sherman Act applies the law to *every* contract, combination, and conspiracy in restraint of trade. If interpreted strictly, the Act might thus be held to prohibit an agreement between firms controlling an insignificant share of a market, to prevent one small competitor from merging with another, and even to forbid normal contractual relationships. It is obvious that the Act cannot be so interpreted. The rule against restraint of trade was not so interpreted at common law.

The common law distinguished between ancillary and nonancillary restraints. An ancillary restraint is incidental to a legal purpose; it may occur, for instance, when a person selling a business, a partner withdrawing from it, or an employee leaving it undertakes to preserve its value by refraining from competition with its purchaser, a remaining partner, or a former employer. Here the courts came to apply a rule of reason, enforcing such restrictions when they were limited in duration and extent, and refusing to do so when they were not. Nonancillary restraints, on the other hand, are those suppressing competition in a market as a whole. And

[22] *U.S.* v. *Addyston Pipe & Steel Co.*, 175 U.S. 211 (1899).

[23] *Northern Securities Co.* v. *U.S.*, 193 U.S. 197.

[24] *U.S.* v. *American Tobacco Co.*, 221 U.S. 106 (1911).

[25] *U.S.* v. *Union Pacific Railway Co.*, 226 U.S. 61 (1912).

[26] *U.S.* v. *Eastern States Retail Lumber Assn.*, 234 U.S. 600 (1914).

[27] *Thatcher Mfg. Co.* v. *FTC* and *Swift & Co.* v. *FTC*, 272 U.S. 554 (1926); *Arrow-Hart & Hegeman Electric Co.* v. *FTC*, 291 U.S. 587 (1934). See above, p. 63.

here, though some American courts followed English precedents in applying a rule of reason, more of them did not.

In the earliest cases brought before the Supreme Court under the Sherman Act, it was argued that the rule of reason should apply. For many years, however, this contention was rejected by the Court. In a decision handed down in the Trans-Missouri case in 1897, Justice Peckham held that Congress had not intended merely to give statutory effect to common-law precedents and found, accordingly, that the Act was not confined to unreasonable agreements but applied, as it said, to every agreement in restraint of trade, even though it may have been valid at common law.[28] In his decision in the Addyston Pipe case in 1898, Judge Taft took a different line. It was the intention of Congress, he said, to adopt the principles of the common law. But the rule of reason, at common law, was confined to restrictions that were ancillary to lawful contracts and did not apply to nonancillary restraints on competition, since these restraints were made unlawful by their purposes.[29] Under either interpretation, the rule of reason was not to be employed.

So the law stood for twenty years, until Chief Justice White handed down the decisions of the Supreme Court in the Standard Oil and American Tobacco cases in 1911.[30] In each of these cases the Court upheld the government. But it went on, in an obiter dictum, to write the rule of reason into the law. Justice White agreed with Judge Taft that Congress had intended to follow the common law. But he found, by going back to English precedents, emphasizing consistent American decisions, and ignoring many inconsistent ones, that the rule of reason had applied to nonancillary as well as to ancillary restraints. The purpose of the Sherman Act, he said, "was not to restrain the right to make and enforce contracts . . . which did not unduly restrain interstate or foreign commerce, but to protect that commerce from being restrained by methods . . . which would constitute an interference, that is, an undue restraint."[31] The Act applied, he admitted, to every agreement in restraint of trade, but this meant every unreasonable agreement, since reasonable agreements did not involve restraint. And, arguing further that Section 2 of the Act was complementary to and therefore must be harmonized with Section 1, he went on to apply the rule of reason, not only to restraint of trade, but also to monopolization and attempts to monopolize.

To both of these decisions, Justice Harlan appended vigorous dissents, saying, in the Tobacco case, that

> . . . the Court, in accordance with what it denominates the "rule of reason," in effect inserts in the Act the word "undue" which means the same as "unreasonable," and thereby makes Congress say what it did not say, what, I

[28] *U.S.* v. *Trans-Missouri Freight Assn.*, 166 U.S. 290.

[29] *U.S.* v. *Addyston Pipe & Steel Co.*, 85 Fed. 271.

[30] *Standard Oil Co. of N.J.* v. *U.S.*, 221 U.S. 1; *U.S.* v. *American Tobacco Co.*, 221 U.S. 106.

[31] *Standard Oil Co. of N.J.* v. *U.S.*, 221 U.S. 1, 59.

think, it plainly did not intend to say, and what, since the passage of the Act, it has explicitly refused to say. . . . In short, the Court, now, by judicial legislation, in effect amends an Act of Congress relating to a subject over which that department of the Government has exclusive cognizance.[32]

But Congress, instead of reversing the Court, limited the application of the Clayton Act, passed three years later, to cases in which the lessening of competition might be substantial, and the rule of reason came to be accepted and employed, thereafter, in interpreting the law.

Is this development to be commended or condemned? It is evident that the word "every" could not be taken literally. Even Justice Peckham had not found all agreements among competitors to be illegal, holding that those which failed to affect the competitive character of a market did not involve restraint of trade. But the door was opened wider by Justice White. Under the terms of his decision, the Court may find that agreements and combinations suppressing competition in a market, being reasonable, are immune. And no criteria for separating the reasonable from the unreasonable are supplied. The meaning of the law is thus uncertain; its application may be lax or stringent, depending on the judgment of the Court. But some uncertainty is inescapable, given the nature of the problems with which the law must deal. Its very vagueness, moreover, endows the Act with greater flexibility, permitting its adaptation to changing needs. Where judges look with favor on monopoly, the rule of reason may be open to abuse; where they believe in competition, it may have its use.

AGREEMENTS AMONG COMPETITORS

From the beginning the Court has upheld the government, with only minor exceptions, in cases brought against overt agreements involving price fixing—whether direct or indirect—control of output, market sharing, and the exclusion of competitors by boycotts or other coercive practices. Here the rule of reason has rarely been applied. Behavior that was held, before 1911, to restrain trade is still held to do so. In cases involving the price reporting and statistical activities of trade associations, however, interpretation has been less consistent and the legal status of such activities is still unclear. In another group of cases, where conspiracy, instead of being proven by overt agreement or formal organization, must be inferred from identity of behavior, the Court has come increasingly, in recent years, to uphold the law. The leading decisions in each of these areas will now be reviewed.

Simple Conspiracies

The earliest cases involving restrictive agreements among competitors were those of the Trans-Missouri Freight Association in 1897,[33] the Joint

[32] *U.S.* v. *American Tobacco Co.*, 221 U.S. 106, 192.

[33] *U.S.* v. *Trans-Missouri Freight Assn.*, 166 U.S. 290.

Traffic Association in 1898,[34] and the Addyston Pipe & Steel Company in 1899.[35] In the Trans-Missouri and Joint Traffic cases, groups of railroads had fixed and enforced freight rates. In the Addyston case, six producers of cast iron pipe had assigned certain markets to each of their number and determined the allocation of contracts elsewhere by operating a bidding ring. In all three cases the defendants argued that their restrictions were required to prevent ruinous competition and that the resulting rates and prices were reasonable. And, in each case, the Court rejected this defense, holding the arrangements to be illegal in themselves.

These precedents were followed faithfully for twenty years, decisions being rendered against collusive bidding by purchasers of livestock,[36] exclusion of competing railways from a terminal,[37] the use of patent licenses to fix the price of bathtubs,[38] and the operation of a boycott by retail lumber dealers.[39] In 1918, in a decision of limited significance, the Court refused to condemn a rule adopted by the Chicago Board of Trade requiring those buying and selling grain outside of trading hours to do so at the price at which the market closed.[40] In 1923 it decided against the government in a case involving control of the output of hand-blown window glass.[41] Under the terms of an agreement between the National Association of Window Glass Manufacturers, representing fifty firms, and the National Window Glass Workers, a union of skilled glass blowers, operation of the plants in this industry was limited to 4½ months in the year, half of them being open during one period and half during another, the workers moving from plant to plant. The Court's acquiesence in this arrangement is explained by the fact that it was devised to meet the peculiar problems of a declining trade in a dying industry. The plan reduced costs by enabling plants to operate, for short periods, at full capacity, assured employment to labor, and eased the transfer of resources from the field. The case does not appear to have involved a serious departure from precedent.

The leading decision on restrictive agreements came in 1927 in the Trenton Potteries case.[42] Firms producing four fifths of the domestic output of vitreous enamel bathroom fixtures had agreed to fix prices and to sell exclusively through jobbers. The Court was emphatic in its refusal to accept the reasonableness of the prices fixed as a defense:

> The aim and result of every price-fixing agreement, if effective, is the elimination of one form of competition. The power to fix prices, whether reason-

[34] *U.S.* v. *Joint Traffic Assn.*, 171 U.S. 505.

[35] *Addyston Pipe & Steel Co.* v. *U.S.*, 175 U.S. 211.

[36] *U.S.* v. *Swift & Co.*, 196 U.S. 375 (1906).

[37] *U.S.* v. *Terminal R.R. Assn.*, 224 U.S. 383 (1912).

[38] *U.S.* v. *Standard Sanitary Mfg. Co.*, 226 U.S. 20 (1912).

[39] *U.S.* v. *Eastern States Retail Lumber Assn.*, 234 U.S. 600 (1914).

[40] *Chicago Board of Trade* v. *U.S.*, 246 U.S. 231.

[41] *National Assn. of Window Glass Mfrs.* v. *U.S.*, 263 U.S. 403.

[42] *U.S.* v. *Trenton Potteries Co.*, 273 U.S. 392.

ably exercised or not, involves power to control the market and to fix arbitrary and unreasonable prices. The reasonable price fixed today may, due to economic and business changes, become the unreasonable price of tomorrow. Once established it may be maintained unchanged because of the absence of competition. . . . Agreements which create such potential power may well be held to be in themselves unreasonable or unlawful restraint, without the necessity of minute inquiry, whether a particular price is reasonable or unreasonable as fixed, and without placing on the government in enforcing the Sherman law the burden of ascertaining from day to day whether it has become unreasonable. . . .[43]

The purpose of the law, said the Court, is to protect the public by maintaining competition. Every agreement to fix prices, however reasonable, is therefore to be condemned.

Doubts concerning this position were raised, however, by the Court's decision in the Appalachian Coals case in 1933.[44] In this case 137 companies, producing a tenth of the bituminous coal mined east of the Mississippi River and around two thirds of that mined in the Appalachian territory, had set up a joint agency to handle all their sales. The Court recognized that this arrangement established common prices for the firms involved, but it went on to find that the industry was seriously depressed, that competition in the sale of coal had been subject to various abuses, and that the selling agency did not control enough of the supply to enable it to fix the market price. It therefore concluded that: "A cooperative enterprise, otherwise free from objection, which carries with it no monopolistic menace, is not to be condemned as an undue restraint merely because it may affect a change in market conditions, where the change would be in mitigation of recognized evils and would not impair, but rather foster, fair competitive opportunities."[45] On this basis, the arrangement was allowed to stand.

This precedent, had it been followed in later cases, would substantially have modified the meaning of the law. In its decision in the Socony-Vacuum case[46] in 1940, however, the Court reaffirmed the rule of Trenton Potteries. This case involved an agreement, described in Chapter 4,[47] under which the major oil companies in ten midwestern states raised and maintained the price of gasoline by purchasing marginal supplies from independent refineries. The Court again rejected the defense that the price established was no more than fair. Said Justice Douglas:

Any combination which tampers with price structures is engaged in an unlawful activity. Even though the members of the price-fixing group were in no position to control the market, to the extent that they raised, lowered, or stabilized prices they would be directly interfering with the free play of

[43] *Ibid.*, pp. 397–98.

[44] *Appalachian Coals, Inc.* v. *U.S.*, 228 U.S. 344.

[45] *Ibid.*, pp. 373–74.

[46] *U.S.* v. *Socony-Vacuum Oil Co.*, 310 U.S. 150.

[47] See above, p. 76.

market forces. The Act places all such schemes beyond the pale. . . . Under the Sherman Act, a combination formed for the purpose and with the effect of raising, depressing, fixing, pegging, or stabilizing the price of a commodity in interstate or foreign commerce is illegal *per se*. . . . Whatever economic justification particular price-fixing agreements may be thought to have, the law does not permit an inquiry into their reasonableness. They are all banned because of their actual or potential threat to the central nervous system of the economy.[48]

The ruling of the Court could not have been more sweeping; any such agreement, even though affecting a minor portion of the market, was forbidden; any manipulation of prices, whatever its purpose, was against the law.

The Court was not troubled by its inconsistency. The oil agreement, it said, had the purpose and effect of controlling market prices; the coal agreement did not. But the two cases are not so easily to be reconciled. In coal the decision permitted a minority to fix prices; in the words of the oil decision, price fixing—even by a minority—was condemned. The contrast is to be explained, in part, perhaps, by the fact that there had been changes between 1933 and 1940 in the composition of the Court, in the prosperity of the country, and in the attitude of the public toward monopoly; in part, by the fact that bituminous coal had been produced by many small firms engaged in active competition, while oil had been refined by large concerns whose pattern of behavior was that of oligopoly. The Appalachian case must be regarded as an exception, the Socony-Vacuum case as a restatement of the general rule.

The government has been highly successful in cases brought against restrictive agreements under the Sherman Act.[49] It should be noted, moreover, that the Court has long upheld the authority of the Federal Trade Commission to proceed against such agreements under Section 5 of the Trade Commission Act.[50] It is in this area that interpretation has been most consistent in supporting the enforcement of the law.

[48] *U.S.* v. *Socony-Vacuum Oil Co.*, 310 U.S. 150, 221–26.

[49] In a suit brought against seventeen investment banking houses, the government charged that they had conspired to fix prices, not by operating underwriting syndicates, but (1) through agreements among members of syndicates to maintain offering prices during periods of distribution; (2) through agreements authorizing syndicate managers to repurchase securities selling below their offering prices during such periods; and (3) through agreements between underwriters and distributors with respect to resale prices. In a decision handed down in *U.S.* v. *Morgan* (Civil No. 43–757, District Court of the U.S., Southern District of N.Y., October 14, 1953), Judge Harold R. Medina dismissed the complaint on the ground that the government had not proved its case. In an accompanying dictum, he then went on to say that limitation of competition among the members of an underwriting syndicate would not violate the Sherman Act because such members are not competitors but are joint venturers in a common enterprise. This reasoning is dubious. If adopted in other cases, it would provide a convenient loophole for violators of the law. See "The Investment Bankers Case: The Use of Semantics to Avoid the Per Se Illegality of Price Fixing," *Yale Law Journal*, Vol. LXIII (1954), pp. 399–407.

[50] *FTC* v. *Pacific States Paper Trade Assn.*, 273 U.S. 52 (1927).

Trade Association Activities

During the twenties four cases came before the Court involving the price and other statistical reporting activities of trade associations in the hardwood lumber, linseed oil, maple flooring, and cement industries. In all four cases the associations concerned were engaged in collecting and disseminating data on production, stocks, orders, sales, and shipments, in preparing and circulating reports on prices and terms of sale, in operating delivered pricing systems, and in holding meetings where prices and production were discussed. In none of the cases was there explicit evidence of agreement as to price and production policy. In the Hardwood and Linseed cases[51] decided in 1921 and 1923, the plans were held to be illegal; in the Maple Flooring and Cement cases[52] decided in 1925, they were not. Said the Court, in the Hardwood case: "Genuine competitors do not make daily, weekly, and monthly reports of the minutest details of their business to their rivals. . . . This is not the conduct of competitors but . . . clearly that of men united in an agreement, express or implied, to act together and pursue a common purpose under a common guide. . . ."[53] And in the Linseed case: "With intimate knowledge of the affairs of other producers . . . the subscribers went forth to deal with widely separated and unorganized customers. . . . Obviously, they were not *bona fide* competitors; their claim in that regard is at war with common experience."[54] But in the Maple Flooring case the Court decided: "that trade associations . . . which openly and fairly gather and disseminate information . . . without, however, reaching or attempting to reach any agreement or any concerted action with respect to prices or production or restraining competition, do not thereby engage in unlawful restraint of commerce."[55] Such activities, said the Court, are not to be condemned "merely because the ultimate result . . . may be to stabilize prices or limit production through a better understanding of economic laws and a more general ability to conform to them."[56]

How is the shift in the Court's position to be explained? The plans that were followed in the two sets of cases differed in detail. The prices that were reported in the Hardwood and Linseed cases were those to be charged in future transactions, firms making quotations were identified, and reports were withheld from customers. In the Hardwood case, moreover, the information provided was accompanied by interpretive comments and strong suggestions as to policy. And in the Linseed case adher-

[51] *American Column and Lumber Co.* v. *U.S.*, 257 U.S. 377; *U.S.* v. *American Linseed Oil Co.*, 262 U.S. 371.

[52] *Maple Flooring Mfrs. Assn.* v. *U.S.*, 268 U.S. 563; *Cement Mfrs. Protective Assn.* v. *U.S.*, 268 U.S. 588.

[53] 257 U.S. 377, 410.

[54] 262 U.S. 371, 389–90.

[55] 268 U.S. 563, 586.

[56] *Ibid.*, p. 584.

ence to quoted prices was required. In the Maple Flooring case, on the other hand, prices were reported for past transactions, sellers were not identified, and the reports were given wide publicity. Here, as in the Cement case, it was noted that members retained their freedom to take such action as they chose.

The plans adopted by the Maple Flooring and Cement associations, however, were not as innocent as they seemed. The former group prepared and distributed estimates showing the average cost of producing each of the grades and dimensions of flooring, and both groups compiled and circulated common freight rate books. The activities of both associations were designed to implement delivered pricing systems. And under these systems, with the base price built on the reported costs or established through price leadership, overt agreement as to prices was not required. This fact, however, was not made known to the Court.

The government's case was poorly prepared: the prosecution confined itself to showing that the practices followed in the later cases resembled those found in the earlier ones. The defense presented evidence to show that the effects of these practices, however restrictive elsewhere, were not restrictive here. And this evidence was not refuted by the government. No agreement to control output or to fix prices was charged or proved. The Court rendered its decision accordingly: "We realize that such information, gathered and disseminated among the members of a trade or business, may be the basis of agreement or concerted action to lessen production arbitrarily or to raise prices. . . . But in the absence of proof of such agreement or concerted action . . . we can find no basis in the gathering and dissemination of such information . . . for the inference that such concerted action will necessarily result. . . .[57] None of these decisions was generalized; each of them was limited to the facts of a particular case.

The next trade association program to come before the Court was that of the Sugar Institute. The program was an elaborate one, having as its purpose the elimination of all indirect methods of competition and the requirement of adherence to the seller's reported price. The association standardized terms of sale, limited cash discounts, classified purchasers, and forbade long-term contracts, sales on consignment, quantity discounts, and allowances for returned bags, storage, and advertising, together with many other practices. It imposed a boycott on distributors performing both brokerage and wholesaling functions. It eliminated certain consignment points and ports of entry for sugar, operated a delivered pricing system, and published a common freight rate book. It reported to its members on the production, sales and stocks of individual refiners, and to its customers only on total production, sales, and stocks. It reported filed prices to buyers and sellers alike, but forbade departure from these prices without filing prior notice of the change. There was no evidence of

[57] *Ibid.*, p. 586.

agreement as to prices themselves, but such agreement was clearly facilitated when every other aspect of each transaction had been standardized.

In 1934 the District Court found this program to be in restraint of trade and, while refusing to dissolve the Institute, issued an injunction prohibiting further adherence to 45 specific practices, including those relating to the operation of the delivered pricing system and the standardization of other aspects of a sale. It required that buyers be given access to statistics on production, sales, deliveries, and stocks, and to "any other statistical information of a similar character," enjoined the practice of reporting and disseminating future prices, and forbade agreement to adhere to the prices that were filed. Two years later the Supreme Court affirmed the decision of the lower court, with two exceptions. It permitted "any other statistical information of a similar character" to be kept in confidence. And, finding that prior announcement of prices conformed to the established practice of the industry, it ruled that future prices might be filed. "The unreasonable restraint which defendants imposed," said the Court, "lay not in advance announcements, but in the steps taken to secure adherence without deviation to prices and terms thus announced."[58] Agreement to observe filed prices was enjoined.

Cases involving trade association activities brought by the Antitrust Division since the Sugar Institute decision (including one against the National Container Association, whose program was described in Chapter 4) have usually been settled by consent decrees. A number of orders issued by the Federal Trade Commission, however, have been appealed to the courts. In most cases the Commission has been upheld. In the case of the Salt Producers Association, the exchange of statistics facilitated adherence to a system of voluntary quotas governing production and sales.[59] The Maltsters Association had standardized commodities and terms of sale, circulated statistics among sellers but withheld them from buyers, and operated a Chicago-plus system of delivered pricing.[60] The Milk and Ice Cream Can Institute had standardized products and discounts, circulated daily reports, and administered a delivered pricing plan.[61] The Crepe Paper Association, too, had operated a system of zone pricing.[62] In all of these cases the association activities were held to violate the law.

In one case, however, the Commission was reversed. Under a plan administered by an agent of the Tag Manufacturers Institute, the manufacturers reported tag specifications, prices, and terms of sale to the agent, who compiled and circulated the data among the sellers, also making it available—nominally, at least—to buyers. Sellers were not required to

[58] *U.S.* v. *Sugar Institute,* 15 F. Supp. 817 (1934); *Sugar Institute* v. *U.S.*, 297 U.S. 553 (1936) 601.

[59] *Salt Producers Assn.* v. *FTC,* 134 F. 2d 354 (1943).

[60] *U.S. Maltsters Assn.* v. *FTC,* 152 F. 2d 161 (1945).

[61] *Milk and Ice Cream Can Institute* v. *FTC,* 152 F. 2d 478 (1946).

[62] *Fort Howard Paper Co.* v. *FTC,* 156 F. 2d 899 (1946).

adhere to reported prices, but new prices and sales below list prices had to be reported daily, and failure to report was penalized by collecting fines. The Commission ordered the plan to be abandoned, holding that it lessened competition.[63] The Court of Appeals reversed the order, finding that the price reports were confined to past transactions, that they were open to the public, and that adherence to reported prices was not required.[64] The decision followed the Maple Flooring precedent. The Commission did not appeal.

The courts, in general, have refrained from passing on particular elements of a trade association program, directing attention rather toward the consequences of the program as a whole. They have refused to generalize their rulings, confining each decision to the case in hand. As a result, the legality of particular practices and programs may be unclear. It would appear, however, that such programs are lawful when they limit price reports to past transactions, preserve the anonymity of individual traders, make data available to buyers as well as sellers, and permit departure from the prices that are filed. Practices and programs may be viewed with disfavor where future prices are reported, traders are identified, information is withheld from buyers, and discussions are held, statements issued, and recommendations made on price and production policies. Such programs are certain to be condemned when they involve elaborate standardization of the conditions surrounding a sale and require adherence to a filed price.

Interlocking Directorates

Section 8 of the Clayton Act, forbidding interlocking directorates between competing corporations, has been productive of little litigation. Violation has been among the offenses charged in antitrust suits and Commission complaints, but in most cases the directors in question have resigned before the issue came to trial. In a survey conducted in 1947, the Antitrust Division found 1,500 persons holding directorships in more than one concern. Here, again, where Section 8 appeared to be violated, the directors usually resigned.[65] In 1952 suits were brought and complaints issued in a number of cases. One of these, involving multiple directorships in Sears Roebuck and competing companies, was carried to the courts. The government was upheld by the district court[66] and the interlock was broken. The decision was not appealed.

The provisions of Section 8, however, can readily be circumvented. Controlling stockholders or officers of one corporation can serve as directors of another. Members of the same family or partners in the same bank-

[63] *In re Tag Manufacturers Institute*, 43 FTC 499 (1947).

[64] *Tag Manufacturers Institute* v. *FTC*, 174 F. 2d 452 (1949).

[65] Victor H. Kramer, "Interlocking Directorships and the Clayton Act," *Yale Law Journal*, Vol. LIX (1950), pp. 1266–75.

[66] *U.S.* v. *Sears Roebuck*, 111 F. Supp. 614 (1953).

ing house can serve as directors of competing concerns. Directors of two corporations that compete with one another may sit together, in a different field, on the board of a third. And there is no legal barrier to interlocks between potential competitors.[67] As a means of preserving competition, therefore, Section 8 is of little practical effect.

Conscious Parallelism of Action

It has long been recognized that unlawful agreement may be proven, in the absence of witnesses or documents, by circumstantial evidence. "It is elementary," said the Supreme Court in the Eastern States Lumber case in 1914, "that conspiracies are seldom capable of proof by direct testimony, and may be inferred from the things actually done."[68] In several cases in recent years the Court has gone even further, holding that knowing participation in a common course of action, without proof of agreement, may constitute conspiracy. In the Interstate Circuit case in 1939 the operator of a chain of movie houses in Texas had entered into separate contracts with eight distributors of films, agreeing to show their pictures for an admission charge of 40 cents, on condition they not be rented later to be shown for less than 25 cents or run on a double bill. There was no evidence that the distributors had consulted one another or agreed among themselves. But such evidence said the Court, "was not a prerequisite to an unlawful conspiracy. It was enough that, knowing that concerted action was contemplated and invited, the distributors gave their adherence to the scheme and participated in it. . . . Acceptance by competitors, without previous agreement, is sufficient to establish an unlawful conspiracy under the Sherman Act."[69] A similar position was taken in the Masonite case in 1942. Here, a manufacturer of hardboard had signed an agency agreement with each of his competitors, authorizing them to distribute his product and fixing the prices at which they could sell. And here, again, there was no evidence of agreement among the other companies. But the Court found the plan to be illegal, holding that each of them must have been "aware of the fact that its contract was not an isolated transaction but a part of a larger arrangement."[70]

In these cases there was evidence that plans had been proposed by Interstate and Masonite; the inference of conspiracy among the other companies was drawn from their adherence to these plans. In the second American Tobacco case, a criminal suit against the three leading producers of cigarettes, decided in 1946, no such proposal was in evidence. Statistics of purchases, sales, and prices were relied upon for proof. In buying tobacco, it was shown, these companies had purchased fixed shares of the supply, each of them paying the same price on the same day. In

[67] See *Report of the Federal Trade Commission on Interlocking Directorates* (Washington: Government Printing Office, 1951).

[68] *Eastern States Retail Lumber Assn.* v. *U.S.*, 234 U.S. 600, 612.

[69] *Interstate Circuit Co.* v. *U.S.*, 306 U.S. 208, 226–27.

[70] *U.S.* v. *Masonite Corp.*, 316 U.S. 265, 275.

selling cigarettes, they had adopted identical price lists, changing their prices simultaneously. In other practices, too, there was striking uniformity. But the case, says William Nicholls, "was probably unique in that there was not a whit of evidence that a common plan had even been contemplated or proposed. The government's evidence was admittedly wholly circumstantial. The fact of identity of behavior was offered as the basis for inferring both the existence and the elements of the alleged common plan and the defendants' knowledge of that plan. Each was alleged to have acted similarly with the knowledge that the others would so act, to their mutual self-interest."[71] But the character of the evidence did not deter the Court. Conspiracy, it said, "may be found in a course of dealings or others circumstances as well as in an exchange of words."[72] The companies were found, accordingly, to be in violation of the law. The decision, says Nicholls, "brought wholly tacit, nonaggressive oligopoly wholly within the reach of the conspiracy provisions of the Sherman Act."[73]

Conspiracy has also been found by the Supreme Court in cases where firms have agreed to identical provisions in the licenses granted them by the owner of a patent[74] and in cases brought under the Trade Commission Act where each of the members of an industry has adhered to a delivered pricing system in the knowledge that all the others would do the same.[75] The significance of these decisions will be considered in the chapters which follow.

In recent years the Federal Trade Commission and the courts have appeared to retreat from the doctrine of conscious parallelism. Early in 1953 the Commission ordered manufacturers of lead pigments to discontinue matching prices through adherence to a system of zone delivered pricing, inferring conspiracy from the existence of price identity. Commissioner Mason dissented, saying, "No one claims the evidence has to show one secret meeting in a smoke-filled room, or any number of meetings, nor do all the conspirators have to be present at any one time and sign their names in blood. But a charge of conspiracy must mean something besides a handle on which to hang an order. . . . In my opinion, some kind of overt act which implements a meeting of the minds is a "must" in a conspiracy. . . ."[76] With a shift occurring shortly in the Commission's membership, this is now said to be the view of a majority. Later in the year the government's suit against the investment banking companies was dismissed by

[71] William H. Nicholls, "The Tobacco Case of 1946," *American Economic Review*, Vol. XXXIX, No. 3 (1949), pp. 284–96, esp. p. 285.

[72] *American Tobacco Co.* v. *U.S.*, 328 U.S. 781, 810.

[73] Nicholls, *op. cit.*, p. 285.

[74] *U.S.* v. *Line Material Co.*, 333 U.S. 282 (1948); *U.S.* v. *U.S. Gypsum Co.*, 333 U.S. 364 (1948).

[75] *Triangle Conduit and Cable Co.* v. *FTC*, 168 F. 2d 157 (1948); *Bond Crown and Cork Co.* v. *FTC*, 176 F. 2d 974 (1949).

[76] *New York Times*, January 16, 1953.

Judge Harold R. Medina, who brushed aside the charge that markets were shared through conventional adherence to historical relationships between bankers and borrowers, finding no evidence of conspiracy.[77] In 1954, in the suit against the major meat packing companies, another district judge ruled that the government could not present evidence relating to the period before 1930 in support of its charge that the packers were now habitually sharing markets in accordance with a pattern that had been created through overt agreement some fifty years ago. At the government's request, the case was then dismissed "without prejudice."[78] In the same year, the Supreme Court handed down a decision rejecting the contention of a motion picture exhibitor in suburban Baltimore that film distributors had violated the Sherman Act by severally restricting first runs to downtown theaters and providing features to suburban houses only for later runs after lengthy clearances. Said Justice Clark: "This Court has never held that proof of parallel business behavior conclusively establishes agreement or, phrased differently, that such behavior itself constitutes a Sherman Act offense. Circumstantial evidence of consciously parallel behavior may have made heavy inroads into the traditional judicial attitude toward conspiracy; but 'conscious parallelism' has not yet read conspiracy out of the Sherman Act entirely."[79] The doctrine, thus, has not been repudiated. But it is likely to be used more sparingly in the near future than in the recent past.

Intra-Enterprise Conspiracy

Conspiracies in restraint of trade have been found to exist not only between independent enterprises but also between the corporations in an integrated structure that is under common ownership, each of them being regarded as a separate person within the meaning of the law. In 1941 General Motors and its subsidiary, the General Motors Acceptance Corporation, were held to have violated the Sherman Act when G.M. required its dealers to finance installment sales of automobiles through G.M.A.C., thus excluding competitors from the financing business.[80] In 1947 in the Yellow Cab case, a manufacturer of taxicabs had acquired control of companies operating cabs in several cities and required them to purchase their cabs from him, excluding other manufacturers from the market and preventing the operating companies from buying where they chose. The Court rejected the defense that sales within a corporate family cannot involve conspiracy. An unreasonable restraint, it said, "may result as readily from a conspiracy among those who are affiliated or integrated under common

[77] *U.S.* v. *Morgan*, Civil No. 43–757, District Court of the U.S., Southern Dist. of N.Y., Decision by Judge Medina, October 14, 1953.

[78] *New York Times*, March 18, 1954.

[79] *Theater Enterprises, Inc.* v. *Paramount Film Distributing Corp.*, 346 U.S. 537, 540.

[80] *General Motors Corp.* v. *U.S.*, 121 F. 2d 376, certiorari denied, 314 U.S. 618.

ownership as from a conspiracy among those who are otherwise independent."[81]

These precedents were followed in later cases. In 1948 in the Griffith case, a company operating a chain of movie houses was found to have conspired with its subsidiaries when it pooled their buying power to bargain for choice pictures, first runs, and long clearances in regions where it had competitors.[82] In 1951 the Calvert and Seagram companies, though under common ownership, were found to be conspiring when they fixed a maximum resale price for whisky.[83] And in the same year the Timken Roller Bearing Company was held to have conspired with its British and French subsidiaries to divide the roller bearing markets of the world.[84]

In one case the courts were asked to find that a single company had conspired with itself. Motorola, Inc. had refused to renew the franchise of one of its dealers. The dealer sued for triple damages, charging that the refusal involved restraint of trade. The court held that the fact that Motorola was a single company constituted a complete defense, dismissing the contention that the company had conspired with itself to restrain trade in its own products as "absurd."[85]

The government lost a major case involving a charge of intraenterprise conspiracy in 1954. Here the defendants were du Pont, General Motors, and U.S. Rubber. The government had contended that the du Pont company, together with members of the du Pont family and certain family corporations, had acquired stock in General Motors and U.S. Rubber for the purpose and with the effect of controlling these companies and employing its control to obtain exclusive markets—preventing du Pont's competitors, for instance, from selling paint to General Motors or tire fabrics to U.S. Rubber. The district court held that the government had failed to prove its case. The evidence, it said, did not show that the du Ponts had sought or exercised control of the other companies or that du Pont had received any preference in their purchases. Dismissing the charge of conspiracy for want of evidence, the court did not attempt to discuss the legal principles that it involved.[86] The government appealed.

[81] *U.S.* v. *Yellow Cab Co.*, 332 U.S. 218, 227. The Supreme Court reversed the lower court on the point of law and remanded the case for trial on the facts. The lower court acquitted Yellow Cab, finding no intent to monopolize. The Supreme Court allowed this decision to stand (*U.S.* v. *Yellow Cab Co.*, 338 U.S. 338, 1949). In a similar case (*U.S.* v. *National City Lines*, 186 F. 2d 562; certiorari denied, 341 U.S. 916) decided in 1951, General Motors, Mack Truck, Firestone, Phillips Petroleum, and Standard Oil of California were found to have conspired to monopolize when they jointly furnished capital to two holding companies operating bus lines in 45 cities in return for ten-year exclusive contracts for busses, tires, and petroleum products.

[82] *U.S.* v. *Griffith*, 334 U.S. 100.

[83] *Kiefer-Stewart Co.* v. *Joseph E. Seagram & Sons*, 340 U.S. 211.

[84] *Timken Roller Bearing Co.* v. *U.S.*, 341 U.S. 593.

[85] *Nelson Radio and Supply Co.* v. *Motorola, Inc.*, 200 F. 2d 911, 914; certiorari denied, 345 U.S. 925 (1952).

[86] *New York Times*, December 4, 1954.

COMBINATION AND MONOPOLY

Combination is more effective than agreement as a method of eliminating competition and obtaining a monopoly. Collusive agreements are constantly tending to break down; they are unenforceable at law. Combinations, on the other hand, are permanent; subsidiary units are effectively controlled. In the history of the Sherman Act, however, the suits against agreements are many, while those involving combinations are comparatively few. Decisions handed down by the Supreme Court in such cases numbered only fourteen from 1895 to 1927; from 1927 to 1948 there were none. In these cases, moreover, the rule of the law has been less clear and less consistent than in those involving agreements among competitors.

In the E. C. Knight case in 1895, discussed above, the Court refused to break up the American Sugar Refining Company on the ground that manufacturing was not commerce, thus raising serious doubts concerning the application of the law. These doubts, however, were soon to be dispelled. In the Northern Securities case in 1904 the law was applied to a holding company. And in the Standard Oil and American Tobacco decisions in 1911, despite the enunciation of the rule of reason, each of these concerns was broken into several parts.

Following its decision in the Northern Securities case, the Court proceeded to uphold the government in every suit where railway combinations were involved. In the St. Louis Terminal case in 1912[87] it enjoined the railroads owning a terminal from denying access to their competitors. In the Union Pacific case[88] in 1912, and again in the Southern Pacific case[89] in 1922, it required the defendants to divest themselves of stock in other lines. And in the Reading and Lehigh Valley cases[90] in 1920 it broke up combinations that enabled these roads to control a number of anthracite mining companies. There was no evidence in any of the cases where divestiture or dissolution were required that the defendants had obtained a monopoly, that they had sought to do so, or that they had engaged in predatory practices.

In its approach to manufacturing, however, the Court displayed more tolerance. It placed its emphasis, in the Standard Oil and American Tobacco decisions, not on the fact of combination or even on the actual attainment of monopoly, but on the monopolistic intent of the defendants and on their use of unfair tactics in eliminating competition and excluding new competitors. And in the United Shoe Machinery case[91] in 1913 it refused to find a merger of three concerns, controlling 95 per cent of the

[87] *U.S.* v. *Terminal R.R. Assn.*, 224 U.S. 313.

[88] *U.S.* v. *Union Pacific R.R. Co.*, 226 U.S. 61.

[89] *U.S.* v. *Southern Pacific Co.*, 259 U.S. 214.

[90] *U.S.* v. *Reading Co.*, 253 U.S. 26; *U.S.* v. *Lehigh Valley R.R. Co.*, 254 U.S. 255.

[91] *U.S.* v. *Winslow*, 227 U.S. 202.

output of shoe machinery, to be in violation of the law. Each of these companies, said the Court, had been given a legal monopoly by its patent rights, and the machines they made were not competitive but complementary. This case, perhaps, was limited in its significance. But three years later a lower court refused to break up the American Can Company, controlling nine tenths of the output of tin cans, because the defendant "had done nothing of which any competitor or consumer of cans complains or anything which strikes a disinterested outsider as unfair or unethical."[92] In its decision in the U.S. Steel case in 1920 the Supreme Court revealed a similar complacency. It was the doctrine contained in this decision that, for the next twenty-five years, granted virtual immunity to monopolistic combinations in manufacturing.

The Good Trusts

The United States Steel Corporation, created in 1901, was a combination of twelve concerns, themselves resulting from earlier combinations of 180 separate companies. It was the largest merger in the nation's history, extending vertically from mining to fabrication and horizontally to all the types of steel mill products, and controlling, at its inception, around two thirds of the output of the industry. When this colossus came before the Court, it still controlled one half of the supply of steel. But in a 4 to 3 decision, with two of its members abstaining, the Court found that the combination did not violate the law.[93]

The majority reasoned as follows: (1) The organizers of the Corporation had intended to monopolize the industry, but they had not succeeded in doing so and, recognizing their failure, had abandoned the attempt. The law was directed, said Justice McKenna, not against an expectation of monopoly but against its realization. Its specific prohibition of attempts to monopolize was thus ignored. (2) Admittedly, the Corporation had conspired with other companies, in earlier years, to fix the price of steel. But this only served to prove its lack of monopoly. The practice, moreover, had been abandoned; the evidence showed that the industry was now competitive. The monopolistic character of the Pittsburgh-plus delivered pricing system was not explained or understood. (3) The decision was thus confined to a narrower issue: the legal status of a combination controlling half of an industry. Certainly the Corporation was big and powerful. But, said the Court, "the law does not make mere size an offense. It . . . requires overt acts and trusts to its prohibition of them and its power to repress and punish them."[94] (4) The question, then, was whether the Corporation had abused its power. Had it acted, by itself, to fix monopolistic prices? Had it excluded others from the market? On the contrary, said the Court, its behavior was exemplary: "It resorted to none of

[92] *U.S.* v. *American Can Co.*, 230 F. 859, 861 (1916).

[93] *U.S.* v. *U.S. Steel Corp.*, 251 U.S. 417 (1920).

[94] *Ibid.*, p. 451.

the brutalities or tyrannies that the cases illustrate of other combinations. It did not secure freight rebates; it did not increase its profits by reducing the wages of its employees . . . , by lowering the quality of its products, nor by creating an artificial scarcity of them; . . . it did not undersell its competitors in some localities by reducing its prices there below those maintained elsewhere . . . ; there was no evidence that it attempted to crush its competitors or drive them from the market."[95] In short, though the Corporation was big, it was not bad. And, accordingly, it was not dissolved. The law was thus held by the majority of the Court, as Justice Day remarked in his dissent, to be "intended merely to suppress unfair practices."[96]

When this decision was announced, the government withdrew its appeals in several pending cases, including the one against American Can. The issue of size was presented to the Court again in 1927, however, when the government sought to break up the International Harvester Company. This concern, a combination of five producers of agricultural implements and machinery, controlled 85 per cent of the output of such equipment when it was established in 1902, and 64 per cent when it was brought before the Court. Its leadership in setting prices was followed by the other members of the industry. These facts, however, did not impress the justices. Six of them, with three abstaining, adhered to the precedent set in the case of U.S. Steel. The law, they said, "does not make the mere size of a corporation, however impressive, or the existence of unexerted power on its part, an offense, when unaccompanied by unlawful conduct in the exercise of its power."[97] Price leadership was rejected as offering evidence of monopoly. In the words of the opinion, "The fact that competitors may see proper, in the exercise of their own judgment to follow the prices of another manufacturer, does not establish any suppression of competition or show any sinister domination."[98] International Harvester, like U.S. Steel, was a good trust.

When these decisions are taken together with the Court's refusal, in the Thatcher, Swift, and Arrow-Hart & Hegeman cases,[99] to enforce the prohibition of security acquisitions contained in the Clayton Act, it appears that the laws against monopolistic combinations were virtually nullified. And this was true for nearly a quarter of a century. In 1932 Justice Cardozo suggested, in another case involving Swift & Co., that mere size might be illegal "if magnified to the point at which it amounts to a monopoly."[100] But it was not until the Aluminum case was decided, in 1945, that a sharp change occurred in the interpretation of the law.

[95] *Ibid.*, p. 441.

[96] *Ibid.*, p. 464.

[97] *U.S.* v. *International Harvester Co.*, 247 U.S. 693, 708.

[98] *Ibid.*, pp. 708–9.

[99] *Thatcher Mfg. Co.* v. *FTC, Swift & Co.* v. *FTC*, 272 U.S. 554 (1926); *Arrow-Hart & Hegeman Electric Co.* v. *FTC*, 291 U.S. 587 (1934). See above, pp. 63, 109.

[100] *U.S.* v. *Swift & Co.*, 286 U.S. 106, 116.

Monopolization Illegal Per Se

The government brought suit against the Aluminum Company of America in 1937, charging that it had monopolized the manufacture of virgin aluminum and the sale of various aluminum products, in violation of Section 2 of the Sherman Act, and asking that it be broken into several parts. The monopoly, originating in a basic patent now expired, had been extended and preserved, according to the government's complaint, by resorting to oppressive tactics, including the elimination of competing fabricators by squeezing the spread between the price charged them for crude aluminum and the prices offered customers for finished goods. After a trial that ran for more than two years the District Court found Alcoa not guilty and the government appealed.[101] When the justices who had previously been connected with the prosecution disqualified themselves, however, the Supreme Court could not muster a quorum of six to hear the case. The judicial code was then amended by Congress to enable a Court of Appeals to serve, in such circumstances, as a court of last resort. The case was certified to the Court in the second circuit and the decision of this court, having the effect of a Supreme Court ruling, was rendered by Judge Learned Hand in 1945.[102]

The Court found that Alcoa manufactured more than nine tenths of the virgin aluminum ingot used in the United States, the rest coming in from abroad, and concluded that this was "enough to constitute a monopoly."[103] It then considered the argument that the power conferred by this monopoly, though it existed, had not been exercised. This distinction, said the Court, "is . . . purely formal; it would be valid only so long as the monopoly remained wholly inert; it would disappear as soon as the monopoly began to operate; for, when it did—that is, as soon as it began to sell at all—it must sell at some price and the only price at which it could sell is a price which it itself fixed. Thereafter the power and its exercise must needs coalesce."[104] The doctrine of the Steel and Harvester cases, that the mere existence of unexerted power is no offense, was thus explicitly reversed. Price fixing was found to be inherent in monopoly. The acquisition of market power became the test of illegality. The double standard of interpretation, which condoned the single-firm monopoly while holding agreements among competitors to be unlawful, was rejected as "absurd."

Alcoa had attained its position, however, not by combining with others, but by reinvesting its earnings and expanding its capacity as the market grew. Was this against the law? The Sherman Act does not forbid monopoly as such; it prohibits the act of monopolization and attempts to monopolize. It did not follow from the company's position, said the Court,

[101] *U.S.* v. *Aluminum Co. of America*, 44 F. Supp. 97 (1942).

[102] *U.S.* v. *Aluminum Co. of America*, 148 F. 2d 416.

[103] *Ibid.*, p. 424.

[104] *Ibid.*, pp. 427–28.

"that it 'monopolized' the ingot market; it may not have achieved monopoly; monopoly may have been thrust upon it."[105] But Alcoa might have avoided this development:

> It was not inevitable that it should always anticipate increases in the demand for ingots and be prepared to supply them. Nothing compelled it to keep doubling and redoubling its capacity before others entered the field. It insists that it has never excluded competitors; but we can think of no more effective exclusion than progressively to embrace each new opportunity as it opened, and to face every newcomer with new capacity already geared into a great organization, having the advantage of experience, trade connections, and the elite of personnel.[106]

To retain monopolistic power merely by growing with the market was thus to violate the law. Nor could the fact of monopolization be excused by the absence of intent to monopolize. To read Section 2 of the Sherman Act "as demanding any 'specific' intent makes nonsense of it, for no monopolist monopolizes unconscious of what he is doing. So here, 'Alcoa' meant to keep, and did keep, that complete and exclusive hold upon the ingot market with which it started. That was to 'monopolize' that market, however innocently it otherwise proceeded."[107] The defense of good behavior was likewise unavailing. The Court condemned the use of squeeze tactics in the past and enjoined their repetition in the future but made clear that it was holding Alcoa guilty of monopolization "regardless of such practices." The firm was not found to be abusing its position at the time of the trial, but a verdict for the government was held not to require the proof of such abuse. Congress, said the Court, "did not condone 'good trusts' and condemn 'bad' ones; it forbade all."[108] The antitrust laws were not intended merely to regulate business practices. It was one of their purposes "to perpetuate and preserve for its own sake and in spite of possible costs, an organization of industry into small units which can effectively compete with each other."[109]

Judge Hand's decision is a landmark in the interpretation of the law. It made a clean break with the Steel and Harvester precedents. It resurrected Section 2 of the Sherman Act. It opened the way to enforcement of the law against monopolization as well as against conspiracy. But the decision was not without its own peculiarities. Its finding of monopoly was based upon assumptions that were highly dubious. By excluding aluminum scrap in measuring the market for raw materials and including not only the ingots Alcoa sold to others but also the ingots it consumed itself, Alcoa's share of the market was found to stand at 90 per cent. But scrap competes with ingots and was excluded on the ground that it had been derived from products made from ingots that Alcoa had once produced,

[105] *Ibid.*, p. 429.
[106] *Ibid.*, p. 431.
[107] *Ibid.*, p. 432.
[108] *Ibid.*, p. 427.
[109] *Ibid.*, p. 429.

though evidence was lacking that Alcoa controlled the scrap supply. Had scrap been included in measuring the market, Alcoa's share would have stood at 60–64 per cent. And if Alcoa's consumption of its own ingots had been excluded, its share of the open market would have stood at 33 per cent. By adopting the first of these definitions of the market, the Court was enabled to make a finding of monopoly. For it went on to hold that 90 per cent "is enough to constitute a monopoly; it is doubtful whether 60 or 64 percent would be enough; and certainly 33 percent is not."[110] But when it wrote these words, the Court took away with one hand what it had given with another. The scope that it left for its doctrine, enunciated so clearly and so forcefully, was small indeed. For if this rule were followed, the firms that could be convicted under Section 2 of the Sherman Act would be few and far between.

Two other points should be noted. In holding expansion with the market through reinvestment of earnings to constitute monopolization, the Court created a precedent under which ordinary business foresight might be questioned and desirable improvements held in check. And in finding the preservation of smallness for its own sake to be a purpose of the law, it gave hostage to those who would use it, not to preserve competition, but to preserve the weak competitor. These issues will receive consideration later on.

The doctrine enunciated by Judge Hand in the Aluminum case was explicitly endorsed by the Supreme Court, in 1946, in the second American Tobacco case, discussed above. In this case three sellers, rather than a single seller, were involved. But the Court held that they could be convicted of monopolization, under Section 2 of the Sherman Act, without proof that they had abused their power. Possession of power and the intention to use it were all that was required. Intent, however, could be inferred from identity of behavior. The existence of power was all that needed to be proved. In the words of the decision, "the material consideration in determining whether a monopoly exists is not that prices are raised and that competition actually is excluded, but that power exists to raise prices or to exclude competition when it is desired to do so."[111] The ghost of the steel decision was thus laid by the Supreme Court itself.

The Court returned to the issue of monopolization in the Griffith case, involving the chain of movie houses, in 1948. Said Justice Douglas: "It is not always necessary to find a specific intent to restrain trade or build a monopoly. . . . It is sufficient that a restraint of trade or monopoly results as the consequence of a defendant's conduct or business arrangements. . . . Monopoly power, whether lawfully or unlawfully acquired, may itself constitute an evil and stand condemned under Section 2 even though it remains unexercised."[112]

[110] *Ibid.*, p. 424.

[111] *American Tobacco Co.* v. *U.S.*, 328 U.S. 781, 811.

[112] *U.S.* v. *Griffith*, 334 U.S. 100, 105–7.

Monopolization Judged by Its Effects

The courts have never repudiated the doctrine enunciated by Judge Hand in the Aluminum case. But their decisions in later cases have softened it. In a 5 to 4 decision in the Columbia Steel case[113] in 1948, the Supreme Court refused to prevent Columbia, a subsidiary of U.S. Steel with 13 per cent of the fabricating capacity on the Pacific coast, from acquiring the largest independent fabricator in the area and thus increasing its share of the business to 24 per cent. The Court said that it would break up combinations established for the purpose of restraining trade and also those involving an unreasonable restraint, and that it would consider, in judging reasonableness, the share of a market brought under control and the vigor of the competition that remained, but would not specify a percentage to be used in the future as a test. In the case before it, however, it found Columbia's expansion to be legitimate and its control of a fourth of the market to be reasonable. The view of the minority was expressed by Justice Douglas in his dissent:

> Industrial power should be decentralized. It should be scattered into many hands so that the fortunes of the people will not be dependent on the whim or caprice, the political prejudices, the emotional stability of a few self-appointed men. The fact that they are not vicious men but respectable and social minded is irrelevant. That is the philosophy and the command of the Sherman Act. It is founded on a theory of hostility to the concentration in private hands of power so great that only a government of the people should have it. The Court forgot this lesson in [the Steel and Harvester cases]. . . . The Court today forgets it when it allows United States Steel to wrap its tentacles tighter around the steel industry of the West.[114]

It should be noted, however, that the position of the majority may have been influenced by the fact that the Department of Justice had agreed, in 1946, to the purchase by U.S. Steel of the government's war-built plant at Geneva, Utah, giving it half of the ingot capacity in the Pacific states, and thus appeared, in the case of Columbia, having swallowed the Geneva camel, to be straining at a gnat.

In 1950, in the district court to which Judge Hand had returned the Aluminum case for the preparation of a remedy, Judge Knox announced his decree. He first laid down a general rule:

> In determining the extent of permissible power that is consistent with the antitrust laws in a particular industry, the following factors are relevant: the number and strength of the firms in the market; their effective size from the standpoint of technological development, and from the standpoint of competition with substitute materials and with foreign trade; national security interest in the maintenance of strong productive facilities, and maximum scientific re-

[113] *U.S.* v. *Columbia Steel Co.*, 334 U.S. 495.

[114] *Ibid.*, p. 536.

search and development; together with public interest in lowered costs and uninterrupted production.[115]

Aluminum, said the Court, must compete with other materials made by large concerns. Dismemberment of Alcoa's research staff and its managerial personnel would lessen its ability to do so. Success in interproduct competition "can be achieved only by companies that are rich in resources, and which are capable of undertaking extensive scientific and market experimentations. At the present juncture, the weakening of any aluminum producer would lessen the buoyancy of the industry as a whole."[116] The Court therefore denied the government's request that Alcoa be broken in two, finding its remedy in provisions requiring the company to license other domestic producers under its patents and to sever its ties with Aluminium, Ltd. of Canada, thus opening the way to competition from other firms.

In 1953, in another district court, Judge Leahy dismissed another suit against du Pont. In this case the government had charged that the company had monopolized the production of cellophane. Defining the market as limited to cellophane alone, the government held that du Pont accounted for the bulk of the supply. Defining it to include all such packaging materials, the court found cellophane to be in competition with waxed paper, glassine, and metal foils. The company had pioneered in developing the product. It had engaged in no predatory practices. It had increased its sales by reducing its price. Said Judge Leahy, "There has been no monopolization or conspiracy or attempt to monopolize shown. The record reflects not the dead hand of monopoly but rapidly declining prices, expanding production, intense competition stimulated by creative research, the development of new products and uses and other benefits of a free economy. Du Pont nor any other American company similarly situated should be punished for its success."[117]

More significant than the foregoing decisions was the one handed down by Judge Wyzanski in the United Shoe Machinery case of 1953.[118] Here, as in the Aluminum case, the company was found to have violated Section 2 of the Sherman Act by monopolizing the industry. But the reasoning of Judge Wyzanski differed from that of Judge Hand. The offense of attempting to monopolize, he said, requires evidence of intent; the offense of monopolizing does not. The means employed, in themselves, may be lawful; the result may be monopolization, which is not lawful. United's business practices—such as leasing rather than selling its machines and making long-term contracts on exclusive terms—were not

[115] *U.S.* v. *Aluminum Co. of America*, 91 F. Supp. 333, 347.

[116] *Ibid.*, p. 416.

[117] *U.S.* v. *du Pont,* 118 F. Supp. 41.

[118] *U.S.* v. *United Shoe Machinery Corp.*, 110 F. Supp. 295. For an analysis of this decision, see L. S. Keyes, "The Shoe Machinery Case and the Problem of the Good Trust," *Quarterly Journal of Economics,* Vol. LVIII (1954), pp. 287–304.

per se immoral or illegal. But the company had not achieved and maintained its overwhelming strength solely by virtue of its "ability, economies of scale, research, and adaptation to inevitable economic laws." Instead, given its dominant position, its business practices, however legal in themselves, had operated to exclude competitors from the field. Judge Wyzanski, thus, did not find monopolization to be illegal as such. But he imposed on the monopolist a stricter standard of conduct than that applying to competitive concerns. The former, he said, must be denied the right to follow practices in which the latter may safely be permitted to engage. His remedy, accordingly, was not to dissolve the company, but to require it to sell as well as lease its machines, shorten its leases, modify their terms, and grant licenses under its patents to its competitors. The decision was appealed by the company and was upheld in 1954 by the Supreme Court.[119]

Vertical Integration

In a number of cases coming before the courts over the years, the combination in question has been vertical rather than—or as well as—horizontal. In the Yellow Cab and other cases described above, bringing transactions between holding companies and their subsidiaries within the purview of the law, it appeared that the Supreme Court might be prepared to question vertical integration as such. But this has not been the rule. In the Paramount case in 1948, the Court said that vertical integration might become illegal if it were undertaken "to gain control over an appreciable segment of the market and to restrain or suppress competition,"[120] or if the integrated company possessed the power and the intent to exclude competitors. But it was careful to state that it did not hold such integration to be illegal per se. In the Columbia Steel case in the same year, U.S. Steel was allowed to acquire control of an additional fabricator on the Pacific Coast. "It seems clear to us," said the Court, "that vertical integration, without more, cannot be held violative of the Sherman Act."[121]

In several cases, however, disintegration has been required. In each of these cases it appeared that the dominant position occupied by a company at one stage of production gave it an unfair advantage over its competitors at another. In the Reading and Lehigh cases[122] in 1920, where companies owning railroads and coal mines had discriminated against other mining companies in providing railway service, the combinations were dissolved. In the Swift case, where a meat packing house had extended its operations backward into the stockyards and forward into the distribution of foodstuffs to the detriment of its suppliers and competitors, a consent decree entered in 1920 required it to withdraw from both these fields. In 1932 when the company asked that the decree be modified to permit it to en-

[119] 347 U.S. 521.

[120] *U.S.* v. *Paramount Pictures*, 334 U.S. 131, 174.

[121] *U.S.* v. *Columbia Steel Co.*, 334 U.S. 495, 525.

[122] *U.S.* v. *Reading Co.*, 253 U.S. 26; *U.S.* v. *Lehigh Valley R.R. Co.*, 254 U.S. 255.

gage in distribution, the Supreme Court refused.[123] In the Pullman case in 1943, where a company that manufactured sleeping cars and also operated all such cars in use on American railroads, employed its control of the market to exclude competitors from the manufacturing business, divorcement of the two functions was required.[124] And in the A&P case, where the company was found in 1946 to be employing its wholesale produce subsidiary, the Atlantic Commission Company, to obtain discriminatory advantages over its competitors, a consent decree accepted in 1954 provided that ACCO be dissolved.[125]

The most important disintegration decree in recent years is that in the Paramount case. This case involved five of the major producers of motion pictures who also operated first-run theaters in the larger cities and chains of smaller theaters throughout the country. The government charged that these concerns had favored their own houses in supplying films, and had required block booking, minimum admission charges, and protracted intervals between successive showings in leasing films to others, thus making it difficult for independent producers and distributors to compete. It sought the separation of production and exhibition, the elimination of block booking, and the prohibition of other coercive practices. The lower court enjoined the practices complained of and required that films, instead of being booked in blocks, be leased through competitive bidding. The Supreme Court found this remedy to be inadequate, insisting also that production and exhibition be divorced.[126] The reorganizations were completed by 1952, the five companies being broken into ten: five of them producers and five operating chains of theaters. As a result, markets have been opened to independent producers and films made more readily available to independent exhibitors.[127]

The issue of vertical integration was raised again by a suit against A.T.&T. and its manufacturing subsidiary, the Western Electric Company. The government charged that the combination excluded other manufacturers from the market for telephonic equipment and asked that it be dissolved. The case was still pending at the end of 1954. Its significance will be considered at greater length in Chapter 20.

Antimerger Policy

Until 1950, as we have seen, Section 7 of the Clayton Act relating to intercorporate stockholdings was rendered ineffective by adverse decisions of the courts. In that year Congress passed the Celler Antimerger

[123] *U.S.* v. *Swift & Co.*, 286 U.S. 106.

[124] *U.S.* v. *Pullman Co.*, 50 F. Supp. 123.

[125] *U.S.* v. *N.Y. Great A.&P. Tea Co.*, 67 F. Supp. 626 (1946); affirmed 173 F. 2d 79 (1949); Civil Action 52–139, District Court of the U.S., Southern District of N.Y., Consent Decree, January 19, 1954. The significance of this case is discussed at length in Chapter 14.

[126] *U.S.* v. *Paramount Pictures*, 334 U.S. 131 (1948).

[127] On the effects of this decision, see the paper by Simon N. Whitney in the *Papers and Proceedings of the American Economic Association* to be published as a supplement to Volume XLV of the *American Economic Review* in May 1955.

Act amending Section 7 to forbid acquisitions of assets as well as shares where the effect "may be" not only to "tend to create a monopoly" but also merely to "lessen competition" if it does so "substantially." Here, as elsewhere in the Clayton Act, the impact of the law will turn upon the meaning given by the enforcement agencies and the courts to the words "may" and "substantially."

By the end of 1954 the Federal Trade Commission had undertaken a comprehensive study of current corporate mergers, seeking to distinguish between those that might lessen competition and those that had such purposes as diversification, vertical integration, and the strengthening of weaker competitors. In three cases the Commission had issued complaints. In one, Pillsbury Mills had acquired two other milling companies, raising its share in a market for flour-base mixes from 16 per cent to 45 per cent. In another, the Crown-Zellerbach Corporation had bought another paper company, increasing its output of Kraft paper from 50 to 70 per cent of that produced on the Pacific Coast. The third case involved a merger between Luria Brothers of Philadelphia and other dealers in iron and steel scrap. In a preliminary opinion in the Pillsbury proceedings, the Commission had found a prima facie case that competition might be substantially impaired.[128]

In three instances where large automobile manufacturers had merged —Kaiser and Willys, Nash and Hudson, and Packard and Studebaker— the enforcement agencies had entered no complaint, probably feeling that the combinations would increase the ability of these concerns to compete with General Motors, Chrysler, and Ford. But when Bethlehem Steel proposed to merge with Youngstown Sheet and Tube, bringing its share of the industry's capacity to a fifth of the total, the Department of Justice disapproved.[129]

One case had reached the courts. The Hamilton Watch Company brought suit under Section 7 to prevent the Benrus Watch Company from acquiring and voting its shares. An injunction was granted by a district court on the ground that potential harm to competition had been shown, and this decision had been upheld by a court of appeals.[130]

These were but straws in the wind. The final effect of the antimerger law is still to be seen.

THE STATE OF THE LAW

The state of the law as to restrictive agreements among competitors is fairly clear. The following classification of agreements that are probably illegal is presented by Corwin Edwards:[131]

[128] *In re Pillsbury Mills, Inc.*, Docket No. 6000, Remand, December 28, 1953.

[129] *New York Times*, October 1, 1954.

[130] *Hamilton Watch Co.* v. *Benrus Watch Co.*, 114 F. Supp. 307; affirmed 206 F. 2d 738 (1953).

[131] Corwin D. Edwards, *Maintaining Competition* (New York: McGraw-Hill Book Co., Inc., 1949), pp. 41–42. Reproduced with permission.

I. Exclusion of competitors from the market.
  A. Agreement to preempt or deprive others of access to facilities for doing business . . . or to afford such access to others only upon discriminatory terms. . . .
  B. Agreement upon exclusive or preferential dealing arrangements designed to impair access by competitors to markets.
  C. Agreement not to use specified channels of distribution, or to make exclusive use of certain designated channels.
  D. Agreement to undertake discriminatory price cutting designed to destroy competition.
  E. Agreement to exact discriminatory prices or terms that prevent or destroy competition.
  F. Agreement to require the purchase of certain goods or services as a condition of supplying others.
  G. Discriminatory patent pools designed to destroy nonparticipants.

II. Restriction of output or of purchases.
  A. Agreement to restrict production, sales, or inventory accumulations.
  B. Agreement to restrict purchases or imports.
  C. Agreement not to construct or acquire additional equipment.
  D. Agreement not to use new processes or not to produce, sell, purchase, or use new types of materials or equipment.
  E. Agreement to limit research.
  F. Agreement to shut down or destroy existing equipment, or to acquire equipment from competitors for such purposes.
  G. Agreement not to produce low-cost products.
  H. Agreement to limit the quality or durability of goods sold or the extent of services rendered.

III. Division of markets.
  A. Allocation of territories in which to sell or purchase.
  B. Allocation of customers.
  C. Rotation of bids or orders.
  D. Agreement on proportion of total sales or purchases to be made by each concern.
  E. Allocation of products to be made or sold or processes to be used.

IV. Price Fixing.
  A. Agreement upon selling bids or prices.
  B. Agreement upon and enforcement of resale prices (except as specifically exempted by law).
  C. Agreement upon purchase prices to be paid.
  D. Agreement to fix price differentials, discounts, or important terms of sale or to designate groups of customers who shall be eligible for discounts.
  E. Agreement to add arbitrary charges to sale prices or to make arbitrary deductions from purchase prices.

V. Elimination of opportunity or incentive to compete.
  A. Agreement to sell through the same agents.
  B. Agreement to pool profits.

VI. Coercion. Agreement to use boycotts and other coercive devices to further any of the foregoing restraints.

Restraint of trade among separate companies, whether accomplished through informal agreement, through formal organization, or through habitual identity of behavior, has been attacked successfully by antitrust.

With respect to monopolization, the law has been less certain. Where market power has been obtained by a single firm, the courts have faltered and enforcement frequently has failed. For a generation, though agreements among competitors were held to be illegal, combinations possessing even greater power escaped correction, unless it was plain that their power had been abused. This judicial schizophrenia had a curious result. Firms once convicted of conspiracy for entering agreements were allowed to go untouched when they proceeded to combine.[132] A statute that had been designed to prevent and break up combinations was so distorted, through interpretation, as to offer them encouragement.

In principle, at least, the law's dichotomy has been corrected by the decisions handed down since 1945. Monopoly as such is legal where it has been "thrust upon" the monopolist. Attempts to monopolize may be held illegal where intent to monopolize can be shown. Monopolization itself may be held illegal, and here no proof of intent is now required. Possession of monopoly power may be found unlawful, even though the power was lawfully acquired. Such power may be condemned, even though it has never been abused. If it has the effect of barring the entry of others to a market, it may be held to violate the law.

This shows progress. But important questions remain. What is monopoly power? According to the courts, it is to be judged by the monopolist's share of the market and the strength of the remaining firms. But what share of a market is illegal? Just where, along the range of possible substitutes, are the boundaries of the market to be drawn? By what rule is the law to measure the ability of others to compete? Clear criteria are lacking. And in their absence, the legality of particular combinations is still quite unpredictable.

The force of the law depends upon the effectiveness of the remedies which it applies. Where competitors have agreed, the courts have long been vigorous in striking down restraints. Where a single firm has possessed a monopoly, they have increasingly shown themselves willing so to limit its powers and reform its practices as to open the way to the entry and growth of possible competitors. But they are still reluctant to break up close-knit combinations and will do so only where it appears that there is no other solution to be found. Whatever the judges may have said, the hand of the law has fallen more heavily on those who have conspired, more lightly on those who have monopolized.

[132] See *Report of the Federal Trade Commission on the Merger Movement* (Washington: Government Printing Office, 1948), pp. 9–14.

SUGGESTIONS FOR FURTHER READING

For a summary of the cases instituted under the Sherman Act, presented chronologically and indexed by name and subject matter, see *The Federal Antitrust Laws* (New York: Commerce Clearing House, 1952). Among the many accounts of the interpretation of the law during its first fifty years, one of the best is Milton Handler, *A Study of the Construction and Enforcement of the Federal Antitrust Laws*, T.N.E.C., Monograph No. 38 (Washington: Government Printing Office, 1941). The major decisions of the following years are analyzed in Joel B. Dirlam and Alfred E. Kahn, *Fair Competition: The Law and Economics of Antitrust Policy* (Ithaca: Cornell University Press, 1954), chaps. iii and v. Interpretation during both periods is discussed, and lengthy excerpts from the leading decisions are included in Andreas G. Padandreou and John T. Wheeler, *Competition and Its Regulation* (New York: Prentice-Hall, Inc., 1954), chaps. xv–xviii incl. See also M. A. Adelman, "Effective Competition and the Antitrust Laws," *Harvard Law Review*, Vol. LXI (1948), pp. 1289–1350, and George W. Stocking, "The Rule of Reason, Workable Competition, and the Legality of Trade Association Activities," *University of Chicago Law Review*, Vol. XXI (1954), pp. 527–619. In order fully to appreciate the decisions of the courts, it is desirable to read through some of the leading cases. The full text of most of the decisions cited in the preceding chapter will be found in the *United States Reports*. The texts, or excerpts therefrom, will also be found in the following casebooks: Milton Handler, *Cases on Trade Regulation* (Chicago: Foundation Press, 1937) and *Supplement to Cases and Other Materials on Trade Regulation* (Brooklyn: Foundation Press, 1947); S. Chesterfield Oppenheim, *Cases on Federal Antitrust Laws* (St. Paul: West Publishing Co., 1948) and *Recent Cases on Federal Antitrust Laws* (St. Paul: West Publishing Co., 1951); Louis B. Schwartz, *Free Enterprise and Economic Organization* (Brooklyn: Foundation Press, 1952); Heinrich Kronsten and J. T. Miller, Jr., *Regulation of Trade: A Case and Textbook* (New York: Fallon Law Book Co., 1953). For current decisions, follow *United States Law Week* (Washington: Bureau of National Affairs) or *Trade Regulation Reports* (New York: Commerce Clearing House).

Chapter 6 PATENTS, COPYRIGHTS, AND TRADE-MARKS

To encourage the advancement of technology, government grants patents to inventors. To promote the creative arts, it records the copyrights of authors, artists, and composers. To prevent sellers from misrepresenting the origin of their goods, it registers trade-marks. In each of these cases it establishes a monopoly—a monopoly that could not exist unless protected by law. As a result, competitors are prevented from employing the patented process, reproducing the copyrighted material, or using the registered mark. The policies that find expression in the patent, copyright, and trade-mark laws are thus in conflict with the policy embodied in the antitrust laws. In some cases this conflict may not be serious: a copyright applies to but one among the many expressions given to ideas; a patent may cover a process for which there are alternatives; a trade-mark may be attached to goods that are in competition with others of their kind. But elsewhere the conflict may be serious indeed: a collection of patents may enable their owner to monopolize an entire industry; a name belonging to a single seller may be the only one by which the product of an industry is known. It is in such cases that the exclusive rights conferred by government create a problem of peculiar difficulty for antitrust.

THE PATENT GRANT

A patent was originally called a letter patent, the word coming from the Latin *patere* meaning "to be open," and was thus an open letter in which the sovereign informed his subjects that he had granted someone a monopoly in some field of trade. In England this power was so abused by the Crown that it was proscribed by Parliament in the Statute of Monopolies in 1624. But an explicit exception was made in the case of monopolies granted to inventors, and the letter patent, known simply as a patent, came to be confined to such privileges. A patent today is an exclusive right conferred on an inventor, for a limited period, by a government. It authorizes him to make, use, transfer, or withhold whatever may be patented. This he might do in any case; what the patent adds is the right to exclude others or to admit them on his own terms. Without a patent, he might attempt to preserve a monopoly by keeping his invention secret; to get a patent, it must be disclosed.

The policy of promoting invention by granting temporary monopolies to inventors, a policy that had been followed in England for nearly two centuries, was written into the Constitution of the United States. The framers of the Constitution did not mention patents, but they did empower the Congress, in Article I, Section 8, Paragraph 8, "To promote the progress of Science and useful Arts, by securing for limited Times to Authors and Inventors the exclusive Right to their respective Writings and Discoveries. . . ." This power was not denied to the states, but it came in practice to be exercised by the federal government alone. It is upon this authority that the American patent system is based.

The Patent System

Congress passed the first patent law in 1790, offering protection to all inventors of novel and useful processes and devices who would disclose their nature in sufficient detail to "enable a workman or other person skilled in the art of manufacture . . . to make, construct . . . or use the same." Under this law a committee composed of the Secretary of State (Thomas Jefferson, himself an inventor of some note), the Secretary of War, and the Attorney General granted 57 patents during the next three years. In 1793 a second law relieved the cabinet officers of this burden, authorizing the Department of State to issue patents to everyone who might register inventions, without questioning their novelty or usefulness, leaving their validity to be determined by the courts. This act resulted in a flood of worthless patents and clogged the courts with litigation. It was superseded in 1836, by a third law which set up a Patent Office under a Commissioner of Patents, required that applications be examined to determine whether the inventions claimed were really new, and provided that patents should be issued only when such inventions were deemed by the Commissioner to be "sufficiently useful and important." The American patent system still rests upon the foundations established by the Act of 1836.

Patents have been obtainable in the United States since 1790 on any useful "art, manufacture, engine, machine," since 1793 on a "composition of matter," since 1842 on "ornamental designs," and since 1930 on botanical plants, and on improvements to any of them. The law thus covers processes of production (art, manufacture), the implements employed in such processes (engine, machine), and the products resulting from them (manufacture, composition of matter, and botanical plants). It covers, as a "composition of matter," not only such chemical products as dyestuffs, plastics, and synthetic fibers, but also foods and medicines—products to which the patent privilege is not generally extended under the laws of other countries. Patents on "ornamental designs" may relate to the design of the article itself or to designs that are incorporated in it or affixed to it. Such designs, however, may be protected more cheaply and for longer periods by obtaining copyrights. Fashions, in which the element of design is important, are neither patented nor copyrighted, not because the law excludes them, but because they change too rapidly to be protected by the usual legal processes. Patents are not granted on methods of doing business, or on fundamental scientific discoveries. But otherwise the law is generous in its coverage.

Patents are issued to individuals, not to corporations. Under the law, a patent is granted only to a person called "the sole and true inventor." But patent rights can be transferred to others through assignment. An inventor may sell his rights in an invention he has already made. Or he may accept employment under a contract which binds him to transfer his rights in any invention that he may come to make. In the usual case, he will file his assignment along with his application for a patent, and the corporation that employs him will be the assignee. In legal theory, patents are issued to individual inventors; in practice, they are owned by corporations.

The territorial scope of a patent is limited to the jurisdiction of the country that grants it. An American who wishes to protect his invention in other countries must take out patents under their laws. Foreigners may likewise take out patents in the United States. A patent may be exploited in one country, in another, or in both, and rights in different countries may be assigned to different firms. Products that are patented may not be imported in violation of domestic patent rights.

In England in 1643 the duration of a patent was fixed at 14 years, a period sufficient to enable a craftsman to train two successive groups of apprentices. This term was adopted in the first patent law in the United States. In 1861, however, an effort to extend the term to 20 years resulted in a compromise that fixed it at 17, and 17 years is still the nominal duration of the monopoly conferred by the patent grant.

In most other countries the patent holder is required to put his invention to work. In some countries this requirement is absolute. In others, it may be waived if the holder can show good cause or prove that a reasonable effort has been made. Failure to work an invention may be penalized by revocation or by the requirement that it be licensed to others. Licensing may also be required where enforcement of one patent would prevent the development of an invention covered by another, where refusal to license would prejudice the trade of other groups, and where the output of patented goods falls short of meeting public needs. No such obligations attach to patents issued by the United States. Within the limits laid down by the courts, the owner of a patent may refuse to work it, work it himself and refuse to license it to others, or license it on such terms as he may choose. In the lightness of its requirements, as in the breadth of its grants, the American patent law is noted for its liberality.

How Patents Are Issued and Validated

It is the function of the Patent Office merely to accept or to reject the applications that are brought before it. Each application must describe, with some precision, the nature of the invention that is claimed. This description takes the form of drawings or formulae accompanied by exposition couched in technical phraseology; no working models have been required since 1890. The monopoly awarded to an applicant will be confined within the boundaries of his claims. These claims are usually formulated by a patent lawyer employed by the inventor or, more often, by the corporate assignee. Their preparation is an art in itself. The broader they can be made, without appearing to be limitless, the wider will be the area of the monopoly. The less informative they can be made, without appearing to withhold essential facts, the less is the likelihood that the technology involved will be disclosed to possible competitors. When the application, thus carefully prepared, is submitted to the Patent Office, it must be accompanied by a $30 fee; when the patent is obtained, another $30 must be paid. The fee or salary of the patent lawyer is the major cost of patenting.

Applications are not made public by the Patent Office. Persons who may hold patents on similar inventions are not informed of the proceedings. Persons who might be injured by a grant of monopoly are not notified. Agencies of government charged with the maintenance of competition are not represented. Interests adverse to the grant are given no opportunity to protest. Whether a patent shall be issued is a matter for the Patent Office alone to decide.

An invention is not supposed to be patented unless it is new and useful and actually works. But the number of applications presented to the Patent Office is so large, and the resources available for handling them are, by comparison, so small, that rigorous standards of appraisal cannot, in practice, be maintained. The Office does not undertake to determine whether an invention is workable: it has no laboratories or testing bureaus of its own; it lacks the funds and the time required to seek the technical advice of private agencies. With respect to usefulness, it adheres to the standard established by Justice Story in 1817. The word "useful," he said, "is incorporated in the Act in contradistinction to mischievous or immoral."[1] An invention is thus presumed to be useful unless there is evidence that it would do positive harm. "There is no provision," says Corwin Edwards, "for proof that the invention has actually been made or that it accomplishes anything, and no provision for skilled technical appraisal of the place which the invention occupies in the developing technology of which it is a part."[2] Nor is there real assurance that the invention covered by a

[1] *Lowell* v. *Lewis,* 15 Fed. Cases, 1018, 1019.

[2] Corwin D. Edwards, *Maintaining Competition* (New York: McGraw-Hill Book Co., 1949), p. 219.

patent is even new. An examiner, in one of the seventy specialized divisions of the Patent Office, searches the file of earlier patents and scientific publications in every case. But, in the words of Walton Hamilton,

> . . . a hurried survey, in terms of mechanical likeness to what has gone before, is the most that can be given. . . . The group of examiners has annually to pass upon a minimum of 60,000 applications, a load which runs to 12 per person per week . . . the usual item involves an extended research into an intricate body of technology, yet only a few hours can be given to it. . . . The examiner can note the claim, glance at the specifications, conduct a casual inquiry, draw upon his experience for anything in point, and allow or reject the application. If he certifies a true invention, the patent issues, without appeal, review, or further ado. . . .[3]

If the examiner rejects an application, it may be carried to the Board of Appeals in the Patent Office where, in a third to a half of the cases, he is likely to be reversed. If the examiner is sustained, the applicant may go on to the Court of Customs and Patent Appeals where his chance of obtaining a patent may be one in five. Out of this process, there emerged an average annual crop of 22,000 patents during the eighties and the nineties, more than 35,000 from 1900 to 1920, more than 46,000 in the twenties and thirties, around 35,000—with somewhat more rigorous standards prevailing—in the forties, and more than 50,000 in 1951. In this flood of claims to monopolistic rights, granted as carelessly as must be the case, there will be many that will overlap.

The Patent Office does not guarantee its product. It does not warrant that the patentee is the true inventor or insure that his claim will be upheld. If he is sued for infringing another patent, he can argue that his own is different or superior. But the Patent Office will not come to his assistance. It leaves to him the burden and the cost of his defense. All that it gives him is a claim upon which he himself can enter suit. If another uses his invention without permission, he can seek an injunction and ask for damages. But the defendant may counter with a patent of his own, or may argue that the plaintiff's patent covers a process or a product that has long been common property. The resolution of such conflicts is the duty of the courts.

Judges have had their training, not in physics, chemistry, and engineering, but in the law. They are seldom expert in industrial technology. But they must decide whether a patent covers a real invention, whether it was issued to the true inventor, and whether it has been infringed. And it is their judgment that determines the existence, the ownership, and the scope of the patent monopoly. Invention of the telephone was claimed by Daniel Drawbaugh, Elisha Gray, and Alexander Graham Bell. Gray's patents were acquired by the Bell interests when their suit again Western Union was

[3] Walton Hamilton, *Patents and Free Enterprise*, T.N.E.C. Monograph No. 31 (Washington: Government Printing Office, 1941), p. 125.

settled out of court, and the telegraph company withdrew from the telephone industry. Drawbaugh's telephone was invented in 1869 and put to work in 1871; Bell's was patented in 1876. When Bell's suit against Drawbaugh reached the Supreme Court, two judges did not sit, three voted for Drawbaugh and four for Bell. It was on this foundation that the telephone monopoly was built.[4] More often, however, the courts have found that the plaintiff's patent was not infringed or that it was lacking in validity. Among 109 infringement suits brought before the Supreme Court from 1900 to 1945, 26 were found to be based on valid patents that had been infringed, 23 on patents that were valid but not infringed, and 60 on patents that were void.[5] It is a rare patent, however, that is taken to court, and an even rarer one that is appealed to the higher courts. The currency that is issued by the Patent Office thus passes at face value, save in those cases where the courts have found it to be counterfeit.

Monopoly and the Advancement of Technology

The concept of invention on which the patent law is based is that of a heroic feat of isolated genius, to be called forth by the promise of monopoly. But invention, in fact, is not heroic. It is a social process. It springs from the common fund of technical knowledge which is part of the social heritage. Technology grows by accretion. Each new contrivance is evolved from something already known. The novel feature is usually slight, when taken in relation to the whole. An invention is not so much a creation as a growth. Its nature is determined less by the ingenuity of the inventor than by the make-up of the material culture in which he finds himself. Given a problem to be solved, normal curiosity, and freedom to experiment, invention is almost certain to occur. The sole and true inventor is a fiction of the law. Some other man, if not Fulton, would have thought of combining the steam engine and the boat. The automobile was a product, not of a solitary genius, but of the common knowledge of the age.

Nor can inventive activity be attributed exclusively, or even largely, to desire for monetary gain. No one can say what actuated the inventors of the wheel, the wedge, the lever, the pulley, the mill, the screw, the drill, the lathe, the keel, the oar, the sail. Certain it is, however, that these contrivances emerged from cultures where the patent was unknown. Many men in later times have been driven to construct devices which could bring them no possible profit. Leonardo da Vinci, Benjamin Franklin, Thomas Jefferson never left off inventing things, never attempted to turn their inventions to practical account. Taussig, who studied the lives of the great utilitarian inventors found that they, too, "were constantly experimenting on all sorts of schemes, promising and unpromising; sometimes

[4] *The Telephone Cases*, 126 U.S. 1 (1887).

[5] E. Burke Inlow, *The Patent Grant* (Baltimore: Johns Hopkins Press, 1950), pp. 142–43.

with money-making intent, sometimes in the spirit of scientific research, and sometimes merely in sport." With these men, "schemes and experiments begin in childhood, and persist so long as life and strength hold. It matters not whether a fortune is made or pecuniary distress is chronic. There is increasing interest in new dodges, increasing trial of new devices. . . . It would seem that no satisfaction from pecuniary success or worldly recognition equals the absorbed interest of trial, experiment, novel problems, happy solutions."[6] The nature and the motivation of invention have been something other than the law assumes.

The patent system was established in an agricultural and handicraft economy. The first patents were awarded for a plow of cast iron, a cradle to be used in cutting grain, and improvements on the tools employed by artisans. Inventions were put to work by the inventors who developed them. Following the industrial revolution, with machine production, the factory system, and the growth of corporate enterprise, the process of invention underwent a striking change. Technology grew in scale and in complexity. Scientific knowledge came increasingly to be specialized. Invention came to require elaborate and costly equipment and to depend for its success on organized research. Corporations began to build their own laboratories and to hire their own technicians, putting them to work inventing for a salary. As an improvement emerged from a corporate laboratory, one of its employees was designated to play the part of the sole and true inventor when a patent was obtained. But the profits of the patent monopoly did not accrue to him. They belonged to his employer to whom the patent was assigned. And this is the basis on which the great majority of new inventions are made and patented today.

This change has given to the patent system a new and entirely different rationale. Research is costly and the commercial development of innovations may demand substantial sums. The ideas that succeed must provide the revenues to pay for those that fail. If competitors were straightway free to imitate the successes and avoid the failures, sharing in the profits of innovation without contributing to its costs, it would be less worth while to make the investments that are required to finance invention and to assume the risks that are involved. It is the temporary monopoly afforded by the patent that encourages the investments and justifies the risks. The patent system thus finds its function less in the stimulation of invention than in the promotion of corporate research and development.

PATENTS AND COMPETITION

The patent system serves a useful purpose; it is also subject to abuse. Patent monopolies have been sought and granted on supposed inventions that have contributed little or nothing to the advancement of technology.

[6] F. W. Taussig, *Inventors and Moneymakers* (New York: Macmillan Co., 1915), pp. 21–23.

Patent procedures have been so manipulated as to extend the duration of exclusive rights beyond the legal term of 17 years. The scope of patent protection has been extended horizontally to monopolize unpatented goods and vertically to control successive stages of production and distribution. In some cases ownership of patents that cover the whole of an industry's technology has been concentrated in the hands of a single firm. In other cases common control has been established by cross-licensing or through the operation of a patent pool. In both, litigation has been deliberately employed as a method of eliminating and excluding competitors. Patent owners have failed to work their patents, refused to license them to others, or granted licenses on restrictive terms. Patent licensing has been employed as a means of controlling the output, dividing the markets, and fixing the prices of entire industries. In the present section consideration will be given to each of these perversions of the patent law.

Patents Without Inventions

The volume of patents has clearly been greater than the quantity of significant invention. Patents have been granted on mere gadgets, on contrivances expressing the lowest order of mechanical ability, and on ideas involving little in the way of novelty. Patents have covered an indentation on the head of a screw, an eraser on the end of a pencil, rubber hand grips on bicycle handlebars, a bosom or dickie sewn onto the front of a shirt, the use of flat cord instead of round cord in the loop at the ends of suspenders, and the use of an oval rather than a cylindrical shape in a roll of toilet paper. Of the successive patents used by the United States Gypsum Company to control the production of gypsum wallboard, the first was issued in 1912 to cover the process of closing the edges of the board by folding the bottom cover sheet around them and then affixing the top cover sheet, the second in 1920 to cover the process of closing the edges by imbedding the ends of both covers in the body of the core, and the third in 1935 to cover the use of starch in producing the core, a process that had been in use since 1924.[7] The patent that gave the Johns-Manville Corporation a monopoly of the business of insulating previously constructed buildings by blowing mineral wool into the space between the outer and the inner walls was one that applied, not to the manufacture of the wool itself, nor to the machinery used in blowing it, but to the process of "providing openings to afford access to the air spaces" in existing structures, "inserting the outlet end of a conduit through said openings, and forcing through the said conduit comminuted heat insulating material . . ."; in short, it was a patent on the idea of blowing through a hole.[8] Four patents obtained by a professor at the University of Wisconsin, and used by the Wisconsin Alumni Research Foundation in collecting

[7] Clair Wilcox, *Competition and Monopoly in American Industry*, T.N.E.C. Monograph No. 21 (Washington: Government Printing Office, 1940), pp. 161–63.

[8] *Ibid.*, pp. 164–65.

royalties from the producers of various foodstuffs, covered the process of increasing the Vitamin D potency of such foodstuffs by exposing them to ultra violet light produced by an artificial source such as a quartz mercury vapor lamp. When these patents were challenged, the Court of Appeals found them to be invalid, observing that it had long been common practice to expose milk and olive oil to the rays of lamps and to cut alfalfa hay and the meat of coconuts and leave them in the sun.[9] The invention, apparently, had been anticipated in the first chapter of the Book of Genesis. When such patents reach the courts, they will rarely be allowed to stand. But until they do, they continue to afford a basis for industrial monopoly.

Extending the Boundaries of Monopoly

The normal duration of the legal monopoly conferred under the patent system is not 17 years but around 20. An invention may be worked for a year before a patent is applied for, and the usual application remains pending in the Patent Office for three years more. The period of pendency may be further extended by the withdrawal and amendment of applications and through the initiation of interference proceedings by the Patent Office when two applications appear to cover the same ground. The Fritts patent, covering the method by which a sound track is implanted on a film, was applied for in 1880, kept pending for 36 years, and issued in 1916, thus affording its owners legal protection for more than half a century. The duration of monopoly may also be prolonged by dividing a complicated invention into several parts—the steps in a process, the elements in a compound, or the sections of a machine—and applying for separate patents at judicious intervals. The patents owned by the Hartford-Empire Co., covering a machine used in the manufacture of glass containers, after being held in pendency for 15 years, were issued successively in 1925, 1928, 1931, and 1937, the final one expiring 44 years after the first application was received. During the life of a basic patent, its owner will seek to develop and patent improvements. He will also be the only buyer to whom patents on improvements made by others can be sold. When one grant of monopoly has expired, another will be ready to take its place. During its period of patent protection, moreover, a firm may have developed a productive organization, market outlets, control over materials, and a monopoly of skilled personnel that will make it difficult, if not impossible, for others to enter the field when its patents have expired. The patent system, in its operation, thus involves a longer tenure of power than that envisaged by the framers of the law.

The monopoly power afforded by patents has been extended in space as well as in time. Monopoly has been extended horizontally from one patented product to another and from patented to unpatented goods. Whether by contract or by persuasion, the shoe manufacturer who has

[9] Testimony of Wendell Berge before Subcommittee on War Mobilization, Committee on Military Affairs, U.S. Senate, October 21, 1943.

leased one of his machines from the United Shoe Machinery Corporation has also obtained the rest of his machinery and supplies from United Shoe, the canner who has leased his canning machinery from American Can or Continental has also bought his cans from the same concern, and the office that has leased an International Business Machine has ordered its tabulating cards from IBM. Monopoly has also been extended vertically from one stage of production and distribution to the next. The Hartford-Empire patents covered a machine used in making glass containers, but they were used not only to monopolize the container machinery business but also to cartellize the container industry itself. Machines were leased to manufacturers of jars and bottles and each of them was licensed to turn out a certain quantity of a certain product and sell it in a certain market at a certain price. The jars and bottles were not patented, but their production and sale was effectively controlled. Under its patent on tetraethyl, the Ethyl Gasoline Corporation forbade licensed refiners to sell antiknock gasoline to any but licensed jobbers. By fixing prices through its jobber licenses, it controlled the distribution as well as the production of this gasoline. Under its patent on multifocal lens blanks used in making spectacles, the Univis Lens Co. licensed wholesalers to grind and polish glasses, prescription retailers to prescribe and fit them, and finishing retailers to grind, polish, and fit, thus controlling the prices charged not only for the patented blanks but also for their subsequent processing and servicing. In these and other cases, extension of the boundaries of patent monopoly has been found to be illegal. But, in the meantime, the profits of wider monopoly have been obtained.

The Monopolization of Patent Monopolies

Not only does a single patent confer a monopoly, but many related patents may be accumulated by a single firm or brought together by agreement among a few or many companies. The large corporation will usually obtain a steady flow of patents through assignments from its own employees, supplemented by purchases from others. United Shoe, with 500 men in its research division and 25 patent lawyers on its legal staff, is said to have acquired nearly 4,200 patents between 1930 and 1947 and to have had 400 patent applications pending and 450 other inventions on hand in 1947.[10] Among 450 corporations covered by a report made by the Patent Office in 1939, there were 112 that held more than 100 patents and 15 that held more than 1,000.[11] General Electric was said at that time to control more than 8,000 patents and A.T.&T. was reported to own more than 9,250 and to hold licenses under some 6,000 others.[12] Concen-

[10] *U.S.* v. *United Shoe Machinery Corp.*, Civil Action 7198, District Court of the U.S., District of Mass., Complaint, December 15, 1947.

[11] Temporary National Economic Committee, *Hearings*, Part III, p. 1128.

[12] Thurman Arnold, *Bottlenecks of Business* (New York: Reynal & Hitchcock, 1940), p. 27; Federal Communications Commission, *Telephone Investigation*, 1938, pp. 243–45.

tration of patent ownership, on such a scale, may place in the hands of a single firm control over each of the possible methods by which a good may be produced, enabling it to monopolize the whole technology of a major industry.

Where a few large corporations hold patents that overlap, each is likely to share its rights with the others through cross-licensing. Such agreements may call for exclusive or nonexclusive licensing, and may cover future as well as present patent rights. The companies participating will usually agree to refrain from attacking the validity of patents held by other members of the group. Where the participants are engaged in different industries, each of them may be given an exclusive right, in his own field, to all of the patents that are involved. The agreement that settled the contest between Bell and Western Union in 1879 divided the communications industry, leaving the telegraph to Western Union and giving the telephone to Bell. Some years later, A.T.&T. entered into a series of agreements with General Electric and its then subsidiary, RCA, giving each interest an exclusive territory within which to exploit the patents owned by both. The first of these agreements, in 1920, gave radiotelegraphy and the manufacture of radio receiving sets to GE, wire and wireless telephony and the provision of wire facilities for radio broadcasting to A.T.&T. A second agreement, in 1926, gave radio broadcasting and other wireless services to RCA, wireless telephony and all wire services to A.T.&T. The third agreement concluded in connection with the dismissal of an antitrust suit in 1932, made the exclusive licenses nonexclusive, but left the existing division of territory undisturbed. Where the participants in a cross-licensing arrangement are engaged in the same industry, all of the technology in the field may thus be brought under unified control. It was a series of treaties between Hartford-Empire and each of the major producers of glass containers that enabled the Hartford company to establish its dominance over the container field. With patents monopolized by agreement, unified licensing was employed to regiment the entire industry.

In industries where essential patents are controlled by many firms, they may be brought together in a common pool. Under such an arrangement, patents may be assigned to a trade association or to a corporation set up for the purpose, and licenses granted to each of the participants under all of the patents in the pool. Licenses may be restricted or unrestricted; royalties may be collected and distributed, or patents may be licensed royalty free. A pool may be confined to patents relating to a single product or may include all those important to an industry. It may be limited to older patents, sharing the earlier inventions, but leaving to innovators, for a time, the advantage of exclusive use. But whatever its characteristics, the patent pool in every case will centralize control over a substantial segment of industrial technology.

Cross-licensing and patent pooling may be employed either to liberate competition or to intensify monopoly. Under such arrangements, improvements resulting from invention are made available to all of the participants and costs are reduced by eliminating litigation within the group. If unrestricted licenses are granted to all applicants on reasonable terms, outsiders are afforded access to the industry's technology. In the automobile industry, since 1915, patents have been pooled and licenses freely given without restriction and without charge. Ford, though not belonging to the pool, has also issued unrestricted licenses royalty free. Patents covering all but the more recent inventions are thus thrown open to the entire industry, and smaller and newer firms may use them without contributing inventions of their own. Since the pool was first established, no manufacturer of automobiles has appeared as plaintiff or defendant in an infringement suit. But agreements combining patents may also be administered with less liberality. A pool controlling all of the inventions in an industry will be the only purchaser of future patents and the only source of patent licenses. By refusing to license, by charging exorbitant royalties, and by drawing upon the combined resources of its members in prosecuting and defending patent suits, it may eliminate outsiders from the field. By including in its contracts provisions which restrict the quantity a licensee may produce, the area in which he may sell, and the prices he may charge, it may regiment an entire industry. Whether cross-licensing and patent pooling make for competition or for monopoly depends therefore upon the purposes for which they are established and the way in which they are administered.

The Use and Abuse of Patent Powers

Under American law the patentee is not required to work his patent. As a consequence, the law may be employed not to promote but to retard the introduction of advances in technology. It has frequently been charged —and as frequently denied—that new inventions are deliberately suppressed. While proof is not sufficient to support this charge, it is certain that patents outnumber the inventions that are put to work. Among 3,777 patents obtained by United Shoe Machinery from 1930 to 1947, only 363 have been employed in producing new machines, 685 covered various features of old models on which the basic patents had expired, and 2,729 were said to be "paper patents which United has never purported to commercialize."[13] But failure to commercialize a patent need not involve suppression of technology. A patent may cover a process that is less efficient than the one employed or a product whose sale would not repay the costs of its development. Among the 9,255 patents held by A.T.&T. in 1935, less than half were in use; of the rest, according to the company, 1,505 were awaiting further development and possible application, 2,126 were kept from use by the availability of superior alternatives, and 1,307 by the

[13] *U.S.* v. *United Shoe Machinery Corp., loc. cit.*

absence of public necessity.[14] The company's judgment as to these matters may well have been influenced, however, by the fact that it already had substantial sums invested in equipment embodying an earlier technology. It is said, in fact, to have postponed the introduction of improvements that would render such equipment obsolete.[15] Under active competition, the rate of change is determined by the market. Under the patent monopoly, it is determined by the patentee. Insofar as suppression of patented inventions does occur, it clearly defeats the fundamental purpose of the patent law.

The patent holder may fail to work his patent himself; he may refuse to license others to do so. Production of military aircraft was held up during World War II until a small manufacturer was finally persuaded to license other companies to make a patented metal fastener.[16] Resort to atabrine as a substitute for quinine was impeded by the fact that its production, under I. G. Farben's American patent, had been limited to a single licensee. The Hartford Empire Co. consistently refused to grant licenses to firms which undertook to enter into competition with its established licensees.[17] According to a policy memorandum taken from its files, the company "licensed the machines only to manufacturers of the better type, refusing many licensees who we thought would be price cutters. . . ." This policy was quite acceptable to manufacturers of the better type. "With the plans we now have," wrote one of them, "there is certain to be a curtailment of the promiscuous manufacture of milk bottles. . . ."[18]

The patentee who grants a license gives some one else the right to share in his monopoly. He promises, in effect, that he will not bring suit against the licensee. Licenses may be granted to one firm or to many. They may permit the licensee to produce and sell in any quantity, in any market, and at any price, or they may sharply restrict his liberty. Output may be limited by imposing quotas or by charging graduated royalties. Hartford Empire's contract with the Florida Glass Co. provided "that the licensee shall not produce in any calendar year . . . more than 21,000 gross of such bottles."[19] The licenses granted the Stanley Elevator Company, under patents owned by Otis and Westinghouse, permitted that concern to sell no more than 20 elevators in any year.[20] Under its contract with General Electric, Westinghouse formerly paid a royalty of 1 per

[14] Federal Communications Commission, *op. cit.*, p. 234.

[15] *U.S.* v. *Western Electric Co.*, Civil Action No. 17–49, District Court of the U.S., District of New Jersey, Complaint, January 14, 1949, pp. 51–62.

[16] Testimony of Thurman W. Arnold, Committee on Patents, U.S. Senate, April 25, 1942.

[17] Joseph Borkin and C. A. Welsh, *Germany's Master Plan* (New York: Duell, Sloan and Pearce, 1943), Chap. 12.

[18] Wilcox, *op. cit.*, pp. 76–77.

[19] *Ibid.*, p. 75.

[20] *Ibid.*, p. 252.

cent on lamp sales which did not exceed 25.4 per cent of the combined sales of the two concerns and 30 per cent on sales made in excess of this share.[21] License contracts may authorize each licensee to sell in a different

Lucille Corcos in *Fortune*

FREE ENTERPRISE IN OUR TIME: THE CLOSED PATENT POOL

market, thus giving each of them a regional monopoly. Hartford's contract with the Northwestern Glass Co. permitted the latter to sell its wares only in Oregon, Idaho, Montana, and Alaska; the contract with the Laurens Glass Works directed that concern to sell its bottles to two buy-

[21] *Ibid.*, p. 104.

ers in Spartansburg, South Carolina.[22] This has been the usual pattern adopted by international cartels. Here, exclusive rights under patents owned by the participants have been granted to a European firm in Western Europe, to a British firm in the Commonwealth, and to an American firm in the United States, and each of them has thus excluded the others' goods from its own territory. A patent holder may also undertake to fix the prices that are charged by subsequent distributors. Thus, U.S. Gypsum required its licensees to sell on a delivered basis under a multiple basing point system and to observe the minimum prices which it prescribed. Masonite licensed competing manufacturers of hardboard and fixed the prices they could charge.[23] And General Electric designated more than 80,000 distributors as agents, thus controlling the retail price of lamps.[24] In each of these ways, the patentee imposes restraints on competition. In some cases he may overstep the bounds of legality. In others, he may be within his rights. The alternative to restrictive licensing, it should be remembered, may be no licensing at all.

Patent Warfare

Large firms have sometimes undertaken to fortify a position of monopoly by accumulating an arsenal of patents to be used in attacking possible competitors. Their lawyers have flooded the Patent Office with a constant stream of applications to cover every process, every machine, and every product that their technicians have invented or might conceivably invent. According to Alfred Kahn: "The great research laboratories are only incidentally technological centers. From the business standpoint they are patent factories; they manufacture the raw material of monopoly. Their product is often nothing but a 'shot-gun,' a basis for threatening infringement suit and scaring off competitors; or a 'scare-crow,' a patent which itself represents little or no contribution but seems . . . to cover an important part of a developing art and hence permits threat of suit."[25] Hartford Empire, according to its policy memorandum, applied for patents designed "to block the development of machines which might be constructed by others for the same purpose as our machines, using alternative means" and for other patents "on possible improvements of competing machines so as to 'fence in' those and prevent their reaching an improved stage."[26] In addition to "blocking" and "fencing" patents, there are "umbrella," "accordion," and "drag-net" patents, drawn up with claims so broad, so expansible, and so effective as to cover and seize upon extensive areas of industrial technology. The practice followed by some

[22] *Ibid.*, p. 76.

[23] *Ibid.*, pp. 161–64.

[24] *U.S.* v. *General Electric Co.*, 82 F. Supp. 753 (1949).

[25] Alfred E. Kahn, "Fundamental Deficiencies of the American Patent Law," *American Economic Review*, Vol. XXX (1940), pp. 475–91.

[26] Wilcox, *op. cit.*, p. 74.

concerns has been described by a member of the patent bar: "As a competitor comes out with a new machine . . . they look through all their pending applications, which may run into several thousand, and see if they can't find some similarity, no matter how far-fetched . . . then they will write claims into the pending application covering this competitor's machine, and in a short time come out with a patent, make charges of infringement, and bring suit. . . ."[27]

Litigation has been deliberately employed as a weapon of monopoly. Between 1877 and 1893, when the first Bell patent expired, the telephone company initiated more than 600 infringement suits.[28] Patent warfare was similarly employed to build the power of National Cash Register, Eastman Kodak, and United Shoe Machinery.[29] Hartford Empire, in later years, repeatedly brought suit against competing manufacturers of container machinery, against the purchasers of such machinery, and against concerns that undertook to produce containers with their own machines. The experience of a producer who unsuccessfully sought to obtain a license to make milk bottles in Texas is a case in point:

MR. COLEMAN: We were sued for infringement of some 9 to 10 claims. I don't recall at the present time.

MR. COX: Tell us about the outcome of that litigation.

MR. COLEMAN: We naturally were finally forced to hire a patent attorney. We had to acquire the services of a Texas attorney, and I think there are some two or three patent attorneys in the State. They brought us into court in April of 1935, as I recall. Well, when I arrived at San Angelo and met them there in the hotel, I can conservatively say there was half a train load of attorneys and equipment. There were motion picture projectors and attorneys all over the place. I don't know anyone of the Hartford legal staff that was not there. They were prepared to give us a nice battle. Well, I had only one attorney, and he was considerably lost in that crowd. I wish you might have seen his face that morning. So I promptly asked for a recess until the afternoon, in order to see if we couldn't settle the case out of court.

MR. COX: Did you settle the case out of court?

MR. COLEMAN: We were able to settle the case out of court; yes, sir. . . .

MR. COX: Is that Knape-Coleman Co. operating today?

MR. COLEMAN: No, sir; it is not.[30]

In patent warfare there is no assurance that the adversary with the better claim will be victorious. Litigation is costly and the outcome is likely to favor the party with the longer purse. Suits may be brought in different jurisdictions and under many different claims. A firm may see its markets vanish as suits are brought against its customers. Such litiga-

[27] Testimony of G. H. Willitts, *Hearings before the Committee on Patents, House of Representatives* (1932), pp. 69–72.

[28] Hamilton, *op. cit.*, p. 89.

[29] Floyd L. Vaughan, *Economics of Our Patent System* (New York: Macmillan Co., 1925), pp. 149–52.

[30] Wilcox, *op. cit.*, p. 77.

tion, moreover, may drag on for years. Its victim may well conclude that capitulation is preferable to bankruptcy. When Eastman Kodak sued the Boston Camera Co. in 1894, obtaining a temporary injunction against the sale of Boston's wares, Eastman was finally adjudged the real infringer, but Boston had by then been broken and was thereupon absorbed.[31] When the predecessor of the Aluminum Company of America sued the Cowles Brothers and was found, after ten years, to have infringed their patents, they agreed to accept a cash settlement and retired from the field.[32] In many other cases, suits have been settled before the courts have passed upon the rival patent claims. A weaker firm with a valid patent may thus sell out to a stronger firm with a patent of dubious validity. Or it may recognize the latter's patent as valid, take out a license, and agree to abide by its terms. Exclusive rights thus tend to gravitate to large concerns, regardless of the legal status of their claims.

PATENTS AND THE COURTS

Most of the problems outlined in the preceding section have been presented in cases brought before the courts. Decisions in such cases have dealt with the standard of patentability; with the right of the patentee to suppress his invention, to deny licenses to others, and to grant one or more licenses on restrictive terms; with his efforts to extend his monopoly to other products and to later stages of production, to control output, to divide markets, and to fix prices; with cross-licensing; and with the operation of patent pools. In general, the earlier decisions were favorable to the patent holder. But the courts have come increasingly, in recent years, to limit the scope and check the abuses of patent monopoly.

The Standard of Patentability

Until 1835 no patent was found invalid for want of novelty. Thereafter a succession of cases involving patents on gadgets led to the development of a judicial standard of patentability. In 1850 the Supreme Court held that a doorknob made of clay or porcelain rather than metal or wood was "the work of the skilled mechanic, not that of the inventor."[33] This distinction continued to govern the decisions handed down for the better part of a century, and patents were upheld if they were deemed to embody a degree of skill that was greater than that of the artisan. But as invention came increasingly to be the product of corporate research, the standard of patentability was raised. And finally, in the Cuno case[34] in 1941, the Court held that usefulness and novelty in a wireless lighter "does

[31] Hamilton, *op. cit.*, p. 47.

[32] George W. Stocking and Myron W. Watkins, *Cartels in Action* (New York: Twentieth Century Fund, 1946), p. 221.

[33] *Hotchkiss* v. *Greenwood*, 11 How. 248.

[34] *Cuno Corp.* v. *Automatic Devices Corp.*, 314 U.S. 84.

not necessarily make the device patentable." Said Justice Douglas: "Under the statute, the device must not only be 'new and useful,' it must also be an 'invention' or 'discovery' . . . That is to say, the new device, however useful it may be, must reveal the flash of creative genius, not merely the skill of the calling. If it fails, it has not established its right to a private grant on the public domain."[35] The standard thus became one that distinguished, not between the skill of the mechanic and that of the inventor, but between mere skill and the flash of genius. This standard has been denounced as resting on subjective judgment. But in this it does not differ from the earlier one. Whether an invention is patentable depends, and has always depended, on the opinion of the courts. But the courts have come increasingly to weigh the public interest against the claims of the patentee.

The widening gulf between the standard of invention accepted by the Patent Office and that adopted by the bench is illustrated by the decision handed down in the Supermarket Equipment case[36] in 1950. The patent in question covered a rack used to slide packages along a counter to the cash register in grocery stores. Said the Court:

> This counter does what a store counter has always done—it supports merchandise at a convenient height while the customer makes his purchases and the merchant his sales. The three-sided rack will draw or push goods put within it from one place to another—just what any such rack would do on any smooth surface—and the guide rails keep it from falling or sliding off from the counter, as guide rails have ever done. Two and two have been added together, and still they make only four. . . . The function of a patent is to add to the sum of useful knowledge. . . . A patent for a combination which only unites old elements . . . withdraws what is already known into the field of its monopoly and diminishes the resources available to skillful men. . . .

And Justice Douglas added the final word: "The fact that a patent as flimsy and as spurious as this one has to be brought all the way to this Court to be declared invalid dramatically illustrates how far our patent system frequently departs from the constitutional standards which are supposed to govern."

The Obligation of the Patentee

The courts have long regarded the patent as a form of private property and have accordingly upheld the right of the patentee to withhold his invention from use. "His title," said a lower court in the Button Fastener case[37] in 1896, "is exclusive, and so clearly within the constitutional provisions with respect of private property that he is neither bound to use his discovery himself, nor permit others to use it." And this position was

[35] *Ibid.*, p. 91.

[36] *Great Atlantic & Pacific Tea Co.* v. *Supermarket Equipment Corp.*, 340 U.S. 147 (1950).

[37] *Heaton-Peninsular Button Fastener Co.* v. *Eureka Specialty Co.*, 77 Fed. 288.

endorsed by the Supreme Court in the Paper Bag case[38] in 1908, when the owner of an unused patent was held to be entitled to an injunction against infringement. More recently the courts have come to speak of a patent as a privilege dependent on the fulfillment of a public purpose.[39] But the right of nonuse is still supported by the law. "A patent owner is not . . . under any obligation to see that the public acquires the free right to use the invention. He has no obligation either to use it or to grant its use to others." So said the Supreme Court in the Hartford Empire case in 1945.[40]

Tying Contracts

Many decisions of the courts have dealt with the efforts of a patentee to extend the scope of his monopoly beyond the boundaries of the patent grant. In some cases the patentee has sought to prevent a competitor from selling an unpatented product for use in a patented combination. In the first of these, the Morgan Envelope case[41] decided in 1893, the Court held that the plaintiff, having sold a patented machine, could not be granted an injunction restraining Morgan from selling an unpatented replacement part. In 1909, however, in the Leeds & Catlin case,[42] the Court held an unpatented record to be an integral part of a patented phonograph, licensed to users by the Victor company, and found that Victor's patent was infringed by the sale of Leeds & Catlin's records. This position was emphatically reversed by the Court's decision in the Mercoid Case[43] in 1944. Mercoid had been sued by Minneapolis-Honeywell when it sold an unpatented switch to be used in connection with a patented combination of thermostats in controlling furnace heat. The Court found no infringement, holding Honeywell's effort to extend the scope of its patent to be illegal per se. "An unpatented part of a combination patent," said Justice Douglas, "is no more entitled to monopolistic protection than any other unpatented device."

In other cases the patent holder has included in his license contracts provisions requiring his licensees to purchase some other product that he has for sale. Before the passage of the Clayton Act such tying contracts were upheld. In the Button Fastener case, already mentioned, the court found a provision requiring those using the fastener to purchase the staples that fed it to fall within the constitutional guarantee of freedom of contract. In the Dick case[44] in 1912, the Supreme Court permitted Dick to bind the purchasers of a mimeograph machine to buy from Dick their stencils, paper, and ink, holding that a patentee could impose whatever

[38] *Continental Paper Bag Co.* v. *Eastern Paper Bag Co.*, 210 U.S. 405.

[39] *Cf. Special Equipment Co.* v. *Coe*, 324 U.S. 730 (1945).

[40] *Hartford Empire Co.* v. *U.S.*, 323 U.S. 386.

[41] *Albany Paper Co.* v. *Morgan Envelope Co.*, 152 U.S. 425.

[42] *Leeds & Catlin* v. *Victor Talking Machine Co.*, 213 U.S. 325.

[43] *Mercoid Corp.* v. *Minneapolis–Honeywell Regulator Co.*, 320 U.S. 680.

[44] *Henry* v. *A. B. Dick Co.*, 224 U.S. 1.

restrictions he might choose. And in the United Shoe Machinery case[45] in 1913, the Court found leases tying one machine to others to be a lawful exercise of patent rights. It was these decisions that led to the inclusion of Section 3 in the Clayton Act. And it was under this section, forbidding tying contracts, that Dick accepted a Federal Trade Commission order, in 1917, requiring it to cease and desist, and that the tying clauses in United Shoe Machinery leases were found by the Court, in 1922, to be in violation of the law.[46] In an earlier case, however, the Motion Picture Patents case[47] decided in 1917, the Court had already reversed the Dick decision, finding a contract that tied the lease of a patented projector to the sale of unpatented films to be illegal under the provisions of the Sherman Act.

Since the Clayton Act was passed, the Court has consistently refused to permit the patentee to extend his monopoly to cover other goods. Following its decision in the United Shoe Machinery case, it struck down contracts, in 1928, requiring radio manufacturers licensed under RCA patents to buy their tubes from RCA;[48] in 1931, requiring licensees of a patented dry ice container to purchase dry ice from the patentee;[49] in 1936, requiring lessees of International Business Machines to buy their tabulating cards from IBM;[50] in 1938, requiring users of a patented method to control the curing of concrete to obtain an unpatented ingredient from the patentee;[51] and in 1945, requiring the purchase of rivets by lessees of patented riveting machines.[52] In these cases, the contracts were found substantially to lessen competition, within the meaning of the Clayton Act, because the patentee dominated the market for the process or product to which the unpatented commodity was tied. In the lower courts, however, tying contracts have been invalidated in cases where the patentee was far from having a monopoly. And this position was upheld by the Supreme Court in the International Salt case[53] in 1947, when it held that a contract requiring the users of a patented salt dispenser to purchase salt from its producer was unreasonable per se. It is evident that the courts will not now tolerate the use of tying clauses, under any circumstances, to extend the boundaries of a patent monopoly.

A similar issue was raised by the Eastman Kodak case which was

[45] *U.S.* v. *Winslow*, 227 U.S. 202.

[46] *United Shoe Machinery Corp.* v. *U.S.*, 258 U.S. 451.

[47] *Motion Picture Patents Co.* v. *Universal Films Mfg. Co.*, 243 U.S. 502.

[48] *Lord* v. *Radio Corp. of America*, 24 F. 2d 505, certiorari denied, 278 U.S. 648.

[49] *Carbice Corp.* v. *American Patents Development Corp.*, 283 U.S. 27.

[50] *International Business Machines Corp.* v. *U.S.*, 298 U.S. 131.

[51] *Leitch Mfg. Co.* v. *Barber Co.*, 302 U.S. 458.

[52] *Judson Thompson* v. *F.T.C.*, 150 F. 2d 952; certiorari denied, 326 U.S. 776. These precedents have been followed by the lower courts. In *U.S.* v. *American Can Co.*, 87 F. Supp. 18 (1949), contracts tying the sale of tin cans to the lease of patented can-closing machinery were held to violate the Clayton Act.

[53] *International Salt Co.* v. *U.S.*, 332 U.S. 392.

settled by a consent decree in 1954. The company had followed the practice of selling amateur color film at a price which included a charge for finishing, tying the sale of the film itself and the business of providing finishing services. Under the terms of the decree, Eastman agreed to sell the film alone, thus admitting competitors to the finishing business.[54]

Restrictive Licenses

Before the Sherman Act was passed, the courts had consistently upheld the inclusion of restrictive provisions in patent licenses.[55] In the first such case to follow the enactment of the law, the National Harrow case[56] decided in 1902, the Supreme Court held that its provisions did not impair the freedom of the patentee. Six manufacturers of harrows had set up National Harrow to hold their patents and to fix the price of harrows through its licenses. The issue presented to the Court, however, related not to the legality of patent pooling but only to that of restrictive licensing. On this point, despite the Sherman Act, Harrow's monopolistic arrangements were held to be permitted by the patent laws. "The very object of these laws," said Justice Peckham, "is monopoly, and the rule is, with few exceptions, that any conditions which are not in their very nature illegal . . . will be upheld by the courts. The fact that the conditions in the contract keep up the monopoly or fix prices does not render them illegal. . . ."

Where a patent owner grants a license to use a patented machine or process or to make and sell a patented product, the courts have generally upheld his right to limit the licensee to a certain geographic area[57] or a certain field of industry,[58] to restrict his output,[59] and to fix the price that he may charge when he sells the patented goods. The leading decision on the latter point was handed down by the Supreme Court in the General Electric case[60] in 1926. One of the issues raised in this case related to the right of General Electric, under its basic patents on the electric lamp, to fix the prices charged by Westinghouse. This right was upheld by the Court, and license contracts fixing a licensee's prices on patented products are still permitted by the law. In other circumstances, however, provisions fixing prices may be adjudged illegal. The right of a patentee to fix the prices charged for unpatented products made by patented processes or on patented machines is highly dubious.[61] His right to control the price at

[54] *New York Times,* December 22, 1954.

[55] *Mitchell* v. *Hawley,* 16 Wall. 544 (1872); *Adams* v. *Burke,* 17 Wall. 543 (1873).

[56] *Bement* v. *National Harrow Co.,* 186 U.S. 70.

[57] *Providence Rubber Co.* v. *Goodyear,* 9 Wall. 788 (1869).

[58] *General Talking Pictures Corp.* v. *Western Electric Corp.,* 304 U.S. 175 (1938).

[59] *Rubber Tire Wheel Co.* v. *Milwaukee Rubber Works Co.,* 154 F. 328 (1907), 210 U.S. 439 (1908).

[60] *U.S.* v. *General Electric Co.,* 272 U.S. 476.

[61] *Barber Coleman Co.* v. *National Tool Co.,* 136 F. 2d 339 (1943); *Cummer-Graham Co.* v. *Straight Side Basket Corp.,* 142 F. 2d 646 (1944).

which patented products, once sold by him or his patentees, are resold by others has generally been denied.

Surrender of title to a patented good has long been held to terminate the patentee's authority over its subsequent use and sale.[62] In the case of *Bauer* v. *O'Donnell*[63] in 1913, it was held that O'Donnell had not infringed the patent on Sanatogen bought from Bauer when he resold it for less than the price that Bauer had printed on the package. The Victor company then undertook to control the resale price of phonographs by licensing consumers to use them and sued Macy's for infringement when it cut the price. In its decision, handed down in 1917, the Court found no infringement of Victor's patent, holding the licensing arrangement to be a subterfuge.[64] General Electric then designated retailers of its lamps as agents, shipped lamps to them on consignment, and retained title until they were sold. The legality of this method of fixing resale prices was brought before the Court as a second issue in the General Electric case in 1926 and was then upheld. In later cases, however, control of resale prices under patents has again been found to violate the law. In the Ethyl Gasoline decision[65] in 1940, the company's effort to control the price of gasoline by confining its sale to licensed jobbers was held to go beyond its patent rights. And in the Univis case[66] in 1942, an agency system, similar to that employed by General Electric, which fixed the prices charged by finishers and distributors of patented eyeglass lenses, was found to be in violation of the Sherman Act.

Restrictive licensing has also been held to be illegal when employed for the purpose of eliminating competition among many licensees. In the Masonite case[67] in 1942, the Court found the series of agency contracts whereby Masonite fixed the prices charged by each of its competitors for patented hardboard to involve concerted action to restrain trade. And in the Gypsum case[68] in 1948, it condemned the establishment of common prices for manufacturers of gypsum board through provisions contained in separate contracts for patent licensing. In this case the government had asked the Court to reverse the rule of the General Electric decision permitting a patentee to fix the prices that might be charged by a licensee. Four of the judges were willing to do so; the rest were not. But all of them agreed that the General Electric precedent "gives no support for a patentee, acting in concert with all members of an industry, to issue substantially identical licenses . . . under which industry is completely regi-

[62] *Bloomer* v. *Millinger*, 1 Wall. 340 (1863); *Mitchell* v. *Hawley*, 16 Wall. 544 (1872); *Keeler* v. *Standard Folding Bed Co.*, 157 U.S. 659 (1895).

[63] 229 U.S. 1.

[64] *Straus* v. *Victor Talking Machine Co.*, 243 U.S. 490.

[65] *Ethyl Gasoline Corp.* v. *U.S.*, 309 U.S. 436.

[66] *U.S.* v. *Univis Lens Co.*, 316 U.S. 421.

[67] *U.S.* v. *Masonite Corp.*, 316 U.S. 265.

[68] *U.S.* v. *U.S. Gypsum Co.*, 333 U.S. 364.

mented." When each of several licensees accepts restrictive terms on the condition or with the knowledge that others will do so, they are guilty, in the eyes of the Court, of conspiracy in restraint of trade.

Cross-Licensing, Patent Pools, and Concentration of Patent Ownership

Cross-licensing and patent pooling have never been held to be illegal per se. But their employment as a means of eliminating competition among patent owners and licensees has usually been condemned. In the leading case on patent pooling, the Standard Sanitary case[69] decided in 1912, where patents covering the production of enameled iron bathtubs and other sanitary wares had been pooled with a trade association, the inclusion in licenses issued to firms producing 85 per cent of the output of such wares of provisions restricting output, fixing prices and discounts, and controlling channels of trade was held to violate the Sherman Act. A similar arrangement was found to be illegal, a few years later, in the Motion Picture Patents case.[70] In the Standard Oil of Indiana case[71] in 1931, however, a pool controlling patents covering methods of cracking gasoline was allowed to stand. But here the Court was impressed by the fact that many other cracking processes remained outside the pool, that licensees under the pooling arrangement did little more than half of the cracking of gasoline, and that cracking provided only a fourth of the total supply. The pool, thus faced with competition, was found to be powerless to fix prices and was therefore held to be within the law. In the Hartford-Empire case[72] decided in 1945, Hartford had employed the patents in its pool to dominate completely the glass container industry, curtailing output, dividing markets, and fixing prices through restrictive licenses; the Court found in Hartford's behavior, as a whole, convincing evidence of unlawful conspiracy. In the National Lead case[73] in 1947, a cross-licensing agreement that divided markets and fixed the prices of titanium pigment was likewise held to be against the law. In the Line Material case[74] in 1948, the Court was even more emphatic in its condemnation of a plan that eliminated competition through cross-licensing. Here, each of two small companies producing patented fuse cutouts had licensed the other and fixed the prices it might charge. Their agreement to do so was held to be illegal per se. "This price fixing scheme," said the Court, "does far more than secure to inventors 'the exclusive right' to their discoveries. . . . It gives them a leverage on the market which only a combination, not a pat-

[69] *Standard Sanitary Mfg. Co.* v. *U.S.*, 226 U.S. 20.
[70] *U.S.* v. *Motion Picture Patents Co.*, 225 F. 800 (1915); 247 U.S. 524 (1918).
[71] *Standard Oil Co. (Indiana)* v. *U.S.*, 283 U.S. 163.
[72] *Hartford Empire Co.* v. *U.S.*, 323 U.S. 386.
[73] *U.S.* v. *National Lead Co.*, 332 U.S. 319.
[74] *U.S.* v. *Line Material Co.*, 333 U.S. 287.

ent by itself, can create." And in the Besser case[75] in 1952 the court held joint action by patentees in refusing licenses, bringing infringement suits, and threatening to sue to be in violation of the law.

In the Line Material case, as in the Gypsum case, four judges were ready to repeal the rule of the General Electric case of 1926 that permitted GE to control the quantities produced and the prices charged by Westinghouse, but this fell short of a majority. In the meantime, the government had started a second suit against GE. The basic patents on the electric lamp had expired and GE had undertaken to perpetuate its control of the industry by employing later patents on such parts of the lamp as the filament and the frosting on the bulb. To this end, it had formed a patent pool with Westinghouse and granted licenses to four other producers, controlling the output and the prices of all six companies. These arrangements, while similar to those approved in 1926, though involving different patents and a larger number of licensees, were found by a district court in 1949 to violate both sections of the Sherman Act. General Electric, said the court, had conspired with its licensees and had "unlawfully monopolized the incandescent electric lamp industry in the United States."[76]

While action to monopolize patents and to control them by agreement has frequently been found illegal, the ownership of many patents by a single company, until recently, was held to be within the law.[77] The issue was raised again, however, in the United Shoe Machinery case,[78] decided in 1953. Here, the government had charged that the company "has been for many years, and is now, engaged in a program of engrossing all patents and inventions of importance relating to shoe machinery for the purpose of blanketing the shoe machinery industry with patents under the control of United and thereby suppressing competition in the industry."[79] The court found that the company held nearly 4,000 patents, about 95 per cent of them the product of its own research, only 5 per cent purchased from others. It found no evidence that the patent right had been abused. United had put a third of its patents to work; it had not suppressed the others or used them to threaten possible competitors. It had not offered or been asked to grant licenses, but it had not refused to do so. It had not resorted to litigation as a means of harassing competitors but had acted in good faith in bringing infringement suits. It had adopted certain policies, however, that operated to handicap competitors. It had refused to sell its machines, making them available only on long-term leases. It had included in its leases provisions that discriminated against customers who might

[75] *Besser Mfg. Co.* v. *U.S.*, 343 U.S. 444.

[76] *U.S.* v. *General Electric Co.*, 82 F. Supp. 753.

[77] *U.S.* v. *Winslow*, 227 U.S. 202 (1913); *Transparent Wrap Machine Corp.* v. *Stokes & Smith Co.*, 329 U.S. 637 (1947); *Automatic Radio Mfg. Co.* v. *Hazeltine Research, Inc.*, 339 U.S. 827 (1950).

[78] *U.S.* v. *United Shoe Machinery Corp.*, 110 F. Supp. 295.

[79] *U.S.* v. *United Shoe Machinery Corp.*, Civil Action No. 7198, District Court of the U.S., District of Mass., Complaint, December 15, 1947.

install competing machines. It had required them to use its own machines at full capacity on all the shoes they made. It had entered into blanket contracts covering not only the lease of machines but also the provision of supplies and services. None of these policies was held to be illegal per se. But their combined effect, given United's dominant position in the field, was found to prove monopolization, in violation of Section 2 of the Sherman Act.

Concentration of patent holdings was involved in three other cases that were pending at the end of 1954. The Western Electric Company, the manufacturing subsidiary of A.T.&T., was charged with monopolizing the production of telephonic apparatus and equipment "by acquiring substantially all basic patents in the field of wire telephony. . . ."[80] International Business Machines, according to the government, had "systematically acquired developments, inventions, and patents . . . relating in any way to tabulating machines" and had "opposed the procurement by others of patents . . . by . . . systematically engaging in interference or opposition proceedings in patent offices throughout the world . . . employing 'fencing in' and 'blocking off' tactics against competitors . . ." and "systematically preempting the services of inventors. . . ."[81] The Radio Corporation of America, owning or controlling about 10,000 patents in the field of radio and television, was charged with following a deliberate policy of monopolizing research and patent rights in this field.[82] Depending upon the outcome of these cases, monopolization of patents through research and assignment and through purchase may be held to be illegal, as is the monopolization of other forms of property.

Remedies in Patent Cases

Employment of patents to eliminate competition has long been limited by decisions that found no invention or no infringement, refused to enforce the terms of license contracts, or enjoined the restrictive practices of patentees. In recent years, where patent holders have violated the antitrust laws, the courts have imposed more stringent remedies. The decree of the district court in the Hartford-Empire case[83] required the company to license all applicants under its patents, royalty free. This decree was modified by the Supreme Court, in a 4 to 3 decision, to permit the collection of reasonable royalties, on the ground that their refusal would involve unconstitutional confiscation of the defendant's property. But the Court agreed, for the first time in history, to compulsory licensing.[84] In the National Lead case two years later, the government asked the Court to

[80] *U.S.* v. *Western Electric Co.*, Civil Action No. 17–49, District Court of the U.S., District of N.J., Complaint, January 11, 1949.

[81] *U.S.* v. *International Business Machines Corp.*, Civil Action No. C–72–344, District Court of the U.S., Southern District of N.Y., Complaint, January 21, 1952.

[82] *Business Week*, November 27, 1954, p. 29.

[83] *U.S.* v. *Hartford Empire Co.*, 46 F. Supp. 541 (1942).

[84] *Hartford Empire Co.* v. *U.S.*, 323 U.S. 386 (1945).

go beyond this precedent, reversing its position on the need for royalties. The Court, again by a 4 to 3 vote, refused to do so, but approved compulsory licensing, and intimated that it might agree to the elimination of royalties if this were the only way in which competition could be restored.[85] In the United Shoe Machinery case in 1953, the District Court directed the company to sell its machines as well as lease them; to eliminate discriminatory provisions and full-capacity clauses from its leases, limiting their term to five years; to discontinue making blanket contracts for machinery, supplies, and services; and also to grant licenses under its patents at reasonable royalties.[86] In 1954 this decree was affirmed by the Supreme Court.[87]

Royalty-free licensing was first required, by a district court, in the case of the General Electric Company in 1953. Following the company's conviction in a criminal suit in 1949, the government asked that it be required to dispose of half of its productive facilities; to abandon the agency system under which it controlled the prices charged by its distributors; to dedicate to public use all of its existing patents covering the manufacture of electric light bulbs and parts; and to grant licenses under future patents in this field, on a reciprocal basis, at reasonable royalties. The court refused to dismember the company or to ban the agency system, but it did order the licensing of patents, with future patents to be made available at reasonable royalties and existing patents royalty free.[88]

Similar provisions have been incorporated in a number of consent decrees. More than thirty such decrees, accepted during the forties, provided for the licensing of all applicants and more than twenty of them for licensing without royalties. Decrees with this provision were accepted by Standard Oil of New Jersey, the Aluminum Company of America, Merck & Co., A. B. Dick, Libbey-Owens-Ford, Owens-Corning Fiberglas, Eastman Kodak, and American Can, thus freeing hundreds of patents on synthetic rubber and gasoline, fabricated magnesium, pharmaceutical products, mimeographing equipment, flat glass, Fiberglas, motion picture color film, and canning machinery. Under the typical decree, existing patents must be licensed royalty free and future patents at reasonable royalties. Royalty charges are determined by agreement between the patent owner and the licensee or, failing this, are established by the courts.

In recent years decrees in antitrust cases have called not only for the licensing of patents but also for the provision of necessary know-how. Owens-Corning Fiberglas was thus required to furnish its licensees, at nominal charge, with written manuals describing its machinery, materials, and processes. American Can was directed to provide any applicant, at cost,

[85] *U.S.* v. *National Lead Co.*, 332 U.S. 319 (1947).

[86] *U.S.* v. *United Shoe Machinery Corp.*, 110 F. Supp. 295.

[87] *United Shoe Machinery Corp.* v. *U.S.*, 347 U.S. 521.

[88] *U.S.* v. *General Electric Co.*, 115 F. Supp. 835.

with "detailed working drawings, specifications of materials, prescribed production methods, and assembly blueprints," and if this should prove "inadequate to enable him satisfactorily to manufacture and assemble the machines and equipment covered thereby" to supply "further information, as the case requires, either (a) in writing, or (b) by making available a reasonable number of technical personnel for consultation . . . or (c) by permitting such applicant or his representative to visit defendant's machine shop where such machines and equipment are manufactured to observe the manufacture thereof."[89] Eastman Kodak agreed to provide other finishers of amateur color film with manuals describing its processing technology, to keep the manuals up to date by issuing annual supplements, and to provide technical representatives to assist competitors in using the methods described.[90] And General Electric was ordered to take similar steps to provide other manufacturers with the know-how required for the production of electric lamps.

The power of the patent monopoly has also been weakened by judicial decisions on two other points. Until recently, a person taking out a license under a patent was prevented, by the doctrine of estoppel or by the terms of the license contract, from questioning its validity. But in the Sola case[91] in 1942, the Supreme Court held that a licensee was not estopped from attacking a patent. And in the Katzinger case[92] in 1947, it freed a licensee from price control on the ground that a patent was invalid, even though his contract forbade him to question its validity. In a number of other cases,[93] during the forties, the Court permitted defendants in infringement suits to show that patents had been used to violate the antitrust laws, and it then refused, on that ground, to enforce them. The patents, though not invalidated, were rendered ineffective, and their usefulness as an instrument of monopoly was destroyed. In still another case, decided in 1952, a Court of Appeals awarded triple damages to a plaintiff who had previously appeared as a defendant in an infringement suit, to compensate him for the resulting loss of sales, on the ground that the patent owner was a monopolist and had brought the infringement suit as a means of furthering his monopoly.[94] Here, as elsewhere, the courts have moved to prevent abuses of the patent grant.

[89] *U.S.* v. *American Can Co.*, Civil Action 26345-H, District Court of the U.S., Northern District of Cal., Final Judgment, June 22, 1950.

[90] *New York Times*, December 22, 1954.

[91] *Sola Electric Co.* v. *Jefferson Electric Co.*, 317 U.S. 173.

[92] *Katzinger Co.* v. *Chicago Metallic Mfg. Co.*, 329 U.S. 394.

[93] *Morton Salt Co.* v. *G. S. Suppiger Co.*, 314 U.S. 488 (1942); *B. B. Chemical Co.* v. *Ellis*, 314 U.S. 495 (1942); *Mercoid Corp.* v. *Mid-Continent Investment Co.*, 320 U.S. 661 (1944). The revision of the patent code enacted by Congress in 1952 contained a paragraph (271-d) which may be so interpreted as to limit the power of the courts to refuse enforcement of a patent on the ground of its misuse.

[94] *Kobe, Inc.* v. *Dempsey Pump Co.*, 198 F. 2d 416.

PATENT REFORM

Many proposals have been advanced for the reform of the patent system, both through changes in the procedure whereby patents are granted and validated, and through changes in the substance of the patent law. Minor changes in procedure were made by Congress in 1939, following the disclosure of numerous abuses in hearings before the Temporary National Economic Committee,[95] and further changes in detail were made when the law was recodified in 1952. But these reforms are insignificant when compared with those effected by the courts. Judicial action has gone far toward protecting the public interest against abuses of the patent grant. There are many patents, however, that are never brought before the courts. And there may still be need for revision of the patent laws.

Checking the Multiplicity, Duration, and Concentration of Patents

The number of patent monopolies might be reduced by legislative changes in the standard of patentability. Patents might well be confined to inventions representing really significant advances in technology or granted only to persons who could show that substantial sums had been spent on research and development. Designs might better be left to protection through copyrights. And the patent privilege might be withdrawn from foods and medicines. The multiplicity of patents might also be reduced through changes in procedure. Patent applications might be published and hearings given to competitors, consumers, and antitrust officials in opposition to the patent grants. The Patent Office might be equipped with a larger staff at higher salaries and thus enabled to take more time and exercise more skill in passing on applications. Larger appropriations for this purpose might be financed by increasing patent fees. All of these measures, or any of them, should operate to check the excessive creation of legal monopolies.

The seventeen-year life of the patent is an anachronism, growing out of a handicraft economy and bearing no functional relation to the requirements of machine technology. There is no reason why the duration of protection should be the same in every case. The period permitted might well be related to the time required to recover the sums invested in research and development. Or basic inventions might be distinguished from mere improvements, major inventions from minor ones, and different terms allowed for each. The actual tenure of monopoly might at least be shortened by dating a patent from the day of application, or by checking delaying tactics and speeding up procedures in the Patent Office to lessen the period of pendency.

[95] The period of use before application and the period during which an application might be amended were each cut from two years to one; the privilege of dropping and renewing applications was abolished; the time allowed for answering Patent Office queries was reduced; the interference procedure was somewhat simplified.

It has also been suggested that the monopolization of patent monopolies might be prevented by limiting the number of patents that may be assigned to a single holder, or by taxing accumulations of patents progressively. Such measures, however, would be crude in application, making no distinction among holdings that are used to monopolize a market, those that serve to strengthen one of many large competitors, and those that are made available to all the members of an industry. These measures could operate only to reduce investments made by larger corporations in industrial research and thus to hamper the advancement of technology. Where large accumulations of patents are used to monopolize an industry, the courts stand ready, under the antitrust laws, to provide a remedy by giving sanction to compulsory licensing.

Checking the Abuse of Patent Powers

Patent abuses, already checked by the decisions of the courts, might well be further checked by certain changes in the patent laws. Exclusion of a patent owner from a market might be prevented by forbidding the entry of infringement suits against his customers until a judgment has been obtained against the owner himself. The differential advantage that patent litigation gives to stronger firms might be reduced by providing simpler means of determining validity and by requiring the Patent Office to bear the cost of defending its grants. The use of patent agreements to circumvent the antitrust laws might be discouraged by requiring that they be filed with the Patent Office, the Department of Justice, or the Federal Trade Commission, and made available to both enforcement agencies. The suppression of patents might be prevented by providing that those withheld from use for a certain period be invalidated or thrown open to compulsory licensing. The inclusion of restrictive provisions in patent licenses might conceivably be forbidden or the terms of such provisions limited by law. Such measures, however, would prevent the patent owner who wished to retain a monopoly in one field from licensing his patent for use in another and might close access to technology, in many other cases, by discouraging the issuance of licenses. If this were to be avoided, control of license contracts would have to be supplemented by compulsory licensing.

Compulsory licensing, as a general policy, would have serious disadvantages. It might impair the incentive to make substantial investments in research. It might make for secrecy, preventing the disclosure of advances in technology. Since the policy could be defeated by demanding exorbitant royalties, it would also be necessary to regulate these charges in accordance with some standard of reasonableness. This problem, of course, is not insoluble, as is shown by the experience of the courts in fixing royalties under antitrust decrees. But compulsory licensing, if it were general, would involve a heavy burden of administrative action and judicial review. Such a requirement, moreover, would work both ways, not only compelling the stronger competitor to license the weaker one, but also compelling the weak to license the strong. It may be doubted that protection of the public interest necessitates its general use.

There are cases, however, in which compulsory licensing may be desirable. It has proved to be a useful remedy where violators of the antitrust laws have been brought before the courts. It may be required, under the Atomic Energy Act, to prevent firms holding patents on nonmilitary uses of atomic energy from barring access to this new field of industrial activity.[96] It might well be demanded where monopoly would imperil public health or safety or national security. It might be employed, after a proper interval, to prevent continued nonuse of patented technology. In this case, one argument against the requirement does not apply; the burden of fixing royalties would be slight. If it is true, as defenders of the patent system have always argued, that no inventions of commercial value are suppressed, there would be no requests for licenses. But if suppression does occur, the threat of compulsory licensing would induce the owner of an idle patent to put it to use. The public would derive the benefits that flow from new technology. And this is the purpose that the patent system was designed to serve.

Government Research and Patent Policy

Before World War II, two thirds of the nation's research was financed by private industry, a sixth by universities and research foundations, and a sixth by government. During the war research expenditures were doubled and the share of government grew to more than three fourths. Publicly financed research is now pre-eminent, not only in the fields of military science and atomic energy, but also in those of transportation and communications, agriculture, and public health. In part, this research is carried on by salaried employees in public agencies. In much larger part, it is conducted by private industries and nonprofit organizations under public contracts. The inventions that result from this research are patented, and the use of patents, in this case, raises important issues of public policy.

Should inventors on the public payroll or those employed under public contracts be required to assign their patents to the government or merely to grant the government unrestricted licenses royalty free, retaining monopolistic rights in other fields? The first of these alternatives has been adopted by the Atomic Energy Commission, the Department of Agriculture, and the Tennessee Valley Authority, the second by the army and the navy. Nine tenths of the contracts let during World War II left patent rights in the hands of private contractors. This policy has serious disadvantages. Where public employees are allowed to retain their patents, they may be tempted to keep their findings secret and unduly to emphasize the patentable aspects of their work. Where private contractors are permitted to do so, they may seek to participate in research when it

[96] The patent provisions of the atomic energy laws are discussed in Chapter 28.

leads to commercially valuable patents and refuse to co-operate when it does not. In this case, moreover, the favored contractor is given an unfair advantage over his competitors. And since these contracts are awarded, in the main, to larger firms, market power is further concentrated and monopoly reinforced. In either case it is improper for inventions financed by public funds to be made a source of private gain. All rights to patents on such inventions should therefore be assigned to the government.

Where patents are owned by the government, a policy must be adopted with respect to licensing: shall licenses be exclusive or nonexclusive; shall they be restricted or unrestricted; shall royalties be charged? Exclusive licensing would force the government to select one among many applicants, conferring a special favor or offsetting it by charging royalties. Restrictive licensing would necessitate continued supervision of the licensees. Royalties would compel the public to pay a second time for inventions it had financed by paying taxes. Licensing on this basis, moreover, would carry with it an obligation to detect and prosecute infringers. It has been the usual policy of government, therefore, to issue licenses to all applicants, imposing no restrictions, and charging no royalties.

COPYRIGHTS

The right of an author to control the publication of his writings was recognized at English common law and was sanctioned by Parliament in 1710. The American Congress was authorized by the Constitution to give protection to authors as well as to inventors; it passed its first copyright law in 1790. This law, as subsequently amended, was codified in 1937. It applies not only to writers, but also to composers, artists, photographers, dramatists, and producers of motion pictures. It covers not only the right to print, reprint, and copy, but also the right to translate, to dramatize, novelize, or put on film, to record music, broadcast it, or perform it in public for profit, to exhibit a movie, or to produce a play. A copyright may be obtained by affixing a notice to a published work and depositing two copies with the Copyright Office at the Library of Congress, accompanied by a $2.00 fee. In the case of unpublished works, a copy or photograph may be deposited; in the case of movies, the title, a written description, and sample prints. The process is merely one of registration; no examination is undertaken and no legal assistance is required. A copyright, when registered, runs for 28 years and may be renewed for another 28. Its owner may bring suit against infringers, seeking an injunction and the recovery of damages. Willful infringement for profit is a criminal offense, punishable by a fine of $1,000, imprisonment for a year, or both.

Copyrights and Competition

The consequences of legal monopoly may be serious in the case of patents; they are less so in the case of copyrights. A patent gives exclusive rights in an idea; a copyright covers only the particular form in which an idea is expressed. A patent may enable its owner to monopolize all the products of an industry; no such power is conferred upon the holder of a copyright. Basic patents have covered all aluminum, all telephones, all glass containers, and all electric lamps. Copyrights do not cover all books, all music, all pictures, or all plays. Each of them is confined to one among many items in a field that is actively competitive.

There is one provision of the American copyright law, however, through which competition is impaired. Since 1891 copyrights have been denied to books in the English language (with a minor exception) unless they are printed in the United States from type set on plates made in the United States. This provision is more restrictive than a tariff; it places a complete embargo on such books. It was designed to relieve American printers of the necessity of meeting foreign competition. It is harmful to the interests of American authors and publishers. The provision prevented the United States from becoming a party to the copyright convention concluded at Berne in 1886, under whose terms books printed in one member country are automatically afforded protection in all the others. As a result, American books (unless simultaneously published abroad) can be copied and sold in other countries without payment of royalties. A new General Universal Copyright Convention was negotiated under the auspices of the United Nations Educational, Scientific, and Cultural Organization at Geneva in 1952. Under this treaty, each country will extend to the authors and publishers of every other country the same treatment it accords its own. Here, again, American ratification would require repeal of the manufacturing clause. Such action would be of benefit to all Americans except the members of the printing trades.

Copyrights have been used in a few cases, as patents have in many, to afford a legal basis for the extension of monopoly. Publishers have sought to maintain resale prices by bringing infringement suits against booksellers. Movie producers have employed block booking contracts to tie the sale of one copyrighted film to that of another. Competition among exhibitors of such films has been restricted by including identical terms in licenses. Competition between newspapers has been impaired by excluding publishers from membership in the Associated Press. The market for rights to commercial performances of music has been monopolized by the American Society of Composers, Authors, and Publishers.

The principal source of revenue from a piece of music is not the right to print or record it but to perform it for profit. With a piece of popular music, such performances may number in the tens of thousands. But popularity is ephemeral; demand may disappear as quickly as it came. In the absence of organization, composers and lyricists would find it difficult to collect the royalties to which they are entitled. As individuals they lack the means to detect and prosecute infringement and would be at a serious disadvantage in bargaining with such powerful interests as the radio and television networks and the motion picture companies. It was to provide them and their publishers with an instrument for collective action that ASCAP was established in 1914. The Society admitted to membership the authors and composers of five or more copyrighted works. It was managed by a self-perpetuating board of directors, half of them representing this group and half the publishers. The Society shortly came to enjoy a virtual monopoly of music rights. All copyrights were assigned to ASCAP; all license contracts were negotiated by ASCAP; all royalties were collected and pooled by ASCAP; the payments made to members depended on ASCAP's appraisal of the commercial value of their works.

In 1932 the Society started charging radio stations a fixed percentage of their gross time sales. In 1941 it demanded that the networks pay it 7½ per cent of such revenues. They refused to do so, and the ensuing deadlock lasted for 10 months. During this period, ASCAP withheld the right to broadcast almost all of the music written during the preceding 50 years. The networks retaliated by setting up Broadcast Music, Inc. as an alternative source of supply, and this has come to be a serious competitor. The dispute was finally settled, with ASCAP getting 2¾ per cent of the networks' gross time sales. By 1953 the Society's membership included nearly 3,000 composers and lyricists and 565 publishers. It had a field staff of 108 men, with offices in all of the states, and was collecting royalties from some 20,000 licensees (including night clubs, dance bands, and the like) running to $17 million a year.[97]

ASCAP has been charged, from time to time, with various monopolistic practices. It has discriminated among its licensees in charging royalties and among its members in distributing them. It has refused to license the broadcasting of individual compositions, insisting on blanket licenses. It has sought to collect royalties, not only from the networks for transcribing music, but also from individual stations for putting it on the air; not only from the producers of musical films, but also from their exhibitors. It has entered into exclusive cross-licensing arrangements with similar societies in other countries, thus adding to the scope of its domestic rights. By monopolizing thousands of legal monopolies, it has acquired and exploited market powers that go far beyond those accorded by a single copyright.

Copyrights and the Courts

The decisions of the courts on the abuse of copyrights run parallel to those in which abuse of patents is involved. In the Bobbs-Merrill case[98] in 1908, and again in the American Publishers case[99] in 1913, where Macy's had resold books for less than listed prices, it was held that this did not infringe the publishers' copyrights. In the Paramount case[100] in 1948, the practice of tying one copyrighted film to another by booking them in

[97] *Business Week*, October 10, 1953, pp. 136–44.

[98] *Bobbs-Merrill Co.* v. *Straus*, 210 U.S. 359.

[99] *Straus* v. *American Publishers' Assn.*, 321 U.S. 222.

[100] *U.S.* v. *Paramount Pictures*, 334 U.S. 141.

blocks was found to be in violation of the law. In the Interstate Circuit case[101] in 1939, the inclusion of identical provisions in license contracts between producers and exhibitors was held to prove conspiracy in restraint of trade. And in the case of the Associated Press[102] in 1945, the fact that AP dispatches were protected by copyright did not deter the court from directing the association to stop refusing access to its services. With respect to ASCAP, however, enforcement of the antitrust laws has proved to be more difficult.

In 1941 ASCAP entered a plea of *nolo contendere* in a criminal suit brought under the Sherman Act and paid a fine of $35,000. At the same time it accepted a consent decree in a civil suit. Under the terms of this decree, the Society was ordered to admit the holders of a single copyright to membership, to provide for the election of directors, and to permit its members to issue independent licenses. ASCAP, however, was still to fix the license terms and collect the royalties. The Society was forbidden to charge for station broadcasts of transcriptions on which network royalties had already been paid. And it was required to license individual compositions separately. This provision was weakened, however, by its failure to specify reasonable royalties.[103] In 1949, following a private suit,[104] ASCAP was enjoined from making further charges for the exhibition of films on whose production royalties had been received. And this action led to the revision of the earlier consent decree. The Society was now ordered not only to include the right of exhibition with that of production but also to facilitate the licensing of individual compositions by offering them at reasonable royalties. Upon a showing that it favored composers of serious music in distributing its payments, a government proposal that it be forbidden to discriminate among its members was dropped. The freedom of ASCAP to abuse its monopoly has been limited. But the monopoly itself is undisturbed. To break it up would be to leave its members at the mercy of powerful interests. To ignore it would tip the balance of power the other way. Between Scylla and Charybdis the law steers an uncertain course.

TRADE-MARKS

Suits to enjoin the infringement of trade-marks were entertained at common law, and statutory protection was subsequently given to such marks by legislatures of the states. The first federal trade-mark law, enacted in 1870, was found to be unconstitutional in 1879, since Congress had not been given power to protect trade-marks along with patents and

[101] *Interstate Circuit* v. *U.S.*, 306 U.S. 208.

[102] *Associated Press* v. *U.S.*, 326 U.S. 1.

[103] *U.S.* v. *ASCAP*, Civil Action No. 13–95, District Court of the U.S., Southern District of N.Y., Civil Decree and Judgment.

[104] *Alden-Rochelle, Inc.* v. *ASCAP*, 80 F. Supp. 888.

copyrights, or to regulate commerce within the states.[105] A new law, passed in 1881, provided for the registration of trade-marks used in foreign trade, enabling their owners to obtain protection abroad and to prevent imports where they were infringed. Another, passed in 1905, provided for the registration of marks used in interstate commerce and gave their owners access to the federal courts. But infringement suits were still decided in accordance with the laws of the several states. It was not until the Lanham Act was passed in 1946 that Congress moved to bring all trade-mark actions affecting interstate or foreign commerce within the purview of the federal law.

The Act provides for the entry, on a Principal Register at the Patent Office, of trade-marks in the form of words or symbols used to distinguish the goods of a single seller, service marks in the form of devices used to identify a seller of services, certification marks that cover the goods or services of several sellers, and collective marks applied to sales made by the members of an association, such as a co-operative. It also provides for the entry, on a Supplemental Register, of names descriptive of goods and places; such marks are not accorded exclusive rights in the United States but may be used in obtaining rights abroad. An application for registry must be accompanied by specimens of the mark, a description of the goods to which it is attached, a statement covering its past use, and a fee of $25. Registry will be denied to marks that resemble those already in use, to those that are deceptive, immoral, or scandalous, and to those that represent the flag or insignia of a state or nation, reproduce the name, portrait, or signature of a living person without his permission or those of a dead president without the permission of his living widow, or disparage public institutions or beliefs. Where two persons claim similar marks, the Patent Office will hold hearings for the determination of priority. Once a mark is registered, an injured person may institute proceedings for its cancellation and may appeal an adverse decision in the Patent Office to the Court of Customs and Patent Appeals. Under the present law, however, marks cannot be contested after they have stood on the Register for five years. Initial registration is for twenty years and may be renewed, upon application, for further terms of like duration. Registry is not essential to the validity of a mark; it establishes no rights not previously recognized by law. What it does is to provide the registrant with prima facie evidence of ownership. Enforcement, as in the case of patents and copyrights, is through private infringement suits.

Trade-Marks and Competition

It is the purpose of a trade-mark, when widely advertised, to take a product out of competition by establishing strong consumer preference. In an industry that is highly competitive, this consequence may not be

[105] *The Trade-Mark Cases,* 100 U.S. 82.

serious. But in one that is dominated by powerful firms, the investment that would be required to gain acceptance for competing brands may bar new entry to the field. It is the cost of advertising, more than any other factor, that checks potential competition in the sale of cigarettes. When a mark is owned by a monopolist, moreover, it may serve to reinforce his power and to prolong his tenure of monopoly. A product may be protected by a patent and a trade-mark; the patent will expire, but the monopoly it has created may be perpetuated by the mark. During the life of the patent, the name given the product by its producer may have become the only one by which it can be bought. The customer who wants transparent glycerinated cellulose hydrate regenerated from viscose is likely to ask for cellophane. Where names have thus become generic, to be sure, the courts have held for the defendants in infringement suits. But litigation is a costly business: the patent on shredded wheat expired in 1912; the name was not found to be in the public domain until 1938; the case of *Kellogg* v. *National Biscuit*[106] had dragged through the courts for more than a quarter of a century. It is not every defendant who can afford to invest such sums to establish his right to compete.

Trade-marks have been used successfully, where patents and copyrights failed, in the maintenance of resale prices, this practice having been approved by state and federal laws. They have been used to implement discriminatory pricing: methyl methacrylate was sold by Rohm & Haas to manufacturers as Lucite and Crystalite at 85 cents per pound, and to dentists as Vernonite and Crystalex at $45 per pound. They have been used in controlling output: companies licensed to produce at graduated royalties under U.S. Pipe and Foundry patents were required to stamp their products with the trade name "deLavaud." They have been used to obtain exclusive markets: General Electric persuaded procurement agencies to establish specifications requiring Mazda bulbs, permitted Westinghouse to use the name, but denied its other licensees the right to do so.[107] Trade-marks have also been used to effect a division of markets among the members of international cartels. Here, a mark is advertised throughout the world, each participant is given the exclusive right to use it in his own territory, and anyone who oversteps the boundaries assigned to him is driven back by an infringement suit. In this way, such names as Mazda, Mimeograph, Merck, and Timken, and the trade-marks of Electric Storage Battery, American Bosch, New Jersey Zinc, and S.K.F. have been used in the establishment of regional monopolies.[108]

Trade-Marks and the Law

The Lanham Act was passed in 1946 after many years of agitation by trade associations and the trade-mark bar. The law contains a number of

[106] *Kellogg Co.* v. *National Biscuit Co.*, 305 U.S. 111.

[107] See S. Timberg, "Trade Marks, Monopoly, and the Restraint of Competition," *Law and Contemporary Problems*, Vol. XIV (1949), pp. 323–61.

[108] *Ibid.* See also B. Diggins, "Trade Marks and Restraints of Trade," *Georgetown Law Journal*, Vol. XXXII (1944), p. 113.

provisions that may be open to abuse. It permits concurrent registration of the same or similar marks by more than one concern, thus making possible their use as a device for sharing markets. It provides for the use of a mark by "related companies" when one "legitimately" controls the other and allows the owner of a mark to assign it when disposing of the good will or "part of the good will" of a business, thus opening the way to production and price control through restrictive licensing. The law approves certification marks, thus inviting attempts to exclude competitors from the market by refusing to certify their wares. These sections of the Act are certain to be cited in defense of practices attacked by antitrust. Their real significance, however, is still to be determined by the courts.

The bill that passed the House was criticized by the Department of Justice, and amendments were added in the Senate to meet the objections that were raised. As the law now stands, incontestible registry is denied to common descriptive names; a mark may be cancelled if it has become the common name of a product on which a patent has expired; a person sued for infringement may defend himself by showing that a mark has been used to violate the antitrust laws; the Federal Trade Commission may bring proceedings for the cancellation of marks that are so employed. These provisions have been denounced and their repeal demanded by various associations representing the trade-mark interests, but as yet, the provisions remain untouched.

Monopolistic practices involving trade-marks have been enjoined in many cases by the courts. Contracts maintaining the resale price of trade-marked goods were held to be unlawful in the Dr. Miles case[109] in 1911; their subsequent legalization will be discussed in Chapter 14. Decisions were rendered against the use of trade-marks to promote discriminatory pricing in the Rohm & Haas case[110] in 1948, against their use in controlling output in the Pipe and Foundry case[111] in the same year, and against their use in excluding competitors from markets in the General Electric case[112] in 1949. In a number of cases involving the sharing of markets for trade-marked goods by international cartels, decided from 1945 to 1950, the courts found such arrangements to be in violation of the Sherman Act, rejecting trade-mark licensing as a defense. Trade-marks, said the court in the Timken case[113] cannot be made "a tool to circumvent free enterprise. . . ."

Cartel agreements involving trade-marks have been canceled and their renewal enjoined.[114] Participants in such arrangements have been for-

[109] *Dr. Miles Medical Co.* v. *John D. Park & Sons Co.*, 220 U.S. 373.

[110] *U.S.* v. *Rohm & Haas*, Civil Action No. 9068, District Court of the U.S., Eastern District of Pa.

[111] *U.S.* v. *U.S. Pipe and Foundry Co.*, Civil Action No. 10772, District Court of the U.S., District of N.J.

[112] *U.S.* v. *General Electric Co.*, 82 F. Supp. 753.

[113] *U.S.* v. *Timken Roller Bearings Co.*, 83 F. Supp. 294 (1949).

[114] *U.S.* v. *Merck* & *Co.*, Civil Action No. 3159, District Court of the U.S., District of N.J., Final Judgment, October 6, 1945.

bidden to grant their foreign partners exclusive rights to use their marks abroad, to deny them the right to sell in the American market, and to interfere with imports into the United States.[115] In a few cases, defendants have accepted consent decrees that required them to dedicate their trade-marks to public use; this has been done by A. B. Dick with respect to "Mimeograph." The decree in the case of S.K.F. went even farther, the American subsidiary agreeing to adopt a distinctive trade-mark for use in export markets and to advertise it in competing with its Swedish parent for sales outside of the United States.[116] No such stringent remedies have been applied, however, where trade-marks have supported purely domestic monopolies. The exclusive right to a name that has been widely advertised is a valuable form of property and one that the government has been reluctant to attack. In the American Tobacco case in 1946, the leading manufacturers of cigarettes were found to be guilty under the Sherman Act. But in this case, unlike others, dissolution was not requested because it could not have been effected without destroying names that are now worth many millions: Camel, Chesterfield, and Lucky Strike.

SUGGESTIONS FOR FURTHER READING

The most interesting discussion of the patent problem is that of Walton Hamilton, *Patents and Free Enterprise*, T.N.E.C. Monograph No. 31 (Washington: Government Printing Office, 1941). Further illustrations of the restrictive use of patents are given in Clair Wilcox, *Competition and Monopoly in American Industry*, T.N.E.C. Monograph No. 21 (Washington: Government Printing Office, 1940), pp. 72–78, 104–8, and 160–65; and in George W. Stocking and Myron W. Watkins, *Monopoly and Free Enterprise* (New York: Twentieth Century Fund, 1951), chap. xiv. There is an excellent analysis in Corwin D. Edwards, *Maintaining Competition* (New York: McGraw-Hill Book Co., 1949), pp. 216–48. Those who have time to go farther should consult the special issues of *Law and Contemporary Problems* for Autumn, 1947, and Spring, 1948, dealing with "The Patent Problem," and the following books: Floyd L. Vaughan, *Economics of Our Patent System* (New York: Macmillan Co., 1924); Morris D. Forkosh, *Economics of American Patent Laws* (New York: New York University School of Law, 1940); George E. Folk, *Patents and Industrial Progress* (New York: Harper & Bro., 1942); L. I. Wood, *Patents and Antitrust Laws* (New York: Commerce Clearing House, 1942); W. B. Bennett, *The American Patent System* (Baton Rouge: Louisiana State University Press, 1943); Harold G. Fox, *Monopolies and Patents* (Toronto: University of Toronto, 1947); and E. Burke Inlow, *The Patent Grant* (Baltimore: Johns Hopkins University Press, 1950).

[115] *U.S.* v. *Electric Storage Battery Co.*, Civil Action No. 31–225, District Court of the U.S., Southern District of N.Y., Final Judgment, November 24, 1947; *U.S.* v. *American Bosch Corp.*, Civil Action 20–164, District Court of the U.S., Southern District of N.Y., Final Judgment, June 4, 1948.

[116] *U.S.* v. *S.K.F. Industries, Inc.*, Civil Action No. 9862, District Court of the U.S., Eastern District of Pa., September 29, 1950.

The copyright system is discussed in the report of the *Conference on the Arts, Publishing, and the Law* (Chicago: University of Chicago Law School, 1952), and in the issue of *Law and Contemporary Problems* for Spring 1954 on "Literary and Artistic Products and Copyright Problems." The story of ASCAP is told in *Business Week*, October 10, 1953, pp. 136–44. The standard sources on the law of copyright are: L. H. Amdur, *Copyright Law and Practice* (New York: Clark Boardman Co., 1936); H. G. Ball, *The Law of Copyright and Literary Property* (New York: M. Bender & Co., 1944); and H. A. Howell, *The Copyright Law* (Washington: Bureau of National Affairs, 1948). On the law relating to trademarks, see "Trademarks in Transition," the issue of *Law and Contemporary Problems* for Spring, 1949.

Chapter 7 EXCLUSION AND DISCRIMINATION

Two monopolistic practices, in particular, have been specifically attacked by the antitrust laws: the use of tying and exclusive contracts, and discrimination in price. These practices have a double significance. They affect the ability of one producer to compete with another in obtaining access to markets. They also affect the ability of one distributor to compete with another in obtaining and reselling supplies of goods. The way in which the applicable provisions of the law are enforced and interpreted will therefore determine the nature of competitive opportunities at the successive stages of production and distribution.

EXCLUSIVE CONTRACTS

Tying and exclusive contracts have been used, as was shown in Chapter 4, to obtain and extend a position of monopoly. Under the Sherman Act, such contracts were canceled, in certain cases, by consent decrees and enjoined by decisions of the lower courts. But in the Dick and Shoe Machinery cases, as has been seen, monopolies obtained through tying contracts were allowed to stand. It was the position taken by the Supreme Court in these cases that led to the inclusion of Section 3, outlawing such contracts where their effect "may be to substantially lessen competition," in the Clayton Act. These contracts have since been attacked more often under this Section and less often under the Federal Trade Commission Act and the Sherman Act.

Tying Contracts

In the first order of the Federal Trade Commission to reach the Supreme Court, in the Gratz case[1] in 1920, a tying contract was involved. Gratz was the principal sales agent of Carnegie Steel, a subsidiary of U.S. Steel and the major producer of ties for binding cotton bales. He was also an agent for a company producing nearly half of the jute bagging used to wrap such bales. By refusing to fill orders for ties unless accompanied by orders for equivalent supplies of bagging, he compelled dealers to turn to

[1] *FTC* v. *Gratz,* 235 U.S. 421.

him for both commodities. The Commission, however, did not seek to prove that this arrangement substantially lessened competition or tended to create a monopoly in violation of the Clayton Act, but charged instead that it was an unfair method of competition, within the meaning of Section 5 of the Trade Commission Act. The Court rejected this contention, interpreting the latter Act so narrowly as to confine Commission orders to practices found "heretofore" to be unfair. Since tying contracts, as such, had not been held to be illegal, the order in the Gratz case was reversed. This interpretation of the Trade Commission Act, as we shall see in Chapter 10, has since been abandoned by the Court.

The Commission has issued orders against tying contracts in a number of cases, under Section 3 of the Clayton Act. But it is through suits instituted by the Department of Justice or by private litigants that the issue has been brought before the Court. In most of these cases one of the products tied by contract was protected by patent rights. Here it was obvious that the patented product was monopolized and that contractual arrangements tying another product to it tended to create a monopoly of the latter as well. In all such cases, as was seen in Chapter 6, the tying provisions have been condemned. A similar arrangement was outlawed by the Court in 1948, when it enjoined block booking in the motion picture industry. It is thus clear that contracts so tying one good to another as to extend the boundaries of monopoly will almost invariably be held to violate the law.

In a recent case brought under the Sherman Act, however, a tying contract was allowed to stand. The *Times-Picayune* was the only morning paper in New Orleans. It also published an evening edition, and here it had a competitor. The paper refused to sell advertising space in its morning edition alone, but required advertisers to purchase space in its evening edition as well. The government sued to break the tie, and the case was finally appealed to the Supreme Court. In its decision, the Court laid down the rule that a tying contract is illegal per se when a seller has a monopoly in the tying product and when a substantial volume of commerce in the tied product is thus restrained. But it went on to find that the *Times-Picayune* had no monopoly, having reached this curious conclusion by defining the market to include all three dailies instead of separating the morning and evening markets and recognizing the *Times-Picayune* monopoly in the morning field. Under the former definition, the contract was held to be legal.[2] Under the latter, following the Court's own rule, it would have been enjoined.

Exclusive Dealing

Most of the orders issued by the Federal Trade Commission under Section 3 of the Clayton Act involve exclusive dealerships. And these have

[2] *Times-Picayune Publishing Co.* v. *U.S.*, 345 U.S. 594 (1953). See also "Definition of the Market in Tying Arrangements," *Yale Law Journal*, Vol. LXIII (1954), pp. 389–98.

been reversed, in several cases, by the courts. Three of these decisions were handed down in 1923. In the Pearsall case[3] it was found that a manufacturer marketing oleomargarine under exclusive contracts controlled only 1 per cent of the output of the product, and it was therefore held that his contracts did not tend to give him a monopoly. In the Curtis case,[4] where schoolboys delivering the Curtis publications were forbidden to carry other magazines, it was found that the company did not sell its publications to the boys, but employed them as its agents, and it was held that Section 3 did not preclude exclusive agencies. In the Oil Pump cases[5] the Commission had issued 27 orders against refining companies who leased to retailers of gasoline, at nominal rentals, tanks and pumps marked with their brand names, prohibiting their use in storing and selling gasoline produced by their competitors. This arrangement, however, did not prevent dealers from installing other tanks and pumps to handle other brands. And, though the cost of financing such installations handicapped independent refiners, the Court held that exclusion of their product from equipment financed by their competitors did not substantially lessen competition or tend toward monopoly. An exclusive contract of a different type was found not to be illegal in a private suit involving General Motors in 1936.[6] General Motors had forbidden dealers in Buicks and Chevrolets to use parts produced by other manufacturers in making repairs or even to offer them for sale. The Court found, however, that competition in the sale of parts had not been lessened and held that the company's contracts were needed to protect its warranty and preserve its goodwill.

In the Pearsall and Curtis suits, the government's case was obviously weak. In the Oil Pump and General Motors cases, the circumstances were unusual. In all other suits to come before the Court, exclusive dealerships have been enjoined. And here, since such arrangements are made illegal only where their effect "may be to substantially lessen competition or tend to create a monopoly," decisions have turned upon interpretations of this phrase.

Before 1947, in all of the cases where the rule against exclusive contracts was enforced, the seller employing such contracts dominated the markets in which he sold. In the Standard Fashion and Butterick cases[7] in 1922 and 1925, firms making two fifths of the dress patterns sold at retail excluded their competitors from the best stores in the cities and from the only outlets available in many smaller towns. In the Q. R. S. Music case[8] in 1926, a company selling through exclusive dealers controlled more than

[3] *B. S. Pearsall Butter Co.* v. *FTC*, 292 F. 720.

[4] *FTC* v. *Curtis Publishing Co.*, 260 U.S. 568.

[5] *FTC* v. *Sinclair Refining Co.*, 261 U.S. 463.

[6] *Pick Mfg. Co.* v. *General Motors Corp.*, 299 U.S. 3.

[7] *Standard Fashion Co.* v. *Magrane-Houston Co.*, 258 U.S. 346; *Butterick Co.* v. *FTC*, 4 F. 2d 910, certiorari denied, 267 U.S. 602.

[8] *FTC* v. *Q.R.S. Music Co.*, 12 F. 2d 730.

half of the output of player piano rolls. In the Eastman Kodak case[9] in 1927, a firm producing more than nine tenths of the motion picture film made in the United States entered into an agreement with its customers, through an association of laboratories making motion picture prints, forbidding them to purchase film imported from abroad. In the Carter Carburetor case[10] in 1940, the principal manufacturer of carburetors gave discounts to dealers who bought exclusively from him and denied them to those who bought from his competitors. In the case of the Fashion Originators' Guild[11] in 1941, an association of dress manufacturers, whose 176 members made three fifths of the dresses sold at retail for $10.75 and up, sought to prevent "design piracy" by signing contracts with 12,000 retailers forbidding them to buy from imitators. In all of these cases, exclusive dealing was enjoined on the ground that its use by a dominant seller had substantially lessened competition and tended toward monopoly. In more recent cases, a less rigid criterion has been employed.

The Test of Substantiality

In the International Salt case, mentioned in Chapter 6, where a contract tying the sale of salt to the lease of a patented salt dispenser was found to be illegal in 1947, the Supreme Court went on to say that

> . . . it is unreasonable, *per se*, to foreclose competitors from any substantial market. . . . The volume of business affected by these contracts cannot be said to be insignificant or insubstantial and the tendency of the agreements to the accomplishment of monopoly seems obvious. Under the law, agreements are forbidden which "tend to create a monopoly," and it is immaterial that the tendency is a creeping one rather than one that proceeds at full gallop; nor does the law wait for arrival at the goal before condemning the direction of the movement.[12]

This reasoning was applied to exclusive dealerships in the Standard Oil of California case in 1949.[13] Standard Oil, producing 23 per cent of the gasoline sold in 7 western states, contracted with some 6,000 independent dealers, handling less than 7 per cent of the gasoline sold in the area, to fill all of their requirements for petroleum products and, in some cases, for tires, tubes, batteries, and other accessories. The lower court held Standard's contracts to be illegal on the ground that competition is substantially lessened when competitors are excluded from "a substantial number of outlets."[14] Standard appealed and the Supreme Court, in a 5 to 4 decision, affirmed the lower court's decree. The positions taken by the different judges illustrate the nature of the issue involved. Justice Douglas in a

[9] *FTC* v. *Eastman Kodak Co.*, 247 U.S. 619.

[10] *FTC* v. *Carter Carburetor Corp.*, 112 F. 2d 722.

[11] *Fashion Originators' Guild* v. *FTC*, 312 U.S. 457.

[12] *International Salt Co.* v. *U.S.*, 332 U.S. 392, 396.

[13] *Standard Oil Co. of California* v. *U.S.*, 337 U.S. 293.

[14] *U.S.* v. *Standard Oil Co. of California*, 78 F. Supp. 850, 857.

separate dissent argued that the requirements contracts should have been permitted, since they were "relatively innocuous as compared with the virulent growth of monopoly power" resulting from the probable alternatives: conversion of the exclusive dealerships into agencies or outright purchase of their businesses. Under these arrangements, he said, "independents are swallowed up by the trusts and entrepreneurs become employees of absentee owners. Then there is a serious loss in citizenship. Local leadership is diluted. He who was a leader in the village becomes dependent on outsiders for his action and policy. Clerks responsible to a superior in a distant place take the place of resident proprietors beholden to no one."[15] The exclusive contract, he felt, "at least keeps the independents alive." Justice Jackson, speaking for three members of the Court, took a different line. Exclusive contracts, he said, must be judged by their effect; they are illegal only when their effect "may be to substantially lessen competition," and here no evidence of this effect was introduced. The decree, therefore, was "but a guess in the dark," lacking "an adequate basis on which to upset long-standing and widely practiced business arrangements."[16] The majority thought otherwise. It is enough, said Justice Frankfurter, to prove "that competition has been foreclosed in a substantial share of the line of commerce affected." Standard's contracts created "a potential clog on competition" and it was the purpose of Section 3 of the Clayton Act to remove such an impediment "wherever, were it to become actual, it would impede a substantial amount of competitive activity."[17]

The issue of substantiality was not presented by the next case to come before the courts. The contracts of the American Can Company, tying the sale of cans to the lease of can-closing machinery and excluding other sellers of cans for five-year terms, were found illegal by a lower court.[18] The company owned 54 per cent of all can-closing machinery and sold 46 per cent of all cans. This was obviously a substantial share. The tying clauses were forbidden and the exclusive provisions were limited to one-year terms.

In two more cases, however, the issue arose again, and the courts followed the precedent of Standard Oil. In the Richfield case,[19] the company's exclusive contracts with filling stations on the Pacific coast were condemned, even though it accounted for but 3 per cent of the gasoline sold in the area. And in the Motion Picture Advertising Service case,[20] the Supreme Court upheld a Commission order reducing from five years to

[15] *Standard Oil Co. of California* v. *U.S.*, 337 U.S. 293, 319.

[16] *Ibid.*, p. 322.

[17] *Ibid.*, p. 314.

[18] *U.S.* v. *American Can Co.*, 87 F. Supp. 18 (1949).

[19] *U.S.* v. *Richfield Oil Corp.*, 99 F. Supp. 280 (1951), sustained *per curiam* 343 U.S. 922 (1952).

[20] *Motion Picture Advertising Service Co.* v. *FTC*, 334 U.S. 392 (1953).

one the duration of exclusive contracts between the producers and the exhibitors of advertising films, despite Justice Frankfurter's complaint that no real evidence had been presented concerning the effect of the contracts on competition in the field.

In the light of these decisions it might appear that exclusive arrangements are close to being outlawed per se. But there are signs that point the other way. In suits brought against the leading manufacturers of farm machinery, the government charged that their insistence that dealers give "adequate representation" to all the items in their lines, while not enforced by contracts, was nonetheless in violation of the Sherman Act. In one of these suits, involving J. I. Case Co.,[21] it was held by a district court that coercive methods might not lawfully be used in obtaining exclusive dealerships but that exclusive dealing was not unlawful as such. The suit against Case was dismissed for want of sufficient evidence of coercion. And thereupon the other suits were dropped. The Federal Trade Commission, during the Eisenhower administration, has continued to proceed against exclusive contracts. In 1954, for instance, it issued orders forbidding the use of such contracts by leading producers of motorcycles[22] and cosmetics.[23] But it dismissed an action involving a minor producer of hearing aids on the ground that substantial injury to competition had not been shown.[24] And it remanded another case for further investigation on the ground that the effect on competition had merely been asserted and not supported by evidence.[25] The Commission, thus, is refusing to avail itself of the latitude afforded it by the decisions of the Supreme Court. It is not holding exclusive contracts to be illegal per se, but is confining its orders to cases in which substantial injury or the probability of such injury to competition in a market as a whole can actually be shown.

PRICE DISCRIMINATION

The sale of goods and services to different buyers at different prices is a common practice. Doctors, dentists, and undertakers customarily adjust their charges to the size of the customer's purse. Department stores sell merchandise at one price on the upper floors and at another in the basement. Railroads charge different rates to different shippers for hauling a ton a mile, and public utilities vary their charges for a cubic foot of gas or a kilowatt hour of electricity. Farmers are paid one price for milk distributed to consumers and another for milk sold to producers of butter and cheese. Exporters sometimes charge lower prices abroad than they do in the United States. Manufacturers and wholesalers classify their cus-

[21] *U.S.* v. *J. I. Case Co.*, 101 F. Supp. 856 (1951).

[22] *In re Harley-Davidson Motor Co.*, Docket 5698 (1954).

[23] *In re Revlon Products Corp.*, Docket 5685 (1954).

[24] *In re Maico Co., Inc.*, Docket 5822 (1954).

[25] *In re Insto-Gas Corp.*, Docket 5851 (1954).

tomers and sell to each class at a different price. Discounts are commonly provided for promptness of payment and for purchases in quantity.

Differentiation in prices frequently involves discrimination in the treatment accorded to different buyers; it does not invariably do so. The costs incurred in making different sales may differ; where prices are varied accordingly, the seller does not discriminate. Discrimination occurs most clearly when the same goods, of the same quality, are sold in the same quantity, at the same time, under the same conditions, and on the same terms, to different buyers at different prices. But it also occurs where costs differ and prices do not, and where differences in price are not proportionate to differences in cost. Discrimination may take the form of variation in the price itself, or the form of variation in the discounts accompanying a uniform price. It may also appear in differences in the quality of the goods and the character of the services provided by sellers and in the allowances made by sellers for services rendered them by buyers. Discrimination, in general, may be said to exist where all but one of the variables of different sales are identical, and also—if more than one variable differs—where the differences in one are not proportionate to those in another.

If markets were perfect, discrimination would be impossible, since every purchaser would buy at the lowest price and on the most favorable terms. If a seller is to discriminate, his market must therefore be divided into segments and each of them dealt with separately. This may be accomplished in a variety of ways. Buyers at different locations are separated by transportation costs and, in the case of international trade, by artificial barriers. Customers are segregated according to the use they make of goods or services: those who drink milk are segregated from those who make it into butter, those who burn electricity at home from those who burn it in factories, those who ride in Pullman cars from those who ride in coaches, and those who ship lumber from those who ship television sets. Purchasers are separated by the time of day, the day of the week, or the season of the year: movies cost less in the daytime and long-distance calls at night; golf courses have lower rates on weekdays than on week-ends; resort hotels are cheaper out of season, coal in the summer, and furs at the August sales. Consumers are segregated by ignorance and by variations in prestige, the same product being sold at different prices under different labels or in different shops. Distributors are classified according to the functions they perform and different discounts are given to those who sell at wholesale and at retail. In these and other ways, discrimination is made possible.

Forms of Discrimination

Discrimination may be open or secret, systematic or sporadic, permanent or temporary; it may be apparent in a structure of prices that is publicly announced and consistently adhered to over a long period of time; it may result occasionally from bargains struck in making individual sales. Discrimination may be purposive: it may be practiced by a monopolist who seeks to maximize his revenues by charging high prices where demand is inelastic and low prices where it is not, by a would-be monopolist who seeks to drive his rivals from local markets, or by a competitor who meets the different prices found in each part of his market or quotes the lower price required to make a sale; it may be designed to reduce costs by encouraging prompt payment, large orders, and off-peak use, to promote a new product, to invade a new market, or to expand sales by experimenting with elasticity of demand. Discrimination may be incidental; this is the case when a seller conforms to a delivered pricing system in his industry. It is the purpose of such a system to enable all sellers to charge identical prices at any destination. But the seller who conforms may charge some buyers more and others less for freight than the amounts he actually pays; his net return will be greater on the former sales than on the latter; in short, he will discriminate among his customers. Discrimination, in this case, is open, systematic, and permanent; but it is incidental to the purpose of monopoly.

The consequences of discrimination cannot be said to be always good or always bad. A number of cases may be distinguished for the purpose of analysis:

1. Discrimination by a single firm possessing a monopoly.
   a) In the absence of public regulation.
   b) Where rates and services are regulated by a public agency.
2. Discrimination by one of many sellers in an industry.
   a) Where incidental to collusion in fixing prices.
   b) Where undertaken independently.
      i. Where it affects competition between the seller and his competitors.
      ii. Where it affects competition between the buyer and his competitors.

Discrimination by monopolists and its regulation by public authorities will be discussed in Chapter 19, the discrimination incidental to delivered pricing systems in Chapter 8. It is with purposive discrimination, undertaken independently by sellers facing competition, that we are here concerned.

The Uses and Abuses of Discrimination

The discount structures of sellers serve a variety of purposes. Discounts for cash cut costs by reducing the amount of credit that must be extended in making sales. Discounts based on the functions performed by buyers afford to wholesalers and retailers the margins that enable them to supply the seller with marketing services that he might otherwise be compelled to provide himself. Discounts based on the size of a single purchase encourage larger orders and thus reduce the cost involved in selling, accounting, collecting, packing, and delivery. Discounts related to the quantity purchased over several months may also cut costs by making possible the forward planning of production, maintaining output in off seasons, stabilizing operations, and reducing investment in inventories. Services rendered to buyers or allowances made to buyers for services rendered by them may pay for themselves by promoting sales. If concessions are justified by savings realized by sellers, they are not fairly to be called discriminatory. But large buyers may use superior bargaining power to exact concessions that are not so justified. And here discrimination will occur.

Discrimination may be judged by its influence on competition at either of two levels: that of the seller or that of the buyer. In either case, its consequences may be good or bad. At the seller's level, competition may be eliminated as prices are cut, in one market after another, and raised again when local rivals have been driven from the field. But competition may be strengthened where discrimination is employed to introduce new products, enter new markets, or feel out lower levels of demand, and where it is used to meet the lower prices of competitors. For reductions thus introduced and copied will eventually be generalized. "Sporadic, unsystematic discrimination," says Morris Adelman, "is one of the most powerful forces of competition in modern industrial markets. Like a high wind, it seizes on small openings and crevices in an 'orderly' price structure and tears it apart."[26]

The framers of the Clayton Act were concerned primarily with the effect of discrimination on competitors of the firm that gives a lower price, those of the Robinson-Patman Act with its effect on competitors of the firm receiving it. At this level, discrimination may strengthen or weaken competing channels of distribution by affecting the relative costs of different distributors. It may prevent equality of opportunity by giving an undeserved advantage to the larger buyer or to the smaller one. It may promote efficiency or subsidize inefficiency by favoring the buyer whose costs are low or the one whose costs are high. If opportunity is to be equalized and efficiency encouraged, the seller must recognize, in the prices charged each buyer, the savings to which the manner of his purchases entitles him. To do more would be to handicap the weak. To do less would be to handicap the strong. In the one case, monopoly would be promoted. In the other, the weak competitor would be protected, but competition itself would be impaired.

Discrimination Under the Clayton Act

Section 2 of the Clayton Act made it unlawful "to discriminate in price between different purchasers of commodities . . . where the effect

[26] M. A. Adelman, "Effective Competition and the Antitrust Laws," *Harvard Law Review,* Vol. LXI, pp. 1289–1350, esp. pp. 1331–32.

of such discrimination may be to substantially lessen competition or tend to create a monopoly *in any line of commerce*." It provided, however, that this should not apply to discrimination "on account of differences in the grade, quality, or quantity of the commodity sold, *or* that makes only due allowance for differences in the cost of selling or transportation," or to discrimination "made in good faith to meet competition," and should not prevent sellers "from selecting their own customers in bona fide transactions and not in restraint of trade." The words here given in italics assumed particular importance in the subsequent interpretation of the law.

In the Mennen case in 1923 and in the Nabisco case in 1924, the phrase "in any line of commerce" was given a meaning so narrow that orders issued by the Federal Trade Commission were reversed. Mennen had refused to give its wholesale discount to a co-operative organization of retail druggist buying in equal quantities. National Biscuit had allowed the units of a chain to pool their purchases in claiming quantity discounts but refused to permit the members of an association of retailers to do so. The Commission found, in these cases, that discrimination had lessened competition with the favored distributors. The courts held, however, that the distributors were in a different line of commerce from Mennen or Nabisco, and found that competition with these concerns was not impaired.[27] This interpretation was reversed in the Van Camp case in 1929. American Can had refused Van Camp a discount granted another packing company and Van Camp had sued for treble damages. The Supreme Court found for the plaintiff, holding that "any line of commerce" included the line where Van Camp competed with the other purchaser.[28] The Commission was encouraged by this decision to issue an order in a pending case against the Goodyear Tire and Rubber Company.

Goodyear had supplied Sears Roebuck with tires like those sold elsewhere under a different trade-mark and with a different tread. Its price for filling all of Sears' requirements was cost plus 6 per cent. To get the contract it had also paid a bonus in cash and Goodyear stock. After making allowance for differences in cost due to the quantities purchased and for savings in selling expenses, the Commission found that Goodyear's discrimination in favor of Sears ran between 12 and 22 per cent of the price at which it sold to other distributors, enabling Sears to undersell them at retail by 20–25 per cent. The Commission issued its order in 1933, contending that the difference in Goodyear's prices could not be justified by differences in cost. The final decision on Goodyear's appeal was not handed down until 1939, three years after the passage of the Robinson-Patman Act. It turned on a single word: "or." This word, said the court, made the phrase "on account of differences in . . . grade, quality, or

[27] *Mennen Co.* v. *FTC*, 288 F. 774, certiorari denied, 262 U.S. 759; *National Biscuit Co.* v. *FTC*, 299 F. 733, certiorari denied, 266 U.S. 613.

[28] *Van Camp Co.* v. *American Can Co.*, 278 U.S. 245.

quantity" completely independent of the phrase "makes only due allowance for differences in . . . cost," and thus permitted *any* difference in these factors to justify *any* difference in price.[29] The decision made it clear that discrimination could not have been prevented under the provisions of the Clayton Act.

This weakness of Section 2 was corrected when it was superseded in 1936 by the Robinson-Patman Act. Another one was not. The proviso preventing application of the law to sellers "selecting their own customers" is still available as a defense for powerful producers who may confine their sales to fabricators or distributors adhering to suggested policies or may coerce their weaker customers by threatening to withhold supplies. Railroads and public utilities are required to serve all comers. Manufacturers, even though controlling the bulk of an industry's output, are not.

Provisions of the Robinson-Patman Act

The Robinson-Patman Act contains a criminal and a civil section. The former makes three offenses punishable by fine and imprisonment. They are (1) charging different buyers different prices on sales that are otherwise identical, (2) selling more cheaply in one part of the country than in another, and (3) selling "at unreasonably low prices," whenever either of the latter things is done "for the purpose of destroying competition or eliminating a competitor." The first of these offenses is so narrowly defined as to be of little practical importance. The second is definite, but the third is vague: when are prices "unreasonably low"? The condition attached would make enforcement, if ever attempted, extremely difficult. It is only in the most flagrant of cases that a court would be likely to find in a cut in prices the purpose of "destroying competition or eliminating a competitor." It is in its civil section that the Act has been significant.

The law deals in part with specific forms of discrimination and in part with discrimination in general. Section 2-c forbids the seller to pay a broker's commission to the buyer himself or to an intermediary under his control. This prohibition is absolute: no exceptions are allowed. Section 2-d forbids the seller to make an allowance for services rendered him by the buyer unless it is made available to the latter's competitors "on proportionally equal terms." Section 2-e forbids the seller to furnish the buyer with facilities or services "not accorded to all purchasers on proportionally equal terms." Allowances, facilities, and services must thus be made proportionate to something, but what this may be the law does not attempt to say. These specific prohibitions serve to prevent evasion of the broader provisions of Section 2-a dealing with discrimination in general.

Section 2-a makes it illegal to discriminate in price, not only where

[29] *Goodyear Tire and Rubber Co.* v. *FTC,* 101 F. 2d 620, certiorari denied, 308 U.S. 557.

the effect may be, as in the Clayton Act, "substantially to lessen competition or tend to create a monopoly," but also where it may be "to injure, destroy, or prevent competition with any person who either grants or knowingly receives the benefit of such discrimination, or with the customers of either of them." The new wording, it should be noted, does two things: it adds *injury to competitors* to the test of illegality, and it locks the door that had been opened by the courts in the Mennen case and closed in the Van Camp case. The section also changes the defense that may be offered by a seller charged with discrimination: (1) he may show that the differentials in his price "make only due allowance for differences in the cost of manufacture, sale, or delivery resulting from the differing methods or quantities in which such commodities are . . . sold or delivered," and (2) he may show that his lower price "was made in good faith to meet" not competition, as in the Clayton Act, but "an equally low price of a competitor." The first defense writes into law the principle that the Federal Trade Commission sought vainly to establish in the Goodyear case. The second permits discrimination to match a lower price, but not to undercut it.

The Act authorizes the Commission to fix limits beyond which discounts for larger quantities may not be given, even though justified by differences in cost, "where it finds that available purchasers in greater quantities are so few as to render differentials on account thereof unjustly discriminatory or promotive of monopoly." And it makes it unlawful for buyers "knowingly to induce or receive" a prohibited discrimination in price.

The Policy of the Robinson-Patman Act

In general, it is the principle of the Robinson-Patman Act that differences in price should be proportionate to differences in cost. But however sound this principle may be in theory, it is difficult to apply in practice. Discounts may be defended if they make only due allowance for differences in the cost, per unit of output, of manufacture, sale, or delivery resulting from differences in methods of sale or delivery or in the quantities involved. But it is no easy matter to distinguish the costs that result from such differences. Savings in the cost of selling and delivering by different methods and in different quantities may readily be shown. But savings in the cost of manufacture are more difficult to prove.

May the lower cost of overhead per unit that results from larger output be credited to buyers placing larger orders? May more overhead be charged against goods that must be produced when a plant is running at full capacity and less against those that may be made in periods when demand is slack? May it be assumed, in fixing the price required to obtain an order, that the extra costs involved are all that need to be considered, overhead having been recovered, in whole or in part, on other sales? Or must overhead be allocated uniformly, and the unit cost of production determined by dividing total output into total expenditures? These are matters on which cost accountants may honestly disagree; accountants for sellers may take one position, those for the Federal Trade Commission another. Problems of accounting theory will thus be presented for solution to the Commission and the courts. And these problems are not easy ones to solve.

In many respects the law departs from the principle that relates differences in price to differences in cost. In some cases it permits discrimination; in others, it even requires it. Sellers may legally discriminate among consumers, and among business buyers who do not compete with one another: spark plugs, for instance, are sold to automobile manufacturers at 6 cents each, to wholesalers at 24 cents, and to retailers, in varying quantities, at 32 cents to 39 cents. Sellers may also charge identical prices where costs differ, or give discounts that fail to reflect real differences in cost; it is illegal to discriminate in favor of the firm that buys in bulk, but legal to discriminate against it. Discrimination, moreover, is required when a broker's commission is denied a buyer who himself performs a broker's services, when allowances or services are withheld though they would pay for themselves by promoting sales, and when the Federal Trade Commission fixes limits beyond which discounts for quantity cannot be given though fully justified by differences in cost.

The Robinson-Patman Act was designed to reduce the buying advantages of the chain stores and other mass distributors. It was thus intended, not to prevent discrimination in general, but to prevent discrimination in favor of larger buyers and to permit or require discrimination in favor of smaller ones. It was concerned less with the maintenance of competition than with the survival of small competitors.

The consequences of the law cannot be measured. By requiring that discounts be justified by actual rather than potential differences in cost, it may discourage price reductions that could profitably be made. By outlawing the practice of setting lower prices, in some part of a market, to test the possibility of increasing sales, it may prevent reductions that would soon be generalized. By denying the mass distributor advantages he formerly obtained, it may keep his costs and prices higher than they otherwise would be. But these influences may be offset in other ways. Concessions once given in one form may now be given in another. Discounts as large or larger than those once granted may still be justified by differences in cost. The mass distributor may buy a plant's whole output or manufacture a product for himself; here, costs may be cut but no discrimination is involved. The law has been used not only to handicap the chains, but also to check the advantages obtained by agencies buying collectively for independent firms. If anything, it has helped the A&P by driving it into the supermarket business. Whether it has operated, on balance, to strengthen or weaken competition, it is impossible to say.

THE LEGAL STATUS OF DISCOUNTS

Local price discrimination has been held by the courts to be illegal under the Robinson-Patman Act as it was under the Clayton Act.[30] Discounts for cash have raised no question of legality since they are generally available to all buyers on equal terms. Half of the orders issued by the Federal Trade Commission, under the amended law, have forbidden the payment of brokerage; wherever these orders have been appealed, the Commission has been upheld. A few orders relate to the provision of allowances and services, and here some progress has been made toward clarifying the uncertain meaning of the law. But it is in connection with the many orders issued under Section 2-a, dealing with discrimination in general, that the more important issues of interpretation have occurred. The application of the law to discount structures will be considered in the remainder of this chapter, its application to the discrimination inherent in delivered pricing systems in the next.

Brokerage

Payment of brokerage has been found to be illegal in a number of different circumstances. In the A&P case, the commissions once paid to A&P had been converted into quantity discounts or outright reductions in price. The company sought to justify this procedure in terms of cost, showing that its agents in the field not only served its purchasing department, but also gave advice to sellers and aided them in disposing of their surpluses, and contending that sellers had been saved the cost of employing brokers' services. But the court rejected this defense, finding the prohibition of such payments to be absolute.[31] In the Webb-Crawford case, where the owners of a wholesale grocery company were also partners in a brokerage concern, it was held that collection of commissions through a dummy was in violation of the law.[32] In these cases brokerage had given an advantage to a single buyer. In others, however, it had been passed on to the benefit of many small concerns.

In the Biddle case, an independent intermediary sold market information and purchasing services to 2,400 clients, passing on to them in lower prices the commissions it obtained.[33] In the Oliver case, another company performed a similar service for 300 wholesale firms.[34] In the Quality Bakers

[30] *Porto Rican American Tobacco Co.* v. *American Tobacco Co.*, 30 F. 2d 234, certiorari denied, 279 U.S. 858 (1929); *Muller & Co.* v. *FTC*, 142 F. 2d 511 (1944); see also the decision handed down by the Supreme Court on December 6, 1954 in the case of *L. L. Moore* v. *Mead's Fine Bread Co.*

[31] *Great Atlantic and Pacific Tea Co.* v. *FTC*, 106 F. 2d 667 (1939), certiorari denied, 308 U.S. 625 (1940).

[32] *Webb-Crawford Co.* v. *FTC*, 109 F. 2d 268 (1940), certiorari denied, 310 U.S. 638 (1940).

[33] *Biddle Purchasing Co.* v. *FTC*, 96 F. 2d 687 (1938); certiorari denied, 305 U.S. 634 (1938).

[34] *Oliver Bros.* v. *FTC*, 102 F. 2d 763 (1939).

case, brokerage was collected and transmitted by an agency set up by 70 wholesale bakers to make co-operative purchases of flour, equipment, and supplies.[35] In the case of the Modern Marketing Service, an agency making purchases for members of the Red and White organization of wholesale and retail grocers passed on to them commissions obtained from such suppliers as Proctor & Gamble, Quaker Oats, Morton Salt, and Diamond Match.[36] In all of these cases, payments that were helpful, not to mass distributors, but to small independent dealers, were prohibited.

When the Commission issued a similar order in 1952 against the District Grocery Stores, a co-operative buying for 275 retailers in Washington, D.C., Commissioner Mason recorded a dissent. Here, he said, was a little merchant who wanted to "make like a big company" with "savvy such as his rivals, the chain stores, had." The Commission "had no business suing the corner grocers." Its order was "immoral and oppressive" and he was "heartily ashamed of any connection with its restriction on free enterprise."[37] But whatever the force of Mr. Mason's logic, his colleagues were supported by the law.

Allowances and Services

Sections 2-d and 2-e of the Robinson-Patman Act forbid the seller to allow discounts to the buyer for merchandising services rendered him by the buyer, or himself to render merchandising services to the buyer, unless such allowances or services are made available to all buyers "on proportionally equal terms." This does not mean that allowances must actually be made or services rendered to all buyers. It does mean, according to decisions made by the Commission, that they cannot be given secretly; their availability must be publicly announced. Their terms cannot be such as to confine them to a few big buyers; they must be made available to all. Allowances, moreover, may be made only for services actually rendered, and they must not be substantially in excess of the cost of these services to the distributors or their value to the manufacturers.

The Commission has issued several complaints under these sections, but few of them have resulted in orders and even fewer have been carried to the courts. In the Corn Products case, a company producing dextrose had spent $750,000 in advertising the candy manufactured by one of its customers but had spent little or nothing in promoting the sales of other firms. The Commission's order to cease and desist was upheld by the Supreme Court.[38] In the Elizabeth Arden cases, demonstrators had been provided to retailers of cosmetics on the basis of criteria that included not only the quantities they purchased, but also the size and character of their stores, with the result that a tenth of the company's customers obtained

[35] *Quality Bakers* v. *FTC*, 114 F. 2d 393 (1940).

[36] *Modern Marketing Service* v. *FTC*, 149 F. 2d 970 (1945).

[37] *New York Times*, January 7, 1952.

[38] *Corn Products Refining Co.* v. *FTC*, 324 U.S. 726 (1945).

the services of demonstrators and nine tenths of them did not. It was found that these services had not been provided on proportionally equal terms.[39] The courts have thus upheld the Commission in requiring that services provided to any buyer must be made effectively available to all.

Allowances and services must be given "on proportionally equal terms." But proportional to what? Here, the Commission has adopted no clear rule. There are various possibilities. One is proportionality to the dollar volume of sales. Another is proportionality to the cost to the buyer of the services rendered by him to the seller. Still another is proportionality to the value of such services to the seller. For a time, it appeared that legality could be assured only by conformity to the first of these tests. But a recent Commission decision involving the big soap companies shows this to be untrue. These concerns made one allowance in their price per case to buyers who advertised their soap in newspapers, a smaller allowance to those who advertised it in handbills, and a still smaller allowance to those who featured it in store displays. These allowances were not proportionate to the quantities of soap sold to buyers in each group. But they were given for services actually rendered and were not substantially in excess of the cost of these services to the distributors or their value to the manufacturers. And on this basis the Commission found them to be within the law.[40]

The Test of Illegality

The prohibitions contained in the foregoing sections of the law are unqualified. But other forms of discounts, covered in Section 2-a, are illegal only where their effect "may be substantially to lessen . . . or to injure, destroy, or prevent competition. . . ." The burden of proof, under this test, depends upon the meaning that is given to the word "substantially," as we saw in discussing the interpretation of Section 3. But it is influenced also by the meaning that is given to the word "may" and to the word "competition" itself. These words were defined in a decision handed down by the Supreme Court in the Morton Salt case in 1948.

Prior to this decision the meaning attached to the word "may" in the phrase "where the effect . . . may be" was that given to it by the Court in the Standard Fashion case[41] in 1922. It was not the purpose of Congress, said the Court, "to prohibit the mere possibility of the consequences described. It was intended to prevent such agreements as would . . . probably lessen competition. . . ."[42] The word "may," according to this dictum, means probability.

[39] *Elizabeth Arden Sales Corp.* v. *Gus Blass Co.*, 150 F. 2d 988 certiorari denied, 326 U.S. 793 (1945); *Elizabeth Arden, Inc.* v. *FTC*, 156 F. 2d 132 (1946), certiorari denied, 331 U.S. 806 (1947).

[40] *In re Lever Bros., Proctor & Gamble, Colgate-Palmolive-Peet*, Dockets 5585, 5586, and 5587, complaints dismissed, January 4, 1954.

[41] *Standard Fashion Co.* v. *Magrane-Houston Co.*, 258 U.S. 346.

[42] *Ibid.*, pp. 356–57.

In its decision in the Corn Products case[43] in 1945, the Court reiterated this position, saying that "the use of the word 'may' was not to prohibit discriminations having 'the mere possibility' of these consequences, but to reach those which would probably have the defined effect. . . ."[44] But it also went on to say that "the statute does not require that the discriminations must in fact have harmed competition, but only that there is a reasonable possibility that they 'may' have such an effect."[45]

It was the latter phrase that was taken as a precedent by Justice Black who spoke for the Court in the Morton Salt case.[46] A "reasonable possibility," he said, is all that need be shown.[47] Justice Jackson dissented, finding in the Corn Products precedent "one of those inadvertencies into which the most careful judges sometimes fall." The law, he said, had been intended by Congress and interpreted by the Court to require a "reasonable probability" of injury.[48] But this was now the view of a minority.

The same decision defined the meaning of injury to "competition." The competition found to be injured by Morton's discounts was not the vitality of competition in general, but "the competitive opportunities of certain merchants." Congress, in passing the Robinson-Patman Act, "was especially concerned with protecting small businesses." The new law "was intended to justify a finding of injury to competition by a showing [in the words of a Senate report] of 'injury to the competitor victimized by the discrimination.' "[49]

This interpretation made for easier enforcement of the law. Probability requires some proof; possibility may be assumed. Injury to particular competitors is more readily to be shown than injury to competition in a market as a whole. But this standard also permits the law to be applied —as its framers had intended—in cases where competitors might possibly be injured but competition itself be unaffected or its vigor actually increased.

In recent years, however, the courts and the Commission have both retreated from the rule of Morton Salt. In 1951 a Court of Appeals reversed a Commission order against the discount structure of the Minneapolis-Honeywell Co., finding insufficient evidence of injury to competition. Said the Court, "We construe the Act to require substantial, not trivial or sporadic, interference with competition to establish the violation of its mandate."[50] And this position was sustained by the Supreme Court in 1952.[51] The Commission, too, has gone back to the earlier

[43] *Corn Products Co.* v. *FTC*, 324 U.S. 726.

[44] *Ibid.*, p. 738.

[45] *Ibid.*, p. 742.

[46] *FTC* v. *Morton Salt Co.*, 334 U.S. 37 (1948).

[47] *Ibid.*, p. 46.

[48] *Ibid.*, p. 58.

[49] *Ibid.*, pp. 46, 49.

[50] *Minneapolis-Honeywell Co.* v. *FTC*, 191 F. 2d 786 (1951).

[51] 344 U.S. 206 (1952).

standard. It dismissed a complaint against the General Foods Corporation in 1954, on the ground that the evidence did not show that the company's discounts had injured or were likely to injure competition, holding that a "reasonable probability" of such injury must be affirmatively proved.[52]

The Cost Defense

Differences in price are not unlawful if they "make only due allowance for differences in the cost of manufacture, sale, or delivery resulting from the differing methods or quantities in which . . . commodities . . . are sold or delivered." The seller charged with discrimination may therefore defend himself by presenting a statement of costs. The FTC has promulgated no rules with respect to acceptable principles of cost accounting. But until recently it has not hesitated to reject estimates of cost that have been offered in defense of differences in price.

The Commission has permitted discounts to be justified by savings in the costs of selling and delivering. It has declined, however, to recognize savings in the cost of manufacturing. It has adopted average total cost rather than marginal cost as its standard, requiring the cost of producing to fill an order to be computed by dividing total output into total expenditures, not by determining the added expenditure that it entails. Overhead, in other words, must be allocated uniformly to all the units sold. Though particular orders may reduce the unit cost of output by making it possible to schedule production over longer periods, to buy materials when they are cheapest, to continue operations when demand is slack, and to avoid the risks involved in carrying inventories when manufacturing for stock, these savings are not accepted in defense of a lower price.

The Commission has put the whole burden of proof on the seller, assuming differences in cost to be nonexistent until they are proven to be otherwise. Where certain of the savings claimed have appeared to be excessive or speculative, it has not merely disallowed these items, but has rejected the accounts as a whole. Where savings have been demonstrated, it has rejected them as not applying to the particular prices involved. And, on the other hand, it has accepted large differences in cost as justifying small differences in price.[53]

It now appears, however, that the Commission is prepared to take a more liberal line. In 1953 its new chairman, Edward F. Howrey, appointed a committee under Professor H. F. Taggart of the University of Michigan to prepare a report on the cost accounting principles involved in "due allowance," looking toward the eventual provision of

[52] *In re General Foods Corp.*, Docket 5675, complaint dismissed, April 27, 1954. Where distributors handle many different items, it would be difficult to show that competition among them had been injured by differences in the discounts offered on a single one. In their interpretation of the law, the FTC and the courts have therefore adopted a narrower concept of injury. It is held, accordingly, that the test relates, not to competition in general, but to competition in the sale of a particular commodity.

[53] See M. A. Adelman, "The Consistency of the Robinson-Patman Act," *Stanford Law Review*, 6: 3–22 (1953).

guidance to business. In 1954 the Commission accepted a defense in which Sylvania Electric Products figured the savings made on larger sales of tubes by averaging them over 600 types of tubes instead of computing them separately for each type. And in a concurring opinion, Chairman Howrey expressed his opposition to any "rigid mechanical" interpretation of the cost proviso, calling for a "rule of reason approach" coupled with "a reexamination of the problem of cost analysis" under the Act.[54]

Buyers' Liability

The prohibition of Section 2-a applies not only to sellers but also to buyers who "knowingly" induce or receive an unlawful discrimination in price. This provision came before the Supreme Court in the Automatic Canteen case[55] in 1953. The Automatic Canteen Company leased candy dispensing machines to distributors and sold them candy for distribution, doing more than half of this business. It obtained discounts from 80 among 115 candy manufacturers, insisting on getting lower prices than those paid by its competitors. The FTC ordered the company to cease and desist from demanding these concessions. The company asserted that its lower prices were justified by the sellers' lower costs. The Commission asked for proof. The company replied that it could not reasonably be expected to prepare analyses of the costs of its suppliers. The Supreme Court agreed. The knowing receipt of a lower price, it held, did not in itself violate the Act. Knowledge that the lower price was unjustified would do so. But here, the burden of proof was on the Commission, not on the company.

This decision all but destroyed the principle of buyers' liability. When it was announced, the Commission dropped all of the pending actions in which this principle was involved. Buyers can still be prosecuted where they knew that their discounts could not be justified. But such knowledge will be difficult to prove.

Quantity Discounts

Quantity discounts, as such, were held by the Supreme Court, in the case of Bruce's Juices, not to be unlawful.[56] But such discounts have been prohibited, in many cases, by the FTC. The Commission has forbidden larger discounts on orders placed by chains and co-operative buying agencies where deliveries are made to separate stores, finding no savings in the cost of delivery and inadequate justification in the costs of production and sale.[57] It has likewise forbidden discounts based on the quantities pur-

[54] *In re Sylvania Electric Products, Inc.*, Docket 5728 (1954).

[55] *Automatic Canteen Co.* v. *FTC*, 346 U.S. 61.

[56] *Bruce's Juices* v. *American Can Co.*, 330 U.S. 743 (1947).

[57] *In re Simmons Co.*, 28 FTC 727 (1939); *In re Standard Brands*, 30 FTC 1117 (1940); *In re Sherwin Williams Co.*, 36 FTC 25 (1943).

chased over periods of time, without regard to the size of individual orders or deliveries, holding that cumulative purchases cannot be shown to cut the seller's costs.[58] The Commission has also ordered U.S. Rubber to desist from making larger concessions on tires and footwear manufactured under private brands than on like products bearing its own name, thus disposing of the issue that had been raised, under the Clayton Act, in the Goodyear case.[59] Here, again, evidence of savings in the cost of manufacture was not allowed to justify a lower price.

The Commission has sometimes found that discounts related to quantities delivered to one place at one time are justified by differences in cost.[60] But even these discounts, in the circumstances of the Morton Salt case, were found to be in violation of the law. Morton's price per case of salt was $1.60 for less than carload lots and $1.50 for carloads of 1,035 cases each and was $1.40 for 5,000 cases and $1.35 for 50,000 cases when these were bought within a single year. Nominally the lower prices were equally available to all of the company's customers. But the only ones who bought enough salt in a year to get it for $1.35 were five large grocery chains. Independent retailers, competing with the chains, obtained supplies from wholesalers who had been required to pay $1.40 or $1.50. The Commission held these differences to be injurious to competition. It found the carload as well as the cumulative discounts to be unjustified by differences in cost. And it ordered the company to desist from selling to retailers at prices lower than those charged wholesalers whose customers compete with them. This order was sustained by the Supreme Court in the decision handed down in 1948.[61]

Quantity Limits

The Robinson-Patman Act authorizes the Federal Trade Commission to fix limits beyond which discounts for larger quantities may not be given, where "purchasers in greater quantities are so few as to render differentials on account thereof unjustly discriminatory or promotive of monopoly." For fifteen years after the law was passed this authority was not exercised. But under pressure from independent dealers and members of Congress, hearings on a proposed order limiting discounts in the sale of tires and tubes were announced in October, 1949. Among 48,000 dealers making purchases from 27 manufacturers, the Commission found that 63, in the largest volume bracket, bought automobile tires for 26–30 per cent less than the prices paid by the smallest dealers, and truck tires for 32–40

[58] *In re H. C. Brill Co.*, 26 FTC 666 (1938); *In re American Optical Co.*, 28 FTC 169 (1939); *In re Simmons Co.*, 29 FTC 727 (1939); *In re Standard Brands*, 30 FTC 1117 (1940).

[59] *In re U.S. Rubber Co.*, 28 FTC 1489 (1939) and Order in Docket 4972 (1950).

[60] *In re Kraft-Phenix Cheese Corp.*, 25 FTC 537 (1937); *In re American Optical Co.*, 28 FTC 169 (1939).

[61] *FTC* v. *Morton Salt Co.*, 334 U.S. 47.

per cent less. Half of the business of distributing tires and tubes was in the hands of two per cent of the distributors. The Commission held the industry's discount structure to be "unjustly discriminatory" and "productive of monopoly" and issued an order in January, 1952, forbidding its members to grant larger discounts for quantities greater than a single carload of 20,000 pounds.

Goodyear appealed, contending that the lower prices offered larger dealers were voluntarily set to cover costs and yield a profit, that smaller dealers could enter the market and survive and grow, and that their share in the sale of tires and tubes had not declined for many years. It argued, too, that concentration is lower, the rate of entry higher, the life of enterprises longer, the share of them making profits larger, and the rate of failure lower in this field than in other retail businesses. It concluded, therefore, that the industry's discounts were not "unjustly discriminatory or promotive of monopoly." At the end of 1954 a district court had refused to consider the case on the ground that Goodyear had not as yet been injured, a court of appeals had ordered it to hear the case on its merits, and no decision had yet been announced.

Functional Discounts

Where buyers are not in competition with one another, discrimination between them is not in violation of the law. The Commission, accordingly, has never issued an order against a functional discount as such, but has explicitly held such discounts to be legitimate.[62] In actions brought against the leading producers of spark plugs, Commission attorneys argued that the low price charged automobile manufacturers made it difficult for other producers to break into the original equipment market, and were thus injurious to competition. These prices, however, were said to be required to keep the automobile companies from making plugs themselves. And the higher prices charged distributors made it easier for new concerns to enter the market for replacement plugs. There was no evidence that competition had, in fact, been harmed. The Commission dismissed the cases in 1953.[63]

The immunity afforded to functional discounts creates the possibility that sellers might evade the law relating to quantity discounts by establishing special customer classes for the purpose of granting discounts that could not be justified by differences in cost. The Commission has thus been forced to pass upon the methods by which customers are classified. In general, it has held that classifications may not be arbitrary, that they must conform strictly to the nature of the operations undertaken by different types of customers, and that buyers at the same level—such as independent retailers, mail order houses, and chain stores—must be put

[62] *In re Simmons Co.*, 29 FTC 727 (1939); *In re Standard Brands*, 30 FTC 1117 (1940); *In re Caradine Hat Co.*, 39 FTC 86 (1944).

[63] *In re Champion Spark Plug Co.*, Docket 3977, case dismissed, 1953.

in the same class.[64] In this case discounts granted may not exceed the savings shown in costs.

Where a customer performs more than one function, as in the case of one who sells at wholesale and at retail, it is necessary to determine which of the relevant discounts may be granted on his purchases. Here, the Commission has ruled that the larger discount allowed for any function may be applied only to the portion of an order for which that function alone is performed, and it has been upheld in this position by the courts.[65] This principle, however, is difficult to enforce, since the seller, in applying different discounts to different portions of a sale, must take the buyer's word as to the quantities that will be handled in different ways, and the buyer has a strong incentive to overstate the quantity on which the higher discount will apply. The rule, moreover, is open to criticism, since it denies the split-function dealer the discount which he should receive for performing the wholesale function on that part of his purchases that he retails himself.

This question was involved in an order issued by the Commission against the Standard Oil Company of Indiana.[66] Standard operated no service stations itself. It sold gasoline in tank wagon lots to retailers and in tank car lots to jobbers who resold it in tank wagons to retailers. It gave the jobbers a discount of 1½ cents a gallon. All of them made some sales at retail. One of them—Ned's in Detroit—operated exclusively as a cut-rate retailer. The Commission held that Standard was practicing illegal discrimination because its price to service stations was higher than its price to jobbers, or higher than the jobbers' price to service stations. It ordered Standard to deny the discount to jobbers on the part of the gasoline they sold at retail. It thus required the discount to be withheld from Ned's and required Standard to police the activities of the other distributors. The order operated to maintain a rigid stratification of functions in distribution, preventing Ned's and others from reducing the retail price of gasoline by combining the functions of wholesaler and retailer. It was reversed by the Supreme Court on other grounds in 1951[67] and was renewed by the Commission, in modified form, in 1953.[68]

The Good Faith Defense

The seller charged with illegal discrimination has two defenses available. One is that the differences in his price were justified by differences in cost. The other is that his lower price "was made in good faith to meet

[64] *In re Pittsburgh Plate Glass Co.*, 25 FTC 1228 (1937); *In re American Oil Co.*, 29 FTC 857 (1939); *In re Sherwin-Williams*, 36 FTC 25 (1943).

[65] *Southgate Brokerage Co.* v. *FTC*, 150 F. 2d 607 (1945); *Standard Oil Co. (Indiana)* v. *FTC*, 173 F. 2d 210 (1949).

[66] *In re Standard Oil Co. (Indiana)* 41 FTC 263 (1945); 43 FTC 56 (1946).

[67] *Standard Oil Co. (Indiana)* v. *FTC*, 340 U.S. 231.

[68] Docket No. 4389, Modified Order (1953).

an equally low price of a competitor." The Federal Trade Commission, in the past, has seriously impaired the cost defense. It has also undertaken to whittle down the good faith defense. This was the issue on which the Commission was reversed by the Supreme Court in the Standard Oil of Indiana case in 1951.

Standard first had sought to justify its lower price to Ned's and other jobbers by presenting evidence as to its costs. This was rejected by the FTC. The company then advanced the defense that its price had been made "in good faith" to meet the offers made by its competitors. The Commission did not question this fact but contended that competition had none the less been injured. Standard replied that proof of meeting the price of a competitor afforded a complete defense. The Court of Appeals supported the Commission, holding this defense to be procedural rather than substantive, serving merely to shift to the Commission the burden of proof.[69] Under this ruling the Commission could charge discrimination, the respondent could advance the good faith defense, and the Commission would then be required to prove that competition had actually been harmed. The ruling was reversed, however, by the Supreme Court.[70] Good faith, said the Court, is a substantive defense. It can be refuted only by proving the absence of good faith. This might be done by showing that the competitor's lower price was itself known to be unlawful, or that his offer was not genuine, being made collusively for the purpose of excusing the defendant's price. But such matters are difficult to prove.

In 1953 the Commission issued its modified order against Standard of Indiana, again requiring that the discount be discontinued.[71] Now, however, it attacked Standard's good faith defense on another ground. This defense, it said, could be used only to justify occasional price matching in particular instances. But Standard's discounts were a part of its established price structure and were regularly given to all of the buyers in a favored class. Here, the Commission had the advantage of precedents. In the Cement case in 1948 the Supreme Court had rejected good faith as a defense of basing-point pricing, denying that it "permits a seller to use a sales system which constantly results in his getting more money for like goods from some customers than he does from others."[72] And in the Minneapolis-Honeywell case, decided by a Court of Appeals in 1951 and upheld by the Supreme Court in 1953, it was held that the defense could not be used to justify the company's regular schedule of quantity discounts.[73] The modified order against Standard Oil has not been tested in

[69] *Standard Oil Co. (Indiana)* v. *FTC*, 173 F. 2d 210 (1949).

[70] *Standard Oil Co. (Indiana)* v. *FTC*, 340 U.S. 231.

[71] Docket No. 4389, Modified Order (1953).

[72] *FTC* v. *Cement Institute*, 333 U.S. 683, 725.

[73] *Minneapolis-Honeywell Co.* v. *FTC*, 191 F. 2d 786 (1951), certiorari denied, 344 U.S. 206 (1952).

the courts. But in setting limits to the good faith defense, the Commission would now appear to be on solid ground.

COMPETITION: SOFT OR HARD?

Laws such as the Robinson-Patman Act and the resale price maintenance acts (to be discussed in Chapter 14) have been designed not so much to maintain competition as to preserve individual competitors. They have thus been criticized as making for "soft competition" in contrast to the "hard competition" demanded by the Sherman Act. Under a policy of hard competition, control of price discrimination would still be required. But the pattern of control would differ in important respects from that provided by the present law.

The test of illegality of quantity discounts, contained in the Robinson-Patman Act, would have to be changed from injury to a competitor to injury to competition in general, and the probability rather than a possibility of such injury would have to be shown. The principle of justifying differences in price by showing differences in cost would be retained. But accounting rules would have to be adopted permitting discounts to be given wherever there were real savings in costs, and these would include savings in the costs of manufacturing as well as in those of selling and delivery. The good faith defense would continue to be available, as now, not to afford immunity to systematic discrimination (such as that involved in the delivered pricing systems to be discussed in Chapter 8), but to justify the discrimination that is involved in sporadic cuts to meet the lower prices of competitors. The provisions of the Act relating to brokerage, advertising allowances, and services would have to be changed to permit such concessions but to prevent their use to evade the rules governing quantity discounts by relating them to the cost and the value of the services involved. The power to limit quantity discounts, where justified by lower costs, would have to be repealed.

Thus amended, the Robinson-Patman Act could be made entirely consistent with the policy of maintaining competition. As it stands today, it is not.

SUGGESTIONS FOR FURTHER READING

On the exclusion of competitors from supplies and markets, see Corwin D. Edwards, *Maintaining Competition* (New York: McGraw-Hill Book Co., 1949), chap. vi. On exclusive and tying contracts, see John Perry Miller, *Unfair Competition* (Cambridge: Harvard University Press, 1941), chap. x; Andreas G. Papandreou and John T. Wheeler, *Competition and Its Regulation* (New York: Prentice-Hall, Inc., 1954), chap. xx; and Joel B. Dirlam and Alfred E. Kahn, *Fair Competition: the Law and Economics of Antitrust Policy* (Ithaca: Cornell University Press, 1954), chaps. iv and vi.

The economics of price discrimination is discussed in A. R. Oxenfeld, *Industrial Pricing and Market Practices* (New York: Prentice Hall, Inc., 1951), pp. 232–53; in Joel Dean, *Managerial Economics* (New York: Prentice-Hall, Inc., 1951), pp. 503–41; and in Fritz Machlup, *The Political Economy of Monopoly* (Baltimore: Johns Hopkins Press, 1952), pp. 136–63. The law with respect to discrimination is considered in Miller, chaps. vii, viii, and ix, which carries the story up to 1941, briefly in Papandreou and Wheeler, chap. xxi, and recently and fully in Dirlam and Kahn, chaps. iv, vii, and viii. See also M. A. Adelman, "The Consistency of the Robinson-Patman Act," *Stanford Law Review*, Vol. VI (1953), pp. 3–22; *Lectures on Federal Antitrust Laws* (Ann Arbor: University of Michigan Law School, 1953), pp. 109–46, and *Robinson-Patman Act Symposium* (New York: Commerce Clearing House, 1946, 1948).

For current developments in these fields, follow *Business Week* and *United States Law Week.*

Chapter 8

DELIVERED PRICING

The forms of discrimination discussed in the preceding chapter arose, in the main, in cases where buyers fulfilled different functions or made their purchases in different quantities. Another form—geographic price discrimination—arises from the fact that sellers and buyers are often located at different points. In such a case the cost of goods at the buyer's destination includes not only the price of the goods themselves but also the charge that is made for their delivery. And it is this cost that is significant in making sales. As a consequence, a seller who seeks to extend the boundaries of his market or to compete for sales in markets that are nearer other sellers, may himself bear part or all of the charge for freight. In doing so he will realize less on sales made far away than on those made near at home. Accepting different net returns on sales to different destinations, he will discriminate between customers.

Such discrimination may be of small significance where goods are high in value and the cost of their delivery forms a small part of the price the buyer pays. Its importance may be great, however, where goods are so heavy or so bulky in relation to their value that the cost of transportation is a large part of the final price. Even here the consequences of discrimination will not be the same in every case. Where sellers act independently, making deliveries to different markets and accepting different net returns, competition in the markets where they sell may be increased. But where they act in concert, whether by explicit agreement or in accordance with a tacit understanding, discrimination may be incidental to arrangements whereby competition is inhibited. It is only in cases such as this that geographic price discrimination has come into conflict with antitrust.

GEOGRAPHIC PRICE STRUCTURES

Prices may be quoted either at the point where goods originate or at the point where they are delivered. Those quoted on the former basis are usually called "f.o.b. mill" or "f.o.b. shipping point" prices, since the seller, in this case, customarily agrees to deliver goods without charge to the conveyance provided—at his plant or at the nearest dock or railway station—by the buyer or a common carrier, i.e. to place them "free on board." Prices quoted at destinations are called "delivered prices" and include the cost of moving goods to the buyer's place of business or to the dock or station nearest him.

Prices quoted on a delivered basis usually involve discrimination; those quoted f.o.b. usually do not. But this is not invariably the case. Delivered pricing may sometimes be nondiscriminatory, and f.o.b. pricing may sometimes discriminate. The effects of various methods of pricing are revealed, as will be seen, not by the form of a seller's quotations, but by a comparison of the sums he realizes in making different sales.

Pricing Methods of Individual Sellers

An individual seller may independently adopt any one of a variety of geographic pricing practices. His choice will be influenced by the nature of his product, by the cost of transporting it to different markets, and by the character of competition in his trade. The resulting structure of prices will vary from case to case.

1. A seller may charge a uniform f.o.b. mill price. If he does so, buyers at different locations will incur different costs in purchasing his goods, and a buyer at any one location will find that his goods are more or less costly than those of his nearby or remote competitors. But the seller's return on every sale, regardless of the buyer's location, will be the same. He will not discriminate.

Alternatively, a seller may quote delivered prices but compute them by making a uniform charge for goods and adding, in every case, the precise amount he has paid for freight. The structure of his prices will, consequently, be the same as that described above. Though selling on a delivered basis, he will not discriminate. His policy will differ from that of the previous seller in only one respect; he retains title during transit and files with the carrier any claims for possible damages.

These methods of pricing are likely to be used both where goods are so low in value, in relation to their weight, that transportation costs confine their sale to local markets, and where goods are so high in value that transportation costs are not significant. They are also found where sellers are under no pressure to meet the figures at which buyers can obtain goods from nearby competitors. This will be the case where all of the sellers in a trade are located at the same center; where transportation rates are so adjusted that a buyer making purchases from sellers at different locations pays the same freight; where each of several sellers offers a highly differentiated product; and where a single seller possesses a monopoly. F.o.b. pricing has been employed in selling many goods, including textiles, leather, apparel, staple foodstuffs, standard drugs, household furniture, automobiles, and agricultural machinery.

2. A seller may quote the same delivered price at every destination in

the United States. In this case the seller's price will include a charge to cover his average expenditure for freight. But this charge will be lower than the freight he pays on sales made far afield and higher than he pays on those made near at hand. His net return will vary, from sale to sale, with the distance of the buyer from his plant. In this sense he will discriminate.

Or a seller may quote a uniform f.o.b. price but make allowances for transportation, permitting his customers to deduct from their bills the full amount of freight that they have paid. Here, again, prices at different destinations will be the same, but the seller will collect less from those who are remote and more from those who are nearby. Though selling f.o.b., he will discriminate.

Such practices, known as "postage-stamp pricing," are used where goods are high in value and freight is relatively unimportant and particularly where the seller of a branded product that is nationally advertised desires to maintain a uniform resale price. They have been employed in selling such goods as hardware, tires and tubes, typewriters, electrical appliances, branded foodstuffs, drugs, cosmetics, soft drinks, candy bars, and cigarettes.

3. A seller may divide the country into zones, charging the same delivered price at every destination in a zone, but raising this price from zone to zone to cover the average cost of freight. He may pay the actual freight himself or direct the buyer to pay it and deduct it from his bill. In either case, the seller's average net return will be the same in every zone. But he will allow less freight than is paid at the farther boundary of a zone and more than is paid at the nearer one. At every boundary, moreover, he will allow less to buyers on the nearer side than he does to others just across the line. Within each zone and along each boundary, he will discriminate.

Zone pricing is likely to be used where the cost of transporting branded goods is so great as to prevent their sale throughout the country at a uniform delivered price. If freight is not too high, one price may be charged at all points east of the Mississippi or the Rockies and another at all points to the west. Where freight is more significant, however, zones may be greater in number and smaller in size. Zone pricing has been employed in selling such goods as refrigerators, washing machines, electric ranges, glass containers, paper products, paints, and business furniture.

4. A seller may meet the price at which a competitor closer to a market will make deliveries there. To do so, he may quote a delivered price that covers freight from his competitor's mill but pay the higher freight from his own mill. Or he may quote an f.o.b. price, or a delivered price that covers his own freight, and permit his customer to deduct from his bill the amount by which his freight exceeds that charged on shipments made by his competitor. In either case he is said to "absorb" freight. Where this is done, prices at different destinations will vary, but a buyer

at any one of them may obtain goods at the same price from a distant seller as from a closer one. The seller's return, however, will differ from sale to sale, being lower where he absorbs freight and higher where he does not. Insofar as he follows this practice, he will discriminate.

A seller may absorb freight occasionally in order to make particular sales. He may do so temporarily in order to find employment for idle capacity. He may adopt freight absorption as a general policy. The practice is likely to be found in trades where products are standardized and sellers numerous, where investment is heavy and fixed costs high, and where the charge for transportation is a large part of the delivered price. It has been followed, among others, by sellers of lumber, bituminous coal, and gasoline.

Pricing Systems of Whole Industries

Delivered pricing systems may be said to exist where identical methods of delivered pricing are customarily followed in considerable detail by all of the members of an industry. They include single basing point systems, multiple basing point systems, systems involving what is known as the universal equalization of freight, and those establishing uniform price zones. Each of these systems may now be described.

1. Under a single basing point system, though production is carried on by different sellers at different points, the same location is used as the

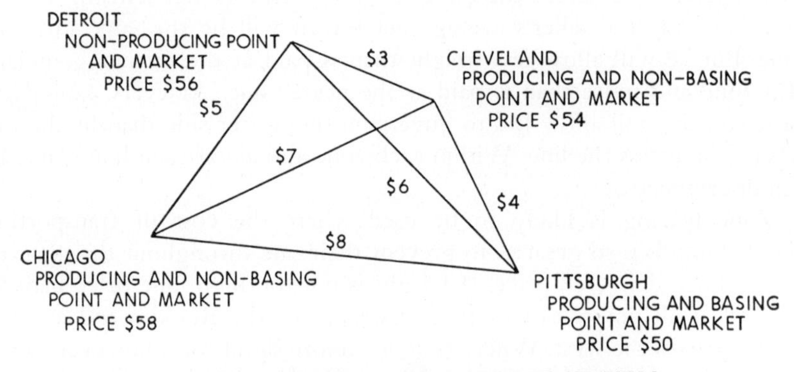

FIG. 1. SINGLE BASING POINT SYSTEM

point of origin by every seller in computing the freight to be added to his base price in determining his delivered price. This system was once known to steel as Pittsburgh-plus, to corn syrup and malt as Chicago-plus, to cast iron soil pipe as Birmingham-plus, and to maple flooring as Cadillac-plus. Where it is used, delivered prices will vary from destination to destination. But if the base prices adopted by all sellers are identical, the delivered prices charged on any sale at any destination by all sellers, however distant, will also be identical. Given a common base price of $50 per ton, a single basing point at Pittsburgh, and the structure of freight rates

TABLE 1

SALES FROM CHICAGO TO PITTSBURGH, CLEVELAND, DETROIT, AND CHICAGO

	Pittsburgh	Cleveland	Detroit	Chicago
Base price	$50	$50	$50	$50
Plus freight from Pittsburgh	0	4	6	8
Delivered price	50	54	56	58
Minus freight from Chicago	8	7	5	0
Mill net realization at Chicago	42	47	51	58
Freight absorption	8	3	..	..
Phantom freight	..	..	1	8

assumed in Figure 1, the mills at Pittsburgh, Cleveland, and Chicago would all charge $50 in Pittsburgh, $54 in Cleveland, $56 in Detroit, and $58 in Chicago.

Under this system, a seller who ships by rail from the basing point will not discriminate. Since he will pay for freight to every destination the exact amount that he has charged, his net return on every sale will be the same. The non-basing point seller, however, will discriminate. He will pay more than he charges for freight in selling to markets closer to the basing point, and less than he charges in selling to markets closer to himself. His net return will vary with the destination of his sales. Consider, in Table 1, the case of the seller located at Chicago. The seller realizes $16 more at Chicago than he does at Pittsburgh. He does so because he pays $8 more freight than he charges at Pittsburgh and charges $8 more than he pays at Chicago. In the first case, he absorbs the difference in freight. In the second, he realizes what is known as "phantom freight." It is the freight absorption and the phantom freight involved, in varying amounts, in sales at different destinations that accounts for the discrimination in the structure of his net returns.

2. Under a multiple basing point system, two or more centers are used as points of origin in computing freight, but there are one or more centers of production that are not so employed. Here, the delivered price at any destination is the lowest one obtained by taking the base price of the product and adding the charge for freight from each of the surrounding basing points. On any sale, the place from which this charge is lowest is known as the governing basing point. As sales are made at different destinations, the governing basing point will shift from place to place. Here again prices differ from destination to destination, but if the base prices used by all sellers are identical their delivered prices at any destination will be the same. If we modify our previous illustration by assuming that a second basing point is established at Chicago and a base price of $50 fixed there, the resulting structure of prices would be that shown in Figure 2. In this case, Pittsburgh is the governing basing point for Cleveland, and Chicago for Detroit.

Here, as under the previous system, the non-basing point seller discriminates by collecting phantom freight when he sells in his own vicinity and absorbing freight when he sells in the vicinity of a basing point. But under this system there is no seller who does not discriminate. When he sells in the territory where his basing point governs, the basing point seller will pay the same amount he has charged for freight. But whenever he

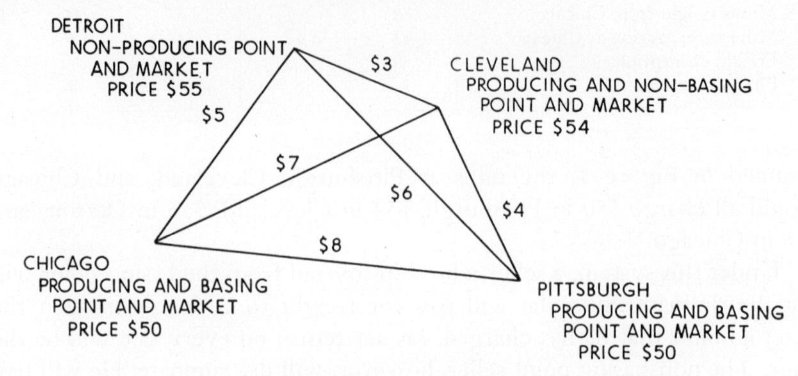

FIG. 2. MULTIPLE BASING POINT SYSTEM

sells where another point governs, he will absorb freight. Under a multiple basing point system, there is no seller, such as the one at Pittsburgh under Pittsburgh-plus, whose net return on every sale will be the same. Variations are shown in Table 2. Here Cleveland discriminates by absorbing

TABLE 2

MILL NET REALIZATIONS, FREIGHT ABSORPTION (−) AND PHANTOM FREIGHT (+) EXPERIENCED BY MILLS AT PITTSBURGH, CHICAGO, AND CLEVELAND

	Pittsburgh	Chicago	Cleveland
In making sales at:			
Pittsburgh.	$50	$42 (−8)	$46 (−4)
Chicago	42 (−8)	50	43 (−7)
Cleveland	50	47 (−3)	54 (+4)
Detroit	49 (−1)	50	52 (+2)

freight and collecting phantom freight, Pittsburgh and Chicago discriminate only by absorbing freight. Cleveland realizes $11 more when it sells at home than when it sells in Chicago, but the extremes of discrimination have been somewhat reduced by establishing Chicago as a second basing point.

Multiple basing point systems have been used in selling steel, cement, lead, pulp, lumber, sugar, and other heavy goods. Under the system that is used in pricing sugar, seaboard cities where cane sugar is imported and refined are used as basing points, and prices at inland cities are computed by adding freight from these points. Though refineries producing sugar from beets are located at a score of centers in the mid-continent, none of them is used as a point of origin in the calculation of a price.

3. The practice known as systematic freight equalization involves adherence to a plenary basing point system, in which every producing point is a basing point. Under such a system, every seller determines his delivered price at any destination by adding the base price and the freight rate

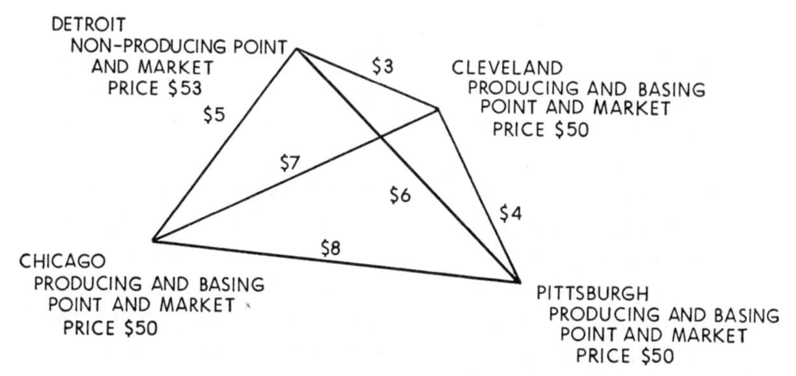

FIG. 3. PLENARY BASING POINT SYSTEM

on shipments from each of the nearby sellers and taking the lowest total as his own. Properly speaking, the practice is one of price equalization, since the charge for the goods themselves as well as that for their delivery is equalized. In this case, as in the previous ones, prices at different destinations will differ, but those charged by all firms selling at any one destination will be the same. The character of this system may be shown by further modifying our illustration to establish Cleveland as a basing point, as well as Pittsburgh and Chicago. If a base price of $50 is adopted at each of these points, the structure of delivered prices will be that shown in Figure 3.

Plenary basing point systems have been used in the sale of salt, binder twine, milk cans, bottle caps, lime, gypsum plaster, window glass, and other building materials, and many heavy chemicals. Under such a system, the returns received by every seller will differ with the destinations of his sales. Since there are no non-basing points, however, no seller will collect

TABLE 3

MILL NET REALIZATIONS AND FREIGHT ABSORPTION EXPERIENCED BY MILLS AT PITTSBURGH, CHICAGO, AND CLEVELAND

	Pittsburgh	Chicago	Cleveland
In making sales at:			
Pittsburgh	$50	$42 (−8)	$46 (−4)
Chicago	42 (−8)	50	43 (−7)
Cleveland	46 (−4)	43 (−7)	50
Detroit	47 (−3)	48 (−2)	50

phantom freight by always charging for delivery from other locations than his own. A seller will discriminate only by absorbing freight, in varying amounts, as he sells in markets that are closer to his various competitors. This may be shown by recurring to our illustrative case (Table 3). One other fact should be noted: the difference between the highest and the lowest realization, which was $16 in the first case and $11 in the second, is now $8. By eliminating the non-basing point, the extent of discrimination is further reduced.

4. A zone pricing system is a variant of the systems that are built on basing points. Under such a system, where common zones are recognized by all the sellers in a trade, delivered prices for each zone are computed by taking a base price and adding to it the average charge for freight from a basing point to each of the destinations within its boundaries. As a result, prices are uniform throughout each zone but differ from zone to zone, and the prices charged by every seller at any destination are the same. Here, again, the non-basing point seller discriminates by realizing more when he sells at home and less when he sells near a basing point. But here, as in the case of zone pricing described above, every seller, including those at basing points, also discriminates among the destinations in each zone and between those lying along its boundaries. Zone pricing systems have been used in the sale of linseed oil, fertilizers, corn products, clay sewer pipe, power cable, and electrical machinery.

Implementing Delivered Pricing Systems

In those industries where delivered prices have regularly been matched by all sellers, the practice has usually been facilitated by some sort of an agreement or understanding with respect to many, if not all, of the factors that influence the prices that are charged. The possibility that variations in price may result from differences—whether deliberate or inadvertent—in the methods of selling and pricing employed by different members of the industry is thus removed.

The prices quoted to any buyer by different sellers would differ if any of them failed to sell on a delivered basis or to make an identical charge for delivery. This would be the case, for instance, if a seller at a non-basing point were to give buyers the option of taking title at his plant and themselves providing for transportation, since nearby buyers would thus be enabled to obtain goods more cheaply from him than from his more distant competitors. It would be the case if a mill at one basing point were to permit a buyer to take title at some location where another point governed the delivered price and to divert a shipment to a destination at which its own price was governing, since the buyer might thus get goods for less money from the mill permitting such diversion than from those refusing to do so. It would also be the case if sellers were to employ different methods of computing freight, using different basing points, different price zones, different types of carriers, or rate books issued by different railroads. The seller who figured freight from a nearer basing point, or pushed zone boundaries outward, would quote a lower delivered price. The seller who charged for delivery by highway or waterway would quote a lower price than the one who charged for delivery by rail. And since the rate structures of different railways differ in detail, a seller who used the rate book issued by one road might charge less than one who used that issued by another.

Under delivered pricing systems, therefore, it has been the usual practice to quote prices only at destinations, refusing to give title at the points where goods are produced, or charging for freight even where buyers are permitted to haul them away in their own trucks. It has been usual for sellers to insist on delivery to final destinations, refusing to make allowances for diversion in transit. It has also been usual for sellers to recognize the same centers as basing points and to adopt the same zone boundaries, whether by formal agreement or by simple acquiescence in the leadership of larger firms. Sellers have customarily calculated their charges for delivery from common basing points on the assumption that goods will move exclusively by rail, collecting phantom freight where they are actually transported by highway or by waterway. In doing so, moreover, they have employed common freight books prepared by their trade associations in place of the schedules issued by the railroads themselves. And they have continued to use these books, after freight rates have been altered, until their associations have authorized a change. It is by methods such as these that the identity of the transportation charge included in each delivered price has been assured.

Prices could vary, of course, though charges made for delivering goods were identical, if those made for the goods themselves were not. Such variations would occur if different sellers were to use different base prices in calculating a delivered price. They would also occur if sellers were to make different adjustments for departures from the standard sizes and qualities for which base prices are announced, or if they were to offer different discounts, allowances, guarantees, or supplementary services. In basing point industries, however, the latter possibility has usually been removed by standardizing every element of a sale that might permit an indirect reduction of a price. In steel, for instance, there was open agreement on the "extras" that are added to the prices of standard products and the "deductions" that are subtracted from them in arriving at the prices of nonstandard goods. In cement, there was agreement on specifications, discount structures, and allowances for returned bags. It is only with respect to the base price itself that existence of agreement has always been denied. But this price, too, has usually been fixed through consultation or through leadership. Indeed, if this were not the case, there would be little point in seeking to control every other factor affecting the calculation of a delivered price. For it is in their contribution to the identity of prices charged at any destination that delivered pricing systems find their real significance.

THE NATURE AND ORIGIN OF BASING POINT SYSTEMS

Ever since World War I, the essential character of basing point pricing systems has been a subject of continued controversy. The Federal Trade Commission has attacked these systems, finding them to be in violation of the antitrust laws. Basing point industries, on the other hand, have defended them, presenting arguments designed to show that they are vigorously competitive. At the same time, economists have differed as to the causation of such systems, one school holding that they are highly artificial, resulting from deliberate collusion among sellers, another contending that they are quite natural, arising from the economic characteristics of the industries where they are found. We turn now to some of the pros and cons of these debates.

Competitive or Monopolistic?

The most complete statement of industry's case for basing point pricing is contained in a volume prepared by the United States Steel Corporation for presentation to the Temporary National Economic Committee in 1940.[1] The Corporation's argument, in major outline, runs somewhat as follows: (1) The basing point system should not be judged by the standard of perfect competition, since " 'perfect competition' is an abstraction, and exists nowhere,"[2] (2) When the steel industry has adhered to this system, however, it has been perfectly competitive. This is shown by two facts: (*a*) The prices quoted by different sellers have revealed the identity "which would result from 'perfect competition' in a single market at any one time."[3] (*b*) Each buyer has been enabled to deal with many sellers; under f.o.b. pricing, he would have been limited to one or a few, a situation which "certainly does not correspond to the assumptions of . . . 'perfect competition.' "[4] (3) The competitive character of the system has been shown, however, not by the industry's adherence to it, but by its departure from it: "It is not a fact that identical delivered prices are universally charged by all producers, particularly in times of low demand. Price cutting is frequent, and since it is not announced it is not immediately met. If such price cutting continues, it becomes known and other producers, if they wish to be competitive . . . must meet the lower prices."[5] (4) The industry's behavior, though imperfectly competitive,

[1] United States Steel Corp., *T.N.E.C. Papers.* Vol. III, *The Basing Point Method,* published by the Corporation, 1940.

[2] *Ibid.,* p. 21.

[3] *Ibid.,* p. 36.

[4] *Ibid.,* p. 85.

[5] *Ibid.,* p. 34.

has been "the natural result of basic economic conditions. . . ."[6] The location of production facilities, in particular, "has been due to the fundamental economic traits of the steel industry . . . rather than to any pricing system."[7] (5) Abandonment of the system, however, "would necessarily result . . . in widespread dislocation. . . ."[8]

Whatever the validity of these arguments, it will be noted that they are wanting in consistency. If perfect competition is nonexistent, it cannot be claimed that the basing point system is perfectly competitive. If competition is to be proved by departures from the system, it is not to be shown by adherence to it. And if the system had not influenced industrial location, its abandonment would not be likely to result in widespread dislocation. Certain of these arguments, however, must be examined in greater detail. Those designed to prove that the system is competitive will be discussed in the present section. The influence of the system on industrial location will be considered later on.

Let us take first the argument that identity of the delivered prices charged by different sellers proves the basing point system to be competitive. It is true that such prices have usually been identical. During the thirties, when the purchasing agent for the Fort Peck Dam opened 10 sealed bids for reinforcing bars, each of them was for $253,633.80.[9] When the Navy Department opened 59 bids for steel pipe, each of them was for $6,001.83.[10] And when the Army Engineers opened 11 bids for cement at Tucumcari, New Mexico, each of them was for $3.286854 a barrel, identity being carried to the sixth decimal place.[11] Again in 1947, when the Illinois Department of Highways asked for bids on cement to be delivered in each of the 102 counties in the state, those submitted by 8 companies were identical for each of the 102 deliveries.[12] Such identities cannot be attributed to mere chance. The mathematical probability of accidentally arriving at those reported in Illinois has been computed as 1 in 8 followed by 214 zeros, a possibility that is even more remote than the random selection of a single electron from the entire universe.[13] Identical prices may be a product of competition. They are more likely to reveal the presence of monopoly.

Under active competition, identity is a goal toward which prices are always moving but at which they seldom arrive and never stay. When one seller charges more than another, buyers shift their purchases. When a

[6] *Ibid.*, Foreword and pp. 22–31.

[7] *Ibid.*, p. 49.

[8] *Ibid.*, p. 94.

[9] *New York Times*, February 20, 1939.

[10] *Annual Report of the Attorney General*, 1937, pp. 37–38.

[11] *Aetna Portland Cement Co.* v. *FTC*, 157 F. 2d 533 (1946), esp. p. 576.

[12] *Congressional Record*, May 31, 1950, p. 7961.

[13] *Ibid.*, computation by Professor C. O. Oakley of Haverford College as reported by Senator Paul H. Douglas.

seller discriminates, charging one buyer more than another, the buyer so adjusts his operations as to obtain the lower price. Wherever prices differ, traders buy in the markets where goods are cheap and sell in those where they are dear. As a result of these forces, prices tend toward identity. But any seller can initiate a change. And constant change prevents identity from being attained or, if attained, from being preserved. Under a basing point system, on the other hand, identity of prices is an actuality. Buyers find no advantage in shifting their purchases. They cannot undermine discrimination by qualifying for a lower price. Traders cannot profit by buying in the cheaper markets and selling in the dearer ones. It is not through these forces that identity is achieved. Under such a system, moreover, most sellers take no initiative with respect to price. Changes, whether upward or downward, are usually announced by only one concern. As a result, identity of prices may persist for months and years at a time. Identical prices, when so attained and so preserved, give evidence not of competition but of agreement in restraint of trade.

So, too, with the argument that a basing point system brings many sellers within the reach of every buyer. This is indeed the case. But this does not prove that such a system fosters active competition. In fact, it proves the opposite. If firms selling heavy goods were really to compete, each one, enjoying lower transportation costs to points within its own vicinity, would undersell its distant rivals at these points. Those shipping by water would undersell those shipping by rail. Under basing point pricing, however, sellers forego the competitive advantage inherent in more favorable locations. Those who are not at basing points, though close to buyers in their own localities, make no attempt to underbid those who are far away. Those who are located on waterways include in their prices a charge for all-rail freight. Sellers at every center of production adhere to prices that enable outsiders to enter markets that would otherwise belong to them alone. This behavior, however, is said by the Corporation to be competitive: ". . . mills at a considerable distance from a basing point . . . behave competitively and naturally when they charge their customers a price which realizes that advantage. . . . They can scarcely be expected to offer lower prices. . . ."[14] "If the mill is the only one which can reach the destination by water, there is no competitive reason why it should give the benefit of the lower transportation cost to the customer. In fact, if it did so, it would be following some non-competitive principle."[15] Competition, in this view, consists merely in meeting another's price, never in taking business away from him by undercutting it. But such forbearance would appear to most observers to betoken a reluctance to compete. If any buyer, under a basing point system, can obtain deliveries from every seller, it is because the absence

[14] U.S. Steel Corp., *op. cit.*, p. 59.

[15] *Ibid.*, p. 66.

of competition, under such a system, has resulted in a level of prices so high that everybody can afford to sell everywhere.

The argument just considered carries as its corollary the contention that f.o.b. pricing would result in the creation of a series of regional monopolies. According to the Corporation, ". . . freight rates would set up a wall between different producers and their markets, greatly limiting the area over which competition now takes place . . . buyers would be reduced to purchasing from the nearest mill . . . there would be very little or no choice . . . any single producer located at a distance from all other mills would have a virtual monopoly. . . . An isolated producer . . . would be able to charge high prices to consumers in his own area."[16] It is true, of course, that the consumer, under f.o.b. pricing, is likely to buy at the nearest mill. He does so to save freight. It is not true that he is prevented from buying from other mills. He may do so if he is willing to pay more freight. He certainly is not at the mercy of a monopolist. If a local mill makes all the sales made in its own vicinity, it is because its price, plus freight, is lower than the price, plus freight, of its nearest competitor. A monopolist exploits his position by charging more. The local mill retains its position only so long as it charges less. This is successful competition, not monopoly.

It remains to consider the argument that the basing point system, in steel, is proved to have been competitive, not because the industry always adhered to it, but because it frequently departed from it. It is true that such departures have occurred. In times of slack demand, particularly, secret concessions were generally made. In 1939, for instance, when the industry was operating at 51 per cent of its capacity, 85 per cent of the sales of hot rolled sheets were made below the quoted price. In such times, it should be noted, it is the larger buyer who obtains the lower price. In good times, on the other hand, adherence to the system has been virtually complete. In 1942, when operations were at 98 per cent of capacity, only 6 per cent of the sales of sheets were made below the quoted price.[17] But these facts, though interesting, are irrelevant. For even if violations of the system were shown to be habitual, they would not prove the system itself to be competitive.

Leaders of basing point industries have sometimes been more candid than the foregoing discussion would suggest. Thus, one trustee of the Cement Institute wrote to another in 1934:

> Do you think any of the arguments for the basing-point system which we have thus far advanced will arouse anything but derision in and out of government? I have read them all recently. Some of them are very clever and ingenious. They amount to this, however: that we price that way in order to

[16] *Ibid.*, pp. 79, 84, 86.

[17] Study by the Bureau of Labor Statistics, reported in *Iron Age*, April 25, 1946, pp. 118 *ff*.

discourage monopolistic practices and to preserve free competition, etc. This is sheer bunk and hypocrisy. The truth is . . . that ours is an industry above all others that cannot stand free competition, that must systematically restrain competition or be ruined.[18]

And President Fairless, of U.S. Steel, was equally frank when he testified before the T.N.E.C.: "We will concede . . . that if base prices as announced were followed in every transaction, and that the nearest basing point to the consumer governed, and that the rail freight was added from that point, and the delivered price arrived at in that manner, there wouldn't be any competition in the steel industry. It would be a one-price industry, pure and simple."[19]

Natural or Artificial?

With respect to the origin of basing point systems, there have been two opposing schools of thought. The first school, basing its analysis on the logic of competitive pricing, has held such systems to be an outgrowth of collusion. In a competitive market, according to this analysis, the rivalry of buyers and of sellers will tend to eliminate discrimination, since no buyer will continue to pay more than another and no seller will continue to accept less from one buyer than from another. Under basing point systems, however, discrimination persists, since buyers who are near at hand continue to pay more—in prices minus freight—than those who are far away, and sellers continue to accept less on distant sales than they could realize by making sales at home. It is clear, from this behavior, that such systems are not a product of competition. They must have originated, therefore, in conspiracy.[20]

The second school, applying the theory of oligopoly, has held that basing point pricing could evolve spontaneously, each seller who adopts it acting independently. According to this view, fewness of sellers always inhibits aggressive competition with respect to price, since any cut may instantly be matched, and the cutter's share in an industry's sales may not increase. An oligopolist, therefore, is unlikely to take initiative in reducing prices unless he feels certain that his industry's total sales will be enhanced. For if they are not, competition will be unprofitable and, if carried too far, may well prove to be ruinous. In the particular circumstances encountered in basing point industries, moreover, a seller who doubts his

[18] *Aetna Portland Cement Co.* v. *FTC*, 157 F. 2d 533 (1946), Respondent's Brief, p. 127.

[19] *Hearings before the T.N.E.C.*, Part 27, p. 14, 172, January 26, 1940.

[20] See F. A. Fetter, *The Masquerade of Monopoly* (New York: Harcourt, Brace & Co., 1931), "The New Plea for Basing Point Monopoly," *Journal of Political Economy*, Vol. XLV (1937), p. 577, "Exit Basing Point Pricing," *American Economic Review*, Vol. XXXVIII (1948), p. 815; Vernon A. Mund, *Open Markets* (New York: Harper & Bro., 1948), "The Freight Allowed Method of Price Quotation," *Quarterly Journal of Economics*, Vol. LIV (1940), p. 232, "Monopolistic Competition and Public Price Policy," *American Economic Review*, Vol. XXXII (1942), p. 727; Fritz Machlup, *The Basing Point System* (Philadelphia: Blakiston Co., 1949).

ability to make more sales by cutting prices will find that he can do so by absorbing freight. And this will offer him a happier alternative. A price cut would apply to every sale he made. As a result, if sales did not expand, his total revenues would fall. Freight absorption, on the other hand, reduces his return on but a fraction of his sales. And if his mill net realization on each such sale exceeds his marginal cost, it will enlarge his total revenues. Discrimination, therefore, comes about quite naturally. And adherence by sellers to a delivered pricing formula manifests nothing more than a rational adaptation to the facts of their environment.[21]

This analysis, it must be admitted, finds considerable support in the conditions found in industries where systems of basing point pricing have been employed. Take the case of steel, for instance: (1) The industry's technology requires production on a scale so great that capital costs obstruct new entry, giving the market to a few large firms. (2) Demand fluctuates with the cycle, leaving idle capacity when business activity declines. (3) Heavy investment carries high fixed costs, tempting each producer to put this capacity to work by reducing his price. (4) The industry's product is highly standardized and is bought in such quantities that a small difference in price may lead to a substantial shift in sales. In these circumstances, a lower price is almost certain to be met by one's competitors. Such a price, therefore, will not be advantageous unless it increases sales throughout the industry. (5) The demand for steel, however, is said to be inelastic. For one thing, the possibilities of substituting steel for other materials or other materials for steel are limited. For another, the demand for steel is derived, in the main, from the demand for goods in which steel is used. A reduction in its price may not be reflected in the prices of these goods. Or if it is, the cost of steel may be so small a part of their prices that a reduction will not affect the volume of their sales. In any case, the demand for these goods, too, is said to be low in elasticity. Machinery and equipment made of steel may find no market in depressions, however low their price. Many consumers' goods made of steel are luxuries and thus dispensable. Most of these goods are durable and the purchase of replacements may therefore be postponed. Sales may thus be unresponsive to a change in price. (6) But price cutting, though futile, might conceivably be carried to lengths that would prove to be disastrous. To make a particular sale, a seller would find it worth his while to quote any price that would more than cover his marginal costs. But such a price would fall far short of his average total costs. And if extended

[21] See J. M. Clark, "Basing Point Methods of Price Quoting," *Canadian Journal of Economics and Political Science*, Vol. IV (1938), p. 477, "Imperfect Competition Theory and Basing Point Problems," *American Economic Review*, Vol. XXXIII (1943), p. 283, "The Law and Economics of Basing Points," *American Economic Review*, Vol. XXXIX (1949), p. 430; C. R. Daugherty, M. G. de Chazeau, and S. S. Stratton, *The Economics of the Iron and Steel Industry* (New York: McGraw-Hill Book Co., 1937), Vol. I, chap. xii; Vol. II, chap. xxii; Arthur Smithies, "Aspects of the Basing Point Problem," *American Economic Review*, Vol. XXXII (1942), p. 705.

for any length of time to a major part of his output, it might well drive him into bankruptcy.

These conditions explain why firms producing steel are unlikely to engage in vigorous competition with respect to price. They do not explain why avoidance of competition took the form of quoting prices for delivery from a common basing point. This development may be attributed, in part, to the fact that changes in the geographic pattern of demand for steel may be rapid, while changes in the pattern of production must be slow. The location of construction projects, in particular, constantly shifts from place to place. Steel mills, on the contrary, are rooted to the ground. Production can move to growing markets only as new facilities are built. In the meantime, if all sales were made f.o.b. mill, one section of the country would be short of steel while another had a surplus of capacity. The basing point system solved this problem by establishing a structure of prices that enabled sellers tied to fixed locations to adjust their shipments to the movement of demand. The emergence of similar systems in other industries selling heavy building materials suggests that basing point systems usually originated in situations where such adjustments were required.[22]

It does not follow, however, that such systems are products of nature rather than works of art. In no case have they come alive full-blown, like Venus rising from the waves. There have been meetings held, agreements entered into, organizations formed, and rules laid down. The evidence of collusion is explicit and voluminous. The proceedings before the Federal Trade Commission in the case of the cement industry ran to 49,000 pages of testimony and 50,000 pages of exhibits.[23] The documentation with respect to steel is equally detailed, the system in this industry being identified, in its early years, with formal pooling arrangements and with a series of dinners, held between 1906 and 1911, at which Judge E. H. Gary, then president of U.S. Steel, presided over discussions of pricing policy. Nor has the subsequent quotation of identical prices been purely spontaneous, as the elaborate paraphernalia of standard prices and terms of sale, delivery to destination, all-rail freights, and common freight rate books, described above, will testify. Adherence to delivered pricing systems has been enforced, moreover, by the imposition of penalties. In the cement industry, any producer who cut his price might be punished by having his competitors quote a still lower price, using his plant as a basing point. Since he would make all of his sales from this point and each of them would make but few, they could thus inflict a serious loss on him at small cost to themselves. According to the Supreme Court, "In one instance, where a producer had made a low public bid, a punitive base point price

[22] See George J. Stigler, "A Theory of Delivered Price Systems," *American Economic Review*, Vol. XXXIX (1949), p. 1144.

[23] For a summary of this evidence, see George W. Stocking and Myron W. Watkins, *Monopoly and Free Enterprise* (New York: Twentieth Century Fund, 1951), pp. 193–216.

was put on its plant and cement was reduced 10¢ per barrel; further reductions quickly followed until the base price . . . dropped to 75¢ per barrel, scarcely one-half of its former base price of $1.45. Within six weeks . . . capitulation occurred and the recalcitrant joined a portland cement association. Cement in that locality then bounced back to $1.15, later to $1.35, and finally to $1.75."[24] In the steel industry, too, said the Federal Trade Commission in 1941, "the potential punishment for any serious attempt to violate the basing point system is price raiding that soon brings the rebels to terms."[25] If basing point pricing were a spontaneous outgrowth of natural causes, as some economists have argued, it would scarcely have been necessary to go to such lengths to insure that its requirements were observed. It is true, of course, that the conditions found in basing point industries do not make for active competition. But it does not follow that each member of such an industry will independently evolve the same sophisticated pricing formula. The theory of oligopoly shows that oligopolists are unlikely to compete. It does not prove that they are unlikely to conspire.

EFFECTS OF BASING POINT PRICING

Two of the consequences of basing point pricing have been described in defining the practice itself: (1) every seller quotes the same price at any destination, and (2) each seller (save those at a single basing point) discriminates by accepting different returns on sales to different destinations. Each of these consequences is the necessary complement of the other. Both of them are inherent in the very nature of the systems that have been employed. There are other effects of these systems, however, that remain to be explored. How have they influenced (1) the provision and the utilization of productive capacity, (2) the location of industrial facilities, (3) the organization of industry, and (4) the level of costs and prices? It is to these questions that we now turn.

The Question of Idle Capacity

It has frequently been charged, by critics of basing point pricing, that industries pursuing this practice have forced consumers of their products to bear the cost of carrying a considerable volume of surplus capacity. It has been pointed out, for instance, that facilities standing idle in cement varied from 15 per cent of capacity in 1924 to 77 per cent in 1933, and in steel from 80 per cent in 1932 to 35 per cent in 1939, and that such industries have been able to break even when operating at a minor fraction of capacity. This situation might conceivably be attributed to either one or both of two causes: (1) to the fact that these industries had built more capacity than potential demands would justify, and (2) to the fact that

[24] *FTC* v. Cement Institute, 333 U.S. 683 (1948) 710.

[25] T.N.E.C. Monograph No. 42, *The Basing Point System*, p. 7.

they had failed to put capacity to work fulfilling such demands. The first of these points relates to investment policy, the second to pricing policy.

With respect to investment, two questions may be raised. First, has new construction in basing point industries kept pace with the growth of demand, has it run ahead, or has it lagged behind? Second, how has the volume of such construction been affected by delivered pricing practices? On neither question is there a consensus to be found. The amplitude of facilities is necessarily a matter of judgment. Provision for the future is an issue, too, in which hindsight enjoys notorious advantages. Producers of steel, denounced during the depression for having built too much capacity, found themselves denounced with equal vigor during and after the war, for having failed to build enough. The influence of basing point pricing on capacity is equally obscure. Insofar as the practice checked consumption by raising prices, growth was retarded. But insofar as it promised higher profits, growth was encouraged. To the extent that basing point systems promoted concentration of ownership, they also furthered concentration of investment decisions. But this development may have led either to a cautious avoidance of overexpansion or to a program of expansion designed to forestall the emergence of new competitors. The net effect of these conflicting forces is unknown.

An answer to the problem of pricing policy is also hard to find. It is clear that demand for products such as cement and steel will fluctuate with the business cycle. It is clear, too, that facilities for the manufacture of such products cannot be expanded and contracted with accordion-like simplicity. If these facilities are adequate to meet the needs of a boom, some of them are likely to stand idle during a slump. In this situation, how is the volume of unused capacity to be minimized? Should prices be raised in prosperity and reduced in depression? Or should they be kept close to the same level in good times and bad? Insofar as demand is elastic, flexible prices would tend to reduce the capacity required during booms by checking purchases and to put more capacity to work during slumps by encouraging them. But insofar as demand is inelastic, they would not. Flexibility might even induce speculative buying on the rise and speculative withholding of purchases on the fall, thus carrying production higher and lower than it otherwise would go. Stability of prices, on the other hand, does nothing to check demand in booms or to stimulate demand in slumps. On the contrary, it may reduce stability of output and make for greater fluctuations in the volume of industrial activity. But it may also serve to lessen speculation by removing the expectation that prices are about to rise or fall. Basing point industries, like other oligopolists, have usually chosen stable prices. Perhaps this choice has been wrong. But it cannot be shown conclusively that a greater utilization of capacity would have been achieved if they had chosen flexibility.

Basing point pricing may have operated to make capacity larger and utilization smaller than they would otherwise have been. But since neither of these results can be demonstrated, the charge that the practice created a burdensome surplus of capacity must be recorded as unproved.

The Location of Industry

The location of productive facilities is influenced by the comparative costs involved in reaching markets and in assembling raw materials. It may also be affected by the pricing system that an industry employs. In the case of cement, markets are most important, since limestone is widely scattered and abundant in supply. The pricing system, moreover, cannot affect the location of markets, since this is determined by the situation of construction projects where the product finds its major use. In the case of steel, materials have exercised a stronger pull, since iron ore and coking coal are concentrated geographically and the costs of transporting them are high. Location of the markets, on the other hand, depends in part on the location of the mills. Where steel is used in construction, to be sure, its market moves about from place to place. But steel is also used in making fabricated goods. And fabricators, in selecting their locations, compare the freight involved in making shipments with that included in the price of steel. Where the former is higher, they settle near their markets. Where the latter is higher, they settle near the mills. They may be attracted to any mill, whatever its location, if steel is sold f.o.b. But where fabricators have crowded around the mills in one city and avoided those in another, it is clear that a basing point system has been employed.

Under such a system, a fabricator who settled near a mill at a non-basing point would have to pay for steel a price that covered phantom freight. His rivals at a basing point, however, would get their steel at the base price free of freight. He could not afford to absorb freight to compete near them. But they could afford to do so to compete near him. As a result, fabricators would settle only at a basing point. By doing so, they would enlarge the market at such a center, attracting new mills and leading mills already built there to expand. The location of mills and of fabricators, interacting, would both contribute to the same result.

Basing point pricing influences the location of the mills themselves in other ways. The system makes it unnecessary for them to settle near the market, since it eliminates competition in the delivered price. It attracts them to non-basing points, however, by holding out the prospect of collecting phantom freight. The major producers may find it profitable to build at these locations. But independent firms may be deterred from doing so by fear that the majors would shortly turn them into basing points. On balance, the system is likely to make for geographic concentration of capacity. Under a single basing point system, in particular, mills tend to settle at the basing point, since this is the one point in the country from which they can ship in every direction without absorbing freight. An artificial inducement to settlement at Pittsburgh was thus added to the natural advantages of that location by the institution of Pittsburgh-plus.

Basing point pricing serves to retard adjustment of industrial location to the steady migration of demand. It keeps mills at work in older centers by enabling them to reach the newer markets, and delays construction of capacity in regions where demand has grown. In this respect, of course, it is not without advantages, since it may be cheaper to produce and ship from existing plants that would otherwise be idle than to build new plants to do the job. But the system does more than this. By giving wider markets to firms located at a basing point, it induces further expansion there. And by keeping prices higher in areas around non-basing points, it puts a brake on their industrial development. The growth of the South and the West was long retarded in this way by Pittsburgh-plus. The expansion of cities located on waterways has likewise been hampered by the practice of charging all-rail freight. The economic fortunes of whole regions may thus have been affected by industrial pricing policies.

The Structure of Industry

The influence of basing point systems on the number of firms and the extent of concentration in industries that have used them is a matter of dispute. On the one hand, it is said that such systems have operated to discourage the entry of new firms and the growth of smaller ones, particularly in outlying markets, by making it clear that any price they might announce, in developing these markets, would be met—automatically and immediately—by every other seller in the industry. On the other hand, it is noted that basing point pricing has usually been incidental to price leadership and that, typically, where a price leader has held an umbrella over a market, other firms have entered and expanded and the leader's share of the market has declined. This is what happened, under single and multiple basing point systems, in the case of steel. United States Steel accounted for two thirds of the ingots produced in 1901 and for only one third of those produced in 1938. It appears, therefore, that such systems, while prejudicial to entry and growth in outlying regions, are consistent with increasing numbers and declining concentration in an industry as a whole. It may be questioned, however, whether the community stands to gain from these developments so long as they are not reflected in competition with respect to price.

The Level of Costs and Prices

Basing point systems may influence the level of prices by affecting the costs of production or distribution or the margin of profit. Their influence on the costs of production, however, is not clear. By permitting mills to sell in wider markets, such systems may have enabled them to attain a larger scale of operations and thus a lower unit cost. But under a single basing point system this advantage is confined, in the main, to mills located at the basing point. And where multiple basing points are used, the advantage is offset by the fact that a seller not only gains business when he ships toward others, but also loses it when others ship toward him. The reduction of costs may be retarded, under either of these systems, by the absence of competitive pressures and penalties. It is even possible that inefficiency may be sheltered and improvements in efficiency impeded by maintaining basing points at locations where costs are high and refusing to establish them at locations where costs are low.

While the influence of basing point pricing on the costs of production is open to question, its influence on the costs of distribution is beyond dispute. By eliminating competition in price, it increases expenditures on salesmanship. By enabling sellers to ship to distant markets, and by making it possible for buyers—without incurring greater costs—to make their purchases from distant firms, it increases expenditures on freight. Transportation is used where it is not needed. Goods are hauled into cities where they could have been produced. Cross-hauling is encouraged, the same goods moving in opposite directions over the same route at the same time. More costly methods of transport are used where cheaper methods are available. Goods that could move by water are moved instead by rail. All of this is wasteful, and all of it makes for higher costs.

These systems also make for higher margins of profit by preventing competition in price. Indirect price cutting is discouraged by standardization, direct price cutting by the practice of always meeting the lowest delivered price. Each seller is deterred from initiating a cut at his own base by the knowledge that such action would be futile, since his share of the market could not thereby be increased. No seller is deterred, however, from raising the price at his base, knowing that his share of the market will not suffer, since every other seller will do the same. The higher costs occasioned by these systems are thus accompanied by higher margins and the resulting level of prices is therefore higher than it otherwise would be.

ALTERNATIVES TO BASING POINT SYSTEMS

In passing judgment on single or multiple basing point systems, it would be well to consider them in the light of their alternatives. The major possibilities are three. The first is to abolish phantom freight by making every producing point a basing point and requiring freight to be computed by the mode of transport used, or by the cheapest of those available, while still permitting sellers systematically to equalize freight—and prices—at destinations, and thus to discriminate among their customers. The second is completely to outlaw geographic price discrimination, forbidding freight absorption as well as phantom freight by requiring that all sales be made f.o.b. mill. The third is to adopt an intermediate position, requiring that buyers be given the option of taking delivery at the mill, but permitting a seller to absorb freight, whenever he wishes, to make a distant sale. Each of these alternatives will be examined in its turn.

Systematic Freight Equalization

As compared with a single or multiple basing point system, one in which every producing point is made a basing point possesses certain possible advantages. If the base price at each of the former non-basing points were to be raised to offset the reduction in freight, the structure of prices would be the same as it had been before. But if this is not done, the elimination of non-basing points will remove an artificial handicap to the development of these areas and facilitate the gradual adjustment of industrial location to the migration of demand. And if the all-rail freight requirement is abolished, it will also do away with an impediment to the growth of cities located on waterways. Since freight must be absorbed in making sales near any distant mill, such sales will be less frequent and the wastes involved in needless transportation will thereby be reduced. The necessity of freight absorption will also limit the punitive invasion of markets and thus afford to independent firms a better opportunity to enter and survive.

The effect of such a system on the margin of profit and the level of prices, however, is less clear. The removal of traditional barriers to independent action may encourage producers to exercise initiative in pricing. And the abandonment of artificial aids to uniformity, such as common freight rate books, should also make for differences. But other sellers may still wait for a leader to announce any changes in base prices. And each of them may adopt as his own, at any destination, the lowest price that is quoted there. As a result, quotations will continue to be identical. And the level of prices may be as high and as rigid as before. Phantom freight will be eliminated. But systematic discrimination will still be practiced through variations in the amount of freight absorbed.

Compulsory F.O.B. Mill Pricing

The remedy for the evils of basing point pricing advocated by its severest critics is the requirement that each seller make all of his sales at a uniform price at the door of his mill, leaving to the buyer the arrangements for delivery. This requirement would do away with geographic price discrimination, giving the same return on every sale. It would confine each mill to a regional market, avoiding the wastes of cross-hauling, and reducing the costs of competitive salesmanship. It would also cut costs by enabling the buyer to employ cheaper modes of transport where they were available. F.o.b. pricing would permit the economic location of new industrial facilities and promote the adjustment of capacity to shifts in the location of demand. It might do so, however, at some cost, hastening the construction of plants in newer markets while condemning those in older regions to partial idleness.

Those who advocate compulsory f.o.b. pricing argue that it would make for active competition. It is not certain, however, that this would be the case. The number of sellers in an industry might not be increased. Plants would be built at new locations, but they might not be built by new concerns. A smaller company, confined to a local market by the prohibition of freight absorption, might find it difficult to survive. A larger one, with greater resources and with its market geographically diversified, would be likely to have greater staying power. The smaller firm might be absorbed by the larger one, and concentration, instead of declining, would increase. The industrial pattern would still be that of oligopoly.

Under f.o.b. pricing, each center of production would have an exclusive market where its price plus freight was lowest, competing with others only where their markets overlapped. It could compete, not by absorbing freight, but only by reducing its base price. This action would extend the boundaries of its market and enlarge the areas in which it challenged its competitors. A seller at such a center might well assume that those at rival centers would retaliate. He would also realize that any reduction in his price, instead of being confined to a few transactions, would apply to all his sales. For both these reasons, he would hesitate to make a cut. Under the circumstances, competition is not to be avoided by precisely equalizing costs at destinations, since delivery methods and charges are beyond control. But markets may be roughly shared by fixing their boundaries through agreement on base price relationships. And, given oligopoly, it is not unlikely that agreement will be obtained.

It may be questioned, moreover, whether the prohibition of all freight absorption would be wise. When a producer has capacity standing idle, it is economical for him to absorb freight in competing for a sale as long as his mill net realization covers his marginal cost. And when new business is not to be had nearby but is obtainable far away, it seems unreasonable to forbid him to go after it. It should be remembered, too, that discrimination may serve as an entering wedge for competition. It may be used, not only to meet another's prices, but also to undercut them. To outlaw it completely would be to sacrifice one of the principal methods through which real rivalry in markets may occur.

F.O.B. Prices with Sporadic Freight Absorption

Under the third alternative, though sales would normally be made f.o.b. and buyers would always be given the option of taking title at the mill, a seller would be permitted to absorb freight, upon occasion, in competing for a distant sale. This alternative has more to commend it than either of the other two. It avoids the worst consequences of basing point pricing without incurring those of pricing f.o.b. It removes the artificial obstacles to economy in the selection of industrial locations and modes of transportation. It permits new plants to be constructed in areas of new demand. But it also permits old plants to follow the market by absorbing freight, leaving no useful capacity stranded in mandatory idleness. It allows for some cross-hauling but wastes less transportation than do systems using basing points. It makes for diversity in costs, where markets overlap, by providing for different methods of delivery. And it works against market sharing through a frozen pattern of base price differentials by permitting one seller to invade another's market by absorbing freight. It thus preserves the function of discrimination as a means of undermining an established price. Of the possible methods of pricing, this affords the greatest opportunity for competition and the least assurance for monopoly.

BASING POINT SYSTEMS AND THE LAW

A basing point system might come into conflict with the antitrust laws in several different ways. First, it might be found to depend upon collusive agreement or conscious parallelism of action and thus to reveal a conspiracy in restraint of trade in violation of Section 1 of the Sherman Act. Or if imposed upon an industry by a dominant firm, it might be held to disclose an attempt to monopolize in violation of Section 2. In either case action would be brought by the Department of Justice under the provisions of the Sherman Act. Second, basing point pricing, involving the avoidance of competition through adherence to a common course of action, might be characterized as an unfair method of competition under Section 5 of the Federal Trade Commission Act. In this case action would be initiated by the F.T.C. Third, the geographic price discrimination resulting from such a system might be found to be injurious to competition and thus to be in violation of Section 2 of the Clayton Act as amended by the Robinson-Patman Act. And in this case action might be taken by either agency. However, though basing point systems had been in use since 1880, and the Sherman Act available since 1890, no decision was handed down by the Supreme Court in any case that clearly questioned the legality of such a system until 1945. To explain this delay it is necessary to review briefly the history of the government's relation to the principal basing point industries, steel and cement.

A Half-Century of Indecision

Basing point pricing had its origin in 1880 when three independent producers began quoting delivered prices that were identical with those charged by the Carnegie company for steel beams. The practice was applied experimentally to a few products until 1890. By 1900 it had been extended to every concern and (with the exception of rails, which are picked up by the railways at the mills) to every product in the field. In 1901 the United States Steel Corporation was organized, and from then on the level of prices was effectively controlled, first through open agreements, then through the Gary dinners, and finally through price leadership. From 1901 to 1903 most steel was sold on a zone price basis. But thereafter all products but rails were priced at Pittsburgh-plus. In 1917, during World War I, the War Industries Board ordered the industry to establish a Chicago base. But the order was rescinded within a year at the suggestion of one of the members of the Board. His name was E. H. Gary.[26] In 1910 the Department of Justice had entered suit against the Corporation charging it with illegal combination and monopolization of the industry. In 1915 this case was appealed to the Supreme Court, but the Court's decision was delayed until 1920 by the war. When it came, as we have seen, three judges held that the Corporation had violated the Sherman Act and four held that it had not. But the striking thing to note, in this connection, is the failure of the government to present any evidence concerning the basing point system or even to raise the issue of conspiracy. The nature and the significance of basing point pricing simply were not understood.

In 1919, immediately after the war, fabricators in the West and the South began to organize and to carry complaints to the Federal Trade Commission concerning the prices they were forced to pay for steel. In 1920, when the government returned the railways to their owners, a 40 per cent increase in freight rates pushed these prices even higher by adding to the plus in Pittsburgh-plus. Protests mounted, resolutions condemning the basing point system were passed by the legislatures of 11 states, and 32 states joined in organizing the Associated States Opposing Pittsburgh-Plus.[27] In response to this pressure, the Commission issued an order, in 1924, directing U.S. Steel to cease and desist "from quoting for sale or selling . . . rolled steel products upon any other basing point than that where the products are manufactured or from which they are shipped." The Corporation then filed a statement promising to obey the order "insofar as it is practicable to do so"[28] and proceeded to set up a multiple basing point system in place of Pittsburgh-plus. The new system aided fabricators in the West and in the South by establishing bases at Chicago and Birmingham. But for many years, these gains were offset, in part, by making base prices higher at these centers than at Pittsburgh. Prices east of Pittsburgh were still Pittsburgh-plus; those west of Chicago were Chicago-plus. The Corporation plainly failed to obey the Commission's order. But the Commission made no attempt to have it enforced.

In 1933, under the provisions of the National Industrial Recovery Act (to be discussed at greater length in Chapter 13), the antitrust laws were suspended and a so-called code of fair competition was approved for steel as for other industries, by President Franklin D. Roosevelt. This code was administered by a Code Authority consisting of the Directors of the American Iron and Steel Institute. In this body, it should be noted, U.S.

[26] F. A. Fetter, *The Masquerade of Monopoly*, pp. 153–54.

[27] *Ibid.*, p. 157.

[28] FTC, *Practices of the Steel Industry*, 73d Cong., 2d Sess., Senate Doc. 159, p. 61.

Steel and Bethlehem Steel had more than half of the votes. The code required all producers to adhere to the multiple basing point system, charging all-rail freight, and empowered the Code Authority to pick the basing points, to publish an official freight rate book, and to issue a book prescribing uniform extras and deductions. The code further required producers to file their base prices and to wait ten days before making them effective, and it gave the Code Authority the power to investigate these prices, to find them unfair, and to direct producers to file new ones, or if they failed to do so, to tell them what their prices must be. The code, in effect, gave to U.S. Steel and Bethlehem the legal right to fix the price of steel. And it provided that other firms, if they departed from this price, should be fined $10 per ton on the steel they produced. As a result, the industry could not obey the Federal Trade Commission's order without violating the NRA code. And it could not adhere to the code without disobeying the FTC.

This situation persisted until the NRA was found to be unconstitutional in May of 1935, and the FTC order again came into force. The industry, however, continued to employ the multiple basing point system throughout the following decade. In 1938, when the Wheeler-Lea Amendment to the Trade Commission Act made all outstanding orders final unless appealed within sixty days, the Corporation filed an appeal. A decision in this case was again delayed, first by agreement, and secondly by the outbreak of another world war. And during the war, ironically enough, the mechanism afforded by the basing point system was used by the Office of Price Administration in establishing, not minimum prices, but maximum prices for steel.

In the case of cement the story is much the same. Here, in 1902, a multiple basing point system was established by the first of a series of trade associations with the help of Universal Atlas, a subsidiary of U.S. Steel. In 1912 the efforts of a second association to enforce the system through patent licensing agreements were abandoned when a circuit court held the patents to be void. In 1925, as we have seen, the activities of a third association were held by the Supreme Court to be within the law.[29] In this case the Department of Justice had shown that the prices charged at destinations were identical. But the Court had been impressed by the defendant's argument that identity of prices revealed the presence of active competition. And the Department had not charged that the basing point system had been employed as a means of carrying out a price-fixing conspiracy. From 1933 to 1935, as in the case of steel, the industry's system was legalized and enforced by a trade association acting as a code authority. Here, too, the system remained in force after the demise of NRA. In 1937, however, the Federal Trade Commission issued a complaint against the Cement Institute and 74 cement producers, following it in 1943 with an order to cease and desist from:

[29] See above, p. 115.

1. Quoting or selling cement at prices calculated or determined pursuant to or in accordance with the multiple basing-point delivered-price system; or . . . any other plan or system which results in identical price quotations or prices for cement at points of quotation or sale. . . .
2. (*a*) Refusing or declining to quote or sell cement at the location of the producing mill. . . .
   (*b*) Refusing . . . to allow purchasers to provide transportation by any means, at any cost, or to any place they may desire. . . .
   (*f*) Quoting or selling cement at delivered prices which systematically include a common-carrier transportation factor greater or less than the actual cost of such common-carrier transportation from the point of shipment to destination.
   (*g*) Quoting or selling cement at delivered prices which systematically include a freight factor representing transportation by a common carrier having higher rates than the means of transportation actually employed. . . .
   (*j*) Collecting, compiling, circulating or exchanging information concerning common-carrier transportation charges . . . to be used as a factor in the price of cement. . . .
3. Discriminating in price . . . by systematically charging and accepting mill net prices which differ by the amounts necessary to produce [identical] delivered costs to purchasers. . . .[30]

The system thus outlawed by FTC was then being used by OPA in fixing ceiling prices for cement. The industry appealed the Commission's order, and in 1946 the Court of Appeals upheld it in part and reversed it in part. The government then appealed, and the final decision of the Supreme Court was handed down in 1948, after price control had been abandoned.

The cement order was a major move in a general campaign against basing point pricing which included orders against producers of corn products, malt, milk cans, crepe paper, rigid steel conduits, and bottle caps. A complaint was also issued, in 1947, against the American Iron and Steel Institute and 101 steel companies, the earlier action in that industry having been confined to U.S. Steel. The corn products cases were the first to reach the courts.

Basing Points before the Courts

The Corn Products Refining Co., with one plant making glucose at Chicago and another at Kansas City, sold this product to manufacturers of candy on the basis of Chicago-plus. The same practice was followed by other producers, including the A. E. Staley company of Decatur, Illinois. Each of these concerns was charged with price discrimination injurious to competition in violation of Section 2*a* of the Clayton Act. Corn Products and Staley appealed the Trade Commission's orders, and in 1945 the two

[30] FTC Docket No. 3167.

cases were finally decided by the Supreme Court on the same day.[31] The Court held that Corn Products at its Kansas City plant and Staley at Decatur had discriminated between customers, absorbing freight on some sales and collecting phantom freight on others, and that this discrimination had injured competition among candy manufacturers by helping those located near Chicago and harming those nearer Kansas City, Decatur, and other non-basing points. The Court also rejected the defense, advanced under Section 2*b* of the Clayton Act, that Staley's lower prices near Chicago were made "in good faith to meet the equally low prices of a competitor," finding that such prices had been quoted systematically. Individual adherence to a single basing point system was thus held to be in violation of the law.

In other decisions, handed down by a Court of Appeals in 1945 and 1946, the FTC was upheld in orders issued, not only under the Clayton Act, but also under Section 5 of the Trade Commission Act, and involving not only a single basing point system, used in selling malt,[32] but also a plenary basing point system for milk and ice cream cans,[33] and a zone pricing system for crepe paper.[34] In each of these cases, the Court suggested that agreement to avoid competition, in violation of Section 5, might be inferred from the characteristics of delivered pricing systems in themselves. "On the face of the situation," said the Court in the milk can case, "it taxes our credulity of belief, as argued, that petitioners employed this system without any agreement or plan among themselves." But in 1946 the same court refused to sustain the Commission's cement order, holding the evidence insufficient to support the charge of illegal agreement under the Trade Commission Act and, though finding the collection of phantom freight under a multiple basing point system to be unlawful under Section 2*a* of the Clayton Act, nevertheless permitting the freight absorption inherent in the same system to be justified under Section 2*b*. The Government appealed.[35]

In a sweeping decision, handed down in the Cement Institute case in 1948, the Supreme Court reversed the lower court, sustaining the Commission at every point.[36] The concerted maintenance of a basing point system, said the Court, "is an unfair method of competition prohibited by the Federal Trade Commission Act."[37] The Commission's finding of illegal agreement was supported by evidence "that the industry's Institute actively worked, in cooperation with various of its members, to maintain the multiple basing point delivered price system; that this pricing system is

[31] *Corn Products Refining Co.* v. *FTC*, 324 U.S. 726; *FTC* v. *A. E. Staley Manufacturing Co.*, 324 U.S. 746.

[32] *U.S. Maltsters Assn.* v. *FTC*, 152 F. 2d 161 (1945).

[33] *Milk and Ice Cream Can Institute* v. *FTC*, 152 F. 2d 478 (1946).

[34] *Fort Howard Paper Co.* v. *FTC*, 156 F. 2d 899 (1946).

[35] *Cement Institute* v. *FTC.*, 157 F. 2d 533.

[36] *FTC* v. *Cement Institute*, 333 U.S. 683.

[37] *Ibid.*, p. 720.

calculated to produce, and has produced, uniform prices and terms of sale throughout the country; and that all of the respondents have sold their cement substantially in accord with the pattern required by the multiple basing point system."[38] The system, being injurious to competition, was also held to be unlawful under the Clayton Act, since "a pricing system involving both phantom freight and freight absorption violates Section 2*a* if . . . prices are computed for products actually shipped from one locality on the fiction that they were shipped from another."[39] The defense advanced under Section 2*b* was again rejected on the ground that prices had been matched "as a practice rather than as a good faith effort to meet individually competitive situations."[40] Collective adherence to a multiple basing point system was held to be against the law.

Another case involving such a system came before a Court of Appeals in 1948. Here, the FTC had issued an order against fourteen manufacturers of rigid steel conduit, a form of pipe used as a shield for electrical wiring. Here, again, the order was brought under Section 5 of the Trade Commission Act. But in this case, the Commission had based its action on two separate counts. In the first count, as in previous cases, it charged the companies with conspiracy. But in the second, it contended that they had individually violated the Act "through their concurrent use of a formula method of making delivered price quotations with the knowledge that each did likewise. . . ." The second count was thus directed, not against agreement to use the basing point system, but against the use of the system as such. The court upheld the Commission on both points, finding strong evidence of agreement, but also going on to hold that concurrent use of a basing point system might be regarded as an unfair method of competition in itself.[41] The decision was appealed but was allowed to stand when the Supreme Court divided 4 to 4 in 1949, presenting no opinions on the case.[42] Another order, directed against the use of a plenary basing point system in the sale of bottle caps, was sustained by a Court of Appeals in 1949, the Court's decision suggesting strongly that the Commission would be upheld in drawing an inference of collusion wherever identical prices, resulting from common adherence to a system of delivered pricing, could be found.[43]

These decisions, in cement and other industries, led eventually to settlements in steel. In 1948 United States Steel signed a decree affirming and enforcing the order that had been issued by the Federal Trade Commission in 1924. And in 1951 the American Iron and Steel Institute and its members accepted an order, based on the complaint issued in 1947, for-

[38] *Ibid.*, p. 716.

[39] *Ibid.*, p. 724.

[40] *Ibid.*, p. 725.

[41] *Triangle Conduit & Cable Co.* v. *FTC*, 168 F. 2d 157.

[42] *Clayton Mark & Co.* v. *FTC*, 336 U.S. 956.

[43] *Bond Crown & Cork Co.* v. *FTC*, 176 F. 2d 974.

bidding them to participate in "any planned common course of action, understanding, or agreement" to refuse "to sell and deliver any steel products f.o.b. at the plant," to compile and exchange lists of base prices, extras and deductions, and freight factors for use in computing prices, or to fix or maintain prices "in accordance with any system or formula which produces identical price quotations or prices or delivered costs." The order, however, specifically permitted delivered pricing or freight absorption "when innocently and independently pursued, regularly or otherwise, with the result of promoting competition," and rejected identity of delivered prices at any destination as necessarily affording proof of violation of the law.[44]

Basing Points before the Public

The decision of the Supreme Court in the cement case evoked a storm of protest. Leaders of basing point industries were joined by members of Congress and by columnists, commentators, and editorial writers in viewing with alarm. Hearings were held, between October, 1948 and January, 1949, by a subcommittee of the Senate, under Capehart of Indiana, to discover how badly business would be harmed. It was argued again, in all seriousness, that basing point pricing makes for competition and f.o.b. pricing for monopoly. It was said that f.o.b. pricing would lead to higher prices, that it would help big business and hurt little business, and that it would turn thriving industrial centers into ghost towns as industry moved away. And it was insisted that the decision might be interpreted as requiring f.o.b. pricing, that it had created uncertainty and confusion as to the meaning of the law, and that legislative "clarification" was required. Some of these points necessitate a further word.

In the summer of 1948 the demand for cement and steel exceeded the supply. Producers could get business close at home and were already refusing to fill the orders they received from distant customers. Under these circumstances, f.o.b. pricing would increase their revenues. On July 1, the cement industry abandoned the basing point system and started quoting prices f.o.b. On July 7, the steel industry followed suit. The prices of cement and steel immediately rose. They rose because each producer, instead of taking his former mill net realization as his new f.o.b. price, continued quoting his old base price. And this was higher, since freight absorption had normally exceeded phantom freight. In steel, for instance, freight had been absorbed on as much as 70 per cent of the volume sold. But this was not the explanation given to the public. The higher prices were blamed, instead, upon the stupidity of the Commission and the Court. And crocodile tears were shed as prices rose and profits grew.

The solicitude for small business shown by basing point apologists was equally disingenuous. A parade of little-business men appeared at the

[44] FTC Order 5508, issued August 16, 1951.

Capehart hearings to answer questions put on the assumption that the Court's decision would forbid them to absorb freight, requiring them to quote all prices f.o.b. Such a requirement, they testified, would mean ruin for them and riches for their powerful competitors. And a few big-business men, following after, sadly agreed. The decision should be reversed, they said, because it would be so harmful to little business and so favorable to them. They had maintained their basing point systems over the years, apparently, as a species of philanthropy.

There was testimony, too, that industry would be forced to migrate, moving out of many centers, but—inexplicably—into none. It was true, of course, that abandonment of basing point pricing would affect industrial location. But it could not do so quickly. As long as demand exceeded supply, in every region, fixed facilities would be kept at work. And even if demand should fall, their owners could reach a shifting market by absorbing freight. If freight absorption were forbidden, surplus capacity might be stranded in older centers, and prices and earnings at such locations might decline. But in the case of steel, for instance, this very development should discourage fabricators already in such a center from leaving and encourage new ones to come in. It is only as the market expands, and as additional facilities are built in newer centers, that relocation gradually occurs. Within 3 years after the Court's decision, 52 new cement plants had been started or planned in 28 states,[45] and steel capacity was growing more rapidly in Cleveland and Detroit, in the South and the West, and along the eastern seaboard than at Pittsburgh and Chicago. But the prophecy of ruin for the older centers appeared to have been slightly exaggerated, as Mark Twain once observed of a report that he was dead.

The attack on the Commission and the Court was based in large part on the contention that all freight absorption had been prohibited. But this contention was disproved by the words of the Court itself: "Most of the objections to the order appear to rest on the premise that its terms will bar an individual cement producer from selling cement at delivered prices such that its net return from one customer will be less than from another, even if the particular sale be made in good faith to meet the lower price of a competitor. The Commission disclaims that the order can possibly be so understood. Nor do we so understand it. . . ."[46] The Commission, moreover, has repeatedly asserted that it has never acted "to prohibit or interfere with delivered pricing or freight absorption when innocently and independently pursued with the result of promoting competition," and that it does not intend to do so.[47] But despite these disclaimers, there were still complaints of confusion and uncertainty. And, in truth, confusion was

[45] *Congressional Record*, March 31, 1951, p. 4564.

[46] *FTC* v. *Cement Institute*, 333 U.S. 683, 724.

[47] See, for instance, statements issued on October 12, 1948, June 10, 1950, August 16, 1951, and December 3, 1951.

created by conflicting statements from members of the Commission and its staff, by contradictory sentences taken out of context from the Court's decision, and even by inconsistent appraisals offered by economists.[48] But the complaints were based, in part, at least, on the fact that the meaning of the law was all too clear. The independent, sporadic absorption of freight to meet the lower prices of competitors was legal, even though involving discriminatory variations in a seller's net returns. The independent absorption of freight, even though persistent, was legal unless injury to competition could be shown. And where freight was an insignificant part of the delivered price, or where customers at different locations did not compete with one another, no such showing could be made. But the collusive and sustained observance of complex and rigid systems of delivered pricing had been found to be in violation of the law. And this was the major source of complaints of confusion and demands that the law be "clarified."

It must be admitted, however, that there remained, between the independent behavior that clearly was legal and the collective behavior that clearly was not, an area of some uncertainty. Suppose that an industry offered no evidence of meetings, correspondence, or conversation leading to agreement on a common pricing policy. Suppose that it had no non-basing points, no all-rail freight requirement, no common freight rate book. But suppose that the delivered prices quoted by one firm were matched, first by another, then by a third, and then by a fourth, first occasionally, then frequently, and then invariably. At what stage in this process would the line be crossed between legality and illegality? This was a hypothetical question that could only be answered by decisions rendered by the courts from case to case.

Behind this question lay the possibility that basing point industries might come again to match delivered prices if the machinery of collusion could be rendered less conspicuous. Their ability to do so would depend upon the nature of the proof required to win a case. On this point, however, the decisions rendered by the courts by 1949, were quite discouraging. In the Morton Salt case, as we have seen, the Supreme Court had held that the Federal Trade Commission need only show a reasonable *possibility* of injury to competition. In the Standard Oil of Indiana case, a lower court had decided that the defense of good faith in meeting competition, instead of being absolute, was only procedural. And under the second count in the rigid steel conduit case, it had been ruled that conspiracy might be inferred from the characteristics of delivered pricing systems in themselves. If prices were safely to be matched, therefore, some legislative "clarification" was required.

[48] See, for instance, F. A. Fetter, "Exit Basing Point Pricing," C. D. Edwards, "Basing Point Decisions and Business Practices," and J. M. Clark, "Law and Economics of Basing Points," *American Economic Review*, Vol. XXXVIII (1948), pp. 815–43, and Vol. XXXIX (1949) pp. 430–48.

Basing Points before Congress

Early in 1949 the Capehart committee, now under Senator Johnson of Colorado, dropped its bill to amend the laws affecting delivered pricing in favor of one sponsored by Senator Myers of Pennsylvania creating a two-year moratorium on further prosecutions of basing point industries. The stay was professedly designed to afford the Supreme Court an opportunity to dispel the confusion then existing by rendering a clear decision in the rigid steel conduit case. But on the day the Meyers bill was reported to the Senate, the Court revealed its 4 to 4 split, recording no opinion on the case. A bill embodying permanent amendments was then presented by Senator O'Mahoney of Wyoming, modified in both houses, sent to conference committee, and finally passed by the House of Representatives in October, 1949.

In the form in which it passed the House, the O'Mahoney bill amended Section 5 of the Federal Trade Commission Act to say that "It shall not be an unfair method of competition . . . for a seller, acting independently, to quote or sell at delivered prices or to absorb freight: Provided, That this shall not make lawful any combination, conspiracy, or collusive agreement . . . involving the use of delivered prices or freight absorption." It amended Section 2*a* of the Clayton Act by adding "That it shall not be an unlawful discrimination in price for a seller, acting independently, (*a*) to quote or sell at delivered prices if such prices are identical at different delivery points . . . or (*b*) to absorb freight to meet the equally low price of a competitor in good faith except where the effect . . . *will* be to substantially lessen competition." It amended Section 2*b* by providing "That a seller may justify a discrimination other than a discrimination which *will* substantially lessen competition by showing that his lower price . . . was made in good faith to meet the equally low price of a competitor."[49] And it further amended the Clayton Act by so defining the phrase "Where the effect may be substantially to lessen competition" as to require a showing of reasonable *probability*.[50] At first glance, these amendments may appear to have been fairly innocent. But they would have had the effect of reversing the Morton Salt and rigid steel conduit decisions and destroying the advantage gained by the decision of the lower court in the Standard Oil of Indiana case. They would have handicapped the government in the prosecution of delivered pricing systems by placing upon it, through the words shown in italics, a heavier burden of proof.

Senate action on the O'Mahoney bill was delayed by a determined fight waged in October, 1949, in January, 1950, and again in May, 1950 by Senators Douglas, Kefauver, Long, Morse, and Hill. In the course of these debates, the character and consequences of basing point pricing

[49] The infinitive, split in 1914, united in 1936, was to be split again in 1949.

[50] 81st Cong., 1st Sess., S. 1008. Italics supplied.

were explained in considerable detail. The bill, with minor modifications, passed the House by a voice vote and the Senate by a vote of 43 to 27. It was vetoed by President Truman on June 16, 1950.[51]

In January, 1951, the Supreme Court reversed the Court of Appeals in the Standard Oil of Indiana case, making good faith an absolute defense. As a result, a defendant in a price discrimination case need only show that he met a competitor's lower price. The government then must prove, not that his action may have injured competition, which would be easy, but that he acted in bad faith, which might well be impossible. The decision thus made it more difficult to win a case. But it was handed down by a divided court and might not always stand. In 1950 Congress had been asked to reverse the Court. In 1951 it was urged to uphold it. A bill was introduced into the Senate, by McCarran of Nevada, amending the Clayton Act to write the Court's decision into the text of the law itself. But the report that accompanied the bill went even farther, making it clear that the identity of delivered prices achieved under a plenary basing point system was held to be lawful, and asserting that no adverse inference could be drawn from evidence as to its duration, frequency, regularity, or rigidity. This effort to legalize basing point pricing, by indirection, was again opposed, in July and August, 1951, by Senators Douglas, Kefauver, and Long. The bill passed the Senate but was not reported to the House. Similar measures were introduced by Senators McCarran and Capehart in 1952, 1953, and 1954, but each of them died in committee. Congress thus failed to change the wording of the law.

In 1953, however, President Eisenhower appointed new members to the Federal Trade Commission, giving it a Republican majority, and this majority made important changes in the Commission's policy. The FTC now takes the position that the good faith defense should be absolute. It directs its attention to cases where it is not merely possible but probable that competition will be injured by illegal practices. And it does not regard parallelism of action as affording sufficient evidence of conspiracy. With this approach, the Commission is less likely to be vigorous in prosecuting delivered pricing systems in the future than it has been in the past.[52]

Until 1953 the demand for steel was strong, and the industry continued selling f.o.b. at its mills. In that year, however, demand slackened and surplus capacity appeared in certain areas. On October 1, 1953, United States Steel announced that it would again absorb freight. Other companies shortly followed suit. But the basing point system was not reestablished. Each mill continued to make sales f.o.b. or on a delivered basis including actual freight. The absorption of freight was limited to particu-

[51] The story of this legislation affords an excellent case study in practical politics. It has been well told by Earl Latham in *The Group Basis of Politics* (Ithaca, N.Y.: Cornell University Press, 1952).

[52] See *New York Times,* June 20, 1953; *Business Week,* July 4, 1953 and August 1, 1953.

lar orders where it was needed to enable mills to compete in making distant sales.[53]

Discrimination is again practiced. It remains to be seen whether freight absorption will again become so general and so habitual as to effect a systematic matching of prices at each point of delivery. Certainly such a practice will be more difficult in the future than it was in the past. The all-rail freight charge and the common rate book have been abandoned. More than half of the steel shipped in 1953 moved by truck, not only by common carriers whose rates are published, but also by contract carriers and private trucks whose rates and costs are not. Under these circumstances, it will not be easy to match delivered prices invariably and instantly. It is clear, moreover, that phantom freight and non-basing points are things of the past. Goods can now be shipped by the most efficient and economical mode of transport. Artificial handicaps to industrial location have been removed. And this is a substantial gain.

SUGGESTIONS FOR FURTHER READING

The two best sources for general reading on delivered pricing are Fritz Machlup, *The Basing Point System* (Philadelphia: Blakiston Co., 1949), and the issue of *Law and Contemporary Problems* for Spring, 1950 on "Delivered Pricing." The steel industry's defense of the basing point system is set forth by the United States Steel Corporation in *T.N.E.C. Papers*, Vol. III, *The Basing Point Method*, published by the Corporation in 1940. This material, together with a reply by the Federal Trade Commission, is reproduced in T.N.E.C. Monograph No. 42, *The Basing Point Problem* (Washington: Government Printing Office, 1941). The most succinct objective analysis of the economic consequences of different geographic pricing systems is Carl Kaysen, "Basing Point Pricing and Public Policy," *Quarterly Journal of Economics*, August, 1949, pp. 289–315. The influence of the basing point system in steel on the economic development of the Southern states is treated in George W. Stocking, *Basing Point Pricing and Regional Development* (Chapel Hill: University of North Carolina Press, 1954). The leading decision on the subject, which is well worth reading, is the one handed down by Mr. Justice Black in *FTC* v. *Cement Institute*, 333 U.S. 683 (1948). The significance of this decision is discussed by a number of lawyers in *Law and Contemporary Problems*, Spring, 1950, pp. 181–271, and by two economists, Frank A. Fetter and Corwin D. Edwards, in the *American Economic Review* for December, 1948, pp. 815–43. The story of the subsequent effort to legalize basing point pricing is well told by Earl Latham in his article in *Law and Contemporary Problems*, Spring, 1950, pp. 272–311, and in his book *The Group Basis of Politics* (Ithaca, N.Y.: Cornell University Press, 1952). The probable future pricing pattern in steel is considered by Marvin J. Barloon in "Institutional Foundations of Pricing Policy in the Steel Industry," *The Business History Review*, Vol. XXVIII (1954), pp. 214–35.

[53] See *Business Week*, September 15, 1953; *New York Times*, October 4, 1953.

Chapter 9 ENFORCEMENT OF ANTITRUST

There have been two approaches to the task of maintaining competition. The first is that of litigation: the prosecution of violators of the law. The second is that of administrative regulation: the establishment of rules to govern future conduct. The first approach was taken by the Sherman Act and has been followed by the Antitrust Division. The second was taken by the Federal Trade Commission Act and has been followed by the FTC. It is with the character of these two approaches and the organization and procedure of these two agencies that the present chapter is concerned.

MAINTAINING COMPETITION THROUGH LITIGATION

When the Sherman Act is violated, it is expected that a public prosecutor or a private plaintiff will bring suit, asking that penalties be imposed, remedies provided, or payment of damages required. The role played by the private suit, however, is a minor one. Enforcement must be sought, in the main, through cases brought by the government. The success or failure of enforcement will depend, therefore, upon the character of the organization established to detect and prosecute violations, the adequacy with which it is staffed and financed, the policies it adopts, and the procedures it employs. The outcome of enforcement will depend, too, upon the nature of the processes of litigation and the effectiveness of the penalties and the remedies to which they lead.

The Antitrust Division

The sums appropriated by Congress for the enforcement of the Sherman Act have always been small. For the first 13 years, no separate appropriation was made, the work being undertaken by the Department of Justice as a part of its general activities. The Antitrust Division was not established until 1903. Thereafter, its annual appropriation ran around $100,000 until 1908, below $300,000 until 1935, and under $800,000 through 1939. The figure did not reach $1,000,000 for 50 years. Then it rose, to $1,300,000 in 1940, to $2,300,000 in 1942, to $3,400,000 in 1949, and to $3,750,000 in 1951. But it is still small when compared with the character of the Division's responsibility, with the sums spent by defendants in antitrust suits, and with those spent by the government on less important activities. Since a single suit may cost anywhere from $100,000 to $500,000, the modest size of the Division's appropriation has seriously limited the number that could be brought. In some years, curiously enough, these appropriations have been surpassed by fines collected from violators. In 1941, for instance, $1,325,000 was paid out and $2,690,000 taken in. The difference of $1,365,000 accrued, however, not to the Antitrust Division but to the Treasury.[1]

The size of the Division's appropriation has been reflected in the size of its staff. Under Theodore Roosevelt, it had 7 lawyers. Under Woodrow Wilson, it had 18. Under Harding, Coolidge, and Hoover, it had 25. It was not until 1939 that the number reached 200, not until 1949 that it approached 300. And this was still a microscopic figure in the federal bureaucracy. Counsel for the government in antitrust cases have usually found themselves outnumbered by counsel for the defense. In the Hartford-Empire case, the Antitrust Division had 5 lawyers and the defendants 30. In the motion picture cases, the Division had 10 and the defendants 50. In the Madison oil case, the respective numbers were 5 and 103. In 1950 the salary range for antitrust lawyers was between $4,150 and $9,975 per year, the average payment standing at $7,081. Counsel for the defense might well get 10 times more than this. Though salaries have been raised, the discrepancy persists. As a result, perhaps, the rate of turnover in the personnel of the Division has been high. From 1903 to 1953, moreover, there were 23 assistant attorneys general in charge of antitrust, an average of 1 for each 2 years. Even when a national administration has undertaken vigorously to enforce the law, it has been handicapped by paltry appropriations, scanty staffs, low pay, rapid turnover, and shifting leadership.

But vigorous enforcement has not always been administration policy. In 2 years under Benjamin Harrison, 7 cases were brought. In Cleveland's second term, there were 8. Under McKinley, there were only 3. Theodore Roosevelt, known as a trust buster, started 44 suits in 2 terms. Taft started 90 in 1. Wilson also started 90; his good beginning was interrupted by World War I. Under 3 years of Harding there were 50 cases, under 5 years of Coolidge 83, under 4 years of Hoover only 38; during these administrations, according to Charles Stevenson, head of an industrial engineering firm in New York, "industry enjoyed, to all intents and purposes, a moratorium from the Sherman Act, and, through the more or less

[1] Committee on Small Business, House of Representatives, *United States versus Economic Concentration and Monopoly* (Committee Print, 1946), pp. 47–51, 252–53; and *Antitrust Law Enforcement* (81st Cong., 2d Sess., House Report No. 3236, 1951), pp. 50–51.

THE DEFENDANTS (SEATED) AND THEIR LAWYERS (STANDING)

effective trade associations which were developed in most of our industries, competition was, to a very considerable extent, controlled. The Department of Justice acted with great restraint and intelligence and only enforced the Sherman Act against those industries who violated the laws in a flagrant and unreasonable manner."[2] Up to the late thirties, says

[2] Quoted by Corwin D. Edwards in *American Economic Review*, Vol. XXX suppl. (1940), p. 167.

Courtesy *Life* Magazine © Time, Inc.

IN THE DU PONT—GENERAL MOTORS CASE 1952–54.

Corwin Edwards, "prosecutions were merely symbolic in character. In any one year, from half a dozen to a dozen instances of law violation were arbitrarily selected for investigation and trial. . . . With all available resources committed . . . the prosecution of a few lawbreakers became in effect a guarantee of immunity to the rest."[3] This has been described by

[3] Corwin D. Edwards, *Maintaining Competition* (New York: McGraw-Hill Book Co., 1949), p. 293.

Paul T. Homan as " 'token' or 'ritual' enforcement, a system of 'selective justice' in which it is hoped a few 'examples' will have a sufficiently deterring effect."[4]

As a part of the New Deal, inaugurated under Franklin D. Roosevelt at the depth of the Great Depression in 1933, the antitrust laws were suspended and agreements to restrain trade were given enthusiastic approval as a means of promoting industrial recovery.[5] In 1935, however, the National Industrial Recovery Act was found to be unconstitutional and, in 1937, the administration reversed its policy, proceeding with equal enthusiasm to the vigorous enforcement of antitrust. This campaign, opened by Robert H. Jackson—later Attorney General and Associate Justice of the Supreme Court—was carried forward by Thurman Arnold who served as Assistant Attorney General from 1938 to 1943. It was Arnold who had commented cynically on the history of antitrust in a satire published shortly before he took charge:

> "Bigness" was regarded as a curse because it led to monopoly. . . . At the same time specialized techniques made bigness essential. . . . In order to reconcile the ideal with the practical necessity, it became necessary to develop a procedure which constantly attacked bigness . . . and at the same time never really interfered with combinations. Such pressures gave rise to the antitrust laws. . . . The same pressures made the enforcement of the antitrust laws a pure ritual. . . . Since organizations were demanded, attempts to stop their growth necessarily became purely ceremonial. . . . The antitrust laws remained as a most important symbol . . . a great moral gesture. . . .[6]

Within a few months, the author of these words had espoused antitrust with evangelistic fervor and was proceeding to enforce the law of 1890 with a zeal that led some wag to rechristen it the Thurman Act.[7] The scope and the vigor which he gave to the work of the Antitrust Division was carried over, in some measure, into later years. By 1950 a thousand suits had been brought by the Department of Justice under the Sherman and Clayton Acts. But of these, 500 had been instituted during the first half-century, 500 during the last decade. Enforcement, on a significant scale, is a phenomenon of recent times.

With the advent of the Eisenhower administration, there was some speculation that enforcement would be cut back to the level of earlier days, but this did not prove to be the case. Under Judge Stanley N. Barnes, who was appointed Assistant Attorney General in charge of the Antitrust Division, some pending suits were dropped, but others were pushed, and new suits were instituted at an undiminished rate, the defendants including

[4] Paul T. Homan, "Notes on the Antitrust Law Policy," in *Readings in the Social Control of Industry* (Philadelphia: Blakiston Co., 1942), pp. 226–62, esp. p. 247.

[5] This experience will be discussed in Chapter 13.

[6] Thurman W. Arnold, *The Folklore of Capitalism* (New Haven: Yale University Press, 1937), pp. 207–8, 211, 217.

[7] See Thurman W. Arnold, *The Bottlenecks of Business* (New York: Reynal & Hitchcock, 1940).

a number of important companies: American Smelting and Refining, the three big manufacturers of soap, United Fruit, and RCA. Approval was denied for the proposed merger of Bethlehem Steel and Youngstown Sheet and Tube. Investigations were begun in the liquor and automobile industries. A committee was appointed, under the chairmanship of Judge Barnes and Professor S. Chesterfield Oppenheim of the University of Michigan Law School, to prepare a report on antitrust policy. Among its 57 other members, most of them lawyers or economists, there were staunch defenders as well as vigorous critics of antitrust. Whatever the final verdict, it was clear that the jury had not been packed.

Preparing a Case

Thurman Arnold's major contribution to antitrust procedure was the inauguration of industry-wide investigations leading to a series of related suits. One such program, covering restraints in urban housing, involved the simultaneous presentation of evidence to grand juries in eleven cities and the subsequent institution of around a hundred suits against manufacturers and distributors of building materials, and general contractors, subcontractors, and labor unions in the building trades. Similar campaigns were directed against restraints among processors of foodstuffs, holders of patents, and participants in international cartels. In most cases, however, the Antitrust Division has taken action, not on its own initiative, but on the basis of complaints brought to it by a company's competitors, its suppliers, or its customers. This procedure, obviously, has its limitations, since complaints are not received in cases where these groups have been intimidated or where all of those participating in an illegal arrangement are contented with the way it works. Nor does every complaint lead to the initiation of a suit. Some cases are dropped and others picked for prosecution in accordance with such considerations as may influence the Division in its choice. As a result, enforcement is haphazard and sporadic, rather than systematic and sustained.

The Division must accumulate a convincing body of evidence if it is to win a case. But it has no investigators of its own. For this purpose it is

THE LAWYERS FOR THE GOVERNMENT IN THE DU PONT—GENERAL MOTORS CASE, 1952–54.

Courtesy *Life* Magazine © Time, Inc.

dependent on the Federal Bureau of Investigation. When a case is pending, it submits a written memorandum to the FBI, outlining the information that is sought. The Bureau, following its usual routine, gathers the data through its local agents, none of whom is trained to meet the particular requirements of antitrust. The resulting materials are then assembled and forwarded to the Division in a written report. As a method of industrial research, and even as mere detective work, the procedure leaves something to be desired. As Wallace and Douglas have put it: "The clean-cut lads of the F.B.I. deserve the respect and admiration of the country. But when they are sent out . . . to find evidence of a price-fixing conspiracy, they are likely to return empty handed. The reason is that their innocent routine is to search business files for evidence which is usually not there. Even if the evidence had once been there, counsel would almost surely have made management aware of its risky significance."[8] Files may have been stripped, witnesses silenced, and evidence destroyed. To piece a case together from the fragments that remain may well require a specialization of training and a co-ordination of effort that the FBI does not provide.

If a case appears to have some substance, litigation may be started and further evidence obtained once it is under way. When a criminal suit has been taken to a grand jury, books and records can be subpoenaed and witnesses compelled to testify. In a civil suit, too, procedures are available whereby documents may be obtained and testimony taken prior to a trial. But these procedures are less effective than the subpoena, and criminal indictments are therefore sought as a means of obtaining evidence in cases where civil actions would otherwise suffice. To correct this situation, it has been suggested that the Attorney General be given the right, upon specific authorization by a court, to subpoena documents and compel testimony in a civil suit. In any of these cases, the Division will sue first and investigate afterward. Then, having assembled its evidence, it will go to court.

The Case at Law

It is by no means easy to win an antitrust suit. In a civil action guilt must be established by a preponderance of evidence. In a criminal suit it must be proven beyond a reasonable doubt. The evidence, however, may be largely circumstantial; documentary proof may be wanting and witnesses reluctant to testify. The complexities of business organization and practice may be difficult for the prosecution to explain and for the jury and the judge to understand. The defendants may be eminently respectable, members of the best clubs, active in charitable enterprises, and pillars of the church. The course of conduct of which they are accused may appear to be quite normal. The jury may hesitate to convict, the

[8] Robert A. Wallace and Paul H. Douglas, "Antitrust Policies and the New Attack on the Federal Trade Commission," *University of Chicago Law Review*, Summer, 1952, p. 18. See also, Committee on Small Business, *Antitrust Law Enforcement*, pp. 56–59.

judge to provide appropriate remedies. A trial, moreover, may drag on for many months. The trial of the Aluminum Company in the District Court ran from June 1, 1938 to August 14, 1940. The judge, when asked on a second occasion by the same attorney to grant a day's adjournment at the birth of a child, warned that such favors were not to be expected when grandchildren began to come along.

Litigation has its shortcomings as an instrument of public policy. The matter at stake in a trial is the behavior of an industry in the future. The matter discussed is the evidence of its wrongdoing in the past. Whatever the substance of a case, the prosecution must seek a conviction, the defense an acquittal. And the outcome will be influenced by the technicalities of the law. The procedure has been best described by Hamilton and Till:

> It brings to the settlement of questions of economic order the processes, hazards, confusions, evasions, circumlocutions, delays, of the legal folkways. . . . Persons competent in the habits of industry must give way to those skilled in the techniques of legal combat. . . . The opposing champions are well versed in demurrer, interlocutory motion, the tactics of seeking or avoiding a general engagement. They are less at home with overhead cost, Pittsburgh-plus, the fiction of the quoted price. . . . The staging of the question as an adversary proceeding sets lawyer against lawyer. . . . Every move, every witness, every fact, every document becomes a counter in a legal game. "The record" has come to do vicarious duty for an analysis of the industry in operation; and every item, favorable to one side, can win admission only against the heavy cross-fire of the other. Every procedural device which may arrest or speed action, flank or snipe the verbal minions of the enemy, color the conduct on parade with innocence or guilt is called into play. . . . Again and again the attorney and the witness raise their antiphonal voices; the counsel for the adverse party chants the approved formula "incompetent, irrelevant, and immaterial"; the judge from the loft above interjects a responsive "sustained" or "overruled"; and the loser, who intends to fight another day, comes in dramatically with "exception". . . . It takes the final summing up of the lawyers to bring the jury back to the dominant legal issue. And somehow antitrust as an instrument of public policy has gotten lost in the scuffle.[9]

The case presents peculiar difficulties to the judge:

> Now there appear before him for judgment defendants who are among the leaders of American business, whose names are household words, whose salaries run into staggering figures. The distinguished members of the American bar come into his court, great in repute, learned in the law. . . . The judge must be as knowing as they; if possible, he must win their respect and acclaim; above all, amid the treacherous moves of litigation, he must save his face. . . . He is expected to have a critical mastery of corporate finance, marketing practice, industrial structure; to have a sound grasp of physics, chemistry, electro-dynamics, in fact the fundamentals of all the mechanical

[9] Walton Hamilton and Irene Till, *Antitrust in Action,* T.N.E.C. Monograph No. 16 (Washington: Government Printing Office, 1940), pp. 59–62.

arts. . . . In a word, he must be alike omnicompetent in law and in industry —an expert in the multiplex of affairs and disciplines which converge upon the case. . . . In the face of his own ordeal, his tendency is to retire somewhat from the domain of industrial reality and to fortify his judicial performance with a meticulous observance of the technicalities. . . . Even the judge himself becomes an obstacle to bringing into sharp relief the pattern of the industry and its points of restraint.[10]

Judges have long been supplied with law clerks to assist them in working through the legal issues presented by a case. But it was not until 1945 that they were authorized, by a modification in the rules of judicial procedure, to employ economists as expert witnesses to aid in analyzing the facts. This practice is as yet uncommon. It was first adopted when Judge Charles E. Wyzanski, Jr. of the District Court in Boston engaged Carl Kaysen of Harvard University to work on the United Shoe Machinery case.

The decision in a civil case may be appealed by either party, the conviction in a criminal case by the defense alone. The appeal is taken on the basis of error, and error is concerned exclusively with points of law. In the words of Hamilton and Till, "The jurists who must correct error—and are presumed not to err themselves—live in a rarified atmosphere where they never see a litigant, observe a witness, or smell the sweat and blood of battle. In their forum quarreling persons are the abstract 'appellant' and 'appellee'; industrial problems, legal contentions; actuality, verbal currency."[11] Here, again, the highly developed skills that are brought to bear on questions of economic policy are those, not of economic analysis, but of the law.

Between the date when an offense occurs and the date when the last court has spoken its final word there may be a span of many years. There is delay until a suit is brought, delay until a decision is rendered by a District Court, delay until it has been reviewed by a Court of Appeals, further delay until the case has been rejected or reviewed by the Supreme Court, and still further delay until the District Court has prepared a remedy. The U.S. Steel Corporation was formed in 1901, sued in 1912, and finally acquitted in 1920. The Aluminum Company was sued in 1937, found innocent by a District Court in 1942, found guilty by a Court of Appeals in 1945, and finally served with an injunction by the District Court in 1951. While its legality is discussed at leisure, monopoly may persist. And when, at long last, it is found unlawful, it may have assumed another guise.

The Private Suit

The possible award of threefold damages in private suits was designed, not only to punish violators of the law, but also to encourage those who

[10] *Ibid.*, pp. 71–72.
[11] *Ibid.*, p. 73.

were injured to sue. But, even with this encouragement, the number of such suits has not been large. Litigation is costly; the resources of the plaintiff may be small and those of the defendant large; to start a suit involves assumption of a serious risk. The burden of proof, moreover, is heavy. The plaintiff must establish (1) that the antitrust laws have been violated, (2) that the violation has caused him injury, and (3) that the injury has amounted to a certain sum. As prima facie evidence on the first point, he may present the decision of a court in a case brought by the government. But the government moves slowly. And where, as in the usual case, it accepts a consent decree or a plea of *nolo contendere*, there is no admission or finding of guilt. The defendant, moreover, may seek to rebut the prima facie case resulting from a conviction. And, if he does, the plaintiff must prove again that the defendant has broken the law. A bill presented to Congress in 1950 would have made the final judgment in a public suit conclusive rather than prima facie evidence of guilt, thus strengthening the private plaintiff's hand. It failed to pass.

Damage suits can supplement, but not supplant, the efforts of enforcement agencies. Such suits are brought on the initiative of private litigants. They cannot be expected to assure the comprehensiveness and the continuity that are required in the administration of the law.

Enforcement could be strengthened, however, if the government itself were permitted to sue for damages when injured, as a purchaser, by conspiracies or combinations in restraint of trade. Some years ago the Procurement Division of the Treasury, after receiving identical bids on three different purchases of tires, required those bidding on a fourth transaction to warrant that their bids had not resulted from agreement. As a result, the prices fell, and the government brought suit to recover the difference between those paid on the earlier and later purchases, a matter of $350,000. In the Cooper case in 1941, however, the Supreme Court found for the defendants, holding that the government was not a "person" within the meaning of the section of the law that authorizes "any person" to bring suit for damages.[12] A bill authorizing the government to recover actual (rather than treble) damages in such cases was passed by the House of Representatives in 1950 but was not acted upon by the Senate.

Criminal Penalties

When the government wins a criminal suit, the penalties that are applied cannot, in themselves, have much force as a deterrent. Imprisonment is rare; the fines imposed are usually insignificant. From 1890 until 1946, defendants sentenced to prison numbered 198. But, of these, 108 were members of the labor unions, 75 were petty racketeers, 8 were wartime spies, and only 7 were businessmen. In the latter cases, moreover, the sentences were suspended. No important industrialist has ever spent a day in jail for violation of the Sherman Act. The typical outcome of a criminal

[12] *U.S.* v. *Cooper Corp.*, 312 U.S. 600.

suit has been a plea of *nolo contendere* followed by a small fine. Fines levied in this way, and upon conviction, in 226 cases involving businessmen and organizations up to 1946, amounted to $9,250,000, the average fine per guilty defendant standing at only $2,000.[13] The total of all the fines imposed on the defendants in a particular case may be much higher, the figure having reached $105,000 in the case of the Aluminum Company, $175,000 in the case of the A&P, and $312,000 in that involving the 3 largest manufacturers of cigarettes. But such penalties become insignificant when compared with the earnings of the companies concerned. Antitrust fines from 1936 to 1948, taken as a percentage of net profits in 1948, amounted to .001 per cent for General Motors, .017 per cent for du Pont, .037 per cent for Alcoa, and .113 per cent for A&P.[14] A bill that would have increased the statutory penalty from a maximum of $5,000 to one of $50,000 passed the House in 1950 but did not reach the floor of the Senate.

The real punishment in a criminal case is to be found less in the sentence imposed by the court than in the cost of the defense and in the unfavorable publicity attending an indictment and a trial. When the government brought suit against a number of manufacturers of paints and varnishes, most of the defendants entered pleas of *nolo contendere* and paid fines of $1,000 to $5,000 each. But the Glidden company contested the action and, in 1951, was found to be not guilty. The cost of its defense, however, is said to have exceeded $100,000.[15] An antitrust suit is frequently derided by a powerful defendant. But it cannot be shrugged off as unimportant, since it may impair the good will of an enterprise and be damaging to its prestige. And this, in itself, may deter some of those who otherwise would break the law.

But a criminal penalty, whatever its severity, does not provide a remedy. Defendants may be fined but an industry's structure and its practices left unchanged. In its case against the major cigarette companies, decided by the Supreme Court in 1946, the government won a sweeping victory,[16] and the heaviest fines in the history of antitrust were imposed. But the companies were left in predominant possession of the market, and their methods of buying tobacco and selling cigarettes were not perceptibly disturbed. The suit, in the opinion of William H. Nicholls, who has analyzed its outcome, may have brought somewhat lower cigarette prices in the short run. But market sharing and price leadership still appeared to be the rule.[17] If behavior that violates the law is to be corrected, civil remedies must be sought.

[13] Committee on Small Business, *United States versus Economic Concentration and Monopoly*, pp. 257–61.

[14] *Hearings before the Committee on the Judiciary, House of Representatives, on H.R. 6679* (81st Cong., 2d Sess.), pp. 13, 38.

[15] *Business Week*, January 12, 1952, p. 156.

[16] Cf. above, pp. 119–20.

[17] William H. Nicholls, *Price Policies in the Cigarette Industry* (Nashville: Vanderbilt University Press, 1951), chap. xxviii.

Injunctions and Decrees

The outcome of a civil suit not dropped by the government nor dismissed by the court is an injunction or a decree. An injunction is negative in character. It is an order of the court admonishing the defendants no longer to do particular illegal things that they had previously done. The guilty are not punished for their past misdeeds but are merely told to go and sin no more. The threat of an injunction, therefore, can have little force as a deterrent. But such an order, once issued, carries the sanction of possible prosecution for contempt of court. The government, moreover, may bring both a criminal and a civil suit, seeking punishment through the one, correction through the other.

A court decree is positive in character, requiring that certain things be done. A decree may order the abolition of a trade association, the liquidation of a holding company, the reorganization of a corporate combination, or the sale of controlling shares of stock. Short of this, it may break the grip of a monopoly by compelling it to take such action as selling rather than leasing patented machines or granting patent licenses to its competitors. Violators of decrees, too, may be punished for contempt.

Both measures are limited in scope and in effect. They apply only to the parties that are named and to the particular matters that are described. An injunction can forbid only those practices that have been found to violate the law. Although one firm has been ordered to abandon a practice, another may continue to use it until this firm, too, has been prosecuted and enjoined. Although one practice has been prohibited, another practice may be used to achieve the same result until another suit is brought and another injunction obtained. The rules that are issued by the courts cannot be taken as a general code to govern business conduct. They cannot anticipate wrongdoing and forbid it in advance.

Injunctions and decrees, however, have been effective in their application, case by case. Injunctions have been successful in breaking up restraints where markets have been controlled through artificial devices and contractual relationships. They have put an end, in many instances, to exclusive dealing, tying contracts, and discriminatory pricing, and have outlawed procedures through which identity of delivered prices has been obtained. Court decrees, too, have gone far toward preventing the restrictive use of patent rights. When the critics of antitrust complain of its impotence, these real achievements are ignored.

But it may well be questioned whether remedies falling short of corporate disintegration will prove sufficient where markets are dominated by a few large firms. For here, as George J. Stigler told a committee of the Congress in 1950, the courts have merely advised the oligopolists to forget that they are oligopolists. But such advice does not destroy the forces that inhibit competition. It does not attack the fundamental bases of restraint. In Stigler's words, "One and only one policy will deal effectively with such oligopolistic industries: the policy of increasing the number of firms and eliminating the dominance of one or a few. . . . On the preventive side, we should prohibit the formation of oligopolies by mergers of competitive firms. On the corrective side, we should make dissolution the normal method of eliminating restrictive practices in oligopolistic industries."[18]

Dissolution, Divestiture, and Divorcement

In markets that are shared by a few large firms, the restoration of effective competition may call for a rigorous application of the three D's of antitrust: dissolution, divestiture, and divorcement. These three measures are closely allied. Dissolution breaks up a combination into several parts. Divestiture requires defendants to dispose of physical assets, securities, or other forms of property. Divorcement comes as a consequence of divestiture. In common usage, however, the terms are interchangeable.

Dissolution has been sought in a minority of suits. It was ordered in less than a hundred cases from 1890 to 1950. In most of these, moreover, the unit dissolved was not an industrial enterprise but a trade association or a common selling agency. The list of actual combinations dissolved is not a long one. It includes, in the earlier years, a number of railroads, the oil, tobacco, and gunpowder trusts, the meat packing and stockyard companies, and concerns making corn products and photographic equipment and supplies. In 1932 General Electric and Westinghouse were ordered to relinquish their control of RCA. In 1943 the National Broadcasting Company was required to sell its Blue Network which became the foundation for the American Broadcasting Company. In 1944 the Pullman subsidiary that operated sleeping cars was separated from the one that manufactured them. And in 1948, after several years of unsuccessful experimentation with milder methods of restoring competition to the motion picture industry, the large producers were divorced from the large exhibitors. In some of these cases, horizontal combinations were broken up; in others, vertical; in still others, both.

The difficulties presented by dissolution, though great, are not insuperable. It is relatively easy to abolish a trade association or a common sales agency, difficult for one corporation to dispose of its stock in another, more difficult to liquidate a holding company, and even more difficult to divide a single corporation into several parts. In all but the first of these cases important property interests are involved. And in the latter ones, painstaking corporate reorganizations are required. But the problems involved are capable of solution, as has been shown by the experience of the Securities and Exchange Commission under the Public Utility Holding Company Act.

[18] *Hearings before the Subcommittee on Study of Monopoly Power, Committee on the Judiciary, House of Representatives* (81st Cong., 2d Sess.), Serial 14, Part 4 A, pp. 994, 996.

In antitrust, however, what man hath joined together the courts still hesitate to put asunder. In the absence of flagrant abuse they are loath to modify established rights of property. Unable to forsee the consequences of disintegration, they are reluctant to risk impairment of efficiency. In the aluminum case, when it finally came back to the district court for the preparation of a remedy, the government asked that Alcoa be broken into two separate, fully-integrated firms. But the court refused. Between the day in 1945 when Judge Hand found Alcoa to possess an illegal monopoly and the day in 1950 when Judge Knox handed down his final decree, the government had sold to Reynolds and Kaiser war-built factories that enabled them to establish two new integrated companies, and Alcoa's share in the output of virgin aluminum had dropped to half. The court did not find competition so effective that relief was not required. It sought to strengthen Reynolds and Kaiser by striking from Alcoa's patent contracts a provision requiring them to license Alcoa under any patents that they might obtain. And it sought to introduce a fourth competitor into the American market by severing the ties of personal stock ownership that bound Alcoa and Aluminium, Ltd. of Canada. But Alcoa was not split in two. Aluminum, said the court, is vital to national defense. It must compete with other materials made by large concerns. Dismemberment of Alcoa's research staff and its managerial personnel would lessen its ability to do so.

In several other cases, such as those involving United Shoe Machinery and General Electric, the courts have found companies to be in violation of the Sherman Act and have granted sweeping remedies, but have denied the government's request that they be dissolved. In the cigarette case, where the companies were convicted in a criminal suit, the government itself failed to follow through by entering a dissolution plea. Each of the large producers had three or four separate plants. Dissolution, therefore, was a physical possibility. But each of the companies had sold all or most of its output under a single brand name. The names could not be passed on to any of the successor companies, since the ones receiving them would enjoy an unfair advantage over all the rest. They could not be abolished, since they were the major assets of the industry. The position of the convicted companies was therefore left undisturbed.[19] The government and the courts have been forthright in their condemnation of monopoly, faltering in their application of remedies. It is this contrast between word and deed that has turned notable legal victories, such as those in aluminum and cigarettes, into economic defeats.[20]

Where dissolution has been effected, its consequences have been open to dispute. In the case of Standard Oil, dissolved in 1911, the holding company distributed among its stockholders, on a pro rata basis, the shares of

[19] Nicholls, *loc. cit.*

[20] See Walter Adams, "The Aluminum Case: Legal Victory—Economic Defeat," *American Economic Review*, Vol. XLI (1951), pp. 915–23.

its subsidiaries. Though the successor companies were nominally independent, their owners were identical. These companies, moreover, were organized along state lines. A community of interest was thus maintained within a group of regional monopolies. The court's decree did serve, however, to discourage open collusion and to encourage the entry of new competitors. As time passed, the concentrated stockholdings were dispersed through inheritance and sale; new firms emerged, and the dominance of the Standard companies declined. In 1931 the decree was modified by a District Court to permit the merger of two of these concerns—Standard of New York and Vacuum Oil—on the questionable ground that the industry, by then, was "genuinely competitive."[21] In the case of the tobacco trust, also dissolved in 1911, the constituent companies making each of the major products were so divided that no one of the successors would account for more than a third of the supply. But here, again, the stocks controlling these concerns were left in the same hands. Nicholls concludes, however, that the dissolution "did usher in a decade of product innovation and price competition which was strongly in the public interest" before the industry "settled down into the pattern of non-price competition."[22]

In recent years, the government has sought to avoid the principal weakness of the earlier dissolution proceedings by requesting that the ownership, control, and management of each of the successor companies be completely and perpetually separated from the ownership, control, and management of any of the others. The government lost the suit in which it sought to sever the ties which bound the du Pont company and members of the du Pont family, on the one hand, and General Motors and U.S. Rubber, on the other. But the remedy it sought in this case still serves to illustrate the thoroughness of its new approach. It asked (1) that the company be forbidden to distribute its GM stock to its own stockholders, but required to sell it on the market and pay them cash, (2) that members of the family be forbidden to purchase this stock, (3) that they be required to sell their own stock in GM and U.S. Rubber, (4) that all of the defendants be perpetually enjoined from holding stock in any of the others, and (5) that General Motors and U.S. Rubber be forbidden to elect to their directorates anyone who had been a director, an officer, or an employee of du Pont.[23] If there were any loopholes left in this proposal, they were not visible to the naked eye.

The Consent Decree

No provision has ever been made by Congress for the settlement of antitrust suits through consent decrees, though such decrees were recog-

[21] *U.S.* v. *Standard Oil Co.* (N.Y.), 47 F. 2d 288.

[22] Nicholls, *op. cit.*, p. 409.

[23] *U.S.* v. *du Pont*, District Court of the U.S., S.D. of Ill., Civil Action No. 490–1071, Complaint, June 30, 1949.

nized by implication when they were mentioned in the Clayton Act. The first consent decree was accepted in the case of the Otis Elevator Company in 1906. Since that time, more than half of the civil suits filed by the government have been settled in this way. The proportion has been even higher in more recent years. As a source of antitrust law, the consent decree today is fully as important as are the decisions of the courts.

A consent decree usually emerges from a protracted series of secret, informal negotiations between lawyers representing the Antitrust Division and counsel for the defense. In such negotiations, as in any case of bilateral bargaining, differences are gradually narrowed as proposals lead to counterproposals and these to counter-counterproposals until agreement is finally attained. The settlement resulting from this process is taken by each side as the best it can get. It is then accepted by a District Court —usually without examination or questioning—and is issued in the same manner and, in general, with the same effect as any other court decree.

The method has much to commend it. It is less expensive than litigation. It has greater flexibility. It permits decrees to be drafted in conformity with the peculiar characteristics of particular industries. It may go beyond the negative provisions of the law to shape affirmative remedies. It sometimes obtains acceptance for reforms more sweeping than those that would have been demanded by the courts. The royalty-free licensing of patents, for instance, before it was required in the General Electric case, had been incorporated in a number of consent decrees. But the method also has its dangers. The negotiations are conducted in private. No record of the proceedings is disclosed. If representatives of the government were to become corrupt or incompetent, offenders might be let off lightly without the facts becoming known. Approval by the court, in the absence of any basis for appraisal, affords no guarantee against abuse. The consent decree, depending on the manner of its use, may either strengthen or relax enforcement of the law.

In December, 1954, the Antitrust Division revealed an innovation in its procedure when it announced a consent decree accepted by the Eastman Kodak Company on the day the case was filed with the court. Here, the terms of the settlement were negotiated before bringing suit and the costs of litigation were saved. This procedure has its advantages both for government and for business. But it remains to be seen whether it can be brought into general use.

Policing the Courts' Decrees

Antitrust decrees, throughout the years, have not been systematically enforced. The Antitrust Division has lacked the money and the staff to follow them up and check on the observance of their terms. Cases have been regarded as closed when the last court has spoken, save in the rare instances where dissolution or divestiture have been required. The provisions of a decree may have become obsolete, but they have not been altered unless the defendants have come into court and asked that they be liberalized. They may have been ignored, but no action has been taken unless someone who was injured has complained. Up to 1951 only eight defendants had been sued and half a dozen fined for contempt of court in cases involving violation of an antitrust decree. A beginning was made toward more careful preparation of decrees and more adequate supervision of compliance with their terms when a Judgments and Judgment Enforcement Section was set up within the Antitrust Division in 1949 and a separate staff assigned to this work.

MAINTAINING COMPETITION THROUGH ADMINISTRATIVE PROCESSES

The judicial process as a method of maintaining competition has obvious weaknesses. It is cumbersome, inexpert, confusing, and frequently ineffective. It was not designed to serve as an instrument of industrial control. The proposal is therefore made, from time to time, that antitrust be removed from the arena of litigation and placed in the hands of an administrative agency, composed of men possessing an intimate knowledge of business, serving as impartial experts, and empowered to issue regulations, industry by industry, forbidding industrial combinations and business practices that would tend to restrain trade or promote monopoly. Such an agency could act speedily, skillfully, and flexibly. It would seek, not to punish, but to prevent. As a safeguard to business, its regulations would be subject to judicial review. But administrative rather than judicial processes would be adopted initially as being more appropriate to the nature of the task at hand.

The proposal is not a new one. Something of the sort is involved, of course, in the practice of giving advisory opinions and in the negotiation of consent decrees. But it is in the Federal Trade Commission that the closest approach to administrative enforcement of competition has been made.

The Federal Trade Commission

It should be remembered that the great bulk of the Federal Trade Commission's time and energy has been directed toward protecting consumers against small-business men, and small-business men against their competitors, in cases where no problem of maintaining competition or preventing monopoly was involved. Up to 1946 only 15 per cent of the Commission's cases had dealt with such problems, and in later years more than half of these had been concerned with exclusive contracts and price discrimination and less than half with conspiracies and combinations in restraint of trade.[24] Among the latter, however, were the cases involving

[24] Committee on Small Business, *United States versus Economic Concentration and Monopoly*, p. 20.

delivered pricing in steel, cement, and other industries that were more important than their relative number would suggest. Here, the Commission launched an effective drive against one of the principal instruments of large-scale monopoly.

As first envisaged the Commission was to have been a vigorous agency, composed of experts, equipped with economic and legal staffs, given broad powers to investigate and report on business organization and practices, and authorized to issue orders that would have the force of law. It was to bring the skill of the specialist and the flexibility of the administrative process to the solution of the problems of monopoly. It was to explore the frontiers of legality and to break new ground in the development of policy. At no time during the life of the Commission, however, have these hopes come close to being realized. The recent criticisms of its record have been harsh in the extreme. According to a group of experts on public administration, reporting to ex-President Hoover's commission on governmental reorganization in 1949,

> The Commission has been hampered by inadequate funds, hostile court rulings, mediocre appointments. Its operations, programs, and administrative methods have often been inadequate. . . . As the years have progressed, the Commission has become immersed in a multitude of petty problems; it has not probed into new areas of anti-competitive practices; it has become increasingly bogged down with cumbersome procedures and inordinate delays in disposition of cases. Its economic work—instead of being the backbone of its activities—has been allowed to dwindle almost to none. The Commission has largely become a passive judicial agency, waiting for cases to come up on the docket, under routinized procedures, without active responsibility for achieving the statutory objectives. . . . With notable exceptions, appointments to the Federal Trade Commission have been made with too little interest in the skills and experience pertinent to the problems of competition and monopoly, and too much attention to service to political party.[25]

The Small Business Committee of the House of Representatives, commenting on the situation in the Commission in 1951, spoke of "the generally low level of morale among its employees," citing as evidence

> The internal strife and office politics that pervade the agency. . . . The many small cliques and groups whose chief interest is in personal authority and advancement. . . . The pronounced feeling of unrest and dissatisfaction in many segments of the Commission. . . . The presence of numerous "prima donnas," persons who are looking for personal glorification and who seem to have scant appreciation of the need of teamwork. . . . Among the older employees an attitude of indifference toward the work of the agency, a reluctance to face new issues, and a determination that one's own little domain shall not be disturbed. . . .[26]

[25] Commission on Organization of the Executive Branch of the Government, *Task Force Report on Regulatory Commissions* (Washington: Government Printing Office, 1949), pp. 119–25.

[26] Committee on Small Business, *Antitrust Law Enforcement*, p. 18.

And James M. Landis, a former Commissioner, serving in 1951 as Chairman of the Committee on Cartels and Monopoly of the Twentieth Century Fund, registered his dissent from the Committee's recommendation that the Commission be strengthened, in the following words: ". . . Reference must be made to what I would call the utter bankruptcy of the Federal Trade Commission. As a practical matter, the deterioration of that Commission has gone beyond redemption. If duties of this kind are to be thrust on some agency, there is really only one thing to do, and that is to wipe out the F.T.C. completely and start afresh."[27]

These criticisms, it must be admitted, are not without some foundation in fact. The Commission, instead of taking vigorous action, has functioned passively, as if it were a court, waiting for outsiders to bring complaints. Its procedures have been clumsy and time-consuming. Cases have lingered on its docket for months and years. One fourth of those settled in the fiscal year 1950 had been pending more than five years; less than a fifth had been handled within a year. There was a backlog of nearly 2,000 unsettled cases at the end of fiscal 1949.[28] The initiative, informality, and dispatch supposedly inherent in the administrative process have not, as yet, been seen.

Much of the responsibility for these shortcomings can be laid at the doors of the Congress. The appropriations made for the work of the Commission ran around $500,000 a year until 1918, around $1,500,000 until 1920, and below $1,000,000 until 1929; they were below $2,000,000 until 1934, below $3,000,000 until 1947, and did not reach $4,000,000 until 1951. At the end of fiscal 1950, the agency had only 650 employees, with fewer than 300 lawyers, less than 100 of them engaged in antimonopoly work. In one case, where the respondents were represented by 102 law firms, the Commission itself was represented by one principal attorney and two part-time assistants. Congress has thus expected the FTC to keep watch on American business with the aid of a corporal's guard.

The White House has been equally indifferent. No sooner had the Commission been established, under Woodrow Wilson, than the attention of the administration was diverted by World War I. The Harding, Coolidge, and Hoover administrations were unsympathetic. William E. Humphrey, appointed by President Coolidge in 1925, dominated the Commission until 1933. The function of the agency, in his view, was less to police the activities of business than to promote its interests. Shortly after Franklin D. Roosevelt was inaugurated he asked Commissioner Humphrey to resign. When the Commissioner refused to do so, the President removed him. Humphrey appealed to the courts and, after his death, the Supreme Court held that the President lacked the power of removal, save for the causes specified in the Trade Commission Act: "inefficiency,

[27] George W. Stocking and Myron W. Watkins, *Monopoly and Free Enterprise* (New York: Twentieth Century Fund, 1951), p. 548.

[28] Committee on Small Business, *Antitrust Law Enforcement*, pp. 19–23.

neglect of duty, or malfeasance in office."[29] Thereafter, the Roosevelt and Truman administrations showed little interest in the FTC. A succession of lame duck appointments set a pattern of mediocrity from which a full recovery was never made.

With the Eisenhower administration, the Commission was given an infusion of new blood. Under Chairman Edward F. Howrey there were important changes in policy. The Commission backed away from the doctrine of conscious parallelism of action and from per se findings of illegality, confining its antimonopoly actions to cases in which collusion could be proved rather than inferred, and judging such practices as exclusive dealing by their probable—not by their possible—effects. At the same time it eased up on enforcement of the "soft competition" provisions of the Robinson-Patman Act. An internal reorganization was effected. The number of pending cases was sharply reduced. A start was made on checking compliance with outstanding orders and requiring regular compliance reports.

Investigations and Publicity

Section 6 of its basic statute gave the Commission power (1) on its own initiative "to gather and compile information concerning, and to investigate from time to time the organization, business, conduct, practices, and management of any corporation engaged in commerce," to require such corporations to file annual and special reports, and to publish such information, "except trade secrets and names of customers, as it shall deem expedient in the public interest," and (2) "upon the direction of the President or either House of Congress to investigate and report the facts relating to any alleged violations of the antitrust Acts. . . ." The Commission, in the opinion of its sponsors, was to possess "full inquisitorial powers." Its investigatory function was held to be an integral part of the regulatory process. Business conduct was to be controlled, not only by legal action, but also, in Woodrow Wilson's phrase, by "pitiless publicity."

In its discharge of this responsibility, however, the Commission has been handicapped, first, by decisions of the courts and, second, by acts of Congress. Its ability to make investigations on its own initiative was limited by the decision of the Supreme Court in the Claire Furnace case[30] in 1927. Here, the FTC had sought to require the periodic submission of data by members of the iron and steel industry, a score of companies had obtained an injunction to prevent it, and the Commission had appealed. The Court held that the Commission could not itself appeal for enforcement of requests for information but could only submit them to the Attorney General for whatever action he might choose to take. The Com-

[29] *Humphrey's Executor* v. *U.S.*, 295 U.S. 602 (1935).

[30] *FTC* v. *Claire Furnace Co.*, 274 U.S. 160.

mission's power to investigate antitrust violations, in response to a Congressional resolution, was curtailed by the Court's decision in the American Tobacco case[31] in 1924. In this case the FTC had asked for information in accordance with a Senate resolution, the company had refused to give it, and the Commission had asked that disclosure be enforced. The Court refused, noting that the Senate had not alleged a violation of the law, and holding that the guarantee against unreasonable searches and seizures contained in the Fourth Amendment to the Constitution, would be abrogated if the government were to conduct "fishing expeditions into private papers on the possibility that they may disclose evidence of crime."[32] This limitation was removed, however by a sweeping decision handed down by the Court in the second Morton Salt case[33] in 1950. In this instance, the Commission had brought suit against Morton for refusing to heed its request for a report on the company's compliance with its order (upheld in the first Morton Salt case in 1948) against illegal discrimination in price. The Commission's authority to demand information, for any purpose within its duties, was upheld by a unanimous court: ". . . An administrative agency charged with seeing that the laws are enforced . . . has a power of inquisition . . . which is not derived from the judicial function. It is more analogous to the grand jury, which does not depend on a case or controversy for power to get evidence but can investigate merely on suspicion that the law is being violated, or even just because it wants assurance that it is not." Where the Court has given, however, the Congress has taken away. Since 1935 the Independent Offices Appropriation Bill has carried a rider prohibiting the use of the Commission's appropriation to finance an investigation of an antitrust violation unless authorized by a joint resolution of both houses accompanied by an allotment of special funds. The Commission can still act on its own initiative, but the sums provided for this work are small. A serious obstacle to publication exists, moreover, in the statutory limitation on disclosure of the "names of customers." Release of reports has been prevented, on this ground, in cases of major industries where these names were common property.

The studies made by the FTC, throughout the years, have been uneven in quality. Some of them have been superficial and apologetic; others have been searching and significant. Studies of general economic interest have dealt with national wealth and income, industrial concentration, the merger movement, interlocking directorates, and international cartels. Studies of business practices have covered open price reporting, delivered pricing, resale price maintenance, and the behavior of chain stores. Studies of particular industries have included among others: copper, motor vehicles, petroleum, pipe lines, and electrical utilities. They have also included,

[31] *FTC* v. *American Tobacco Co.*, 264 U.S. 298.

[32] *Ibid.*, p. 306.

[33] *U.S.* v. *Morton Salt Co.*, 338 U.S. 632.

in response to agricultural interests, a number of those from whom the farmers buy or to whom they sell: farm machinery, fertilizer, flour milling, meat packing, and the distribution of milk and dairy products, and fruits and vegetables. The information provided by such investigations has led to the enactment of a number of important statutes, the outstanding example being that of the 78-volume report on the electrical utility industry which laid the foundation for the Public Utility Holding Company Act of 1935.

Cease and Desist Orders

The only formal action that the FTC can take is to issue an order to cease and desist. Such an order has serious weaknesses. It is purely negative in character. It can forbid a practice that is in itself illegal; it cannot forbid one that would otherwise be lawful on the ground that it is an integral part of an unlawful plan. It can tell respondents what they are not to do; it cannot require them to take affirmative action to rectify past wrongs or to afford assurance against future ones. The order is strictly limited in scope. It is confined to a particular offense by a particular offender in a particular case. It leaves the respondent free to offend in a different way, and leaves his neighbor free to offend in the same way, until an order has been issued in another case. No matter how often a practice has been condemned, further offenses cannot be punished until each procedural step has been taken again and again.

The penalty for violating the Trade Commission Act, as it now stands, is a fine of not more than $5,000 per day, collected by entering a civil suit. The penalty for violating the Clayton Act is punishment for contempt of court. Before these penalties can be imposed, however, it must be established, in independent proceedings, that two successive violations of the Trade Commission Act or three successive violations of the Clayton Act have occurred. Under the former Act, if an order is not appealed to a court, it becomes effective in sixty days; if it is appealed and sustained, it is confirmed by an injunction; in either case, a defendant may then be punished for a single repetition of his offense. Under the Clayton Act, however, the Commission must prove a first violation before it can issue an order, a second before it can obtain an injunction, and a third before a violator will be punished for contempt. There seems to be no good reason why the simpler procedure now provided in the Trade Commission Act should not also apply to the Clayton Act. One repetition of an offense should be enough.

During most of its life the Commission has made little effort to determine whether its orders have actually been observed. When issuing them, it has directed respondents to submit reports on their compliance within sixty or ninety days. Its authority to do so was upheld by the Supreme Court in the second Morton Salt case in 1950, and the defendants in this case were subsequently fined a total of $80,000 for refusal to report. But a single report is all that has been demanded; nothing has been required in later months or years. In fiscal 1950 reports were received on compliance with 85 new orders but none on compliance with more than 4,000 older orders that were still in force. When reports have been received, examined, and filed, it has been assumed that compliance has been obtained. The Commission has rarely moved to punish violations unless outsiders have brought renewed complaints. Its appropriation and its staff have been too small to enable it to make an independent check regularly. A Compliance Division was set up in 1947 and a comprehensive investigation of compliance with outstanding orders was finally inaugurated in 1954.

Stipulations and Trade Practice Conferences

From the time of its formation up to June 30, 1950, the FTC had handled more than 44,000 cases. Of these, some 33,000, or about three fourths, had been dismissed or dropped; some 4,000 had resulted in the issuance of orders; more than 7,000 had been settled through informal processes. The use of formal orders has declined, both relatively and absolutely. From 1936 to 1941, 1 case in 5 had led to an order; from 1946 to 1951, only 1 in 10. In the earlier period, 254 orders were issued yearly; in the latter, only 69. Increasing reliance was being placed on other methods of effecting settlements.[34]

Most important among these methods is the stipulation. This is a document signed by an actual or potential respondent in which he agrees to abstain from illegal practices. A comparable device is the letter or affadavit of discontinuance, in which an offender gives assurance that he has abandoned the use of such practices. When any of these papers is accepted, a case is closed without the imposition of a penalty. This procedure is more likely to be adopted, it should be noted, in cases of practices that deceive consumers and those of unfair methods of competition in petty trade, where the problem of monopoly is not involved. Here, in the view of the Commission, informal settlement is quicker and cheaper than the issuance of formal orders and may be equal in effectiveness.

The other informal procedure used extensively by the Commission is the formulation of codes of trade practice by industrial conferences. The first of these conferences was held in 1919. By 1950, trade practice rules were in effect for 168 different industries. It is the purpose of this procedure to enlist the voluntary co-operation of business in avoiding resort to practices that would violate the law. To this end, the Commission has encouraged the adoption of trade practice rules, in certain cases, by dropping pending complaints, and by approving, in Group II, rules condemning practices that are not illegal but that the industry believes to be unfair. In its Group I Rules, however, it has merely codified existing law and shown its application to the circumstances of specific industries. And these are the only rules that it promises to enforce. But compliance is not po-

[34] Committee on Small Business, *Antitrust Law Enforcement*, p. 24.

liced, and violators are prosecuted only as complaints may happen to come in.

The Commission has always professed enthusiasm for this procedure, contending in 1941 that it had led to "the wholesale abandonment and prevention of unfair methods of competition, trade restraints and abuses"[35] and in 1952 that it "often effects immediate and simultaneous correction of trade abuses which might otherwise require prosecution of protracted suits."[36] The basis for these conclusions is unknown. It is possible, of course, that the discussion and circulation of trade practice rules may have some educational value. But it is unlikely that profitable practices will be abandoned voluntarily. And there is always danger that the program may be employed to give the color of official endorsement to practices that involve restraint of trade. Unless held in check, the Commission's trade practice conference work might come increasingly to diverge from the main direction of Commission policy.

Political Vulnerability

Litigation, with all its faults, has one outstanding advantage: it is familiar, it is understood, it is clothed with prestige; as a consequence, it is accepted, if not with enthusiasm, at least with tolerance. The prosecutors and the courts are likely to be permitted to do their work. An administrative agency, by contrast, is peculiarly vulnerable to political attack. If inert, lenient, and ineffective, its placid existence may be undisturbed. But if vigorous in the performance of its duties, it will be headed for trouble. Its powers may be curtailed, its appropriation slashed, its administrators refused confirmation, its personnel subjected to persecution, its very existence jeopardized.

When the Supreme Court upheld the orders issued against basing point pricing, in 1948, the hue and cry was raised against the FTC. It was said that the Commission had exceeded its authority, that it had usurped the prerogatives of Congress, that it was embracing alien ideologies. In an article published in 1952, the basing point lawyer who served as counsel to the Capehart committee denounced the Commission for concealing its objectives, for creating confusion, and for embarking on crusades for f.o.b. pricing, against functional pricing, and against good faith competition, and demanded that it be dismembered, its antitrust function being transferred to the Department of Justice and its research functions to the Department of Commerce.[37] The clock was thus to be turned back to the days before World War I.

If the Federal Trade Commission comes to grief, it will not be because

[35] Federal Trade Commission, *Control of Unfair Competitive Practices through Trade Practice Conference Procedure*, T.N.E.C. Monograph No. 34 (Washington: Government Printing Office, 1940), p. 14.

[36] Federal Trade Commission, *Annual Report, 1951*, p. 70.

[37] William Simon, "The Case Against the Federal Trade Commission," *University of Chicago Law Review*, Vol. XIX, p. 297. See also Robert A. Wallace and Paul H. Douglas, *loc. cit.*

it has been too lax, but because it has been too tough. If it values survival, an agency thus attacked is likely to draw in its horns. It will be interesting to follow the future policies of the FTC.

THE NEED FOR UNIFICATION OF POLICY

The authors of the Federal Trade Commission Act intended that the Commission should play a major role in the enforcement of antitrust. At the request of the court, in an antitrust suit, the Commission was to serve as a master in chancery to prepare a tentative decree. At the request of the Attorney General, it was to draw up plans for the reorganization of illegal combinations. And upon such a request, or at its own initiative, it was to investigate and report on compliance with antitrust decrees. None of these functions has ever been performed, since the requests that were contemplated have never been forthcoming, and the Commission has been unwilling to enter where its presence has not been desired. The integration of the two agencies of enforcement, clearly contemplated by Congress, has not occurred. As a result, in the words of the House Committee on Small Business, "The anti-trust program today is being conducted in a series of isolated skirmishes under two separate forces and two separate commands."[38] Formal liaison was established between the Commission and the Antitrust Division in 1948, and one agency or the other now obtains priority in particular actions through a system of clearances. Overlapping is thus avoided but omissions are not. Some offenders may escape entirely. Whether others are made the objects of cease and desist orders or criminal suits will depend upon the chance that FTC or Justice was the first to take a case. Each agency formulates its own program. If the two coincide, it is by accident rather than design. In the absence of central direction, it is not surprising if antitrust is characterized by inadequacy of coverage, errors in timing, and inconsistency of policy.

This inconsistency goes beyond the relations between the Department of Justice and the FTC. The policy of antitrust is one among many. Those promoting monopoly through patents and tariffs or restraining competition in labor, agriculture, and small business have conflicting purposes. Certain industries have been exempted from antitrust. In others, antitrust is supposedly enforced by separate agencies—the Secretary of Agriculture, the Federal Reserve Board, the Interstate Commerce Commission, the Federal Power Commission, the Federal Communications Commission, the Securities and Exchange Commission, and the Civil Aeronautics Board—each of them a law unto itself. Here and elsewhere, where services and rates are regulated by public agencies, this regulation may be narrower in scope than the exemption granted from the Sherman Act. There are also administrative decisions made by other agencies of government that affect the maintenance of competition: decisions, for instance, that govern the

[38] Committee on Small Business, *Antitrust Law Enforcement,* p. 70.

letting of contracts, the granting of loans, and the disposition of public property. Competition is affected, too, by measures adopted by state and local agencies, and these measures may be influenced by decisions of the federal government. But nowhere in this government is there an officer, or even an interagency committee, charged with responsibility or given authority to look at national policy as a whole, to draw up a comprehensive program, to co-ordinate the programs of separate agencies, to resolve conflicts, or to eliminate inconsistencies.

The voices that speak for competition, in the federal government, are a long way down the line. The special interests of business, labor, and agriculture are represented in the President's cabinet; the general interest in maintaining a free economy is not. Antitrust would be more effective if policy were unified and given expression in the upper councils of the government.

But the successes and the failures of the policy will depend, in the last analysis, upon the character of its popular support. Antitrust was once a great crusade; it is no longer. Every pressure group—big business, little business, labor, and agriculture—gives lip service to competition in general. But each of them asks for an exception when it is expected to compete. The consumer, on the other hand, is uninformed, unorganized, and even indifferent. The problem of monopoly seems less urgent when standards of living are rising, even though they might have risen even more. Public attention is claimed, and political action demanded, by many another worthy cause. And so there is no lobby at work in Washington turning on the heat for antitrust. The wonder, therefore, is not that the policy has been less than wholly successful, but that it has succeeded so largely as it has.

Opinions differ as to the wisdom of the policy of maintaining competition and as to the effectiveness with which it has been carried out. Opinions differ, too, concerning the many proposals for its reform. These are matters to which we shall return in Chapters 30 and 31, after the alternatives to this policy have been examined and appraised.

SUGGESTIONS FOR FURTHER READING

Corwin D. Edwards closes his book *Maintaining Competition* with an excellent chapter on "Administration." An entertaining and illuminating account of the work of the Antitrust Division is that by Walton Hamilton and Irene Till, *Antitrust in Action*, T.N.E.C. Monograph No. 16 (Washington: Government Printing Office, 1940). For an appraisal of the effectiveness of particular antitrust decrees see: William H. Nicholls, "The Tobacco Case of 1946," *American Economic Review*, Vol. XXXIX, No. 3 (1949), pp. 284–97; Walter Adams, "The Aluminum Case: Legal Victory—Economic Defeat," *American Economic Review*, Vol. XLI (1951), pp. 913–23; and the papers by Simon N. Whitney and James W. McKie on the decrees in the motion picture and tin can cases in the *Papers and Proceedings* of the American Economic

Association, to be published as a supplement to Vol. XLV of the *American Economic Review* in May, 1955. A critical appraisal of *Antitrust Law Enforcement by the Federal Trade Commission and the Antitrust Division, Department of Justice* by the Select Committee on Small Business of the House of Representatives is contained in House Report No. 3236, 81st Cong., 2d Sess. (1951). On the Federal Trade Commission, see also The Commission on Organization of the Executive Branch of the Government, *Task Force Report on Regulatory Commissions* (Washington: Government Printing Office, 1949), chap. xii.

PART III

Supplementing Competition

Chapter 10 PROTECTING CONSUMERS AND INVESTORS

The maintenance of competition protects the community against the evils of monopoly. But it affords no protection against the harm that may be done by competitors. Competing sellers and competing buyers may not be equally well informed, and those who possess information may take advantage of those who lack it. Sellers and buyers may not be equally able to bargain, and those who have this ability may impose upon those who do not. Sellers seeking present profits and buyers seeking present satisfactions may waste scarce natural resources, thus impairing the well-being of future generations and endangering their security. Government is therefore concerned, not only with the preservation of competition, but also with the ways in which men compete. So laws have been enacted to equip traders with accurate information, to equalize their capacity for bargaining, and to safeguard future needs against present wastes. Thus government has sought to facilitate the operation of free markets and to protect them against abuse. And it has acted, too, to give encouragement to producers by adopting measures that are designed to promote voluntary participation in various forms of productive activity.

The next three chapters, constituting Part III of this book, are concerned with governmental programs that supplement individual initiative as a stimulator, and competition as a regulator, of business. The present chapter deals with measures that protect buyers—consumers of goods and services, depositors in banks, and purchasers of insurance policies, stocks, and bonds—against fraud and deception on the part of sellers. The next chapter has to do with measures adopted in the interest of producing groups—business, agriculture, and labor—for the purpose of promoting production, protecting weaker sellers against stronger buyers, and equalizing bargaining power. Chapter 12 is devoted to the conservation of natural resources. The discussion of the protections afforded to investors and to workers is comparatively brief. These subjects are treated more fully in texts that deal with banking, insurance, corporation finance, and the economics of labor. They are outlined here, however, in order to indicate their relevance to the present analysis.

THE CONSUMER AND THE LAW

The large enterprise, as a buyer, whether it be a business organization, a public institution, or an agency of government, is unlikely to be defrauded or deceived by other enterprises, as sellers, since it customarily places little or no reliance on any representation that they may make. Instead, it employs skilled purchasing agents who specialize in the goods it buys, lays down specifications to govern quality and performance, and conducts tests in its own laboratories to make sure that the specifications are met. The ultimate consumer, however, does not do his buying in this way. His purchasing agent—the housewife—is usually selected for her competence in other fields. The goods that he must buy are so many, so varied, and so complex that he can scarcely expect her to become an expert on all—if on any—of them. He cannot hope to establish his own specifications or to make his own tests. He is rarely in a position to judge quality or performance or even, perhaps, to protect himself against short measure and short weight. He must rely, therefore, upon the representations that are made by the manufacturers who produce the goods he buys and the merchants who distribute them. As a result, he may be persuaded to purchase articles that are harmful or dangerous or simply worthless, to accept one quantity or quality in the guise of another, and to pay far more for what he gets than it is really worth. Placing his confidence in the word of the seller, he may often be protected by the latter's interest in preserving a reputation. But he may sometimes be defrauded and deceived. And it is against fraud and deception that action has been taken, over the years, at common law and through legislation by local, state, and federal governments.

The Consumer at Common Law

Centuries ago, the position of the consumer, at common law, was encompassed within the meaning of the phrase *caveat emptor:* "Let the buyer beware." Under this rule, the buyer was held to be able to protect himself and was therefore denied damages if he brought suit. The doctrine was developed, however, in cases involving the purchase of familiar articles, displayed in plain sight, so that an appraisal of their value could be made. As time passed, it ceased to fit the facts. Goods became less simple and markets more impersonal; spot transactions gave way to the conclusion of contracts for future performance; the buyer was forced to rely increasingly upon the seller's honesty. This change was given recognition by the courts, and *caveat emptor* came to be modified by the legal rules of fraud, warranty, and negligence.

Under the rule of fraud, contracts were invalidated, at an early date, where it was shown that one of the parties had been tricked into signing different terms than he had thought, and damages came to be awarded where it could be proved that sellers had willfully made statements that they knew to be false. Proof of fraud was by no means easy to establish. But actions under the other rules were more readily sustained. Warranty was held to be expressed in written or oral statements made by a seller or his agent at the time of sale, or implied where goods were sold for future delivery; and if goods were not as represented, the buyer was upheld in refusing to accept or pay for them, or in keeping them and suing under his contract, asking damages for its breach or demanding performance in accordance with its terms. Under the rule of negligence, it was held that a seller was bound to reveal to buyers any defects hidden in his product of which he knew or should have known, and a buyer injured by his failure to do so might recover damages.

The consumer was thus afforded some protection at common law. But the law was curiously inconsistent in its results. In two cases, decided by the same court in the same year:

> The unfortunate woman who swallowed a tack in a blueberry pie lost her case because her lawyer proceeded in tort, alleging and failing to prove negligence. The slightly less unfortunate woman who broke a tooth on a bean-like stone in an order of baked beans won because her lawyer, though equally unable to prove negligence, had drawn up his papers on the basis of breach of warranty.[1]

The common law, moreover, applied only to injury in the past; it contributed little to the prevention of injury in the future. And it was called into play only when buyers were sufficiently harmed and angered, and sufficiently well-to-do, to take the initiative and bear the cost involved in bringing suits. If the consumer is really to be protected, prohibitions against fraud and deception must be written into statutes, accompanied by penalties, and enforced by public officials at public expense.

State and Local Regulations

State and local governments have long assumed responsibility for the supervision of weights and measures. In the usual case, a state official issues regulations establishing specifications and tolerances for all weights, measures, and weighing and measuring devices, such as gasoline pumps and merchants' scales. Local officials inspect all new devices and test all old ones once or twice a year. Devices found to be accurate are sealed or stamped and those found to be inaccurate are seized and destroyed. Persons convicted of giving short weight or measure may be fined or jailed. Compliance with legal standards, however, is less than universal. The funds provided for administration are usually meager. The fines imposed are small and jail sentences are rare. Honesty in weights and measures is to be attributed more to voluntary observance of the laws than to the vigor with which they are enforced.

[1] Nathan Isaacs, "The Consumer at Law," *Annals of the American Academy of Political and Social Science*, Vol. 173 (1934), pp. 177–87, esp. p. 178.

Measures adopted by the states to protect the safety and the health of the consumer are so numerous that it is possible to do no more than indicate their general character. The production, possession, and sale of narcotics is usually regulated; the sale of drugs without a doctor's prescription is forbidden; and the sale of poisons is controlled. Adulteration and misbranding of foods and drugs is generally prohibited, as is the use of arsenic in spraying fruits and vegetables. Inspection of meat and fish and the pasteurization of milk are made compulsory. The sale of second-hand bedding is restricted, and the sterilization of hair and feathers used in new bedding is customarily required. Standards of cleanliness, enforced by inspection, are established for food-dispensing establishments—such as dairies, canneries, bakeries, meat markets, and restaurants—and for clinics, dispensaries, barber shops, and swimming pools. Standards of professional competence are employed in granting and refusing licenses to physicians, dentists, midwives, nurses, pharmacists, optometrists, and chiropodists. And the list is not by any means complete.

The states have acted, too, to protect the consumer against financial loss. From the establishment of standard weights and measures, they have gone on to prescribe standard containers for certain products—such as fruits, vegetables, milk, and cream; standard weights for others—such as a loaf of bread or a ton of coal; and standards of quality for still others—such as fertilizers, butter, and eggs. They have required that packages be so labeled as to show the weight of their contents and that certain goods, such as animal feeds, be so labeled as to reveal their composition. Most states have made it a criminal offense to obtain money under false pretenses. Most of them have adopted a uniform sales act, prescribing a standard form for sales contracts and defining the obligations of warranty. Many states have enacted a model statute forbidding the publication of advertisements containing untrue, deceptive, or misleading statements of fact, and several others have forbidden such misstatements where they are made willfully with intent to deceive. In neither case, however, is there any pretense that such laws have been enforced.

Action has also been taken to protect small borrowers. Institutions making small loans, such as personal finance companies, industrial banks, credit unions, and remedial loan societies, have been brought under the jurisdiction of banking departments in most states. In earlier years, necessitous and uninformed borrowers were cruelly exploited by loan sharks. They were charged exorbitant rates of interest and kept continually in debt with threats of attachments of wages and personal property. The small loans business is now controlled, however, by a Uniform Small Loan Law which has been adopted by three fourths of the states. Under this law, lenders are licensed, the rates that they may charge are limited, and their ability to obtain repayment by attaching wages and property is curbed. Small loans are still costly, but the ethics of the lenders have been greatly improved.

Federal Regulations

Since 1872, federal law has prohibited the use of the mails to defraud. Each year, inspectors for the Post Office Department investigate cases where glasses have been fitted by mail, fake cures sold to sufferers from cancer, tuberculosis, and other serious ailments, and money collected for worthless insurance policies, stocks in nonexistent mining ventures, and the clearance of title to mythical estates. The Department grants a hearing to any person accused of such practices and, if it finds him guilty, may issue a fraud order, instructing postmasters not to cash money orders made out to him or to deliver letters addressed to him, but to return them instead to their senders, stamped "FRAUDULENT!" Serious cases may be turned over to the Department of Justice for criminal prosecutions, leading to fines up to $1,000 or imprisonment up to five years or both. Fraud orders are issued and convictions obtained by the hundreds every year. But the Post Office can exclude no more than a minor fraction of illegal letters from the mails. Lacking the right of censorship, it acts upon complaint. In many cases the victims of fraud do not complain. And where they do, the swindler named in an order need only change his name and address to resume his business.

Congress was given power, by the Constitution, to enact laws establishing standards of weight and measure. In general, it has failed to do so, leaving this responsibility to the states. In 1836 it directed the Secretary of the Treasury to provide the states with copies of the standards used in collecting customs duties, and these were adopted, without exception, by the states. In 1901 it created the National Bureau of Standards, assigning it the function, among others, of serving as a custodian of the prototypes against which standards used by the states may be checked. Congress has acted, in a few cases, however, to establish compulsory standards of measurement, defining the ampere, volt, watt, and other electrical measures in 1894, the barrel as a unit of dry measure in 1915, and other containers for fruits and vegetables in 1916 and 1928.

The federal government has gone farther in providing for the establishment of standards relating to the composition, quality, and performance of various goods. Congress fixed standard grades for apples sold in barrels in 1912, and for turpentine and rosin in 1923, and also enacted a standard definition for butter in 1923. It gave official sanction to the standards for drugs contained in various professional compendia in 1906 and 1938 and authorized the Food and Drug Administration to establish, for foodstuffs, minimum standards of quality in 1906 and minimum standards of identity in 1938. It empowered the Secretary of Agriculture to establish standard grades for cotton in 1914, for grains stored in public warehouses in 1916, for perishable agricultural commodities in 1930, for tobacco in 1935, and for other agricultural products in 1936. The use of such grades is usually required in organized commodities markets, where goods are bought unseen and contracts made for future delivery. Elsewhere, in general, they need not be used; but if they are, misrepresentation of the grade of goods is forbidden by law.

Congress has enacted a number of other laws forbidding sellers to misrepresent their goods or requiring the disclosure of information concerning character and quality of the goods. The misbranding of foods and drugs was forbidden by the Food and Drugs Act of 1906, the misbranding of cosmetics and therapeutic devices by the Food, Drug, and Cosmetic Act in 1938. Misrepresentation was among the unfair methods of competition outlawed by the Federal Trade Commission Act in 1914 and among the deceptive acts or practices outlawed by the Wheeler-Lea Act in 1938. Disclosure of identity, composition, quality, or the presence of harmful ingredients was required in the case of drugs in 1906, insecticides and fungicides in 1910, seeds in 1912, animal viruses, serums, and toxins in 1913, horse meat in 1919, caustic poisons in 1919, substandard canned goods in 1930, alcoholic beverages in 1935, foods in 1938, wool products in 1939, human viruses, serums, and toxins in 1944, and fur products in 1951.

The sale of certain goods has been subjected to more stringent controls. The sale of adulterated foods, drugs, and cosmetics is prohibited. Importation of substandard tea was barred in 1883, of diseased animals in 1890, of adulterated seeds in 1912, of substandard viruses, serums, and toxins in 1913, of honeybees—unless from regions approved by the Secretary of Agriculture—in 1922, of impure milk in 1927, and of meat unfit for food, or that from countries with rinderpest or foot and mouth disease, in 1930. The interstate sale of milk or cream containing fats other than butter fats was forbidden in 1923. In a few cases, federal inspection services have been set up. Under the Sea Food Act of 1934, establishments processing sea foods may, if they wish, be inspected by the Food and Drug Administration and may then advertise the fact that their products have been prepared under its rules. Inspection of certain other goods is compulsory. Under the provisions of the Meat Inspection Act of 1907, slaughtering, packing, and canning plants are inspected by the Department of Agriculture. Animals are inspected before, and carcasses after, slaughter; diseased meat is destroyed and pure meat stamped "U.S. Government Inspected" and released for sale. Approval before sale is also required in the case of viruses, serums, and toxins and, under the food and drug laws, in the case of new drugs, antibiotics, and coal tar colors used in foods, drugs, and cosmetics.

Consumer Representation in Government

As consumers, men want to get more for their money. And so they desire a larger output of goods high in quality and low in price. As producers, men want to get more money. And they may do so, at times, by curtailing output, impairing quality, and raising price. As consumers, all men are interested in having a bigger pie. As producers, each of them is interested in getting a bigger slice, even if it means a smaller pie. The producer interest is a special interest that sets one group against another. The consumer interest is a general interest that all men have in common. But the interest of producers in the revenue to be derived from a particular good is strong. And however great the consumer's interest in goods in general, his interest in the quality and cost of a particular good is likely to be weak. As a result, producer interests are effectively organized for political action, and the consumer interest is not.

This situation is reflected in the organization of the federal government. There are departments in the government to represent the interests of agriculture, commerce, and labor, but none to represent the interest of the consumer. This interest is served, to be sure, by certain of the existing bureaus, commissions, and other agencies. But nowhere is it recognized as such.

During the early days of the New Deal, when new administrations were established to promote recovery from depression by curtailing output and increasing prices, units were set up within the administrations to safeguard the consumer's interest. By executive action, a Consumer's Advisory Board was attached to the National Recovery Administration and a Consumers' Counsel to the Agricultural Adjustment Administration in 1933. By act of Congress, a Consumers' Counsel was attached to the Bituminous Coal Commission in 1935. These agencies were staffed with able, sincere, and hard-working people. But, by and large, their influence on policy was negligible. Where they engaged in consumer education, they were tolerated. But where they objected to administrative decisions, they appeared to the administrators, who were acting under heavy pressure from producer groups, to be stupid nuisances or willfull obstructionists. And, lacking effective political support, they could safely be ignored. With the approach of World War II, a Consumer Division was set up in the Council of National Defense. But when the war came, it had quietly disappeared.[2]

If consumer representation is really to be effective, it must be backed by political force. This backing can be provided, in part, by organizations of purchasing agents for state and municipal governments, universities and hospitals, mail order houses, chain stores, and department stores. But it must be accompanied by organized pressure from the purchasing agents who do the buying for the American home—from housewives acting through the women's clubs.

THE FOOD AND DRUG ADMINISTRATION

For nearly half a century the federal government has undertaken to protect consumers against impurities in foods and drugs. Today, the food and drug laws are taken for granted. But for decades, their enactment was

[2] See Persia C. Campbell, *Consumer Representation in the New Deal* (New York: Columbia University Press, 1940).

bitterly opposed by the industries concerned. The need for such legislation first became apparent about 1880 with the growth of large-scale food processing industries, concealing foods in cans where their quality could not be judged, and employing harmful substances to improve their appearance and to preserve them for sale in mass markets, and with the development of a patent medicine industry, dispensing dangerous and habit-forming drugs. The first bill calling for regulation was introduced in Congress in 1890, and during the next twenty-five years, nearly 150 other bills were introduced. But the public was apathetic, the opposition determined, and the bills were shelved. Then public attention was captured as the problem was dramatized. Dr. Harvey W. Wiley, the chief chemist of the Department of Agriculture, organized within his staff a "poison squad," whose members volunteered to eat foods currently being offered for sale, and reported to the press, from day to day, on the state of their health. Upton Sinclair wrote a novel, *The Jungle*, picturing the filth found by his characters in the Chicago packing plants and describing the sale of diseased cattle as clean meat. Samuel Hopkins Adams published a series of articles in *Collier's* exposing the patent medicine business. At last, the country was aroused. The General Federation of Women's Clubs organized and directed a widespread and effective drive for the enactment of a law. The Pure Food and Drugs Act, drafted by Dr. Wiley, was finally passed in 1906, when Theodore Roosevelt was President. Enforcement of the law was assigned to the Department of Agriculture, and Dr. Wiley was put in charge.

The Food and Drugs Act of 1906

The Act forbade adulteration and misbranding of foods and drugs sold in interstate commerce. Food was defined as adulterated if it contained decomposed or putrid animal or vegetable substances or parts of diseased animals, if it had been so mixed or colored as to conceal its inferiority, if ingredients had been added that made it injurious to health, or if valuable constituents had been removed and others substituted or mixed with it so as to impair its quality or strength. Candy was said to be adulterated if it contained various mineral substances, poisonous colors or flavors, liquors, drugs, or other harmful materials. Drugs were adulterated if they fell below the standards laid down in the United States Pharmacopoeia or the National Formulary or any other standards under which they were sold. Foods and drugs were declared to be misbranded if their packages or labels bore statements which were "false or misleading in any particular," if one was sold under the name of another, if the contents of packages had been removed and others substituted, or if the presence of certain narcotics or stimulants was not revealed. Food was also misbranded if its weight or measure was not plainly shown; drugs, if their packages or labels bore false claims of curative effects. The law authorized the seizure and forfeiture of adulterated or misbranded foods and drugs and made adulteration or misbranding a misdemeanor punishable by a fine of not more than $200 for the first offense, and a fine of not more than $300 or imprisonment for not more than one year, or both, for each subsequent offense.

As passed, the law was a substantial achievement; in operation, it proved to have a number of serious weaknesses. It failed to cover the growing trade in cosmetics or the sale of therapeutic devices such as sun lamps, orthopedic shoes, bust developers, and electric belts. It exempted foods sold under proprietary names and those labeled as compounds, imitations, or blends. Since it gave the Food and Drug Administration no authority to establish standards of identity for foods, it handicapped the Administration in proving that they were misbranded. Since it failed to authorize inspection of food processing plants, it prevented action to improve the conditions under which foodstuffs were prepared. The law did not control false advertising claims; it applied only to the statements made on the package containing the food or drug or the label affixed to it. In 1911, moreover, the Supreme Court held that the prohibition of statements that were "false or misleading in any particular" was limited to statements of fact concerning the identity of quality of a product and did not extend to claims concerning its beneficial effects.[3] This decision led to the adoption of a corrective amendment in 1912. But the amendment, through the efforts of the patent medicine lobby, forbade statements that were both "false and fraudulent," thus imposing on the Administration the burden of proving fraudulent intent. The law was administered by a small staff with an inadequate budget, operating under continuous pressure from the manufacturers whom it was supposed to regulate. Convictions were difficult to obtain, prison sentences were rare, and the fines imposed were so small as to amount to little more than a modest license fee.

A drive for stronger legislation got under way in the twenties and the thirties with the publication of a large number of books on the abuses of advertising, beginning in 1927 with *Your Money's Worth* by Stuart Chase and F. J. Schlink. In its office in Washington, the Food and Drug Administration set up a museum that came to be known as the Chamber of Horrors. Here, in a series of exhibits, could be seen samples seized from foods on public sale—filthy candy, decayed fruit, worm-eaten nuts, butter full of maggots, and raisins infested with insects; samples of patent medicines to cure every known disease, with testimonials from their users, accompanied by copies of their death certificates; and samples of cosmetics—eyelash beautifiers containing poisonous aniline dyes, hair removers containing thallium acetate, and hair tonics, freckle removers, ointments and salves containing mercury or other dangerous ingredients —together with photographs of women who had been blinded, paralyzed, or permanently disfigured by their use.

[3] *U.S.* v. *Johnson*, 221 U.S. 488.

In 1933, Rexford G. Tugwell was appointed Assistant Secretary of Agriculture by President Franklin D. Roosevelt and shortly thereafter sponsored the enactment of a new law. Associations of food, drug, patent medicine, and cosmetic manufacturers raised a slush fund of $500,000, lined up the press, attacked the Tugwell bill as un-American, and denounced Tugwell himself as a subversive character. By such tactics, the lobbyists succeeded in delaying action for five years. In the autumn of 1937, however, a drug manufacturer who wished to distribute sulfanilimide in liquid form added a deadly poison—diethylene glycol—as a solvent and put it on the market as Elixir Sulfanilimide, making no effort to test the mixture for toxicity. Of the 240 gallons made, the first 6 sold were found to be the certain cause of 73 deaths in 15 states and the probable cause of 20 others. At the same rate, distribution of the entire batch would have killed 3,720 people. The Food and Drug Administration seized the remaining stock and prosecuted the manufacturer. But it would have been powerless to act before the tragedy occurred. The shock of this experience contributed heavily to the enactment of a new law in 1938.[4]

The Food, Drug, and Cosmetic Act of 1938

The Act of 1938 strengthened the earlier definitions of adulteration and misbranding. Food was now defined as adulterated if it contained any poisonous or deleterious substance, if it was colored with coal tars not approved by the Food and Drug Administration, if it was prepared under conditions that might result in contamination with filth or injury to health, or if it was packed in containers composed of substances that might make it injurious. Candy could no longer contain metallic trinkets or other inedible materials. The wording that defined misbranding to cover statements that were "false or misleading in any particular" was restored. Under an amendment adopted in 1930, the Administration had been authorized to establish standards of "quality, condition and/or fill of container" for canned goods, and such goods were said to be misbranded if failures to meet these standards were not disclosed. Now, the Administration was empowered to set up minimum standards of identity and fill for all foodstuffs, and disclosure of failure to meet them was required. The exemption formerly granted to foods sold under brand names was withdrawn, and for foods, as for drugs, it was provided that the ingredients of those departing from established standards must be shown. Foods and drugs were both defined as misbranded if their containers were so made or filled as to mislead the purchaser. For drugs, moreover, the law required inclusion on the label of directions for use and warning against misuse.

The scope of the law was extended to cover cosmetics and therapeutic devices. A cosmetic was declared to be adulterated if it "is or may be

[4] See Stephen Wilson, *Food and Drug Regulation* (Washington: American Council on Public Affairs, 1942).

injurious" under customary or prescribed conditions of use, and to be misbranded—as with foods and drugs—if its label bore statements that were "false or misleading in any particular." Here, again, deceptive containers were forbidden. But the rules for cosmetics were less stringent than those for foods and drugs. Soaps were exempted. In the case of hair dyes, the use of coal tar colors was permitted if their labels stated that they might irritate the skin, gave directions for making skin tests, and warned that use on eyebrows and eyelashes could lead to blindness. In general, no provision was made for the establishment of standards, and the disclosure of ingredients was not required.

The law was strengthened, however, in other ways. The government was authorized to inspect factories producing foods, drugs, devices, and cosmetics. Where the processing of foodstuffs might involve a risk of contamination so serious as to menace public health, it was empowered to license manufacturers and to establish standards of sanitation as a condition for granting licenses. Drug concerns developing new drugs were required to obtain approval from the Food and Drug Administration before putting them on sale, and the Administration was authorized to deny approval to drugs that had not been tested and to those that were found to be unsafe. Penalties for violation of the law were increased to $1,000 or a year's imprisonment or both for an unwitting or negligent first offense, and to $10,000 or three years or both for offenses involving intent to defraud or mislead. At the same time, the advertising of foods, drugs, and cosmetics was brought under the supervision of the Federal Trade Commission by the Wheeler-Lea Act, discussed below.

The Food and Drug Administration (FDA) was removed from the Department of Agriculture in 1940 and placed within the Federal Security Agency, now the Department of Health, Education and Welfare. Its annual appropriation, in the early fifties, ran around $5 million. In 1950, it had a few more than a thousand employees, two fifths of them in Washington and three fifths in the field, less than a fourth of them engaged in inspection work. In the case of meat, regulated under the Meat Inspection Act by the Department of Agriculture, each carcass must be inspected before it can be sold. In the case of antibiotics and coal tar dyes the FDA follows a similar procedure, passing judgment on a sample from every batch. But for other products, its samples are very small. No more than a tenth of the establishments processing or storing foods, drugs, and cosmetics can be inspected in any year, and no more than 0.1 per cent of the output of these products can be analyzed. Here, as elsewhere, the resources provided by Congress are too small to enable the enforcement agency to do a really thorough job.

The Administration suffered an unexpected reversal in December, 1952 when the Supreme Court denied it the right to inspect factories without the permission of their owners, on the ground that the Act of 1938 had been drafted so clumsily that the intended power was not conferred. Since most violations have been uncovered through plant inspections, this decision seriously handicapped enforcement of the law. President Eisenhower, in his first message to Congress, recommended enactment of an amendment to restore the Administration's power. This was opposed by the manufacturers. But a measure permitting inspection "at reasonable times," upon written notice, was adopted in 1953. The victory, however, was a paper one. The Administration's appropriation was so sharply cut that its staff was reduced to less than 800. With some 96,000 establishments engaged in processing and storing foodstuffs, it was able, on this basis, to inspect no more than 0.1 per cent of these establishments in any year and to get around to each of them no oftener than once in twelve years.[5]

In 1951, the Administration's inspectors seized and condemned more than 23 tons of filthy foods on every working day. Its staff rejected a fifth of the applications made to introduce new drugs, recalled a number of dangerous drugs from the market, and checked on warehouses to make sure that drugs were kept at temperatures that would preserve their potency. The agency was also required to prevent some 60,000 to 70,000 retailers from selling drugs without prescriptions. After hearings by the FDA, persons found to be in violation of the law are turned over to the Department of Justice for prosecution. Among 349 criminal cases in 1951, fines ranging from $1,000 to $9,000 were collected in 56 cases, and prison sentences averaging 16 months were imposed on 22 defendants; of these, however, 18 were placed on probation and only 4 served time.[6]

Unsafe Foods and Cosmetics

With the continued growth of food processing industries, producing on a large scale for distribution to mass markets, there has been increasing use of chemicals in bakery products, salad dressings, peanut butter, ice cream, soft drinks, and many other foods. Chemicals are added for a variety of purposes: to facilitate processing, to compensate for the loss of nutrients—vitamins, proteins, and minerals—in processing, to prevent deterioration or preserve an appearance of freshness, and to improve color or taste. Where the FDA establishes a standard that excludes a chemical from a product, the use of the chemical may be discontinued or, if continued, must be acknowledged on the label. And where it can be proved that a chemical has injured the consumers of a product, its use can be stopped. But chemicals can still be introduced into the nation's food supply without making prior tests to determine whether they are safe. Among 704 chemicals so used in 1950, the FDA and the Public Health Service found that 428 were known to be safe; the safety of the other 276 was unknown.[7]

[5] *New York Times*, January 28, 1954.

[6] Food and Drug Administration, *Annual Report, 1951.*

[7] Select Committee to Investigate the Use of Chemicals in Foods and Cosmetics, *Report on Food*, June 30, 1952 (82d Cong., 2d Sess., House Report 2356) p. 4.

For many years, flour was bleached with nitrogen trichloride to make it white, and the use of this chemical was continued for several years after it was discovered, in 1946, that dogs fed bread baked from flour so treated developed canine hysteria. Nutritive elements are still removed in the process of preserving flour for commercial distribution and then restored, in part, in the process of "enriching" bread with chemicals. Bread has also been given a more enduring appearance of softness by the use of emulsifying agents such as the polyoxyethylene stearates. In 1952, after ten years of preliminary research and hearings that included 3,000 exhibits and covered 17,000 pages of testimony, the FDA established standards of identity for five varieties of bread. Its right to do so was attacked by the chemical companies who manufactured the emulsifiers, but their complaint was rejected by the Supreme Court in 1953. The new standards ruled out some 30 ingredients, including the chemical softeners. Under the law, however, these ingredients could still be used if their presence was noted on the wrappers of substandard bread.

Chemicals are also used extensively in the manufacture of cosmetics, where they are known not only to serve as irritants and sensitizers producing dermatitis but also to have caused a number of more serious injuries. There are cases on record, in recent years, of death from a cold permanent wave lotion, of impairment of vision from a shampoo, and of disfigurement from the use of lacquers on the hair and fingernails. Here, again, chemicals may be used without pretesting and their use cannot be forbidden until injury is proved.

A committee was appointed by the House of Representatives in 1950 to investigate the use of chemicals in foods and cosmetics. Following protracted hearings, it rendered its report in 1952. Finding existing provisions of the law inadequate to protect the public, it recommended that manufacturers be required to obtain approval from the FDA before introducing chemicals into foods and cosmetics, as they have been required, since 1938, to obtain approval before marketing new drugs. In the case of cosmetics, the Committee also recommended that listing of ingredients on labels be required, that the exemption granted to soaps be removed, and that the use of the more harmful varieties of coal tar dyes be prohibited.[8] No action had been taken on these recommendations at the end of 1954.

THE FEDERAL TRADE COMMISSION

From 1914 to 1938, the great majority of the orders issued by the Federal Trade Commission (FTC) were directed, not against monopolistic practices, but against methods by which one small competitor injured another. Respondents were ordered, in some cases, to cease and desist from espionage, malicious interference, disparagement, inducing breach of contract, commercial bribery, and similar practices. More often, they

[8] *Ibid.*, pp. 25–27, and *Report on Cosmetics*, June 17, 1952 (82d Cong., 2d Sess., House Report 2182), pp. 8–13.

were ordered to abandon misrepresentation. Orders against misrepresentation served to protect consumers. But this was not their legal purpose. Under the law, as it then stood, they were issued to safeguard competitors against deceitful diversion of patronage. Any protection that they might afford to consumers was purely incidental. Since the adoption of the Wheeler-Lea amendment in 1938, however, Section 5 of the Trade Commission Act has forbidden, not only unfair methods of competition, but also deceptive acts or practices, and four new sections—12 to 15, inclusive, supplementing the Food, Drug, and Cosmetic Act of 1938—have authorized the Commission to move against dissemination of false advertisements of these commodities. Prevention of misrepresentation is thus a major part of the Commission's work, accounting for two thirds of the cases with which it deals.

Preventing Misrepresentation

The number of cases in which the FTC has taken action against misrepresentation runs into the thousands. Orders have been issued repeatedly, over the years, involving practices such as these:

1. Misrepresenting the character, composition, or quality of goods: passing off one good as another—cotton as linen, rayon as silk, woodchuck as mink, rabbit as seal, gumwood as mahogany, and veneers as solid wood—selling imitations as originals, seconds as prime quality, adulterated goods as pure, and secondhand goods as new.
2. Misrepresenting the geographic origin of goods: giving the impression that quality is high by claiming a familiar source, such as Havana for cigars not made in Cuba and Panama for hats not made in Panama.
3. Falsely claiming endorsement of goods: suggesting that impartial and responsible persons have investigated and approved their quality—describing goods, for instance, as "Government Issue" or "U.S. Regulation" when they are not, or intimating that they have been endorsed by the Boy Scouts or the Red Cross.
4. Misrepresenting the usefulness of goods: making false statements concerning the curative powers of patent medicines, the corrective properties of various devices, or the beautifying effects of cosmetics, or failing to disclose the potential harmfulness of drugs.
5. Misrepresenting the real price of goods: advertising an article sold only in combination with others as "FREE," indicating that goods are being sold below cost when they are not, or suggesting that bargains are being offered by first marking prices up and then marking them down.
6. Misrepresenting the nature of the seller's business: claiming a status that implies a higher quality or a lower price, as is the case, for instance, when blenders of whiskey claim to be distillers, when manufacturers of clothing describe themselves as weavers, and when dealers in furniture parade as manufacturers.

The Commission has also proceeded against another method of sales promotion that would appear to be socially undesirable, ordering manufacturers of penny candies to cease and desist from providing retailers with selling schemes, accompanied by advertising displays, whereby the quantity or price of candy obtained by school children was determined by chance. Here, though no misrepresentation was involved, it was held that inculcation of the gambling spirit was harmful, that children were unable to protect themselves, and that scrupulous manufacturers might be forced to adopt the practice in order to avoid the loss of sales to their less scrupulous competitors.

Unfair Methods and the Courts

In general, the Commission's authority to issue orders against misrepresentation has been upheld when these orders have been appealed to the courts. In the Winsted Hosiery case[9] in 1922, the Supreme Court upheld an order against a manufacturer who sold socks containing little or no wool under such names as cashmere, merino, worsted, and wool. In the Royal Milling case[10] in 1933, it upheld an order directing a concern that merely mixed and blended flour to desist from representing itself as a milling company. In the Algoma Lumber case[11] in 1934, it supported the Commission in ordering a number of West Coast lumbermen to discontinue the practice of describing yellow pine as "California White Pine." And in the Keppel case,[12] in the same year, it sanctioned an order against the sale, in interstate commerce, of candy to be resold through lotteries. In the Standard Education Society case[13] in 1937, the Court upheld an order requiring the publisher of an encyclopaedia to stop representing that sets were being given free to selected buyers for advertising purposes and that payments asked of them covered nothing but the cost of periodic looseleaf supplements. And in 1941, the Supreme Court refused to review decisions of a lower court upholding the Commission in ordering Ford and General Motors to desist from claiming that their interest rate on installment sales was 6 per cent when, in fact, the 6 per cent was figured on their original loans, ignoring monthly payments, and the actual rate of interest on balances remaining unpaid was 11½ per cent.[14]

But the Commission has not always been so fortunate when it has appeared before the courts. The law itself is clear enough. In plain words, "unfair methods of competition in commerce are hereby declared unlawful" and action is authorized "if it shall appear to the Commission that a proceeding by it . . . would be to the interest of the public. . . ." But

[9] *FTC* v. *Winsted Hosiery Co.*, 258 U.S. 483.

[10] *FTC* v. *Royal Milling Co.*, 288 U.S. 212.

[11] *FTC* v. *Algoma Lumber Co.*, 291 U.S. 67.

[12] *FTC* v. *R. F. Keppel & Bro.*, 291 U.S. 304.

[13] *FTC* v. *Standard Education Society*, 302 U.S. 112.

[14] *General Motors Corp.* v. *FTC*, 114 F. 2d 33 (1940), certiorari denied 312 U.S. 682 (1941); *Ford Motor Co.* v. *FTC*, 120 F. 2d 175 (1941), certiorari denied 314 U.S. 668 (1941).

the Supreme Court has curbed the Commission, from time to time, by holding that a method it has proscribed was not "unfair," that it was not harmful to "competition," that it was not "in" commerce, or that action against it was not in the public interest.

In the Gratz case[15] in 1920, where an order had been issued against a contract that tied the sale of bagging to the sale of baling ties, the Court held that the use of a tying contract (though it might be illegal under the Clayton Act) was not an unfair method of competition, within the meaning of the Trade Commission Act, since the words *unfair methods* "are clearly inapplicable to practices never heretofore regarded as opposed to good morals because characterized by deception, bad faith, fraud, or oppression, or as against public policy. . . ." The law was thus amended by the insertion of the word "heretofore" and the principle established that the Commission could not issue orders against new forms of unfairness, but could act only where it could find a precedent in common or statute law. This interpretation stood until the Court handed down its decision in the Keppel case[16] in 1934: "We cannot say that the Commission's jurisdiction extends only to those types of practices which happen to have been litigated before this Court. Neither the language nor the history of the Act suggests that Congress intended to confine the forbidden methods to fixed and unyielding categories." The restrictive rule of the Gratz case was thus reversed after nearly fifteen years.

In the Raladam case[17] in 1931, the Commission had ordered the makers of Marmola to cease and desist from claiming that the product could be safely administered or that it would reduce obesity. The Court agreed that the advertising was unfair and the Commission's action in the public interest but held the order invalid on the ground that "competition" had not been damaged, since there was no evidence of the existence of truthful manufacturers of slenderizing preparations who might be harmed by Raladam's mendacity. The Commission was thus denied the right to protect consumers against misrepresentation where it was the general practice in a trade. This position was reversed in a second case involving the Raladam Company[18] in 1942. But the loophole had already been plugged by Congress when it passed the Wheeler-Lea Act in 1938.

Two other decisions, imposing limits on the Commission's powers, still stand. In the Klesner case[19] in 1929, where each of two small merchants in Washington, D.C., called his store "The Shade Shop" and the Commission had ordered one of them to desist, the Court reversed the order on the ground that the controversy was a private one, to be settled

[15] *FTC* v. *Gratz*, 253 U.S. 421.

[16] *FTC* v. *R. F. Keppel & Bro.*, 291 U.S. 304.

[17] *FTC* v. *Raladam Co.*, 283 U.S. 643.

[18] *FTC* v. *Raladam Co.*, 316 U.S. 149.

[19] *FTC* v. *Klesner,* 280 U.S. 19.

by a private suit, and that no "specific and substantial" public interest was involved. In the Bunte case[20] in 1941, the Court reversed an order against a manufacturer who was making candy in Illinois for sale by lottery in Illinois, on the ground that his activity, while it affected commerce, was not "in" commerce, as the law required. These decisions have been regretted as limiting the Commission's jurisdiction. But they may also have the advantage of directing its attention from a multitude of petty cases to a smaller number of more important ones.

The Wheeler-Lea Act

The Wheeler-Lea Act of 1938 not only amended Section 5 of the Federal Trade Commission Act to make "unfair or deceptive acts or practices" unlawful. It also established new controls over the false advertising of foods, drugs, cosmetics, and corrective or curative devices. It empowered the Commission to ask a district court to issue a temporary injunction to prevent dissemination of a false advertisement, pending the completion of its own action in the case. And it made dissemination of such advertisements a crime, punishable by a fine up to $5,000 or imprisonment up to six months or both for the first offense, and by fine up to $10,000, or imprisonment up to a year, or both, for a subsequent offense, if it could be shown either (1) that the use of misrepresented products had been injurious to health, or (2) that misrepresentation was undertaken with intent to defraud or mislead. The law thus provides more methods of dealing with falsehood in the advertising of foods, drugs, devices, and cosmetics than in the advertising of other goods. In general, the Commission may employ the familiar procedures of stipulation, complaint, order, and suit to obtain the imposition of a civil penalty where an order has been disobeyed. Here, it may also seek an injunction or turn a case over to the Department of Justice for prosecution. But the difficulty of proving that misrepresentation caused injury, or that it was intentional, is such that criminal suits are likely to be few.

A different standard is established for judging falsehood in advertising under the Wheeler-Lea Act than for judging misbranding under the Food, Drug, and Cosmetic Act. A good is misbranded if its label is "false or misleading in any particular." An advertisement is false if it is "misleading in a material respect." The latter standard is obviously weaker than the former one. But the law also provides that advertisements shall be judged not only by statements made but also by those "suggested," and by the extent to which they fail to reveal "material" facts. The force of the law thus turns on what statements or suggestions, and what omissions, are to be regarded as "material." Depending on the judgment of the courts, the amount of misrepresentation permitted under this standard may be large or small.

[20] *FTC* v. *Bunte Bros., Inc.*, 312 U.S. 349.

Controlling Advertising

The staff of the Division of Investigation in the Federal Trade Commission currently examines advertisements in 50 mail order catalogues, 500 newspapers, and 450 to 500 other periodicals, checks radio and television continuities, and monitors broadcasts over 2,600 stations and 4 networks. The survey of advertising is conducted on a sampling basis, involving examination of each periodical three times a year and of scripts used by broadcasters from one to three times a year. Among the hundreds of thousands of items examined in a year, some 30,000 may be questioned; but, of these, as few as 200 may lead to the initiation of a case. A larger number of cases have their origin in outside complaints. When action is undertaken, an inquiry is first made by correspondence. If the matter cannot be settled in this way, it is referred to one of the Commission's field offices for an investigation and report. Samples of the advertiser's products may then be obtained and turned over to technical agencies of the government—such as the Food and Drug Administration, the Public Health Service, or the Bureau of Standards—for analysis. Where evidence of misrepresentation is thus developed, the Commission may go forward with a case.

In the great majority of instances, actions against false or misleading advertisements are dropped when the Commission receives assurance, through a letter, an affidavit, or a stipulation, that the statements to which it has objected will no longer be made. Under stipulation with the Commission, in recent years, various manufacturers have agreed, for example, to desist from representing:

that Beau-T-Form Maternity Garments enable a woman to maintain the youthfulness of her figure during pregnancy, eliminate the discomforts of pregnancy, or promote easy or safe delivery;

that Nurserytyme crib mattresses will keep a baby's spine straight, materially help a child develop properly, or have an appreciable effect on a child's future health;

that "Start," a gasoline additive, eliminates the risk of frozen gas lines in automobiles and insures easy starting in cold weather;

that Plasta Starch can be relied upon to double the life of fabrics or increase their wearing life by any definite length of time;

that antihistamine preparations are effective in preventing colds;

that J-O Paste will rid the premises of rats and that rats consuming the product will leave the premises to die;

that the Toni twin's hair was waved by the twin herself and not by a hairdresser;

that Fashion-Glo Bust Cream will beneficially affect the structure and firmness of the breast; and that Ever-Seal caskets afford the body permanent protection against the elements.[21]

A much smaller number of cases goes on through the mill of complaint, hearing, and formal order. The Commission, in recent cases, has ordered certain concerns, among many others, to desist from representing:

that Herbold Pomade will color the roots of the hair and prevent the hair from becoming gray;

that Imdrin is an adequate, effective, or reliable treatment for any kind of arthritis, rheumatism, neuritis, sciatica, gout, neuralgia, or bursitis, will cure these ailments, correct their underlying causes, or arrest their progress;

that Carter's Little Liver Pills will have any therapeutic action on any condition, disease, or disorder of the liver; that it will increase or beneficially influence the formation, secretion, or flow of bile; that it is a cure, remedy, or competent or effective treatment of those conditions in which an individual feels "down and out," "blue," "down in the dumps," "worn out," "sunk," "all in," "mean," "low," "cross," "tired," "miserable," "grouchy," "cranky," "peevish," "fagged out," "grumpy," or "run-down";

that Nu Maid Margarine provides the user with increased pep, energy, vitality, vigor, strength, or endurance;

that Ipana will prevent pink toothbrush;

that Lucky Strikes—or the smoke from them—contain less nicotine or less acid than other leading brands; that they are easy on the throat; or that they provide protection against throat irritation or coughing; and

that smoking Camels encourages the flow of digestive fluids, increases the alkalinity of the digestive tract or aids digestion in any respect; that their use relieves fatigue or creates, restores, renews, gives, or releases bodily energy; that their use does not affect or impair the "wind" or physical condition of athletes; that the smoke from Camels is soothing, restful, or comforting to the nerves, or that it protects one against nerve strain; and that Camels never leave an after taste.[22]

The number of cases to reach the courts is very small. In 1951, there were five actions in which the FTC was seeking civil penalties. Of these, the most important was the one in which it asked that the Thomas company be fined $290,000 for repeated violations of its order to abandon the claim that it could grow hair on bald heads.

The effectiveness of the Commission's effort to check falsehood in advertising is open to question. The usual case is closed by a stipulation, which is nothing more than a slap on the wrist. An order carries no pen-

[21] See Stipulations in Dockets 7890 and 7944 (1949), 8042–8049 and 8072 (1950), 8111, 8115, 8117, and 8142 (1951), and 8299 (1952).

[22] See Orders in Dockets 4861 (1949), 4795, 4922, 5353, and 5691 (1950) and 4287, 4970, and 5733 (1951).

alty for past deceptions and does nothing to prevent future ones. A criminal action is virtually unknown. When cases have been appealed, the courts have tended to accept a good bit of misrepresentation as a matter of course. In the Ostermoor case[23] in 1927, a lower court reversed the Commission's order against an advertisement that pictured the filling of a mattress, when liberated, as fanning out to many times the thickness of the mattress itself. Said the court, ". . . the slightest pictorial exaggeration of the qualities of an article cannot be deemed to be . . . a misrepresentation . . . The time-honored custom of at least merely slight puffing . . . has not come under a legal ban." And this precedent has been followed in more recent cases, the courts permitting one concern to advertise a "perfect" lubricant that will operate a car for an "amazing" distance,[24] and another to represent a cure for obesity as "easy," "simple," and "safe."[25] When cases are won and sanctions imposed, moreover, they apply only to the company that makes the advertised product, not to the advertising agency that prepares the misleading copy, to the publisher who prints it, or to the station that broadcasts it. And then the advertiser need only drop the old campaign and embark upon a new one as deceptive as the last. The Commission cannot require the publication of retractions. It cannot censor copy in advance. And it can scarcely be expected to keep pace with the inventive copy writers in the advertising agencies. The control that it exerts may moderate some of the more serious abuses of advertising. But it is not to be described as rigorous.

In 1952 the Commission undertook to curb misrepresentation in the advertising of cigarettes by seeking an injunction under the provisions of the Wheeler-Lea Act relating to foods and drugs. In this it was unsuccessful, the District Court and the Court of Appeals both holding that cigarettes did not come within these provisions, being neither foods nor drugs. In 1953, under the Eisenhower administration, the Commission abandoned its effort to control cigarette advertising through the Wheeler-Lea Act, turning from compulsion to persuasion. In September, 1954, it invited the industry to adhere voluntarily to a detailed code of advertising standards requiring, for example, that advertisements should not claim "directly or by implication that cigarette smoking in general or the smoking of any brand of cigarette" is "not harmful" or "nonirritating," should not "refer to the throat, larynx, lungs, nose, or any other part of the body," and should not use any word, term, or illustration "in such a way as to represent or imply medical approval."[26] Whether its invitation will be accepted remains to be seen.

The Commission's new majority reversed another policy when it abandoned the attack on the use of the word "Free." Formerly, this word

[23] *Ostermoor & Co.* v. *FTC*, 16 F. 2d 962.

[24] *Kidder Oil Co.* v. *FTC*, 117 F. 2d 894 (1941).

[25] *Carlay Co.* v. *FTC*, 153 F. 2d 493 (1946).

[26] FTC, *News Summary*, No. 15, October 19, 1954.

had been held to be deceptive where any conditions had to be complied with in order to obtain an article described as "Free." On this basis, an order had been issued against the Book-of-the-Month Club and the Club had appealed it to the courts. Now, the Commission ruled that the word "Free" could be used, even though conditions were attached, if the conditions were fully disclosed. The order against the Club was modified accordingly.[27]

STANDARDS, GRADES, AND LABELS

Consumers' goods may be identified either by brand names attached to them by sellers, or by standards developed by semiofficial or official agencies. The two methods of identification are not to be confused. Standards are established by scientists and technicians. They are set forth in terms of a product's physical characteristics, its composition, performance, and quality. They may take the form of a single minimum, below which sales may be legally forbidden or disclosure of inferiority required, or a number of grades whereby differences in quality are recognized. Conformity to standards and departure from them are communicated to the buyer through informative labeling. Brand names, on the other hand, are invented by sales promoters and advertising men. They are designed to catch the buyer's eye and ear and to remain in his memory. They need not reveal the physical characteristics of a product and may even misrepresent them: Palmolive—no palms, no olives; Grape Nuts—no grapes, no nuts. They need not even identify the maker; many brand names are owned by wholesalers or retailers. The seller who stakes his reputation on a name has an incentive to maintain the quality of his product. But there is no assurance that he will always do so; impairment may go undetected and the worsened product may be still sold under the familiar name. Brand names are communicated to the consumer through national advertising. By calculated employment of the arts of applied psychology—appeals to the instincts of sex and mother love, to fears of ill health and unpopularity, to hopes for business success and social prestige—they are surrounded with an aura of desirability. The informative label enlightens; the advertisement persuades.

It is only where goods are sold to the ultimate consumer that branding and advertising are significant. And it is here that the fight over public standardization, grading, and labeling has taken place. Industrial equipment and materials are bought on specification. Agricultural commodities are traded in accordance with official grades. Products that farmers buy —seeds, fertilizers, insecticides, and the like—are required to bear informative labels. But here, the activities of government have been invited and supported by the traders and the farmers themselves. In the special case of alcoholic beverages, informative labeling was but a part of the

[27] FTC, *News Summary*, No. 18, December 7, 1953.

larger program of taxation and of distribution through state stores that followed the abandonment of prohibition. For other consumers' goods, however, laws requiring standardization, grading, and labeling have usually been enacted in the face of bitter opposition, even in cases where abuses were notorious and where public health and safety were at stake.

Present Requirements

Standards of weight and measure and standard sizes for containers have been set up, as we have seen, by state and federal governments. Standards of quality, usually for goods bought or sold by farmers, have also been established by certain of the states. Standards of identity for drugs have been given official sanction by Congress, and the Food and Drug Administration has been authorized to prescribe minimum standards of quality for canned goods and standards of identity for all foods, together with standards of container fill. Observance of these standards is not obligatory, but departure from them must be disclosed. In the case of sea food, adherence to official standards is optional, but cannot be claimed unless public inspection has been requested and its requirements satisfied. Legal grades have been established, under various authorizations, for many goods, principally agricultural commodities. In certain transactions, the use of such grades is required. In most cases however, the only requirement is that conformity with a grade shall not be falsely claimed.

With respect to labeling, requirements vary from case to case. It is usually provided that true weight and measure must be shown. For alcoholic beverages, and for animal feeds, disclosure of composition is required. For drugs, composition need be shown only if they depart from standards established by law. But here, as with cosmetics, caustic poisons, insecticides and fungicides, the presence of dangerous ingredients must be revealed, and warnings must be given and instructions provided for their proper use. For foods, failure to satisfy minimum standards must be disclosed. For most products, however, the law contents itself with the negative provision that misrepresentation is not to be allowed. But there are three other cases in which affirmative disclosures are required.

Under the Wool Products Labeling Act of 1939, labels must be affixed to products containing wool (with certain exceptions, such as carpets, rugs, and upholstery) showing the percentages of new wool, reused or reprocessed wool, and other fibers or fillers that are used. Refusal to provide this information is made punishable by fine or imprisonment, and falsification is made a violation of Section 5 of the Federal Trade Commission Act. Enforcement is by the Commission. In 1951, inspectors examined 25,000,000 products in 12,000 establishments, discovering 14,000 violations that were settled informally and 14 that led to orders to cease and desist. It has been the purpose of the law not so much to protect consumers against misrepresentation as to protect wool growers against the competition of other fibers and weavers of woolens against the competition of other goods.

Under the Fur Products Labeling Act, passed in February, 1951, the Federal Trade Commission was directed to hold public hearings to determine the true English names of furs and to issue a Fur Products Name Guide by February, 1952. Sellers were required to use these names on labels attached to fur products after August, 1952, and also to state whether the furs contained in such products were new or used, if they had come from bellies, tails, or paws, and if they had been dyed or bleached. The program was launched with the co-operation of the Master Furriers' Guild. If the law can be enforced, it promises a revolution in the practice of the trade.

The Flammable Fabrics Act was passed in 1953 after a number of persons had been seriously burned as a result of the ignition of garments made of synthetic materials. Under the provisions of this law, which took effect in June, 1954, the production or distribution of any article of apparel which is "so highly flammable as to be dangerous when worn" is made illegal under the Federal Trade Commission Act. The Commission may institute proceedings to enjoin the manufacture or sale of such articles and to confiscate existing stocks. Willful violation of the law is made punishable by fine and imprisonment. Producers and distributors cannot be prosecuted if the one from whom they bought a fabric has provided them with a guaranty that it passes certain tests of flammability. The tests have been devised by the National Bureau of Standards and the testing procedures prescribed by the FTC. To aid in enforcement, producers of flammable fabrics are required to keep swatches of each class sold and to maintain full records of their sales.

The Experience of OPA

Official standards and informative labels would enable the consumer to protect himself against misrepresentation and, upon occasion, to obtain a higher quality for a lower price. But any effort to require their wider use would surely face an uphill fight. The sums invested in the advertising business—by advertisers, by advertising agencies, and by advertising media—are very large. Those who have made such investments are quick to defend themselves against any movement that appears to threaten the basis of their livelihood. And standardization, grading, and informative labeling seem to the advertising business to carry such a threat. It is the purpose of branding and advertising to afford the seller a modicum of monopoly. To this end, his goods are sheltered from competition by creating an impression that they are somehow unique, by surrounding them with an atmosphere of mystery, and by preventing their comparison with others of their kind. Objective standards and informative labels, on the other hand, would tell the consumer exactly what he was getting, direct his attention to quality and performance, and facilitate comparisons. And if such standards were generally available, the consumer might come to rely upon them more and to believe in advertising less. So standardization, grading, and informative labeling are resisted when they are proposed. And this resistance is powerful, since advertising supports the major media of mass communication—newspapers, magazines, radio, and television—through which opinion on issues of public policy is formed.

During World War II as part of a program designed to curb inflation, an Office of Price Administration (OPA) was established and empowered to fix maximum prices for particular goods. In order to identify the goods to which these prices applied, and to prevent evasion of its regulations by deterioration of quality, the OPA made use of existing standards—developed by private or public agencies—where they were available, and set up standards of its own where they were not. In the spring of 1943, it established grades of quality for rayon hosiery and for canned fruits and vegetables. And here, as elsewhere, it required informative labeling.

The case of rayon hosiery was a special one. Before the war, it had accounted for less than 3 per cent of all the hosiery sold. But now, with silk and nylon withdrawn from civilian markets, it accounted for the whole supply. And the prices of rayon stockings had gone up by leaps and bounds. OPA therefore issued a regulation fixing maximum prices, defining Grade A hosiery in terms of quality of yarn and character of construction, and permitting manufacturers to charge more for stockings that met this standard than for those that did not. The regulation also required that the grade, gauge, price, and maker's name or trade-mark be stamped on the welt of each stocking sold. At the same time, the Office established grades for canned goods, designated as *A*, *B*, *C*, and *D*, ordered that the 1943 pack should be graded, and required that each can should be labeled with its grade.

The reaction to these moves was instantaneous and violent. Industry demanded action of Congress. Investigations were undertaken simultaneously by four committees of the Senate and the House. Representatives of the hosiery manufacturers, the canners, and related business interests expressed themselves without restraint. Senators and Congressmen took up the hue and cry. Members of the staff of OPA, it appeared, were long-haired professors, visionary theorists, crackpots, and reformers, men who had never carried a precinct or met a payroll, who sought to destroy free enterprise and representative government in America and establish socialism or communism in their stead. Business demanded, therefore, that the OPA be purged. And this was done: the economists who had taken responsibility for the hosiery and canned goods regulations resigned, and Congress disposed of several others by providing that none of the funds allotted to the agency could be used to pay the salaries of price administrators unless they were qualified for the work by experience in business, industry, or commerce. An amendment sponsored by Senator Robert A.

Taft, and enacted in July, 1943, forbade OPA to employ standards of quality in setting ceiling prices unless such standards were generally in use, or were required by other agencies, or were the only method whereby prices could be controlled. And it flatly prohibited requirement of grade labeling. Labeling requirements were thereupon removed from twenty regulations. The battle to inform the consumer was lost.

PROTECTING THE CONSUMER'S SAVINGS

When the consumer saves, he is likely to put his money in a bank, to buy a life insurance policy, or to purchase stocks or bonds. In each of these cases, he must depend upon the competence and the integrity of those with whom he deals. His bank might be mismanaged, its assets stolen; he cannot himself examine its books or inspect its vaults. His insurance company might gamble with his savings; he cannot check on its investment policies. His insurance contract might carry, in small type, provisions that would limit his potential benefits; lacking the knowledge to analyze it, he is likely to take the agent's word. The new issues of stocks or bonds offered him by security salesmen might represent no actual undertaking, might not be backed by genuine assets, or might be seriously overpriced. The market on which he buys and sells old issues might be so rigged that he would pay more and take less for them than they were worth. If his corporation prospers, the earnings that should come to him might be diverted to insiders. If it goes bankrupt, the assets that should be his on reorganization might be so shuffled as to go to someone else. If he were to attempt to diversify his risks by buying shares in an investment trust, he might find it run by bankers as a dumping ground for issues that the market had refused. Stocks and bonds, like foods and drugs, may be adulterated and misbranded. And the buyer of securities, like those who purchase other goods, may be ill equipped to protect himself against the seller who misrepresents his wares. It is for these reasons that government has moved, first at common law and then through state and federal legislation, to safeguard the interests of investors by preventing fraud, by regulating banks, insurance companies, and the securities markets, by defining the responsibilities of corporate directors, officers, and trustees, and by controlling the processes of bankruptcy.

Bank Deposits

Depositors in banks are protected by government in many ways. Freedom to set up national banks is limited by the federal government and freedom to set up state banks, under varying standards, by the several states. The operations of national banks are supervised by the Comptroller of the Currency, the Federal Reserve System, and the Federal Deposit Insurance Corporation (FDIC); those of state banks by state banking departments and also, where such banks have joined them, by the Federal Reserve System and the FDIC. Banks must render periodic reports and are visited without warning by examiners who go through their books and make sure they have the assets that they claim. Savings banks are usually required to confine their investments to specified categories of securities. Commercial banks are given greater freedom of selection, but the volume of their lending and the size of the reserves that they must hold to meet their obligations are subject to detailed controls. These controls are designed, not only to stabilize the volume of industrial activity, but also to protect the interests of depositors. Under laws passed in the thirties, moreover, the quality of the assets held by national banks is safeguarded by compelling them to divorce affiliates engaged in distributing securities, by forbidding any bank to lend more than a tenth of its capital and surplus to a single borrower, and by limiting the loans a bank may make to any of its officers. The dissipation of banking resources through competition for business is prevented by prohibiting the payment of any interest on demand deposits and of interest at more than a specified rate on time deposits. Depositors in national banks and in state banks that have joined the system are protected, finally, by insurance of their deposits with the FDIC.

Protection is extended, also, to depositors in building and loan associations. Associations chartered by the states are subject to supervision by the state banking departments. Those chartered by the federal government are supervised by the Home Loan Bank Board. Accounts in the state associations may be insured by the Federal Savings and Loan Insurance Corporation. Those in the federal associations must be so insured.

Life Insurance

Since 1894, insurance companies have been regulated by the states. Since 1905, moreover, such regulation has come to be pervasive and detailed. For it was in 1905 that Charles Evans Hughes, directing the investigation of the Armstrong Committee into the practices of companies in New York State, disclosed a series of abuses—manipulating insurance funds, making excessive payments to officers, reporting fictitious assets, and refusing to pay legitimate claims—that led to the widespread enactment of stronger laws. Some states have established separate insurance departments. But most of them assign this function to the agency that regulates state banks, building and loan associations, and small loans companies. In general, the states control admission to the insurance business, prescribe forms for policies, supervise financial operations, and provide for the settlement of disputed claims. In an effort to assure responsibility, companies, brokers, and agents are required to obtain licenses and those who cannot satisfy administrative standards are excluded from the field. To check misrepresentation, policy forms are simplified and standardized, or limited to those that the administrator may approve. To insure financial soundness, the states require the maintenance of adequate reserves, check on the value of assets, and control investment policy. In some states, funds may be invested only in authorized securities; in others, in any securities that are not disapproved. Disputed claims are usually settled by the courts, but some states seek to save the time and cost of litigation by providing machinery to arbitrate disputes. Typically, the states enforce their controls by requiring companies operating within their borders to make deposits of securities, by calling for annual reports, and by conducting periodic and special examinations of company accounts.

Stocks and Bonds

Use of the mails to distribute fraudulent securities has been prohibited by federal law since 1872. The provisions of this law, the methods employed in its enforcement, and its resulting limitations were all described above. The distribution of securities has also been regulated by the states since 1911, when Kansas passed the first of the so-called "blue-sky" laws, to prevent promoters, in the words of one legislator, from selling shares "in the bright blue sky itself." Such laws had been enacted by all the states except Nevada by 1933. In a few states, these laws merely provide that the fraudulent sale of securities shall be a criminal offense, empower the Attorney General to prosecute offenders, and authorize the courts to grant injunctions and to impose penalties. In most cases, however, the laws require dealers in securities to obtain licenses, excluding nonlicensed dealers from the trade. They also require that securities themselves be registered before they can be sold within a state. Registrants must file extensive information, and registry may be denied where issues are fraudulent or registration statements falsified.

These laws have afforded scant protection to investors. The funds provided for their enforcement have rarely been adequate to finance a real analysis of the statements that are filed. Little effort has been made to censor security prospectuses, the only documents that buyers see. The laws do not prevent mismanagement of corporations, once their securities have been sold. Nor do they regulate the subsequent transfer of these securities. Many transactions escape control, moreover, since the jurisdiction of state authorities does not extend to sales across state lines. It remained for Congress to make the first effective provision for the protection of investors when it enacted the securities laws in the early years of the New Deal.

THE SECURITIES AND EXCHANGE COMMISSION

The speculative boom that followed World War I came to an abrupt end with the stock market crash in October, 1929. In the course of the next few years, the value of stocks listed on the New York Exchange fell from $89 billion to $15 billion and the value of bonds listed from $49 billion to $30 billion, representing a total loss to investors—on paper, at least—of $93 billion. At the same time, purchasers of stocks in public utility holding companies, investment trusts, and other ventures, and buyers of bonds issued by real estate promoters, foreign corporations, and foreign governments, took further losses as the issuers went bankrupt or defaulted on the payments that were due. Holders of stocks in the Insull companies, one of the great utility empires, lost nearly $750 million. Holders of shares in 22 investment trusts saw their value drop from $560 million to $50 million. Americans who bought debentures issued by Ivar Kreuger, the Swedish match monopolist, recovered $10 million on the $250 million they had paid. At the depth of the depression, three fifths of the real-estate mortgage bonds outstanding, two fifths of the bonds of foreign corporations, and a third of those of foreign governments were in default.

This financial debacle led to a series of investigations: to hearings before the Senate Committee on Banking and Currency, running to 12,000 pages of testimony and exhibits, on the practices of commercial banks, investment bankers, and the stock exchanges; to an inquiry by the Federal Trade Commission, filling more than 70 volumes, on the practices of public utility holding companies; and, subsequently, to studies by the Securities and Exchange Commission dealing with the practices of trustees who held the securities backing corporate bonds, and with those of investment advisers and investment trusts. Out of these investigations there came startling disclosures of misrepresentation, manipulation, incompetence, and irresponsibility on the part of many who had been conspicuous as leaders in finance. It was revealed:

1. That investment affiliates, set up by certain large commercial banks, had sponsored dubious securities, conducted high-pressure selling campaigns among the banks' depositors, pushed the sale of the banks' own shares, and speculated in these shares themselves;
2. That investment bankers had misrepresented the securities they sold, had concealed significant facts, and had dressed the market, buying some of these securities to make them appear more valuable than they really were; that they had discriminated among investors, offering lower prices to preferred lists of favored purchasers; and that they had obtained excessive margins for themselves;
3. That traders had manipulated the stock market, acquiring securities and forming pools which drove their prices up, by circulating favorable publicity through tipsters and financial columnists, by making wash sales (nominal transactions in which no securities changed hands) and by matching orders (buying through one broker and selling through another) both at steadily rising quotations, thus creating the appearance of an active market, then unloading their holdings at the peak of prices, withdrawing their support, even reversing their operations, and possibly buying again when prices had declined;
4. That promoters had employed the holding company as a means of pyramiding control over public utility properties; that this control had been used to inflate the valuations and the costs, to raise the rates, and

to siphon off the earnings of the operating companies; and that pyramiding, not only of control, but also of profits and losses had erected, upon a sound industrial foundation, a superstructure of highly speculative securities;

5. That trustees of securities held as backing for corporate bonds had failed to protect the bondholders' interests; that they had permitted the debtor in the Kreuger case, for instance, to withdraw superior securities and substitute inferior or even worthless ones; that they had inserted provisions in trust indentures designed to relieve them of responsibility;
6. That investment trusts, organized and run by investment bankers, had been forced to absorb securities for which the bankers could find no other market, to make needless purchases and sales in order to yield the bankers a commission, and to pay the bankers excessive fees for managing thir affairs; and that investment advisers, like sellers of securities, had sometimes had interests, adverse to those of their clients, which they had failed to disclose.

These revelations, reported in the press in circumstantial detail, gave rise to insistent demands for financial reforms. And Congress, in the next few years, enacted a series of laws that were tailor-made to prevent abuses of the types that had been found. Commercial banks were required to divorce their investment affiliates, as has been mentioned, by the Banking Act of 1933. Public offerings of new securities were brought under the control of the Federal Trade Commission by the Securities Act of 1933. The stock exchanges were subjected to regulation by the Securities Exchange Act in 1934, and the Securities and Exchange Commission (SEC) was established to take over the administration of both these laws. The Commission's authority was extended to cover public utility holding companies in 1935, trustees of security issues in 1939, and investment trusts and investment advisers in 1940. This body of legislation was enacted in the face of vigorous opposition from the business community. As time has passed, however, it has come to be accepted as a matter of course.

The Public Utility Holding Company Act finds its greatest significance in strengthening state regulation of public utility rates, and will be discussed, in that connection, in Chapter 20. The provisions of the other laws administered by the SEC are briefly summarized below.

The Securities Act

Where securities worth more than $300,000 are publicly offered for sale in interstate commerce or through the mails, the issuer must file a registration statement with the SEC, disclosing the information the investor needs to enable him objectively to appraise their value. In the case of corporate securities, he must disclose the provisions of the corporation's charter, outline its capital structure, explain the relation of the new security to others then outstanding, describe the scope and character of the company's business, tell how the funds raised by the new issue are to be employed, reveal any material contracts to which the corporation is a party, list its directors and officers together with the sums that they are paid, describe any cases in which such persons have had an interest in things the company has bought, list the principal holders of the company's stock, list those who have options to purchase its securities, tell what stock has been given for services or properties other than cash, name the underwriters of the issue, reveal the size of their commissions, and show the yield of the security to the issuer as well as its cost to the purchaser. In the case of foreign bonds, similar information is required, including data on the purpose for which the funds are to be used, the legal status of the issue, the financial condition of the borrower, and his past record in making payments on his debts.

The SEC makes a thorough examination of registration statements and security prospectuses. And where it finds that false or misleading statements have been made or material facts withheld, it may issue an order suspending a security's sale. But this is the extent of its responsibility. The Commission does not undertake to advise investors as to the merits of securities. It has no power to prevent the sale of any stock or bond, however dubious, as long as full disclosure has been made. Its function is merely to insure that sellers tell the truth, the whole truth, and nothing but the truth.

Where securities are covered by the law, sale without registration is made a criminal offense. In addition, purchasers of securities who suffer losses are permitted to bring civil suits against those who signed the registration statements and, if they can prove that their losses resulted from falsification or concealment, are entitled to return the securities and recover the money paid, plus interest, minus any earnings received, or to collect damages equal to the sums lost on securities they have sold. Individuals signing a registration statement—directors, underwriters, appraisers, accountants, and engineers—can avoid personal liability by showing that they exercised reasonable care in judging and confirming its validity. But liability cannot be avoided by the issuing corporation itself. Suits for recovery must be brought within three years of the original sale of the securities concerned and within one year of the discovery that misrepresentation had occurred.

The Securities Exchange Act

The Securities Exchange Act of 1934 had three major purposes: (1) to restrain stock market speculation by empowering the Federal Reserve authorities to establish, and the SEC to enforce, regulations governing the amount of credit that can be extended by banks to stock exchange members, dealers, and brokers, and by brokers to their customers; (2) to prevent manipulation of the market by giving the SEC the power to regulate trading practices; and (3) to protect investors in corporations by requiring the publication of various reports. Provisions directed toward the second of these purposes are outlined in the present section. Those directed toward the third will be considered later.

Stock exchanges, dealers and brokers, and listed securities are required to be registered. A number of manipulative devices—market pools, wash sales, and the dissemination of false and misleading information—are flatly prohibited. Other trading practices, such as price pegging (buying securities so that quoted prices will not fall), short selling (contracting to deliver securities the seller does not possess), dealing in options ("puts" and "calls" that give one party the privilege of requiring another, respectively, to buy or sell securities at a stated price), and trading by stock exchange members for their own accounts, are made subject to regulation by the SEC. An exchange that violates the law or rules laid down by the Commission may be fined up to $500,000, or closed temporarily or permanently by having its registration suspended or withdrawn. Members or officers of an exchange, when found to be in violation, may be suspended or expelled. Corporations that fail to obey the law and regulations may have their securities denied the trading privilege by suspension or cancellation of registry. Persons found guilty of willful violation may be fined up to $10,000 or imprisoned up to two years or both. Persons responsible for misrepresentation, in statements filed with the Commission, may be sued by investors who have suffered losses and, unless they can prove they acted in good faith, may be forced to pay them actual damages. The SEC is also authorized by the Act of 1934 to lay down rules to govern trading in over-the-counter markets, and by the Maloney Act of 1938 to supervise the regulation of such trading by associations of investment bankers, dealers, and brokers.

Since its establishment, the Commission has played a leading role in bringing about reorganization of the New York Stock Exchange and the New York Curb Exchange. It has kept trading on the exchanges under continuous surveillance and has investigated promptly any irregularities that have occurred. It has also periodically inspected transactions between dealers and brokers and their customers. In 1940, the Commission was upheld by a Court of Appeals in expelling one market operator and suspending two others from trading privileges.[28] The danger that investors will be defrauded through manipulation of the exchanges has virtually disappeared.

The Trust Indenture Act

Investigations made by the SEC in its early years led to the enactment of laws extending the Commission's authority to trustees of securities backing corporate bonds and to investment advisers and investment trusts. The Trust Indenture Act of 1939 is designed to exclude from trusteeship of a corporate mortgage anyone who has an interest adverse to that of holders of the corporation's bonds, and to prevent trustees of such securi-

[28] *Wright* v. *SEC*, 112 F. 2d 86.

ties from avoiding legal responsibility. The law sets up standards of eligibility for trustees and requires them to make full disclosure of the terms of trust indentures. It defines the obligations that trustees must assume. And it empowers the SEC to regulate the operations in which they are permitted to engage.

The Investment Company and Investment Advisers Act

This Act, passed in 1940, requires investment trusts and investment advisers to register with the SEC. It provides that two fifths of the directors of an investment trust must be independent of security underwriters, brokers, or advisers, and forbids such trusts to use their funds to finance affiliated bankers or security distributors. It authorizes the Commission to supervise transactions between the trusts and affiliated interests, to regulate the charges made for managing their affairs, and periodically to inspect their books. The law also forbids investment advisers to defraud their clients, to make profit-sharing arrangements with them, or to assign their contracts to other persons without their consent, and requires any adviser who acts as a principal in a transaction to inform his client of the fact. Violations of the law are made a criminal offense, punishable by fine and imprisonment.

Appraisals of the SEC

In the early days of the Commission's life, it was often charged that its registration requirements were so onerous as to discourage the issuance of new securities. But this complaint is now less often heard. Aside from its involvement in the Public Utility Holding Company Act, the Commission has enjoyed greater freedom than most regulatory agencies from political attack. In carrying out its responsibilities, it has sought the co-operation of the financial community. Its first members were men of outstanding ability. Its prestige, for many years, has been high. In 1949, one of the task forces of the Hoover Commission on the organization of the government reported that the SEC "has combined knowledge of the field, judgment and reasonable consistency of policy with freedom from partisan political pressures. The Commission on the whole has been notably well administered. Even its critics concede that its staff is able and conscientious, and that the Commission generally conducts its work with dispatch and expedition. . . ." In sum, the task force found the SEC to be "an outstanding example of the independent commission at its best."[29] In 1952, however, a committee of the House of Representatives could say only that the Commission had done "a pretty good job" in protecting investors.[30] And in 1954, a former Commissioner complained, in a letter to the *New York Times*, that the Commission's budget had been slashed and its

[29] Commission on Organization of the Executive Branch of the Government, *Task Force Report on Regulatory Commissions* (Washington: Government Printing Office, 1949) p. 144.

[30] *New York Times*, December 6, 1942.

staff cut (from 1,700 in 1941) to about 700: "less than the number of employees in a single large brokerage office." As a result, he said, new offerings of securities were subject to needless delay, control over investment companies was shaky, and the laws controlling the activities of brokers and dealers were widely flouted.[31]

THE INVESTOR AND THE CORPORATE INSIDER

The modern corporation is characterized by wide diffusion of nominal ownership and narrow concentration of actual control. If the capitalization of a corporation is all in voting common stock, control can be exercised by one share more than half of those outstanding. If it is half in voting common and half in nonvoting preferred, control can be exercised by one share more than a fourth. If the capitalization is one third common, one third preferred, and one third bonds, control lies with those who hold a bit more than a sixth of it. This would be true if more than half of the common were required for control. But such is rarely the case. Many shares are held by persons who make no effort to exercise control—by speculators who are constantly shifting their holdings, by investment institutions seeking only to diversify their risks, by scattered owners whose activities are limited to cashing their dividend checks and signing their proxy certificates. Control may thus be held by those who own a quarter of the common, representing but a twelfth of the total investment, or an eighth representing a twenty-fourth, or even less. In practice, control over the largest corporations is exercised, through operation of the proxy machinery, by minority stockholdings or by self-perpetuating managements with as little as 5 per cent or even 1 per cent of the outstanding shares. In some cases, moreover, concentration has been facilitated by the issuance of common stock with no vote and other classes of stock with multiple votes, and carried even further by pyramiding through successive layers of holding companies.

The danger in this situation is that the few who are in control will so employ their power as to divert the earnings of a corporation from its many owners to themselves. This has been done, in the past, in a variety of ways. Managements have voted themselves huge salaries and secret bonuses. Directors and officers have borrowed from their corporations at low rates of interest, bought from them at low prices, and sold to them at high prices. Insiders, possessing information that was not supplied to others, have profited by selling their stock before a dividend was to be passed and by purchasing stock before a dividend was to be declared. Dividends have been withheld and surpulses accumulated, in one year; payments that should have gone to holders of noncumulative preferred stock have been distributed, instead, to holders of common, in the next. Earnings have been diverted, too, by enabling insiders to acquire more shares, at

[31] Letter from J. Howard Rossbach, *New York Times*, April 22, 1954.

favorable prices, when prospects improved, and by denying to other owners the right to buy such issues and thus to maintain their proportionate claim to dividends. And these manipulations have been shielded by impublicity; by the issuance of no reports, of delayed reports, of inadequate reports, and of reports that have misrepresented the finances of the companies concerned.

When corporations have gone through bankruptcy, there have been further opportunities for gain. Reorganization was effected, until 1933, through receiverships established by courts of equity. It was not the duty of a receiver to reorganize a bankrupt company, but only to keep it in operation and to conserve its assets while reorganization plans were prepared by its creditors. For this purpose, protective committees were set up to represent the interests of investors holding different classes of securities, such holders were invited to deposit their securities together with proxy powers, and reorganization committees were then appointed to formulate and propose specific plans. When such a plan was approved by a court, the process was completed by transferring the bankrupt's property to a new corporation through a foreclosure sale.

In these procedures, inside interests were often dominant. They would select a person sympathetic to the company's management to act as its receiver and persuade a friendly judge to appoint him to the post. They would take the initiative in setting up committees that nominally represented the interests of investors, in soliciting proxies, and in obtaining the deposit of securities. They would lead reorganization committees to propose new plans designed to keep them in control. Investors would be advised to accept securities of smaller value than those they previously held. New securities, with superior rights, would be floated to raise additional capital. And the very bankers who had distributed the earlier issues would handle the new flotations and pocket generous commissions on the deal. Profits would also be made by persons using inside information for trading in the company's securities. Excessive fees would be collected, with the approval of the court, by the receiver, by committee members, by bankers serving as depositaries, and by lawyers representing the many groups concerned. And when the receivership had ended, investors would again find themselves in possession of a crippled enterprise, saddled with debt, and left in control of those who had ruined it before.

It was to protect financial lambs, thus shorn and reshorn, that further controls were adopted in the early years of the New Deal. And these controls, it should be noted, have gone some distance toward preventing the repetition of abuses that were all too common in the past.

Checking the Diversion of Earnings

The courts have shown a disposition, since the thirties, to hold corporate directors to a stricter standard of accountability. The position of a director has come increasingly to be likened to that of a trustee. And the fiduciary relationship has been held to require, not only fidelity to the interests of stockholders, avoiding personal gain at their expense, but also the exercise of considerable care and diligence in protecting them against loss. Instead of escaping responsibility merely by pleading that they had acted in good faith, directors have been held to liability for negligent mismanagement.

Concentration of control and diversion of earnings have also been checked by legislation. The issuance of nonvoting common stock has been forbidden by several states and, in cases of corporate reorganization, by Congress in the Chandler Bankruptcy Act of 1938. Pyramiding of control through the holding company device, in the case of public utilities, has been limited by the Public Utility Holding Company Act of 1935 and subjected to regulation by the SEC. This law and others already mentioned contain provisions that make it easier for investors to protect themselves against insiders whose interests may differ from their own. Publication of informative reports is required, by the Securities Act of 1933, of corporations making public offerings of new securities. It is also required, by the Securities Exchange Act of 1934, of all firms whose securities are listed on a registered exchange. Solicitation of proxies by such companies, under the latter act, must conform to rules laid down by the SEC. Proxy statements must be truthful; proposals advanced by stockholders who oppose the management must be included and submitted to a vote. Speculation by insiders in the shares of their own concerns is handicapped by provisions, contained in the Securities Exchange Act, the Public Utility Holding Company Act, and the Investment Company Act, that apply to directors, officers, and owners of a tenth or more of the stock in any corporation covered by these laws. Such persons are forbidden to sell the stock of their companies short. They are required to make frequent reports on changes in their ownership. And if any of them makes a profit by buying his company's stock and selling it within six months (or by selling the stock and rebuying it), his gain can be recovered for the company through a suit brought by the company itself or by any of its stockholders. Diversion of earnings by transactions between concerns within a holding company structure is also prevented, in the case of public utilities, by provisions of the Act of 1935 that make all such transactions subject to approval by the SEC.

As a result of the statutes and decisions that made directors and officers more liable to suits, a movement developed, during the forties, to indemnify them for the costs incurred in their defense. Enabling laws were enacted by several states and corporate bylaws were amended to make such restitution possible. These provisions do not apply, however, where directors or officers have been dishonest or negligent. Here, liability is still maintained.

Bankruptcy and Reorganization

Where debtors are able to pay their debts, government stands ready to enforce the contracts they have made. But where, through incompetence or misfortune, they have lost their ability to pay, such contracts cannot be enforced. Here, government serves as an umpire, safeguarding the interests of debtors and creditors alike. It refuses creditors the right to seize all of a debtor's assets, depriving him of the means of self-support and denying him an opportunity to make another start. It forbids the debtor to hide his assets, to change their location, or to transfer their ownership in an effort to defraud his creditors. It prevents one creditor from taking possession of assets to which another has an equal claim. In some cases, it liquidates the debtor's assets and seeks to distribute the proceeds, with an even hand, among his creditors. In others, it attempts to effect a compromise that will lighten the debtor's burden by persuading his creditors to extend the maturity and reduce the size of their claims. Where the debtor is a corporate enterprise, it may undertake to keep the business in operation and to improve its prospects by reorganizing its financial structure, easing its debts but giving the holders of each of its securities an opportunity to participate fairly in its future returns. These things are done, through the courts, under the provisions of the bankruptcy laws.

Congress was given power, by the Constitution, "to establish uniform laws on the subject of Bankruptcies." During most of the nineteenth century, however, it left this matter to the several states. Three federal laws were passed but soon repealed, the first lasting from 1800 to 1802, the second from 1841 to 1843, and the third from 1867 to 1878. A permanent federal bankruptcy law was not enacted until 1898. This law endured, without significant amendments, for nearly forty years. It provided not only for liquidation and distribution of a debtor's assets but also for an agreement scaling down his debts, and the latter procedure was frequently employed in settling cases involving small concerns. But the law made no provision for the reorganization of larger corporations and such reorganizations came increasingly to be effected through equity receiverships. It was the exposure of abuses that had grown up under this system that led to the amendment of the Bankruptcy Act during the thirties, most notably by the Chandler Act of 1938.

The Chandler Act applies to industrial and utility corporations and prescribes the procedure that must be followed if the debts of such a corporation exceed $250,000 and it is to be reorganized. The law limits the activities of insiders and provides extensive safeguards for other holders of securities. It requires the court to appoint a disinterested person as trustee, excluding from this post all creditors, stockholders, directors, officers, and employees of the company, its lawyers, and its bankers. It requires all those who seek to represent the interests of investors to file sworn statements and empowers the court to supervise their operations and to pass upon the compensation they receive. It charges the trustees with sole responsibility for formulating the plan of reorganization and presenting it to the court, after notifying the interested parties and considering whatever proposals they may make. It directs the court to hold a hearing on the trustee's plan and, where a corporation's debts exceed $3 million to obtain an opinion from the SEC. When the plan is approved by the court, the law provides that it shall be submitted to the company's creditors and stockholders, together with the court's opinion and the Commission's report. If creditors with two thirds of the company's debt and owners with half of its stock agree, the plan then goes into effect.

Reorganization procedure for railroads is governed by amendments adopted in 1933 and 1935 and differs in detail from that described above. Here, the law manifests somewhat less concern for the safety of the investor, and the preparation of opinions on reorganization plans is assigned to the Interstate Commerce Commission rather than the SEC.

Further Controls Proposed

Further proposals for corporate reform, in the interest of investors, have been made from time to time. Some of them call for a general strengthening of controls, to be accomplished, according to one approach, through adoption by the states of a uniform incorporation law with provisions bringing the standards of the weaker laws up to those of the best, or, following another approach, through enactment by Congress of a law that would require any corporation above a certain size and operating in interstate commerce either to take out a federal charter or to obtain a license from the federal government. Other proposals seek to reduce the concentration of voting power, by requiring, for instance, that preferred stockholders and bondholders be given the right to vote, at least on certain issues and in certain contingencies, or by curtailing the use of the holding company device in other industries as well as in public utilities. Still other proposals are directed toward providing the investor with fuller information and more effective representation by such means as the creation of independent committees of shareholders to make investigations and reports, public auditing of corporate accounts, election of minority members to boards of directors through cumulative voting, and appointment of public members to such boards. None of these proposals is under serious consideration at the present time. But they indicate the direction that reform might take if financial scandals were again to be disclosed.

SUGGESTIONS FOR FURTHER READING

The classic on conditions leading to the enactment of the food and drug laws is Upton Sinclair's novel, *The Jungle*, available in several editions. Exposures of the sort that led to the legislation of 1938 are contained in: Stuart Chase and F. J. Schlink, *Your Money's Worth* (New York: Macmillan Co.,

1927), F. J. Schlink and Arthur Kallet, *100,000,000 Guinea Pigs* (New York: Vanguard Press, 1933), F. J. Schlink, *Eat, Drink, and Be Wary* (New York: Covici, Friede, Inc., 1935), Arthur Kallet, *Counterfeit* (New York: Vanguard Press, 1935), T. Swann Harding, *The Joy of Ignorance* (New York: W. Goodwin, Inc., 1932) and *The Popular Practice of Fraud* (New York: Longmans, Green & Co., 1935), and Mary C. Phillips, *Skin Deep* (New York: Vanguard Press, 1934). Persisting dangers are described in the reports of the Select Committee to Investigate the Use of Chemicals in Foods and Cosmetics (82d Cong., 2d Sess.; House Reports 2182 and 2356, 1952). The legislative history of the food and drug laws is presented in Stephen Wilson, *Food and Drug Regulation* (Washington: American Council on Public Affairs, 1942), and their provisions are analyzed in the Winter, 1939, issue of *Law and Contemporary Problems*, dealing with "The New Food, Drug, and Cosmetic Legislation." A running account of the work of the Food and Drug Administration is given in its *Annual Report*, which may be obtained from the Department of Health, Education, and Welfare, Washington 25, D.C.

The work of the Federal Trade Commission in preventing misrepresentation is well described in Harry L. Purdy, Martin L. Lindahl, and William A. Carter, *Corporate Concentration and Public Policy* (2d ed.; New York: Prentice-Hall, Inc., 1950), chap. xxii. A current account of the Commission's activities is given in its *Annual Report* and in its weekly summary of press releases, which is available upon request. Decisions worth reading affecting this phase of the Commission's work are those in the Winsted, Algoma, and Keppel cases, cited above. Current decisions are reported in the *United States Law Week.*

The principal work on consumer standards is Jessie V. Coles, *Standards and Labels for Consumer Goods* (New York: Ronald Press Co., 1949). See also Samuel P. Kaidanovsky, *Consumer Standards*, T.N.E.C. Monograph 24 (Washington: Government Printing Office, 1941).

The literature exposing the exploitation of investors is voluminous. The sale of fraudulent securities is described in Watson Washburn, *High and Low Financiers* (Indianapolis: Bobbs-Merrill Co., 1932), high-pressure distribution of securities by bankers in Julian Sherrod, *Scapegoats* (New York: Brewer, Warren, and Putnam, 1931), manipulation of the securities exchanges in A. Newton Plummer, *The Great American Swindle* (New York: A. N. Plummer, 1932), investment trust abuses in John T. Flynn, *Investment Trusts Gone Wrong* (New York: New Republic, Inc., 1930), and all of these matters in the report of the Committee on Banking and Currency on *Stock Exchange Practices* (73d Cong., 2d Sess.; Senate Report 1455, 1934). The classic cases of exploitation of investors by corporate insiders are those of the Erie, the Union Pacific, and the Central Pacific. The first of these stories is told by Charles Francis Adams in "A Chapter of Erie," reproduced in F. C. Hicks, *High Finance in the Sixties* (New Haven: Yale University Press, 1929); the second, under the heading of the Credit Mobilier scandal, in any American history; the third by Oscar Lewis in *The Big Four* (New York: A. A. Knopf, 1938). Some of the cases in which corporations were defrauded by their directors and officers, during the twenties, are summarized in W. Z. Ripley, *Main Street and Wall Street* (Boston: Little, Brown & Co., 1927), in I. M. Wormser, *Frankenstein, Inc.* (New York: McGraw-Hill Book Co., 1931), and in John T. Flynn, *Graft in Business* (New York: Vanguard Press, 1931). Cases in which insiders profited from corporate reorganizations are described in B. J. Reis, *False Security* (New York: Equinox Cooperative Press, 1937), by Max Lowenthal in *The Investor Pays* (New York: A. A. Knopf, 1933) and in "The Case of the Missouri Pacific," *Harper's Magazine*, December, 1934, and by Morris Markey in "Boy, Go Out and Get Me a Shingle" in the *New Yorker* for August 3, 1935.

The laws that regulate banks, insurance companies, corporations, and the securities markets are summarized in Ford P. Hall, *Government and Business* (3d ed.; New York: McGraw-Hill Book Co., 1949), chaps. xiii, xiv, xx, xxiii. For a fuller discussion, see the standard texts on banking, insurance, and corporation finance, particularly H. G. Guthman and H. E. Dougall, *Corporate Financial Policy* (New York: Prentice-Hall, Inc., 1948), H. E. Hoagland, *Corporation Finance* (New York: McGraw-Hill Book Co., 1947), and W. H. Husband and J. C. Dockeray, *Modern Corporation Finance* (3d ed.; Homewood, Ill.: Richard D. Irwin, Inc., 1952).

Chapter 11 AIDING BUSINESS, AGRICULTURE, AND LABOR

Government not only acts to safeguard the interests of buyers—consumers and investors; it also takes action on behalf of sellers—businessmen, farmers, and laborers. The measures it adopts to protect consumers and investors are usually in the general interest; prevention of fraud and misrepresentation is beneficial to the whole community. But the buyer's interest and the general interest are not completely to be identified. Consumers may feel themselves to be well served by a steady flow of supplies that is maintained in the face of violent fluctuations in prices and in the incomes of producers. Consumers and investors may be content with low prices or high profits resulting from child labor, from dangerous working conditions, from long hours, low wages, and the denial of security. In the general interest, it may be deemed desirable to moderate extremes in the fluctuation of prices, to insure the welfare of labor, and to promote and preserve equality in bargaining. Where the interests of consumers and producers are in conflict, the general interest may require a compromise.

Measures adopted in the interest of sellers, usually in response to pressure from organized producer groups, are invariably presented to the public in terms of their contribution, whether real or merely nominal, to the general interest. Some of them undoubtedly may be so justified; others may or may not; still others quite certainly cannot. Each of them must be appraised in the light of its purposes and its results. It is possible, however, to distinguish among measures of several different types. (1) There are measures that aim, by extending public assistance, to promote the development and maintenance of certain socially desirable forms of productive activity. These include many types of aid to business and agriculture. (2) Other measures are designed to improve the operation and insure the integrity of markets, without influencing the substance of the transactions that may occur. Examples are the securities legislation, described in Chapter 10, and the laws relating to stockyards, commodities exchanges, and employment offices. (3) Still other measures seek to protect the honest seller against the dishonest one, preventing the use of unfair methods of competition and raising the general level of competitive behavior. Much of the work of the Federal Trade Commission is a case in point. (4) There are measures, too, that serve to protect a weaker seller against a stronger buyer, acting on his behalf when he lacks the power to protect himself. In this category are the laws controlling the labor of women and children and safeguarding workers in general against the hazards of industry. All of these measures leave the allocation of resources to be determined, in the main, by the forces of supply and demand operating in free markets. They may be regarded, along with measures adopted for the protection of consumers and investors and for the conservation of natural resources, as merely supplementing competition as a regulator of productive activity. In this sense, they are discussed below.

But government's aid to groups of sellers does not stop here. In other cases, such aid tends to distort the allocation of resources, to abandon reliance on competition as a regulator, or to mitigate its force. (5) Under some measures, public assistance is employed as a means of conferring special favors on particular producing groups, diverting resources to them and away from the producers of other goods. This is true of many of the subsidies provided to business and to agriculture. The line between this category and the first of those given above, it should be noted, is not an easy one to draw. (6) Other measures are intended to aid the weaker seller in his dealings with the stronger buyer by enabling him to obtain equality of bargaining power. This is the purpose of the laws permitting the formation of agricultural co-operatives and labor unions and requiring collective bargaining. Here, reliance on competition as a regulator is abandoned. Instead of equalizing the power of buyers and sellers by forcing the former to compete, government seeks to do so by allowing the latter to combine. (7) There are measures, finally, that accord a favored position to certain sellers, sheltering them from the full force of competition, or granting them the privilege of uncontrolled monopoly. Included here are many of the laws enacted in the interest of farmers and small businessmen. The nature and consequences of these laws will be considered in Part IV of this book which deals with the policy of moderating competition. Logically, consideration of the measures that fall into the two preceding categories should also be postponed to that part. But for convenience in exposition, these are included in this chapter along with other measures adopted by government on behalf of business, agriculture, and labor.

AID TO BUSINESS

Business has always depended, of course, upon functions fulfilled for it by government: upon the provision of legal status for the business unit, the maintenance of a monetary system, the establishment of standards and grades of quantity and quality, the enforcement of contracts, the protection of creditors in bankruptcy, the preservation of order, the guardianship of public health and safety, and the assurance of national security. But the contribution of government to the prosperity of business has gone far beyond this: to the provision of commercially valuable services, to the extension of credit, and to the grant—over the years—of billions upon billions of dollars in subsidies.

It was the view of Alexander Hamilton, propounded in 1791 in his famous *Report on the Subject of Manufactures*, that public aid to private industry would promote the economic development of the country and thus would operate, indirectly, to enhance the well-being of its inhabitants. And this philosophy, embraced first by the Whigs and adopted later by the Republicans, dominated the formulation of public policy for more than a century. Business was the earliest recipient of public favors and it has been by far the largest one. It was not until the years of the Great Depression and the New Deal that assistance came to be extended, on anything approaching a comparable scale, to other groups in the community.

Government Services

One of the more important of the many services rendered by government to business is that of providing it with useful information. State and federal governments—particularly the latter—are the principal source of the statistical reports that are used by businessmen in their daily operations. The *Statistical Abstract of the United States*, its annual issue running to more than a thousand pages of fine type, serves as little more than an index to the vast quantities of statistics that are collected, analyzed, and published periodically by the Bureau of the Census and other offices of the Department of Commerce, by the Bureau of Mines, the Bureau of Agricultural Economics, the Bureau of Labor Statistics, the Bureau of Internal Revenue, the Interstate Commerce Commission, the Securities and Exchange Commission, the Federal Reserve System, and many other public agencies. Economic trends are reported regularly by such publications as the *Survey of Current Business*, the *Federal Reserve Bulletin*, and the *Monthly Labor Review*. Special studies, covering many phases of business activity, are listed in each number of the *Monthly Catalogue of Government Documents*. Maps, charts, and other aids to navigation are published by the Coast and Geodetic Survey. Estimates of prospective crops are released by the Crop Reporting Service. And weather forecasts —of great importance not only to agriculture but also to shipping, aviation, and other businesses—are issued daily by the Weather Bureau.

Government also carries on research and releases its findings for commercial use. The Geological Survey and the Bureau of Mines, the Forest Service, and the Fish and Wildlife Service, together with similar agencies in many states, function in effect as laboratories for the mining, lumbering, and fishing industries. The Tennessee Valley Authority has developed new chemical fertilizers and given its formulas to the fertilizer industry. The National Bureau of Standards engages in physical research, conducts tests, and establishes industrial standards when requested to do so by two thirds of the members of a trade. The Atomic Energy Commission already is providing radioisotopes for industrial research and will come increasingly to authorize commercial applications of its various discoveries.

Other services of commercial value rendered by government are the promotion of foreign sales, the protection of foreign investments, and the assurance of greater safety in the transportation of men and goods. Business is assisted in making sales in foreign markets through the efforts of the Department of Commerce at home and those of the consular service abroad. The interests of American firms with funds invested in other countries, when they are threatened by discriminatory legislation, by controls that prevent the transmission of earnings, or by failure to provide adequate, prompt, and effective compensation in the event of nationalization, are represented through diplomatic channels by the Department of State. The safety services of government, rendered through such agencies as the Coast Guard, the Civil Aeronautics Administration, the Interstate Commerce Commission, and various state and local authorities, include the provision of aids to navigation by water and by air, the inspection of all forms of transportation equipment, the enforcement of qualifications for transport personnel, the regulation of traffic, the maintenance of rescue facilities, and the investigation of accidents. These services, in the main, may be regarded as merely promotional in character. They do not seriously affect the allocation of resources or interfere with the regulatory power of competition.

Protection against Unfair Competition

When the courts developed rules condemning unfair methods of competition as violations of the common law, and when the Congress forbade employment of such methods, in Section 5 of the Federal Trade Commission Act, it was not so much their purpose to protect the consumer as to serve the interest of business by protecting the scrupulous businessman against his unscrupulous competitor. Protection of the consumer was not explicitly made a function of the Commission until the Wheeler-Lea Amendment was passed in 1938. But protection of business has been its duty both before and since.

The Commission's procedures have already been discussed in some detail. At this point, it is sufficient to note how they have been employed on behalf of business. A number of orders issued by the Commission have directed businessmen to cease and desist from molesting their competitors in a variety of ways: by spying on them and stealing their trade secrets, by threatening them with litigation, by spreading false rumors about their credit, by disparaging their products, by inducing their customers to break contracts, and by bribing purchasing agents and salesmen to obstruct the distribution of their competitors' goods. The number of such orders has not been large, and some of them have been reversed upon appeal. But the Commission has also sought to prevent deceitful diversion of patronage by misrepresentation of the nature of a seller's business or the origin, character, or price of his goods. Its orders, for instance, have forbidden one seller to represent his products as those of another by simulating the latter's mark or name—Mentholanum for Mentholatum, Schafner for Schaeffer, and Goodwear for Goodyear. And such orders, issued in larger numbers, have invariably been upheld. This activity serves to raise the general plane of competition. But it leaves the guidance of production to the market. It preserves the function of honest competition as a regulator of business.

Government Loans and Guarantees

Many agencies have been set up by the federal government—most of them during the Great Depression—to lend money to private enterprises, to insure the funds deposited with private lenders, and to guarantee repayment of their loans. Some of these agencies have served their purpose and have terminated their activities or still are doing so. But a score of them remain, leaving the government a major factor in financing agriculture, housing, shipping, and export trade, and important as a source of credit for other industries.

The government does not lend money directly to builders or to buyers of houses. But it does maintain a variety of programs whereby the funds available for housing are substantially increased. By granting federal charters to local savings and loan associations, it adds to the number of enterprises that lend to purchasers of homes. Through the Federal Savings and Loan Insurance Corporation, it enables these and other associations to attract and hold more savings by insuring the funds deposited with them. Through the Federal Home Loan Bank System, it provides a reserve of credit for such associations, enabling them to meet increased withdrawals or to expand their loans. Through the Federal Housing Administration, it insures loans made by banks and other private lenders for the construction and repair of individual houses, and guarantees mortgages on large-scale rental-housing projects. Through the Public Housing Administration, it makes grants to aid local governments in clearing slums and building low-rent housing for low-income families. And through still other agencies, it provides housing for defense workers and finances the purchase of homes by veterans. The low-rent housing program involves substantial subsidies. On some of the other programs, the government bears the costs of administrative overhead. But in the main, its housing activities support themselves. And they make a heavy contribution to the prosperity of the construction industries.

The government provides the funds that finance the merchant marine and a major part of the country's export trade. Through the Federal Maritime Board, it lends to shipping companies, at 3½ per cent interest for 20 years, three fourths of the prices they pay when they buy new ships. Through the Export Import Bank, it makes loans (and also guarantees and participates in loans made by private banking interests) to American exporters and to foreign firms and governments to finance the purchase of American goods. Through this medium and through other intergovernmental loans and grants, it has provided the dollars to maintain American exports at the level reached in the years that have followed World War II.

Aside from housing, shipping, and export trade, the government employed the Reconstruction Finance Corporation (RFC) for many years as its major instrument in making loans to industry. This body was established, on a temporary basis, in 1932, to check financial disaster by extending emergency aid to such enterprises as railroads, banks, and insurance companies. But its life was repeatedly extended and its powers enlarged. During the thirties, it was employed to finance relief and recovery programs; during the war, to finance the procurement of strategic materials and the construction of industrial facilities. In 1948, its powers were again enlarged, enabling it to lend to any state or local government, to any public agency, to any financial institution, and to any business enterprise in the United States. By 1950, its loans had reached an annual rate of nearly 5,000 in number and nearly $500 million in amount, and had been extended to a great variety of undertakings in manufacturing, commerce, and the service trades. And since the RFC was not supposed to lend where private credit was available, its activities may be assumed to have provided business with funds that it would otherwise have been unable to obtain. The Corporation's life was ended in 1954 and a Small Business Administration, with limited lending powers, was set up in its place.[1]

Insofar as government financing of business pays its own way, this activity may be classified as promotional. But insofar as it is deliberately provided at a loss, it involves a subsidy. And this tends to bring more resources into the subsidized industries than they would otherwise obtain.

Subsidies to Transportation

In some cases, government has gone beyond the extension of credit and the provision of other services to the subsidization of private enterprise. It has undertaken to promote the development of transportation, in particular, by contributing heavily to the construction of railways and by providing highways, waterways, and airways at public expense. American railroads, during the nineteenth century, were the recipients of grants amounting to 183 million acres of public lands, some of them valuable mining and timber properties. They were also aided by cash contributions, by tax exemptions, and by governmental subscriptions to their securities. The growth of the trucking industry was stimulated, during

[1] On these programs, see Commission on the Organization of the Executive Branch of the Government, *Task Force Report on Lending Agencies* (Washington: Government Printing Office, 1949).

the earlier part of the twentieth century, by heavy public expenditures on highway construction, the motor carriers being subsidized by the failure of governments to compel them to pay enough in taxes to cover their contribution to highway costs. But assistance to railroad and trucking companies has only a historical significance. Large transportation subsidies are now confined to carriers by water and by air.

The shipping industry is subsidized in many different ways. First, it is sheltered from foreign competition. The coastwise and intercoastal trade has been reserved, since the founding of the republic, to ships flying the American flag. All goods carried overseas for the army or the navy and half of the cargoes financed by government loans or by grants to other countries must be hauled in American ships. Second, shipping in general and shipping on inland waterways in particular have benefited by the billions of dollars spent by federal, state, and local governments on the improvement of harbors, the dredging and canalization of rivers, and the construction of canals—these waterways and related facilities being provided to shipping companies at no charge or at a fraction of their cost. Third, the transoceanic companies have been enabled to acquire ships on terms that have cut their capital costs. And fourth, their costs of operation have been subsidized.

The transoceanic lines have been provided with ships at bargain prices and supplied with the money to pay for them. Ships that were built for the government have been sold to private operators at a few cents on the dollar. After World War I, 220 ships that had been built for $516 million were sold for $41 million. After World War II, 1,950 ships built for $4,561 million were sold for $1,719 million.[2] The construction of new ships is also subsidized. Under the Merchant Marine Act of 1936, the government may contribute, as a "construction differential subsidy," the difference between the cost of building vessels in American and in foreign yards. This contribution is nominally limited to a third of total cost. But where there is "convincing evidence" that American yards cannot compete on this basis, it may be raised to half. And where a ship is designed to include features that increase its potential usefulness for national defense, the fraction may be even higher. The liner "United States" was built at a cost of $76,800,000. Of this, $43,900,000 was put up by the taxpayers and only $32,900,000 by the United States Lines.[3] In such a case, moreover, three fourths of the price a company must pay may be loaned to it by the government, these loans being made on terms that themselves involve a subsidy. And finally, of the fourth the company puts up, some or all may have been left in its hands by legislation that exempts the profits of subsidized shipping companies, when placed in reserves for new construction, from both the corporate income tax and the excess profits tax.

[2] Blair Bolles, *How to Get Rich in Washington* (New York: Dell Publishing Co., 1952), p. 112.

[3] *New York Times*, April 2, 1953.

The operation as well as the construction of ships is subsidized. For many years, the subsidy was hidden in excessive payments made for carrying the mails. Under the Merchant Marine Act of 1936, however, it was brought into the open. An "operating differential subsidy" has since been paid to cover the difference in cost assumed to be involved in operating under the American rather than a foreign flag. Until 1952, this subsidy was confined to ships sailing regularly on established routes. In that year, the law was amended to extend it to all ships making transoceanic voyages. In the seven prewar years 1937–42, the total net operating subsidy (after certain repayments) was $17 million. In the seven postwar years 1947–52 (after the program had been suspended and renewed) the comparable figure was $203 million. In 1953, prospective subsidies were running between $65 million and $70 million a year.[4]

Commercial aviation, too, is subsidized. More than a billion dollars have been invested in airports, almost all of it by federal, state, and local governments. In addition, the federal government has spent hundreds of millions on airway facilities: beacons, markers, radio beams, emergency landing fields, weather reporting facilities, traffic control equipment, instrument landing systems, and the like. The companies using these facilities are not expected to repay their costs. These companies are supported, moreover, by payments for carrying mail designed to enable them, along with other revenues, to cover their operating costs. The size of these payments has been determined, since 1940, by the Civil Aeronautics Board (CAB), but the subsidies involved were borne, until 1953, by the Post Office Department, contributing many millions to its annual deficit. In 1953, responsibility for paying the subsidies was transferred, by Executive Order, from the Post Office to the CAB.

The subsidies to transportation have obviously affected the allocation of resources in the economy. Subsidies given the railroads, in the early years, greatly speeded their construction by diverting to this purpose resources that otherwise would have been used in other ways. Those now provided to shipping and to aviation enable these industries to attract more capital and labor than they could otherwise command and divert to carriers by water and by air some traffic that might be moved more economically by rail.[5]

Subsidies to Other Industries

Subsidies to industries other than transportation are always hidden rather than direct. Subsidization is involved, of course, when foreign competitors are excluded from the American market by the tariff and when out-of-state or out-of-town competitors are excluded from regional or local markets by restrictive statutes or ordinances. Here the subsidy, in-

[4] *New York Times*, November 9, 1953.

[5] On public aids to transportation, see Truman C. Bigham and M. J. Roberts, *Transportation* (2d ed.; New York: McGraw-Hill Book Co., 1952), chap. xxii.

stead of being distributed by the government, is paid by the consumer in a higher price. And this, indeed, is the method of subsidization that has been most generally employed. But business enterprises have also been subsidized in other ways, notably (1) by exempting them from taxes, (2) by selling goods and services to them for less than they are worth, and (3) by buying goods and services from them for more than they are worth.

Exemption from business and property taxes, for five, ten, or fifteen years, has been employed by state and local governments as a means of attracting new industries. Six states have authorized their subdivisions to issue tax-exempt securities to build and equip factories for rental to new concerns, who can then deduct their rents from income in computing the federal corporate income tax. Reduction of liability under the corporate income tax has also been used by the federal government to encourage mining operations and to stimulate construction of new industrial capacity. Not only may mining companies deduct the costs of exploration and development in determining taxable income, but they are also given the option of making arbitrary deductions for depletion of wasting assets (at rates that run from 5 per cent of gross income for some minerals to 23 per cent for sulfur and 27½ per cent for oil) instead of deducting for actual depletion throughout the assets' estimated life. Corporations constructing facilities deemed essential to production for national defense have been granted permission, during the first and second World Wars and again under the Revenue Act of 1950, to deduct a fifth of the cost of such facilities from taxable income each year for five years, instead of making smaller deductions throughout their lifetime, as would otherwise have been required. If tax rates continue high, a corporation that adopts this practice may postpone tax payments but not escape them, since it will be unable to write off the cost of new facilities in their sixth and later years. But if tax rates fall below their wartime peaks, its gain will be substantial, since it will minimize its liability in years when rates are high, postponing it to years when rates are low. Percentage depletion and accelerated amortization, as they are called, have excused some concerns from taxes that others were required to pay, and have thus operated, in effect, to provide a subsidy.

Goods have frequently been sold by government to business for less than they were worth. During the nineteenth century, valuable mining and timber lands were not only given to railroads but sold to others for a song. More recently, plants built for $20 billion during World War II, and materials acquired at $40 billion remaining in the hands of the government at the end of the war, were sold at but a fraction of their cost. In the case of iron and steel, for instance, 116 units costing $750 million went for $260 million or about 35 cents on the dollar.[6] In disposing of surplus

[6] *Iron and Steel Plants, Disposal Status as of December 31, 1950* (Washington: General Services Administration, 1951).

materials, the emphasis was on speed, not price. Airplanes were sold for less than the value of the gasoline left in their tanks, and brand-new machinery, never uncrated, was sold for scrap. Insofar as the prices paid for such goods fell short of actual market values, their purchasers were subsidized.

So, too, with the sale of public services. When government engages in lending, guaranteeing, and insuring operations, the fees it charges frequently fail to cover its total costs, the administration of such programs being financed by the taxpayers. Government has subsidized private forestry, not only by supporting research and education, but also by providing it with fire protection, with planting stock, and with technical assistance for less than cost. Government has subsidized the livestock industries by permitting sheep and cattle to graze in national forests and on other public lands for fees below those charged on private ranges. It has subsidized the publishers of newspapers and magazines by delivering their products at a loss. In 1950, for instance, the cost of this service was $242 million, the postage paid $42 million, and the subsidy $200 million.[7] In the postman's bag, as he staggers up the street, are pounds of periodicals containing editorials that denounce the government for doing many things, but not (it may safely be assumed) for cutting the costs and contributing to the profits of publishers.

Government also subsidizes business by buying goods and paying more for them than they are worth. Under the Buy American Act of 1933, procurement officers must purchase goods produced in the United States unless their price exceeds the price of goods produced abroad by more than a specified percentage. Contracts for war production have usually been let, under the pressure of emergency requirements, not through competitive bidding, but on the basis of cost-plus-a-fixed-fee or cost-plus-a-percentage-of-cost. In both cases, profits may have been increased by padding costs, and in the latter, in particular, the incentive to do so was obviously strong. Under many contracts, high prices have been reduced through renegotiation. Wartime profits, in general, have been subject to the excess profits tax. But it is still likely that the government, on a major part of its procurement, has paid substantially more than a competitive price. At the end of World War II, moreover, the emphasis in settling terminated contracts was not on economy but on speed. As a result, the settlements were generous, a few of them involving fraud, but more providing a substantial subsidy.[8]

In the case of one product, the government has not only paid an excessive price but has been compelled to buy supplies for which it has no need. From 1878 to 1903, under the Bland-Allison Act and the Sherman Silver Purchase Act, the Treasury was required to buy specific quantities of silver each month, and the metal thus acquired was added to the stock

[7] *New York Times*, February 28, 1951.

[8] Bolles, *op. cit.*, chap. iii.

of money. In 1933, under the Thomas Amendment to the Agricultural Adjustment Act, purchases again were authorized; and in 1934, Congress directed that they be continued until silver should provide a third of the metal backing for the currency. In 1932, the market price of silver had stood at 24.5 cents per ounce. In 1934, the Treasury's buying price was set at 50 cents, in 1939 at 71.11 cents, and in 1946 at 90.5 cents. For many years, the whole domestic output has been diverted to the government, the silver used by industry being imported at lower prices from abroad. The metal is dug from the ground in the mountain states only to be buried again at West Point, New York. There, it is utterly useless, contributing nothing to the value of the currency. The sums paid for it, now running into the billions, represent nothing but a subsidy to the mining industry. In all of these cases, the allocation of resources is distorted. As a result of governmental intervention, more of some goods and less of others are produced than consumers would freely choose.

AID TO AGRICULTURE

Government, in the United States, has aided agriculture for a century and more. Since the Great Depression, government assistance has taken the form, predominantly, of measures designed to raise the prices of the things the farmer sells. This has been done by restricting imports and by subsidizing exports, by curtailing the quantities produced or marketed, and by making loans or purchases. But government has also extended aid in other ways. It has stimulated agricultural settlement, financed agricultural research and education, provided irrigation services, encouraged agricultural co-operation, regulated livestock and commodities markets, provided agricultural credit, ameliorated rural poverty, promoted rural electrification, and insured the farmer's crops. The programs that seek to aid agriculture by raising prices will be discussed, in some detail, in Chapters 15 and 16. Those that extend aid without manipulating prices are considered, more briefly, below.

Promotional Activities

Government has promoted agriculture by selling land to farmers at low prices and by giving it away, by constructing irrigation projects, by building farm-to-market roads, and by providing rural mail delivery. Until 1819, land was sold at $2.00 an acre, first in tracts of 640 acres, then 320, and finally 160. In 1819, the price was cut to $1.25 and the acreage to 80. Under laws enacted in 1830 and 1841, squatters were given preemptive rights. And under the Homestead Act of 1862, farm families were given title to 160 acres each if they settled on the land and cultivated it for a period of five years. In 1902, the size of homesteads was increased to 320 acres where settlers undertook to irrigate arid land; in 1916, it was raised to 640 acres in the case of grazing lands. In 1902, also, the government began to make more land available by building irrigation works. By 1950, more than 4 million acres had been reclaimed and opened to settlement.

In agriculture, too, research and education have been carried on almost exclusively by government. In 1862, when it passed the Homestead Act, Congress also set up the Department of Agriculture, and passed the Morrill Land-Grant College Act, donating land to the states for agricultural colleges. And it subsequently extended federal aid to the states, under the Hatch Act of 1887, for agricultural experiment stations and, under the Smith-Lever Act of 1914, for agricultural extension work. The Department of Agriculture, with more than 80,000 employees, now functions as a gigantic agricultural service agency. Research in soil chemistry and plant and animal biology, in the improvement of fertilizers and feeds, in the control of pests and diseases, and in other aspects of agricultural technology is conducted by the Department and by the state experiment stations. Education in agricultural methods is provided to students by the land-grant colleges, and is carried to the farmer, through farmers' institutes, through demonstration projects, and through instruction on the farm, by thousands of county agents employed jointly by the Department and the colleges.

In all of these programs, it has been assumed that the general interest would be served. The settlement of the country has been hastened. The production of foods and fibers has been enlarged. But this has been done by granting subsidies to farmers at the expense of other taxpayers. The allocation of resources to agriculture has not been left for the market to decide.[9]

Irrigation

The earliest irrigation projects were built and operated through private enterprise, and the first irrigation laws were designed to encourage this type of activity. With the passage of the Newlands Act in 1902, however, a Bureau of Reclamation was established in the Department of the Interior, and the construction of irrigation systems became a function of the federal government. The first of these systems were small, being confined to the single purpose of irrigating agricultural land. In later years, however, the Bureau came to undertake gigantic projects, such as those at Hoover Dam on the Colorado and at the Grand Coulee on the Columbia, involving not only irrigation but also power production, navigation, and flood control. By 1950, the Bureau was operating 43 projects in 17 western states, providing water to 2,200,000 acres and supplementing the supply on 2,500,000 more.

Under the Newlands Act, public land was temporarily reserved for irrigation and then reopened to entry, with homesteads limited to the size required to support a family, no more than 160 acres being made available

[9] On the homestead policy, see Rainer Schickele, *Agricultural Policy* (New York: McGraw-Hill Book Co., 1954), chap. xx.

in any case. In the region of the Grand Coulee, land was purchased by the government and resold to settlers, with similar limits on size. Such limits were designed to spread the benefits of irrigation, but they are said to have forced the division of land, in many cases, into holdings too small to be operated with real efficiency. The Bureau recovers its construction costs in annual installments, the settlers thus obtaining title to water rights. An alternative arrangement permits delivery of water as a service for an annual charge, but this is little used. The government has sought to prevent speculators from profiting by selling land at prices which reflect the value of irrigation while leaving purchasers to meet the installments required to pay for the facilities. Since 1926, no sale of irrigable land has carried water rights until half of these charges have been paid, unless the Bureau has first approved its price as containing no increment of value based on irrigability.

It is difficult to tell how far the users of public irrigation services may have been or may be subsidized. Irrigation has yielded revenues in the form of prices and rentals for public lands and payment for water rights. After an initial period of development, the farmer is expected to repay the cost of building distribution facilities in annual installments reaching over forty years. But the farmer's contribution may or may not equal his benefits. Information on some projects is incomplete because they have already been written off. Others still have many years to run. With multipurpose projects, moreover, cost cannot be definitely ascertained. The part of the investment in a dam that is to be charged to irrigation rather than to flood control, navigation, or hydroelectric power is a matter of judgment. To the extent that irrigation has been required to meet its proper share of this joint cost—whatever that may be—it has paid its own way. To the extent that this share has been charged, instead, to power and other purposes, irrigation has been subsidized.[10]

Agricultural Co-operation

Government has encouraged the formation of co-operative associations to engage in the processing and marketing of agricultural commodities. In the absence of such associations, the farmer would be at a disadvantage in disposing of his crops. Agricultural products are usually sold in markets where sellers are small, scattered, and numerous, and buyers large, concentrated, and few. Many of these products are perishable; producers are, therefore, under pressure to sell them before they deteriorate. The buyer is thus in a position to depress the seller's price. For some products, moreover, as is the case with milk, the payments made depend on measurements of quantity and quality applied by the buyer at the time of delivery, or on the uses to which various quantities may be put. And here, in the absence of organization, the seller might be defrauded by false reports. Co-operation has been developed as a means of equalizing bar-

[10] On irrigation policy, see Roy E. Huffman, *Irrigation Development and Public Water Policy* (New York: Ronald Press Co., 1953).

gaining power and protecting the producer's interest. Co-operatives serve as common selling agencies, assembling, sorting, grading, packing, storing, and distributing agricultural products in wholesale quantities. In some cases they have gone further, engaging in the manufacture of foodstuffs —such as butter, cheese, and ice cream—in retail distribution, and in other merchandising activities.

The act of combining in a co-operative was formerly held to violate the antitrust laws of certain states. But in 1914, in the Clayton Act, Congress declared that this form of organization, as such, was not in violation of the Sherman Act. And during the twenties, a uniform statute permitting co-operatives and prescribing their legal structure was enacted by many of the states. Under this law, the return that could be paid on an association's capital was limited, and each owner of its shares was given a single vote. In 1922, in the Capper-Volstead Act, Congress exempted the usual business activities of bona fide co-operatives from the antitrust laws, and empowered the Secretary of Agriculture to prevent monopolistic abuses by adopting a procedure like that of the Federal Trade Commission, involving public hearings and the issuance of orders to cease and desist. And in 1926, the Cooperative Marketing Act set up a division in the Department of Agriculture to conduct research and carry on educational work in co-operative marketing, gave the co-operatives permission to assemble, interpret, and disseminate trade statistics, and again empowered the Secretary of Agriculture to prevent abuse. In 1934, under another law, similar arrangements were established for fisheries. At the present time, there are some 10,000 co-operatives with 6 million members, such organizations handling a fourth of the agricultural commodities produced in the United States.[11]

The significance of these arrangements varies from product to product. Where producers are geographically concentrated, as they are in the cases of fruits, vegetables, nuts, and milk, a co-operative may possess monopolistic powers. And the Secretary of Agriculture, who has here been given jurisdiction, is likely to look on its activities with greater sympathy than the Antitrust Division might have shown. But where producers are widely scattered, as is the case with the great staple crops, co-operatives are unlikely to control enough of the supply to dictate the price. In one case, the laws exempting co-operatives from antitrust may grant a license to monopoly. In another, they may serve merely to permit an equalization of bargaining power. But in either case, they extend to agriculture a privilege that is denied to industry. Except for Appalachian Coals, joint selling agencies, under the Sherman Act, have been held to be illegal per se.

Regulation of Livestock Markets

Many regulatory laws have been enacted, by state and federal governments, to protect the farmer from injury and to insure the integrity of

[11] Schickele, *op. cit.*, p. 424.

the markets where his goods are sold. Loss from insect pests and plant and animal diseases has been reduced by prohibiting the importation and the domestic transportation of infested plants and diseased animals. Damage from caustic poisons, from insecticides, fungicides, and rodenticides, and from viruses, serums, and toxins has been prevented by requiring sellers to make disclosures of composition and quality. Misrepresentation in the sale of fertilizers, feeds, and seeds has likewise been checked by requiring informative labeling. The distribution of agricultural products has been promoted and the operation of agricultural markets facilitated by establishing standards and grades of quantity and quality. Manipulation of these markets, to the detriment of the farmer, has been prevented by subjecting the stockyards and the commodities exchanges to public control.

The stockyards, located in the larger midwestern cities, provide facilities for the unloading, care, and feeding of livestock, pending their sale. They also serve as central markets where animals are weighed and bought and sold, where information is supplied, and where other market services are performed. At one time, growers accompanied their cattle to market, cared for them there, and handled their sale. Later on, these services came to be provided by commission houses, and growers shipped to them, receiving payment through the mail. A shipper's return was the price obtained for him by an agent, hundreds of miles away, minus the agent's commission and the charges made for stockyard services. The price might be set too low, the charges too high; growers became dependent on the honesty of the commission men. Stockyard facilities, first established by the railroads, were later purchased by the major packing companies. The packers became the landlords—as well as the customers—of the commission men, controlled their use of livestock pens, and their access to other market services. This situation was subject to abuse, and there is evidence that it was abused. In a report[12] published in 1918, the Federal Trade Commission found that the packing companies had paid high prices to stimulate large shipments and had then withheld purchases until prices fell and shippers, burdened with mounting costs of yard services, were forced to sell; that they had also depressed prices by entering into collusive agreements with commission men; that they had further reduced the grower's return by delaying switching and unloading, thus causing shrinkages in weight; and that stockyard owners and commission men alike had made excessive charges for their services. To eliminate these abuses, the Commission recommended public ownership and operation of the stockyards as the only effective remedy. This recommendation was not adopted. But in 1920 the packers accepted a consent decree requiring them to sell their holdings in the stockyards to an independent company. And in 1921, Congress subjected the livestock markets to regulation under the Packers and Stockyards Act.

[12] Federal Trade Commission, *Meat Packing Report*, 1918.

This law transfers jurisdiction over trade practices, in the case of packing companies, from the Federal Trade Commission to the Department of Agriculture, authorizing that Department to prevent unfair, deceptive, and unjustly discriminatory methods, manipulation of prices, and restraint of trade by conducting investigations, making complaints, holding hearings, and issuing orders to cease and desist. The Act also provides for the regulation of stockyards, market agencies, and dealers using these facilities. Stockyard owners and agencies are required to render reasonable services and to charge just, reasonable, and nondiscriminatory rates. They must file their charges with the Department and open them to public inspection and they may not depart from the figures they have filed without prior notice. The Department may suspend these filings and if, after a public hearing, it finds a charge to be unjust, unreasonable, or discriminatory, may prescribe the charge that can be made. This legislation follows the usual pattern of public utility regulation, to be discussed at length in Part V of this book. Its constitutionality was upheld by the Supreme Court in 1922.[13]

Regulation of Commodity Exchanges

Agricultural products that can be standardized and graded are bought and sold on organized exchanges, often being traded sight unseen. There are ten major commodity exchanges in the United States, some of them providing for trade in produce, imported foodstuffs, and raw materials, two of them specializing in cotton, and three in grain, the most important being the Chicago Board of Trade. These bodies are membership associations managed by governing boards. They supply facilities for trading, collect and disseminate market information, adopt and enforce trading rules, and provide for the adjustment of disputes. Trading on the commodities exchanges is much like that on the securities exchanges, save that here the element of speculation is enhanced. Transactions include not only trade in commodities already harvested and placed in storage, but also contracts for future delivery of commodities that are yet to be grown. Such contracts have their uses: a manufacturer who has bought an agricultural material for processing can protect himself against the loss that would result from a drop in its price by hedging, i.e., by making a contract for future delivery of a similar quantity of the material to serve as an offsetting bet. But hedging depends on the existence of an active futures market, and this depends, in turn, on the presence of traders who specialize in speculation. And here, as in the securities markets, speculation is subject to abuse. Speculators may manipulate the market, driving prices up to sell high when they have bought low, driving prices down to buy low when they hold contracts that enable them to sell high. In the first case, farmers are unlikely to object; in the second, they are certain to do

[13] *Stafford* v. *Wallace*, 258 U.S. 495.

so. When the prices of grain declined, in the months that followed World War I, the farmers held that speculation was to blame. And it was this view that first led to the enactment of legislation bringing the commodities exchanges under public control.

The Future Trading Act of 1921 effected this control by imposing a tax, at 20 cents a bushel, on contracts for the future delivery of grain, but exempting such transactions on exchanges that were registered with, and regulated by, the Secretary of Agriculture. This law was invalidated by the Supreme Court on the ground that it went beyond the constitutional limits of the taxing power.[14] The Grain Futures Act of 1922, based on the commerce power, was upheld.[15] Under its provisions, a Grain Futures Administration, consisting officially of the Secretaries of Agriculture and Commerce and the Attorney General, collected information on the dealings of speculators and undertook to prevent the dissemination of false information, but did little more. It remained for the Commodity Exchange Act of 1936 to extend the scope of control and to increase its effectiveness.

The present law, administered by a Commodity Exchange Authority in the Department of Agriculture, covers future trading in a number of different commodities. Exchanges and traders must register and submit reports. The dissemination of false and misleading information and the use of manipulative devices, such as wash sales and market corners, are prohibited. The Authority is empowered to put a brake on speculation by setting limits on the futures contracts of individual traders and on the extent to which a market may rise or fall in a single day. It polices trading on the exchanges, issues orders to check violations, and may enforce them by suspending or revoking registrations, by withdrawing trading privileges, and by appealing to the courts to impose penalties involving fines and imprisonment.

Regulation of the stockyards and the commodity exchanges does not attempt to control the total volume of transactions or to fix the prices at which goods are bought and sold. These are left to be determined by the forces of demand and supply. Such regulation was undertaken in the interest of the farmer. But by assuring the honesty of markets, it serves the interest of the trader, the merchant, and the processor as well.

Agricultural Credit

Like other industries, agriculture has need for various forms of credit: long-term credit to finance the purchase, enlargement, and equipment of farms; credit for shorter periods to finance the purchase of feed, seed, fertilizer, and other supplies, and the processing and marketing of agricultural commodities. Unlike other industries, however, agriculture long had difficulty in obtaining loans. Credit was adapted to the needs of manufacturing and commerce. The funds available to farmers were scarce and

[14] *Hill* v. *Wallace*, 259 U.S. 44 (1922).

[15] *Board of Trade* v. *Olsen*, 262 U.S. 1 (1923).

the rates of interest charged were high. The farmers therefore turned for assistance to the federal government.

The government has come to play a major role in the provision of agricultural credit. In the main, it has done so by promoting the development of co-operative lending agencies. Long-term credit is supplied through a system of twelve regional land banks, set up in 1916 under the Federal Farm Loan Act to make loans on mortgages that were acquired and endorsed by local farm loan co-operatives. The capital of the land banks, originally subscribed by the federal treasury, has since been purchased and is now owned by the co-operatives. Credit for shorter periods is supplied by three separate systems, set up by federal law with funds provided by the government. A system of twelve intermediate credit banks, one in each of the land bank districts, was established in 1923 to rediscount paper originating in loans made by commercial banks or by co-operatives to finance such purchases as those of livestock and agricultural equipment. A parallel system of twelve production credit corporations, with a central corporation in Washington, was set up in 1933 to finance the creation of local production credit associations and to supervise their operations. These associations, now around 500 in number, make loans for periods of one to three years to cover the purchase of feed, seed, fertilizer, machinery, and other expenses of operation. They obtain most of their loan funds from the intermediate credit banks, having come to be the banks' chief customers. The associations are co-operatives, nearly nine tenths of their stock now being owned by their members. The intermediate credit banks and the production credit corporations, however, are still owned by the government. A third system, set up in 1933 under government ownership, includes a central bank and twelve district banks for co-operatives and makes loans to finance the activities of such associations in processing and marketing agricultural commodities. All of these agencies were brought under the supervision of a Farm Credit Administration in the Department of Agriculture in 1933.[16]

All of these credit operations have been subsidized to some extent, administrative overhead being charged to the taxpayer and rates of interest established that failed to cover full costs. The land banks, however, have passed into private ownership and now stand on their own feet. The other systems go far toward paying their own way. But there is still an element of subsidy.

Aid to Low-Income Farmers

The forms of credit made available through the agencies just described still fail to meet the needs of farmers in the lowest income groups. Public

[16] On the various forms of agricultural credit, see Harold G. Halcrow, *Agricultural Policy of the United States* (New York: Prentice-Hall, Inc., 1953), chap. xxii, or G. W. Forster and M. C. Leager, *Elements of Agricultural Economics* (New York: Prentice-Hall, Inc., 1950), Part IV.

loans for feed and seed were occasionally made to such farmers, before 1933, to tide them over during periods of drought and similar emergencies. But it was not until the Great Depression that aid came to be extended on a major scale. Beginning in 1933, the Federal Emergency Relief Administration made relief disbursements to rural as well as to urban people who were found to be in need. In 1935, the Resettlement Administration was established to construct subsistence homestead projects, to move farm families onto better lands, and to promote rehabilitation of such families by making grants and loans. In 1937, this agency was superseded by the Farm Security Administration, set up under the Bankhead-Jones Farm Tenant Act. The FSA was authorized to assist lenders and borrowers in readjusting the terms of existing debts, and itself to make direct loans to farmers who could not obtain funds elsewhere. Loans to enable farm tenants, farm laborers, and sharecroppers to obtain ownership of farms were made at 4 per cent interest, to be paid off in forty years, with annual installments adjusted to the farmer's ability to pay, being reduced in bad years and raised in good. Loans were also made, for periods of five to seven years, to provide subsistence and to finance the purchase of livestock, equipment, and supplies. The FSA supervised borrowers to insure that its loans served the purpose for which they were made. The agency set up local offices in more than 2,000 counties, to assist in debt adjustments, to make and administer loans, to help farmers work out farm plans, and to give them instruction in farm management. By employing something akin to social case-work methods, it succeeded in putting thousands of rural families on their feet. The FSA also established programs of group medical care and operated a number of camps for migratory laborers.

During World War II the scope of these activities was reduced. In 1946, the FSA was superseded by another agency, the Farmers' Home Administration. This body is empowered to handle all grants and loans made to farmers with low incomes, including those for the purchase and enlargement of farms, the construction and improvement of farm homes, the provision of water facilities, the co-operative purchase of machinery, operating expenses, and emergency needs. Since 1948, it has been authorized to insure mortgage loans made by private lenders. This power has served to double the credit it has made available. Its own outstanding loans amounted to $300 million in 1951.

The aid extended by these agencies has been restricted by legal provisions requiring its apportionment among the states on the basis of farm population and tenancy, and limiting the loans that can be made to individual borrowers. In some cases, this has had the effect of holding farms to a size that is too small for real economy. Observers of the program are agreed that the record of repayments is remarkably good. At present, the interest paid on the outstanding loans comes close to covering their cost.

But the expenses of administration are still borne, in part, by the taxpayer.[17]

Rural Electrification

As late as 1935, only a tenth of the farms in the United States had electricity. By 1951, more than four fifths of them had been electrified. Half were served by private companies and half through public agencies. But the initiative that brought about the change was taken by the government. The private companies had long been reluctant to extend their lines into sparsely populated rural areas. They were encouraged to do so by the example set them by the Rural Electrification Administration.

The REA, first created by executive order in 1935, was given statutory authority in 1936. Its primary function has been that of making loans to co-operative associations set up to build and operate electrical facilities. But it has also provided these associations with legal, construction, engineering, and other advisory services. Its loans have usually financed the erection of transmission and distribution lines to carry purchased power. In some cases, however, they have also covered generating plants. The co-operatives are given legal preference in purchasing power from projects operated by the federal government. Title to the facilities financed by REA is held by these associations. The loans are being paid off, at 2 per cent interest, over periods of 35 years. And when payments are completed, the properties will pass into debt-free private ownership.

The program has been a highly successful one. There were nearly a thousand electric co-operatives in 1951, serving more than 3,500,000 customers. Electricity has been carried to the farms, costs and rates have been cut, and consumption has been increased. Payments are running ahead of schedule. But interest charges have not been high enough to cover all of the government's expenditures; the gains achieved have thus been subsidized.[18]

Crop Insurance

A farmer's crop may fall off seriously in any year through no fault of his own. He may plant the same seed with the same fertilizer on the same land and cultivate it in the same way. But his yield may be diminished by forces that he is powerless to control: by drought, flood, freezing temperature, wind, hail, plant disease, and insect pest. His risks of loss are like those met in other fields by purchasing insurance policies. But insurance companies have not attempted to provide indemnities against declines in yields resulting from hazards other than wind and hail. They have lacked

[17] On these programs, see Halcrow, *op. cit.*, chap. xxiii, and Schickele, *op. cit.*, chap. xxi.

[18] See Eli W. Clemens, *Economics and Public Utilities* (New York: Appleton-Century-Crofts, 1950), chap. xxiv, and Halcrow, *op. cit.*, chap. xxiv.

both the data required to determine risks and the assurance of breadth and diversity of coverage. All-risk crop insurance was therefore unavailable until it was provided by the federal government.

The Federal Crop Insurance Corporation (FCIC) was established in 1938. It first wrote insurance on wheat in 1939 and on cotton in 1941. Its losses, in its early years, were heavy. In 1943, Congress provided for its liquidation. In 1944, however, Congress renewed the program, permitting the insurance of certain crops, in a limited number of counties, on an experimental basis. Later on, provision was made for contracts covering several crops.

The FCIC has experimented with a number of different insurance plans. A farmer may insure a crop at 50 or 75 per cent of his average yield during the ten previous years. Premiums and indemnities may be fixed in physical units, such as bushels or pounds, or they may be converted into dollars and cents. Premiums are based on estimates of risk, but a different premium may be fixed for each farm or a common premium fixed for all of the farms in a county. In the latter case, the rates of individual farmers may be reduced on the basis of favorable experience. Indemnities are paid when the yield of a crop falls below the level at which it is insured. Under multiple-crop contracts, indemnities are based on average yields.

The system is supposed to break even over the years, the profits of the good years compensating for the losses of the bad. In fact, however, the FCIC lost money until 1947 and went into the red again in 1949, its premiums being only three fourths as large as its benefits. Operations are on a small scale, with a small fraction of the farmers covered and a small fraction of the acreage in any crop insured. There is an adverse selection of risks, farmers on poor land coming in and farmers on good land staying out. Premiums are too low or indemnities too high. But if premiums were to be raised or indemnities to be reduced, coverage would decline still further and the selection of risks would become even more unfavorable. A solution to this problem may be found by experimenting with other plans. A better balance of risks might be obtained by selling insurance for whole areas rather than farm by farm. And premiums might be put on an actuarial basis by insuring in accordance with inches of rainfall. As the Corporation gains in experience, it may be able to keep its premiums and benefits in balance. But it is not expected to cover its administrative costs. Here, again, the farmer is being subsidized.[19]

AID TO LABOR

Legislation on behalf of labor had its origin, more than a century ago, in humanitarian efforts to check the obvious abuses of industrialism. Chil-

[19] *Halcrow,* op. cit., chap. xxvi, Geoffrey S. Shepherd, *Agricultural Price and Income Policy* (Ames: Iowa State College Press, 1952), chap. xi, and Theodore W. Schultz, *The Economic Organization of Agriculture* (New York: McGraw-Hill Book Co., 1953), chap. xix.

dren had been employed in mines and factories, which stunted their growth and deprived them of educational opportunity. Women had been put to work, for long hours and at night, under conditions that were harmful to morals and at tasks that impaired their strength. Men, too, had been exposed to industrial accident and occupational disease, working in surroundings that imperiled their safety and their health. Correction of these abuses was the purpose of the early labor laws.

In later years, such legislation has been concerned, more largely, with wages and hours, with labor organization and collective bargaining. It has come to be recognized that workers, when acting independently, are at a disadvantage in dealing with their employers. To the worker, the job is vital; to the employer, though labor is needed, the individual laborer is not. Without reserves to support him during prolonged negotiations, the worker must shortly come to terms; the employer can better afford to wait. The worker lacks market information and negotiating skill; the employer possesses both. In such a situation, a fair bargain is not to be obtained. It has thus appeared that workers whose bargaining power is weak must be defended, or that equality of bargaining power must be assured. As a consequence, laws have been enacted to protect unorganized workers against low wages and long hours, to establish the right of workers to organize, and to lay down rules to govern collective bargaining.

Protection for Women and Children

Child labor laws, in the United States, date from a statute adopted in Massachusetts in 1842 establishing a ten-hour day for children under 12 years old employed in factories. From this beginning, the states went on gradually to extend and tighten their regulations, excluding children from certain employments, requiring attendance at school, raising age limits, reducing hour limits, and establishing minimum wages. Today such laws are found in all the states, a typical statute requiring school attendance until 16 and forbidding employment in factories or stores (during school hours or at night) before 16 and in mines before 18. Where employment is permitted, the laws fix maximum hours and half of them provide for a minimum wage. In general, agriculture, domestic service, and street trades are exempt, and provision for enforcement is inadequate. More than 2 million boys and girls of school age were found to be employed in 1952.[20]

This legislation has long been upheld by the courts on the ground that children, being unable to protect themselves, are entitled to protection by the state. But when Congress first attempted to reinforce it by enacting federal laws, its efforts were obstructed by decisions that denied their constitutionality. The first of these laws, adopted in 1916 to prevent the transportation of products of child labor in interstate commerce, was

[20] Report by National Child Labor Committee, *New York Times*, November 27, 1952.

found in 1918 to violate the commerce clause.[21] The second, passed in 1919, imposing a tax upon such products, was held in 1922 to exceed the taxing power.[22] A constitutional amendment was submitted to the states in 1924, giving Congress the power to "limit, regulate, and prohibit the labor of persons under 18 years of age," but vigorous opposition by manufacturing and agricultural interests prevented its ratification. From 1933 to 1935, child labor was prohibited by the codes adopted under the National Industrial Recovery Act, to be discussed in Chapter 13. And since 1938, the employment of children under 16, or under 18 in hazardous occupations, has been forbidden in industries covered by the Fair Labor Standards Act. This law was held to be constitutional in 1941,[23] a quarter of a century after Congress first attempted to bring child labor under federal control.

The first statute to regulate the employment of women, in this country, was enacted by New Hampshire in 1847. Such legislation, too, was gradually extended, beginning with laws establishing maximum hours, going on to forbid the use of women in occupations that would endanger their morals, their safety, or their health, and providing finally for the determination of a minimum wage. Under the earliest minimum wage law, adopted by Massachusetts in 1912, observance of the wages fixed was voluntary. Under the laws that followed, it was made compulsory. By 1950, there were statutes fixing maximum hours for women in 41 states, the District of Columbia, and Puerto Rico, and statutes fixing minimum wages in 26 states, the District of Columbia, Puerto Rico, Alaska, and Hawaii. The constitutionality of the maximum hour laws was upheld by the Supreme Court in 1908;[24] but that of the minimum wage laws was denied in 1923[25] and again in 1936,[26] being finally established when the Court reversed its position in 1937.[27] In 5 states, the minimum wage is fixed by statute; in 21, by an administrative agency. Here, different minima are fixed for different occupations. The laws have their greatest significance in retail distribution and in the service trades.

Protection against Industrial Hazards

The states have long sought to protect men as well as women and children against the risks of industrial accident and occupational disease. Beginning with Massachusetts in 1877, they have enacted laws calling for the installation of safety appliances, the inauguration of safety inspections, and the adoption of other precautions against accidents; laws regulating

[21] *Hammer* v. *Dagenhart*, 247 U.S. 251.

[22] *Bailey* v. *Drexel Furniture Co.*, 259 U.S. 20.

[23] *U.S.* v. *Darby*, 312 U.S. 100.

[24] *Muller* v. *Oregon*, 208 U.S. 412.

[25] *Adkins* v. *Children's Hospital*, 261 U.S. 525.

[26] *Morehead* v. *N.Y. ex rel. Tipaldo*, 298 U.S. 587.

[27] *West Coast Hotel Co.* v. *Parrish*, 300 U.S. 379.

dangerous processes and forbidding the use of harmful materials; and laws requiring certain standards of sanitation, ventilation, and illumination. Such laws now typically provide for the establishment of rules and regulations by an administrative agency and for their enforcement by periodic inspection of industrial facilities. In few states, however, is adequate provision made for the financing of inspection services.

Protection is also afforded by laws prohibiting the employment in certain occupations—such as tunneling under air pressure—of men who lack the strength to do the work; by laws requiring the observance in other occupations—such as truck driving—of periods of rest; and by laws establishing maximum hours in many hazardous industries. An Oregon law limiting hours for men employed in mines and smelters was upheld by the Supreme Court in 1898.[28] But a New York law limiting hours in bakeries was held to be unconstitutional in 1905.[29] The constitutionality of state maximum hour laws was finally established, however, in 1917 when the Court upheld a second law enacted in Oregon applying both to women and to men employed in manufacturing.[30]

Alongside this legislation there has developed a comprehensive program of social insurance, beginning half a century ago with enactment by the states of laws establishing employer's liability and providing for workmen's compensation in the event of industrial accident, and culminating, under the provisions of the Social Security Act of 1935, as amended in 1939, in the creation of systems of unemployment insurance by the states and a system of old age and survivorship insurance by the federal government. These systems are largely financed by taxes imposed on the employer. Insurance against the risks of labor has thus been made a cost to be covered in the price of goods. Analysis of this program would go beyond the scope of the present book. It is sufficient here to note its extent and its significance.

Maximum Hours and Minimum Wages

Maximum hours and minimum wages have been fixed by law, not only to protect women and children, and men employed in hazardous trades, but also to combat depression and to raise the level of wages for workers in general. It was assumed, during the thirties, that a ceiling over hours would increase employment by spreading the work among more employees, and that a floor under wages would contribute further to recovery by enlarging purchasing power. It was this reasoning, however dubious, that was used to justify the maximum hour and minimum wage requirements of the National Industrial Recovery Act (NIRA). In later years, such requirements came to be defended as a means of establishing fair standards of employment, protecting workers who lacked the power to

[28] *Holden* v. *Hardy*, 169 U.S. 366.

[29] *Lochner* v. *New York*, 198 U.S. 45.

[30] *Bunting* v. *Oregon*, 243 U.S. 426.

protect themselves. In this context, however, the limitation of hours took on a different character. Work beyond the hours fixed, instead of being forbidden, in the interest of safety and health, was merely penalized by requiring that time-and-a-half be paid for overtime. Maximum hour requirements thus came to serve as a means of increasing take-home pay.

General wage and hour laws were enacted in many other countries, beginning with New Zealand in 1894 and Australia in 1896, before they were adopted in the United States, and they had been enacted by a few of the states before they were adopted by the federal government. But American experience with such legislation has been derived, in the main, from laws that were passed by Congress during the thirties. Under the Davis-Bacon Act of 1931, contractors on federal construction projects were required to pay their employees the wages prevailing in their respective localities. Under the Walsh-Healey Act of 1935, all employers with government contracts exceeding $10,000 were required to observe prevailing rates. Under the NIRA, from 1933 to 1935, wage and hour provisions were written into the codes that governed private industries. Under the first Guffey Act, in 1935 and 1936, they were maintained for the bituminous coal industry. The Merchant Marine Act of 1936 empowered the Maritime Commission to fix minimum wages for the officers and crews of subsidized ships. And the Sugar Act of 1937 empowered the Secretary of Agriculture to set such minima for workers employed by subsidized producers of sugar beets. A comprehensive law, and a lasting one, was finally obtained when the Fair Labor Standards Act was adopted by Congress in 1938 and was upheld by the Supreme Court, in a unanimous decision, in 1941.[31]

The Fair Labor Standards Act applies to men and women employed in occupations in or affecting interstate commerce, save those specifically exempted, such as administrative and professional personnel, outside salesmen, workers rendering personal services, and those producing or processing agricultural commodities. It covers about half of the labor force. As originally written, the law cut maximum hours from 44 in 1938 to 40 in 1940, and raised minimum wages from 25 cents an hour in 1938 to 40 cents in 1945, providing procedures that enabled particular industries to approach the latter figures with greater rapidity. In 1949, the law was amended, raising the minimum wage to 75 cents. These requirements are administered by the Wage and Hour Division in the Department of Labor. If an employer pays less than the minimum wage or less than time-and-a-half for overtime, the Division will usually collect the difference and turn it over to his employees. But if he does not co-operate, it may sue to recover. And after a second offense, it may ask that he be fined up to $10,000, or imprisoned up to six months, or both.

It is the purpose of wage and hour laws to obtain for the worker better

[31] *U.S.* v. *Darby,* 321 U.S. 100.

terms of employment than he could have demanded, acting alone. To appraise the consequences of these laws, however, would require a lengthier analysis than can be undertaken here. These consequences may be favorable to labor, or unfavorable, or negligible, depending on the characteristics of the limits that are set and of the changing situations to which they are applied. It may be noted, however, that the Fair Labor Standards Act has never been put to a critical test. In a period of growing demand and rising prices, its requirements have not been difficult to meet.

In establishing minimum standards for labor, through laws controlling the employment of women and children, requiring provision for health, safety, and security, and setting moderate limits on hours and wages, government sets a plane for competition, as it does in checking unfair methods of competition, through the work of the Federal Trade Commission. It may curtail the supply of goods and services that would have been produced under substandard conditions of employment. But it leaves wide latitude for the operation of competition as a regulatory force.

Employment Exchanges

One of the media through which workers and jobs are brought together is the private employment agency. Such agencies, in the past, have sometimes engaged in unfair practices. They have misrepresented wages and working conditions to applicants for jobs. They have bribed foremen to discharge workers so that they might collect additional fees from new recruits. When jobs have been scarce, their charges have been extortionate. Employment agencies, like the securities and commodities exchanges, have therefore been subjected to public control. Most states require such agencies to obtain licenses and to post bonds that will assure their responsibility in the event of suits for damages. Many states regulate agency operations, forbidding misrepresentation, requiring full disclosure, and demanding the return of fees where jobs do not materialize and where workers are shortly discharged through no fault of their own. And some states have fixed the fees the agencies may charge. Such a law, enacted in New Jersey, was held to be unconstitutional by the Supreme Court in 1928. But this position was reversed in 1941. The states now have unquestioned power to regulate.[32]

The private agencies have been dwarfed, during the past twenty years, by the development of a comprehensive system of public employment offices. Such offices were first set up by individual states, beginning with Ohio in 1890. A bill designed to increase their number by extending federal aid was vetoed by President Hoover in 1931. But a similar measure, the Wagner-Peyser Act, was signed by President Roosevelt in 1933. This law promoted the creation and expansion of state employment office systems by providing federal grants to cover half of their costs, and set up

[32] *Ribnik* v. *McBride*, 277 U.S. 350 (1928); *Olsen* v. *Nebraska*, 313 U.S. 236 (1941).

the United States Employment Service to co-ordinate their activities. During World War II the offices were taken over by the federal government; but in 1946 they were returned to the states, with their expenses to be borne entirely by the federal treasury. The employment office system serves the interests of both employers and employees. It participates in the payment of unemployment insurance benefits. It provides information concerning labor supplies and employment opportunities. It contributes to proper placement and eases the movement of workers from job to job.

In these activities, as in the regulation of the securities and commodities exchanges, government seeks merely to insure the integrity of markets. It does not fix prices, leaving this to the forces of demand and supply.

Fair Employment Practices

Beginning with New York State in 1945, nine states and several cities have enacted laws forbidding discrimination in employment on the basis of race, creed, color, or national origin. These laws apply to discrimination by employers in hiring, firing, promoting, and determining compensation, by labor unions in admitting members, and by employment agencies in classifying and referring employees. Under such laws, a worker who suffers from discrimination may file a complaint with an administrative agency. An effort will then be made to obtain an adjustment through conciliation. If this fails, the agency is empowered to hold a public hearing and issue an order directing an offender to cease and desist from discriminatory practices. Such orders can be enforced by the courts.

The agencies concerned have proceeded with caution. Few cases have resulted in an order, and fewer have been carried to the courts. Reliance has been placed, in the main, on conciliation and the enlistment of voluntary support. But substantial progress is said to have been made in the enforcement of the laws.[33]

These laws are more social than economic in their significance. But they fall in the same category as others respecting conditions of employment. They affect the plane of competition. But, in the main, they leave the operation of the market undisturbed.

Policy Toward Labor Organization

Government may affect the content of the wage bargain, not by prescribing its terms, but by influencing the relative strength of the bargainers. It may oppose the organization of labor, thereby depressing wages. It may promote organization, thus raising them. Or it may seek to equalize the bargaining power of employers and workers, leaving wages to be determined by a test of skill and strength. But it cannot ignore the problem. A policy toward the organization of labor is not to be escaped.

The history of this policy, in the United States, falls into three periods:

[33] Monroe Berger, "Fair Employment Practices Legislation," *Annals of the American Academy of Political and Social Science*, Vol. 275 (1951), pp. 34–40.

(1) the years before 1932, during which government put its weight on the side of the employer; (2) the years from 1932 to 1947, when it shifted its weight to the side of the worker; and (3) the years since 1947, in which it has appeared to be groping toward a middle ground. An adequate discussion of these developments would require a book in itself. All that can be done here is to indicate the direction of the change.

Until 1842, the courts held the mere existence of a labor organization to constitute an illegal conspiracy. In that year, the Supreme Court of Massachusetts set a new precedent, holding that questions of legality were raised, not by unions as such, but by the character of their activities.[34] Thereafter, the courts sought to distinguish between legal and illegal strikes, according to their purposes, and between lawful and unlawful uses of the boycott and forms of picketing. In general, unions were tolerated. But the law gave no protection to the right of workers to organize. Employers were not required to recognize the unions or to engage in collective bargaining. On the contrary, they were permitted to obstruct unionization and to interfere with union activities. And they did so, by requiring workers, as a condition of employment, to sign "yellow dog" contracts which forbade union membership, by spying on their workers, by discharging union members, and by circulating black lists to prevent them from obtaining other jobs. For many years, moreover, government gave the employers its positive support. Union meetings were forbidden by local authorities and union organizers driven out of town. Company police were clothed with legal authority. Sweeping injunctions were issued by the courts, ostensibly to protect the property of employers, but actually to handicap the workers by jailing their leaders for contempt. Local and state police and federal troops were used in breaking strikes. Though unions were legal, they were kept from growing strong.

This policy was sharply changed, beginning in 1932. In that year, Congress passed the Norris–La Guardia Act, outlawing the "yellow dog" contract and restricting the freedom of federal courts to employ the injunction as a means of preventing the organization of labor or the successful prosecution of a strike. In 1933, in Section 7-A of the National Industrial Recovery Act, Congress explicitly recognized the right of employees "to organize and bargain collectively through representatives of their own choosing" and forbade employers to interfere with this process, or to require that workers join a company union or refrain from joining an independent union in order to get a job. And in 1935, when the NIRA was found to be unconstitutional, Congress passed the Wagner Act, reaffirming the right of organization and collective bargaining, forbidding a number of "unfair labor practices" whereby employers might attempt to interfere, and setting up a National Labor Relations Board with power to issue orders directing employers to cease and desist from such practices.

[34] *Commonwealth* v. *Hunt,* 4 Metcalf 111.

The constitutionality of the new law was upheld.[35] The policy was effective: union membership increased from less than 3 million in 1933 to more than 15 million in 1947.

A third period dates from the passage of the Taft-Hartley Act in 1947. This law, coming after a series of major strikes and succeeding rounds of wage increases, represented a reaction from the prolabor provisions of the Wagner Act. It was highly controversial, being raised as an issue in two national elections. It was long, complicated, clumsy, and in some respects unworkable. But it did give a new direction to public policy. Unlike the Wagner Act, it spoke not only of union rights but also of union responsibilities. And its list of unfair labor practices included both those of employers and those of unions of employees. It sought to protect the union member against the union, the union and the employer against each other, and the public against both. The imperfections of the Act made clear the need for its revision. But its major significance remained: it represented a first step, if a faltering one, toward a position of neutrality.

In dealing with the labor market, government does not attempt to maintain competition as a regulator. In practice, it cannot hope to make the demand side of the market effectively competitive. As an alternative, it has therefore adopted the policy of permitting labor to develop countervailing power. It has weakened the force of employer monopsony, not by breaking it up, but by supporting the growth, on the other side of the market, of labor monopoly.

Settlement of Industrial Disputes

The outcome of disputes between employers and unions may be left to a trial of strength. But such disputes may drag on for weeks and months. And in the meantime, essential services are interrupted, to the detriment of the community as a whole. To prevent this, government is forced to intervene.

The history of such intervention cannot be recited here. A word may be said, however, concerning its major forms. These are conciliation and mediation, investigation and publicity, and arbitration—voluntary and compulsory. Under the first of these, government seeks to bring the disputants together and to assist them in resolving their differences, but does not itself attempt to influence the result. Similarly, when it conducts investigations and publishes reports, government may maintain a scrupulous neutrality. But it may also slant its publications in an effort to enlist support for an outcome it desires. When it acts as an arbitrator, government itself determines the substance of the agreement. But the significance of its action depends upon whether acceptance of its decision is voluntary or compulsory. If it is voluntary, government must seek to arrive at terms that will be mutually acceptable. But if it is compulsory, government may

[35] *NLRB* v. *Jones & Laughlin Steel Corp.*, 301 U.S. 1 (1937).

favor the employer, or the worker, and compel the other one to acquiesce. In the other cases, the outcome depends upon the forces of the market. Here, it rests upon authority.

GOVERNMENT AND GROUP PRESSURES

When government assumes a new function at the behest of a group of producers, it may be questioned whether it is the public interest or only a private interest that is being served. When sellers persuade the state to exclude their rivals from the market, and to grant them monopolistic privileges, the answer is fairly clear. But the question also arises when public assistance is provided to promote the development and maintenance of particular forms of productive activity, and when measures are adopted to protect the seller who is weak against the buyer who is strong.

Fitzpatrick in *St. Louis Post-Dispatch*

NEW NATIONAL ANTHEM

We have seen how public services, loans, and subsidies have been extended to businessmen and farmers, how farmers and workers have been encouraged to organize to attain equality of bargaining power, how unorganized workers have been safeguarded, and how industrial disputes have been brought to settlement. It remains to consider whether government, under political pressure from producer groups, can be relied upon to fulfill such functions with strict impartiality.

The Economics and Politics of Subsidies

Subsidies are neither to be approved nor condemned indiscriminately. Some of them serve the common interest; others do not. A number of questions must be asked in every case: (1) Is the purpose for which the subsidy is paid a worthy one? (2) Granted the worth of the purpose, is the subsidy really needed? (3) Granted the need for the subsidy, is it charged to the consumer or to the taxpayer? (4) However financed, is the subsidy hidden or provided openly? (5) However provided, what are its probable effects?

Worthiness of purpose, of course, is a matter of judgment, and is not to be determined by a scientific rule. It would generally be agreed, however, that many of the purposes for which subsidies have been provided are highly worthy ones—the opening of the West, the circulation of periodicals, the construction of low-rent housing, the insurance of crops, and the support of industries required for national defense. It would be agreed, too, by almost everyone except the mining interests, that no public purpose is served by paying fancy prices for silver dug up in the West to be reburied in the East. But the desirability of many other subsidies is open to debate. Why, for instance, should shipping companies be subsidized?

The case for an American merchant marine rests on two arguments: economic advantage and national security. The economic argument has been pretty well exploded. A big national-flag fleet is not needed to protect shippers against exorbitant freights and discriminatory practices: plentiful world tonnage and active competition will take care of that. Nor is it needed to promote sales abroad or to deliver exported goods: shipping companies are common carriers, not merchandisers; their ships are not to be compared, as they often are, to the delivery wagons of a retail firm. The interest of shippers is in good service and low freights. If these can be provided better under foreign flags, business gains nothing from a forced expansion of American lines. On the contrary, if other nations are denied the opportunity to earn American dollars by selling shipping services, it will be just that much harder for them to buy American goods.[36]

The security argument clearly justifies the payment of subsidies, in peacetime, to maintain facilities for building ships that will be needed in time

[36] Clair Wilcox, "Merchant Marine II: The World View," *Fortune*, December, 1944, p. 168.

of war. But the justification for subsidizing the operation of ships is not so clear. The merchant fleet available for our defense at the outbreak of war will consist of those ships found in or entering our harbors and those of our allies. The enemy fleet will comprise those ships found in or entering enemy ports. And this regardless of the flags they fly. Operation under the American flag would not appear to be required for national security. But in this case as in others, if an effective lobby is maintained on Capitol Hill, a dubious purpose will not prevent a subsidy from being paid.

When we ask whether a subsidy is really needed, the answer turns on economics rather than politics. Here, again, the shipping subsidies may be used to illustrate. American shipyards, it would seem, cannot compete on an equal basis with those of other countries. Ships are usually made to order, in small numbers. Standardization and mass production, in which Americans excel, are rarely feasible. Costs in the United States have been twice as high as those abroad. If the domestic industry is to build for companies engaged in foreign trade, it must be subsidized. The need for an operating subsidy, however, is open to dispute:

> It is part of the folklore of the shipping trade—reiterated with an insistence that evokes some skepticism—that this subsidy is required solely to offset the higher wages paid under the American flag. It is true that American wages have been half again as high as foreign wages in the Atlantic trades. But payrolls are only 10 to 15 percent of operating costs. The difference in wages, therefore, can be no more than 4 or 5 percent of such costs. Moreover, there are some costs where the advantage runs the other way. Fuel oil, for instance, is cheaper here than abroad. Insurance, port expenses, and cargo-handling costs are roughly the same for U. S. and foreign lines. The cards are not all stacked against the operator of American ships. . . .
>
> Costs might be cut and revenues increased in many ways. Before the war, a typical freighter spent two weeks at sea and two in port. It was earning money only half the time. If the average turnaround could be cut in half, income would thus go up by a third. On the usual voyage, moreover, the pay load ran from three-fifths to two-thirds of capacity. If ships could sail full and down, revenues would be between 50 and 55 percent higher. Ship design, port facilities, cargo-handling devices, and the packaging of freight might be improved. There is room for scientific study of operating methods; shipping has been little explored by efficiency experts and management engineers. More thought might also be devoted to merchandising shipping services; foreign traders complain that the American lines make less effort to meet their needs than the British, the Norwegians, and the Dutch.[37]

With better management, the operating subsidy might not be needed. But where political pressure is applied, Congress may not insist upon convincing proof of need. In this case, instead of dropping the subsidy, it amended the law in 1952 to enlarge its scope.

If a subsidy is to be paid, for whatever reason, it is desirable that it be

[37] *Ibid.*, pp. 204–5.

financed, not by the consumer, but by the taxpayer. When subsidies are paid by the consumer in higher prices—as is the case with those provided by the tariff and by the program of agricultural price supports, discussed in Chapter 15—the incidence of the burden is regressive, the higher prices resting lightly on those whose incomes are large and heavily on those whose incomes are small. When subsidies are provided directly by the government, on the other hand, their cost can be distributed among the taxpayers in accordance with their ability to pay.

However it is financed, a subsidy should not be hidden, but provided frankly and openly. Recipients prefer the hidden subsidy. Its existence can be obscured, its cost concealed. Being collected indirectly, it may require no formal justification, no annual round of hearings, reports, debates, and votes. And thus it stands a better chance of a protracted life. By the same token, the public interest demands an open subsidy, one that is plainly labeled and understood, that must be defended and appropriated year by year. Such a subsidy cannot survive in the absence of knowledge and consent. In this respect, the payments to shipping are almost the only ones that cannot be criticized.

Finally, even though subsidies are provided openly, on proof of need, for desirable purposes, they may have unfortunate effects. Since they come, not from the market, but from the public purse, they may divert the attention of managements from the cultivation of customers to the cultivation of Congressmen. Being paid, in general, when losses are incurred and not when profits are shown, they reward incompetence and penalize efficiency. Instead of encouraging the producer to stand on his own feet, they invite him to lean upon the state. Rather than progress, they make for lethargy.

Government as Equalizer, Arbitrator, and Protector

Government has sought to aid producers, in certain cases, by improving the operation and insuring the integrity of the markets where they sell, and by setting up public markets where private markets were inadequate. It has acted, as we have seen, to regulate stockyards, commodities exchanges, and employment agencies, and to establish a system of public employment offices. Here, it has left essential decisions to the market, preserving its own neutrality. But government has also encouraged the organization of sellers into agricultural co-operatives and labor unions, to assure them equality of bargaining power. Where bargaining has been disorderly, and where sellers and buyers have been deadlocked, it has undertaken to settle their disputes. Where sellers have been unable to organize, as is the case with women and children, it has itself prescribed the terms on which their services might be sold. And here, since it influences and makes important decisions, and is subject to political pressures, government may experience difficulty in maintaining a position of impartiality.

Where government has encouraged sellers to organize, it has done so because it had no hope that it could protect them by forcing buyers to compete. So it has acquiesced, instead, in the development of countervailing power, ranging monopoly against monopsony. And where competition, on either side of the market, is not to be attained, there is much to be said for such a policy. But there are also dangers to be recognized.

If the power of buyers and sellers can be equalized, they will be unable to exploit one another, but they may combine to exploit someone else. Co-operative associations may protect the milk producer against the milk distributor, but the two may join hands to make the housewife pay a higher price for milk. The United Mine Workers may protect the miners against the operators, but the two may agree to restrict the supply and raise the price of coal. This is likely to occur, particularly, in periods when inflation makes it easy for the buyer to pass on his higher cost in a higher price. If the consumer is to be protected against this outcome, competition must be maintained or prices regulated in the market where the buyer subsequently sells.

When organization is permitted, there can be no certainty that equality of power—and nothing more—will be attained. In the case of labor, for instance, monopoly may undercompensate or overcompensate for monopsony. Unions may stay weak where employers are strong; grow strong where employers are weak. Though the balance is shifted, imbalance in bargaining may persist. If it is clear, moreover, that workers or employers are to be strengthened by public action, each will attempt to influence the state. And it is scarcely probable that government, under such pressures, will adhere to its purpose of equalizing market powers. More likely, it will shift its weight from one side to the other as the contending forces push and pull. More will be given, first to wages, then to profits, and then to both—and the consumer left to pay the bill. There is no assurance, in this process, that workers or employers will be treated fairly, or that the public interest will be served. There are inequalities of power, not only in markets, but also in politics.

Where government serves as a mediator or is voluntarily accepted as an arbitrator of industrial disputes, it must act impartially, since it lacks the authority to impose its will. But where arbitration is made compulsory, the impartiality of the arbitrator is not to be assumed. If the political power of employers and employees is evenly divided, he can preserve his position by dividing his decisions, throwing half of them to one side and half to the other. But if power is unequal, he is likely to favor the side that controls his appointment, his budget, and his legal authority. Employers and workers will therefore strive to capture the arbitral machinery. And decisions will go to those who win the votes.

So, too, with laws fixing minimum wages, maximum hours, and other conditions of work. In the main, such legislation has been motivated by humanitarian interests and has been confined to the establishment of minimum standards for the protection of women, children, and men who are unorganized. But these laws, too, where used to control the terms of employment in general, can provide a focus for the politics of power.

SUGGESTIONS FOR FURTHER READING

For a general discussion of governmental aids to business, see either Merle Fainsod and Lincoln Gordon, *Government and the American Economy* (New York: W. W. Norton & Co., 1941), chap. iv, or Harold D. Koontz, *Government Control of Business* (Boston: Houghton Mifflin Co., 1941), chap. xxix. An impression of the current scope of such aids may be obtained by glancing through the *United States Government Organization Manual* or the section of the *Congressional Directory* that summarizes the official duties of federal agencies. Various subsidies to business are described in Blair Bolles, *How to Get Rich in Washington* (New York: W. W. Norton and Dell Publishing Co., 1952).

The story of aid to agriculture is told in detail in Murray R. Benedict, *Farm Policies of the United States, 1790–1950* (New York: Twentieth Century Fund, 1953). The various forms of such aid are analyzed in Harold G. Halcrow, *Agricultural Policy of the United States* (New York: Prentice-Hall, Inc., 1953), chaps. xxii–xxvi, and in Rainer Schickele, *Agricultural Policy* (New York: McGraw-Hill Book Co., 1954), chaps. vi–viii and xx–xxiv.

A comprehensive survey of governmental control of working conditions is contained in H. A. Millis and R. E. Montgomery, *Labor's Progress and Some Basic Labor Problems* (New York: McGraw-Hill Book Co., 1938) and in Glenn W. Miller, *American Labor and the Government* (New York: Prentice-Hall, Inc., 1948). Government policy toward the organization of labor is discussed in Sumner Slichter, *The Challenge of Industrial Relations* (Ithaca, N.Y.: Cornell University Press, 1947), in George W. Taylor, *Government Regulation of Industrial Relations* (New York: Prentice-Hall, Inc., 1948), and in Harry A. Millis and Emily C. Brown, *From the Wagner Act to Taft-Hartley* (Chicago: University of Chicago Press, 1950).

The case for a policy of supporting countervailing power as an alternative to competition is presented by J. K. Galbraith in *American Capitalism* (Boston: Houghton Mifflin Co., 1952), particularly chaps. ix–xi. Professor Galbraith's thesis is attacked and defended in the *Quarterly Journal of Economics*, Vol. LXVII (1953), pp. 469–92, and in the *American Economic Review*, Vol. XLIV, No. 2 (May, 1954), pp. 1–34.

Chapter 12 CONSERVING NATURAL RESOURCES

In most of the industries where producers compete in seeking profits their competition may be relied upon to protect the public interest. In the exploitation of natural resources, however, this is not the case. Here, competing producers may cut the trees off hillsides, permitting the rains to wash the topsoil from farm lands, to shoal streams and clog reservoirs, and to flood the cities in the valleys below. They may scramble for petroleum, blowing natural gas into the air, flooding the pools with water, and leaving much of the oil underground. They may draw heavily upon supplies of water for use in agriculture or industry, lowering the water table for a whole community. In cases such as these the general welfare is endangered, and action to conserve resources must be taken by government.

Here, again, the consumer interest and the public interest may diverge. The consumer may acquiesce in wasteful methods of exploitation if they provide him, at the moment, with a large supply at a low price. The public interest takes a longer view. It is concerned not only with the present generation, but with the next and with those to follow. It measures today's convenience against tomorrow's need. If this interest is to be served, pressure from producers and consumers must be offset by pressure from enlightened and unselfish groups. Posterity does not vote; its welfare depends upon the prudence of those who do.

THE NEED FOR CONSERVATION

When the first white men came to this continent, resources were so abundant in relation to needs that no thought had to be given to economy in their use. What man desired was his for the taking, and whatever was taken, there was more to take. And so, for more than two centuries, natural wealth was wasted recklessly. It was converted into private fortunes. It was destroyed for the pleasure of destroying it. In time, as population expanded and as levels of living rose, requirements increased and resources grew scarce. It came to be realized that profligacy was no longer possible. And out of this realization came the popular demand that waste be prevented and natural wealth conserved. The conservation movement had its origin in the abuses of the past.

The Rape of a Continent

Three centuries ago half of the land that now comprises the United States was in timber—unbroken tracts of virgin forest stretching for hundreds of miles, dense stands of white pine to the north, yellow pine to the south, and softwoods in the far west, with giant trees centuries old, measuring from 5 to 10 feet through and towering 200 and even 300 feet into the air. Between the forests lay the grasslands of the Great Plains with deep layers of fertile soil built up over the ages as grasses rotted where they died. Everywhere, save in the deserts, water was plentiful, its surface flow controlled, its underground sources replenished by moisture-holding roots and leaves. The streams ran clear; rivers, lakes, and oceans teemed with fish. Plains and forests abounded with wildlife; great herds of buffalo, elk, and antelope roamed the prairies; countless flocks of wild fowl crossed the skies. Beneath the surface lay rich deposits of minerals: metals readily accessible, coal in quantity, oil and gas held in vast reservoirs waiting only to be tapped.

Upon this natural paradise the white man fell with weapons of destruction, chopping, plowing, and shooting his way from east to west. The forests he regarded as a nuisance, felling giant trees to clear the land for planting, stripping them to get bark for tanning, burning them to get lye for soap. For generations he cut the forests clean, leaving dry slash to burn and scorch the soil, sparing no trees to scatter seeds and start new growth. By 1850 the center of logging had moved from Maine to New York, by 1860 to Pennsylvania, by 1870 to the region of the Great Lakes, by 1900 to the pineries of the South, by 1930 to the Pacific Coast. What axe and fire did to the forests, the plow, cattle, and sheep did to the hillsides and the plains. Plowing and overgrazing destroyed the grasses, removing the soil's protective cover, exposing it to wind and water, and leaving it to blow and wash away. The rain, instead of renewing stores of water underground, increasingly ran off the surface. Rivers were yellowed with silt, poisoned with industrial wastes, turned into open sewers. Fish were destroyed by pollution of the inland streams, by overfishing of the lakes and seas. The giant sturgeon of the Chesapeake Bay were slaughtered for their roe, their bodies thrown to rot along the shore. The numbers of birds and animals were reduced by the destruction of their natural habitat—the cutting of forests, the plowing of grasslands, and the drainage of swamps. Wildlife was eliminated, too, by trap and gun, to provide food and clothing, to protect crops and livestock, and merely for the pleasure of the sport. The egret was killed for its plumes, thousands of buffalo for their tongues, and elk to get two teeth to dangle from a chain. Methods of mining were equally destructive: the more accessible deposits were taken, the richer veins exploited, the poorer ones allowed to go to waste; gas was blown away and oil left underground.

Our resources, as a consequence, have been depleted. Nine tenths of our virgin timber has been cut. Great stands have been turned into inferior second growth, or into worthless brush, unsightly stumps, and bare rock. Nearly a third of our topsoil has washed or blown away. Erosion is said to have destroyed or seriously impoverished some 280 million acres of crop and range land, an area equal to that of six midwestern states.[1] The water table has been lowered; in the arid West and the industrial East, particularly, populations have approached the limits of supply. Pollution, moreover, has made it necessary to draw water from great distances and to spend millions in purifying it for use. Important fisheries have been exhausted; catches have declined; species once plentiful have all but disappeared. Many forms of wildlife have been extinguished, among them the passenger pigeon, the great auk, the heath hen, and the Labrador duck; others would be extinct if not protected by the law. Minerals, too, have been moving toward exhaustion at a rapidly quickening pace. For most of them consumption in the United States since World War I has been greater than that in all the world in all the years before. From 1900 to 1950 the annual use of all materials increased five times, the use of crude oil thirty times. In that half century more copper, lead, and zinc was taken than was left in known reserves. Once self-sufficient in the basic metals, we must now import to satisfy our needs. The cream has been skimmed from our resources; the day when they could be taken for granted has long been past.

The Conservation Movement

The demand for conservation of natural resources came first from geographers and foresters, from nature lovers and sportsmen, and from citizens aroused by evidence of wanton waste. It concerned itself, primarily, with preservation of the forests and with protection of wildlife and fisheries. The first measure adopted by Congress in this field, in 1871, created a Commissioner of Fish and Fisheries. The second, in 1872, established the Yellowstone National Park, to provide "for the preservation, from injury or spoliation, of all timber, mineral deposits, natural curiosities or wonders within said park, and their retention in their natural condition" to serve "as a public park or pleasuring ground for the benefit and enjoyment of the people." This was followed, in 1888, by a law facilitating the irrigation of arid lands; in 1890, by one creating Yosemite National Park; and in 1891, by one that authorized the President to issue proclamations withdrawing public lands from entry, to be held as forest reserves. Such withdrawals were subsequently made by Harrison, Cleveland, and

[1] This estimate has frequently been cited by the Soil Conservation Service of the U.S. Department of Agriculture.

McKinley; a forestry bureau was set up in the Department of Agriculture in 1897, and Gifford Pinchot was appointed as its chief in 1898.

It was through the crusading zeal of Pinchot, in the administration of Theodore Roosevelt, that conservation was made a national issue. "The forest and water problems," said Roosevelt in his first message to Congress, "are perhaps the most vital internal questions of the United States." A number of important measures followed. More national parks were created. The forest reserves were greatly enlarged. In 1902 Congress provided for the construction of irrigation projects by the federal government; in 1903, for the creation of national wildlife refuges; in 1905, for the establishment of the Forest Service; in 1906, for the protection of Alaskan fisheries. In 1907 the movement was given further impetus by the report of the Inland Waterways Commission, showing the relation between forests, water supply, and stream flow; in 1908, by a conference of governors at the White House, by the establishment of a National Conservation Commission, and by the endorsement of conservation measures in the platforms of both major parties.

Carried forward under Taft and Wilson, the movement received a setback when public attention was diverted by World War I, and when Albert B. Fall, Secretary of the Interior in the Harding administration, was convicted of accepting bribes to turn the navy's oil reserves at Elk Hills, California and Teapot Dome, Wyoming over to private companies. Interest was again aroused, however, during the thirties, when drought and wind filled the air with clouds of dust, and when the "Okies," driven from the Dust Bowl of the Great Plains, set forth upon the trek to California described by John Steinbeck in *The Grapes of Wrath*. Now a second crusader appeared, under a second Roosevelt, this time preaching the gospel of conservation of the soil. Through speeches, magazine articles, and motion pictures like *The Plow That Broke the Plains* and *The River*, Hugh H. Bennett took his message to the people. Through the Soil Conservation Service of the Department of Agriculture, established under his leadership, he left his mark upon the land. The New Deal will be remembered, too, for the Taylor Grazing Act—marking the first attempt to prevent overgrazing on the public range—for extension of the system of national parks and monuments, for the work of the young men enrolled, during the Great Depression, in the Civilian Conservation Corps, for reforestation, and for the inauguration of great projects—beginning with the TVA—for reclamation, rehabilitation, and flood control. The presidents to go down in history as the great conservationists will be the two Roosevelts.

The public interest in conservation again lagged during and after World War II. There were still a score and more of national organizations representing the interests of their members in the parks and forests, in wildlife, birds, and fisheries, and in other forms of natural wealth. Significant reports were issued by the President's Water Policy Resources Commission in 1950 and by the President's Materials Policy Commission in 1952. But the people were apathetic. The war had made heavy inroads on their natural resources, but they still enjoyed prosperity. Materials might be exhausted, but they were confident that science would produce synthetic substitutes. Public regulation came to be viewed with suspicion. A drive to sabotage the Taylor Grazing Act succeeded. A protracted struggle between state and federal governments for the control of offshore oil did not appear to raise a ripple of concern. The fight for conservation had not been finally won. In the words of Luther H. Gulick:[2]

> . . . we still have the appalling and needless waste of land erosion with every heavy rain; we still have streams of wealth and future sustenance running away to the ocean in muddied yellow and red; we still have tens of millions of acres of destructive, ignorant, and selfish farming; whole mountainsides of poor and destructive forest management; and millions of acres of idle and deteriorating land. This is to many the saddest area of American failure, not primarily because it curtails our wealth in future years, but because it lays bare a poverty and selfishness of spirit, an aesthetic degradation, a lack of modesty before nature, an evasion of responsibility to future generations.

Future Requirements and Resources

The United States will be confronted, in the years that lie ahead, with the problem of maintaining a growing population, at a rising level of living, on a base of limited resources. By 1975 the country's population will approach or pass 200 million. Its gross national product, increasing at the rate of 3 per cent per year, should then be double that of 1950. To support production at this rate its annual consumption of materials must rise by more than half. It may need less than 20 per cent more timber and 40 per cent more food and fibers. But its requirement for minerals will rise by 90 per cent, for water to be used in industry by 170 per cent, and for electricity by 260 per cent. And both materials and power must come from resources that have finite limits, some of them largely exhausted, others approaching exhaustion at a rapid rate.[3]

Natural resources may be divided, according to the nature of the problems presented by increasing requirements, into three major groups: (1) those that are inexhaustible, such as solar energy and water power, (2) those that are exhaustible but replaceable, such as forests, grasslands, wildlife (if not exterminated) and the fertility of the soil, and (3) those that are exhaustible and irreplaceable, such as minerals (including metals and fuels) and the soil itself. The minerals may be further divided into (*a*) those that are relatively plentiful in the United States, such as coal,

[2] Luther H. Gulick, *American Forest Policy* (New York: Duell, Sloan & Pearce, 1951), p. 38.

[3] See President's Materials Policy Commission, *Resources for Freedom* (Washington: Government Printing Office, 1952), Vol. I.

and (*b*) those that are relatively scarce, such as oil and gas. With respect to the first group of resources no need for conservation will arise. With respect to the second, the need is for avoidance of waste in exploitation and attention to renewal of supply. It is principally in the third category, and particularly in its second subdivision, that there is danger of serious shortages.

But sober judgment, even here, supports no prophecy of doom. If materials grow scarce they may be imported—at least in peacetime—from abroad. With intensified effort and with new techniques of exploration, further deposits may be disclosed at home. With improved methods of recovery, more may be obtained from known reserves. Deposits of lower grade may be exploited, synthetic substitutes developed, and more plentiful materials employed in place of scarcer ones. By reclaiming scrap the same materials may be used again and again. Supplies may be stretched, moreover, through greater economy in use. The problem to be faced in the future will not be that of unsatisfied wants but that of rising costs. This problem should be soluble, though difficult. But for its solution continued attention to conservation will be required.

The Meaning of Conservation

Conservation has two different meanings. According to the first, it is enforced nonuse, requiring the present generation to abstain from exploiting natural resources so that they may be preserved for exploitation by other generations later on. According to the second, it is avoidance of waste. But waste also has two meanings. The one is expressed in physical terms: in this sense, waste occurs whenever resources are lost that might have been recovered by the most efficient methods available, even though their value may fail to cover the necessary cost. The second meaning is economic: here, waste is said to occur when resources are lost whose value would have covered the cost of saving them.

Conservation, conceived of as nonuse or as avoidance of physical waste, may be appropriate in certain cases: the preservation of the redwoods, of wilderness areas, of wildlife, of natural curiosities and national monuments, and of resources required, at any cost, for national defense. But it is not appropriate for forests, soils, and waters, or for minerals, in general, as was shown by the President's Materials Policy Commission in its report in 1952:

> Most thoughtful persons agree that conservation is a good idea, but there are wide differences as to how best—and how much—to protect the future claimants against the nation's treasure of resources. . . . One popular fallacy is to regard our resource base as a fixed inventory which, when used up, will leave society with no means of survival. A related fallacy is that physical waste equals economic waste: the feeling that it is wasteful to use materials in ways that make them disappear. This attitude can lead to devoting a dollar's worth of work to "saving" a few cents worth of waste paper and old string.

These fallacies together lead to a hairshirt concept of conservation which makes it synonymous with hoarding. A sound concept of conservation, in the view of this Commission, is one which equates it with efficient management—efficient use of resources and of manpower and materials: a positive concept compatible with growth and high consumption in place of abstinence and retrenchment. . . .

Conservation is something very different from simply leaving oil in the ground or trees in the forests on the theory that by sacrificing lower value uses today we will leave something for the higher value uses of tomorrow when supplies will be scarcer. Using resources today is an essential part of making our economy grow; materials which become embodied in today's capital goods, for example, are put to work and help make tomorrow's production higher. Hoarding resources in the expectation of more important uses later involves a sacrifice that may never be recouped; technological changes and new resource discoveries may alter a situation completely. It may not be wise to refrain from using zinc today if our grandchildren will not know what to do with it tomorrow. But following a course of conservation which, as here suggested, weighs economic factors carefully, is very different from the eat, drink, and be merry philosophy which sees no point in judicious self-restraint and no cause to worry over posterity's welfare.[4]

True conservation, then, may be defined as the management of publicly owned resources and the supervision of privately owned resources in the general interest. In various cases it may involve the preservation of unique resources for continued enjoyment or insurance against emergencies, the development of new resources through drainage, irrigation, and similar activities, the restoration of damaged resources and the prevention of future damage through reforestation, improvements in cultivation, and the like, and the maintenance of renewable resources by making renewal coincident with use. In every case, including that of nonrenewable resources, it requires avoidance of economic waste.

THE PUBLIC DOMAIN

The areas comprising the public domain of the United States were acquired, first, by cession to the federal government of lands extending to the Mississippi claimed by the thirteen original states, and then, in 1802, by purchase of claims to lands beyond the Mississippi from France. They were subsequently extended by the purchase of Florida from Spain in 1819, the occupation of the Northwest Territory in 1846, and the cession of vast southwestern regions by Mexico in 1848, supplemented by purchase from Mexico in 1853. Title to many of these lands was confirmed through conquest and through treaties with the Indian tribes. In this way, a century ago, the federal government came to own 1,442 million acres, or three fourths of the area then within the boundaries of the United States.

[4] *Ibid.*, p. 21.

These holdings were further augmented by the purchase of Alaska, involving another 378 million acres, from Russia in 1867.

Having come into possession of such vast areas, the government was faced with the following problems. Should its lands be held or disposed of? If held, how should they be administered? If disposed of, what should be the terms? Of the 1,442 million acres that once constituted the public domain, 1,030 million acres, or more than half of the nation's continental area, aside from Alaska, have been transferred from federal ownership, while 412 million acres, or a fifth of this area, together with most of the land in Alaska, remain in federal hands. Policy in the disposal and in the reservation of public lands will be discussed in this section. Policy in the administration of such lands will be considered, in connection with the discussion of particular resources, later on.

Disposal of Public Lands

Some sales of public land were made to settlers, for as little as 75 cents an acre, before the federal government was formed. But disposition on a major scale did not occur until the public domain had been established and surveyed, laid out in townships, and divided into sections of 640 acres each. Thereafter, the dominant policy was that of transferring ownership to state governments and to private interests. Large tracts of land were given to the states to encourage education, reclamation, and other public activities, and to railroad companies to promote the nation's economic development. Until 1862, aside from such grants, disposal of public lands was regarded mainly as a source of revenue. Sales were made at first in tracts of a section each, then in half sections, in quarter sections, and finally in eighths. The price stood at $2.00 an acre until 1820 and at $1.25 from 1820 on. Under the Homestead Act of 1862 emphasis shifted from the provision of revenue to the promotion of settlement. In accordance with laws enacted in 1830 and in 1841, squatters had long been granted prior purchase rights. But now, title to a quarter section might be obtained, without payment, by five years occupancy and improvement of the land. The people were thus invited to help themselves, and land was divided among them on the basis of first come, first served.

This policy, already generous, was later made even more so. Under the Timber Culture Act of 1873 an individual was authorized to obtain 160 acres of land by planting trees on 40; under the Timber and Stone Act of 1878, by planting trees on 10. Under the latter law, moreover, he was entitled to purchase a quarter section of valuable timber land on the Pacific Coast for $2.50 per acre. Under the Desert Land Act of 1877 one who promised to irrigate arid land was permitted to buy 640 acres, and later 320 acres, at $1.25 an acre. In 1909 a homesteader was enabled to acquire a half section of such land, and in 1916 a full section, without charge. In 1912, too, the period of occupancy required under the Homestead Act was reduced from five years to three.

The provisions of these laws, though lenient, were frequently ignored. The public domain was not adequately policed. The conditions governing its exploitation were not effectively enforced. Land was occupied without registry. Timber was cut, for decades, over wide areas, by trespassers. Title to tracts many times the size of a quarter section, or a section, was obtained through dummy entries by railroad, lumber, and mining companies. Great stands of timber and rich deposits of minerals were thus turned over to private interests for as little as $1.25 an acre or, under the Homestead Act, for nothing at all.

Reservation and Extension of Public Lands

With the growth of the conservation movement, from the end of the nineteenth century, there came to be increasing support for the view that the public lands remaining, instead of being turned over to homesteaders or left open to unregulated grazing, should be reserved for public uses and administered by agencies of government. Earlier, reservations had been made for occupancy by the Indian tribes and for the establishment of Yellowstone and Yosemite parks. But the policy of reservation really dates from 1891, when Congress authorized the President to issue proclamations reserving forest lands. Under this authority 46 million acres were reserved by Harrison, Cleveland, and McKinley; 148 million by Theodore Roosevelt. Reservations came to be made, too, by Congress itself or by the Executive under enabling acts, for other national parks and monuments, for wildlife refuges, for irrigation projects, and for power sites. And finally, after 1934, more than 142 million acres of range lands were withdrawn from alienation under the Taylor Grazing Act.

Not only has the public domain increasingly been closed to private ownership; its size has been augmented by purchases from private owners and by private gifts, amounting to 50 million acres or more. The homestead laws are still on the books. But, outside Alaska, there is little land now open to entry. And, save for unsuspected mineral wealth, this land is virtually valueless.

The policy of reservation has always met with vigorous local opposition. Ninety-six per cent of the land remaining in the public domain lies within the borders of eleven western states. And here it comprises more than half of the total area. The states concerned complain that federal ownership of their resources deprives them of needed revenues. The government has met this argument, in part, by sharing with the states the monies it collects from licensees who operate on public lands. But the real basis for opposition is a fundamental one. The lumbering, grazing, and mining interests desire to have the public domain offered for sale, or at least turned over to the states, so that they may exploit it with fewer restraints than would be imposed by the federal government.

For this reason, the reservation of public lands is constantly under attack. During the Hoover administration, a commission appointed to study the problem endorsed a proposal that the lands be given to the states. Under Franklin D. Roosevelt, when the Jackson Hole National Monument was set up in Wyoming, incorporating 32,000 acres given by John D. Rockefeller, Jr., Congress voted to rescind the reservation and was prevented from doing so only by a pocket veto. And during the Truman administration, efforts to take away the President's power to withdraw further lands from entry were defeated only when they had aroused the resistance of beneficiaries of reclamation projects, recreational interests, sportsmen, and conservationists. Under Truman and Eisenhower, too, a comparable issue was presented by the dispute between the coastal states and the federal government over the control of offshore oil.

The Submerged Coastal Lands

Along the nation's coasts and stretching out to sea from the low tide mark there lies a strip of land that is under relatively shallow water, known as the continental shelf. In width it averages some thirty miles, varying from narrow ledges to sections in the Gulf of Mexico that reach as far as 250 miles before they drop into the deeps. For three miles out this area has been held by international law to fall within our national boundaries. But until recently it has not mattered whether it belonged to the federal government or to the states. In practice, the states have regulated the taking of clams, oysters, shrimps, crabs, sponges, and other forms of marine life from these waters and the federal government has acquiesced. But no real issue of ownership was raised until the thirties when rich deposits of oil were discovered in the Pacific off the coast of California and in the Gulf of Mexico off the shores of Texas and Louisiana. It was this discovery that gave rise to protracted controversy over title to the tidelands, so called despite the fact that the right of the states to areas between the high and low tide marks had never been a matter of dispute.

The states concerned enacted laws asserting their ownership of offshore oil. By this authority they licensed drilling and collected royalties. Bills claiming federal ownership were introduced in Congress from time to time but failed to pass. Then, in 1945, President Truman issued a proclamation asserting the supremacy of federal rights, and the Attorney General brought suit against the state of California asking for invalidation of its law. In 1946, while this case was pending, Congress passed a quitclaim bill relinquishing the lands in question to the states. The bill was vetoed and the veto was sustained. Then, in 1947, the Supreme Court handed down its decision, denying title to California without giving it clearly to the federal government, but asserting that the latter "has paramount rights in and power over that belt, an incident to which is full dominion over the resources of the soil under that water area. . ."[5] The government then sued the states of Texas and Louisiana and, in 1950, was

[5] *U.S.* v. *California,* 332 U.S. 19, 38–39.

again upheld. But Congress, instead of providing for administration of the offshore lands, proceeded again to give them to the states. In 1952 it passed a second quitclaim bill, characterized by the President as "robbery in broad daylight—and on a colossal scale." Again the bill was vetoed and again the veto stood.

The issue was now carried into the presidential campaign, the Democrats and Governor Stevenson supporting the position of the federal government, the Republicans and General Eisenhower supporting the claims of the states. The Republicans won the election, but Mr. Truman fired a parting shot. Four days before he left office, in January, 1953, he issued an executive order setting aside the submerged coastlands as a naval petroleum reserve. This move proved ineffective. The new Congress, following weeks of hearings and a month of Senate debate, voted to transfer to the coastal states title to those offshore lands that lay within their "historic boundaries." And guarding against the possibility that this might be held unconstitutional, Congress also transferred the right of control over exploitation of the resources within these boundaries. The "historic boundaries" were not defined, their determination being left to future litigation. It was assumed, however, that they lay three leagues (or 10½ miles) from the low water mark in the case of Texas and the west coast of Florida and three miles in the case of other states. Within these borders, the order creating an oil reserve for the navy was revoked. Beyond them, the other Truman order, issued in 1945, was reaffirmed. This order asserted that resources of the sea bed and the subsoil of the Continental Shelf "appertain to the United States" and are subject to its control but carefully refrained from interfering with the freedom of the seas by claiming sovereignty over the waters above. It thus appeared that most of the proven reserves—and perhaps a sixth of the potential reserves—of offshore oil had been given to the coastal states. The new law was signed by President Eisenhower on May 22, 1953.

The issues in this dispute—aside from those of tradition, sentiment, and historic legal rights—were two. First, the coastal states desired to obtain the revenues, running into billions of dollars, that would be paid as royalties on offshore oil. Their opponents offered to give them three eighths of such royalties outright and to use the other five eighths in financing federal grants to the states for education, in which they would also have a share. But the coastal states were not satisfied with three-eighths-plus of the revenue; they wanted it all. The issue, thus, was whether this source of income should be used to benefit the people of all the states or those of a few. The Congress decided, by 56 to 35 votes in the Senate and by 278 to 116 in the House, that it should go, not to all 48 states, but to 3 or 4. Second, the Truman order had sought to conserve the supply of oil, an asset of crucial importance for national defense. It could be argued, of course, that conservation—in the sense of checking economic waste—could be insured as effectively by the coastal states as by the federal government. But it could scarcely be contended that conservation—in the sense of holding present supplies for later use—would be practiced with equal caution by the states. It is only the federal government, bearing responsibility for military security, that could be expected to maintain a petroleum reserve. The states, acting individually, with no such responsibility, would be more likely to succumb to the temptation of immediate royalties. The issue here was that of meeting the needs of national defense. All doubts on this score were resolved by the Congress and the President in favor of the states.

The constitutionality of the new law was challenged by the states of Rhode Island and Alabama, and was upheld by the Supreme Court on March 15, 1954 on the ground that the right to dispose of property belonging to the United States "is vested in Congress without limitation."[6] Both state and federal governments then proceeded to grant leases within their respective domains. But the location of the boundary between them was still in dispute. Was the three-mile or three-league boundary of a state to be measured from the low-water mark existing today or from that existing when it joined the Union? Was it to be measured from the mainland or from outlying islands? Was it to run in a straight line or was it to follow the indentations of the shore? The law did not say. To settle these questions, further litigation or legislation would be required.

FORESTS

The forests of the United States have long been treated as if they were mines to be exhausted rather than lands to be kept producing annual crops. Careless logging has destroyed the smaller trees and left the ground covered with slash and brush, inviting fires that have killed the seed trees and burned the soil itself. Clear cutting, too, has killed the seed trees and the seedlings, and comparatively little replanting has been done. Methods of lumbering have been improved, in recent years, and some of the more flagrant wastes reduced. But disease still destroys a billion cubic feet of wood a year and fire destroys a half a billion more. Half of the timber cut and sawed is wasted in the process: one fourth of the material contained in a tree is left in the woods; another fourth is left at the mill. The annual growth still runs behind the annual cut, being less than half of that needed to satisfy future demands. Forest conservation, therefore, requires increased disease and fire protection, improved techniques and greater care in logging, fuller utilization of the wood that is taken, and replanting at twice the rate that presently obtains.

If timber is to be regarded not as a mineral but as a crop, the forests must be so managed that their yield will be sustained. A tree suitable for pulpwood can be grown in from 15 to 40 years; one suitable for lum-

[6] *Alabama* v. *Texas, Louisiana, Florida, California,* Supreme Court of the United States, October Term 1953, decision dated March 15, 1954.

ber will take from 50 to 80 years. To obtain the greatest possible output, in the long run, those trees—and only those trees—should be taken that are ripe for use. And for every tree that is cut, another should be planted to take its place. If 50 years were the period required for growth, one fiftieth of a stand would be cut and one fiftieth replanted every year. The harvest would thus be reaped, but the forest would remain. This is the meaning of sustained yield management.

The possibilities of conserving the forests depend upon the character of their ownership. There are some 450 million acres of commercial forest land in the United States. Of this, one fourth is publicly owned, one fifth (some 90 million acres) being owned by the federal government. Three fourths is private property. Of this land, 15 per cent is in large tracts held by pulp and lumber companies. The rest is in scattered patches, half of it in wood lots on several million farms. For the public forests, adoption of conservation measures is merely a matter of good management. For private holdings, it may require the imposition of controls. Where holdings are large, controls are clearly feasible. Where holdings are small and scattered, they are difficult to enforce.

Administration of Public Forests

The timber in the national forests is not withheld from use, but is exploited in accordance with the sustained yield principle. Standing timber is sold to private loggers on the basis of competitive bids. Contracts may specify the types and sizes of trees that are to be taken, or government foresters may mark the trees that are to be cut. Contractors are forbidden to injure the remaining trees and are required to dispose of all inflammable slash. Operations are policed by the foresters and observance of regulations is enforced.

Two criticisms are made of federal forest policy. The first has to do with the size of the permitted cut. The government's fifth of the commercial forest land contains two fifths of the standing timber. But it accounts for only one tenth of the annual cut. The private forests are being seriously depleted. But the public forests are not being drawn upon as extensively as sustained yield management should allow. Trees that are overripe are still allowed to stand, impeding the surrounding growth. The difficulty here, in part at least, is that of inaccessibility.

A second issue has arisen, in the Pacific Northwest, in connection with the building of access roads. For many years the government confined itself to selling timber rights, and the major lumber companies built the railroads, and later the dirt roads, over which the logs were hauled. Then the government itself began to build better all-purpose forest roads. As a result, many smaller loggers were enabled to reach the timber and haul it away by truck. The number of bidders increased and prices tended to rise. The larger companies have therefore denounced the construction of public roads as socialistic and demanded that it be stopped. The smaller ones, on the other hand, have demanded that more such roads be built. The question here is not whether or how the trees are to be cut, but at what price and by whom.

State Regulation of Private Forests

The standards of private forestry in the United States, though greatly improved in recent years, still leave much to be desired. When the United States Forest Service examined cutting practices on private lands in 1945, it found less than a tenth of the operations up to good forest standards, only a third fair enough to maintain a reasonable stock of growing timber, and two thirds poor or destructive. On many of the larger properties, owned by pulp and lumber companies, the practices were good. Trained foresters were employed and timber was treated as an annual crop. But on the smaller patches, where most of the trees are found, the practices were generally poor. Timber, when sold, was cut clean and little replanting was done.

Most of the timber states, particularly those in the North and the West, now have well supported forestry departments. All of the states have laws designed to protect their forests against fire and disease. Some of them also seek to regulate private forest practices. In 1951, there were sixteen states with laws promoting improvement in methods of lumbering. In some cases these laws provided for the issuance of rules by state officials. In others, they left establishment of standards to local committees of lumbermen. In most cases the laws were regarded as "educational" in character; penalties for noncompliance, though authorized, were not imposed. In New Hampshire, compliance with public regulations was purchased through a tax device. Instead of paying the property tax on the value of all their timber, owners were given the option of being exempt from taxes on the timber they left standing and paying taxes only on the timber that they cut. The severance tax was fixed at 10 per cent, but owners found to be meeting public standards were taxed at only 7 per cent. In only a few states, notably Oregon and Washington, were mandatory regulations established and enforced. Here, cutting was forbidden below a certain diameter, retention of seed trees was ordered, and replanting was required. The constitutionality of such legislation was upheld by the Supreme Court of the United States, in a case involving the Washington statute, in 1949.[7]

Federal Regulation of Private Forests

The federal government has no authority directly to regulate private forest management. But it has sought indirectly to promote the adoption of conservation practices. It has aided the states in forest research and education, in fire protection and pest control, and in the provision of planting stock. Under the provisions of the Norris-Doxey Act of 1937,

[7] *Dexter* v. *Washington*, 338 U.S. 863.

it has encouraged the improvement of forestry in rural areas, particularly on farm wood lots. Thus, by 1950, it had established 230 co-operative forest management projects in 36 states. Each of these projects, covering 3 to 5 counties, was provided with a resident forester who rendered technical assistance to wood lot owners, advising them on cutting, planting, management, and marketing. Under the provisions of the Sustained Yield Act of 1944, the government has also sought to influence the practices employed on larger private forest lands. This law permits the Forest Service to grant long-term exclusive contracts for cutting trees in public forests to operators who will agree to the establishment, under federal supervision, of sustained yield units that will include adjacent private properties. Such agreements, running from 50 to 100 years, are designed to purchase conformity with conservation practices by giving private operators the assurance of continued timber supplies. This plan, however, has not fulfilled its purpose. Only one agreement (on the Olympic Peninsula in Washington) had been concluded by 1952. The smaller operators have opposed the program on the ground that it will grant the larger ones perpetual monopolies within the public forests. The larger operators, on the other hand, have hesitated to accept extension of federal supervision to the methods used on private lands.

Conservationists have often contended that forest resources are to be conserved only by taking more forest lands into public ownership, and agencies such as the Forest Service and the National Resources Board recommended, during the thirties, that some 200 million acres be added to existing public forest areas. In later years, attention has shifted to means of increasing public control over private cutting practices. Bills introduced in Congress have provided for the establishment of national standards, for federal grants to enable the states to enforce them, and for federal enforcement where the states might fail to act. The report of the President's Materials Policy Commission, in 1952, recommended that, for a period of 5 years, the federal government aid the states in enforcing their own standards, and that if, at the end of this period, state regulation was still inadequate, Congress enact legislation authorizing federal control. Whether state co-operation should thus be coerced, and whether enforcement, on this basis, would be effective, is still a matter of dispute.

SOILS AND WATERS

Conservation of the soil aims to prevent exhaustion of fertility and the loss of the soil itself by controlling methods of grazing and cultivation. Conservation of water seeks to maintain an adequate, pure, and steady supply by retarding the runoff, preventing pollution, and controlling floods. Conservation also enlarges the area available for cultivation by irrigating arid land. Since grazing is largely done on the public domain, it is subject to regulation by the federal government. Cultivation, being done on private lands, is influenced indirectly by the law. Control of water usually involves a drainage basin that extends beyond the boundaries of a single state. State programs to prevent pollution thus require federal support. And large-scale projects designed to hold water in storage, to provide for irrigation, and to prevent floods have been constructed by federal agencies and financed by federal funds.

Administration of Public Grazing Lands

During the nineteenth century, ranchers turned their livestock loose to graze on public lands. They obtained no permits, observed no rules, and paid no fees. Legally they were in trespass, but no attempt was made to keep them off. As the public domain was sold and given to settlers, the better half of the range lands, producing two thirds of the feed, was taken into private ownership. The poorer half, producing a third of the feed, remained in public hands. This half was still grazed, without permission, regulation, or payment. In some cases, ranchers even sought to fence it, holding that years of uncontested trespass conferred proprietary rights. Control of grazing in national forests was finally inaugurated in 1900, control of grazing on the public range in 1934. Ranchers still drive their herds into the forests and onto the range lands for part of every year. But now permits must be obtained, regulations observed, and payments made.

Priority in obtaining permits for grazing in the forests is given to those whose stock has grazed there in the past. But permits are granted as a privilege, not a right. They are limited to ten years, are not transferable, and may be revoked. Holders of permits must obey the regulations of the Forest Service. The length of the grazing season and the numbers of livestock admitted are rigidly controlled. The season is shortened and the numbers curtailed, if need be, to protect the forest floor. A fee is charged per animal unit per month in accordance with a formula based on the prices of cattle and sheep in relation to the prices of other goods. The resulting figure is lower, however, than the charges made for grazing on private lands. And the Forest Service cares for and improves the range.

Under the Taylor Grazing Act of 1934, the remaining public range lands, amounting eventually to 142 million acres, were withheld from alienation, and provision was made for their administration by a Grazing Service in the Department of the Interior. Grazing districts were created and advisory boards of local stockmen established to co-operate in making grazing rules. Permits were granted to cover specified numbers of livestock during certain months of the year. Priority was given to past users, and the permits were confined to those who could feed and water stock in the months when it was off the range. These rights, unlike those granted by the Forest Service, were transferable and could thus be capitalized and sold. The fees charged were nominal: 8 cents per head for cattle and horses, one fifth as much for sheep and goats. The Grazing Service was to undertake reseeding and improvement of the forage on the range.

Under pressure from stockmen, control of grazing has repeatedly been subject to political attack. During the forties Senator McCarran of Nevada launched an investigation of Grazing Service "bureaucracy" that ran for seven years. As a result, the agency's appropriation was cut from more than $1 million in 1945–46 to around $500,000 in 1947–48 and its staff from 250 to 86, leaving but 50 men to supervise 142 million acres of grazing lands. In effect, the senator's campaign repealed the Taylor Grazing Act, delivering the grazing districts into the hands of the local boards of stockmen and leaving the Washington office too weak to exercise control. This served the special interest of the users of the range, but sacrificed the general interest in the conservation of the soil. In 1946 Representative (later Senator) Barrett of Wyoming, inspired by McCarran's example, started a similar investigation of the Forest Service, directed toward transferring control of grazing in the forests to local livestock boards. And again in 1953 and 1954, a bill sponsored by Representative Hope and Senators Thye and Aiken and supported by President Eisenhower would have made forest grazing permits permanent and transferable and permitted their holders to construct improvements, excluding newcomers and establishing private property rights on forest lands. Both efforts failed; a storm of opposition was aroused. The conservationists fought to save the forests, but not to save the soil.[8]

Soil Conservation

On land that is under cultivation, the techniques of conservation include the preservation of fertility through fertilization and crop rotation, and the preservation of the soil itself—against wind erosion by planting trees to serve as windbreaks, and against water erosion by terracing sloping fields, by planting crops on the contour, by planting strips of sod-forming grasses and legumes between intertilled crops, by planting wide grassed runways to retard the runoff, by building check dams and diversion channels, and by rotating crops to leave absorbent organic matter in the soil. Farmers cannot be ordered to adopt these practices, but they may be persuaded to do so by undertaking educational programs and by purchasing co-operation with public funds. And this is what the federal government has done. For many years, it has carried on research and education through the Department of Agriculture, the state experiment stations and agricultural colleges, and the agricultural extension service. During the thirties, it initiated two more programs, the first under the Soil Conservation Act of 1935, the second under the Soil Conservation and Domestic Allotment Act of 1936.

[8] See E. Louise Peffer, *The Closing of the Public Domain* (Stanford, Cal.: Stanford University Press, 1951), chap. xv, and articles by Bernard De Voto in *Harper's Magazine* for January and June, 1947, January and July, 1948, and August, 1954.

The Act of 1935 established the Soil Conservation Service (SCS), and this agency, under H. H. Bennett, embarked upon a program of setting up demonstration projects and providing technical assistance, on a voluntary basis, to combat erosion of the soil. To this end, it sought and obtained the co-operation of the states. Thus, laws were passed by all the states permitting farmers to organize soil conservation districts and administer them as units of local government. At the request of such a district, the technicians of the Soil Conservation Service will make a survey and draw up a work plan for the district and for each of its farms, classifying the land according to its suitability for cultivation and showing the proper use for every field. Working together, a technician and a farmer will determine how to fertilize his soil, how to rotate his crops, where to terrace, where to plant on the contour, where to plant in strips, and where to drain. On the basis of his plan, the farmer will conclude an agreement with the conservation district which then may help him to obtain equipment, fertilizers, planting stock, and seeds. By majority vote, the farmers in a district may establish mandatory land use regulations. Voluntary co-operation, however, is the general rule. By 1951 more than 2,300 districts had been created, including three fourths of the farm land in the country, and 4,800,000 farmers were participating in the program. Under Roosevelt and Truman, the SCS was organized into seven regional offices, each with its staff of soil technicians. Early in the Eisenhower administration, the Secretary of Agriculture, Ezra Taft Benson, proposed to abolish the regional setup, turning the administration of the program over to the states, and leaving its technicians to seek employment with the state agricultural colleges and experiment stations. The proposal proved to be unpopular. The Service was reorganized, but a modified regional structure was retained. The morale of the staff, however, was said to have been seriously impaired.[9]

The Soil Conservation and Domestic Allotment Act of 1936 was employed by the New Deal as a means of maintaining agricultural incomes after the Agricultural Adjustment Act of 1933 was found to be unconstitutional. Under the Act of 1933, "benefits" had been paid to farmers who co-operated in raising prices by curtailing the acreage of certain basic crops. Under the new law, "conservation payments" were made to farmers who co-operated in conserving the soil by restricting their planting of "soil-depleting" crops. Under both laws, the crops in question were the same. The Agricultural Conservation Program was thus set up alongside the Soil Conservation Service, and local committees of farmers were created to participate in its administration. The program was continued by the Agricultural Adjustment Act of 1938. During World War II, foods and fibers grew scarce and emphasis was shifted from curtail-

[9] See H. H. Bennett, "Land in Peril," *The Nation*, May 23, 1953, pp. 436–37, and Bernard De Voto, "Conservation: Down and on the Way Out," *Harper's Magazine*, August, 1954, pp. 66–74.

ment of output to soil-conserving practices. Attention has been directed, however, less toward the prevention of erosion than toward the preservation of fertility. Farmers have been paid for doing things they would have done in any case, i.e., for adopting such profitable practices as liming their fields and planting winter cover crops. The payments, made with the approval of the local committees, have gone to some 3 million farmers at the rate of some $250 million a year. This is five times the size of the $50 million annual appropriation of the SCS.

The two programs overlap. The work of the Soil Conservation Service is intensive, being concerned with long-run conservation plans. The Agricultural Conservation Program is extensive, being concerned with annual practices. The former does more for conservation. The latter costs more money. But, in its local committees, it has powerful political support.

Water Conservation

Water has many uses. Without withdrawal from streams or natural reservoirs, it provides a habitat for fish, places for recreation, channels for navigation, and means for the disposal of human and industrial wastes. Withdrawn, it quenches thirst, promotes sanitation, irrigates crop lands, supports livestock, generates electricity, and contributes heavily to industrial operations, cooling, washing, and grading materials and products, and entering into a growing number of chemical processes. In the West, water is used more largely for irrigation; in the East, for industry.

To be available for withdrawal uses, water must be captured and controlled. Of an average annual precipitation of 30 inches in the United States, however, 21½ inches evaporate, 8½ inches run off, and only one inch of this is intercepted and consumed. In the country as a whole, five sixths of the water used is taken from the surface, one sixth from under ground. The arid West, however, depends more heavily upon the latter source. Here, the shortage of water is acute. Population has outrun supply, and the water table has fallen as competitive pumping has drawn off water more rapidly than it has been replaced. Many of the populous industrial areas of the country, too, are approaching the limits of pure water supplies. Streams are polluted, their flow diminished, water tables lowered, and ground waters ruined (along the coasts) by the incursion of salt from the seas. As a result, water for urban and industrial uses must be drawn from greater distances and freed of impurities at constantly increasing costs.

In this situation, men have sought to add to the supplies of water, attempting to precipitate rainfall by seeding clouds from aeroplanes, and considering the possibility of pumping water from the sea and removing its salt to make it fit for use. The President's Materials Policy Commission suggested, too, in 1952, that it might become necessary to practice greater economy in use, recycling water for repeated uses, rationing users in accordance with a system of priorities, asking industry to adopt techniques that call for smaller quantities, reserving purer water for more important purposes, and leaving contaminated water for employment where purity is not required. The water conservation measures so far adopted by government have been confined, however, to the provision of irrigation works, discussed in Chapter 11, the abatement of stream pollution, the improvement of soil and forest practices on watersheds, and the construction of storage reservoirs.

Relatively little progress has been made in the abatement of pollution. Streams have been filled with sediment, with industrial wastes, and with raw sewage. Less than half of the cities in the East have sewage treatment facilities; those with a third of the urban population have none. Cities treat and use the waters that have been polluted by those that lie along the streams above them, and in turn discharge their sewers into the waters used by those below. Most states have laws designed to check pollution, but few have power to compel the treatment of urban and industrial wastes. States acting alone, moreover, are handicapped by the fact that rivers flow across state lines. Interstate or federal action is required.

Under the Water Pollution Control Act, passed by Congress in 1948, the Public Health Service prepares plans for interstate streams, seeks the enactment of uniform state laws, co-operates with state authorities, works with interstate agencies where they exist, and encourages their formation where they do not. It may declare any pollution of interstate waters that endangers the health of persons in another state to be a public nuisance, and may recommend its control. If pollution continues, it may then take steps that can terminate in a federal suit against an offender if the state concerned gives its consent. The Act also provides for federal loans, up to $250,000 at 2 per cent, to finance a third of the cost of sewage treatment works. But there is no real power of compulsion. And, weak as it is, the law has not been carried out. The Congress has not made adequate provision for its administration; it has never appropriated the funds required for making loans. If pollution is to be prevented, the law must be strengthened and the sums provided for its enforcement increased.

River Valley Development

Not only may water be short in quantity and low in quality; its flow may be irregular, dried river beds alternating with disastrous floods. Floods are not completely to be prevented: rains may fall on frozen or saturated ground and snows may melt more rapidly than they can be absorbed. But damage from floods can be substantially reduced, and this has long been a responsibility of government. To protect the properties on river banks, levees and flood walls have been built and river channels have been deepened and enlarged. These measures, however, are of limited effect. A levee or a flood wall—if it holds—may save a sheltered area. But it will do so by diverting flood waters to unprotected lands across and down the stream. Channel improvement may carry the waters past a city only to spread them on the lands below. If floods are really to be controlled, waters must be held upstream to be released more gradually.

Under natural conditions, this is what occurred. The forest cover delayed the melting of the snow, checked evaporation, cut the velocity of the wind, held the soil in place, and held the water in the soil. The grass cover, too, held soil and water. The runoff was retarded, underground reservoirs were replenished, and floods were checked. With the coming of civilization, these defenses were destroyed. Clear cutting of timber disclosed the forest floor to sun, wind, and rain. Careless logging left skid trails and invited fires. Overgrazing killed the seedlings and packed the earth, destroying its absorptive power. On the grasslands, too, overgrazing and careless cultivation removed the spongelike cover and exposed the soil. The hillsides and the lowlands were eroded, soil washed and blown away. Now the water, instead of sinking into the ground, evaporated and ran off. The water table was lowered; the valleys were inundated with recurring floods. To hold back the floods, it now is necessary to improve the management of forests and soils along the watersheds. Forest conservation and soil conservation are fundamental to any program of water conservation. These are not three separate problems, but three parts of a common one.

Flood waters may also be held in check by building storage dams. But dams, if big enough, will serve more purposes than flood control. Stored water may be used to irrigate dry land. Released when needed, it may keep a river at the depth required for navigation. Captured as it falls, it may generate electric power. By raising and lowering the water in an artificial lake, the larvae of mosquitoes can be killed and public health improved. In and around such lakes, moreover, are opportunities for fish and wildlife and sites for recreational activities. The water thus controlled is needed, too, for drainage and for domestic and industrial use. These purposes may come in conflict; irrigation competes with navigation, production of power with flood control, the damming of rivers with the preservation of fisheries. If such conflicts are to be resolved, priorities must be established, and this can be done only by a common authority. The jurisdiction of such an authority, moreover, must be broad. For, in managing watersheds, controlling water levels, regulating stream flow, and allocating water among competing uses, a drainage basin must be treated as a whole.

A drainage basin normally extends beyond the boundaries of a single state. Disputes over the sharing of water in interstate rivers have therefore been carried for decision to the federal courts. But states have also solved their common problems in other ways. Officials of adjacent states have adopted common policies in the control of small streams. States have enacted identical laws, such as those providing for soil conservation districts. They have passed reciprocal laws: New York, New Jersey, Pennsylvania, and Delaware, for instance, have set up an Interstate Commission on the Delaware River Basin (INCODEL) to plan and recommend co-ordination of the work of state and federal agencies in supplying water, abating pollution, and controlling floods. States have also entered into compacts, approved by Congress under the provisions of the Constitution (Article I, Section 10), to govern the division of waters in interstate rivers and to establish common planning and administrative agencies. On the Rio Grande since 1939, and on the Upper Colorado since 1949, water has been apportioned by an interstate commission with a chairman appointed by the President. On the Ohio since 1940, a commission representing eight states and the federal government has had advisory and administrative powers for the prevention of pollution. Interstate agencies in another field have assumed still heavier responsibilities. Since 1921 the construction and operation of terminal and transportation facilities in the port of New York have been administered by the Port of New York Authority. And since 1949 similar functions in the area of St. Louis, together with the formulation of plans for water supply, sewage disposal, and land use, have been assigned to a bi-state agency. Each of these bodies serves a special purpose; none of them administers a comprehensive program of river valley development. The only body with such jurisdiction is an agency of the federal government: the Tennessee Valley Authority.

In the Columbia and the Missouri river valleys, a number of federal agencies have long been engaged in irrigation, flood control, hydroelectric power, and other water conservation activities. The efforts of these agencies are loosely co-ordinated by voluntary interagency committees. But these bodies are lacking in statutory authority and administrative power. It is generaly recognized that more effective organization is required. But the form of this organization has become a political issue, particularly in the case of the Missouri.

The Missouri Basin comprises a sixth of the land in the United States, including part or all of ten states. Comprehensive plans for its development were prepared by General Lewis A. Pick of the Army's Corps of Engineers and W. Glenn Sloan of the Bureau of Reclamation. These were combined in the Pick-Sloan Plan in 1944, and initiation of the projected public works was authorized by Congress in the Flood Control Act of that year. The plan involves 138 major projects for flood control, irrigation, and hydroelectric power, including 1,500 miles of levees, 5 big dams, and hundreds of smaller ones, together with forest and soil conservation, navigation, recreation, public health, and similar activities. To co-ordinate these activities, bills establishing a Missouri Valley Authority, on the model of the TVA, have frequently been presented to Congress. But these have always been opposed by the governments of the states concerned. The states, in turn, have proposed the creation of a joint commission, under an interstate compact, with ten votes for the states and ten for the federal government. The first solution is open to question, in this case, because extensive works, administered by existing agencies, are already under way; the second because it would give the states co-ordinate powers in supervising federal agencies engaged on federal projects financed by federal funds. The Missouri Basin Survey Commission, in its monumental report on *Missouri: Land and Water*, issued in 1953, recommended the establishment, by the federal government, of an administrative body with power to plan and direct the work of all the governmental agencies engaged in developing the land and water of the valley.

WILDLIFE AND FISHERIES

All of the states have departments or commissions for the conservation of fish and game whose activities are financed in part by the sale of hunting and fishing licenses and in part by grants of funds derived from federal taxes on fishing tackle, guns, and ammunition. Such agencies maintain wildlife refuges and hunting preserves, operate fish hatcheries, and stock the lakes and streams, each spring, with fish. They regulate hunting and fishing by sportsmen and the taking of seafoods such as lobsters, oysters, clams, and shrimp by commercial fishermen. State laws forbid the hunting of certain species (quail, wood duck, canvasback, and redhead) and control the time when others may be taken, the methods that may be used, the sex and size that may be killed or kept, and the quantities that hunters or fishermen may take. Hunting and fishing are permitted at certain seasons but not allowed at others, particularly during breeding times. The caliber and load of guns is regulated; the use of live decoys, bait, ferrets, fires, snares, nets, and dynamite, and the shooting of wildfowl at night are prohibited. Limits are established for the sportsman's kill or catch, both for the day and for the hunting or fishing season as a whole. These regulations are enforced by game wardens and violators may be punished by fine and imprisonment.

The federal government has also contributed to the conservation of wildlife and fisheries. In 1900 Congress made it a federal offense to transport in interstate commerce animals killed in violation of state laws. In 1903 the first national wildlife refuge was established at Pelican Island in Florida. In 1913 the United States concluded a treaty with Canada for the protection of migratory birds. The Fish and Wildlife Service now operates nearly 300 refuges, some of them for big game and smaller animals, most of them providing food and cover for waterfowl and other birds. Fishing in coastal waters is regulated by the states, and here local interests have come into conflict, since state laws differ and fish and fishermen may cross state lines. But the federal government has not intervened. In the extraterritorial waters off the coast of Florida it has controlled the taking of sponges since 1906, regulating the operations of divers, the character of their equipment, and the sizes they may take. In Alaska it has controlled the salmon fisheries since 1924. The government has also entered into treaties controlling fishing in international waters. Since 1911 the seals of the Pribilof Islands have been protected by such a treaty and the size of the herd, once cut from 3 million to 150,000, has been restored. Since 1935 treaties have governed the killing of whales, once pursued and taken, in all sizes at all seasons, by factory ships. Similar agreements have been concluded between the United States and Canada for the conservation of fisheries in the Great Lakes and in the Pacific Northwest. Such measures, though to their ultimate advantage, have usually been adopted in the face of opposition by local fishing interests.

MINERALS

Mineral resources include the metals (iron, the ferrous alloys, copper, lead, zinc, bauxite, and other non-ferrous ores), the mineral fuels (coal, oil, and gas), and many other valuable materials: stone, clay, gypsum, salt, sulfur, graphite, fluorspar, phosphates, potash, and the like. Deposits of these materials are exhaustible and irreplaceable. For some of them (such as iron, nickel, molybdenum, coal, limestone, clay, gypsum, salt, phosphates, and potash) the supply in North America is large enough to satisfy foreseeable demands. In the case of coal, the United States has 40 per cent of the world's known reserves and has mined less than 3 per cent of its supply. But for some minerals (such as manganese, chromite, tungsten, tin, antimony, mica, quartz crystals, and industrial diamonds) deposits are lacking or deficient. For others (iron, copper, lead, zinc, etc.) depletion of domestic supplies has necessitated increasing reliance on imports. And now the United States, though it produces half of the world's output of petroleum, is also importing oil from overseas.

Declining supplies lead to higher prices and these, in turn, make for greater economy in production and in use. Where minerals essential to national defense are not available in ample quantities, however, action by government may be required. Materials may be bought abroad and held in strategic stockpiles. They might well be withheld from less important uses and allocated to more important ones. Recovery from scrap, resort to lower grade deposits, and development of substitutes might be encouraged by paying subsidies. Government might undertake, moreover, to reduce the wastes involved in extraction and processing. So far, however, aside from oil and gas, it has not attempted to influence mineral technology.

There are wastes in mining. Recovery of ore from open pits, as with iron and copper, is virtually complete. Recovery of coal by stripping runs from 75 to 95 per cent. But recovery from underground operations is only partial. Poorer veins are not worked; material is left in walls or pillars or abandoned as the roof caves in. In the case of coal, one half is taken and the other half is lost. But the physical waste is not all economic waste. For most of the material lost would have been recovered if the price were high enough. To improve the extraction of such materials, government has relied upon the forces of the market place.

Aside from safety requirements, the public regulation of methods of mining has been confined, almost exclusively, to oil and gas. Upon these minerals the United States now depends for more than half of its supply of energy, for its lubricants, and for raw materials for its industries. Essential in time of peace, they are vital to the nation's defense in time of war. And it is in the extraction of oil and gas that the most serious wastes of mining have occurred. Government has therefore acted to conserve supplies by regulating methods of mining on private land, where 95 per cent of the oil and gas is produced, and on public land, where five per cent is produced.

Wastes in Mining Oil and Gas

Deposits of crude petroleum are found, at depths varying from a few hundred to several thousand feet, in reservoirs of irregular shape lying between successive folds of rock. In these deposits oil occurs with gas and water, the three being separated in accordance with their specific gravities: the gas above, the water below, and the oil between. When the rock that seals a reservoir is punctured by drilling, the oil is forced to the surface by the pressure of expanding gas. If wells are so placed, in relation to the conformation of the underlying strata, as to make full use of this pressure, a maximum of oil and gas will be recovered at a minimum of cost. But if they are not, the gas may be permitted to escape, its pressure will be wasted, and the oil will have to be brought up, at higher cost, by pumps. A pool of oil, moreover, is a geologic unit. If wells are properly spaced, and rates of flow adjusted, gas pressure can be so distributed as to economize its use. But if wells are close together and operated independently, gas and its pressure may both be thrown away. For economy in exploitation, a pool should be under common management.

Between the boundaries of a pool of oil, created some millions of years ago and lying a mile or more beneath the surface of the earth, and the property lines drawn on the surface sometime within the last century or two, there is no necessary relationship. Under Roman law and under the Napoleonic Code, the title to land pertained only to the surface; subsurface rights were retained by the state. Under English law, however, since the time of Queen Elizabeth I, ownership of the surface has been held to carry with it ownership of everything that lies beneath. And this doctrine was carried over into the law of the American colonies and the United States. When metals or coal were found beneath a man's land, therefore, it was clear that they belonged to him. But oil and gas do not stay put; they move from place to place. And so, when they were found, it was necessary for the courts to decide whether they belonged to the man who owned the land around a well or to his neighbors. Conflicting precedents were available. One was the doctrine of riparian right which gave those owning lands that touched on running streams an equal interest in the preservation of their flow. A second was an English rule, dating from 1843, giving the owner of a water well the right to withdraw percolating waters from beneath the ground. A third was the law of capture, giving ownership of wildlife to those who should reduce it to possession. Of these, the courts rejected the first and chose the other two. Fugacious minerals, they reasoned, are similar to percolating waters, to prowling beasts and migratory birds. Let a man seize them as they cross his land and they belong to him.

It followed from this rule that a landowner could drill for oil wherever he pleased, as often as he pleased, and as speedily and as carelessly as he pleased, without regard to the geology of the underlying reservoir, in order to take its wealth before it could be taken by the owners of adjacent lands. Or, in leasing rights to another, he could provide for termination of the lease if the latter failed to drill and operate his wells in such a manner as to withdraw the greatest possible amount of oil. The consequences of the law of capture may be illustrated by the sketch below. If the section of a pool shown here were to be exploited as a unit, with a view to assuring maximum recovery at minimum cost, drilling would proceed slowly, wells being placed in accordance with the conformation of the reservoir, spaced to take full advantage of gas pressure, and carefully cased to prevent water from flooding the pool. There would be no well on the land of C. The gas trapped at this point would be used to drive the oil up

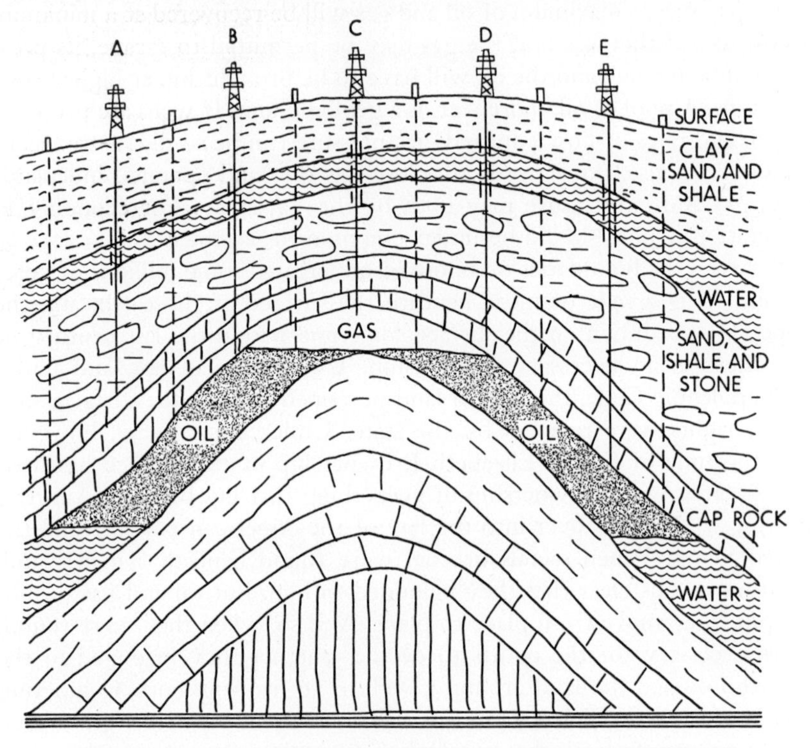

CROSS-SECTION SKETCH SHOWING THE OCCURRENCE AND MINING OF OIL AND GAS

through the wells of B and D. Assume, however, that property lines are drawn as indicated by the markers on the surface and the dotted lines below. Now C, sinking a well, strikes gas. He finds no market for it in his vicinity. He cannot store it. And if he leaves it underground, it will go to work producing oil, not for him, but for B and D. So he blows it off, in order to reach the oil. All of the owners move so swiftly that they cannot drill with care. Most of them case their wells effectively to seal off water. But D, as shown by the broken lines, does not. So water from above now floods the pool. Water also advances from below. It could be held back, and more oil pumped out, if A and E would pump in air. But they have no incentive to do so, since the costs would be charged to them and the profits collected by B, C, and D. So gas is thrown away, oil mixed with water and left underground. The situation has been even worse than that depicted here. For wells have been drilled, not at the center of each man's property, but to offset one another at its outer limits, the feet of derricks all but touching along the boundaries.

The wastes resulting from competitive exploitation are numerous. First, there are those involving an actual loss of gas and oil: the venting and flaring of gas that could have been captured and used as a fuel, the waste of natural gasoline mixed with the gas, the destruction of oil through carelessness by flooding and by fire, the abandonment of recoverable oil, and the loss through runoff, seepage, and evaporation of oil stored above ground. Second, there are wastes in costs that are higher than they need to be; such costs are involved in the use of capital and labor to construct offsetting wells, to make and install pumps to do the work that could have been done by gas, and to build tanks for storing oil that could have been left in storage underground. And third, there are the wastes involved when scarce, exhaustible materials are produced in such quantities that they are put to inferior uses instead of being held for more important ones: when oil, for instance, replaces coal in heating buildings and driving locomotives instead of being held as a fuel for motor vehicles and aeroplanes, and when gas is used in making carbon black. Great progress has been made, in recent years, in reducing many of these wastes. Less gas is blown off, more oil recovered. And natural gas (two thirds of it from gas wells, a third from oil wells) is now being piped from the Southwest to northern and eastern markets in quantities approaching those consumed at home. But wastes persist, and steps directed toward prevention have been taken by the oil-producing states.

Conservation of Oil and Gas

Laws were enacted at an early date to prevent some of the more obvious forms of waste. Pennsylvania, in 1878, required that wells be plugged upon abandonment, and Indiana, in 1891, prohibited the flaring of natural gas. Similar laws were passed, during the nineties, by other states, but none was vigorously enforced. Real regulation dates from the enactment of a statute by Texas in 1919, giving the Railroad Commission of that state authority to issue orders preventing physical waste. By 1940, conservation laws had been passed by all of the major oil-producing states. Under these laws, typically, waste is condemned and regulatory powers conferred upon administrative agencies. Of these, the most important (in the order of the volume of output within their jurisdiction) are the Texas Railroad Commission, the California Division of Oil and Gas, the Louisiana Commissioner of Conservation, and the Corporation Commissions of Oklahoma and Kansas.

The rules issued by these bodies cover such matters as the spacing of wells, the methods of drilling, casing, shooting, and plugging wells, the flaring of gas at the wellhead, the open storage of oil, and the establishment of oil-gas and oil-water ratios. They may also require repressuring of pools with air, gas, or water to achieve secondary recovery. The rules governing spacing may establish, as drilling units, areas that can be drained most economically by single wells, may permit a well to be drilled in the center of such a unit and forbid drilling along its boundaries, and, where different owners hold title to land within a drilling unit, may require them to pool their interests in a single well. Such regulations are policed by the requirement of permits for drilling, by supervision of drilling operations, by field inspections, and by gas-oil ratio and pressure tests. There is no question that these measures have produced results. The grossest wastes have been stopped; the flaring of gas has been sharply reduced and the recovery of oil substantially increased. But it cannot be said that waste has been ended and the final goal of conservation reached.

Conservation requires unitization: the careful determination of the boundaries of a reservoir, the location of wells in accordance with its geological peculiarities, and regulation of the flow from each well to maintain pressure throughout the field. To this end, the law of capture must be abandoned, a pool placed under common management, and property owners assigned proportionate shares in total royalties. But unitization, in general, is not compulsory. In some states, as has been noted, pooling of interests in a drilling unit may be required. But this principle is not usually extended to an entire field. In some states, too, voluntary unitization agreements have been exempted from the antitrust laws. But agreement here must be unanimous: if one landowner holds out, the project fails. In Oklahoma, a unitization order can be issued if owners of land covering more than half of a pool request it, and will become effective unless owners of more than 15 per cent of the land object. In Louisiana, the Conservation Commissioner may require unitary operation in any field where independent operations would lead to waste. But in Texas and California, where production is greatest, no such authority exists.[10]

[10] See Blakeley M. Murphy, ed., *Conservation of Oil and Gas* (Chicago: American Bar Assn., 1949).

Control of Mining on Public Lands

For purposes of control, minerals found on public lands fall into three groups. Uranium, under the Atomic Energy Act of 1946, is reserved to the federal government. Oil, gas, coal, phosphates, sodium, potassium, and sulfur may be exploited by private operators in accordance with the terms of leases granted under the Mineral Leasing Acts, the first of which was passed in 1920. Access to other minerals found on the public domain is still governed by the Mining Law of 1872. Under this law, one who locates such minerals can claim possession of a tract of twenty acres by setting up markers on its boundaries, and may obtain a patent recording his title by paying $5 an acre and spending $500 on development. This procedure, once intended to afford a stimulus to exploration, no longer bears a significant relationship to the production of minerals. Most claims are unpatented, and here no more than 2 per cent of the properties are being mined. Even where claims are patented, there are mines on only 15 per cent. The law is being used, in fact, to obtain possession of lands for lumbering, grazing, and recreational purposes. The location procedure is obsolete, is subject to serious abuse, and should be dropped. Subsurface rights should be governed by leasing. Discovery of minerals should not give title to the surface. Those who have used alleged discoveries as a pretext for appropriating surface values should be dispossessed.

Under the Mineral Leasing Act, as it now stands, the Secretary of the Interior is empowered to grant leases for the exploitation of oil and gas and certain other minerals on public lands. Where there is no known geologic structure containing such minerals, he may grant exclusive rights to conduct explorations in designated regions for limited periods at a moderate charge. Where oil and gas are known to exist, however, leases are granted on the basis of competitive bids. Such leases give access to land only insofar as it is needed for mineral operations; they require lessees to avoid damage to timber and interference with forage and to prevent soil erosion and water pollution. They also provide for regulation of the spacing and drilling of wells. Where a pool lies under private as well as public lands, the Secretary may enter into voluntary unitization agreements with private owners. Where a pool lies entirely within the public domain, or where a prospective lessee of public land holds title to adjacent private land, he may require unitization as a condition of granting a lease. Drilling operations are inspected and the provisions of leases enforced by the Geological Survey.

NATIONAL CONSERVATION POLICY

In the field of conservation, as elsewhere, the nation lacks a comprehensive definition of policy. Different measures, adopted by different legislative bodies at different times, do point toward a common goal: promotion of the general welfare by avoiding economic waste in the exploitation of natural resources, by renewing renewable resources, by restoring damaged resources and preventing further damage, by developing new resources, and by preserving unique resources for further enjoyment and use. But this objective, instead of being articulated, must be inferred.

In organization, too, co-ordination is lacking. The Forest Service and two agencies dealing with the soil—the Soil Conservation Service and the Agricultural Conservation Program—are in the Department of Agriculture. But the Bureau of Land Management is in the Department of the Interior, as is the Fish and Wildlife Service, the National Park Service, and the Office of Indian Affairs. Different bureaus in different departments, operating under different statutes, are applying different policies in managing adjacent lands. Two agencies are engaged in river valley development: the Bureau of Reclamation and the Army's Corps of Engineers, one in Interior and the other in the Department of Defense. In this situation, there is danger both of duplicated effort and of failure to develop resources for multiple use. To improve administration, a minority of the Hoover Commission for governmental reorganization proposed, in 1949, that all conservation activities be brought together in a Department of Natural Resources. The majority, however, recommended only that all land activities, including those of the Bureau of Land Management, be assigned to Agriculture, and all water activities, including those of the Army Engineers, to Interior. Extractive industries, in general, have opposed the concentration of authority, fearing that stricter standards of conservation would prevail.

Clear definition was also wanting in the national security aspects of conservation policy until the President's Materials Policy Commission submitted its report in 1952. The Commission recommended, in the event of war, that demand for strategic materials be curbed by eliminating nonessential uses, economizing in military use, and promoting the development of substitutes, and that dependable supply be increased by encouraging exploration both at home and abroad, by setting up pilot plants for the advancement of processing techniques and stand-by facilities for emergency use in working lower-grade materials, by importing and stockpiling foreign materials, and by maintaining in-the-ground reserves of scarce domestic materials through measures designed to curb their extraction, i.e., through conservation by nonuse.[11]

It is clear that political pressure from organized producers will militate against these policies. There will be pressure to subsidize high-cost domestic sources of supply in peacetime by buying at home for stockpiles instead of buying abroad at lower costs. Such high-cost sources, in the

[11] PMPC, *op. cit.*, Vol. I, chap. xxvii–xxx.

Commission's judgment, had better be held in reserve for use in an emergency and stockpile dollars spent where they will buy the most. There will be pressure, too, to encourage domestic exploration and development (and to maintain domestic prices and profits) by excluding foreign materials through high tariffs and restrictive quotas on imports. There are already duties, ranging from 2 per cent to 68 per cent of value, on such strategic materials as copper, lead, zinc, tungsten, fluorspar, manganese, and aluminum. And there are recurrent demands for quotas on imports of petroleum. But barriers to imports, instead of adding to supplies, serve only to speed exhaustion of irreplaceable resources that might better have been kept in storage underground. They would almost seem to be designed to give assurance, in case of war, that the enemy shall have strategic materials while America shall not. "The overriding national interest," said the Commission, "points clearly to the desirability of eliminating the obsolete tariff barriers to the entry of materials into the United States."[12]

SUGGESTIONS FOR FURTHER READING

A brief survey of America's natural resources is contained in J. F. Dewhurst and Associates, *America's Needs and Resources* (New York: Twentieth Century Fund, 1947), chap. xxiii, a more complete survey in the National Resources Board, *Report, December 1, 1934* (Washington: Government Printing Office, 1935), and a later one in the President's Materials Policy Commission report, *Resources for Freedom* (Washington: Government Printing Office, 1952). The methods of conservation of each of the major types of natural resources are discussed in A. F. Gustafson and Others, *Conservation in the United States* (Ithaca, N.Y.: Cornell University Press, 1939), in Guy-Harold Smith (ed.), *Conservation of Natural Resources* (New York: John Wiley & Sons, 1950), and in a special issue of the *Annals of the American Academy of Political and Social Science* for May, 1952, on "The Future of Our Natural Resources." Students are also referred to *The Conservation Yearbook*, published annually.

On the history and administration of the public domain, the most recent and readable books are Marion Clawson, *Uncle Sam's Acres* (New York: Dodd, Mead & Co., 1951), and E. Louise Peffer, *The Closing of the Public Domain* (Stanford, Cal.: Stanford University Press, 1951). With respect to forests, Robert Marshall, *The People's Forests* (New York: Smith & Haas, 1933), presents a strong plea for conservation, and Luther H. Gulick, *American Forest Policy* (New York: Duell, Sloan & Pearce, 1951), makes the latest and clearest report. A popular presentation of the case for conservation of the soil is Paul B. Sears, *Deserts on the March* (New York: Simon & Schuster, 1937). The standard work in the field is Hugh H. Bennett, *Soil Conservation* (New York: McGraw-Hill Book Co., 1939). Those interested in the grazing problem should consult Marion Clawson, *The Western Range Livestock Industry* (New York: McGraw-Hill Book Co., 1950) and Mont H. Saunderson,

[12] *Ibid.*, p. 79.

Western Stock Ranching (Minneapolis: University of Minnesota Press, 1950). The operation of the soil conservation program is described in W. Robert Parks, *Soil Conservation Districts in Action* (Ames: Iowa State College Press, 1952); the political conflicts involved in the program are discussed in Charles M. Hardin, *The Politics of Agriculture* (Glencoe, Ill.: The Free Press, 1952). On water policy, see the report of the President's Water Resources Policy Commission, *A Water Policy for the American People* (Washington: Government Printing Office, 1950); on irrigation policy, Roy E. Huffman, *Irrigation Development and Public Water Policy* (New York: Ronald Press Co., 1953); and on river valley development, Charles McKinley, *Uncle Sam in the Pacific Northwest* (Berkeley: University of California Press, 1952), and the report of the Missouri Basin Survey Commission, *Missouri: Land and Water* (Washington: Government Printing Office, 1953). The wastes that have occurred in the production of oil are best described in George W. Stocking, *The Oil Industry and the Competitive System* (Boston: Houghton-Mifflin Co., 1924), chaps. vii–x, and in John Ise, *United States Oil Policy* (New Haven: Yale University Press, 1926), chaps. xiv–xvii. The latest and most authoritative description of measures adopted for conservation in this field is Blakeley M. Murphy (ed.), *Conservation of Oil and Gas* (Chicago: American Bar Assn., 1949).

PART IV

Moderating Competition

Chapter 13 DEPARTURES FROM ANTITRUST

Although the maintenance of competition has long been the policy of the United States, expressed in the common law since colonial times and embodied in statutory law for more than half a century, it has not been followed with consistency. There have been other policies, some of them pursued for many years, others adopted during the Great Depression of the thirties, that restrained competition and made for monopoly. There have been periods of national emergency, of depression and war, when the policy of maintaining competition has been abandoned and the antitrust laws temporarily suspended in whole or in part. From time to time, moreover, particular groups have been exempted from the provisions of antitrust. In some cases these groups have been subjected to alternative forms of control. In others, they have been given a virtual license of monopoly. Several of these departures from the policy of preserving competition will be outlined in the present chapter; others will be examined, at greater length, in the chapters which follow.

POLICIES INCONSISTENT WITH ANTITRUST

Policies inconsistent with antitrust have been pursued by federal, state, and local governments. The conflict between the patent system and the antitrust laws was discussed, in some detail, in Chapter 6. The tariff has excluded foreign competitors from American markets for more than a century. Federal policies with respect to taxation, procurement, labor, and agriculture have restrained competition during the past two decades. State corporation laws have facilitated corporate combination. State laws and local ordinances have excluded outsiders from state and local markets and from entry into sheltered trades. In some cases restraint of competition has been an incidental consequence of measures adopted for other purposes. In others, as with the laws restricting access to markets, it has been deliberate.

State Corporation Laws

Until the middle of the last century, most corporations obtained their charters through specific enactments by state legislatures. By 1850, however, many states had adopted general incorporation laws, and by 1875 such laws provided the usual method of incorporation. Until 1889 these laws did not permit one corporation to control another by owning its shares. In that year New Jersey amended its law to authorize such holdings. Other states, competing for the business of selling corporate charters, shortly followed suit. No limits were placed upon the purpose of intercorporate stock ownership or on its scope.

The new laws facilitated corporate combination and concentration of control. To effect a combination it was no longer necessary to persuade the owners of a corporation's assets to vote in favor of their sale. Control could be obtained more simply and more cheaply by acquiring a majority or a working minority of its voting stock. In this way competing companies could be brought under common ownership, they could be linked through common subsidiaries, and a single company could spawn subsidiaries of its own. Holding companies could be pyramided, layer upon layer, with control concentrated at the apex and extended over a widening base. Control could be exercised, moreover, to withhold dividends and reinvest earnings, thus contributing to further growth. All of these developments have made for size and for monopoly. A policy that came to be embodied in state incorporation laws, contemporaneously with the passage of the Sherman Act, has thus run counter to the purposes of antitrust.

Tax Policy

Competition has also been restricted by taxation. In some cases, the effect was intended. This was true, for example, of the federal tax formerly imposed on oleomargarine, of the tax imposed on bituminous coal producers who did not adhere to the minimum prices fixed by the government under laws enacted in 1935 and 1937, and of state taxes on chain stores. In other cases the effect, though inadvertent, has been the same. Consider, for instance, the impact of taxation on the cigarette industry. Here, the larger producers maintain their dominant position by spending large sums on advertising. In computing net income for the purposes of the federal income tax, these expenditures can be deducted as a cost. If they were taxed, they would be less heavy and the competitive opportunities of smaller producers would be improved. Another tax has clearly worked to handicap the smaller firms, but none the less has been retained. The federal excise tax on cigarettes, together with taxes imposed by many states, contributes largely to their final price. This tax is proportionate to quantity rather than to value. It falls as heavily (more heavily, percentagewise) upon the cheaper brands as on the more expensive ones. It thus obscures the difference in their price. If the tax were made proportionate to value, this difference would be increased. The position of the cheaper brands would be improved and the leadership of Camel, Lucky Strike, and Chesterfield would be challenged by strong competitors. Despite this fact, however, the Congress has repeatedly refused to change the basis of the tax. The anticompetitive effect of this tax, therefore, is not an accident.[1]

There are several other ways in which the present structure of federal taxes may operate to discourage the establishment of new firms, to hamper the growth of small firms, and to promote the combination of existing firms. The personal income tax, with its steeply progressive rates, makes it difficult for people in the upper brackets to accumulate the surplus funds required to start new businesses. It discourages investment in the stocks of new, uncertain undertakings, favors investment in bonds and in the shares of old, established firms. It prevents expansion of small concerns through reinvestment of earnings, where they are organized as individual proprietorships or partnerships. The fact that capital gains are taxed at a lower rate than the larger incomes may stimulate investment in enterprises whose future growth appears to be assured. But it may also induce the owner of a family business to have it sold during his lifetime, to a large competitor, who can offer an exchange of shares or ready cash. The tax on corporate income, at a high flat rate, obstructs the growth of smaller firms more seriously than that of larger ones. It permits the diversified company to offset high returns on one product with low returns or losses on another, an alternative that is not open to the single-product firm. It discourages the reinvestment of earnings, the principal means by which the growth of smaller firms can be financed. It does this, first, by reducing the profits to be expected from reinvestment, and second, by reducing the earnings from which such reinvestment can be made. At the same time it prevents the smaller company from financing expansion by selling securities on the market, since it impairs the attractiveness of corporate shares. The tax does permit a corporation to carry the losses of one year forward or backward, for two years, to offset the profits of another. And this reduces the weight with which it falls on risky undertakings. But it affords no aid to new concerns. The corporate income tax thus presents a greater impediment to newer and smaller firms than to older and larger ones. The estate tax, finally, may force the aging owner of a family enterprise to offer it for sale. And, if he does, a large competitor is likely to be the purchaser. None of these effects was intended by the framers of the tax laws. But all of them may discourage competition and promote monopoly.[2]

Procurement Policy

When government is suddenly compelled to embark upon a large new program of expenditure, as is the case, for instance, when it must mobilize for war, it is likely to make its purchases, in disproportionate amounts,

[1] See William H. Nicholls, *Price Policies in the Cigarette Industry* (Nashville: Vanderbilt University Press, 1951), pp. 415–23.

[2] See J. Keith Butters and John V. Lintner, *Effect of Federal Taxes on Growing Enterprises* (Boston: Graduate School of Business Administration, Harvard University, 1945).

from larger firms. During World War II, in the United States, 100 companies obtained 67 per cent of the prime war supply contracts and 10 of them obtained 30 per cent. The top 100 companies had 51 per cent of the new war facilities that were privately financed and 75 per cent of those that were privately operated and publicly financed. Twenty companies received 50 per cent of the government's industrial research contracts, and 10 of them received 37 per cent. An effort was made, through the Smaller War Plants Corporation and similar agencies, to encourage the placement of contracts with smaller firms. But concentration of government business remained the general rule. So, too, with the contracts let by the Atomic Energy Commission, during and since the war. Here, construction and operation of extensive facilities has been confined to an handful of large concerns, and experience in the development of a whole new area of technology has given them a head start over their possible competitors.

All this is understandable. Big companies have established reputations for competence and reliability. They have their representatives in Washington. They keep themselves informed concerning government requirements. They make their offers at the proper time and place and in the proper form. They approach public officials on the basis of personal acquaintanceship. Procurement agencies, by dealing with them, can cover more ground and do it in a shorter time. Small suppliers, by contrast, are numerous, scattered, and unknown. They must be recruited, instructed, and supervised. To put them to work requires a larger organization, consumes more effort, and involves delay. It is not surprising that the market leaders get the lion's share of the business. But this means that they move farther ahead while their smaller rivals lag behind. Procurement policy, directed toward other objectives, thus makes for concentration and monopoly.[3]

Labor Policy

It has been the policy of the United States since 1933 to promote and protect the organization of labor. This policy was first embodied in the National Industrial Recovery Act. It was reaffirmed and elaborated in 1935 in the National Labor Relations Act. Under the terms of this law, employers were required to grant recognition to labor unions and to engage in collective bargaining. The methods by which some employers had attempted, in the past, to prevent the organization of labor were outlawed as "unfair labor practices." No comparable obligations or limitations were placed on unions. The law was amended, however, in 1947, by the Labor Management Relations Act, known as the Taft-Hartley Act, to prohibit unfair practices on the part of unions as well as employers. The new statute became a focus of political controversy. It was long, detailed,

[3] See Corwin D. Edwards, "Antimonopoly Policy during Rearmament," *American Economic Review,* May, 1952, pp. 404–17.

complicated, in part unworkable, and in part said to be unjust. The issues it raised do not concern us here. The law did attempt to approach a balance between the rights and duties of employers and those of employees. And—what is significant for our purposes—it retained the principle of union recognition and collective bargaining.

Is collective bargaining consistent with the policy of maintaining competition? When businessmen combine and agree to control the supply of goods and services in order to raise their prices, their action is condemned as a conspiracy in restraint of trade. When workers combine and agree to control the supply of labor in order to raise their wages, why should the same rule not apply? Freedom to organize is avowedly designed to afford labor equality of bargaining power. But bargaining power for labor means ability to influence wages through control of supply. And there is no way to tell when this power is equal—and no more than equal—to the power of employers to influence wages by controlling demand. Nor is there any reason to suppose that labor will always be content with mere equality. Endorsement of collective bargaining, it must be admitted, departs from the concept of free markets. Instead of creating a situation in which many sellers may deal with many buyers, it accepts monopoly as a counterweight for monopsony.

This policy, however, is inescapable. The market for labor differs from that for manufactured goods and services. In the latter, sellers who compete are unlikely to be weaker than the buyers with whom they deal. In the former, they are almost certain to be so. Industry is not to be so atomized that no employer has an advantage in dealing with his employees. In the market for goods, moreover, sellers who combine are likely to be stronger than buyers. In the market for labor, too, a union that covers a highly competitive industry may have greater strength than many small employers. But unions that face large employers, or associations of employers, are unlikely to have such power. Policy in the market for labor may therefore differ justifiably from that adopted in the market for goods. Labor organization, moreover, serves other than economic ends: it recognizes the dignity of the individual, contributes to health and welfare, preserves and strengthens the institutions of democracy. Requirement of union recognition must be accepted, then, as an established policy. But its influence may sometimes reach from the market for labor to that for goods. And here it may come into conflict with the policy of antitrust.

Unions may raise costs by requiring the employment of unneeded labor and by limiting the amount of work that may be done. They may retard economic progress by preventing the use of new machinery, methods, and materials. They may exclude outsiders from a market by withholding the supply of labor. They may enforce agreements to fix prices, curtail output, and divide markets by applying the sanction of the strike. If they act solely in their own interest, without agreement with employers, such measures are not held to violate the Sherman Act.[4] But if they conspire with employers to impose such restraints, the law is held to apply.

There is another way, however, in which combination in the sale of labor may affect competition in the sale of goods. Where different unions deal with the employers in an industry, and where a single union makes different contracts with each of them, such competition may be unimpaired. But where a union bargains with all of the firms in an industry, and where all of its contracts are made in identical terms, the labor element in costs becomes uniform and rigid, and competition based on differences in wages disappears. When employers agree on common wages, they are also likely to agree on prices whereby the wages can be paid. Wage rates, moreover, may be established at levels that some concerns cannot afford. These producers will go out of business, and production will be concentrated in the hands of those that may remain. Wage levels, finally, may be set so high as to discourage the entry of new competitors, and exclusive occupancy of a market by the parties to a wage agreement may thus be assured. In these ways, unionization may restrain competition, not only in the market for labor, but also in the market for goods.

Agricultural Policy

American agricultural policy since 1929 has sought to maintain the prices of agricultural products at levels higher than those that would result from the interplay of the forces of demand and supply in free markets. To this end the government has made loans and purchases, taken supplies off the market, diverted them to noncommercial uses, and dumped them abroad, encouraged farmers to restrict the quantities produced and marketed, approved agreements fixing prices and controlling sales, and compelled producers and distributors to adhere to their terms. These are the techniques of monopoly. If adopted by businessmen, they could be prosecuted as restraints of trade. Here, they are approved as methods of approaching "parity." The parity concept, and the methods employed in supporting agricultural prices will be examined in Chapters 15 and 16. At this point, it suffices to point out that the policies now applied to business and to agriculture are not only inconsistent; they are antithetical.

Barriers to International Trade

The United States has imposed duties on imports throughout its history. But its emphasis until the Civil War, was on a tariff for revenue. Thereafter, rates were raised by Republican administrations, reduced by Democratic administrations, and raised again by the Republicans for the purpose of protecting domestic producers against their foreign competi-

[4] *U.S.* v. *Hutcheson,* 312 U.S. 219 (1941).

tors. Duties reached their highest point under the Hawley-Smoot Tariff Act of 1930. They have been steadily reduced under the Reciprocal Trade Agreements Act since 1934. But duties on many products are still prohibitive. There were 500 rates that stood at 50 per cent or more in 1953, those on coal tar dyes running to 300 and 400 per cent and those on certain watch parts to 800 per cent. Nor are duties themselves the only barrier. Imports are obstructed by the methods of customs administration. Tariffs are raised by putting goods in classes that bear higher rates and by overstating the values to which the rates apply. Marks of origin are required to be affixed in ways that add unreasonably to costs. Importers are discouraged by excessive red tape and interminable delays. Sanitary regulations are sometimes used to exclude products that are not so much contaminated as competitive. In some cases, internal taxes and regulations have been so devised as to discriminate against imported goods. Procurement agencies, under rules adopted pursuant to the Buy American Act of 1933, are forbidden to buy abroad unless the domestic price exceeds the foreign price by more than a specified percentage. Rigid quotas are imposed on imports of cane sugar to protect domestic beet growers, and quotas are applied to other agricultural imports, from time to time, to prevent them from undercutting supported prices.

The trade policy of the United States is less restrictive than it was 25 years ago. It is less restrictive than that of most other countries, where quota systems and exchange controls, governing the use of foreign monies, are the general rule. But it is still inconsistent with America's position as the world's greatest creditor, with her interest in retaining export markets, and with her need to build and hold an alliance for the preservation of her national security. And it is inconsistent with the maintenance of competition.

Barriers to imports exclude foreign competitors from the domestic market. They make it easier for domestic producers to obtain and perpetuate monopolies and to enforce restrictive agreements. Where rivalry does arise, they protect high costs at home against the competition of lower costs abroad. They exact from the consumer, in a higher price, a profit for monopoly and a subsidy for inefficiency. They are foreign to basic principles of market freedom and private enterprise.

Barriers to Nonlocal Trade

The federal constitution forbids the imposition of duties on trade between the states. In the case of alcoholic beverages, however, the Twenty-first Amendment (abolishing national prohibition) permits state governments to restrict imports as a means of regulating the liquor business. Many states have used this power not so much to check the consumption of intoxicants as to prevent producers outside their borders from competing with local maltsters, brewers, vintners, distillers, and growers of hops, grapes, and grains. In the case of other goods, as well, though no such exception has been made, legislators have discovered various means of protecting producers located in one state or city from the competition of those located in another.

Many states have protected local dairy interests by forbidding the sale of yellow margarine and by imposing heavy taxes on the production and sale of uncolored margarine. They have protected local nurseries by employing their horticultural laws to curtail the importation of nursery stock. In 1939, the federal government was imposing quarantines against 11 plant diseases and insect pests, the states against 239. Some states, through grading and labeling requirements, have restricted imports of chickens and eggs. Florida has defined "fresh dressed poultry" as poultry slaughtered in Florida; and Florida, Georgia, and Arizona have each defined "fresh eggs" as eggs laid within the state. A number of states maintain rigorous standards in grading fruits and vegetables and exclude those falling in the lower grades. Georgia has empowered its agricultural authorities to embargo out-of-state fruits and vegetables when they believe the domestic supply to be sufficient for the markets of the state. State laws have handicapped out-of-state truckers. Some states have discriminated against trucks that come in loaded, prepared to sell, in favor of those that come in empty, prepared to buy. The Buy American Act has its counterpart in state law. Nearly every state requires that some sort of preference be shown to residents in making public purchases. State agencies and institutions have thus been forced to hire local labor, award contracts to local bidders, and purchase supplies from local firms. City councils have taken similar action. Urban markets for fluid milk have been closed to all producers but those whose dairies have been inspected and approved by local health authorities, a measure that limits competition when applications for inspection are refused. Building ordinances, likewise, though ostensibly designed to eliminate hazards to health and safety, have contained provisions which operate to exclude from local markets materials produced by outsiders and to compel builders to use materials produced by local firms.

These measures have the same defects as do the barriers to international trade. In fact, they may be more harmful, since the area they leave open to freedom of competition is a smaller one. As we move from "Buy American" through "Buy Indianan" and "Buy Middletown" to "Buy Main Street," the consequences differ, not in kind, but in degree.

Barriers to Certain Occupations

Entry into professions affecting public health and safety—medicine, nursing, pharmacy, and the like—has long been regulated by the states. Qualifications have been established, examinations given, and licenses required. Over the years, this form of control has gradually been extended until, today, there are as many as 75 trades where entry is restricted by law. All of the states require licenses of accountants, architects, attorneys, chiropodists, dentists, embalmers, engineers, nurses, optometrists, osteopaths, pharmacists, physicians, teachers, and veterinarians, and most of them license barbers, beauticians, chiropracters, funeral directors, surveyors, and salesmen of insurance and real estate. A number of states also license such tradesmen as plumbers, dry cleaners, horseshoers, tree surgeons, automobile salesmen, and photographers. Altogether, there are more than 1,200 occupational license laws, averaging 25 per state.

Many of these laws have been enacted, not in response to popular demand, but at the behest of organized producer groups. "The shoe fitter's responsibility is the very foundation of a child's health," read an advertisement published in the daily papers of New York in 1953. ". . . the Juvenile Shoe Guild is actively campaigning for state licensing of children's shoe fitters." The boards that administer the laws are usually composed entirely of members of the trades concerned. In some cases, the governor must appoint licensed practitioners; in others, a trade association picks the board. The powers of these bodies differ. Some are advisory: qualifications are established, examinations given, and licenses issued and revoked, in name, at least, by public officials. Others have complete authority. In general, the states exercise little or no control. In only 18 of the 48 states is the licensing function centralized in a supervisory agency.[5]

Some of these laws are doubtless needed to protect public safety, health, and morals. But many of them are obviously designed to limit competition. And all of them can be diverted to this end. The standards established for admission to a trade may be unnecessarily severe. Extensive educational requirements have been set up for barbers and ten years of experience or a college degree asked for plumbers. Licensing may be employed as a means of defining the jurisdiction of competing trades. Some states have refused to license drug stores to freeze ice cream or to serve meals. Others have confined the sale of such products as bicarbonate of soda, witch hazel, iodine, and Epsom salts to licensed pharmacists. In North Carolina, the installation of tile has been limited to licensed tile contractors and other contractors excluded from the field. These statutes, finally, may be used to enforce agreements with respect to price. In Nebraska, under a law enacted in 1937, automobile dealers were licensed, and "willfully or habitually making excessive trade-in allowances" was declared to be a sufficient ground for denying or revoking licenses.

Many of these laws are inconsistent with the policy of maintaining competition. If this policy is to prevail, such laws should be repealed. Where consumers need to be informed concerning the qualifications of tradesmen, the issuance of certificates should usually suffice. Uncertified

[5] "Occupational Licensing Legislation in the States," *State Government*, December, 1952, pp. 275–80.

practitioners should not be excluded from a trade. Where licensing is really needed, the states should assume responsibility for preventing its abuse.

SUSPENSION OF ANTITRUST IN DEPRESSION

Between 1929 and 1932 the national income of the United States fell from $90 billion to $40 billion. The Federal Reserve Board's index of industrial output fell from 110 to 58. By 1933 nearly 15 million workers were unemployed. By March 4, 1933, every bank in the country had been closed. On that day Franklin D. Roosevelt was inaugurated President. The new administration immediately embarked upon an ambitious program designed to effect reform, provide relief, and promote recovery. To the last of these ends, the banks were reopened and bank deposits guaranteed. The dollar was devalued to encourage export trade. Public expenditures were increased: money was distributed to persons on relief and paid out in wages to those employed on public works. Farm incomes were enlarged, by paying subsidies and by curtailing output to raise prices, on the assumption that the prices farmers received had fallen too far in relation to the prices farmers paid. It was in this context that the National Industrial Recovery Act was signed into law on June 16, 1933.

It was the avowed purpose of the new law to stimulate recovery by increasing consumer demand. Demand was to be increased by increasing purchasing power. Purchasing power was to be increased by increasing employment and raising wages. Employment was to be increased by establishing maximum hours. Wages were to be raised by establishing legal minima and by requiring union recognition and collective bargaining. To enable businessmen to pay higher wages to more workers, they were to be protected against "chiselers" (i.e. competitors) who might undercut their prices. And to afford them this protection, the antitrust laws were to be suspended. Codes of "fair competition" were to be drawn up, industry by industry, setting forth the maximum hours and the minimum wages, guarteeing collective bargaining, and establishing the rules whereby the chiselers were to be controlled. But prices were not to be raised. Said Mr. Roosevelt:

> I am fully aware that wage increases will eventually raise costs, but I ask that managements first give consideration to the improvement of operating figures by greatly increased sales to be expected from the rising purchasing power of the public. . . . If we now inflate prices as fast and as far as we increase wages, the whole project will be set at naught. We cannot hope for the full effect of this plan unless, in these first critical months, and even at the expense of full initial profits, we defer price increases as long as possible.[6]

[6] As quoted in L. S. Lyon and Others, *The National Recovery Administration* (Washington: Brookings Institution, 1935), p. 758.

Such was the logic of the law, described by the President as "the most important and far-reaching legislation ever enacted by the American Congress."

The new program was not conceived by the President's academic advisers, the so-called "brain trust." It had its origin in a deal between organized labor and organized business. Labor had long sought maximum hour and minimum wage limits, union recognition, and collective bargaining. Business was seeking the right of "self-government," meaning freedom to make and enforce rules restricting competition, to be obtained by suspending the prohibitions of antitrust. Gerard Swope, President of the General Electric Company, had published a widely discussed plan for a nation-wide "coordination of production and consumption" through legalized co-operation in controlling prices and methods of competition. The United States Chamber of Commerce had issued a report proposing revision of the antitrust laws to permit similar programs of economic planning. According to the Chamber's president, Henry I. Harriman, "The time has come when we should ease up on these laws and, under proper governmental supervision, allow manufacturers and people in trade to agree among themselves on these basic conditions of a fair price for the commodity, a fair wage, and a fair dividend."[7] When it passed the National Industrial Recovery Act, the Congress heeded this advice.

NIRA and NRA

The law specified that all the codes must provide for maximum hours, minimum wages, and collective bargaining. Beyond that, it left initiative in formulating their provisions to trade associations, requiring only that such groups truly represent their trades, do not restrict admission, and do not eliminate or oppress small competitors. When codes were approved by the President, violation of their terms became an unfair method of competition, punishable as a misdemeanor by a fine of $500 for each offense. All practices permitted were exempted from antitrust.

The National Industrial Recovery Act was administered by the National Recovery Administration. At its head, during the first year, was General Hugh S. Johnson, a former cavalry officer. Beneath him were 55 deputy administrators, most of them businessmen, each of them responsible for a different segment of industry. Advising these officials were a research division, a legal division, and three advisory boards, representing the interests of industry, labor, and the consumer. This organization, set up almost over night, proceeded at high speed to codify labor standards and trade practices throughout American industry.

The program was launched with a great fanfare. Pending the completion of the codes, a President's Re-employment Agreement, containing minimum labor standards, was signed by more than two million employ-

[7] 73d Cong., 1st Sess., House of Representatives, Ways and Means Committee, *Hearings on National Industrial Recovery*, p. 134.

ers. These firms were permitted to display the emblem of the Blue Eagle at their places of business and to affix it to their goods. The public was invited, in effect, to boycott those who failed to do so. In the meantime, the work of drafting the codes got under way.

Trade Associations and Code Authorities

At the beginning, the NRA had no policies to govern the character of the provisions offered and accepted for inclusion in the codes. The first drafts were drawn up by the trade associations. They were a product of negotiation between these associations and organized labor, each conceding terms to the other in return for agreement to the terms that it sought for itself. These drafts were discussed informally with the deputy administrators, who acted not as guardians of the public interest but merely as arbitrators of disputes. Later drafts went to public hearings where the proposed provisions could be criticized. Then, when needed modifications had been made, the final drafts were handed to the deputies. If the Industry and Labor Advisory Boards had found them acceptable, they were approved. If the Consumers' Advisory Board had objected, its protest was ignored. The industry and labor boards had organized backing; the consumers' board did not. When the codes were approved by the deputies, they were rubber stamped by the administrator and the President and given the effect of law.

The codes were administered by bodies known as code authorities. These bodies were largely composed of or selected by trade associations. The personnel and the policy of the authorities were controlled by trade associations. In three cases out of four, the code authority secretary and the trade association secretary bore the same name and did business at the same address. Code administration was usually financed by mandatory assessments against each of the firms in an industry. In the garment trades, collection of the levy was assured by the requirement that a label purchased from the code authority must be sewn in every garment sold. The program thus involved a virtual delegation to trade associations of the powers of government, including in some cases, the power to tax.

The NRA undertook, in its own words, "to build up and strengthen trade associations throughout all commerce and industry."[8] It conferred new powers and immunities on strong associations, invigorated weak associations, aroused moribund associations, consolidated small associations, and called some eight hundred new associations into life. It sought to employ these agencies as instruments in the promotion of industrial recovery. But many of the provisions which it permitted them to write into their codes were ill designed to achieve this end. In order that the significance of these provisions may be understood, it would be well, first, to examine their prototypes in the character and activities of European cartels.

[8] NRA Bulletin No. 7, January 22, 1934.

Cartels

A cartel is an association of independent enterprises in the same or similar branches of industry, formed for the purpose of increasing the profits of its members by subjecting their competitive activities to some form of common control. Membership in such an association is usually voluntary, although in some cases it has been required by law. The members remain under separate ownership, retaining their freedom of action with respect to matters which are not included, and surrendering it only in respect to matters which are included, within the scope of their agreement. The distinguishing characteristic of the cartel is the fact that this agreement invariably requires the substitution of common policies for independent policies in the determination of price and production.

Cartel types, differentiated according to the methods which they employ, fall into four major categories. In the first are those associations that attempt to control the conditions surrounding a sale: standardization cartels, engaged in the simplification and standardization of products; term-fixing cartels, devoted to the regulation of such matters as conditions of delivery, time of payment, discounts, options, free deals, return privileges, quality guaranties and guaranties against price declines. In the second category are those associations that undertake to fix prices: trade-mark cartels that unite the producers of branded goods in boycotts directed against distributors who undercut the stated resale price; calculation cartels that promote the adoption of common methods of cost accounting, common estimates of cost, and common margins of profit; minimum-price and uniform-price cartels that circulate lists of prices, hold meetings for the discussion of prices, set up committees to issue detailed schedules of prices, and police their members to enforce adherence to such prices. In the third category are those associations that undertake to distribute among their members particular productive activities, sales territories, and customers: specialization cartels that assign to certain members the exclusive right to produce certain varieties of an industry's products; zone cartels that assign to certain members the exclusive right to sell in certain markets; customer-preservation cartels that reserve for each member the exclusive right to sell to his former customers; and order-allocation cartels that decide in the case of each submission of bids which member's bid shall be lowest. In the fourth category are those associations that undertake to award each member a fixed share of the business: plant restriction cartels that limit the number of hours during which plants may be operated, limit the number of machines that may be employed, and prohibit the installation of new machines; fixed-production-share cartels and fixed-marketing-share cartels that assign quotas to each of their members and impose, upon those who produce or sell more than their quotas permit, fines whose payment is guaranteed by previous deposits; production-equalization cartels and marketing-equalization cartels that assign production or marketing quotas and either operate equalization pools, making collections from those who exceed their quotas and payments to those who fail to attain them, or readjust quotas in succeeding periods, reducing the shares of those who exceed them and increasing the shares of those who keep within them; profit-sharing cartels that operate profit pools, collecting part or all of their members' profits and redistributing them upon some predetermined basis; and cartels called syndicates that employ common agencies, either to negotiate sales for their members and allocate orders among them, or to distribute part or all of their output, fixing terms and prices, assigning quotas, and dividing profits. The methods employed by a single cartel may place it within more than one of these categories. Cartels of all types attempt to regulate the terms of sale; term-fixing cartels are merely those that confine themselves to this activity. But few cartels stop here; the tendency has been to move on from those forms of control that are mild and simple to those that are stringent and complex.

In a few industries, in a few countries, cartelization has been required by law. Elsewhere, the enforcement of cartel arrangements depends upon persuasion backed by various forms of economic pressure. Cartels are in a position to discipline their members by revoking licenses granted under patents which they hold in a common pool, by imposing fines against money which they hold on deposit, and by withholding payments from equalization pools, profit pools, sales receipts, and other funds which they control. They can compel outsiders to become members or even drive them out of business by offering loyalty discounts to customers who do not deal with them, by boycotting suppliers who sell to them and customers who buy from them, and by making exclusive contracts with suppliers and with customers which cut them off from access to materials and markets.[9]

Codes of Fair Competition

The NRA approved 557 basic codes, 189 supplementary codes, 109 divisional codes, and 19 codes entered into jointly with the Agricultural Adjustment Administration—a grand total of 874. The codes spelled out more than a thousand different kinds of provisions for the regulation of 150 different types of competitive practices. In addition to the mandatory labor provisions, they set forth rules condemning a number of trade practices that had long been held to be unfair. Here, the authors drew upon the texts of trade association codes of ethics, trade practice conference agreements with the Federal Trade Commission, and orders issued by the FTC. Thus the codes denounced various forms of misrepresentation, forbade defamation of competitors, inducing breach of contract, and

[9] This section is reproduced, in abbreviated form, from Clair Wilcox, *Competition and Monopoly in American Industry*, T.N.E.C. Monograph No. 21, pp. 215–17.

commercial bribery, and prohibited design piracy, espionage, vexatious litigation, and the enticement of employees. These provisions added little to existing law. They were in the tradition of established policy.

But the codes did not stop here. They went on to control terms of sale, prices, markets, production, capacity, and the channels of distribution. In the name of fair competition, they required adherence to practices that the Federal Trade Commission and the courts had held to be unfair. They perverted the concept of unfairness in competition by extending it to competition itself. Industry by industry, they were designed by a majority to curb the competitive propensities of an obstreperous minority. Item by item, they copied the pattern of the European cartel.

Control of Terms of Sale

All of the codes contained provisions which governed the terms and conditions of sale, subjecting to detailed regulation in various combinations such matters as quotation, bid, order, contract, and invoice forms, bidding and awarding procedures, customer classifications, trade, quantity, and cash discounts, bill datings, credit practices, installment sales, deferred payments, interest charges, guaranties of quality, guaranties against price declines, long-term contracts, options, time and form of payments, returns of merchandise, sales on consignment, sales on trial or approval, cancellation of contracts, trade-in allowances, advertising allowances, supplementary services, combination sales, rebates, premiums, free deals, containers, coupons, samples, prizes, absorption of freight, delivery of better qualities or larger quantities than those specified, sale of seconds and of used, damaged, rebuilt, overhauled, obsolete, and discontinued goods, the payment of fees and commissions, and the maintenance of resale prices. In general, these provisions were designed to affect the allocation of business between trades and among the firms within a trade and to prevent the granting of any indirect concession which would operate to reduce a price.

Control of Prices

More than 85 per cent of the codes contained some provision for the direct or indirect control of price. A dozen of them permitted the code authorities to establish minimum prices without regard to costs of production and without approval by the NRA. The code for the bituminous coal industry, for instance, stated that "the selling of coal under a fair market price . . . is hereby declared to be . . . in violation of this code. . . . The fair market price of coal . . . shall be the minimum prices . . . which may be established . . . by the respective code authorities." Another two dozen codes empowered the authorities to fix prices equal to the "lowest reasonable" costs of a "representative" firm, to become effective when approved by NRA. In iron and steel, and in a few other industries, the codes legalized basing point systems of delivered pricing, specifying each of the elements of the pricing formulas and prescribing their use. In iron and steel, moreover, the code provided that

> The board of directors shall have the power . . . to investigate any base price for any product . . . filed by members of the code. . . . If the board of directors, after such investigation, shall determine that such base price is an unfair base price . . . the board of directors may require the member of the code . . . to file a new list showing a fair base price. . . . If such member of the code shall not . . . file a new list . . . the board of directors shall have the power to fix a fair base price. . . .

In the paper tag industry, too, a price reporting provision was employed as a method of fixing a common price. The code for this industry forbade producers who did not file prices to sell below the lowest price filed by any of their competitors. In practice, prices were filed by a single large concern.

The fixing of prices was usually less overt. Some 200 codes permitted code authorities to establish minimum prices only to prevent "destructive price cutting" and to do so only in the event of an "emergency." These limitations, however, had little significance. The concepts were never clearly defined. "An emergency," it was said, "is something that is declared by a code authority." As the coal dealers put it, "We have always had an emergency in retail solid fuel." The code for this trade became effective on February 26, 1934; the authority declared an emergency on March 1, 1934, and proceeded to fix prices based on the "lowest reasonable costs" of selling coal. Emergencies were also declared in several other trades, affording their members an opportunity to arrive at "cost determinations" which could be used to justify high minimum prices. The history of NRA gives evidence that they made the most of this opportunity.

In the codes for the wholesale and retail trades, price fixing took the form of provisions for "loss limitation." In some cases, these provisions forbade the distributor to sell goods for less than they cost him. In others, they required him to add a markup based upon some estimate of distribution costs. In still others, they compelled him to charge a price set by the producer or by the wholesaler from whom he bought. It is likely that provisions of the second type and it is certain that those of the third type involved something more than the mere limitation of loss.

The type of price fixing provision which was most widely adopted, under NRA, was that which provided for "cost protection." Three fifths of the codes prohibited sales below "cost." The effect of such a provision would depend, of course, upon the standard of cost that was employed. If a firm were forbidden to sell below its own cost, it might be undercut by a lower-cost competitor. If it were forbidden to sell below the cost of its lowest-cost competitor, the provision would not serve to raise the prices of the trade. If it were forbidden to sell below an average cost computed for the trade, the result would depend on the method of computation. Did all firms report or was a sample used? If the latter, was the sample representative? Were the reports honest, or were they padded? Was the average a simple one or was it weighted? If the latter, were the proper weights applied? Was the figure taken as representative a mean, a median, or a mode? Were the reports and the computations taken at face value, or were they subjected to an independent audit? Depending on the answers to these questions, the prices set by this provision would be high or low.

More than half of the codes provided for the establishment of a standard costing system. More than fifty of them forbade sales below some average of cost, the rest forbade sales below the seller's individual cost. In many cases the procedure followed in the determination of an average cost led to the establishment of an arbitrary minimum price. In the printing industry, the code authority collected data from 200-odd printers among some 17,000 and issued "cost determination schedules" in the form of catalogues which set forth minimum prices rather than costs. In the paint industry, the authority sent questionnaires to 160 among some 2,000 firms, rejected 34 of the 74 replies, and employed the 40 remaining (which included no data on certain of the industry's products and no returns from some of its more important members) in arriving at figures which were said to represent "the lowest reasonable cost of manufacturers, large and small, throughout the industry." So, too, with the adoption of a common formula for use in the determination of individual costs. In the limestone industry, the code authority prescribed itemized costs for successive operations that added up, in every case, to a uniform total. In the trucking industry, the authority drew up a schedule of costs in dollars and cents, and truckers whose rates fell below the resulting figures were charged with violation of the code. This procedure was known to the industry as "cost education." In some cases, finally, the code provided not only for uniform costs but also for a uniform markup. Thus, the code of the waterproofing industry forbade its members to sell below "allowable cost" plus a "reasonable" percentage to be determined by the code authority, and the code of the brick industry forbade selling below "direct factory cost" plus an item called "weighted average indirect allowable cost," this item being stated by the code authority in terms of dollars at a figure which was uniform throughout the industry.

Two thirds of the codes provided for the establishment of open price reporting systems. Most of these systems were of a character that would probably have been outlawed under the earlier decisions of the courts. Nearly half of them gave no information to buyers. Most of them required the filing of identified price lists. Most of them also required sellers to adhere to the prices they had filed until new filings became effective, and three fourths of them required a waiting period before a new filing was permitted to take effect. In many cases the price reporting systems afforded a convenient medium through which the price fixing provisions could be policed.

Allocation of Markets

A number of codes contained provisions which were designed to effect an allocation of markets among the members of a trade. Some of them prohibited freight allowances, thus preventing sellers from entering distant markets by absorbing freight. Others prohibited "dumping," forbidding firms to sell outside their "normal market areas" at prices lower than those "customarily" charged within such areas and granting code authorities the power to determine which areas were "normal" and which prices "customary." Still others divided the country into zones and forbade producers located in one zone to sell in another below the prices charged by producers located there. Thus the code for the salt-producing industry provided that "the minimum prices established in any marketing field by any producer in that field shall be the lowest prices at which any producer shall sell in that field. . . ." Such provisions, in effect, set up a tariff wall around each of the designated areas.

Control of Production

Ninety-one codes provided for the restriction of output and the distribution of available business among the firms in a trade. A few codes limited the size of inventories, compelling manufacturers to confine their operations to the volume permitted by current sales. Sixty codes, most of them in the textile industry, imposed limitations on the number of hours or shifts per day, or the number of hours or days per week, during which machines or plants might be operated, thus curtailing production and allocating the resulting volume of business on the basis of capacity. A half dozen codes, including those for the petroleum, lumber, copper, and glass container industries, provided for the limitation of production in accordance with estimates of total demand, and for the assignment of production quotas on the basis of present capacity or past production or sales.

Control of Capacity

Some fifty codes imposed limitations upon the construction, conversion, or relocation of productive capacity, or made some provision for the imposition of such limitations. In some cases, the provision of new facilities and the inauguration of new services were forbidden. The code for the iron and steel industry provided that "it is the consensus of opinion in the industry that, until such time as the demand for its products cannot adequately be met by the fullest possible use of existing capacities for producing pig iron and steel ingots, such capacities should not be increased. Accordingly . . . none of the members of the code shall initiate the construction of any new blast furnace or open hearth or Bessemer steel capacity." A number of transit codes forbade the opening of new routes or the extension of existing ones. In other cases, additions to capacity required the permission of the code authority or the approval of the NRA, thus giving these bodies control over entry to the industry and the relative growth of different companies.

Control of the Channels of Distribution

The codes for the wholesale and retail trades were designed, in general, to check the development of competing channels of distribution. They established mandatory markups and so defined the trades as to include the mass distributors. They limited the discounts that could be given to distributors buying in quantity. They established customer classes and specified the discounts that should be given to each class. They required, for instance, that a discount of only 25 per cent be given to retailers and a discount of 50 per cent to wholesalers. They forbade manufacturers to assume distributive functions or to sell their goods to certain classes of distributors. They specified the customers that might be served by wholesalers and those that were reserved to retailers. These provisions were enforced against manufacturers and wholesalers by rules forbidding distributors to buy from those who disobeyed their terms.

Penalties

Adherence to code requirements was enforced not only by penalties provided in the law, but also by sanctions established in the codes. The requirements imposed on manufacturers by distributors and on wholesalers by retailers were enforced by organized boycotts. Twenty-six industries bound their members to pay "liquidated damages" into the treasury of the code authority in the event of a violation. The iron and steel code contained the following provision:

> Recognizing that the violation by any member of the code of any provision (dealing with base prices, delivered prices, or terms of sale) will disrupt the normal course of fair competition in the industry and cause serious damage to other members of the code and that it will be impossible fairly to assess the amount of such damage to any member of the code, it is hereby agreed by and among all members of the code that each member of the code which shall violate any such provision shall pay to the Treasurer . . . as and for liquidated damages the sum of $10 per ton of any products sold in violation of any such provision.

In this case, as in others, it appears that the "liquidated damages" were really fines imposed on violators of the code rather than payments made to injured parties to reimburse them for losses actually sustained.

The End of NRA

It soon became clear that the power conferred upon the trade associations by the law had been abused. Despite the President's plea that price increases be postponed, business had made the most of its monopolistic opportunities. Complaints began to be heard. They came not only from customers, when prices had been raised, but also from competitors when their opportunities had been curtailed by the restraints imposed upon them by their industries. In the spring of 1934 the President appointed a committee, under the eminent lawyer, Clarence Darrow, to investigate. The committee's report condemned the whole undertaking, denouncing it as "monopoly sustained by government" and as "a regimented organization for exploitation." In the fall of 1934, General Johnson was replaced by an administrative board of seven members, including representatives of business, labor, and the consumer. Thereafter, NRA policy was radically revised. Provisions of the sort that had been written into the earlier codes were no longer granted. Applications for the approval of activities requiring specific sanction were denied. But the new policy was not applied to the existing codes. They were allowed to stand.

As written, the law was due to expire in the summer of 1935. The President asked Congress to extend its life for two more years. Hearings were held by the Senate, and it appeared that the powers conferred by the law, if extended at all, would be sharply modified. While Congressional action was still pending, the Supreme Court handed down its decision on the Schechter case.[10] The Court was unanimous. The law involved an unconstitutional invasion of intrastate commerce and an unconstitutional delegation of legislative power. The NRA was put to death on May 27, 1935.

An Appraisal of NRA

NRA must be given credit for the improvement of labor standards in the United States. The codes initiated the maximum hours, minimum wages, and prohibition of child labor that were continued, in 1935, by the Fair Labor Standards Act, and the union recognition and collective bargaining that were continued by the National Labor Relations Act. The code authorities manifested little interest in enforcing the labor provisions of the codes, confining their attention to the suppression of competitive practices. But the NRA itself undertook enforcement of these provisions, and here it attained a modicum of success.

The trade practice provisions of the codes were administered most effectively in industries that had not been vigorously competitive: those that were disciplined by powerful trade associations or dominated by a few large firms. Here, the legal sanction was not needed; suspension of the antitrust laws was all that was required. In more competitive industries, however, where firms were small and numerous and trade associations weak, enforcement of the codes was difficult if not impossible. And here they tended to break down.

The National Industrial Recovery Act contributed little, if anything, to recovery. The substitution of action—even if ill-advised—for inaction

[10] *Schechter* v. *U.S.*, 295 U.S. 495 (1935).

may have made for a restoration of confidence. The building of floors under wages and prices may have convinced businessmen that the bottom had been reached. But prices rose more rapidly than wages, checking the expansion of purchasing power. Industrial prices rose with agricultural prices, thus preventing the restoration of the balance that the Agricultural Adjustment Act was designed to achieve. The price increases, adding to costs, may well have discouraged ventures that business would otherwise have regarded as feasible. It is certain that they did so in the vital construction industries. Other measures adopted by the New Deal undoubtedly stimulated business activity: the agricultural program, devaluation, and deficit spending. But it was the conclusion of the economists of the Brookings Institution that the "Recovery" Act itself "on the whole retarded recovery."[11]

The NRA did serve one useful purpose. It provided the country with a demonstration of the character and the consequences of cartelization. It showed that industry, when given the power of "self government," could not be trusted to exercise it in the public interest; that enterprise would be handicapped and vested interest protected, progress obstructed and stagnation assured. It showed that businessmen, if given a blank check to be filled out, would proceed to commit economic suicide, pricing themselves out of the market and encouraging consumers to turn to substitutes: to oil when the price of coal was boosted and to mechanical refrigerators when the price of ice was raised. It showed, moreover, that enforcement of limitations on competition required a greater degree of regimentation than business was prepared to take, and that supervision adequate to protect the public interest would require an enormous organization, to be supported at a heavy cost.

It is probable that the NRA was like a vaccination, giving the United States a mild case of the cartel disease and immunizing it against the disease itself. It is certain that—as long as this experience remains in memory—there are few who would welcome its return. If American industry, in general, is again to be cartelized, the movement will have to take a different form.

The Philosophy of Cost Protection

One idea persists. Admittedly such practices as price fixing, market sharing, production control, and curtailment of capacity are reprehensible. But is not cost protection to be justified? Surely, sale below cost must be maliciously destructive and its prohibition, therefore, must be reasonable.

This view is based upon a false assumption as to the essential character of "costs." It assumes that costs are objective figures, scientifically ascertained by impersonal accountants, and set forth in precise terms on which all accountants would agree. But this is not the case. Costs are purposive;

[11] Lyon and Others, *op. cit.*, p. 873.

they are instruments of business policy. Cost accountants are employed by managements and will show whatever it may be that managements want shown. Costs are based on judgments and judgments may differ. There may be different opinions, first, as to what should be included in costs: how much overcapitalization, how much obsolete capacity, how large an expenditure on sales promotion and public relations, what level of executive salaries. Opinions may differ, second, on how to measure the items that are included in costs. Are raw materials to be charged at the prices paid for those used in a product, at the prices paid for the last ones purchased, or at current replacement cost? Is a particular expenditure to be charged to the costs of operation or to the cost of capital? Is capital to be entered at its original cost or at its reproduction cost? Is it to be depreciated by writing off an equal sum during each year of its estimated life, larger sums in the beginning that taper off in later years, or larger sums in years when business is good? And, by the way, how estimate an asset's estimated life? Opinions may differ, finally, as to the distribution of overhead costs among joint products. Should they be made proportionate to material costs or labor costs or both, related to power consumed, machine hours used, or floor space occupied, or allocated in accordance with any one of several other principles? As men's judgments differ, so will their estimates of costs. To forbid sales below cost, therefore, is to set as a minimum price a figure that is not objective but is one that accountants can manipulate.

The cost protection philosophy, moreover, ignores the economic function of cost and price. It assumes that cost is immutable and price adjustible; that cost, therefore, must always be taken as cause and price as effect. And this assumption, too, is false. For cause and effect may operate the other way around. If price falls below cost, it is possible that cost may be reduced. New materials may be employed, new methods discovered, wastes eliminated, and efficiency increased. The cost of capital may be reduced, by writing down excessive valuations, or by putting overvalued assets through the wringer of bankruptcy. This, after all, is the disciplinary function of the cost-price relationship. If price were never permitted to fall below cost, there would be no business failures, no compulsion to adjust production to changing demands, no penalty for waste and inefficiency. Business, under a system of private enterprise, is driven by the carrot of profit and by the stick of loss. Cost protection would leave the carrot, but it would take away the stick.

SUSPENSION OF ANTITRUST IN WARTIME

The conditions that characterize a war economy are the opposite of those encountered in depression. There is growing demand and full employment. There are shortages and inflationary pressures. Prices are rising more rapidly than costs and profits are going up. But here, too, there are demands for relief from antitrust. It is said that businessmen, to further the war effort, must enter into agreements for the conservation of scarce resources and the allocation of scarce facilities and supplies. And it is argued that they cannot devote their full energies to war production if their attention is diverted by antitrust proceedings before the Federal Trade Commission and the courts. Suspension of antitrust becomes the price of willing co-operation in the prosecution of the war.

In World War II, the Chairman of the War Production Board was given authority, by Section 12 of the Small Business Mobilization Act of 1942, to certify to the Attorney General that "the doing of any act or thing, or the omission to do any act or thing, by one or more persons" was essential to the war effort and was thus in the public interest. Thereafter the matters covered in such certificates were exempt from antitrust. More than 200 of these certificates were issued during the war. There is no evidence that the power to grant immunity from prosecution was seriously abused. But the power was so sweeping that the opportunity for abuse was clearly there.

An arrangement was also worked out during the war, by which, at the request of the war agencies, antitrust actions already under way could be postponed. In response to such requests 33 cases were deferred by the Department of Justice and several others, whose number was not published, by the Federal Trade Commission. The suits that were postponed involved large companies and important issues. "It was evident from the beginning," says Corwin Edwards, "that deferment jeopardized the success of the government in these cases, since it involved the probability that memories would grow dim, that some witnesses would die, and that the whole subject matter would come to seem remote and unimportant because of the passage of time."[12] How serious a handicap this may have proved to be, it is impossible to say.

The Defense Production Act of 1950, adopted following the outbreak of war in Korea, authorized the President—or officials to whom he delegated his power—to exempt from the antitrust laws activities found "to be in the public interest as contributing to the national defense." These officials, however, were required to consult with the Attorney General and the Chairman of the Federal Trade Commission before requesting an exemption and to obtain the approval of the Attorney General for any request that they might make. The antitrust authorities could thus prevent an exemption by raising objections and the Attorney General could do so by withholding his consent. No provision was made for the postponement of cases already under way.

EXCEPTIONS TO ANTITRUST

A number of industries and business practices have been exempted, over the years, from the provisions of the antitrust laws. In some cases monopoly has been accepted as inevitable or desirable and government has

[12] *American Economic Review*, May, 1952, p. 407.

undertaken the regulation of rates and services. This is true of transportation and public utilities, whose control is discussed in Part V. In other cases it has appeared that the members of a trade, far from possessing the powers of monopolists, are at a disadvantage in bargaining. And here, instead of attempting to restore competition to both sides of the market, Congress has approved the principle of bilateral monopoly. This solution, already discussed in the case of labor, has also been adopted in that of agricultural co-operatives. It could be applied, with equal logic, to situations sometimes found in manufacturing industries and in the distribution trades. In still other cases, industries have appeared to be chronically distressed. The demand for their products has declined, substitutes have displaced them, changing technology has made established methods obsolete, and competition has induced recurring bankruptcies. Here, the obvious remedy would be to ease migration from the field. But Congress, instead, has sought to afford relief by permitting such industries to curtail output, share markets, and fix prices. Bituminous coal and certain agricultural commodities, to be discussed in later chapters, will illustrate the point. And finally, there are cases where exemptions are to be explained by the ability of well organized trades to exert political power. There are businessmen who take the view that competition, though desirable for others, is not appropriate for themselves. And there are politicians who give lip service to the maintenance of competition but are open to persuasion that exceptions should be made. The legalization of resale price maintenance will be described in Chapter 14.

Labor and Agriculture in the Clayton Act

In a number of cases brought under the Sherman Act, the courts have condemned certain restrictive activities of labor unions and agricultural co-operatives. It was argued, before 1914, that some of these decisions raised doubts concerning the right of such bodies to exist. There was also hope, among unions and co-operatives, that legislative approval of their existence might be interpreted as endorsing their activities. So, in response to the demands of labor and agriculture, the following provision was written into Section 6 of the Clayton Act: "Nothing contained in the antitrust laws shall be construed to forbid the existence and operation of labor, agricultural, or horticultural organizations, instituted for the purposes of mutual help and not . . . conducted for profits, or to forbid or restrain individual members of such organizations from carrying out the legitimate objects thereof; nor shall such organizations, or the members thereof, be held or construed to be illegal combinations or conspiracies in restraint of trade under the antitrust laws." This provision clearly exempted unions and co-operatives per se. But it was not interpreted to grant complete immunity. The exemption was expressly limited to the "legitimate objects" of such groups. And these objects were not held to include restraint of trade.

Agricultural and Fisheries Co-operatives

The exemption afforded to agricultural co-operatives was broadened by the Capper-Volstead Act in 1922. Under this law, "farmers" are permitted to employ such associations as common agencies in sorting, grading, and packing their crops, in producing such foodstuffs as butter, cheese, and canned goods, in marketing their output, and in fixing prices and terms of sale. This privilege is confined to associations operated for mutual benefit, each of whose members has a single vote or whose dividends are limited to eight per cent per year, and whose supplies are drawn predominantly from within their membership. One other safeguard is provided: "If the Secretary of Agriculture shall have reason to believe that any such association monopolizes or restrains trade . . . to such an extent that the price of any agricultural product is unduly enhanced," he may issue a complaint, hold a hearing, and issue an order to cease and desist which, upon noncompliance, he may request the Attorney General to enforce.

This exemption has not been held to permit co-operatives to conspire with other distributors, to fix resale prices, or to discriminate unlawfully among their customers. But it is none the less a sweeping one, enabling co-operatives to make exclusive contracts with hundreds of farmers, to combine in the establishment of common marketing agencies, and even to attain positions of monopoly. It encompasses not only farming operations but also manufacturing establishments engaged in processing agricultural commodities. The safeguard embodied in the law affords but scant protection against abuse. No criterion is established by which to judge whether prices have been "unduly" enhanced. The Secretary of Agriculture, moreover, may be expected to view the activities of agricultural co-operatives with a not unsympathetic eye. It should be noted, too, that such associations were authorized by the Cooperative Marketing Act of 1926 to collect, disseminate, and interpret trade statistics, an activity that has brought many a trade association into conflict with antitrust.

Under the Fisheries Cooperative Marketing Act of 1934, an exemption similar to that of the Capper-Volstead Act was extended to fishermen. Here, the authority to serve complaints and issue orders if prices were "unduly" enhanced was conferred upon the Secretary of Commerce, to be transferred in 1939 to the Secretary of the Interior. But here a different situation exists. Fisherman, typically, are independent proprietors, holding title to their boats and selling their catch to fish dealers and canners. Some of them have financed their boats by mortgaging them to the canners and some of them may work part-time as laborers in the canneries. In general, fishermen have not availed themselves of the privilege of forming co-operatives. More often, they have come together in labor unions, sometimes combining with cannery workers, to bargain with the fish dealers and canners. But the substance of their bargains relates, not to wages for their labor, but to the price of the product which they sell. In 1949, however, it was held that fishermen could not claim exemption from antitrust as members of labor unions, since their relation to the purchasers of fish was not that of employees.[13] The way remains open, however, to obtain exemption by establishing fisheries co-operatives. And here, as in agriculture, there is danger of abuse.

Under the provisions of the agricultural marketing agreements legislation of the 1930's, co-operatives were further authorized to enter into agreements with the processors and distributors of agricultural commodities to control their sale and price, and the Secretary of Agriculture was empowered to order them to do so. This legislation, providing for the establishment of both voluntary and compulsory cartels, will be considered in Chapter 16.

Agreements and Combinations in Transportation and Communications

Transoceanic shipping rates have customarily been fixed by agreement among the ship lines of different countries meeting in shipping conferences. Under the Shipping Act of 1916, American lines participating in these agreements were granted exemption from the antitrust laws. The Act required that the agreements be filed with the U.S. Shipping Board and authorized the Board to modify or cancel rates, in services touching American ports, that it found to be discriminatory or unfair, and to disapprove American participation in agreements that would be detrimental to the commerce of the United States. This function was inherited by the U.S. Maritime Commission and subsequently by the Maritime Board. The law thus sanctions international shipping cartels. But competition in rates —given the general policy of maintaining national merchant fleets— would be likely to degenerate into competition in subsidies. As a matter of economics, cartelization is undesirable. But as a matter of diplomacy, it may be a lesser evil than economic warfare. In such a situation, however, there is need for regulation. And effective regulation is prevented by the absence of an international regulatory agency.

The combination of competing companies, when approved by the Interstate Commerce Commission, was permitted by Congress in the case of railroads in 1920, telephone companies in 1921, motor carriers in 1935, and water carriers in 1940. The combination of air lines, and rate agreements and pooling arrangements among such lines, when approved by the Civil Aeronautics Board, were permitted in 1938. The combination of the Western Union and Postal Telegraph companies, with the approval of the Federal Communications Commission, was made possible by an Act of Congress in 1943. In each of these cases the resulting combinations were subject to the jurisdiction of a regulatory agency.

The latest exemption afforded to transportation is that provided to

[13] *U.S.* v. *Local 36, I.F.A.W.A.*, 177 F. 2d 320.

traffic associations by the Reed-Bulwinkle Act of 1948. Railroad rates had been regulated by the Interstate Commerce Commission since 1887, motor carrier rates since 1935. But the Commission acted only on the cases that were brought before it and, in practice, reviewed less than 1 per cent of the specific rates. Presumably each carrier was to take the initiative in fixing its charges. But, for many years, all changes in rates had been submitted to traffic associations set up by the carriers for this purpose and were not made effective unless approved. The Supreme Court had held, repeatedly, that the antitrust laws applied to the railroads. So, in 1944, the Department of Justice brought suit against a railroad traffic association under the Sherman Act. The railroads thereupon demanded exemption. Congress complied; the Bulwinkle Bill was passed, vetoed by President Truman, and passed over his veto. As a result, carriers may now apply to the ICC for approval of agreements respecting rates and fares. The antitrust authorities may present their objections to the provisions of such agreements before the ICC. The Commission may require that the agreements be terminated or modified. If it approves them, they are exempt from antitrust. But the law provides that the associations shall not prevent an individual carrier from exercising initiative in changing rates. And it requires them to report to the ICC on their activities. It may be doubted, however, that these provisions will suffice to insure substantial competition in the establishment of rates by surface carriers.

Export Trade Associations

In 1918 Congress passed the Webb-Pomerene Act, exempting from the antitrust laws any "association entered into for the sole purpose of engaging in export trade," thus legalizing combinations for making sales abroad. The Act expressly forbade the members of such associations to interfere with the exports of nonmembers or to take joint action in making sales in the domestic market, warning them not to "enter into any agreement, understanding, or conspiracy or do any act which artificially or intentionally enhances or depresses prices within the United States . . . or which substantially lessens competition within the United States or otherwise restrains trade therein." Associations were directed to file their charters, bylaws, agreements, and other data with the Federal Trade Commission and to make periodic reports to that body. The Commission was not authorized to issue orders to cease and desist from violations of the law, but it was permitted to investigate association activities and to recommend readjustments that would bring them within the scope of the exemption.

Webb-Pomerene associations have numbered something more than a hundred, about fifty of them being in existence at any one time. Normally they have handled less than a tenth of the goods exported from the United States. Most of the earlier associations were operating agencies, making sales abroad, allocating orders at home, assembling and shipping goods, making collections, and remitting payments to their members. It was generally assumed that mere price and quota agreements were not permitted by the law. In 1924, however, in response to a letter from a group of silver producers, the FTC declared that an association need not "perform all the operations of selling its members' product to a foreign buyer" but might be engaged solely "in allotting export orders . . . and in fixing prices at which the individual members shall sell. . . ." From that time, most associations have left to their members the work of making sales, shipping goods, and collecting payments, confining themselves to the task of fixing prices or assigning quotas or both.

For more than twenty years, the supervision of these associations by the Federal Trade Commission was only nominal. The documents required by law were kept on file and the names of the associations and the value of their exports were reported annually. This work was the responsibility of a single Commission employee. In 1940, the Commission took its first formal action, effecting a readjustment of the activities of the Pacific Forest Industries. At the same time the Temporary National Economic Committee exposed abuses on the part of associations exporting copper, sulfur, and potash. And beginning in 1944 the Commission launched a series of investigations leading to readjustments in the phosphate and other industries.

The Webb-Pomerene Act did not say whether export trade associations might participate in international cartels. But in its silver letter, the FTC asserted that it saw no reason why such an association "might not adopt a trade arrangement with non-nationals reaching the same market, providing this market was not the domestic market of the United States. . . ." A number of associations joined in cartel agreements on the strength of this interpretation of the law. In 1939, however, the Department of Justice initiated a campaign against cartel abuses. And in 1945 in its decision in the case of the Alkali Export Association, the Supreme Court held that the association's participation in such arrangements was illegal, since the Webb-Pomerene Act was intended to promote competition rather than collusion in the markets of the world.[14]

A number of arguments have been advanced in support of this exemption: (1) By combining, exporters can reduce the cost of making foreign sales; they can save money on advertising, selling, and handling, on freight, insurance, storage, and the like. (2) Combination will enable small American exporters to compete more effectively with larger ones. (3) Foreign sellers are united in cartels. Americans would find it difficult to compete with them if they, too, were not permitted to combine. (4) Foreign buyers are also cartelized. In the absence of combination, American sellers would be at a disadvantage in bargaining.

If associations actually engaged in physical operations, the first of these arguments would have some validity. But most of them do not. If associations were usually composed of smaller firms, the second argument also would have some point. In practice they have been formed more fre-

[14] *U.S.* v. *Alkali Export Assn.*, 325 U.S. 196.

quently by larger companies. The third argument is dubious. The cartelization of foreign sellers should not make it difficult for Americans to sell abroad. Quite the contrary: cartels raise prices and this should make it easier to compete. The last argument, too, is open to question. Foreign buyers may be cartelized, but the American firms that have combined to deal with them have seldom been weaklings needing help.

It may be doubted, finally, that firms can combine when selling abroad and compete with undiminished vigor when selling at home. The vigilance exercised by the Federal Trade Commission may not suffice to keep the right hand of industry from knowing what the left hand is doing. Competitors with common offices, adopting common policies, may not attain the singleness of purpose that the law assumes.[15]

Insurance

In 1920 Congress exempted from the antitrust laws combinations of marine insurance companies. The share of marine insurance carried with American companies was a minor one, and the action was designed to encourage their development. The exemption was complete; no administrative approval was required. Presumably, however, such combinations would face the competition of foreign insurance companies.

For many years it was held that the business of writing domestic insurance policies was intrastate in character and therefore was not covered by the Sherman Act. In 1944, however, the Supreme Court found that the operations of fire insurance companies involved the transmission of communications, documents, and money in interstate commerce and concluded that the Sherman Act applied. The insurance interests then sought complete exemption from the law. In this they were not wholly successful. The McCarran Act, passed in 1945, suspended enforcement of the antitrust laws against rate agreements among insurance companies for a period of three years, making the antitrust laws applicable thereafter, but only "to the extent that such business is not regulated by state law." The effect of this action was to stimulate enactment, by the states, of laws regulating insurance rates. There are certain collusive practices, moreover, such as agreements among insurance companies not to file lower rates and boycotts denying reinsurance privileges to those who do so, which can still be prosecuted under the Sherman Act.

Exceptions to State Antitrust Laws

The legislatures of the several states have granted numerous exceptions under their respective antitrust laws, acting on behalf of farmers, retailers, and the local service trades. In most states there are laws permitting agricultural marketing agreements and in many there are laws providing for the establishment of minimum prices for milk. In all but three of the states

[15] See *Report of the F.T.C. on the Operation of the Export Trade Act*, T.N.E.C. Monograph No. 6, Part III (1940); American Economic Assn., "Consensus Report on the Webb-Pomerene Law," *American Economic Review*, December, 1947, pp. 848–63.

the maintenance of resale prices has been legalized, and in many of them merchants have been forbidden to sell at prices that fall below their costs. At one time or another a number of states have authorized the establishment of minimum prices in barbering, shoe repairing, laundering, cleaning and dyeing, and other service trades. These exemptions apply, in the main, to fields that would normally be highly competitive. Their effect is to be felt in local markets for consumers' goods and services.

Exceptions and the Maintenance of Competition

In national policy the maintenance of competition is still the general rule. Permissive monopoly is still regarded as exceptional. The trades exempted are less important than those still subject to the law. In some cases, however, the exceptions granted have not been accompanied by alternative controls. In others, the controls provided have been devised to serve the interests of particular groups rather than those of the community as a whole. In still others, controls appear to be designed to serve the public interest. But the regulatory agencies reflect the attitudes of the industries they are supposed to regulate. Or the methods of regulation do not afford an adequate substitute for the safeguards of competition. If the policy of maintaining competition is to prevail, many of the present exceptions should be repealed. And where exceptions are justified, they should be conditioned, as an alternative, on the acceptance of effective controls.

SUGGESTIONS FOR FURTHER READING

The public policies that are inconsistent with antitrust are discussed in Fritz Machlup, *The Political Economy of Monopoly* (Baltimore: Johns Hopkins Press, 1952), chaps. vii–x incl., and in George W. Stocking and Myron W. Watkins, *Monopoly and Free Enterprise* (New York: Twentieth Century Fund, 1951), chaps. xii and xiii. For criticism of labor monopoly, see also Henry C. Simons, "Some Reflections on Syndicalism" in the *Journal of Political Economy* for March, 1944, or in his *Economic Policy for a Free Society* (Chicago: University of Chicago Press, 1948); and Charles E. Lindblom, *Unions and Capitalism* (New Haven: Yale University Press, 1949). On the National Recovery Administration, an excellent short account is given by Merle Fainsod and Lincoln Gordon in chap. xvi of *Government and the American Economy* (New York: W. W. Norton & Co., 1941 and 1948). Fuller statements are contained in the report of the Committee of Industrial Analysis on the NRA, published in 1937 as House Document No. 158 of the 75th Cong., 1st Sess.; and in Leverett S. Lyon and Others, *The National Recovery Administration* (Washington, D.C.: Brookings Institution, 1935). Exceptions to the antitrust laws are discussed in Corwin D. Edwards, *Maintaining Competition* (New York: McGraw-Hill Book Co., 1949), chaps. iii, vi, and vii; and in Vernon A. Mund, *Government and Business* (New York: Harper & Bros., 1950), chaps. xiii and xiv.

Chapter 14 CURBING COMPETITION IN DISTRIBUTION

One of the principal fields in which both state and federal governments have departed from the policy of maintaining competition is that of wholesale and retail distribution. The members of these trades are numerous and, when organized, politically powerful. Every legislator has scores, hundreds, or even thousands of grocers, druggists, and other tradesmen in his district. When any of these groups speaks with a single voice, he listens. And when the voice demands suppression of competition, he is likely to agree that competition should be suppressed. The result is seen in the body of legislation with which this chapter is concerned.

THE COMPETITIVE STRUGGLE

In the absence of public intervention the distributive trades are highly competitive. There is no obstacle to entry to the field. Capital requirements, particularly in retailing, are low. The necessary equipment is inexpensive and may be bought at second hand. Stocks of goods are abundant; sources of supply are numerous and widely scattered; credit is readily available. Labor may be provided by unskilled workers hired at low wages, by the retailer himself, and by members of his family. The processes of distribution are simple. Technical training and managerial experience are not required. New types of distributive agencies are continually springing into life. The field is in a constant state of flux.

In the United States in 1948 there were more than 2,000,000 establishments engaged in distribution, more than 240,000 of them in wholesaling and nearly 1,770,000 in retailing. Among the retail outlets, less than a tenth belonged to chains; more than nine tenths were operated by one-store firms. There were 402,000 food stores, 188,000 filling stations, 56,000 drug stores, and 35,000 hardware stores. In liquor, candy, women's clothing, dry goods, furniture, and household appliances, the outlets numbered around 30,000 each; in men's clothing around 25,000; in jewelry, auto supplies, shoes, and notions around 20,000; in tobacco and flowers around 15,000. There were 2,500 department stores and more than 20,000 general stores.[1] There is competition between stores of the same type and between stores of different types: drug stores compete with hardware stores, hardware stores with auto supply stores, auto supply stores with variety stores, variety stores with candy stores, candy stores with food stores, food stores with tobacco stores, and tobacco stores with drug stores. Wholesale markets, in general, are national or regional; retail markets are local. But even in the latter case the number of competitors usually is large. Hard roads and automobiles, moreover, have brought the local merchant into competition with the door-to-door salesman, the roadside stand, the supermarket, the department store, and the specialty shop. And even in isolated communities he must compete with Sears Roebuck and Montgomery Ward.

Changing Patterns of Distribution

In the nineteenth century the trading post and the peddler gave way to the general store, the general store to the specialized store. The channel of distribution then established ran from the manufacturer through the wholesaler to the retailer and on to the consumer. In the twentieth century, this channel was by-passed with increasing frequency as the manufacturer began to sell directly to the retailer and even to the consumer, until 25–30 per cent of his goods came to be distributed in this way. The principal factor in this development was the growth of the large-scale retailer: the mail order house, the department store, and the chain. Of these the most important was the chain. In 1948 mail order houses handled little more than 1 per cent of retail sales, department stores around 8 per cent, chain stores around 30 per cent. This form of organization grew rapidly during the 1920's, most notably in the grocery business. By 1929 the A&P had 15,418 stores, Kroger had 5,575, and Safeway 2,340.[2] Thereafter the number of their stores declined, A&P being down to 4,600 in 1949. But this development reflected the displacement of smaller stores by larger ones. Supermarkets, introduced during the thirties and expanded during the forties, came to handle more than a third of the grocery business. Many of these establishments were under independent ownership. But the chains held their ground: A&P, Kroger, and Safeway sold 17 per cent of the groceries in 1935 and 18 per cent in 1951.[3]

The mass distributor has made life more difficult for the manufacturer, the wholesaler, and the independent retailer. He has bought directly, eliminating the wholesaler. He has demanded substantial discounts on his purchases, threatening otherwise to enter production in competition with the manufacturer. When making goods for himself and when buying them from others, he has sold them under his private brand. He has re-

[1] *U.S. Census of Business, 1948, Retail Trade.*

[2] Charles F. Phillips and Delbert J. Duncan, *Marketing: Principles and Methods* (2d. ed.; Homewood, Ill.: Richard D. Irwin, Inc., 1952), p. 164.

[3] *Business Week*, June 28, 1952, p. 43.

duced prices at retail by introducing the methods of self-service and cash and carry, and by seeking his profit in a small margin on a large turnover, thus undercutting the independent retailer. Sometimes, to attract customers, he has sold well-known goods at a loss, annoying both their manufacturers and their other distributors.

His suppliers and his rivals have shaped their tactics accordingly. The manufacturer has sought to secure the loyalty of the consumer by spending large sums to advertise his brand. The wholesaler, too, has branded and advertised the goods he handles. And he has attempted to bind his customers to him by organizing voluntary chains. The independent retailer, finally, has formed co-operative buying groups in an effort to claim the discounts obtainable by purchasing in quantity. He has copied the methods of self-service and cash and carry. And he has aligned his fortunes with those of the manufacturer and the wholesaler by pushing the sale of national brands. But neither the wholesaler nor the retailer has been content to rely on methods such as these. Instead, they have turned to the states and to the federal government for help.

The Attack on the Mass Distributor

One of the first steps taken on behalf of the independent merchant was to impose an artificial handicap on the mass distributor by subjecting him to a discriminatory tax. Beginning in the 1920's, laws taxing chain stores were enacted in 29 states. This tax was typically imposed on every store in a chain at a rate which rose with the number of stores maintained within a state, the maximum levy ranging from $100 in Wisconsin to $500 in Idaho and $750 in Texas. In Louisiana, however, the rate rose with the number of stores in a chain, wherever located, reaching a maximum of $550 on each outlet maintained within the state by chains operating more than 500 stores. This was upheld as a valid method of classification by the Supreme Court of the United States[4] and was copied by a number of other states. Bills were introduced in Congress calling for the imposition of federal taxes at higher rates but failed to pass. One of them, sponsored by Representative Wright Patman of Texas, coauthor of the Robinson-Patman Act, would have taxed each store in a chain of more than 500 stores at the rate of $1,000 multiplied by the number of states in which the chain was operating. At the time, this would have imposed on the A&P a levy of $450 million, or roughly half of its gross revenue. The chain store taxes failed to accomplish their purpose. Instead of destroying the chains they made them more efficient, resulting in the elimination of less profitable units and stimulating the development of supermarkets. The taxes were dropped by 15 states, being found unconstitutional by some and repealed by others. By 1953 only 14 such laws remained.

A second approach was to reduce the buying advantages of the mass

[4] *A.&P.* v. *Grosjean*, 301 U.S. 412 (1927).

distributor. This was attempted in the provisions of the NRA codes that denied the wholesaler's discount to retailers and limited quantity discounts and advertising allowances. It was continued in the Robinson-Patman Act in 1936. This law was drafted by the counsel for an association of wholesale grocers. Its effect, as we have seen in Chapter 7, has been to handicap the competitors of the old-line wholesaler, not only the chain store, but also the wholesale co-operatives and other buying agencies that serve the independent retailer. Suppliers are forbidden to pass on to distributors savings that result from the elimination of brokerage services in making a sale. They may not render services to distributors or pay distributors for services rendered them, unless such services or payments are available "on proportionally equal terms" to all. Different prices may be charged for different quantities insofar as they make only due allowance for differences in cost. But the discounts thus obtainable are limited by the methods permitted in the computation of cost. And the Federal Trade Commission may establish limits beyond which differences in price are forbidden even though justified by differences in cost. One of the first orders issued under the Robinson-Patman Act involved the A&P. In this case the Supreme Court upheld the brokerage section of the law and enjoined the A&P from accepting a broker's discount. But the attack on the buying advantages of the chain did not stop here. In 1949 the Department of Justice initiated a civil suit asking that the company be dissolved as an illegal combination under the provisions of the Sherman Act. The issues presented by this suit are considered, in some detail, below.

A third method of protecting the independent merchant has been that of restricting the freedom of the mass distributor to reduce the prices at which he sells. There were provisions in the NRA codes permitting resale price maintenance, forbidding sales below cost, and requiring the addition of a minimum markup. Now, resale price maintenance has been legalized by most states and the federal government, and minimum markup laws enacted by many of the states. The significance of this legislation is to be considered in the last two sections of the present chapter.

THE A&P CASE

The Great Atlantic and Pacific Tea Company was founded in 1859. Ninety years later it was a gigantic holding company with retail subsidiaries operating close to 5,000 stores in more than 3,000 cities in 40 states, with manufacturing subsidiaries producing a minor but substantial share of the goods it sold, and with wholesale subsidiaries making its purchases. Of the latter the most important was the Atlantic Commission Company, a broker dealing in fruits and vegetables not only for A&P but also for other distributors. The company was handling less than 7 per cent of the groceries sold in the United States, but more than half of those sold in a few cities, and more than a third of those sold in a good many others.

It had served as a pioneer in introducing new techniques of distribution, improving sanitation in the sale of foodstuffs, making seasonal foods available throughout the year, local foods available throughout the country, and foods once consumed only by the rich available to all. It had kept its margin low, receiving this commendation in 1946 from Judge Walter Lindley in a federal district court: "To buy, sell, and distribute to a substantial portion of 130 million people one and three-quarters billion dollars worth of food annually at a profit of 1¼ cents on each dollar is an achievement one may well be proud of."[5] In 1949 the company realized a profit of $33.3 millions on sales of $2.9 billions, a margin of 1.1 per cent.[6]

In 1944 the government initiated a criminal suit against the A&P under the Sherman Act. In 1946 the company was found guilty by Judge Lindley and fined $175,000.[7] On appeal the conviction was sustained,[8] and A&P paid its fine, not carrying the case to the Supreme Court. Thereupon, in 1949, the government brought a civil suit, asking that the company be enjoined from illegal practices in buying and selling and that it be dissolved, cutting off its manufacturing activities, abolishing its central purchasing agencies—including ACCO—and splitting its retail operations into seven parts.

Practices in Selling

The government's complaint centered on the sales policies, the buying advantages, and the vertical integration of the A&P. With respect to selling, it charged that the company engaged in temporary, local price cutting, deliberately taking losses to drive out competition in some areas and recouping them by charging higher prices in others. It was said, too, that the company undertook to expand its volume by selling below cost, instead of computing prices by first determining its costs and then adding a margin of profit.

It is true that the prices charged by A&P have varied from store to store. The company admits that, from market to market, it meets the prices charged by its competitors. It may even make deeper cuts in markets where cuts are being made by other stores. As a result its prices will be lower where its competition is tougher. The scope of its operations and the magnitude of its financial resources, moreover, are such as to enable it to carry particular outlets for long periods at a loss. But there is no evidence that the company has increased its share of the market by employing geographic price discrimination to drive out local competitors. And if losses were deliberately incurred in some areas, it would be difficult to find others where they could be recouped. In every market where the A&P operates it has to face competitors.

[5] *U.S.* v. *N.Y. Great A.&P. Tea Co.*, 67 F. Supp. 626.

[6] See feature story in *Time*, November 15, 1950, pp. 89 ff.

[7] *U.S.* v. *N.Y. Great A.&P. Tea Co.*, 67 F. Supp. 626 (1946).

[8] 173 F. 2d 79 (1949).

It is true, too, that the company has reduced its margins and its prices in an effort to increase its sales. And in this it has succeeded. With larger volume, costs have been reduced and aggregate profits have been increased. But such behavior is scarcely to be criticized. Competitive sellers are normally to be expected to expand their sales by taking advantage of elasticity of demand. To insist on cost-plus pricing, as the government appeared to do, is not to promote competition but to stifle it.

"Defendants," said the government in its complaint, "have regularly undersold . . . competing retailers. . . ." And A&P published its reply in full-page advertisements in more than 2,000 daily and weekly newspapers throughout the United States: "To this charge we plead *guilty*. We confess that for the past 90 years we have constantly stepped up the efficiency of our operations in order to give our customers more and more good food for their money." But this exchange was not entirely fair to the government. "Defendants," said the complaint, "by coercing and receiving unlawful buying preferences, have become enabled to and have regularly undersold . . . competing retailers. . . ."[9] The emphasis was on the company's advantages in buying.

Advantages in Buying

The A&P has always sought, in one way or another, to buy at prices lower than those that were paid by its competitors. Before the Robinson-Patman Act was passed, it demanded a broker's discount. When this was outlawed, it asked that the prices it paid be cut by a similar amount. When this was forbidden by the FTC, it announced that it would buy only from suppliers who would sell direct and not through brokers. The company insisted on substantial allowances for advertising the products it handled and on discounts for other services it rendered their producers. Operating its own warehouses, it induced suppliers to add to their charges when making store-door deliveries to its competitors. But whatever the form of these concessions the important thing is that they enabled A&P to obtain its goods at a lower price.

This gave the company an advantage. But was it an unfair advantage? Or did the government seek to subject the company to an unfair handicap? A&P performed a broker's services; it was denied a broker's commission. It provided suppliers with advertising and other services; the allowances it could receive on this account were limited. It bought in quantity; whether its discounts involved discrimination required analyses of its suppliers' costs. But all these matters were fully covered by the Robinson-Patman Act. Why go beyond this to seek the company's dissolution under the Sherman Act?

The government charged that A&P obtained its preferential prices by coercing its suppliers. It was said to do so by threatening to manufacture

[9] Civil Action 52–139, S.D. N.Y., September 15, 1949.

for itself. There is no question that the company's buyers were tough traders. And it is certain that their position was strengthened by the availability of an alternative. But opinions differ as to whether their operations were properly to be described as coercion or merely as successful bargaining. It is interesting, too, to note the identity of those who were said to be coerced. In some cases, they were large and powerful processors. Here, the mass distributor exacted concessions from oligopolists to pass them on, at retail, in a lower price. If this be coercion, consumers would welcome more of it. In other cases, to be sure, the suppliers were small concerns. But, in general, A&P bought no more than a tenth of the foodstuffs sold in national markets and no more than a fifth of those sold in regional markets. If suppliers disliked its offers, they could sell to someone else.

Vertical Integration

The government's final complaint had to do with the vertical integration of A&P. In selling the products of its factories, the company was said to charge higher prices to its competitors than to its own outlets, employing the higher profits made on the former sales to offset the lower profits or losses realized on the latter. Its retail operations were thus held to be subsidized by its gains from manufacturing. It would seem, however, that the company was justified in charging less when distributing goods through its own outlets, since this process entailed none of the costs of soliciting business and transferring ownership. There is doubt, moreover, that its factories really subsidized its stores.

Strictly speaking, the A&P did not "sell" and its stores did not "buy" the goods A&P made itself. The figure that it entered in its books, when making such a transfer, was an accounting fiction, not a market reality. By reducing this figure it could have eliminated the apparent profits of its factories and augmented the profits of its stores. And, as a result, the charge that the former operation was being used to subsidize the latter could no longer have been made. This charge could have been brought, with equal logic, against any integrated firm. For it was the government's contention that the use of profits realized by one subsidiary to offset the losses incurred by another is an abuse inherent in integration. Certainly, such a practice is inherent. But it may be questioned whether it is an abuse.

A similar issue was presented by the activities of the Atlantic Commission Company. But here there were further charges. ACCO served both as a purchasing agent for A&P and as a broker handling shipments made by suppliers to the competitors of A&P. The two functions were said to be inconsistent, and the company's dual position was said to have been abused. As a broker, ACCO should have devoted itself solely to the interests of its clients. But, as a purchasing agent, it sought to get fruit and vegetables of better quality at lower prices for A&P. The company sought also to induce suppliers of produce to sell through it exclusively and to induce jobbers to buy through it exclusively. And insofar as it succeeded, it cut its rivals off from other sources of supply. It was this division of interest and abuse of power that was emphasized by the district court in its decision in the criminal case. But ACCO never came close to obtaining a monopoly. So one might ask, if its customers were really victimized, why they failed to take their business elsewhere. It would appear, if ACCO had not served them, that they would have been no better off.

The Central Issue

The growth of A&P and similar chains has made the grocery business more competitive. It has improved the methods and cut the costs of distribution. It has given the consumer a better product at a lower price. And this is precisely what competition is supposed to do. The chains, moreover, carry no threat of monopoly. Their share of the business is a minor one and it has not increased for many years. New competitors have entered the market, with new methods, and the door stands open to the entry of many more. The purpose of the government's suit, therefore, was not to enforce competition or to prevent monopoly. It was to protect the independent grocer against the competition of the chains. The attack was on the advantages of size. The legal issue was whether these advantages so seriously restricted the competitive opportunities of small merchants as to constitute restraint of trade. The issue of public policy was whether the small competitor should be protected at the risk of impairing the vigor of competition, or competition preserved at the risk of harming the small competitor.

The Consent Decree

The civil suit was settled by a consent decree in January, 1954.[10] The government accepted less than it had asked. The retail chain was not broken up. The manufacturing operations were not cut off. But A&P was enjoined on several points. (1) In selling, the company was forbidden to fix a low markup for particular stores with the purpose of eliminating local competition by having them operate at a loss. Such intent, however, is not to be inferred from the mere fact of operation at a loss. It must be proved if the company is ever to be convicted of violating the decree. And this will not be easy to do. (2) In buying, A&P was forbidden to require its suppliers to stop selling food to its competitors through brokers, to stop offering discounts to these competitors, and to raise the prices charged them. And it was further forbidden to obtain discounts by combining the quantities purchased by 2 or more of the 37 units in which it groups its stores, except in certain cases where savings in costs may be shown. (3) With respect to integration, A&P agreed to dissolve the Atlantic Commission Company. And it was forbidden, thereafter, to buy any food for competitors or to sell any food to competitors, except that processed in its own plants.

[10] *Ibid.*, Consent Decree, January 19, 1954.

The decree, in its detail, subjects A&P to many limitations that do not apply to its competitors. It remains to be seen, however, whether it will constitute a serious handicap. Many observers take the view that the dissolution of ACCO did the company more good than harm. In 1954 for the first time, the total sales of A&P passed the $4 billion mark.

RESALE PRICE MAINTENANCE

Resale price maintenance is an arrangement under which the seller of a product identified by a brand name or trade-mark sets a minimum price below which the buyer may not go in making a subsequent sale. The person who sets the price may be the producer or a distributor of the product in question. The persons whose prices are thus to be controlled are those who sell the product at retail. It is the purpose of the practice to prevent retailers from competing in the prices charged for branded goods.

Freedom to maintain resale prices was first sought by manufacturers. Certain retailers had sold well-known branded goods at low prices as a means of attracting customers. Other dealers, when meeting these prices, obtained small margins on such goods. This threatened to make their distribution unprofitable, and manufacturers feared that dealers might fail to push them or even drop them from their stocks. They therefore sought to insure the loyalty of their distributors by preventing reductions in price.

Before the 1930's, resale price maintenance had repeatedly been condemned by the courts, being held both to violate the Sherman Act and to be an unfair method of competition under the Federal Trade Commission Act. Producers had attempted to obtain legal sanction for the practice by bringing infringement suits against those who undercut the prices printed on their products, charging violation of patents and copyrights, and by entering into contracts with their distributors, but to no avail.[11] There were but two methods of maintaining resale prices that the courts allowed (1) Manufacturers could refuse to sell to price cutters.[12] Indeed, their freedom to do so was guaranteed by Section 2 of the Clayton Act, which gives to "persons engaged in selling goods, wares, or merchandise in commerce the right to select their own customers in *bona fide* transactions and not in restraint of trade." But refusal to sell could not be used to enforce an illegal agreement to maintain a resale price.[13] And it could not be carried to the extent of spying on distributors and threatening to withhold supplies.[14] (2) Producers were permitted to fix the prices at which

[11] See *Bobbs-Merrill Co.* v. *Straus*, 210 U.S. 339 (1908); *Dr. Miles Medical Co.* v. *John D. Park & Sons Co.*, 220 U.S. 373 (1911); *Bauer* v. *O'Donnell*, 229 U.S. 1 (1913); *Straus* v. *Victor Co.*, 243 U.S. 490 (1917).

[12] *U.S.* v. *Colgate & Co.*, 250 U.S. 300 (1919).

[13] *U.S.* v. *A. Schroeder's Son, Inc.*, 252 U.S. 85 (1920).

[14] *Beechnut Packing Co.* v. *F.T.C.*, 247 U.S. 441 (1922).

their products could be sold by agents.[15] But agency could not be used as a mere subterfuge; the permission was limited to cases where an agent did not take title but acted solely on behalf of his principal. The maintenance of resale prices was thus severely circumscribed by law. And the Federal Trade Commission had undertaken to prevent the practice by issuing scores of complaints and orders to cease and desist.

As time went on, manufacturers lost interest in fixing the prices at which their goods could be resold. A substantial portion of their output came to be marketed, at cut prices, by mass distributors. And these concerns possessed the alternative—if prices were set too high—of entering into competition by producing under private brands. It was therefore desirable for the manufacturer to retain the favor of the price cutter as well as that of the dealer who wanted prices maintained. So he retreated into neutrality, abandoning his efforts to change the law.

The initiative was now taken by trade associations representing the interests of independent retailers, with the National Association of Retail Druggists in the lead. Until 1931 repeated attempts to get bills permitting resale price maintenance through Congress had ended in failure, and the practice had been approved by New Jersey but by no other state. Then the retailers' associations started moving on the legislatures. And within a few years price maintenance had been legalized by nearly all of them, under the euphemism of "fair trade."

State Fair Trade Laws

The first of the new laws was enacted in California in 1931. It exempted from the state's antitrust act any contract wherein the seller of a branded product bound the buyer, when reselling it, to charge the price the former specified. The law proved ineffective because retailers who did not sign contracts undercut the prices charged by those who did. An amendment was therefore adopted in 1933, incorporating a provision known as the non-signer's clause: "Wilfully and knowingly advertising, offering for sale, or selling any commodity at less than the price stipulated in any contract entered into pursuant to . . . the Act, whether the person so advertising, offering for sale or selling is or is not a party to such a contract, is unfair competition and is actionable at the suit of any person damaged thereby."[16] Contracts maintaining resale prices were thus made binding, not only on retailers who had signed them, but also on those who had refused to do so. The terms of a contract accepted by a single dealer might thereby be made to govern the prices charged by every dealer in the state.

The California law, including the non-signer's clause, was shortly copied by other states. The validity of such enactments was upheld by the

[15] *U.S.* v. *General Electric Co.*, 272 U.S. 476 (1926).

[16] *California Statutes*, 1933, chap. 250.

Supreme Court of the United States, in 1936, in the case of *Old Dearborn Distributing Co.* v. *Seagram Distillers Corp.*[17] The manufacturer, said Justice Sutherland, had made a substantial investment in advertising his brand. The good will thus acquired was a species of property that belonged to him. When he made a sale, he parted with his product, but not with his good will. When distributors cut his prices, they impaired his good will and thus inflicted damage on his property. Prevention of such damage was a proper subject for legislation. And then came this clincher: "There is nothing in the Act to preclude the purchaser from removing the mark or brand from the commodity—thus separating the physical property, which he owns, from the good will, which is the property of another—and then selling the commodity at his own price, provided he can do so without utilizing the good will of the latter as an aid to that end."[18] The laws that had been enacted at the behest of retailers were thus justified in terms of the rights of manufacturers. The decision stimulated the spread of retail price fixing. By 1941 all the states but Missouri, Texas, and Vermont—a fourth exception being the District of Columbia—had fair trade laws.

More than half of these laws followed the California act, most of the others being based on a model statute drafted by the National Association of Retail Druggists. Under both drafts, a first seller not only may bind a second one but may also require him to bind a third. According to the California pattern, prices may be fixed by the producers of branded products or, failing this, by their wholesale distributors. The N.A.R.D. model confines this power to the owner of a trade-mark and to distributors to whom he delegates authority. This draft permits producers to bind themselves to refuse to sell, both to price cutters and to those who buy from them. It also copies Justice Sutherland, explicitly permitting distributors to undercut established prices if identifying brands have been removed.

The laws place no limit on the level at which a seller may set a resale price. They make no reference to the costs of distribution or to the reasonableness of the margins that may be allowed. The contracts they authorize, however, are confined to those involving vertical agreements among manufacturers, wholesalers, and retailers. Horizontal agreements among producers or among distributors are usually forbidden. A product, to be covered, must be "in free and open competition" with similar goods produced by other firms.

Exceptions to price-fixing requirements are typically made to permit reductions when selling damaged goods, closing out a line, liquidating a business, or making a sale under the order of a court. Enforcement is not by public officials. The laws are not criminal statutes. In general, they carry no penalties. What they do is merely to exempt resale price main-

[17] 299 U.S. 183.

[18] 299 U.S. 183, 195.

tenance contracts from state antitrust laws, giving persons injured by violations of such contracts the right to bring suit for injunctions and damages. Adherence to fixed prices, therefore, is privately policed.

Fair Trade in Operation

The statutes legalizing resale price maintenance were whipped through the legislatures at breakneck speed. There is no record of hearings having been held in forty states. There is no transcript of hearings available in any state. The California law was supposed to contain a provision authorizing a producer to require "any dealer" to maintain a stipulated price. The text enacted, however, was garbled. Instead of "any dealer," it read "in delivery," so that the authorization made no sense. The care with which the laws were considered is indicated by the fact that this version was passed by the House and the Senate and signed by the governor, not only in California, but also in Arizona, Iowa, Louisiana, New Jersey, New York, Pennsylvania, and Tennessee. The N.A.R.D. held the hoop and cracked the whip. The legislators and the executives obediently jumped.

High-pressure tactics were used, too, in persuading reluctant manufacturers to enter into contracts, at prices providing margins that distributors desired. Committees of distributors visited the manufacturers, reviewed the contracts they proposed to issue, and discussed the adequacy of the margins they allowed. In the drug trade the goal was a margin of 33⅓ per cent, i.e., a markup of 50 per cent. Manufacturers, in turn, received assurance that the prices being set by their competitors were equal to their own. Nominally they did not join in horizontal agreements. The effect, however, was the same. There were rewards for those who co-operated and penalties for those who did not. Retailers' associations circulated white lists of manufacturers who signed contracts, advising dealers to push their goods, giving them window and counter displays, special advertising, and extra sales effort. They issued black lists of those who failed to sign, the black lists carrying with them the threat of boycotts. When the makers of Pepsodent refused to enter contracts, "Pepsodent went under the counter in practically every California drug store . . . and . . . clear across the country. . . . Rapidly, other brands . . . forged ahead. . . . Result: a few months later, Pepsodent returned to the fold. . . ."[19]

There was similar co-operation in enforcement. Fair trade committees, set up by the druggists, distributed lists of contract prices, sought to persuade individual druggists to abide by them, policed the trade to discover price cutters, and turned them over to manufacturers for prosecution. In Connecticut, the committee agreed "to police all contracts . . . through the service of a well-organized group of 65 investigation and enforcement

[19] *Business Week*, August 28, 1937, pp. 37, 44.

captains, located in strategic points throughout the state, under a full-time director of enforcement. . . ." Under this arrangement, when price cutting was reported to a captain, "he first contacts the dealer complained of in an effort to have him increase his price. If this procedure fails . . . the director of enforcement . . . authorizes the captain to make several purchases from the dealer . . . in the presence of a witness. Affidavits as to the purchases are then made and sent to the manufacturer involved, whose problem it then becomes to have the dealer increase his price." This system worked so well, according to the secretary of the committee, that "it has not been necessary to warn any dealer a second time."[20]

The Miller-Tydings Act

The fair trade laws permitted resale price maintenance when both of the parties to a contract were in the same state. But such contracts were held to violate the federal antitrust laws when the parties were in different states. And the great bulk of branded goods sold at retail had moved across state lines. If resale prices were to be maintained it was necessary to amend the federal laws. This was accomplished in 1937 by attaching a rider to the District of Columbia Appropriations Act, which was passed just before the Congress adjourned. President Roosevelt was thus forced either to accept the rider or to deprive the District government of the revenues required to finance its activities. He therefore recorded his objection to the substance of the measure and to the manner of its enactment but signed it into law.

Such was the origin of the Miller-Tydings Amendment to the Sherman Act. The amendment exempted from the federal antitrust laws interstate contracts fixing resale prices within those states where intrastate contracts had been legalized. As a result, the Federal Trade Commission and the Department of Justice could still prosecute persons attempting to maintain resale prices in three states and the District of Columbia, but not in the other 45 states. The law applied only to products "in free and open competition" with others of the same type, and forbade agreements between manufacturers, between wholesalers, or between retailers.

The validity of this amendment was not successfully called into question until 1951. In that year, the Supreme Court handed down its decision in the cases of *Schwegmann Bros.* v. *Calvert Corp.* and *Schwegmann Bros.* v. *Seagram Distillers Corp.*[21] Schwegmann operated a supermarket in New Orleans. The state of Louisiana had a fair trade law, including a non-signer's clause. Calvert and Seagram made contracts with other retailers of whisky in the state, fixing the price of fifths at $4.24. Schwegmann refused to sign and sold them at $3.35. Calvert and Seagram sued and Schwegmann appealed. The Court held that the Miller-Tydings Act ap-

[20] Federal Trade Commission, *Resale Price Maintenance* (Washington: Government Printing Office, 1945), p. 244.

[21] 341 U.S. 384.

plied only to those distributors who had accepted interstate contracts. The Act contained no reference to the non-signer's clauses in the state laws, and therefore did not permit control of the prices at which non-signers resold goods brought in from other states. In the words of Justice Douglas, "Contracts or agreements convey the idea of a cooperative arrangement, not a program whereby recalcitrants are dragged in by the heels and compelled to submit to price fixing." Such a program, he said, "is not price fixing by contract or agreement; that is price fixing by compulsion; that is not following the path of consensual agreement; that is resort to coercion."

The Schwegmann decision knocked the prop from under the structure of fair trade. Within a week R. H. Macy & Co. of New York announced reductions in the prices of some 6,000 branded goods. Gimbel Brothers met the cuts. Macy's went lower, and other stores joined in. A major price war was under way. In one day prices were cut as much as 30 per cent. Palm Beach suits went from $29.95 to $16.87, Underwood typewriters from $92.50 to $65.99, Waterman fountain pens from $3.95 to $1.59, and Bayer aspirin from 59 cents to 4 cents. Such prices produced a buying wave that rivaled the Christmas rush. Battalions of police were assigned to keep the crowds of shoppers in control. The contagion spread to Detroit, Denver, New Orleans, and 40 other cities. No cuts were reported, however, in 80, including Boston, Philadelphia, Cleveland, Chicago, and Los Angeles.[22] The warfare came to an end, within 6 weeks, when stocks had been exhausted and manufacturers refused to replenish them. Some cynics took the view that merchants had employed price cuts as a method of advertising and had welcomed them as a means of disposing of swollen inventories. In any case they had proved to be costly. Prices soon moved back toward their earlier levels. And Macy's announced a change in its traditional policy of undercutting other stores by 6 per cent: "We endeavor, with reasonable exceptions which include goods price-controlled by the manufacturer, to save our customers at least six percent for cash."

The price war afforded the proponents of fair trade a dramatic illustration of the need for Congressional action to undo the damage that the court had done. Bills were introduced with the potent backing of the American Fair Trade Council, representing the manufacturers of branded goods, and the Bureau of Education on Fair Trade, organized by the druggists to represent their interests and those of other associations of distributors. The enactment of these bills was opposed at public hearings by Schwegmann and Macy, by the Department of Justice and the American Bar Association, by organizations of labor and agriculture, and by many other groups. But the druggists had not forgotten how to get results. Congress was overwhelmed with letters, telegrams, phone calls, and delegations of visitors. The McGuire-Keogh Fair Trade Enabling Act passed

[22] Survey by Dun & Bradstreet, reported in *Congressional Record*, July 1, 1952, pp. 8937–39.

the House by a vote of 196 to 10 and the Senate by a vote of 64 to 16. It was signed by President Truman on July 14, 1952.[23]

The McGuire-Keogh Act

The new law is an amendment to Section 5 of the Federal Trade Commission Act. Like the Miller-Tydings Act, it exempts from all the antitrust laws interstate contracts fixing resale prices within the states where intrastate contracts are allowed, confines this exemption to products "in free and open competition," and forbids agreements between competitors. But it goes beyond this to permit the enforcement of interstate contracts against all of the dealers in a state when such contracts have been signed by any one of them. In short, it reverses the Schwegmann decision by extending the federal exemption to cover the non-signer's clause.

After this law was enacted, Eli Lilly & Co. fixed a resale price of $2.83 on a bottle of insulin. Schwegmann sold it for $2.08. Lilly sued, under the Louisiana law, and was granted an injunction by the state court. Schwegmann appealed to the federal courts, contending that the non-signers provisions in the state and federal laws were unconstitutional. He lost his case in the Court of Appeals[24] and carried it to the Supreme Court of the United States. In October, 1953, this body refused him a hearing.[25] A year later, in October, 1954, the Court refused to review the decisions of lower courts upholding the New York, New Jersey, and federal laws in cases appealed by Sam Goody, a dealer in phonograph records, and S. Klein, a department store operator in New York and Newark.[26] Fair traders were jubilant, as is indicated by the advertisement that is reproduced on the following page. Refusal to review, however, does not affirm the validity of a decision of a lower court. But it does permit it to stand.

This is not the end. Further litigation is exploring the limits of the laws and questioning their validity. A loophole was opened in the Wentling case,[27] where it was held that a mail-order house in Philadelphia, while bound by contracts signed by retailers in Pennsylvania, could not be forced to sell at prices set in contracts with those in other states, since the laws of those states did not apply outside their borders. Sales by mail across state lines are thus beyond the reach of the non-signers clause, and mail-order houses set up in the District of Columbia or in states without fair trade laws are apparently free of resale price controls. The laws of several states have been sustained, but those of Arkansas, Georgia, Florida, Michigan, and Nebraska were found to be unconstitutional by the supreme courts of those states and that of Utah by a lower court in that state during 1953, 1954, and the early months of 1955. A petition by an

[23] For the President's statement on signing the bill, see *New York Times,* July 15, 1952.

[24] *Schwegmann* v. *Eli Lilly & Co.*, 205 F. 2d 788 (1953).

[25] 346 U.S. 856.

[26] *New York Times,* October 26, 1954.

[27] *Sunbeam Corp.* v. *Wentling,* 185 F. 2d 903 (1950).

Thanks to 9 wise men...

the law of the jungle can no longer decide the price of what you buy!

Never forget October 19th.

You won a great victory that day.

The United States Supreme Court rejected a suit that would destroy fair dealing. Nine men of wisdom made the living profit, like the living wage, the law of the land.

Thanks to these men of justice, Fair Trade is on the books—to stay. It will serve us all, protect us all against the slashing tactics of those for whom a hunger for sales is justification for ruthlessness.

The man who makes the goods you buy need never again fear that his product will be cheapened against his will. The value he takes pains to create cannot be destroyed.

You will always be able to recognize the good product from the inferior. Too often in the past, an "amazing saving" masked poor quality to make the so-called saving possible.

The retailer you trust and the wholesaler who serves him can be sure of the profit that promises more than mere survival. Unprotected by Fair Trade, many small business men had been cut so perilously close to "break-even" by jungle-pricing that one slump could destroy them.

When profits make sense, they make wage raises possible and jobs more secure. For sane profits build sound business, and this is the basis of growth.

For these reasons, and more, men of foresight are celebrating October 19th and America's good fortune that men of such wisdom sit on our highest tribunal. For us at Doeskin Products, this decision has a special significance. We have held steadfastly to the principle of Fair Trade in the face of the most aggressive price competition.

We are fortunate that our products had the quality to sustain your support. But we have kept apart from jungle tactics because we believe that a distribution system based on a fair profit is the only way to keep America sound.

It assures the worker his job and his future. It gives the consumer faith instead of doubt.

It keeps America in business.

DOESKIN PRODUCTS, INC.

MAKERS OF DOESKIN FACIAL TISSUES • BATHROOM TISSUES AND PAPER NAPKINS

11 West 42nd Street, New York 36, N. Y.

association of retail jewelers requesting the Federal Trade Commission to take action to compel price-cutting discount houses to comply with the requirements of the fair trade laws was rejected by the Commission in 1955 on the ground that such action would be inconsistent with the spirit and purpose of antitrust.[28]

There is continuing action, too, on the legislative front. Efforts will be made to close the Wentling loophole, to bring fair trade to the states that do not have it, and to tighten the laws of those that do. In Georgia a second law was passed and found unconstitutional. But in Michigan, in

[28] See *Business Week*, February 19, 1955.

1953, a fair trade bill was defeated by the legislature. And in Vermont, the Senate rejected such a bill by a vote of 21 to 8. The Bureau of Education on Fair Trade still has its work cut out for it.

The Case Pro

The case for resale price maintenance is based upon a criticism of the loss leader. A leader is a well-known product with a well-known price that is sold below this price for the purpose of attracting customers. A loss leader, properly speaking, would be a leader that was sold at a loss. But it is seldom clear, when the term is used, whether it is taken to mean that a product is being sold at less than the markup customary in the trade, at less than the seller's markup on other goods, at less than invoice cost plus distribution cost, or simply at less than invoice cost. In the first two cases, there would seem to be no ground for criticism, since there is no reason why all dealers should use the same markup or why any dealer should apply the same markup to all his goods. If loss means sale at less than invoice cost plus distribution cost, the term is robbed of precision by the uncertain judgments involved in computing distribution cost. If loss means sale below invoice cost, however, the meaning is precise. But is such a practice to be condemned? Loss-leader selling is simply an alternative method of sales promotion. A dealer, seeking to increase his sales, might spend his promotional money either on advertising or on selling something for less than it cost. In the first case the consumer would get a picture on a billboard; in the second, a product at a lower price. Why should the one be permitted and the other prohibited?

First, say the advocates of fair trade, because the loss leader harms the consumer. When an article is sold by other dealers for $3.50 and by Macy, say, for $1.79, the consumer gets the false impression that comparable savings are to be obtained on everything in Macy's store. So, along with the leader, he is induced to buy a lot of other goods on which he does not save a cent. Price cutting, moreover, is inconvenient, since it forces the customer to higgle over his purchases. The maintained price, on the other hand, protects the consumer by preventing deception. And it saves his time by obviating the necessity of higgling. It may be doubted, however, that the consumer is deceived as often by actual bargains as he is by advertising. And this is an activity that the fair traders, for all their zeal in fighting misrepresentation, do not propose to touch. Loss-leader prices, moreover, are stated and adhered to by the seller, leaving no room for bargaining. And the convenience of maintained prices, in general, may well be offset by their height.

Second, it is said, loss-leader selling is harmful to the manufacturer. The case usually cited is that of the Ingersoll watch, "the watch that made the dollar famous."

> Some retailers throughout the country decided to use the Ingersoll watch as a loss leader. They began to sell it for less than a dollar. The price went down and down as competition increased, until it was finally selling for 57

cents, far below the wholesale price. The retailers who were selling it at that price were making up their losses on sales of other merchandise in their large stores. . . . Small business retailers were forced to drop the Ingersoll dollar watch. They could not sell it if they charged more than 57 cents, and they could not afford to sell the watch at that price and take the loss involved in each sale. The result was that the manufacturer lost his market and was forced out of business.[29]

The watch, presumably, had lost its usefulness as a leader for the larger stores. And, since consumers had been led to value it at 57 cents, it could never again be sold for a dollar. The end of Ingersoll occurred some time before World War I. But the case, according to fair traders, is not unique. Indeed, they say, "the annals of American manufacturing are replete with examples of products which have been price-slashed out of existence."[30] The Federal Trade Commission however, has professed its inability to identify such products. And further doubt is cast upon the statement by the curious apathy of the manufacturer. For the manufacturer, with his very survival at stake, is content to leave it to the retailer to bear the brunt of the battle for fair trade.

The loss leader, finally, is said to be harmful to the retailer. Price cutters feature different articles, each of them shifting from one to another. Small dealers are forced to meet their prices on line after line. And, in doing so, they are driven inexorably toward bankruptcy. Price maintenance, runs the argument, is needed to keep the little merchant alive. And, in fact, there may be instances where this is true. If the book department at Macy's, for instance, were to cut its prices on best sellers, the small book dealer might find it difficult to survive. But there is no evidence that substantial numbers of merchants have been put out of business by loss-leader competition alone. And it is significant that small stores are to be found in the District of Columbia and in Missouri, Texas, and Vermont.

It should be noted, finally, that resale price maintenance goes far beyond the prevention of selling at a loss. This purpose could be accomplished by forbidding sales below invoice cost or by requiring a minimum markup to cover distribution cost. But the fair trade laws permit the establishment of a uniform markup bearing no relation to cost. They seek to eliminate all possibility of competition at the retail level by enforcing a minimum price.

The Case Con

Resale price maintenance is to be criticized, first, because it facilitates price fixing agreements among manufacturers. The legal provisions re-

[29] Senate Small Business Committee, quoted in *Congressional Record,* July 1, 1952, pp. 8935–36.

[30] Committee on Small Business, House of Representatives, *Fair Trade: the Problem and the Issues* (82d Cong., 2d Sess., House Report No. 1292, 1952), p. 38.

quiring that products be "in free and open competition" and forbidding horizontal understandings are really without effect. Each maker of competitive products may sign a different contract with a different distributor. But none of them will do so until the distributors assure him that the price he sets is the same as that established by his rivals. Manufacturers need not conspire with one another. But the result is as it would be if they did.

Second, fair trade suppresses competition in retailing. It denies the consumer the lower prices made possible by greater efficiency, by larger volume, by simpler service, by cheaper equipment and lower rents. It compels the low-cost seller to charge as much as the high-cost one, the high-turnover seller as much as the one whose turnover is low, the cash-and-carry store as much as one providing credit and delivery, the store in a slum as much as the shop on Park Avenue. And this is accomplished, under the aegis of the law, without giving the appearance of conspiracy.

Third, the system tends to freeze the channels of distribution, retarding the advancement of technology. To preserve the independent merchant, it deprives the mass distributor of his principal appeal. By preventing tough competition in price, it makes for soft competition in the form of advertising and salesmanship, costly facilities, and nonessential services. "The crux of the problem of resale price maintenance," concluded a committee set up to study the problem in Canada, "is whether the consumer should reap the benefits of the most efficient forms of retailing or . . . should be forced to pay more in order to make retailing . . . a more comfortable occupation. . . ."[31]

Consequences of Fair Trade

When the fair trade laws were enacted, the average level of retail drug prices rose. But manufacturers, in general, did not adopt their nominal resale prices as those to be legally maintained. Instead, they sought to fix on figures high enough to satisfy the independent retailers and low enough to hold the business of the mass distributors, tending to set them between the highest and the lowest previously charged. The legal minima then became the actual prices in both types of outlets. And, as a result, prices rose in downtown department stores, cut-rate stores, and chains, but fell in smaller independent outlets in outlying neighborhoods and in small towns. The increases, however, outweighed the declines, and the general level rose.

Characteristically, for drugs and liquors, prices in markets where they are fixed are higher than those in markets where they are free. Among 117 drug items checked in 1948, in Maryland and the District of Columbia, 29 cost a seventh less, 38 cost a quarter less, and 35 cost a third less in the District. The average cost of 54 drug items was 16.2 per cent less in St.

[31] *Resale Price Maintenance, An Interim Report of the Committee to Study Combines Legislation* (Ottawa, 1951), p. 16.

Louis, Missouri than in East St. Louis, Illinois.[32] In 1952 a fifth of Schenley whisky sold at $4.32 in Maryland and Virginia and at $3.23 in Washington, D.C., and Gillette razor blades sold at 98 cents and 87 cents, Bayer aspirin at 59 cents and 46 cents, Ipana toothpaste at 47 cents and 37 cents, Phillips milk of magnesia at 39 cents and 34 cents, and Ex-Lax at 28 cents and 19 cents, respectively.[33] Drugs sold for 12 per cent less and liquor for 16 per cent less in St. Louis than in East St. Louis.[34] And the average price for 208 different items was 17 per cent lower in the four price-free jurisdictions than in the 45 where prices were maintained.[35]

It may be questioned whether price maintenance has really aided the independent retailer. Margins may be raised. But higher prices, by cutting the volume of sales and by increasing the costs of selling, may limit total profits. Price competition, suppressed on certain goods, may merely shift to others whose prices cannot be controlled. Private brands, at low prices, may be offered by mass distributors, and the independent, bound by his contracts, may find himself unable to compete. High margins, moreover, may attract newcomers to a trade. Gross profit margins on food items run around 18 per cent, those on drug and toilet items around 30 per cent. As a result, the number of food stores carrying drugs and toiletries rose from 37 per cent to 85 per cent of all such stores in the 10 years ending in 1952.[36] Drug and toilet items have been added, too, by other types of retailers. So the druggists' volume must be shared with growing numbers of competitors. Resale price maintenance alone, it seems, will not suffice. In England after this system was adopted, the numbers of merchants selling proprietary medicines increased so rapidly that the chemists requested their makers to restrict their distribution to members of the chemist's trade. In the United States the N.A.R.D. may well come to demand, in time, that the sale of all drugs and toiletries be confined by law to registered pharmacists.

For the manufacturer the gains from fair trade are even more dubious. If he resists the pressure of the retailers' association and refuses to maintain resale prices, he may be excluded from independent outlets. If he yields and enters into contracts, he will be under further pressure to increase the independent's margin by setting his prices high. If he sets them too high, he may cut his volume. And he may provoke increasing competition from private brands. While insuring the loyalty of the independent, he may lose his outlet through the mass distributor.

Scope and Enforceability

Resale price maintenance can do neither as much good nor as much harm as the arguments for and against it would suggest. There are limits

[32] *Fortune*, January 1949, p. 70.

[33] *Congressional Record*, May 7, 1952, p. 4986.

[34] *Ibid.*, July 1, 1952, p. 8914.

[35] *Ibid.*, p. 8912.

[36] *Business Week*, February 16, 1952, pp. 158 ff.

to its applicability. And, even where it is applicable, there are difficulties in its enforcement.

Resale prices can be maintained only in the case of goods that are standardized, branded, and easily identifiable, that are widely used and frequently purchased, and whose cost to the consumer is neither insignificant nor very large. They cannot readily be maintained where the cost of raw materials is a major part of total costs and where this cost is subject to substantial and repeated fluctuations. Price maintenance, thus, appears to be inapplicable to clothing, furniture, hardware, jewelry, and notions, and to such foodstuffs as meat, flour, sugar, and canned fruits and vegetables. It has been used, mainly, in the cases of drugs, cosmetics, liquor, tobacco, and books, together with such other products as electrical appliances, auto accessories, photographic equipment, phonograph records, and sporting goods. And these do not add up to more than 10 per cent, by value, of the products sold at retail in the United States.

Maintained prices can be evaded in many different ways. Goods may be offered, under the permitted exceptions, as having been damaged, or as belonging to lines that are being dropped. Price cutters may offer premiums, coupons, gifts, bonuses, bargain combinations, and special deals. Prices on costly appliances such as refrigerators and television sets are particularly difficult to enforce. Prices may be cut, in effect, by making liberal trade-in allowances: the purchaser of a vacuum cleaner may be allowed $20 for his old broom. Retailers regularly give discounts on expensive items to employees, friends, and steady customers. Manufacturers and jobbers make sales at retail, charging less than the retail price. Discount houses, operating openly in major cities, offer electrical appliances, household equipment, and other price-maintained goods at 10–20 per cent below the standard price. It was estimated in 1954 that such outlets, with an annual volume of $25 billion, were making 18 per cent of the retail sales in the United States.[37] In such a situation, it may be questioned how much of an effort the manufacturer is likely to make to enforce the prices he may fix. One manufacturer is reported to have invested in enforcement activities as much as $1 million a year. But even this may not suffice. In 1948 the General Electric Company hired detectives to purchase its products from discount houses in New York, brought suits, and obtained injunctions. But the houses continued to operate. Such concerns must be on guard against making sales to spotters, must expect to be taken to court, and must be prepared to pay an occasional fine. But with substantial profits obtainable when sales are made at a markup of 33 per cent instead of 66 per cent, this may be treated as a minor cost. Most manufacturers will continue to supply them; they buy in quantity and pay cash.[38]

[37] Estimate by United States Chamber of Commerce, *New York Times*, November 5, 1954.

[38] Edward M. Brecher, "Discount Houses," *Consumers' Union Reports*, Vol. XIV (1949), pp. 343 ff., 420 ff., 469 ff.; Ralph S. Alexander and Richard M. Hill, "What to Do about the Discount House," *Harvard Business Review*, Vol. XXXIII (1955), pp. 53–65.

MINIMUM MARKUP LAWS

There are several lines, as has been seen, where retailers get little or no protection from the fair trade laws. This is true, in particular, of groceries. The costs of many foodstuffs are subject to fluctuations that make it difficult to maintain a set price. The outlets offered by chain stores and supermarkets are highly attractive to manufacturers. And these distributors can push their private brands. As a result, grocers have found it difficult to obtain price maintenance contracts. They have therefore sought legal protection against the price cutter in another way. The product of their efforts is to be found in the provisions of a number of state laws known as Unfair Practices Acts, Unfair Sales Acts, Fair Sales Acts, and the like. Some of these laws are broader in scope than others. But all of them require the retailer to add a minimum markup to the invoice or replacement cost of the goods he sells.

Such laws had been enacted by 31 states, beginning with an amendment to California's Unfair Practices Act in 1935, and they were still in effect in 28 states in 1948. Some of them had copied the California act; others, a draft prepared by a wholesale grocers' association. In purpose, these statutes are like the fair trade laws. In method, they differ in several respects. They apply to all goods sold by the trades they cover, not merely to branded products that compete with others of their kind. They are mandatory rather than permissive. They require no initiative of producers, involve no contracts, and control the dealers covered without asking their consent.

Statutory Provisions

These laws, in general, forbid a dealer to make a sale for less than his invoice or replacement cost, whichever is lower, plus a markup designed to cover his operating costs. Some of them specify that an arbitrary figure, such as 6 per cent, shall be added. Others require the addition of a figure to cover the "cost of doing business" and define this cost, as in the California law, to include "the following items of expense: labor (including salaries of executives and officers), rent, interest on borrowed capital, depreciation, selling cost, maintenance of equipment, delivery costs, credit losses, all types of licenses, taxes, insurance, and advertising"; they provide for the computation of such cost through the medium of cost surveys to be made by associations of retailers. In either case the sum that results must be accepted by the courts as affording presumptive evidence of a seller's costs. And one who is prosecuted must bear the burden of proving that his costs, in fact, are not so high.

The prohibition of sales below cost is limited to those made with the intent of destroying competition or injuring a competitor. But the force of this limitation is weakened, in some of the laws, by making the fact of such sales presumptive evidence of intent. Exemptions are provided for seasonal and perishable commodities, for damaged or deteriorated goods, for closing-out or liquidation sales, and for sales made by order of a court. An exception is also made for sales below cost "in good faith" to meet the lower, lawful price of a competitor. But here, the seller may be required to prove that the price he met was not itself in violation of the law.

The statutes are enforced, not only by private suits for injunctions or damages, but also, at the request of a retailer or a trade association, by criminal prosecution at public expense. Violation is usually made a misdemeanor, punishable by fine or imprisonment or both. The states, with minor exceptions, have established no special agencies of enforcement. Administration has been left almost entirely in the hands of private groups.

Trade Association Law Making

The laws are usually explicit in enumerating the items that must be included in computing costs. But they provide no standards to govern the competence or the fairness of the groups that make the computations. In Montana and Utah state trade commissions conduct the cost surveys. But in other states such surveys are made by retail trade associations. A method commonly employed is that of mailing return postcards asking retailers their cost of doing business and fixing a figure on the basis of the cards returned, or that of holding a meeting where markups are discussed and a figure selected by agreement as representative of costs. In southern California the Food and Grocery Bureau sent questionnaires to 4,000 retail grocers in 1936, received replies from 200, and used this random sample as its basis in fixing a markup of 6 per cent, raising the figure on the basis of a similar survey in 1939 to 8 per cent.[39] In San Francisco the Retail Grocers Association, using postcard questionnaires, adopted a markup of 6 per cent in 1937, raised it to 8 per cent in 1938, and to 10 per cent in 1939.[40] In 1940, at a meeting of grocers in western Washington, "after some discussion, it was agreed to set the minimum mark-up at ten percent instead of the six percent we had been working on up to that time."[41] And at a meeting of the Colorado Food Distributors Association, the president asked association members to raise their hands if their costs were less than 12 per cent. No hands went up. The minimum markup was fixed at 12 per cent.[42]

Enforcement of markups as well as their computation is left, in the main, to the trade associations. These bodies assess their members to obtain funds for police work. They watch advertisements, employ shoppers, and call on price cutters to persuade them of the error of their ways. If violations are repeated, they ask the district attorney to prosecute. With

[39] Federal Trade Commission, *op. cit.*, pp. 858–59.

[40] *Ibid.*, pp. 854–55.

[41] *Northwestern Merchant,* April, 1940, quoted in Vernon A. Mund, *Government and Business* (New York: Harper & Bros., 1950), p. 457.

[42] *Business Week,* December 28, 1940, p. 18.

the burden of proof weighing heavily on the defendant, this usually suffices to bring him into line. If not, he may face the ultimate penalties of fine and imprisonment.

The activities of trade groups under these statutes have brought them into conflict with the federal antitrust laws. The Federal Trade Commission has issued orders and the Antitrust Division has initiated suits against collusion in fixing markups and coercion in enforcing them. And their efforts have been upheld, almost invariably, by the courts. But the decisions have been confined to particular offenses. The cases have not been so presented as to require the courts to pass on the validity of the laws themselves. Where the states have specified a markup, the laws might be found valid. But where they have delegated this authority to trade associations, they might be held to be without effect. In interstate commerce federal authority is supreme. The antitrust laws, unless amended, should thus take precedence over inconsistent legislation by the states.

Fair Trade and Unfair Sales

Some of the criticisms of the fair trade laws apply with equal logic to the minimum markup laws. Both involve collusion to coerce competitors. Both raise prices, shelter inefficiency, and obstruct progress. Both are difficult to enforce. Insofar as they succeed, both tend to defeat themselves by evoking added competition. Unlike the fair trade laws, however, the minimum markup laws relate the prices they fix to some standard of costs. In doing so, they raise all of the theoretical and practical difficulties of cost protection that were discussed in Chapter 13. But it must be noted that the markups actually established under these laws have not been high. With druggists asking markups of 50 per cent, under fair trade laws, and with grocers making average markups of 18 per cent, the mandatory figures of 6, 8, 10, and 12 per cent set under the markup laws seem moderate indeed. At this level the laws leave ample room for competition in price. They prevent extremes in price cutting, but little more. If loss-leader selling is to be forbidden, minimum markups (set by statute rather than by trade associations) would be far less objectionable than the contracts that are written in the name of fair trade.

THE PRESERVATION OF COMPETITORS

In the field of distribution, the threat of monopoly comes, not from big business, but from little business. It is the large concern that has been the tough competitor. It is the small merchant, combining with others in groups to exert political pressure, who has sought to make sure that competition will be soft. It is at his behest that legislatures have harnessed competition, so that life may be easier for the small competitor. Quite clearly, the policy is self-defeating. New forms of competition are discovered and new competitors arise. But whether the policy succeeds or fails, a question remains: can it be justified?

Certainly, there is inequality in competition between the large, diversified distributor and the small, specialized one. The large concern has greater bargaining power than the small one and thus can purchase at a lower price. The diversified concern, by drawing on other resources, can sustain losses where its specialized competitor would be destroyed. The gains of size and diversity are shared with the consumer, bringing him more goods for less money, as competition is supposed to do. But if the small and specialized distributor cannot survive the struggle, there may be other values that are lost. It is possible that smallness and independence, though inefficient and costly, should be preserved for their own sake. Perhaps the little merchant in the village should be protected from the chain so that he may fulfill the responsibilities of civic leadership. Perhaps the little bookstore should be defended against the book department at Macy's so that it may serve as an educational agency. But if this is to be the policy, it should not be permitted to masquerade under the name of competition. It should be adopted in full awareness of the price that the consumer will be forced to pay.

SUGGESTIONS FOR FURTHER READING

The competitive struggle in the distribution trades is well outlined by Nathaneal H. Engle in *Problems of Small Businesses*, T.N.E.C. Monograph No. 17 (Washington: Government Printing Office, 1941), chap. xvi; and by A. D. H. Kaplan in his *Small Business: Its Place and Problems* (New York: McGraw-Hill Book Co., 1948), chap. viii. For a fuller discussion, see Charles F. Phillips and Delbert J. Duncan, *Marketing: Principles and Methods* (2d ed.; Homewood, Ill.: Richard D. Irwin, Inc., 1952). The issues involved in the A&P case are analyzed by Morris A. Adelman in "The A&P Case: A Study in Applied Economic Theory," *Quarterly Journal of Economics*, Vol. LIII (1949), pp. 238–57; and in "The Great A&P Muddle," *Fortune*, December, 1949, pp. 122 ff.; and by Joel B. Dirlam and Alfred E. Kahn in "Antitrust Law and the Big Buyer: Another Look at the A&P Case," *Journal of Political Economy*, Vol. LX (1952), pp. 118–32, in "Integration and Dissolution of the A&P Company," *Indiana Law Journal*, Vol. XXIX (1953), pp. 1–27, and in *Fair Competition* (Ithaca, N.Y.: Cornell University Press, 1954), pp. 77–81, 166–69, 211–16, and 234–41. The best brief presentation of facts and arguments on the fair trade laws is that prepared for the Select Committee on Small Business of the House of Representatives, *Fair Trade: The Problem and the Issues* (82d Cong., 2d Sess., House Report No. 1292, 1952). The authoritative references on resale price maintenance are Ewald T. Grether, *Price Control Under Fair Trade Legislation* (New York: Oxford University Press, 1939), and *Report of the Federal Trade Commission on Resale Price Maintenance* (Washington: Government Printing Office, 1945). The minimum markup laws are discussed by Grether and the FTC and, more recently, by Richard H. Lovell in "Sales Below Cost Prohibitions," *Yale Law Journal*, Vol. LVII (1948), pp. 391–425. See also Robert Tannenbaum, *Cost Under the Unfair Practices Acts* (Chicago: University of Chicago Press, 1949). Current developments are reported in *Business Week*.

Chapter 15 AGRICULTURAL PARITY AND PRICE SUPPORTS

There are about 5,500,000 farms and 23,500,000 people living on farms in the United States. As a percentage of the total population, farm folk have declined, dropping from more than 90 per cent in 1800 to 35 per cent in 1900 and to around 15 per cent at the present time. As a political force, however, they have more than held their own. Under the provisions of state and federal constitutions, agriculture is overrepresented in the legislature of each of the states and in the Congress of the United States. In the Senate, for instance, New York with 15,000,000 people has two votes, while 18 rural states with a comparable population have 36 votes. The farmers, moreover, are organized. There are four general organizations—the American Farm Bureau Federation, the National Grange, the National Council of Farmer Cooperatives, and the National Farmers Union—and a number of special product groups, the National Cooperative Milk Producers' Federation standing second only to the Farm Bureau in size and power. There are local, county, and state committees elected by farmers to give advice on the administration of the government's agricultural programs. And the Department of Agriculture itself, largely staffed with former members of these bodies, functions effectively as a pressure group. As a result, the political power of agriculture exceeds that of business or labor. And this power has been used to force adoption of those policies that the farmer has conceived to be in his particular interest.

THE AGRICULTURAL ECONOMY

In the absence of public intervention, the producers of most agricultural commodities would be powerless to fix the prices at which they sell. In agriculture as a whole and in each of its branches, producing units are numerous, the typical unit is small, and the degree of concentration in production is low. Each of the major crops is grown on hundreds of thousands, a few of them on millions, of farms, and these numbers may readily be increased. Four farms in five consist of less than 200 acres and represent an investment of little more than $10,000 in land and buildings, machinery, and livestock. For any of the major crops, the eight or ten largest producers account for but a minor fraction of 1 per cent of total output. None of them controls a part of the supply large enough to enable him, by curtailing output, appreciably to affect the price. No group of farmers, acting in concert, is likely to control enough of a supply to enable it to fix a price, since curtailment of output, by holding out the promise of higher returns, would encourage nonparticipation among its members and stimulate expansion among outsiders. The agricultural economy, if left to itself, is a competitive economy.

The Structure of Agricultural Production

The picture brought to mind by the word "farm" is that of an enterprise of moderate size producing several familiar commodities such as corn, wheat, cotton, tobacco, hogs, cattle, poultry, milk, and eggs. But among the 5,500,000 units called farms there is great diversity in the nature of the product, in the character of the processes of production, in the degree of specialization, and in the scale of operations. The term comprehends the production of feed grains and livestock in the Corn Belt, of wheat on the Great Plains, of cotton and tobacco in the South, and of range livestock in the Southwest. It covers the dairy farms of New England, the Middle Atlantic, and the Lake States, the truck farms along the Atlantic Coast and the Gulf of Mexico, the citrus groves of Florida and California, and the apple orchards of Virginia and Washington. It includes the producers of ducks on Long Island, sugar cane in Louisiana, and tree nuts on the Pacific Coast. With a hundred different crops, grown under widely differing conditions, there is no such thing, in actuality, as a typical farmer or an average farm.

For the purposes of the Census, a farm is defined as a tract of land where agricultural operations are performed, measuring more than three acres or selling commodities worth more than $150 per year. The definition thus includes suburban homes whose occupants have industrial employment and do a little farming on the side. Nearly a third, or around 1,700,000, of all farms fall in this category, their operations being part time or nominal. More than two thirds of all farms, or about 4,000,000, are operated by their owners, some of them debt free, others encumbered with mortgages. Less than one third, or about 1,500,000 are operated by tenants, rents being paid by some of them in cash, by others in shares of agricultural products. The latter group is divided, in turn, into those who have their own equipment and plan their own operations, and others, called sharecroppers, numbering close to 350,000, who contribute nothing but their labor and are paid not in wages but in shares of the crop. A few thousand farms, finally, are operated by salaried managers.

The ideal form of organization for American agriculture, according to the quadrennial platforms of each of the political parties, is that of the family farm. This is usually defined as an enterprise of such a size that it can be financed, managed, and operated, with little or no hired help, by a farmer and the members of his family. Here, the farmer is owner, manager, and worker, his residence is both a home and an office, his wife and children are partners and fellow laborers. His income from farming and other sources may go into a common pool; his operating costs and his living expenses may be met from the same account. The family farm thus differs in character from other businesses. It combines a productive enterprise with a mode of life.

When nominal and part-time farms, sharecroppers, and large-scale operations are eliminated from consideration, there remain about 3 million units that might be classified as family farms. But many of these afford little more than subsistence to the farmer and his family. Two fifths of the farms in the country account for but a tenth of the agricultural products that are marketed. The other three fifths, numbering around 3 million, account for nine tenths. This is commercial agriculture. And it is to serve the interests of commercial agriculture, in the main, that agricultural legislation has been devised.

The Economic Efficiency of Agriculture

There have been striking gains in the productivity of American agriculture in recent years. New seeds have been developed, as in the case of hybrid corn; the breeds of livestock and poultry have been improved. Better methods of cultivation have been adopted; more machinery has been introduced; more fertilizers and insecticides have been employed. As a result there have been sharp increases in output per farmer, yield per acre, eggs per hen, and pounds of milk per cow. But this progress has not been general. If the best methods in use were commonly adopted, the output of land now under cultivation might well be double what it is today. The work of the agricultural experiment stations and the agricultural extension services has reached some farmers; it has not begun to reach them all.

Farming in the United States, according to Theodore W. Schultz, "does not come anywhere near meeting the standard of efficiency set by the American economy. Instead it has all the earmarks of being highly inefficient, falling far behind most other major industries."[1] Measured in terms of value added per worker, manufacturing is two and one half times as productive as agriculture in the western states and four times as productive in the South.[2] Compared with agricultural productivity in other countries, too, that in America is low. The value product here is only half as high as in Australia and New Zealand. On half of our farms, it falls below that realized in England, Denmark, Holland, and elsewhere in western Europe. "One has to go to the very backward agriculture of

[1] Theodore W. Schultz, *Production and Welfare of Agriculture*, (New York: Macmillan Co., 1949), pp. 50–51.

[2] *Ibid.*, p. 57.

eastern Europe," says Professor Schultz, "to find productivity as low as it is on fully half of the farms in the United States."[3]

The reasons for such inefficiency are plain. In some cases, farmers are uneducated and the land they farm is barren. In many more, farms are too small to permit the economical employment of agricultural machinery. The price of land is often so high as to make it difficult for farmers to purchase tracts that are adequate in size. Farms that once were big enough have sometimes been divided through inheritance. For some crops, moreover, farms that are of family size, whatever their price, are still too small. As a result, too little capital and too much labor are employed, and production falls far short of optimum efficiency. With more machines and fewer men, the productivity of agriculture could be raised, the cost of foods and fibers reduced, and workers by the hundreds of thousands released from the farms to add to the output of industry.

The Farmer and the Market

It is the function of prices to guide producers in allocating resources to the production of various goods. Where more is demanded, rising prices are supposed to call forth more production; where less is demanded, falling prices are supposed to warn producers to contract. In agriculture, however, this function is performed imperfectly. When the farmer is deciding what quantities of what commodities to plant, the prices he has to guide him are those obtained for crops produced the year before. These prices are not likely to be repeated; they were the consequence of conditions that are subject to change. A high price for one commodity may have resulted from a drought; the season ahead may be a rainy one. A low price for another may have been caused by a bumper crop; in the coming harvest yields may fall. Where a price is high, other farmers may increase their plantings and drive it down; it might be wiser not to go along. Where a price is low, others may contract their acreage and drive it up; the farmer who plants as much as ever may do very well. Production, therefore, responds but slowly to changes in price relationships. And the individual farmer may miss the market every time, never producing more or less until everyone else decides to do the same.

The prices of agricultural commodities fluctuate more violently than prices of manufactured goods. This fact is to be attributed, in the main, to the relative inelasticity of their demand and supply. Where demand and supply are elastic, changes in price are limited. When price goes up, demand contracts, supply expands, and the rise is checked. When price goes down, demand expands, supply contracts, and the decline is stopped. With agriculture it is otherwise. For some commodities, such as meats and fruits, demand is fairly elastic. But for most, a change in price does not result in a proportionate change—or anything approaching a proportionate

[3] *Ibid.*, p. 60.

change—in the amount consumed.[4] Foods, in general, are necessaries. If prices are high, consumers may eat less, but they will still eat. If prices are low, consumers may eat more, but most of the money they save will be spent for other things. So, too, with supply. When prices, in general, go up, agricultural output is increased. Workers leave the farms, attracted by the higher returns obtainable in industry. But farmers increase their investment in land, fertilizer, and machinery. When prices fall, however, output is maintained. With unemployment, workers drift back to the farms. And farmers continue to produce. Interest, rent, and taxes must be paid. Land, equipment, and family labor can be put to work without expense. They might better be employed than left in partial idleness. Replacement and repair of buildings and machinery can be postponed. Fertilization can be skimped. As long as the cost of seed and feed remains below the price at which an individual farmer sells his output, he can maximize his income by producing at full capacity. And, unless the law forbids it, this is what farmers in general will do. It follows that supply is relatively elastic but demand inelastic as prices rise and that both are inelastic as prices fall. As a result, increases in price are only partially arrested, and declines are allowed to go unchecked. So swings from low to high and high to low are both repeated and extreme.

The Farm Problem

For agriculture as a whole, the problem presented to public policy is not that of relative poverty. Proponents of agricultural legislation have made much of statistics that purport to show that people on farms have incomes only half as high per capita as those received by non-farm groups. But this quotient of low income has been obtained by overstating the number of farm folk in the divisor and understating the aggregate farm income in the dividend. The divisor has been inflated by including people who work in town and live on suburban tracts that the Census classifies as farms. The dividend, on the other hand, has been deflated by excluding the farmer's income from non-farm sources and by underestimating the rental value of the farm house and the value of food produced and consumed on the farm. When the necessary corrections have been made, it is found that family income, outside the southern states, is as high for farm as for non-farm families. Indeed, in Iowa and other midwest states in recent years, incomes in agriculture have exceeded those in industry.[5]

In commercial agriculture, there are millions of farmers whose incomes compare favorably with those of successful business or professional men.

[4] See Harold G. Halcrow, *Agricultural Policy of the United States* (New York: Prentice-Hall, Inc., 1953), pp. 71–72. Studies of the demand for farm products are summarized as showing elasticities between 0.1 and 0.3 for wheat, cotton, tobacco, milk, sugar, and potatoes, around 0.5 or 0.6 for feed grains, and from 0.6 to 3.0 for meats and fruits.

[5] See Geoffrey S. Shepherd, *Agricultural Price and Income Policy* (Ames: Iowa State College Press, 1952), chap. ii.

But in agriculture, as elsewhere, income is distributed unequally. There are many thousands of farm families whose level of living falls below the minimum standard required for health and decency. These families are concentrated geographically, most of them in the states of the Southeast. Here, on farms that are small and ill-equipped, there are ignorant farmers working infertile soil. Here, in many counties, medical care is inadequate and schools are poor. And here the birth rate is the highest found in the United States. The problem of rural poverty, thus, is mainly one of promoting migration, raising productivity, and improving health and education in the South. It is not one of raising the level of income for agriculture as a whole.

In general, the trouble with the farmer's income is not its level but its undependability. Supply is uncertain: the same acreage, cultivated in the same way, may yield more one year and less the next; a crop as a whole may be good, but on particular farms that crop may be destroyed by drought, flood, hail, disease, or pests. Demand is unreliable: foreign markets may be closed; business depression may cut the quantities of foods and fibers that will be consumed at home. These are forces that the farmer is powerless to control. But they may drive his income down to levels that impair his standard of living, prevent him from paying his taxes, the installments on his machinery, and the interest on his mortgage, and finally deprive him of his farm. It is the fear of such a disaster, more than anything else, that has brought the farmer to a point where he is now unwilling to entrust his fortunes to the market, abandoning governmental supports. And this fear has its basis in the bitter experience of the past.

FORERUNNERS OF PARITY

The two decades before World War I were a golden era for American agriculture. Markets grew as industry expanded. On the farms, prices and incomes rose. Prosperity was sustained uninterrupted for the longest period the farmer had ever known. With the outbreak of war, production of foodstuffs in western Europe suffered, and supplies from the Argentine and Australia were cut off by a shortage of shipping. The United States was called upon to feed her allies. Farm prices rose sharply, farm output was expanded, and farm debt grew as new acres were bought on credit and the prices of crops were capitalized in the price of land. When the war ended, the farms of Europe came back into production and shipments from Argentina and Australia were resumed. Markets disappeared and prices dropped.

American agriculture did not participate in the prosperity that followed the war. And when the Great Depression struck, agriculture went from bad to worse. Demand at home collapsed and prices continued to fall. The cash income of farmers dropped from $11 billion in 1929 to $5 billion in 1933. Farm families suffered hardships, and farms were lost through sales for delinquent taxes and foreclosures of mortgages. In 1927 a National Farmer's Holiday Association was formed and, in 1932, this body declared an embargo on deliveries of agricultural products until prices should rise, laying virtual siege to Council Bluffs and Sioux City, with all roads blocked, incoming wagons overturned, and milk cans emptied onto the ground. In one Iowa county, mortgage agents were bound with rope and dragged across the county line behind a speeding car. In Iowa, too, foreclosure sales were thronged with silent men, armed with pitchforks and shotguns, and farmers bought their farms back with a single bid, while a noose dangled ominously from a nearby tree. It was in this experience of prolonged and deepening depression that government support of agricultural prices had its birth.

"Protection"

The first method of increasing prices to be adopted after World War I was that of raising tariffs on imports of agricultural commodities. This was done under President Harding in 1921 and 1922 and again under President Hoover in 1930. The method was effective for some products, such as sugar and wool, where consumption exceeded domestic production and foreign producers competed in the American market. Here, it aided a minority of farmers at the expense of farmers as a whole. As consumers, farmers were forced to pay more for the protected foods and fibers. As exporters, they found their markets closed by the inability of their customers to earn dollars with which to buy, and by the erection of barriers abroad in retaliation for those erected by the United States. For the great export crops—cotton, tobacco, wheat, pork and its products, and many others—the tariff was completely ineffective. Here, production exceeded consumption. And where duties were imposed, they served only to keep out competing supplies that never had come in. For agriculture as a whole, "protection" turned out to be a gold brick. If prices in general were to be boosted, it was clear that another method would have to be found.

"Making the Tariff Effective"

Attention now turned to the invention of devices that would make it possible to sell an export crop at a higher price at home than that obtainable abroad. There were several of these plans. Under all of them, the American market was to be isolated by a tariff, with duties equal to the difference between domestic and foreign prices. And the domestic prices were to be supported by reducing the quantities of agricultural products sold in the United States and dumping American surpluses on the other markets of the world. Since protection was generally regarded as legitimate, this was called "making the tariff effective." It did not make the tariff effective. What it did was to create another mechanism of quite a different kind.

The most important of these proposals, known as the McNary-Haugen plan after its sponsors, Senator McNary of Oregon and Representative Haugen of Iowa, was embodied in a series of five bills that were introduced in Congress beginning in 1924. The first three bills failed of enactment; the fourth and fifth were vetoed by President Coolidge in 1927 and 1928. The plan underwent various modifications in its successive drafts. But in its final form, it provided for the establishment of a government export corporation with a large revolving fund, to be used in purchasing agricultural products in the American market in quantities sufficient to raise domestic prices to the levels desired. The stocks thus accumulated would then be sold abroad at the world price. The money lost in the process would be recovered by imposing a tax, known as an equalization fee, on the sales made at home. In the case of wheat, for instance, where a tariff of 42 cents a bushel had been imposed, a crop of 800 million bushels might be selling at the world price of $1.30. The corporation would enter the market, buying 200 million bushels, say, at $1.72, thus bidding up to that figure the price obtained for the whole crop, increasing its value by 42 cents times 800 million bushels or $336 million. The corporation would lose 42 cents times 200 million bushels or $84 million on its sales abroad. This would have to be deducted, in an equalization fee, from the gain in the value of the crop. But the farmers would still be $252 million to the good.

Another means to the same end was the export debenture plan, introduced in Congress but finally dropped when President Hoover declared that it would be vetoed if passed. Under this proposal, exporters of agricultural products would be given government debentures having a value equal to the difference between the world price and the desired domestic price. These could be sold, at face value minus a small discount, to importers of other goods who then would be permitted to use them in paying customs duties. Exporters thus would tend to bid up the price of an entire crop by paying the world price plus the debenture value for the part of it that would be sold abroad. Customs revenues would fall, but no costs would be incurred in buying and selling commodities or in imposing and collecting equalization fees.

A third device was called the domestic allotment plan. This plan would have raised domestic prices by restricting the freedom of farmers to sell their crops in the domestic market. Each farmer was to be given an allotment, based on past production, and forbidden to sell in larger quantities for use at home. Here, too, the resulting surpluses were to be dumped abroad. But this scheme required the establishment of even more elaborate administrative machinery than the others.

Each of these plans, by raising prices, would tend to increase production and decrease consumption in the United States, thus creating larger surpluses for export, depressing the world price, and largely defeating its purpose by reducing the related domestic price. Each of them would be regarded by other nations as an act of economic warfare, would lead to retaliation, and thus would deprive American agriculture and industry of markets overseas. President Hoover, rejecting this approach, held that the farm problem was to be solved, not by fixing prices, but by promoting the orderly marketing of agricultural commodities.

"Orderly Marketing"

The Agricultural Marketing Act of 1929, adopted during the early months of the Hoover administration, sought to place agriculture "on a basis of equality with other industries . . . (1) by minimizing speculation, (2) by preventing inefficient and wasteful methods of distribution, (3) by encouraging the organization of producers into effective associations . . . (4) by aiding in preventing and controlling surpluses in any agricultural commodity, through orderly production and distribution. . . ." Its purpose was to be effected, in the main, by promoting the establishment of co-operative marketing associations, owned and controlled by farmers, to handle agricultural commodities. These associations were to stabilize prices by buying when crops were large and selling when crops were small. They were authorized to set up stabilization corporations for the storage of temporary surpluses. The Act created a Federal Farm Board, with a revolving fund of $500 million, and empowered it to support the associations in their activities.

The Board began its operations in the fall of 1929. Faced with declining prices, it developed a program of loans and purchases, dealing principally in cotton and wheat, but also in wool, mohair, grapes, raisins, dairy products, and a dozen other commodities. It acquired cotton at 16 cents a pound and wheat at $1.15 to $1.25 a bushel. By the summer of 1931, cotton had fallen to 6 cents and wheat to 39 cents, and the Board was holding 3,500,000 bales of cotton and 257,000,000 bushels of wheat. Its revolving fund no longer revolving, the Board then announced that it would make no further loans or purchases. The harvest of 1931 produced a bumper crop, and prices fell to the lowest levels of the century. In this market the Board started to unload. Altogether, its losses ran somewhere between $300 million and $400 million. A large part of its holdings was donated to the Red Cross for distribution as relief. The agency was finally abolished in 1933.

The experiment was a failure. The Board did not succeed in stabilizing prices. It checked their fall by entering the market, then speeded it by pulling out. The one thing accomplished was to transfer the losses incurred through falling prices from producers and handlers to the taxpayer.

The failure is readily explained. Stabilization through storage is feasible where funds are ample and surpluses are shortly followed by shortages. The Farm Board's funds were limited, and it dealt in commodities that were always in surplus and never in short supply. Even this might work, however, if production would be controlled. The Board did appeal to farmers to kill off part of their livestock, plough under part of their cotton, and curtail their acreage of other crops. But it had no authority to compel them to do so. And its exhortations were ignored. Production was maintained and prices continued to fall.

"Equality for Agriculture"

In 1921 George N. Peek and Hugh S. Johnson of the Moline Plow Company published a pamphlet under the title of *Equality for Agriculture* in which they set forth a plan to raise the prices of agricultural commodities to levels that would bear the same relation to the prices of other goods as that existing in the years before the war. This was soon adopted as the objective of the McNary-Haugen bills and other price-raising plans. Kept alive in the thinking of farm economists and politicians, it was rechristened as "parity" in 1933 and embraced as the goal of New Deal farm policy.

Parity, under the new program, was to be sought through loan, purchase, and storage operations like those of the Farm Board. But the Farm Board debacle was not to be forgotten. Nor were surpluses to be dumped abroad, as proposed by the McNary-Haugen, export debenture, and domestic allotment schemes. Instead, production was to be controlled. For this purpose, however, the government was to adopt the machinery of the domestic allotment plan. And its activities were to be financed by a tax resembling the McNary-Haugen equalization fee. So, by drawing on past experience and incorporating elements from past proposals, the New Deal put together a program designed to raise farm prices in the name of parity.

PRICE SUPPORTS IN DEPRESSION

During the past two decades the farm program of the federal government has undergone repeated changes in detail. But in broad outline it has remained the same. Its objective has always been stated as some form of parity. It has always made provision for supporting prices by loans and purchases and for the disposition of surpluses. The lending function has been performed, since 1933, by the Commodity Credit Corporation, first set up by executive order and operated, in effect, as a subsidiary of the Reconstruction Finance Corporation, but later transferred to the Department of Agriculture and given statutory authority. The law has always permitted producers and handlers of agricultural commodities to enter into agreements controlling their sale, and has empowered the Secretary of Agriculture to make participation in such arrangements compulsory. This part of the program, confined in practice to commodities produced or consumed within limited geographic areas, will be considered in Chapter 16. And finally, some form of provision has always been made for control of the quantities of the major commodities that may be produced or marketed. It is with parity, loans and purchases, disposal of surpluses, and control of production and marketing that the remainder of the present chapter is concerned.

Controlling Production by Contract, 1933

The Agricultural Adjustment Act of 1933 took as its purpose the restoration of parity, which it defined as the establishment of "prices to farmers at a level that will give agricultural commodities a purchasing power with respect to articles farmers buy equivalent to the purchasing power of agricultural commodities in the base period . . . August, 1909—July, 1914," with later base dates adopted for tobacco and, subsequently, for a few other commodities. It denominated as "basic" seven commodities: wheat, cotton, corn, hogs, rice, tobacco, and dairy products, a list that was shortly extended to include a half a dozen more. For these commodities, the Secretary of Agriculture was empowered to curtail production by entering into voluntary contracts with farmers under which each of them would agree to restrict his acreage of a particular crop or his breeding and feeding of a specific type of livestock to a fixed percentage of the quantities obtaining in a base period. And the Secretary was further authorized to make payments, in the form of rentals for acres taken out of production or other benefits in cash, to those farmers who were willing to co-operate. Farm income was thus to be enhanced in two ways: (1) by higher prices resulting from curtailment of output, and (2) by checks drawn on the Treasury of the United States. The law provided for funds to make these payments by imposing a tax on the processors of the basic commodities, such as ginners of cotton, millers of wheat, and packers of meat. It also permitted the use of such funds to promote the expansion of markets and the disposal of surplus commodities.

The government proceeded at once to put its instruments to work. In 1933, the Commodity Credit Corporation started making loans on cotton and corn. These were "nonrecourse" loans, made at 10 cents a pound on cotton and at 45 cents a bushel on corn, the cotton being in storage in warehouses, the corn in cribs on the farms. If prices went above 10 cents and 45 cents, the farmer could pay off his loan, repossess his crop, sell it, and pocket the difference. If prices fell below these figures, he could default on his payment, keep the money loaned him, and let the government take the loss. From his point of view, the proposition was "Heads, I win; tails, you lose." What was involved in the lending operation, in reality, was the establishment of a minimum price.

Some commodities were diverted from their normal markets, during the early years of the program, by making purchases for distribution to persons on relief. In 1933, with a pork surplus threatening, the government bought 6,200,000 little pigs and 222,000 pregnant sows, distributing part of this stock through relief agencies, turning part of it into grease and fertilizer, some of which was dumped in the Mississippi when tankage facilities were overtaxed. But there was relatively little subsidization of exports. The major emphasis was on production control.

For cotton and tobacco, in 1933, with heavy surpluses in sight, the government's first contracts required the planters to plough under a portion of their growing crops. For other commodities and in later years, the contracts controlled the number of acres to be planted by individual farmers and the heads of livestock to be produced. In 1934 their acreage of wheat was cut 15 per cent, corn 20 per cent, and cotton 35 per cent, their litters of pigs 25 per cent, and other products in varying amounts. Persuaded by official propaganda and tempted by cash benefits, farmers signed contracts to cover half of the acreage of corn, three fourths of that of wheat, cotton, and tobacco, and three fourths of the output of pork. The program was thought to be successful. There was a moderate decline in the output of cotton, tobacco, and other crops, a sharp decline in the output of wheat and corn. But in the latter case, the reduction was to be attributed principally to a serious and widespread drought.

Prices rose, and the CCC escaped disaster. The loan rate on cotton was increased from 10 cents to 12 cents, and the agency accumulated a substantial stock. But the corn loans paid off. For this good fortune, some credit must be given to control of acreage, a great deal more to lack of rain.

Controlling Production by Taxation, 1934–35

Voluntary production control has a fatal weakness. As prices rise, it becomes increasingly advantageous for farmers to refuse contracts, cashing in on the high prices established through the curtailments effected among their neighbors by themselves producing in unlimited quantities. And as their output grows, the prices are reduced. To prevent this, the insiders are likely to demand that the outsiders be compelled to participate by having penalties imposed on those who do not. And this is what was done with cotton and tobacco in 1934 and with potatoes in 1935.

Under the Bankhead Cotton Control Act of 1934, the government was to fix the total quantity that might be marketed each year and to assign quotas to individual growers on the basis of past output. Each grower who signed a contract was to receive tax exemption certificates to cover his quota. Cotton sold in excess of quotas, bearing no such certificates, was to be subject to a tax equal to half of its price. This penalty was designed to force growers to accept contracts and to keep their sales within the amounts fixed. The plan was to take effect when two thirds of the growers participating in a referendum should vote affirmatively. In accordance with these provisions, a referendum was held and the plan was approved. Under the Kerr-Smith Act, a similar pattern of control was applied to tobacco at the same time.

The Potato Control Act of 1935 set up an even more elaborate scheme to curtail the production and sale of potatoes. Quotas in the allowable total of production were to be established for every state and county and for 3 million individual farms. Potatoes were to be sold in uniform packages meeting specifications to be published by the Commissioner of Internal Revenue. Every package was to bear a tax stamp. Each farmer was to be given stamps to cover his quota. For every bushel of potatoes sold outside a quota, the stamps required were to cost 45 cents. The sale or the purchase of unpackaged or unstamped potatoes was made punishable by a fine of $1,000, by imprisonment for one year, or both. No funds were provided to enforce the law; it was repealed before it took effect.

Production control evoked a great deal of derision in its early years. One wag wrote a letter to a newspaper:

> Mr. B— has a friend who received a government check this year for not raising hogs. So B— now proposes to get a farm and go into the business of not raising hogs; says in fact not raising hogs appeals to him very strongly. Of course he will need a hired man and that is where I come in. I write you as to your opinion of the best kind of farm not to raise hogs on, the best strain of hogs not to raise, and how best to keep an inventory of the hogs you are not raising. His friend who got the $1,000 got it for not raising 500 hogs; now we figure we might easily not raise 1,500 or even 2,000 hogs, so you see the possible profits are only limited by the number of hogs we do not raise. . . .[6]

The plow-under in cotton and tobacco was said to have run into difficulty because the mules were obstinate; they had always been whipped for stepping on growing crops and were slow to learn the economics of the

[6] *New Republic*, October 24, 1934, p. 309. The program seemed ridiculous, too, to Ogden Nash:

> Higgledy, piggledy, my black hen,
> She lays eggs for gentlemen.
> Gentlemen come every day
> To count what my black hen doth lay.
> If perchance she lays too many,
> They fine my hen a pretty penny;
> If perchance she fails to lay,
> The gentlemen a bonus pay.
>
> Mumbledy, pumbledy, my red cow,
> She's cooperating now.
> At first she didn't understand,
> That milk production must be planned.
> She didn't understand at first
> She either had to plan or burst.
> But now the government reports
> She's giving pints instead of quarts.
>
> Fiddle-dee-dee, my next-door neighbors,
> They are giggling at their labors.
> First they plant the tiny seed,
> Then they water, then they weed;
> Then they hoe and prune and lop,
> Then they raise a record crop;
> Then they laugh their sides asunder
> And plow the whole kaboodle under . . .

New Deal. It was also suggested that the potato problem might be solved by coating the tax stamps with potato paste and hiring the unemployed to affix them, thus doing away with unemployment, malnutrition, and the potato surplus at a single stroke. But this was before parity and price supports had achieved unquestionable respectability.

Controlling Production by Soil Conservation, 1936

In January, 1936, in the Hoosac Mills Case, the Supreme Court held the production control provisions of the Agricultural Adjustment Act of 1933 to be unconstitutional on the ground that the processing tax was employed, not to serve the general welfare, but in the interest of a particular group, and that the benefit payments it financed were used to purchase conformity with a program which the powers delegated to Congress by the Constitution gave it no authority to enact.[7] Upon the recommendation of the President, the cotton, tobacco, and potato control measures were repealed. The administration then cast about for a method by which its program could be continued without running afoul of the Court. The result was the Soil Conservation and Domestic Allotment Act of 1936.

It was the purpose of this law not only "to promote the conservation and profitable use of agricultural land," but also to re-establish "the ratio between the purchasing power of the net income per person on farms and that of the income per person not on farms that prevailed during the five-year period August, 1909—July, 1914." The goal was stated as income parity rather than price parity, but it was still parity with a prewar base. Administration of the conservation program was delegated to state agencies and to county and local committees. Farmers were invited to submit adjustment plans to these committees and $500 million was appropriated to enable the Treasury to keep on paying benefits, doing so now upon proof that these plans had been carried out. Payments were made for such soil-building practices as applying fertilizer and turning green manure. They were also made, in accordance with the domestic allotment plan, for taking specified portions of acreage out of soil-depleting crops and putting them into soil-conserving crops. The soil-depleting crops, by some coincidence, were the very ones whose output the government had previously been seeking to curtail. The soil-conserving crops were unmarketable grasses and legumes.

The law was a hurried stopgap. It was concerned less with conserving the soil than with conserving the program of benefit payments for production control. For this purpose, however, it was a clumsy instrument. It was followed by a second Agricultural Adjustment Act in 1938.

Controlling Marketing by Quotas, 1938

The new law went back to the definition of parity price adopted in 1933, but provided that interest on farm mortgages, taxes on farm real

[7] *U.S.* v. *Butler*, 297 U.S. 1.

estate, and freight rates must be taken into account in computing the parity ratio, thus setting the figure at a higher level. It directed the Commodity Credit Corporation to make nonrecourse loans on corn, wheat, and cotton at 52 per cent to 75 per cent of parity whenever supplies should rise above certain levels or prices fall below certain levels. Price-pegging, for these crops, was thus made mandatory rather than permissive. In accordance with these provisions, loans were made on wheat and cotton at 52 to 57 per cent of parity and on corn at 70 per cent. The CCC had thus acquired 13 million bales of cotton (equivalent to a year's supply) by 1939, some 700 million bushels of corn (or twice a normal carry-over) by 1940, and 600 million bushels of wheat (more than double the holdings that ruined the Hoover Farm Board) by 1942.

The disposal of surpluses had been financed since 1935 with funds provided for this purpose from customs revenues. This work, initiated by the Surplus Commodities Corporation, was taken over by the Surplus Marketing Administration in 1940. This agency continued to turn surplus foods over to state relief agencies. In addition, it developed a food stamp plan, under which such foods were sold to persons on relief at prices lower than those charged other customers. And it distributed further surpluses to children by inaugurating a program of contributions to school lunches.

The Act of 1938 directed the Secretary of Agriculture to prepare annual acreage allotments for corn, wheat, cotton, tobacco, and rice. And whenever the output of any of these commodities should exceed the quantity normally produced by a specified percentage, it required him to fix the total quantity that could be marketed. If two thirds of the growers approved the plan in a referendum, the total would then be broken down into quotas for every state, county, and farm. Commodities produced in excess of the quotas could not be sold, bartered, given away or fed to stock, but had to be destroyed or stored. Farmers who kept within their quotas were eligible for commodity loans, for soil conservation payments, and for parity payments based on their allotted acreage. Those who exceeded their quotas were penalized by a heavy tax. The compulsion applied to cotton and tobacco in 1934 was thus made available for controlling the other crops as well. Since marketing controls were not established unless approved by two thirds of those voting in a referendum, the procedure was said to be a democratic one. But the cards were stacked to produce a favorable vote: if quotas for a crop were disapproved, the government would not support its price.

This pattern of control was upheld by the Supreme Court, first on the ground that the marketing quotas controlled commerce rather than production,[8] and later on the ground that production on individual farms affected prices in nation-wide markets, and that the regulation of such prices was within the power of Congress.[9] The Act of 1938, a culmination

[8] *Mulford* v. *Smith*, 307 U.S. 38 (1939).

[9] *Wickard* v. *Filburn*, 317 U.S. 111 (1942).

of a series of measures designed to solve the problem of agricultural depression, was still in operation when World War II brought back prosperity.

PRICE SUPPORTS IN PROSPERITY

From 1939 to 1945, while wholesale prices on non-farm commodities rose 28 per cent, the prices paid to farmers rose 112 per cent. While national income as a whole rose 129 per cent, income from farming rose 165 per cent. While dividend payments went up 23 per cent, the weekly earnings of factory labor 104 per cent, and the per capita income of persons not on farms 99 per cent, per capita income from farming went up 220 per cent. In 1945, the ratio of farm to non-farm income per capita, on the 1909–14 base, stood at 151; compared with city folk, farmers were half again as well off as they had been in the golden era before World War I.[10] The gross cash income of farmers, down to $5 billion when the farm program was inaugurated in 1933, went above $25 billion in 1946 and above $30 billion in 1947 and 1948. The parity ratio, with 100 as its goal, stood at 113 in 1946, at 115 in 1947, and at 110 in 1948. The farmer had obtained everything he had asked for, and a great deal more. But parity and price supports had taken root. They were here to stay.

Wartime Goals and Controls

With the coming of war, surpluses gave way to shortages, falling prices to rising prices, deflation to inflation. There was need for a sharp reversal in policy. The problem now was to increase supply, restrain demand, and put ceilings over prices. Responsibility for rationing and price control was assigned to the Office of Price Administration. But the Emergency Price Control Act of 1942 forbade the administrator to put ceilings over the prices of agricultural products until they had passed 110 per cent of parity, the price on October 1, 1941 or December 15, 1941, or the average price from 1919 to 1929, whichever was the highest. The farmers' friends in Congress saw to it that the prices of agricultural commodities were controlled with less severity than those of other goods. But the controls were not without effect; farm prices rose precipitately when they were removed in the summer of 1946.

There were not only ceilings over prices; there were floors under them. But price supports were now used, not to increase farm incomes, but to encourage farmers to divert production from crops that were needed less to those that were needed more. In 1941 the Secretary of Agriculture announced the levels at which the government intended to support the prices of hogs, dairy products, chickens, and eggs. Thereafter, such action came to be taken as a matter of course, being extended to

[10] Murray R. Benedict, *Farm Policies of the United States, 1790–1950* (New York: Twentieth Century Fund, 1953), pp. 450–52.

scores of other commodities. Announcements designed to stimulate output were made in advance of seeding and breeding time. The prices announced were supported by loans and purchase guarantees. In most cases, they were obtained in the market. If not, they were made good by government purchases. With an army to feed, it was easy to dispose of any surplus that might be acquired. The advance announcement of guaranteed prices was popular with farmers. And it was approved by economists, since it employed the pricing mechanism to guide production, the purpose they believed it ought to serve.

In May, 1941, Congress raised the mandatory loan rate on basic commodities to 85 per cent of parity. In June, 1941, in the Steagall Amendment to the Commodity Credit Corporation Act, Congress extended this level of support to all commodities whose output the Secretary of Agriculture had requested farmers to increase. In October, 1942, it raised the mandatory supports to 90 per cent of parity (later boosting that for cotton to 92½ per cent) and required that they be maintained for two years after the President should declare the war to be at an end. President Truman made this declaration on December 31, 1946, thus terminating the postwar price commitment on December 31, 1948. The government was aided in meeting this commitment by prosperity at home and by its policy of extending aid to other countries by financing their imports, including those of American agricultural commodities. But as the end of 1948 approached, it was clear that new legislation would be required.

Supports: Flexible or Rigid?

New farm laws were enacted in 1948 and 1949, the first by a Republican Congress, the second by the Democrats. Both accepted without question the goal of parity and the principle of mandatory price supports. Both made changes in the computation of parity. And both reflected a struggle between those who wished to make price supports flexible—so that overproduction of some crops could be checked by reducing the supports and production of others stimulated by raising them—and those who wished to preserve rigidity. In the first group were the grain and livestock growers, the Farm Bureau, and the Grange. In the second, were the cotton growers and (in 1949) the Farmers' Union. In both cases, the Senate voted for flexibility and the House for rigidity. And in both cases, the final measure was a compromise.

The Agricultural Act of 1948 undertook to modernize the price parity formula, still tied to the 1909–14 base. During the previous thirty to forty years, the demand for wheat and other field crops and the cost of producing them had declined. The demand for livestock, dairy products, fruits, and vegetables had risen and the cost of producing these commodities had not declined. The old parity formula, however, kept the prices of the former products high and those of the latter products low, thus discouraging the transfer of resources from the first group to the second. The law therefore established a new formula for parity. This formula still retained the 1909–14 ratio between farm and non-farm prices as the goal for agricultural prices as a whole. But it modified this standard, in the case of individual products, by making allowance for past changes in demand and cost. In short, the law moved away from a formula that was obsolete toward one more nearly in accordance with reality. But the change was not to take effect at once. A transitional parity, figured at the old rate minus 5 per cent each year, was to apply until the new parity was higher.

The Act of 1949 retained the two methods of computation. But it raised the new parity figure by requiring the inclusion of farm wages in figuring the prices farmers pay. And it postponed abandonment of the old formula until 1953, providing that parity should be determined, in the meantime, by making both computations for every product and adopting the higher figure of the two. Subsequently, Congress continued this procedure to 1956, putting off the change in formulas for three years more.

In the Act of 1948 the principle of flexibility was introduced by making the height of the required supports to vary inversely with the size of prospective supplies. Thus, if prospective supplies were normal (i.e., equal to last year's consumption, plus probable exports, with an allowance for carry-overs) prices were to be supported at 75 per cent of parity. If they were below normal, supports would rise to a maximum of 90 per cent of parity at 70 per cent of normal. If they were above normal, supports would fall to a minimum of 60 per cent of parity at 130 per cent of normal, with higher levels permitted only if acreage allotments or marketing quotas were in effect. The law thus broke with the principle of rigid supports. But flexibility was put off until 1950; basic crops were to be supported at 90 per cent of parity in 1949.

The Act of 1949 again moved, in principle, from rigidity to flexibility. But it narrowed the range and raised the level of supports, fixing 75 per cent of parity (instead of 60 per cent) as the support to be provided when supplies were 130 per cent of normal, and 90 per cent of parity (instead of 75 per cent) as the support when supplies were normal. The law, moreover, fixed high and rigid supports for the next few years, postponing such flexibility as it permitted until 1953. In 1952, Congress acted again, this time postponing flexibility to 1955. As a matter of economics, Congress took the position that supports should be flexible. As a matter of politics, it feared that flexibility would be unpopular.

The farm program that the Eisenhower administration inherited in 1953 may now be summarized. (1) Price parity was the goal, with parity to be computed according to two formulas, both on a 1909–14 base, and the higher price obtained to be taken as governing. (2) For the purpose of determining price supports, commodities were divided into three classes. (*a*) Basic commodities—wheat, corn, cotton, tobacco, rice, peanuts—had to be supported at 90 per cent of parity. (*b*) Designated nonbasic commodities—wool and mohair, honey, tung nuts, milk and milk products—had to be supported at varying degrees of parity: 75 to 90 per cent for the dairy products and 60 to 90 per cent for the others. (*c*) Other products, including meats, fruits, and vegetables, could be supported at any figure up to 90 per cent of parity—these supports were not mandatory, but with other supports required it was difficult to avoid them. In 1953 the government was supporting 25 different commodities. (3) Products were still being purchased with funds allotted from customs revenues, to be dumped abroad, given to public institutions or private charities, or distributed through school lunches. (4) The quantity of commodities reaching the market was controlled in two ways. (*a*) Acreage allotments could be established for any commodity when supplies reached a certain level. The lowest figure to which plantings could be cut was fixed by law at 55,000,000 acres for wheat and 17,500,000 acres for cotton. Compliance with allotments was voluntary but non-co-operators were not eligible for full price supports. (*b*) Marketing quotas had to be proposed for basic crops when supplies were more than 20 per cent above normal. If they were disapproved by more than a third of the growers voting in a referendum, prices would be supported at only 50 per cent of parity. In the case of tobacco, there would be no support. If quotas were approved, growers exceeding them were taxed at 50 per cent of the loan rate for corn, cotton, wheat, and peanuts, at 50 per cent of parity for rice, and at 40 per cent of the previous season's average price for tobacco.

Subsidies: Visible or Hidden?

In 1949 a number of changes in farm policy were embodied in a plan proposed by Charles F. Brannan, Secretary of Agriculture in the Truman cabinet. Under this plan parity would have been computed by employing a complicated formula built on a ten-year moving base that started with the years 1939–48 when the buying power of farm income was at an all-time high. And farmers would have been promised 100 per cent of this new parity. In 1950 this would have put them at a level 25 per cent above that realized during the war. The plan thus called for rigid guaranties at figures far higher than any that the farm organizations or the farm bloc in Congress had ever ventured to propose. The Secretary then went on to divide agricultural commodities into two classes: those that could be stored and those that could not. Growers of storable commodities were to obtain their guaranteed returns in the form of prices supported by nonrecourse loans and government purchases as before. But for the perishables, something different was proposed. This was the heart of the Brannan Plan and the feature that plunged it into the center of violent controversy.

The proposal was that the prices of goods that could not be stored should not be supported, but that such goods should be sold in the market for whatever they would bring, and that the difference between the market price and parity should be paid to the farmer directly in the form of a subsidy from the federal treasury. The problems created by storage of perishable commodities were thus to be avoided: there would be no pressures to dispose of growing stocks, no losses from spoilage, no scandalous wastes. The plan appeared, moreover, to have a strong political appeal: it promised high prices to farmers and low prices to consumers. Its cost to the taxpayer was not calculated. In public discussion this aspect of the proposal was played down.

There is much to be said for direct payments as an alternative to price supports. No generalization can be made about the comparative cost of the two methods to the government. With direct payments, to be sure, no handling or storage charges are incurred. But the comparative cost will depend, too, upon the elasticity of the demand for the particular commodities involved, direct payments being costlier where demand is inelastic and cheaper where it is elastic.[11] There is no question, however, that the cost of direct payments to the community as a whole is less than that of price supports. With this method, all goods move into consumption; none of them spoil in storage; none of them are destroyed. In their effect on the distribution of income, too, direct payments are to be preferred. Here, subsidies need not be paid to every producer in proportion to his sales; the subsidies paid the largest producers can be limited. And with the burden of financing the subsidies borne by the taxpayer rather than the consumer, its incidence is less regressive. Direct payments have the final advantage of making for better international relations. They avoid the practice—common under price supports—of using the markets of other countries as a dumping ground.

The Brannan Plan was embraced by the CIO on behalf of organized labor, by the Farmers' Union, and by President Truman. It was emphatically rejected by the Farm Bureau and the Grange, by the Republicans in Congress, and by most of the Democrats. There were two principal reasons for the opposition. The first was the visibility of the subsidy. The idea of making direct payments was not a new one. Parity payments had been made before the war. These and other payments, since 1933, have averaged more than $500 million a year. But farmers still feel that prices obtained in the market are earned, even though the market has been rigged for them by the government. It offends their pride to be offered a subsidy—in any form that can be recognized. Moreover, when subsidies are brought into the open, there is danger that they will be cut off. Secondly, it appeared that the high prices promised would stimulate production, that the large quantities requiring subsidization would inflate the costs of the program, and that these costs could not be met unless strict controls were imposed on the quantities produced and sold. It was feared,

[11] Where demand is inelastic, price can be substantially increased by purchasing a small quantity of a crop, and the loss incurred in disposing of such a quantity will not be great. Where demand is elastic, however, the price cannot be substantially increased without purchasing a large quantity, and such a quantity cannot be disposed of without incurring a heavy loss.

therefore, that the plan would lead to further interference with the farmer's freedom by a growing agricultural bureaucracy. The Brannan plan never came within sight of enactment. But it did serve to illuminate the issues raised by agricultural subsidies.

Republican Farm Policy

In his major speech on farm policy during the presidential campaign, General Eisenhower made obeisance to parity. "I firmly believe that agriculture is entitled to a fair, full share of the national income," he said. "And a fair share is not merely 90 per cent of parity, but full parity." And this goal was to be achieved "in ways that minimize government control and protect farmers' independence."[12] In his first message to Congress, President Eisenhower again affirmed his allegiance to "full parity of income" as a goal, to be sought "in ways that minimize governmental interference in the farmer's affairs, that permit desirable shifts in production, and that encourage farmers themselves to use initiative in meeting changing economic conditions."[13] Mr. Eisenhower did not explain how parity was to be achieved without controls or interference. During the campaign he had denounced the "moral bankruptcy" of the Brannan Plan. Now, he promised to support farm prices at 90 per cent of parity, as the law required, until 1955.

On February 11, 1953, the new Secretary of Agriculture, Ezra Taft Benson, made a speech before the Central Livestock Association in St. Paul, Minnesota. His views as to policy broke sharply from those that had prevailed for twenty years:

> Price supports should provide insurance against disaster . . . and help to stabilize national food supplies. But price supports which tend to prevent production shifts . . . and which encourage uneconomic production and result in continuing heavy surpluses and subsidies should be avoided. . . . Farmers should not be placed in a position of working for government bounty rather than producing for a free market. . . . Futhermore, inefficiency should not be subsidized. . . . Relief programs should be operated as such—not as an aid to the entire agricultural industry. Emergency programs should be terminated as soon as the emergency is over.

This opinion, said the Secretary, was based on an old-fashioned philosophy "that it is impossible to help people permanently by doing for them what they could and should do for themselves . . . that you cannot build character by taking away man's initiative and independence. . . . It is doubtful if any man can be politically free who depends upon the state for sustenance. A completely planned and subsidized economy weakens initiative, discourages industry, destroys character, and demoralizes the people."[14] Coming from the Department of Agriculture, this was news. But the economic and political facts that faced the Secretary were stubborn ones.

[12] *New York Times*, September 7, 1952.

[13] *New York Times*, February 2, 1953.

[14] *Congressional Record*, February 13, 1953, pp. 1098–99.

Demand was falling: the foreign aid that had financed two thirds of American farm exports was being tapered off; production had recovered abroad. Supply was large: farm output was a third greater than it had been before the war. Surpluses were growing; farm prices were falling. Mr. Benson soon found himself in the business of making loans and purchases and cutting back the production of basic crops.

In the fall of 1952 Secretary Brannan had started supporting butter at 90 per cent of parity. By April 1, 1953, the government had 125 million pounds in storage and was buying more than 2 million pounds a day. Secretary Benson extended the support, not dropping it to 60 per cent, as the law permitted him to do, but keeping it at 90 per cent for another year. In the spring of 1954, with 270 million pounds of butter on hand, the Secretary braved a storm of opposition and cut the price supports on dairy products from 90 to 75 per cent of parity. But the surpluses of these and other products continued to mount. More than $6 billion was tied up in agricultural products at the end of the fiscal year 1954. Of this, $2,337 million was in outstanding loans; $3,668 million in outright ownership.[15] Normal storage facilities were exhausted; commodities were stored in the holds of the reserve fleet of old Liberty ships, in unused airplane hangars, and in abandoned movie theaters. Storage costs alone ran over $250 million a year. In March, 1954, at the President's request, Congress raised the borrowing power of the Commodity Credit Corporation from $6,750 million to $8,500 million, an amount that exceeded the farmer's annual cash receipts from all the basic crops. In June, he asked that it be raised to $10 billion.

In the summer of 1953, with the supply of wheat nearly 50 per cent above normal, the Secretary was compelled to propose controls. Under existing law, he could have cut the 76,800,000 acres then in production back to 55 million. But Congress raised this minimum to 62 million and the Secretary proclaimed quotas at that level. In a referendum held in August, 1953, the quotas were approved by a vote of nine to one. In October, the Secretary proclaimed quotas for cotton, cutting acreage from 24,500,000 to 17,900,000, a figure which Congress subsequently raised to 24,500,000. In December, these quotas, too, were approved by a vote of nine to one. The government thus came again to interfere with the independence of wheat and cotton farmers for the first time in a dozen years. By the middle of 1954 some 30 million acres had been taken out of the production of these and other crops. The strictest controls in history had been imposed.

The Act of 1954

On January 11, 1954, President Eisenhower sent a message to Congress recommending the adoption of a "new farm program." The major elements in the program were these: (1) Of the government's holdings of commodities, $2,500 million's worth was to be set aside in a reserve that

[15] *New York Times,* September 17, 1954.

might be used for aid abroad or relief at home, but not sold commercially. (2) The flexible provisions of existing law, setting price supports at 75–90 per cent of parity, were to be allowed to take effect in 1955. The new parity formula, also in accordance with existing law, was to be allowed to take effect in 1956. Downward adjustments from old to new parity, however, were to be gradual, being made after 1956 at the rate of 5 per cent per year. (3) Wool, unlike other commodities, was to be sold in the market for what it would bring. The subsidy to wool producers was to take the form of a direct payment, equal to the difference between the market price and 90 per cent of parity.

The new program was not really new. The proposed set-aside had little meaning, since the commodities in question would not have been sold commercially in any case. A bookkeeping device, it permitted further additions to the surplus by pretending that part of the surplus did not exist. The flexible supports would have taken effect in 1955 and the new parity formula in 1956 without new legislation. The wool proposal bore a striking resemblance to the Brannan plan. But presumably it was free of the taint of moral bankruptcy.

A new law, based on these proposals, was passed by Congress and signed by the President on August 28, 1954. It was hailed as a victory for the Administration. The set-aside was provided. The new parity was permitted to take effect in 1956, with gradual adjustments thereafter. The wool plan was adopted, with the amendment that subsidies might be paid up to 110 per cent of parity. The real fight in Congress, again, was on flexibility versus rigidity of supports. This fight the Administration won in principle but not in actuality. The new law provided for supports for basic crops at 82½–90 per cent of parity. If no law had been passed, flexibility would have become effective at 75–90 per cent of parity.

THE MECHANISM OF PRICE SUPPORTS

By now, the pattern of price supports should be familiar. It includes: (1) the computation of price goals for farm products in terms of 1909–14 purchasing-power parity, (2) a program of mandatory and permissive loans and purchases designed to maintain farm prices at fixed percentages of parity, (3) provision for the disposition of resulting surpluses, and (4) control of the quantities of commodities produced and sold. Each of these elements of the program will now be subjected to further analysis.

Parity Price

The concept of parity was put in a nutshell by a cattle raiser interviewed on Edward R. Murrow's television program, "See It Now": "If a man could take a bushel of corn to town in 1912 and sell it and buy him a shirt, he should be able to take a bushel of corn to town today and buy a shirt."[16] This, indeed, is the general idea. But in operation it is not as simple as it seems.

The processes involved in the computation of a parity price may be illustrated by showing how the price for wheat was determined on January 15, 1952:

1. Compute the old parity as follows:
   a) Determine the average price of the commodity during its base period. For wheat, the base period was 1909–14 and the average price, per bushel, during this period was $0.884
   b) Compute an index of prices paid by farmers, taking those paid in 1909–14 as 100. This is called the parity index. In January, 1952, it stood at . . . 277
   c) Multiply (*a*) by (*b*) and divide by 100. The old parity price for wheat is . $2.45
2. Now compute the new parity as follows:
   a) Determine the average price received by farmers for the commodity during the preceding ten years. For wheat, this was $1.740
   b) Compute an index of the average prices received by farmers for all agricultural commodities during the same ten years, using the prices received in 1909–14 as 100. In January, 1952, this index stood at 235
   c) Divide (*a*) by (*b*). This gives an "adjusted base price" for wheat of . . $0.740
   d) Compute an index of prices paid by farmers, including the wages of farm labor, taking the prices paid in 1909–14 as 100. In January, 1952, this index stood at 287
   e) Multiply (*c*) by (*d*) and divide by 100. The new parity price for wheat is . $2.12
3. Take the higher of the two parity figures as the effective parity price. For wheat this is $2.45

(If the computation were illustrated by certain other commodities, such as livestock, fruits, and dairy products, the new parity would have been higher.)

In addition to computing the parity index and parity prices, the Department of Agriculture also computes a general parity ratio. This is the ratio of the index of prices received by farmers to the index of prices paid.

Parity price is said to be a just price. But, at best, the figure rests on fallible human judgment. And, at worst, it is subject to deliberate manipulation. Parity can be raised by shifting the base date from 1909–14 to some other period when price relationships were more favorable, and this has been done in the case of certain commodities. It can be raised by boosting the index of prices paid, and this was done when Congress required, at one time or another, that interest, taxes, freight rates, and wages be added. Before 1950 this index included 170 commodities used in farm production and in farm family living. Since then, it has included 337. Each of these commodities is given a weight in making the computation. The index of prices received includes 48 agricultural commodities, each of which is given its own weight. The height of a parity price is influenced by the items chosen for inclusion in these indexes and by the weights assigned them. These decisions are made by the statisticians of the Department of Agriculture.

In the depression parity was a distant goal, to be approached in the fullness of time. During the war it became a figure that had to be exceeded

[16] *The Reporter*, April 14, 1953, p. 23.

before inflation could be restrained. Since the war it has been employed to fix, and to justify, the levels at which prices have been guaranteed. Parity is a convenient instrument. It is also a sacred symbol. The office-holder or candidate, outside the cities, who takes parity in vain will do so at the risk of his political life.

Loans, Purchases, and Storage

Storage operations have often been advocated as a means of stabilizing prices, i.e. reducing the amplitude of price fluctuations over time. If this were its purpose, the government would attempt to estimate the prices that would achieve a long-run equilibrium between supply and demand, establish a price range below and above this level, buy when prices fell under the lower limit, and sell when they rose over the upper one. Supplies would thus be withdrawn from the market and put into storage in seasons when output was large, released from storage and returned to the market in seasons when output was small. The farmer would enjoy a stabler price, the consumer a steadier supply. The government would aim to break even, its profits covering its costs.

Under the price support program, the purpose has been a different one. Lending, buying, and storing have been employed, not to stabilize prices, but to raise them. Congress has repeatedly hoisted the parity figure, hoisted the percentage of parity to be assured by supports, and made supports mandatory rather than permissive. And with prices thus set above the equilibrium level, production has been encouraged, stocks have been accumulated, and these accumulations have been unloaded at a loss. From its establishment in 1933 up to June 30, 1954, the aggregate loss incurred by the Commodity Credit Corporation was $1,540 million. But the figure was kept so low by good luck rather than by good management. On three occasions the Corporation was enabled to rid itself of excessive holdings at good prices by purely fortuitous events: in 1934, by the drought; in 1942, by World War II; in 1950, by the war in Korea. It is possible that disaster might continue to bail the Corporation out, striking once in a decade, but it would not be prudent to count on it.

The costs of storage vary with the character of the commodities involved. They are lower for durable products and higher for perishable ones. Cotton can be kept for years if stored in a dry place. Grain can be kept for two or three years before it begins to deteriorate. But meat, eggs, dairy products, fruit, and vegetables spoil rapidly, require refrigeration, and cannot be kept in growing quantities without excessive costs. It is with such commodities that the government has had its unhappiest experience. From 1943 to 1950 it was required to support the price of potatoes, first at 90 per cent and finally at 60 per cent of parity. Of the potatoes acquired, less than a tenth were transferred to schools and relief agencies, more than nine tenths going into livestock feed, alcohol, flour, starch, and spoilage. Millions of bushels were dumped to rot or covered with kerosene and burned. Other millions were dyed blue, to keep them out of commercial channels, and sold back to farmers at a pittance for use as feed and fertilizer. The government's loss on potatoes alone was $600 million. In 1951 Congress withheld supports and, for a time, potatoes enjoyed the unique distinction of being the only crop on which supports were forbid-

THAT OLD REPROBATE!

Alexander in the Philadelphia *Evening Bulletin*

den. But authority was restored and purchases resumed in 1954. In the case of dairy products, the government's holdings on September 10, 1954 included 447 million pounds of butter, 428 million pounds of cheese, and 233 million pounds of dried milk, acquired at a cost of more than $500 million. Another fiasco was in the making with enough butter in sight to grease the ways for battleships. The government's loss on all commodities during the fiscal year 1954 was $419 million. Its potential loss on the commodities it held at the end of the year was more than $1 billion.[17]

[17] *New York Times*, September 17, 1954.

Surplus Disposal

When the government sets a price above the level that would balance demand and supply, it creates a surplus. If the surplus is not to be destroyed, it must be disposed of in some other way. The method of disposition most popular with Congressmen is dumping abroad. This gives the foreign consumer American foods and fibers at low prices at the expense of the American consumer and taxpayer. But subsidized competition is resented by the foreign producer. This, in itself, would not bother the Congressmen. But economic aggression evokes retaliation, closes foreign markets to American exporters, and endangers international diplomacy. These difficulties can be avoided if surpluses are dumped at home.

Distribution through welfare agencies, charitable institutions, and school lunches has much to recommend it. Certainly, it is better to use supplies in this way than to destroy them or to subsidize their competition with commodities produced abroad. More food is made available to needy persons and to growing children, and some of the funds available for the care of these groups can be stretched to cover other purchases. But nutrition, which should be the goal of feeding programs, is here subordinated to the purpose of raising agricultural prices. If milk and oranges are fortunately in surplus, the dietary balance of the beneficiaries may well be improved. But if potatoes are in surplus, the needy and the young may be stuffed with them even though their diets already contain more carbohydrates than they need. If nutrition were really the objective, a different approach would be required.

Foods and fibers are also diverted to industrial uses and employed as animal feeds. It is possible that continued research in these areas may come, in time, to create new demands. But, in the main, this method of disposal serves but to replace materials produced at low cost with those produced at high cost.

Control of Supply

With support prices set high, the losses incurred through surplus disposal can be kept within limits only if supply is controlled. This may be done by restricting the quantities that may be produced or sold. The controls applied to production are of limited effectiveness. Acreage can be reduced, but this cannot be expected to bring about a proportionate reduction in output. Farmers will retire their poorest acres and retain their best ones. They will use better seeds, plant them closer together, apply more fertilizer and insecticides, and devote more labor to each acre. The land that is kept idle will be more productive when brought back into use. And, finally, there is the weather. In determining the volume of agricultural production, Mother Nature is far more influential than Uncle Sam.

The controls applied to marketing are more effective. With heavy penalties for sales exceeding quotas, supplies can be kept down. And with products unsalable, production will be reduced. But when the output of one crop is curtailed, farmers use their land and labor to produce another. Or they may put their land in pasture and raise more livestock. New surpluses appear and these, in turn, must be controlled. The process logically can end, in the phrase of Henry A. Wallace, only when every ploughed field has its permit sticking to its post. Administration of such controls requires a vast bureaucracy supported at a heavy cost.

PRICE SUPPORT POLICY APPRAISED

The farm program of the past two decades may be appraised in terms of its basic philosophy, its economic logic, and its possible results. Is parity ethically justifiable? Is the support of product prices an appropriate means to the end of farm welfare? Is it more likely to help or to harm the farmer in the long run? The program may also be appraised in terms of actual experience. What has it cost the taxpayer and the consumer? How has it affected agricultural productivity? How has it influenced the allocation of resources within agriculture and between agriculture and the rest of the economy? By the first test, the program must be condemned. By the second, it does not come off so badly.

The Ethics of Parity

Parity is presented as a precise statistical expression of ultimate justice in the distribution of income among producing groups. Some doubt is thrown on the purity of the concept by the brazen way in which its statistics have been manipulated by the Congress. But it is still maintained that farmers as a group should get the same share of the nation's income, and that farmers as individuals should stand in the same relationship to non-farmers, as they did in some period in the past. In view of the disproportionate gains realized by farmers over the past two decades, it would be difficult on this basis, to justify the continued maintenance of price supports. When agriculture pleads hardship, one recalls the caption under the picture of the Illinois farmer in *Life:* "That's my son's Buick; I drive a Cadillac." But even if statistics showed that the farmers' share in income had declined, it would not follow that the government should undertake to increase it.

It is nonsense to argue that the share of income going to any group should always remain the same. And this holds for farmers as it does for lamplighters, glass blowers, and livery stable keepers. As technology advances and income grows, the share of a single industry should decline. A steady shrinkage in the fraction spent for foods and fibers, in particular, is the mark of a progressive community. There are few who would argue that the farmer's share in income should have been frozen at the 45 per cent or so that he received in 1790, or at the 30 per cent he received in 1860. There is no greater logic in the contention that it should be frozen at the 15 per cent he gets today. If the farmer's relative worth to society is declining, there is no ethical principle to support the proposition that his relative income should be maintained. And the farmer has no better claim to such protection than any other group in the community.

The parity to which the price supports are tied, moreover, is not one of income per farmer, but rather one of price per hundredweight, per bushel, and per pound. Parity, said the cattle man, means that a bushel of corn should always buy a shirt. Here, the concept of justice attaches itself to a relationship among inanimate objects. Morality is said to require that the values at which such objects exchange should always be the same. This is to say that a television set should always bring ten suits of clothes. Such a proposition is recognized at once as fallacious. But if not a TV set, why a bushel of corn? If the demand for a product or the cost of producing it goes down, it should command less of other products in return. It has no moral claim to more. To grant such a claim is to pervert the pricing mechanism, helping the producers of one product, hurting the producers of another, and harming the consumers of both.

Parity cannot be justified as establishing justice between farmers and non-farmers or between agricultural products and other goods. In operation, it creates inequities among farmers themselves. The parity formula is more favorable to some crops than to others. If all were supported at the same percentage of parity, there would be inequities. But the percentages of support, also, are varied. And these variations find their sole explanation in differences in political power.

The benefits of the program are not distributed on the basis of need. The larger incomes resulting from higher prices and governmental payments are proportioned to the farmer's scale of operations. The poor farmer gets little. The rich farmer gets much. Checks drawn on the Treasury and paid to individuals have run into hundreds of thousands of dollars. The consumer and the taxpayer have footed the bill.

The moral pretensions of this program must be stripped away. A group possessing great political power cynically employs this power to force a transfer of income from others to itself. It surrounds this operation with a cloak of respectability. The cloak is parity.

Confusion of Means and Ends

The ultimate objective of agricultural policy should be that of improving the well-being of farm families. The method employed by agricultural policy has been that of fixing the prices of farm products. But if the goal is welfare, this method of approaching it is not appropriate. Welfare would better be approached directly, through the improvement of social services. With price fixing as the method, the most aid is given to those who need it least, the least to those who need it most. Prices, as instruments, are properly employed in serving quite a different purpose. Their goal should be that of effecting economy in the allocation of resources—within agriculture and between agriculture and other industries. But prices, whose function should be purely instrumental, have come to be regarded as objectives in themselves. And policy has been distorted by accepting means as ends.

As demand falls, and as costs fall, prices also should fall. And this decline should warn producers to divert resources to the production of other goods. When prices are supported at levels unjustified by demand and cost, this does not happen. Producers keep on turning out commodities that are wanted less instead of shifting to the production of those that are wanted more. And, as a result, resources are wasted and the advancement of levels of living is restrained.

This is what tends to happen under the program of price supports. In agriculture a free economy is displaced by a planned economy. Resources are allocated, not in accordance with the dictates of the market, but in response to the pushes and pulls of politics. The logical consequence is malallocation, in agriculture itself, and in the community as a whole. The accidental price relationships of the historic past are congealed within a rigid mould. The alteration of taste and the improvement of technology are willfully ignored, as if agriculture should be impervious to change. As a result, instead of providing the consumer with the foods he wants, the farmer is encouraged to keep on producing foods that have to be given or thrown away. And instead of moving into industry, where their labor would be highly productive, workers are invited to remain in agriculture where it is not.

There is waste, too, where production is tied to fixed locations by acreage allotments and marketing quotas. Here, the use of a historic base prevents expansion on lands where yields are high and permits continued cultivation of acreage that ought to be retired. So larger quantities of fertilizer are needed, and the community gets a smaller product at a higher cost.

The Long-Run Prospect

There is no assurance that the program, in the long run, will succeed in accomplishing its purposes. There is danger that the farmer will price himself out of the market. And where he does not, there is danger that what is gained in the higher prices charged for crops will be lost in other ways.

By insisting that the price of cotton be maintained at an artificial level, the American planter has acted to deprive himself of his former share of the market, both abroad and at home. He has encouraged the expansion of competitive acreage in South America, Africa, and Asia. From 1932–33 to 1938–39, before exports were financed by appropriations for foreign aid, consumption of American cotton outside the United States declined 46 per cent, while consumption of foreign-grown cotton increased 69 per cent. The prices obtained, by law, for cotton have also tended to stimulate the substitution of competitive materials. Cotton's place has been taken in part by rayon, not only in apparel but also in tire fabrics. In 1935 rayon had none of this market; in 1945 it had half. Cotton has been superseded by paper, too, in products such as towels, napkins, tissues, packages, and bags. From 1930 to 1940, its share in sugar packaging dropped from 90 per cent to 55 per cent; from 1925 to 1942, its share in cement bagging dropped from 83 per cent to 27 per cent.[18] Long faced with increasing competition, the cotton grower has seemingly been bent on self-destruction. Confronted now with the development of new synthetic fibers, the wool grower exhibits a similarly suicidal bent. So, too, with the dairy farmer. In 1940 butter had nine tenths of the market for spreads, and oleomargarine only a tenth. By 1952 the per capita consumption of butter had dropped 47 per cent, that of margarine had risen 310 per cent; the two divided the market half and half. Yet with creamery butter retailing at 85 cents a pound and margarine at 29 cents, producers persuaded the Secretary of Agriculture to support the price of butter at 90 per cent of parity.

In cases such as these an artificial level of prices cannot permanently be maintained. In others, this may be possible. But the advantage obtained by the farmer may be dissipated by attracting new entrants or by inflating the value of land. With tobacco, for instance, from 1935 to 1947, acreage increased by 30 per cent, but the number of allotments increased by 50 per cent. More farmers crowded in to share the higher price and each of them got less of the augmented income for himself. Where an advantage remains, it is capitalized in determining the prices charged for land. In 1946, without a quota, tobacco land was selling for $40 an acre. With a quota, it was selling for $500 to $1,000 more.[19] Here, the capital value of the added income resulting from the quota is appropriated by the man who owned the land at the time when the quota was imposed. The farmer who subsequently buys the land pays for the value of the quota as he would for any other form of property. Thereafter, though price is inflated by monopolistic restriction of output, he receives but a competitive return.

Results in Practice

The total cost of the farm program to the taxpayer from 1933 to 1951, including the losses of the CCC, the customs revenues spent on surplus removal, special subsidies for sugar and wheat, and direct payments for soil conservation and production adjustment (but not including administrative expenses) is estimated at something more that $10 billion.[20] It has thus run around $600 million a year. This is about 3 per cent of the annual

[18] *Looking Ahead With Cotton*, U.S. Department of Agriculture, Miscellaneous Publication No. 584 (1945), pp. 8–17.

[19] See John E. Mason, "Acreage Allotments and Land Prices," *Journal of Land and Public Utility Economics*, May 1946, pp. 176–81.

[20] Halcrow, *op. cit.*, pp. 277–78; Rainer Schickele, *Agricultural Policy* (New York: McGraw-Hill Book Co., 1954), pp. 279–81.

value of agricultural output. It is between 1 and 2 per cent of the federal budget. The program, obviously, has not driven the country into bankruptcy.

The cost would have been greater had not the CCC been bailed out, on three occasions, by drought and war. The fact that stocks were on hand in these emergencies is sometimes cited as an achievement of the program. The argument would have some validity if the stockpiling had been planned. It was a consequence, however, not of foresight but of foolhardiness.

It is difficult to estimate the cost of the program to the consumer. The prices of some products in some years have been raised. And the increases have been pyramided as the products have passed on through the hands of wholesalers and retailers. But this effect has been offset, in some measure, by other developments. There has been a marked advance in agricultural productivity. From 1925–29 to 1949–53, output per man hour on the farms nearly doubled and output per acre rose by more than a fourth.[21] And during the forties, instead of declining, total output rose. These developments were a consequence of heavy investments in improved technology. And these investments have been attributed, by some observers, to the confidence inspired by price supports. They may also be attributable, in larger measure, to the fact that demand, during the war years, was strong, with prices well above parity and controls on output not applied.

In practice the program has not prevented a desirable shift of labor from agriculture to industry. Nor is it likely to do so. Price supports are of greatest benefit to the farmer whose productivity is high, and he is not the one who should leave the farm. They are of little benefit to the one whose productivity is low. They offer little impediment, therefore, to his movement into industry. Price supports, moreover, have not prevented a reallocation of resources within agriculture. But this is because prices, during most of the years since the program was inaugurated, have been above the supports. The effect of supports, when operative, has doubtless been to discourage and delay some shifts that would otherwise have taken place.

AGRICULTURAL REFORM

Among the critics of agricultural policy, there are a few who would go back to *laissez faire*, leaving the farmer at the mercy of the market. But this view is politically unrealistic and is not widely held. Agreement is fairly general that some form of governmental intervention is required. As to particular programs, opinions differ widely. But most economists would accept the view that base-period price parity should be abandoned, that the effort to set the prices of particular commodities above the long-

[21] D. Gale Johnson, "Competition in Agriculture: Fact or Fiction," *American Economic Review*, Vol. XLIV, No. 2 (1954), pp. 107–15, esp. p. 108.

run equilibrium level should be dropped, and that government should address itself to agriculture's fundamental problems: rural poverty, price uncertainty, and income instability.

Reducing Rural Poverty

The farmers at the lower end of the income scale suffer from several disabilities: their farms are too small; they have not been trained in modern methods of cultivation; they lack the capital with which to acquire needed equipment and supplies. They and their families do not have access to medical and educational facilities equivalent to those provided in the cities. If these farmers are to be aided two things are required: many of them should be encouraged to migrate from rural to urban areas; those who remain should be helped to raise their productivity.

The mobility of rural people can be increased by providing better education for children and training for adults, by promoting the industrialization of backward rural areas, as was done in the Tennessee Valley, by providing information concerning employment opportunities, and by making loans to cover moving costs. The productivity of poorer farmers can be raised by improving medical and educational facilities through federal grants in aid to states for use in needy areas, by loans to finance the purchase of larger farms and better equipment, and by a program of instruction in farm management such as that developed by the Farm Security Administration. If rural poverty is to be reduced, this is the way to do it, not by boosting the prices at which the wealthy farmer sells his crops.

Reducing Price Uncertainty

To improve the dependability of prices as a guide for the farmer to follow in planning his production, a number of economists have proposed that the government adopt a permanent program of forward pricing. Under such a program Congress would delegate authority to a board of experts who would make careful estimates of demand and supply for agricultural commodities, determine what prices would bring these forces into equilibrium, and announce them in advance of seeding or breeding time. The government would then guarantee that these prices would actually be obtained on the quantities produced that season. When the board's estimates were accurate the government would not have to make good on its guarantee. But if demand should prove to be smaller or supply larger than the board had assumed, the government could make good in one of two ways. It could buy commodities and store them until the price in the market had been bid up to the forward price, taking its stocks into consideration when it computed the supplies available in the coming year. Or it could stay clear of the market, making direct payments to farmers to cover the difference between the market price and the forward price. Such payments might conceivably be balanced, when prices obtained exceeded those promised, by collecting a tax.

The program proposed is similar to the one that was used to guide production during the war. Forward pricing, however, would bear no relation to base-period parity. The plan is not designed to raise prices or incomes. Its sole purpose would be that of enabling the farmer to base his decisions on the certain prices of the future rather than the uncertain prices of the past.

Such a proposal raises many questions. Would the experts selected to set the forward prices be skillful enough to keep the government's commitment within manageable bounds? Could they be insulated against the pressures of politics? Could farm organizations and Congressmen be persuaded to give them the freedom they would need to do an honest job? The answers can be found only by giving the plan a further trial.

Reducing Income Instability

If there is a gradual decline in the prices of particular crops or in farm income as a whole, this is a development to which the farmer should be expected to adjust. But the real problem of agriculture is not that of orderly adjustment to gradual change. It is that of sudden and violent deflation. This may be caused by the collapse of demand in a business depression. It may be caused by a change in supply. Depression is what the farmer fears most. It is this fear that excuses parity price supports. If it could be removed, they might conceivably be dropped.

The causes of depression lie outside of agriculture, in the instability of the industrial economy. The cure of depression, likewise, is outside agriculture, in the broader area of monetary and fiscal policies. If the industrial economy could be stabilized, the major problem of agriculture would be solved. But assuming that depressions are not prevented, how can their impact on the farmer be reduced?

One cause of fluctuations in farm income is changes in supply. A crop as a whole may be normal while on certain farms the same crop is destroyed by drought, flood, wind, hail, or pests. Or the size of a whole crop may fluctuate, yielding a high price on a small output in one year, a low price on a large output in the next. In the first case, the remedy is crop insurance, discussed in Chapter 11. In the second, it is storage. Here, economists have proposed that commodities be bought when crops are large and sold when crops are small, not to raise prices, but solely to stabilize supplies. In the case of feed grains, such operations could reduce fluctuations in their prices, in the resulting cost of producing livestock, and in the supply and price of meat. With these commodities and with others, storage could also lessen fluctuations in the incomes of producers. But here, again, there is danger that politics would destroy its value as a stabilizer by using it, as before, to obtain a higher price.

A second cause of fluctuations in farm income is changes in demand. Such changes may be countered in a variety of ways. One possibility would be to maintain the demand for agricultural products, during depressions, by subsidizing domestic consumption. This was done, to some extent, during the Great Depression, through food distribution and the food stamp plan. A second proposal, made by several economists, calls for contracyclical contributions, in cash, to agricultural incomes. Under one version of this proposal, such payments would make up part or all of the difference between the price of crops before and during a depression. This has been criticized as establishing a new form of parity that would interfere with the functioning of forward prices in directing production. Under a second version, this difficulty is avoided by basing payments, not on prices, but on the difference between predepression and depression incomes. This, however, would have the effect of placing farmers in a more favorable position than non-farmers during a slump. A final method would put a floor, not under money incomes, but under real incomes, by making payments to support them at a level below their long-run average, financing these payments by imposing taxes on farmers during periods of prosperity. This plan resembles the system of unemployment compensation that cushions the decline of labor income during depressions. It merits further consideration as a stabilizer of agricultural purchasing power.

SUGGESTIONS FOR FURTHER READING

A good description of the characteristics of the agricultural economy is presented by Harold G. Halcrow in *Agricultural Policy of the United States* (New York: Prentice-Hall, Inc., 1953), Part I. An excellent analysis of the problems of agriculture is that by Geoffrey S. Shepherd in his *Agricultural Price and Income Policy* (Ames: Iowa State College Press, 1952), chaps. i, ii, iii, and v. See also Theodore W. Schultz, *Production and Welfare of Agriculture* (New York: Macmillan Co., 1949), chaps. v, vii, and xii, and Rainer Schickele, *Agricultural Policy* (New York: McGraw-Hill Book Co., 1954), chaps. x and xix.

The authoritative history of agricultural policy is Murray R. Benedict, *Farm Policies of the United States, 1790–1950* (New York: Twentieth Century Fund, 1953). A good account, in briefer compass, is presented by Schickele in his chaps. xii, xiii, and xv. The objectives of parity and price supports are discussed by Schickele in chap. xi. The arithmetic of parity is set forth in the Department of Agriculture's *Parity Handbook* (82d Cong., 2d Sess., Senate Doc. 129, 1952). Storage programs are analyzed in Halcrow, chap. xviii, and in Shepherd, chaps. vii to x; surplus disposal plans in Halcrow, chap. xx, Shepherd, chap. xii, and Schickele, chap. xiv; production and marketing controls in Halcrow, chap. xix, Schickele, chap. xii, and Schultz, chap. xiii. On the reduction of rural poverty, see Halcrow, chap. xxiii, Schickele, chap. xxi, and Shepherd, chaps. xvii–xix; on crop insurance, Halcrow, chap. xxvi, Shepherd, chap. xi, and Schultz's *The Economic Organization of Agriculture* (New York: McGraw-Hill Book Co., 1953), chap. xix.

Critical appraisals of farm policy are contained in Schultz's *Redirecting Farm Policy* (New York: Macmillan Co., 1943), and in his *Production and Welfare of Agriculture*, chaps. i–iv; also in O. B. Jesness (ed.), *Readings on*

Agricultural Policy (Philadelphia: Blakiston Co., 1949), chaps. v, x, xi, and xvii, and in a statement by thirteen distinguished agricultural economists called *Turning the Spotlight on Farm Policy* (Chicago: The Farm Foundation, 1952). Minority reports in partial defense of present policy are entered by J. K. Galbraith and D. Gale Johnson in the *American Economic Review,* Vol. XLIV (1954), pp. 40–52, and Vol. XLIV, No. 2, pp. 107–15. Programs for agricultural reform are presented in Shepherd, chaps. vi–xix, in Jesness, chaps. xii–xvi, in Schickele, chap. xvii, in Schultz, *The Economic Organization of Agriculture,* chap. xx, and in Oscar Heline and Donald R. Kaldor, *A Framework for Long-Range Agricultural Policy* (Washington: National Planning Association, Pamphlet No. 72, 1950). See also D. Gale Johnson, *Forward Prices for Agriculture* (Chicago: University of Chicago Press, 1947) and the prize essays in a contest on "A Price Policy for Agriculture" sponsored by the American Farm Economic Association, published in the *Journal of Farm Economics* for November, 1945.

Chapter 16 COMPULSORY CARTELS

In the last three chapters we have seen how government has responded to pressures brought to bear upon it by industries where producers are numerous and well organized. In all of the cases examined it has adopted measures designed to lessen competition. In some of them it has undertaken to protect established enterprises against the effects of a decline in demand, or against the emergence of new competitors. In many, its action dates from the Great Depression and was first intended as a temporary measure of relief. Under the NRA such relief took the form of freedom to establish cartels. For industry in general this freedom was shortly terminated by the Supreme Court. But for particular industries it had been afforded by other legislation or was re-established, after the Schechter decision, by new enactments. This was true of bituminous coal from 1935 to 1943. It is still true of the production of crude petroleum and sugar and of the sale of agricultural commodities produced within limited geographic areas, such as fruits, nuts, and vegetables, or sold within limited markets, such as milk. In these industries, competition in production or in price has been or may be forbidden, and the restrictions imposed are enforced by government itself. Here, though it calls them by different names, the United States has embraced compulsory cartels.

FIXING COAL PRICES

The government undertook to establish minimum prices for bituminous coal during a period of depression when demand was low. It abandoned the undertaking during a period of prosperity when demand was high. But restoration of its powers has been proposed in bills introduced in Congress since the end of World War II. And, in another slump, the pressure for re-enactment of such a measure might well prove irresistible.

The moving force behind this legislation was that of organized labor. Wages are close to two thirds of the costs incurred in mining coal. Wage rates are set in collective bargains negotiated with the coal operators by the United Mine Workers of America. When the industry competes, there is danger that prices will be cut so low that these wages cannot be paid. By putting a floor under prices, however, government may enable the operators to keep on paying wages at the rates that their contracts require. This was the purpose of the coal laws that were passed in 1935 and 1937. During the war, with operators prosperous and wage contracts kept, the power to fix prices was permitted to expire. In the early postwar years, with demand sustained by a high level of industrial activity and with supply controlled by union limitations on the length of the work week, it was not needed. But whenever falling demand and growing competition should threaten the level of prices and wages, it would doubtless be demanded once again.

Bituminous: The Sick Industry

For a score of years economists have used the term "sick industry." And the industry they have invariably used to illustrate the concept is bituminous coal. Here is an industry that has come close to satisfying all of the requirements of the definition of pure competition. The product cannot be differentiated; its heating value is measured in standard British thermal units. Producers are numerous: from year to year, 5,000 to 6,000 concerns operate 6,000 to 9,000 mines, each producing a thousand tons or more, with other thousands of companies operating on a smaller scale. No firm or group of firms controls enough of the output to enable it to influence the price substantially. Production can easily be expanded. Half of the world's coal is in the United States. Deposits of bituminous are widely scattered; title to workable seams is distributed among thousands of owners. Much of the supply is so readily accessible that mines can be opened quickly and at small expense. There is no barrier to the entry of new concerns and the development of new properties. Any person or group who can muster a moderate amount of capital is free to join the industry. Bituminous has long been actively competitive. It has also been chronically sick.

Coal's major customers are the railroads, the public utilities, and the manufacturers of steel. As oligopsonists, these buyers are able to play off one supplier against another in an effort to depress the price. Their demand for coal, moreover, is relatively inelastic. For one thing, the cost of coal is but a small part of their total costs, and the price at the mine is but a part of the price they pay. For another, demand for their own products is similarly inelastic and their prices are fairly inflexible. A reduction in cost is unlikely to be reflected in these prices. And even if it were, it might not substantially affect their output or the amount of coal that they would buy. A cut in the price of coal, therefore, does not result in a proportionate increase in sales. The demand for coal varies less with its price than with the volume of business activity.

The supply of coal is quick to expand but slow to contract. Rising prices encourage operators to increase the output of existing mines, to reopen abandoned mines, and to bring new areas into production. Falling prices do not result in a comparable reduction in the number of operators or in the volume of output. It may cost more to stop producing than to produce at a loss. Fixed charges must be met. Property taxes, for instance, are levied on the value of the deposits, not on the quantities removed. A mine once opened cannot be closed without expense. It must be ventilated to prevent the accumulation of dangerous gases, pumped to prevent flooding, and timbered to prevent cave-ins. Coal once produced cannot be stored at the mine without additional cost. It must be handled twice, is subject to deterioration, and may be lost through fire. Operators therefore tend to produce as much as they can sell and to sell as much as they produce.

With demand down and supply maintained, prices drop. But labor and capital remain within the industry. The miners are highly specialized; their work is skilled. Living in isolated settlements, they often lack alternative opportunities. For these and other reasons, they are lacking in mobility. Equipment, too, is specialized and cannot be moved. Investments can be liquidated through bankruptcy, and this occurs. But the real capital remains, to be kept in operation at a lower level of cost. Now losses may be avoided and profits earned. But eventually supply will again outrun demand, and the industry will be headed for another round of bankruptcies.

This has been the story of bituminous. And it may be doubted that anyone has gained. The prices paid by consumers have been low, but they have fluctuated widely and supplies have been interrupted by repeated strikes. The wage rates paid to labor have been high, but employment has been irregular and annual incomes have been low. The work has been hazardous, and the workers, living in company towns, were long denied the exercise of civil liberties. As for the operators, losses have exceeded profits for decades at a time, and investments have been put through the wringer again and again.

Like agriculture, bituminous coal enjoyed no share in the prosperity that followed World War I. Demand declined as users turned to other sources of fuel—petroleum, natural gas, and falling water—and as they learned to reduce the quantities of coal consumed in generating power. In 1918, coal met 70 per cent of the demand for energy; in 1937, only 45 per cent. At the same time, the supply of coal increased. New mines were opened in the South, where rich deposits still remained unworked. Here, the structure of freight rates made it possible for operators to compete in northern markets, mechanization kept their costs down, and the lack of unionization enabled them to obtain labor at less than the union rate. Here, though demand was declining, expansion appeared to be profitable. As a result, the average price of coal at the mines dropped from $3.75 in 1920 to $1.78 in 1929. The number of miners employed dropped from 700,000 to 500,000. The industry as a whole lost money in every year from 1920 to 1934. Three operators out of 5 were in the red in 1929.

With the coming of depression, the situation went from bad to worse.

In 1932 the average realization on coal at the mine was down to $1.31. The number of miners was down to 400,000, the number of days of work down to 146 per year, the average annual wage down to $662. The power of the union was broken; the number of miners paying dues was down to 15 per cent. Four firms out of 5 were operating at a loss. The industry ended the year with a deficit of more than $50 million. It was in this situation that minimum prices came to be fixed for coal.

From Competition to Cartelization

The first step taken to aid the industry was the formation of a private cartel. In 1931 a common sales agency, called Appalachian Coals, Inc., was set up by 137 companies controlling three fourths of the coal produced in Virginia, West Virginia, Kentucky, and Tennessee. The agency was to allocate orders among its members and to call for a reduction in output if prices were deemed too low. When sued by the Department of Justice for violation of the Sherman Act, it was acquitted by the Supreme Court on the ground (1) that it handled only 12 per cent of the coal mined east of the Mississippi and was therefore in no position to control the prices in the markets where it sold, and (2) that it imposed a reasonable restraint on competition in an industry that was suffering acute distress.[1]

The solution of voluntary cartelization was never given a real test. For in 1933 the whole industry was brought under compulsory control by the NRA. The code for bituminous coal contained the required provisions establishing maximum hours and minimum wages and guaranteeing collective bargaining. And this was highly significant, since the minimum wages reduced the differential that favored expansion in the South, and labor organization—shortly increasing union membership from 15 per cent to more than 90 per cent—promised to eliminate it altogether. In addition, the code improved the lot of labor by prohibiting many practices that had proved to be injurious, both at the mines and in the company towns. For the operators, it contained the usual trade practice provisions and authorized the establishment of minimum prices.

In providing for price fixing, the government sought to centralize the power in a national authority. But the industry resisted, and the final result was a compromise. Code authorities representing the operators were set up in five geographic divisions. The power to fix minimum prices was delegated to marketing agencies or trade associations or, failing this, to the code authorities. The only guidance given was the requirement that the prices must be "fair." The NRA was permitted to appoint a nonvoting member to each of the authorities and was empowered to veto the prices that were fixed. During its lifetime, it was moving toward the development of pricing criteria and the co-ordination of minimum prices set by different regions for sales in common markets. But its work was not com-

[1] *Appalachian Coals, Inc.* v. *U.S.*, 288 U.S. 344 (1933).

pleted when it was brought to an end by the Schechter decision in 1935. The prices set under the code were observed for a few months. But in 1934 they began to break under the pressure of interregional competition. And by 1935 the whole structure had been virtually destroyed. It was clear that prices could not be enforced if they were set on a basis of regional autonomy.

When the NIRA was found to be unconstitutional, in May 1935, Congress moved swiftly to re-enact controls for coal. A bill introduced by Senator Joseph Guffey of Pennsylvania provided not only for labor safeguards and price fixing, but also for curtailment of production. Under this bill, the government would have borrowed $300 million, purchased coal deposits, and withheld them from development. It would have imposed a tax of 10 per cent on sales of coal, using two fifths of the proceeds to service its bonds. The other three fifths were to be used in retraining surplus miners and transferring them to other industries.

In the Bituminous Coal Conservation Act of 1935, known as the Guffey-Snyder Act and signed in August of that year, control of production was dropped. The only appearance of conservation in the final measure was in the title at its head. In effect, the law revived the NRA code, providing for central supervision over regional price determinations and making other changes in detail. It never came into full operation, its constitutionality being challenged as soon as it was signed.

In May, 1936, the Supreme Court held the Act of 1935 to be invalid on the ground that its labor provisions exceeded the powers of Congress to regulate commerce, since commerce is "a thing apart from the relation of employer and employee."[2] The price-fixing provisions were also invalidated, but only on the ground that they could not be extricated from the other sections of the law. The Court thus hinted broadly that it would have upheld them had they stood alone. Congress took the hint; within three weeks a bill was introduced that dropped the regulation of labor but continued the price-fixing machinery. It was not passed, however, until the next session. The Guffey-Vinson bill became the Bituminous Coal Act of 1937. The constitutionality of this law, too, was questioned, but it was upheld by the Supreme Court, in an eight to one decision, in 1940.[3]

The Second Guffey Act was to be administered by a National Bituminous Coal Commission, this body being converted in 1939 into a Bituminous Coal Division in the Department of the Interior. It provided for the establishment of maximum as well as minimum prices and created a Consumers' Counsel to represent the interest of consumers in the price-fixing process. These provisions, however, were little more than window dressing. The real purpose of the law was that of putting a floor under prices. Sale below minimum prices was made illegal, and conformity was enforced by imposing a discriminatory tax of 19½ per cent on the sales made by producers who failed to co-operate.

[2] *Carter* v. *Carter Coal Co.*, 298 U.S. 238, 303.

[3] *Sunshine Anthracite Coal Co.* v. *Adkins,* 310 U.S. 381.

The Price Fixing Experiment

Under the terms of the Act, the process of fixing prices was to proceed by five steps:

1. The Commission was to determine the weighted average cost of producing coal in each of 23 producing districts and in each of 10 minimum price areas. This figure would cover all of the mines in a district but might differ from district to district in an area. When determined, the cost estimates were to be submitted to district boards elected by the operators.
2. Each board was then to propose minimum prices for each kind, quality, and size of coal produced in the district, with differentials applying to market areas, customer classes, and seasons of the year. These prices were to meet four standards. They were to be so calculated (*a*) as to yield "a return per net ton for each district in a minimum price area . . . equal as nearly as may be to the weighted average of the total costs, per net ton, . . . of the tonnage of such minimum price area," (*b*) to "reflect, as nearly as possible, the relative market value of the various kinds, qualities, and sizes of coal," (*c*) to be "just and equitable as between producers," and (*d*) to "have due regard for the interests of the consuming public."
3. The Commission was to review these proposals, district by district, and to approve, disapprove, or modify them, returning them to the district boards.
4. The boards were to co-ordinate their prices where coal produced in different districts competed for sale in common market areas. In doing so, they were required (*a*) to be "just and equitable" as between districts, (*b*) to give due weight to the relative values of different grades and sizes of coal, in different uses, at different times, within these markets, and to the competition of other fuels, (*c*) to preserve "fair competitive opportunities," and (*d*) to keep the return per net ton in every minimum price area as close as possible to "the weighted average of the total cost per net ton" of the area.
5. The resulting prices were then to be submitted to the Commission which was empowered to review them, rejecting or modifying them or putting them into effect.

This was to be the normal procedure. But if the district boards should fail to act, the Commission was authorized to do so. And once the minimum prices had been established, it was to raise or lower them whenever the weighted average cost of producing coal should rise or fall by more than two cents per ton.

Under pressure from the union and the operators, the Commission hastened to fix its prices, taking short cuts through the maze of requirements set up by the law. It made tentative cost findings and directed the district boards to employ them as a basis for price proposals. When the boards failed to co-ordinate their prices in common markets, it did the job itself. It issued its final schedule of prices, in December, 1937, without holding formal hearings or attempting to present a justification of the action that it took. The legality of this procedure was immediately questioned, the courts were flooded with requests for injunctions, and the schedule was revoked in February, 1938.

The Commission—and later, the Division—then proceeded with a meticulous regard for the requirements of due process. It held public hearings to determine whether sales were in interstate commerce. It spent months on its computation of costs, holding preliminary hearings, issuing findings of fact and formal determinations, and then holding final hearings within each area. It devoted further months to hearings on the price proposals submitted by the district boards. When the boards failed to coordinate their prices, it again undertook the task. But now it worked out an elaborate classification of kinds, grades, and sizes of coal, and made a painstaking study of the sources of every type of coal that was sold in each of the country's market areas. On this basis it prepared a tentative schedule of prices, holding hearings throughout the summer and fall of 1939, and issuing its official schedule in the summer of 1940, to take effect in October of that year.

The Division's final action established minimum prices for every type of coal produced in every region in the United States and sold in every market at every season for every type of use—about 400,000 separate prices in all. At the time, it raised the general level of prices by about 11 cents a ton. The job was not completed until three years after Congress had passed the law. By then, the world was again at war. The demand for coal was growing and its price was rising, along with those of other goods. The schedule of prices, prepared at such great pains, was no longer needed to keep prices from going down. But it was very useful in keeping prices from going up. It was used for this purpose by the Office of Price Administration throughout the war. And this, in fact, was the only use it ever had.

The Possible Results

Would the plan have worked in normal times? Nobody really knows. It is clear that the procedures established were cumbersome, that adaptation to changing conditions would necessarily be slow, and that producers might be forbidden to cut their prices when demand was falling and supplies were large. If coal could not be sold, it is likely that violations would become so common that the structure would break down. With sellers numbering in the thousands and transactions in the hundreds of thousands, and with methods of evasion readily at hand, it may be doubted that minimum prices could be enforced. For the undertaking to succeed, government would have to control production as well as price.

If the plan could have worked, how would it have affected the industry's efficiency? Again, nobody knows. If costs would have been estimated closely, the principle of basing minimum prices on a weighted average should have afforded an incentive for efficiency, eliminated inefficient operators, and concentrated operations in the more efficient mines. But here, as elsewhere, estimates of cost could be padded. And there would doubtless have been pressure to add a margin of profit in fixing a minimum price. If the level of prices were thus increased, high-cost producers would have been sheltered and excessive resources kept in the industry.

Under the Guffey Acts, prices were to be set by law at a level that would enable the operators to pay the wages required in their contracts with the union. Since the war they have been maintained by limiting production through union control of the length of the work week. In either case, the higher wages and prices have another obvious effect. They stimulate the substitution of other fuels and the mechanization of mining, thus depriving operators of markets and miners of jobs. And they make their contribution to conservation by checking the consumption of coal, which is plentiful, and increasing the consumption of oil and gas, which are not. As far as the union is concerned, a deliberate choice appears to have been made against more jobs at low pay, in favor of fewer jobs at higher pay. By 1952 oil and gas were providing 62 per cent and coal only 34 per cent of the nation's energy and the number of miners was again down to 400,000. As oil and gas approach exhaustion and their prices rise, coal will reclaim a growing share of the market as its own. In the meantime its hope seems to lie in the development of economical means of liquifaction, gasification, and conversion into electricity for transmission by wire from the mouth of the mine.

The Anthracite Cartel

Anthracite coal differs from bituminous in many ways. It is used, in the main, for space heating in urban centers in the East. Almost all of the hard coal mined in the United States comes from an area of 480 square miles in northeastern Pennsylvania. Control of these deposits has long been concentrated in the hands of a few concerns. The industry has not suffered from the chronic illness that has afflicted bituminous. Until recent years, its owners charged a monopoly price and secured a monopoly profit. But then, like bituminous, it began losing business to oil and gas. And so, to prevent increasing competition among its members, the industry turned for help to the Commonwealth of Pennsylvania.

Since 1939, under the provisions of the Pennsylvania Commerce Act, a committee consisting of three representatives each of the hard coal operators, the United Mine Workers, and the Commonwealth has met each week at Harrisburg to decide how much coal shall be produced in the coming week. The committee's decision is based on a report of market requirements obtained by telephone from a group of fourteen coal sales executives meeting in New York. The permissible production is then divided among the 50 companies participating in the plan in accordance with their former shares in total sales. Seven companies account for two thirds of the output in the group, the other 43 for the remaining third. In 1949 there were 57 operators remaining outside the plan, but they did not produce significant amounts. Legally, participation is voluntary. But any mine could easily be shut down: by the union, through a strike, or by the Commonwealth, on the ground that safety regulations were not observed. So far, the application of these sanctions has not been required.[4] The industry has been content to divide up whatever share of the market is left it, instead of seeking, through product improvement and price competition, to keep a bigger share for coal.

PETROLEUM PRORATIONING

In the operation of pipe lines and refineries, the oil industry has often revealed the characteristics of monopoly. But in the production of crude petroleum, it has been competitive. Here, production is more highly concentrated than in the case of bituminous coal, the major companies normally accounting for half of the supply. But the number of independent producers runs into the thousands, known reserves are substantial, improvements in mining are enlarging recovery, and exploration is constantly going on. When a new field has been opened, as we saw in Chapter 12, competitive exploitation has led to a prompt expansion of output without regard to the current state of demand. As a result, substantial discoveries have depressed the price of crude.

In such a situation, producers formerly sought to protect their prices and incomes by entering into voluntary agreements for the control of output. But such agreements tended to break down as outsiders kept on producing and insiders either withdrew or failed to keep their word. Not only were the agreements unenforceable; they might be held to violate the Sherman Act. The industry has therefore undertaken to legalize its restrictions and to enforce them by enlisting the coercive power of government. The result has been a body of state and federal legislation setting up an elaborate system of prorationing. This is producer legislation, designed to serve a producer interest. In the oil states and in the nation, its enactment is a tribute less to the political power of the major oil companies than to that of organizations representing the thousands of independent producers of petroleum.

Development of State Prorationing

The first law designed to maintain the price of oil by curtailing production was enacted in Oklahoma in 1915. The law forbade "economic waste" as well as physical waste, and defined it as production in excess of

[4] Clair Wilcox, *Competition and Monopoly in American Industry*, T.N.E.C. Monograph 21 (Washington: Government Printing Office, 1940), pp. 181–92; *New York Times*, April 19, 1949.

"reasonable market demands." It authorized the state's Corporation Commission to determine allowable output and to prorate it among well owners in proportion to the potential capacity of their wells. The law was enacted to reduce an oversupply of oil. But the growth of demand in World War I did away with the surplus, and the plan was not put into effect. The law is significant, however, as the one that set the pattern for prorationing.

With the coming of depression in the thirties, the demand for oil declined. This experience, in itself, was unfamiliar to the industry. At the same tme, moreover, lush new fields were brought into production. Output in east Texas jumped from nothing in 1930 to more than a million barrels a day in 1931, an amount exceeding the total output of Oklahoma or California. Prices plummeted: the average price of Mid-Continent crude (36° gravity) fell from $1.229 a barrel at the beginning of 1930 to $.239 in the summer of 1931, sales being made, in some cases, for less than a dime. Under a law passed in 1919 the Texas Railroad Commission had the authority to reduce physical waste but not to control economic waste. But something had to be done. Acting without waiting for Congressional approval, the governors of Oklahoma, Kansas, and Texas made a compact to restrict production, and set up an advisory committee to determine the output that each of their states was to be allowed. In Oklahoma the proration law was resurrected and the Corporation Commission put to work dividing the state's allotment among its wells. In Texas also, though legal authority was wanting, the Railroad Commission began prorationing. The orders issued by these bodies were resisted. In both states, they were enforced by declaring martial law. In 1932 the Supreme Court declared this measure to be invalid.[5] But it upheld the Oklahoma statute on the assumption that prorationing was a method of conservation, thus coming within the power of the state.[6] Texas amended its earlier law of authorize prorationing. And within a few years, most of the other oil-producing states had fallen into line.

The typical proration law prohibits waste, defines it to include not only physical but also economic waste, defines the latter as production in excess of "reasonable market demand," and empowers a state commission to restrict output and apportion that allowed among fields and among producers in a pool. The only important oil state to lack such a statute is California. And here, a similar program has been administered by a voluntary committee of oil producers.

State action, taken by itself, has two serious weaknesses. It provides no method for determining the size of the total market or the shares to be allotted to individual states. And it affords no means of compelling the states to keep within their shares. A single state, if its output were substantial, could destroy the program by refusing to co-operate. To com-

[5] *Sterling* v. *Constantin*, 287 U.S. 378.

[6] *Champlin Refining Co.* v. *Corporation Commission of Oklahoma*, 286 U.S. 210 (1932).

plete the structure of control, and to insure its effectiveness, the oil producers have therefore turned for help to the federal government.

Development of Federal Regulation

In 1924, when it was feared that national security might be endangered by a shortage of oil, President Coolidge set up a Federal Oil Conservation Board to consider means whereby waste might be prevented and supplies conserved. Within a few months production had mounted, stocks had accumulated, and prices had dropped. The Board therefore turned its attention to methods of restriction. In a series of reports issued during the following years, it proposed the adoption of an interstate compact to control supply. When the industry presented a plan to share world markets with foreign producers and to set up a quota system in the United States, the Board was sympathetic, but the Attorney General expressed the opinion that the plan would violate the Sherman Act and it was not put into effect. In 1930, however, the Board set up a Volunteer Committee on Petroleum Economics to make estimates of future consumption, based on facts supplied it by the Bureau of Mines, and to recommend output quotas to the states.

In 1933 this lead was followed under the NIRA. The program adopted for the oil industry imposed controls at every stage of its operations: production, refining, and marketing. To regulate supplies, limitations were placed on imports, on withdrawals from storage, and on the output of crude. The industry's code provided for periodic determination by a federal agency (the Bureau of Mines) of the amounts required to balance consumer demand, for allocation of these amounts among the producing states, and for prorationing among pools and wells by state authorities. And where the states should fail to limit output, it authorized the federal government to act.

Unlike the other codes, this one was not turned over for administration to the industry. Nor was it entrusted to the NRA. Instead, the code was placed under Harold L. Ickes, then Secretary of the Interior, who served as Petroleum Administrator, and was managed by officials of his department, with a committee of oil producers serving in an advisory capacity. In this case, the abuses experienced in many other industries did not appear. But the code did provide the oil producers with the mechanism they required to establish a nation-wide system of production control.

The Recovery Act itself did more than this. In Section 9-*c*, it empowered the President to prohibit interstate shipments of petroleum that had been produced in violation of state laws. "Hot oil," turned out in excess of state quotas, was to be excluded from interstate commerce, and restriction of output was thus to be enforced. In 1933 the President required that oil offered for shipment be covered by affidavits in which the sellers swore that it had been produced within their quotas. In 1934, when this system had broken down, he set up a Federal Tender Board to issue certificates of clearance that had to be shown before petroleum or its products were permitted to move across state lines. This system worked. But in January, 1935, the Supreme Court found Section 9-*c* to be unconstitutional, on the ground that it involved an invalid delegation of power, since the authority conferred on the President was not accompanied by standards adequate to govern its use.[7] In the next month Congress restored the executive's power to prohibit interstate shipments in excess of state quotas by passing the Connally Hot Oil Act. The new law contained procedural safeguards, and was upheld by a Circuit Court of Appeals in 1936.[8] Unquestioned before the Supreme Court, its constitutionality has since been assumed.

In May, 1935, the Schechter decision destroyed the petroleum code along with the codes administered by NRA. But the nation-wide system of controlling production survived. The Bureau of Mines continued to make its estimates of demand. In August, 1935, Congress approved an interstate compact among the oil-producing states. And the regulation of interstate shipments was continued under the Connally Act.

The Present Pattern of Control

The production of crude petroleum has now been controlled, for many years, in the following way: (1) The Bureau of Mines makes monthly forecasts of consumer demands for gasoline, fuel oil, and other petroleum products, translates these forecasts into an estimate of the demand for crude, and divides this total into separate estimates for the producing states. It then transmits its estimates to the regulatory agencies of the states. Legally, no state need follow them. Actually, all of them do. (2) The state agencies, co-operating through the Interstate Oil Compact Commission, consider the Bureau's estimates and agree as to how they are to be put into effect. (3) Each of these agencies prorates the total for its state among its own fields, pools, and wells. (4) The federal government, under the hot oil law, prevents interstate shipments in violation of state quotas. Each of these steps requires a further word.

The Bureau of Mines makes two important estimates: one showing the total demand for petroleum and one showing the demand for petroleum from each state. The first is an estimate of the quantity that will be bought at the prevailing price. It does not show how much less would be bought if the price were raised or how much more would be bought if it were reduced. It assumes the legitimacy of price fixing, accepting without question the proposition that price should be taken as given and supply adjusted to demand. The estimates for the several states, though presented as estimates of demand, are really nothing of the sort, since there is no such thing as a demand for oil produced in a particular state. They are production quotas, based on past output or present capacity. As such, they

[7] *Panama Refining Co.* v. *Ryan,* 293 U.S. 388.

[8] *Griswold* v. *President of the United States,* 82 F. 2d 922.

are necessarily arbitrary in character, replacing the dictates of the market with the judgments of public officials and the expedients of politics.

The Interstate Oil Compact, first approved in 1935 and periodically renewed without amendment ever since, appears to serve the purpose of conservation. Its twenty signatories agree to enact and continue laws designed to prevent the physical waste of oil and gas. And Article V of the document forswears any intention "to authorize the states joining herein to limit the production of oil or gas for the purpose of fixing the price thereof. . . ." But the Compact authorizes the Commission to recommend "coordination of the exercise of the police powers of the several states . . . to promote the maximum ultimate recovery from the petroleum reserves of said states . . ." and commits each of these states to enact or continue laws providing "that oil produced in violation of its valid oil and/or gas conservation statutes . . . shall be denied access to commerce. . . ." The meaning is plain. And, in fact, the interstate compact, while of little significance in promoting conservation, has served as a convenient instrument in carrying out the program of production control.

In establishing quotas for individual producers, the states have sought to assure each claimant his fair share of the wealth in a pool. But they have found no wholly satisfactory method of achieving this result. At first, quotas were fixed on a flat basis per well. But this was unfair unless the wells in a field were evenly spaced and pressure throughout the reservoir was uniform. It rewarded the owner who had drilled a large number of wells and penalized the one who had not. And it required that pressure be kept under one tract to drive up oil on another. Under a second method, quotas were based on the potential output of each well, and the potential was measured by running at full capacity. This gave larger quotas on tracts where pressure was greater. But the process of measurement was wasteful. And this method, like the other, put a premium on the duplication of wells. A third basis of allocation made the quota for each well proportionate to the area it drained. This did away with the incentive to drill additional wells. But it discriminated among owners unless reservoir conditions under tracts of equal size were uniform. More recently, a number of other formulas have been developed, combining these factors in various ways and taking account of such matters as the thickness of oil sands, the permeability of subsurface strata, the fluidity of deposits, volumetric displacement within reservoirs, and differences between static and flowing bottom-hole pressures. But allocations are not based on technical considerations alone. Small producers are numerous and politically powerful, and the formulas employed are always modified to provide a minimum quota for every well. Under such an arrangement in Texas in the thirties, some wells were cut back to 2 per cent of their capacity while 75 per cent of the output in one field and 98 per cent in another was produced under flat per-well allowances. When the quotas were challenged, however, they were upheld by the Supreme Court of the United States on the ground that the state commission could legitimately adopt any method of allocation it might choose.[9]

In its control of interstate shipments, the federal government enforces the restrictions imposed by the states, whatever they may be. The President is authorized by Section 4 of the Hot Oil Act to suspend the operation of the law if he should find that the amount of petroleum moving in interstate commerce had been so sharply curtailed as to cause a "lack of parity" between supply and demand. But the standard thus established is a vague one, and no such finding has ever been made. With respect to the control of oil production, the federal government has abdicated its responsibility for policy.

Stabilization and Conservation

The objective of prorationing is stabilization, not conservation. The two are not identical. Conservation, it will be remembered, has various meanings: (1) postponement of consumption, (2) complete recovery, and (3) recovery wherever price will cover cost. Stabilization also has different meanings. Nominally, it seeks only to moderate the fluctuations in a price. In practice, it seeks a higher level.

Does stabilization contribute to conservation? In some respects, it does. By restricting the supply of oil and raising its price, it may check inferior uses at present and hold larger reserves for superior uses in the future. By keeping stripper wells in operation, it may insure a larger ultimate recovery. By curtailing flush flows, it saves the costs involved in storage above ground. But these advantages could be obtained in other ways. And here, they are offset by the fact that stabilization causes waste. When total output is made to depend upon the quantity that can be sold at a fixed price, it bears no necessary relation to the quantities required for economical recovery. When every well receives a quota and spacing is not subjected to rigorous control, excessive drilling is encouraged, there is needless duplication of investment, and the efficiency of production is impaired. Real conservation, as we saw in Chapter 12, requires the unitary operation of a pool. But prorationing differs from unitization. It is concerned with equity among property owners, not with maximum recovery at minimum cost. Insofar as stabilization makes for conservation, it does so incidentally and accidentally. Its real objective is a higher price.

During most of the time that oil production has been cartelized, demand has been large and prices have been strong. There is little doubt, however, that the plan would support the price of oil in a depression; unlike the one adopted for bituminous coal, it provides for control of supply. The danger is not that prorationing will fail to work but that it will work too well. Producers may go too far in boosting prices. And consumers may insist that prices be controlled. This has happened to other industries

[9] *Railroad Commission* v. *Rowan & Nichols Oil Co.,* 310 U.S. 573 (1940).

possessing monopoly power. There have been signs, from time to time, that it may happen to oil.

SUGAR QUOTAS

The United States has always consumed more sugar than it has produced, importing a major part of its supply, some of it from Hawaii, Puerto Rico, the Virgin Islands, and the Philippines, but more from Cuba, where production is large and costs are relatively low. Sugar beets and cane are grown by less than 3 per cent of the farmers on the mainland. But these farmers are located in 19 states and influence the votes of 38 senators. For many years, they have been sheltered from foreign competition by barriers to imports.

During the nineteenth century, the tariff on sugar was not set at a level designed to protect domestic production. Sugar was admitted duty free from Hawaii after 1875, from Puerto Rico after 1902, from the Philippines after 1914, from the Virgin Islands after 1917, and at a preferential rate of 20 per cent below the general tariff from Cuba after 1903. Around the turn of the century, protective duties were imposed, bringing the rate on sugar in general up to 1⅔ cents a pound and that on Cuban sugar up to 1⅓ cents. After World War I the world production of sugar expanded and its price fell steadily. The United States increased its duties in 1921, in 1922, and again in 1930, the rate set on sugar in general rising to 2½ cents and that on Cuban sugar to 2 cents. These rates cut the share of foreign producers (mostly Cuban) in the American market from 54 per cent to 30 per cent, increasing the share of other off-shore producers from 25 per cent to 45 per cent and that of domestic producers from 21 per cent to 25 per cent. In 1931, under the leadership of Cuba, an agreement was negotiated among the principal countries exporting sugar whereby they cut their output in half. But prices were not improved, since contraction in these areas was largely offset by expansion elsewhere. From 1930 on, the relative position of Cuban producers was worsened and that of American producers improved.

In a series of trade agreements concluded between 1934 and 1948, the duty on Cuban sugar was successively cut to .9 cents, to .75 cents, and to .5 cents. And under the Philippine Trade Act of 1946, duties are to be reimposed on Philippine sugar, beginning at 5 per cent of the full rate in 1954 and rising 5 per cent per year until they reach 100 per cent of the full rate in 1973. But the tariff is no longer of major significance. The right to produce sugar and sell it in the American market has come to be controlled in another way.

The Sugar Acts of 1934 and 1937

Under the Jones-Costigan Act of 1934, the Secretary of Agriculture was directed to make an annual estimate of the quantity of sugar required for consumption in the United States and to establish quotas to govern imports and domestic production. The division of the market between foreign and domestic producers was to be determined by selecting as a base the three years within the period 1925–34 that the Secretary deemed to be "most representative." Under pressure from domestic interests, the Secretary came to the conclusion that the three years that followed the enactment of the Smoot-Hawley Tariff Act in 1930 were "most representative" and based his quotas on the market shares resulting from that law. The domestic quota was divided among producing areas, the area quotas between cane and beet producers, the beet quotas among beet factory districts, and cane and beet quotas among individual growers. Sugar was made a basic commodity under the first AAA, production was controlled by contract, and rental or benefit payments were made for reductions in output, being financed by imposing a processing tax. This was the usual pattern under the AAA. In this case, however, farmers receiving benefits were required not only to curtail production but also to eliminate child labor and to observe such minimum wages as the Secretary might require.

The Act of 1934 was not specifically invalidated when the Supreme Court outlawed the first AAA in 1936. But Congress moved quickly to eliminate its production controls and processing tax and to bring sugar cane and beets under the Soil Conservation Act, with import quotas and domestic subsidies maintained. In the next year a second quota law was passed, following the earlier pattern with differences in detail.

Under the Sugar Act of 1937, the Secretary of Agriculture was still required to make his annual estimate of demand. But the division of the market between foreign and domestic producers was now written into the law. The former were given 29 per cent of the market, the Philippines 15 per cent, and other insular and domestic producers 56 per cent. And the law provided further that the latter share should never fall below 3,715,000 tons. An excise tax of .5 cents a pound was imposed on imports and domestic output to finance the payment of subsidies. And now quotas were imposed on refined as well as raw sugar and on that coming not only from foreign countries but also from islands under the American flag. The only purpose of this provision was to protect mainland refineries.

In 1937, too, an international agreement was concluded among the major sugar producing and consuming countries. Under its terms the producing countries agreed to limit their exports and the consuming countries agreed to maintain their imports by controlling domestic production. The import quotas assigned the United States were those established under the Sugar Act. During World War II the quota system was suspended. Sugar from the Philippines was cut off. Its share in the American market fell to virtually nothing. That of Cuba rose to 45 per cent. The quota system and the international agreement were re-established after the war.

The Sugar Act of 1948

Under the Act of 1948, which continues in effect until 1957, the Secretary of Agriculture is again directed to make an annual estimate of domestic demand. In doing so, he is required to consider (1) the amount consumed during the preceding year, (2) the state of inventories, (3) changes in population, (4) the level and trend of consumer purchasing power, and (5) the relation between changes, since 1947, in the price of refined sugar and in the general cost of living as shown by the consumer's price index of the Bureau of Labor Statistics. The law also divides the market, now giving domestic areas and the Philippines absolute quotas totaling 5,418,000 tons and providing that requirements in excess of this amount shall be divided between Cuba and other countries in the ratio of 96 per cent to 4 per cent. (This division was modified in minor detail, but not in principle, by an amendment passed in 1951.) Subsidies are still paid to domestic growers of cane and beets for controlling output and observing minimum labor standards. From 1942 to 1952, such payments averaged $56 million a year.

When quotas were reimposed under the present law, the shares of domestic producers were again increased, that of the Philippines restored, but to a smaller figure than before, and that of Cuba cut back from the level it had reached during the war. The quota for Cuba and other foreign countries is now a residual one, their share in the American market fluctuating with the Secretary's estimates of requirements. At 8,000,000 tons, Cuba gets 31 per cent; at 7,500,000 tons, she gets 28 per cent. Domestic producers are insulated against fluctuations in the market. Foreign producers are promised the gains of prosperity—and asked to bear the risks of depression.

Everything depends upon the Secretary's annual determinations of demand. The standards provided in the law are vague enough to leave him considerable latitude. Hearings are held, at which consumers propose that the figure adopted be large so that the price of sugar may be low and domestic producers propose that the figure be small so that the price may be high. The Secretary then presumably selects a figure that will bring political forces into balance and proclaims it to be the consumption requirement for the coming year. Here, as with petroleum, it is assumed that price and demand are fixed and that supply alone is adjustable.

The Sugar Act establishes a rigid cartel. With other crops, quotas cannot be imposed unless supplies are abnormally large and two thirds of the growers voting in a referendum have given their consent. But here, commodities can never be produced without an allotment or produced in greater quantities than the allotments may allow. The law subsidizes a tiny minority of American farmers, enabling them to waste the nation's resources by remaining in a high-cost industry. It harms the consumer by raising the price of sugar. It harms producers in Cuba and other countries by closing a major part of the American market to low-cost supplies. But the sugar growers are organized, the consumers are not, and Cubans do not vote in the United States.

AGRICULTURAL MARKETING AGREEMENTS

One part of the farm program that was inaugurated by the Agricultural Adjustment Act of 1933 was not discussed in Chapter 15. Under the provisions of that law, the Secretary of Agriculture was authorized to enter into agreements with the processors and distributors of farm products for the purpose of regulating their sale, and such agreements were exempted from the antitrust laws. The Secretary was also empowered to bring recalcitrant handlers into line by requiring them to obtain licenses. Doubts arose, however, concerning the constitutionality of the licensing provision and it was little used. After the Schechter decision the program tended to break down. In 1935, however, Congress amended the law to drop the licensing feature and in its place, empower the Secretary to make agreements binding by issuing formal orders. Thereafter, the agreement and order procedure came to be used in handling many nonbasic crops, particularly horticultural specialties. In 1936 this part of the program was not affected by the Supreme Court decision that invalidated the production control and processing tax provisions of the Act of 1933. But Congress proceeded, in the next year, to give it a permanent foundation in the Agricultural Marketing Agreement Act of 1937.

The Act of 1937 empowers the Secretary of Agriculture to enter into marketing agreements and to issue marketing orders. The persons whose activities are regulated by such agreements and orders are the handlers (processors and distributors) of agricultural commodities. The controls imposed thus apply not only to producers' co-operatives that handle their members' products but also to individual proprietors, partnerships, and corporations engaged in manufacturing and marketing. Agreements take the form of contracts between the Secretary and individual handlers; they do not apply to those who do not accept them. But orders are binding on all handlers of a commodity, whether they agree to them or not. Agreements function as voluntary cartels, orders as compulsory cartels.

Agreement and Order Procedures

The issuance of agreements and orders proceeds through the following steps: (1) Producers, acting through their co-operatives, agree upon a program and present it to the Secretary of Agriculture. (2) The Secretary holds public hearings, considers the evidence presented pro and con, and prepares an agreement. (3) If the agreement is to be accepted voluntarily, he submits it to the handlers for signature. If compulsion is required, he puts it to a vote. (4) If two thirds of the producers and half of the handlers involved accept it (or three fourths and four fifths, respectively, for California citrus fruits), he issues an order. And with producer approval, he may also issue an order even though the handlers disapprove.

Agreements and orders have been used principally for commodities produced in limited areas or sold in limited markets, where they could be more easily negotiated and their provisions more readily enforced. Such controls have frequently been applied to fruits, nuts, and vegetables and, less often, to products such as tobacco, potatoes, soybeans, hops, honey bees, and naval stores. The most important commodity covered—always by orders—is milk. In 1950 there were 35 orders in effect for milk, and around 30 agreements and orders for all of the other commodities.

For milk, the orders are administered by a public official appointed by the Secretary of Agriculture. For the other commodities, agreements and orders are administered by committees elected by growers and handlers of the commodities concerned. In neither case is any representation accorded to consumers. Violations of orders are reported to the Department of Justice for action. Enforcement is affected through civil suits for injunctions or triple damages and through criminal prosecutions leading to fines of $50 to $500 for each violation, each day being counted as a separate offense.

Controls for Regional Crops

Agreements and orders for products other than milk may not fix prices directly. But they may contain trade practice provisions similar to those found in the NRA codes. And they sometimes require that prices be filed and forbid sales below filed prices until after the expiration of a waiting period. The method usually adopted, however, is that of influencing price by controlling supply.

Supply has been controlled in three principal ways. (1) Daily or weekly shipments have been regulated so as to even out the rate at which commodities move to market. This has been done in the case of perishables, such as citrus fruits. Here the whole supply is sold, but sales are regularized to avoid gluts and scarcities. The fluctuation of prices is reduced; their general level is not substantially increased. Producer incomes are stabilized; dealers are assured steadier supplies; consumers are deprived of an opportunity to buy at bargain prices during periods of surplus. (2) The supplies of several commodities have been controlled by regulating their quality so as to prevent the shipment of substandard grades, sizes, and maturities. In this case rejects are withheld from the market and diverted to inferior uses or destroyed. Producer prices and incomes are likely to be increased, and consumers are clearly denied an opportunity to buy the less expensive grades. (3) For certain more durable commodities, the quantity that can be sold during a season has been fixed and each producer given a quota related to a historic base. Here, surpluses have been diverted to other uses or pooled in storage for future sale. Such arrangements raise prices to consumers. And, in the short run, where demand is inelastic, they increase the incomes of producers. But, in themselves, at the prices fixed, they afford no solution to the long-run problem of imbalance between demand and supply. Whatever the method used, the purpose is to improve the position of the producer at the expense of the consumer. A producer-oriented department runs the program; the consumer has no voice in the controls.

Hog Cholera Serum and Virus

Thirty-five firms manufacturing and distributing hog cholera serum and hog cholera virus operated, from 1933 to 1935, under an NRA code which permitted them to fix the prices at which they sold. When the NRA was brought to an end by the Schechter decision, Congress amended the Agricultural Adjustment Act to empower the Secretary of Agriculture to issue a marketing order covering the handlers of these commodities. The code was then converted into an order and has since continued in effect. It establishes standards to govern the quality of serum and virus products and requires the maintenance of reserve stocks. But it permits the makers and handlers of these products to operate as a cartel, exempt from antitrust.

MILK MARKET CONTROLS

Because milk is heavy and bulky in relation to its value, its transportation cost is high. Because it is easily contaminated and affords a medium favorable to the growth of bacteria, city governments require that dairies be inspected and that milk sold in its original form be pasteurized. The region from which a city draws its milk, known as its milkshed, is therefore limited in size both by the economic factor of transportation cost and by the political one of inspection requirements. Entry into the business of distributing milk is also limited by the cost of pasteurization facilities. The urban market for fluid milk is thus a sheltered one, lending itself to the application of private and public controls. About two fifths of all milk is consumed in fluid form. Three fifths is sold to manufacturers who turn it into butter, cheese, ice cream, and concentrated and powdered products. In these forms, it can be shipped more cheaply, lasts longer, and carries less of a threat to public health. This market for milk is therefore a wide one and is less readily subjected to control.

Milk is essential to a balanced diet, particularly for growing children. Experts in nutrition assert that consumption per capita should average a pint a day. The demand for milk has a high degree of income elasticity, rising and falling with prosperity and depression. But it is said to have a low degree of price elasticity, sales falling less than proportionately when prices are increased and rising less than proportionately when prices are reduced. Price elasticity is lowest among the upper income groups, where milk is delivered to the home, and where it is used for drinking; it is highest among the lower income groups, where milk is bought at stores, and where it is used for cooking. Consumption is fairly steady throughout the year, falling but 5 per cent below and rising but 5 per cent above the annual average.

Dairying is the most important single source of agricultural income. Milk is produced commercially on nearly 2 million farms, most of them in states near urban centers in the East and Middle West. Its supply remains about the same from year to year, depending upon the number of cows and the output per cow. A higher price does not quickly increase the number of cows: three years elapse from the time a cow is bred until her heifer begins to give milk. A lower price does not reduce the number; cows could be slaughtered, but the price of meat is also likely to be low. Changes in price, moreover, have little effect on bovine physiology. The supply of milk fluctuates with the seasons, rising as much as a third above the yearly average in the spring when calves are born and cows are put out on green pasture, and falling as much as a fourth below it in the fall. With consumption in urban markets varying little, the surplus produced in the spring is sold to manufacturers.

Urban Milk Markets

Most of the milk sold in a typical city is distributed by two or three large concerns. In many cities these concerns are subsidiaries of two great holding companies: National Dairy Products and Borden's. As sellers, the distributors behave as oligopolists. They compete in the duplication of delivery services, in brand names, advertising, and salesmanship. They seldom compete in price. Despite the fact that supply varies widely from season to season, the price of milk remains the same throughout the year. And every company delivering milk to the doorstep charges the same amount.

Where price competition has entered the market, it has come from delivery through stores. Here, a substantial saving in cost is possible. In New York City in 1948 the consumer paid 24.8 cents a quart for milk delivered at his home, 12.55 cents going to the farmer and 12.25 cents to the distributor. He paid 22.1 cents for milk bought at stores, 12.5 cents going to the farmer and 9.6 cents to the distributor.[10] His saving of 2.7 cents a quart was to be attributed, not to a difference in profit, but to the lower cost of distributing through stores. But since the large distributors have invested heavily in delivery facilities they have generally sought to check store sales. To this end, they have urged adoption of regulations fixing retail prices, forbidding the sale of milk over the counter at a price lower than that charged for delivery, and discriminating against paper containers, the use of which facilitates its sale through stores. And in this they have been

[10] *Report of the New York Milkshed Price Committee* (New York: Market Administrator, New York Metropolitan Milk Marketing Area, 1949), p. 57.

supported by members of the milk wagon drivers' union, whose jobs depend upon retention of the high-cost system of home delivery.

In buying milk the large distributors appear as oligopsonists. Its sellers are thousands of dairy farms. Unorganized, the farmer would be at a disadvantage in making his sale; organized, he can bargain collectively for better terms. Milk producers have therefore established co-operative associations and, through these associations, have entered into negotiations with distributors for the purpose of determining the farmer's price. Such associations now control the bulk of the milk that is offered for sale in all the major markets in the United States.

These associations have served the milk producer in another way. The payments he receives are based upon an f.o.b. price at the city plant, which is subject to deductions for haulage, terminal, and other charges. They depend, also, upon the quality of his milk and the uses to which it is put. Distributors might defraud the farmer by deducting from his payments transportation and other charges in excess of those actually incurred, by understating the quality of his milk, and by misrepresenting the shares going into different types of use. It is the function of the co-operatives to prevent such abuses by inspecting company records and accounts.

Milk Price Structures

For the purpose of fixing the prices to be paid producers, milk is classified according to use. Class I, which brings the highest price, contains milk that is sold fresh for consumption in fluid form. The other classes, which bring less, contain milk that goes through various manufacturing processes before it is consumed. Class I milk would normally bring more than other milk because transportation charges restrict its supply and sanitary precautions add to its cost. But these factors alone do not explain its higher price. Distributors are willing to pay more for Class I milk because they can charge more for it. And they can charge more because demand in the urban market is inelastic, because supply is under their control, and because inspection and pasteurization requirements protect them from the entry of competitors. Distributors cannot pay as much for milk in other classes because the markets where they sell it are highly competitive and they cannot control its price. The structure of milk prices is thus deliberately discriminatory, with markets separated and prices adjusted to variations in the conditions of demand and supply. In theory the farmer receives different prices for different gallons of identical milk depending upon where they are ultimately sold. In practice he gets a single price, known as a blended price, which is an average of the prices for the different classes weighted by the quantities sold in each class.

The classified price plan is usually supplemented by a pooling arrangement. If a distributor were to sell more of one farmer's milk and less of another's in Class I and were to pay them accordingly, the former would receive a higher and the latter a lower blended price. This is prevented by the establishment of individual handler pools. Under such an arrangement, the blended price is computed by weighting the class prices in proportion to all of the distributor's sales, and the price he pays to every farmer is the same. But another difficulty remains. Different distributors may sell different fractions of their milk in various classes. A farmer may therefore get a different blended price from one distributor than his neighbor gets from another one. This is prevented by the establishment of market-wide pools. Here, the blended price is computed by weighting the class prices in proportion to all of the sales in the market, and the price paid by every distributor to every farmer is the same. Standing alone, this arrangement might be unfair as among distributors, since the fractions sold by different distributors in different classes might not be the same. All of them would pay the market average in buying milk, but some of them might get more and some of them less than the market average in selling it. To meet this situation, a market-wide pool is usually accompanied by an equalization pool, with distributors who sell more than the market average in Class I paying in, and those who sell less drawing out. As a result, each distributor not only pays the market average on his purchases but also gets the market average on his sales.

This pattern is further complicated by the fact that farmers are often paid in accordance with the provisions of a "base rating" or "base and surplus" plan. Under such a plan, each farmer is assigned a quota corresponding to his low production during the fall and winter months and is paid throughout the year at the Class I price for "base" milk, produced within his quota, and at a lower price for "surplus" milk, produced in excess of his quota. As a result, the prices paid to different farmers will differ. And this is the purpose of the plan. But the returns realized by different distributors may also differ, since one will pay a higher average price for milk than another if his producers' bases are larger in relation to his Class I sales. Here, again, the problem is solved by setting up an equalization fund, with distributors whose Class I sales exceed their producers' bases paying in and those whose producers' bases exceed their Class I sales drawing out.

The base-and-surplus plan was designed, originally, to reduce seasonal fluctuations in supply by giving farmers an incentive to even out the freshening of their cows. But it has also come to be employed, at times, as a means of restricting and allocating output and excluding new producers from the field. By refusing to revise quotas from year to year, thus compelling farmers who have expanded output to accept a lower price for their additional supply, producers' associations have sometimes checked production and imposed pecuniary penalties on those who sought to obtain a larger share of the market. By refusing to assign quotas to newcomers, thus depressing the prices that can be obtained for months or years, they have sought to monopolize markets, discouraging the entry of competitors.

Public Intervention in Milk Markets

Producers of milk fared better than other farmers in the decade that followed World War I. The prices of dairy products were above parity from 1921 to 1929. The break in prices, with depression, was less severe for these products than for other agricultural commodities. In March, 1933, the index for farm products in general stood at 55, that for dairy products at 73. But prices were down and producers were dissatisfied. They were also well organized. In state capitals and in Washington their pleas for aid fell on sympathetic ears.

More than half of the states enacted temporary or permanent milk control laws beginning in 1933. These laws typically conferred upon some state agency—usually a milk control board composed, in most cases, of representatives of producers and distributors—the power to promulgate rules and regulations governing the production, transportation, processing, handling, storage, and sale of milk and its products; to define and designate milksheds and marketing areas; to fix minimum producer, wholesale, and retail prices; to grant licenses to persons engaged in the industry; and to refuse or revoke licenses for violation of its orders. It was the purpose of these measures, in general, to increase the incomes of producers by underwriting the prices negotiated between producer associations and distributors, by regulating output, and by obstructing entry, and to maintain the margins of distributors by fixing resale prices and by preventing the development of competing methods of sale. The power of a state government to fix prices for milk was upheld by the Supreme Court of the United States in the Nebbia case in 1934.[11]

Action was also taken by the Agricultural Adjustment Administration. Consideration was given, for a time, to the possibility of restricting production through contracts and benefit payments, as had been done with other commodities. But this plan was dropped in favor of control through marketing agreements. Such agreements had been established for fifteen markets by the end of 1933. In general, they gave legal effect to collective bargains establishing producer prices, checked output and obstructed entry by adopting the base-and-surplus plan, and enlisted the co-operation of distributors by fixing retail prices and by imposing handicaps on their unorthodox competitors. The base-and-surplus plan was eliminated from the agreements in 1934. The effort to control retail prices was abandoned and distributors were compelled to adhere to the agreements through the use of the licensing power. In 1935 the licensing provision was dropped from the law and orders were substituted for licenses. And in 1937 rules governing the federal regulation of milk markets were spelled out in detail in the Agricultural Marketing Agreements Act.

[11] *Nebbia* v. *New York,* 291 U.S. 502.

Under this law, the federal government can regulate markets when interstate commerce is involved. It can act only by order, and only when two thirds of the producers consent. It cannot limit the size of a milkshed (although local health authorities still may do so). Its orders must classify milk according to use and prescribe the method of fixing the price of each class. They may provide either for an individual-handler pool or for a market-wide pool, but in the latter case they must also provide for the equalization of returns. The prices set in an order must equal parity or, in the discretion of the Secretary of Agriculture, an amount which he deems adequate to insure "a sufficient quantity of pure and wholesome milk." They must also reflect the price of feeds and other economic conditions which affect supply and demand. And they must be in the public interest. The parity standard has not been significant; since 1937 the price of milk has been well above parity. The other standards are so vague as to leave the Secretary free to adopt any price upon which producers and distributors agree. Enforcement of such prices through federal orders was upheld by the Supreme Court in the Rock Royal case in 1939.[12]

Federal Milk Market Orders

Milk markets are usually under federal orders where cities are located near state borders and where milk is drawn from more than one state. Most of the great urban markets for milk were under federal orders in 1950, those of California, Connecticut, and New Jersey being the exceptions to the general rule. Each of the 35 orders then in effect delineated the market area it covered, defined the classes of milk, set forth the price of each class or the formula to be used in computing it, described the manner of pooling, required the presentation of reports on the quantities of milk that were sold for different uses, prescribed the method of payment, and provided for the auditing of distributor records and accounts. Each of the orders provided, further, for the appointment of a market administrator and for the imposition of assessments to cover the costs of administration.

Prices, under such orders, have been fixed in two principal ways: by administrative determinations following public hearings, and by adjustment in accordance with the provisions of a formula. Under the first of these methods, there have been delays in adapting prices to changing conditions, since alterations cannot be made without new hearings, and the hearing procedure is costly, cumbersome, and time consuming. Under the second, adaptation is continuous and automatic, and hearings need be held only to consider the provisions of the formula. But this method also has its difficulties. Factors that are relevant to the price of milk must be agreed upon and the data they call for must be obtained. The formula may have to be set aside to meet conditions that arise in an emergency, such as a sudden drought. Producers are likely to accept a formula when it puts

[12] *U.S.* v. *Rock Royal Cooperative, Inc.*, 307 U.S. 553.

their prices up; they are less likely to do so when it puts their prices down. And in this case, its operation may be superseded by administrative action fixing prices at a level higher than its terms would justify.

The price of Class I milk in all the major markets is now fixed by formula. Under the formulas that have had the longest and widest use, this price is determined by taking as a base the price currently paid for milk by manufacturers of dairy products and adding a differential to cover the extra costs of transportation, sanitation, and handling involved in supplying milk for Class I use. The advantage of this procedure is that it adjusts the price in the sheltered Class I market to changes in demand and supply by relating it to the price in the market for manufacturing milk where these forces have free play. As a result, the Class I price is not maintained at a level that diverts a growing share of milk to other classes, depressing their prices, and thus causing the blended price of milk to fall.

In recent years the competition of margarine has driven down the price of butter and hence the price that butter manufacturers will pay for milk. As a result, the formulas that have tied the price of Class I milk to that of manufacturing milk have lost their popularity. Beginning with Boston in 1948 and New York in 1950, several of the major milk markets have adopted new formulas in which the Class I price is cut loose from that of manufacturing milk and related to other factors such as the cost of feed and labor, the prices of other agricultural products, the general level of commodity prices, and the volume of consumer purchasing power. Under the New York formula the Class I price is raised when the share of milk going to other markets contracts and lowered when it expands, thus keeping it from getting too far out of line. But under none of these formulas will it be possible to keep the blended price from falling as the price of manufacturing milk goes down.

All of the formulas are modified by adjustments designed to lessen seasonal fluctuations in supply and by premiums for higher quality and for convenience of location. Where milksheds overlap, moreover, farmers may find that differences in the formulas used make it advantageous for them to ship first to one market and then to another.

State Milk Controls

State milk control laws have been repealed or allowed to expire by a number of the states that enacted them after 1933. There were 17 such laws in effect in 1953. These laws are used where the milkshed for a market lies entirely within the boundaries of a single state. They may be used in preference to federal orders where producers or distributors desire to impose restrictions that federal orders do not permit, such as production control and retail price fixing. And they may also be used as a supplement to federal controls. A price for producers throughout a milkshed may be fixed by a federal order and the retail price in the market fixed by the state. Such an arrangement may be demanded by distributors as a condition for their acceptance of the producer prices that the federal order may require. Where a market has operated under both federal and state orders, their provisions have been made consistent and the same person has been appointed as administrator by federal and state governments.

In general, the procedures followed in preparing state milk orders and the provisions of the orders themselves are similar to those adopted under federal controls. But some of the states have also gone on to control the production of milk and to limit the entry of new producers. Under a quota system established in Oregon in 1933,

> . . . certain milk producers were given the exclusive right to supply a given market with fluid milk and cream. . . . Up to about mid-1939 the individual producer who was allotted a quota owned that quota in about the same way that he owned other real or personal property. . . . Recent orders of the milk control board place rather rigid limitations upon the right of the individual producer to sell or transfer his quota. These regulations were the result of criticism of the board which arose from the fact that producers were selling their quotas to other producers. This was taken to be an indication that the board was creating valuable property rights by granting certain producers monopoly privileges. . . . The quota under the new regulation is, in general, attached to the farm or to the herd and equipment rather than to the man. . . .[13]

Under the new regulation, of course, a farmer could still cash in on the capital value of his quota when he sold his farm or herd. In some states, entry to markets is restricted through the use of a base-and-surplus plan. In Virginia no producer may sell in a market without a base, new applicants for bases must present satisfactory evidence that additional milk is needed, and the State Milk Commission will not grant bases to exceed annual Class I sales by more than 5 per cent.[14]

Fourteen of the seventeen milk control laws in effect in 1953 provided for the fixing of prices at retail. In most cases, such prices are fixed on the basis of informal investigations by state authorities and statements of a general character presented by distributors at public hearings. In California, they are based on painstaking studies of the costs of distribution.[15] But this procedure raises all of the problems that we have found to be implicit in efforts to establish minimum prices on the basis of calculations of cost. In fixing prices the state boards usually set them as high for sales across the counter as for home delivery or limit the difference between the two. They forbid quantity discounts and sales in large containers. And

[13] Don S. Anderson, "Regulation of Fluid Milk Marketing in Oregon," in *Economic Standards of Government Price Control*, T.N.E.C. Monograph 32 (Washington: Government Printing Office, 1941), Part II, chap. ii, pp. 107–8.

[14] Maynard C. Conner, *The Milk Market Control Law in Virginia* (Blacksburg, Va.: Agricultural Experiment Station, Bulletin 444, June 1951), pp. 30–33.

[15] See J. M. Tinley, *Public Regulation of Milk Marketing in California* (Berkeley: University of California Press, 1938), chaps. vi–ix.

(except in Massachusetts and Virginia, where the courts have forbidden it) they require dealers to charge a cent more per quart when they sell milk in paper containers than when they sell it in bottles. If these measures help the farmer, they do so indirectly. It is their purpose to protect the orthodox distributor against his lower-cost competitors.

Effects of Milk Controls

The programs of milk control adopted by the federal government and by the states have been designed to maintain the incomes of producers and distributors at the expense of consumers. In accordance with the usual procedure, consumers have been privileged to present statements at public hearings. But these statements, in most cases, have been confined to expressions of the opinion that prices should be low, while those prepared on behalf of producers' associations by accountants and statisticians have been replete with tables, charts, and graphs which demonstrate convincingly why prices should be high. The decisions that follow these hearings, moreover, are made by officials who owe the very existence of their agencies and their jobs to the producer pressure groups. Under the circumstance, the hearing accorded to consumers can be little more than a matter of form.

Federal and state controls doubtless assure the farmer a higher price than he would otherwise receive for Class I milk. But they may not give him a higher blended price, since less of his milk may be sold in Class I and more in the other classes than would be the case if the market were not controlled. State controls maintain the margins of distributors and thus make sure that a higher Class I price is reflected in a higher retail price. By checking the introduction of less expensive methods of distribution, they keep the price of milk at a figure substantially higher than that consumers otherwise would have to pay. One consequence of these controls has been to increase the sale of canned and powdered milk, since the controls force those who consume fresh milk to subsidize those who consume milk in other forms. Another consequence has been to hold per capita consumption of fresh milk in the United States to a half pint per day, or only half of the amount required for dietary needs. Consumption, moreover, is unequally distributed, being highest in the upper-income groups where there are fewer children per family, and lowest in the lower-income groups where there are more. Whatever the program has done for producers and distributors, it has not contributed to the health and strength of the next generation of Americans.

Milk markets, however, cannot be freed of all controls. The farmer sells his milk to oligopsonists. He must therefore be permitted to organize and to bargain collectively. In the public interest, moreover, the bargaining process must be supervised by government. In markets under federal orders, the procedure employed in fixing the producer's price is a proper one. The requirement of public hearings is designed to prevent abuses.

The use of formulas permits flexibility in administration. The formulas, of course, should not attempt to divorce the price of Class I milk from the underlying forces of supply and demand but should be so devised as to respond to changes as they occur. One thing more is needed: the consumer interest should be represented more effectively. This might be accomplished by creating a consumer's counsel or empowering some other public official to argue the consumer's case. It might also be accomplished by voluntary organizations, such as the League of Women Voters, acting in the consumer's interest. The further measures, adopted under state laws, to protect distributors from competition, preserve their methods of doing business, and maintain their margins, are harmful to producers and consumers. They should be repealed.

It has sometimes been proposed that producers be paid more and consumers charged less by reducing the margins of distributors. In accordance with such proposals, this would be done in two quite different ways. Following one approach, home delivery would be maintained as the method of distribution, but its cost would be cut by eliminating competition. This would be done either by establishing private monopolies and regulating their charges or by having milk delivery made a function of city governments. The other approach would reduce the cost of distribution by making it more competitive, abandoning retail price control, prosecuting restraint of trade in urban markets under the antitrust laws, and keeping the door open to new types of distributors and to new developments in technology.

In support of the first proposal, it is contended that monopoly could cut the cost of distribution almost in half by eliminating competitive solicitation of customers, excessive differentiation of products, and duplication of delivery routes, by permitting more extensive use of automatic machinery, and by employing equipment more nearly at full capacity.[16] The wisdom of this proposal, however, is open to dispute. Past experience, in other fields, both with the public regulation of private monopolies and with the administration of municipal enterprises, has not been such as to raise high hopes for efficiency and economy in the monopolistic distribution of milk. This experience is to be reviewed in the next two Parts of this book.

The competitive approach would encourage new developments in technology. And such developments are on the way. Not only does margarine compete with butter; vegetable fats compete increasingly with butter fat in making ice cream. Methods may be invented to can or dehydrate milk without losing its flavor. A way has already been found to concentrate the product, cutting its bulk and weight by two thirds. By reducing the cost of transportation, this could bring more producers within reach of the urban consumer, thus cutting the producer's price.

[16] See W. P. Mortenson, *Milk Distribution as a Public Utility* (Chicago: University of Chicago Press, 1940).

In this way, and also by reducing the cost of distribution, it could cut the retail price. Unless artificial barriers are imposed to prevent it, changing technology may well break down the complex of restraints within the Class I market on which the present structure of controls depends.

SUGGESTIONS FOR FURTHER READING

The economic difficulties experienced by the bituminous coal industry during the twenties are well described by Walton H. Hamilton and Helen R. Wright in *The Case of Bituminous Coal* (New York: Macmillan Co., 1926). The history of public regulation is outlined in Glen L. Parker, *The Coal Industry* (Washington: American Council on Public Affairs, 1940). The price-fixing experiment is described fully by Ellery B. Gordon and William Y. Webb in Part III of *Economic Standards of Government Price Control*, T.N.E.C. Monograph 32 (Washington: Government Printing Office, 1941), and more briefly but adequately by Eleanor Poland in Leverett S. Lyon and Victor Abramson, *Government and Economic Life* (Washington: Brookings Institution, 1940), Vol. II, chap. xxiv.

A description and history of oil prorationing is given in Blakeley M. Murphy (ed.), *Conservation of Oil and Gas* (Chicago: American Bar Association, 1949). This activity is appraised by Myron W. Watkins in *Oil: Conservation or Stabilization* (New York: Harper & Bros., 1937), by Myron W. Watkins and Aaron Director in chap. xxv of Lyon and Abramson, and by Northcutt Ely in *Readings in the Social Control of Industry* (Philadelphia: Blakiston Co., 1942), pp. 318–62. A more recent discussion is that of Eugene V. Rostow, *A National Policy for the Oil Industry* (New Haven: Yale University Press, 1948), Part II.

The earliest sugar controls are described in John E. Dalton, *Sugar: A Case Study of Government Control* (New York: Macmillan Co., 1937). Material relating to the Act of 1937 is presented in Joshua Bernhardt, *The Sugar Industry and the Federal Government* (Washington: Sugar Statistics Service, 1948). The Act of 1948 is reproduced and summarized in *Sugar: Facts and Figures, 1952* (Washington: U.S. Cuban Sugar Council, 1952).

Experience with agricultural marketing agreements is discussed by Geoffrey S. Shepherd in *Agricultural Price Control* (Ames: Iowa State College Press, 1945), Part III; and by Floyd F. Hedland in the *Journal of Farm Economics*, XXXII (1950), 1006–15.

The structure of urban milk markets is interestingly described in Walton H. Hamilton *Price and Price Policies* (New York: McGraw-Hill Book Co., 1938), and is analyzed at greater length in J. M. Cassels, *A Study of Fluid Milk Prices* (Cambridge: Harvard University Press, 1937). A more recent study is R. W. Bartlett, *The Milk Industry* (New York: Ronald Press, 1946). An excellent brief account is given by Joel B. Dirlam in Walter Adams (ed.), *The Structure of American Industry* (New York: Macmillan Co., 1950). Procedure in issuing federal milk market orders is described in Carl McFarland, *Milk Marketing Under Federal Control* (New York: Milk Industry Foundation, 1946). The operation of such orders up to 1940 is appraised by Warren C. Waite in T.N.E.C. Monograph 32, cited above, Part II, chap. i.

Subsequent experience is considered in the Market Research Reports of the Dairy Branch, Production and Marketing Administration, Department of Agriculture, Washington. See, particularly, Robert W. March, *The Pricing of Surplus Milk in the Chicago Market* (1949), Edmond S. Harris, *The Philadelphia Milk Supply* (1950), Glenn W. Freemyer, *Milk Supply Problems in the St. Louis Market* (1950), Edmond S. Harris and Joel L. Blum, *Federal Regulation of Milk Marketing in the Duluth-Superior Area* (1951), Edmond S. Harris, *Milk Marketing Plans in the Kansas City, Mo. Area* (1952) and Alexander Swartz, *Federal Regulation of the Minneapolis–St. Paul Fluid Milk Market* (1952). An illuminating discussion of the problems involved in the development of pricing formulas is contained in the *Report of the New York Milkshed Price Committee* (New York: Market Administrator, New York Metropolitan Milk Marketing Area, 1949). The operation of state milk control laws up to 1940 is analyzed by Don S. Anderson and R. K. Froker in T.N.E.C. Monograph 32, Part II, chaps. ii–vi. The control systems of particular states are outlined in J. M. Tinley, *Public Regulation of Milk Marketing in California* (Berkeley: University of California Press, 1938); Earl Warner, *The State Milk Control Agencies in New England* (Burlington, Vt.: Agricultural Experiment Station, Bulletin 565, 1941); and Maynard D. Conner, *The Milk Market Control Law in Virginia* (Blacksburg, Va.: Agricultural Experiment Station, Bulletin 444, 1951).

PART V

Substituting Regulation for Competition

Chapter 17 THE TASK OF REGULATION

It has been the general policy of government in the United States to maintain a competitive economy. Exceptions have been made, as we have seen, to moderate the force of competition in a number of highly competitive industries. Exceptions have also been made in the case of certain industries where monopoly has appeared to be inevitable and even desirable. Here, deprived of competition as an instrument of discipline, government has sought to protect the interests of consumers by itself undertaking to regulate rates and services.

The industries thus treated fall into two broad groups. In the first are those supplying water, electricity, gas, telephone and transit services in local markets, together with those transmitting electricity and gas and providing communication by telephone and telegraph over long distances. Such industries are known as public utilities. They include many different companies. But each of these companies sells in a market where it possesses a monopoly. It can therefore be handled as a separate unit, its rates fixed with some precision at a level that will cover its costs and yield it a desired return. In the second group are industries providing interregional transportation: railroads, oil pipelines, motor carriers, water carriers, and airlines. The firms in these industries do not possess complete monopolies. Each type of carrier competes with many of the others and most of them compete among themselves. Such firms cannot be treated separately; where they compete, their rates must correspond. Their costs, however, may not be the same. As a consequence, their earnings will differ, one receiving more, another less. In this case, regulation cannot yield precise results. But in both cases, the methods it uses are the same.

The problems that are common to all industries where rates and services are regulated will be considered in this chapter and the two that follow. Those that are peculiar to public utilities will be discussed in Chapter 20, those peculiar to transportation, in Chapters 21 and 22. One other industry—radio and television broadcasting—has been singled out for regulation on a permanent basis, but for quite a different reason and in quite a different way. This story will be told in Chapter 23. In wartime, finally, government has temporarily displaced the market as a regulator for the whole economy. Its experience in doing so will be recounted in Chapters 24 and 25.

THE RATIONALE OF REGULATION

Regulation of rates and services was based, at the outset, on the assumption that the economic characteristics of the regulated industries were such as to set them apart from other businesses. These industries, it appeared, were naturally monopolistic. Their services were indispensable. They performed, as it were, a public function. The people, with no alternatives, depended upon them. Yet they operated as private enterprises, conducted for profit. Being free of competition, they could exploit their powers to the public detriment. Government was, therefore, compelled to intervene to safeguard the public interest. Regulation was thus a substitute for competition. Where competition was impossible, its purpose was to bring the benefits that competition would have brought.

Such was the logic of regulation. Even at the beginning, it was oversimplified. And with the passage of time, important amendments were required. But the logic still contains a core of truth.

Characteristics of Regulated Industries

In most of the industries subjected to regulation (railroads and public utilities, for instance, but not motor or water carriers) operations must be conducted on a large scale in order to attain low unit costs. Plants are huge and highly specialized, involving heavy investments and high fixed charges. They may be built in anticipation of demand. And until demand develops, their capacity will be but partly used. Plants must be big enough, in any case, to satisfy demand at its peak. The service they produce cannot be stored. In off-peak periods, therefore, capacity stands idle. But whatever the volume of output, fixed charges have to be met. In such a situation, cost per unit will diminish as volume is increased: the part of this cost that varies with output (materials, wages, etc.) may be unaffected, but the part that is constant (interest, administration, etc.) will decline. Volume may be increased by reducing rates. There is therefore a strong incentive to compete in price. But such competition may become destructive. For it will always be to the advantage of a company to keep on cutting prices—if it must do so to keep from losing business—as long as they continue to cover its variable costs and contribute something toward its overhead. Price warfare, if carried far enough, will drive an industry into bankruptcy, impairing its capacity to serve. More likely, this fate will be averted by combination or by agreement as to rates. These industries, thus, are said to be natural monopolies. And, as such, they are set apart for special treatment by the state.

As a justification for regulation, however, this argument has been overemphasized. The railroads, after the Civil War, did engage in rate wars. But among the public utilities such warfare has been the exception rather than the rule. In both cases, combination and agreement have been usual. But, in this, the regulated industries are not unique. The steel industry, for instance, and the automobile industry involve large-scale production, heavy investment, and high fixed costs. They may have idle capacity and be tempted to put it to work by competing vigorously in price. Here, again, such competition could become destructive. And here, too, this outcome has been forestalled by combination and agreement, whether explicit or merely understood. This is the familiar pattern of oligopoly. The argument just recited could be used with equal force to justify the regulation of any industry where plants are costly and firms are few. The distinction between those that are regulated and those that are not must be made on other grounds.

In the case of public utilities there are other bases for monopoly. With most of them competition is confined by local market boundaries. It is limited, too, by the fact that their facilities must be located in city streets. There is a physical limit to the number of tracks that can be laid upon a street, the wires that can be strung above it, and the mains that can be buried below it. There is an even narrower limit to public tolerance of the nuisance that would be involved in duplicating such facilities. Some services, moreover, are of such a nature that competition would be undesirable. Urban transit is more convenient where cars are pooled and where connections can be made. Telephone service is more convenient where all subscribers are connected through the switchboards of a single company. Under such circumstances, monopoly is to be preferred.

But this alone does not explain control of rates and services. For competition has been lacking in other industries where regulation is unknown. The explanation lies, rather, in the buyer's disadvantage in bargaining. With steel, for instance, purchases are made, not by the ultimate consumer, but by oligopsonists who are able to protect themselves. With automobiles, they are made by the consumer, but they are nonessential, infrequent, and can be postponed. The availability of used cars, moreover, and variations in trade-in values afford him numerous alternatives. He does not demand protection by the state. With utility services, however, it is otherwise. They are essentials bought continuously by many small consumers. For them, the need is urgent and is not postponable. And there are no acceptable alternatives. The buyer must meet the seller's terms or go without. It is this that sets the public utilities apart, explaining why regulation is required.

Elsewhere, however, this explanation does not suffice. For transportation, though increasingly competitive, is increasingly controlled. Between those industries that are regulated and those that are not, no hard and fast line can be drawn by the economist. Nor has such a line been drawn by the courts.

Legal Status of Regulated Industries

For many years, as we saw in Chapter 2, the Supreme Court attempted to permit regulation where it seemed to be needed and to forbid it where it did not by placing in a separate category those industries that it found to be "affected with a public interest." For nearly half a century, from its decision in *Munn* v. *Illinois* in 1877 to that in the Wolff Packing Company case in 1923, the Court enlarged this category, being liberal in approving regulatory powers. But during the next decade, it tightened up, repeatedly striking down the efforts of the states to regulate. There is, however, no clear principle by which to distinguish the cases in which the legislatures were upheld from those in which they were reversed. The tests of public interest most often mentioned by the Court were the essentiality of the service provided and the absence of competition in providing it. But neither of these criteria was followed with consistency. The rule of the law, in effect, was that an industry was affected with a public interest if the Court said so and was not if it said not.

Then in 1934 the Court handed down its decision in the Nebbia case, permitting the state of New York to fix a minimum price for milk even though the business of producing and distributing milk had none of the usual characteristics of a public utility. The doctrine of affectation with a public interest was thus discarded. As the law now stands, an industry can be regulated whenever the legislature decides to act. If some rates are controlled, it is because the people have demanded action. If others are uncontrolled, it is because they have not.

Purposes of Regulation

The crux of regulation is control of rates. The general level of rates is controlled to prevent monopolists from charging monopoly prices and obtaining monopoly profits, to promote wide use of the service, and to insure continued progress by requiring that gains in efficiency and advances in technology be passed on in lower rates. The structure of rates is controlled to prevent discrimination that would be unduly favorable to some consumers and unduly prejudicial to others. Service also must be controlled, to guarantee its availability and to make sure it is adequate in quantity and acceptable in quality. Otherwise, the ground gained in reducing rates might well be lost. If the quantity and quality of service are to be maintained, the financial stability of the regulated enterprise must be preserved. Rates cannot be set so low as to impair its credit. And its financial operations must be controlled. For all of these purposes, finally, it is necessary to regulate company accounts. For it is only through accurate accounting that control of rates and services and finances can be effectively administered.

THE REGULATORY COMMISSIONS

Industries have been regulated by the terms of decisions handed down by courts at common law, by the terms of franchises granted by cities and charters granted by states, and by the terms of ordinances enacted by city councils and statutes enacted by state legislatures. Each of these methods proved ineffective, as was seen in Chapter 2. Control by the courts was spasmodic and negative in character, coming only when suits were brought and injury was proved. Control by franchises and charters was clumsy and inflexible. Control by ordinances and statutes had the same defects. The states eventually turned, therefore, to regulation by commissions. These were semi-independent agencies operating under general legislative powers. They were to have the advantages of expertness, flexibility, and impartiality. They came to be the characteristic means by which rates and services are controlled.

The first commissions, with jurisdiction over railroads, were set up in the New England states before the Civil War. Their powers, however, were largely advisory. Railroad commissions with mandatory powers were first established in the Midwest in the early seventies. Their authority was soon curtailed. But such commissions were set up by many states in the years that followed. And in 1887 Congress established the Interstate Commerce Commission. Thereafter, the regulation of railroads passed largely into the hands of the federal government.

Commission regulation of public utilities was slower to develop. These services, in general, came later than the railroads. Abuses, until notorious, went unrecognized. Legislatures, in the absence of public clamor, were slow to act. Except for a board set up at the instance of gas producers in Massachusetts in 1885, utility commissions date from the early years of the present century. The first of them were set up in 1907 under Governor Robert M. Lafollette in Wisconsin and Governor Charles E. Hughes in New York. Thereafter, in some states, the railroad commissions were given jurisdiction over public utilities. And in others, they were abolished and utility commissions set up in their place. By 1920 utilities had been brought under commission control in more than two thirds of the states. But the commissions were often limited in jurisdiction and in power. The need for regulation outran the ability to regulate. Then, after the market crash of 1929 and the financial scandals that followed, the state commissions were strengthened, their jurisdiction extended and their powers increased.

Today there are commissions in all the states, most of them known as public utility or public service commissions, a few of them still as railroad commissions, and a few others as corporation commissions or commerce commissions. There are also five federal commissions with authority over transportation and interstate utilities. The commission form of regulation is well entrenched.

The State Commissions

Among the state commissions, in 1954, all but 2 or 3 had jurisdiction over motor carriers and telephone and telegraph companies; 42 had jurisdiction over electric light and power, 41 over water, 40 over manufactured gas, 38 over natural gas, 45 over street railways, 33 over gas pipelines, and 26 over oil pipelines.[1] In general, the commissions had been given power to control rates, fixing them at reasonable levels and preventing undue discrimination, and to control the quantity and the quality of services. About three fourths of them were authorized to regulate utility finances, and all of them were empowered to control the methods of accounting and to require reports.

In size, the commissions range from 1 member in Oregon and North Carolina to 7 in South Carolina; the usual number is 3. Their members are appointed by the governor in 31 states, most of them in the North, chosen by the legislature in 2, and elected by the people in 15, the latter being in the South and West. The qualifications required by law are few: membership usually must be bipartisan and members must be citizens and residents without financial interests in the regulated industries. But the members need not have training or experience in engineering, economics, accounting, or law. Few commissioners, in fact, have had technical competence. Elections are won through other qualities, and appointments are often made as a reward for political services. The salaries paid commissioners are low. In 1954 there were 4 states that paid around $15,000 (New York, New Jersey, Pennsylvania, and California) and four that paid $5,000 or less (Delaware, Kentucky, Montana, and North Dakota). The median salary was $8,500.[2] These figures, obviously, do not compare to the payments made to officials of the regulated industries. The tenure of commissioners, finally, is short. The terms fixed by law run from 2 to 10 years; the term in three quarters of the states is 6 years. Some commissioners are reappointed, but most of them serve a single term or even less.

Some of the commissions are organized along functional lines, with divisions for rates, engineering, accounting, financial, and legal work, others are organized into separate divisions for different utilities, and still others into some combination of the two. The stronger commissions are staffed with technical experts, with fair salaries and some assurance of tenure. But, in general, the staffs are far too small to do a thorough job. Appropriations are inadequate: in 1947 the total appropriated to 48 commissions was but $15,500,000, and of this $7,000,000 went to four commissions (New York, California, Pennsylvania, and Illinois), leaving only

[1] *Book of the States 1954–1955*, (Chicago: Council of State Governments, 1954), p. 423.

[2] *Ibid.*, p. 422.

$8,500,000 for the other 44, an average of less than $200,000 apiece.[3] A utility corporation may spend far more than this to fight a single case. Litigation by the companies is financed by those who pay their rates. The commissions, too, are so financed: since 1930 their funds have come increasingly from levies imposed on the utilities.

The commissions have been given a measure of independence. Their membership is bipartisan, their terms are so staggered that no governor, in his own term, can appoint a majority, and their members cannot be removed without serious cause. But this independence may be little more than nominal. A governor can select from the minority party a member who is sympathetic to his views. If the governor serves a second term, he can appoint a majority of the commissioners. The legislature controls a commission's powers, its appropriation, and its very existence, being able to reorganize or abolish it at any time. Governors and legislators who favor the utilities may therefore influence the commissions. And the commissions may attempt to assure their preservation by allying themselves with the interests they are supposed to regulate.

Commission Procedure

Much of the work done by the Commissions originates in complaints made by consumers. These deal, in the main, with the availability and quality of service, the accuracy of meters, and the application of different items in the schedule of rates. Such matters are handled informally, adjustments being obtained, in most cases, without undue delay. The commissions, however, make little effort to inform consumers concerning their availability to perform this service. Most consumers, in fact, are unaware that such commissions exist.

More important cases have to do with the general level of rates. During periods when costs have been falling, such cases have been originated by complaints from city officials, large industrial users, or other consuming groups. Most commissions have the power to make investigations and institute proceedings on their own initiative. But many of them have lacked the will or the ability to do so, acting as if they were judicial bodies passively waiting for complaints. This attitude of impartiality has served the interest of the utilities, since consumers have usually lacked the knowledge and the resources that would enable them to bring a case. During periods of inflation, however, when costs are rising, requests for increases in rates are brought by the companies. And here, delay in action or refusal to act may work to their disadvantage, serving the consumer interest.

Rate-level cases may be handled informally or formally. Reductions have sometimes resulted from negotiations between commissioners and utility officials. In some instances, formal action has been avoided as long

[3] Eli W. Clemens, *Economics and Public Utilities* (New York: Appleton-Century-Crofts, Inc., 1950), pp. 412–13.

as there was any hope of obtaining an informal settlement. But concessions are more likely to be obtained if there is some prospect that formal measures will be used.

Formal cases take more time, require more work, and cost more money. They involve procedures that are specified by law, elaborated in administrative rulings, and subject to judicial review. Public notice must be given and formal hearings held. Witnesses may be subpoenaed and compelled to produce records and documents. Some commissions have left complainants to their own resources. Others have assisted them by conducting investigations and introducing evidence. Cases are prepared and argued by one division of a commission's staff; initial decisions may be made by an examiner; final decisions are made by the commission itself. These decisions must be accompanied by formal findings of facts. They may lead to orders requiring changes in rates and services. Such orders cannot be enforced by the commissions themselves. If not accepted, they must be taken to the courts.

The Federal Commissions

There are five federal commissions with jurisdiction over interstate transportation and utility services. Of these, the Interstate Commerce Commission was the first. Set up in 1887, it now controls railroads, oil pipelines, interstate motor carriers and water carriers, and a number of other transportation agencies, such as freight forwarders and express companies. It is the largest of the commissions, its budget being larger than the total for commissions in all but two of the states. The Federal Power Commission, first set up in 1920 with three cabinet officers as members, was reorganized in 1930 with full-time independent membership. It now has jurisdiction over power projects on navigable rivers and interstate transmission of electricity and natural gas. The Federal Communications Commission, established in 1933, took over the regulation of interstate telephone and telegraph services from the ICC and that of radio and television from the Federal Radio Commission of 1927. The Securities and Exchange Commission, organized in 1934 to supervise the securities markets, was given power in 1935 to regulate the finances and the corporate relationships of public utilities. The Civil Aeronautics Board, created under legislation passed in 1938, has the jurisdiction that its name implies. The Federal Maritime Board, successor in 1950 to the U.S. Maritime Commission of 1936 and its predecessor, the U.S. Shipping Board of 1916, now has control of international shipping but has no jurisdiction over domestic carriers. International aviation is under the CAB, international telecommunications under the FCC. But it is only with the domestic responsibilities of the commissions that we are now concerned. It should be noted, too, that regulatory functions are performed by some of the regular departments of the government. The regulation of packers and stockyards and commodities exchanges by the Department of Agriculture is a case in point. This activity was described in Chapter 11 and what was said there need not be repeated here.

The ICC has eleven members, the FCC has seven, and the FPC, the SEC, and the CAB each has five. Membership is bipartisan and members can have no financial interest in the industries they control. No other qualifications are established in the laws. Appointments are made by the President for terms running from five to seven years. The salaries paid, while generally somewhat higher than those paid by the states, are still inadequate to attract and hold the sort of talent that the work requires. The tenure of members of the ICC is fairly long; reappointment is common, commissioners serving, on the average, for thirteen years. With the other agencies, however, this is not the case, members of the SEC and the CAB usually serving only three years and those of the FCC only three and a half.[4] Appropriations made for the work of the five federal commissions are roughly double those made for the commissions of the forty-eight states. The federal commissions, in general, are larger, their staffs running over 1,000 in the case of the SEC and the FCC and over 2,000 in the case of the ICC. Staff members were found by the Hoover Commission, in 1949, to be well qualified and consciencious.[5] But here, again, the government cannot compete with the salaries paid by the regulated industries.

The federal commissions have been criticized for failing to consider their programs as a whole, to plan their action in advance, or to formulate and announce their governing criteria, their time being taken in handling the daily load of case work. They have succeeded, however, in maintaining a reputation for impartiality. The independence of the commissions is safeguarded by their bipartisan character and their long and overlapping terms. The President cannot remove members of the ICC or the CAB except on proof of inefficiency, malfeasance, or neglect of duty. No such protection is extended, however, to members of the FPC, the FCC, or the SEC.

Each of the commissions, at one time or another, has come under political attack. A usual charge is that these agencies serve as both prosecutor and judge. To curb their powers, two proposals have been made. One would destroy the independence of the agencies, subordinating each of them to some department in the executive branch. The other would separate the functions of prosecutor and judge, assigning the executive branch the former and confining the commissions to the latter. Neither of these proposals has commended itself to the Congress. The independence of the commissions has been preserved. And the segregation of functions has been accomplished within the agencies themselves.

[4] Commission on Organization of the Executive Branch of the Government, *Task Force Report on Regulatory Commissions* (Washington, D.C.: U.S. Government Printing Office, 1949), p. 24.

[5] *Ibid.*, p. 23.

RATES AND EARNINGS

The regulation of rates has two aspects: control of the rate level and control of the rate structure. The former has to do with the size of a corporation's earnings. Here, the commissions are concerned that the return yielded by the rates be neither so high as to exploit consumers nor so low as to discourage investors. The rate structure has to do with the particular rates paid for different units of service by different classes of customers. Here, the problem is discrimination. The regulated industries are not forbidden to discriminate. But the commissions must take care lest the manner of discrimination be unfair or unreasonable, favoring some customers and harming others.

The Rate Level

The general level of rates should be high enough, first, to cover the current costs of operation and, second, to yield a proper return on the money invested in facilities. This return should be high enough to do two things. Looking backward, it should be fair to investors, avoiding impairment of the value of their property. Looking forward, it should preserve the credit standing of the regulated company so that it will be able to attract the capital it will need if its service is to be maintained, improved, and expanded in response to consumer demand. If earnings do more than this, the company will obtain monopoly profits at the expense of its customers. If they do less, its service will fall short in quantity and will decline in quality.

Control of the rate level involves three different processes. First, it is necessary to control operating expenses. These expenses are the largest sum that must be covered in the rates. If they are inflated, through dishonesty or inefficiency, the rates will be too high. To prevent this, methods of accounting must also be controlled. Second, it is necessary to determine the rate of return on investment that is to be taken as fair to consumers and investors and as adequate for the maintenance of credit. This rate is expressed as a percentage of the value of a company's property. Third, it is necessary to determine this value. This process involves the estimation of construction costs and the deduction of depreciation. Here, again, control of accounting is required, since inflation of the rate base would necessitate the allowance of larger earnings and higher rates. Methods of valuation differ, as do methods of allowing for depreciation. It is here that the major controversies over regulation centered for nearly half a century.

The commissions operate within the limits of the Constitution as it is interpreted by the courts. In its Fifth Amendment, the Constitution forbids the federal government to deprive any person of property without due process of law. In the Fourteenth Amendment, it imposes a similar prohibition on the states. The word "person," as we saw in Chapter 2, has been interpreted to mean corporation, the word "property" to mean corporate earnings and the value of corporate investment, and the words "due process" to comprehend not only the procedure followed in setting rates but also the adequacy of the rates themselves. The courts thus undertook to review the rates that the commissions set. Their concern, primarily, was to protect investors. Their attention was focused upon the adequacy of earnings. And in judging earnings, the issues brought before them usually related, not to the percentage adopted as a fair rate of return, but to the method used in measuring the rate base. The matter of valuation thus became the heart of the problem of controlling rates. It is only in the past decade that the courts have left this matter to the discretion of the regulatory agencies.

Even now, control of rates is neither continuous nor tight. No effort is made to eliminate excessive earnings the moment they appear. Earnings are examined on complaint, or on commission initiative, perhaps no oftener than once in a decade. In the meantime, if demand has grown and costs have declined, returns that are excessive may be realized and retained. There is no assurance, however, that earnings will be adequate. As costs rise, commissions may be slow to grant corresponding increases in rates. And as demand falls, earnings may fall whatever the rates allowed. Surpluses are not seized and deficits are not made up as they appear.

Control looks backward rather than forward. Prices are fixed for future sales, but no effort is made to estimate the possible effect of different prices on the volume that can be sold, or the effect of volume on unit costs. It may be that equal revenues or even greater revenues could be obtained through the larger sales resulting from a lower price. It may be that larger sales would lead to lower costs by increasing the utilization of existing capacity, or by permitting operation on a larger scale. It is thus possible that adequacy of earnings is consistent with the provision of more service to more customers. But when the commissions compute total revenue, they multiply the new price by the old volume. And when they compute earnings, they subtract the old costs. Demand and costs are assumed to be frozen. The dynamics of production are ignored. Control, thus exercised, is negative rather than affirmative.

These, in general, are the problems that must be faced in considering control of the level of rates. They are to be discussed in greater detail in Chapter 18.

The Rate Structure

The regulated company is a monopolist or a semimonopolist. It sells the same service to different classes of buyers. But it does not charge them all the same price. In part, the differences in price can be explained in terms of differences in cost. But, in large part, they cannot. And here, the company discriminates. Being a monopolist, it seeks to maximize its revenues by charging more where demand is strong and alternatives lacking, less where demand is weak and alternatives available. If such discrimination were forbidden, sales might well be smaller, costs higher, and prices therefore higher for consumers as a whole. Discrimination, thus, may be desirable, but it is also dangerous. The seller who discriminates may willfully favor one buyer over another, giving the former an unfair advantage and placing the latter under an unfair handicap. In regulated industries, therefore, the extent of discrimination that is practiced cannot be left to the companies but must be controlled by the commissions and the courts. The problems encountered in regulating the structure of rates will be considered in Chapter 19.

SERVICE, SAFETY, AND EFFICIENCY

"Service and efficiency," writes J. M. Clark, "are coordinate parts of any attempt to control prices; first, because it does the buyer no good to pay a lower price if the quality or quantity he gets for his money is lowered in the same proportion, giving him gas, for instance, of four-fifths the former heating power for four-fifths the former price. Second, it does the buyer no good to compel the producer to accept half the former net earnings if he gets in exchange a management half as efficient, for the poor management will add more to the costs of operation than the regulating commission can take away in reduced earnings."[6] In practice, the commissions have devoted some attention to quantity and quality of service and safety of operation but little to efficiency of management.

Quantity of Service

The quantitative controls over service are those relating to entry, extension, and abandonment. Where city streets are used, a company wishing to enter a utility industry must obtain a franchise from the city government. In all regulated industries, moreover, an entrant must apply to the relevant commission for a "certificate of public convenience and necessity." By denying certificates, it is thought, a commission can prevent speculative construction, overcapacity, and ruinous competition, thus assuring financial stability and continued service at regulated rates. But it may also impede progress by protecting old investments against the challenge of new technology.

A company with no competitors may be slow to expand its service even though demand has grown. Under regulation, however, expansion may be required. A commission cannot compel a concern to extend its operation into new territories. And it will take no initiative in ordering extensions within a region where operations are already under way. But it is likely to act, upon complaint, to force the concern, within this region, to extend to new customers the service it has been providing to older ones.

[6] J. M. Clark, *Social Control of Business* (New York: McGraw-Hill Book Co., 1939), p. 337.

It may not issue such an order where an extension would entail a substantial loss. But it may do so even though some loss would be incurred.

A commission cannot prevent a company from abandoning all its operations. But commissions can and do prohibit partial abandonments. This problem has been of small importance to the utility commissions, since they have been dealing, in the main, with expanding industries. It has been of great importance, however, to the ICC. Branch lines of railroads have become unprofitable as a result of exhaustion of resources, relocation of industry, and the increasing competition of motor carriers. The Commission has therefore been faced with many requests for abandonment. It has granted some but denied others even though the branches had to be operated at a loss. Commissions may hesitate to require unprofitable extensions. But they are even more reluctant to deprive consumers of service they already have.

Quality of Service

The regulatory commissions are usually empowered to prescribe reasonable standards of service, requiring the regulated companies to conform. With most public utilities, these standards may include such matters as continuity of service, accuracy of meters, deposits and repayments, methods of billing, and the treatment of complaints. They may also define the quality of service in terms of technical dimensions and establish permissible limits of variation. For water, there may be standards of purity and pressure; for electricity, limits to variation in voltage; for gas, standards of heat content measured in British thermal units, limits to the percentage of impurities, and requirements as to the amount and steadiness of pressure. Telephone service, conceivably, could be controlled by limiting the number of subscribers on a line, specifying the amount and quality of equipment to be provided, reducing interference in transmission, and shortening the time required in completing calls. Urban transit, finally, might be governed by standards of cleanliness, ventilation, lighting, and heating of cars, frequency of service, adherence to schedules, and adequacy of rush hour service in terms of the ratio of seats to passengers and the number of square feet provided per standee.

The danger of prescribing service standards is that technology will be frozen, progress impeded, and managerial initiative impaired. This is a danger that the utility commissions have been able to avoid. In practice, little has been done in the way of developing and enforcing standards of quality. The utilities take the initiative, the commissions intervening only on complaint. On the whole the results appear to be good. With most utilities the quality of service is high.

The railroads are a special case. The ICC has been given extensive powers with respect to such matters as car supply, switching service, interconnection of carriers, interchange of traffic, the establishment of through routes and joint rates, and the joint use of terminals. The exercise of these powers, moreover, involves an administrative undertaking of considerable magnitude.

Safety

Along with service, regulation has to do with safety. This is true of all utilities. Prevention of explosion from gas leaks and of fire from unguarded wiring is a matter of public concern. Assurance of safety will bulk large in any program for industrial applications of atomic energy. But safety has been most important, to date, in the regulation of transport industries. Requirements are established, for all types of carriers, governing such matters as the character of equipment, the use of safety devices, the qualifications and hours of employees, the transportation of explosives, speed, and the investigation of accidents. Detailed regulations applying to railroads control the length of trains and the size of crews, provide for boiler inspection and the elimination or protection of grade crossings, and require the use of block signals, automatic couplers, and power brakes. It is in the case of aviation, however, that safety comes first of all. The safety work of the Civil Aeronautics Administration and the Civil Aeronautics Board will be described in Chapter 22.

Efficiency

Under private enterprise, efficiency and progress are normally evoked by the promise of profit and the penalty of loss. But where rates and earnings are regulated, the profit incentive is weakened or diverted to other ends. In the case of transportation, a common rate is fixed for all of the carriers in a group. The carrier with lower costs earns more; the one with higher costs earns less. So some incentive is retained. But if the group as a whole reduces its costs, its rates will be cut. And if it increases them, its rates will be raised. In the case of public utilities, moreover, this procedure is applied to the individual firm. If regulation is tight, earnings cannot be enlarged by cutting costs. Let management be diligent in this cause, then rates will be reduced. Let it be indolent, then rates will be increased. There is no incentive to efficiency. Earnings, however, may be enlarged in other ways. The rate base can be expanded by unnecessary and extravagant investment. Operating expenses can be padded, property valuations inflated, and regulation obstructed by ceaseless litigation. But here, the profit incentive runs against the public interest.

If regulation were tight, efficiency would have to be sought through detailed supervision of operations. Orders would have to be issued and performance checked. The regulatory agencies would have to duplicate the central functions of management. In fact, however, regulation is not tight. With rate reductions lagging behind cost reductions, sometimes for many years, there is still an incentive to efficiency. But this incentive persists, not where regulation works well, but where it fails to work.

In principle, earnings should be related to efficiency. One way of doing this, which has sometimes been attempted, is to tie the percentage of return to the level of rates, raising it as rates are cut and cutting it as rates are raised. But this procedure has its limitations. Rates might be cut, not by reducing costs but by impairing service. Close control of standards of service would therefore be required. Costs and rates might be raised, not by inefficiency but by causes that managements were powerless to control. The only alternative is to develop standards of efficiency in physical terms, together with methods of measurement by which performance can be appraised. But this is something that no commission has tried to do.

CORPORATE FINANCE AND INTERCORPORATE RELATIONS

Control of the finances of regulated companies is designed to protect consumers and investors by preventing overcapitalization, by maintaining a proper balance in capital structures, and by averting defeat of the purposes of regulation through various intercorporate relationships. It involves the power to disapprove security issues, to forbid combinations, and to supervise intercorporate transactions. In 1920 authority over the finances of railroads was given to the ICC. But until 1930 such authority with respect to public utilities was either lacking or was little exercised. Since that time, however, financial controls have been imposed by most of the states and by a number of federal agencies. Such controls are crucially important. Not only are they needed in themselves; they may also be employed in support of other regulatory activities. A request for approval of an issue of securities may afford an occasion for review of rates and services. Permission may be given on condition that rates be cut or services improved. Where these matters are settled through negotiation, a commission's power over security issues provides it with a stronger hand in bargaining.

Control of Capitalization

The base to which a percentage return is applied in computing a company's earnings is the value of the property it employs in rendering its service, not the value of its outstanding stocks and bonds. One might suppose, therefore, that overcapitalization would not matter, since the company's rates would not be affected if it were overcapitalized. But this, in fact, is not the case. Overcapitalization creates strong pressure for funds to use in paying interest and dividends. These funds may be obtained by charging high rates or giving poor service. The overcapitalized company is certain to seek high rates. If it is held to a fair return on its actual assets, it may have little or nothing left, after paying interest, to distribute in dividends. In this case, its stock will decline in value and it may be unable to raise further capital by selling new securities. With rates held down, the company may obtain the funds required for dividends by setting aside inadequate reserves for depreciation or by skimping maintenance. In either case, service eventually will suffer. Confronted with such a situation, a commission is likely to set rates at a level that will permit the payment of dividends on watered stock, preserving the company's credit and its ability to serve.

There is little that can be done about overcapitalization in the past. When companies go through bankruptcy and must be reorganized, however, water can be squeezed out, and the value of securities limited to the actual value of properties. In some cases, short of bankruptcy, voluntary revaluations may be obtained. But prevention of overcapitalization, in the main, has to do with new issues of securities, floated to finance new enterprises, combinations, and expanded operations by existing companies.

In controlling new issues, the commissions are concerned with their purposes, their size, and the cost of their distribution. Issues are not approved unless for necessary purposes and in amounts required to satisfy these purposes. Expenditure of the proceeds is supervised to make sure that they are used for the purposes approved. The costs of distribution are limited by fixing the minimum prices to be received by the issuers, by fixing the margins to be retained by the underwriters, and in some cases by requiring the placement of issues through competitive bidding.

Many railroad and utility companies have long had close relationships with particular banking houses, invariably employing these houses to market their securities. This practice has been defended on the ground that it assures the borrower sound advice and responsible service. It has been attacked on the ground that it gives the banker an excessive margin and the borrower a smaller share of the investor's dollar than he would otherwise receive. In 1926 competitive bidding for certain railway securities was required by the ICC. In 1939 and 1941 competitive bidding for issues under their jurisdiction was required by the FPC and the SEC. Similar requirements have been made by some of the state commissions. But this is not the general rule.

The Capital Structure

Regulation concerns itself not only with aggregate capitalization but also with the relative proportions of different types of securities and the terms on which they are issued. If too large a part of a company's capital is in the form of bonds, its fixed charges will be high and it will be less able to weather a depression. Its ability to meet future needs by borrowing will also be impaired. The commissions are therefore likely to limit the share of bonds, usually to half or thereabouts of total capital. To preserve a company's ability to raise new capital through sales of common stock, they may also maintain the value of outstanding common by limiting the fraction of preferred.

Protection of investors is an end in itself. But it is also undertaken to maintain a company's credit and thus its capacity to render service. The SEC and some of the state commissions now protect bondholders by regulating the provisions of bond indentures. They may attempt to insure the availability of funds to pay interest and principal by limiting the distribution of dividends and by requiring the accumulation of sinking funds. They may safeguard the value of mortgaged properties by specifying the provisions to be made for maintenance and depreciation. The commissions may also protect stockholders by preventing an inequitable distribution of voting power. To this end, they may forbid the issuance of nonvoting shares and of shares with multiple or contingent voting rights. In reorganizations, finally, the ICC and the SEC attempt to make sure that the relative rights of all classes of security holders are observed.

Combinations and Intercorporate Controls

One corporation may obtain the assets of another by leasing them or by getting a controlling interest in the latter's stocks. Two or more corporations may be combined, in fact, through outright merger. Or a third corporation may combine them, in effect, by controlling their shares. All these forms of combination and acquisition of control are now subject to regulation, in one way or another, by public agencies. In the case of transportation, elimination of competition was forbidden, until 1920, under the Sherman Act. But it has been permitted, since that time, upon approval by the ICC and, in the case of airlines, by the CAB. In exercising supervision over these matters, the agencies concern themselves not only with the effect of their action on competition in service but also with its effect on the financial strength of the carriers and on the welfare of investors in their securities. When combination is permitted, total capitalization and the character of the capital structure can be controlled.

The most serious problems of intercorporate relationship are those created by the holding company. This device has been used, in many cases, as a means of defeating the purposes of regulation. The holding company votes the controlling shares in a subordinate operating company, elects its directors, and chooses its management. It then enters into business transactions with the operating company, borrowing from it, lending to it, and selling it properties, goods, and services. None of these transactions is the result of arm's-length bargaining. The holding company may borrow at a low rate of interest and lend at a high rate. It may charge exorbitant prices for properties, equipment, and supplies, and for construction, financing, management, and other services. By so doing, it pads the costs of the operating company and enlarges the base upon which earnings are allowed. As a result, so long as holding company charges are beyond the reach of the commissions, they must be covered by raising operating company rates. The holding company, moreover, may seek to enhance its revenues by forcing the operating company to make inadequate provision for depreciation and maintenance and thus to pay larger dividends, impairing its ultimate strength. If regulation is to be effective, it is obvious that holding companies must be controlled. Before the thirties, such control was either lacking or seriously inadequate. In 1933 the ICC was given jurisdiction over railroad holding companies. In 1935 the SEC was given extensive powers with respect to public utility holding companies. The state commissions, too, were granted new authority. The holding company loophole was nearly if not entirely closed.

Interutility Competition

Regulation, in its origin, was justified by the absence of competition. Regulated industries, in general, are not supposed to be competitive. But many of them compete with industries offering alternative services: the railroads, pipelines, motor carriers, water carriers, and airlines with one another, gas with electricity, and the telephone with the telegraph. Such competition raises problems for the rate makers. And it poses a basic issue of policy: should combination of competing media be permitted or should competition be required?

In the case of transportation, as we shall see, the competition of other carriers is regularly taken into account in fixing rates. But with public utilities, this is not the case. Gas and electricity, telephone and telegraph, each stands on its own feet. As a result, when the earnings of one are high, its rates may be cut, thus making it difficult for the other to survive. Such a policy, however, would appear to be desirable. If competing services are on an equal footing, it gives the larger share of the market to the one with lower costs.

The states, in general, have permitted common ownership of gas and electric services. This arrangement is defended as reducing the costs of management, selling, billing, and collecting, and as permitting the use of each service for the most economical purposes. It is criticized as removing a possible incentive to improve service and cut rates, and as permitting the postponement of innovations so as to protect investments in existing plants. The SEC, in the process of reorganizing holding company systems, has generally put gas and electricity under separate managements. The ICC and the CAB, with power to permit the combination of unlike carriers, have rarely done so. There has been combination within the telephone and telegraph industries, but not between the two. In the main, the federal commissions have sought to preserve competition between different media. An exception must be noted, however, in the case of the FCC. This agency has given radio licenses to newspapers, FM licenses to AM stations, TV licenses to radio stations, and also to motion picture companies. The problems presented here will be discussed in Chapter 23.

ACCOUNTS AND REPORTS

A commission must be equipped with accurate and informative accounts if it is to succeed in assuring reasonable rates, satisfactory service, and financial stability. To control the general level of rates, it needs to know operating expenses and the value of investments. To control the rate structure, it needs to know the costs of different types of service. To pass judgment on proposals for extension and abandonment, it needs information on the revenues and costs of particular operations. And to prevent overcapitalization, it requires information on all corporate assets and liabilities. If accounts were falsified or obscure, the commission would be seriously handicapped. Control of accounts, therefore, is essential to provide support in every other phase of its activities.

Abuses in Accounting

If operating expenses are padded without detection, the allowance made for them in fixing the level of rates will be too great, and rates and earnings will therefore be too high. This padding may be done in several ways. Accounts may not be properly segregated. Money spent in the interest of investors may be charged to consumers. Transactions with affiliated interests may not be properly identified. Expenditures for capital improvements may be included, in the guise of maintenance, in operating accounts. Excessive sums may be set aside each year in reserves for various purposes. Money spent in replacing worn-out equipment, though already covered in past contributions to depreciation reserves, may be charged again as current costs. In all of these ways, rates may be pushed up and elements of profit concealed in expense accounts.

If the rate base is padded, the amount of earnings that is added to expenses in fixing rates will be magnified. Here, again, a number of methods may be used. Properties may be entered at figures exceeding their actual cost. Intangible items may be included: good will, franchise value, and value as a going concern. Properties may be sold back and forth among the members of a holding company system at ever increasing prices. Or their values may be written up without bothering to make a sale. Depreciation that has been charged to operating expenses may not be deducted from the valuation of assets. Property long since retired may be kept on the books. And rates will be boosted accordingly.

Through improper accounting, too, financial stability may be endangered by paying excessive dividends. Fictitious surplus accounts may be set up and dividends apparently declared from surplus when really paid out of capital. Insufficient charges may be made for depreciation and dividends paid though adequate provision for the replacement of worn-out property has not been made. Under retirement accounting, so called, no charges may be made for depreciation in bad years, keeping earnings and dividends high, and heavy charges made in good years, keeping earnings low and providing a justification for higher rates. Here, again, regulation will suffer a defeat.

Control of Accounting

For many years, companies subjected to regulation resisted supervision of their accounts as an invasion of privacy. But in this they were not upheld by the courts. Power to prescribe the form of accounts and the methods of accounting was eventually granted to all of the commissions, both federal and state. But there was no uniformity in the systems first prescribed. As a result, some companies had to keep several sets of books to conform to the differing requirements of different agencies. It was difficult to examine company accounts. And it was almost impossible to compare the operations of different concerns, private and public, large and small, and to appraise their relative efficiency. A movement toward the adoption of uniform systems finally got under way. Systems prescribed for gas and electric companies by the FPC and for telephone companies by the FCC, in the middle thirties were approved by the National Association of Railroad and Utilities Commissioners. Within the jurisdiction of the federal agencies, the systems took effect at once. In the states, their use awaited approval by the state commissions and adoption by the regulated companies.

The new systems went into complete detail, laying down clear accounting principles. They prescribed the categories to be used in classifying expenditures, distinguishing those chargeable to investors and to consumers, segregating those involving affiliated interests, and differentiating capital costs from operating costs. They required that property be entered in the books at its cost to the persons first devoting it to public service, thus eliminating subsequent write-ups in its value. They forbade retirement accounting, requiring instead that equal sums be set aside for depreciation in good years and in bad. In these and other ways, they sought to provide the regulators with a solid footing in facts.

All commissions require annual reports, prescribe their form, and specify the material they must contain. Some commissions examine the manner in which accounts are kept and check the accuracy of reports, making field audits from time to time. Others lack the resources with which to make such audits. And still others decline to make them, holding this to be an unwarranted invasion of the privacy of management. Accounting powers are universal, accounting systems adequate, but accounting requirements indifferently enforced.

SUGGESTIONS FOR FURTHER READING

The matters discussed in this chapter are covered at greater length in several texts on public utilities. See Emery Troxel, *Economics of Public Utilities* (New York: Rinehart & Co., Inc., 1947), chaps. i–x and xxi, particularly chaps. ii and x, and Eli W. Clemens, *Economics and Public Utilities* (New York: Appleton-Century-Crofts, Inc., 1950), chaps. iii, xvii, xix, and xx. An older volume is Irston R. Barnes, *The Economics of Public Utility Regulation* (New York: F. S. Crofts & Co., 1942), see chaps. iii, vi, viii, xx, and xxi. An excellent survey of public utility regulation is that by Ben W. Lewis, included as chap. xxi in Leverett S. Lyon and Victor Abramson (eds.), *Government and Economic Life* (Washington, D.C.: Brookings Institution, 1940). In this connection, it would also be worth while to read chap. xiv on "Types of Control" and Chap. xxi on "Regulation, Service and Efficiency" in J. M. Clark, *Social Control of Business* (2d ed.; New York: McGraw-Hill Book Co., 1939).

Chapter 18 THE RATE LEVEL

A number of different objectives might be sought by government in controlling the general level of rates in regulated industries. First, government might undertake to strike a balance between the interests of consumers and those of investors, fixing rates that would be low enough to prevent extortion of monopoly profits from the consumers but high enough to avoid injustice to the investors. Second, it might seek to promote the widest possible use of regulated services, setting rates at the lowest level consistent with the earnings required to attract the needed capital. These two objectives are not the same, since extortionate profits can be prevented not only where rates are low and volume large but also where rates are high and volume small; and also since earnings sufficient to attract new capital may differ from those required to compensate investors in the past. Third, government might attempt to increase consumption by encouraging the reduction of costs and rates through improvements in efficiency and progress in technology. And fourth, it might employ its control of rates as a means of stabilizing economic activity, raising them to retard a boom and reducing them to cushion a slump. In practice, however, only the first of these goals has been sought. Regulation has had to do, not with expansion of use, promotion of efficiency, advancement of technology, or stabilization of the economy, but solely with the question of earnings. At times, it has emphasized the interest of consumers; at other times, the interest of investors. But always, the balance of these interests has been the focus of its concern.

Thus motivated, control of the rate level requires the establishment of rates that, when multiplied by the expected volume of output, are calculated to yield enough revenue to cover all of the costs of operation and, in addition, to provide whatever earnings the regulators may find necessary and desirable. In measuring the adequacy of earnings, two factors are used: the value ascribed to the property of a regulated company, known as the rate base, and a percentage of this value, known as the rate of return. Establishment of the rates that will be required to yield the necessary revenues, at the volume assumed, thus involves three processes: (1) determination of the costs of operation, (2) determination of the rate base, and

(3) determination of the rate of return. Each of these processes is discussed in one of the major parts of this chapter.

Rates, under this procedure, are fixed on a cost-plus basis. But costs, supposedly, are supervised. Efficient management is expected, and honest accounting is required. Return on investment, moreover, is not guaranteed. The regulators may overestimate future demand and underestimate future costs. Conditions may change and earnings, consequently, may fall short. But the shortage will not be made up by the government. Regulation, on the other hand, may underestimate demand and overestimate costs. And here, the surplus earnings that result will not be taken away. Control of earnings, finally, has to do with earnings as a whole; its limits do not apply to dividends. The interest paid on bonds and the dividends on preferred stock may be well below the rate of return allowed. From the sum remaining, therefore, dividends may be paid on common stock at a rate that is well above the one allowed. The declaration of dividends is sometimes supervised to safeguard the financial soundness of a company, but not to limit the profits of the owners of its shares.

COVERING THE COSTS OF OPERATION

Quantitatively, the costs of operation are more significant than the return allowed on investment. They add up to the largest sum that must be covered in fixing rates. In the case of public utilities, they may range from more than half to as much as three fourths of total revenues; in the case of railroads, from two thirds to more than four fifths. These costs include all types of operating expenses, plus annual charges for depreciation, plus taxes. Typically, operating expenses may run around 60 per cent of revenues, depreciation around 5 per cent, and taxes around 10 per cent. Each of these categories will be considered in one of the sections that follow.

Operating Expenses

The need for controlling operating expenses might be questioned on the ground that regulated companies will find it in their own interest to keep expenses down. But this is not invariably the case. Expenditures made on behalf of investors may be charged to consumers. Managements may profit by voting themselves high salaries and substantial bonuses. Holding companies may gain by forcing their subsidiaries to purchase goods and services at excessive prices. In some cases, the groups controlling regulated companies may be incompetent. In others, they may be dishonest. To guard against such possibilities, expenses of operation must be supervised.

The legality of such supervision has long been recognized by the courts. In a railroad case[1] decided in 1892, the Supreme Court asserted

[1] *Chicago & Grand Trunk Railway Co.* v. *Wellman,* 143 U.S. 339.

that the legislative power was not "subservient to the discretion of any railroad corporation which may, by exorbitant and unreasonable salaries, or in some other improper way, transfer its earnings into what it is pleased to call 'operating expenses.' "[2] For a time during the twenties, the Court restricted the power of commissions to regulate expenditures. In the Southwestern Bell case of 1923,[3] it forbade the Missouri Commission to question the payments made by Southwestern to its holding company, A.T.&T., saying, "The Commission is not the financial manager of the corporation, and it is not empowered to substitute its judgement for that of the directors of the corporation; nor can it ignore items charged by the utility as operating expenses unless there is an abuse of discretion in that regard by the corporate officers."[4] This rule would have made it virtually impossible to control the expenses resulting from intercompany transactions within a holding company system. It was revised, however, in the Illinois Bell decision[5] of 1930, the Court permitting the Illinois Commission to reject the costs incurred through intrasystem purchases of goods and services. And in 1936, in a case involving the regulation of stockyard charges by the Secretary of Agriculture,[6] the Court gave broader scope to cost control, explicitly approving the Secretary's rejection of certain expenditures on the ground that they were unwise. Said Justice Roberts, "The contention is that the amount to be expended for these purposes is purely a question of managerial judgement. But . . . regulation cannot be frustrated by a requirement that the rate be made to compensate extravagant or unnecessary costs for these or any purposes."[7]

In practice, the commissions have not been vigorous in controlling costs. None of them has promulgated rules or established standards to govern expenditures. Only three or four of them have the power to require that budgets be submitted in advance. And even these lack budgetary control; they cannot prevent unwise expenditures from being made. Most commissions examine the reports that are periodically submitted on expenses incurred in the past. And if certain items seem improper, they may warn the companies concerned that they will not include them in computing future rates. But regulation may be so lax that the warnings will be ineffective. When rates are formally contested, expenses may be questioned. In such cases, however, the company will present its accounts as a record of established facts. And the representatives of the public will seldom be equipped to challenge the propriety of the items they contain.

[2] *Ibid.*, p. 346.

[3] *Southwestern Bell Telephone Co.* v. *Public Service Comsn. of Missouri*, 262 U.S. 276.

[4] *Ibid.*, p. 289.

[5] *Smith* v. *Illinois Bell Telephone Co.*, 282 U.S. 133.

[6] *Acker* v. *U.S.*, 298 U.S. 426.

[7] *Ibid.*, pp. 430–31.

Upon occasion, certain items may be disallowed. But such control, at best, is indirect and weak.

Where it is exercised, the supervision of expenditures is selective. The prices and wages paid for goods and services bought in the open market are accepted as given. Inquiry is confined to matters where the interests of consumers and investors are obviously in conflict, and where the prices paid do not result from arm's-length bargaining. Questions may be raised, for instance, concerning the propriety of charging to consumers the costs of institutional advertising, political contributions, donations to charity, and other public relations activities, and the costs of litigation, particularly when it is designed to prevent reductions or to obtain increases in rates. Questions might also be raised concerning the legitimacy of salaries and bonuses, though this is seldom done. In recent years, however, commissions have inquired into transactions between affiliated corporations that might produce inflated costs. In some cases, intercorporate contracts must be submitted for approval. In others, the reasonableness of intercorporate payments must be proved. Certain expenses incurred by distributors of gas and electricity are regulated, moreover, by federal agencies: the wholesale prices charged for interstate transmission by the FPC, and holding company charges by the SEC. But no such control has been applied to the charges made by A.T.&T., the telephone holding company.

If the commissions were really to undertake to eliminate extravagant and unnecessary costs, they would have to go much further than they have gone in analyzing expenditures. In doing so, they might employ statistics of costs as a tool, comparing the expense ratios of different companies (expenses as a percentage of revenues), their expenses per unit of output, and their expenses per customer. Such comparisons would have to be used with some discretion, since conditions affecting the costs of different companies are not the same. But they would at least afford a point of departure for further analysis. A few commissions have used statistics as a tool but only to a limited extent. In general, these agencies have concerned themselves with the honesty but not with the wisdom of expenditures.

The commissions have usually taken the view that decisions respecting the wisdom of expenditures lie within the province of management. They have refused to substitute the judgment of regulators for that of managers. But the line they have sought to draw between regulation and management is unreal. The substantive problems with which the two must deal are the same. If regulation is to fulfill the function of competition as a disciplinarian, it must invade the sphere of management. Where it refuses to do so, there is no safeguard for the public interest. This is the inescapable dilemma of regulatory control.

Depreciation as a Cost

Depreciation has been defined by the National Association of Railroad and Utilities Commissioners as "the expiration or consumption, in whole or in part, of the service life, capacity, or utility of property resulting from the action of one or more of the forces operating to bring about the retirement of such property from service."[8] Physical depreciation is caused, through the passage of time, by forces such as wear and tear, rust, rot, and decay. Functional depreciation may come sooner: when facilities are rendered obsolete by innovations in technology, made inadequate by growth in demand, or condemned by changes in legal requirements. Depreciation may also result from contingencies such as disasters, accidents, and the disappearance of supplies: as, for instance, when exhaustion of natural resources deprives railroads of the traffic they were built to haul. Whatever its cause, depreciation involves destruction of the value of facilities used in the process of providing service. Unless the plants of regulated companies are to deteriorate, these facilities must be replaced. And provision for their replacement is properly to be charged to consumers as a cost of the service they receive.

Provision for maintenance, also, is a cost. But the two are not the same. Maintenance keeps facilities in good condition as long as they are kept in use. It supplies machines with necessary parts. It covers buildings with paint. But it does not provide the funds with which to replace the machines when they must be retired or the buildings when they must be torn down and rebuilt. This is the function of the depreciation charge.

Provision for replacement has been made in two quite different ways: through retirement accounting and through depreciation accounting. The former has been favored by the regulated companies, the latter by the regulatory agencies. Under retirement accounting, replacements are not charged to operating costs until they are actually made. Under depreciation accounting, reserves for replacement are built up by annual charges during the life of the facilities. Retirement accounting is said to be more flexible. And it is: it enables companies to make earnings look worse than they are in good years by making substantial replacements, thus forestalling possible demands for reductions in rates; it enables them to make earnings look better than they are in bad years, thus maintaining dividends at a higher figure than could be paid if the steady decline in the service value of facilities were recognized. This method of accounting permits managements to indulge in fair weather finance, enjoying profits today while jeopardizing financial strength tomorrow. It has therefore been rejected by all of the commissions. Depreciation accounting, with annual charges to meet declining values, is now generally required.

The size of the depreciation charge depends on three factors: (1) the difference between the cost of the facilities concerned and their probable salvage value, (2) the number of years during which this sum is written off, and (3) the method used in distributing the sum among these years. The facilities may be valued at their replacement cost or at their original

[8] National Association of Railroad and Utilities Commissioners, *Proceedings*, 1944, pp. 82–83.

cost. In the former case, the annual charge will fluctuate as prices change. In the latter, it can be stable. And this is what the commissions have preferred. At one time, the Supreme Court required that valuations be made at replacement cost,[9] but this decision has since been reversed.[10] Original-cost accounting is now the general rule. Salvage values are estimated and deducted. The length of depreciation periods is determined by engineering estimates of life expectancy. In practice, a separate charge is not computed for each item of property, but items are classified and an average charge applied to all those falling in each class. The provision for depreciation can be distributed over time, finally, in three different ways: (1) it can start high and decline from year to year, (2) it can start low and rise, and (3) it can remain the same. The first of these methods has theoretical advantages, but its use is prevented by practical difficulties. The choice has been between the other two.

Under the second method, a sinking fund is set up on a company's books and equal sums assigned to it each year. It is assumed that the fund is invested and interest earned. In practice, it is reinvested in the business, but interest is credited to it, compounding annually. As the fund grows, the interests payments rise. The total contributions for depreciation are therefore on a rising scale. These contributions are so computed that the basic payments plus the compound interest will be equal to the cost of assets at the time they are retired. Under the third method of distributing charges, equal amounts are assigned to a depreciation reserve each year. This reserve, too, is usually reinvested in the business. But it is not credited with interest. The annual contributions add up to the cost of the property retired. In either case, the capital costs of depreciating facilities are gradually transferred to operating costs. The sinking fund method is more complicated, the straight line method simpler. The latter is preferred by the commissions and is more widely used.

Depreciation has two related aspects: it is charged to operating costs; it must also be deducted from the rate base. Under the sinking fund method, the part of the fund attributable to interest has come from the owners of the company and has not been charged to operating costs. It is therefore not deducted from the base. But under the straight line method, all of the payments assigned to depreciation reserves are covered in costs; the full amount of accrued depreciation should therefore be deducted from the base. Otherwise, consumers would be paying for the same thing twice: once in costs and again in the return still allowed on an investment that has been charged to costs. Where accrued depreciation is deducted, the balance of interest between consumers and investors is not materially affected by differences in the size of the annual depreciation charge. If the charge is higher, consumers will pay more in costs and less in earnings. If it is lower, investors will get less in costs and more in earnings.

[9] *United Railways and Electric Co.* v. *West,* 280 U.S. 234 (1930).

[10] *FPC.* v. *Hope Natural Gas Co.,* 320 U.S. 591 (1944).

The Problem of Obsolescence

Changes in technology and shifts in demand may be as important as wear and tear in necessitating the retirement of facilities. But the rate of physical depreciation can be estimated, with some accuracy, by engineers, while the speed of obsolescence cannot be foreseen. As a consequence, no separate allowance is made for obsolescence in depreciation accounting. This factor is assumed to be covered in the general depreciation charge.

Failure to provide specifically for obsolescence may delay the introduction of improved equipment into regulated industries. Under competition, a firm is compelled to introduce improvements when its competitors do so. Under monopoly, too, it may choose to introduce them, being free to set its prices at levels that will recover the cost of the old equipment and cover depreciation charges on the new. But under regulation, such freedom is lacking. The regulated company cannot raise its rates without permission. It may not be permitted to charge enough to recover the cost of outmoded facilities if it retires them. It is therefore likely to keep them in use. The installation of new equipment may be postponed for many years until the old wears out. And, in the meantime, consumers will be denied the benefits that might have come from the advancement of technology.

This impediment would be removed, of course, if the depreciation of abandoned equipment were stopped, leaving it in the rate base. And this is done, in effect, when such equipment is defined as stand-by capacity and kept on the books. But this solution of the problem is unsatisfactory, since it compels consumers to pay a return, in perpetuity, on investments that have no use. A better procedure would be to permit obsolete equipment to be amortized while the equipment that replaced it was being depreciated at the normal rate. Amortization might be swift, full cost being recovered by the company before any benefits were passed on to consumers. Preferably, it would be slower, costs being recovered more gradually and some benefits accorded to consumers at an earlier date.

In practice, most commissions have done little or nothing about the recovery of investments in obsolete facilities. Regulation, as it is administered, thus operates to impede adoption of improvements in technology.

Taxes

In making rates, taxes—with but minor exceptions—are included in operating costs and deducted from revenues in determining earnings. This procedure has been required since 1922 by a decision of the Supreme Court.[11] It applies not only to taxes on property and on output, which normally are regarded as costs, but also to taxes on net income, which are not.

With respect to the first group of taxes, the question to be asked re-

[11] *Galveston Electric Co.* v. *Galveston,* 258 U.S. 388.

lates to their desirability as a source of public revenue. There can be no objection, to be sure, to imposing as heavy a burden on industries that are regulated as is borne by those that are not. But legislative bodies do not always stop at this point. They find in regulated services a convenient source of income and employ their producers, in effect, as tax collectors. In this way they unduly burden the consumers of such services and discourage the allocation of resources to the satisfaction of their wants. Here, policy in taxation is made without regard to its effect on regulation, and an artificial handicap is imposed on regulated industries.

With respect to taxes on net income, a different question is raised. Such taxes, generally, are supposed to be computed on the basis of earnings remaining after costs have been deducted from gross revenues. Their treatment, in this case as costs, favors investors in regulated companies, excusing them from taxes that investors in other industries are required to pay. It is true that unregulated companies may sometimes succeed in shifting their income taxes, in part at least, to consumers. But such shifting is not invariable or complete, and it is not endorsed by law.

Not only are rates raised when taxes on net income are treated as costs. High rates are kept high. They produce high earnings. These produce high taxes. And these must be covered again in costs. Excessive rates are thus perpetuated automatically. If this anomaly in regulation is to be corrected, such taxes must be excluded in computing operating costs.

FIXING THE RATE BASE

The process of determining the size of the rate base is known as valuation. Commissions and courts have often spoken of this process as one of finding the value of investments. As a matter of fact, these bodies do not find value; they make it. Companies that are regulated differ sharply in this respect from those that are not. In the latter case, value is not established by public authority. It is the result of market processes. The value of a company's property is determined by taking the revenue produced by the sales made at the price fixed in the market, deducting the costs incurred in the process, and capitalizing the remaining profits at the prevailing rate of interest. In the case of regulated companies this cannot be done. For the price on which the value is based is not fixed in the market; it is set by the regulators themselves. If they put it high, value will be high; if they put it low, value will be low. Value, in the commercial sense of the term, cannot be used as a basis for fixing rates. It is a consequence of prices, not a cause. Value for rate making is quite a different thing. It is established by regulation. It rests, not on the prices of products, but on estimates of the cost of productive properties. What we are concerned with, here, is not commercial value but the size of the rate base and the process by which it is fixed.

This process includes many steps. First, values must be assigned to forms of property that are tangible and reproducible, such as buildings and machines. A line must be drawn between items to be included as used and useful and those to be rejected as not. A decision must be made as to the costs to be employed in assigning values, whether those originally incurred, those required to reproduce the property, or something in between the two. Costs must be obtained from company books and records or an inventory taken and the items priced. A method must be adopted for computing depreciation, the computation made, and the resulting figure deducted from the cost of this part of the property. Second, a value must be assigned to land, an asset that is tangible but not reproducible. Here, a method of pricing must be determined and applied. And finally, decisions must be made as to the allowance of values for intangible assets. And where allowances are made, the values must be assigned.

In this process there are many opportunities to inflate the rate base and thus to increase permitted earnings by raising rates. Items may be improperly included: equipment not used or useful kept on the books, or various intangibles allowed. The items included may be overpriced: extravagant payments recognized, property transfers between affiliated corporations accepted at face value, facilities priced on the basis of imaginary costs of reproduction, and land priced not at what it cost but at what it would bring. These are the problems with which this part of the chapter is concerned.

The Judicial Rule of Fair Value

For half a century, in fixing the rate base, the commissions were dominated by the courts. In 1877, in its decision in the case of *Munn* v. *Illinois*,[12] the Supreme Court had taken the position that rate making was a legislative rather than a judicial function. But in 1886 it reversed this position, asserting that rates fixed under legislative authority were subject to judicial review and might be set aside if they were found, in violation of the Fifth or Fourteenth Amendments, to deprive investors of their property without due process of law.[13] And in 1894 for the first time it nullified the rates established by a state commission.[14] But the court set up no standard by which to judge the reasonableness of commission valuations until it handed down its decision in the famous case of *Smyth* v. *Ames*[15] in 1898.

The state of Nebraska had passed a law in 1893 setting up a Board of Transportation and giving it power to fix the rates charged for hauling freight. The railroads challenged the rates fixed by this body, claiming denial of due process. Some of these roads had been built during and after the Civil War when prices were much higher than in later years. The railroads contended, therefore, that they were entitled to a return on their

[12] 94 U.S. 113.

[13] *Stone* v. *Farmers' Loan and Trust Co.*, 116 U.S. 307.

[14] *Reagan* v. *Farmers' Loan and Trust Co.*, 154 U.S. 362.

[15] 169 U.S. 466.

original cost. William Jennings Bryan was the lawyer for the state. He sought to defend the contested rates by arguing that the railroads' property should be appraised at the lower level of reproduction cost. Thus, the issue was joined between two principles of valuation. And, since prices were falling, the companies embraced original cost and the government, reproduction cost.

The Supreme Court found the rates to be confiscatory on either basis. And then it went on, in a dictum not essential to its decision, to discuss the valuation of investments in regulated industries. This dictum later came to be of great importance, providing a basis for judicial review of rates for nearly fifty years. Said Justice Harlan:

> We hold . . . that the basis of all calculations as to the reasonableness of rates to be charged by a corporation . . . must be the fair value of the property being used by it for the convenience of the public. And, in order to ascertain that value, the original cost of construction, the amount expended in permanent improvements, the amount and market value of its bonds and stocks, the present as compared with the original cost of construction, the probable earning capacity of the property under particular rates prescribed by statute, and the sum required to meet operating expenses, are all matters for consideration, and are to be given such weight as may be just and right in each case. We do not say that there may not be other matters to be regarded in estimating the value of the property. What the company is entitled to ask is a fair return upon the value of that which it employs for the public convenience. On the other hand, what the public is entitled to demand is that no more be exacted from it . . . than the services rendered . . . are reasonably worth.[16]

This statement merits careful analysis. Rates, if they are to stand, must be high enough to afford a fair return on a fair value of invested capital. But fair return and fair value are not defined. Some of the items to be considered in determining fair value are enumerated. These include: (1) operating expenses, (2) earning capacity, (3) the market value of stocks and bonds, (4) original cost and money spent on improvements, and (5) "the present as compared with the original cost." And, lest something may have been forgotten, "We do not say that there may not be other matters to be regarded. . . ." Of the matters mentioned, however, (1) operating expenses are irrelevant, having nothing to do with the determination of the rate base; (2) earning capacity and (3) the market value of stocks and bonds are logical absurdities, since these depend upon the rates that are being fixed; (4) original cost and (5) present cost, while relevant and logical, are inconsistent, since the values to which they lead are far apart. What is fair value: original cost or present cost or some compromise between the two? The Court does not say. Both must be considered, and each must be given "such weight as may be just and right. . . ."

[16] *Ibid.*, pp. 546–47.

Some of the errors in the doctrine of *Smyth* v. *Ames* came to be corrected in the next few years. Operating costs were quietly dropped from the factors to be considered in appraising property. Earning capacity[17] and the value of stocks and bonds[18] were rejected as factors by the Court. Deduction for depreciation, overlooked by Justice Harlan, was added to the "matters to be regarded" in 1909.[19] Original cost and present cost remained as determinants of value.

It should be noted that the rule of *Smyth* v. *Ames*, in its time, was not calculated to justify excessive rates. Consideration of construction costs afforded a wholesome corrective to the tendency to set rates at levels that would validate inflated capitalizations. And consideration of "the present as compared with the original cost" provided a check for use in cases where original cost had been too high. The conversion of this rule into a device for raising rates was the work of later years.

Judicial Emphasis on Reproduction Cost

Until World War I, regulated companies sought valuations based on original cost, while regulators favored reproduction cost. Then, with wartime inflation, prices soared and reproduction cost mounted. For many companies it came to be twice as high as original cost. As a result, the protagonists changed sides. The companies now contested commission orders in the courts, seeking to increase their profits by getting valuations based on reproduction cost. And the commissions defended their orders, basing their valuations on original cost. This controversy dominated regulation for the next twenty years, monopolizing the attention of the companies, the commissions, and the courts.

Until 1926 the Supreme Court took a middle ground. Its dicta seemed to favor reproduction cost. It insisted that this factor be considered. But it said that reproduction cost should not be given exclusive weight. And its decisions approved rates based on valuations that had given the factor minor weight. In one case, where prices had risen 110 per cent, it accepted a valuation that had been raised 33 per cent.[20] In another, where prices had risen 100 per cent, it rejected a valuation that had been raised 25 per cent.[21] The Court, however, was divided. The majority, under the leadership of Justice Butler, a railroad lawyer appointed to the Court by President Harding, came to give increasing emphasis to reproduction cost. The minority rejected this position. Its leading spokesman, Justice Brandeis, a well-known liberal appointed by President Wilson, wrote a series of dis-

[17] *Minnesota Rate Cases*, 230 U.S. 352, (1913).

[18] *Knoxville* v. *Knoxville Water Co.*, 212 U.S. 1 (1909).

[19] *Ibid.*

[20] *Galveston Electric Co.* v. *Galveston*, 258 U.S. 388 (1922).

[21] *Southwestern Bell Telephone Co.* v. *Public Service Commission of Missouri*, 262 U.S. 287 (1923).

senting opinions in which he argued that valuations should be based on prudent investment, i.e., on that part of the original cost that was prudently incurred. In this he was followed by other jurists, commission members, and academic authorities. The controversy thus came to be centered upon the respective merits of prudent investment and reproduction cost.

The high-water mark of reproduction cost valuation came with the Court's decision in the case of *McCardle* v. *Indianapolis Water Co.* in 1926. The original cost of the company's property was $10 million. Its reproduction cost was estimated at $22 million. The state commission allowed $15 million. The company claimed $19 million. The Court held that rates based on any valuation below $19 million would be confiscatory. At a return of 7 per cent this permitted earnings of $1,330,000. Of this, some $525,000 was required to pay interest on bonds and dividends on preferred stock, leaving more than $805,000 to be paid on an original investment of $250,000 in common stock, an annual yield of more than 300 per cent. Said Justice Butler: ". . . in determining present value, consideration must be given to prices and wages prevailing at the time of the investigation; and, . . . there must be an honest and intelligent forecast as to probable price and wage levels during a reasonable period in the immediate future." And again, "It is well established that values of utility properties fluctuate, and that owners must bear the decline and are entitled to the increase."[22]

In the O'Fallon case,[23] which followed in 1929, the Court repeated the fair value formula, setting aside the valuation of railroad properties that had been made over many years by the Interstate Commerce Commission, with meticulous care and at great expense, on the ground that insufficient consideration had been given to reproduction cost. But here, as elsewhere, the Court refused to say how much consideration of this factor was required.

The commissions, thus, were left in the dark. They had to allow a fair return on a fair value. But they had no way of telling what value the Court would accept as fair. Fair value, as Ben W. Lewis has remarked, was "the unpredictable product of incalculable considerations."[24] The Court found it by going into a trance, "embracing revelation as its technique of rate value determination."[25] In an effort to satisfy the undisclosed requirements of the law, the commissions undertook "to accord consideration to a modified reproduction cost figure as one among an assortment of irreconcilable elements to be transmuted into 'fair value' by the alchemy of mystic

[22] *McCardle* v. *Indianapolis Water Co.*, 272 U.S. 400, 408.

[23] *St. Louis and O'Fallon Railway Co.* v. *U.S.*, 279 U.S. 461.

[24] Leverett S. Lyon and Victor Abramson (eds.), *Government and Economic Life* (Washington, D.C.: Brookings Institution, 1940), p. 694.

[25] *Ibid.*, p. 699.

judgement,"[26] arriving finally at a figure which bore "no derivative relation to any figures in evidence and no ascertainable relation to any functional purpose of rate making."[27]

The Economics of Reproduction Cost

The argument usually advanced in support of reproduction cost valuation was that it was needed to keep earnings in regulated industries in line with those in other industries and with changes in the cost of living. Other earnings rise during prosperity; if investors are to be treated fairly under regulation and the credit of regulated industries maintained, their earnings should be permitted to keep pace. And this can be accomplished by making changes in valuations to correspond with changes in construction costs.

So went the argument. There are questions that might be raised concerning the need for keeping earnings in line. But these will be considered later on. At the moment it is sufficient to point out three flaws. (1) The investor is said to be entitled to a constant return in goods and services. To provide it, his earnings in dollars should be adjusted in accordance with changes in the index of living costs. Reproduction cost valuation adjusts it in accordance with changes in the index of construction costs. The two are not the same. (2) It is not proposed that interest on bonds or dividends on preferred stock be changed as prices change. Dividends on common stock, under this method of valuation, will therefore change more than prices do. Assume a company with a valuation of $10 million and a return of 6 per cent, producing earnings of $600,000. On $3 million of bonds at 4 per cent, it pays $120,000. On $3 million of preferred stock at 5 per cent, it pays $150,000. It has $330,000 left. On $4 million of common stock, it can pay 8¼ per cent. Assume that the price level doubles. The company is revalued at $20 million. With its return still at 6 per cent, it now earns $1,200,000. It still pays $270,000 on its bonds and its preferred stock. But it now has $930,000 left for its common. This gives it a yield of 23¼ per cent. Prices have doubled, but dividends on common stock have tripled. (3) If the investor's earnings need to be kept in line with changing prices, this can be done, without touching the rate base, by varying the rate of return. In the case just given, earnings were raised from $600,000 to $1,200,000 by raising the valuation from $10 million to $20 million while leaving the rate of return at 6 per cent. The same result could have been obtained by leaving the valuation at $10 million and raising the rate of return to 12 per cent. Why not do it this way? The answer is not hard to find. Public opinion would be outraged if the rate of return to investors in regulated industries were doubled, advancing it to such a height. But it does not complain when the same effect is achieved through revaluation.

[26] *Ibid.*, p. 701.

[27] *Ibid.*, p. 692.

For here, it does not realize what is going on. The companies center their attention on the rate base rather than the rate of return because valuation is a mystery and earnings can thus be boosted with greater ease.

Consider the uncertainties inherent in the concept of reproduction cost. (1) What is it that is being reproduced: a modern replacement for an old plant, the old plant in its original condition, or the old plant as it stands today? The assumption made in the McCardle case was that the company, starting fresh, would build its old plant in its depreciated condition,[28] a purely imaginary procedure in which sane managements are unlikely to engage. (2) Under what conditions is reproduction to occur: those originally existing or those existing at the present time? If the former, are allowances to be made to cover the possible cost, today, of cutting paths through forest long since razed, and hauling supplies by horse and wagon rather than train or truck? If the latter, are sums to be allowed for tearing down the buildings that might conceivably be standing where a railroad has its lines, or for ripping up and then relaying pavements that did not exist when a water company first laid its mains? Company lawyers have lively imaginations. And though the more absurd of their inventions have been rejected by the courts, a certain residue remains. (3) What methods of reproduction are to be assumed: simultaneous rebuilding of the whole plant involving large-scale operations and employing modern techniques, or piecemeal reconstruction on a small scale with techniques no longer in use? The latter assumption is the usual rule. And here, again, a procedure is imagined that no sane management would countenance. (4) What prices are to be taken as representing reproduction cost: the spot prices of a particular day, the average prices of a recent period, or figures based on forecasts of the future? If spot prices, they change from day to day; the chosen day may not be representative. If average prices, they may be raised or lowered by changing the selected period. If either, the costs computed are those of the past and not the future. But if future prices are to be employed, valuation becomes a matter of guesswork, with the companies, presumably, guessing high and the commissions guessing low. Yet it was said by Justice Butler, speaking for the Court in the McCardle case, that forecasts of future prices should be made.

The case against reproduction cost valuation is conclusive. The principle facilitates manipulation of the rate base, capitalizing imaginary costs. The value it yields is uncertain, the estimates of companies and commissions being millions of dollars apart. The value is also unstable, being out of date before the valuation is completed and fluctuating widely over time. The valuation process is expensive, involving investigation and litigation respecting matters that could be taken, from existing records, as established facts. The process occasions protracted delays, cases dragging through the commissions and the courts for months and years. When costs

[28] *McCardle* v. *Indianapolis Water Co.*, 272 U.S. 400 at 417–18 (1926).

are falling, adjustments in rates are thus postponed and excessive earnings retained, to the benefit of the investor. But when costs are rising adjustments may be slow, too. And here, the investor will suffer; his enthusiasm for reproduction cost will wane. The principle works in only one direction: it is supported when prices rise but not when they decline.

Original cost valuation has none of these infirmities. The value it yields is definite and understandable, showing the actual sum invested in the business. This value is stable, affording a firm foundation on which the structure of regulation may be reared. If it is decided that earnings should be varied as prices change, this can be done, without disturbing the rate base, by altering the rate of return. Original cost valuation is simpler, quicker, and cheaper. It is not devoid of opportunities for controversy. Opinions may differ, for instance, as to actual investment versus prudent investment and as to investment cost versus first cost. Actual investment would accept at face value the figures shown on a company's books; prudent investment might reduce or eliminate certain items as dishonest or extravagant. Investment cost would accept as given the prices paid for productive facilities; first cost would ignore the prices set in transfers between affiliated companies, employing those paid when the facilities were first devoted to the public service. These differences are important, but in comparison with those arising under reproduction cost they are small. And finally, original cost is easily kept up to date. It is necessary only to add the cost of improvements and deduct the accrued depreciation shown on the books from year to year. Properties do not have to be revalued every time there is a change in rates. Action is speeded, and the expenses of regulation are reduced.

Judicial Abandonment of Reproduction Cost

During the thirties and the forties the Supreme Court moved away from reproduction cost. In the Los Angeles Gas and Electric case[29] in 1933, and in the Pacific Gas and Electric case[30] in 1938, the Court accepted valuations made by the California commission on the basis of original cost, holding the method employed to be within the discretion of that agency. And in the Natural Gas Pipeline case[31] in 1942, the Court upheld an order by the Federal Power Commission substantially reducing pipeline rates. The order was a temporary one, based on the company's own valuation, and did not raise the issue of original versus reproduction cost. But in the course of its opinion, the Court had this to say: "The Constitution does not bind rate-making bodies to the service of any formula or combination of formulas. Agencies to whom this legislative power has been delegated are free . . . to make the pragmatic adjustments which

[29] *Los Angeles Gas and Electric Corp.* v. *Railroad Commission,* 289 U.S. 287.

[30] *Railroad Commission* v. *Pacific Gas and Electric Co.,* 302 U.S. 388.

[31] *Natural Gas Pipeline Co.* v. *FPC,* 315 U.S. 575.

may be called for by particular circumstances."[32] And the significance of the decision was emphasized in a concurring opinion by Justices Black, Douglas, and Murphy:

> . . . we think this is an appropriate occasion to lay the ghost of *Smyth* v. *Ames,* . . . which has haunted utility regulation since 1898. . . .
>
> As we read the opinion of the Court, the Commission is now freed from the compulsion of admitting evidence on reproduction cost or of giving any weight to that element of "fair value." The Commission may now adopt, if it chooses, prudent investment as a rate base—the base long advocated by Mr. Justice Brandeis.[33]

In the next case, Justice Douglas spoke for the majority.

The FPC had ordered the Hope Natural Gas Company to reduce its rates by something more than 60 per cent. Among other things, the company had contended that it should be allowed a return of 8 per cent on a reproduction cost of $66 million. The Commission had allowed it a return of 6½ per cent on an original cost of $33 million. Its action was upheld in 1944, in a five to three decision, by the Court. Said Justice Douglas: "Under the statutory standard of 'just and reasonable,' it is the result reached and not the method employed which is controlling. . . . It is not the theory but the impact of the rate order which counts. If the total effect of the rate order cannot be said to be unjust and unreasonable, judicial inquiry . . . is at an end."[34] In this case, the total effect of the order did not appear to be unjust. The company had accumulated substantial reserves. It could borrow new money by selling bonds at 3 per cent. At the rates set, it would still be able to pay 8 per cent on its stock. This satisfied the Court: "Rates which enable the company to operate successfully, to maintain its financial integrity, to attract capital, and to compensate its investors for risks assumed certainly cannot be condemned as invalid, even though they might produce only a meager return on the so-called 'fair value' rate base."[35] The rule of fair value was thus brought to an end. What was put in its place?

Clearly, the Court did not go back to the position of *Munn* v. *Illinois.* It gave more latitude to the commissions, but it retained the right of review. Commission orders, it said, will be upheld if their results are reasonable. But how are the Commissions to know whether the Court will find them so? Certain results were mentioned; among them, the ability of a company to attract capital. But the Court did not say that these were the only results to be considered. And it gave no criteria by which they might be judged. Just where is the line to be drawn, for instance, between a return that enables a company to attract capital and one that does not? The

[32] *Ibid.,* p. 586.

[33] *Ibid.,* pp. 602, 606.

[34] *FPC* v. *Hope Natural Gas Co.,* 320 U.S. 591, 602.

[35] *Ibid.,* p. 605.

Court left the development of standards to the commissions. But it will test the results of their work by standards of its own. And these standards are doubtless yet to be formulated and never to be divulged. The Court has relaxed its grip on regulation. But it has left the regulators in the dark.

The decision in the Hope case is none the less a landmark. It disposes of reproduction cost. It shifts attention from the rate base to the rate of return. It puts less emphasis on the need for earnings to preserve the values of the past and more on their function in maintaining service in the future. The decision removes an impediment to effective regulation created by the federal courts. Consideration of reproduction cost is still required, however, by statutes as interpreted by the courts in several states.

The Task of Valuation

Where the property in the rate base is valued at its original cost, the figures required may be obtained in one of two ways: they may be found in a company's books, or they may be computed by taking an inventory and then multiplying the items by the prices that were current at the time they were bought or built. The first of these methods obviously is less costly. But it cannot be used where records, for any reason, are unavailable or unreliable. This difficulty may be encountered where facilities were constructed before accounting was brought under commission control. It has less significance where construction has been more recent and accounts kept in accordance with commission rules. An original cost rate base, once obtained, can be kept up to date by reference to current accounts. An initial valuation based on reproduction cost can be made only by taking an inventory and multiplying the items in the list by present prices. It can be kept up to date, however, by employing an index of construction costs.

Inventories are taken by company engineers. Commissions may check them, by field inspections, if they have the funds to do so. More likely, they will accept them as they stand. Differences arise, however, concerning the inclusion of particular items. Rates are supposed to afford a return only on property that is used and useful in the regulated service. Facilities that have been dismantled or abandoned, together with those that are not related to the service, should therefore be excluded. But here, the judgments of the companies and the commissions may not be the same. The companies are likely to argue that obsolete equipment must be retained as stand-by capacity for use in case of need. The commissions may differ. Usually, however, the judgment of management is taken for granted. There has been little litigation on this point. Differences can arise, also, concerning the possible exclusion of certain expenditures as imprudent. But here, again, few cases have been carried to the courts.

The cost of materials and equipment and that of the labor employed in construction does not give the full measure of the investment in facilities. Money has also been spent on other matters incidental to going into business: organization, legal services, engineering, supervision, and interest, insurance, and taxes during construction. If these expenditures have not been charged to operating costs, their inclusion in the rate base is usually allowed by law. In the past, lump sums were allowed to cover such items, usually running around 15 per cent of the total value of a plant. In recent years, however, allowances have generally been limited to figures supported by showings of actual cost.

The remaining steps in the process of appraising fixed assets are the deduction of depreciation and the addition of the value of land, which are discussed below. An addition is also made for a current asset: working capital. Working capital is required to bridge the gap between the time when a company pays for what it buys and when it collects for what it sells. It may be measured by subtracting current liabilities from current assets, or by adding up the operations requiring outlays of cash. The question of working capital comes up in every rate case, but the problem presented is a minor one.

Deduction of Depreciation

The fact that depreciation must be deducted to determine present value has been recognized by the courts since 1909.[36] But the method of computing the amount to be deducted has long been in dispute. The commissions have looked on depreciation as an accounting matter, favoring deduction of the full amount shown (under straight line accounting) in the depreciation reserve. The companies have argued that depreciation is an engineering matter, equipment retaining its value as long as it can be operated efficiently, and that deductions should therefore be based on engineering estimates, nothing being deducted unless deterioration in efficiency is observed. In the history of regulation this dispute has ranked second only to that between original cost and reproduction cost.

The procedure favored by the commissions is the sounder of the two. It recognizes the steady exhaustion of capacity for service, due to all forms of depreciation, and provides for the regular amortization of investment in facilities. It is simple and inexpensive. And it insures logical consistency in the treatment of depreciation as an operating expense and as an item in the capital accounts. The procedure supported by the companies, on the other hand, has a number of defects. It takes no account of the fact of obsolescence or other forms of functional depreciation involving a decline in value that is not reflected in a loss of efficiency. It does not even recognize the full extent of physical depreciation, since equipment, instead of deteriorating slowly, may break down all at once. The procedure is complicated and costly, requiring appraisals by engineers. And it is illogical, requiring consumers to pay a return on an investment that they have already paid for in operating costs.

The companies have sought to have their cake and eat it too. When operating costs were under discussion, their experts have testified that

[36] *Knoxville* v. *Knoxville Water Co.*, 212 U.S. 1.

their properties were depreciating at an alarming rate. And when the rate base was being fixed, the experts have testified again—and with a straight face—that scarcely any depreciation was to be observed. In both cases, it has been their purpose to raise the level of rates: first, by inflating operating costs; and second, by inflating the base on which a fair return must be allowed. And in the past, the Supreme Court has crowned their efforts with success.

In the New York Telephone case[37] in 1926, Justice Butler, speaking for the majority, rejected the commission's effort to deduct accrued depreciation, saying: "The revenue paid by the customers for service belongs to the company. . . . Customers pay for service, not for the property used to render it. Their payments are not contributions to depreciation . . . or to capital of the company."[38] And in the McCardle case, he went on to approve the limitation of deductions to observed depreciation: "The testimony of competent valuation engineers who examined the property and made estimates in respect of its condition is to be preferred to mere calculations based on averages and assumed probabilities."[39] A few years later, however, the Court retreated from this position. In the Lindheimer case[40] in 1934, the Illinois Bell Telephone Company, with more than $48 million in its depreciation reserve, admitted less than $16 million as observed depreciation. Here, the Court recognized the relation between the annual charge for depreciation and the depreciation reserve, regarding both as excessive when measured by observed depreciation. And it proposed that the charge be reduced in fixing rates. But it did not accept the depreciation reserve as the proper measure of deductions for depreciation. Nor has it ever done so, explicitly. In the Hope case, however, the Court declared itself to be concerned only with the results, not with the methods of regulation. Since 1944, therefore, the commissions have been free to deduct the full reserve for depreciation in fixing the rate base.

Land

Land is of minor importance in the valuation of most transportation industries and municipal utilities. It is of major importance, however, in the cases of railroads and gas companies. Land differs from other items in the rate base, having no cost of production. But the dispute between original cost and present cost has been repeated in fixing a value for its cost of acquisition. And here, the decision went, at the outset, to the advocates of present cost.

In the Minnesota rate cases[41] in 1913 the Supreme Court permitted railroad land, acquired as a gift or at low prices, to be entered in the rate base at the market value of adjacent land, thus allowing investors an annual re-

[37] *Board of Pub. Util. Commissioners* v. *N.Y. Telephone Co.*, 271 U.S. 23.

[38] *Ibid.*, pp. 31–32.

[39] *McCardle* v. *Indianapolis Water Co.*, 272 U.S. 400, 416 (1926).

[40] *Lindheimer* v. *Illinois Bell Telephone Co.*, 292 U.S. 151.

[41] 230 U.S. 352.

turn upon the unearned increment. The railroads asked for even more. On the assumption that they would be forced to pay more than market value if acquiring their lands at present, they proposed that the value be computed by using a multiplier that would take this factor into account. But this was farther than the Court was willing to go.

Until 1954 the Federal Power Commission determined interstate pipeline rates by deducting from the figure at which the pipeline companies sold their gas another figure to cover the costs they incurred in producing it. In computing the latter figure, it valued the companies' gas lands on the basis of original cost. And in so doing, it was upheld, in 1934, by the Court.[42] The Commission abandoned this procedure, however, in 1954, accepting the price that is paid to independent producers as the cost of gas to the pipeline companies. The way was thus opened for the companies to realize an unearned increment in the value of their lands.[43]

Intangibles

Not content to increase their earnings by overpricing tangible assets, regulated companies have also attempted further to inflate the rate base by adding intangibles: good will, franchise value, water rights, leaseholds, and value as a going concern. Inclusion of most of these items has long been rejected by the commissions and the courts. Good will is a capitalization of earnings that exceed a competitive return. To include it in the rate base would be to admit the failure of regulation to control the profits of publicly created and protected monopolies. So, too, with franchise value. Where a city has made a charge for a franchise, the sum invested belongs in the rate base. But this is rarely the case, franchises normally being granted as gifts. Inclusion of this item would require the public to pay a return, in perpetuity, on an appraisal of its generosity. The same is true of rights to the use of flowing water possessed by irrigation, power, and water companies.

The leases held by gas companies, permitting exploitation of deposits under private lands, are a special case. They have usually been bought and paid for. Their cost is properly recognized in valuing company properties. When gas is discovered, however, their value will rise. Should the increase be reflected in the valuation? Such a practice would afford an incentive to exploration—a stronger incentive, probably, than is required. It would also grant the companies an unearned increment on which to base an annual return. The Federal Power Commission, in connection with its determination of pipeline rates, has valued leaseholds, not at the price they would bring in the market, but at their original cost. And in this it was upheld in 1945 by the Supreme Court.[44]

[42] *Dayton Power and Light Co.* v. *Pub. Util. Commission*, 292 U.S. 290.

[43] This matter is discussed at greater length in Chapter 20.

[44] *Colorado-Interstate Gas Co.* v. *FPC*, 324 U.S. 581; *Panhandle Eastern Pipe Line Co.* v. *FPC*, 324 U.S. 625.

Going-concern value, supposedly, represents an amount by which the value of a plant that is in operation exceeds that of an identical plant that is not. But no reasonable measure of this value has ever been devised. A figure could be obtained, of course, by capitalizing excess earnings. But this, too, obviously, would be nothing but good will under a different name. So various rationalizations have been attempted. Going-concern value has been said to cover the costs of reproducing a business, apart from its physical facilities: creating an organization, recruiting and training personnel, developing administrative procedures, opening up a market, and educating customers. It has also been said to compensate a company for the losses it may have suffered in the early years of its development. But neither of these notions is really tenable. The costs said to be involved in reproducing a business have already been covered in operating expenses; to write them into the rate base would be to count them twice. The losses of previous years should scarcely be compensated if the excess profits of those years are not recoverable. And such losses, in any case, are not properly to be capitalized. There is something to be said for a policy of averaging earnings over time. But this cannot be retroactive. And it is better to be accomplished, not by manipulating the rate base, but by varying the rate of return. Going-concern value, in short, is purely hypothetical. It is the most intangible of all of the intangibles. Like the others, it capitalizes the amount by which earnings are permitted to exceed a reasonable return. But unlike the others, it has some plausibility.

Going-concern value has been recognized by the courts, accepted by the commissions, and generally included in valuations until recent years. In the Knoxville Water Company case[45] in 1909, the Supreme Court said that there was an "added value of the plant as a whole over the sum of the values of its component parts, which is attached to it because it is in active and successful operation and earning a return."[46] And in the Des Moines Gas Company case[47] in 1915, the Court found this "element of value in an assembled and established plant, doing business and earning money, over one not thus advanced" to be "self-evident."[48] In accordance with these and similar decisions, the commissions long followed the practice of making an arbitrary allowance for going value, usually adding 10 per cent, more or less, to the value of physical facilities in arriving at the rate base. After 1933, however, the Supreme Court shifted its position. In the Los Angeles Gas and Electric case,[49] decided in that year, the Court upheld the California commission in rejecting an allowance of $9 million claimed by the company as going value. And in the Dayton Power and Light

[45] *Knoxville* v. *Knoxville Water Co.*, 212 U.S. 1.

[46] *Ibid.*, p. 9.

[47] *Des Moines Gas Co.* v. *Des Moines*, 238 U.S. 153.

[48] *Ibid.*, p. 165.

[49] *Los Angeles Gas and Electric Co.* v. *R.R. Comm.*, 289 U.S. 287.

case[50] in 1934, it rejected a similar claim, saying that this intangible "is not something to be read into every balance sheet as a perfunctory addition."[51] As a result, the commissions no longer add a separate allowance for value as a going concern. But they may still be influenced by the concept when they fix the value of physical facilities.

FIXING THE RATE OF RETURN

In determining the earnings that are to be permitted, the rate of return is fully as important as the rate base. But it has received far less attention from the commissions and the courts. Under the decision in the Hope case, however, it is possible to hold the rate base steady. And if this is done, earnings will be influenced only by varying the rate of return. Attention should thus be shifted to the rate of return as an instrument for effecting the purposes of earnings control. Here, a number of problems will arise. How determine the rate of return required to attract new capital? In fixing this rate, should each year be treated separately, or should returns be averaged over time? Should the level of rates and earnings be kept steady throughout the business cycle or raised and lowered as other prices and profits rise and fall? And, finally, should the rate of return be varied to afford an incentive to efficiency? These are the problems discussed below.

Fair Return in Practice

In its decision in the case of *Smyth* v. *Ames*, the Supreme Court listed the matters to be considered in determining fair value, but made no effort to define a fair return. In the Willcox case[52] in 1909, the Court remarked that a fair return is not the same in all cases but varies with circumstances, localities, and differences in risk. And in the Bluefield Waterworks case[53] in 1923, it went on to say that such a return

> . . . must be determined by the exercise of a fair and enlightened judgement, having regard to all relevant facts. A public utility is entitled to such rates as will permit it to earn a return . . . equal to that generally being made at the same time and in the same general part of the country on investments in other business undertakings which are attended by corresponding risks and uncertainties; but it has no constitutional rights to profits such as are realized or anticipated in highly profitable enterprises or speculative ventures. The return should be reasonably sufficient to assure confidence in the financial soundness of the utility and should be adequate, under efficient and economical management, to maintain and support its credit and enable it to raise the money nec-

[50] *Dayton Power and Light Co.* v. *Pub. Util. Comm. of Ohio*, 292 U.S. 290.

[51] *Ibid.*, p. 309.

[52] *Willcox* v. *Consolidated Gas Co.*, 212 U.S. 19.

[53] *Bluefield Waterworks and Improvement Co.* v. *Public Service Comm.*, 262 U.S. 679.

essary for the proper discharge of its public duties. A rate of return may be reasonable at one time, and become too high or too low by changes affecting opportunities for investment, the money market, and business conditions generally.[54]

Here, as in *Smyth* v. *Ames*, the Court listed a number of factors for consideration. But it did not define them or indicate their relative weights. How, for instance, are other undertakings "attended by corresponding risks and uncertainties" to be identified? Under what circumstances is "confidence in the financial soundness" of an enterprise assured? When is the judgment employed in combining such factors to be regarded as "fair and enlightened"? The Court has provided no answers to these questions since 1923.

In principle, the rate of return allowed by the commissions and the courts has supposedly been set to equal that obtainable in other industries with comparable risks. In practice, this standard is not usable. Competitive industries have greater risks. There are unregulated industries with comparable risks, but they enjoy the profits of monopoly. In neither case can the rate of earnings be adopted here.

The return allowed to regulated companies may well be lower than that obtained in other fields. In general, the service sold by these concerns is an essential one, and their sales are steady, growing, and assured. The government grants them a monopoly, protecting them against the entry of competitors and against competition in rates. By regulating their finances, it gives assurance to investors that their savings will be safe. For all these reasons, the companies should be able to market their securities at a low rate of return. The rate, however, must be higher than that obtainable on riskless investments, such as government bonds. For these industries are not entirely free of risk. Through natural hazards (earthquakes, landslides, wind storms, floods, and fires) they may suffer losses not entirely covered by insurance. In business depressions, their revenues may decline. With shifts in industrial location, their markets may disappear. And with new developments in technology, they may encounter the competition of substitutes produced by other industries. The return allowed them is not guaranteed. This return, therefore, may be less than that obtainable in other ventures and must be more than that paid by the government. But this leaves considerable latitude for the determination of a rate.

The rate actually allowed by the commissions and the courts has been conventional or arbitrary, bearing no apparent relation to any statement of principles. It has usually been based on expert testimony, with little pretense of economic analysis. There has been no real study of the conditions governing investment decisions, the character of alternative investment opportunities, or the expectations that must be satisfied if new investments are to be made. Bankers and brokers, appearing for the compa-

[54] *Ibid.*, pp. 692–93.

nies, have given their opinion that future risks are likely to be great and that earnings, consequently, must be high if securities are to be sold. Witnesses for the public have pointed out that risks, in the past, have been small, and that the rate at which money can be borrowed is low. The commissions and the courts have then exercised their "enlightened judgement," coming up with a figure that they have rarely attempted to explain. Usually, this figure has fallen somewhere between 5½ and 8 per cent. The allowed return has differed from industry to industry and has varied over time. Among municipal utilities, it has recently been lowest for water companies, higher for electric, gas, and telephone companies, and highest for street railways. This return has been reduced as the cost of money, in the market, has declined. During the twenties, for public utilities in general, it was cut from around 7½ per cent to 7 per cent; during the thirties, to 6 per cent; and during the forties, to 5½ per cent.[55] But the adjustment was tardy and inadequate. While the cost of money fell by 50 per cent, the return allowed to regulated industries was cut by only 20 per cent. Here, as in determining operating costs and fixing the rate base, the consumer was overcharged.

The Attraction of Capital

In its decision in the Hope case, the Supreme Court suggested, as a test of the adequacy of earnings, the ability of a company to attract new capital. The importance of assuring this ability is not to be denied. If regulated undertakings are to keep pace with growing demand, modernize their equipment, and improve their facilities, they must be able to obtain more money from investors by selling bonds and stocks. In itself, this fact affords no standard by which the adequacy of earnings can be judged. Capital may be attracted at low rates or at high ones. But if the rate set is lower or higher than is needed for the purpose, regulation has failed. To serve as a standard, it is necessary to take the lowest rate that will insure the needed investment. But how is this rate to be identified? The Court did not say. If the commissions are to use this standard, they must develop measures of their own.

When emphasis is placed on the attraction of new capital, the character of the capital structure must be taken into account. In the past this has rarely been done. A certain return has been fixed for the investment as a whole. The return on bonds and on preferred stock has been fixed by contract between the company and the investors. The return on common has been a residue, depending upon the relative magnitude of the three types of securities. Assume a company capitalized at $5 million and allowed a return of 6 per cent, or $300,000, with bonds outstanding at 4 per cent and preferred stock at 5 per cent. If the company has $1 million

[55] See Eli W. Clemens, *Economics and Public Utilities*, (New York: Appleton-Century-Crofts, Inc., 1950), pp. 233–34.

in bonds, they get $40,000. If it has another $1 million in preferred stocks, they get $50,000. There is $210,000 left for $3 million of common, a return of 7 per cent. But if the company has $2 million in bonds, they get $80,000. And if it has $2 million in preferred stocks, they get $100,000. This leaves $120,000 for $1 million of common, a return of 12 per cent. Failure to consider the character of the capital structure thus has two undesirable effects. It encourages overissuance of bonds and preferred stocks, burdening companies with fixed charges and making them highly vulnerable to contractions in demand. And it forces consumers to pay the holders of common stocks a higher return than they would otherwise obtain.

In fixing a rate of return that will be sufficient to attract the necessary capital, a distinction should be made among types of securities, and each type given the return that it requires. In the case of bonds and preferred stocks already outstanding, this return is easily determined. It has been fixed by contract and is printed on the securities themselves. In the case of new issues, the return required will be fixed by the state of the market. And the terms of such issues, in general, are under commission control. It is only with respect to common stock that determination of an adequate return is difficult.

A standard of capital attraction looks toward the future, as the standard of fair value looked toward the past. The rate required to sell securities today may differ from that obtaining when earlier issues were sold. In the case of bonds and preferred stock, this fact is taken into account. Older issues may bear one rate and newer issues a different one. But in the case of common stock, this is not the case. All holders of common get the same return. This return must be high enough to meet the expectations of investors in the future. May it ignore the expectations of investors in the past? Their money is already in hand. If the required return has fallen, it will yield them less than they had been permitted to expect. But there will be nothing for them to do but accept the smaller dividends or sell their shares and pocket the loss. Such a policy, however, would be less than fair. Considerations of equity are not to be forgotten. The rate of return, therefore, cannot be set with a view to the future alone. The treatment accorded past investments, moreover, may affect the decisions of those whose capital is sought today.

Fairness to former investors and attraction of new ones may not lead to the same return. A rate set for one of these purposes is likely to be too high or too low for the other. This dilemma could be avoided if common stocks were classified and given different rights to share in earnings, or if they could be issued at different prices and then paid the same dividends. But such arrangements have been subject to abuse and are now prohibited by law. John Bauer has proposed that common stocks, like other securities, be placed on a contractual basis, each issue bearing its appropriate return.[56] The proposal has obvious advantages. Old investors would be treated fairly, receiving what they had been permitted to expect. New shares would bear whatever rate was required to effect their sale. The amount of earnings needed would be definite. But there are also disadvantages. The risks that still remain in regulated industries prevent a fixed return on common stock. The return, of course, could be guaranteed. But in this case the function of taking risks would be assumed by government. A fixed return, moreover, would remove a possible incentive to efficiency. The holders of common would have no more reason to interest themselves in management than those of other securities. The normal functions of ownership would virtually disappear. A single rate of return for common stock, both old and new, would seem to be inevitable.

In the future, increasing emphasis is likely to be placed on the attraction of new capital. How is this to be assured? Eli W. Clemens has suggested that the ratio of dividends or earnings on a company's stock to the price at which it sells in the market be taken as a guide. The market value of its securities could then be related to the prudent investment value of its facilities, in accordance with this ratio, by adjusting its total earnings. Suppose a company's stock is earning $60,000 and selling for $1,200,000, the ratio being 5 per cent. Suppose its prudent investment value is $1,000,000. The price of the stock can be cut to this figure, yielding the 5 per cent investors apparently require, by reducing its earnings to $50,000. Thereafter, the price can be kept at $1,000,000 by adjusting earnings, reducing them if it rises and increasing them if it falls. The company's credit will thus be protected and the salability of its securities assured.[57]

Where the rate of return is related to the quantity and character of a company's securities, as is here suggested, its finances must be controlled. Otherwise, a claim for larger earnings might be created by overcapitalization. It might be based on a capital structure so burdened with fixed charges that dividends on common stock were imperiled and its value depressed. Or it might even be supported by deliberately withholding dividends to drive this value down. Such practices must be prevented if the regulation of earnings is to be precise.

Expansion of investment depends not only on the ability of companies to attract new capital but also on their desire to do so. This desire is affected by the rate of interest, to which the commissions and the courts have given their attention. But it is also affected, and to a greater extent, by expectations as to future revenues and costs, a matter which regulation —so far—has ignored. Investment is discouraged by uncertainty, encouraged by certainty. And these depend, in part, on regulatory policies. Capital may be made available by fixing a proper rate of return. But a greater

[56] John Bauer, *Transforming Public Utility Regulation* (New York: Harper & Bros., 1950), chap. x.

[57] Clemens, *op. cit.*, pp. 241–43.

stimulus might be given to investment by adopting clear policies, announcing them in advance, and adhering to them with consistency.

The Earnings Period

The period employed in controlling earnings is a single year. The volume sold in the previous year is multiplied by the prospective rates, the costs of that year are deducted, and the remaining income is taken as a percentage of the rate base. But the realization of this percentage is not assured. The commissions do not attempt to forecast the future. And if they did, they might not succeed. Demand may prove to be larger and costs smaller than they have assumed, or vice versa. Earnings may therefore be higher or lower than they have planned. But rates are not adjusted, in the next year, to compensate for these discrepancies. Earnings are not averaged, surpluses recaptured, or deficits made up. Each year is taken as sufficient in itself.

This procedure was required, until the thirties, by the decisions of the Supreme Court.[58] It is open to serious criticism. Where consumers, through miscalculation by the commissions, have been forced to pay rates that have yielded more than a fair return, the surplus should not go to the companies. And where investors, conversely, have failed to realize a fair return, they should not be compelled to bear the loss. Where earnings fluctuate, securities are made more speculative and the cost of obtaining capital higher than they need to be. And where earnings are uncertain, managements are reluctant to experiment with price reductions that might prove advantageous to consumers and investors alike.

The alternative to discontinuous control of earnings is continuous control, taking a longer period and balancing the good years with the bad. Under such a policy, a reserve fund with maximum and minimum limits could be established. The excess earnings of one year would be paid into the fund. The deficient earnings of another would be supplemented by drawing on it. If the fund exceeded the maximum set, rates could be cut. If it fell below the minimum, they could be raised. Consumers and investors would both thus be protected against miscalculation by the commissions. Securities would be made less speculative and the cost of capital reduced. With recovery of possible losses assured, an obstacle to experimentation with lower rates would be removed.

Whatever the law, it is likely that commissions have always been influenced by past earnings in determining future rates. But there are only two or three places where plans have been adopted that provide for continuous control.[59] There is reason, in recent decisions, to believe that

[58] *Knoxville* v. *Knoxville Water Co.*, 212 U.S. 1 (1909); *Galveston Electric Co.* v. *Galveston*, 258 U.S. 388 (1922); *Georgia Rwy. and Power Co.* v. *Comm.*, 263 U.S. 625 (1923); *Pub. Util. Commrs.* v. *New York Telephone Co.*, 271 U.S. 23 (1926).

[59] These plans are described in Emery Troxel, *Economics of Public Utilities* (New York: Rinehart & Co., Inc., 1947), pp. 403–18.

further extension of the principle would meet with the approval of the Court.[60]

Policy in the Business Cycle

Adjustments to changes in the general level of prices, it was argued above, might better be made through the rate of return than through the rate base. It remains to consider whether such adjustments should be made at all. Should the prices fixed for regulated services and the earnings allowed investors in such services be held steady during prosperity and depression or kept in line with prices and earnings in other industries?

In the past, prices and earnings have not been completely rigid. Prices have been adjusted in response to changes in operating costs, and the rate of return has been modified in response to changes in interest rates. But the costs of regulated industries are relatively inflexible. Adjustments to changes have been tardy. And modifications in the rate of return have been slow and small. Prices and earnings, in these industries, have been less flexible than in other fields. Their prices have not kept pace with other prices. Their earnings have not been governed by changes in the cost of living or in the earnings obtainable elsewhere.

The relative rigidity of these prices may make for greater instability. When they are maintained in depression, investors get more and consumers are left with less than would otherwise be the case. But, of the two, investors have the lower propensity to spend. The effect of maintaining their incomes is therefore deflationary. On the other hand, when these prices are maintained in prosperity, investors get less and consumers are left with more than otherwise. And since consumers have a higher propensity to spend, the effect is inflationary. By altering these prices, during the successive phases of the business cycle, regulation could make some contribution toward reducing the fluctuations in business activity. By cutting prices in depression, shifting income from investors to consumers, it could help to cushion the slump. And by raising prices in prosperity, shifting income from consumers to investors, it could help to check a boom. If control were to be adapted to this purpose, investors would be given a low return in depression, a high return in prosperity, a fair return when averaged over the cycle as a whole. The importance of such a policy, however, is open to question. The possible variation in prices would not be large. The greatest cut possible in a depression would be the amount of dividends plus the annual depreciation charge. It is unlikely that all of this would be taken. And only a part of that taken would be shifted from money saved to money spent. The contribution to recovery would probably be small. So, too, with the effect of an increase in price during

[60] *United Railways and Electric Co.* v. *West*, 230 U.S. 234 (1930); *Lindheimer* v. *Illinois Bell Telephone Co.*, 292 U.S. 151 (1934); *FPC* v. *Hope Natural Gas Co.*, 320 U.S. 591 (1944).

prosperity. Greater flexibility is probably desirable. But its significance as a stabilizer should not be overemphasized.

Two arguments are advanced in support of a policy of raising earnings during prosperity. The first is ethical: to be fair to investors, earnings should be kept in line with the prices of consumers' goods so that their real income will remain the same. The second is economic: earnings must be kept in line with those in other industries if capital is to be obtained. The ethical argument is untenable. The holders of bonds and preferred stocks are not paid in dollars of constant purchasing power. The holders of common stocks were never promised such a return. They have no real claim for preferential treatment. It should be noted, moreover, that investors advance this argument only when prices rise, never when they fall. The test of the economic argument is to be found in the market. The bonds and the preferred stocks of regulated companies, presumably, will be floated at prices that will sell them. The only question that arises is whether common can be sold. It is possible that investors will continue to buy shares that yield a smaller but a steadier return than that obtainable elsewhere. If so, earnings need not be increased. But it is also possible that the comparative yield of shares in regulated companies may be regarded so unfavorably that their market value will decline. In this case, if new shares are to find buyers, the rate of return should be increased.

Incentive to Efficiency

Under the present pattern of control, no effort is made to effect adjustments in the rate of return so as to afford an incentive to efficiency. The same rate is allowed to companies that are well managed and to those that are not. If a company obtains a larger return than that allowed, it may keep the excess. And, with rate reductions lagging, this situation may persist for years. An incentive is thus afforded for cutting costs. But if rate reductions were prompt, this incentive would be substantially reduced. And if earnings control, instead of being discontinuous, were made continuous, averaging the good years with the bad, it would disappear.

An incentive could be provided if the commissions were to divide the surplus earnings resulting from efficiency between consumers and investors, granting a higher rate of return where managements succeed in cutting costs. But such a program would not be easy to administer. Surpluses might be due to causes other than improvements in efficiency: to errors made by the commissions in their calculations, or to increases in demand or reductions in cost for which managements were not responsible. It would be necessary to identify the gains resulting from efficiency. And for this purpose, standards of performance and methods of measurement would have to be devised. The application of such standards would be difficult. And it would take the commissions a long way into the domain of management.

Rewards for efficiency would not be questioned in the courts. But penalties for inefficiency would be appealed. And here, the standards and measurements employed would have to be submitted to review. The prospect is one that would not be welcomed by the companies, the commissions, or the courts themselves. An even more serious obstacle to the imposition of such penalties is to be found in their effect upon the ability of a company to attract new capital. A reduction in earnings would make it harder to sell securities. It would thus perpetuate antiquated methods and obstruct investments required in the public interest. The rate of return could be increased to reward efficiency, but it could not well be cut to penalize inefficiency.

THE RECORD OF RATE LEVEL CONTROL

Among the possible purposes of rate level control, regulation has shown little interest in the expansion of output and use, in the promotion of efficiency, or in the stabilization of economic activity. Its sole function has been that of striking a balance between the interests of consumers and investors, preventing the extortion of monopoly profits while preserving the ability of regulated companies to attract new capital. Of these two objectives, it is clear that the latter has been served. Where monopoly has persisted, as in the case of telephone, gas and electric services, regulated companies have encountered no difficulty in selling their securities. But in preventing excessive earnings, regulation has had but limited success. In general, the rate of return obtained by regulated monopolies has been well above that required to pay interest on bonds and to maintain a market for preferred and common stocks.[61]

The hand of regulation has been lax. Operating expenses have not been tightly controlled. Income taxes have been covered as a cost. Intangibles have been included in the rate base. Land has been overvalued. Facilities have been overpriced. Depreciation, already covered as an expense, has not always been deducted in the valuation of depreciated property. The rate of return allowed has been arbitrarily determined and set at a higher level than would have been required. And where earnings have exceeded this allowance, the surplus has been left with the regulated companies. Judged by the standards of the competitive market, regulation has fallen short. Competition, where it is present, affords a sterner discipline.

SUGGESTIONS FOR FURTHER READING

The problems relating to control of the rate level are discussed at length in the texts cited at the end of the previous chapter, and in John Bauer, *Transforming Public Utility Regulation* (New York: Harper & Brothers, 1950). The control of operating costs is considered in Clemens, chap. vi; in Troxel,

[61] See Clemens, *op. cit.*, pp. 235–39.

chap. xi; in Barnes, chap. xviii; and in Bauer, chaps. v and xii. The basic work on valuation is J. C. Bonbright, *The Valuation of Property* (2 vols.; New York: McGraw-Hill, 1937). This problem is covered in Clemens, chaps. vii, viii; Troxel, chaps. xii, xiii, xiv; Barnes, chaps. xi–xiv and xvi–xvii; and Bauer, chap. ix. The problem of depreciation is analyzed in Clemens, chap. ix, and in Troxel, chaps. xv, xvi. On the determination of the rate of return, Troxel's chaps. xvii–xix, inclusive, are excellent. See also Clemens, chap. x; Barnes, chaps. xiv–xv and xvii; and Bauer, chaps. iv and x. The objectives and standards of price level control are discussed by Donald H. Wallace in *Economic Standards of Government Price Control*, T.N.E.C. Monograph No. 32 (Washington, D.C.: U.S. Government Printing Office, 1941), pp. 411–31 and 493–504. An interest-proposal that the method of control be changed to provide for pricing on the basis of marginal cost is analyzed by Troxel in his chap. xx.

Chapter 19 THE RATE STRUCTURE

If a company were to sell its services at a uniform price per unit, without allowing for the differences in cost or in demand involved in making different sales, regulation could concern itself exclusively with problems of the rate level, ignoring those presented by the rate structure. But when a company classifies its services, charging different prices to different customers, and when it grants discounts to those who buy in greater quantities, the structure as well as the level of rates becomes a matter of concern. The rate level has to do only with total revenues, costs and earnings: with assurance of equity in the relationship between investors as a group and consumers as a group. The rate structure has to do with particular charges: with equity in the relationships among consumers. Earnings that are fair both to investors and to consumers, as a whole, may be produced by rates that are differentiated in a variety of ways. One pattern of differentiation may be neutral in its effect upon competition among concerns that buy a common service, such as electric power or the movement of freight; another may give one competitor an unfair advantage and place a second under an unfair handicap. One pattern may require all customers to contribute, on an equitable basis, to the costs incurred in serving them; another may grant one group a subsidy and subject a second to a tax. The attention of regulators must therefore be directed, not only to the revenue produced by a company's rates, taken as an aggregate, but also to the rates themselves, taken individually; not only to the propriety of the earnings that they yield, but also to the consequences that flow from the ways in which they are related, one to another.

BASES OF PRICE DIFFERENTIATION

Differences in rates are based, in part, on differences in cost. It may cost less to serve one class of customers than another, to sell in larger quantities than in smaller ones. Differences in rates are also based, more largely, on differences in demand. Rates are set low where demand is elastic: where customers have less need for a service or less ability to pay for it, and where they can provide it for themselves or obtain it from a company's competitors. Rates are kept high where demand is inelastic: where the buyer's need and ability to pay are great, and where the seller possesses a monopoly.

If rates are proportioned to costs, some buyers will pay less than others, but the seller will not discriminate. Where his customers engage in competition, his position will be one of strict neutrality, affording none an artificial advantage, imposing on none an artificial handicap. As among consumers, he will play no favorites, subsidizing none and taxing none. But differences in rates may not be proportionate to differences in cost. At times they may be smaller; more often they will be larger. And here, discrimination will occur.

In part, discrimination is unavoidable. For it is usually impossible precisely to determine unit costs. Some costs are clearly identified with output and can readily be charged to particular kilowatt-hours or ton miles. This is true, for instance, of direct labor and of fuel. But other costs are jointly incurred in rendering different types of service. They do not vary directly with output, but decline in significance as output grows. These are the costs of capital—interest and depreciation—and administrative overhead. Where investments are heavy, as with railroads and electrical utilities, such costs are large. As a matter of accounting they must be allocated among the different units of service. But there is no correct way in which this may be done. The process of allocation necessarily involves an exercise of judgment. Whatever the result, it is open to dispute. Even if companies sought to make their rates proportionate to their costs, therefore, it would be impossible to tell for certain whether they had succeeded or failed.

Discrimination is not only inadvertent; it is also purposive. By discriminating among its customers, a company may expand its sales and enlarge its revenues. It may effect a fuller utilization of its facilities, spread its fixed costs over more units of output, and thus reduce its unit costs. Through larger revenues and lower costs, it may seek greater profits. Regulation, of course, is designed to keep profits within bounds. But for regulators, too, discrimination has its uses. It may be needed to enable a company to cover its costs and obtain a fair return on its investment. It may contribute to a lower general level of rates and to a wider use of regulated services. It may be employed to encourage uses that are thought to be socially desirable and to discourage those that are not.

Differences in Cost

In moving goods by rail, it can readily be shown that one ton is costlier than another. Goods that are bulky in relation to their weight take up more space than those whose density is high, goods that are irregular in size and shape more space than those that can be stacked. Goods that must be loaded by hand cost more than those that can be loaded mechanically.

Goods that require special equipment or services, such as refrigeration for fruit or watering for livestock, cost more than those that do not. Since railroads assume the risk of loss or damage, valuable goods cost more than cheap goods, small articles (being easily stolen) more than large ones, and fragile articles (being easily broken) more than sturdy ones. Since shippers themselves load goods moving in carloads, such shipments cost the railroads less than those in less-than-carload lots. And since regularity of movement permits economy in operation, goods moving in steady volume cost less than those that move sporadically.

It can be shown, too, that one mile is costlier than another. Terminal costs are as high for short hauls as for long hauls. Line costs may be higher, since short hauls involve fewer cars per train, poorer loading, and more frequent stops. Costs per mile, therefore, decline with distance, being lower for the longer hauls. Costs may even be unlike for equal distances. They are higher in the mountains than on the plains, in floodlands than on safer ground, and in the wintry North than in the sunny South. A mile costs more where traffic is sparse than where it is plentiful. It costs more where goods move in the direction of heavy traffic than where they move in the direction of empty cars.

In the sale of electricity, likewise, it can be shown that one kilowatt-hour costs more than another. The costs of this service, as they are presented by accountants, are divided into three categories: output costs, customer costs, and demand costs. Output costs are those incurred in the operation of a plant: the costs of labor, fuel, materials, and supplies. They vary with the volume of production. Customer costs are those incurred in reading meters, sending and collecting bills, keeping accounts, and the like. They vary with the number of customers. Demand costs are also known as readiness-to-serve costs. They are the overhead costs of capital and management involved in providing a plant that is large enough to meet the peak demand that may be made on it at any day and hour. They are thus a function of capacity. Differences in total cost per kilowatt-hour cannot be attributed to output costs, since they are roughly the same for each unit produced. They can be attributed, to some extent, to customer costs, since these costs decline, per kilowatt-hour, as a customer's consumption grows. Such differences, however, are not large enough to be of major significance. It is in demand costs, therefore, that the explanation for differences in cost per kilowatt-hour is mainly to be found. Investment in electric plants is heavy and overhead costs, accordingly, are high. The investment required depends upon the peak demand. A kilowatt-hour taken at the peak adds to the overhead; one taken at another time does not. The cost of the first, therefore, is higher than that of the second.

Utility accountants, in their analysis of costs, speak of the load factor of a utility system, the load factor of an individual customer, and the diversity factor of the system as a whole. The system's load factor is its average load expressed as a percentage of its peak load. Thus, if the average load over a period is 6,000 kilowatts and the peak at any moment is 9,000, the load factor is 66⅔ per cent. The customer's load factor is his average consumption expressed as a percentage of his maximum consumption. The system's diversity factor is determined by adding up the maximum demands of all of its customers, whenever they occur, and dividing this sum by the maximum demand made on the system as a whole at any one time. Thus customer A may take one kilowatt at 8:00 A.M., customer B two kilowatts at noon, and customer C three kilowatts at 4:00 P.M., a total of six kilowatts; the maximum demand made on the system at any hour, however, may be three kilowatts; the diversity factor, therefore, is 2.

The average cost per kilowatt-hour will be reduced if the system's load factor can be raised. This may be accomplished in two ways: by improving the load factor of each customer or by raising the diversity factor. The customer's load factor may be improved by encouraging him to increase his consumption, using more power at off-peak hours. The diversity factor may be raised by attracting groups of customers whose maximum demands will be scattered, also coming at off-peak hours. Thus there is in the nature of utility costs a basis for differentiating rates, setting them at different levels for different classes of customers and reducing them as a customer buys in larger quantities.

Differences in Demand

The differentiation of rates is to be explained, in larger measure, by differences in demand. For some classes of customers and for some quantities of service, demand is relatively inelastic; for others, relatively elastic. In the first case, more money can be obtained if rates are kept high; in the second, if they are made low. Where a seller, by charging a single price, can make sufficient sales to keep his facilities fully employed and obtain sufficient revenue to cover his costs and earn a fair return, he will not be likely to discriminate among his customers. But a price set low enough to maintain full production may not yield sufficient revenue to cover costs. And one set high enough to cover costs may leave capacity in idleness. In such a case, the seller will find it to his advantage to discriminate.

Consider the monopolist whose situation is depicted in Table 1. The sales that he can make and the revenue he can obtain by selling all of his output at various prices are shown in the first three columns. His total costs are shown in the fourth. These include both the costs of capital and management that remain fixed whatever the volume of output and the costs of operation that vary with the quantity produced. And, for the sake of simplicity, they are assumed to include a fair return on the investment in the plant. The final column shows the resulting profit, in excess of a fair return, or the resulting loss. The monopolist, if he sells at a single price, will choose the one that will yield him the greatest profit. In this situation, he will charge $6.00 and produce 400 units. Let us assume, however, that his plant is big enough to turn out 2,000 units or more. He could sell this quantity at $2.00, but here he would not cover his costs. He could cover his costs at $5.00, but here he would be left with idle capacity. Suppose, however, that the seller discriminates. The result is shown in

TABLE 1

AN UNREGULATED MONOPOLIST SELLING AT A SINGLE PRICE

Price	Sales	Total Revenue	Total Cost	Profit or Loss
$9.00	100	$ 900	$1,400	−$ 500
8.00	200	1,600	1,750	− 150
7.00	300	2,100	2,050	50
6.00	400	2,400	2,300	100
5.00	500	2,500	2,500	0
4.00	700	2,800	3,000	− 200
3.00	1,000	3,000	3,400	− 400
2.50	1,400	3,500	4,100	− 600
2.00	2,000	4,000	5,000	− 1,000
1.50	2,800	4,200	6,400	− 2,200
1.00	3,600	3,600	8,000	− 4,400

Table 2. Here, the prices, sales, and costs shown are the same as those in Table 1. But the seller divides his customers into separate groups and collects a different price from each. His total revenue is increased, as shown. And the resulting profit or loss (aside from a fair return) is sharply

TABLE 2

AN UNREGULATED MONOPOLIST DISCRIMINATING IN PRICE

Price	Sales	Sales in Each Class	Revenue from Each Class	Total Revenue	Total Cost	Profit or Loss
$9.00	100	100	$ 900	$ 900	$1,400	−$ 500
8.00	200	100	800	1,700	1,750	− 50
7.00	300	100	700	2,400	2,050	350
6.00	400	100	600	3,000	2,300	700
5.00	500	100	500	3,500	2,500	1,000
4.00	700	200	800	4,300	3,000	1,300
3.00	1,000	300	900	5,200	3,400	1,800
2.50	1,400	400	1,000	6,200	4,100	2,100
2.00	2,000	600	1,200	7,400	5,000	2,400
1.50	2,800	800	1,200	8,600	6,400	2,200
1.00	3,600	1,200	1,200	9,800	8,000	1,800

changed. Here, again, the monopolist will seek the greatest profit. But he will obtain it by creating a number of customer classes, charging those in the top group as much as $9.00 and selling to those in the bottom group for as little as $2.00. With such a scale of prices, he can operate close to full capacity. And he can raise his extra profit from $100 to $2,400.

Such discrimination cannot be practiced unless it is possible to divide the market, separating one sector from another, so that those charged the higher rate cannot buy in the low-rate sector, and so that those buying at the lower rate cannot resell in the high-rate sector. With transportation and public utilities, however, such a division is readily achieved. For these industries sell services, rather than transferable goods, and control their use by delivering them as they are consumed. If a railroad charges more for hauling textiles than for hauling coal, the textile manufacturer cannot get the lower rate by having his goods loaded onto coal cars. And if a gas or electric company charges a householder more than it charges a manufacturer, the householder cannot get the lower rate by connecting his dwelling with the factory's pipes or wires.

Discrimination is not without its limits. No group can be made to pay more than it believes the service to be worth. At higher prices, business would be diverted or destroyed. A ceiling is set, therefore, by what the traffic will bear. No sales will be made, on the other hand, for less than the added costs of labor, fuel, and supplies (the marginal variable costs) that they entail. Otherwise, the seller would make them at a loss. A floor is thus established by his out-of-pocket costs. Within these limits, however, the latitude for variation may be wide.

From his sales as a whole, the seller must recover not only the variable costs of operation but also the fixed costs of capital and administration. These costs are jointly incurred in serving all classes of customers. But they need not be charged equally against each unit sold. From some sales, it may be possible to recover a good bit more than average total costs; from others, a good bit less. As long as he gets something (above his variable costs) to contribute to his fixed costs and his profits, it will be worth the seller's while to cut his price, where he must do so, in order to obtain additional customers or to sell in larger quantities. He will therefore fix his charges, for different customers and for different quantities, in accordance with his judgment as to elasticity of demand. Where demand appears to be elastic, he will ask less toward overhead and profit; where it seems to be inelastic, he will take more.

The Case for Discrimination

Discrimination may have certain marked advantages. First, it may bring about a fuller employment of facilities and a wider consumption of services. Thus, in Table 2 we saw that output was raised from 400 units to 2,000 units. Second, discrimination may result in lower prices for all consumers. The price reductions in the lower groups need not be offset by price increases in the upper groups. At every level in the scale, including the highest, the price charged can be lower than would be the case if the seller did not discriminate. But this gain is unlikely to be realized unless rates and earnings are controlled.

Let us refer again to Table 2. Here, the monopolist obtained $2,400 beyond the fair return that we assumed to be included as a cost. He did so by taking from each class of customers all that the traffic would bear.

He cut some prices from $6 to $5, $4, $3 and $2; he raised others from $6 to $7, $8, and $9. Now let us assume that rates are regulated. The regulatory agency limits earnings to a fair return. If the law were to prohibit discrimination, the price fixed would be $5, as is shown in Table 1, and 500 units would be produced and sold. But suppose the law permits discrimination. The results are shown in Table 3. Here, again, the prices, sales, and costs are the same as those previously shown. As in Table 2, consumers are classified and a different price charged in each class. But here, a fair return is obtained from a scale of prices that begins at $1.50. The volume of output is raised to 2,800 units. And every price in the scale, up to the top price of $3.00, is well below the $5.00 that would have to be charged if discrimination were not allowed. The customer who pays $3.00 is not harmed when the same service is sold to another for $1.50. On the contrary, he is helped, since this enables him to save $2.00 himself.

It is on this basis that discrimination has long been permitted in railroad and public utility rates. If the railroads, for instance, were to establish a

TABLE 3

A REGULATED MONOPOLIST DISCRIMINATING IN PRICE

Price	Sales	Sales in Each Class	Revenue from Each Class	Total Revenue	Total Cost	Profit or Loss
$3.00	1,000	1,000	$3,000	$3,000	$3,400	−$400
2.50	1,400	400	1,000	4,000	4,100	− 100
2.00	2,000	600	1,200	5,200	5,000	200
1.50	2,800	800	1,200	6,400	6,400	0
1.00	3,600	1,200	1,200	7,600	8,000	− 400

uniform rate per ton at a figure that would cover average total costs, they would not improve the position of shippers whose commodities now bear the higher rates. In fact, they would worsen it. For producers of heavy and bulky low-value goods, that are now carried at low rates, could no longer afford to ship them. The volume of traffic would decline. All of the railroads' fixed charges would have to be met by the traffic that remained. The rates paid by high-value traffic would have to be raised. Shippers who now pay high rates should therefore be happy that other shippers are served at low rates.

For discrimination to be so justified, however, certain conditions must obtain. First, there must be a heavy investment entailing high fixed costs and a substantial amount of capacity standing in idleness, so that costs per unit can be reduced by spreading the fixed costs over a larger volume of output. Second, the lower rates must be needed to get business that would not otherwise exist. Third, they must be high enough to cover variable costs and contribute something to overhead. And fourth, the whole scale of rates must be regulated to keep earnings reasonable and to keep discrimination within bounds.

DISCRIMINATION IN PRACTICE

The rate structures of most industries rendering transportation and public utility services are highly differentiated. The differences found in them are based, in part, on differences in cost. But they are to be explained, in larger measure, by differences in demand. In the railroad and electric industries, in particular, discrimination is deliberate and detailed. The railroads discriminate among commodities and among hauls, charging more overhead to one ton or mile and less to another. The utility companies discriminate among customers, according to the uses made of their service and the quantities consumed, collecting more where they can get it and less where they cannot. Discrimination, in these industries, is a settled policy, practiced by the companies and accepted by the law.

Railroad Rates

Passenger fares show relatively little discrimination. Higher fares are charged in parlor and Pullman cars and lower fares on commutation trains. But the principle of classifying service, so common in Europe, is little used in the United States. Circuitous lines meet the fares of direct lines for service between competitive points, and discounts are sometimes offered on round trips. But, in general, the railroads charge a uniform fare per mile. They practice discrimination, chiefly, in the structure of rates for freight.

There are some 5,000 different commodities that are hauled in carload lots. These appear as some 25,000 commodity descriptions when differences in packing and manner of shipment are taken into account. There are freight stations at some 35,000 locations in the United States. Goods can move between these stations by scores or even hundreds of different routes. As a result, if rates were specified item by item and haul by haul, there could be tens of millions of separate rates. The structure of rates has been simplified, however, in two ways. First, the railroads have adopted systems of classifying commodities. Three standard systems were developed before 1890 by committees representing the carriers: one known as the "Official Classification" in the northeastern states, one in the South, and one in the West. There were seven regular classes in the Official Classification, twelve in the Southern, and ten in the Western, identical commodities being differently classified in the three regions. In 1952, however, the regional classifications were superseded by a uniform classification in the area east of the Rocky Mountains. Under such systems, particular commodities packed in particular ways are assigned to particular classes and all commodities in the same class pay the same rate. Second, the computation of rates for different distances is also simplified. Rates based on cost would be less than proportionate to distance, as we have seen, since long hauls cost less per mile than short hauls. But distance rates are not made to conform precisely to differences in cost. Instead of being tapered mile by mile, they are reduced in mileage blocks. Rates may also be established between key points and blanketed back to intermediate points. And rates for several points of origin or destination may be combined in common groups. In spite of these devices, the structure of rates remains a complicated one. There are some 75,000 freight tariffs in use in the United States. And a single tariff may run to more than a thousand pages of fine type.

The rate structure discriminates among commodities. Goods in lower classes move at fixed percentages of the Class 1 rates: those in Class 2 at 85 per cent, those in Class 3 at 70 per cent, and so on, goods in the lowest class paying as little as 13 per cent. But discrimination does not stop here. Less than 5 per cent of the freight hauled is required to pay the class rates. Around 10 per cent of it moves on "exception ratings" which are set from 20 to 25 per cent below the corresponding class rates. These ratings have been established in recent years, largely for the purpose of meeting the competition of motor carriers in hauling lightweight, valuable goods. Around 85 per cent of all freight moves at "commodity rates." These apply to the transportation, in large quantities, of specific commodities between specific points. Ton for ton, they are set far below other rates. This has long been done to make possible the movement of heavy, bulky, low-grade goods and, in particular, to meet the competition of water carriers. In the structure of rates as a whole, therefore, the differences between commodities are great. And these differences bear little relation to differences in cost. In a study made in 1948 the Interstate Commerce Commission compared the carload revenues from certain commodities with the full cost of hauling them, including overhead and return on investment, and found, for instance, that copper ore was hauled at 41 per cent of cost, logs at 43 per cent, gravel and sand at 61 per cent, cattle at 77 per cent, and coal at 81 per cent, while sugar was charged 124 per cent of cost, paint 151 per cent, cheese 158 per cent, automobiles 169 per cent, and cigarettes 207 per cent.[1] The differences in the rates charged for transporting such commodities depend, not on differences in cost, but on differences in the elasticity of demand.

The rate structure discriminates, too, among hauls. Some discrimination is incidental to the practice of simplifying the structure by using distance blocks, relating rates to key points, and grouping points of origin and destination; more is a consequence of the policy of so fixing rates on particular hauls as to meet those charged by competing carriers and so fixing rates for particular locations as to equalize their competitive opportunities. Thus, a circuitous line will match the rate charged between two points by a direct line, and a railroad will match the rate charged between ports by a water carrier, maintaining higher rates at other points. And where two producing points are at unequal distances from a common

[1] Cited in D. Philip Locklin, *Economics of Transportation* (4th ed.; Homewood, Ill.: Richard D. Irwin, Inc., 1954), p. 144.

source of raw material or a common market for their product, the more distant point will be given the same rate as the nearer one. These differences have nothing to do with costs: rates are lower where demand is made elastic by competition, higher where it is not.

The Rates of Other Carriers

Among other carriers, discrimination has been a serious problem only in the case of oil pipelines. These lines are owned and operated by the major refiners. But they also carry oil to independent refineries. In this situation there is danger that the majors may handicap the independents by charging high rates or imposing unreasonable restrictions on their services. The problem presented is a special one, having to do with competition in the oil industry. It is to be discussed in Chapter 22.

With water and motor carriers, variable costs are more important and fixed costs less important than with railroads. There is therefore less temptation to discriminate. The water carriers follow the commodity classifications adopted by the railroads, setting their rates at a fixed percentage below those charged by rail. For distance, their rates per mile decline more sharply than do those by rail. The motor carriers use fewer classes than the railroads. Their rates tend to be set at or near the level of rail rates, declining less sharply on longer hauls. But quantity discounts are given, not only for truckloads, but also for shipments larger than truckloads, to compete for traffic that might otherwise be moved by rail.

In air passenger service the principle of classifying customers has been adopted, lower fares being charged for coach flights than for first-class flights. The service differs, but the reduction in fares is greater than the saving in costs. In air express and air freight there is little commodity classification. Arbitrary minimum charges are made for small shipments and for short hauls. Beyond this, rates increase with distance in large mileage blocks.

Electric Rates

In the early years of the service, electricity was sold at a uniform rate per kilowatt-hour. Then, as producers sought to extend their operations, they began to discriminate. In order to sell to groups who were unable or unwilling to buy at the established rate, they classified their customers, fixing a lower rate for the new customers, maintaining the higher rate for the older ones. And in order to encourage greater consumption by present customers, they fixed lower rates for larger quantities, maintaining the higher rate for smaller ones. As a result, the structure of electric rates came to be highly differentiated. Different classes were established for residential use, commercial light and power, industrial power, etc., and rates were differentiated from class to class. Within each class, moreover, consumption was divided into blocks, measured in kilowatt-hours, and rates were reduced in succeeding blocks. Thus, the average rate per kilowatt-hour charged for residential use might be 4 cents, for commercial use 3 cents, and for industrial use, 1½ cents. And among residential users, the charge for the first 50 K.W.H. per month might be 5 cents per K.W.H.; for the next 150 K.W.H., 3 cents; and for everything above 250 K.W.H., 2 cents. As a consequence of these distinctions, the spread between the upper and lower rates came to be substantial, industrial users being favored over residential users and large consumers over smaller ones.

The differences thus created have persisted to the present time. In general, they correspond to differences in the elasticity of demand. Big industrial users have the alternative of generating their own power; their demand, therefore, is highly elastic; their rates are low. Other users lack this alternative; their demand is less elastic; their rates are higher. Householders can use gas rather than electricity for cooking; for this purpose their demand is elastic; the additional kilowatt-hours used in cooking fall in the quantity blocks where rates are low. Householders, on the other hand, are unlikely to substitute gas, kerosene, or candles for electricity in lighting; their demand for this purpose is inelastic; the hours used in lighting fall in the first block where rates are high. Both customer classes and quantity blocks are set up by the utility companies on the basis of their judgment of what the traffic will bear.

The companies deny that they discriminate, defending their rates by presenting analyses of costs. Output costs (for labor, fuel, etc.) are distributed among customers in proportion to their consumption as measured by meters. Customer costs (for billing, collecting, etc.) are charged equally to each customer. And demand costs (for the investment necessitated by readiness to serve) are also calculated for individual customers. These costs may be measured by the number of rooms in a customer's house, the number of switches he can turn on, the number of appliances he uses, or, more precisely, by a meter that records his consumption at its peak. The different costs may be shown separately on the consumer's bill. This is done, sometimes, under two-part or three-part rates, which are used most often in the sale of commercial and industrial power. Such systems, however, appear to be complicated and are employed less often in billing householders. Here, a one-part rate is generally used, but it is graduated downward in successive blocks. The recovery of customer costs may be assured by making a minimum charge (say $1.00 a month) though nothing is consumed, or by making a flat charge for the first block consumed (say $1.00 for the first 10 K.W.H.). Or it may be assumed that customer costs are recovered from the high rate charged in the first block. It is assumed, too, that demand costs are recovered in the earlier blocks. And it is therefore held that rates in these blocks must be high, while rates in later blocks—since they need cover only output costs—may properly be low.

This sort of analysis, however, is open to serious question. There can be no objection to the practice followed in allocating output costs and little objection to that followed in allocating customer costs, provided such costs are not padded. But demand costs are a different matter. These are really the overhead costs of capital. They are jointly incurred in rendering the different classes and quantities of service. There is no correct method of allocating such costs among these classes and quantities. Any method employed will depend upon the judgment of the person who adopts it. And his judgment is likely to be influenced by his purposes. The methods of allocating demand costs used by public utility companies have been designed to justify differences in rates by a showing of corresponding differences in costs, and thus to support the contention that the companies do not discriminate.

The differences in the rates charged different classes of consumers were first defended on the ground that they corresponded to differences in their responsibility for peak demand. Householders, supposedly, paid high rates because they turned on their lights at the peak. And manufacturers got low rates because they operated their factories off the peak. In time, however, this argument ceased to serve. With the introduction of electrical appliances, householders came to use more power off-peak. And with the growth of industrial consumption, manufacturers created new peaks of their own. But the companies continued to charge high rates for residential use and low rates for industrial use, whether on the peak or off. A different rationalization was required.

The utilities now employ what is known as the non-coincident demand method of allocating overhead. For this purpose, they compute an aggregate maximum demand by adding together the separate maximum demands of all classes of buyers, although these demands may come at different times. Then they determine the percentage of this aggregate that is attributable to each class. And then, finally, they distribute their overhead costs in accordance with these percentages.

The method is based upon two fallacies. First, it involves circular reasoning. The differences in demand that are used as a guide in allocating costs are not independent of differences in rates, but are themselves determined by these differences. The companies first fix the rates they want to charge. These rates, in turn, affect the quantities demanded. These quantities are then used to govern the distribution of costs. And the costs are presented, finally, to justify the rates. Q.E.D. Second, the method ignores the factor of diversity. The concept of maximum coincident demand for a utility system as a whole is meaningful. The concept of aggregate non-coincident maximum demands of customer classes is not. A company does have to build a plant big enough to meet the peak of coincident demand. It does not have to build one big enough to meet the aggregate of non-coincident demands. For such demands, by definition, occur at different times. If a customer's maximum comes at the same time as the system's maximum, he may properly be charged with some responsibility for the size of the investment that is required. But if it comes at any other time, he cannot. The so-called demand costs assigned to individual customers result from an arbitrary allocation of system overhead and are not logically to be justified.

The differences found in the structure of electric rates are discriminatory, since they do not correspond to real differences in cost. Discrimination, moreover, has been introduced into the structure in another way. The utility companies hesitated, at first, to promote expansion of use by cutting rates to old subscribers, fearing that the demand of such users might be so inelastic that their contribution to revenue would decline. In time, however, the companies discovered a method of promoting wider use through rate cuts without risking a decline in revenue. This is known as the objective rate plan. Under this plan, the customer is offered two schedules of rates: the old one at its former level and a new one—the objective rate—at a lower level. His bill in the same month of the preceding year is taken as a base. If he adds so much to his consumption that his present bill, at the lower rate, is larger than his base bill, he pays the present bill. If he fails to do so, he pays the base bill. In other words, he pays for his actual consumption at the new rate or for his base-period consumption at the old rate, whichever yields the higher bill. This device enables the companies to experiment with elasticity of demand without disturbing the existing structure of rates. It enables them, in effect, to have their cake and eat it too. The plan has one great advantage: by showing that demand is elastic, it may lead to outright reductions in rates. In the meantime, however, it makes for discrimination: the customer who increases his monthly bill gets a lower rate per kilowatt-hour than the one who does not.

The Rates of Other Utilities

The pattern of gas rates is similar to that of electric rates. Customers are classified and rates are varied in accordance with differences in the elasticity of demand. Lower rates are charged, for instance, for industrial than for domestic use, and for space heating than for cooking and water heating where competition is not so stiff. Overhead is allocated on the basis of non-coincident demands. Consumption is measured by meters and rates adjusted downward in successive blocks. But the pattern is simpler than with electricity, and the differentials involved are not as great. This may be attributed, in part, to an important difference in the character of the two services. Electricity must be produced as it is used; gas can be manufactured or imported and kept in storage. With gas, therefore, operations can be carried on with greater regularity. The load factor is less important, and there is less need to improve it by manipulating rates.

Rates for water are even simpler than those for gas. Consumers are usually classified, consumption metered, and rates reduced in later blocks. But water companies are less interested than other utilities in promoting consumption. The load factor is not important. There are limits to available supplies. And most of the companies are owned and operated by city governments.

Rates for urban transportation service are the simplest of all. A single fare, for any distance at any hour, is typical. But this does not avoid discrimination. Long hauls cost more than short hauls. Fares adjusted to costs would increase with distance, in successive zones. In other countries this is usually the case. In the United States, however, the single fare discriminates against the short-haul rider in favor of the long-haul one. In this industry, moreover, the load factor is highly important. The service has high peaks at rush hours and long periods between them when the plant is only partly used. Efforts have sometimes been made to improve this situation by selling passes at low fares, to be honored only during off-peak hours. But discounts are also given for weekly passes and for quantity purchases of tokens that are available for on-peak use. In general, transit fares discriminate against the off-peak user in favor of the on-peak one. The companies would gain if they could differentiate their fares by distance and by time of day. They retain the single-fare system because it is less expensive to administer.

In considering telephone rates, a distinction must be made between toll service and local exchange service. Differences in toll rates conform to differences in costs. Such rates vary with distance and duration. They are lower on station-to-station than on person-to-person calls. And they are lower off-peak, at night and Sundays, than on-peak during business hours. Local rates, however, bear little relation to costs. Aside from coin box service, rates are not proportioned to the number or the duration of calls. Nor are they lowered during off-peak hours. Rates are differentiated, rather, in accordance with differences in the elasticity of demand. Business users are charged more than domestic users because they find the service indispensable. Subscribers are charged more for single-party lines because they are willing to pay for added convenience. They are charged less for multiple-party lines because low rates are needed to bring about the widest possible use of the service. And the more widely the service is used, the more valuable it will be to those who can be made to pay the higher rates. The structure of telephone rates is deliberately discriminatory. And no effort has been made to conceal this fact beneath the cloak of an arbitrary allocation of costs.

REGULATION OF RAILWAY RATE STRUCTURES

When it is said that a regulatory agency "fixes" rates, this does not mean that the agency takes the initiative in setting each of the many particular rates that go to make up the rate structure. Such rates are initiated by the companies themselves. Railroad rates, for instance, are originated by the railroads. Proposed changes are filed with the Interstate Commerce

Commission. Unless the Commission suspends them, in response to protests or upon its own motion, they take effect in thirty days. Shippers may always complain concerning particular rates, and the Commission will review them. But the rates that come to it for action, though large in number, are probably less than 1 per cent of all those in effect. And when it acts, the Commission takes the other rates in the structure for granted, never questioning the propriety of the pattern as a whole.

The Interstate Commerce Act contains a number of provisions with respect to the structure of rates. Section 1 of the Act requires that the rates charged on particular goods and between particular points be "just and reasonable," and that the systems used in classifying goods be "just and reasonable." Section 2 prohibits discrimination between persons, and several other sections outlaw specific forms of such discrimination. Section 3 covers other forms of discrimination, making it illegal for a carrier to give any "undue or unreasonable preference or advantage" or to impose any "undue or unreasonable prejudice or disadvantage." Section 4 applies to a particular form of discrimination between places, forbidding a carrier, without express permission of the ICC, to charge more "for a shorter than for a longer distance over the same line, in the same direction, the shorter being included within the longer distance." Section 6 requires that rates be published and adhered to and forbids changes in rates without prior notice.

These requirements were first applied to the railroads. They have since been copied in regulating other carriers. But the ICC, in their enforcement, has concerned itself mainly with the structure of railroad rates. For it is here that the problem of discrimination has been most serious.

Particular Rates

A shipper may complain that the rate charged for a particular commodity or a particular haul is unjust or unreasonable, in violation of Section 1 of the Interstate Commerce Act. Such a complaint does not allege discrimination: it has to do, not with the relation between one rate and another, but with the propriety of a rate in and of itself. But the ICC has no absolute standard by which justice and reasonableness may be judged. It does not attempt, for instance, to determine the cost of carrying a particular commodity or making a particular haul. Instead, it compares the rate that has been questioned with some other rate in the structure, taking as its standard an analogous commodity or a haul of equal length.

The Commission will approve a difference in rates if it can be justified on either of two grounds. First, it may be shown that it corresponds to a difference in costs. Here, it should be noted, the determining factor is not the absolute cost of handling a particular shipment, but the difference in the cost of handling two. Second, a difference in rates may be justified by a difference in the value of the service to shippers. Thus, the Commission has long held that it is just and reasonable to charge more for handling finished goods than for handling raw materials and more for valuable goods than for cheaper goods. And since 1933 the agency has taken elasticity of demand into account under an amendment that requires it to consider the effect of rates upon the movement of traffic. In a few cases, finally, the Commission has based its decisions upon considerations of public welfare, approving lower rates, for instance, to encourage the shipment of such commodities as fertilizers and building materials. But this is the exception rather than the general rule.

When it finds a rate to be unreasonable, the ICC prescribes a maximum that may be charged. Before 1915 the Supreme Court permitted such maxima to be set low for particular goods, provided a railroad was able to obtain a fair return on its business as a whole. Thereafter, the Court held that maxima could not be set below the full cost of the service rendered, including overhead, since this would deprive the roads of property without due process of law.[2] In 1953, however, the Court appeared to return to its earlier position, not explicitly reversing its previous decisions, but holding that "the Due Process Clause should not be construed as a bar to the fixing of noncompensatory rates for carrying some commodities when the public interest is thereby served."[3] The railroads may not charge more than the maximum rates that are prescribed; they may charge less. But here, too, their freedom is limited. The ICC has power to fix minima as well as maxima. It may permit a road to set a rate at a figure that fails to cover its full costs. But it requires that all rates be reasonably compensatory. To this end, it forbids the setting of any rate at less than out-of-pocket costs. A just and reasonable rate, therefore, is not a specific figure but is one that comes within the limits that may be prescribed, not rising above a maximum that may cover or more than cover fully-allocated costs, not falling below a minimum that covers only out-of-pocket costs.

Classification Systems

The three major systems of classifying commodities for the purpose of establishing class rates—the Official Classification in the Northeast, the Southern, and the Western—were developed by the railroads in these regions before the turn of the century and were influenced by the economic conditions prevailing at the time. In each region the roads undertook to establish the structure of rates that would maximize their revenues. And this led to the adoption of different principles of classification and to the establishment of different rates for the same goods. The Northeast was a manufacturing region, and here the classification was so arranged as to encourage the exportation of manufactured goods. The South and the West were exporters of foodstuffs and raw materials, and here, with rates set low for such commodities, the roads augmented their revenues by

[2] *Northern Pacific Railway Co.* v. *North Dakota*, 236 U.S. 585 (1915).

[3] *Baltimore & Ohio Railroad Co.* v. *U.S.*, 345 U.S. 146, 150.

setting them high for manufactured goods. As a result, class rates were higher in the South and much higher in the West than in the Northeast, though the cost of hauling goods was actually lower in the South and only moderately higher in the West. These discrepancies in the geographic structure of rates persisted for many years. They made it easier for manufacturers in the Northeast to ship to the border states and to the South and West, harder for those in the South and West to ship to the border states and to the Northeast. They thus afforded an artificial advantage to industry in the Northeast and imposed an artificial handicap on industry in the South and West.

With the beginning of large-scale industrial development in the South and West during the thirties, the geographic discrimination in the classification systems came under vigorous attack. Complaints were made by the State of Georgia, by the Tennessee Valley Authority, and by the Antitrust Division. The fight was carried to the ICC, to the courts, and to the Congress. Action was opposed by the manufacturing interests and the railroads in the Northeast and by the railroads in the South and West. But in the Transportation Act of 1940 Congress provided explicitly that railroad rates should give no unreasonable preference to any region, district, or territory. In 1945 the ICC found the three existing classification systems to be unreasonable and issued a temporary order raising class rates in the Northeast and reducing them in the South and West, pending hearings on the establishment of a uniform classification for the country as a whole. Its action was challenged by the railroads but was upheld by the Supreme Court in 1947.[4] A uniform classification was then prepared and was finally put into effect, in the territory east of the Rocky Mountains, in 1952. It is too early to appraise the consequences of this reform, but presumably it will encourage the location of industry in accordance with factors other than discriminatory elements in the structure of railroad rates.

Control of Discrimination

Railroads have discriminated in three ways: between persons, between commodities, and between places. Discrimination between persons was once extensive. It is now forbidden by law. The grosser abuses of the past have clearly been eliminated. Rebates are no longer given to favored shippers at the expense of their competitors. There may still be some favoritism in the performance of service. But when it is disclosed, it is enjoined. Discrimination between commodities and between places is not forbidden as such but only when it is undue or unreasonable. The establishment of limits to govern such discrimination is one of the principal functions of the ICC.

Cases are brought before the Commission as complaints are presented by shippers paying higher rates. If he is to obtain a favorable decision, a complainant must show three things: (1) that there is a competitive re-

[4] *State of New York* v. *U.S.*, 331 U.S. 284.

lationship between his own commodity or location and the one that enjoys a lower rate, (2) that he has suffered (or is likely to suffer) serious injury as a result of the difference in rates, and (3) that the same railroad charges the two rates and would be able to correct the situation by changing one or both of them. The railroad, on the other hand, may argue that the difference in rates is nondiscriminatory, corresponding to a difference in costs. Or it may defend discrimination by presenting evidence that its service is more valuable to one shipper than to another, or that it encounters competition in serving the one and not the other. If the Commission fails to find undue discrimination, it will allow the rates to stand. But if it makes such a finding, it will order the railroad to remove the discrimination, permitting it to do so by reducing the higher rate, by raising the lower rate, or by doing both.

Cases involving discrimination between commodities arise where goods that may be substituted for one another compete in the same market and where competition between fabricators is affected by the relation of rates on raw materials to those on finished goods. With respect to substitutes, the Commission usually requires comparable rates. It has acted, for instance, to forbid higher rates for benzol than for gasoline, for linseed oil than for cottonseed oil, and for lard substitutes than for lard. With respect to raw materials and finished products, the relationship of rates may affect the location of industry, giving plants that are close to raw materials an advantage over those that are close to markets, or doing the reverse. The fortunes of different flour mills, for instance, will depend upon the rates fixed for wheat and flour, and those of different packing houses upon the rates fixed for livestock and meat. In such cases the Commission tends to eliminate any artificial advantage or disadvantage by relating differences in rates to differences in costs. In either type of case, however, exceptions may be made, the railroads being allowed to fix lower rates on commodities where they face competition than on those where they do not.

Discrimination between places had been built into the structure of freight rates long before the Interstate Commerce Act was passed. In the Northeast, rates were generally related to distance. But in the South, they were so established as to meet the competition of water carriers to various ports, and these ports served, in turn, as basing points in fixing rates to inland towns. As a result, rates throughout the South declined as traffic approached a waterway. On transcontinental traffic, moreover, rates were computed by taking the water rates from Atlantic to Pacific ports and adding to them rail rates for hauling goods back toward the East. Transcontinental rates therefore declined as traffic moved on toward the Pacific coast. The Act forced a revision of this structure. Under its provisions, the ICC has adopted the principle of relating rates to distance. But it has permitted many exceptions to this general rule.

Cases of place discrimination fall into two categories. Those involving a higher charge "for a shorter than for a longer distance over the same line, in the same direction, the shorter being included within the longer distance" come under Section 4 of the Act, known as the long-and-short-haul clause. All other such cases come under Section 3, which deals with discrimination in general. Long-and-short-haul discrimination is forbidden unless expressly permitted by the ICC. In Section 4 cases, therefore, the burden of proof is on the railroad that seeks relief from this provision of the law. In Section 3 cases, however, the procedure is the same as that for discrimination among commodities. A shipper who complains of a higher rate than that charged at another place must show that the two places are in competition, that he is injured by the difference in rates, and that the same railroad charges both rates and has the power to change them. And the railroad may defend itself by showing differences in the cost of service, in the demand for service, and in the competition faced on the two hauls. The considerations that influence the Commission's decisions in cases brought under either Section are much the same.

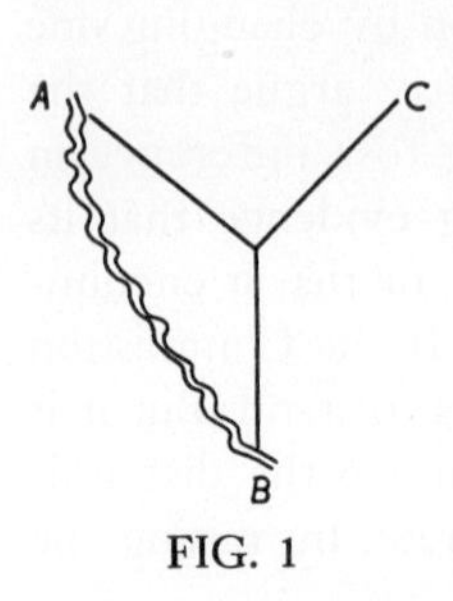

FIG. 1

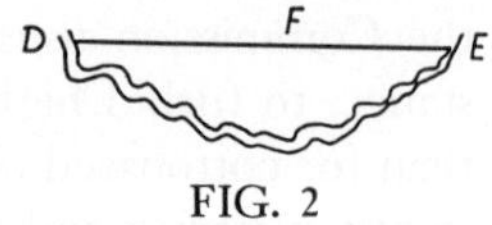

FIG. 2

Discrimination may be permitted where there is competition between railroads and other carriers, between two railroads, or between two producing areas obtaining their raw material from a common source or selling in a common market. Thus, as shown in Figure 1, a railroad that runs from *A* to *B* may be permitted to meet the low rate of a water carrier operating on the river between these points without fixing an equally low rate on the equidistant haul from *C* to *B*. And, as shown in Figure 2, a railroad that runs from *D* to *E* may be permitted to meet the rate of a water carrier between these points, even though it would then be charging more for the shorter haul from *D* to *F* than for the longer haul from *D* to *E*. Similarly, as shown in Figure 3, railroad *W* that follows a circuitous route from *G* to *H* may be permitted to meet the rate of railroad *X* that follows a direct route, without fixing an equally low rate for the equidistant haul from *I* to *H*. And, as shown in Figure 4, railroad *Y* may be permitted to meet the rate of railroad Z from *J* to *K*, even though it would then be charging more for the shorter haul from *J* to *L* than for the longer haul from *J* to *K*. And finally, as shown in Figures 5 and 6, a railroad that serves the competing industrial centers *M* and *N* that draw their raw materials from the common source *O* or sell their product in the common market *O* may be permitted to reduce the rate at *M* to the figure charged at *N*.

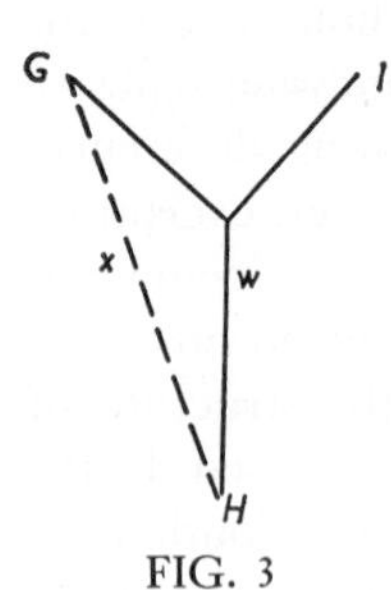

FIG. 3

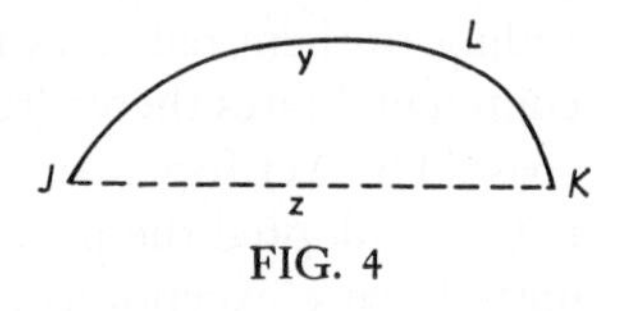

FIG. 4

Such discrimination has its limits. A railroad may fix a lower rate for one of two equidistant hauls or for a longer than for a shorter haul only when it is forced to do so to meet competition that arises from some natural advantage, such as that of a water carrier or a shorter rail line. Thus, as shown in Figure 7, railroad *W* will not be permitted to charge lower rates between *P* and *Q* where it competes with railroad *X*, a line of equal length, than between *R* and *Q*, where it has no competitor. And, as shown in Figure 8, railroads *Y* and *Z* will not be permitted to charge less for the longer haul from *S* to *T* than for the shorter hauls from *S* to *U* and *V*, merely because they compete at *T* and not at *U* and *V*. A railroad may be permitted to equalize the competitive opportunities of different places, as was done in Figures 5 and 6. But it cannot be required to do so. Thus, the producers at *M* have no legal right to demand that their rate be made the same as that at *N*. And opportunities can be equalized only by offsetting natural disadvantages, not by canceling natural advantages. In the cases shown in Figures 5 and 6, the railroad may reduce the rate at *M* to the level of that at *N*. It may not raise the rate at *N* to the level of that at *M*.

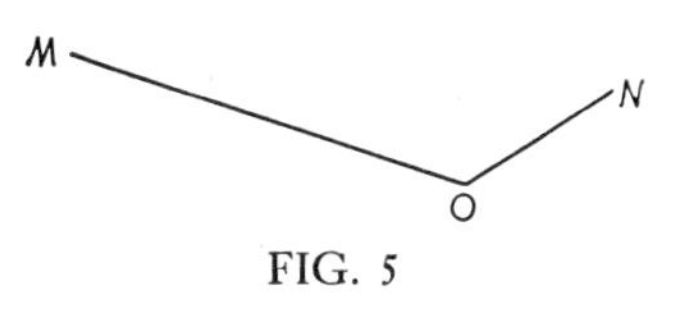

FIG. 5

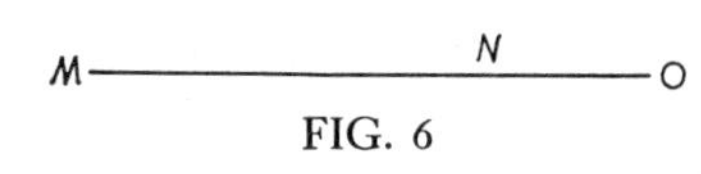

FIG. 6

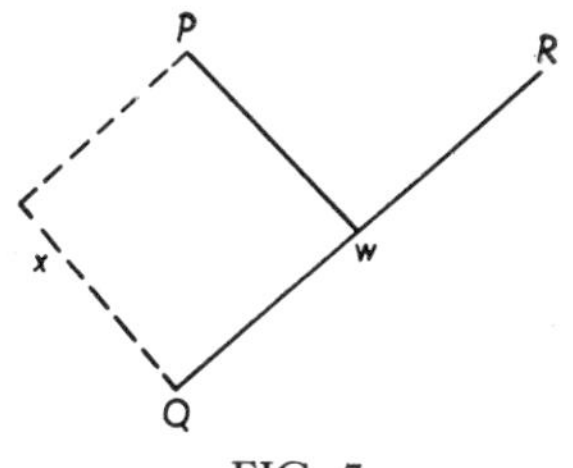

FIG. 7

The decisions made by the ICC and reviewed by the courts, in cases such as these, determine when discrimination will be permitted and when it will not. But the line thus drawn between legality and illegality is not always clear. The limits of discrimination, at any time, will depend upon the composition and the judgment of the Commission and the courts.

Consequences of Discrimination

Discrimination among commodities, where it involves the establishment of lower rates for goods that otherwise would not move at all, may be of general benefit. It is of benefit to the carriers, since it enables them to enlarge their revenues, make fuller use of their facilities, reduce their unit costs, and improve their position with respect to earnings. It obviously benefits the producers of commodities that pay the lower rates. It even benefits the producers of those that pay the higher rates, for if the low-rate traffic did not move, they would have to pay all the overhead costs and provide all the earnings by themselves, and their rates

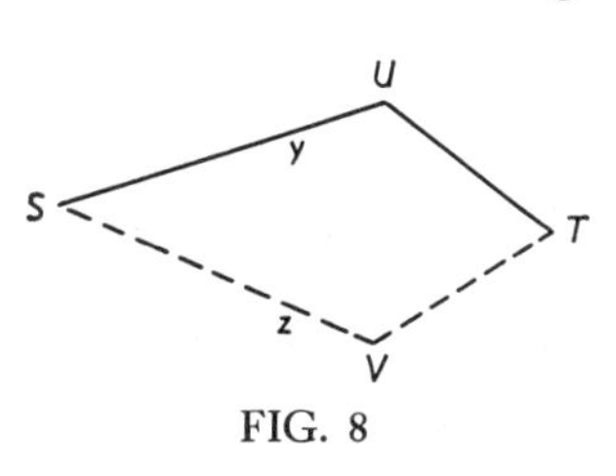

FIG. 8

would be higher still. It benefits the community as a whole, since goods are thus made generally available that otherwise would be confined to local areas.

Discrimination among commodities, however, is frequently designed, not to increase the volume of traffic, but merely to divert existing traffic from one carrier to another. Discrimination between places, also, usually has this effect. Such discrimination may benefit a particular carrier, enabling a railroad, for instance, to obtain traffic that would otherwise have moved by water or by highway or over another line. It obviously benefits the commodities and the places that enjoy the lower rates. It may even be said to benefit those that pay the higher rates. Thus, in Figures 1–4, the people of *C*, *F*, *I*, and *L* are better off than they would be if the railroads serving them got none of the traffic between the competitive points, and were therefore forced to turn to them for more of the revenue required to cover costs and provide a fair return. But it cannot be said that such discrimination is of benefit to the community as a whole. What one carrier gains, another loses. The discriminating carrier gets more traffic and more revenue; the competing carrier gets less. With the former, costs and rates will be lowered. With the latter, they will be raised. The practice, moreover, has a social cost. It obstructs the allocation of traffic among different media in accordance with their relative economy. And it results in wasteful transportation by roundabout routes.

Discrimination between places has another effect. It exerts a powerful influence on the location of industry. Where the disadvantage of distance from materials and markets is offset by lower rates, one community (such as *M* in Figures 5 and 6) may grow in importance while another (such as *N*) may be denied the growth it would otherwise have attained. Production may thus be diverted from more economic to less economic sites.

The less desirable consequences of discrimination are to be attributed to the competitive character of the transport industry. If transportation were monopolized, goods would not be moved by rail where water was cheaper or by circuitous routes where direct routes were available. Nor would a transport monopoly, under public regulation, be so likely to promote the development of one community at the expense of another. But where transportation is provided by many different carriers, each of them must be given an opportunity to go after competitive business and to develop new sources of revenue. And the forms of discrimination thus permitted will lead to waste. Competition, however, may have offsetting advantages. This question will be considered again in Chapter 22.

REGULATION OF PUBLIC UTILITY RATE STRUCTURES

With regard to the structure of rates, the laws that regulate public utilities usually follow the pattern of those that regulate railroads, requiring that particular rates be just and reasonable, that they be published, observed, and not changed without prior notice, and that discrimination be not unjust, unreasonable, or undue. But the state utility commissions have given much less attention to rate structures than has the ICC. Among the many possible structures that might serve equally well to cover costs and provide investors with a fair return, they have made no effort to discover and adopt the one that would best serve the public interest. Instead, they have left the initiative in fixing particular rates to the companies, accepted the pattern of rates established, subjected it to little scrutiny, and made little effort to have it modified.

Where the commissions act, it is usually in response to complaints. In such cases they must draw a line between the unreasonable discrimination that the law forbids and the reasonable discrimination that it allows. In doing so, however, they have developed no clear principles, but appear to have been guided, rather, by vague conceptions of equity. The commissions have frequently insisted that rate forms be simple and understandable. They have sometimes checked the multiplication of consumer classes and have even limited the differentials between them. In general, however, they have accepted classifications and differentials that have been based on differences in the elasticity of demand. Typically, they have compared the rate structure of one company with that of another and have held discrimination to be reasonable if it conformed to the customary pattern. The commissions have said that the establishment of particular rates is necessarily a matter of business judgment. But they have set up no standards in accordance with which such judgment must be exercised.

The commissions have generally held that differences in rates should be related to differences in costs. And they have sought to prevent the rate for any class from being set below its incremental or out-of-pocket cost. But they have laid down no rules to govern the allocation of overhead. Instead, most of them have accepted, without question, the theory of company accountants that allocates overhead in accordance with the proportionate responsibility of different customers for non-coincident demand. The commissions, moreover, have tended to favor discrimination where it has had the effect of expanding consumption and bringing about a fuller utilization of productive capacity. They have thus approved the creation of low-rate classes, the reduction of rates in successive quantity blocks, and the adoption of objective rate plans. As a result, the wide differentials established between classes, and between large and small users within these classes, have been allowed to stand. In the case of electricity, particularly, the low rates go to big business, where demand is elastic and where protection by government is not required. The high rates go to small business and to householders, where demand is inelastic and where such protection is really required. The law thus fails to give to those who need it most the aid it was intended to provide.

This failure is to be attributed to three main causes. First, the commissions have been compelled to devote most of their energy to the struggle over the level of rates and have had little of it left to spend in reforming the structure of rates. Second, they have been deceived by the methods of accounting that are employed to justify discrimination, not understanding the principles of demand on which discrimination is really based. And third, they have been deterred from overhauling the structure of rates by the fact that many of its parts have come to be deeply embedded in business expectations. Reformation of the structure, according to different principles, would be helpful to those whose rates were lowered and to the community in general. But it would be harmful to those whose rates were raised and would therefore be politically unpopular.

The last of these difficulties could have been overcome by revising the structure gradually rather than suddenly. When costs fall, the general level of rates can be lowered. When they go up, it must be raised. On such occasions, the structure of rates can be so modified as to make it less discriminatory. When the general level is lowered, the higher rates in the structure can be reduced more, the lower rates less, and the differentials narrowed. When the general level is raised, the higher rates can be raised less, the lower rates more, and the differentials narrowed. But this has not been done. When the rate level has been changed, all the rates in the structure have moved together. The pattern of differentials has been preserved. The opportunity to lighten the impact of discrimination has been thrown away.

SUGGESTIONS FOR FURTHER READING

The problems of the rate structure and its regulation are discussed in a number of the volumes cited at the end of the previous chapters. The theory of discrimination is considered by Wallace in Part IV, chap vii of his T.N.E.C. Monograph, by Troxel in his chaps. xxiv, xxv, and xxvi, and by Clemens in his chap. xi. It is also treated in Philip D. Locklin, *Economics of Transportation* (4th ed.; Homewood, Ill.: Richard D. Irwin, Inc., 1954), chap. viii, and in Truman C. Bigham and Merill J. Roberts, *Transportation* (2d ed.; New York: McGraw-Hill Book Co., 1952), chap. xii. Railroad rate structures are described in Locklin, chap. ix, in Bigham and Roberts, chap. xvi, in Russell E. Westmeyer, *Economics of Transportation* (New York: Prentice-Hall, Inc., 1952), chaps. xi, xii, and xiii, and in Marvin L. Fair and Ernest W. Williams, Jr., *Economics of Transportation* (New York: Harper & Bros., 1950) Part III. Public utility rate structures are described in Clemens, chaps. xii, xiii, and xiv, in Barnes, chap. x, in Troxel, chaps. xxvii and xxviii, and in Bauer, chap. xiii. The regulation of railway rate structures by the Interstate Commerce Commission is discussed by Locklin in chaps. xix–xxiii, incl., by Bigham and Roberts in chaps. xiii, xiv, and xv, and by Fair and Williams in chap. xxix. On the regulation of public utility rate structures, the chapters by Troxel, cited above, are particularly good.

Chapter 20 REGULATION OF PUBLIC UTILITIES

In some states regulation of companies rendering one or another of the public utility services is left to local governments. In most cases, however, responsibility for such regulation is entrusted to state commissions. In the case of gas and electricity, local and state controls have been reinforced, since the middle thirties, by controls exercised by two federal agencies: the Federal Power Commission and the Securities and Exchange Commission. In the case of telegraph and telephone services, interstate operations are regulated, and state regulation of intrastate operations is supplemented, by the Federal Communications Commission. The present chapter is concerned with regulation of public utilities by the state and federal commissions, with particular reference to gas, electric, telegraph, and telephone services.

CONTROL BY THE STATES

In a few states, notably New York, Wisconsin, Illinois, and California, utility commissions have earned a reputation in the past for vigor and effectiveness. But, by and large, the verdict of scholars on the performance of such bodies has damned them with faint praise. In the opinion of Ben W. Lewis, "The record of public utility regulation generally since 1907 is neither impressive, nor yet too disheartening."[1] According to Emery Troxel, "Although state commission regulation of utility industries is an improvement on what local governments and franchises can provide, it is still . . . far short of good social control."[2] And in the words of John Bauer, "The wonder is that regulation has worked as well as it has. Although far from satisfactory, it has not been a complete and unmitigated failure. While the commissions have not measured up to high standards, perhaps they have done, in the main, the best they could under all the circumstances. They have carried on their work in an easygoing, nonalert

[1] Leverett S. Lyon and Victor Abramson (ed.), *Government and Economic Life* (Washington, D.C.: Brookings Institution, 1940), p. 744.

[2] Emery Troxel, *Economics of Public Utilities* (New York: Rinehart & Co., Inc., 1947), p. 87.

way, but they have seldom deliberately flouted the public interest. . . ."[3] Certainly, regulation has not proved to be really adequate as a substitute for competition in fulfilling its functions of preventing monopoly prices and profits, checking discrimination, reducing costs, inducing technical progress, and promoting wider use of utility services. The limited effectiveness of the state commissions and some of the reasons for their failures will be discussed below.

Effectiveness of Regulation

It is virtually impossible to measure the results of utility regulation. Standards by which to measure service are difficult to develop and apply. Rates are quoted for standard units, but the meaning of comparisons between regulated and unregulated companies is obscured by differences in the structure of rates. In the case of electricity, for instance, the average charge per kilowatt-hour is affected by the methods used in classifying service and by the relative importance of different classes in total output. Comparisons can be made, of course, in terms of monthly bills for like quantities of like services. But their significance will still be open to dispute. Rates are affected by many factors other than the mechanism of control. There are differences in costs of generation between plants that are large and small, hydro and steam, close to coal and at a distance; differences in costs of transmission where plants are near to consumers and where they are far away. In comparing private and public plants, moreover, it must be remembered that the bases for computing costs are not the same.

With this caution, certain generalizations may be made concerning electric rates. These rates have varied greatly from state to state and from city to city, the highest figures being twice the lowest ones. Rates have been lower where they were regulated by state commissions than where they were not. But rates charged for private power, under regulation, have generally been higher than those charged for public power. Private companies have cut their rates when faced with the example of public competition. And, at the lower level, consumption and earnings have increased. The force of example has thus been more effective as a regulator than the force of law. "Practically up to this moment," wrote John Bauer in 1950, "electric rates have remained generally excessive and consumers have not got the benefits of regulation as intended."[4]

Regulation, of course, is not designed to force rates down to the lowest level that will cover costs and yield a fair return, but merely to prevent

[3] John Bauer, *Transforming Public Utility Regulation* (New York: Harper & Bros., 1950), pp. 137–38.

[4] *Ibid.*, p. 127. For a careful study of comparative rates around 1940 see *Electric Power and Government Policy* (New York: Twentieth Century Fund, 1948), pp. 210–37.

the return from being too high. Even here, it has often failed. In the twenties, according to surveys made by the Federal Trade Commission and by legislative committees in New York and Pennsylvania, many gas and electric companies were realizing 20–30 per cent per annum on their actual investment and a few as much as 50 or 100 per cent or even more.[5] From 1920 to 1930 earnings per share of utility stocks quadrupled as demand grew and costs declined. The increasing prices of such stock revealed that investors would provide capital for a return much lower than the one they then obtained. But the commissions rarely attempted to eliminate excessive profits by reducing rates. During the thirties, however, substantial reductions were made. But as late as 1948 the Twentieth Century Fund, reporting on a study made around 1940, asserted that "many state regulated electric utilities are earning profits which may be regarded as unreasonable," and thus found "a basis for the widespread feeling . . . that state regulation in general has failed to achieve its primary purpose."[6]

In the case of telephones, regulation of the general level of rates, according to Bauer, "has in fact been far less effective than that of the other local utilities."[7] The commissions have been ill-equipped to cope with the complexities of technology, corporate organization, and interstate relationships found in this industry. They have been more reluctant here than elsewhere to inquire into the reasonableness of rates.

Evidence as to the ineffectiveness of regulation has come, in the main, from a period when growth in demand and changes in technology resulted in falling costs. During this period, delay in adjusting rates preserved excessive earnings. Adjustments were therefore obstructed by the utilities. In the future, however, with the economies of scale already realized, with labor organized to press for higher wages, and with continued inflation raising the prices of equipment and supplies, the trend of costs may be reversed. In such a situation, applications for rate increases will be filed by the utilities and vigorously pressed. Action, consequently, may be speeded. But some delay is likely to persist. And in this case, instead of going up, earnings will go down. Regulation may be made effective by its very ineffectiveness. The danger is that earnings, in some cases, may be so depressed that the credit of utility companies will be affected and their service impaired.

Not only have rates and earnings been high in the past; there has been excessive discrimination in favor of large users of gas and electricity and against the small householder, as we saw in Chapter 19. With telephones, however, this is not the case.

[5] These studies are summarized in Clair Wilcox, *Competition and Monopoly in American Industry*, T.N.E.C. Monograph No. 21 (Washington, D.C.: Government Printing Office, 1940), pp. 94–95.

[6] Twentieth Century Fund, *op. cit.*, p. 244.

[7] Bauer, *op. cit.*, p. 337.

Shortcomings of State Commissions

The state commissions have done little to control the quality of utility services, in general leaving initiative to the companies and acting only on complaint. Most of them have manifested little interest in the structure of rates, accepting cost analyses advanced to rationalize discrimination, or entrusting the formulation of particular charges to the discretion of managements. All of them have been concerned with the level of rates. But few have sought to control operating expenses, the largest element in the rate level, by passing on them in advance. All have prescribed accounting systems, essential to rate control, but few have attempted to enforce them by audits in the field. Few have undertaken to develop criteria of equity or efficiency to govern earnings. And none has sought to maximize consumption by reducing rates to the lowest level that would yield a fair return. Instead, attention has been centered, in the past, on determining and preserving the value of utility properties. Some commissions, in making valuations, have accepted reproduction costs. Others, while giving such costs little weight, have made obeisance to the courts by going through the mumbo jumbo of the valuation ritual. Energy has been diverted from the purpose for which the laws were passed and the commissions formed.

Formal action is through a rate case. Some commissions initiate such cases. Others are passive, waiting for cases to be brought. In these proceedings the contest between the company and the consumer is not an equal one. The company is represented by able lawyers, well paid, fortified with facts, and supported by a staff of expert witnesses. In some states the commission assists the consumer in preparing his case. In others, it does not. In both, his lawyers are poorly paid and inadequately re-enforced. And if the consumer wins, the company can appeal—and appeal—and appeal. In the past protracted litigation has been the rule. One telephone case, begun in 1921, was not decided until 1934.[8] In such a situation, the commissions despaired of making progress through formal procedures and sought to salvage what they could by entering into negotiations with the companies.

Negotiation is faster and cheaper than litigation. And it may lead to cuts in rates. But there is no assurance that it will always protect the public interest. The negotiators meet behind closed doors; no record of their proceedings is released. The outcome will depend upon the zeal of the contending parties and on their skill in bargaining. The commission has certain advantages: it can threaten formal action, appeal to public opinion, or deny requests for extensions or abandonments or for the issuance of new securities. But the companies have the support of greater knowledge, financial resources, and staying power. They are therefore unlikely to concede as much as the law would have required. The rates agreed to may still be well in excess of costs; the profits they yield may be exorbitant.

[8] *Lindheimer* v. *Illinois Bell Telephone Co.*, 292 U.S. 150.

As the Power Committee of the Twentieth Century Fund remarked, "there is something fundamentally wrong with a system in which matters of such public moment are handled by public bodies in informal, and nearly always secret, conferences with interested executives."[9]

Most of the state commissions confine themselves to keeping up with the daily load of work, as Bauer put it, "in an easy-going, nonalert way." Few of them attempt to formulate their policies or to plan their programs in advance. Few of them undertake significant research. The commissions, says Troxel, "seem to be apathetic and do not press for funds, statutory powers and other means of improvement." The typical commissioner "appears more satisfied with things as they are than with good regulatory effects, more interested in his politics than his knowledge and expertness. In general, the states are sending nice political-minded boys to do a job that calls for wise and determined men."[10]

Causes of Failure

Responsibility for the failures of regulation cannot be charged to the commissions alone but must be shared by the courts, the legislatures, the executives, and the public at large. It was the courts that asserted their right to review the work of the commissions, stripped them of necessary powers, and reversed their decisions, always to the end of preventing or canceling reductions in rates. The explanation for their action is not far to seek. According to Bauer, "the judges had been appointed extensively from prominent lawyers with successful corporation practice, who were heavily impregnated with private business perspectives. They had little consciousness of the public aspects of industry and little concern for the protection and advancement of public interest. Throughout the judicial domain, the dominant attitude was one of guardianship toward property and of vigilance against legislative and administrative encroachments."[11] It was thus by judicial action that the emphasis in regulation was shifted from the protection of consumers to the protection of property.

The legislatures have impeded regulation by denying the commissions adequate jurisdiction, powers, and funds. Even yet there are states where the control of particular services is left to local governments, where valuations must be based on cost of reproduction, and where power to control depreciation effectively is denied. In many states commissions cannot control security issues or other financial practices. And in most states they cannot require submission of budgets prior to action on expenditures. The courts, moreover, were given their opportunity to negate the work of the commissions by the failure of the legislatures to include clear standards in the laws. The commissions were simply instructed to establish rates at reasonable levels, but reasonableness was not defined. The door to judicial

[9] Twentieth Century Fund, *op. cit.*, p. 757.

[10] Troxel, *op. cit.*, p. 88.

[11] Bauer, *op cit.*, p. 125.

interpretation thus was opened wide. The Congress, too, contributed to the defeat of regulation by failing for many years to act to bring interstate transactions and holding company operations under control.

The errors of courts and legislatures have been matched by those of the executives. Governors have made poor appointments, filling commissionerships with political hacks, unqualified by experience or interest for the work. In some cases they have even appointed men chosen by the utilities or have otherwise discouraged real enforcement of the law. By selling the consumer down the river, they have obtained political support.

And finally, the fault lies with the public: with consumers and with voters generally. No group has been organized to make sure that the commissions have adequate jurisdiction and powers, that they are well staffed and financed, that they act with vigor and dispatch. One reason is that the problem has not seemed to be serious. Utility rates are a small part of the consumer's budget; for many years, instead of being raised, they were reduced—the trouble was merely that reductions in rates did not keep pace with reductions in costs. Utility services, moreover, have been good and getting better. This is not the sort of situation in which people are stirred to act. Another reason for public apathy, however, is to be found in the propaganda efforts of the utilities.

In hearings conducted by the Federal Trade Commission in the early thirties, trade associations of gas and electric companies were shown to have spent millions of dollars every year to influence public opinion. These bodies fed news and editorials to the press and used their control of advertising to prevent unfavorable publicity. They supplied friendly speakers for public meetings and kept unfriendly speakers from getting a hearing. They provided teaching materials to schools and colleges and sought to censor textbooks that they disapproved. They planted their propaganda in labor unions, granges, women's clubs, churches, and Sunday schools. According to one of their officials, they employed every means of communication but skywriting. And so they spread the word that public ownership was bad, that private enterprise was good, and that tighter regulation was not required.[12] It took financial scandals of the greatest magnitude to overcome the confidence that they created and to arouse consumers from the lethargy this confidence induced.

Since the disclosures of the thirties, the utilities have been more discreet. But, according to Bauer, they have continued their efforts to influence regulation.

First, they have maintained close and insistent political connections with both major parties. Second, they have watched constantly for their own inter-

[12] The evidence taken from utility records and presented by utility witnesses is summarized in Irston R. Barnes, *The Economics of Public Utility Regulation* (New York: F. S. Crofts & Co., 1942), chap. xxiii. The story is told more fully in Jack Levin, *Power Ethics* (New York: Alfred A. Knopf, 1931), and in Carl D. Thompson, *Confessions of the Power Trust* (New York: E. P. Dutton & Co., 1932).

est along the entire political front so as to get favorable actions and avoid unfavorable. Third, they have watched and promoted, or opposed, appointments, not only to the commissions but to the technical staffs. Fourth, they have sponsored favorable legislation and headed off unfavorable. Fifth, they have participated in quasi-public organizations and through them extended their influences into the communities and into political channels. Sixth, they have used extensive advertising and other means of publicity to stimulate favorable attitudes, and to prevent unfavorable news articles and editorial comments; seldom have newspapers printed squarely the public side in utility controversies. Seventh, the companies have kept close contact with the commissions, spreading graciousness and lures for their private advantage.

"While originally the companies were vigorously opposed to regulation," says Bauer, "they have come not only to accept it but largely to convert it into an instrument of protection for themselves."[13]

FEDERAL CONTROL OF ELECTRICITY

The Federal Power Commission was set up under the Water Power Act of 1920 to control the construction and operation of hydroelectric projects on navigable streams, jurisdiction over such waters under the commerce clause of the Constitution, as interpreted by the courts, belonging to the federal government. As originally constituted, the Commission was composed of the Secretaries of War, Interior, and Agriculture. This structure proved to be unwieldy, the cabinet members being occupied with other duties and the Commission's work being delegated almost entirely to its staff. In 1930 the law was amended to reorganize the body, providing for the appointment of five full-time commissioners, with bipartisan representation and five-year overlapping terms. Under Title II of the Public Utility Act of 1935, the Commission's jurisdiction was extended to cover the wholesale transmission of electricity in interstate commerce, and the body was authorized to draw up plans for regional power systems, to require interconnections, and to investigate and report on electric costs and rates. Under other legislation, the Commission was directed to pass upon the rates charged by certain federal hydro projects. And under the Natural Gas Act of 1938, it was empowered to regulate the interstate transmission and sale for resale of natural gas. In 1953 the agency had a staff of 630 and an appropriation of $4 million. Its activities relating to electricity will be discussed in this section. Its work in regulating natural gas, demanding the lion's share of its attention, will be considered in the next.

Control of Hydro Projects

Until 1920 licenses permitting the development of power on navigable rivers were granted by special acts of Congress. Such licenses were given

[13] Bauer, *op. cit.*, p. 137.

in perpetuity, without charge, and with no provision for subsequent regulation of the licensees. Valuable rights were thus squandered without regard for the national interest. This situation was vigorously denounced by Theodore Roosevelt. But it was not corrected until the passage in 1920 of the Water Power Act.

Under this law, responsibility for granting licenses is given to the FPC. In making such grants the Commission is to consider how the projects proposed would affect the use of water for other purposes, such as irrigation, navigation, and flood control. And it is to give priority to applications made by state and local governments. Licenses are to run for fifty years, whereupon they may be renewed or granted to other applicants or the federal government can take over the properties involved, by mutual consent or by condemnation, paying a price that covers net investment exclusive of intangibles. Licensees must pay an annual rental to cover the costs of administration and the use of public lands. They must provide for other water uses and for the maintenance of their own facilities. After twenty years they must make annual payments into an amortization reserve. Licensees must conform to regulations imposed upon them by the states and by the FPC. The Commission is empowered to govern methods of accounting. And where no state agency exercises jurisdiction, it may regulate rates, services, and financial practices.

Since federal authority is limited to navigable waters, the Commission's power to control certain projects has been questioned on the ground that the streams involved were not navigable. But here, the courts have been liberal, defining navigability to cover streams that carry no commercial traffic and streams that might be navigated if they were improved, and even permitting the FPC to control the construction of dams on non-navigable tributaries of navigable streams.[14] Under these interpretations, the Commission's jurisdiction has been broad.

In granting licenses, the Commission has examined projects in relation to the development of river basins as a whole and to all the purposes that such development must serve. It has usually preferred projects making full use of the potential power to those allowing part of it to go to waste. It has favored public bodies over private applicants and firms that had contracts for the sale of power over those that did not. It has refused to grant licenses permitting the development of an entire watershed by a single company. But it has required applicants to present plans for interconnection with other lines.

The Commission has done little to regulate its licensees. It has prescribed a uniform system of accounting that not only must be used by companies under its jurisdiction but also has been approved by the association of state commissioners and adopted by many of the states. It has thus been influential in improving accounting practices, requiring proper-

[14] See *Appalachian Power Co.* v. *U.S.*, 311 U.S. 377 (1940).

ties to be valued at their original cost and depreciation to be handled by making annual contributions to reserves. Its engineers have periodically inspected all projects under construction and in operation to insure compliance with license terms. And it has enforced the law's requirement regarding amortization. But the Commission has rarely regulated rates, finances, or services. The mere existence of state commissions, however impotent, has sufficed to stay its hand.

Under the laws establishing some (but not all) of the federal hydro projects, the rates charged for power must be approved by the FPC. These rates must cover the separable costs of producing power and some part of the joint costs involved in providing facilities for this and other purposes. Here, the principal problem facing the Commission is that of finding a proper basis for the allocation of joint costs. This is a matter whose significance will be considered at some length in Chapter 26.

Control of Interstate Activities

In the thirties, nearly a fifth of the electricity consumed in the United States had moved across state lines. State commissions fixed the rates at which out-of-state companies sold to local consumers. But they were powerless to fix those at which out-of-state generators made sales in quantity to local distributors. When the Rhode Island commission attempted to fix the price that a Rhode Island generator charged a Massachusetts distributor, the Supreme Court held that neither state had jurisdiction over interstate commerce in electricity.[15] As a result, where current was generated in one state and distributed in another, the rates charged by the distributing company could not really be regulated, since the price that it paid for its power was beyond control.

This loophole was closed by Title II of the Public Utility Act of 1935. The FPC was given jurisdiction over electricity transported across state lines and sold for resale. It thus became a utility regulator as well as a conservation agency. Where the states lacked power, it was authorized to regulate rates and earnings, prescribe methods of accounting, and control financial operations, combinations, and the transfer of facilities. Upon complaint by a state, the Commission was empowered to order improvement of interstate service. And it was also authorized to regulate discrimination in price between localities.

Where the Commission's jurisdiction under this law has been questioned, it has been upheld, in general, by the courts. But the agency has not been active in fixing rates. Few complaints have been filed, cases heard, and orders handed down. Here, again, the Commission's greatest contribution has been its system of accounts.

Two other activities are carried on under the Act of 1935. The Commission conducts research and publishes reports, including statistics on

[15] *Rhode Island Public Utilities Commission* v. *Attleboro Steam and Electric Co.*, 273 U.S. 83 (1927).

electrical utilities, a compilation of rate schedules, and annual comparisons of typical monthly bills for different classes of service in all communities with more than 2,500 inhabitants, affording a basis for comparing the results of different types of operation: hydro and steam, large and small, private and public. It also studies the nation's prospective demand for power and its potential supplies and draws up plans for regional power systems involving the co-ordination of separate facilities. The Commission encourages voluntary interconnections, and has exercised its power to order connections made and energy sold or exchanged in times of emergency. It is the nearest thing to a planning and co-ordinating agency for power to be found in the United States.

National Power Policy

The work of the FPC under the Act of 1935 must be considered in the context of New Deal power policy. In Title I of the same Act, utility holding companies were subjected to regulation by the SEC. At the same time large-scale multipurpose federal projects involving the generation and transmission of hydroelectric power were being established in the valleys of the Tennessee, the Columbia, and many other streams. The generation and distribution of power by local governments was being encouraged by federal grants and loans. The extension of service into rural areas was being promoted by the Rural Electrification Administration, through long-term low-interest loans to co-operatives. Preference was being given to municipalities and co-operatives in the sale of federal power. Taken together, these programs were designed to make state regulation more effective by closing existing loopholes, to regulate private operations indirectly by setting an example in the sale of public power, to reduce the cost of power to the consumer, to make it generally available, and to increase its use. The control of holding companies will be considered later in this chapter. The federal power projects will be discussed, at some length, in Chapter 26. At this point, it may merely be noted that the power policy of the New Deal, unlike some of its other policies, was consistent, straightforward, and highly effective.

With the election of a Republican administration in 1952, the pendulum began to swing the other way. Federal projects were curtailed and greater encouragement given to private companies. These changes, too, will be discussed in Chapter 26.

FEDERAL CONTROL OF NATURAL GAS

Natural gas, obtained as a by-product in the search for oil, was wasted for many years, being blown off, burned, or devoted to inferior industrial uses in the vicinity of the oil fields. Little of it was shipped across state lines. Then, in the thirties, big new oil and gas fields were developed in regions remote from markets for gas. And, at the same time, the introduction of seamless steel pipe and other improvements in pipeline construction extended the distance over which gas could be economically transported from around 200 miles to 1,000 miles or more. High-pressure pipelines were built from the fields in the South and West to the cities in the North and East. By 1954 more than half of the gas was moving in interstate commerce, being carried into 43 of the states. Gas was providing a fourth of the nation's energy. A fifth of it was manufactured, four fifths natural. Of the natural gas sold, three fourths went to industrial users, one fourth to 7 million householders who provided the gas companies with the larger part of their revenues.

The gas industry falls into three divisions: production, transportation, and distribution. Gas is distributed to consumers by local utility companies, whose operations are regulated by state or city governments. It is transported by pipeline companies, some of the lines being owned by producers and some of them by distributors. It is produced by oil and gas companies, a score of them, roughly, being corporate giants conducting integrated operations, some thousands of them being independents selling their output in the field. The pipeline companies produce a fifth of the gas they carry, obtain four fifths of it from the independents. Of the industry's three stages, distribution involves the largest costs, transportation far less, and production least of all. When the consumer pays 75 cents for a thousand cubic feet of gas, 47 cents may go for distribution, 22 cents for transportation, and only 6 cents for the gas itself. But the cost of gas to the pipeline company and the company's charge for transportation enter into the costs of local distributors and must be reflected in their rates.

Until 1938 state and local authorities were powerless to control the price that distributors paid for imported gas. Interstate pipelines, the Supreme Court held, were beyond their reach.[16] As a result, they were confined to regulating distribution charges. Controlled gas rates floated on top of the uncontrolled prices charged at the city gates. This escape, similar to the one found until 1935 in the interstate transmission of electricity, was closed by the Natural Gas Act of 1938.

The Natural Gas Act

The Act of 1938 brought the interstate transmission of natural gas and its sale for resale under the control of the FPC. The Act exempted the production and gathering of gas and its retail distribution. It established the usual pattern of rate control, requiring the pipeline companies to publish and adhere to their charges, giving prior notice of prospective changes, and empowering the Commission to suspend such changes, to

[16] *West* v. *Kansas Natural Gas Co.*, 221 U.S. 229 (1911); *Haskell* v. *Kansas Natural Gas Co.*, 224 U.S. 217 (1912); *Public Utilities Comsn.* v. *Landon*, 249 U.S. 236 (1918); *Pennsylvania* v. *West Virginia*, 262 U.S. 553 (1923); *Barrett* v. *Kansas Natural Gas Co.*, 265 U.S. 298 (1924).

fix "just and reasonable" rates, and to eliminate "undue" preferences. It also authorized the Commission to prescribe and enforce methods of accounting and to ascertain the "actual legitimate cost" of pipeline properties. As amended in 1942 the law requires the companies to obtain certificates from the FPC for interstate construction, acquisitions, extensions, and abandonments, and gives the Commission limited power to order extensions. The law carries no authority to regulate financial practices or combinations. And, unlike the Act of 1935 relating to electricity, it confers no power to order interconnections and makes no provision for studies directed toward the possible unification of facilities.

The Commission's jurisdiction has frequently been questioned, but it has been given broad scope by the courts. In 1942 the Supreme Court held that an order requiring an intrastate subsidiary of an interstate pipeline to make an extension was properly to be issued, not by a state commission, but by the FPC.[17] In 1945 it held that the exemption from control of production and gathering did not prevent the Commission from including the value of producing and gathering facilities in the rate base when fixing the transportation charges of integrated companies.[18] In 1950 it upheld the right of the Commission, at the request of the city of Cleveland, to ascertain the cost of transporting gas from the southern border of Ohio through the pipes of the East Ohio Gas Co., a large distributor, and incidentally to determine the value of the company's facilities, though they were all confined within the state.[19] And in the Phillips case in 1954, the Court found it to be the Commission's duty to fix the price that pipelines pay independent producers for their gas, holding that exemption of the functions of production and gathering did not involve exemption of subsequent sales.[20] Interpretation has thus carried the Commission's jurisdiction forward to cover the distribution of gas and backward to cover its production. But part of what the Court has given, the Congress has taken away.

In the East Ohio case, the ownership of a long-distance high-pressure pipeline was divided at the border of the state, East Ohio operating the last 650 miles. This stretch was regulated by the Ohio state commission, it valuation being computed, in accordance with Ohio law, on the basis of reproduction cost. When the city of Cleveland asked the FPC to find the cost of transporting gas from the state line, its valuation was $35 million lower, being based on original cost. Adoption of the lower figure would have reduced the price the company could charge consumers in Cleveland for their gas. The utility interests, with the support of the state

[17] *Illinois Natural Gas Co.* v. *Central Illinois Public Service Co.*, 314 U.S. 498.

[18] *Colorado Interstate Gas Co.* v. *FPC*, and *Canadian River Gas Co.* v. *FPC*, 324 U.S. 581.

[19] *FPC* v. *East Ohio Gas Co.*, 338 U.S. 464.

[20] *Phillips Petroleum Co.* v. *Wisconsin*, *Texas* v. *Wisconsin*, and *FPC* v. *Wisconsin*, Supreme Court of U.S., October Term, 1953, Nos. 280, 281, 418, June 7, 1954.

utility commissioners, therefore undertook in 1952 to have the Natural Gas Act amended to deny the FPC any jurisdiction over pipelines that are wholly intrastate. The bill failed of passage in that year, but it was enacted and signed by President Eisenhower in 1954. As a result, consumers in Ohio and elsewhere were deprived of the Commission's aid in determining the cost of gas, and separation of ownership at state lines was offered other pipeline companies as an approved method of evading the federal law.[21]

Fixing the Price of Gas

It is in the regulation of pipelines that the FPC has done its most important work. And it is here that it has been most violently attacked. The Commission has made substantial reductions in pipeline rates. In doing so, it has adhered to the principle of making valuations at original cost. It was the Commission's defense of this principle that led to the decision of the Supreme Court in the Hope Natural Gas Co. case in 1944, repudiating the fair value doctrine of *Smyth* v. *Ames* and breaking its hold on the regulation of gas and other utilities. To determine the rates charged for transporting gas, moreover, the Commission has had to start with the price of gas at the city gate, and then subtract from it the cost incurred or the price paid in obtaining gas in the field. It has thus not only become involved in regulating the transportation of gas but also in fixing the price of gas itself. And this has stirred up a hornet's nest of politics.

Where an integrated company produces the gas it transports, the FPC subtracts the value of the gas in determining the transportation charge. Here, the issue that arises is how this value is to be fixed. There are two alternatives: one is to use the price that is paid to independent producers; the other is to use the production costs of the integrated companies. The first alternative has serious disadvantages. As the price of gas goes up, it permits the pipeline companies to realize an unearned increment in the value of their producing properties. And, now or later, this price may not be set in a free market but determined by the companies themselves. Originally, therefore, the Commission adopted the second alternative, computing the cost of producing gas by taking the companies' operating expenses and adding a return of 6 per cent on their producing properties, valued on the basis of depreciated original cost. In 1954, however, this policy was reversed in a case brought before the Commission by the Panhandle Eastern Pipeline Co. Gas produced and transported by the pipeline companies is now valued at the price they pay to independents.

Another issue, long bitterly contested, relates to the Commission's power to regulate this price. The extent to which production had really been exempted by the law was called into question, after 1945, by the decisions of the courts. The Commission therefore considered whether it should attempt to fix the producer's price. Some of its members opposed such action; others—among them, Chairman Leland Olds—tended to

[21] See *Congressional Record,* July 2, 1952, pp. 9153–56; July 5, 1952, pp. 9611–13.

favor it. In 1949, when Olds was nominated for another term by President Truman, he was attacked by the oil and gas interests, being charged with subversive sentiments, and the nomination was turned down. In 1950 a bill explicitly denying the FPC authority to fix the price of gas was introduced in Congress by Senator Kerr, an Oklahoma oil man. The bill was supported by influential Democrats from the producing regions of the Southwest, opposed by Senator Douglas of Illinois and others from the consuming areas of the North and East. When enacted, it was vetoed by President Truman, and the veto was sustained. The President thereupon appointed his friend, Mon Wallgren, to the chairmanship of the Commission. And in 1951, under Wallgren's leadership, the Commission decided, in the Phillips case, that it lacked the power to fix the price of gas. In effect, the purpose of the Kerr Bill was achieved and that of the President's veto was reversed.

The Phillips Petroleum Company was the largest of the independent producers of gas. The company had raised its price and had been brought before the FPC upon complaint by the state of Wisconsin and the municipalities of Milwaukee, Kansas City, and Detroit. These plaintiffs now appealed. And in June 1954, in a five to three decision, the Supreme Court held that Phillips was a natural gas concern within the meaning of the Natural Gas Act and that the Commission should therefore determine whether its prices were just and reasonable.[22] Thus, for the first time in history, the Court directed a regulatory agency to increase the scope of its activities. And the FPC was faced with the unwelcome task of fixing the prices charged by thousands of independent producers of gas. In July, 1954, the Commission issued an order freezing the wellhead price of natural gas sold for interstate transmission, requiring producers to apply for certificates and to file their prices, and asserting its power to control future increases.

This development is certain to be fought. Renewed efforts to exempt producers' prices from the Natural Gas Act are likely to be made, this time with greater success. An FPC request for $300,000 to enable it to administer its new controls was smothered in the Appropriations Committee of the Senate in 1954. Producing interests are turning also to the state legislatures, seeking laws that will permit the establishment of minimum prices for gas. Such legislation has already been enacted in Kansas and Oklahoma and is under consideration in Texas. In accordance with its decision in the Panhandle case, moreover, the FPC will recognize these prices, once they are fixed. But support for minimum prices is not unanimous. Industries and utilities buying gas oppose them. The pipeline companies fear that they may be caught in a squeeze as the states raise the price at which they buy and the FPC forbids or postpones increases in the price at which they sell. And the big oil companies see in minimum

[22] *Phillips Petroleum Co.* v. *Wisconsin, loc. cit.*

price fixing an entering wedge for more extensive regulation. The outcome, here, remains in doubt.

The Problem of Conservation

Gas is limited in quantity, exhaustible, and irreplaceable. It should therefore be used with economy. Today, however, consumption is increasing and much of the supply is directed into inferior uses where coal would suffice. Gas is employed, for example, as a raw material and as a fuel for industry when it might better be saved for residential purposes. The FPC can do little to correct this situation. It has not been given power to control the use of gas directly. But it can exert its influence indirectly through its power over price. Thus, by permitting producers and pipeline companies to charge high prices, at the expense of the consumer, it could slow down the rate of consumption and curtail less essential uses. It is often in the name of conservation, therefore, that the industry argues for policies that would make its prices—and its profits—high. Such arguments are plausible but misleading. If gas needs to be economized, this can be done without exploiting the consumer or giving unearned profits to the gas companies. The purpose can be served better by taxing or by directly controlling the rate and the kinds of use.

Involved in the problem of conservation, there are also conflicts of interest between regions. The urban areas of the North and East want large quantities of cheap gas. The producing states of the Southwest would prefer to keep the gas at home to provide a foundation for greater industrial development. The interest of the first group can be served by making pipeline rates low; that of the second by making them high. The FPC, of course, has been given no mandate to govern the allocation of resources among different regions in the United States. But regional interests may none the less attempt to influence its policies.

FEDERAL CONTROL OF HOLDING COMPANIES

Utility companies were first established on a small scale in local markets. In time these companies came to be combined in larger units. And eventually numbers of them were brought together, through ownership of stock, by holding companies. Some of these concerns performed no management function, serving merely to diversify investment risks. Others, however, provided their operating subsidiaries with a great variety of managerial services. Some of them controlled operating companies located in contiguous territories, where services could be co-ordinated through interconnections of facilities. But others exercised control over widely scattered properties, where unification of services was not a possibility. There were not only holding companies controlling operating companies, but also superholding companies controlling holding companies. And, in some cases, the holding company structures were several stories high. This development had its most rapid growth in the years that followed World War I. By 1932 sixteen top holding companies controlled more than three fourths of the electricity produced in the United States.

The combination of operating companies frequently has advantages. Where physical integration is possible, the combined markets may be served with a smaller investment in facilities; costs may be reduced by operating on a larger scale, and by improving capacity, load, and diversity factors; savings may be realized through economies in using fuel and labor, and by standardizing and exchanging equipment and supplies. Where properties are scattered, too, a larger enterprise may find it easier to sell securities and to borrow money from the banks. A holding company, moreover, may operate on a scale that enables it to employ experts in many fields of management that smaller operating companies could not afford. And it may provide its subsidiaries with skilled supervision, technical advice, and a great variety of managerial services. But the growth of holding companies cannot be explained on these grounds alone. There were profits to be obtained in their promotion and operation. There were personal fortunes to be built. And this had little or nothing to do with the enhancement of efficiency.

Holding Company Abuses

An outstanding characteristic of the holding company structure was pyramiding: of control, of profits, and of losses. Let us see, first, how this structure facilitated the pyramiding of control.

1. Assume that there are 64 operating companies, each capitalized at $4,000,000, divided as follows: $2,000,000 in 4 per cent bonds, $1,000,000 in 5 per cent preferred stock, and $1,000,000 in common. The total investment in these properties is $256,000,000. Each operating company can be controlled with half of its common, requiring an investment of $500,000. All 64 can be controlled with $32,000,000. This is ⅛ of the total investment.
2. Now divide the 64 operating companies into 16 groups of four each. Over each group set up a Father Holding Company. Each Father controls each of its operating companies with $500,000; all four with $2,000,000. It is capitalized at $2,000,000; of this, $1,000,000 is in 5 per cent preferred and $1,000,000 in common. Each Father company can thus be controlled with $500,000. All 16 can be controlled with $8,000,000. The controlling share is 1/32 of the total investment.
3. Now divide the 16 Father companies into four groups of four each. Over each group set up a Grandfather Holding Company. Each Grandfather controls each of its Father companies with $500,000, all four with $2,000,000. Half of its capitalization of $2,000,000 is in 5 per cent preferred and half in common. Each Grandfather can thus be controlled with $500,000; all four of them with $2,000,000. This is 1/128 of the total investment.
4. Now set up a Great-Grandfather Holding Company to control the four

Grandfather companies. It does so with an investment of $2,000,000. Its capitalization of $2,000,000 is half in 5 per cent preferred and half in common. It can be controlled with $500,000. This is 1/512 of the total investment.

5. Finally, set up a Great-Great-Grandfather Holding Company. Capitalize it at $500,000. Sell half of it in 5 per cent preferred. The half that remains is 1/1,024 of the total investment. The investing public puts up $255,750,000. John Dough puts up $250,000 and runs the show.

If anything, this illustration understates the case. A larger part of the total capitalization could be in nonvoting securities. Control could be obtained with less than half the common. The money needed to buy the stock of one company could be borrowed, putting up the stock of another as security. The number of holding companies between the controlling interest and the operating properties could be multiplied indefinitely. In the Associated Gas and Electric structure there were twelve layers. In the Insull empire, one of the operating companies was controlled, at the top, by an investment of one two-hundredths of one per cent.

It is easy to see how such a structure pyramided profits. To return to our illustration:

1. Assume that the 64 operating companies are allowed a return of 6 per cent. On $256,000,000, this gives them $15,360,000. Of this amount, 4 per cent must be paid on $128,000,000 in bonds, or $5,120,000. Then 5 per cent must be paid on $64,000,000 of preferred, or $3,200,000. This leaves $7,040,000 to be distributed as dividends on $64,000,000 of common, a return of 11 per cent.
2. Half of this, or $3,520,000 goes to the 16 Father companies. They pay 5 per cent on $16,000,000 of preferred, or $800,000. This leaves them $2,720,000 to distribute on $16,000,000 of common, a return of 17 per cent.
3. Half of this, or $1,360,000 goes to the four Grandfather companies. They pay 5 per cent on $4,000,000 of preferred, or $200,000. This leaves them $1,160,000 for $4,000,000 of common, a return of 29 per cent.
4. Half of this, or $580,000 goes to the Great-Grandfather Company. This company pays 5 per cent on $1,000,000 of preferred, or $50,000. This leaves it $530,000 for $1,000,000 of common, a return of 53 per cent.
5. Half of this, or $265,000, goes to the Great-Great-Grandfather Company. It pays 5 per cent on its $250,000 of preferred, or $12,500. It has $252,500 left for John Dough. On his investment of $250,000, he makes more than 100 per cent.

This may explain why the control of a holding company structure was regarded as a prize. But pyramiding also had its risks. Let us assume that a mild recession brings a moderate reduction in the revenues of the operating companies. They still cover all of their expenses. But instead of earning 6 per cent on their investment, they earn only 4 per cent. What happens?

THE INSULL UTILITY HOLDING COMPANY SYSTEM, 1932

INSULL-HALSEY STUART INTERESTS
Insull Family
Corp. Sec. Co. of Chi. Voting Trust
Officers and directors of
Corporation Securities Co. of Chicago
and
Insull Utility Investments, Inc.

46.9%(1)
15.2%(1)
25.7%
11.5%
0.3%
25%
75%
100%

Corp. Securities Co. of Chi.

Insull Utility Investments

Corporation Syndicate Inc.

100%

Second Utilities Syndicate

Public Service Trust

100%

Insull Son & Co.

100%
100%
25%

Insull Son & Co. of Canada

Insull Son & Co. Ltd.

Natural Gas Co. of America

2.1%(2)
9.3%(2)
4.3%(2)
12.4%(2)
5.2%(2)
23%(2)
10.6%(2)
12.6%(2)

Public Service Co. of No. Ill.

Commonwealth Edison Co.

Peoples Gas Light & Coke Co.

Middle West Utilities Co.

P.S. Subsidiary Corp.
(Owning investments in-)
Peabody Coal Co.
Chi. No. Sh. & Mil. RR
Chi. Aur. & Elg. Corp.
P.S. Co. of No. Ill.
Chi. Dist. El. Gen. Corp.
Super-Power Co. of Ill.
Ill. Lt. & P. Co.
Real Estate and misc.
Western United Corp.
Midland United Co.
No. Am. Lt. & P. Co.
McHenry Co. Lt. & P. Co.
Calumet City P. S. Co.
Utils. Service Co.

Waukegan Generating Co.

Commonw. Subdy. Corp.
(Owning investments in-)
Ill. No. Utils. Co.
Western United Corp.
P. S. Co. of No. Ill.
Midland United Co.
Chi. Dist. El. Gen. Corp.
Super-Power Co. of Ill.
Peabody Coal Co.
Ill. Mid. Ry. Co. (100%)
Chi. Rapid Tr. Co.
Chi. No. Sh. & Mil. RR
Chi. Aur. & Elg. Corp.
Commonw. Edison Co.
Utility Securities Co.
Real estate, ind. & misc.

Chi. Rapid Tr. Co.
Leases Chi. Jc. RR Co.
Ill. No. Utils. Co.

Chi. Dist. P. Line Co.
Utils. Oil & Ref. Co.
Ogden G. Co. (leased under cont. to pur.)
Peoples G. By-P. Corp.
Ind. Nat. G. & O. Co.

Mich. & Adams S.D.Vlts. Inc.
Peoples G. Stores Co. Inc.
Peoples G. Subdy. Corp.
Nat. G. Inv. Co.
Texoma Nat. G. Co.

Central Illinois P. S. Co.
Chi. Joliet El. Ry. Co.
Dellwood Park Co.
Chi. & Joliet Transp. Co.
Southern Ill. Ry. & P. Co.

The Kentucky Securities Corp.
Lexington Ice Co., Inc.
Kentucky Coach Co.
Consolidated Coach Corp.
Blue Grass Park Co.
Lexington Utilities Co.
Kentucky Tract. & Term. Co.

Miss. Valley Utils. Inv. Co.
owns investments in--
American Central Utils. Co.
American P. S. Co.
Central & Southwest Utils. Co.
Commonwealth Edison Co.
Corp. Secur's. Co. of Chicago
Insull Utils. Investments, Inc.
Midland United Co.
National P. S. Corp.
New England Industries, Inc.
North American Lt. & P. Co.
Peabody Coal Co.
Southern Nebraska P. Co.
Southwestern Gas & El. Co.
Southwestern Lt. & P. Co.

Western United Corp.
Jointly contr. by
P. S. Co. of No. Ill.
and C. E. Co.
Aur. Elg. & Fox R. El. Co.
Western Un. G. & El. Co.

Peabody Coal Co.
Controlled through voting trust by
Commonwealth Ed. Co.
Peoples G.Lt. & Coke Co.
P. S. Co. of No. Ill.
Middle W. Utils. Co.

Super-Power Co. of Ill.
(Jointly controlled by
C. E. Co. 30%
P.S.Co. of No. Ill. 25%
C. I. P. S. Co. 25%
N. A. L. & P. Co. 20%)

Chi. Dist. Gen. Co.
(Jointly controlled by
C. E. Co. 40%
P.S.Co. of No. Ill. 30%
No. Ind. P. S. Co. 20%
P. S. Co. of Ind. 10%)

National Electric Power Co.

National Public Service Corp.
Electric Mgt. & Eng. Corp.

New England P. S. Co.

84 William St. Corp.
Jersey Central P. & Lt. Co.
Lakewood Water Co.

Central Vt. P. S. Corp.
Lyman Falls Power Co.
Bucksport Water Co.
Salmon Falls Water Co.
Grovetch El. Lt. Co.
Swans Falls Co.
P. S. Co. of New Hamp.
Manchester Street Ry.

Northwest Utilities Co.
Lake Superior Dist. P. Co.
Northwestern P. S. Co.
Wisconsin P. & Lt. Co.
Mauston El. S. Co.
So. Beloit W. Gas & El. Co.

Kentucky Utilities Co.
Old Dominion P. Co.
Old Dominion Ice Corp.

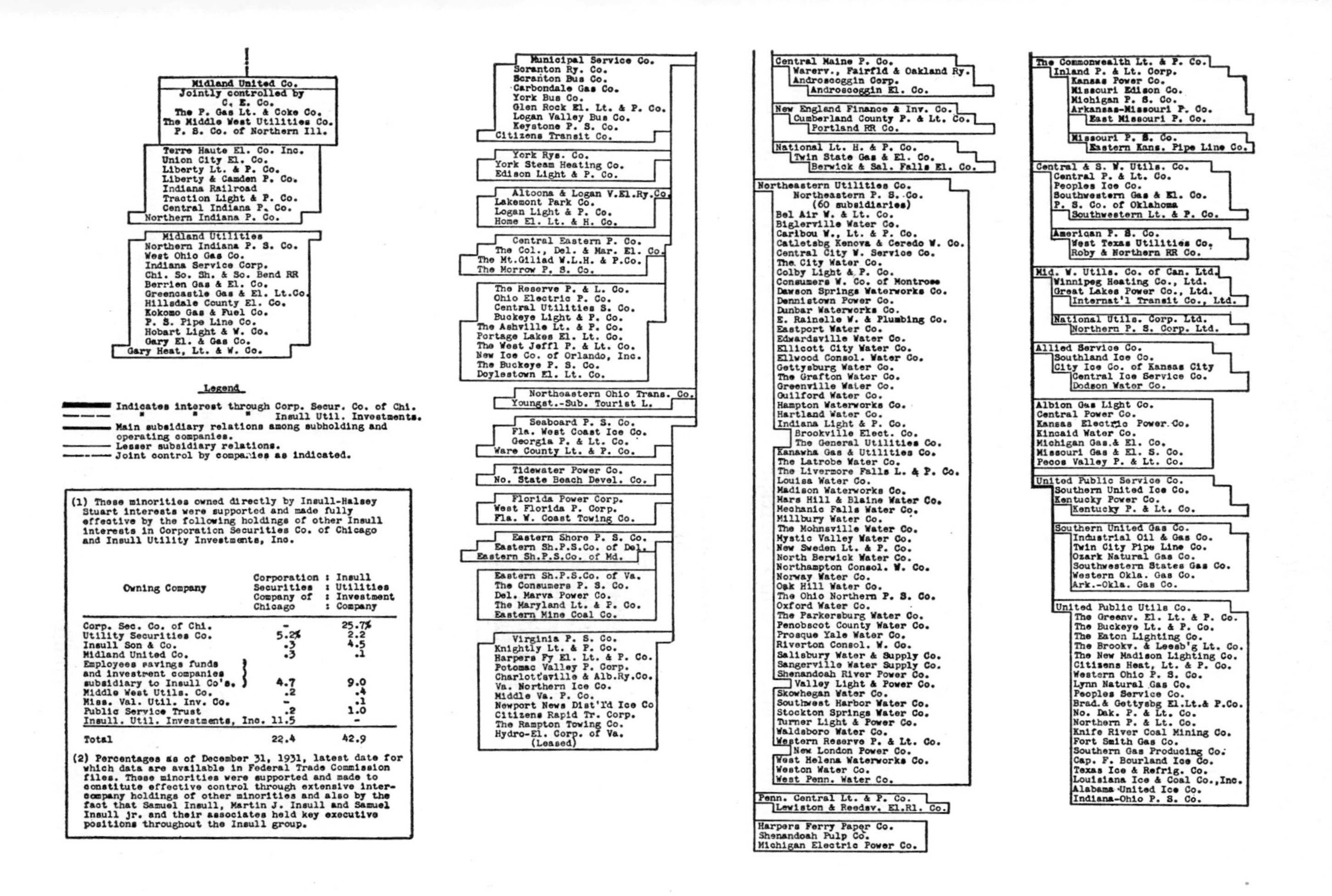

(1) These minorities owned directly by Insull-Halsey Stuart interests were supported and made fully effective by the following holdings of other Insull interests in Corporation Securities Co. of Chicago and Insull Utility Investments, Inc.

Owning Company	Corporation Securities Company of Chicago	Insull Utilities Investment Company
Corp. Sec. Co. of Chi.	-	25.7%
Utility Securities Co.	5.2%	2.2
Insull Son & Co.	.3	4.5
Midland United Co.	.3	.1
Employees savings funds and investment companies subsidiary to Insull Co's.	4.7	9.0
Middle West Utils. Co.	.2	.4
Miss. Val. Util. Inv. Co.	-	.1
Public Service Trust	.2	1.0
Insull. Util. Investments, Inc.	11.5	-
Total	22.4	42.9

(2) Percentages as of December 31, 1931, latest date for which data are available in Federal Trade Commission files. These minorities were supported and made to constitute effective control through extensive inter-company holdings of other minorities and also by the fact that Samuel Insull, Martin J. Insull and Samuel Insull jr. and their associates held key executive positions throughout the Insull group.

1. The 64 companies get $10,240,000. They pay $5,120,000 on their bonds, and $3,200,000 on their preferred. They have $1,920,000 left for their common, a return of 3 per cent.
2. Half of this, or $960,000 goes to the Father companies. They pay $800,000 on their preferred. They have $160,000 for $16,000,000 of common, a return of 1 per cent.
3. Half of this, or $80,000 goes to the Grandfather companies. They cannot meet the dividends on their preferred, let alone their common.
4. The income of the Great-Grandfather company and that of the Great-Great-Grandfather company is zero. They pay no dividends. They cannot even pay their bills. The companies go bankrupt. The house of cards comes tumbling down.

The holding company operators thus did something that would have seemed to be impossible: they took control of an industry that was guaranteed a legal monopoly of a necessary service and turned it into a highly speculative enterprise. From the soundest investment in the market, they converted utility shares, at the upper levels, into counters in a game of chance.

In this situation, there was an insistent drive for dividends. These could be obtained, in one way, through higher rates. Every dollar by which rates were changed was reflected in the dividends of the upper holding companies. These companies, therefore, were vigorous in resisting rate reductions and ingenious in finding ways by which rates could be increased. To this end, they padded the valuations of the operating companies, by making excessive charges for construction services, by causing properties to be sold back and forth at rising prices, by failing to make deductions for depreciation, and by writing up the value of the assets on the books. Dividends could be obtained, too, by reducing charges against income. And here, the holding companies indulged in fair-weather finance, neglecting to maintain their operating properties, failing to set aside reserves for depreciation, and building up fictitious surpluses. Dividends were thus paid out of capital, and the strength of the underlying enterprises was impaired.

The holding companies made money not only by collecting dividends but also through intercompany transactions. They borrowed money from the operating companies and loaned money to them. They handled the sale of their securities. They sold them equipment and supplies. They set up subsidiaries to provide them with engineering and managerial services. The prices paid in these transactions did not result from arm's-length bargaining. The officers of the operating companies depended on the officers of the holding companies for their jobs. If they were asked to pay excessive prices, they did not complain. They did as they were told. In this way, holding company profits were hidden in operating company costs. And they were covered, of necessity, by the state commissions in setting the level of rates.

The Holding Company Act

Until 1930 the state commissions, in computing operating company expenses, were denied the right to disallow payments made to holding companies unless they could show them to be fraudulent. In that year the Supreme Court held, in the Smith Case,[23] that the commissions could look into the cost to the holding companies of the goods and services that they supplied, thus shifting to them the burden of proof. Thereafter, more than half of the states gave their commissions some power over holding company activities. Intrastate holding companies were brought under control. But the larger holding company systems were beyond the reach of the individual states.

In 1928 the Federal Trade Commission had been directed by Congress to investigate electric and gas utilities. In 1935 it published its final report, summarizing more than seventy volumes of hearings and exhibits. Many holding company abuses were thus brought into glaring light. At the same time the largest holding company systems—Associated Gas and Electric, Insull, and Foshay in Minneapolis—had come down in ruins, scores of others were bankrupt, in receivership, or in default, and hundreds of thousands of investors had seen their savings disappear. The country was ripe for reform.

The Public Utility Act of 1935 had two parts. Title II was the law, discussed above, giving jurisdiction over interstate transmission of electricity to the FPC. Title I was the Public Utility Holding Company Act. This was the most stringent corrective measure ever applied to American business. It went beyond any other in requiring the reorganization of corporate structures and in forcing divestment of property. It made the Securities and Exchange Commission a potent regulator of electric and gas holding companies. Wherever abuses had been disclosed, it provided powers of control.

The Act defined a holding company as one holding 10 per cent or more of the voting stock of another holding company or an operating company or having a "controlling influence over the management or policies" of such companies. It exempted those that were entirely intrastate or were predominantly operating companies with contiguous properties. The companies covered were required to register with the SEC and to file a statement showing all of the significant details of their structure and operations. The other provisions of the law fall into five categories. (1) The most severe provision was that of Section 11 (*b*) (2), generally known as the "death sentence," which provided for the elimination of the third and upper layers in the holding company structures, permitting Father and Grandfather companies, but forbidding Great-Grandfathers, Great-Great-Grandfathers, and remoter generations in the sequence of control. (2) Section 11 also empowered the SEC to effect the simplification of the

[23] *Smith* v. *Illinois Bell Telephone Co.*, 282 U.S. 133.

remaining holding company structures through financial reorganization. The law then provided for the regulation of the reorganized concerns, authorizing the SEC to control (3) the operations of holding companies, (4) the dealings of their officers and directors, and (5) their relations with their subsidiaries.

To effect reorganizations, the companies were invited to prepare and submit their own plans. The Commission was then to hold hearings, approve or reject the proposals, or order them modified. In the absence of company initiative, it could prepare the plans itself. To force their adoption, it was required to obtain an order from a court. The Commission was instructed to confine each holding company organization to a single system of integrated operating companies and other businesses economically necessary or reasonably incidental thereto. It was authorized, however, to permit a holding company to control more than one system if (1) such control was needed to preserve substantial economies, (2) the systems were contiguous, being located on both sides of state or national borders, and (3) the resulting structure would not be so large as to impair local management, efficient operation, and effective regulation. In reorganizing corporations, the Commission was directed to do away with complications in their capital structure and to eliminate inequities in the distribution of voting power.

The regulatory powers conferred upon the SEC were extensive. Holding companies were required to follow methods of accounting prescribed by the Commission. They were required to obtain the Commission's approval before buying or selling assets or floating securities. They were forbidden to contribute to campaign funds or to engage in hidden lobbying activities. Their officers and directors were required to file their stockholdings and to make reports on changes. Profits realized on their dealings were made recoverable at law. Bankers were denied directorates unless such appointments were approved by the SEC. Holding companies were forbidden to borrow money from operating companies; their loans to these companies were subjected to control. Holding companies were forbidden, too, to perform various services for operating companies. For this purpose, mutual service companies, subordinate to the operating companies, were to be formed. All intercorporate contracts within a holding company system were brought under Commission control. And the Commission was further authorized to protect the operating companies against exploitation by controlling the declaration of dividends.

Holding Companies under the SEC

The constitutionality of the Holding Company Act was promptly challenged. The Electric Bond and Share Company refused to register, the SEC brought suit to compel it to do so, and the registration requirement was upheld by the Supreme Court.[24] The North American Company resisted reorganization, arguing that the disintegration provisions of the Act

[24] *Electric Bond & Share Co.* v. *SEC*, 303 U.S. 419 (1938).

exceeded the powers conferred on Congress under the commerce clause and violated the Fifth Amendment by depriving the company of property without due process of law. This argument was rejected by the Court.[25] The American Power and Light Company then contested the simplification of its corporate structure, advancing the previous arguments and also contending that the law involved an unconstitutional delegation of legislative power. Again, the Court did not agree.[26] The SEC thus found itself on solid ground.

The Commission approached its task with caution. It was not until 1940 that voluntary disintegration plans were submitted and formal proceedings begun. By 1951 the Commission had undertaken the reformation of corporate structures including more than 200 holding companies and nearly 2,000 other companies. In 1952 it reported that 85 per cent of the job was done.[27] In the upper levels some holding companies had reduced their holdings of operating company voting stocks to less than 10 per cent, becoming investment companies. Others had merged with their subsidiaries. Still others had distributed their holdings to their stockholders or had sold them in the market and distributed cash, thus liquidating their affairs. Here, the duty of the SEC was plain: the upper levels had to go. Elsewhere, however, its task was more difficult.

Where were holding company systems to be dissolved and where allowed to stand? The Commission was strict in its enforcement of the principle of integration. It favored a compact system, confined to a single area, its facilities interconnected or capable of interconnection, its operations co-ordinated, and its management unified. It opposed the common control of electricity and gas, and the operation of companies providing other services, unless they could be shown to bear a functional relationship to the provision of electricity or gas. In permitting a holding company to control more than one utility system, it required that all three of the conditions laid down in the law be satisfied: (1) such control must be needed to preserve substantial economies *and* (2) the systems must be contiguous, *and* (3) they must be small enough to permit local management, efficient operation, and effective regulation. In this way the many-tiered holding company systems with widely scattered properties were eliminated and the simpler, closely-integrated systems were preserved. In the main, local utilities were restored to local managements. There are about twenty regional holding company systems remaining under Commission control.

The method by which divestment was to be effected had not been specified by law. Here initiative was left to the companies. Some holding companies sold their properties to other holding companies, to independent operators, or to local governments. Some sold their security holdings

[25] *North American Co.* v. *SEC*, 327 U.S. 686 (1946).

[26] *American Power & Light Co.* v. *SEC*, 329 U.S. 90 (1946).

[27] *Report of the SEC to the Subcommittee on Monopoly of the Select Committee on Small Business, U.S. Senate*, 83d Cong., 2d Sess., Subcommittee Print No. 4, 1952.

on the market. Some divided them among the owners of their shares. Whatever the method, it was supervised by the SEC, strict watch being kept on the expenses incurred, the fees collected, and the prices paid.

Along with the simplification of holding company systems went reorganization of the capital structures of individual companies. Here, the Commission scaled down overcapitalization, eliminating write-ups, required competitive bidding for new securities, and strengthened depreciation reserves. It retired excessive debt and insisted on a substantial equity in common stock. It ordered inclusion in bond indentures of provisions to protect the holders of the bonds. And it sought to protect the rights of stockholders by insuring an equitable distribution of voting power. The reorganizations brought about by the SEC were not effected at the expense of the investor. Indeed, corporate finances were strengthened and the market value of utility shares was raised.

This sweeping reorganization of the electric and gas utility industries was a significant accomplishment. It did not in itself make the regulation of rates and services effective. But it removed a major obstacle to control. More than this, it showed that the problems encountered in dissolving corporate combinations are not insoluble, and thus provided a lesson for the critics of the Sherman Act.

Control of Intercorporate Transactions

Most state commissions now have authority over contracts between operating companies and other companies in holding company systems. In some states such contracts must have commission approval before they become effective. In others, they must be filed and may be disapproved. In general, the commissions pass judgment on the character of the services that are to be rendered and the charges that are to be made. They do not permit such charges to be fixed as a percentage of operating revenues but limit them to figures that do no more than cover the costs incurred and provide a reasonable return on the capital employed by companies rendering intercompany services. The expenditures and earnings of such companies, moreover, are subject to regulation by the SEC. Control of service charges, however, is less than rigorous. Intercompany contracts are presumed to be reasonable, and the commission that would hold them to be otherwise must bear the burden of proof. Control by the states, in most cases, is indirect, charges being influenced only by disallowing excessive amounts as expenses to be covered in fixing the level of operating company rates. Control by the SEC, in practice, does not go far beyond the requirement of periodic reports.

FEDERAL CONTROL OF COMMUNICATIONS

In 1910, under the Mann-Elkins Act, the rates of companies providing interstate and foreign telephone, telegraph, and cable services were subjected to regulation by the Interstate Commerce Commission. This body was concerned primarily with railroads and took little interest in the communications industries, acting only in response to complaints. In a quarter of a century only fourteen cases were brought before it, ten of them dealing with telegraph and cable services and only four with telephones. In 1927 regulation of radio broadcasting was entrusted to a Federal Radio Commission. The broadcasting companies, however, did not have the status of common carriers and the Commission was not empowered to control their rates. In 1934 these functions were brought together under the Federal Communications Commission, a new bipartisan agency with seven members serving seven-year terms, set up under the Federal Communications Act. The Commission's major attention, since its establishment, has been devoted to radio and television. Its activities in this area will be described in Chapter 23. It is only with the Commission's work in regulating common carriers that we are here concerned.

In this field the usual pattern of control applies. Rates must be just and reasonable, must be published and observed, and notice given prior to a change. The FCC can suspend proposed changes, upon complaint or at its own initiative, and can prescribe maxima and minima. There may be no unjust discrimination in rates or services. Certificates must be obtained for entry, and the FCC may require extensions, interconnections, and through rates, and determine the division of such rates between participating companies. Accounts are subject to control, appropriate methods of valuation may be employed, and means of providing for depreciation may be prescribed. The Commission has jurisdiction over combinations and may prohibit interlocking directorates. It has no authority, however, over security sales or corporate reorganizations, and no control over intercompany contracts or the declaration of dividends.

The Telephone Holding Company

Almost all of the telephone business in the United States is in the hands of one concern: the American Telephone and Telegraph Company. This enterprise is an outgrowth of a series of companies that were set up after 1875 to exploit the telephone patents of Alexander Graham Bell. At that time the Western Union Telegraph Company was also providing telephone service, using the patents of Elisha Gray. The Bell interests brought suit for infringement and the two groups came to an agreement under which they divided the field, Bell taking the telephone and Western Union the telegraph. Bell then proceeded to obtain control of local telephone companies, through patent licenses and purchases, acquired the Western Electric Company, the leading manufacturer of telephonic equipment, and set up A.T.&T. to develop long-distance services. In 1893 and 1894 the basic patents expired, and a number of independent companies entered the field. In the meantime, however, Bell had fortified its position by obtaining patents on particular aspects of the art. Now, it declared war on its rivals, instituting hundreds of infringement suits, refusing to supply equipment or to provide long-distance service, and undercutting rates. Through a reorganization effected in 1899, A.T.&T. emerged as the parent company. Within ten years its dominance of the telephone business was assured. In 1909 the company sought also to take over the telegraph business by acquiring a controlling interest in Western Union. But the Department of Justice objected, and in 1913 the company relinquished its control. At the same time it agreed to provide long-distance service to independent local companies. In 1920 Congress acted to permit further acquisitions of telephone properties, with the approval of the ICC. Thereafter, the telephone monopoly became well nigh complete.

In 1939 A.T.&T. owned 93 per cent of the voting stock in 21 associated telephone companies, whose operations covered the entire area of the United States. Directly, or through its subsidiaries, it controlled more than half of the voting stock in 181 concerns. From its office in New York the company controlled between 80 and 90 per cent of the nation's local telephone service and 98 per cent of its long-distance lines. Through its manufacturing subsidiary, Western Electric, it accounted for 90 per cent of the nation's output of telephonic equipment. The president of A.T.&T. was empowered to vote its stock in the operating companies and to select the directors and officers of these concerns. The parent company was thus in direct and complete control of the entire telephone system.[28]

A.T.&T. is now the biggest corporation in the country and probably in the world. Its business operations are greater in magnitude than those of many cities and states. In 1952 the company had more than a million stockholders and around three quarters of a million employees. It provided local service, through its subsidiaries, to 40 million telephones, and long-distance service, through its own operations, to 48 million. Its assets were close to $13 billion, its gross income $4 billion, its net income $400 million.

The company receives its income, in the main, from dividends paid it by the associated telephone companies, from charges it makes for the services it renders them, from the earnings of its long-distance lines, and from the profits of Western Electric. This income is derived ultimately from the rates paid by subscribers to telephone service. The corporate structure of the telephone system is much simpler than that of the other utility holding company systems described above. But the relation of the parent company to its subsidiaries is much the same. And A.T.&T. has the same ability as other holding companies to render regulation ineffective by determining their policies.

[28] Federal Communications Commission, *Investigation of the Telephone Industry in the United States*, 76th Cong., 1st Sess., House Doc. 340 (1939), pp. xxiii–xxv, 21, 24, 65, 103–22.

The Telephone Investigation

In 1935 the FCC was directed by Congress to investigate the telephone industry. The inquiry was extensive: the basic record included 8,500 pages of testimony, 2,000 exhibits, and 77 staff reports. The Commission's final report was published in 1939. It disclosed no such financial scandals as those found by the FTC in the electrical industry. But it did give evidence that A.T.&T. had taken advantage of its opportunity to increase its profits, at the expense of the consumer, by padding the operating expenses and the property valuations of the associated companies. With telephones, as with electricity, regulation by state commissions had thus been robbed of its effect.

The Commission found that the parent company, in prescribing methods of accounting, had required its subsidiaries to include in operating expenses depreciation charges known to be in excess of actual requirements but had forbidden them to deduct more than a part of depreciation reserves in arriving at the valuation of their properties. Annual charges for depreciation had not been reduced by an amount sufficient to compensate for the increasing length of life of the telephone plant. These charges were close to a fifth of the expenses involved in operating the system and thus significantly affected the consumer's bill. Reserves, built up out of such charges, represented more than 25 per cent of the investment in the telephone plant. But only "observable" depreciation was deducted in determining the rate base, and the depreciation "observed" amounted to only 5–10 per cent, instead of 25 per cent, of property values. To the extent to which reserves, accumulated from rates paid by subscribers, were not deducted from the base upon which further rate payments were computed, the subscribers were compelled to pay the companies a return on money which they themselves had contributed.[29]

The fee that A.T.&T. collected for the services it rendered the associated companies, then set at 1½ per cent of their gross income, included many items that were not properly allocable to such services. The company required its subsidiaries to support the research and patenting activities of the Bell Laboratories through which it not only developed improvements in the art of telephony, but also obtained patents which were designed to preserve its monopoly in the telephone business and in the manufacture of equipment, and to enable it to extend its operations into industries outside the field of telephonic communication. The new patents, though largely financed by the associated companies, belonged to A.T.&T. The company licensed firms outside the system to use them, collected royalties, and retained the resulting income, refunding nothing to the subsidiaries whose contributions had paid for the research. Not only this; A.T.&T. charged the associated companies for the use of the very inventions whose development their previous payments had financed and

[29] *Ibid.*, chap. xi.

employed the resulting revenue to develop further inventions for whose use it collected a further fee. The patent policy of the parent company thus affected the costs of its subsidiaries and influenced the rate which the telephone subscriber was required to pay.[30]

A.T.&T. handled the financing of the whole system. It made advances to the associated companies, supplied them with the capital which they required, and charged them for the costs incurred in the process. Year after year, the company collected interest at a fixed rate, neither altering its charge with fluctuations in the rates charged by other lenders nor permitting its subsidiaries to borrow from other sources of supply. In computing its fee for financing the company included the dividend which it paid on its own stock. This dividend was fixed at a rate far in excess of that required to obtain money in the open market. It was a distribution of profit, not a cost of doing business. Its size was attributable, in large measure, to the absence of effective regulation. Its inclusion in the costs of the associated companies was scarcely to be justified.[31]

The facilities employed by A.T.&T. and by its subsidiaries in rendering long-distance service so overlapped that it was impossible to determine either the reasonableness of the tolls charged or the fairness with which the resulting revenues were divided. The FCC came to the conclusion that tolls were either too high or were so divided as to favor unfairly the parent company.[32]

A.T.&T., finally, was found to have established standards and issued instructions which compelled the associated companies to purchase practically all of their apparatus, equipment, and plant materials from Western Electric. Six small independent producers of such supplies, subsisting largely on the business which Western gave them, were in no position really to compete with it. Since Western obtained its orders without competitive bidding, it was not forced to sell at a competitive price. The company's cost accounts did not afford an authentic basis for testing the reasonableness of the prices which it set upon specific products. Its prices, moreover, bore no apparent relation to its own statement of costs. Both costs and prices for many items were above those reported by independent firms. Western Electric profits had never been subject to any sort of public control. From 1882 to 1936 the company realized a net income on cash paid-in capital that exceeded 20 per cent in 41 years, 50 per cent in 25 years, and 100 per cent in six years. The FCC concluded that excessive charges had been made by Western, entering into the operating expenses and property valuations of the associated companies, and thus compelling the state commissions to fix rates that yielded them something more than a fair return.[33]

[30] *Ibid.*, chaps. vi, vii, viii.

[31] *Ibid.*, chap. xv.

[32] *Ibid.*, chap. xii.

[33] *Ibid.*, chaps. x, xviii.

Telephone Regulation

Intrastate telephone rates are subject to regulation by state commissions in nearly all the states; interstate rates to regulation by the FCC. But no agency has the power to regulate the Bell Telephone Laboratories, Western Electric, or A.T&T., to fix their charges, to control their costs, or even to prescribe the form of their accounts. Since the Supreme Court handed down its decision in the Smith case in 1930, the commissions have been permitted to inquire into the nature of the services rendered by these companies, to judge the reasonableness of their charges, and to disallow unreasonable charges as expenses to be covered in fixing rates. In practice, however, none of these agencies is able to obtain the information or to make the findings that would be required. Dealings between the operating companies, on the one hand, and the holding company and its research and manufacturing subsidiaries, on the other, are not controlled.

To make telephone regulation effective, two different approaches have been proposed. The first would disintegrate the holding company system, introducing an element of competition into the determination of operating company costs. This is the approach that was taken by the Antitrust Division of the Department of Justice in 1949 when it filed a complaint under the Sherman Act, asking that Western Electric be divorced from A.T.&T. and split into three separate companies, that A.T.&T. be compelled to grant licenses to other manufacturers under its patents, at reasonable royalties, and that all manufacturers be required to make their sales by competitive bidding.[34] John Bauer, while questioning the antitrust action, proposes that A.T.&T. be required to dispose of its nontelephonic activities and suggests that the public interest would be better served if research and development, as well as manufacturing, were opened to competitive organizations, such as General Electric and Westinghouse.[35] Under the second approach, intercompany transactions in the holding company system would be supervised in the telephone industry as they are in the electric and gas industries. To this end, the FCC recommended only that it be authorized to prescribe the cost accounting methods to be used by manufacturers of telephonic equipment. Bauer would go much farther, extending federal regulation to all sales of goods and services by Western Electric, Bell Laboratories, and A.T.&T., fixing their charges to cover their costs and provide a fair return on the investment in their properties.

Another difficulty in regulating telephone rates is created by the common use of facilities in intrastate and interstate business. Here, the state commissions have followed the lead of A.T.&T. in segregating the two types of operation, making allocations, in accordance with complicated formulas, between the local companies and its own Long Lines. These

[34] *U.S.* v. *Western Electric Co.*, District Court of the U.S. for the District of N.J., Civil Action No. 17–49, *Complaint*, January 14, 1949.

[35] Bauer, *op. cit.*, pp. 335–36.

formulas are necessarily arbitrary in character and the resulting allocations are not independently verified. In practice they are said to have worked to the disadvantage of the local companies. This difficulty could be avoided if the commissions were to abandon the principle of segregation, basing their rates on all the facilities and operations of the local companies. The revenues received from subscribers and the payments made to the Long Lines for interstate messages, at rates controlled by the FCC, could then be covered in the current accounts of the local concerns. In this way, coordination of state and federal regulation could be better attained.[36]

The FCC, despite its preoccupation with radio and television and the limitation of its powers respecting common carriers, has had some influence in controlling the telephone industry. It has aided the state commissions by prescribing accounting systems that require valuation on the basis of original cost and control the methods of providing for depreciation. These requirements were resisted, at first, by the Bell companies but were soon upheld by the Supreme Court.[37] The Commission has also succeeded in persuading A.T.&T. to make a number of reductions in interstate rates and to allocate less of the revenue derived from interstate business to its Long Lines and more to the local companies. But these changes have not been effected through precise determinations of operating costs and returns on investment. They have been brought about by negotiation: A.T.&T. has seen that its rates were high and has agreed to cut them.

Telegraph Regulation

Until 1943 telegraph service in the United States was rendered by two concerns: Western Union and Postal Telegraph. Western Union had four fifths of the business, Postal Telegraph one fifth. The former company had certain advantages. It operated the stock market ticker service. It had contracts giving it exclusive rights to string its wires along railroad tracks and to locate its offices in terminals and office buildings. These arrangements, however, were under attack by the Antitrust Division. The company made money during prosperity, incurred losses in years of depression. Postal was bankrupt and in receivership. The FCC recommended that the two firms be allowed to merge. Enabling legislation was enacted and the merger was effected in 1943.

The telegraph business has encountered increasing competition from other media: the development of air mail, the improvement of two-way communication by telephone, and the teletype service operated by A.T.&T. The division of fields between the telephone and telegraph interests has operated to the advantage of the former. A.T.&T. has enjoyed steady earnings; Western Union has not. The company has been slow to modernize its equipment. The quality of its service has declined. Costs have risen: more labor is required to effect communication by telegraph

[36] *Ibid.*, pp. 338–42.

[37] *A.T.&T. Co.* v. *U.S.*, 299 U.S. 232 (1936).

than by telephone, and wages have gone up. Three fourths of the company's income is derived from its operations in 150 cities. But it is forced to maintain its service in 4,000 smaller places, conducting it largely at a loss. The FCC has acted favorably on numerous requests for elimination of local offices and reduction of hours, and has approved substantial increases in rates. But the industry's prospects are still unpromising.

Two different solutions are suggested. One is to permit the telephone company to take over the telegraph business, creating a communications monopoly. The other is to strengthen Western Union by transferring to it the teletype business now operated by A.T.&T. The latter solution is permitted by the law passed in 1943, has been recommended by a committee of the Senate, and has been proposed from time to time by Western Union. It would give the company all of the means of record communication, raise its revenues by a third, and thus increase its ability to compete.

FEDERAL-STATE RELATIONSHIPS

In the laws enacted by Congress and in the policies adopted by the federal commissions efforts have been made to co-ordinate the activities of state and federal agencies. Joint boards of state and federal commissioners may be established to confer on common problems where jurisdictions overlap. Joint investigations may be conducted and joint hearings held. There may be common decisions on basic policies. In the case of telephones, for instance, the FCC conferred with the National Association of Railroad and Utilities Commissioners in promulgating its accounting regulations, in making allocations between intrastate and interstate operations, in eliminating disparities between intrastate and interstate rate structures, and in working out the division of interstate revenues between the local companies and the Long Lines of A.T.&T. The federal commissions have also functioned, in effect, as service agencies to the state authorities. The FPC, for instance, may act upon request to determine the cost of producing and transmitting electricity and gas. And it may make the members of its staff available to serve as expert witnesses. The effectiveness of the state commissions may thus be enhanced.

But federal intervention is not always welcomed. The state commissioners may fear that their agencies will decline in importance with the growth of federal power. They have before them the example of the railroads, where nearly all authority has been taken over by the ICC. They have also seen the way in which the FPC has extended its jurisdiction over navigable rivers and over the production and distribution of gas. And they have resented the imposition of federal regulations in areas where state and federal jurisdictions overlap. The state commissions, moreover, are more likely than the federal agencies to be subservient to the industries they are supposed to regulate. As a result, the laws establishing federal bodies are sometimes so drafted, in response to local pressures, as seriously to circumscribe their powers. And the commissions of the states are even found intervening, on the side of the utilities, in litigation with those of the federal government. Where the respective powers of the state and federal agencies are in dispute, the companies will be found, almost invariably, supporting the position of the states.

RATE REGULATION IN OTHER FIELDS

Two other cases of rate regulation should be mentioned in passing. State governments regulate the rates charged by fire and liability insurance companies. The federal government regulates those charged by stockyards and livestock agencies.

Insurance Rates

The right of the states to regulate insurance companies was upheld by the Supreme Court in 1914.[38] For many years, however, the companies were permitted to join in the operation of rating bureaus for the purpose of establishing common rates. They were not prosecuted for such activity under state antitrust laws, and little effort was made to control the rates they fixed. Then a group of fire insurance companies in the southeastern states was sued by the federal government for violating the Sherman Act. And in 1944 the Supreme Court held that insurance was in interstate commerce and was subject to the federal law.[39] Thereupon, in 1945, Congress suspended the application of the Sherman Act to insurance for the next three years, affording the states an opportunity to strengthen their regulations, and provided that it should apply thereafter only "to the extent that such business is not regulated by state law." As a result, the insurance companies, in co-operation with the National Conference of Insurance Commissioners, worked out bills for rate fixing and urged their enactment on the states. Today, fire insurance rates are controlled in all the states; liability insurance rates in a few.

In some respects, the regulation of insurance companies resembles that of public utilities; in others, it differs. In both cases, entry into business is controlled, the level of rates is regulated, and discrimination is curbed. Supervision of insurance companies, however, is not given to an independent commission, but is entrusted to the head of a state department, usually known as an insurance or banking commissioner. Valuations are made, but the assets involved are not physical properties but holdings of securities, and they are valued not for the purpose of fixing rates but to assure the maintenance of adequate reserves. With insurance, moreover, there is greater control of the form of contracts and the investment of funds.

Three different procedures are followed in fixing rates. In a few states, the insurance commissioner, after holding public hearings, establishes the

[38] *German Alliance Insurance Co.* v. *Lewis*, 233 U.S. 389.

[39] *U.S.* v. *Southeastern Underwriters Assn.*, 322 U.S. 533.

rates himself. In most states, however, the rates are prepared by the rating bureaus and proposed by the companies. In some cases membership in the bureaus is voluntary; in others, it is compulsory. With some states the rates proposed take effect when they are approved by the commissioner. With others, they take effect unless they are disapproved.

In general, it cannot be said that these controls are rigid. The power to formulate rates is largely delegated to the rating bureaus. The purchasers of policies are afforded neither the protection of competition nor that of really effective regulation.

Stockyard Rates

The rates charged for stockyard services are regulated, under the Packers and Stockyards Act of 1921, by the Department of Agriculture. The conditions that led to the enactment of this law, and the nature of its provisions, were discussed in Chapter 11.

SUGGESTIONS FOR FURTHER READING

An objective appraisal of state utility regulation is contained in *Electric Power and Government Policy* (New York: Twentieth Century Fund, 1948), chap. iv. The shortcomings of regulation are discussed in John Bauer, *Transforming Public Utility Regulation* (New York: Harper & Bros., 1950), Part I.

Federal regulation of electric and gas utilities is described in the texts cited previously: in Troxel, chap. v; in Clemens, chap. xviii; and in the Twentieth Century Fund report, pp. 163–99. See also James C. Bonbright, *Public Utilities and National Power Policies* (New York: Columbia University Press, 1940), and Robert D. Baum, *The Federal Power Commission and State Utility Regulation* (Washington, D.C.: American Council on Public Affairs, 1942). "The Regulation of Natural Gas" is the subject of Vol. XIX, No. 3 of *Law and Contemporary Problems* (Summer, 1954). For current developments, see the annual reports of the Federal Power Commission, and the magazine *Public Utilities Fortnightly*.

Federal regulation of holding companies is discussed by Troxel in chap. viii, and by Clemens in chap. xxi. The authoritative source on holding company abuses is the report of the Federal Trade Commission, *Utility Corporations*, 70th Cong., 1st Sess., Senate Doc. 92, Parts 72-A and 73-A (Washington, D.C.: U.S. Government Printing Office, 1935). It is instructive to set beside this the text of the Public Utility Holding Company Act of 1935. On the enforcement of this law, see the reports of the Securities and Exchange Commission.

Federal regulation of the telephone industry is discussed by Bauer in chap. xvi. The authoritative study of this industry is Federal Communications Commission, *Investigation of the Telephone Industry in the United States*, 76th Cong., 1st Sess., House Doc. 340 (Washington, D.C.: U. S. Government Printing Office, 1939). On policy with respect to the regulation of the telephone and telegraph industries, see also the report of the President's Communications Policy Board, *Telecommunications, a Program for Progress* (Washington, D.C.: U.S. Government Printing Office, 1951). For current developments, follow the annual reports of the Federal Communications Commission.

Chapter 21 REGULATION OF RAILROADS

It is in the case of railroads that the federal government first undertook to regulate the operation of a private business. It is here that government has had its longest experience as a regulator and its greatest powers, that its regulatory activities have been most extensive, most intensive, and most detailed. It is here that regulation has been most effective and attended by the greatest measure of prestige. The story of this experience therefore has particular significance. An account of the changing relationship between the government and the railroads is given in this chapter. An account of public regulation of other transport media and of national policy respecting transportation as a whole will be presented in the next.

PUBLIC AID TO RAILWAYS 1850–70

In its first stage, the policy of government toward railroads was to promote construction. Its motivation was solely that of opening up the country and speeding its settlement. To this end, assistance was provided by local, state, and federal governments. Local and state aid took the form of purchases of stock at figures above its market value, loans at low rates of interest, guarantees of railroad bonds, donations of cash, land, equipment, materials, and labor, and exemption from taxes. Federal aid took the form of grants of right of way through the public domain and freedom to use materials on the domain, such as timber and stone; of low-interest loans; and, more important, of extensive gifts of public lands. From 1850 on, 72 such transfers were effected, more than 130 million acres being involved. Most of this went to a few transcontinental lines, two thirds of it to the predecessors of five of the present roads. In some cases, receipts from land grants covered a major part of the construction costs. As a consequence of public aid, roads were built before there was traffic to support them. Fortunes were made through financial manipulation by their promoters, and heavy losses were sustained by those who bought their shares. But the country was opened and its settlement assured.

Estimates of the total of public aid vary, according to the basis of computation, from $600 million to $1,500 million. Against these sums, however, an offset must be made. Railroads receiving land grants were required, thereafter, to carry freight for the government at reduced rates. And this obligation was not suspended until 1946. It is possible that the government by that time had saved as much on transportation costs as it had spent on public aid.

STATE REGULATION OF RAIL MONOPOLY 1871–87

During the years of railroad building, little thought had been given to the possible need for regulation. Several roads were built in every section of the country, and it was assumed that competition between them would protect the public interest. But competition proved, instead, to be ruinous. And it led, shortly, to collusive agreements among the railroad companies. The level of rates was raised, and discrimination was practiced between persons, between products, and between communities. The public attitude toward the railroads changed from benevolence to hostility. Shippers demanded protection. And for this, they turned first to the legislatures of the states.

The Emergence of Monopoly

The economic characteristics of the railroad business were such as to lead the roads into destructive competition. Their investment in plant and equipment was large. The annual cost of this investment was high. This cost, in the short run, was fixed, not varying with the volume of traffic. Operating expenses, too, were largely fixed: plant and equipment had to be maintained and administrative charges met whether volume was large or small. Fixed costs, as a fraction of total costs, in the railway industry, may be as low as a fourth or a fifth when capacity is fully used. But they may be as high as half or two thirds when utilization is incomplete. With overexpansion, in the early years, much capacity stood idle and fixed costs were high. There was pressure, therefore, to increase volume by reducing rates. Greater volume, though at lower rates, might lead to greater earnings, since fixed costs could thus be spread over more units, and total unit costs, thereby, would fall. Rate cuts, however, might not stop at total unit costs. To obtain a particular shipment, rather than lose it to a competitor, it would be advantageous to keep on cutting the rate as long as it yielded enough to cover the variable costs involved—for extra fuel and labor—and contributed something toward meeting overhead. If a minor part of a railroad's traffic were carried on this basis, its revenues might thus be maximized. But if a major part were so handled, it would be headed for bankruptcy. And this is what happened during the sixties and the seventies. Rate wars, breaking out among the roads between the Atlantic and Chicago, between Chicago and the Pacific, and in the South, carried rates to a fraction of their former levels and threatened the industry with disaster. Monopolistic agreements were the result.

Agreements among the railroads first took the form of understandings with regard to rates. When these proved ineffective, they were superseded by market-sharing arrangements known as pools. These were of two major types: traffic pools and money pools. Where traffic was pooled, competitive shipments were divided among the participating carriers in accordance with agreed percentages, the distribution being effected by employing certain large shippers (such as Swift, Armour, and Standard Oil) as "eveners," granting them rebates on their rates, and so directing their shipments that quotas would be filled. Where money was pooled, shipments were not controlled, but earnings from competitive traffic were divided into shares on which the railroads had agreed. In either case, competition was ended and rates were raised. And with monopolistic pricing thus established, discrimination was widely practiced as a means of maximizing total revenues. All shippers were affected by the higher rates, and some shippers were unfairly handicapped by favors granted their competitors.

Resentment against the railroads, arising during the seventies, was strongest among the farmers of the Midwest, and was given expression through the granges. Farm prices had been falling as a result of overexpansion, and high freight rates were blamed. It was felt that the farmer would get more of the sums paid in the market if the railroads hauling his crops there were required to take less. Dissatisfaction was created, too, by discrimination, by losses resulting from financial manipulation, by political scandals, and by the arrogance of railroad managements. The granges therefore demanded action, first by the states and then by the federal government.

The Granger Laws

Common carriers had long been given a special status at common law in judgments handed down on cases brought before the courts, being required to serve all comers at reasonable rates, avoiding discrimination among those whose circumstances were the same. The railroads had also been subjected to control through the provisions of their charters and through the activities of state commissions which had been set up, in some cases, as early as the thirties and the forties. But these methods were ineffective: the courts did not act unless a plaintiff carried through a suit; the charters were limited and inflexible; the commissions were confined to such matters as appraising property taken under eminent domain, reporting on charter violations, and enforcing safety laws. Until the granger laws were passed in the early seventies, there was no real control over rates.

Such laws were enacted in Illinois, Iowa, Wisconsin, and Minnesota between 1871 and 1874. In general, they either fixed maximum rates at low and rigid levels, or set up a commission and empowered it to fix these rates at levels which were reasonable. The laws were upheld by the courts. But they were bitterly attacked by the railroads, being held responsible for bringing on the business depression of 1873. Within a few years they had been repealed or replaced. But the setback for regulation was only temporary. New laws were enacted during the eighties, establishing state commissions with substantial powers. By 1887 commissions were in operation in 25 states.

During these years, the farmers had been pressing, too, for action by the federal government. Such action was finally precipitated by a decision handed down by the Supreme Court in the Wabash case[1] in 1886. The Wabash railroad had been found guilty of violating the law of Illinois by charging more for a shorter haul from one town in Illinois to New York than it charged for a longer haul from another. The Court reversed this verdict on the ground that the shipments in question could not be regulated by the state, since the Constitution gave exclusive jurisdiction over interstate commerce to the federal government. Where traffic was confined within its borders, a state could act. But where it crossed state lines, the Congress alone had power.

FEDERAL REGULATION OF RAIL MONOPOLY 1887–1917

In 1872 a committee known as the Windom committee was appointed by the Senate to investigate the possibility of reducing the cost of transportation from the Midwest to the East. In 1874 this body made its report, charging that rail rates were extortionate and recommending that the government own and operate some railroads as a means of controlling the charges made by their competitors. No action was taken. In 1885 the Senate appointed a second committee—the Cullom committee—to consider proposals for federal regulation. In 1886 the report of this committee condemned discrimination in railroad rates, urged legislation to control it, and recommended that a commission be established to enforce its terms. In 1887, following the Wabash decision, this proposal was enacted into law.

The Act to Regulate Commerce, 1887

The Interstate Commerce Act, as it came to be known, initially applied to common carriers transporting passengers or property in interstate or foreign commerce wholly by rail or, in cases of continuous movements under common control, partly by rail and partly by water. The law forbade the pooling of traffic or earnings. It required that the rates established by carriers be "reasonable" and "just," leaving the definition of these terms ultimately to the courts. It also required that rates be published and adhered to and that prior notice be given before they were increased. The Act contained a number of provisions designed to limit

[1] *Wabash, St. Louis & Pacific Railway Co.* v. *Illinois,* 188 U.S. 557 (1886).

discrimination. It prohibited rebates to favored shippers and (with minor exceptions) all other forms of discrimination among persons. It curbed discrimination among commodities and among places by forbidding carriers to give "any undue or unreasonable preference or advantage" or to impose "any undue or unreasonable prejudice or disadvantage," leaving it to the courts again to determine when discrimination was undue or unreasonable. The law specifically attacked one form of discrimination between places, forbidding the railroads—unless granted special permission to do so—to charge more for a shorter haul than for a longer haul, when the one was contained within the other, over the same line in the same direction. This prohibition was qualified, however, by the proviso that the two hauls be "under substantially similar circumstances and conditions."

The Act created an Interstate Commerce Commission and set forth its powers. The Commission was authorized to undertake investigations upon complaint by shippers or upon its own initiative. It was empowered to compel witnesses to testify, to demand the production of books and documents, to prescribe uniform systems of accounting, and to require annual reports. Where it found that the law had been violated, the Commission was authorized to issue an order directing the carrier in question to cease and desist from the illegal activity. If its order was not obeyed, it could apply for an enforcing order to a federal court. In such proceedings the Commission's findings of fact were to be taken as prima facie evidence. Carriers were made liable for damages sustained as a result of violations of the Act, and the Commission was empowered to determine the amount of such damages. Certain violations, such as the granting of rebates, were made punishable by fine and imprisonment, and here the Commission was to assist in prosecuting cases brought before the courts.

Emasculation of the Act of 1887

The new commission made a good beginning toward enforcement of the law. But its efforts were soon obstructed by the courts. When it found a rate to be too high, the Commission specified the rate that should be charged. But the Supreme Court held, in 1897, that it had no power to do so.[2] As a result, a rate that was found unreasonable could be cut a fraction of a cent and maintained at this level until another case was brought, the process being repeated again and again. The Commission was thus deprived of any real power over the level of rates. So, too, with discrimination. The law provided that the testimony of a witness could not be held against him in a later suit. But when action was taken against the granting of rebates, a shipper refused to testify, claiming protection against self-incrimination under the Fifth Amendment to the Constitution. And in this he was upheld.[3] The evidence required for preventing personal dis-

[2] *ICC* v. *Cincinnati, New Orleans, and Texas Pacific Railway Co.*, 167 U.S. 479.
[3] *Counselman* v. *Hitchcock*, 142 U.S. 547 (1892).

crimination was thus made difficult to obtain. Enforcement of the prohibition of higher rates for shorter than for longer hauls was also blocked. This prohibition applied only "under substantially similar circumstances and conditions." And the Supreme Court, in another case[4] decided in 1897, held that competition between railroads and between trading centers was a factor in making conditions dissimilar. Since this competition was the source of most long-and-short-haul discrimination, its prevention was thus brought to a halt. The Commission's orders, finally, were not binding in themselves but had to be taken to the courts for enforcement. Here, decisions were delayed for months and years. In the meantime, rates found to be unreasonable continued in effect. The Commission's rulings were thus ignored, and shippers were discouraged from bringing new complaints.

The ICC, throughout its second decade, found itself confined, in the main, to conducting research and making advisory reports. The law was amended in 1893 to compel witnesses to testify without risk of self-incrimination, and in 1903 to give suits brought under its provisions priority in the courts. It was amended, too, by the Elkins Act of 1903 to make recipients of rebates as well as railroads and their officers and agents liable in cases of personal discrimination. But the Commission was not granted real powers until the passage of the Hepburn Act in 1906 and the Mann-Elkins Act in 1910.

Strengthening the ICC 1906–10

The Hepburn Act undid some of the damage that had been done by the courts. (1) It authorized the Commission, when rates were found to be unreasonable, to specify the legal maxima. (2) It contained many provisions designed to prevent personal discrimination. It gave the Commission jurisdiction over industrial railroads and private car lines and empowered it to control divisions of rates and charges made for switching and for special services rendered by shippers and by carriers. It forbade free passes, except to railway employees. It increased the liability of recipients of rebates and the criminal penalties that could be imposed. (3) The law forbade railroads to haul (except for their own use) goods they had themselves produced. This provision, known as the commodities clause, was designed to remove the advantage in car service and rates enjoyed by railroad-owned anthracite mines over their independent competitors. (4) The law sought to prevent railroads from refusing to interchange traffic with water carriers by empowering the Commission to require the establishment of joint routes, to fix joint rates, and to determine how they should be divided. (5) The law strengthened the ICC in other ways. It required that all accounts be kept in such forms as the Commission might prescribe. It provided heavy penalties for delay and falsification in the submission of reports. And it made the Commission's orders effective after

[4] *ICC* v. *Alabama Midland Railway Co.*, 168 U.S. 144.

thirty days, with noncompliance punishable thereafter by a fine of $5,000 per day, thus putting on the railroads the burden of appealing to the courts.

The Mann-Elkins Act made other significant changes in the law. (1) Under the Act of 1887, the ICC had been unable to pass upon a rate until after it had been put into effect. When rates were rising and complaints were numerous, this meant that unreasonable charges could be collected for many months before the Commission was able to act. When action was finally taken, moreover, these charges would have been passed on in product prices and restitution was therefore difficult if not impossible to effect. The new Act corrected this situation by giving the Commission power to suspend proposed increases, for a stated period, while it considered their legality. The burden of justifying higher rates was thus put on the carriers. (2) When one rate was cut, under the original Act, the railroads could compensate for the reduction by raising another. Now the Commission was empowered, on its own motion, to consider the schedule of rates as a whole. (3) The Commission was also authorized to control the system used in classifying freight. And finally (4) the loophole found by the court in the long-and-short-haul prohibition was closed. The phrase "under substantially similar circumstances and conditions" was dropped from the law. The effectiveness of the prohibition was thus restored, and the formulation of policy to govern exceptions was left, in the main, to the ICC.

The new laws rehabilitated the Commission. Its orders, in general, came to be accepted by the courts. Other legislation followed. In 1912 the railroads were forbidden to own or operate vessels passing through the Panama Canal. In 1913 the ICC was directed to determine the value of railway properties. In 1917 it was authorized to require the roads to establish reasonable rules to govern the provision of freight cars and, if need be, to prescribe such rules itself. Concerning the valuation act, a further word should be said.

The Railway Valuation

The Act of 1887 had provided that rates should be reasonable and just. The Supreme Court had held, in the case of *Smyth* v. *Ames* in 1898, that reason and justice required the allowance of a fair return on a fair value. But the value of the railroads was unknown. Until the Hepburn and Mann-Elkins Acts were passed, this did not matter, since the ICC had been left with little power over rates. But with regulation strengthened, the need for determining value was recognized.

The Valuation Act of 1913 directed the Commission to ascertain the value of every railroad in the United States. For each piece of property, other than land, used by each road it was to determine the original cost to date, the cost of reproduction, and the cost of reproduction less depreciation. In the case of land, it was to determine value both at the time of its dedication and at the time of its valuation. And to these sums, it was to add a proper value for intangibles. A tentative value, as of 1913, was to be announced. If there were protests, public hearings were to be held. A final value was then to be adopted and thereafter kept up to date.

The initial valuation was expected to take three years. In the end it took almost twenty and cost more than $50 million. In 1933 the work of bringing the 1913 valuation up to date was still to be done. And by this time, as we shall see, the requirement that rates be fixed to yield a fair return on a fair value had been dropped.

State and Federal Jurisdiction

As the power of the ICC increased, that of the state commissions declined. In the Wabash case the Court had drawn a line between interstate and intrastate traffic, assigning the one to the federal government and the other to the states. But points of conflict remained: the two types of traffic were intermingled, the rates charged for one affecting those that could be charged for the other. When intrastate rates were set at levels that disturbed the pattern of interstate rates, the ICC ordered them changed, and the issue of jurisdiction was carried to the courts. In the Shreveport Rate Case,[5] decided in 1914, the Texas commission had fixed rates for traffic from Dallas and Houston to northeast Texas that were lower than those fixed by the ICC for traffic from Shreveport, Louisiana, and the ICC had issued an order rescinding the intrastate rates on the ground that they were unduly preferential to Dallas and Houston and unduly prejudicial to Shreveport. Its power to do so was upheld by the Supreme Court. The Commission was thus given jurisdiction over intrastate as well as interstate rates whenever an influence on interstate commerce could be shown. And in nearly all important cases such a showing could be made. In fixing rates, the state commissions were, therefore, relegated to a minor role.

The state commissions have not abandoned the field of transportation. They regulate intrastate carriage by highway, waterway, and air. They exercise some control over safety and service on the railroads. And they still fix rates where lines are wholly intrastate. But in every phase of railway regulation, for forty years, the dominance of the ICC has been assured.

MANAGERIAL SUPERVISION OF RAIL MONOPOLY 1918–33

Up to World War I, regulation took the form of judicial action designed to protect shippers against extortion and discrimination. The ICC exercised no affirmative authority over railway management. It was charged with no positive responsibility to maintain railway earnings. With the coming of war, service broke down, and the government was forced to operate the railroads, paying them a fixed return. When the war ended,

[5] *Houston, East and West Texas Railway Co.* v. *U.S.*, 234 U.S. 342.

new legislation was required. Arrangements had to be made to effect the reversion to private operation. Gaps in the regulatory structure had to be closed. There was need, for instance, for more effective control of service and for authority to regulate the issuance of securities. Attention had to be given, too, to the financial needs of the railroads. New capital was sought, but earnings were declining and credit was impaired. There followed a complete revision of the law, increasing the powers of the Commission and charging it with new responsibilities. A different phase in the history of regulation was begun.

Government Operation 1918–20

When America entered the war in 1917 the demand for railway service was substantially increased. Men, materials, and equipment had to be moved, in quantity and without delay, to army camps, to war industries, and to Atlantic ports. The railroads, under their separate managements, proved to be incapable of doing the job. Each of them sought profit for itself. It therefore hoarded cars when they were needed on other lines. It routed shipments over its own tracks and through terminals when other lines made it possible for terminals to be by-passed. As a result, the movement of supplies was impeded by car shortage and terminal congestion; the breakdown of transportation threatened to prevent successful prosecution of the war. The government took over the railroads on December 28, 1917.

The United States Railroad Administration operated the railway system as a single unit. It eliminated needless duplication of facilities and services. It pooled rolling stock and used it where there was the greatest need. It economized equipment, establishing priorities for freight and insuring that cars were fully loaded by fixing sailing days. It speeded service, making shipments by the shortest routes and by-passing crowded terminals. It succeeded in moving the men and the materials that were required to win the war. And this was its purpose.

The government paid each railroad company a rental for its properties. It undertook to maintain these properties, returning them in as good condition as it found them, and to make necessary improvements for which the roads would pay. The management of operations, subject to government orders, was left to the officials of the roads. Whether the railroads were better off or worse off after this experience is a matter of dispute. The government, certainly, lost money. But this was because it failed to raise its rates, as wages and other costs increased. The record affords little or no evidence concerning the desirability of public ownership. It does show, however, that unification can make for greater efficiency.

Transportation Act of 1920

The provisions of the Transportation Act of 1920 fall into three categories: those that were designed to facilitate a return to private operation, those that involved a further extension of the powers and duties of the ICC, and those that represented a major departure in regulatory policy. It is only with the second and the third that we are here concerned.

The Commission was given new authority over service, securities, and rates. It was empowered to order unification in the event of an emergency, to require joint use of terminals, and to establish rules respecting the use of locomotives and cars. Its permission was required before a railroad could build a new line or extend an old one, abandon service on all its lines or any part of them, or obtain new capital by selling its securities. As a means of preventing destructive competition and discrimination, the Commission was authorized to establish minimum as well as maximum rates. And in finding a rate unreasonable, it was empowered to fix, not merely a maximum, but the exact rate that should be charged. The Act also reinforced the long-and-short-haul clause, giving statutory effect to policies that the Commission had followed in granting exceptions to its general rule.

In other provisions the Act departed from previous policy. It recognized that the task of fixing rates for railroads differs from that of fixing rates for public utilities. Every gas or electric company has a monopoly in the community it serves. Separate rates can be set for each of them at a level that will guarantee it a fair return. Most railroads, however, compete with other roads at various points along their lines. Different rates cannot be fixed for different roads. If this were done, the road with the higher rates would get no business. Rail rates, therefore, must be set at a common level. But common rates, applied to different roads, will not yield similar returns. The roads may differ as to volume of traffic, conditions of cost, and structure of capital. One may be strong, another weak. When rates are set for both, the one may prosper, but no profit for the other can be guaranteed. It was to the solution of the problem presented by this situation that the attention of those who framed the Transportation Act of 1920 was turned.

The Act set up a new rule to govern the making of rates, directing the ICC to fix them "so that carriers as a whole (or as a whole in each of such rate groups or territories as the Commission may from time to time designate) will, under honest, efficient, and economical management . . . earn an aggregate annual net railway operating income equal, as nearly as may be, to a fair return upon the aggregate value of the railway property of such carriers. . . ." Congress set 5½ per cent as the figure to be taken as a fair return for the first two years, authorizing the Commission in its discretion to raise it to as much as 6 per cent. Several things should be noted about this rule. It required the ICC to look into the honesty, efficiency, and economy with which the railroads were managed. It imposed on the Commission an affirmative obligation with respect to railway earnings. But it did not guarantee that the roads as a whole would actually realize the profit that the rates were intended to provide. And it did not guarantee that any road, taken by itself, would make ends meet. The problem of the strong and weak roads still remained.

Three solutions were attempted. (1) Under a provision known as the recapture clause, a road that earned more than 6 per cent on the value of its property in any year was permitted to keep half of the excess, putting it in a reserve fund from which it could pay interest and dividends. But it was required to turn the other half over to the ICC to be placed in a revolving fund from which loans (at 6 per cent interest) could be made to weaker roads. (2) The Commission was directed, in determining how rates on joint hauls should be divided, to give special consideration to the need of weaker roads for revenues. (3) Combination, once forbidden, was now encouraged. The ICC was empowered to permit pools, if they would improve service and reduce costs, and to permit one railroad to control another, if it appeared that the public interest would be served. It was instructed to prepare a plan for consolidation of the railroads into a limited number of competitive systems of approximately equal strength. Thereafter, it was to approve combinations that conformed to its plan and disapprove those that did not. In all of these ways, the railway system as a whole was to be strengthened, the weak roads being aided or absorbed at the expense of the strong.

Results of the Act of 1920

The transitional provisions of the Act of 1920 and those that strengthened the Commission were successful. The new rule of rate making and the efforts to solve the strong-and-weak road problem were not. Despite the obligation imposed on the ICC to fix rates that would yield the roads from 5½ to 6 per cent on their investment, their average earnings did not reach this figure, and the rule was supplanted in 1933. The recapture clause, the division of joint rates, and the combination program did not succeed in strengthening the railway system by bringing the stronger roads to the support of the weak.

The power of the government to capture excess earnings, when challenged, was upheld by the Supreme Court.[6] But the plan worked badly. The weaker roads got little aid from money for which they had to pay as much as six per cent. The stronger roads curtailed the profits subject to recapture by increasing their expenditures. With earnings computed as a percentage of property values, they contested the Commission's valuations in the courts. The major consequence of the plan was litigation. Acknowledged to be a failure, it was repealed in 1933.

The provision directing the ICC to favor the weaker roads in dividing joint rates was also upheld by the Court.[7] This plan, too, proved to have its limitations. Divisions were possible only where carriers made connections and were significant only where traffic was interchanged in sub-

[6] *Dayton–Goose Creek Railway Co.* v. *U.S.*, 263 U.S. 456 (1924).

[7] *New England Divisions Case*, 261 U.S. 184 (1923).

stantial quantities. The share of a joint rate left to a stronger road could not be cut so far as to be confiscatory. Such a road, moreover, might reduce joint hauls by inducing shippers to route their goods in other ways. And a weak road might hesitate to offend a strong one by insisting on a larger share. The plan was doubtless of some assistance. But it lacked the strength to solve the problem in itself.

In 1921 the ICC published a tentative plan for consolidation of the railroads, held hearings on it, and issued its final plan in 1929. This called for the creation of two systems in New England, a line along the Atlantic coast, a system in the South, five trunk lines from the Atlantic to Chicago, five regional systems in the central and northwestern states, and five transcontinental lines from Chicago to the Pacific, a total of nineteen. These systems were to realize some of the advantages of unification. They were to compete with one another in rendering service. And each of them was to be strong enough to earn a fair return at a common level of rates. Combinations in accordance with this plan were not to be required. But where voluntarily proposed, they were to be approved. Such combinations, however, did not occur. The shareholders of the stronger roads displayed an understandable reluctance to risk curtailment of their earnings by taking on the burdens of the weaker ones. The major systems, on the other hand, were eager to absorb the strongest of the shorter lines. The combinations they sought, in general, were not according to the plan. But these were the combinations that actually occurred. The ICC had been given no jurisdiction over holding companies, and consolidation was effected by setting up such companies to purchase railroad shares. This loophole was closed in 1933 when the law was amended to give the Commission authority over all combinations, however achieved, including those effected through holding companies. But there were still no proposals for mergers conforming to the pattern the Commission had proposed. And finally in 1940 the requirement that combinations conform to a plan drawn up in advance was dropped from the law. Thereafter, with consolidations as with other acquisitions of control, the Commission could grant approval when it appeared to be in the public interest. The project of creating a score of competing railway systems, comparable in strength, was thus abandoned.

The Hoch-Smith Resolution, 1925

After World War I, the prices of agricultural products fell. The farmers again sought to get a larger share of the price paid at the market by obtaining lower freights. Failing to persuade the ICC, they turned to Congress. In response to this pressure a resolution was passed in 1925 declaring it to be Congressional policy, when rates were fixed by the Commission, that "the conditions which at any time prevail in our several industries should be considered insofar as it is legally possible to do so, to the end that commodities should freely move." The resolution directed the

Commission to investigate the railway rate structure, determining how it affected different regions and products, in view of their comparative prices, and to make such changes as might be required. Specifically, it directed the Commission to put the rates on agricultural commodities at the lowest lawful level possible.

This action did not have a determining influence on railway rates. When the ICC cited it, in support of a reduction in an agricultural rate, and a railroad appealed, the Supreme Court held[8] that the resolution was to be regarded as an expression of hope, not as a mandatory rule of rate making. But the resolution does show how political pressure may be used to influence the structure of rates.

The Depression and the Railroads

The railroads were hard hit by the depression of the thirties. Car loadings fell off; from 1929 to 1932 gross revenues were cut in half. If their capitalization had been in stocks, the roads would have been in a better position to sustain this loss. But 56 per cent of their capitalization, in 1932, was in bonds, bearing an average interest charge of 4.58 per cent. In many cases, though operating costs were covered, interest could not be paid. By 1938 as many as 111 railroads, with more than 30 per cent of the country's mileage, had become insolvent and were in receivership. Railway bonds had been a major outlet for conservative investment. Nine tenths of them were held by institutional investors: savings banks, insurance companies, university endowments, and the like. The railway problem thus became, not that of protecting the shippers against the railroads, but that of protecting the holders of railroad securities against financial loss.

Several things were done to meet this situation. In 1932 the Hoover administration set up the Reconstruction Finance Corporation and empowered it to make loans to the railroads, among others. In the next ten years such loans reached a total of $850 million, enabling many roads to stave off bankruptcy. In 1933 Congress sought to facilitate the reorganization of railway companies by adding a new section (Section 77) to the Bankruptcy Act of 1898. This measure was amended, in detail but not in principle, in 1935 and again in 1936. Under its terms, delay was to be prevented, investors protected, and sounder financial structures attained. The ICC was empowered to prevent the exploitation of bankrupt railroads by controlling the costs of reorganization. And its approval was required for the adoption of reorganization plans. In 1933, also, Congress embodied emergency provisions in a statute making major changes in railroad law.

The Emergency Transportation Act of 1933 included sections, mentioned above, repealing the recapture clause and bringing holding companies within the jurisdiction of the ICC. It replaced the 1920 rule of rate making with a new rule that will be discussed below. It also sought to

[8] *Ann Arbor R.R. Co.* v. *U.S.*, 281 U.S. 658 (1930).

improve the financial condition of the railroads by reducing their costs. To this end, the Act provided for the appointment of a Federal Coordinator of Transportation, to be chosen from the members of the ICC, and for the creation of regional committees representing railway managements. These agencies were to cut costs by eliminating wastes and by reducing duplication of facilities and services. A serious limitation was imposed, however, upon their powers. No action could be taken that would reduce the volume of railway employment or the wages of any railway employee. The results of the program were meager. The committees could not agree upon economies to be effected. The Coordinator made some valuable reports. But he did little co-ordination. The make-work limitation in the law, adopted to satisfy labor, tied his hands behind his back.

SUPERVISION OF TRANSPORT COMPETITION 1933—

For sixty years the regulation of railroads was based on the assumption that they possessed monopolistic powers and that shippers therefore required protection against exorbitant and discriminatory rates. In regulating rates it was further assumed that substitutes for railway service were not available and that rates could therefore be set at whatever level might be required to enable the roads to cover their costs and obtain a fair return. With the emergence of increasing competition from other carriers—by pipeline, highway, waterway, and air—these assumptions lost validity. Many shippers, by substituting other modes of transport, were now able to protect themselves. And increases in rates, instead of yielding an assured return, might lead to a decline in revenues. This was a fundamental change, and one to which policy had to be adjusted. The process of adjustment began in 1933.

Emergence of Competition

From 1916 to 1939 the railroads' share of intercity freight ton-miles dropped from more than 77 per cent to less than 63 per cent; their share of intercity passenger miles from 98 per cent to less than 9 per cent. By 1953 their share of freight had fallen to 55 per cent. Here, the greatest gainers were the pipelines and the trucks. In the case of passenger traffic, 85–90 per cent is now carried by private automobiles. And for the remaining 10–15 per cent the railroads must compete with buses and aeroplanes. In 1953 passenger travel by air was almost double that by Pullman car, and the passenger revenues of the largest airlines were greater than those of the largest railway companies. The situation is even worse than these figures would indicate, since the railroads have tended to lose the part of their business that paid them best and to keep the part that paid them least. They have lost to the highways valuable merchandise on which the rates were high, retaining commodities moved in bulk on which the rates are low. They have lost to the airlines long-distance, first-class passenger traffic which was profitable, retaining commutation traffic which is not. They have suffered, too, from the development of Diesel and hydroelectric power, since oil moved by pipe and electricity moved by wire compete with coal, the bulk of which is moved by rail.

The competitors of the railways have certain marked advantages. The pipelines have lower costs. So do the water carriers, though their service is slow and subject to interruption. The airlines have greater speed, but at a greater risk. The motor carriers have lower costs on short hauls, higher costs on long hauls. But they have greater flexibility, giving faster service and superior convenience, avoiding the costs of packing and rehandling by operating from door to door.

Faced with such competition, the railroads might have retained a larger share of traffic by introducing improvements of their own. Buses and trucks might have been used to a greater extent as feeders, supplementing instead of substituting for movement by rail. Door-to-door service might have been developed at an earlier date, and packing and handling reduced by loading standard containers or trailers on flat cars for longer hauls. Freight might have been speeded and passenger service made more attractive and more convenient. In all of these respects, improvements came twenty years too late. The railroads sought, rather, to increase their revenues by obtaining permission to raise their rates. Instead of improving their competitive position, they worsened it. They suffered the effects of managerial inertia, ingrained through long years of monopoly and regulation.

The 1933 Rule of Rate Making

The new rule of rate making, contained in the Emergency Transportation Act of 1933, recognized that competition had created greater elasticity in the demand for railway services, and that earnings, therefore, could no longer be assured by raising the level of railway rates. It directed the ICC, in fixing rates, to "give due consideration, among other factors, to the effect of rates on the movement of traffic; to the need, in the public interest, of adequate and efficient transportation service at the lowest cost consistent with the furnishing of such service; and to the need of revenues sufficient to enable the carriers, under honest, economical, and efficient management, to provide such service." The rule still required the Commission to look into the honesty, economy, and efficiency with which the railroads were managed. But it no longer contained an affirmative obligation to provide the railroads with a fixed return. After thirty-five years of regulation based upon the doctrine of fair value, and after twenty years of costly valuation work, it abandoned value as a factor to be taken into account. The new rule was functional in character, providing for rates that would attract business, assure adequate service and cover its necessary cost, and establish earnings at a level required to insure railway credit, so that new capital could be obtained. In introducing these factors into its consideration, the rule accorded a broad new area of discretion to the ICC.

The rule was amended, by the Transportation Act of 1940, in one important respect. In considering the effect of rates on the movement of traffic, the Commission was instructed to confine itself to movement "by the carrier or carriers for which the rates are prescribed." It was thus made clear that the rates of one type of carrier were not to be adjusted to influence the movement of traffic by another.

Extension of Control to Other Carriers

Up to 1935, pipelines and some ships operated by railroad companies were the only carriers other than railroads controlled by the ICC. Carriers by water and by air were subject to some safety regulation by the federal government. And these, together with motor carriers, were subject to safety regulation and to some economic regulation by the states. Common carriers by water on the Great Lakes and in the coastwise and intercoastal trades were subject to the jurisdiction of the United States Shipping Board. But other carriers on these waters and all carriers on other inland waters were uncontrolled. Air service was supervised, to some extent, by the Postmaster-General and the rates paid for carrying mail were fixed by the ICC. But aviation, otherwise, was free of economic regulation. And the federal government had no power of any sort over the railroads' most serious competitor: the motor carrier.

The next few years were marked by a significant expansion of federal control. In 1935 interstate motor carriers were brought within the jurisdiction of the ICC. In 1938 carriers by air were subjected to economic regulation under a Civil Aeronautics Board. In 1940 all interstate transportation by water was brought within the jurisdiction of the ICC. In all of these cases, the familiar pattern of control, developed over the years through experience with the railroads, was applied, with minor changes in detail, to the other carriers. In the case of motor and water carriers, the 1933 rule of rate making was adopted without change. In the case of aviation, it was modified in one respect, directing the CAB, in fixing rates, to consider the need of each company, taken separately, rather than that of the industry as a whole, for revenue sufficient to enable it to provide adequate and efficient service.

The extension of control to these carriers was caused by factors differing radically from those that explained its application, a half century earlier, to the railroads. At that time shippers had complained of poor service, high rates, and unjust discrimination. But now shippers were well satisfied with the treatment they were receiving at the hands of carriers by highway, by water, and by air. The pressure for regulation came not from consumers but from producers. It had its origin, not in the abuses of monopoly, but in the fact that competition was hard to take.

Transportation Act of 1940

The railroad problem had now become a transportation problem, and regulation had moved on from railroads alone to transportation as a whole. This change was recognized by the statement that was put at the head of the Interstate Commerce Act by an amendment contained in the Transportation Act of 1940. It was then declared to be the policy of Congress

> . . . to provide for fair and impartial regulation of all modes of transportation subject to the provisions of the Act, so administered as to recognize and preserve the inherent advantages of each; to promote safe, adequate, economical, and efficient service and foster sound economic conditions in transportation and among the several carriers . . . to the end of developing, co-ordinating, and preserving a national transportation system by water, highway, and rail, as well as other means, adequate to meet the needs of the commerce of the United States. . . .

All forms of transportation were to be developed. Regulation was to be impartial. The emphasis was on the system as a whole. And this still stands as the expression of national transportation policy.

The Act of 1940 made certain changes, already mentioned, in the law. It eliminated the requirement that combinations conform to a prior plan. It modified the rule of rate making. It brought water carriers under the jurisdiction of the ICC. In addition, the Act made a number of other changes in substance and in procedure. It amended the long-and-short-haul clause in further detail. It made clear the power of the ICC to prevent discrimination among regions and directed the Commission to examine the interterritorial structure of rates. And it put the burden of proof on the carriers in proposing reductions as well as increases in rates.

The Railroads in World War II

The railroads, in 1941, had 25 per cent fewer freight cars, 30 per cent fewer passenger cars, and 32 per cent fewer locomotives than in 1914. With larger cars, multiple tracks, and more tracks in yards and sidings, their carrying capacity, in the two years, was about the same. But the volume of freight that had to be handled in World War II was nearly twice as great as the volume handled in World War I. More freight was moved by highway and by air. But expansion of motor traffic was limited by shortages of trucks, parts, and tires. And the volume of air cargoes was relatively insignificant. Coastwise water traffic was sharply curtailed as ships were sunk, and until more pipe lines could be built the railroads had to carry oil from the producing regions to the refineries. The great bulk of the wartime freight was moved by rail. And this was done by the railroads themselves; operation by the government was not required.

How is this performance to be explained? For one thing, cars were moving west as well as east, carrying full loads both ways. For another, the ICC possessed substantial powers to deal with an emergency. And the Office of Defense Transportation was given authority to issue orders designed to insure effective use of rail facilities. But some of the credit for the achievement must also be given to the railway managements.

The war brought several years of high earnings. The railroads emerged from the period with their debts reduced and their financial position substantially improved. But their costs rose in the postwar inflation. And they were again confronted with increasing competition from other carriers.

Railway Rate Bureaus

Changes in the general level of railway rates cannot be made without the approval of the ICC. And changes in the structure of rates may be ordered by the Commission in response to complaints. But individual rates are initiated by the roads themselves. In taking such action, each road might act independently. In practice, it does not. For many years, particular changes have been effected through the medium of trade associations known as rate bureaus. A road or a shipper proposing a new rate takes his proposal to one of these bureaus. The proposal then goes to a public hearing, followed by a committee decision, subject to a series of appeals. The final action of the bureau takes the form of a recommendation to the carriers concerned. Legally, each of them retains the right to make a change, even though the bureau disapproves. In practice, none of them is likely to do so. Rates will not be changed unless competing roads agree. This procedure, long followed by the railroads, has also been adopted by other types of carriers.

In 1944 the Department of Justice brought a suit against the Western Association of Railway Executives, the American Association of Railroads, and a number of western roads, charging that the establishment of rates through bureaus was in violation of the Sherman Act; and the state of Georgia brought another suit in which the legality of such activities was attacked. In the light of existing precedents, there was little doubt that the bureaus would be held to violate the law. The railroads therefore turned to Congress for exemption. The Reed-Bulwinkle Act, granting their request, was passed over the veto of President Truman in 1948.

The new law made rate agreements subject to approval by the ICC. It left shippers free to carry complaints to the Commission, and authorized the Attorney General to take cases before that agency. The law was defended as maintaining order in the making of rates and bringing all aspects of the process within the jurisdiction of a single body. It was attacked as assigning further responsibilities to a body that lacked the ability and the inclination to discharge them in the public interest. The Commission could scarcely begin to review the thousands of individual rates on which the bureaus might act. And it was less likely than competition to force reductions in such rates.

THE INTERSTATE COMMERCE COMMISSION

The Interstate Commerce Commission has steadily grown in scope, in power, and in the character of its responsibilities. From railroads and rail-controlled water carriers, its jurisdiction was extended in 1906 to oil pipe-lines, express companies, sleeping car companies, industrial railroads, private car lines, and refrigeration and storage services; in 1910 (until they were transferred to the FCC in 1934) to telephone, telegraph, and cable companies; in 1933 to railway holding companies; in 1935 to motor carriers; in 1940 to all domestic water carriers; in 1942 to freight forwarders (middlemen who collect small consignments, consolidate them into truck-loads or carloads for shipment, and unload and deliver); and in 1948 to rate bureaus. Starting with feeble powers, it has been given effective control over service, finances, accounts, and the level and structure of rates. Once semijudicial in character, it has come to be charged with a considerable measure of managerial responsibility. Its permission must be obtained for entry, extension, abandonment, pooling, combination, and the issuance of securities. It can issue orders with respect to safety devices and practices, require joint routes and determine the division of joint rates, require joint use of equipment, and demand unification of facilities in time of emergency. Under the rate-making rule of 1933, it is directed to exercise business judgment as to the expediency of raising or lowering rates. Monopoly in transportation has given way to competition. But regulation, instead of being abandoned, has taken on new force.

Organization and Procedure

When first established the ICC had five members; this number was increased to seven in 1906, to nine in 1917, and to eleven in 1920. Appointments are made by the President with the approval of the Senate for overlapping terms of seven years. Members have often been reappointed as their terms expired. Both political parties must be represented, but no other qualifications for membership are provided by law. In practice, according to the Task Force of the Hoover Commission on governmental organization, "appointments have been of mixed quality. Not a few have been political. . . . The Commission has always had a nucleus of very able members, but appointees have only rarely been the best men available."[9]

The Commission is headed by a chairman, selected by its members, each of them being chosen in turn to serve for a single year. The magnitude of its task is such as to necessitate considerable delegation of authority. In 1917 the law was amended to authorize the creation of divisions of three members each to hear and decide cases subject to rehearing

[9] Commission on Organization of the Executive Branch of the Government, *Task Force Report on Regulatory Commissions*, 1949, pp. 84–85.

by the full commission. In 1933 the agency was empowered to delegate functions to individual commissioners and to boards of employees. In 1940 provision was made for the establishment of divisions to hear appeals.

Critics of the Commission's administration still find it to be overburdened, poorly organized, and too big to fulfill its duties with efficiency. The docket of cases is a heavy one, as many as 4,000 formal complaints and another 2,000 informal complaints awaiting action at a single time. In 1950 the Commission's staff numbered more than 2,000 and its budget ran over $11 million. The Commission itself is organized into five divisions, its staff into fifteen bureaus, some of them set up according to the functions they perform (safety, service, valuation, etc.) and others according to the mode of transport they control (motor carriers, water carriers, and freight forwarders). The Hoover Commission found the eleven-man executive to be a cumbersome device for administration and recommended that the chairman be designated by the President, for a longer term, and given administrative responsibility. Its Task Force found the pattern of organization to be an impediment to the disposition of cases involving intercarrier competition, resulting in the adoption of conflicting policies, and recommended that it be overhauled.

Many grievances brought to the Commission are disposed of informally. And the Commission's procedure in formal cases is said to be simpler than that of the courts. But action is slow, the settlement of ordinary complaints commonly taking from one to two years. And the procedure is criticized as being legalistic, inflexible, and ponderous.

The Marasmus of the ICC

Compared with other regulatory agencies, the ICC has been fairly free from political interference. In its time it has enjoyed considerable prestige, having a reputation for expertness and impartiality. In recent years, however, the Commission has come to be described as railroad-minded. And it is said to have lost its basis in popular support.

This criticism was discussed, pro and con, in a series of articles published in the *Yale Law Journal* in 1952 and 1953, beginning with an article by Samuel P. Huntington called "The Marasmus of the ICC,"[10] a marasmus being defined by Webster as a "progressive emaciation and general wasting due to enfeebled constitution rather than any specific or ascertainable cause." The Commission, said Huntington, has ceased to be impartial, identifying the public interest with the railroad interest, and favoring railroads over motor carriers and water carriers in controlling service and fixing rates. It has been consistently supported by the railroads before Congress and the public, its independence defended and its expansion urged. It has lost the support of shippers, the confidence of motor and water carriers, and the respect of Congress and the courts. Allying

[10] *Yale Law Journal,* LXI (1952), 467–509. See also LXII (1953), 171–226, 561–74; LXIII (1953), 44–63.

itself with the industry it was set up to regulate, it has forfeited its past prestige.

The evidence adduced in support and in refutation of this indictment runs into many pages of detail that cannot be evaluated here. It may be noted, however, that changes in the position of the ICC have not occurred in a vacuum, but have been caused by changes in the nature of the problems with which it has had to deal and in the policies that Congress has written into the law. It should be noted, too, that the railroads are not entirely satisfied with regulation as it stands.

The Commission and the Railroads

The railroads are under tight control. The ICC is authorized to inquire into the honesty, efficiency, and economy with which they are managed, a function which—if really fulfilled—would involve a virtual duplication of managements. This is not done. But, as things are, decisions that in other industries are left exclusively to management must here be shared with the Commission. On crucial issues of business policy—the desirability of expanding or contracting operations, of raising or lowering rates—the Commission may reject the judgments of management and substitute its own. Or it may delay action while deciding what position it shall take. In either case, the consequences may be serious.

Under the 1933 rule of rate making, the ICC must consider the effect of rates on the movement of traffic. In doing so, it has made its own guesses as to elasticity of demand. In this connection, it has given weight to the competitive position of the railroads, their public relations, and the state of the nation's economy. During depression, it has undertaken to estimate how changes in rates would affect the confidence of business. During prosperity, it has sought to judge how they would influence inflationary trends. All these are matters respecting which judgments may differ. If the Commission rejects the views of management, the consequences may be good or bad: where its judgment is superior, the railroads will gain; where its judgment is inferior, they will lose. But when losses occur, nobody can be held responsible: the stockholders of the railroads may complain, but their directors have a perfect alibi, and the members of the ICC are out of reach. This situation has led to the proposal that the Commission be deprived of its power to fix a maximum level of rates, a suggestion that will be considered at the end of Chapter 22.

In most cases, the Commission has finally accepted the views of management. But many months have elapsed before it has done so. And in the meantime, costs have risen while revenues have lagged. Losses have been incurred and railway credit has been impaired. The funds required for improvement have not been obtained. But here, again, the railway managements cannot be held accountable, neither can the members of the ICC.

The delay attending Commission action has led to proposals for reform. A bill introduced in Congress in 1954 would amend the law to require an interim ruling within sixty days of an application for a rate increase, and a final ruling within another sixty days. In making its interim ruling, the Commission would be forbidden to consider the effect of rates upon the movement of traffic, basing its decision solely on the trend of costs.

SUGGESTIONS FOR FURTHER READING

The historical development of government regulation of railroads is presented in greater detail in a number of the standard texts on the economics of transportation cited at the end of Chapter 19: in Locklin, chaps. x–xv; in Westmeyer, chaps. v–ix; in Bigham and Roberts, chaps. vii–x; and in Fair and Williams, chaps. xxiv and xxv. A good chapter by Charles L. Dearing, carrying the story up to 1940, is included in Vol. II of *Government and Economic Life* by Leverett S. Lyon and Others (Washington, D.C.: Brookings Institution, 1940). The authoritative work on the ICC is I. L. Scharfman, *The Interstate Commerce Commission* (New York: Twentieth Century Fund, 1931), published in four vols. For a more recent appraisal of the Commission, pro and con, see the series of articles by Samuel P. Huntington and others in the *Yale Law Journal*, LXI (1952) 467–509; LXII (1953) 171–226; and LXIII (1953) 44–63. Delays in rate decisions and the way they have affected railroad earnings are discussed in Charles L. Dearing and Wilfred Owen, *National Transportation Policy* (Washington, D.C.: Brookings Institution, 1949), chap. xiii. The story of increasing competition in transportation is well told in a Report to Executives in *Business Week*, March 20, 1954, pp. 102–20.

Chapter 22 NATIONAL TRANSPORTATION POLICY

Government does two things with respect to transportation: it promotes and it regulates. It promotes the development of various modes of transportation by extending public aid. It regulates all modes of transportation, controlling entry, combination, services, and rates. Transportation policy, as distinct from railroad policy, must comprehend all types of carriers. And it must include promotion as well as regulation. In regulation, the nation's policy, as enunciated by the Congress, is one of impartiality. In promotion, however, each type of carrier is considered separately; no effort is made to adopt a program that will be comprehensive in itself or consistent with impartial regulation. It is the purpose of this chapter, first, to outline the methods employed in promoting and regulating modes of transportation other than railroads—pipelines, motor carriers, water carriers, and air carriers—and second, to consider the problems involved in developing a comprehensive and consistent policy for transportation as a whole.

OIL PIPELINES

The products moved by pipelines are gas, crude petroleum, and petroleum products. In moving gas, other carriers do not compete. This business, like the transmission of electricity, finds its significance in connection with the regulation of public utility rates, and was discussed in that connection in Chapter 20. In moving petroleum and its products, the pipelines do take traffic that might be handled by other carriers. Nearly a fourth of the crude petroleum is moved by tankers and three fourths by pipe, only 2 per cent by road and by rail. The cost of movement by pipe is so low (less than a fifth of that by rail) that truckers and railroads make no effort to compete. Pipeline costs are lower, too, for petroleum products, but here the differential is less and other carriers take part. In neither case, however, do the railroads complain that pipeline competition is unfair. For the pipelines, unlike their other competitors, are not subsidized.

The real problem raised by the petroleum pipelines is how they affect competition, not in transportation, but in the oil industry. Most of the trunk lines that carry petroleum from the fields to the refineries are owned by the major integrated oil companies. The situation gives the integrated company an advantage over the independent producer and the independent refiner. If it charges itself a high rate for transporting its own oil to its own refineries, it does not reduce the profitability of its operations as a whole. But when it charges the independent producer the same rate for carrying his oil to an independent refinery, it augments its profits at his expense. High pipeline rates may induce the independent producer to sell his output to the integrated concern, depress the price which he obtains, and make it unprofitable for him to compete in the business of production. High pipeline profits can be used to finance the refineries of the integrated concern and thus make it difficult for the independent to compete in the business of refining.

The relationship between the major oil companies and their pipeline subsidiaries is similar to that which once obtained between the anthracite coal companies and the anthracite-carrying railroads. Congress, in the Hepburn Act of 1906, prohibited common carriers from transporting commodities in the production of which they had an interest. In the same Act, Congress gave oil pipelines the status of common carriers and made their rates subject to regulation by the ICC. But it specifically excluded these concerns from the provisions of the commodities clause.

The common carrier status of the pipelines is nominal rather than real. At first the companies refused to accept oil produced by others and insisted on buying it in the field. Carrying no oil but their own, they argued that they were not covered by the law. This position, however, was rejected by the Supreme Court in 1914.[1] Thereupon, the companies excluded independents from their lines by establishing high minimum tender requirements, refusing to accept shipments that fell below a stated figure, such as 100,000 barrels, and by charging high rates. The lines were used predominantly to carry oil to the refineries of the majors located near the markets. The refineries of the independents were built near the fields. As a result, nine tenths of the oil that moves through pipelines still belongs to the owners of the lines.

The ICC has shown little vigor in regulating the pipelines. In 1922 and again in 1940 it reduced minimum tender requirements. In 1935 it announced the results of an investigation of pipeline rates, finding the rates of twenty-one companies to be excessive. The companies reduced their charges and no further action was taken. There have been few other cases involving rates. Producers have either accepted the prices offered by the pipelines or sold to the independent refineries. In any case they have lacked the inclination or the courage to appeal to the ICC. In 1941 the Department of Justice brought suit against the integrated companies, charging that their receipt of pipeline dividends constituted acceptance of rebates in violation of the Elkins Act of 1903. The case was settled by

[1] *The Pipe Line Cases*, 234 U.S. 548.

a consent decree, under which the companies agreed to limit their dividends to 7 per cent of their valuation, thus accepting an indirect incentive to reduce their rates. Divorcement of the business of transporting oil from the business of producing and refining it, though frequently proposed, has never been enacted into law. Such action would have turned the pipelines into common carriers. Short of this, discrimination could have been limited by more vigorous action by the ICC. As matters stand, the lines function, in the main, as plant facilities, and the industry has adjusted its operations accordingly.

MOTOR CARRIERS

The most serious competitors of the railroads are the motor carriers. Their competition, according to the railroads, is unfair. The railroads must provide their own ways, buying the land, building the roadbed, tunnels, and bridges, laying the track, meeting the costs of maintenance, paying interest on their investment, and contributing through property taxes to the support of every county and city they pass through. The motor carriers, on the other hand, operate on ways acquired, constructed, and maintained at public expense, having no investment to make and no property taxes to pay. As users of the highways, to be sure, they are subject to other taxes that are levied to meet the costs of construction and maintenance. But the railroads contend that the motor carriers do not pay their share of these costs. And the motor carriers argue, just as vigorously, that they do. On this issue, the opinions of experts are in conflict and a final judgment cannot be made.

Meeting Highway Costs

It may be doubted that intercity transportation should be required to meet all highway costs. Roads have other uses: they give access to land, facilitate community services, and promote performance of many of the functions of government. They raise property values and thus increase tax-paying ability. Local roads, particularly, are properly to be financed from general revenues. But intercity highways are used primarily for long-distance transportation, and their users might well be expected to defray their costs. Before World War I, all highway costs were met, in the main, by taxes on property. But since that time, they have been met increasingly by levies on users: motor license fees, gasoline taxes, and the like. In 1951 three fourths of the money spent by states on highways came from these sources, the rest being borrowed or obtained in the form of grants from the federal government. When allowance is made for the other purposes served by highways, it is generally agreed that operators of motor vehicles, as a whole, now bear a fair share of their costs. But this burden must be divided again between private vehicles and commercial carriers. Do trucks and buses pay their part of user costs? On this point, authorities disagree.

Two methods have been employed in measuring user costs. In accordance with one, it is assumed that trucks and buses should bear the same costs as other vehicles plus the extra costs incurred in making highways wider and stronger on their account. Using this method, the Federal Coordinator of Transportation made a study in the thirties and came to the conclusion that vehicles for hire (with the sole exception of light trucks) met more than their fair share of user costs.[2] Under a second method, such costs are determined by measuring the use made of the highways in terms of some unit such as gross ton miles. Employing this method, the Board of Investigation and Research set up under the Transportation Act of 1940 concluded that automobiles, light trucks, and light buses paid their way, but that heavy trucks, tractor-trailer combinations, and large intercity buses did not.[3] This conclusion, however, is open to question. In determining the damage done to highways, wheel and axle loads are more significant than gross ton miles, and heavy trucks and buses have more wheels and axles than lighter ones. New estimates are being made in terms of these units. But here, again, the methods of measurement are in dispute.

The Motor Carrier Industry

The railroads (aside from those operated as industrial facilities in lumbering, mining, and manufacturing) are all of them common carriers. With motor vehicles, this is not the case. Such vehicles must be divided, first, into private carriers and carriers for hire. Of all the trucks on the road, 85 per cent are in the first category and only 15 per cent in the second. But the private carriers account for less than half of the ton miles hauled and the carriers for hire account for more than half. The latter group must be divided, again, into contract carriers and common carriers. The contract carrier hauls goods in quantity, under special contract, for a single large shipper or, at most, for a very few. It is only the common carrier who holds himself out to serve the public generally. Contract carriers account for more than a tenth of the trucking firms and more than a tenth of intercity tonnage hauled for hire, common carriers for nearly nine tenths.

The trucking industry is characterized by large numbers of small concerns. Nearly 20,000 certificates and permits for interstate operation were outstanding in 1952. There are a few large companies, with revenues running into the millions. But nine tenths of them own fewer than ten trucks and nearly half of them own only one or two. In the absence of public intervention, the industry would be highly competitive. Entry is easy; the cost of the capital required is low. With railroads, investment in plant is twice as great as annual revenue. In trucking, it is but a fifth as great.

[2] Federal Coordinator of Transportation, *Public Aids to Transportation*, Vol. IV (Washington, D.C.: U.S. Government Printing Office, 1940).

[3] Board of Investigation and Research, *Public Aids to Domestic Transportation*, chap. iv, 79th Cong., 1st Sess., House Doc. No. 159 (1944).

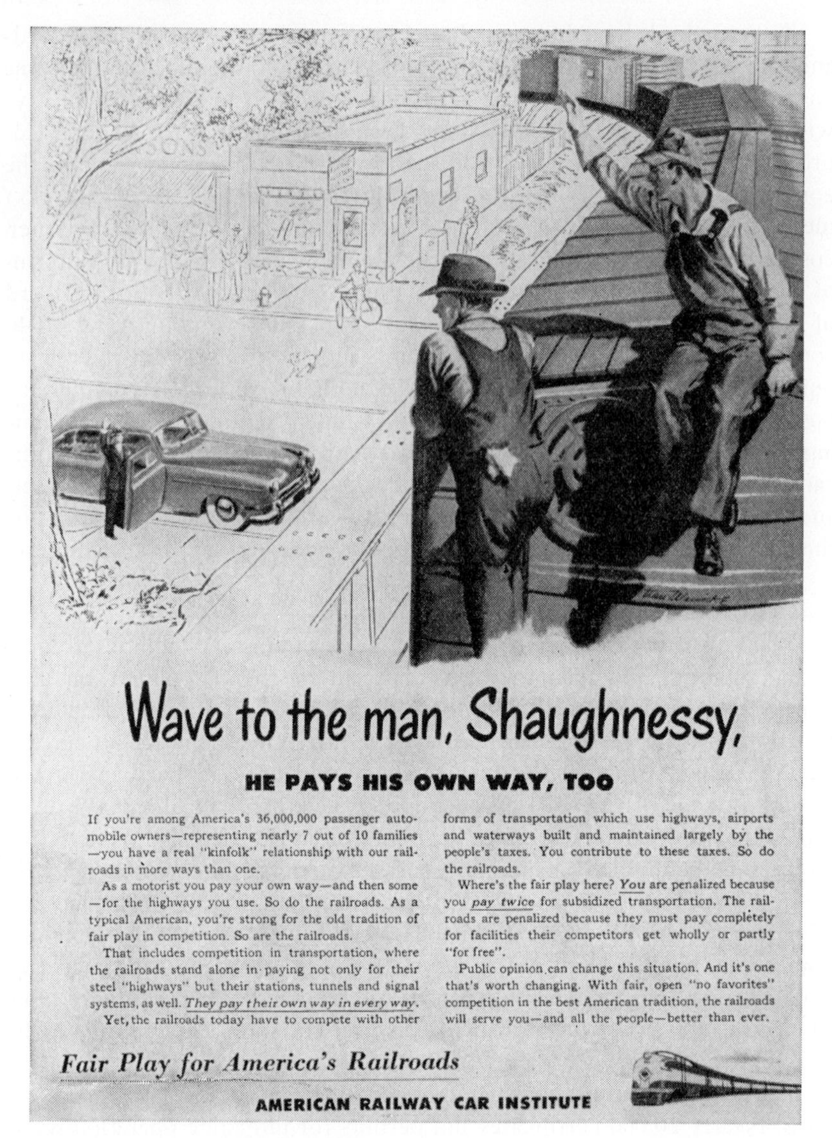

Fixed costs, accordingly, are low. Of annual expenses, only a tenth are constant; nine tenths vary with the amount of business done. There is little temptation to increase volume by cutting rates. There is little likelihood of destructive competition leading to monopoly.

Regulation by the States

For many years the states have regulated motor carriers in order to control the use of their roads and to insure safety. To this end they have established standards governing the width, length, height, and weight of vehicles, their lights, brakes, and other equipment, the speed at which they

TRUCK TAXES HELP BUILD 'EM ALL!

In 1948, the total construction cost of all the highways, roads and streets built throughout America was $1,531,000,000.

In 1948, the trucks paid—in special highway-use taxes, including Federal Excise taxes—more than $1,089,000,000.

You need no slide rule to discover that truck taxes alone amount to more than two-thirds of the Nation's total highway construction-cost bill.

Nor do you need to be told what truck taxes mean to *you.*

* * *

Figure it out for yourself.

Today, and for years past, hundreds of thousands of trucks and tractor-trailer combinations are taxed all the way from $1,000 to $3,000 and more *EACH, PER YEAR,* in special "highway-use taxes" for the right to run over the roads.

What's more, some of the large express highways these truck taxes help build and maintain are actually forbidden to truck traffic. Also, hundreds of thousands of miles of country roads are virtually never used by commercial trucks; are used by farm trucks primarily.

So bear in mind, that *in addition* to paying for the roads they use to bring you everything you eat, buy, use or wear—the trucks also help pay for the roads, streets and highways which the motoring public uses almost exclusively.

HOW TRUCK TAXES HELP MAINTAIN MISSOURI'S HIGHWAY SYSTEM

With much of our highway pattern laid out, we have entered a period where maintenance and renewal of Missouri's highways is assuming major importance.

Truck taxes in Missouri play a major role in paying for highway maintenance. In 1948 Missouri spent $______ for repair and renewal of the state administered road system according to figures from U. S. Bureau of Public Roads. In the same year truck taxes totalled $______ or ____% of this entire cost.

And, bear in mind, that the greatest volume of most highly-taxed truck traffic runs over *only* a small fraction of the total Missouri street and highway mileage.

MISSOURI BUS & TRUCK ASSN.
118-A East High Street, Jefferson City, Mo.
and
THE AMERICAN TRUCKING INDUSTRY
American Trucking Assn.,
1424 16th St., N.W., Washington 6, D. C.

may be driven, the age of their drivers, and the number of hours that a driver may work. Beginning in the twenties, the states also undertook to regulate the business of common carriers, requiring certificates of convenience and necessity for entry and applying controls, in varying degrees, to services, rates, accounts, and securities. They soon found, however, that the carriers could evade their regulations by operating under contracts. They sought, therefore, to bring contract carriers under control. At first, the courts resisted their attempts. But the state of Texas hit upon the device of requiring permits rather than certificates of public convenience and necessity for contract operations. And the Supreme Court, in a case decided in 1932,[4] allowed its law to stand. All but one or two of the states now require certificates of common carriers and permits of contract carriers and regulate their services and rates.

In the case of highways, unlike that of railways, intrastate business is still within the exclusive jurisdiction of the states. And interstate carriers must obey the laws controlling traffic on state highways and pay the taxes levied for their use. But in 1925, when Michigan attempted to exclude an interstate carrier by refusing it the right to operate, the Supreme Court held that regulation of interstate commerce was beyond the power of the state.[5] There was pressure, thereafter, for federal legislation, from the railroads, the bus lines, some truckers, and the state commissions. But it was ten years before a federal law was passed.

Motor Carrier Act of 1935

The Motor Carrier Act of 1935 applies unequally to different carriers. All interstate carriers are subject to such regulations governing safety of operation as the Interstate Commerce Commission may prescribe. But private carriers are under no further control. And many carriers for hire are specifically exempt. Among them are vehicles used in local transit operations, those used incidentally by railways, shipping companies, and airlines, and those owned and operated by farmers and agricultural cooperatives. More important is the exemption, under political pressure, of carriers transporting agricultural commodities, horticultural products, livestock, and fish, but not products that are made from them.

The remaining provisions of the law apply to those contract and common carriers that are not exempt. Both must carry liability insurance. And for both, the ICC is given power to prescribe methods of accounting, require reports, control the issuance of securities where capitalization exceeds $1 million, and approve or disapprove combinations and acquisitions of control. But beyond this, the two are treated differently, the law being looser for contract carriers and tighter for common carriers.

Entry is regulated. A grandfather clause protects the rights of firms in operation before the law was passed. Contract carriers must obtain permits. Common carriers must obtain certificates, for which more stringent conditions are laid down. A company cannot be given the right to carry on both types of operation unless good cause is shown. Dual operation might be abused, affording the carrier an opportunity to discriminate

[4] *Stephenson* v. *Binford*, 287 U.S. 251 (1932).

[5] *Michigan Public Utilities Commission* v. *Duke*, 266 U.S. 570.

by hauling goods for favored shippers under contract at lower rates. The ability to offer both types of service, moreover, would give the operator an advantage over his competitors in soliciting business.

Rates are controlled. Contract carriers must file their minimum charges and may not charge less. The Commission may fix a legal minimum, but not a maximum. Common carriers, on the other hand, are subject to much the same pattern of control as are the railroads. Their rates must be reasonable and not unduly discriminatory. They must be published and observed and notice must be given before a change. The Commission can suspend proposed changes and fix minima, maxima, and specific rates.

The control of common carriers by motor differs in certain respects, however, from the control of carriers by rail. The ICC is specifically denied the power to fix the rates charged on intrastate hauls. It cannot require through routes or joint rates. It cannot prevent the discontinuance of service. And the law contains no long-and-short-haul clause. In one respect, a heavier obligation is imposed: truckers must obtain insurance on the goods they carry; the responsibility of railroads for loss or damage is assumed.

Motor Carriers under the ICC

In 1950 there were close to 200,000 motor carriers with 1,000,000 vehicles under the jurisdiction of the ICC. Of these, most were private carriers or were exempt from all but safety regulation. But there were some 20,000 companies with 250,000 vehicles subject to economic control. To administer the law, the Commission has set up a Bureau of Motor Carriers, with a sizable staff in Washington and in the field. The Bureau's resources, however, are inadequate for the work that it must do. Safety regulations must be prescribed and enforced, and rules established to govern the filing of surety bonds and insurance policies. For many months, the Bureau was engaged in defining its jurisdiction and determining which companies were subject to which controls. It had to distinguish, for instance, between private operations and carriage for hire, between agricultural commodities where haulage was exempt and the products of such commodities where it was not, and between contract carriers and common carriers. It had to pass on thousands of applications for permits and certificates. And in each case, it had to determine whether the applicant fell within the provisions of the grandfather clause. In later years the Bureau has been concerned more largely with controlling new entry, combinations, and rates.

Commission policy with regard to entry is not well defined. Entry is not refused, in general, on the ground that railway service is available. Permits are sometimes granted to contract carriers despite the objection of common carriers. And new certificates are sometimes given to common carriers, enabling them to compete with existing firms. In the case of bus lines, particularly, the desirability of maintaining competition is recognized. But the weight of Commission action lies the other way. Permission for regular transcontinental service has been refused, to keep a truck line from competing with the railroads for longer hauls. Permits have been denied to contract carriers where they would compete with common carriers. In granting certificates, moreover, the Commission has held that existing companies are entitled to carry all the traffic they can handle adequately and efficiently before new entrants are admitted to the field. And it has usually looked with favor on proposals for combination or acquisition of control, holding that costs are likely to be reduced and service improved. On balance, therefore, the effect of Commission action on these matters has been to make the industry less competitive.

So, too, with rates. In passing on requests for changes in the general level of rates, the Commission concerns itself, as with the railroads, not with individual companies, but with the carriers as a whole. But here, its standard is a different one. It does not judge the rate level by measuring the return upon the carriers' investment, since investment in the industry is so small in relation to revenue that rates calculated to yield a fixed return might not suffice to cover costs. Instead, it seeks to insure an operating ratio that will afford a safe margin of revenues over costs, generally holding a ratio of 93 to be reasonable. In passing on complaints with respect to particular rates, the Commission employs the same principles, in the main, that it does with the railroads. But it tends to give less emphasis to marginal costs and more to fully allocated costs. In prescribing the actual rates that must be charged, moreover, the Commission has shown more interest in fixing minima than maxima. Power to fix minimum rates was originally granted, in the case of railroads, to prevent destructive competition leading to monopoly. With motor carriers, such competition is unlikely to occur. But the Commission establishes regional minima, on the basis of proposals made by motor carrier rate bureaus. And in doing so, it is influenced less by motor carrier costs than by competing railway rates. This policy protects the carriers against loss of revenue through competition. It also moderates the competition that the railroads otherwise would face.

WATER CARRIERS

Transportation by water falls into a number of different categories, each of them involving a different type of cargo and carrier. Transoceanic shipping does not compete in the domestic market and will not be considered here. Included in domestic transportation are coastwise oceanic shipping, intercoastal shipping through the Panama Canal, and shipping on the Great Lakes, the Mississippi River system, and other inland waterways. Coastwise shipping, in 1951, carried an eighth as much tonnage as the railways, four fifths of this being in tankers carrying oil. Intercoastal shipping was much smaller in volume; its relative importance has declined.

Carriers on the Great Lakes handled less than a fifth as much as the railroads, most of it being in iron ore, coal, and grain. Carriers on other inland waterways handled less than a tenth as much tonnage as moved by rail.

Public Aid to Waterways

For carriers on the oceans and on the Great Lakes, ways are provided by nature. For those on other inland waters, they are provided by government. For both, harbors are improved and port facilities maintained at public expense. Appropriations for waterways were made, at an early date, by state and local governments. Appropriations have been voted by Congress every year or so for the past century. Improvements have not been made in accordance with any comprehensive plan, the contents of the congressional pork barrel being determined, from time to time, by trading votes. Save for the Panama Canal, all waterways are free of tolls. User charges, comparable to those imposed on motor carriers, are unknown. The rates charged by water carriers, therefore, need cover only the costs of their equipment and its operation. The costs involved in providing their ways, if any, are met by the taxpayer.

Most water carriers, particularly those operating on rivers and canals, are clearly subsidized. But the amount of the subsidy is difficult to compute. In making estimates on an annual basis, expenditures on capital must be distinguished from those on current operation, the rate at which capital is to be depreciated must be determined, a decision must be made on whether to include a charge for interest on the government's investment, and—since improvements in river systems are made not only for navigation but also for irrigation, flood control, and the generation of electric power—it is necessary to decide how much of the capital cost is to be charged to shipping and how much to these other purposes. All of these matters are open to dispute. Estimates as to the extent of subsidization are therefore hazardous. One such estimate, made by the Board of Investigation and Research for the year 1940, set the figure for traffic moving on rivers and canals at 3.1 cents per ton-mile.[6]

The Shipping Industry

The shipping business, like the trucking business, is divided among private, contract, and common carriers. The private carriers transport their own goods, such as petroleum and iron ore, in vessels designed for the purpose. The contract carriers also transport bulk cargoes in specialized craft, often serving under charter or operating as tramps. The common carriers handle specialized or general cargoes, operating on schedule over fixed routes. All three types of carriers use the same waterways and compete for the same business. As in the case of motor carriers, entry is easy, the cost of capital being low. Fixed charges, too, are low. There is little tendency toward ruinous competition, ending in combination and

[6] Board of Investigation and Research, *op. cit.*, p. 21.

monopoly. In the absence of regulation, the industry would continue to be competitive.

Regulation of Water Carriers

Under the Interstate Commerce Act of 1887, the ICC was given jurisdiction over water carriers operated by railroads where continuous shipments were made by water and by rail. Under the Panama Canal Act of 1912, railroads were forbidden to operate ship lines without approval by the ICC and were forbidden absolutely to operate ships using the canal. Under the Shipping Act of 1916, as amended in 1933 and 1938, the United States Shipping Board and its successor, the Maritime Commission, were given authority over common carriers on the Great Lakes and in the coastwise trade and both common and contract carriers in the intercoastal trade. But until 1940 contract carriers, aside from the intercoastal trade, and all carriers on rivers and canals were largely uncontrolled. And such control as existed was divided between the Shipping Board or the Maritime Commission and the ICC.

All this was changed by the Transportation Act of 1940. Jurisdiction over transoceanic shipping alone was assigned to the Maritime Commission (later to the Maritime Board). Jurisdiction over water carriers in interstate commerce was given to the ICC. But the great bulk of such traffic, involving as much as nine tenths of the tonnage was exempted from the requirements of the law. The carriers granted exemption include small craft, ferries, and ships operated incidentally by railroads and trucking companies, all private carriers, contract carriers whose cargoes and vessels are so specialized that they do not compete with common carriers, and common carriers whose cargoes consist of three or fewer commodities in bulk.

Where the law applies, its provisions are similar to those established for motor carriers. Entry is controlled, contract carriers being required to obtain permits and common carriers to obtain certificates. Unless specially approved by the ICC, no company may have both. The rights of those existing when the law was passed are protected by a grandfather clause. Methods of accounting may be prescribed and reports required. Pools and combinations may be approved or disapproved. Jurisdiction over rates charged in intrastate traffic is left to the states. Interstate rates are controlled, the methods differing for contract and common carriers. Both must publish their rates and observe them, giving prior notice of a change. The Commission can suspend proposed rates pending an investigation. For contract carriers, it can fix minimum rates, but not maxima. For common carriers, the familiar pattern applies. Rates must be just and reasonable, without unjust discrimination or undue preference or prejudice. The Commission can fix maxima as well as minima. Here, as with railroads but not with motor carriers, the long-and-short-haul clause is made effective, and through routes with joint rates may be required. As with motor carriers, the Commission cannot prevent abandonment. And here, it is given no power over the issuance of securities.

In its administration of the Act of 1940 the Commission has had to define the groups that are exempt, distinguish between contract and common carriers, and determine the applicability of the grandfather clause. In the few cases where new firms have applied for entry, it has granted permits and certificates over the objection of existing interests, but refused them where it appeared that traffic was not sufficient to support the applicants and those already in the field. In the absence of complaints by shippers, the Commission has had little occasion to prescribe rates.

CIVIL AVIATION

The airlines are the newest competitors of the railroads, carrying the smallest volume of traffic, but showing the most rapid growth. In 1918 the government began to operate air mail routes. In 1926 it began letting air mail contracts to private lines. The development of commercial aviation dates from this time. The growth of the industry was further stimulated by the great volume of traffic created by World War II. From 1940 to 1950 the quantity of mail carried increased five times, passenger miles six times, and express and freight tonnage fifty times. At the end of 1952 commercial airlines were serving nearly 700 cities with 1,250 planes. In that year they accounted for more than a third as many passenger miles as the railroads but for less than .1 per cent as many ton-miles of cargo.

Public Aid to Aviation

Airways, like highways and waterways, are provided by government. An airway is a route, ten miles or more in width, equipped with aids to navigation: beacon lights, radio ranges, communications facilities, weather reports, and emergency landing fields. Under a program initiated in 1948, omnidirectional ranges are gradually being installed to free pilots from the air lanes and permit direct flight. The airway system is maintained and operated by the federal government. No charge is made for its use.

Airports, too, are publicly provided. At the end of 1952 there were more than 2,000 municipal airports in the United States. Construction was first financed by local governments. Federal aid was given, in a haphazard fashion, from 1940 until 1946, when the Federal Airport Act was passed. Under this measure, aid for construction and improvement is extended, on a matching basis, in accordance with a comprehensive plan. The operation of airports is financed, in part, by landing fees, rentals, concessions, and the sale of fuel. But income does not cover interest on investment or depreciation or—in most cases—even maintenance and operating costs.

Commercial aviation is subsidized indirectly by being permitted to use the federal airways for nothing and municipal airports for less than cost. It is subsidized directly through payments designed to equal the amount by which an airline's revenues fail to cover its costs and yield a fair return on its investment. From 1938 to 1953 these payments were made by the Post Office in the form of excessive rates for carrying the mail. The rates were fixed by the Civil Aeronautics Board; the resulting subsidy was hidden, until 1951, in the postal deficit. In 1951 the CAB began reporting the air mail pay and the airline subsidy separately. In that year the pay was $26,500,000 and the subsidy $36,000,000. In 1952 the pay was $33,000,000 and the subsidy $25,000,000.[7] In 1953, under an executive order issued by President Eisenhower, responsibility for paying the subsidy was transferred from the Post Office to the CAB.

The Aviation Industry

On the airways, as on the highways and waterways, there are private, contract, and common carriers. The common carriers are of three types: scheduled carriers and non-scheduled carriers, handling both passengers and cargo, and carriers handling cargo alone. The scheduled carriers operate on established schedules over regular routes between fixed termini. They include two groups: the trunk lines, thirteen of them in 1953, the four largest (American, Eastern, Trans-World, and United) doing three fourths of the business; and the feeder lines, sixteen in number, rendering local services. The non-scheduled lines, known generally as the non-skeds, are not confined to fixed routes and are not supposed to operate with any regularity. In 1952 these included some 1,400 small carriers, such as the operators of air taxi services, and 64 companies operating large planes. There were three all-cargo lines (Flying Tiger, Slick, and U.S. Airlines) in 1953. Airline revenues are obtained primarily by carrying passengers and mail. In 1952 trunk line revenues came 87.6 per cent from passengers, 4.7 per cent from mail, and 5.4 per cent from express and freight; feeder line revenues 45.7 per cent from passengers, 50.4 per cent from mail, and only 1.9 per cent from express and freight, the remainder being miscellaneous.

In their economic characteristics the air carriers lie somewhere between the railroads and the trucking companies. They need make no investment in airways or airports. But planes are costly and depreciate rapidly. The annual cost of capital, therefore, is lower than for railways and higher than for motor carriers. Operating expenses vary with volume, but not directly, since planes are loaded at different fractions of capacity. In the short run, moreover, many other costs are fixed: insurance, taxes, rents, and administration. There may therefore be some tendency toward competition in rates so serious as to endanger service and safety. There may even be some tendency toward monopoly. But entry, unless controlled, is fairly easy. Without regulation it is likely that the industry would be competitive.

[7] Civil Aeronautics Board, *Administrative Separation of Subsidy from Total Mail Payments to Domestic Air Carriers*, 1951 and 1953.

The Pattern of Regulation

Aviation is regulated by many of the states. With respect to safety, such regulation is legally in effect but has been largely superseded, in practice, by federal control. With respect to economic matters, regulation of intrastate flying is left to the states. But commercial flights, in general, cross state lines, bringing the industry as a whole within the jurisdiction of the federal government. Under the Air Commerce Act of 1926, provision was made for regulation in the interest of safety. And under the Air Mail Act of 1934, control over airline service, accounting, and intercorporate relations was given to the Post Office, and power to fix rates for air mail was given to the ICC. Unified and comprehensive federal regulation dates from the Civil Aeronautics Act of 1938.

Under this Act, as it was modified by an executive order issued in 1940, aviation is subject to control by two federal agencies. The Civil Aeronautics Administration, in the Department of Commerce, has two general functions. It promotes aviation, establishing and maintaining the airway system, and planning and administering the airport program. It enforces safety rules, testing aircraft, examining airmen, controlling air traffic, and investigating accidents. The Civil Aeronautics Board, a semi-independent agency composed of five members appointed by the President and also located in the Department of Commerce, is charged primarily with responsibility for economic regulation. It controls entry, establishes routes, regulates rates, and determines air mail payments and subsidies. The Board also prescribes safety rules and investigates accidents.

With respect to safety, all flying is brought within the scope of the Act. With respect to economic matters, however, control is limited to common carriers. The CAB, moreover, is empowered to grant exemptions from control. The law follows the usual pattern of regulation, with certain differences. Entry requires a certificate of public convenience and necessity, the rights of carriers in business when the Act was passed being preserved by a grandfather clause. Abandonment also requires permission, and pooling, combination, and intercorporate relationships are subjected to control. Rates must be just and reasonable, without undue preference or prejudice. They must be published and observed and notice given before a change. Changes can be suspended, and the CAB can fix maximum rates or minima or both. The long-and-short-haul clause does not apply. As in the case of water carriers, no power is given to control the issuance of securities. The CAB has another function that differentiates it from the ICC. It is given authority, like that of the Federal Trade Commission, to prevent unfair methods of competition and unfair or deceptive practices within its jurisdiction by issuing orders to cease and desist.

Air Safety

Responsibility for safety is divided between the CAA and the CAB. The Board promulgates safety rules. The Administration enforces them.

It registers, tests, and rates aircraft. It inspects maintenance facilities. It examines and rates airmen and mechanics. It can reprimand them, suspend them, or revoke their certificates. It controls all traffic in the air. The airline pilot submits his flight plan to the CAA Air Route Traffic Control Center, giving his route number and his altitude. The Center makes sure that no other plane is flying this route at this altitude at this time. It then posts a clearance slip. The pilot must also get a take-off clearance from the CAA traffic tower. In flight, he follows the CAA radio range beam, receives the CAA weather information and keeps reporting his position to the CAA communications center. Upon arrival he may be guided by an instrument landing system or by precision approach radar operated by the CAA. To carry on its work, relating mainly to functions such as these, the Administration had a budget, in 1953, of nearly $140 million, and a staff of nearly 16,000 employees. The CAB, by comparison, is small in size.

Nine tenths of all accidents are investigated by the CAA. But accidents are also investigated by the CAB. This division of responsibility is based upon the theory that the CAA, in its administration of air safety rules, might itself be guilty of negligence and might therefore seek to shift the blame. The Board, accordingly, is authorized not only to promulgate the rules, but also, in case of serious accident, to make an independent investigation and determine responsibility. This body, however, is concerned primarily with economic regulation and lacks the special skills for safety work possessed by the CAA. Better provision for safety might be made if responsibility were centered in the CAA and a completely independent agency established to investigate the causes of accidents.

Control of Supply

Until 1938 there was no legal barrier to entry to civil aviation. Air mail contracts were let by competitive bidding. But any one who wished to operate without a contract was free to do so. Under the Civil Aeronautics Act, entry is controlled by the CAB. The Board may permit some carriers to operate by granting them exemptions, as it has done in the case of the non-skeds. Where carriers are not exempt they must obtain certificates. The certification of lines in existence in 1938 was mandatory. But action on applications covering new operations is within the discretion of the Board. Such applications have included proposals for new trunk lines, for the addition of new routes to old lines, for new feeder lines, and for all-cargo carriers.

In the years since 1938 the Board has granted no application for the creation of new trunk lines. In this respect it has obstructed competition. But it has sought to protect the earnings of existing carriers and thus to preclude the expenditure of larger sums on subsidies. The Board has looked with favor, however, on applications from old lines for new and extended routes. Here, it has sought to strengthen weaker systems and to promote competition by permitting the duplication of service on established routes. But its policy has been criticized as creating systems that cannot be self-supporting and impairing the earning capacity of the trunk lines as a whole. Three of the trunk lines had to be subsidized in 1953; ten were self-sufficient. The Board has also been generous in granting certificates to small carriers providing local and feeder services. And here, again, it has been criticized. With such services, in general, traffic has been sparse, revenues have been inadequate to cover costs, and subsidies accordingly have been high. Of the $25 million paid out in subsidies in 1952, as much as $19 million went to local lines. On some of these lines, the passenger paid as little as a fifth of the cost of his ride. And the lines took local business away from railroads and motor carriers. The Board acted on fifteen applications for all-cargo services in 1949, granting certificates to four concerns. Three of them, still surviving, compete with the cargo services of passenger lines. But the Board's action, in this case, has generally been approved.

The President's Air Coordinating Committee, reporting in 1954, recommended that the government move toward the elimination of subsidies by encouraging the formation of systems that would be capable of self-support. To this end, it proposed that the number of trunk lines be reduced and the weaker lines strengthened through combination, and that feeder lines, where continuation of their service is essential, be absorbed and supported by the larger carriers.[8] The CAB, in its control of combination, has refused to permit the acquisition of airlines by railroads or shipping companies. But it has tended to favor mergers among the airlines themselves. In this matter, however, its authority is merely permissive. As the law stands, combination cannot be compelled.

The most violent controversy with regard to the Board's policies has raged about its exemption of the non-skeds. This exemption was first granted in 1938 and was intended to apply to operations that were irregular in character and limited in extent. After World War II, however, the non-skeds increased in number, providing service with fair regularity on an increasing scale. In 1947 the Board required them to register. In 1949 it discontinued its blanket exemption and required them to apply for exemption individually. In 1951 it limited the number of flights that any one of them could make in any month to three on major routes and eight between fixed points. This ruling, however, evoked such a storm of protest that it was dropped in 1953. Non-scheduled operations have been defended as affording opportunity for small business and providing the competition that led to the inauguration, by scheduled lines, of air coach and air cargo services. They have been attacked as affording inferior safety and skimming the cream off the market to the detriment of the certificated carriers. Clearly, the exemption of large-scale regular services

[8] President's Air Coordinating Committee, *Civil Air Policy*, Washington, D.C., 1954, pp. 6–16.

is inconsistent with the theory of regulation. The President's Air Coordinating Committee recommended that it be stopped.[9]

Control of Rates and Subsidies

The CAB has exercised little control over rates. The airlines, in general, are prevented by the competition of other carriers from putting their rates too high. They might be tempted, however, to put them too low, since any losses they incurred would be made up to them in the form of larger subsidies. The Board did act, in 1947, under pressure from independent cargo operators, temporarily to fix minimum cargo rates, thus protecting the independents from competition by lines that could use their passenger revenues to subsidize their cargo business. It has made no effort to fix a minimum for fares, permitting them to be cut as a means of increasing traffic. Here, it has been less interested in tightening regulation than in promoting the use of the service.

The Board has devoted more attention to determining the amounts to be paid for carrying the mail or distributed as subsidies than to fixing rates and fares. It established two methods of payment for air mail: a service rate and a need rate. The service rate is paid to lines that are self-supporting. It is based on estimates of cost per pound-mile, involving an allocation of joint costs between mail and other services. A common figure is fixed for all of the lines in a group, and those that make a larger profit are allowed to keep it. An incentive is thus afforded for improvements in efficiency. The need rate (paid by the Post Office until 1953) went to carriers that had to be subsidized. It was computed separately for each line by adding together all costs, subtracting all other revenues, and adding a fair return (figured prospectively at 8 per cent and retroactively at 7 per cent) on actual investment. Subsidies paid by the CAB since 1953 have been computed on the same basis. This method of compensation underwrites all losses and affords no incentive to efficiency.

Before money is paid out in subsidies, the CAB is required by the Civil Aeronautics Act to consider the need of each airline for income "under honest, economical, and efficient management." But the Board lacks the management engineering staff that it would need to enable it to determine how efficiently the lines are managed. It does compare statistics of expenditures. And in computing subsidies, it may disallow certain expenditures that have already been made. But it does not really prevent inefficiency. To do so, it would have to be equipped to supervise the work of management in great detail.

REGULATING COMPETITIVE MEDIA

In the beginning the task of regulating the railroads, like that of regulating public utilities, was one of controlling a business possessing monop-

[9] *Ibid.*, pp. 18–21.

oly power. As other types of carriers came to offer serious competition, the familiar pattern of regulation was applied to each of them in turn. But the nature of the problem facing the regulators underwent a fundamental change. Entry could no longer be controlled, combinations judged, and rates fixed, solely with a view to the effect of action on a single type of carrier. Regulation, unless strictly impartial, would influence the allocation of traffic, thus affecting the comparative development of competing services. But impartiality, in the face of conflicting policies regarding promotion, was not to be achieved.

Control of Supply

Control of entry was first undertaken to protect the solvency of a regulated monopoly. It is now practiced to govern the adjustment of supply to demand in a competitive industry. In the cases of pipelines, water carriers, and airlines, this control has not been so employed as to inhibit competition. In the case of motor carriers, it has. Trucking companies have been denied certificates. And where certificates have been granted, they have frequently limited operating rights. Truckers may be confined to carrying certain commodities or classes of commodities. They may be permitted to give full service between two termini but not at intermediate points, to give service only by roundabout routes, or to give full service at some points and limited service at others. The effect is to prevent an economic use of truck space and to require unnecessarily expensive hauls.

Limitations on the supply of trucking service have their defenders. They are said to prevent destructive competition, impairment of service, and instability of rates. They are said, too, to permit attainment of the most economical scale of operation, and co-ordination of different transport services. But each of these arguments is open to question. The character of the industry's costs is such that destructive competition is unlikely to occur. Alternatives are so readily available that service is unlikely to be impaired. Uncertainty as to rates may be harmful to shippers, but this can be avoided by requiring prior notice of changes, rather than eliminating competition from the field. There may not be significant economies in large-scale operation. But if there are, it should be possible for firms to grow in size without the aid of artificial barriers to small competitors. Co-ordination of the services of different transport media can be effected by administrative action. But it could also be effected—and perhaps with greater economy and efficiency—through market processes. Control of the supply of trucking, moreover, has as its purpose protection of investors in the railroads. It operates to freeze technology, preserving outmoded forms of transportation and delaying the development of superior services. One fact, however, should be noted: the damage that regulation can do, in this regard, is limited by its inability to control the private carrier.

Control of supply operates in another way to obstruct adjustment to change. Carriers other than railroads are permitted to confine themselves to traffic they find to be profitable. The motor carriers do not haul goods that are low in value; the water carriers do not take goods in small lots; the airlines discourage unprofitable business by charging high rates. Each of them has the freedom to pick and choose. The railroads, however, are required to keep on handling business that yields no profit or even involves a loss. They must haul low-value goods that will move only at low rates. They must maintain service on branch lines that have ceased to pay their way. They must continue to carry commuters even though they would be better off if the commutation service were dropped. The railroads are thus victims, as well as beneficiaries, of quantitative controls.

Control of Combination

Where rail, motor, and water carriers are concerned, the control of combination is within the jurisdiction of the ICC. Where airlines are involved, it is within the jurisdiction of the CAB. The combination of like carriers and the combination of unlike carriers raise quite different problems. In the first case, the issue is whether to permit the elimination of possible competition in service as well as rates between firms who employ the same technology. In the second, it is whether to permit the elimination of competition, not only in service, but also in rates and in technology.

With respect to the railroads, until 1920 the government pursued two different policies. It recognized the existence of monopoly and regulated rates. But, at the same time, it forbade pooling under the Interstate Commerce Act and combination under the Sherman Act. The two policies were inconsistent. If regulation were effective, there would be little point in maintaining competition. If competition were maintained, there would be little need to regulate. Under the Transportation Act of 1920, this anomaly was brought to an end. Pooling and combination were made permissive, subject to approval by the ICC. And this precedent was followed, in later years, with other carriers.

The combination of unlike carriers may also be approved. But here, in general, approval has been withheld. The ICC has permitted railroads to acquire supplementary motor services but not competing ones. And the CAB has refused to permit control of airlines by surface carriers. In the interest of progress, they have required the different transport media to compete. But such competition makes for optimum economy only when the competitors are put on an equal footing. And this has never been done.

Control of Rates

As monopolists the railroads tended to differentiate their rates in accordance with the value of the services they rendered, charging in each case what the traffic would bear. As a regulator the ICC sought to prevent the rate level from going too high and the rate structure from becoming too discriminatory by fixing legal maxima. With the growth of competition, the pattern of railroad rates began to change. As motor carriers took over goods with higher values that had moved at higher rates, the railroads cut these rates to check the loss. They reduced their less-than-carload rates, graduating these rates by size of shipment, and introducing all-commodity rates for mixed carloads. As water carriers cut into the business of hauling goods with lower values, the railroads cut rates on their competing hauls. For moving such goods in trainloads, they established rates below their carload rates. Where goods could be handled more cheaply by other carriers, they fought to keep them on the rails. Where their competitors were subsidized, they met the rates resulting from the subsidy. The structure of railroad rates was still discriminatory. But the nature of the discrimination had changed. Lower rates were charged on the goods that now could be moved by other carriers; higher rates on the goods that could be moved by rail alone. Insofar as more profitable traffic was lost, rates had to be raised on the traffic that remained. And as rates were raised, the competition of other carriers grew more keen. In this situation, the task of regulation came to be less one of fixing maximum rates than of fixing minima.

As long as the government confined itself to fixing maximum rates, traffic was allocated among the different types of carriers in accordance with the choices of shippers, made in response to the rates that were charged. But as soon as the government began to fix minima, the allocation of traffic came under the influence of public policy. It is the purpose of this policy, as enunciated by Congress, "to provide for fair and impartial regulation of all modes of transportation . . . so administered as to recognize and preserve the inherent advantages of each. . . ." In fixing minimum rates, how is this to be done?

One possibility would be to establish a minimum for each commodity so high that every type of carrier could handle it. Under such a plan, the rates would be set to cover the costs of the carrier whose costs were highest. Inefficiency would be protected; incentive to progress would be removed. Instead of preserving inherent advantages, the plan would preserve inherent disadvantages.

A second possibility would be to fix minimum rates for each type of carrier on the basis of its costs alone. No one of them would be required to raise its rates to give protection to another. Inherent advantages would be preserved. The principle is clear, but its application depends upon the method used in computing costs. (1) If out-of-pocket costs were taken as the measure to be employed in setting individual rates, including no allowance for overhead, there would be no real limit to competition. The carrier with the lowest out-of-pocket costs in the short run would get the business. The one that could operate most economically in the long run might be driven from the field. Its inherent advantages would not be preserved. (2) If costs were fully allocated, each item of traffic being required to carry its proportionate share of the overhead, business would be distributed more economically and inherent advantages preserved. But the railroads would be forbidden to meet the rates of their competitors. Their position would be worsened by denying them the right to discriminate in an effort to insure full use of their facilities. It is desirable that some discrimination be permitted where investments are large and fixed costs high. (3) Another measure lies between these two extremes. Minimum rates can be set to cover the fully-allocated costs of the medium whose costs are lowest. Other carriers can be permitted to reduce their individual rates to this level, provided they cover their out-of-pocket costs. The inherent advantages of the low-cost medium will thus be protected. And other media will be allowed, through discrimination, to compete for business that would keep their facilities in use.

In effect, the last of these measures is the one the ICC has used. Starting with an established structure of rates, it has permitted one type of carrier to meet the rates of another where they are "reasonably compensatory," but has forbidden it, in doing so, to go below its out-of-pocket costs. Its policy thus puts a floor under competition and affords continued opportunity to the medium whose costs are high, but still permits traffic to move at rates set by the medium whose costs are low.

Promotion versus Regulation

If minimum rate making is to be impartial, permitting traffic to be allocated in accordance with inherent advantages, the real costs of each type of carrier must be reflected in its money costs. But insofar as carriers are subsidized, their money costs will not reflect their real costs. Rates will be based on artificial rather than inherent advantages. Traffic will be allocated, not in accordance with comparative economy of operation, but in proportion to the sizes of the subsidies. The effort to achieve impartiality in regulation will be set at naught.

This, in fact, is the case. The railroads have to cover all their costs. Their competitors, save for the pipelines and possibly some of the motor carriers, do not. Heavy trucks and buses may not be required to pay their share of highway costs. Carriers by water and by air are not required to pay for the use of the waterways or the airways. And airlines, in addition, are paid an outright subsidy. As a result, facilities are expanded where costs are high and traffic diverted from carriers whose costs are low.

The promotion of different forms of transportation is subject to no comprehensive plan. Money is voted separately for highways, waterways, and airways without regard to its effect on transportation as a whole. Administration, too, is unco-ordinated. Federal aid to state highways is handled by the Bureau of Public Roads. Improvement of waterways is the work of the Army Corps of Engineers. Airways are provided and federal aid to airports administered by the CAA. Nowhere is there an agency possessing overall responsibility. Nowhere is any effort made to achieve consistency between regulation and promotion in accordance with the stated principles of national transportation policy.

TOWARD ECONOMY IN TRANSPORTATION

Each of the modes of transportation has its particular advantages. Motor carriers are best adapted to moving goods in small quantities, making short hauls, providing feeder services, and meeting the need for flexibility. Water carriers have the lowest costs where freight is hauled in bulk for long distances and speed is not required. The airlines enjoy superiority in carrying passengers and valuable goods for long distances at high speeds. The railroads do best on long hauls in carload lots at intermediate speeds. Here, their scope, speed, and dependability are greater than those of the water carriers, and their costs lower than those of the motor carriers or the airlines. Greater economy would be realized in transportation if each of these media could be given the work that it is best equipped to do. This might be accomplished in one of two ways: administratively, by bringing the several transport media under common control, or through the market, by equalizing competitive opportunities.

Co-ordination of Services

Administrative co-ordination could be effected by transportation companies operating railroads, trucks and buses, ships and planes. For each shipment, the managers of such an enterprise would presumably employ the method that would move it with the greatest convenience and economy. Provision would be made for interconnection of different services at common termini. Trucks and buses would be used for pickup and delivery, supplementing longer hauls by railways, waterways, and airlines. Interchangeable containers could be used, trucks and trailers carried on flatcars, rolling stock loaded onto ships. A complete service could be offered, at the lowest possible cost, adapted to the needs of the customer.

This might be accomplished by a company possessing a national or regional monopoly. With such an organization, savings could be realized, too, through unification of facilities, joint use of equipment, elimination of duplicate services, and the like. But the stimulus of competition would be lacking. Stagnation, rather than progress, might be the result.

The different modes of transportation might also be combined and operated together, in any area, by each of a number of different companies. This form of organization is favored by the railroads. It would preserve competition in service, if not in rates. It would simplify regulation by eliminating the competitive inequality of different carriers. But the plan has one great danger. It might impede the development of carriage by highway, by water, and by air. The transportation companies would be dominated by railroad interests, since their major investment would be in rail facilities. They might well hesitate to employ the other media if these facilities were partly idle. The full costs of hauling a shipment could be lower by truck than by rail, but if out-of-pocket costs were still lower by rail, the truck would not be used. The railroads, moreover, have been notoriously unprogressive. It is mainly through the competition of other media that their service has been improved. If this competition were to be ended, they might sink back into their rut.

Equalizing Competitive Opportunities

If transportation is to be competitive, it is important that the independence of the different types of carriers be preserved. But if traffic is to be allocated among these carriers in accordance with their inherent advantages, they must be put on an equal footing with regard to costs. This might be done in one of two ways. The motor, water, and air carriers could be charged for the use of public facilities. Or the railroads could be given aid that would be comparable to that now given their competitors.

User charges have the advantage of collecting the cost of transportation facilities from the people who use them instead of imposing it on the general taxpayer. Their effect on competition among the different media depends upon the way in which they are computed. Here, there are three possibilities. (1) The other carriers might be asked to pay charges equivalent to the burden borne by the railroads. In this case, they would be expected not only to meet their share of the costs incurred by the government in providing them with facilities, but also to cover costs the government had not incurred: interest on land though no land had been bought, interest on investment though it had been financed in whole or in part by taxation rather than by borrowing, interest at commercial rates though money had been borrowed at government rates, and taxes on property though no such taxes had been paid. This method of computation would protect the railroads, but it would subject the other carriers to an artificial handicap. (2) The users of public facilities might merely be required to pay their own share of the costs actually incurred by the government. Such costs would not include the imputed interest or taxes mentioned above. Their allocation among different purposes (such as flood control, irrigation, power production, and navigation) and among different classes of users (such as automobiles and light and heavy trucks and buses) would be difficult. But once this problem was solved, the subsidization of competing carriers through government outlays would be brought to an end. This, however, would not require the users of public facilities to meet their full economic costs. For these include the cost of capital, not only when borrowed, but also when provided by the taxpayer. (3) User charges could be set to cover economic costs, including interest actually paid by the government and interest imputed, at the same rate, on capital provided by the taxpayer. But even here, the competitors of the railroads would enjoy an advantage. They would have to meet only a part of the cost of jointly used facilities. This cost would include interest but at the low rate paid by government. And it would include no taxes.

If user charges were imposed, it is probable that motor carriers could pay them and continue to compete. But transportation by water and by air would certainly be curtailed. It may be argued that such transportation, even where uneconomic, should be maintained. Water carriers and airlines may be needed for national defense. But so, for that matter, are the railroads. Defense requirements, where legitimate, should be defined with precision, not used in vague justification of haphazard subsidies. And other carriers should not be aided in ways that harm the railroads, which must haul the bulk of the goods that are needed in time of war.

Competition might be equalized, alternatively, by aiding the railroads. The government could purchase their facilities, assuring them continued use. It could then provide ways to all types of carriers without charge, or impose charges that would result in comparable costs. Even if the railroads were required to finance the government's outlay, their fixed costs would be reduced: the interest rate would be lower and there would be no property taxes to pay. This suggestion raises many problems that cannot now be explored. It is opposed by the railroads, who see in it an entering wedge for public ownership.

Less Regulation or More?

The regulation of transportation was undertaken when the railroads were monopolists. Now that the industry is competitive, it may well be asked whether regulation, instead of being extended, should not be dropped. The answer is, in part, that competition is not complete. There are still hauls that can be made only by rail. And though competition has changed the pattern of discrimination, protection against undue discrimination is still required. The railroads, moreover, possess much greater resources than their competitors. In the absence of regulation, they might engage in unfair competition, driving their weaker rivals from the field. They might refuse, for instance, to interchange shipments with other carriers. They might slash rates on competing traffic or establish competing services, conducting them at a loss. With their competitors eliminated, they might then proceed to regain and to exploit their position of monopoly.

Few would propose that regulation be abandoned, but many have suggested that it be relaxed. According to one view, existing powers over the railroads should be retained, but the power to restrict entry into other transport industries and the power to fix minimum rates for these industries should be withdrawn. Greater reliance would thus be placed on competition as a regulator of railroad rates. This proposal assumes, of course, that the problems involved in placing the carriers on an equal competitive footing will somehow be solved.[10] Other observers have proposed that control over the minimum rates charged and over the discrimination practiced by railroads be continued, but that control over maximum rates be dropped, and that the clause in the 1933 rule of rate making requiring the ICC to consider the "effect of rates on the movement of traffic" be repealed. In this view, competition is now sufficiently strong to prevent the general level of rates from going too high. And, in this situation, responsibility for decisions concerning the probable effect of rates on revenues should be returned to railway managements, eliminating duplication of the managerial function with its consequent delays.[11] It has also been urged, with some reason, that carriers be accorded greater freedom to abandon unprofitable services. Alternatives are now so readily available that little hardship would be involved.

Proposals that regulation be tightened are as frequent as those that it be relaxed. It is pointed out, for instance, that railroads are completely covered while many classes of other carriers are exempt: trucks transporting agricultural commodities, livestock, and fish, water carriers transporting a few commodities in bulk, and all but scheduled airlines. It is noted, too, that the control of contract carriers is weak and that of common carriers often incomplete: there is no federal control, for instance, over intrastate traffic by media other than railroads, over the issuance of securities by water carriers and airlines, or over the abandonment of motor or water services. To achieve effective and impartial regulation, it is said, these gaps in the law should be closed. Voluntary consolidation, also, has been a failure. Elimination of the weaker airlines could be effected by withdrawing subsidies. But if stronger railroad systems were to be created and weaker lines absorbed, compulsion would be required. This would doubtless be resisted by investors who stood to lose, and questions of constitutionality would be raised. But it is the only way, short of public ownership, that the sort of consolidation contemplated by the Act of 1920 could be brought about.

Reorganizing Transport Agencies

It is generally agreed that the various federal agencies engaged in promoting the different forms of transportation should be brought together in a single department, perhaps in a Department of Transportation with a Secretary in the President's cabinet. Such a department would be charged with responsibility for planning the development of transportation as a whole. It would also take over the executive functions of other agencies, such as the promulgation and enforcement of safety regulations and car

[10] See James C. Nelson, "The Role of Regulation Re-examined," National Resources Planning Board, *Transportation and National Policy* (Washington, D.C.: U.S. Government Printing Office, 1942), pp. 197–238.

[11] See Charles L. Dearing and Wilfred Owen, *National Transportation Policy* (Washington, D.C.: Brookings Institution, 1949), pp. 272–304, 371–75.

service rules. Its relation to regulatory functions, however, is a matter of dispute. Some students of public administration contend that such functions should be located in the department. Others contend that the independence of the regulatory agencies should be rigidly preserved. The weight of opinion appears to lie with the latter group.

Another point is debated with even greater heat. Should the regulation of civil aviation be turned over to the ICC or should it remain with the CAB? In support of concentrating power in a single agency, it is argued that authority must be comprehensive if policy is to be consistent, regulation impartial, and decisions made in the light of their effect on transportation as a whole. In opposition, it is said that the ICC is overworked, that it is ignorant of the peculiar problems of aviation, and that its sympathies are with the railroads. One's choice in this dispute depends upon his purposes. If the creation of a national transportation system is the goal, it is best to be reached by bringing all types of carriers within the jurisdiction of a single agency. But if the promotion of aviation is to have priority, this is best to be achieved by maintaining the independence of the CAB. So far, the Congress has made the second choice.

SUGGESTIONS FOR FURTHER READING

All of the matters discussed in this chapter are considered at greater length in the standard texts on transportation cited at the end of Chapter 19. The regulation of pipelines is covered by Locklin in chap. xxviii and by Westmeyer in chap. xxx. See also W. A. Prewitt, "The Operation and Regulation of Crude Oil and Gasoline Pipe Lines," *Quarterly Journal of Economics*, LVI (1942) 177–211. The control of motor carriers is discussed by Locklin in chaps. xxix–xxxiii, and by Westmeyer in chaps. xviii–xxii. A more complete study of this subject is Charles A. Taff, *Commercial Motor Transportation* (Homewood, Ill.: Richard D. Irwin, Inc., 1952). For a critical appraisal of public policy respecting highway transportation, see National Resources Planning Board, *Transportation and National Policy* (Washington, D.C.: U.S. Government Printing Office, 1942), pp. 197–237. The control of civil aviation is considered by Locklin in chaps. xxxv–xxxvii, and by Westmeyer in chaps. xxvi–xxx. A fuller text is John H. Frederick, *Commercial Air Transportation* (3d ed., Homewood, Ill.: Richard D. Irwin, Inc., 1951). For a shorter discussion, see Richard Hellman, "The Air Transport Industry," chap. xiii in Walter Adams (ed.), *The Structure of American Industry* (New York: Macmillan Company, 1950). The policies followed in regulating air carriers are criticized in Lucile S. Keyes, *Federal Control of Entry into Air Transportation* (Cambridge: Harvard University Press, 1951), and defended in Civil Aeronautics Board, *The Role of Competition in Commercial Air Transportation*, a report to the Subcommittee on Monopoly of the Select Committee on Small Business, U.S. Senate, 1952. The most recent statement on the subject is *Civil Air Policy* (Washington, D.C.: President's Air Coordinating Committee, 1954). For current information, see the annual reports of the Civil Aeronautics Board.

The promotion of various modes of transportation is treated extensively in Charles L. Dearing and Wilfred Owen, *National Transportation Policy* (Washington, D.C.: Brookings Institution, 1949), Part I, and more briefly in Bigham and Roberts, chap. xxii, and in National Resources Planning Board, *Transportation and National Policy*, pp. 250–78. The fundamental studies of public aid are Federal Coordinator of Transportation, *Public Aids to Transportation* (Washington, D.C.: U.S. Government Printing Office, 1940), and Board of Investigation and Research, *Public Aids to Domestic Transportation*, 79th Cong., 1st Sess., House Doc. No. 159 (1944). The relation between promotion and regulation is discussed by Dearing and Owen in Part II, by Bigham and Roberts in chap. xvii, and by the NRPB report on pp. 102–39. See also Truman C. Bigham, "Regulation of Minimum Rates in Transportation," *Quarterly Journal of Economics*, LXI (1947) 206–11; and Ernest W. Williams, Jr., "The ICC and the Regulation of Intercarrier Competition," *Harvard Law Review*, LXIII (1950) 1349–72. The future of transportation policy is considered by Locklin in chap. xxxviii, by Westmeyer in chaps. xxxii and xxxiii, by Bigham and Roberts in chap. xxiv, by Fair and Williams in chap. xxxvi, by Dearing and Owen in chaps. xvi and xvii, and by the NRPB report on pp. 1–17 and 304–29. Recent official statements are: Secretary of Commerce, *Issues Involved in a Unified and Coordinated Federal Program for Transportation* (Washington, D.C.: U.S. Government Printing Office, 1950), and Senate Committee on Interstate and Foreign Commerce, *Domestic Land and Water Transportation*, 82d Cong., 1st Sess., Senate Rept., No. 1039 (1951). The railroad point of view is presented in *Sound Transportation for the National Welfare* (Chicago: Transportation Association of America, 1953).

Chapter 23 REGULATION OF RADIO AND TELEVISION

In its supervision of companies providing interstate and international communication by telegraph, telephone, cable, and radio, the Federal Communications Commission uses the methods customarily employed in the regulation of common carriers, controlling entry, services, and rates. The Commission also has jurisdiction over radio broadcasting, but here its function is a different one. Entry is rigidly controlled, but for a different reason than with public utilities. In such industries, this control is designed to maintain essential services by preventing destructive competition—resulting from heavy investments and high fixed charges—that would endanger solvency and impair credit. In broadcasting, on the other hand, investments are comparatively small, fixed costs are low, and destructive competition is unlikely to occur. Here, control of entry is necessitated by the fact that the number of channels in the radio spectrum is limited and demand for their use exceeds the supply. Air space must be allocated, but the task is primarily one of making and enforcing traffic rules. The broadcaster's services are scrutinized in granting or denying him the right to use the air, but they are not regulated in detail. Rates are not controlled. The broadcaster serves the consumer without charge; there is no rate to be fixed. He sells time to the advertiser, but here he faces the competition of other stations and other advertising media. There is no need, therefore, to impose on him the obligations of a common carrier or to fix his rates. Among the businesses that are subject to commission regulation, broadcasting stands in a class by itself.

In assigning channels to different applicants, the FCC must consider the relative importance of various purposes: safety at sea and in the air, police and military operations, dispatching of trucks and taxis, telephonic connection with trains and ships and with subscribers in rural areas, communication by amateurs, and experimentation with new devices, as well as educational and commercial broadcasting. All of these require consideration and their respective claims must be weighed, one against the other, in assigning exclusive rights to the use of channels in the air. But it is only with the regulation of public broadcasting that the present chapter is concerned.

BACKGROUND OF REGULATION

Communication by radio dates from the discoveries of Guglielmo Marconi in Italy around the turn of the century and from subsequent developments by Ambrose Fleming in England and by Lee De Forest and E. H. Armstrong, among others, in the United States. The first public broadcast in this country, using the method of amplitude modulation, occurred in 1920 when Westinghouse station KDKA in Pittsburgh announced the election of Warren G. Harding. Other stations were soon established by Westinghouse, General Electric, and A.T.&T. It was assumed, at this time, that broadcasting was to be financed by manufacturers of receiving sets and, perhaps, by educational institutions and city governments. Then, in 1922, commercial broadcasting was inaugurated by the A.T.&T. station, WEAF in New York, and radio shortly became an advertising medium. The first network was set up by A.T.&T. in 1923. Then, following an agreement with GE, Westinghouse, and their patent-holding company, RCA, in 1926, A.T.&T. withdrew from the field, its network being taken over by an RCA subsidiary, the National Broadcasting Company. The Columbia Broadcasting System was set up in the following year. Network domination of the broadcasting business dates from this time. Frequency modulation broadcasting, on a commercial basis, was authorized in 1940, television in 1941, and color television in 1951. The business has grown phenomenally. There were 110 million receiving sets in use in the United States in 1953, including 10 million FM sets and 25 million receiving TV. There were one or more sets in 95 per cent of the nation's homes—75 million of them in 45 million homes—and another 27 million in automobiles.[1] The number of commercial broadcasting stations had increased from 966 in 1943 to 3,668 in 1953. Of these, 2,584 were on AM, 601 on FM, and 483 on TV.[2] Programs were being broadcast in color in twenty cities in 1954 and were planned for forty others in 1955. It was expected that 700–800 television stations would be on the air in 375 cities, reaching nine tenths of the country's population, by the end of 1956.

Interests in Radio

The groups with a stake in radio are many and diverse. They may be identified as follows:

1. The broadcasting stations. A few of them are owned by networks, but nearly 99 per cent are independent. The typical station is a small-scale business. For radio, construction and annual operating costs run around $50,000; for television, from $200,000 to $250,000. The stations obtain part of their revenue by selling time directly to advertisers, part by selling it

[1] Federal Communications Commission, *Nineteenth Annual Report*, 1953, p. 123.
[2] *Ibid.*, p. 111.

to networks. The business is highly profitable. In 1952 the independent AM and combined AM-FM stations made 364 per cent on the depreciated cost of their physical property; the independent television stations made 85 per cent.[3] The broadcaster's most valuable asset is his license, giving him an exclusive right to a portion of the air, which he gets as a present from the government. Stations are bought and sold at figures far in excess of their physical worth, the difference being a capitalization of their monopoly rights. Substantial gains are realized in the process, and vested interests are established, making it almost certain that licenses, once granted, will always be renewed.

2. The networks. There are four national networks and several regional networks in radio, four national networks in television. These concerns operate some forty stations and have contractual relations with more than half of the independent radio stations and with nearly all of the television stations. They buy time from these stations at retail and sell it to advertisers at wholesale. They provide commercial and sustaining programs, originating half of the material broadcast by their affiliates and three fourths of that broadcast during the evening hours. This business, too, is profitable. In 1952 three regional networks made 116 per cent on the depreciated cost of their physical assets. The four national radio networks made 80 per cent. The four national television networks made 20 per cent.[4]

3. A.T.&T. Following its patent agreement with RCA, this company has owned and leased to the networks the facilities over which their programs are carried from station to station for rebroadcasting. Its monopoly in this field contributes a substantial portion of its revenue.

4. The advertisers. These are the merchants and the manufacturers who buy time on local stations and on national networks to sell their wares. In some cases, they merely pay for spot announcements. In others, they finance elaborate shows. Conspicuous among the users of this medium are the makers of branded consumers' goods such as cigarettes, gasoline, and soap.

5. The advertising agencies. These are the concerns that plan the national advertising campaigns, dream up the slogans, compose the commercials, write the scripts for network shows, hire the musicians and the actors, and stage the performances. They arrange for time on the networks, sell programs to the advertisers. This is the origin of the programs that are most widely heard and seen. A few advertisers and a few agencies dominate the networks and the stations, largely controlling what goes on the air.

6. The amusement industry. This includes ASCAP, whose activities in collecting royalties for the owners of music copyrights were described in Chapter 6. It also includes unions of musicians, actors, and technical

[3] *Ibid.*, pp. 114–16.
[4] *Ibid.*

personnel. These groups deal with the stations, the networks, and the advertising agencies.

7. The manufacturers and (8) the distributors of radio and television sets. These companies may have substantial sums tied up in inventories embodying an earlier technology. Their earnings may therefore be threatened by technical change.

9. The repair men. These are the small-scale operators for whose services the consumer pays many millions of dollars a year. Some of them make repairs when none are needed and charge more for their work than it is worth. And the consumer has no defense.

10. The listener and the looker. This is the forgotten man, woman, and child of radio and TV. The advertiser, the agency, the network, and the station try to give him what they think he wants. But the government gives him little thought. Supposedly, he gets his entertainment free. Actually, he does not. His investment—in receiving sets, in electricity, and in repair bills—is many times as large as that of all the other groups combined. And he pays for his programs when he buys the goods they advertise. But the other groups are organized to exert political pressure and the listener-looker is not. As a result, the government serves their interests more than his.

Beginnings of Control

Regulation was first applied to broadcasting under the authority of an Act passed in 1912 which was designed to control the use of air waves in telegraphy and telephony. Under this law, persons transmitting radio messages were required to obtain licenses from the Secretary of Commerce, and operation without a license was made a misdemeanor. As the law was worded, it was not clear whether the Secretary had the power to refuse licenses or was obliged to grant them to all who might apply. But Herbert Hoover, when Secretary, sought to employ this authority to control the number of licensees. He called a conference of broadcasters and negotiated an allocation of frequencies. Under this allocation, the Zenith Radio Corporation of Chicago was put on the same frequency as General Electric and limited to two hours of broadcasting per week. Zenith jumped to another channel and Hoover brought suit to enjoin it from broadcasting. The court decided for the company in 1926 and Hoover appealed to the Attorney-General for a ruling as to his powers. The Attorney-General replied that the Secretary had no authority, under the Act of 1912, to withhold licenses or to designate frequencies, prescribe hours of operation, or limit station power. Hoover therefore abandoned his attempt to regulate the industry. The result was pandemonium. Within the next few months, some two hundred new stations went on the air, each of them using any frequency it chose. Interference was general, and the usefulness of radio as a medium of communication was virtually destroyed. In desperation, the industry turned to the government, demanding public action to bring order out of chaos in the air.

The Radio Act of 1927 forbade broadcasting without a license, set up a Federal Radio Commission to pass on applications for licenses, and authorized it to assign wave lengths, fix hours of operation, and control station power. Licenses were to be granted only where the Commission found that this would serve the "public interest, convenience, or necessity." They were limited to three years and were subject to revocation. The Commission thus held the power of life and death over every station in the industry. But this power was not exercised with a firm hand. By 1927 the commercial interests were thoroughly entrenched. The broadcasting business had become an advertising medium, and the organization of programs had been taken over by the network companies. The Commission did not attempt to alter the established pattern of control. It gave the best channels, the best hours, and the highest power to the commercial interests, assigning poor channels, off hours, and low power for educational broadcasting. It did little or nothing to improve or maintain the quality of broadcast services or to protect the broadcasting privilege against abuse. The Commission's timidity is to be explained, in part, by the fact that its appropriations were small and its tenure uncertain. Its authority was granted by Congress, in 1927, 1928, and 1929, for a year at a time, and was not made permanent until 1930. The agency was abolished when its functions were taken over by the Federal Communications Commission under the Communications Act of 1934.

Radio under the Communications Act

The sections of the Communications Act dealing with radio follow the pattern established by the Radio Act of 1927. The law requires broadcasters to obtain licenses from the FCC and authorizes the Commission to classify stations, prescribe their services, assign their frequencies, determine their locations, and fix their power. It instructs the Commission to bring about an efficient and equitable distribution of radio services among states and communities. Licenses cannot be granted to aliens, to foreign corporations, to domestic corporations controlled by foreigners, to representatives of foreign governments, or to persons found guilty of violating the antitrust laws. The Commission is empowered to inquire into the technical, financial, and moral responsibility of other applicants, the quality of their broadcasting apparatus, the qualifications of their technical personnel, and the value of their services to listeners. The standard governing the issuance of licenses is still that of "public interest, convenience, or necessity." It is the stated purpose of the Act to provide for the use of radio channels by private enterprises "but not the ownership thereof." Licenses cannot be transferred or assigned without Commission approval. They are limited, as before, to three years and may be renewed, modified, or revoked. The broadcasting of lotteries and of obscene, indecent, or profane language is prohibited, and a station that provides time to one candidate for public office is required to afford equal opportunities to rival candidates. But the Commission is forbidden to censor radio programs or to interfere with the right of free speech.

The Commission has occupied itself, in the main, with the problem of allocating air space, and with the difficult issues of policy which this involves. It has granted and renewed licenses and approved transfers of broadcasting properties. It has policed the air to apprehend illegal operators and to enjoin their activities. It has issued rules to govern the relation of stations and networks, has published a study of the character of radio programs, and has sought unsuccessfully to suppress give-away programs as lotteries. But the Commission lacks the resources with which to monitor programs with any regularity. And it has shown great reluctance to interfere with broadcasting operations, rarely employing its power to deny renewal of licenses. Despite its moderation, however, the FCC has been a center of violent controversy. The commercial interests in radio are not harmonious. Whatever the issue before the Commission and whatever its decision, someone is certain to be dissatisfied. As a result, the agency has constantly been subject to political attack.

ALLOCATION OF AIR SPACE

The allocation of air space is necessitated by the fact that the number of broadcasting channels and the number of stations that can use a single channel without interference are strictly limited. Radio broadcasts are carried by electromagnetic waves emitted from an electric circuit in which the magnitude of the current is constantly being changed. The frequency of the waves depends upon the frequency of the oscillations employed, slow oscillations producing long waves with low frequencies, rapid oscillations producing short waves with high frequencies. The frequencies are measured in waves per second, the units of measurement used being kilocycles (thousands of cycles) and megacycles (millions of cycles). The spectrum available for practical use extends from the low frequencies where broadcasts are disturbed by static to the high frequencies where physical limitations make broadcasting increasingly difficult. The standard AM broadcast band has been assigned to the middle frequencies between 550 and 1,600 kilocycles per second. To avoid interference in such broadcasting, it is necessary to give each channel a width of ten kilocycles. There is thus room for 106 channels in the standard band. The number of stations that may occupy these channels depends upon the hours during which they may broadcast and the amount of power they may use. With the power and the hours now permitted, there is room for some 2,600 AM stations in the United States. The number of applicants for AM licenses is many times this figure. The FCC, therefore, must pick and choose. And since licenses are costless and highly profitable, its task is that of giving valuable prizes to a few and denying opportunity to many more. The Commission's problem is the same, as we shall see, when it undertakes to allocate space in the higher frequencies for FM and TV.

The AM Allocation

One question that had to be answered in making the AM allocation was that of station power. At stake here were the issues of monopoly versus competition in broadcasting, availability of service to listeners in different regions, availability of the medium for local uses, and cultural standardization versus cultural diversity. It was the intention of Congress that the industry should be competitive and that every region in the country should be served. But these objectives were in conflict. If the power permitted were low, the number of stations could be large, but listeners in remote and sparsely settled regions would not be reached by broadcasts. If the power were high, every region could be reached, but the number of stations would be small. Broadcasting, moreover, would tend to be concentrated in a few large cities. Matters of state and local interest would not get on the air. Broadcasts would be devoted primarily to making sales in mass markets. Programs would not be designed to meet the needs of rural listeners. Everything would be cast in the standard mold of Broadway and Hollywood.

The Commission might have escaped this dilemma by giving high power in some channels and low power in others. From 1934 to 1939, in fact, it did permit WLW in Cincinnati to broadcast experimentally at 500 kilowatts. But it was felt that high-power stations would be given an unfair advantage over their low-power competitors. So, in 1939, the permission was withdrawn. Under present regulations, stations are divided into three classes: local, regional, and clear channel, the local stations being assigned as much as 250 watts, the regional stations from one to five kilowatts, and the clear channel stations from 10 to 50 kilowatts, some sixty of them operating at the higher power. On this basis, too, the opportunities for earnings are unequal. And regional diversity has not really been protected, since the development of network broadcasting has insured the uniformity that low power was intended to prevent.

Similar issues are encountered in fixing broadcast hours. A radio transmitter emits waves that behave in two different ways: ground waves that travel near the surface of the earth and sky waves that go off into the air. At night, the sky waves are reflected back to earth by the ionosphere. As a result, an AM channel can be used by several stations without interference during the day but not at night. If all stations are permitted to operate around the clock, rural areas will not get clear reception after dark. But if this privilege is given to some stations and not to others, the former will be favored and the latter handicapped. Here, there has been a compromise. By international agreement, certain channels have been reserved for the exclusive use of single stations at night and other stations assigned to these channels have been confined to daytime hours. Reception in rural areas is thus given some protection. But the clear-channel stations are limited in power. They are located, moreover, in major cities, and their programs are designed to appeal to an urban audience. As a result, there are still some parts of the country in which reception is lacking or inadequate and many others in which local interests are not served.

The FM Allocation

In AM broadcasting, sound is transmitted by varying the amplitude of the carrier wave. With frequency modulation, the amplitude of the wave is kept the same and its frequency varied. The band allotted to FM broadcasting is in the higher frequencies between 88 and 108 megacycles per second. Since each FM channel requires a width of 400 kilocycles, there is room in this band for 50 channels, as compared with the 106 available for AM. But high-frequency waves, instead of traveling along the ground, pass off into space. With such waves, also, the elimination of static requires less power. As a result, stations can be located closer together without interference, and more stations can share the same channel. Thus, with 50 channels, it should be possible to have 2,000 stations broadcasting on FM. The introduction of FM, therefore, was expected substantially to increase the number of stations, providing more opportunities for local interests, and making the industry more competitive. Reception of FM, moreover, is superior to that of AM, since it is relatively free from interference and is beyond the reach of most varieties of static.

Commission approval of FM broadcasting was opposed by the owners of existing AM stations. Approval was given, however, in 1940. But despite the superiority of FM reception, the expected growth of this method of broadcasting did not occur. Listeners who had already invested in AM receivers were reluctant to convert. And new buyers found that AM sets were cheaper than FM sets. As a result, the AM stations held the mass audience and the national advertising business, while the independent FM stations reached fewer listeners and sought to support themselves by selling advertising time to local merchants. The number of FM stations reached 1,020 in 1948 but had declined to 601 by 1953.[5] Of these, however, nine tenths were operated by AM broadcasters and employed for the simultaneous transmission of AM programs. Independent FM stations have never been profitable. The 56 on the air in 1952 were operated at an aggregate loss of $1 million.[6] The financial weakness of FM has proved to be advantageous, however, to one group of listeners. Lacking the means to present live programs, a number of FM stations devote a major part of

[5] *Ibid.*, p. 111.
[6] *Ibid.*, p. 115.

their time to broadcasting records of fine music. An audience that would otherwise have been neglected has thus been served.

The TV Allocation

The space originally allotted for television by the FCC fell in the very high frequency band between 54 and 216 megacycles per second. This space overlapped that assigned to FM broadcasts, leaving 12 channels of the width required for TV. There were 37 stations operating in these channels in 1948 and 71 others under construction, a total of 108. Stations were already encountering interference, and the demand for further space was far in excess of the supply. It appeared to be possible, however, to increase the number of channels available by making use of the ultra high frequencies (UHF). But before this could be done, it was necessary to determine the feasibility of UHF broadcasting and to fix the width of channels, the distance between stations, and the amount of power to be used. At the same time, it was desirable to reconsider the allocation of very high frequency (VHF) space to TV. The Commission therefore imposed a freeze on TV, granting no more construction permits and no new licenses. A new allocation was worked out during the next three years and the freeze was lifted in the spring of 1952.

The TV allocation retains the 12 channels in the VHF band and creates 70 new channels, each 6,000 kilocycles wide, located between 470 and 890 megacycles in the UHF band, making 82 channels in all. The distance required between stations differs for different geographic zones, running from 170 to 220 miles for VHF and from 155 to 205 miles for UHF. The power permitted on different VHF channels runs from 100 to 316 kilowatts; that permitted UHF stations is 1,000 kilowatts. On this basis, there is room for 2,051 television stations in 1,275 different communities, 619 of them on VHF and 1,432 on UHF. When the freeze was lifted, there was a land rush of applicants for licenses. The Commission established a system of priorities to govern its consideration of applications, giving first priority to cities more than 40 miles from an existing station and considering these in order of population. In the next 18 months, it authorized 453 new stations, 178 in the VHF band and 275 in the UHF band.

The new allocation, however, is not working out as was expected. The UHF stations are running into the same difficulty as was encountered by FM. Nearly all the television receivers in use in 1953 were built for VHF. Of the new sets produced in that year, moreover, 80 per cent were equipped for VHF alone and only 20 per cent for both VHF and UHF. If the owners of VHF sets are to receive UHF broadcasts, they must invest in converters, additional antennas, etc., and this is an investment that few are willing to make. The UHF stations are thus caught in a vicious circle: lacking an audience, they cannot obtain large advertising revenues; lacking revenues, they cannot finance popular programs; lacking such programs, they cannot attract an audience. As a result, the stations are forced to fight an uphill battle for survival. Some of them have surrendered their licenses. There are many applicants for the few spots still available in VHF, few for the many available in UHF.

This development could have been avoided in a number of different ways. (1) All television stations could have been moved into the UHF band. But this would have rendered most TV sets obsolete and would therefore have been highly unpopular. (2) Some cities could have been assigned exclusively to VHF and others to UHF, instead of putting most of them on both. But this would have favored the owners of sets in the former cities and penalized those in the latter. (3) The power of VHF stations could have been reduced and that of UHF stations increased. But this, too, would have involved discrimination, favoring those closer to VHF stations and penalizing those farther away. A fourth solution has been suggested: the band assigned to FM broadcasts could be taken away and given to television, thus making three more VHF channels available to TV licensees. The only losers here would be the small, weak FM stations and the owners of FM receivers, including the audience for music of high quality. And these interests are less potent, politically, than those who want more programs and more profits from TV.

Air Space for Education

In the Communications Act of 1934, Congress directed the FCC to consider the desirability of reserving a number of radio channels for educational broadcasting. After some consideration, the Commission decided not to do so. It acted, in part, on the assurance of commercial licensees that educational programs would be broadcast by their stations. A Federal Radio Education Committee was established, including broadcasters and educators, for the purpose of promoting such programs. But education was relegated to the poorest hours in the day and was dropped entirely when programs yielding advertising revenue became available. In a few cases educational institutions were granted AM licenses carrying low power. But the great bulk of the AM band was turned over to commercial interests.

Education fared better in the FM allocation, where profits were not so promising and commercial pressures not so intense. In 1953 there were 116 authorizations outstanding for noncommercial stations, 49 of them limited to a power of 10 watts, confining their broadcasts to a college campus or a small college town. Space is still available for education in the FM band. The real struggle over educational broadcasting has centered in the allocation of space for TV.

At hearings held during the freeze on TV licenses, the National Association of Educational Broadcasters asked that a fourth of the TV channels be reserved, supporting its request with detailed evidence of the inferior quality of the programs, the quantities of advertising, and the dearth of educational material being broadcast by commercial licensees.

The National Association of Radio and Television Broadcasters opposed the reservation, arguing that educators were incompetent to produce television programs, that they would not attract a large audience, and that much of the space reserved for them would go to waste. In its final allocation, however, the Commission set aside a tenth of the TV channels for education, providing originally for 242 educational licensees and later for 251, a third of them in the VHF band and two thirds in UHF. This provided three fourths of the cities in the country with educational channels, but left a fourth with none.

Educators have been slow to apply for television licenses. By May 15, 1954, five stations were in operation, 24 other licenses had been granted, and 17 applications were pending, a total of 46; there were no applicants for the two hundred allocations that remained. The major obstacle to educational TV is lack of financial resources. Nonprofit stations are forbidden to meet any part of their costs by selling time to advertisers. They must therefore finance themselves by obtaining grants from school boards, city councils, or state legislatures, and such grants are opposed by commercial broadcasters. The Ford Fund for Adult Education, with an appropriation of $5 million from the Ford Foundation, has offered to give one dollar for every two dollars raised for educational stations, and a National Citizens' Committee for Education in Television has undertaken to enlist public support. If these ventures succeed, education will have some space on the air. If they fail, the pressure to grant the remaining licenses to commercial interests may become too strong to resist.

COMPETITION AND MONOPOLY

It was the policy of Congress, when it passed the Communications Act, to favor competition in radio. This policy was designed to afford opportunities for small business, to deny monopoly profits to licensees, to provide service for all states and communities, and to prevent concentrated control of an important medium of communication. The issue of competition versus monopoly has repeatedly been presented to the FCC. It was raised when the Commission determined the number, power, and control of AM stations, when it considered applications for joint control of AM and FM stations and of radio and TV, when it examined the relationship of stations and networks, and when it decided whether to permit stations to be controlled by owners of competing media: radio stations by newspapers and television stations by motion picture producers or exhibitors. It is to these decisions that we now turn.

Competition among Stations

The Commission has generally sought to maximize the number of broadcasting stations. Wherever possible, it has granted two or more licenses in each community. In doing so, it has been upheld by the Supreme

Court. In the Sanders Case,[7] where a station had contested the granting of a second license in a city, the Court held, in 1940, that radio was not a public utility, that control of entry was not designed to protect licensees against competition, and that the Commission, in granting a license, was not required to consider the effect of its action upon competitors.

The Commission has also sought to prevent concentration in station ownership. It has refused to grant more than one license to a single licensee in the same service (AM, FM, or TV) in the same community. And it has limited the number of stations, wherever located, that it would license to a single broadcaster. In 1951, there were 70 firms controlling two or more AM stations, with 275 stations under multiple ownership, but 2,100 other AM stations were independently controlled. The FCC, however, has not followed the policy of enforcing competition between different types of broadcasting. It was assumed, at one time, that FM licenses would go to large numbers of independent operators. But the Commission eventually yielded to pressure from AM stations, granting more than 90 per cent of the FM licenses to such concerns. So, too, with television: the capital and the enterprise for TV broadcasts have come from the radio industry, and the TV licenses have been granted, in the main, to radio licensees.

Competition among stations is unequal, since some are confined to daytime hours and held to low power, while others are permitted to broadcast around the clock and use much higher power. There are some sixty stations operating on clear channels, a score of them with exclusive rights at night. These stations, using 50 kilowatts, already have a nighttime radius of some 750 miles. They have sought, for years, to have their power increased, enabling them virtually to blanket the country and leaving still less space for stations with weaker power. Most of these stations are owned by or affiliated with the two major networks: NBC and CBS. These interests already enjoy a substantial advantage over their competitors. The requested increase in station power would give them an even greater one.

Stations and Networks

Half of the radio stations in the United States are owned by or affiliated with one of the national networks, providing them with programs that take up half of their time. The FCC has no jurisdiction over the networks as such, but it can influence them indirectly through its power to control the stations they own and those they serve. Following complaints from broadcasters, the Commission launched an investigation of network practices in 1938 and issued a report revealing various abuses in 1941. At that time, NBC and CBS dominated the field, Mutual was struggling for existence, ABC was yet to be created, and independent stations found themselves at a serious disadvantage in bargaining.

[7] *FCC* v. *Sanders Bros. Radio Stations*, 309 U.S. 470 (1940).

The contracts which controlled the relationship between the major networks and their outlets contained provisions which worked to the detriment of competing networks and station operators. They ran for five or ten years and might be renewed by the networks—but not by the stations—on thirty days notice. The network typically took an option on the station's time, obtaining the right to make use of preferred hours for broadcasting. On 28 days' notice it might require the station to sell it any one of the contracted hours, even though this forced the operator to cancel an arrangement with a local customer, thus running the risk of losing his patronage. The network gave no guarantee that it would use the optioned time; in practice, it used only a third of the time that it reserved. It paid for the time it used, but made no payment for its right to use the other two thirds of the station's hours. The station, however, could not reject a program unless it could prove to the satisfaction of the network that the public interest would suffer if it were used. The usual contract forbade a station to accept a program from another network, thus denying it the right to obtain profitable business and preventing new networks from getting a foothold in the industry. It also forbade the station to accept programs from national advertisers for local broadcasting at rates below those which the network charged for the station's time, thus preventing it from competing for national advertising. These provisions were found by the Commission to stifle competition and to make the station a servant of the network rather than an instrument for serving the public interest.

At that time, also, the National Broadcasting Company was operating two networks: the Red and the Blue. It broadcast most of its commercial programs over the Red, calling on the outlets in this chain for three fifths of its optioned time. It provided the outlets in the Blue with sustaining programs, calling on them for less than a fifth of its optioned time. Connection with the Red was profitable; connection with the Blue was not. But the contracts which the company made with its stations did not specify the chain to which they were to be attached. This arrangement gave NBC the power of life and death over its outlets, compelling them to acquiesce in the terms which it prescribed. And it excluded competing networks from access to the stations on the Blue.[8]

The Commission acted to correct these abuses, issuing rules to govern the relationship of networks and stations under its power to grant or withhold station licenses. The new rules limited network contracts to two years. They modified the option clauses, increasing the length of notice required and giving stations greater freedom to reject network programs. They outlawed the exclusive affiliation clause, enabling network affiliates to use programs from other networks and enabling other stations to obtain network programs. They forbade the networks to control the rates charged by their affiliates in competing for advertising business. The

[8] See FCC, *Report on Chain Broadcasting*, 1941.

Commission also sought to compel NBC to divest itself of one of its networks, the Red or the Blue.

The new rules were welcomed by Mutual and by independent broadcasters; they were vigorously resisted by NBC and CBS. In hearings before a committee of the Senate, the companies argued that the rules would cripple if not paralyze broadcasting, threaten the very existence of networks, create anarchy in the air, and encourage the government to socialize the industry. In a suit brought to enjoin enforcement of the rules, they contended that the Commission had exceeded its authority, acted arbitrarily and capriciously, and taken their property without due process of law. This position was rejected by the Congress and the Courts, the Commission's contract regulations being upheld by the Supreme Court in 1943.[9] In the meantime, the Department of Justice had brought suit under the Sherman Act to compel NBC to dispose of one of its networks. The company sold the Blue which became the basis of ABC and, thereupon, the case was dropped.

As a result of these developments, there are four national networks in radio instead of two. ABC was brought into existence, and ABC and Mutual were given a better opportunity to obtain affiliates. Stations, too, were given a better chance to obtain access to networks. The industry became somewhat more competitive. But NBC and CBS retained their dominance. Their prophecies of doom were not fulfilled.

In television, nearly all the stations are affiliated with four national networks: NBC, CBS, ABC, and Du Mont. But here, with stations few in number, their bargaining power has been high, and exclusive affiliation has been the exception rather than the rule. All four networks thus compete for station time. But NBC and CBS, drawing on their radio resources, get more than the other two. The Commission once considered issuing a rule to limit the time a station could take from one network, or one requiring it to take a certain amount of time from each. But it became apparent that a quota system of this sort would hamper rather than foster competition, and the plan was dropped.

Competition between Media

In communication, as in transportation, the question arises as to whether different media should be required to compete with one another or be permitted to combine. This issue first presented itself to the FCC in connection with applications for broadcasting licenses and purchases of stations by owners of newspapers. Radio and newspapers compete, of course, both in the dissemination of news and in the sale of advertising services. It was, therefore, feared that newspaper ownership of broadcasting facilities might result in the suppression of competition and the creation of local monopolies. The Commission made a study of this problem between 1941 and 1944 and finally decided to issue no general rule. In

[9] *National Broadcasting Co.* v. *U.S.*, 319 U.S. 190.

practice, it has tended to favor other applicants where there is only one newspaper in a town. But it has not refused a license to a newspaper where it faces competition, or even where it possesses a monopoly, if it is the only applicant. Nor has the Commission sought to prevent newspapers from purchasing radio properties. As a consequence, a fourth of the AM stations and three fifths of the TV stations are owned by publishers. The competition that exists is between ownership interests rather than communications media.

A similar problem is created by the competition of television with motion picture producers and exhibitors in the entertainment business. The movie interests have substantial investments in production and exhibition facilities. If permitted to control TV, they might seek to protect themselves by retarding the development of their competitor. The Commission has complained that movie producers have refused to release new films and featured players for performance on TV, the producers replying that action forcing them to do so would deprive them of an audience and prevent them from recovering their costs. Movie exhibitors, at the same time, have asked that channels be set aside for TV showings in theaters, such telecasts being unavailable on other receivers. In 1952 the Commission was asked to approve the merger of the American Broadcasting Company with Paramount Theaters. Both companies had resulted from dissolutions in antitrust cases: ABC had been separated from NBC and Paramount Theaters from Paramount Pictures. But the Commission gave its approval, in the hope that the combination would create a stronger competitor for NBC and CBS. Here, again, the competition sought was that of ownership interests rather than entertainment media.

CONTROL OF TECHNOLOGY

The FCC has one responsibility that makes its position unique among regulatory agencies: it controls the rate of technical change. The introduction of each new development in radio depends upon the willingness of the Commission to approve the facilities to be employed, to provide a channel for experimental use, and eventually to assign channels for general broadcasting. This responsibility is inescapable: control of access to the air involves control of the purposes for which it is used. But the responsibility is a difficult one to discharge. Approval of innovations may render existing equipment obsolete. It may commit the industry prematurely to inferior techniques. Refusal to approve, on the other hand is bound to give rise to charges of bureaucratic obstructiveness. Here, as elsewhere, the Commission is sure to be damned if it does and damned if it doesn't.

Introduction of FM and TV

The Commission first had to face the problem of innovation when it approved FM broadcasting. Its AM licensees opposed its action on the ground that large sums had been invested in AM transmitters and receivers whose usefulness would be destroyed. But FM was found to have great technical advantages, and channels were provided for its use.

The problem was raised again by the introduction of TV. Here, the Commission had to decide whether to establish standards for equipment, requiring all broadcasters to conform, or to permit different companies to develop and use facilities of different types. The Commission refused to standardize, fearing to freeze a changing art. It encouraged experimentation, but delayed commercial broadcasting. This, though unpopular, was wise. The relation of receiver and transmitter is that of lock and key. If receivers embodying a particular method of telecasting had been widely sold, the development of other methods might have been foreclosed. The Commission, in seeking to promote improvement of the art, might have found itself presented with a *fait accompli.* So the allocation of channels for commercial broadcasts was postponed. At the same time, the materials that would have been required for television were made unavailable by World War II. By the time the war had ended and commercial telecasting was approved, the research that was basic to its development had been done. The Commission thus gained the advantage of delay without being forced to bear the blame. The Commission's control of technology did not involve it in serious conflict until it was forced to choose between rival systems of introducing color into TV.

Introduction of Color

In 1950 CBS had developed a method of broadcasting in color, known as a field sequential system, involving the use of a spinning, synchronized disc attached to the television receiver and alternately flashing green, red, and blue, which the viewer's brain translated into colored pictures. At the same time, RCA was working on a dot sequential system in which the pictures were formed, as they are in color printing, by a multitude of colored dots. The CBS system was incompatible, i.e., broadcasts in color by this method could not be received on existing sets in black and white. The RCA system would be compatible; broadcasts could be received in black and white. CBS applied for permission to use its system in initiating color telecasts. Its application was opposed by RCA, by NBC, and by most of the other interests in the industry.

Against approval of the application, it was argued that receiving sets in the hands of consumers and those in the stocks of merchants and manufacturers would be made obsolete, and that the industry would be committed, by hasty action, to an inferior method of color broadcasting. In support of the application, it was urged that pictures, being available in color, should be enjoyed without delay. In October, 1950, after 62 days of hearings, 10,000 pages of testimony, and 265 exhibits, the Commission gave its approval for broadcasts in color by CBS. Thereupon, a suit for an injunction was brought by RCA. In May, 1951, the Commission was upheld by the Supreme Court, Mr. Justice Black asserting that its action was not capricious and that the Court would not reverse it on the ground that it might have been unwise.[10] The right of CBS to go ahead was clear. In October, 1951, however, the Office of Defense Mobilization requested the company to postpone development of color on the ground that the materials involved were needed in the Korean War. The company complied.

The television industry took advantage of the respite thus provided to set up a national committee that represented all the interests involved. This body undertook to perfect a method of color casting that would be fully compatible. Its final product, based on the dot sequential system originated by RCA, was presented to the Commission for approval. In December, 1953, the Commission reversed itself, accepting the system for general use. It offered to hold hearings on this decision if there were any objection, but CBS did not object. A superior technique was finally adopted. But it was not the one that the Commission first approved.

PROGRAM CONTENT

Under the terms of the Communications Act, the FCC is specifically denied the power of censorship. But it is also authorized, in granting or renewing station licenses to determine whether the "public interest, convenience, or necessity would be served. . . ." And it is permitted to develop its own criteria in judging the public interest. In passing on applications for new licenses, it may therefore consider the character of program service that is promised. And in passing on applications for renewals, it may consider the character of programs provided in the past. The Commission, thus, may not require a script to be submitted for approval in advance of a performance. But it may refuse renewal of a license on the ground that past performances have failed to serve the public interest. This power, if it were really used, would enable the Commission—for better or for worse—to influence freedom of speech and the quality of programs on the air.

Freedom of the Air

The FCC is forbidden to interfere with the right of free speech. But it does not follow that the air is free. The Commission has not adopted the policy of allocating frequencies to minority groups, but has favored stations that supposedly will serve all groups in the community. Such stations, however, are not regarded as common carriers. Access to the microphone or the TV camera cannot be demanded as a legal right. If a station permits one candidate to broadcast during a campaign, it must offer a similar opportunity to other candidates. But they may not get on the air, lacking the funds to pay the price their rival paid. No station, moreover, is required to give or sell its time to any candidate. A station need not

[10] *RCA* v. *U.S.*, 341 U.S. 412.

broadcast controversial issues. And if it does so—apart from contests for elective office—it is not required by law to give both sides.

The right of access to the air was tested in 1949 when an atheist named Scott demanded the the licenses of certain stations be revoked because they had broadcast attacks on atheism but denied him time to reply. The stations argued that atheistic broadcasts would not be popular, that atheists were but a small minority, and that they therefore had no right to time. This argument was rejected by the FCC:

> If freedom of speech is to have meaning it cannot be predicated on the mere popularity or public acceptance of the ideas sought to be advanced. It must be extended as readily to ideas which we disapprove or abhor as to ideas which we approve. . . .
>
> Every idea does not rise to the dignity of a "public controversy" and every organization, regardless of membership or the seriousness of its purposes, is not *per se* entitled to time on the air. But an organization or idea may be projected into the realm of controversy by virtue of being attacked. The holders of a belief should not be denied the right to answer attacks upon them or their belief solely because they are few in number.

The logic was that of Milton, Voltaire, Jefferson, and Mill. But the Commission failed to carry through. "There is no obligation on the part of a station licensee," it said, "to grant the request of any and all persons for time to state their views on matters in which they may be interested."[11] Scott's petition was rejected on the ground that the controversy was lacking in public importance and that he had not been personally attacked. The way was thus left open for a different decision in any case where the issue was important and the attack personal. On other occasions, the FCC has come to the aid of groups such as co-operatives and labor unions, persuading broadcasters to afford them an opportunity to present their views. But it is not likely to insist, in every case, that the unpopular minority be heard. It may be doubted, for instance, that the Commission would refuse renewal of a license because a station had denied a Communist an opportunity to answer an attack upon his faith.

The question of free speech has also been raised when licensees have used their stations to broadcast their own opinions. Complaints were made in 1941 that a station in Boston owned by the Mayflower Broadcasting Corporation was supporting various causes and candidates to the exclusion of opposing views. After investigation, the FCC issued a decision, saying that the air space allotted to a licensee was part of the public domain and could not be used as if it were his private property. To employ it in the public interest, balanced discussion was required. The station itself was not to be an advocate. This ruling was denounced by the broadcasting industry and, in 1949, after further hearings, it was modified. Under the

[11] Quotations are from the Commission's decision as reproduced in Charles A. Siepmann, *Radio, Television and Society* (New York: Oxford University Press, 1950), Appendix VI.

new decision, licensees are permitted to broadcast their own opinions as long as they allow contrary opinions to be heard. But it is not clear just how this is to be enforced.

A similar problem is raised by commentators sponsored by advertisers. To achieve a proper balance, a station should carry both conservatives and liberals, both isolationists and internationalists. But stations sell time, and advertisers fill the time with any commentators they may choose. The result may be one-sided. But unless someone complains, the FCC is unlikely to know it. And even if a complaint is made, it is unlikely to act.

One danger is that discussion of controversial issues will not be balanced. Another is that they will not be discussed at all. Broadcasters, advertising agencies, and advertisers are all engaged in salesmanship. And salesmen do not lightly run the risk of giving offense to customers. Censorship is forbidden to the FCC, but it may legally be practiced by commercial interests.

The wonder is, in such a situation, that American radio is fairly free. Controversial issues are aired. Opposing points of view are heard. Persons attacked are given a chance to reply. Some subjects may be taboo; criticism of advertising and advertisers is certain to be rare. But criticism of politics and politicians is common. The air, indeed, may well be freer than would be the case if the Commission held a tighter rein.

Quality of Programs

The only provisions of the Communications Act governing the character of radio programs are those that forbid the broadcasting of "any obscene, indecent, or profane language" and "any advertisement of or information concerning any lottery, gift enterprise, or similar scheme, offering prizes dependent in whole or in part upon lot or chance. . . ." No standards respecting the balance of material to be broadcast or the quality of individual programs have been established by the FCC. Determination of the nation's radio and television fare is left to commercial interests. In principle, responsibility for programing lies with broadcasters. In practice, it is abdicated to the advertisers and advertising agencies. It is as if the editorial content of newspapers and magazines were prepared by the people who write their advertisements.

People engaged in selling merchandise are certain to seek the largest possible audience. And in order to obtain it, they are likely to appeal to the lowest common denominator of intelligence, education, and taste. A few good programs are available, but the general quality is low, and instead of rising, it has tended to decline. On most of the wave lengths, most of the time, the air is filled with dance music, vaudeville, quiz shows, giveaways, soap operas, violence, and crime. Such material, certainly, should be available for those who want it. But it should not occupy the air to the virtual exclusion of public affairs, science, philosophy, literature, dramas, ballets, symphonies, and the graphic arts. With other media—books, magazines, newspapers, theater, and movies—some part of the output is addressed to the cultivated minority. But with radio and TV, minority interests and tastes are generally ignored.

In 1929 the National Association of Broadcasters, in its "Standards of Commercial Practice," provided that "Commercial announcements . . . shall not be broadcast between 7 and 11 P.M." In 1937 the Association relaxed its standards to permit a tenth of the time in hour and half-hour programs, a sixth of that in quarter-hour programs, a fifth of that in 10-minute programs, and a third of that in 5-minute programs to be devoted to advertising. Even these limits have rarely been observed. Commercials have come to be too long, running to several minutes of straight sales talk. They are too frequent, sometimes following one another without interruption. They are too obtrusive, being set to music, inserted in the middle of a program, and woven into the program itself. Some of them are offensive, stressing the displeasure caused by constipation, by body odors, and the like. The excesses of advertising on the air today abuse the privilege that is given to broadcasters by the government.

Little has been done by the FCC to raise the quality of programs. In 1946 the Commission issued a report on the *Public Service Responsibility of Broadcast Licensees*, pointing out that the performance of radio stations, by and large, was falling short of the promises they had made when they applied for licenses. Over half the broadcast time was in programs written and produced by advertisers. Sustaining programs were disappearing from the air. Five sixths of the time was devoted to programs taken from networks, or to records, or transcriptions. Local live programs averaged only 13 minutes during five evening hours. Broadcasters were not providing listeners with a balanced offering. They were not serving the interests of their own communities. Advertising abuses were common and serious. The Commission's indictment was sweeping and well documented. But its report concluded lamely with the recommendation that standards be raised (1) by self-regulation in the industry, (2) by college and university stations, (3) by radio critics in newspapers and magazines, and (4) by councils of radio listeners. The Commission itself was not prepared to make use of the powers that it possessed.

In 1949 the Commission issued rules prohibiting give-away shows, under the provision of the law forbidding lotteries. Enforcement was resisted by the networks, the case being appealed eventually to the Supreme Court. The decision turned upon the definition of a lottery. The networks argued that give-away shows were not lotteries since nothing of value was contributed as a consideration by members of the audience. The Commission contended that the time taken from listeners and lookers by the lure of quick and easy riches was a thing of value, constituting a consideration within the meaning of the lottery laws. In a unanimous decision handed down in 1954, the Court held for the networks, saying that the Commission's rules "overstepped the boundaries of interpretation."[12] The Commission's one real attempt to prevent the prostitution of the airwaves thus came to naught.

Revocation of Licenses

The FCC has clear authority to refuse renewal of a license, the law saying plainly that licenses convey no right of property. But the penalty of revocation is so severe that it is seldom used. The Federal Radio Commission did revoke the licenses of two quacks who were broadcasting prescriptions and selling patent medicines over the air. And it took similar action in the case of a Protestant clergyman who used his station to make violent attacks on the Catholic Church and on various citizens of Los Angeles. Upon appeal, this action was upheld.[13] The FCC has refused to renew licenses where applicants have falsified the ownership of stations or turned over to brokers the business of selling time. It has warned broadcasters that licenses might be lost if certain types of programs, such as those dealing with astrology, were continued. But it has moved to revoke a license on grounds of program content in a single case. G. A. Richards, who owned broadcasting stations in Los Angeles, Cleveland, and Detroit, was charged with requiring their commentators to attack Democrats, New Dealers, labor unions, Negroes, and Jews, instructing them in the use of inflection, innuendo, and invective, and avoidance of the libel laws. In 1951, while the case was pending, Richards died, and the Commission renewed the licenses rather than penalize his heirs. In effect, licenses are permanent. Whatever the behavior of the licensee, his rights are automatically renewed. If the Commission were really to supervise his behavior, a lighter penalty would be required.

ALTERNATIVES IN RADIO

Broadcasting may be private or governmental. It may be conducted as a commercial enterprise or as a public service. It may be competitive or monopolistic. In a few other countries, such as Argentina, Chile, and Mexico, radio is in the hands of commercial interests as it is in the United States. In Holland, stations are operated by political and religious groups; in Sweden, by a corporation controlled by the nation's press. In most countries, however, broadcasting is a governmental monopoly or is carried on both by private and by public agencies. The first of these systems is illustrated by Great Britain, the second by Canada.

[12] *FCC* v. *American Broadcasting Co., Columbia Broadcasting System, National Broadcasting Co.*, Supreme Court of the U.S., October Term 1953, Nos. 117, 118, 119.

[13] *Trinity Methodist Church, South* v. *Federal Radio Commission,* 62 F. 2d 850 (1932).

Radio in Britain

Broadcasting in the United Kingdom was initiated by the manufacturers of receiving sets. The industry was taken over by the government in 1927. It has since been managed by the British Broadcasting Corporation, an autonomous agency with its own directors and officers located in the Post Office. The BBC is financed by annual fees paid by the owners of radio and television sets. Since Britain must share the air with European stations, fewer channels are available for English broadcasts than in the United States. The Corporation operates five regional radio stations and three national networks; it has had but one network for TV. Each of the radio networks carries a different type of program; a regional station may substitute its own program to serve local needs. The Corporation has been progressive, leading the American industry in experimentation with television. It has been popular, enjoying widespread public support.

The principal argument for the government monopoly in Britain is its superiority in programing. The BBC seeks to establish higher standards and to achieve greater diversity and better balance than are known in the United States. It broadcasts no advertising. It carries a high percentage of classical music, serious drama, and talks on science, literature, and art. It has gone farther than American radio in preparing broadcasts for the schools. Its children's programs, its newsreels, and its documentaries are better than those in the United States. The Corporation attempts to serve all cultural levels, one of its three networks being confined to programs that are of interest to a small minority. It has deliberately undertaken to raise the level of popular taste, giving its audience what it thinks they ought to have, not what they want; and it edits all speeches before it puts them on the air. To American observers, its programs may seem dull. Certainly, American radio and TV are livelier. And, in discussing controversial issues, they afford a freedom that is unknown on the BBC. But the British people prefer their radio to ours.

In 1952 the government proposed that a second television network be established under an Independent Television Authority to compete with the BBC. The programs on this network were to be produced by private contractors and financed by selling time to advertisers. The proposal aroused a storm of protest, being denounced by elder statesmen, the press, the universities, and the church. Such a measure, it was said, would debase popular taste by dragging British television down to the vulgar level of that in the United States. To quiet the opposition, the government modified its plan. As adopted in 1954, the law permits the ITA to produce some programs itself, financing them partly by revenue from the license fee and partly by selling time directly to advertisers. In general, however, the Authority will sell time to program contractors and they, in turn, will sell time to advertisers. The programs that are broadcast will be produced by the contractors, not by advertising agencies. The Authority is to require that advertisements be limited in length, clearly separated from program material, and introduced only at natural breaks. And it is empowered to censor scripts and to fine producers for violating its rules. In this form the plan does not permit real independence in producing programs. But it should prevent the worst abuses of advertising. The members of the new Authority were appointed in August, 1954, with Sir Kenneth Clark, an eminent art educator, as chairman. The first broadcasts were expected after the middle of 1955.

Radio in Canada

In Canada most broadcasting stations are privately owned. But the only network company—the Canadian Broadcasting Corporation—is owned and operated by the government. The Corporation licenses the private stations, provides them with programs, and supervises their operations; it has a score of stations of its own. The system is financed by license fees. The CBC has three networks, two broadcasting in English and one in French. Some of its programs are taken from the American nets, but four fifths of them originate in Canada. The Corporation provides service to the schools and to the rural areas. It broadcasts more educational material and more good music than is carried by the chains in the United States. Independent stations can put on their own programs and sell time to advertisers. But they cannot affiliate with any network but the CBC. It is the clear intention of the Canadian Parliament to preserve the nation's cultural integrity.

The Future in America

Three things are needed to improve broadcasting in the United States: (1) more nearly complete geographic coverage, with more adequate service for rural areas, (2) elimination of the worst abuses of advertising, and (3) betterment of the content and balance of programs in the interest of a discriminating minority.

Service to areas now neglected could be assured by granting some stations higher power—500 or even 1,000 kilowatts—or by creating more regional stations and giving them clear channels and moderate power. The inequality of earnings that might result could be avoided by auctioning rights to stronger stations instead of giving them away or by taxing such stations and using the revenues thus obtained to support the services of the weaker ones.

The FCC, within its present powers, could eliminate abuses in advertising. The Commission is authorized by law to prescribe the nature of services to be rendered by licensees. In pursuance of this authority, it could issue rules to limit the number and length of commercials, separate them from program materials, and confine them to natural program breaks. Such action would not involve the censorship of programs but merely prevent encroachments on their time.

There is a serious obstacle to improving the general quality of radio and television fare: most of the owners of receiving sets are content to leave the programs as they are. But there remains the problem of the minority that the present system fails to serve. There is an audience in America—and a sizable one—for programs similar in quality to those broadcast on the Third Program of the BBC. But how are they to be obtained?

There are several possibilities. Independent FM stations can be kept alive if their income is supplemented by popular subscription. Nonprofit stations can be operated, at public expense, by city governments or by school boards, city colleges, and state universities. They can be run by private colleges and universities or set up independently and financed by annual giving or by endowment funds. And popular programs, free of advertising, can be provided commercially by Subscriber TV. Under this system a scrambled image is broadcast, to be unscrambled only for those who pay a fee. For this purpose, a variety of methods may be used. Under one, the image is unscrambled by dropping a coin in a box on the receiving set. Under another, this is accomplished by purchasing a punched card and inserting it in a decoding device. Under a third, the picture is obtained by telephone and the charge collected by the telephone company. Each of these methods has been tested experimentally. But commercial application depends upon the allocation of wave lengths by the FCC.

SUGGESTIONS FOR FURTHER READING

Good brief discussions of the problems involved in regulating radio and television are those by E. W. Clemens in *Economics and Public Utilities* (New York: Appleton-Century-Crofts, Inc., 1950), chap xvi, and by Emery Troxel in *Economics of Public Utilities* (New York: Rinehart & Co., 1947), chap. xxiii. The best recent books on the subject are Charles A. Siepmann, *Radio, Television, and Society* (New York: Oxford University Press, 1950), and Llewellyn White, *The American Radio* (Chicago: University of Chicago Press, 1947). Earlier volumes are C. B. Rose, Jr., *National Policy for Radio Broadcasting* (New York: Harper & Bros., 1940), and Thomas P. Robinson, *Radio Networks and the Federal Government* (New York: Columbia University Press, 1943). The best sources of material on the quality of radio and television programs are: the report of the Federal Communications Commission on *Public Service Responsibility of Broadcast Licensees* (Washington: Government Printing Office, 1946), and the Monitoring Studies by the National Association of Educational Broadcasters, Urbana, Ill. See, for instance, their Study No. 6: Dallas W. Smythe, *Three Years of New York Television*, 1954. For an account of the development of the BBC, see R. H. Coase, *British Broadcasting* (Cambridge: Harvard University Press, 1950). For current information on the United States, see the annual reports of the FCC, the magazine *Business Week*, and the columns by Jack Gould in the *New York Times*.

Chapter 24 DIRECT CONTROLS IN WARTIME

Production for national defense, if it takes a minor and a stable share of national output, can be effected through normal market processes without resorting to governmental controls. But a defense effort that demands a substantial share of output, involving a sudden diversion of resources, cannot be guided through market processes alone. The mechanism of prices may still be used. But a war economy, in any country, is likely to be managed through central planning and authoritarian control.

This has been the case in the United States. Production was directed and certain prices were fixed, during World War I, by a Food Administration, a Fuel Administration, and a War Industries Board. Economic activity was controlled, during World War II, by another group of federal agencies, prices and rents being fixed and consumers' goods rationed by an Office of Price Administration, wages regulated by a War Labor Board, materials allocated by a War Production Board, and workers placed by a War Manpower Commission, the activities of these bodies being co-ordinated first by an Office of Economic Stabilization and finally by an Office of War Mobilization. Price and production controls were exercised again, during the war in Korea, by an Office of Price Stabilization and a Wage Stabilization Board under an Economic Stabilization Agency, and by a Defense Production Administration, all of them being subordinate to an Office of Defense Mobilization. Similar agencies, with extensive powers, would undoubtedly be established in the event of another war.

MOBILIZATION AND CONTROLS

If war comes during a depression it may be possible to fulfill the need for munitions, without diverting resources from the production of civilian goods, simply by putting idle plants and laborers to work. But during prosperity, when resources are fully employed, such diversion will be required. If military demands are to be satisfied, other demands will have to be denied. Factories will have to be converted from nonessential to essential uses—from the production of automobiles, for instance, to that of army trucks and tanks. Materials and labor will have to be moved from civilian to military employments—from the construction of grandstands to that of barracks, from the manufacture of hosiery to that of parachutes. In peacetime, such shifts would be accomplished through the market: by paying higher prices for the production of needed goods, thus inducing manufacturers to convert their facilities and enabling them to attract materials and labor by paying higher prices and wages. In wartime, these shifts are accomplished largely through administrative controls.

Why Controls Are Needed

Wartime controls have two purposes: to stabilize prices and to facilitate the diversion of resources to production for defense. War makes for inflation, both in particular prices and in the level of prices as a whole. It suddenly multiplies the demand for certain goods and services that are limited in quantity. And where such bottlenecks occur, prices rise precipitately. These increases are larger than would be required to induce expansion of supply. They add to the cost of the war. And they come to be reflected in the costs and prices of other goods. Price increases, therefore, have to be controlled, even though particular rather than general.

The demand for defense supplies bids up particular prices. But this is not all. The money spent for such goods increases the incomes of producers. And this enlarges their purchasing power as consumers. But the supply of consumers' goods is not increased. With demand up and supply down, the prices of such goods as well as those of war goods will tend to rise. In anticipation of shortages and rising prices, moreover, businessmen may add to demand by making purchases to enlarge their inventories, and consumers, by buying to build up private hoards. As prices rise, the cost of living rises. There then will be demands for higher wages. And with higher wages, production costs will rise. A wage-price spiral, pulled up by growing demands and pushed up by rising costs, will carry prices to ever higher levels. Inflation will pervade the whole economy.

Inflation must be prevented, first, because it is unjust. It reduces the value of money and thus alters the effect of contracts to the benefit of debtors and to the detriment of creditors. It enriches the speculator and punishes the saver. It injures all those whose incomes are fixed in terms of dollars: the aged and the widows with children, who are living on benefits from annuity contracts, insurance policies, and social security accounts. It harms those whose incomes lag as prices rise: white-collar workers, salaried professionals, and government employees. It impairs the financial strength of private education, research, religion, and social services. It effects a wholesale redistribution of wealth and income, giving rise to bitterness and social strife.

Inflation must be prevented, second, so that resources may be devoted to producing war goods in the quantities required. The market works well as an allocator in normal times, when changes are small and gradual. But it works badly in an emergency, when they must be large and sudden. A sharp increase in the prices of war goods may not attract resources to their production. For the prices of civilian goods will also rise. In the former case, demand is temporary and uncertain. In the latter, it is permanent and sure. Producers may therefore prefer to go on making automobiles, say, rather than tanks, even though the price of tanks is high. By bidding up prices, the government may merely add to its expenditures. Inflation, moreover, may even operate to curtail supplies. Owners of scarce materials, expecting prices to rise still higher, may withhold them from the market, hoping to profit on the rise. And workers, demanding higher wages, may stop production by going on strike.

Controls are needed, not only to prevent inflation, but also to guide production. If inflation is held in check by fixing prices, the function of the market as an allocator must be taken over by administrative agencies. And even if it is checked, without price fixing, through monetary and fiscal measures, the operation of the market must be supplemented by other forms of control. Facilities that are not converted voluntarily must be commandeered. Materials withheld by speculators must be seized. And where production is not forthcoming, mandatory orders must be placed. A war cannot be fought and won without controls.

Indirect and Direct Controls

The controls that are used to curb inflation may be indirect or direct. Indirect controls are those that operate to limit civilian demand by restricting total purchasing power. They seek to attack the cause of inflation by reducing the excess of money over goods. These controls are monetary and fiscal. The monetary controls are administered by the Federal Reserve authorities. They check expansion of the money supply by discouraging the extension of credit for nonessential purposes. The fiscal controls are exercised by Congress. They limit the government's contribution to income by postponing nonessential expenditures. And they mop up the excess of purchasing power by raising taxes or, perhaps, by forcing people to save instead of spend. As a result of these measures, the supply of money is kept from outrunning the supply of goods and services. And, insofar as they are effective, the allocation of resources can be left to the market and the use of direct controls kept to a minimum.

Direct controls are those which govern the prices, production, distribution, and consumption of particular goods and services. They include regulations fixing maximum prices, rents, and wages, prohibiting or curtailing the manufacture of certain goods, limiting the purposes for which certain materials may be used, allocating materials among producers, restricting the size of inventories, and rationing consumers' goods. They substitute administrative action for the mechanism of the market, requiring the establishment of new agencies, procedures, and penalties. Insofar as indirect controls are ineffective, more direct controls must be employed. But the two are complements rather than substitutes. The choice between them is one of relative emphasis.

Three Approaches to Stability

The stabilization program that has usually been favored by economists would seek to bring total demand into equilibrium with total supply by emphasizing indirect controls. It calls for tight money and for stiff taxation. It would put war finance on a pay-as-you-go basis, increasing taxes as expenditures increase. Such a program would have marked advantages. It would be simple and inexpensive, avoiding much of the complex and costly paraphernalia of direct controls. It would be flexible, maintaining the normal functioning of markets and responding to free consumer choice. But the program would also have its disadvantages. It would be difficult administratively and next to impossible politically to raise taxes as fast and as far as would be required. Even if taxes were sharply increased, resources would still be devoted to producing luxuries as persons of wealth spent their remaining incomes or drew upon the savings of the past. The program would cancel the influence of monetary incentives in persuading people to enter the labor force, to work overtime, and to increase their efficiency. Dealing only with total demand and supply, it would not break the bottlenecks existing in facilities, materials, or manpower, or prevent the cost-push of inflation starting in such cases from spreading through the whole economy.

A second approach to stability, dubbed the disequilibrium system by J. K. Galbraith,[1] relies more heavily upon direct controls. Under this system, though demand exceeds supply, inflation is held in check by price fixing and rationing. This is what happened, in fact, during World War II. Taxation, in the United States, did not keep pace with public expenditures. The generation of income exceeded the production of purchasable goods and services. But prices were held down, with fair success, by regulations issued by the government. Goods in short supply were rationed. And the money left over was saved. The system worked for a time. But it does not follow that it would work again. In the event of another war spending might be stimulated by the experience of past inflation and saving discouraged by the fact that past accumulations were already large. Patriotic compliance might not be forthcoming; black-market operations might be more extensive and more difficult to control. The system, moreover, has serious disadvantages. It necessitates a large administrative apparatus, highly centralized, costly, and cumbersome. It tends to be rigid, obstructing individual initiative and retarding economic change. It substitutes the pressures of politics for the impersonal judgments of the market place. Inescapable in an emergency, direct controls maintained for many years might threaten the survival of democracy. Despite the measure of success attained by such controls in World War II, most economists

[1] See *American Economic Review*, XXXVII (1947), 287–302.

would still contend that indirect controls should have the greater emphasis.

The obvious shortcomings of each of these approaches have led Edward S. Shaw and Lorie Tarshis to suggest a third.[2] This proposal would not fix the prices of consumers' goods or require the rationing of particular commodities. Instead, it would provide each household with a ration that would limit its total expenditures. The consumer would obtain his ration permit when he paid his income tax. He would then take it to a bank where he would exchange it for ration checks and coupons. These would replace all other currency and could be spent but once. The total of such rations would be held to an amount that would balance current output at stable prices. Inflation would be prevented, but production would be guided, through the mechanism of the market, by free consumer choice. Any income remaining, after taxes, above the consumer's ration would be converted into annuities or non-interest bonds with stable purchasing power, payable after the end of the war. Spending by business on plant and equipment would be controlled directly by the government. But aside from the over-all rationing of consumer expenditures and the regulation of business investment, the economy would be left free. This approach has been elaborated in considerable detail. On paper it has much to recommend it. But it has never been tested in experience.

STABILIZATION CONTROLS

To check inflation in time of war, ceilings are placed on prices, rents, and wages. The prices of war goods are controlled to hold down public expenditures and thus to limit the generation of income by the government. The prices of civilian goods are controlled to stem panic buying, to prevent hoarding, and to hold down the cost of living. Rents are controlled to protect tenants against exploitation, to aid in the recruitment of workers for war plants, and because rents, too, are an important element in the cost of living. The cost of living is held down to limit demands for higher wages. And wages, in turn, are controlled to prevent increases in production costs. The price and wage controls are interdependent, each being required if the other is to work.

Price Control

It is sometimes argued that price control will not be needed if the distribution of raw materials is controlled by allocation and the distribution of consumers' goods by rationing. These processes, it is said, will hold demand in check. And, as a result, prices will not rise. But this is not the case. With prices uncontrolled, suppliers would violate allocation orders to sell to producers who would pay them more. Dealers would build up

[2] See "A Program for Economic Mobilization," *American Economic Review*, XLI (1951), 30–50.

stocks in violation of inventory limits, expecting that prices would rise. Merchants would sell to buyers who had no rations, provided they were paid a higher price. Consumers would sell their rations to one another; prices would mount and the pattern of distribution intended would not be achieved. Allocation and rationing are difficult at best. To be successful, they must be reinforced by price control.

The techniques and the standards of price control, its requisites and its feasibility, are discussed at length in Chapter 25.

Rent Control

The method employed in regulating rents is not to fix them, dwelling by dwelling, at figures designed to cover costs and yield a fair return on a fair value of the properties concerned, a procedure that would be administratively impracticable, but rather to freeze them at the levels obtaining on some date before the war, and subsequently to make adjustments to cover the cost of improvements and to remove obvious inequities. This was the method used by the Office of Price Administration in World War II. The Emergency Price Control Act of 1942 empowered the Price Administrator to designate certain localities as defense rental areas, to recommend action by local governments, and failing such action, to impose federal controls. Under this authority, 650 areas were designated, landlords were required to register, and rents were fixed for 16,000,000 dwelling units, the initial ceilings being set at the levels existing on April 1, 1941. Provision was made in 1947 for decontrol at the option of local governments. The federal powers were restored, however, during the war in Korea in 1951. Federal control was finally abandoned in 1953, save for certain areas where housing shortages were acute and rents were increasing so rapidly as to impair the ability of defense plants to obtain and hold employees. The number of units still covered at that time was only 200,000. But rents in New York and Connecticut were under state controls. And New Jersey, Massachusetss, and Kansas had enabling laws.

Federal rent control was administered through local offices, the burden of handling individual cases being a substantial one. In some 5,000,000 cases, the OPA considered complaints by tenants that rents should be reduced, on the ground that the base-date rental had been falsified, that it had exceeded the rent for comparable quarters in the neighborhood, or that the equipment or services provided had been curtailed. In 1,500,000 cases, it passed on requests from landlords that rents be raised, on the ground that the base-period figures had been abnormally low, that increasing costs had created serious hardships, and that dwellings, equipment, or services had been improved. On new construction, rents were fixed by the Federal Housing Administration, building permits being denied if they were found to be too high. But where dwellings were converted for rental or altered in character, new rents had to be determined by OPA. The right of landlords to evict their tenants was restricted. Suits could be brought where tenants failed to pay their rent, where they used their quarters for illegal purposes or committed nuisances, and where the owners sought, in good faith, to recover the quarters for their own occupancy. In other cases the consent of OPA was first required.

On balance, rent control was a success. Its effectiveness is to be attributed largely to the fact that tenants were familiar with the quality and price of the service they were buying and co-operated willingly in the enforcement of the law. A sharp increase in rents was halted and the level of rents held steady throughout the war. But the program had its weaknesses. Commercial rents were not covered and properties were converted, accordingly, from residential to commercial purposes. Sales of real estate were exempted and owners, instead of renting, sought to sell. Rental ceilings were evaded by fraudulent sales, with small down payments and monthly installments exceeding the previous rents. They were evaded, also, by converting unfurnished apartments to furnished ones at higher figures, by requiring tenants to purchase furniture at exorbitant prices, and by forcing them to make deposits for damages, the deposits never being returned. Control of rents resulted, too, in deterioration of dwellings through neglect of maintenance and refusals to redecorate.

Rent control is popular with tenants and thus has strong political support. It persisted, in the United States, for years after other controls were dropped. It has been continued in France and in Great Britain ever since World War I. But control is unfair to landlords, holding them to a smaller return than that received on funds invested in other fields. It brings about malallocation of dwelling space, since tenants whose families grow smaller hold on to large apartments where the rents are fixed. It discriminates among tenants, favoring those already located as against newcomers who are seeking space. In the long run, it injures the very group it is supposed to aid, since it prevents the supply of rental housing from increasing and may even cause it to decline. Rent control may be needed in a time of acute emergency. But as a permanent policy, it is likely to do more harm than good. The danger is that, once it has been started, it never will be stopped.

Wage Control

Control over wages, like that over rents, is established through a base date freeze, and subsequent increases in wage rates are permitted only when approved by the stabilization authorities. A War Labor Board was created early in World War II for the purpose of settling industrial disputes, but it had no power to prevent wage increases upon which employers and workers had agreed. This power was provided in the Stabilization Act of October, 1942. Under the terms of this Act, wages were frozen at the levels obtaining on September 15, 1942. Altogether, the Board, acting through its regional offices, settled nearly 29,000 wage disputes and handled more than 460,000 applications for wage increases affecting 29,000,000 employees. Wage control was abolished promptly at the end of the war, to be reinstituted for a time during the war in Korea.

The issues presented by wage control relate both to the level and to the structure of wage rates. (1) Should the level of wages be raised to keep pace with increases in the cost of living? Such action would be inflationary. Preferably, the cost of living should be stabilized and the level of wages held down. But weaknesses in price control may render such a policy impossible. (2) Should the level of wages be raised to keep pace with gains in productivity? In peacetime, such gains should be reflected in rates of pay. But under the conditions of wartime, they are less likely to occur, and they are difficult to measure when they do. (3) How should the structure of wages be modified? Here, action may be taken to raise wages that fall below a minimum standard of health and decency, to recognize individual merit, to reward continued services, and to remove abnormal disparities within plants and between plants. But changes should not be made to effect reallocation of labor. If inflation is to be held in check, this function should be fulfilled through manpower controls.

During World War II, the policy with respect to the level of wages first adopted, in dispute cases, by the War Labor Board was that of permitting wages to be raised by 15 per cent to match the rise in the cost of living up to the summer of 1942. After the Stabilization Act was passed, however, such increases were confined to wages that had not already been raised by this amount and no further increases on this account were made. With respect to the wage structure, the Board followed the practice of raising wages where it held them to be substandard, where intraplant disparities required correction, and where individual merit and length of service needed to be recognized. In some cases, it raised them to attract labor into occupations essential to the prosecution of the war. But, in the main, its efforts were directed toward the removal of what were known as interplant inequities. This was done, not by reducing the higher wages, but by raising the lower ones. Such wages were raised to the average level obtaining in the market for the type of labor concerned. As a result, the average itself was raised, creating new inequities and affording a basis for still further claims. The trend of wages, under such adjustments, was steadily upward. But the movement was kept within control. During the war in Korea, on the other hand, the Wage Stabilization Board adopted the inflationary policy of permitting the whole level of wages to rise in step with the cost of living.

Wage controls, at best, do not prevent increases in the worker's take-home pay. They apply only to straight-time hourly earnings. And the pay envelope may be fattened by longer hours and higher rates for overtime. Labor will therefore gain as the rise in weekly wages outruns the rise in living costs. Controls, moreover, may be violated by upgrading through reclassification and promotion, or simply by paying more than the law allows. Enforcement is difficult: violations cannot readily be detected;

they may involve collusion between employers and employees. Wage controls, therefore, cannot be tight. But wages under control will rise less rapidly than those left free. Increases, at least, can be delayed through the obstructions inherent in the workings of bureaucracy.

ALLOCATION CONTROLS

Stabilization controls may check inflation. But they do not solve the problem of directing resources into the fields where they are needed most. They may even hinder reallocation by freezing past relationships. In the absence of other controls, scarce materials and labor, instead of being drawn into production for defense, may still be devoted to nonessential purposes. Supplies that are urgently needed may be seriously delayed. Old customers may be preferred to new ones, and the first orders received may be the first filled. There may also be distortions in the distribution of consumers' goods. Such goods, instead of reaching those who have the greatest needs, may go at worst to those who happen to be favored by distributors, or at best to those who have stood longest in the lines. If the nation's powers are to be employed effectively in the prosecution of the war, controls must be applied to the use of productive facilities, the allocation of materials and manpower, and the distribution of consumers' goods.

Facilities Controls

To secure production in the quantities required for national defense, new facilities must be constructed and old facilities converted to new purposes. Construction of new facilities has been encouraged by accelerated amortization, a practice which permits their cost to be written off, not during their lifetime, but within five years, thus reducing corporate tax liability. Failing this, facilities have been built by the government and leased to its contractors. Conversion of old facilities may be forced by seizure. Such action, however, is infrequent. Plants were seized in cases other than labor disputes on only seven occasions in World War I and eight in World War II. Conversion has been effected in the United States mainly by curtailment or limitation orders, prohibiting the manufacture of nonessential goods or holding it to a fraction of the quantity produced before the war. Facilities thus made idle become available for the production of defense supplies. Such action was taken, for instance, in the case of automobiles during World War II.

Another method of effecting conversion, employed extensively in Great Britain but little used in the United States, is that of concentrating the production of less essential goods in certain plants and freeing others for production for defense. In Britain, during World War II, this was done in more than sixty industries, including textiles, hosiery, shoes, and pottery. In all these fields, production was cut to three fourths or less of the prewar volume and concentrated in nuclear plants. The program raised serious problems: how to select the plants that were kept in operation, how to compensate the owners of those that were closed, and how to preserve for both an equal opportunity to enter civilian markets after the war. But under the pressure of emergency, these difficulties were somehow overcome. In the United States, no parallel program was attempted. The production of civilian goods was rarely cut. And political pressure in support of plants in particular regions and those producing under particular brands would doubtless have been impossible to resist. In this country, in fact, the policy was to encourage production of civilian goods by large numbers of small firms so that larger plants could be converted more completely to production for war.

Materials Controls

Controls over materials are of three major types. Inventory regulations are designed to prevent the hoarding of scarce materials. Conservation and simplification orders are designed to prevent their use for nonessential purposes. And priority and allocation systems are established to insure their use where they are needed most.

Inventory controls were set up by the War Production Board in World War II to limit the stocks of raw materials, semifinished goods, and finished goods that might be held by manufacturers, wholesalers, and retailers. The inventories permitted were related to a prewar base or to the quantities required to maintain operations over a limited period of time. In the case of strategic materials, such as copper and aluminum, they were held to the quantities needed for ninety, sixty, or thirty days. The regulations required that stocks in excess of the limits set be sold to the government. And they prevented the accumulation of further surpluses by withholding priorities.

Conservation orders forbid manufacturers to employ certain materials in the production of certain goods. In World War II, for instance, such orders prohibited the use of copper, aluminum, nickel, zinc, and rubber in making a number of nonessential articles. The manufacture of these articles was still permitted, but only with substitute materials. Simplification orders economize materials by reducing the numbers of models, colors, and sizes that may be produced and eliminating needless gadgets and ornaments. Thus the WPB removed the cuffs from men's trousers and the ruffles from nightgowns, reduced the types of baby carriages from twenty to two or three, and cut the varieties of caskets from sixty-five to fourteen, curtailing the use of metals in linings, handles, and trim. Materials freed from such applications were made available for use elsewhere.

These methods do not insure that materials will be used in producing war goods or essential civilian goods. For this purpose, systems of priorities and allocation are employed. Priority ratings are given to government contractors by the procurement agencies. Producers of scarce materials are required to put orders with high priorities at the top of the pile and fill them first. But there is no assurance that the materials ordered will be supplied. The ratings are qualitative, not quantitative. They are merely hunting licenses, giving the contractors prior claims on such materials as they can find. They are not related to the quantities available. And priorities may be inflated as procurement agencies compete in a scramble for scarce supplies. Thus, a contractor with an A rating may be pushed aside by one with an A-1 or an AA and he, in turn, may have to yield to one whose order bears an AA-1 or an AAA. The contractor's rating, moreover, may get him one material but not another that he needs. If the demand for materials is to be limited to the supply, if materials are to be assembled in the proper combinations, and if they are to be devoted to their most important uses, the flow of these materials must be controlled. For this purpose, a comprehensive system of allocation is required.

This was the experience in World War II. The system of priorities first used by WPB broke down completely. Allocations were established for particular materials in short supply, and these cut off nonessential demands, diverting supplies to more important purposes. But unrelated allocations did not assure delivery, in the proportions needed, of all the materials required for the production of essential goods. To this end, two comprehensive systems of allocation were developed: the Production Requirements Plan in 1942, followed by the Controlled Materials Plan in 1943.

Under the Production Requirements Plan, companies using basic materials applied to the WPB for purchase authorizations. These authorizations were kept within the limits of available supplies. There was no danger, therefore, that orders thus approved would not be filled. But the system had a serious weakness. It applied only to the distribution of materials among their first processors. It did not control the use to which the articles produced by these concerns were ultimately put. The castings for which metal was allocated to foundries, for instance, might be incorporated in nonessential consumers' goods instead of goods required for defense. The allocations were made at the wrong end of the productive process. If materials are to be used where most needed, they must be tied to requirements for finished goods.

This was the method employed by the Controlled Materials Plan, used after 1943 in the allocation of strategic metals: steel, copper, aluminum and their alloys. Here, the process of allocation was vertical rather than horizontal. Allotments were made to the manufacturers of end products on the basis of requirements estimates. They were then passed down the line to intermediate processors and original producers in the form of authorizations to buy controlled materials. The need for finished products thus governed the purposes for which these materials were used. The plan had one drawback. It tended to freeze particular suppliers to particular customers, impairing competition in the markets concerned. But if the process of allocation was to serve its purpose, this was unavoidable.

Fundamentally, the planning and control of production in wartime should involve the following steps: (1) determination of the need for final products both for military and for civilian use, (2) translation of these needs into requirements for materials and manpower, (3) comparison of these requirements with the quantities available, (4) modification of production plans to bring demands within the limits of supplies, (5) allocation of resources in accordance with the pattern of production desired, and (6) enforcement of allocation orders to insure conformity. This process must go on continuously, allocations being tied to production schedules and modified when there are changes in the basic plan. The necessities of warfare, in short, require replacement of free markets by political controls.

Manpower Controls

War not only increases the demand for labor but also reduces the supply by taking millions of able-bodied youths into the armed services. It also occasions shortages of workers with special skills. People must therefore be attracted into the labor force—minors, women, and persons who had retired—and workers must be drawn into those occupations where labor is needed most. This could be done by raising wages, but wage increases would lead to higher costs and prices, creating instability. Or workers might be allocated as materials are. Each employee could be required to carry a ticket and employers with low priorities forbidden to hire men leaving jobs with high priorities. Government inspectors could check on the utilization of labor and require workers to shift from less essential employments to more essential ones. The draft could be made universal and draftees released on furlough to fill particular jobs. But these things are unlikely to be done. Workers cannot be ordered around as materials are without infringement of human liberty. And compulsion, instead of increasing output, may impair morale and reduce productivity. In moving labor from place to place, less stringent measures are likely to be used.

This was the case in the United States in World War II. Workers were released from nonessential activities by curtailment and limitation orders, but were then left free to accept employment where they chose. Young men subject to the draft were granted occupational deferments when possessing special skills. An effort was made to take work to the worker by encouraging placement of contracts in regions where labor was not in short supply. Obstacles to mobility were lessened by providing information through public employment offices and by assuring the maintenance of retirement benefits and seniority rights. Movement to essential occupations was induced by non-wage incentives—good working conditions, housing, and schooling—and by assurance of overtime. In certain areas and in certain industries, the War Manpower Commission experimented with plans that required employees moving from one job to another to obtain certificates of availability or required employers to obtain labor through public employment offices which were to make assignments in accordance wih WPB priorities. But these schemes were largely voluntary and were not effectively enforced.

Rationing

Rationing does for consumers' goods what allocation does for raw materials. It balances demand with supply and controls the distribution of the quantities available. Its purpose is to assure fulfillment of the most important needs and, beyond this, to distribute limited supplies with equity. It can be fairer than reservation of goods by merchants for their favored customers. It will be more convenient than distribution to those who stand in queues. Rationing will afford to every household an equal chance to buy.

It is neither desirable nor necessary to ration all consumers' goods. Some goods will not be scarce. Others, though scarce, will not be essential. Still others, though scarce and essential, will be so difficult to ration that the attempt cannot be made. In general, rationing works best where goods pass through a bottleneck on their way from the point of origin to the point of final use. Here, distribution can be brought under administrative control. But where many small and scattered producers sell directly to consumers, the undertaking may well prove to be unmanageable. The goods to be rationed, therefore, will be those that are scarce, essential, and not impossible to control.

Rationing programs must be prepared in secret and sprung without warning. Public discussion of prospective action would set off a wave of buying that would concentrate supplies in private hoards. The objective of equity in distribution would not be achieved. If rationing is to be orderly, shortages must be anticipated and programs initiated before they appear to be needed. Delay will make the need apparent, lead to runs on stores, and force adoption of programs that cannot be carefully planned but must be hastily improvised.

Rationing programs are of three major types. (1) Certificate rationing is used where goods are very scarce and purchases are made infrequently. Certificates authorize the purchase of a specific quantity of a particular commodity. They are given only on a showing of special need. This method is used in rationing consumers' durables such as automobiles, tires, and stoves. (2) Coupon rationing is used where goods are purchased frequently and ready substitutes are not available. Here, each person eligible for a ration is entitled to buy a certain quantity during a certain period of time. Ration books are distributed containing different coupons to be used for different goods. The size of an individual ration can be varied by changing the value of a coupon or the duration of its validity. This method is used in rationing such commodities as sugar, coffee, and gasoline. (3) Point rationing covers a family of products which are close substitutes. It is used where the rationing of individual items would not be feasible. Here, the values of coupons and products are expressed in points, and the consumer is permitted to spend her points for any product she may choose. If a product sells quickly, its point value can be raised; if it sells slowly, its value can be reduced. Thus supply and demand can be kept in balance for each item in the group. This method is more difficult than the others to administer. It has the advantage of preserving greater freedom of consumer choice. It is used in rationing such products as canned goods, and meat, butter, fats, and oils.

The determination of rations differs from product to product. With durables, distribution is on the basis of need. Automobiles and tires, for instance, go first to physicians, and refrigerators to hospitals. Here, administrative judgment must be employed in establishing priorities, and a separate decision must be made in every case. Some non-durable goods, such as shoes, can be distributed equally. But others require differentiation. Larger gasoline rations must be given to war workers, larger fuel oil rations to families with invalids and infants, larger food rations to nursing mothers and children and persons engaged in heavy work. Special problems are presented by institutional and industrial consumers. Here, rations may be related to the quantities used before the war, but such allotments will soon get out of date. The determination of rations, moreover, is likely to be influenced by political pressures. If such pressures are resisted, the rationing official may find himself out of a job. If they are not, public confidence in the integrity of the system will be impaired.

Rationing is enforced by balancing ration currency, in the form of coupons, with supplies of rationed goods. The retailer collects the currency from consumers and uses it, in turn, to obtain supplies from wholesalers. If he sells without collecting coupons, he cannot replenish his stocks. So, too, with wholesalers buying from manufacturers. Coupons thus flow upstream as goods flow down. At the most convenient bottleneck, the rationing authority checks the currency collected against the goods sold. Here the coupons are withdrawn from circulation and destroyed. In World War II a system of ration banking was developed, dealers depositing ration currency with their banks and drawing checks against ration accounts to use in buying new supplies. In this way distributors were spared the inconvenience of counting coupons and the bookkeeping involved was handled by the banks. Adjustments must be made, where coupons and goods are balanced, for evaporation, shrinkage, pilferage, loss of coupons, and the like. And enforcement officers must be on the lookout for counterfeiters of the ration currency.

In Germany, ration books had been printed and deposited in the post offices for distribution before Hitler marched into Poland. In the United

States, rationing was unprecedented and unplanned. During World War I, the only commodity rationed was sugar. During World War II, rationing was initiated within three weeks after Pearl Harbor, the first program being that for automobile tires. This was improvised by a professor of economics—Ben W. Lewis of Oberlin College—working day and night, scarcely pausing for food or sleep. In the next year, a large rationing organization was built up within the OPA, a major program being launched each month. Administration was carried on through scores of field offices and thousands of local boards, staffed largely with volunteers. Three ration books were printed, 150,000,000 copies of Books I and II being distributed with the aid of teachers through the public schools, those of Book III being distributed through the mails. Two billion ration tokens were manufactured for use in making change. The operation was one of major magnitude. But it covered only a seventh of the consumers' goods sold in the United States. Serious shortages were confined to a few commodities. Most goods, even at the height of the war, remained in adequate supply. Another time, the undertaking might be even more formidable.

On the whole, rationing in World War II must be accounted a success. But it ended, unfortunately, in failure. On the assumption that an increase in rations would be politically popular, even though supplies were inadequate to match them, the ration currency was overissued. As a consequence, when coupons were offered, consumers could not get goods. The system threatened to break down. Then, despite its promise not to do so, OPA invalidated outstanding coupons. Those who had taken its word were injured. Public confidence in the integrity of the system was destroyed. All rationing but that of sugar was abandoned by the autumn of 1945.

CO-ORDINATION OF CONTROLS

Each of the wartime controls can be so administered as to support or to cancel the effect of others. Price and wage controls can be employed to facilitate the proper allocation of materials and labor or so rigidly enforced as to obstruct shifts needed for the prosecution of the war. Controls on materials and manpower can be used to reinforce ceilings on prices and wages or withheld from use however badly needed for stability. Procurement agencies and those responsible for the supply of materials are apt to look upon the stabilization authorities as willful obstructionists. Price and wage controllers are likely to view the procurement and materials officials as determined inflationists. Contention between these groups delays decisions and dissipates administrative energies. The objectives of both are legitimate. Where they come into conflict, they must be compromised. Agencies exercising particular controls must therefore be subject to over-all direction, their purposes thrown into a common balance, and differences between them resolved. This was the function of the Office of War Mobilization during World War II and the Office of Defense Mobilization during the war in Korea.

SUGGESTIONS FOR FURTHER READING

The best general discussion of wartime controls is Donald H. Wallace, *Economic Controls and Defense* (New York: Twentieth Century Fund, 1953). A fuller discussion, including a valuable collection of excerpts from other sources, is Lester V. Chandler and Donald H. Wallace, *Economic Mobilization and Stabilization* (New York: Henry Holt & Co., 1951). An historical account of the economic controls employed in the United States in the Second World War is presented by the Bureau of the Budget in *The United States at War* (Washington: Government Printing Office, undated). An excellent series of articles on the issues raised by wartime controls is contained in the *American Economic Review* XLI (1951) 30–85. The best accounts of rent control and rationing are presented in Harvey C. Mansfield and Associates, *A Short History of OPA*, Chapters 4 and 5 (Washington: Office of Temporary Controls, General Publication No. 15, 1947). Many of these materials are included in the volume by Chandler and Wallace. See also W. Glenn Campbell, Editor, *Economics of Mobilization and War* (Homewood, Ill.: Richard D. Irwin, Inc., 1952).

Chapter 25 COMPREHENSIVE PRICE CONTROLS

Prices have been controlled by the government of the United States during three wars: World War I, World War II, and the war in Korea. Price control in World War I was limited in extent and in duration. Maximum prices were established for wheat, hogs, and sugar by a Food Administration and for coal by a Fuel Administration, acting under statutory powers. Other prices were controlled by the War Industries Board. This was primarily a procurement agency. As such, it bought goods at prices it negotiated with sellers or commandeered them at prices it fixed as fair. And to prevent such goods from being diverted to civilian uses, it also put ceilings over the prices paid for them by other buyers. In doing so, it acted without legal authority, relying for enforcement upon its power to grant or withhold priorities. Most commodities were not subjected to control. And save for sugar and coal, the regulations were confined to the earlier stages of production and distribution, no limits being placed on the prices charged by retailers. The experience lasted but a few months, the war being ended in its second year.

During World War II the function of controlling prices was assigned to a single agency: the Office of Price Administration. This agency was given wide jurisdiction and substantial powers. Its regulations were virtually complete, coming to cover goods and services of nearly every type, and reaching from the producers of raw materials, through processors and fabricators, to wholesale and retail distributors. Most of these regulations were in operation for as much as four years, some of them for more than five years.

Abandoned in 1946, price controls were reimposed in 1951, following the outbreak of war in Korea. An Office of Price Stabilization was set up, on the model of OPA, with similar jurisdiction and powers. Drawing upon the experience of its predecessor, this agency again put ceilings over the prices of nearly all goods and services at each of the stages of production and distribution. But its ceilings were too high to be of real significance. During the latter half of 1950 prices had been inflated by a wave of speculative buying for business inventories and consumer hoards. And it was the level thus established that OPS incorporated in its controls. As a result, when demand subsided, most prices fell below the maxima allowed by law. Controls existed, on paper, for two years. But they were little observed and indifferently enforced. The real experience with price control, therefore, is that accumulated during World War II. And it is with this experience, in the main, that the following discussion deals.

REQUISITES OF PRICE CONTROL

It is not to be supposed that prices can be held in check simply by authorizing an administrative agency to issue orders forbidding them to rise. If prices are really to be controlled, such orders must be supported by consistent action in other fields. They must be supplemented by monetary policies designed to restrain the expansion of credit and by fiscal policies designed to minimize the government's deficit by reducing nonessential expenditures and by increasing taxes. Otherwise, the price controllers will be attempting to hold down the heat by sitting on the mercury in the thermometer while the lenders and the spenders are heaping coals on the flames. Action with respect to prices must be implemented, also, by appropriate action with respect to supplies. If ceiling prices are not to be evaded by deterioration of quality, the goods to which they apply must be identified by standardization and informative labeling. And if prices are not to be inflated by uptrading, i.e., by offering little or nothing in low-price lines and concentrating sales in high-price lines, the flow of materials into these lines must be controlled. Moreover, if ceilings are to be protected against rising costs, it may be necessary to simplify products and to concentrate production. And if they are not to be imperiled by the pressure of unsatisfied demands, such demands must be restrained by allocation and rationing. For these purposes, the price controllers must have the co-operation of the agencies controlling supplies. If denied it, their efforts may be set at naught. Control of the prices paid to businessmen must be accompanied, finally, by control of the prices paid to farmers and the wages paid to laborers, since no one of these groups will be willing to have its share of the nation's income subjected to control unless the share of each of the others is also controlled. For regulation to be tolerable, a balance of group interests is required. Insofar as these supports are granted, the control of prices may succeed. Insofar as they are withheld, it will be bound to fail.

The success or failure of price control will also depend upon the character of the control itself: its scope, its guiding policies, its methods, and the way in which it is enforced. These are the matters with which the present chapter is concerned.

Scope of Price Control

The leading issue in the debate on price control in 1941 was how extensive its coverage should be. Bernard Baruch, who had headed the War

Industries Board in World War I, argued that control should be comprehensive, with all prices, rents, wages and other payments being frozen on a given day and increases forbidden thereafter unless approved by the control authorities. Leon Henderson, who first headed the OPA in World War II, argued that control should be selective, with administrative efforts concentrated on those prices where inflationary pressures were at work and the market left free to allocate supplies of other goods and services. In support of the Baruch proposal it was said that prices are so interrelated that some cannot be fixed if others are left free: that one price is affected, for instance, by another that enters into costs, and that a controlled price cannot compete with an uncontrolled price in bidding for scarce supplies. And it was said that a policy which held some incomes down while permitting others to rise would be unfair. As a matter of economics and ethics, these arguments were sound. The difficulty with the proposal was administrative. The volume of individual adjustments that would be necessitated by a comprehensive freeze could not be handled, and the multitude of prices that would be frozen could not be enforced, until the price administration had been provided with central, regional, and local offices and equipment, had recruited and trained a large staff, had effected its organization and procedures, and had developed its standards and its methods of control. And all this would take time. A system of free markets cannot be converted into one of administered markets overnight. In time, control may be feasible if it is comprehensive. But at the outset, the job will be more manageable if it can be selective.

Selectivity may be necessary in the early days of mobilization. And it may be sufficient during a gradual build-up or a minor conflict when expenditures on defense are relatively small. But if this is to be the policy, which are the prices that are to controlled? Here, there are two views. According to one, attention should be directed toward those goods where the most serious shortages are felt and where the signs of inflation first appear: to the materials and the facilities required for the production of defense supplies. Inflationary pressure in general should be checked by monetary and fiscal action. The greater pressures at bottlenecks of production should be the main concern of price control. Thus, during World War II, the first regulations issued by the OPA put ceilings over the prices of such products as machine tools, metallic scrap, hides and skins, iron and steel, nonferrous metals, cotton yarns, lumber, and coal. According to the other view, the emphasis should be placed on prices that affect the cost of living, since a rise in living costs will evoke demands for higher wages, and a rise in wages will increase the costs of production and necessitate higher prices all along the line. It is assumed, here, that monetary and fiscal action will not be vigorous enough to hold down the prices of consumers' goods by checking the expansion of demand. In both world wars, this proved to be the case. And during the war in Korea, the first regulation issued by the OPS fixed maximum prices, not for materials entering into defense production, but for automobiles. It was the fear of general, rather than specific, inflationary pressures that was then in mind.

In a major war neither of these approaches will suffice. If control starts with industries producing for defense, it will have to be extended to other industries to prevent the diversion of scarce materials. If it starts with primary producers, it will have to be extended to fabricators and to distributors in order to hold down the cost of living and to check the spiral of wages, costs, and prices. If control starts, on the other hand, with cost-of-living items, the rising prices of defense supplies will add to inflationary pressures by necessitating larger public expenditures. The rising profits of defense industries will invite new wage demands. And wage increases for defense workers will lead to wage increases for workers producing civilian goods. Selective control, moreover, will prove to be politically untenable. If the profits of one industry are to be curbed, those of another cannot long be permitted to rise. Wherever it starts, price control is bound to be extended, in time, throughout the whole economy.

Certain prices are likely to be exempted from control. Thus, in 1942 Congress exempted newspapers, press services, books, magazines, motion pictures, radio broadcasting, advertising, insurance, real estate, securities, and professional services. The OPA, for administrative reasons, never attempted to control such items as objects of art, used business and personal effects sold at auction, and processed agricultural commodities, pelts, and furs sold by farmers and trappers for less than $75 per month. And beginning in 1943 it began dropping from control such trivia as pin cushions, shoe horns, music boxes, bird houses, dinner bells, glass flowers, artificial fruit, and novelties made of butterfly wings. It is sometimes argued that all luxury goods should be excluded from control. But such a policy would not be desirable, since it would divert resources to their production and permit their producers to enjoy profits higher than those obtained in other fields.

Guiding Policies in Price Control

If price control is to be effective, three fundamental principles must be observed. First, the use of price as an incentive and as an allocator must be minimized. The task of guiding production and allocating resources must be accomplished by controlling supplies. Otherwise, prices will mount steadily as ceilings are raised in a competitive effort to direct the flow of scarce materials, first this way and then that. Second, escalation must be avoided. Farm prices must not be raised to cover every increase in the parity index. Wages must not be raised to cover every increase in the cost-of-living index. And industrial prices must not be raised to cover every increase in production costs. As long as profits are at a reasonable level, absorption of cost increases should be required. Otherwise, the controllers will not be stabilizing prices, but merely recording their inflationary rise. Third, wherever a fractional addition to supply is needed and the cost of obtaining it exceeds the ceiling price, this cost should be met by fixing a higher price for the needed increment, by subsidizing its production, or by putting all of the output in a common pool and setting a price to cover its average cost. The extra cost of the increment should not be covered by raising the ceiling as a whole. Oherwise, a small addition to supply—say 4 or 5 per cent—may necessitate a large addition to price—say 50 per cent or 100 per cent or more—and this will be pyramided in the costs and prices of producers and distributors who are all along the line. If these principles are followed, the chances of price control may be good. If they are not, its chances will certainly be poor.

Price Control in World War II

The control of prices in World War II dates from the spring of 1940 when a Price Stabilization Division was established in an advisory council on national defense. The Division sought to check inflation by informal methods: suggestions, warnings, and voluntary agreements with businessmen. This was known as the period of jawbone control, when prices were held down with paper clips and rubber bands. The Office of Price Administration was set up, under an executive order, in the spring of 1941. This agency began to issue formal price schedules, though possessing no clear enforcement powers. Congressional hearings on a price control bill dragged on through the summer and the fall. The attack on Pearl Harbor came at the beginning of December. The Emergency Price Control Act was finally passed at the end of January, 1942. The Act gave legal status to the OPA, empowered the Price Administrator to put ceilings over any prices that had risen or threatened to rise, and made his orders enforceable at law.

The Act, however, had serious weaknesses. It forbade the Administrator to regulate agricultural prices until they should exceed 110 per cent of parity or the levels reached during any one of three previous periods, whichever was highest. It required him, when fixing prices for processed goods, to set them high enough to cover the prices established for agricultural raw materials. And it further required him, before fixing agricultural prices, to obtain the consent of the Secretary of Agriculture. The Act made no provision for the control of wages. With the prices of foods and fibers thus freed from control, the cost of living rose. And with wage increases uncontrolled, wages also rose. With incomes growing and costs rising, prices could not be held. It soon became clear that selective control would not suffice.

On April 28, 1942, OPA issued a General Maximum Price Regulation freezing all prices (save those specifically exempt) at the highest levels obtaining in the month of March. Control was thus made comprehensive. But farm prices still were largely free and wages entirely so. The cost of living continued to rise. So did wages. And so, in consequence, did costs and prices all along the line.

On October 2, 1942, Congress passed a Stabilization Act authorizing the Price Administrator to put ceilings over agricultural prices at parity or at the highest figure obtaining in 1942, whichever was higher, and forbidding employers to raise wages without the approval of the War Labor Board. The law also set up an Office of Economic Stabilization to settle disputes arising when the Department of Agriculture or the War Labor Board should ask for higher prices or wages and the OPA for lower ones. But inflation, still, was poorly controlled. The pressure for higher incomes persisted, adjustments were made in the regulations, and the general level of prices continued to rise.

On April 8, 1943, the President issued a "hold-the-line" order, directing the stabilization authorities to hold future wage and price increases to the minimum amounts required by law. In the next month, the OPA established maximum prices for foodstuffs at retail in dollars and cents, reducing the prices of major items and keeping them down by paying subsidies to their processors. This was the turning point in price control. The cost of living was stabilized. Wages were held in check. The index of prices was steadied for the next two years.

With the end of the war, wage controls became inoperative as workers struck for higher hourly rates. Wages rose, and farmers and businessmen sought higher prices for themselves. A bill was passed in 1946 extending price controls. But it was so filled with provisions boosting prices that President Truman vetoed it. For nearly a month, markets were free. Farm prices soared. Then a new bill was passed and signed. Ceilings were again imposed. At this, the farmers struck. Livestock was kept on the farm. Consumers got no meat. The strike succeeded. The ceilings on meat were lifted. And, with this, the structure of controls collapsed.

Price Control in the Korean War

At the end of June, 1950, war broke out in Korea. Three months later, Congress passed the Defense Production Act providing power to control prices, either selectively or comprehensively. The law required that wages also be controlled if prices were. But it forbade the imposition of ceilings on farm prices until they should exceed parity or the levels reached in the month before Korea, whichever was higher. An Economic Stabilization Agency and a Wage Stabilization Board were set up in September, an Office of Price Stabilization in the following January. The ESA began with informal methods. In December it went on from persuasion to compulsion with a specific regulation: the one on automobles. But the requirement respecting wages made selectivity impossible: wages could not be held down in some industries and allowed to rise in others. On January 26, 1951, the ESA issued a general wage-price freeze. But in doing so, as noted above, it set its ceilings, not at the pre-Korea levels, but at the inflated figures obtaining at the beginning of the year.

Thereafter, each major pressure group was assured that its income would be raised as other incomes rose. For agriculture, this was done in accordance with the parity requirement in the law. For labor, it was accomplished by raising wages to cover rises in the cost of living and by permitting escalator clauses in union contracts to take effect. For business the law was amended in the summer of 1951 to require that producers' ceilings be raised to cover all past increases in production costs, and also that the higher prices resulting from this requirement be pyramided and passed on to consumers by permitting distributors to add the same percentage markups that they used before Korea. The principle of cost absorption was thus abandoned. Inflation, instead of being suppressed, was made compulsory. Higher farm prices meant higher food prices. Higher food prices meant higher living costs. Higher living costs meant higher wages. Higher wages meant higher production costs. Higher production costs meant higher prices for the things that farmers buy. This would raise the parity index, then farm prices, then the cost-of-living index, then wages, then production costs, then price ceilings, and so on, and on, and on. In such a situation, the price controllers never really had a chance. The OPS began suspending ineffective regulations in the spring of 1952. The stabilization machinery was liquidated in the spring of 1953.

TECHNIQUES OF PRICE CONTROL

Maximum prices may be established for producers in four different ways. (1) They may be fixed in dollars and cents for all sellers by the pricing agency. (2) They may be frozen at the highest figures obtained by individual sellers in some previous period. (3) They may be computed by individual sellers in accordance with a formula provided by the pricing agency. (4) They may be computed for individual sellers by the agency itself. Maxima may be established for distributors by regulating the margins they can add to acquisition costs or by fixing the prices they can charge. A common margin may be set for all goods or different margins for different goods. Margins or prices may be frozen or specified. And both with producers and distributors, a single maximum may be fixed for all sellers or different maxima for different sellers. Each of these techniques has its advantages and its disadvantages.

Dollars-and-Cents Ceilings

It is frequently difficult or impossible to fix maximum prices in dollars and cents. This can be done most readily where products are standardized, producers few in number, markets well organized, and information readily available. Here, the controllers may adopt the price list of a market leader. They may use the prices reported in a trade journal. Or they may follow a well-established formula in computing the prices they specify. In the case of steel, for instance, in World War II, OPA took the base price quoted by U.S. Steel, applied the industry's standard extras and deductions, used its basing points, and referred to its freight-rate book, thus fixing a definite price for each of the products handled by each of the steel warehouses throughout the United States. In many industries, however, the needed information is more difficult to obtain. Here, the OPA sent questionnaires to producers. Or it made sample studies of production costs. In the case of bituminous coal, as we saw in Chapter 16, it took the elaborate data that had been painstakingly assembled for the purpose of fixing minimum prices and put them to work in fixing maxima.

The dollars-and-cents ceiling has many advantages. It can be made to conform to past price structures and customary pricing practices. Unlike a base-date freeze, it does not perpetuate abnormal base-period relationships. Unlike a freeze or a formula ceiling, it does not require the seller to keep extensive records or to make detailed reports. Since it announces the legal maxima to the buyer and to the enforcement officer, it is hard to evade and comparatively easy to enforce. Its one real disadvantage lies in the fact that its preparation may require a large amount of labor and take a great deal of time. As a result, inflation might get out of hand if the price controllers were to confine themselves to the meticulous development of regulations tailored to meet the needs of particular industries. If action is to be prompt and comprehensive, a cruder instrument will be required.

Freezes

A freeze may be specific or general, applying to a particular industry or to all producers and distributors. In either case, it establishes a ceiling for each good or service sold by each seller by holding him to the highest price he charged for the same good or service during some period in the past. In World War II, for example, the General Maximum Price Regulation (popularly known as the General Max) issued in April set the seller's ceiling at the highest price he charged in March.

This device has certain advantages. A freeze order can be drafted without obtaining detailed information. It conforms automatically to existing price structures and pricing practices. It can be issued promptly. Its coverage can be broad. As a temporary expedient, its use is inescapable. In the long run it can be replaced with tailored regulations. But even in the short run it has serious disadvantages.

If a freeze is really to check incipient inflation, it must be imposed swiftly, without previous warning or public debate. Otherwise, anticipatory increases will be made so that ceilings, when established, may be high. An earlier period might be selected as the base. But political pressures are likely to insure the use of a later one. While a freeze is under discussion, the price controllers will usually seek to prevent increases by appealing to the patriotism of businessmen. Some sellers will co-operate; others will not. Then, when the freeze is finally imposed, the price boosters will be rewarded and the patriots penalized.

A freeze, though easy to prepare, is difficult to administer. It congeals abnormal and fortuitous price levels and relationships, catching some prices at figures established in long-term contracts, in special concessions, in flush seasons, and in clearance sales. Corrections must be made, and this requires administrative action. A freeze leaves certain prices uncontrolled. It covers the case where the same seller sold the same product in the base period. It does not cover a new seller, a new or altered product, or an old seller who has taken on a new product. For these purposes, it must be supplemented by another technique. A freeze, finally, is hard to enforce. The seller will doubtless know what his highest price was in the base period; the buyer probably will not. The seller can be required to post his legal prices and to maintain records for inspection by enforcement officers. But the buyer will not know whether the posted prices are correct. The seller will be burdened with a task involving considerable cost. And the enforcement agency can hope to check but an insignificant fraction of the prices posted with the records kept.

Where a freeze is applied at successive stages of production and distribution, another difficulty is encountered. This was the case, for instance, under the General Max. The retailer's price in March, let us say, was based on the price charged by the wholesaler in February and by the manufacturer in January. By March, these prices had risen. Now, when the retailer bought at his supplier's March price and sold at his own March price, his margin was squeezed. So, too, with the wholesaler. This could not have been avoided by fixing a January base, say, for manufacturers and a February base for wholesalers, since the speed with which different goods move through the channels of distribution is not the same, and intervals fixed for one would not be appropriate for another. The freeze created the squeeze. The squeeze, accordingly, had to be relaxed. This could be done in one of two ways. It could be rolled back by reducing the prices of wholesalers and manufacturers. It could be rolled forward by raising the prices of wholesalers and retailers. It was the intention of OPA to roll the squeeze back. But this proved a difficult thing to do save in those cases where the sellers with lowered ceilings were subsidized by the government. The squeeze, more often, was rolled forward, raising the ceilings established for distributors. A general freeze, it was found, will soon be followed by a thaw.

Formulas

Dollars-and-cents ceilings cannot be established for goods or services that cannot be standardized: for custom-made products, for example, or for building construction or repair work. Nor can freezes be applied to new sellers, to sellers taking on new lines, or to new or altered goods. In such cases, a price regulation will prescribe a formula for sellers to use in computing the prices they may charge. Such formulas specify the factors to be employed in making the computation and show how they must be combined. Under some of them, ceilings are calculated by comparing one item to another one whose price is known; under others, by relating prices to costs.

The principle of comparability was used in fixing prices, under the General Max, where sellers and goods were not the same as they had been in March. If a seller had not sold an item in March, he was instructed to take as his ceiling the price he charged for the "similar" product "most nearly like" it. If he had not sold a similar product, he was told to take the price charged for the item by the "most closely competitive seller." For new goods, where neither of these methods would work, distributors were told to select a "comparable" product, divide its maximum price by its replacement cost, and multiply the resulting percentage by the cost of the item being priced. And manufacturers were instructed, in a later regulation, to take the comparable products with costs just above and just below those of a new good, determine the average markup on these products, and add it to the new good's costs. In each of these cases, the seller was left free to make his own selection of a "similar" product and a "competitive" seller, or to exercise his own judgment as to the comparability of old and new goods. He was thus afforded wide latitude in determining his price.

The cost formulas used in price control range from utter simplicity to extreme complexity. All of them provide for the addition of certain margins to certain basic costs. But some of them merely require the seller to use the same cost factors and the same method of calculation that he did in some base period. And others specify, in considerable detail, how each element of cost is to be computed, how margins are to be determined, and how the two shall be combined. A formula will be loose if it permits cost factors to be priced at current levels, tighter if it requires them to be priced at base-period rates. But even here, it cannot prevent costs from being inflated by increasing the quantities of the factors that are used. A formula will also be loose if it permits margins to be added to costs as percentages, tighter if it requires them to be figured in dollars and cents. Where formulas are used in making estimates, recalculation based on subsequent experience may be required. Where they are used in pricing new lines of standard products, the ceilings once computed may continue to apply. Where goods cannot be standardized, however, a computation must be made for every sale.

Formulas, at best, are feeble instruments. Cost accounting is not a science but an art. Costs are a matter of judgment, and under a formula ceiling the judgment is made by the seller whose price is being fixed. Even if he is scrupulously honest, he is likely to adopt those principles of accounting that make for a higher rather than a lower price. When he announces his ceiling, the buyer has no way of telling whether it is correct. Nor do the price controllers. They may require him to make reports. But they cannot begin to check such reports, in thousands upon thousands of cases, against the sellers' books. Under formula regulations, in general, sellers can set their ceilings where they please, and no one can really say them nay.

Specific Authorizations

Producers of new goods, instead of being permitted to establish their own ceilings, may be required to apply to the pricing agency to have specific prices authorized. This was done, under OPA, in the cases of toys, furniture, and other consumers' durables. Here, the principle employed in fixing prices was that of putting them in line with those of comparable goods. This was accomplished in three different ways. (1) OPA selected the two most nearly similar articles in the seller's line, averaged their markups in percentages and in dollars and cents, and fixed the price of the new item by adding to its costs the lower of the two. (2) OPA fixed a price that would enable the seller to obtain the same percentage return on the new item that he was realizing on his business as a whole. (3) OPA asked for samples or for blueprints and specifications of the new item and compared it with similar articles produced by other sellers, ascertained their ceilings, and fixed a price that would enable the new item to compete. Maximum prices were thus established for 66,000 different products in a single year.

Ceilings thus set by price controllers are likely to be lower than those computed by sellers themselves. But this method, also, has its disadvantages. The goods thus priced were not standardized. There were differences in judgment, between controllers and producers, as to the products taken as a basis of comparison. There were differences, too, concerning the allowances that should be made for such intangibles as style and prestige of trade names. As a result, there was irritation, altercation, and delay. Sellers were handicapped, in planning production, by their inability to discover the prices they would be allowed to charge. Some of them, defiant or discouraged, proceeded to put goods on the market without applying for a legal price. And OPA never found out what they had done.

Differential Pricing

With some goods, where demand is large in wartime, the costs of marginal increments will be much higher than those incurred in obtaining other parts of the supply. Ores brought up from thin seams underground will cost more than those removed from open pits. Products turned out with obsolete equipment will cost more than those produced in modern plants. Goods imported from abroad will cost more than those produced at home. In such cases, the price controllers must decide whether to fix a single maximum price for all of the supply or different maxima for different parts of the supply.

During World War I, the controllers followed the practice of setting a single price. The ceiling for a product was typically placed at a level which was calculated to cover average total unit cost plus a reasonable profit for the bulk-line producer, i.e., the one whose contribution was required in order to obtain 90 per cent of the needed supply. This was supposed to cover the costs of firms producing the remaining 10 per cent and to afford them an incentive to increased efficiency. In some cases, however, a ceiling was set at a level designed to cover costs and provide a profit for the highest-cost producer in the field. Thus, to get a marginal addition to supply, the government fixed a price of 26 cents for copper, the bulk of which was produced at an average cost of 14 to 17 cents.

Such a policy is open to serious criticism. If a single ceiling is set at a level high enough to cover marginal costs, it will be highly inflationary and will yield excessive profits to producers having average costs. On the other hand, a price that is low enough to check inflation and to prevent windfall profits will cut off supplies that are urgently required. And a compromise price, between the two, will do both: it will permit inflation and windfall profits where costs are low and cut off supplies where costs are high. The solution to this dilemma is found in differential pricing.

In World War II, this was the general rule, the regulations issued by OPA providing for differentiation in several ways. Where ceilings were established by freezes or by formulas, they automatically resulted in different maxima for different sellers. Where they were fixed in dollars and cents, high-cost sellers were frequently granted adjustments permitting them to charge higher prices. In a number of regulations, moreover, different prices were fixed for different firms, or sellers were classified and a different price was fixed for each class.

Unless it is supplemented by other measures, differential pricing may force one buyer to pay more than another for the same commodity. Such an arrangement is workable in some cases and not in others. It will work in retail distribution, where different prices have always been charged by different types of outlets. It will work at earlier stages of production if there are buyers who are willing to purchase the higher-priced portions of the supply. This will be the case where buyers sell, in turn, under cost-plus contracts or ceilings. It may also be true with a common ceiling if demand so far exceeds supply that buyers cannot satisfy their needs by shifting to lower-priced sellers, and if the higher prices are an insignificant part of the buyers' costs or can be absorbed in the buyers' profits. A system of multiple prices will not work, however, where buyers must sell, in turn, under a common ceiling, where supply is so far in excess of demand that buyers will shift their purchases to low-cost sellers, where the higher prices are significant in costs, and where profit margins are too narrow to permit them to be absorbed. In such cases, though sellers get different prices, buyers must be given a single price. This may be done in two ways: by subsidizing high-cost sellers and by pooling high-cost and low-cost supplies.

Subsidies

A distinction must be made between the policy of holding prices down by subsidizing every unit of a supply and the policy of holding prices down by subsidizing the marginal units alone. When OPA rolled back the prices of foodstuffs in the spring of 1943, it effected the cut by paying an equivalent subsidy to processors on the entire output of meat, butter, coffee, and other commodities. As a result, the cost of living was reduced, wages were held in line, and inflation was finally checked. But the subsidy cost the government almost as much as the price cut saved the consumer. (The cut was larger at retail than at wholesale because the distributor's percentage markup was added to a smaller base.) When margins are subsidized, on the other hand, the subsidy costs much less than it saves the consumer, since it is paid on a minor part of the supply to hold down prices on the whole supply.

Marginal subsidies were used, in World War II, to cover the extra costs involved in obtaining added supplies: those imported from abroad, those requiring costlier modes of transportation, and those more difficult to produce. The most significant of these arrangements was the premium price plan for copper, lead, and zinc, developed by the late Donald H. Wallace, Professor of Economics at Princeton University. Under this plan, the ceiling price of copper, for instance, was held at 12 cents throughout the war. The metal that could not be produced at this price —about a tenth of the supply—was bought by the government at seventeen cents or twenty-two cents and resold to the industry at twelve cents. The price increases prevented in this way ran into hundreds of millions of dollars, as much as twenty dollars being saved for every dollar spent in subsidies.

The method of equalizing prices by pooling supplies has one advantage over that of paying subsidies. In this case, there is no burden on the Treasury. The government buys the whole supply of a commodity from its producers, paying each of them his own cost plus a profit. It then sells at a price that covers its average cost. It thus holds the ceiling down without incurring a loss. This device was employed extensively in Germany during both world wars. It was used in the United States, during World War I, in fixing the price of sugar and, during World War II, in equalizing the cost of transporting crude oil, by different carriers, from the producing fields to the refineries. It might well have been used in many other cases to hold down prices and public expenditures.

Fixing Retail Prices

The control of retail prices raises a number of important questions. (1) Should the controllers specify the price the retailer may charge or the margin he may add to the price he pays? Where the price is specified, enforcement is easier, but margins may be squeezed as costs increase, and the necessity of making adjustments will impose a heavy burden on the pricing agency. Where control is confined to margins, squeezes are avoided and the burden of administration is minimized, but ceilings are computed by sellers, their accuracy is unknown to buyers and can rarely be checked by enforcement officers. (2) If margins are controlled, should an average figure be set for all of a merchant's business or different figures for different commodities? An average margin would afford great flexibility, leaving the merchant free to raise or lower the price of particular goods. But it would appear to the consumer to involve no control, since final prices would not be fixed. And it would be virtually impossible to enforce, since violations could not be detected until the average margin realized was computed at the end of the year, accountants could not be recruited in the numbers that would be required to audit the retailers' books, overcharges could not be recaptured, and further violations could not be prevented by cutting the margin that violators would be permitted to use. If margin control is to be effective, a separate margin must be fixed for every line in the merchant's stock. (3) Should margins be fixed in percentages or in dollars and cents? Percentage margins conform to business practice, but they are inflationary, increasing in dollars and cents as the costs of the merchant's goods increase. Dollars and cents margins are tighter, but they are harder to establish and to enforce. (4) Should prices or margins be the same for all retailers or different for different retailers? If a single ceiling were set low enough to prevent inflation, it would eliminate small independent merchants and concentrate distribution in department stores, chain stores and supermarkets. If it were set high enough to preserve the independents, it would permit inflation through higher prices for mass distributors. If it were set between the two extremes, it would do both. To check inflation, while preserving existing channels of distribution, retailers must be classified and a different ceiling established for each class.

Control of retail prices in World War II was first established, by the base-date freeze technique, under the General Max. Dollars-and-cents ceilings were fixed in 1943 for all important grocery items in every large community. This was a major operation. First, stores were classified by size. Second, an elaborate study was made to determine the margins normally applied to different items by different classes of stores. Third, certain margins (usually those covering three fifths of the supply) were selected as typical. Fourth, the local offices of OPA discovered the prices paid by each class of store for each of the items involved. Fifth, they added the typical margin to the buying price to fix the selling price. Sixth, they published a schedule setting forth the resulting ceiling for each of the items in each of the classes of stores. This schedule enabled the housewife to check on the legality of every price she paid. In the case of perishables, where costs varied continually, the ceilings thus established were subject to recalculation, week by week. For dry groceries, however, such changes were not permitted. As a result of this control, the retail prices of food, in general, rose less than 2 per cent from June, 1943, to June, 1946. In the case of many other goods, where the General Max was superseded by margin regulations, retail prices rose substantially.

STANDARDS OF PRICE CONTROL

Whatever the techniques used in fixing prices, standards are needed to govern the levels at which they are set. Under a freeze, the level at which prices are caught is likely to be high, raising no question of equity to producers or adequacy of supplies. But under a dollars-and-cents ceiling, prices may be set too low to be fair to producers or so low as to cut off essential supplies. And under either type of regulation, prices once fair and adequate may cease to be so as costs continue to rise. Standards are needed, therefore, to judge the levels at which ceilings are first established, to decide whether they must be raised, and to determine the size of the increase that may be required. And if ceilings once fixed are later to be lowered, standards are also needed to determine which of them are to be reduced and how large the reductions are to be.

Under the Emergency Price Control Act of 1942, the Price Administrator was permitted to establish such maximum prices "as in his judgment will be generally fair and equitable and will effectuate the purposes of this Act," one of these purposes being "to assist in securing adequate production of commodities." The Administrator was further directed to give due consideration to the prices prevailing between October 1 and 15, 1941 and to make adjustments for such relevant factors as increases or decreases in costs and in profits during and subsequent to the year ended October 1, 1941.

In accordance with these provisions, it was necessary for OPA to develop criteria of general fairness and equity. It was clear from the use of the word "generally" that such criteria were to be applied, not to individual producers, but to an industry as a whole. But were they to be applied to all of an industry's operations taken together or to each of its products taken separately? And, in either case, when was a ceiling to be held fair and when unfair? To answer these questions, the Office developed two criteria: an industry earnings standard and an individual product standard, whose provisions are described below. And to insure the maintenance of "adequate production," it established rules for increasing the prices of individual producers even where such increases were not required for general fairness and equity.

Industry Earnings Standard

The fairness of a ceiling can be judged only by its effect upon an industry's profits. But how are profits to be measured—as a return on sales or as a return on investment? Maintenance of the prewar ratio of profits to sales would afford an increasing return on investment as volume grew. And it might necessitate higher prices even though profits were already high. Establishment of a fair percentage return on a fair valuation of an industry's assets would be next to impossible. The problems involved in this procedure have not been solved in more than six decades of railroad and public utility regulation. They could scarcely be settled promptly and simultaneously for all American industries. Determination of a fair return can be avoided, however, by assuring an industry the same return that it had earned before the war. And determination of a fair value can be avoided by measuring this return, not as a percentage, but in dollars and cents. This was the method adopted by OPA.

Under the industry earnings standard, the statutory requirement of general fairness and equity was held to be satisfied as long as the aggregate dollar profits received by an industry on all of its operations, before payment of corporate income and profits taxes, equaled the average profits received in the prewar years 1936–39 inclusive, plus or minus a comparable rate of return on net increases or decreases in investment since that period. Unless profits fell below this level, requests for general price increases were denied and absorption of cost increases was required.

This was the general rule; there were exceptions. Agriculture was granted a more liberal standard by the law. Industries that had been abnormally depressed in the base period were permitted to shift to another base or to charge prices which covered current bulk-line costs. Industries suffering reductions in volume, due to cutbacks in civilian production, were held to prices which covered their current direct costs plus their base-period overhead and profit per unit of output. In the distributive trades, instead of aggregate dollar profits, the measure used was the average peacetime ratio of net profits to sales.

The industry earnings standard was attacked by businessmen who argued (1) that profits should be allowed to grow as output grew, however great the resulting return on investment, (2) that profits should be measured after taxes, so that income and excess profits taxes could be passed on to consumers in a higher price, and (3) that prices should be set high enough to assure each seller a profit, whatever his efficiency. The standard was defended as one that permitted each industry to obtain its normal peacetime earnings, the period selected as a base containing years of high, low, and average prosperity. It was used, moreover, not to fix a limit beyond which profits were not allowed to grow, but one below which they were not to be reduced. Upon appeal, the standard was upheld by the courts. A similar standard (with 85 per cent of the average profits of the best three of the four years 1946–49 as its base) was used by OPS in the Korean war.

Minimum Product Standard

Most producers turn out more than one product and most distributors handle more than one line. Prices are fixed, not for whole industries or trades, but for individual items. And though over-all profits may be adequate to meet the industry earnings standard, the ceilings set on particular items may still be too low to be fair or to maintain supplies. The earnings standard must be supplemented, therefore, by one that deals with products separately.

Under the rule adopted by OPA, the price of a product was held to satisfy the statutory requirement of fairness and equity as long as industry earnings were adequate and the price itself covered out-of-pocket costs (or average manufacturing costs) but not administrative overhead, selling costs, or profits, for the bulk of the output, the bulk line being drawn at three fourths of the supply. In cases where part of a product was turned out by firms producing several lines and part of it by firms producing only one, it was recognized that this rule might be unfair to members of the latter group. Here, the adequacy of earnings was tested by two measures —the industry's profits on the product and the profits of single-line producers—and ceilings were kept high enough to satisfy the lower of the two. In the distributive trades, the product standard required that the ceiling on each line be high enough to cover the cost of doing business but not to yield a profit on that line.

This standard, like the earnings standard, was designed to protect business by preventing the price controllers from setting ceilings too low. But it was none the less attacked on the ground that prices should be high enough to cover full costs and yield a profit on each of an industry's products, whatever its profits on its operations as a whole. Such a policy would have departed from normal business practice, since overhead costs are seldom allocated equally among product lines. It also would have been inflationary, necessitating higher ceilings for products whose producers were enjoying profits many times as large as those they had received before the war. The product standard, like the earnings standard, was sustained by the courts and was adopted, again, by OPS.

Individual Seller Adjustments

Administrative adjustments must often be made in the maximum prices established under general regulations. A dollars-and-cents ceiling may be found to contain errors. A freeze may have perpetuated abnormal price relationships. Such inequities must be corrected, case by case. A ceiling that is generally fair, moreover, may cut off certain segments of supply. It may afford an ample margin to sellers whose base-period prices were high and a meager one to those whose base-period prices were low. It may lead sellers to offer more goods in lines where margins were wide and fewer in lines where they were narrow. A regulation may result in shortages in certain localities. It may eliminate sellers with high costs. In each of these cases, it may be desirable to maintain supply. And it may be possible to do so, without raising the general ceiling, by making adjustments entitling individual sellers to charge more than the ceiling price.

Standards to govern such adjustments were developed by OPA. In cases of local shortage and in those of high-cost sellers, no action was taken unless the supplies in question were deemed to be essential. The difficult problem of developing criteria of essentiality was side-stepped by accepting certification from one of the agencies responsible for military or civilian supply. In these cases, and also in those of low-price producers and low-margin products, upward adjustments required a showing of hardship. The criteria used in determining hardship were similar to those employed—on an industry-wide basis—in determining equity. A producer was held to suffer hardship if his dollar profits before taxes were smaller than those received in the base period, and if his earnings on investment in the base period had not exceeded the average earnings of his industry. He was also held to suffer hardship if his maximum price was below his manufacturing cost, exclusive of selling cost, administrative overhead, and profit. If over-all earnings were inadequate, the ceiling on the seller's product would be raised to cover total unit costs and yield a reasonable profit. If they were adequate, the ceiling would be raised to cover manufacturing costs alone.

Some effort was made by OPA to limit the number of upward adjustments by seeking other solutions to the problem of shortages: by obtaining subsidies for high-cost producers, for instance, and by persuading the supply agencies to curb the shift of production from low-margin to high-margin lines. An effort was also made to minimize the effect of such adjustments by requiring a producer whose over-all profits were ample to offset the higher price allowed on one product by accepting a lower price for another, or by requiring him to show that the higher price would not be passed on to the consumer but would be absorbed by the producers or distributors to whom he sold. In most cases, however, supplies were maintained by raising prices, and the higher prices were neither offset nor absorbed. Even so, the adjustment process led to dissatisfaction. Decisions were delayed, applications were denied, and the increases granted were smaller than those that had been sought. So approval as well as disapproval and action as well as inaction were resented by businessmen.

Price Reductions

The level at which a ceiling is fixed may be too low to be fair to producers; it may also be too high to be fair to consumers. Costs may rise as wages and raw material prices rise and as less efficient labor and equipment are employed; they may also fall with the substitution of cheaper materials, with growth of volume, and with changes in technology. Profits may be limited to prewar levels by refusing to raise prices as costs increase; they may also be limited by reducing prices as costs decline. If administrative action, instead of the market, is to fulfill the function of putting prices up, it should also fulfill the function of putting prices down.

Price reductions were clearly authorized by law in World War II. The Price Control Act said that prices should be "generally fair and equitable" not to producers alone, but presumably to consumers as well. It instructed the Price Administrator to consider the prices prevailing in October, 1941 and to make adjustments for increases or decreases in costs and in profits occurring after October, 1940. This meant that he could reduce a price that had been caught by a freeze at a level higher than that obtaining in October, 1941, unless costs had risen proportionately. It also meant that he could fix a price below the October, 1941, level if costs had fallen and profits risen since October, 1940, and that he could reduce any price he might establish if they should subsequently do so. The OPA standards of fairness and equity would have justified reducing prices wherever profits were larger than those enjoyed in the four years before the war. On October 3, 1942, moreover, the President issued an Executive Order directing the Administrator to determine prices "in such manner that profits are prevented which in his judgement are unreasonable or exorbitant." And on April 8, 1943, in a second order, he instructed the Administrator "to prevent profiteering and to reduce prices which are excessively high, unfair, or inequitable."

Some prices were cut by OPA in 1942 and 1943. An effort was made, following the General Max, to restore the margins of distributors by rolling back the squeeze, but relief was more often obtained by raising the prices distributors charged than by reducing the ones they paid. The prices of foodstuffs were reduced when dollars-and-cents ceilings were established in 1943, but this was done by subsidizing their processors. The price of one product was reduced, in some cases, to offset an increase granted on another one, but such reductions were the exception rather than the rule. And an attempt was made, finally, to reduce prices on the ground that profits were too high. The criterion employed in this connection was not the industry-earnings standard but a looser one (profits on sales in 1941) permitting profits far larger than those received before the war. But the reaction to price cuts, even on this basis, was violent. OPA was charged, in Congressional hearings, with attempting to destroy the profit system, to abolish private enterprise, and to create a socialized economy. The effort to reduce prices sometimes instead of always raising them had been abandoned by 1944.

This was probably inevitable. It is hard enough to keep prices from going up. It is well nigh impossible, politically, to put them down. Ideally, the price controllers should perform the function of the market mechanism, raising some prices and reducing others. Actually, the most they can hope for is to limit the rise of some prices and to keep others from rising at all.

FEASIBILITY OF PRICE CONTROL

Price control in World War II was attended with a considerable measure of success. Prices rose less sharply during this period than they had in World War I. They rose less under OPA than they did before controls were imposed or after they were dropped. The prices that were controlled rose less than those that were not. And prices under controls that were tight rose less than those under controls that were loose. But the success of OPA in holding prices was not as great as a study of index numbers would suggest. For one thing, the indexes reflect the prices of standardized commodities, and these are the ones that are most readily controlled. For another, they do not reveal the inflation implicit in deterioration of quality and in the diversion of production from low-price to high-price lines. Prices were raised indirectly through resort to such devices. They were also raised directly and legally by moving up to ceilings, by taking advantage of formulas, by obtaining individual adjustments, and by getting the legal maxima increased. And they were raised illegally—sometimes inadvertently through ignorance of the regulations and inability to understand their terms; sometimes deliberately through willful violation of the law.

In part, the troubles of OPA are to be attributed to the failure of Congress to support its efforts by taking appropriate action in other fields, and to the statutory limitations within which it was forced to operate. In part, they would seem to be inherent in the very nature of price control. For such an undertaking is bound to encounter serious obstacles—administrative, economic, and political.

Administrative Difficulties

The preparation of regulations, the administration of adjustments, and the enforcement of maximum prices affecting nearly everything bought and sold in the United States is an undertaking of major magnitude. It requires the creation of a far-flung organization with a central office and regional and local branches, with commodity divisions and subdivisions, and with functional specialists in personnel, accounting, law, research, public relations, and the like. It requires the development of procedures that will meet the tests of due process. It calls for a large budget and necessitates the recruitment and direction of a large staff. For OPA, the annual budget for price and rent control and rationing reached $185,000,000 in 1945. The number of persons engaged in these activities exceeded 160,000. Of these, 100,000 were unpaid volunteers serving without compensation on local price and rationing boards. Sixty thousand were paid employees, 36,000 of them working for the local boards, 20,000 in regional and local offices, and 4,000 at the headquarters in Washington. An adequate discussion of the administrative problems presented by such an organization would require a treatise in itself. A word may be said, however, concerning the enforcement of price controls.

Under the Price Control Act of 1942, the Administrator was given ample enforcement powers. He could ask the courts to enjoin violations, bring suits for treble damages, require sellers to obtain licenses and suspend the licenses of violators, or request the Department of Justice to initiate criminal actions leading to fines and imprisonment. In practice, he relied on the injunction, the other methods of enforcement being little used. Action was taken, moreover, in but a tiny fraction of the cases where violations occurred. OPA had fewer than one investigator per county, fewer than the number of game wardens in the United States. It could hope to deal only with a few conspicuous cases, trusting to publicity to exercise a deterrent effect. The Office therefore concentrated on flagrant and persistent violations by manufacturers and wholesalers, leaving enforcement of the retail regulations to the local boards. These boards were more concerned with rationing than with price. But they had price panels whose members checked on retail prices, heard consumer complaints, conferred with retailers, obtained promises of compliance, collected refunds, and turned repeated violators over to the enforcement authorities. All this work was done, it should be noted, by unpaid volunteers.

Enforcement of price controls requires the prosecution of offenders and the imposition of penalties. But general compliance is not to be obtained by these measures alone. It must rest on public understanding and acceptance of the program, on voluntary observance resulting from popular support. To this end, a campaign of education is required. Such a campaign was carried on by OPA. But it was not entirely successful. In some fields the ceilings were quietly disregarded. And the public was tolerant, failing to view an increase in prices as a crime. A price controller is said to have visited a sale of cattle in Texas. "Aren't these prices above the ceiling?" he asked. "Oh, you mean that there OPA," was the reply. "We never had that down here."

Economic Obstacles

With some commodities, control of prices is fairly easy; with others, it is very difficult. The ease with which a price can be controlled depends upon three factors: the characteristics of the commodity concerned, the trend of the costs incurred in its production, and the structure of the market in which it is sold.

Control is easier where goods are standardized, produced in quantity, and sold continuously. It is more difficult where they are unlike, produced one at a time, and sold infrequently. It is hard to control the prices of custom-made goods, of new, altered, and secondhand goods, of seasonal and perishable products, and of goods where varieties are numerous, where the element of style is important, and where models are frequently changed. It is hard, for example, to control the prices of buildings, machine tools, repair services, meals served in restaurants, furniture, toys, used cars, fresh fruits and vegetables, and most forms of wearing apparel.

It is easy to hold onto prices where costs are declining. This may be the case where labor is of minor importance, where cheaper materials can be substituted, where investment is heavy and fixed charges high, and where increasing utilization of capacity reduces overhead per unit of sales. This was the case during World War II, for instance, with steel castings, aluminum, and magnesium. It is difficult to hold onto prices, on the other hand, where labor is a major element in cost, where more expensive materials must be used, where declining volume concentrates overhead, and where increasing volume can be obtained only by resorting to costlier sources of supply—to deeper and thinner veins in mining and to obsolete equipment in manufacturing. It is hard, for example, to hold down the price of lumber and the prices of minerals.

It is easier to control prices, finally, where production is concentrated in the hands of a few large firms, where price leadership and market sharing have been common, where pricing formulas have been followed, and where trade associations have influenced production, prices and terms of sale. Maximum prices were fixed most readily by OPA where minimum prices had been fixed successfully by NRA. It is difficult to control prices, however, where production is carried on by many small firms and where markets are normally competitive. Enforcement of maxima was difficult for OPA where enforcement of minima had been difficult for NRA. It was easy, for instance, to control the prices of steel, cement, and glass containers; hard to control those of forest products, textiles, and personal services.

Political Obstacles

The price controller must operate, of necessity, within the limits imposed on him by politics. He will be handicapped by provisions written into his statute to serve the interests of pressure groups. His appropriation will be inadequate; and if he gives offense, it may be cut. He will be bombarded by Congressional requests for higher prices, some of them polite, some of them insistent, some of them threatening. He will be investigated repeatedly by Congressional committees, his competence questioned, his integrity attacked. His discharge will be demanded; his salary may be stopped. He will be expected to hold down prices with one hand tied behind his back. And if he develops some device for doing so, the law will be amended to forbid its use.

This was the story of OPA. Its original statute exempted labor, impeded control of agricultural prices, and forbade the Administrator to require changes in "the business practices, cost practices or methods, or means or aids to distribution established in any industry." Its first Administrator, Leon Henderson, was dropped when he sought to fix the prices of agricultural commodities. The head of its price department, J. K. Galbraith, was discharged when he set up standards to identify some of the products to which its ceiling prices were applied. Administrative positions on its staff were closed to professional economists (described in Congress as "long-haired professors" who had never "carried a precinct or met a payroll") and turned over to businessmen. Its standards of control were weakened by Congressional action. Under the Bankhead Amendment, enacted in 1944, OPA was required to fix prices that would cover total costs and yield a profit, product by product, for the textile industry. And under the Barkley-Taft Amendment, adopted in 1946, it was required to fix prices on this basis for all industries.

Among items affecting the cost of living, OPA was least successful in controlling the prices of apparel. Here it was faced with the problems of deterioration in quality and diversion of production from low-price to high-price lines. To solve the first of these problems, the Office undertook

Carl Rose in *New York Times Magazine*

to standardize certain articles (notably women's stockings) tying its prices to definitions of quality. This was prevented by the Taft Amendment, enacted in 1943, which forbade the establishment of prices for products "described in terms of specifications or standards, unless such specifications or standards were . . . in general use in the trade or industry affected, or . . . previously . . . required by another Government agency." To discourage uptrading, the Office first forbade any seller to offer any category of garments in a price line higher than the highest one handled in the base period. This was a weak form of control, since it did not prevent sellers from dropping their lower price lines. And it could be evaded by closing a shop and reopening under another name. Even so, its application to retailers was outlawed by Congress in 1944. The Office then issued a regulation requiring manufacturers to maintain the same average prices for each category of garments as they had in 1943, thus forcing them to produce in low-price lines to offset their production in high-price lines. This method of control, too, was forbidden by amendment in 1946.

Price control was similarly handicapped in the Korean war. The law enacted in 1950 hampered the application of ceilings to farm prices, prohibited changes in business practices, forbade the introduction of new commodity standards, and prevented the limitation of retail price lines. And amendments adopted in 1951 required the OPS to raise the prices of manufacturers to cover all past increases in their costs and those of distributors to maintain their traditional margins. One of the prices that OPA had found most difficult to control was that of meat. The ceilings on the large packing houses were well enforced. But livestock was diverted to black-market butchers who sold above the ceiling price. Profiting by this experience, OPS sought to enforce its meat prices by licensing slaughterers, giving each of them a quota based on his 1950 share, and tagging each piece of meat with the slaughterer's license number, thus eliminating black-market operations in this commodity. Thereupon, Congress amended the Defense Production Act to forbid the use of slaughter quotas in fixing the price of meat.

Public Attitudes

In all of this, the members of Congress are not to be too harshly condemned. The representatives of the people were merely representing the people. Price control is bound to be unpopular. As J. K. Galbraith put it:

> No price fixer can avoid working damage on the fortunes of individuals —if not in an absolute sense, then at least in relation to opportunity. His task consists in denying men income they have had or could have had. When such effect is wrought by the free market there is no one to blame, or at most, the onus attaches subjectively to grasping middlemen, insatiable unions, or Wall Street. When a price fixer damages a man's fortune or his hope for one, that individual is left in no doubt as to who is responsible or as to the appropriate object of his dislike.[1]

All regulation is resented. The OPA differed in but one respect. It simultaneously imposed its ceilings upon nearly every price charged by nearly every trade in the economy. It was in action on all fronts and at all times. Its rules and regulations ran into many thick volumes, all of them having the effect of law, none of them written by the Congress itself. No agency that meddles with matters which so intimately affect the daily lives of all Americans can hope to escape abuse. Price control may influence people, but it does not win many friends.

[1] J. K. Galbraith, *A Theory of Price Control,* (Cambridge, Mass.: Harvard University Press, 1952), p. 27.

In time of war, as always, the public is inconsistent. In principle, it demands stability. In practice, it seems bent upon inflation. The seeming paradox is readily explained. All men have a common interest in the prices at which they buy. Each man has a special interest in the price at which he sells. The common interest calls for stability. The special interest calls for inflation. The common interest is unorganized, inarticulate, and impotent. The special interests are organized, vocal, and powerful. Every pressure that is brought to bear upon the Congress is a pressure for higher prices. Thus, agriculture, labor, and industry each contends for a larger share of the nation's income while, within their ranks, each group of farmers, laborers, and businessmen attempts to keep in step with every other.

Successful price control requires a high degree of economic literacy and political responsibility. Given the impetus of patriotism, a program of popular education, and a balance of group interests, it may be made to work. Lacking these, save in a time of the gravest national emergency, its chances will be small.

SUGGESTIONS FOR FURTHER READING

American experience with price control in World War I is outlined in Charles O. Hardy, *Wartime Control of Prices* (Washington: Brookings Institution, 1940). The best account of price control in World War II is that contained in chap. iii of Mansfield, *A Short History of OPA* and reproduced as chap. xviii in Chandler and Wallace, *Economic Mobilization and Stabilization* (both cited at the end of Chapter 24). A more detailed account of the problems arising in price control is presented in other volumes of the series of Historical Reports on War Administration published in 1947 by the Office of Temporary Controls. Of these, the most important are No. 8, *Pricing Techniques* and No. 7, *Pricing Standards,* and on particular industries, No. 6, *Studies in Industrial Price Control* and No. 3, *Wartime Apparel Price Control.* A general discussion of the principles of price control is contained in J. K. Galbraith, *A Theory of Price Control* (Cambridge: Harvard University Press, 1952). The story of price control in the Korean war is told in the relevant sections of the Quarterly Reports of the Director of Defense Mobilization, published by the Government Printing Office during 1951 and 1952. A critical appraisal of this experience is presented in Robert A. Brady, *The Citizen's Stake in Price Control* (Paterson, N.J.: Littlefield, Adams & Co., 1952).

PART VI

Substituting Public for Private Enterprise

Chapter 26 PUBLIC ENTERPRISE IN THE UNITED STATES

The methods employed by government to insure that the activities of business are so conducted as to serve the general interest have included the maintenance of competition, the regulation of private enterprise, and public ownership and operation of industry. Where competition has proved to be unworkable and where regulation has failed, private enterprise has given way to public enterprise. The problems presented by the maintenance of competition and by the regulation of business have been examined in the preceding chapters; those presented by government ownership and operation will be considered in Part VI.

Public enterprise is difficult to define. Some of the activities of government are regarded as examples of such enterprise and others are not. But the line between the two is not an easy one to draw. According to one definition, public enterprise is said to involve provision by government of goods or services that might also be provided privately. But this distinction excludes the postal service, which has always enjoyed a monopoly but is generally thought to be a public enterprise. And it includes the school system, which competes with private education but is not usually designated as a public enterprise. According to the definition that is commonly given, a governmental activity may or may not be called a public enterprise, depending upon how it is financed. Some goods and services produced by government are distributed to users in return for individual payments in the same way as sales are made by private firms. Others are distributed without charge and their costs recovered through taxation. In the first case, government is said to be engaging in enterprise; in the second, it is not. But when the line is drawn here, activities that are otherwise identical may fall on opposite sides. Thus, a road financed by charging tolls will be defined as a public enterprise and one financed by collecting taxes will not. And this is true even though the taxes imposed, such as motor vehicle license fees and taxes on motor fuels, are designed to make collections from users in proportion to the character and quantity of their use. There are servicces, moreover, where the prices charged are not set high enough to cover total costs, their deficits being met through taxation. This has been the case, for instance, with the Post Office and with certain urban transit systems. But self-support cannot be made the test of public enterprise. For, if it were, the same activity would be included in one year and excluded in another, depending upon whether it had operated in the black or in the red. Nor can collection of some part of the cost of a service from its users be made the test. For in this case, a small matriculation or diploma fee would suffice to classify a city college or a state university as a public enterprise, even though its costs were defrayed almost entirely from general revenues.

In the nature of the case, any definition of public enterprise must be arbitrary. No such definition will be attempted here. But in the discussion that follows, little or no consideration will be given to the traditional activities of government such as the provision of roads and streets, police and fire protection, and public education, attention being directed, in the main, to those activities that are business-like in character, involving services that might be provided commercially. It is with the use of public enterprise as an alternative to competition or to regulation that we are here concerned.

The character of public enterprise differs from industry to industry. It differs, first, as to scope. In some cases, as with the postal service, government has monopolized an entire field. In others, as with the generation and distribution of electricity, it has monopolized particular markets but left most markets in private hands. In still others, notably in the fields of banking and insurance, it has entered into competition with private firms. Public enterprise also differs as to form. In some fields, such as the postal service and electric light and power, government has both owned and operated productive facilities. In others, such as atomic energy and synthetic rubber, it has provided facilities that have been operated under contract by private concerns. And in one case, that of the railroads during World War I, it assumed responsibility for the operation of facilities that were privately owned. Examples of each of these types will be given in the pages which follow.

THE GROWTH OF PUBLIC ENTERPRISE

The activities of government have steadily grown in variety and in extent. Services that were once provided by private enterprise have come increasingly to be supplied by public agencies free of charge. Cities, today, provide not only for streets and police and fire protection, but also for harbor facilities, sewage disposal, and the removal of garbage and trash; not only for elementary instruction, but also for school lunches, playgrounds, medical examinations, public clinics, and hospital beds; for colleges, libraries, museums, zoos, parks, bathing beaches, swimming pools, golf courses, and free concerts by bands and orchestras. State governments, too, provide not only for highways and prisons, but also for parks, forests, hospitals, universities, and various programs of social security. The federal government, apart from such activities as the maintenance of national parks, libraries, and museums, does not itself provide free services. But it contributes, through grants in aid, to the provision of such services by the cities and the states.

Services rendered commercially as well as those provided without charge have passed from private into public hands. The operation of city water systems and the provision of water for irrigation are now predominantly governmental responsibilities. And government has entered increasingly into the provision of such services as credit, insurance, housing, and electricity. These developments reflect a striking change, over time, in public attitudes. The trend has clearly been toward giving wider scope to production by agencies of government. But such production plays a minor role in the American economy.

Extent of Public Enterprise

In 1950 national income in the United States—the total earnings of labor and property arising from the current production of goods and services—was $239 billion. Of this, only $23.5 billion, or less than a tenth, was paid out by federal, state, and local governments. And of this, $21 billion originated in the general activities of these governments, and only $2.5 billion, or about a ninth, in activities defined by the Department of Commerce as public enterprises. Of this, again, $617 million, or about a fourth, was paid out by state and local enterprises and $1,891 million, or about three fourths, by federal enterprises. In short, public enterprises accounted for little more than 1 per cent of the nation's income; federal enterprises for about .75 per cent.[1] "Creeping socialism," denounced with such vigor by businessmen and politicians, still had a long way to creep.

Causes of Public Enterprise

The establishment of public enterprises, in the United States, is not to be attributed to socialist ideology. For, in this country, the doctrines of socialism have never been embraced by more than a tiny minority. Nor have such enterprises been created to afford a source of public revenue. In other countries, governments have been financed, in part, by profits derived from state monopolies of products such as tobacco, matches, and salt. But here, state and municipal liquor stores are almost the only example of public enterprises operated for a profit. And even they are justified as means of controlling the use of alcohol.

The real causes of public enterprise in America are many and varied. (1) Productive activities of the greatest magnitude have been undertaken because they were deemed essential to the prosecution of warfare and to national defense. This was the origin of the first dam thrown across the

[1] Department of Commerce, *National Income, 1951 Edition,* pp. 157, 159.

Tennessee River, at Muscle Shoals, Alabama, during World War I. It was the origin of the atomic energy and synthetic rubber plants built during World War II. It explains the great shipbuilding programs undertaken during both world wars. (2) Other activities were inaugurated for the purpose of pulling the country out of the Great Depression. This was the beginning of the Reconstruction Finance Corporation and other lending agencies, of public housing, and of large-scale river valley developments. (3) Some public enterprises have been created because private business saw little prospect of profit in a field. This was the case with the Alaska Railroad, with crop insurance, and with the provision of electricity in small towns and rural areas. (4) In other instances, the cost of an undertaking has been so high and its risks so great that it could not be privately financed. This was true of the Panama Canal and the river valley developments. It would have been true of atomic energy in time of peace. (5) The acquisition of many enterprises has been incidental to undertakings established for other purposes. Dams built to provide water for irrigation have also provided waterpower for the generation of electricity. Operation of the Panama Canal has also involved operation of the Panama Railroad. The maintenance of prisons has necessitated the creation of prison industries. Military, naval, and atomic energy installations have involved the government in providing whole cities, complete with community services, for the housing of its employees. (6) At times, governments have been forced to take over an industry by the breakdown of operations under private management. This has been the case with streetcar and subway systems in certain cities. It was the case with the railroads during World War I.

Under all these circumstances, the inauguration of public enterprises has been less a matter of choice than of necessity. But there are cases where deliberate choices have been made. (7) Some enterprises are designed to conserve the nation's resources: state and national forests, irrigation works, and public administration of grazing lands. (8) Others are related to programs of social welfare: public education, housing, health, and social insurance. (9) In some cases, public ownership and operation have been stimulated by the revelation of abuses under private enterprise and by the failure of regulation to keep rates and earnings from going too high. This was true of electricity in the thirties. Here, the use of public plants as yardsticks by which to measure private operations was one of the arguments advanced for their establishment. (10) There are a few cases where it appears that public enterprise is to be attributed solely to the view that the nature of a service is such as to require its socialization. This doubtless explains monopolization of the postal service by the federal government and of water distribution by many municipalities. But the logic of this policy has not been carried very far. The arguments advanced for public enterprise, in these cases, would seem to apply with equal force to the telephone service and the distribution of milk. It can merely be recorded as a historic fact that socialism has been adopted for communication by mail and not by telephone, for supplying water and not for delivering milk.

Obstacles to Public Enterprise

Expansion of public enterprise has not been hampered by the courts. Where governments obtain property by exercising the right of eminent domain, state and federal constitutions require that the taking be for public use and that just compensation be paid. And where new facilities are built or existing facilities purchased in a voluntary sale, the expenditures must be made for a public purpose or to promote the general welfare. But the courts have seldom obstructed public enterprise by requiring excessive compensation. And they have accepted the judgment of legislative bodies as to public purposes. The Supreme Court of the United States upheld the establishment of a municipal fuel yard by the city of Portland, Maine, in 1917,[2] socialization of banking, grain storing, milling, and other enterprises by the State of North Dakota in 1920,[3] and initiation of a wholesale and retail gasoline business by the city of Lincoln, Nebraska, in 1927.[4] In the words of Chief Justice Taft, a state may engage in "almost any private business if the legislature thinks the state's engagement in it will help the general public and is willing to pay the cost of the plant and incur the expense of operation."[5]

The right of the federal government to engage in the business of generating, transmitting, and distributing hydroelectric power has also been recognized. In the Ashwander case in 1936,[6] when a stockholder in a power company sued to prevent it from selling transmission lines to the Tennessee Valley Authority, the Supreme Court held that water falling over TVA dams was government property, that the government had the right to sell its property, and that it was therefore entitled to acquire facilities that would be useful in making a sale. In the Eighteen Power Companies Case in 1939,[7] when the private companies in the Tennessee Valley sought to restrain the TVA from competing with them in the sale of electricity, the Court refused their request on the ground that their charters and franchises had not granted them monopolistic rights. And in another case in 1941,[8] when the state of Oklahoma sought to prevent the federal government from building a dam on the Red River, the Court rejected its plea, holding that inclusion of power development in the

[2] *Jones* v. *City of Portland*, 245 U.S. 217.

[3] *Green* v. *Frazier*, 253 U.S. 233.

[4] *Standard Oil Co.* v. *City of Lincoln*, 275 U.S. 504.

[5] *Wolff Packing Co.* v. *Court of Industrial Relations of the State of Kansas*, 262 U.S. 522 (1923).

[6] *Ashwander* v. *TVA*, 297 U.S. 288.

[7] *Tennessee Electric Power Co.* v. *TVA*, 306 U.S. 118.

[8] *Oklahoma* v. *Atkinson Co.*, 313 U.S. 508.

project did not derogate from the authority of Congress to build the dam for navigation and flood control. In none of these decisions did the Court explicitly endorse the entry of the federal government into the power business. But it consistently refused to interfere.

Public enterprise has been limited more often by the legislatures than by the courts. In the past, cities were frequently prevented from obtaining the funds required to purchase or construct a utility plant by legal restrictions on their borrowing power. They were forbidden to borrow for other than specified purposes. Their debts were limited to a fixed percentage of the value of their taxable property, or the amount they could borrow in a year was limited to the size of their revenue during the year, or both limitations were applied. In many cases, bonds could not be sold unless the issue was approved by a two-thirds vote. Publicly-owned utilities were also handicapped by being forbidden to sell beyond the city lines. During the thirties, however, many of these restrictions were removed. Cities were authorized to issue bonds outside their debt limits for the purpose of acquiring utility properties, the issues to be serviced from utility revenues. They were permitted to sell utility services beyond their boundaries. Provision was made, too, for the creation of special authorities with broad jurisdiction and added borrowing power. Today, as a result, there are fewer legal barriers to local government enterprise.

The most serious obstacle to a further extension of public ownership and operation lies in the state of public opinion. The American people, in years of prosperity, look upon public enterprise with suspicion and upon private enterprise with admiration or, at least, with tolerance. This may be due, in part, to the persistence and the skill with which propaganda unfavorable to public enterprise has been disseminated by private interests. It is also due, in large measure, to the demonstrated ability of private enterprise to render satisfactory service at an acceptable price.

THE POST OFFICE

The post office is traditionally a public enterprise. The postal service, wrote Adam Smith in 1776, "is perhaps the only mercantile project which has been successfully managed by, I believe, every sort of government. The capital to be advanced is not very considerable. There is no mystery in the business. The returns are not only certain, but immediate."[9] Congress was given the power by Article I, Section 8 of the Constitution "To establish Post Offices and post Roads," and a postal system, including 74 post offices, was established by the first Congress in 1789. The system was originally set up as a separate agency, under the President. In 1829, however, the Postmaster-General was admitted to the cabinet. And in 1872 the Post Office was made a department of the government. Today it is one of the biggest businesses on earth, with more than 40,000 offices,

[9] *The Wealth of Nations,* Book V, chap. ii, Part I.

more than 500,000 employees, and revenues running close to $2,000,000,-000 a year. It has afforded the United States its most extensive experience with the public ownership and operation of a business.

Organization and Administration

The Post Office Department is organized much as a private business would be organized, with responsibility nominally centered in the Postmaster-General and a hierarchy of subordinates responsible to him. But the Department is not run as a private business would be run. It cannot select its own personnel. The upper positions, some 20,000 in number, including first-, second-, and third-class postmasterships, are filled through political patronage, adherents of one party being fired and those of another hired whenever administrations change. The remaining jobs are controlled by the Civil Service Commission; those who fill them can neither be appointed nor dismissed without the approval of that agency. The Department does not set the rates it charges. All rates but those for parcel post are fixed by Congress. Parcel post rates are fixed by the Interstate Commerce Commission. The Department does not determine the amounts it spends. Salaries are fixed by Congress. Appropriations for post office buildings are included in the public works pork barrel. The Post Office makes contracts with private carriers for transportation of the mail. The amounts its pays the railroads are fixed by the Interstate Commerce Commission. The sums it pays the airlines are fixed by the Civil Aeronautics Board. And these have been designed to subsidize the aviation industry. Postal revenues cannot be used to defray the costs of the service; they must be paid into the Treasury. To finance its activities, the Department must present its budget requests to the Bureau of the Budget and to appropriations committees of the House and Senate and have funds voted it by Congress in annual appropriation bills. Funds for the Post Office are broken down, by purposes, into some sixty different appropriations, and each expenditure must be charged against the appropriation under which it has been authorized. The Department's books are checked by the General Accounting Office to make sure that no unauthorized expenditures are made.

The individual postmaster cannot operate his office as if it were a business. He is bound hand and foot by the rules contained in *Postal Laws & Regulations*, a book that weighs nearly three pounds and runs close to a thousand pages. Until recently the Department's administration was highly centralized. Every one of the more than 40,000 postmasters got his instructions directly from Washington and made his reports directly to Washington. However urgent the repairs required in an emergency, the postmaster could not pay for them by transferring money from one account to another without first obtaining permission from Washington. Whatever his need for equipment, he could not buy it without authority from Washington:

The post office at Seattle one time badly needed a tow truck for its own breakdowns. Washington, however, wouldn't approve the purchase. Then the Seattle postmaster learned he could buy an Army-surplus tow truck, new, for $1.00. So he went ahead and bought it? Oh, no. He had to write Washington for approval. But Washington answered: "No." Thought the postmaster then: "I'll buy it myself; give it to the Department." But he couldn't—not without first writing to Washington. And the answer on that too was "No." The number of breakdowns in Seattle didn't require a tow truck, Washington believed; and it was contrary to procedure to allow any local postmaster on the scene to act on his own judgement and initiative.[10]

This situation stood in marked contrast to the pattern of organization that characterized large-scale private industry. If it were operated as a private enterprise, administration of the postal service would long since have been delegated to regional headquarters, and the individual postmaster would have been accorded a larger measure of responsibility. A program of decentralization was finally inaugurated under the Eisenhower administration, the first of fifteen projected regional offices being opened in November, 1953.

When the Post Office was investigated by former President Hoover's Commission on Organization of the Executive Branch of the Government in 1949, it was employing none of the techniques of modern management. It had no management engineering. It was doing no research on the service needs and desires of its patrons, and little or no research on methods of handling and transporting mail. It was giving little formal training to its personnel. Its accounting system was antiquated, its cost controls rudimentary. It had no standards by which to measure performance on the job. Again in 1954, the Advisory Council of the Senate Post Office Committee reported that employee training was inadequate, and supervisor training lacking, that working conditions were "deplorable," and that employee morale was low.[11] To its question, "What is wrong with the Post Office?" the Hoover commission answered, "(*a*) The administrative structure is obsolete and overcentralized. (*b*) A maze of outmoded laws, regulations and traditions freezes progress and stifles proper administration. (*c*) . . . it lacks the freedom and flexibility essential to good business operation."[12]

Efficiency and Progress

The Post Office, over the years, has steadily expanded the scope of its services. Starting with the general delivery window, it went on to urban free delivery in 1863 and to rural free delivery in 1896. Starting with let-

[10] C. Lester Walker, "So They're Re-doing the Post Office," *Harper's Magazine*, June, 1951, pp. 37–45, esp. p. 39.

[11] *New York Times*, January 19, 1954.

[12] Commission on Organization of the Executive Branch of the Government, *The Post Office* (Washington: Government Printing Office, 1949), p. 3.

ters and papers, it took on parcel post in 1913. And, from time to time, it has added such services as registry, special delivery, money orders, postal savings, parcel insurance, c.o.d. collection, and air mail. Measured against the service provided a century or more ago, the Post Office has progressed. But measured against the possibilities, its progress has been slow. In recent years it has even lost some ground. Four or five deliveries a day are common in Europe; six are the rule in Japan. But here, in 1950, deliveries in residental areas were cut from two to one.

The Department has not gone far toward adopting improved methods of handling bulk materials. Much of its equipment is antiquated. The average age of its trucks in 1949 was more than fifteen years. The office in Philadelphia was still using horse-drawn vehicles. Instead of being racked in modern containers and hoisted and hauled with jacks and trucks of modern design, mail was still transported in bags. Instead of being sorted by machine, it was sorted by hand. A sorting machine had been invented by a postal worker in Chicago. But the inventor had not been rewarded. And the machine had not been introduced in other offices because Congress had not appropriated money to cover its cost. Though the burden of door-to-door delivery could have been lessened and delivery speeded by the development of special types of light motorized vehicles, the postman still carried the mail in a sack on his back.

Research into methods of handling has been undertaken in recent years. But there is no assurance that Congress will appropriate the funds that will be needed if the improvements developed are ever to be introduced. The experts who studied the Department for the Hoover Commission remarked that postal officials had sometimes taken initiative within the limits of the conditions under which they had to work. But, they said, "circumstances beyond their control have created a philosophy of management which is sluggish, irresolute, and wasteful rather than imaginative and cost conscious. . . . While it can be shown that over the years postal methods have been improved and costs reduced, it has been an uninspired low-geared effort which progressive business men would regard as mediocre."[13]

Postal Rates and Deficits

For a quarter of a century after the Post Office was established, it was operated as a business and returned an annual profit. But since that time, Congress has emphasized expansion of the service and made little effort to insure that rates shall cover costs. In all but 13 of the 100 years from 1853 to 1953, the Department operated at a deficit. At the end of this period, the deficit was running beyond $700 million a year. And this figure understated the loss, since the Department's accounts included no charge to cover the depreciation of post office buildings. The deficits could always

[13] *Ibid., Task Force Report on the Post Office*, p. 33.

have been wiped out, of course, if somebody had raised postal rates. But the Postmaster-General could not and Congress would not.

The structure of postal rates bears little relation to the costs involved in carrying different classes of mail and in rendering different types of service. Flat rates to all domestic destinations are fixed for letters, post cards, air mail, newspapers and magazines, books, and other materials weighing eight ounces or less. Rates graduated by zones are fixed for parcel post. And separate charges are made for various types of special handling and other services. Some mail is carried free: that sent by members of Congress and by agencies of the federal government, books and records for the blind, and newspapers distributed at post offices in the counties where they are published.

In 1950 every class of mail handled by the Department, except letters, was carried at a loss. And every other service provided, except postal savings, was operated at a loss. Post cards that cost 2.8 cents to handle were carried for 1 cent (and subsequently for 2 cents). Newspapers and magazines, still carried at a rate set in 1879, were responsible for a loss of $200 million. Third-class matter, consisting largely of advertising materials, involved a loss of $123 million.[14] The character of the rate structure discriminated against the letter writer in favor of other users of postal services. And the inadequacy of the rate level forced the taxpayer to subsidize these users, notably the publishers of newspapers and magazines and the distributors of other advertising media.

It would scarcely be desirable to require every service rendered by the Post Office to pay its own way. Routes in remote and sparsely settled regions must be maintained at a loss as a matter of public policy. But it is certainly reasonable to expect the postal service as a whole to support itself. And this would be possible if Congress were to delegate its power to fix rates, or if Congress itself were to raise rates. But rate increases are politically unpopular. In 1953, the Postmaster-General, seeking to reduce a prospective deficit, asked Congress to raise the letter rate from 3 cents to 4 cents and the air mail rate from 6 cents to 7 cents and to increase the rate on newspapers and magazines. But Congress did not act.

FEDERAL BUSINESS ACTIVITIES

In 1949 the Hoover Commission reported that the federal government owned or was financially interested in about 100 important business enterprises. Apart from the Post Office, such enterprises fall into five major categories: (1) carrying on the administration of public lands, (2) lending and guaranteeing loans and providing insurance against a number of different risks, (3) supplying transportation facilities and operating transportation services, (4) supplying manufacturing facilities and engaging in manufacturing, and (5) generating, transmitting, and distributing elec-

[14] Message from President Truman, *New York Times*, February 28, 1951.

tricity. Enterprises in the first four of these categories will be described briefly in the present section. The federal power projects will be examined at greater length in the next.

Administration of Public Lands

The federal government owns more than 400 million acres of land within the forty-eight states, acts as a trustee for 56 million acres owned by the Indian tribes, and holds title to another 365 million acres in Alaska. Aside from the Communist countries, it is the biggest landlord on earth. As a landlord, however, it is unique, taking more interest in the use to which its land is put than in the revenue it yields. Its concern, as we saw in Chapter 12, is with the conservation of resources. In general, the government does not itself engage in the operation of extractive industries. But it does sell rights and services to private interests. And this is a business-like activity.

The national forests, including some 90 million acres of commercial forest lands, are managed by the Forest Service in the Department of Agriculture. The Service sells standing timber to private loggers, supervises logging operations, issues grazing permits, collects fees, and controls methods of grazing. The other public lands are administered by bureaus in the Department of the Interior. The Fish and Wildlife Service is responsible for the management of more than 18 million acres contained in some 200 refuges for waterfowl and 40 refuges for other types of wildlife, and for the propagation of fish in some 100 hatcheries. The National Park Service manages more than 20 million acres, including 28 national parks and around 150 monuments and other sites of natural or historical interest. The Service grants concessions to private enterprises for the operation of tourist facilities. The Office of Indian Affairs acts as a trustee for the 56 million acres of Indian lands. The Bureau of Reclamation controls land held for irrigation, running from 10 million to 15 million acres in different years. It builds and operates dams and ditches, sells land, supplies water, and collects water rents. The Bureau of Land Management administers the rest of the public domain, including more than 140 million acres of range lands. Here, it issues grazing permits and collects grazing fees. The Secretary of the Interior also grants leases to mining companies for the exploitation of oil and gas and other minerals on public lands and collects mining royalties.

This activity is not carried on for profit. But it does afford a test of the capacity of government for large-scale management. And here, the quality of its performance appears to have been high.

Federal Lending Agencies

In 1949 the Hoover Commission found some forty federal agencies, with 300 offices and 35,000 employees, engaged in the business of making loans or providing insurance against various types of risks. Some of these agencies were legacies of the depression and the war. Others had been set up to carry out ambitious programs of social reform. Still others were designed to serve as integral parts of the banking and insurance machinery.

Much of the government's activity in this field has been directed toward broadening the availability of credit to different groups and for different purposes, and increasing the stability of credit, by promoting the formation of mutual institutions controlling central credit reservoirs where risks are pooled. The Federal Reserve System, set up in 1913, conforms to this pattern. Strictly speaking, the system does not afford an example of public enterprise, since each of the Federal Reserve Banks is owned by its member banks and six of its nine directors are elected by the member banks. But the Board of Governors of the system, appointed by the President, selects the other three directors and exercises general control. The pattern was also followed in setting up the system of Federal Land Banks in 1916, to provide long-term mortgage credit to farm loan co-operatives. These banks were initially financed by the government but are now wholly owned by the co-operatives. So, too, with the Federal Home Loan Bank System, created in 1932 to provide a reserve of credit for building and loan associations and other home-financing agencies. The stock of the banks is now owned by member associations; the government contributes no financial support, the Home Loan Bank Board serving only as a supervisory agency. With two other systems of specialized central credit institutions, however, ownership is still in federal hands. These are the Federal Intermediate Credit Bank and its twelve district banks, set up in 1923 to provide credit, for periods running from six months to six years, for clearing and fencing land, planting orchards, buying livestock and farm machinery, etc., and the twelve Production Credit Corporations, created in 1933 to finance local production credit associations making loans, for shorter periods, for the purchase of feed, fertilizer, and the like. Each of these organizations serves financial institutions; none of them lends directly to individual borrowers.

Direct loans are made, however, by a number of federal agencies. Three of them lend to farmers. The Central Bank for Cooperatives and twelve district banks, set up in 1933, make loans to finance the activities of agricultural marketing associations. The Rural Electrification Administration, created in 1935, makes loans to finance the construction and operation of transmission and distribution lines by rural electrification cooperatives. Its program has been successful, delinquencies being few and repayments running well ahead of the scheduled dates. The Farmers' Home Administration, successor in 1946 to a series of units first set up in 1933, makes mortgage loans, production loans, and subsistence loans to small farmers to help them buy their farms, improve their farming operations, and achieve self-support. The Administration is both a lender and an educational agency.

Direct loans are also made to businessmen. For twenty years the Reconstruction Finance Corporation was the largest lender in the United States. Established in 1932 during the Hoover administration, with an initial capital of $500 million, it undertook to avert the spread of bankruptcy by making loans to railroads, banks, and insurance companies. In the Roosevelt administration, the Corporation was employed, during the depression, to finance programs of relief and recovery, and during the war, to finance the production and procurement of essential goods, setting up a number of subsidiaries to carry on its manifold activities. In 1947 the Corporation's power to finance other governmental agencies was terminated. In 1948 it was authorized to make loans to promote small businesses that could not obtain credit through normal channels. According to the investigators who reported to the Hoover Commission in 1949, the Corporation's record during the depression was highly satisfactory and the functions assigned it during the war were well performed.[15] During the Truman administration, however, the RFC came into bad odor as a result of an investigation conducted by Senator J. William Fulbright, Democrat, of Arkansas. It appeared that the quality of the Corporation's management had declined and that dubious loans had been made on the basis of political influence. As a consequence, a bill was passed by Congress and signed by President Eisenhower in 1953 putting the agency into liquidation and ending its life on June 30, 1954. In twenty years, the RFC had made 640,000 loans and had lent or spent $48,750 million. It had suffered defaults on only 1 per cent of its loans, and had paid more than a billion dollars into the Treasury. The assets remaining in its portfolio were valued at $700 million. Over all, its operations had not been conducted at a loss.

The law that killed the RFC created a Small Business Administration, with a revolving fund of $300 million, and authorized it to lend up to $150 million to small firms, to use $100 million to assist such firms in obtaining government contracts, and to lend $25 million to state and local governments for public works and another $25 million for relief from disasters. The funds available for lending were reduced, but the principle of government lending was retained.

Two other agencies make business loans. The Federal Maritime Board makes loans to shipping companies to enable them to purchase ships. The Board is charged with the duty of promoting the American merchant marine; this is but one of its activities. The Export-Import Bank was established in 1934 to finance the expansion of foreign trade. To this end, it has made loans to American traders and to their foreign customers. During and after World War II, the Bank came to be used predominantly as a medium for the extension of intergovernmental loans. Together with

[15] Commission on Organization of the Executive Branch of the Government, *Task Force Report on Lending Agencies* (Washington: Government Printing Office, 1949), pp. 21–22.

other agencies for foreign aid, it promoted economic reconstruction and development, thus losing its business character and becoming, in the main, an instrument of foreign policy.

In some cases, financial agencies have been established by the government to serve as instruments in carrying out programs that have not been expected to pay their own way. Such agencies have administered various types of subsidies. Subsidiaries set up by the RFC distributed money for relief during the depression and provided facilities for production and procured marginal supplies of essential materials at high costs during the war, the losses incurred in the process being canceled by acts of Congress. The Commodity Credit Corporation, as we saw in Chapter 15, is required to make loans to support the prices of agricultural commodities at levels fixed by law, even though substantial losses may result. And the Public Housing Administration is authorized to make both loans and grants to finance the construction and operation of low-rent housing by city governments. Under the Housing Act of 1937, as amended in 1949, the Administration may lend to local authorities as much as 90 per cent of the cost of clearing slums and building housing, and may make grants to cover the difference between the cost of such housing and the rents its tenants can afford to pay. The federal government thus confines itself to subsidization. The housing is built, owned, and operated by municipalities.

Federal Insuring Agencies

Insurance programs were inaugurated during the thirties to serve a number of different purposes. Some of them were designed to restore and maintain confidence in the stability of private financial institutions. The Federal Deposit Insurance Corporation was set up in 1933, with more than half of its stock owned by the government, the rest by the Federal Reserve Banks, its directors being appointed by the President. The Corporation insures deposits up to $10,000 in all banks belonging to the Federal Reserve System and in other banks that choose to be insured. The Federal Savings and Loan Insurance Corporation was established in 1934. All of its stock is held by the Treasury. This Corporation insures accounts in savings and loan associations. Associations chartered by the federal government must carry insurance and those chartered by the states may do so. The Federal Housing Administration, also created in 1934, insures home mortgages that are held by financial institutions. The Federal National Mortgage Association, set up in 1938, buys insured mortgages from such lenders and sells them to institutional and other investors. The functions fulfilled by the last three agencies are calculated to increase the availability of credit for private housing.

The Federal Crop Insurance Corporation was established in 1938 to insure crop yields against all natural risks. It started writing insurance on wheat in 1939 and on cotton in 1941. Until 1947 the Corporation suffered an adverse selection of risks, or its premiums were too low or its indemnities too high—in any case it lost money. By 1943 the losses were so large that Congress voted its liquidation, and no insurance was written on the crops that were harvested in 1944. In that year, however, the program was extended on an experimental basis, being limited to a certain number of counties and confined to those where a certain number of farmers should apply. In 1950 only 6 per cent of the farmers were insured.

In its program for veterans and in its social security system, the federal government administers the largest insurance undertakings to be found on earth. In 1951 the life insurance policies handled by the Veterans' Administration covered 459,000 veterans of World War I and 7,100,000 veterans of World War II. And the old age and survivorship insurance handled by the Social Security Administration covered 89,000,000 persons who had wage credits, 62,000,000 of whom were fully insured. In paying benefits, the operations of these agencies resemble those of private companies. But they are differently financed. With veterans' insurance, as with private insurance, the benefits are covered by the premiums. But the administrative costs are borne by the taxpayer. Under the social security system, individual benefits are related to the wages on which wage and payroll taxes have been paid. But benefits are acquired more cheaply by those retiring in the system's early years than will be the case with those retiring later on. So far, the benefits paid have been exceeded by the taxes collected. As time goes on, however, more people will become eligible for larger benefits and payments will have to be financed, in part, from other sources of revenue. Social insurance, resting on the taxing power, thus differs in character from the insurance sold by private companies.

Federal Transportation Enterprises

The federal government owns and operates two railroads, one in the Panama Canal Zone and one in Alaska. The Panama Railroad Company was acquired in 1904, the purchase being incidental to the construction of the canal. In addition to running a railroad across the isthmus, the company operated a ship line between New York and the Canal Zone and soon came to operate most of the business enterprises in the zone, including fueling plants, terminal services, public utility systems, hotels, restaurants, commissaries, and recreational facilities. Congress invested $7 million in the stock of the company in 1910 and appropriated another $5 million to finance its activities. No appropriations have been made since that time. Up to June 30, 1947, the company had met its costs from its own revenues and had paid $25 million in dividends to the Treasury. In 1948 the railroad company lost its identity, being absorbed by the Panama Canal Company which now operates the canal itself and all other public enterprises in the zone. The Secretary of the Army holds the stock of this company and appoints its directors. The Governor of the Canal Zone serves also as its president. The business undertakings in the zone appear to have been operated with efficiency. The local administration has been accorded a large measure of freedom. The fact that it has possessed a monopoly in a substantial market has also contributed to its success.

Provision for the construction of a railroad to promote the development of the territory of Alaska was made in 1914. The road was built and has been operated by the Department of the Interior. Until the forties, the roadbed, structures, and equipment were primitive in character and operations were conducted at a loss. Between 1945 and 1953 the road was rebuilt and re-equipped at a cost of $75 million. Its ability to cover its costs in the future will depend, of course, upon the extent to which traffic is generated by economic growth.

In addition to making loans and grants to private shipping companies, the federal government has also engaged in the construction and operation of merchant ships. Under the Shipping Act of 1916, enacted during World War I, the United States Shipping Board was authorized to buy, lease, charter, or build vessels and to operate them commercially. The Merchant Marine Act of 1920, passed at the end of the war, provided for the disposal of such vessels. But sales were slow and, for many years, a substantial fraction of the merchant fleet remained in the possession of the Shipping Board. The Merchant Marine Act of 1928 provided for further construction and permitted continued ownership and operation by the government. The Merchant Marine Act of 1936 established a Maritime Commission to supersede the Shipping Board and sought to promote private enterprise in shipping by making loans and granting subsidies. The Commission was also authorized, however, to build ships and charter them to private lines for operation on essential trade routes if these lines were unable or unwilling to provide the ships themselves. The building program then adopted called for the construction of fifty ships a year over a period of ten years. This program was rapidly expanded during World War II. Between 1939 and 1946 the Commission built more than 5,600 ships. At the end of this period the United States accounted for three fifths of the merchant tonnage in the world, most of it being owned by the government. Under the Ship Sales Act of 1946, Congress permitted the sale of war-built ships at a fraction of their cost and, on this basis, hundreds of them were sold to private companies. On June 30, 1951, however, the Maritime Administration (successor in 1950 to the Maritime Commission) still had 2,222 ships. Of these, 1,759 were being held in a national defense reserve, but 463 were in operation, most of them being chartered to private companies or operated by such companies acting as agents for the government. Over the years, the shipping program has been carried forward at a heavy loss. But since this program was designed to contribute to national defense and to subsidize the shipping industry, its success or failure is not to be measured on a commercial scale.

From 1918 to 1953 the government operated a barge line on the Mississippi, Missouri, Illinois, and Warrior Rivers, together with railway switching facilities at Birmingham, Alabama. This undertaking was started during World War I to supplement the overloaded railroads. It was continued after the war as a means of interesting private capital in the development of inland water transport. The line was operated, after 1924, by the Inland Waterways Corporation, located first in the War Department and then in the Department of Commerce. Whether through this example or not, water haulage was in fact promoted, more than a hundred private barge lines being in operation in 1953. But the Corporation itself was not financially successful, making money in twelve years and incurring losses in seventeen, its total loss running to $7 million on an original investment of $20 million. This record is to be explained, in part at least, by the fact that its equipment was antiquated and that Congress required it to continue certain services that were clearly unprofitable. For many years, it was the policy of Congress to sell the line, but there were no takers. Finally, in 1953, a sale was effected, the properties, including some new equipment, going for $9 million to the Federal Waterways Corporation, a private concern.

Federal Manufacturing Enterprises

The government is also involved in manufacturing activities. The navy builds ships and produces paint, rope, ships' stores, and the like. The army and the navy manufacture weapons, ammunition, uniforms, and other military goods. The Post Office makes its own mail bags. Federal prisons operate industries to provide their inmates with employment and to train them for later life. In all of these cases, government produces for its own use. Elsewhere, however, goods made in publicly-owned factories are offered for general sale.

Until 1861 the government had its printing done by private printers. In that year it bought a small print shop a few blocks from the capitol. Today the Government Printing Office, on the same site, is the biggest printing plant on earth, with 33 acres of floor space and 7,000 employees. The Office does $80 million or more of business each year, producing $60 million worth itself and farming the remainder out to private plants. On July 1, Congress provides it with $10 million or more as working capital. The Office then charges the departments and agencies of the government, at cost, for the work it does, meets all of its expenses, and returns its working capital to the Treasury on the thirtieth of June. The Office clears its books each year, always operating in the black. The Superintendent of Documents handles sales, buying documents at cost from the Printing Office and selling them at a markup of 50 per cent. He distributes some 40 million publications a year, returning a substantial profit to the Treasury.

Through the Virgin Islands Company, incorporated in 1934 to provide employment and promote recovery in the islands, the government has gone into the business of producing sugar, molasses, and rum. The refineries and distilleries, purchased from their former owners for $3 million, are owned by the government and operated by the company. The company has lost money on sugar, made money on rum. From 1934 to 1947 its net deficit totaled $60,000. In the same period, however, the government collected $56 million in taxes on rum produced in the Virgin Islands and sold in the United States. If this revenue had been returned to the islands, the enterprise would have contributed substantially to their development.

Two other industries were established by the government during World War II to produce essential materials: rubber and tin. The advance of the Japanese armies in southeast Asia had cut off the major sources of supply. The government therefore invested some $700 million in the construction of 29 synthetic rubber plants, raising the capacity of this industry from around 8,000 tons to more than a million tons a year. At the same time, it built a smelter in Texas City, Texas to produce pig tin from Bolivian concentrates. The rubber plants were operated, under contract, by oil and rubber companies at cost plus a fixed fee. The smelter has been operated by the government, first by the Reconstruction Finance Corporation, and later by a Federal Facilities Federation, its output being allocated in part to industry and in part to a strategic stockpile. In 1954 the Administration recommended that it be closed, but Congress kept it in operation, extending its life to June 30, 1955.

It was always assumed that the synthetic rubber plants would eventually be sold to private owners. But there were serious obstacles to such a sale. Some of the plants were obsolete. All of them were expensive. And synthetic cost so much more than crude that its sale had to be forced by requiring manufacturers of rubber products to use fixed proportions of the two. By 1953, however, synthetic was underselling crude and had captured three fifths of the market; the mixing requirement had been dropped. In that year Congress provided for the sale of the plants. A Rubber Producing Facilities Disposal Commission was appointed by the President. In November, 1953, it called for bids. By June, 1954, when bidding was closed, it had received 75 bids from 35 companies. Under the law, it had until December 27, 1954 to negotiate contracts of sale. These contracts were then to be submitted to Congress for approval. To prevent monopolization of the industry, the law required the Commission to obtain from the Attorney-General and transmit to Congress an opinion on the conformity of its disposal plan to the provisions of the antitrust laws. The sale of the plants was finally effected in 1955.

FEDERAL POWER PROJECTS

For half a century the federal government has been in the business of generating and selling hydroelectric power. It entered this business, as it were, by the back door. Under the Reclamation Act of 1902, the Bureau of Reclamation was established in the Department of the Interior with authority to construct irrigation works. Such works, of course, included dams, and water falling over the dams became a source of power. In 1906, therefore, Congress authorized the Secretary of the Interior to enter into contracts for the sale of this power, directing him, in doing so, to give preference to "municipal purposes." Until the thirties, such operations were few in number and small in scale, attracting little public attention. Beginning with the construction of Hoover Dam on the lower Colorado, however, a number of large-scale projects were initiated, involving irrigation, water supply, flood control, navigation, and incidental power production throughout whole river valleys, notably those of the Colorado, the Tennessee, and the Columbia. Here again, power was a by-product. Water supply and flood control were the major purposes of the development on the Colorado. National defense was the objective for building the first large dam on the Tennessee. Business recovery and re-employment through public works were the primary goals of further construction on the Tennessee and the Columbia. And comprehensive planning for regional rehabilitation and economic development became the all-embracing purpose of the TVA. But in all these cases, the quantity of power involved was very large. And the manner of its disposition thus became a major issue of public policy.

Before the administration of Franklin D. Roosevelt, hydroelectric operations were turned over to irrigation districts, municipalities, and private companies. The sale of power was treated as a source of revenue, being used to help defray the costs of irrigation and other purposes. With the coming of the New Deal, however, the federal government adopted a more aggressive policy. Not only did it build more dams. It bought and built steam plants to "firm up" its supply of hydroelectric power. In 1933 it accounted for 1 per cent of the output of electricity; in 1953, for 13 per cent. The government also bought and built transmission lines and stimulated the purchase and construction of distribution facilities by municipalities and rural co-operatives, making loans and grants to these bodies and giving them a preferential right to purchase federal power. More than this, it no longer sought to profit from its power operations, but adopted rates designed merely to cover costs and to promote expansion of use. And it employed these rates, upon occasion, as a yardstick by which to measure the fairness of rates charged by private companies and the effectiveness of regulation by state commissions, seeking through such comparisons to influence their policies. Power was still but one of the purposes served by multipurpose projects. But power was pushed. And it was this change in emphasis that made the federal power program a major issue of partisan politics.

The Lower Colorado

The developments in the Lower Colorado Valley include Hoover Dam in Boulder Canyon, Davis Dam sixty miles downstream, Parker Dam ninety miles below it, the All-America Canal which diverts the waters of the Colorado to the irrigation of the Imperial Valley of California, and the Imperial Irrigation District of California. The demand for these works came primarily from the people of southern California who sought water supply, irrigation, flood control, and supplementary power. Construction of a dam in Boulder Canyon was authorized by Congress in 1928. Built by the Bureau of Reclamation, it was completed in 1936, being christened Hoover Dam by the Republicans, rechristened Boulder Dam by the Democrats, and re-rechristened Hoover Dam by the Republicans. This structure is 726 feet high and backs up the waters of the Colorado for 115 miles. Its installed power capacity in 1948 stood at 1,034,800 kw. (That of the Niagara Falls Power Co., the largest private hydroelectric installation, was 419,000 kw.) Capacity at the Davis, Parker, and Imperial Valley Dams is much smaller: it stood at 135,000 kw. in 1948 and may ultimately reach 380,000 kw.

When it provided for the construction of Hoover Dam, Congress required the Secretary of the Interior, before installing power facilities, to make contracts for the sale of power that would insure recovery of their cost, with interest. It authorized the Secretary to dispose of power in any one of three ways: (1) by building and operating the power plants, (2) by selling rights to falling water, permitting the purchasers to build and operate the plants, and (3) by building the plants and contracting for their operation by lessees. Of these alternatives, the Secretary chose the third. The government built two power plants. The one on the Arizona side of the river was leased to the City of Los Angeles, the one on the Nevada side to Southern California Edison. The lessees had to build and operate their own transmission lines.

The Act of 1928 required the Secretary to charge the highest price obtainable for power, fixing it on the basis of competitive alternatives. The price initially set in the fifty-year contracts with the two lessees was thus based on the alternative cost of generating steam power at Los Angeles. This price was designed to yield a profit. Of $165 million spent on the project, $25 million was charged to flood control. Revenue from power was to amortize the other $140 million at 4 per cent in fifty years. Investment in generating equipment was to be amortized in ten years. None of the cost of the dam was to be charged to irrigation or water supply. Power consumers were to subsidize these purposes. Under these arrangements, there was no thought of using public competition as a means of reducing private utility rates or increasing the consumption of electricity.

In 1940 the original contracts were modified. Improvements in technology had reduced the alternative cost of generating steam power. Comparison with the lower rates charged for power generated on the Tennessee and the Columbia had given rise to public complaints. The new provisions extended the period for amortizing generating facilities from ten years to fifty and—more important—cut the interest rate from 4 per cent to 3. The price of power from Hoover Dam was thus reduced. But the arrangements otherwise remained the same.

The Tennessee Valley

The first federal installations on the Tennessee River, consisting of two nitrate plants, a steam power plant, and Wilson Dam at Muscle Shoals, Alabama, were constructed to assure the government a supply of nitrates for the manufacture of explosives during World War I. After the war, private companies offered to buy the properties, but their bids were rejected as inadequate. At the same time, Senator George W. Norris, Republican, of Nebraska was urging public operation of the facilities at Muscle Shoals and further development of the resources of the Tennessee. Bills embodying this program were passed by Congress but were vetoed by President Coolidge in 1928 and by President Hoover in 1931. For years, the power and nitrate plants stood idle and the power contained in water falling over Wilson Dam was allowed to go to waste. Then, with the New Deal in 1933, a bill was enacted by Congress and signed by President Roosevelt to carry out the program that Senator Norris had proposed. The first of the new dams to be planned and built under the program was named Norris Dam. The name has not been changed.

The primary purposes of the new law, as set forth by Congress, were flood control and navigation. (The law was amended in 1935 to require provision of a nine-foot channel from Knoxville to the mouth of the Tennessee.) The third purpose stated was that of providing for "the maximum generation of electric power" insofar as this was "consistent with flood control and navigation." It was declared to be public policy to use the plants at Muscle Shoals to "improve, increase, and cheapen the production of fertilizer and fertilizer ingredients." And, more broadly, it was said to be the intention of Congress to conserve and develop the resources of the valley and to promote the economic and social well-being of its people.

To carry out this program, the law created a semiautonomous agency in the form of a corporation, designed to combine the prerogatives of government with the flexibility of private enterprise: the Tennessee Valley Authority. The policies of the Authority, within the law, are determined by a Board of Directors consisting of three members appointed by the President, subject to approval by the Senate, for overlapping terms of nine years. Detailed administration is delegated to a General Manager who is appointed and held responsible by the Board. The Authority is freed from Civil Service regulations in selecting and managing its personnel. Unlike most other federal enterprises, it does not depend on annual appropriations to cover its operating costs, but meets them from its own commercial revenues. The Authority must obtain approval from Congress for new construction, from the Bureau of Budget for its administrative expenses, and from the Treasury for borrowing. Its books are audited by the General Accounting Office. But its operations are not regulated by state or federal utility commissions. And, compared with most federal enterprises, it is generally free of other external controls.

The flood and navigation control facilities of the TVA in 1952 included nine dams equipped with locks on the main stream and nine storage dams on its tributaries. In addition, the Authority exercised control, by agreement, over the storage and release of water at ten dams owned by the Aluminum Company of America. The power facilities at the eighteen multipurpose dams and at nine single-purpose dams and ten steam plants had a capacity of 3,860,000 kilowatts. Additional facilities at these sites and at two more dams and seven steam plants then under construction were expected to bring the capacity of the system to 9,560,000 kilowatts by 1956. The TVA inherited the original dam and steam plant at Muscle Shoals. It bought from private companies one dam on the Tennessee and a number of steam plants and smaller hydroelectric developments. Its first new dams—Norris and Wheeler—were designed for it by the Bureau of Reclamation. The rest of the system it has designed and built itself.

In controlling stream flow and water levels, the TVA has been highly successful. The volume of water in streams and reservoirs throughout the river basin is centrally controlled, being subject to adjustment from day to day and even from hour to hour. Floods are held back from the Tennessee, the Ohio, and the Mississippi; waters are impounded in the winter and the spring and released in the summer and the fall. During the dry season, in earlier years, the Tennessee dropped to a depth of two feet at Chattanooga and a foot and a half at Knoxville. Now an eleven-foot channel is mantained throughout the year, supporting navigation for 630 miles from Knoxville to the river's mouth. Malaria, once common in the region, has virtually been eliminated by raising and lowering water levels by inches to strand the larvae of mosquitoes. Progress has been made in sanitation through the Authority's studies of stream pollution and through the installation, under state laws, of sewage treatment plants. Fishing has been improved, reserves established for wildfowl, and land set aside in parks for recreational purposes.

Aside from its water control activities, the TVA has worked a transformation in the valley that has made it a model which is admired, studied, and copied in the development of backward areas throughout the world. Before 1933 the standard of living in the region was low; per capita income was 40 per cent of the national average. There was little industry, production being predominantly agricultural. The soil was eroded and lacking in fertility. Public facilities for health, education, and recreation were poor. By 1950 per capita income had been raised to 60 per cent of the national average. The availability of power had attracted new industries to the valley. Erosion had been checked through reforestation and the introduction of soil-conserving practices. Dairy herds had been improved by providing better pasturage. Crop yields had been increased

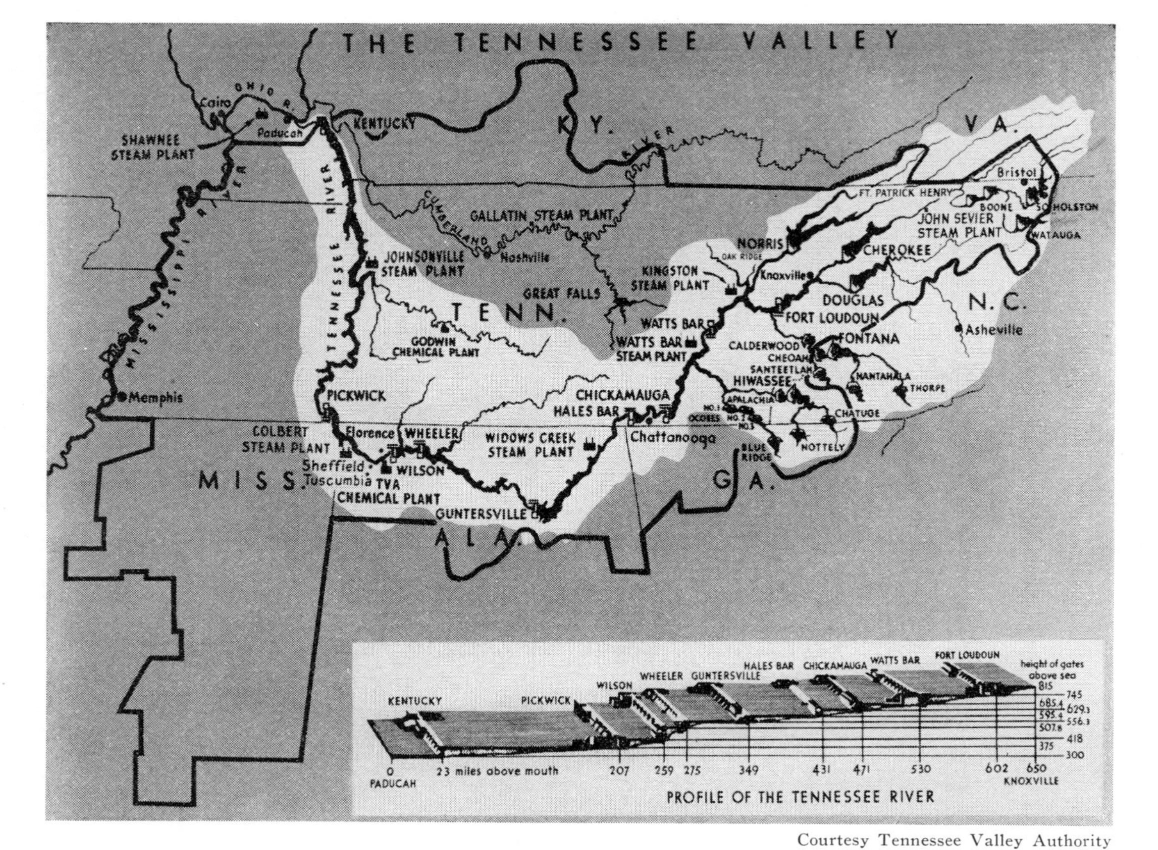

Courtesy Tennessee Valley Authority

THE TENNESSEE VALLEY

The drainage area of the Tennessee River is shown in white. The broad black line encloses the area in which TVA power is sold.

through fertilization. The TVA was engaged in an extensive program of chemical research and in the production and promotion of concentrated fertilizers, its results being made available to farmers everywhere and to other fertilizer manufacturers. In co-operation with state and local agencies, it had contributed to marked improvements in public health, education, and other activities of government. Its success in these undertakings is attested by the virtually unanimous support accorded it by the people of the valley.

The TVA Power Program

Under its enabling act, the TVA was required to give preference to public and co-operative nonprofit bodies in selling power. It was authorized to lease, buy, or build transmission lines to enable it to reach a market. It was instructed to put its power activities on a self-supporting basis. And it was permitted to control the prices at which distributors could resell its power.

In building up its transmission and distribution systems, the TVA encountered determined resistance from private power companies already operating in the region. It did not undertake to duplicate the facilities owned by these companies, seeking instead to buy them out. But its right to enter the power business was challenged (unsuccessfully) in the courts. Its attempt to create demand on the farm through rural electrification co-operatives was handicapped by the construction of spite lines designed to skim the cream from the rural market. Its offer to purchase existing properties at their original cost as determined by an independent audit was rejected as inadequate, their owners demanding prices that would cover the capital value of their earning power. It was this struggle that brought Wendell Willkie, then president of Commonwealth & Southern, to the national prominence that won him the Republican nomination for the presidency of the United States in 1940. The TVA was finally victorious, winning its lawsuits, building up its rural market, and purchasing private facilities at prices between those it had offered and those their owners had asked. In 1950 it was selling power directly to large industrial users and indirectly to 1,250,000 other customers through 50 rural co-operatives and 95 distribution systems owned by local governments. Its problem was not to find a market for its power, but to generate enough power to meet the demands of its market.

The TVA power system is not exclusively hydroelectric, a large part of its energy being generated in auxiliary steam plants. Since the flow of water is regulated to meet the needs of flood control and navigation, the quantity released varies from time to time. At one time there may be too much to put through the turbines, the rest of it washing over the dams; at another, there may be so little that turbines are shut down. The steam plants lessen this irregularity; they "firm up" the supply of power. Here, however, electricity is not a by-product of other activities. And, on this basis, the construction of steam plants has been vigorously opposed by the private utilities. Funds for such construction were denied the TVA by the Republican Eightieth Congress, voted it by the Democratic Eighty-first. Of the 9,500,000 kilowatts of capacity expected to be in operation in 1956, half will be hydro and half steam.

In fixing its rates, the TVA deliberately sought to promote expansion in the use of power. It rejected the usual policy of starting with present costs, setting rates to cover them, and reducing rates only as consumption might increase. Instead, it assumed demand to be elastic and set rates at a level designed to create a market that would enable it to produce at full capacity. Calculating what its costs would be at this volume, it also sought to establish rates that would cover its costs. Whether it actually did so has long been a subject of debate.

There is no question that TVA rates have covered the costs of building and operating the facilities that are used exclusively in generating and transmitting power. But have they also borne a fair share of the joint costs of multipurpose facilities? The answer depends upon one's judgment as to the proper method of allocating such costs. And judgments differ. At the one extreme there is the view, sometimes expressed by private utility interests, that all of the cost of the many dams in the valley should be charged to power and none of it to flood control or navigation. At the other is the view, once said to be held by directors of the TVA, that all of the cost should be charged to these purposes and none of it to power. Between these extremes, a number of theories have been developed to justify the allocation to power of various percentages of the joint costs. Each of these theories is defensible and each of them is open to attack. Choice among them is a matter of judgment. The final decision, inevitably, is arbitrary in character. Under the principle adopted by TVA, joint costs are reallocated from time to time as new facilities are built. In the past, 30 per cent of these costs have been charged to flood control, 30 per cent to navigation, and 40 per cent to power. On this basis, the investment in power facilities, on June 30, 1953, was $803,500,000. Net operating income, from 1933 to 1953, yielded a return that varied between 2.7 per cent and 5.8 per cent of the power investment. Of a total net income of nearly $226,000,000 during this period, $81,000,000 was paid back to the government and nearly $145,000,000 was invested in new power facilities.[16]

In dealing with the distributors who buy its power at wholesale and sell it at retail, the TVA serves, in effect, as a regulatory agency. It supervises their finances, prescribes their methods of accounting, and controls their rates. The Authority has sought to insure that these rates shall be set at levels that are designed, not to yield a profit that will finance the other activities of local governments and reduce their taxes, but to increase the use of power and contribute to the valley's economic development. In

[16] *Annual Report of the Tennessee Valley Authority, 1953*, pp. 9, 24.

1952 residential consumers in the Tennessee Valley bought electricity for less than half of the nation's average rate: 1.35 cents per kilowatt-hour compared with 2.78 cents. And they bought twice as much, per customer per annum, as the nation's average: 3,907 kilowatt-hours compared with 2,091.[17] In less than twenty years the number of farms electrified had been raised from 3 per cent to 80 per cent. The total consumption of power in the valley had grown from 1,500,000,000 kilowatt-hours per year to more than 23,000,000,000, increasing fifteen times. Judged in terms of the purposes for which it was established, the TVA was a success.

The Columbia River

The Columbia River with its tributaries—the most important being the Snake—drains an area of more than 250,000 square miles in the states of Washington, Oregon, Idaho, and Montana. Plans for the development of this basin have called for a series of dams surpassing those of the TVA, with an ultimate hydroelectric capacity of more than 10,000,000 kilowatts. Construction here was started in the thirties to provide relief from unemployment and to contribute to business recovery. Bonneville Dam, on the lower Columbia, was built and has been operated by the Army Engineers, its primary function being that of promoting navigation. The dam is equipped with ship locks and with fish ladders that enable salmon and other fish to swim upstream to their spawning grounds. Its power capacity is over 500,000 kilowatts. The Grand Coulee Dam, on the upper Columbia, has an ultimate capacity of nearly 2,000,000 kilowatts. It is the biggest structure on earth, standing 450 feet high, measuring 4,300 feet at its crest, and creating a lake that stretches for 150 miles to the Canadian border. The dam was built and has been operated by the Bureau of Reclamation; it serves the purposes of stream control and irrigation. Power generated at the dam is used to pump water from the Columbia up into the Grand Coulee, a dry river bed 2–6 miles wide and 27 miles long between cliffs 600 feet high, which affords a natural reservoir whence water is released to irrigate more than 1,000,000 acres of desert land in central Washington. The Army Engineers and the Bureau of Reclamation co-operate in handling these installations as an integrated unit in controlling stream flow and producing power.

The sale of power is assigned to still another agency: the Bonneville Power Administration, established by Congress in 1937 and placed under a single administrator in the Department of the Interior. The administrator is authorized to buy or build transmission facilities and is instructed to "give preference and priority to public bodies and cooperatives." Seattle and Tacoma, two of the largest cities in the region, already had municipal plants. And there has been some growth in distribution by other cities and co-operatives. But most of the power handled by the BPA has been sold to

[17] *Annual Report of the Tennessee Valley Authority, 1952*, pp. 28–29.

private utilities or directly to large industries. The dams on the Columbia were derided as white elephants during the depression. But, along with those on the Tennessee, they provided the energy required to produce aluminum for military aircraft and to create the atomic bomb during the war. Here, again, the demand for power has kept pace with the supply.

Bonneville rates, like those charged by the TVA, are not designed to yield a profit but are expected to cover the separable costs and part of the joint costs involved in producing power. In this case, the task of allocating joint costs has been assigned by Congress to the Federal Power Commission. At Bonneville Dam the FPC has charged half of these costs to power. Here, the power plant, with rates among the lowest in the country, will cover all of its operating costs and pay for itself and for half of the dam at 3 per cent interest within 40 years. At the Grand Coulee, part of the power costs must be charged to pumping for irrigation. But rates are expected to cover the rest of these costs and about a third of the costs of the common facilities.

Proposals have been made at times for the creation of a Columbia Valley Authority. The power potentialities of the region are only beginning to be realized. The multi-agency administrative structure is unduly cumbersome. But opposition by private interests to further public development is strong. So the cumbersome setup is retained. The BPA turns its revenues in to the Treasury. And each of the agencies must go to Congress for appropriations to finance its operations year by year.

Other Federal Projects

Multipurpose dams have been built in a number of other places by the Bureau of Reclamation and by the Army Engineers. Power from dams in Oklahoma and Arkansas is marketed by the Southwestern Power Administration, set up by the Secretary of the Interior in 1943, along the lines of the BPA. Power from dams in several southeastern states is sold by the Southeastern Power Administration set up in 1950. The third largest structure built by the Bureau—next to the Grand Coulee and Hoover Dams—is Shasta Dam, 180 miles north of San Francisco. This is a part of a large project in which the surplus water of the Sacramento River is diverted to irrigate the Central and San Joaquin Valleys of California. Much of the power generated at Shasta is used for pumping. The rest has been sold to a private utility company.

Construction of a number of multipurpose dams in the Missouri Basin, in accordance with the Pick-Sloan Plan, described in Chapter 12, was authorized by Congress in the Flood Control Act of 1944. The plan called for six big dams on the main stream and for many smaller ones. One of the large structures, Fort Peck Dam in Montana, has already been built. Constructed by the Army Engineers, it is the largest earth-filled dam in the world, measuring four miles at its crest. Four other big dams are being built in the Dakotas. In 1952 the government was operating twelve hydroelectric plants in the basin, most of them on a small scale, three of them in connection with the Colorado–Big Thompson project where water is pumped through a tunnel from the western slope of the Great Divide to irrigate land to the east, its fall down the eastern slope of the mountains providing a part of the power required to run the pumps. Eleven more hydroelectric plants were expected to be in operation by 1960. Proposals to create a Missouri Valley Authority have been opposed by private power companies and by local governments. Under the present setup, each installation is handled separately, the Bureau of Reclamation marketing the surplus power.

In two other regions, projects have been proposed but not developed by the federal government. At the International Rapids on the St. Lawrence, the power is to be developed by the State of New York; at Niagara Falls, by the State or by private companies. At Passamaquoddy, on the border between Maine and New Brunswick, it was proposed in the early days of the New Deal to harness the tides in the Bay of Fundy, impounding waters at high tide and using them to generate electricity as they were permitted to recede. The project was started but it was abandoned at an early stage.

New Deal Power Policy

The promotion of navigation on inland waterways has its critics. But there are few who would question the desirability of irrigation and flood control. And when dams are built for these purposes, there are few who would argue that water power thus created should not be used. There are objections, however, to the methods employed in selling such power, to the policies followed in setting rates, to the use of these rates as a yardstick by which to measure those charged by private companies, and to the construction of steam plants to stabilize and expand the power supply.

Under Hoover, the power created at Boulder Canyon was sold at the dam, and the sale was made at a price designed to yield a profit that would subsidize irrigation and flood control. Under Roosevelt and Truman, the federal government built its own transmission lines and encouraged local governments and rural co-operatives to acquire distribution facilities, assisting them financially and assuring them priority in the sale of power. Instead of leaving the field to private enterprise, it actively promoted public ownership. Its rates, moreover, were set at levels that were calculated to maximize consumption. They were designed, not to yield a profit, but to forward economic and social development. This policy, while unpopular with private utility companies, would appear to be defensible. In certain regions it displaced or forestalled private enterprise. And in setting rates it took risks that private enterprise could not afford to take. But it did succeed in promoting regional development in a way that private enterprise would not have done.

Federal power rates have more than covered the separable costs of generating, transmitting, and distributing power. But have they covered total costs? The answer depends upon the method used in allocating the joint costs of multipurpose dams. Under one method, power operations may be shown to have yielded a profit. Under another, they may be shown to have involved a loss. The principles of allocation can be debated at length. But the debate is futile, since no agreement is to be obtained. If dams are to be built in any case, the resulting power may well be priced to cover its separable costs and to maximize its use. The problem of allocation can be ignored.

In the early years of the New Deal, public rates were frequently put forth as a yardstick by which to measure the propriety of private rates. State regulation of private rates was said to be ineffective, and comparison with public rates was offered as a means of tightening control. But such comparisons are open to question. Costs differ from steam plants to hydro plants, from private operation to public operation, from single-purpose projects to those with many purposes. And here the insoluble problem of allocating joint costs becomes a crucial one. As a result, truly comparable figures are not to be obtained. If public rates are low, therefore, it does not follow that private rates should be set at similar amounts. In objecting to the yardstick propaganda of the period, the private companies had a legitimate complaint. It should be noted, however, that the example set by public projects was a salutary one. Low public rates disclosed the existence of a vast potential market. They were copied by private companies. And they led to larger sales and greater profits. The public rates were not fair yardsticks. But public projects, like the TVA, did serve as pacesetters for private industry.

In answer to a question at a press conference in the summer of 1953, President Eisenhower cited the TVA as an example of what he meant by "creeping socialism."[18] In a sense, the characterization was justified. The project is certainly socialistic. And it has moved from place to place. The TVA started with a series of multipurpose dams. To transport incidental power, it built transmission lines. To obtain an assured market, it promoted public ownership of distribution facilities. To avoid duplication, it bought out private companies, thus obtaining a regional monopoly. To "firm up" its power supply, it built steam plants. To keep pace with growing demands, as any private enterprise would have done, it built more steam plants. Far from creeping, it proceeded at a walk or even at a run. The people of the valley thought it was headed in the right direction. The Eisenhower administration disagreed.

Republican Power Policy

In its first session, in 1953, the new Congress sharply reduced the budgets of the Bureau of Reclamation, the Army Engineers, the Rural Electri-

[18] *New York Times*, June 18, 1953.

fication Administration, and the TVA. It canceled all new projects and put a stop to some that were already under way. It refused to appropriate money for a TVA steam plant at Memphis, and forbade the Southwestern Power Administration to use its funds to lease steam plants to "firm up" its power supply. At the same time, the new Secretary of the Interior, Douglas McKay, abandoned his Department's previous plan to build a large multipurpose dam, as a part of the Columbia Valley water control system, in Hell's Canyon on the Snake, and withdrew its objection to the construction of a number of small power dams by private companies. These dams would cost less money and would be completed sooner, but they would add only half as many kilowatts to the hydroelectric capacity of the river system as a whole. In disposing of the power generated at Clark Hill Dam on the Savannah River, the Secretary proposed to turn all of Georgia's share over to a private company which would then be expected to resell it to rural co-operatives in accordance with the preference required by law. At other projects within his jurisdiction, the Secretary observed the preferential rights of public agencies in making current sales, but sold the remaining power to private companies under long-term contracts, thus preventing the public buyers from exercising their rights to enlarge their purchases in the future as their needs grow. These moves were generally interpreted as parts of a concerted effort to curb public enterprise in the generation and distribution of electricity.

On August 18, 1953, Secretary McKay issued an official statement of power policy. The Department, it said, will continue to recommend the construction of generating facilities, emphasizing multipurpose projects which are "beyond the means of local, public or private enterprise." But it holds that "the primary responsibility for supplying power needs of an area rests with the people locally." Accordingly, "it will not oppose the construction of facilities which local interests, either public or private, are willing to provide. . . ." The Department will build and operate transmission lines, but not if "other public or private agencies have or will provide the necessary facilities upon reasonable terms." In making sales, it will give preference to public bodies and to co-operatives. But it will not ordinarily deal with large industrial consumers, selling surplus power instead to private utilities. Wholesale rates will be the "lowest possible . . . consistent with sound business principles." The rates charged by municipalities and co-operatives reselling federal power will be freed of federal control.[19]

Federal power policy became a major political issue in 1954 when President Eisenhower directed the Atomic Energy Commission to enter into the Dixon-Yates contract. The expansion of atomic energy operations had created an added demand for power in the area served by the TVA. Congress, however, had denied the TVA the $100 million it requested to meet

[19] *New York Times*, August 19, 1953.

this demand by building a steam plant at Memphis. Now it was proposed that AEC contract with two utility holding companies (through E. H. Dixon and E. A. Yates, their presidents) to build a private steam plant costing $107 million at West Memphis, Arkansas, and to feed into the TVA transmission lines some 600,000 kilowatts of power to replace like quantities that the TVA would supply to the AEC. This deal was defended as saving the government an immediate capital outlay. It was attacked as saddling the AEC with larger annual costs, as promising the Dixon-Yates combine exorbitant profits, as being effected without competitive bidding, and as being forced on AEC and TVA—supposedly independent agencies—against the better judgment of the members of their boards. Whatever the merits of these contentions, one purpose was clear: to prevent TVA from expanding farther as its market continued to grow. In response to public criticism, the contract was modified to put a ceiling on the Dixon-Yates companies' profits and to enable the government to acquire the new plant at any time within three years. It was then approved by the Joint Congressional Committee on Atomic Energy, all the Republicans voting yes and all the Democrats voting no. In the Congressional elections in November, 1954, the Democrats won control of both houses of Congress. It thus became certain that the Dixon-Yates contract would be investigated and possible that it would not be permitted to take effect.[20]

STATE ENTERPRISE

Early in the nineteenth century, state governments operated banks, built and operated turnpikes and canals, and contributed to the building of railroads. By the middle of the century, however, most of these activities had been abandoned or were being conducted as public services. Again in the 1920's, the state of North Dakota embarked upon an ambitious program of public ownership of banks, grain elevators, flour mills, and other enterprises. But this, too, was dropped within a few years. At present, most states maintain public parks and forests. All states run factories in their prisons, making products such as bags and binder twine for sale to farmers, automobile license plates, and a variety of other goods for public use. A few states have gone into the business of providing housing or have assisted local governments in providing housing for veterans and for lower income groups. But the major enterprises in which the states are now engaged are the provision of transportation facilities, the construction of power projects, the operation of liquor stores, and the maintenance of insurance services.

State Transportation Facilities

The state of New York has long maintained a system of barge canals, 525 miles in length, which it operates at public expense, charging no tolls.

[20] *New York Times,* September 5, October 7, November 11, 1954.

The Commonwealth of Massachusetts, since 1918, has operated the transit system of Boston and neighboring cities and towns. Harbor facilities at ocean ports—wharves, docks, warehouses, and the like—are usually owned by state governments. At New Orleans a State Board of Port Commissioners, formed in 1896, operates grain elevators, coffee terminals, banana conveyors, cranes, derricks, a belt-line railway, a canal, and a free-trade zone where goods can be imported, processed, and exported duty-free. In some cases, an agency has been set up by two or more states to provide the facilities required along a common waterway. Of these, the most important is the Port of New York Authority.

The Port of New York Authority was established, under an interstate compact between the states of New York and New Jersey, in 1921. Its activities are directed by a board of twelve commissioners, six appointed by the governor of each state, to serve for terms of six years, without pay. They are administered by a general manager appointed by the board. The Authority is empowered to plan, lease, buy, or build all types of terminal and transport facilities. It can finance construction by selling bonds, fix and collect tolls, and use its revenues to defray operating expenses and to pay interest and amortize its debts. In 1953 the Authority had around 2,000 employees and assets of $475 million. It was operating some marine terminals, but its major activity was that of providing interurban transportation facilities. In 1930 it acquired the Holland Tunnel, which had been built in 1927, and in the next ten years it built the Lincoln Tunnel and the George Washington Bridge. It also owns three Staten Island bridges, a railroad freight terminal, two truck terminals, a bus terminal, an airport, an office building, and a number of industrial properties. It operates the Newark, LaGuardia, and New York International airports under lease. The Authority has lost money on some of its terminals and other projects, but has covered these losses and made substantial profits by charging high tolls on its tunnels and bridges. These structures cost $266 million. The tolls collected to 1953 reached $427 million. Profits are used to retire debts and to finance expansion. The profit in 1953 was more than $20 million. The Authority is frequently cited as a model of public enterprise. But its success must be attributed, in part, at least, to its monopoly power, its independence, and its freedom from regulation in fixing rates.[21]

State governments have long built and maintained highways, financing this activity in recent years by charging license fees and taxing motor fuels. With the growing demand for multilane superhighways, however, these revenues have proved inadequate, and the states have gone back to the practice, abandoned a century ago, of collecting tolls. The first of the modern toll roads, the Pennsylvania Turnpike, was opened in 1940. By 1952 such highways had been built or were under construction in ten

[21] See Austin J. Tobin, "The Port of New York Authority," *State Government*, September, 1947, pp. 233–39; and William S. Fairfield, "The New York Port Authority, Guardian of the Toll Gates," *The Reporter*, September 29, 1953, pp. 21–27.

other states, and others were projected, the total length running to 3,600 miles and the total investment to more than $3 billion. The roads, in most cases, are planned, built, and operated by semiautonomous agencies similar to the Port Authority. These bodies function as business entities, selling bonds, collecting tolls, and using their revenues to cover their costs and retire their debts. The revenues of the Pennsylvania and New Jersey Turnpikes reached $16 million each in 1952. Whether such roads, in general, will be freed when paid for or maintained as sources of public income remains to be seen.[22]

State Power Projects

Multipurpose projects including the generation and sale of hydroelectric power have been constructed by state governments in Nebraska, Oklahoma, Texas, and South Carolina. The people of Nebraska are served exclusively by publicly-owned electrical utilities. Three large irrigation and power projects were built during the thirties, their lines being connected to form a common pool. A number of towns were operating their own power plants, and lines were being built in rural areas by REA co-operatives. Then, in 1939, a Consumers' Public Power District was formed to acquire the properties of several private companies. And in 1946 the Omaha Public Power District was set up to take over the facilities of the Nebraska Power Co. in Omaha and in many other towns. With this, electricity in Nebraska was completely socialized.

In New York, a state power authority was created by the legislature when Franklin D. Roosevelt was governor in 1931, and the water power within its boundaries was declared to be a resource of the state. The authority was directed to build dams, generate power, and sell it to private companies. But it was not permitted to build, own, or operate large-scale transmission lines. It was thus placed under a serious handicap in bargaining. Until 1954 this body had not built any dams or generated any power. In that year, however, Congress approved American participation in a navigation and power project in the International Rapids of the St. Lawrence. The State Power Authority was designated by President Eisenhower to act for the United States in damming the river, and construction work was started in August, 1954. When the project is completed, New York State will co-operate with the public hydroelectric system of Ontario in generating power. The power potential of the St. Lawrence is estimated at 750,000 kw., that of the Niagara at more than 1,000,000 kw. Here, it had not been finally determined, at the end of 1954, whether the power was to be developed by the state or by private companies. To the extent that the state does come to operate these power plants, the consumer may derive some benefit from lower capital costs. But his gains will

[22] See J. M. Fischer, "The Rebirth of Turnpikes," *Commercial and Financial Chronicle*, November 13, 1952, pp. 6 *ff.*; "Toll Roads and Toll Authorities," *State Government*, June, 1953, pp. 157 *ff.*

be limited by the fact that the power must be sold for transmission and distribution by private companies.

State Liquor Stores

With the repeal of the Eighteenth Amendment in 1933, control of the liquor traffic was returned to the states. Two different methods of control were then adopted: the licensing of private distributors and distribution by the state itself. The latter method was advocated as a means of eliminating private profit from the sale of liquor and thus preventing expansion of consumption by removing the incentive to stimulate demand. Seventeen states went into the business of selling liquor at wholesale, sixteen of them also selling at retail. Three of these states monopolized distribution. The rest permitted some private traffic, usually monopolizing package sales of hard liquor but licensing drinking places and distributors of beer.

State liquor store systems occupy an ambiguous position. They are supposed to serve both as regulators of the use of liquor and as merchandisers of the stuff. The former function has had little of their attention, the latter a great deal. Per capita consumption of intoxicants is somewhat lower in states with public liquor stores than in those without. But nobody knows why. And the trend has been upward in both. The state stores, on the other hand, have been highly profitable. Their earnings, over the years, have run between 12 and 21 per cent of their gross revenues. In 1946 the stores in 16 states took in $807,496,000 and paid $132,345,000 into the state treasuries, a return of 16.4 per cent on sales. State stores do not advertise their products, leaving that function to the manufacturers. But they have not eliminated profit from the liquor business, being operated principally as sources of public revenue.[23]

State Insurance Programs

Since 1936 all of the states have administered compulsory unemployment compensation systems, collecting payroll taxes from employers and paying benefits to the unemployed. These are large-scale operations. But, being a form of social insurance, they differ in character from those conducted by private companies. Since 1911 the states of North Dakota, South Dakota, and Oklahoma have sold hail insurance, and the state of Wisconsin has sold life insurance policies. These operations are similar to those of private companies but on a small scale. Another form of insurance written by state as well as private companies is more important: the compensation of workmen suffering industrial injuries.

Under laws passed since 1911, all states now require employers to make payments to workers in cases of disabling accidents or occupational dis-

[23] See B. Y. Landis, "Economic Aspects of State Alcoholic Beverage Monopoly Enterprises," *Quarterly Journal of Studies on Alcohol*, September, 1948, pp. 258–69, and E. M. Denny, *State Liquor Control* (Salt Lake City: University of Utah, Institute of Government, 1950).

ease. And they further require employers to give proof of their ability to make such payments or to carry insurance to cover their risk. In thirty states, in 1949, such insurance was written only by private companies. But in eighteen states there were state funds. In eleven of these, the state funds competed with private insurers. In seven, they had a monopoly. In the past state funds have had lower costs than the private companies, and monopoly funds have had lower costs than the competitive funds.[24] As a result, the private insurers have lost business to the states.

It is the fear of a similar development in the field of automobile liability insurance that has led insurance companies to oppose the enactment of laws requiring the owners of motor vehicles to be insured. Compulsory insurance might lead to the establishment of state insurance funds. State funds might take business away from private companies by charging lower rates. Or they might be given a monopoly. To prevent this threat to private enterprise in the automobile insurance business, those who use the highways are denied the protection that compulsory insurance would afford.

LOCAL GOVERNMENT ENTERPRISE

Local governments, in the United States, engage in a great variety of activities that might be carried on by private enterprise. All of them maintain elementary and secondary schools. Many of them support colleges, libraries, museums, parks, playgrounds, zoos, golf courses, bathing beaches, and swimming pools. Some of them operate public markets, wharves, docks, coal yards, ice plants, slaughter houses, laundries, and cemeteries. A few run liquor stores, telephone systems, and gas plants. Among cities of more than 5,000 population, in 1953, auditoriums were owned and operated by a sixth, airports by a fifth, incinerators by a fifth, sewage treatment plants by half, and water systems by three fourths.[25] Water was supplied by private companies in Birmingham and Indianapolis, by the government in every other city of any size. In this field, public enterprise is generally accepted. In three others, it has given rise to controversy. These are urban transit, electrical distribution, and low-rent housing, where cities have entered on a substantial scale.

Urban Transit

In six of the twelve largest cities in the United States—New York, Chicago, Detroit, Cleveland, Boston, and San Francisco—the transit systems are publicly owned and operated. In the other six—Philadelphia, Los Angeles, Baltimore, St. Louis, Pittsburgh, and Washington—they are managed by private companies. In Philadelphia, however, the subways are privately operated but publicly owned.

[24] Herman M. Somers and Anne Somers, *Workmens Compensation* (New York: John Wiley, 1954), p. 125.

[25] *Municipal Year Book, 1953*, p. 67.

In some cities transit has been a public enterprise for many years. In others, public ownership has been necessitated by the inability of private companies to make ends meet. The industry, in recent times, has suffered from a steady decline in demand. This development has been attributed, in part, to the five-day work week, longer vacations, and television. It is a consequence, more clearly, of the widespread ownership and use of private automobiles. As riders have shifted from mass to individual transportation, traffic congestion has increased and the quality of transit service has declined. With fewer riders, the quantity of service also has been curtailed. Costs per passenger have risen and fares have had to be increased. And the combination of poorer service and higher fares has contributed to a further contraction of demand. Private operators, in some cases, have been saved from bankruptcy by public subsidies. Or cities, to maintain an essential service, have bought them out.

The financial record of the municipal systems is not a happy one. In 1951–52, Chicago and Cleveland broke even. But Detroit lost $2,300,000, San Francisco lost $2,600,000, and Boston lost $7,800,000. In 1952–53, the deficit in New York was $46,000,000.[26] Behind these figures lies the fact that the Chicago system, operated by a semiautonomous Transit Authority, was required to set fares at a level that would cover its costs, while the New York system, for instance, was not. In Chicago, the fare was 15 cents. In New York, it had been held at 5 cents until 1948 and at 10 cents from 1948 to 1953. Politicians had curried favor with the voters by opposing higher fares and the taxpayers had financed the deficit. In 1953 a New York City Transit Authority was established under state law and required to make ends meet. Its first act was to raise its fare to 15 cents. On this basis it expected to get out of the red and into the black.

Municipal Electric Systems

Among cities of more than 5,000, in 1953, electricity was sold by 21 per cent, being generated and distributed by 9 per cent, and bought and distributed by another 12 per cent.[27] The largest city in the group was Los Angeles. The greatest concentration of such cities was in the Tennessee Valley. Included also were Seattle and Tacoma in Washington, Austin and San Antonio in Texas, Lansing and Kalamazoo in Michigan, Cleveland and Columbus in Ohio, and Kansas City, Missouri, Springfield, Illinois, Ft. Wayne, Indiana, Jacksonville, Florida, and Holyoke, Massachusetts. In some of the cities, municipal systems competed with private companies. In most of them, they had a monopoly.

Public ownership, in this field, grew steadily until the twenties, largely in small towns where private enterprise had not come in. It declined dur-

[26] *New York Times*, March 23, 1953.

[27] *Municipal Yearbook, 1953*, p. 67.

ing the twenties, as many municipal systems were bought up by private concerns or holding companies. This movement was checked during the thirties when the Diesel engine afforded a means of generating power efficiently on a small scale. It was reversed when the federal government began aggressively to promote municipal ownership. From 1933 to 1938 the Public Works Administration financed the acquisition and construction of power facilities, making grants to cover 45 per cent of their cost and loans to cover part or all of the other 55 per cent. And municipalities, along with rural co-operatives, were accorded a preference in the sale of federal power.

Many of the city systems date from this time. They were established in the face of determined opposition from the private companies. Public ownership had long been handicapped by laws limiting the purposes for which cities could borrow, and the amounts they could borrow, or requiring that bond issues be approved by a two-thirds or three-fourths vote, and also by laws forbidding cities to sell beyond their boundaries. Bills to remove these obstacles were opposed by utility lobbies in the legislatures of the states. And when such bills were passed, votes approving bond issues were fought in the cities themselves. In some cases, cities were forbidden to construct their own facilities, being compelled to buy out the owners of private plants. And with their bargaining power thus impaired, they could be forced to pay a higher price. Such tactics, however, were unsuccessful. Municipal ownership gained ground.

The relative efficiency of public and private power systems, in American cities, has been a matter of protracted controversy. It is possible, by a judicious selection of cases for comparison, to construct an argument for either side. And this has frequently been done. But where impartial appraisals are available, the evidence is mixed. When public and private systems, in general, are compared, the former make a poor showing because their average size is smaller, and smaller plants have higher unit costs. Some of the small public systems are poorly run. On balance, however, they do not compare unfavorably with small systems run by private companies. A more significant comparison can be made between public and private systems of greater size.

It is difficult to compare the quality of service, because there are no measures that can readily be applied. But it is possible to compare rates, and here it is found that public rates are usually lower than private rates. The lower rates, moreover, appear to be a consequence of lower costs. When sixteen large public systems and nineteen large private systems were compared for the Twentieth Century Fund, it was shown that the former had slightly higher costs for generation and transmission but substantially lower costs for sales promotion, customer accounting, bill collecting, and general administration, with lower total costs as a result. And the public systems had made adequate provisions for depreciation and, unlike the private systems, had devoted large sums to the retirement of their debts.[28] On the other hand, as is often pointed out, private systems pay taxes and public systems are tax exempt. The latter frequently render free services, such as water pumping and street lighting, to city governments. But the cost of such services may not equal the taxes that private companies are required to pay. The public systems enjoy an even greater advantage in their ability to borrow at a lower interest rate. And this, indeed, may go far toward explaining their lower costs and rates. When all these matters are taken into account, however, the municipal systems appear to have been run with marked success.[29]

Public Housing

Several thousand houses were built by the federal government to provide shelter for war workers during World War I. But the beginning of large-scale public housing in the United States dates from the Great Depression. The government was authorized, under Title II of the National Industrial Recovery Act of 1933, to finance the construction of houses as a means of increasing employment. At first, it confined itself to making loans to private, limited-dividend housing corporations. But progress, through these agencies, was slow. Then the government proceeded itself to buy large tracts of land in cities, often involving the clearance of slums, and to build large-scale housing developments, renting apartments to families in the lower income groups. At the same time, it built a number of homestead projects in rural and suburban areas to care for stranded populations, promote subsistence farming and small industrial developments, and provide subsistence homes within reach of urban employment. And it built three large green-belt towns: Greenbelt, Maryland, Greenhills, Ohio, and Greendale, Wisconsin.

This was emergency action, designed primarily to promote recovery from a deep depression. Other emergencies followed with World War II and the Korean war. The federal government again constructed houses—most of them temporary but many of them permanent—for war workers and military personnel. A long-range housing program was inaugurated, however, with the Housing Act of 1937 and carried forward by the Housing Act of 1949. This program has included some provision for federal aid to rural housing. But its main purpose has been the promotion of slum clearance and low-rent housing in urban areas. And here, municipal governments are expected to play a major part.

Under the long-range program, the federal government has limited its participation to the extension of financial aid. The states (43 of them by 1953) have enacted laws permitting cities to set up public housing authorities. Nearly a thousand of these agencies had been established by

[28] *Electric Power and Government Policy* (New York: Twentieth Century Fund, 1948), pp. 405–9.

[29] See *Ibid.*, pp. 399–437, and E. W. Clemens, *Economics and Public Utilities* (New York: Appleton-Century-Crofts, 1950), pp. 561–75.

1953. The local authorities draw up the plans for slum clearance and housing construction, purchase the land, and enter into contracts with private builders to do the work. When the projects are completed, the authorities operate them, with staffs that include business managers, social workers, and maintenance employees. Dwellings are made available to families with low incomes at rents they can afford to pay. Since demand exceeds supply at the rentals fixed, the quarters must be rationed. Preference is given first to families displaced by slum clearance, and second to families lacking housing or living in substandard dwellings, and, within each of these groups, to veterans. Entry is limited to those with incomes no greater than five times the rentals, and continued occupancy to those whose incomes do not exceed this level by more than 20–25 per cent. Incomes are examined each year and those exceeding these limits are required to move. The median income of tenants in such housing in 1952 was a little over $2,000 a year. The median rent, including heat and utilities, was about $35 a month. The cost, per apartment, was closer to $60 a month. The difference was made up largely by the federal government. Federal aid took two forms. The government made loans to supplement the borrowing power of the local authorities, contributing up to 90 per cent of construction costs. And it made outright grants, thereafter, to meet the operating deficits. Similar grants were made by local governments, usually in the form of tax exemption or the provision of free services. As projects are finally paid for, by amortizing their bonds, it is assumed that the authorities will be able to operate them without further federal help. But the housing involved is obviously provided, not on a commercial basis, but as a form of public charity.

In absolute numbers, public housing is impressive: there were nearly 1,300 projects with close to 300,000 dwelling units under public management at the end of 1952. Relatively, it is of small significance: it provides less than 1 per cent of all dwellings, and accounted for but 5 per cent of the new housing starts in 1952. And authority for further construction has repeatedly been reduced. The Housing Act of 1949 provided for the construction of 135,000 new units per year for the next 6 years. The Congress cut this figure to 50,000 in 1951, to 35,000 in 1952, and to 20,000 in 1953. In a Message to Congress in January 1954, President Eisenhower asked for authority to finance the construction of 140,000 units in four years, at the rate of 35,000 a year. But Congress granted authority for only 35,000 units in a single year, and so hedged this with restrictions that no such number could be built. Further building, on any scale, awaits another depression, or a war, or a drastic reversal of policy. But cities will remain in the business of operating housing by virtue of the projects that have already been built.[30]

The issues raised by the housing program are too involved to be de-

[30] For current information on public housing, see the Annual Reports of the Housing and Home Finance Agency and the Municipal Yearbooks.

bated here. It is evident that public housing has been provided at a loss. This could be avoided, of course, by charging rents to cover costs, accepting tenants with higher incomes, and leaving lower-income groups to crowd into such quarters as were left. But such a policy would sacrifice the social purposes for which the low-rent projects were designed. The loss on housing, as such, could also be avoided by charging commercial rents and paying subsidies directly in the form of contributions to the incomes of the families that were housed. Such a procedure would serve to clarify the financial relationships involved. And for this there is something to be said.

THE FUTURE OF PUBLIC ENTERPRISE

Public opinion, in the United States, has usually opposed government ownership and operation of industry. The growth of such activity in recent times has been a consequence of major crises such as a depression or a war. The only case of socialization to evoke widespread popular support is that of electricity. The only other industry for which public ownership has seriously been urged, from time to time, is railroad transportation. But this proposal has few backers at the present time. The trend today is all the other way. Most popular discussion is concerned, not with the socialization of private enterprise, but with the privatization of public enterprise. And the swing of the pendulum is unlikely to be reversed by anything less than a major depression or another war.

Public Ownership and Operation of Railroads

Many volumes have been filled, over the years, with the pros and cons of public ownership of railroads. The industry has always been one of the first that socialists have proposed to nationalize. And public ownership has also been advocated, at times, by persons other than socialists. In 1874 a committee reporting to Congress recommended that the nation or the states undertake to operate one or more railroads as a means of regulating the services rendered and the rates charged by private lines, thus anticipating by many years the New Deal idea of yardstick control. And from January 1, 1918 to March 1, 1920, beginning in World War I, operation of the railroads was directed by the federal government.

This period is often described as one of government ownership and operation. It is said that the experiment was a failure, and that the inefficiency of public enterprise was thereby proved. But no such view can be supported by the facts. The railroads continued to be owned, during this period, by private stockholders. They continued to be operated by private managements. The government merely required that their facilities be pooled and their services co-ordinated to promote the prosecution of the war. The Railroad Administration lost $1,886 million. It did so because it refrained from raising rates—and thus promoting inflation—while costs were going up. If it had sought to cover costs or to show a profit, this could easily have been done. The real test of the undertaking was in the Administration's ability to reorganize the transport service and direct it toward the winning of the war. And here, it was successful. With respect to the long-run desirability of public ownership and operation, however, the experience proved little either way.

After the war, nationalization was strongly urged by the railroad brotherhoods. The unions' proposal—known as the Plumb Plan for their counsel, Glenn E. Plumb—called for ownership and operation by a federal corporation with a board of fifteen directors, five to be chosen by the workers, five by the managerial employees, and five to be appointed by the President to represent the public. Profits were to be divided between the workers and the government. And whenever they passed a certain point, rates were to be cut. The Plumb Plan enlisted little popular support and was given scant attention by the Congress. With the adoption of the Transportation Act of 1920, it shortly dropped from sight.

During the depression of the thirties, talk of public ownership was heard again. A fifth of the railroads in the United States, and a third of the railway mileage, were in receivership. The industry was supported, to the extent of more than a billion dollars, by federal loans. A Federal Coordinator was established to assist the roads in solving their financial problems by reducing their costs. Joseph B. Eastman, an outstanding member of the Interstate Commerce Commission, was appointed to the job. In his subsequent reports, Mr. Eastman took a fatalistic view. Public ownership, he said, would have advantages and disadvantages. But, in the long run, it probably was unavoidable. The railroads, he felt, would be unable to finance themselves. Being regulated in minute detail, they had already lost their private character. Government, in the circumstances, might as well assume complete responsibility. Accordingly, a plan for public ownership was then set forth.[31] Its adoption, however, was never considered seriously.

Again in 1942, Ralph L. Dewey, writing one of the chapters in the National Resources Planning Board's report on *Transportation and National Policy* argued for nationalization as a means of enabling the railroads to survive the competition of subsidized highways, airways, and waterways.[32] But the Board itself did not endorse the proposal. Public ownership of railroads remained—and still remains—a matter for academic debate.

Public Competition with Private Enterprise

Business organizations, such as the United States Chamber of Commerce and the National Association of Manufacturers, have complained,

[31] See the reports of the Federal Coordinator of Transportation (73d Cong., 2d Sess., Senate Doc. 119, 1934, pp. 13–21, and 74th Cong., 1st Sess., House Doc. 89, 1935, pp. 49–55).

[32] See pp. 278–303 of that report.

from time to time, concerning government competition with private firms. Such competition, they contend, is unfair, since public enterprises may enjoy lower costs and may even be conducted at a loss. Toward the end of the Hoover Administration, a special committee was set up by the House of Representatives to investigate the problem. The committee held extensive hearings and built up a long record of cases, coming to the conclusion that "The entrance of the government into commercial and industrial undertakings, backed by public credit and resources and its military and civilian personnel, for the purpose of competing with the business establishments and the opportunities of livelihood of its citizens is . . . repugnant to our fundamental democratic institutions and aspirations."[33] It therefore recommended that such activities be abandoned and that a standing committee of Congress be established to guard against "unwise and unprofitable encroachments" upon private enterprise. This report was followed by a great expansion of governmental undertakings during the depression and the war. Then, in 1953, another committee of the House held hearings on the same subject, taking four volumes of testimony from witnesses who complained that the federal government was producing some 275 different types of goods and services. The list included such items as anchor chains, brushes and brooms, cleaning and pressing, Diesel engines, furniture, greenhouses, harness shops, ice cream, laundries, mattresses, paint, rope, seeds, tailoring, and woodworking. It appeared to be quite shocking until subjected to analysis.

In some cases, as with the Post Office and atomic energy, government has always had a monopoly. In others, as with crop insurance, private enterprise has no desire to compete. In a few, as with electricity, government has taken over monopolies from private owners. This may be resented, but it is not a case of public competition with private enterprise. There are other goods and services, however, that are produced both by government and by private firms. But some of them are sold in separate markets: low-rent housing to tenants who cannot afford to pay commercial rentals, public loans to borrowers who cannot obtain credit from private lenders. The public and private agencies do not compete. Other things are produced by government for its own use: paint and rope by the navy, mail bags by the Post Office, munitions by the arsenals, and local services in the Canal Zone, in atomic energy towns, and on army posts. Such items are numerous. They make up most of the list compiled by the committee of the House. Perhaps the government should buy these things instead of making them. But the practice complained of here is the common business practice of vertical integration, not competition with private enterprise. Such competition does occur in a few cases: the postal savings system with private savings banks, city colleges and state universities with private institutions, public recreational facilities with the

[33] *Report of the Special Committee Appointed to Investigate Government Competition with Private Enterprise* (72d Cong., 2d Sess., House Report 1985, 1933), p. 18.

commercial amusement industry. But these cases are comparatively rare. The real grievance is not that government has competed unfairly, but that it has excluded private enterprise from certain profit-making opportunities.

The Privatization of Public Enterprise

The direction of movement in the United States today is from public back to private enterprise. This policy is not exactly new. From 1919 to 1933 the Congress sought unsucessfully to find a private buyer for Muscle Shoals. The government sold to private operators, after both world wars, the merchant ships that it had had to build. And it sold to manufacturers, after World War II, plants built for more than $20 billion at but a fraction of their cost. The Truman Administration had tried to sell the Mississippi barge line and had planned to dispose of the synthetic rubber plants. But with the Eisenhower administration, the movement took on speed. In the first two years the barge line was sold, the RFC was liquidated, and arrangements were made for the sale of the synthetic rubber plants. The government put the brakes on public enterprise in electricity. Former President Hoover was asked to head another commission. The first Hoover Commission had shown how the functions of government could be fulfilled with greater efficiency. This one was expected to show what functions could be dropped. Its reports were to recommend the withdrawal of government from fields where goods and services could be supplied by private enterprise.[34]

It was unlikely, however, that public undertakings could be compressed within the lines that had bounded them in 1933. The RFC was gone, but it had left the Small Business Administration as its heir. Mr. Hoover had expressed the view that the objective of public power policy "should be to get the federal government out of the business of generating and distributing power as soon as possible."[35] But President Eisenhower was not prepared to go that far. The TVA, he told his press conference on October 21, 1953, had to be accepted as an historic fact. The sale of the system, he thought, would be a pretty drastic step.[36]

SUGGESTIONS FOR FURTHER READING

There is no recent, comprehensive study of public enterprise in the United States. The most reliable source on federal enterprises is the Commission on the Organization of the Executive Branch of the Government (the first Hoover Commission). The reports of this body on *The Post Office* and *Federal Busi-*

[34] In a report published on March 13, 1955, the Commission recommended a drastic curtailment of the government's lending, guaranteeing, and insuring activities. See *New York Times*, March 14, 1955.

[35] *New York Times*, April 12, 1953.

[36] *New York Times*, October 22, 1953.

ness Enterprises and the reports of its Task Forces on *The Post Office, Lending Agencies,* and *Revolving Funds and Business Enterprises of the Government* were published by the Government Printing Office in 1949. The public power projects, in general, are well discussed in E. W. Clemens, *Economics and Public Utilities* (New York: Appleton-Century-Crofts, 1950), chaps. xxiii–xxviii, and in *Electric Power and Government Policy* (New York: Twentieth Century Fund, 1947), chaps. vii–xi. There is an extensive bibliography on the TVA. The more important titles are: David E. Lilienthal, *The TVA: Democracy on the March* (2d ed.; New York: Harper & Bro., 1953); J. S. Ransmeier, *The Tennessee Valley Authority* (Nashville, Tenn.: Vanderbilt University Press, 1942); C. H. Pritchett, *The Tennessee Valley Authority; A Study in Public Administration* (Chapel Hill, N.C.: University of North Carolina Press, 1943); Herman Finer, *The TVA: Lessons for International Application* (Montreal: International Labor Office, 1944); Henry Billings, *The Power and the Valley* (London: Hart-Davis, 1953) and Gordon R. Clapp, *The TVA* (Chicago: University of Chicago Press, 1955). See also the annual reports of the TVA, particularly those for 1950 and 1953. The best current source on state government enterprises is the magazine *State Government* and the annual *Book of the States;* on local government enterprises, the *Municipal Yearbook.* A good statement of the case for public ownership of railroads is that by Ralph Dewey in National Resources Planning Board, *Transportation and National Policy* (Washington: Government Printing Office, 1942), pp. 278–303. A good statement of the disadvantages is presented in the Federal Coordinator's report (73d Cong., 2d Sess., Senate Doc. 119, 1934), pp. 13–21. A balanced discussion of the subject is contained in D. Philip Locklin, *Economics of Transportation* (4th ed.; Homewood, Ill.: Richard D. Irwin, Inc., 1954), chap. xxvii.

Chapter 27 POLICY IN OTHER COUNTRIES

The pattern of relationships between government and business, in most other countries, differs markedly from the one that has prevailed in the United States. Everywhere, save in the totalitarian economies, many if not all of the controls discussed in the preceding chapters will be found. But the emphasis is not the same. Other countries have passed laws against monopolies and restrictive business practices. But most of them have tolerated and even encouraged cartels. And few have undertaken to insure the maintenance of competition. As in America, most countries have sought to moderate the impact of competition on small producers. In agriculture, particularly, this has been the case. Most countries, also, have regulated banking and corporation finance, enacted laws protecting workers and consumers, and made provision for the conservation of natural resources. In Great Britain the rates and services of railroads have been controlled by administrative tribunals. But elsewhere, agencies comparable to the American regulatory commission are little known. Public ownership and operation, on the other hand, is far more prevalent abroad than in the United States.

In wartime the comprehensive planning and authoritarian control of economic activity has been well-nigh universal. But in peacetime, it has been confined, in general, to the totalitarian states. These included, between the two world wars, Fascist Italy, Nazi Germany and Soviet Russia. They include, today, the Fascist states of Spain and Argentina and the lengthened list of Communist countries: The Soviet Union and its European satellites (Poland, Hungary, Roumania, Bulgaria, Czechoslovakia, and East Germany), Jugoslavia, and Red China. Under fascism, private ownership and operation are permitted but are subordinated to the purposes of the state. Under communism in Europe private property is virtually abolished. All industry, save petty handicrafts, and all commerce and finance are in the hands of governments. Agriculture, though not completely collectivized, is under strict control. The allocation of resources is governed by a common plan, one blueprint being drafted in Moscow to cover Russia and its satellites. In Chinese industry and agriculture, private ownership survives. But here, too, allocation is planned and the plan is carried out by distributing raw materials and finished products through government trading agencies. In all these countries, consumers have lost their power to direct production, managements their freedom to make decisions, and workers their right to organize and bargain collectively. Free markets have given way to political controls. The pattern of economic life thus differs sharply from that found in the United States. In the discussion that follows, therefore, the totalitarian economies are omitted and attention is directed toward the relationships obtaining in economies where markets are relatively free.

THE MAINTENANCE OF COMPETITION

Competition has been favored and monopoly condemned by many nations at some point in their histories. But this policy has never been universal. Some of the measures adopted, moreover, have never been enforced. And others have been modified or repealed. In western Europe —except for France—and in Japan, cartels were always legal. In France the effort to maintain competition was abandoned at the end of the nineteenth century. In Great Britain and elsewhere it disappeared in the Great Depression of the thirties. Since World War II, however, an attempt has been made to decartelize Germany and Japan. And measures designed to curb restrictive business practices have been considered by many countries and adopted by a few, notably by Great Britain in the Monopolies and Restrictive Practises Act of 1948. But Canada is the only country whose policy has run parallel to that of the United States.

Canada

In 1889 the Canadian Parliament made it a misdemeanor to conspire or combine to restrain trade, unreasonably to enhance prices, or unduly to limit productive facilities, restrict production, or lessen competition. In effect, this was the Sherman Act with the rule of reason written in. In 1910 this law was supplemented by the Combines Investigation Act. Under the new measure, upon the complaint of six citizens alleging illegal practices and the order of a court, the Minister of Labor was to appoint three persons to investigate and report. It was hoped that this procedure would be preventive in effect. But criminal prosecutions could still be initiated where it was not. These laws were little used before World War I. In 1919 Parliament created a Board of Commerce with powers (comparable to those of the Federal Trade Commission) to make investigations and reports and to issue orders to cease and desist. The latter provision, however, was held unconstitutional and was dropped in 1923. The administration of the Combines Investigation Act was transferred, in 1935, to a three-man commission which was given authority not only to investigate and report on monopolistic agreements and combinations and unfair business practices, but also to recommend approval of agreements that would prevent wasteful and demoralizing competition without unduly restraining trade. The latter provision, similar in character to that contained in the NIRA, was found to be unconstitutional. In 1937 the commission was abolished and administration of the Act entrusted to a single commissioner.

Under the law as it now stands, conspiracies and combinations in restraint of trade are forbidden by the Criminal Code, investigations are made and reports issued, on his own initiative, by the Commissioner under the Combines Investigation Act, and offenders may be prosecuted by the Minister of Justice or by the Attorney-General of one of the provinces. No provision is made for civil remedies. In recent years, a number of searching reports have been made and suits have been brought involving several major industries.

A committee appointed by the Minister of Justice to study the Canadian legislation reported in 1952. The Committee rejected proposals, similar to those made in the United States, that particular practices held to be illegal be specified by law, and that the government be required to prove that the restraints it prosecutes have actually been detrimental in their effects. It recommended that the function of making investigations and that of appraising the findings and issuing reports be divided between two separate agencies, that a civil remedy be provided in the form of a judicial restraining order, and that offenders be required to file periodic reports on compliance with the courts.[1]

Prewar Tolerance of Monopoly

Measures curbing monopolistic practices have been adopted, from time to time, by many different countries. In France, Turgot's edict of 1776 abolished the guilds of merchants and manufacturers, Chapelier's Act of 1791 prohibited agreements and even meetings for discussion of common interests by masters and their men, and the Penal Code of 1810 forbade manipulation of prices in local markets for commodities. In some thirty other countries, including Spain, Portugal, Greece, Turkey, Egypt, and Iran, the law has condemned interference with such markets through curtailment of supplies, collusive bidding, or other fraudulent activities. In the British Commonwealth, antimonopoly laws of limited significance were enacted in Australia in 1906, New Zealand in 1910, and South Africa between 1906 and 1925. In Mexico, the Constitution of 1917 contained an article forbidding monopolies and denouncing all efforts to stifle competition. Antitrust laws, on the American model, were passed by Argentina in 1923, the Philippines in 1925, Mexico in 1926, Costa Rica in 1932, and Brazil in 1938.

In nearly all countries with patent systems, the laws contain provisions designed to prevent the suppression of patents. In some fifty countries such provisions call for revocation or compulsory licensing if a patent is

[1] See *Report of the Committee to Study Combines Legislation.* (Ottawa, 1952).

not exploited within two or three years. In Mexico the life of a patent may be shortened; and in many other countries, fees are imposed at rates increasing annually to discourage nonuse.

Some of the antitrust laws have been repealed or modified. Others have never been enforced. In 1884 France repealed Chapelier's Act, opening the way to cartelization. And in 1926 it provided explicitly for the recognition of cartels. In 1931 Mexico's antitrust law was superseded by an act permitting agreement and combination with the approval of the government. And since that time, Mexico has encouraged monopoly as a means of promoting industrial development. The law of Argentina was dropped in 1946; it had not been enforced. The laws of Australia, New Zealand, and South Africa have been dead letters. That of Brazil, likewise, has never been enforced. The less developed countries, in general, have been apathetic toward the problem of domestic monopoly.

In most industrial countries, cartels have never been illegal. In France, though once illegal, they have long been legalized. As a result, outside of Canada and the United States, this form of organization has dominated industry and trade. Cartelization enjoyed its longest history and reached its highest development in prewar Germany. Dating from the seventies of the last century, the movement advanced through successive stages with the approval of successive governments until practically every form of business activity that lent itself to cartelization, from the extractive industries, through heavy and light manufactures, transportation, and construction, to the wholesale and retail trades, was organized into one or more cartels. In France, after the eighties, business was brought together in *comptoirs* which functioned variously as joint purchasing offices, common export agencies, zone cartels, quota cartels, and selling syndicates. In Belgium, likewise, cartelization dated from the end of the nineteenth century. Elsewhere in Europe the movement did not assume extensive proportions until after World War I. In many countries cartels were subjected to supervision, activities deemed harmful were discouraged, and those deemed beneficial were enforced by law. In Italy, as in Germany, during the thirties the cartel structure served as an instrument in carrying out the economic policies of the totalitarian state. In Japan, where industrialism had been imposed upon a feudal society, the control of industry, until after World War II, was in the hands of a few great families.

In Great Britain the policy of freedom of trade long impeded the progress of cartelization by compelling British businessmen to meet the competition of foreigners. The abandonment of that policy, with the adoption of the Import Duties Act of 1932, provoked a rapid transition to a predominantly cartelized economy. Ben W. Lewis, writing in 1937, described the "typical British industrialist" in the following words:

> Today, as a member in good standing of a "rationalized" industry, he is allotted a specific percentage of the total business which his industry has decided to handle during the year (and he will pay into a "pool" if he exceeds his

quota and will be compensated if he is "short"); he will consult the industry schedule before pricing his goods and will not deviate therefrom without permission; he will submit his sales contracts to the officials of his industrial association for advance approval and will throw open his books for industry inspection; he will pay a levy to be used by the industry to purchase and destroy "redundant" capacity; and he will deposit with the officers of his association a substantial amount to be forfeited if he is found guilty of noncompliance.[2]

At that time, complete cartels, fixing prices, limiting output, assigning quotas, operating equalization pools, and imposing fines against penalty deposits, controlled the cement, coal, and iron and steel industries, and agreements governing prices, capacity, and output were found in many other fields. Such activity, wrote Dr. Lewis, "is characteristic of all British industry. Wherever the nature of the product or the conditions of production and marketing will permit, price-fixing schemes are in operation or contemplation, and in a large number of cases they are accompanied by devices for controlling and allocating production."[3]

Decartelization in Germany and Japan

The combines and cartels in Germany, and the great family holding companies known as the Zaibatsu together with the cartels in Japan were held responsible by American opinion for complicity with the Axis powers in the initiation and prosecution of World War II. Their continued existence was also felt to carry with it a threat of future aggression. As an occupying power at the end of the war, therefore, the United States pressed for deconcentration and decartelization of German and Japanese industry. In Germany it acted in co-operation with Great Britain and France whose enthusiasm for the program was not great. In Japan it was able to act alone.

In 1947, under U.S. Military Government Law 56, effective in the American zone of Germany, excessive concentrations of economic power were prohibited, German participation in international cartels was forbidden, some 3,000 domestic and international cartel agreements were voided, and laws restricting entry to markets by requiring licenses were annulled. In 1949, under the Occupation Statute, responsibility for the program was assumed by the Allied High Commission. The coal and steel complex of the Ruhr was broken up, the common sales agency for coal being dissolved and the number of steel companies increased from twelve to twenty-eight. The great chemical combine, I. G. Farbenindustrie, was reorganized, creating three chemical companies and six concerns in related fields, its patents and trade-marks being divided among these and other firms. Similar action was taken in other industries. In 1951 the High Com-

[2] Ben W. Lewis, *Price and Production Control in British Industry* (Public Policy Pamphlet No. 25, University of Chicago Press), pp. 1–2.

[3] *Ibid.*, p. 16.

mission announced that it would relinquish its power over industrial organization when the government of western Germany should enact an adequate law of its own. In 1952 and thereafter, antimonopoly legislation was proposed by the administration of Chancellor Adenauer. Under these proposals, combinations and agreements to restrain competition were to be forbidden unless confined to standardization of products or terms of sale or explicitly permitted by a cartel authority. Such permission, moreover, was to be given only for export trade, for schemes that rationalized an industry without fixing prices or curtailing output, and to prevent plants from closing during a depression. The enactment of any such measure has been vigorously opposed by German industrialists, who reject the idea of competition as alien to their philosophy and still profess to find in cartelization their only hope for future strength and stability. It has also been opposed by the labor unions, who see in competition a threat to job security. In the judgment of most observers, German industry will be recartelized within the next few years.

In Japan, under General Douglas MacArthur, Supreme Commander of the Allied Powers, a similar policy of deconcentration and decartelization was pursued. In 1946 the securities of the chief Zaibatsu holding companies were turned over to a liquidation commission and the companies were dissolved. In 1947 the commission was authorized to designate other concerns as involving excessive concentration and to order their reorganization. More than 300 concerns were so designated and thirty of them were reorganized. Six hundred companies were required to divest themselves of holdings of securities. Twelve hundred cartels were dissolved. In 1948, under the guidance of SCAP, the Japanese government enacted an antimonopoly law. This measure prohibited unfair methods of competition and unreasonable restraints of trade, while permitting collective activities of the types allowed in the United States. It was to be administered by a Fair Trade Commission, similar in character to the American FTC. In practice the Commission showed little enthusiasm for its task, busying itself, in the main, with trivia. In 1952 Japan regained its sovereignty. In 1953 it amended the antimonopoly law to permit cartel agreements, with the Commission's consent, in foreign trade, during periods of depression in domestic trade, and where needed to promote the improvement of technology and the reduction of costs. It also legalized resale price maintenance, intercorporate stockholdings, and interlocking managements. Further modifications were in prospect. In Japan, as in Germany, the policy of maintaining competition is unwelcome, having been imposed by an external force. Rejected by business, it has found no basis in popular support.

Postwar Movement against Restrictive Practices

In an effort to promote world-wide economic reconstruction in the years that followed the war, the United States made large loans and grants to other countries, and took the lead in a program of reducing barriers to trade. And since it appeared that the gains achieved in this way might well be offset by a renewal of monopolistic practices, American officials also sought to persuade other nations to adopt measures whereby competition could be maintained. This process of persuasion was carried forward in the course of negotiations dealing with a proposal for an International Trade Organization, the adoption of the General Agreement on Tariffs and Trade, the conclusion of several treaties of friendship, commerce, and navigation, the inauguration and operation of the Marshall Plan for economic aid to Europe, and the development of broader programs of technical co-operation, economic assistance, and military aid. As a result—in part at least—of these efforts, policy toward restrictive business practices came to be reconsidered by thirty countries in various parts of the world. Constitutional provisions conferring power to nationalize private monopolies were adopted by France in 1946 and by Italy in 1947. New regulatory laws were enacted by Great Britain in 1948, by Denmark and South Africa in 1949, by Belgium in 1950, by Austria and India in 1951, and by Sweden in 1953. And further legislation was under consideration in France, Italy, Switzerland, and the Netherlands.

The new laws, in general, do not prohibit combinations or cartels as such, but attempt to insure that their monopolistic powers are not abused. Typically, they seek to influence business policy by providing for the collection of information and the publication of reports. In some cases, they authorize *ad hoc* investigations in the form of special studies or general surveys. In others, they require that information be collected and published on a continuing basis by a special commission or a department of the government. Some of them contemplate further parliamentary action in cases of adverse reports. A few of them require that cartel agreements be registered. This requirement, of course, may be a mere formality. But it becomes important if registration is denied, suspended, or terminated in cases of abuse. In Denmark, Norway, and Sweden, for instance, the requirement appears to have had a regulatory effect.

In 1953 the Swedish Riksdag passed another law, creating a Free Trade Board and giving it two duties to perform. First, it was to undertake to eliminate the harmful effects of restrictive practices, such as price fixing, market sharing, and discrimination, by entering into negotiations with the companies concerned. But it was given no coercive power. Second, the law prohibited resale price maintenance and bidding cartels, and authorized the board to grant or reject applications for exemptions from this rule. Participants in price maintenance schemes and bidding rings not thus exempted are liable to punishment.

The British Monopolies Act of 1948

The British Monopolies and Restrictive Practises (Inquiry and Control) Act of 1948 applies where a third or more of any product is bought or sold by a single enterprise, or by two or more enterprises who have an expressed or tacit agreement to limit competition. It does not apply, however, to the nationalized industries or to private monopolies approved by other laws. The Act creates a Monopolies and Restrictive Practises Commission, consisting of ten members appointed by the Board of Trade, an agency corresponding to the Department of Commerce in the United States. The Commission is charged with the duty of investigating particular industries or business practices referred to it by the Board of Trade and reporting its findings together with recommendations designed to remedy or prevent any practices which it deems to operate against the public interest. In interpreting the public interest, the Commission is instructed to consider the need to achieve:

a) the production, treatment, and distribution by the most efficient and economical means of goods of such types and qualities, in such volume and at such prices as will best meet the requirements of home and overseas markets;
b) the organization of industry and trade in such a way that their efficiency is progressively increased and new enterprise is encouraged;
c) the fullest use and best distribution of men, materials, and industrial capacity in the United Kingdom; and
d) the development of technical improvements and the expansion of existing markets and the opening up of new markets.

The Board of Trade may propose remedial action to companies covered by the Commission's recommendations, and may request the Commission to report on whether and how far its proposals have been carried out. The Ministers responsible for different industries are also empowered to give effect to such recommendations by preparing orders prohibiting restrictive agreements, boycotts, conditional sales, and preferential terms, and presenting them for approval by Parliament. No criminal penalties are provided. But the government or any person who claims injury may bring a civil suit for appropriate relief.

In 1953 the Monopolies Commission had a staff of 54 persons and a budget of £70,000. In its first four years, it had been asked to make twelve investigations and had prepared seven reports. In general, the Commission has not attacked great size in business, but has concerned itself with abuses of the power that size confers. It has not attacked agreements fixing prices, as such, but has criticized the establishment of prices that appear to be unreasonably high. It has approved the maintenance of resale prices by producers but has disapproved their enforcement by collective action. The Commission has denounced measures that limit freedom of entry to markets, such as exclusive dealing, discrimination, and boycotts. And it has condemned production control and quota schemes. Its recommendations, up to 1953, had called for little governmental action, leaving reform to the industries concerned. An order had been issued in a single case. Elsewhere the Board of Trade had confined itself to making proposals for remedies.

The British program has its weaknesses. The Commission's staff and its appropriation are small; its coverage is limited and its progress slow. Penalties are lacking; reliance on persuasion and publicity may not suffice to protect the public interest. But the law does mark a beginning. It makes possible the steady accumulation of knowledge and the formulation of policy through a case-by-case approach. The Commission has the support of both political parties. The only change in prospect is an increase in its size, enabling it to enlarge the volume of its work.

THE PREVENTION OF COMPETITION

In other countries, as in the United States, governments have undertaken to protect producers by suppressing competition during certain periods and in certain industries. Almost everywhere, during the Great Depression of the thirties, restrictions by trade associations were made permissive or compulsory. In some cases, moreover, laws were passed establishing minimum prices or forbidding sales below cost. Where antimonopoly laws have been adopted, export associations, trade unions, and agricultural co-operatives are frequently exempt. Resale price maintenance is disapproved in Canada, Brazil, and Sweden, but permitted elsewhere. And in the production and distribution of agricultural products, throughout the world, prevention of competition is the general rule.

Depression Policies

During the Great Depression, many governments sought to forestall destructive competition by encouraging or compelling trade associations to fix prices, curtail output, and eliminate surplus capacity. In some countries, such measures were limited to certain industries: to coal, textiles, and shipbuilding in Great Britain, to coal, silk, and shoes in France, to dairy products and embroidery in Switzerland. Elsewhere, such restraints were general. In some cases, cartelization was permissive, as it was in Mexico under the Monopoly Act of 1931. In others, cartel restrictions were made binding on all producers if a majority—or two thirds—of them approved. This was true under laws that were passed in Japan in 1931 and in the Netherlands, Belgium, and France in 1935. The Dutch and Belgian laws, however, were little used. And the French law, confined to the silk industry, never took effect. Under legislation enacted in Great Britain, Italy, and Germany, cartelization could be made compulsory. The British legislation, however, was confined to a few industries. And the Italian government never exercised its power to compel participation in cartels. It was only in Germany that such participation was generally required. Here, under a Nazi decree of 1933, the Ministry of Economics was empowered to establish a cartel in any industry, to compel outsiders to join, and to exclude nonmembers from the field. And, thereafter, this power was used in organizing German industry for war. In many countries, cartels survived the depression and the war. But outside of agriculture, they have ceased to be compulsory.

Agricultural Policies

Almost everywhere, during World War I, agriculture was closely controlled. After the war free markets were re-established. But during the Great Depression controls were again imposed. And, since that time they have never been removed. In other countries, as in the United States, farmers are politically powerful. And they have called on governments to protect them against the risks encountered in free markets and the adjustments that the unimpeded operation of such markets would require. As a result, the allocation of resources in agriculture today is generally influenced by agreements among producers or determined by governments themselves.

In one place or another, throughout the world, controls similar to each of those imposed in the United States are to be found. The power to regulate markets is conferred upon producer and distributor cartels and observance of cartel restraints is made compulsory. The prices of basic crops are supported by governments. Commodities are bought and stored. Surpluses are diverted to industrial uses or fed to livestock or to school children. Some of the surpluses are dumped abroad. In a few cases, moreover, products are sold in the market for what they will bring and farmers are paid an outright subsidy. And for various crops in different countries, there are production and marketing controls.

In Great Britain, from World War II until 1954, trade in agricultural products was handled largely by the government. During this period, markets were assured and minimum prices were guaranteed for two to four years at a time, such guarantees being provided for three fourths of the output of the British Isles. In 1954 private trading was restored but prices still were guaranteed. In the case of grains, the government sets a standard price. If the farmer gets less than this in the market, the government gives him the difference between his average realization and the standard price in the form of a subsidy called a "deficiency payment." In the case of eggs and potatoes, minimum prices are fixed and the government makes up the difference on any sales that are made for less. With livestock, minimum prices on individual transactions as well as standard prices, averaged for all sales, are assured. For many years, moreover, boards of producers have been authorized to fix prices, curtail production, and assign quotas. And with some products—milk among them—this is done.

In other countries of the British Commonwealth exports of foodstuffs are handled by governments, shipments being made largely to the United Kingdom on long-term contracts by state trading agencies. In Canada a Wheat Board monopolizes trade in wheat. An Agricultural Prices Support

Board is authorized to establish minimum prices for other products and has done so, on an *ad hoc* basis, from time to time. In Australia domestic prices are fixed at levels designed to cover costs of production. Returns from exports and domestic sales are pooled, producers being paid an average price. In New Zealand the government undertakes to stabilize prices by taxing exports in periods when prices are high and paying subsidies in periods when they are low. In South Africa commodity boards engage in the business of buying, processing, storing, and selling many products, monopolizing foreign sales of some and both domestic and foreign sales of others, and affect the production and sale of other products by establishing quotas and fixing prices.

In western Europe, also, there are extensive controls. Imports of competitive foodstuffs are restricted and domestic production is subsidized. In Belgium and the Netherlands domestic wheat must be mixed with imported wheat in making flour. In the Netherlands, too, semigovernmental monopolies are empowered to fix prices, control production, and regulate trade. In Norway and Sweden the prices of agricultural products are adjusted in accordance with an index of parity. In Norway these prices are related to the cost of living and are raised when wages rise. In Sweden they are related to costs of production, the purpose being to maintain the relation between the farmer's income and his costs that existed in 1938–39. In other countries the agricultural programs are narrower in scope. But almost everywhere the prices paid domestic producers are held at levels higher than those obtaining in other markets of the world.

So, too, with Latin America. In Mexico the production and distribution of various commodities are controlled by government corporations and by producers' co-operatives. In Cuba the sugar industry is rigidly controlled. In Argentina the government monopolizes all trade in wheat and foreign sales of other commodities, determining domestic prices by fixing the amounts that it will pay. Here, exceptionally, the Peron regime deliberately kept these prices down, seeking to finance its other activities by buying low and selling high. As a result, production and exports declined, and the prices paid to farmers had to be raised. In Brazil, on several occasions, beginning in 1906, the government undertook to raise the price of coffee by purchasing supplies and withholding them from the market. During the thirties, new plantings were restricted, and stocks equivalent to three years consumption were burned or dumped at sea. Now, Brazil has lost its dominant position in the coffee market. But the production and sale of coffee and other export crops are still subject to control by marketing monopolies. Prices are fixed, quotas assigned, and exports regulated by government licenses.

INTERNATIONAL AGREEMENTS

Where markets extend beyond national boundaries, competition can neither be promoted nor prevented by the independent action of individual governments. Here, if governments are to exercise control, they must do so through the medium of international agreements. Such an agreement was negotiated, between 1946 and 1948, for the purpose of controlling the practices of international combines and cartels; but failing ratification by the governments concerned, it has never taken effect. Provisions designed to maintain competition are included, however, in the Schuman Plan treaty constituting the European Coal and Steel Community which was ratified in 1952. And numerous agreements have been concluded, from time to time, for the purpose of regulating trade in aquatic and agricultural products and other raw materials. Through international as well as national action, governments have sought to check monopoly in manufacturing and to check competition in the extractive industries.

International Combines and Cartels

Restraints within domestic markets have their counterparts in the restrictions that producers have imposed on international trade. In fact, the two are intimately related. For, unless high tariffs and shipping costs prevent it, monopolistic arrangements in domestic markets may be destroyed by competition from abroad. And, unless domestic markets are effectively controlled, international monopoly may be destroyed by competition at home.

The tightest form of control over world markets is that accomplished through the international combine. In this case, the holding company device is commonly employed to bring under common ownership and management a number of enterprises that have been incorporated to operate in different countries. A looser form of organization than the combine, the international cartel may be equally effective in eliminating competition in world trade. Price-fixing cartels have controlled the rates charged for international services and pegged the prices of goods sold in world markets. Territorial cartels have distributed exclusive sales areas among their participants. Quota cartels have curtailed production and exports and allocated output and export shares. Selling syndicates have handled foreign orders, fixed prices, and apportioned sales. Patent cartels have operated international patent pools, including in their licenses provisions which have enforced a partition of the markets of the world.

Like the domestic cartel, the international cartel operates to bar new enterprise, to obstruct technological improvement, to impair productive efficiency, to check competition, and thus to hold down planes of living. Like the tariff, it operates to restrict trade. But, unlike the tariff, it is set up by businessmen, without public representation or responsibility, for private ends. It thus usurps the authority of governments and delivers the determination of foreign economic policy into private hands.

Control of Restrictive Practices

Where monopoly is to be controlled by international action, the methods used by national governments are not available. Nations are not now ready to confer upon an intergovernmental agency the powers required to break up existing combines or cartels or to prevent new ones from being formed. Nor are they prepared to delegate to such an agency the power to regulate rates and services. Action must therefore be taken by individual governments. And it must rest upon the voluntary co-operation of national states. Such a plan was embodied in the proposed Charter for an International Trade Organization adopted by delegations from more than fifty countries at a United Nations conference in Havana, Cuba, in 1948.

Under the terms of the Charter, each nation belonging to the ITO was to take all possible steps, within its jurisdiction, to insure that commercial enterprises, whether private or public, did not engage in practices which restrained competition, limited access to markets, or fostered monopolistic control in international trade, whenever such practices interfered with the expansion of production or trade. These practices were listed as including such matters as fixing prices or terms of purchase or sale, discriminating against particular enterprises or excluding them from markets, allocating markets, production, customers, sales, or purchases, curtailing output or fixing production quotas, agreeing to prevent the development or application of technology, and extending the use of rights acquired under patents, trade-marks, and copyrights to products or activities not within the scope of such grants. Upon complaint by a member, the ITO was to make an investigation, hold hearings, and if it found that the practices in question had harmful effects, was to request the members concerned to take remedial action and might itself recommend specific remedies. No member was compelled to accept the specific recommendations. But each of them was required to consider such recommendations in determining the action it would take to carry out its general obligation to suppress monopolistic practices. And if a member failed to act, it might be penalized by withdrawal of tariff cuts that had been granted on its goods.

The Havana Charter was not ratified; its chapter on restrictive business practices never took effect. In 1951, however, the Economic and Social Council of the United Nations adopted a resolution recommending that nations adhere to the policy it embodied, and set up a committee to formulate proposals for further international action in the field. In 1953 the committee reported, proposing a revision of the chapter designed to make it effective in itself without the rest of the ITO. No action has been taken since that time.

The Schuman Plan

The European Coal and Steel Community, originating in a plan proposed by Robert Schuman when he was Foreign Minister of France, became a reality in 1953 when a common market for coal, iron ore, scrap, and steel was created in Western Europe by the removal of national barriers to trade in these commodities among France, Belgium, the Netherlands, Luxembourg, Western Germany, and Italy. The Community is governed by a High Authority set up by the six governments. This body, though subject to certain limitations imposed by a Council of Ministers and an Assembly consisting of members of parliaments, possesses some of the attributes of sovereignty. It can issue directives that are binding on individual enterprises and impose fines on those who do not conform. It can levy taxes and pay subsidies. And it can borrow money, make loans, and guarantee loans made by others. These powers are to be used to strengthen the coal and steel industries of the region by retiring inefficient mines and plants, modernizing other facilities, and promoting expansion at points where costs are low. The change is to be gradual, transitional assistance being extended to those displaced in the process of relocation.

The treaty constituting the community contains a number of provisions that are designed to curb the power of private monopoly. It permits associations of producers but forbids: "all agreements among enterprises, all decisions of associations of enterprises, and all concerted practices, which would tend, directly or indirectly, to prevent, restrict or impede the normal operation of competition within the single market, and in particular: (*a*) to fix or influence prices; (*b*) to restrict or control production, technical development or investments; (*c*) to allocate markets, products, customers or sources of supply."[4] The treaty permits existing combinations to stand, but forbids new combinations unless approved by the High Authority, and directs the High Authority to approve them only when they will not enable enterprises "to influence prices, to control or restrain production or marketing or to impair the maintenance of effective competition." Where such combinations do occur, it empowers the High Authority to "order the separation of the enterprises or assets wrongly concentrated or the cessation of common control." And in any cases where enterprises have "a dominant position which protects them from effective competition," it permits the High Authority, after consulting with the government concerned, to "fix the prices and conditions of sale to be applied by the enterprise in question, or establish manufacturing or delivery programs to be executed by it."[5]

These passages have a familiar ring. In spirit, they seem to parallel the provisions of the antitrust laws forbidding agreements and combinations in restraint of trade and those of the public utility laws authorizing administrative regulation of monopolistic rates and services. But the treaty does more than this. It permits freight absorption and can be interpreted to permit the establishment of a basing point system of delivered pricing. In periods when "a serious shortage" exists, it empowers the High Authority to fix maximum prices and to allocate raw materials and finished

[4] *Treaty Constituting the European Coal and Steel Community*, Article LXV.
[5] *Ibid.*, Article LXVI.

products. And in periods when "a manifest crisis exists or is imminent," it empowers the High Authority to fix minimum prices and to establish production quotas.[6] Such actions, however, must be approved by the Council of Ministers.

Two questions are raised by these provisions. Will independent freight absorption operate to make the market more competitive, or will systematic equalization of prices at points of delivery operate to make it less so? Will conditions usually be found sufficiently normal to permit enforcement of the antimonopoly rules, or so abnormal as to justify the use of price and quantity controls? In the former cases, the discipline of the market may be restored. In the latter, it will not. But even here, the powers once exercised by combines and cartels will have been taken over by a public body responsible to governments. The hold of private monopoly on the coal and steel industry of Western Europe has undoubtedly been broken. The High Authority will not permit cartels or combinations controlling prices and production. It is certain to be jealous of its powers.

Intergovernmental Commodity Agreements

Governments have frequently entered into agreements designed to check competitive production and trade in world markets. It has been the purpose of such agreements (1) to conserve seals, whales, and other marine life in international waters, (2) to curb the manufacture and distribution of narcotic drugs, (3) to allocate scarce materials among claimant nations in time of war, and (4) to stabilize or to raise the prices of commodities in the interest of producers. It is only with agreements for the last of these purposes that we are here concerned.

Agreements to control prices have been concluded for different commodities at different times. In the twenties, there were agreements on tin and rubber; in the thirties, on tin, rubber, tea, wheat, and sugar; in the forties, on coffee and wheat; in the fifties, on wheat and sugar. Such agreements are of three major types: (1) long-term multilateral contracts for purchases and sales, (2) arrangements controlling exports, imports, stocks, production, and prices, and (3) plans for international buffer stocks. The first type is represented by the wheat agreements of the forties and the fifties. The second includes most of the other agreements of the past decades. The buffer-stock device, though repeatedly recommended, has seldom been adopted on an international scale.

In the wheat agreements, the nations participating fixed an upper and a lower price. The exporting countries agreed to sell certain quantities of wheat at the upper figure if the market price should rise above it, and the importing countries agreed to buy certain quantities at the lower figure if the price should fall below it. For those inside the agreement, the range of fluctuations in price was limited. For those outside, it was in-

[6] *Ibid.*, Articles LVIII, LIX, LXI.

creased, since the insiders could not raise prices in the free market by buying there when they were low, or reduce prices in the free market by selling there when they were high. The exporting countries placed a bet, in effect, that prices were going to fall. If so, they were protected. But if prices rose, they would have had to sell for less than they would otherwise have been able to get. The importing countries bet that prices were going to rise. And here, they were protected. But if prices fell, they would have to buy for more than they would otherwise have had to pay. There was danger, therefore, that the plan would not work. In practice, when market prices rose above the maximum, the United States continued to deliver, subsidizing its exports and charging its losses to the taxpayer. Since prices did not fall below the minimum, the importing countries were not called upon to honor their commitment to buy. It should be noted, however, that Great Britain, the principal importer, withdrew from the agreement when it was renewed in 1953.

Under commodity control agreements, exports and imports have been restricted through taxation, prohibition, the imposition of quotas, and the requirement of licenses. Subsidies have been paid and loans made to assist producers in withholding their supplies. Governments themselves have bought, stored, and held commodities. Limitations have been imposed upon acreage sown, livestock kept, and minerals developed and, at a later stage, upon crops gathered, livestock slaughtered, and mines worked. In cases where production could not easily be curtailed, portions of a crop have been destroyed. Under some agreements, prices have thus been influenced indirectly. Under others, minimum prices have been fixed.

Such agreements have been subject to serious abuse. Nominally they have been devised for the purpose of stabilizing prices. But the levels at which this stabilization has been attempted have almost invariably been higher than those that could be justified by conditions of demand and supply. Quotas have been allocated on the basis of past performance rather than prospective efficiency. Production has thus been frozen to uneconomic locations; high-cost production has been kept in operation, low-cost production prevented, and average costs increased. Little effort has been made to enhance efficiency, to expand consumption, to promote the diversion of resources into more productive activities. In few cases have importing countries been accorded a voice in the negotiation or administration of an agreement or the interests of consumers taken into account.

Under a buffer-stock scheme, supposedly, violent short-run fluctuations in price would be prevented and gradual long-run adjustments permitted to occur. Trade and production could thus be freed from regulation and resources shifted in response to changes in demand. An international agency would control the market by establishing a range of prices, buying when they fell below the minimum and selling when they rose above the maximum. Its own holdings would be kept small by moving its range of prices to the proper point; the bulk of world trade would be left in private hands. The agency would be established with capital supplied by governments; it would finance its operations by private borrowing. In the long run, it would just break even; its profits and its losses, over time, would cancel out.

In theory, certainly, the plan is sound. In practice, however, it may be doubted that it could be carried out. The buffer-stock agency would be set up and controlled by governments; it would be subject to political pressures; and these pressures would be directed toward assuring producers the highest prices obtainable. Efforts would inevitably be made to set the minimum and maximum figures at levels that would not be justified. Attempts to reduce these figures would encounter determined resistance. The agency's prices, in all probability, would be set too high. As a result, production would be increased, consumption would be curtailed, and stocks would accumulate. Carrying charges would mount; losses would be incurred. From here on, the agency could avoid disaster in only one way. If it were to unload its holdings, prices would fall disastrously. If it were to destroy them or give them away, it would go bankrupt. But gradual liquidation and continued solvency might be possible if production were to be controlled. The scheme thus ends in promoting the very policy it was supposed to prevent. And here, as elsewhere, the consumer bears the cost.

Under the provisions of the ITO Charter, nations would have accepted substantial limitations on their freedom to enter into commodity agreements. Such agreements were to be limited in scope and duration. They were to promote a shift of production to more economic locations and a transfer of resources to more economic employments. They were to afford consuming countries and producing countries an equal voice. And they were to be accompanied, at every stage, by full publicity. These rules were designed to safeguard the interests of consumers, to force adjustments to changing conditions, and to facilitate the early restoration of free markets.

The Charter, as noted above, was never ratified. Committees appointed subsequently to advise the United Nations have looked upon intergovernmental agreements with greater favor, urging their adoption as a means of stabilizing commodity prices. But such agreements are not easy to negotiate. Producers and consumers cannot often agree upon a price. And producers can rarely agree on market shares. It is unlikely, therefore, that such agreements will be numerous.

THE REGULATION OF BUSINESS

Legislation for the protection of consumers, investors, and workers and the conservation of natural resources is found throughout the world, being older and more extensive in certain other countries than it is in the United States. The regulation of rates and services by administrative tribunals, however, is less common abroad than here, since railroads and public utilities are usually owned and operated by governments. Almost everywhere, during World War II, economic activity was subjected to comprehensive controls. When the war ended, many of these controls were dropped. But inflationary pressures persisted and goods continued to be scarce. In some countries, therefore, wartime powers over the allocation of resources were retained. This was true, in particular, under Labor governments in Great Britain and in Norway.

Protective Legislation

Laws regulating the quality of particular foods and beverages were adopted in England, France, and Germany as early as the thirteenth century. Comprehensive laws designed to insure the purity of foods and drugs were enacted in England in 1860, in Germany in 1876, and in France in 1884. Legislation forbidding adulteration and misbranding, enforcing standard weights and measures, requiring grading and inspection of commodities, and regulating trading on commodity markets is now found in nearly every country in the world.

The laws of other industrial countries have always protected investors in corporate securities. In Great Britain and in Europe, the power of incorporation has been exercised by central governments. Debasement of standards through interstate competition has not occurred. In general, promoters are required to provide full information and are held accountable for any statements they have made. Corporations are required to issue adequate reports, and directors are made liable for losses resulting from their misconduct or negligence. Trading on the securities exchanges is subject to strict control. The American legislation of the thirties served merely to afford investors in this country protection of the sort that had long been extended to investors abroad.

Legislation protecting labor dates from the English Health and Morals of Apprentices Act of 1802. Laws limiting the labor of women and children, controlling hazardous occupations, and regulating conditions in factories were enacted first in England and then spread gradually throughout the world. Laws providing for maximum hours and minimum wages, originating in New Zealand in 1894 and in Australia in 1896, were adopted by many other countries in the next thirty years. Social insurance laws were first enacted in Germany: against sickness in 1883, accidents in 1885, and old age in 1889. A law insuring against unemployment was first enacted by Great Britain in 1912. By 1950 more than 20 nations were providing benefits for unemployment and more than 40 for sickness, accidents, old age, and survivorship. Everywhere, outside the totalitarian countries, labor unions are recognized, collective bargaining is practiced, and provision is made for the mediation and arbitration of disputes.

The conservation of natural resources has long been practiced in the more advanced countries of the world. Mineral rights, in Europe, are reserved to governments. Forest services are highly developed and public forests are maintained. Stream pollution is prevented and water resources are rigidly controlled. With resources limited in relation to population, wasteful methods of exploitation were never permitted to go as far as they did in the United States.

Regulation of Monopoly

Experience with the regulation of railways, in Great Britain, ran parallel to that of the United States. A law condemning discrimination was enacted in 1845. But control through judicial processes proved ineffective, as did control by charters and by statutes. In 1873 a Railway and Canal Commission was created and, in 1888, it was given power to determine rates. In 1921 the commission was superseded by a Railway Rates Tribunal. And this body has continued to function, before and since the railroads were nationalized.

In the case of electricity, in Britain, an advisory commission was set up in 1919 to work out plans for the regional integration of local generating and distributing facilities. And in 1926 a Central Electricity Board was created to carry these plans into effect. But these bodies had no authority over rates. For public utilities, in general, the supervision of rates was entrusted to the regular departments of the government. It was only for railroads that the law set up an independent regulatory commission, similar to those established in the United States. And since nationalization, it is only with railroads that the rates set by managements are subject to review.

In Western Europe, likewise, the charges of railroads and public utilities have been supervised, if at all, by the existing ministries. The independent commission has been little used. The comparative absence of regulation is doubtless to be explained by the fact that monopolistic services provided in the United States by private companies have long been provided in Europe through public enterprise.

Comprehensive Planning and Control

In most democratic countries, wartime controls were gradually liquidated after the end of World War II. In a few countries—notably in Great Britain and Norway—they have had a longer life. In Britain, there has been a persisting deficit in the balance of international payments, with imports tending to outrun exports and threatening the adequacy of gold and dollar reserves. As a result, the government has continued to regulate international transactions, controlling foreign exchange, licensing exports and imports, promoting exports, and limiting imports by imposing discriminatory duties and restrictive quotas. Under the Labor government, moreover, Britain took as its objectives, in domestic life, the assurance of full employment, the expansion of social services, and the reduction of inequality. And it pursued these objectives at the cost of inflationary pressures and continued scarcities. To curb inflation, therefore, it retained price controls. And to distribute scarce materials and products, it retained allocation and rationing. But manpower controls were dropped entirely, and all domestic controls were gradually relaxed.

Economic activity is not governed by a comprehensive plan in Great Britain as it is, for instance, in the Soviet Union. The planning staff in Britain, like the Council of Economic Advisers in the United States, prepares estimates of future trends and offers advice as to the direction of public policy. But it issues no directives for industry to carry out. The government, to be sure, possesses extensive powers. But its controls are negative rather than positive. It tells producers what they may not do, not what they must. In Britain, as in other democratic countries, the larger part of economic life is free.

One control, not exercised elsewhere, is important. The government holds a veto on investment. Business cannot raise money by issuing new securities without first obtaining the permission of the Treasury. It cannot construct new plants without first obtaining building permits from the Ministry of Works, the Board of Trade, and the local authorities. It cannot procure materials to build new plants unless its orders are supported by a sponsoring ministry. Control over new investment is thus complete. And it enables the government substantially to influence the future structure and location of industry. This power has been exercised, in the main, with a view to improving Britain's balance of payments by promoting exports and relieving local unemployment by encouraging industry to settle in regions where labor is in surplus.

In Norway, ever since the war, economic activity has been completely planned and controlled. Sweeping powers have been vested by the parliament in an Office of the Price Directorate. This agency prepares annual budgets to govern investment, employment, production, consumption, and foreign trade. It regulates prices, wages, interest, and profits and limits dividends. It tells businessmen what goods to produce, in what quantities, and where they can be sold. It controls quality and can require standardization, modernization, and research. It can prevent the establishment of new enterprises, in any field, and check the expansion of existing firms. In Norway the market has been largely superseded by the state. But the state is not totalitarian; the Price Directorate is still subject to democratic political control.

PUBLIC ENTERPRISE

Public ownership and operation, varying in scope, is found in every country in the world. In certain fields—transportation, communications, and municipal services—outside of the United States, this form of enterprise has long been usual. The movement toward nationalization was speeded, in the twentieth century, by war, depression, and war. World

War I brought communism to Russia. World War II brought it to the countries of Central Europe and to China. The wars and the depression contributed to the spread of public enterprise outside the communist region—in Western Europe and in the underdeveloped areas. Such enterprise, in its present scope, extends from its traditional fields to new industries such as aviation, radio, and television, and to mining, manufacturing, and trade. The tide of nationalization reached its high point during the years of postwar reconstruction in the forties. With disillusionment in the fifties, it started to recede.

Traditional Fields of Public Enterprise

For more than a century governments have monopolized certain industries, operating them as sources of public revenue. From ten to twenty countries, in each case, have thus monopolized tobacco, matches, alcoholic beverages, and salt. In Venezuela, cigarette papers have provided revenue; in Japan, camphor; in India and Thailand, opium. In the Latin countries of Europe and America, in Australia, and elsewhere, governments finance themselves, in part, by conducting public lotteries, having nationalized the gambling industry.

Another long-established field of public enterprise is transportation and communication. Highways and port facilities have been publicly provided everywhere. The railroads of Belgium, Italy, Germany and Switzerland were taken over by governments in the latter years of the nineteenth century. All those of France were taken over by 1937. The railroads of more than fifty countries, including all the major powers but Britain and the United States, were nationalized before World War II. Urban transit systems have been predominantly governmental, as have the subways in all large cities outside the United States, except Madrid. Post offices have always been national undertakings, and the telegraph systems, in most countries, have been developed and operated by the postal authorities. In Germany the telephone service was developed by the state telegraph system. Elsewhere in Europe the telephones were taken over around the turn of the century. By 1950 the service was publicly operated everywhere save in some of the underdeveloped areas and in Brazil, Canada, and the United States.

Public utilities, throughout the world, have long been owned by governments. Water supply, in nearly all large cities, is a public responsibility. Gas and electricity were publicly provided in more than three fourths of the cities of Germany and in half to two thirds of those in Great Britain before 1930. Regional systems for the generation and transmission of electricity were operated by governments in Canada, New Zealand, and South Africa. An authority to develop the power resources of the Rhone was set up in France. The Central Electricity Board, in Great Britain, was given a monopoly of transmission lines by a Conservative government in 1926. The operation of cemeteries, crematoria, and funeral services was undertaken by many cities in Europe, the provision of ice by cities in Italy and England, and the distribution of milk by cities in Italy.

Housing has been supplied by governments for longer periods and in greater quantities in Europe than in the United States. Houses were built by the King of France for silk workers in Paris early in the seventeenth century. In England public housing was first permitted by law in 1851. In Germany and the Netherlands, it dates from 1901. Elsewhere it had its origin in the shortages that followed World War I. In most countries, the governments undertook to stimulate construction by co-operatives, limited-dividend societies, and other private builders by providing subsidies in the form of cheap land, tax exemption, and low-interest loans. But in some cases—notably in the city of Vienna—housing was built and operated by the governments themselves. In Great Britain, between the two world wars, a fourth of the new housing, including virtually all of the rental housing, was constructed by local authorities. After the second war, this program was expanded by the Labor government, four fifths of the new housing being provided through public enterprise.

The Nationalization Movement

The movement toward public ownership was quickened during the thirties and particularly during the forties. It made its appearance not only in the advanced economies of Western Europe, but also in underdeveloped areas throughout the world. Its causes were various. In Britain it found its origin in the tradition of a socialist party, finally come to power, and in proposals for industrial reorganization designed to enhance efficiency. In France it sprang from the syndicalist philosophy that calls for the seizure of power by organized labor and from a desire to punish capitalists who had collaborated with the enemy during World War II. In Italy it began with an effort to protect private enterprises from the consequences of the Great Depression by providing governmental aid. In the underdeveloped areas it gave expression to a world-wide revolt against colonialism and imperialism and to nationalistic demands for economic independence. But however diverse its causes, it led, in every case, to a marked expansion in the scope of public enterprise.

The nationalization program of the Labor Party in Great Britain, effected through measures adopted in 1946, 1947, and 1948, included finance (the Bank of England), Commonwealth communications (civil aviation, cables, and radio), public utilities (gas and electricity), transportation (carriers by rail, by water, and by road), a depressed industry (coal), and another industry that fell into none of these categories (iron and steel). Some of these measures were not controversial. But others, such as those relating to road haulage and to iron and steel, were highly so. The program was carried out by a socialist government. But it was not envisaged as a part of a revolution that would bring about a completely socialized economy. Each case was argued on its merits. And the argument for nationalization ran in terms of its possible contribution to productive efficiency and public responsibility. Coal mining, for instance, was to be made more efficient through reorganization and modernization. The iron and steel industry, already monopolized, was to be made more responsible by transferring its controlling shares from private owners to the government. But Britain was still to have a mixed economy, a fifth of it—more or less—being operated by the state, four fifths of it by private enterprise.

In France the postwar nationalizations included the Bank of France and the four largest commercial banks, the thirty-four largest insurance companies, as much of the coal, gas, and electrical industries as still remained in private hands, the Renault works, and a company manufacturing engines for aeroplanes. In addition, the government extended its participation in mixed companies in a number of different fields: aviation, shipping, motion pictures, broadcasting, news service, chemicals, and petroleum. The French program was inspired by leftists—trade unionists, socialists, and communists—who had played a large part in the resistance movement in France and among the Free French abroad. Nationalization was seen by these groups as affording the means to three ends. It was to promote economic reconstruction. It was to transfer economic power from the capitalists to the workers. And in some cases, such as the Renault works and the aeroplane engine company, it was to punish collaborators. In these cases, the properties were confiscated. But in France, as in Great Britain, compensation was the rule. Today, despite extensive nationalization, the economy of France, like that of Britain, remains predominantly free.

In Italy industries have been made public less by design than by default. An Institute for Industrial Reconstruction, similar to the Reconstruction Finance Corporation in the United States, was set up during the depression of the thirties to extend financial aid to ailing industries. This agency, with its subsidiaries, came to hold the shares of many Italian companies. These holdings, moreover, were continued and increased during and after the war. As a result, the Institute controls a third of Italian industry, owning all or nearly all of the stock in coal mining, shipbuilding, shipping, and motion pictures, a large part of that in iron and steel plants and machine shops, and about a quarter of that in electricity and other public utilities. In addition, the government owns the country's five largest banks, the railroads and the airlines, the telephone, telegraph, and radio systems, and the petroleum industry. Public enterprise, though adopted without reference to any logical pattern, is thus as extensive in Italy as it is in Britain or in France.

Nationalization, in underdeveloped countries, has been directed primarily toward public utilities and minerals. The railway, urban transit, power, and communications systems of these countries have usually been provided by foreign capital. In many cases, the governments of such countries have expelled the foreign owners by buying up their shares. In this way, for instance, Argentina acquired control of its transport and utility systems during and after World War II. Exploitation of the natural resources of underdeveloped countries has also been undertaken by foreigners. In some cases these countries have been treated badly. In others, they have been treated well. But in all cases they have sought to shake off foreign control and to manage their resources by themselves. Thus, foreign oil properties were taken over by Mexico in 1938 and by Iran in 1951, and all future oil developments in Brazil were monopolized by the government in 1953. So, too, the tin companies of Bolivia were nationalized in 1952 and a large part of the land owned by the United Fruit Company was taken by Guatamala in 1953. Here, nationalism has been the motive and socialism has merely been the means.

Among all underdeveloped countries, industrialization and economic independence are major goals of policy. If new industries are not to be created by foreigners, they must be provided or promoted by the governments. Where basic industries—such as transport, communications, and power—are lacking, they must be supplied through public enterprise. And where a shortage of capital prevents the establishment of private enterprises in manufacturing and other fields, the government must sponsor new ventures and underwrite their shares. This is the function, for instance, of an Industrial Development Corporation in Pakistan and a National Development Company in the Philippines. Here, again, nationalism is the motive and socialism but a means. But broad areas of economic activity have thus been passing into governmental hands.

The Scope of Public Enterprise

The fields in which public enterprise is most common, throughout the world, are banking, transportation, communications, and public utilities. In nearly all countries, the central banks are now owned by governments. And in some countries, other banks and insurance companies have been nationalized. Railroads, outside the United States, have long been public undertakings. Aviation, in 1952, was entirely public in fifteen countries, partly public and partly private in seven, and wholly private in twenty-eight. Shipping companies are controlled by the governments of France, Italy, and the Netherlands. A merchant fleet is operated by Argentina; another is jointly owned by Venezuela, Colombia, and Ecuador. Telegraph and telephone services are usually governmental. Radio and television broadcasting, in 1950, was wholly or partly a public enterprise in most countries, including those of Western Europe and the British Commonwealth, being wholly private only in Sweden, in Latin America, and in the United States. Urban transit, gas, and electricity are characteristically provided by governments. And rental housing, in cities, is widely accepted as a public responsibility.

Several governments are engaged in mining, a few in manufacturing, and many more in foreign trade. Great Britain has owned the controlling shares in the Anglo-Iranian Oil Company since 1914. Great Britain, the Netherlands, France, and Italy operate coal mines. And Turkey is in the business of mining coal, copper, chrome, and manganese. Mineral resources have been nationalized by Mexico, Brazil, Bolivia, and Argentina. Oil is produced by Mexico, tin by Bolivia. Sales of nitrates and copper are handled by the government of Chile. Public enterprise in manufacturing is less usual, being confined to a few countries and a few industries. State trading, adopted by some countries during the depression and by most countries during the war, was designed in part to reduce the cost of necessary imports, as in the case of Great Britain. It was designed, in larger part, to increase the prices and the incomes of domestic producers of foodstuffs and raw materials. A substantial part of the world's trade is still carried on by governments.

Denationalization

In Great Britain and in Western Europe, the process of nationalization appears to have run its course. The high hopes held out at the end of the war have failed of fulfillment. Consumers, workers, and politicians alike have been disillusioned. There has been a widespread loss of faith in the benefits of public enterprise. As a result, the proponents of nationalization have come to regard the process as completed and have ceased to urge its extension to other fields. The opponents, moreover, have insisted that the process be reversed. In Great Britain, the Trades Union Congress and the Labor Party, while continuing to pay lip service to socialism, no longer propose that further industries be socialized. And the Conservative government has kept its promise to denationalize iron and steel and the road haulage industry. A bill repealing the nationalization of iron and steel was passed by Parliament in 1952. A bill providing for the sale of the government's fleet of 40,000 lorries was passed in 1953. In the other industries taken over by Labor, however, the Conservatives permitted public enterprise to stand.

SUGGESTIONS FOR FURTHER READING

The laws governing business, up to 1940, in Great Britain, France, and Germany, and in Argentina, Brazil, Chile, and Mexico are described in Temporary National Economic Committee Monograph No. 40, *Regulation of Economic Activities in Foreign Countries* (Washington: Government Printing Office, 1941). Legislation up to 1952 in twenty countries is outlined in the report of the Department of State on *Foreign Legislation Concerning Monopoly and Cartel Practices* to the Subcommittee on Monopoly of the Select Committee on Small Business of the U.S. Senate (82d Congress, 2d Session, Subcommittee Print No. 5, 1952), Part II. The laws of countries belonging to the United Nations are analyzed in United Nations, Economic and Social Council, *Analysis of Governmental Measures Relating to Restrictive Business Practices*, March 30, 1953 (mimeographed), and in Sigmund Timberg, "Restrictive Business Practices," *American Journal of Comparative Law,* II (1953) 445–73. The structure of markets and the laws governing competition and monopoly in Great Britain, Canada, and South Africa, and in France, Italy, Western Germany, Norway, and Denmark, as of 1951, are described in Edward H. Chamberlin (ed.), *Monopoly and Competition and Their Regulation* (London: Macmillan & Co., Ltd., 1954), pp. 3–109, 141–87, and 359–85. The detailed controls obtaining in Great Britain are discussed by Political and Economic Planning in *Government and Industry* (London: Political and Economic Planning, 1952). Experience with the British Monopolies Act of 1948 is considered by PEP in "The Monopolies Commission," *Planning* XIX (1953), 185–200, and by C. D. Harburg and Leo J. Raskind in "The British Approach to Monopoly Control," *Quarterly Journal of Economics,* XLII (1953), 380–407. Foreign agricultural policies are outlined in Karl Brandt, *The Reconstruction of World Agriculture* (New York: W. W. Norton, 1945), in John D. Black and Maxine E. Kiefer, *Future Food and Agriculture Policy* (New York: McGraw-Hill Book Co., 1948), and in the monthly magazine *Foreign Agriculture* published by the Foreign Agricultural Service of the U.S. Department of Agriculture.

The nationalization movement in Great Britain is described in Robert A. Brady, *Crisis in Britain* (Berkeley: University of California Press, 1950), and in Ben W. Lewis, *British Planning and Nationalization* (New York: Twentieth Century Fund, 1952). Nationalization in France is discussed by Henry P. De Vries and B. H. Hoeniger in "Post-Liberation Nationalizations in France," *Columbia Law Review,* L (1950), 629–56, by Adolf Sturmthal in "The Structure of Nationalized Enterprises in France," *Political Science Quarterly,* LXII (1952), 357–77, and by J. M. Jeanneney in Edward H. Chamberlin's *Monopoly and Competition and Their Regulation,* cited above, pp. 471–92.

The story of international negotiations directed toward the control of cartels is told in Clair Wilcox, *A Charter for World Trade* (New York: Macmillan Co., 1949), chap. x; in William Diebold, Jr., *Trade and Payments in Western Europe* (New York: Harper & Bros., 1952), chap. xiv, and in the State Department report cited above, Part III. The text of the Schuman Plan merits careful study. It is given in *The Schuman Plan Constituting a European Coal and Steel Community* (Washington: Department of State, Publication 4173, 1951). Excellent analyses of the significance and the operation of the plan are given by William H. Parker in "The Schuman Plan—A Preliminary Prediction," *International Organization,* VI (1952), 381–95, and by Horst Mendershausen in "First Tests of the Schuman Plan," *Review of Economics and Statistics,* XXXV (1953), 269–88. The different types of intergovernmental commodity agreements are discussed by Joseph S. Davis in *International Commodity Agreements: Hope, Illusion, or Menace?* (New York: Committee on International Economic Policy, 1947), and by D. Gale Johnson in *Trade and Agriculture* (New York: John Wiley, 1950), chap. ix. Negotiations relating to such agreements are described in Wilcox, *op. cit.,* chap. xi. The conclusion of agreements for the purpose of stabilizing international commodity markets is recommended in *Measures for International Economic Stability* (New York: United Nations, Department of Economic Affairs, 1951), chap. ii, and in *Resources for Freedom,* Report by the President's Materials Policy Commission (Washington: Government Printing Office, 1952), Vol. I, chap. xv.

Chapter 28 THE CONTROL OF ATOMIC ENERGY

On August 6, 1945, President Truman announced that an atomic bomb had been exploded over Hiroshima. More than 70,000 people had been killed; as many more had been wounded; a sizable city had virtually been destroyed. On August 9, a second bomb was exploded over Nagasaki. On August 10, Japan surrendered. These dramatic events marked the culmination of an enterprise in which the government of the United States had been engaged for the previous five years. In 1939 Albert Einstein had written to President Roosevelt, informing him that scientists had succeeded in splitting the atom, thus releasing a force of potential military use. In 1940 the government initiated a program of atomic research. In 1942 the first self-sustaining nuclear chain reaction was achieved in a laboratory at the University of Chicago. In the next year work was started on a wartime program that eventually cost nearly two billion dollars. Great plants were built to manufacture bomb materials at secret cities in Tennessee and in the State of Washington. A secret laboratory was built atop a mesa in New Mexico where physicists devised the bomb. On July 16, 1945, the first bomb was exploded experimentally on the desert in New Mexico. Within a month World War II had come to an end. The American people were faced with a new problem. How, now, was the power they had unleashed to be controlled?

THE PATTERN OF DOMESTIC CONTROL

All of the atomic facilities had been built and were owned and operated by the government. There was general agreement that this should continue to be the case. The processes employed were dangerous in themselves; the products were weapons; secrecy was demanded; tight control was required. But what agency should be given authority to exercise control? During the war, the program had been administered by the Manhattan Engineer District, a unit established for the purpose by the Army Corps of Engineers. Now, the question was whether control should be left with the military or turned over to civilians. Atomic energy could be used in weapons. It might also come to be employed for peaceful purposes. Military control might hamper these developments. The May-Johnson Bill, fathered in the Pentagon, would have perpetuated such control. It evoked determined opposition. A committee was appointed by the Senate to work out another approach. Its proposals, embodied in a bill sponsored by its chairman, Senator Brien McMahon of Connecticut, provided for control by an Atomic Energy Commission, composed of civilians, with decisions affecting military uses to be made in consultation with a Military Liaison Committee, any differences between the two bodies being resolved by the President. The McMahon Bill was passed by the Congress with an overwhelming vote. Signed by President Truman, it became the Atomic Energy Act of 1946.

Atomic Energy Act of 1946

The Atomic Energy Commission, set up by the new law, consists of five members appointed by the President, with the consent of the Senate, for terms of five years each, their terms being so arranged that one appointment is to be made each year. The Chairman, designated by the President, receives a salary of $20,000, the other members $18,000 each. The Commission is a policy board, administrative authority being delegated to a General Manager, appointed by the Commission at a salary of $20,000. Detailed operations are carried on by four divisions: Research, Engineering, Production, and Military Applications. The Commission is advised by the Military Liaison Committee and by a General Advisory Committee of civilian scientists. Its work is subject to oversight by a Joint Committee composed of members of the Senate and the House.

The law permits private enterprise in mining the ores—uranium and thorium—from which fissionable materials are produced. But from this point on, every step is kept under strict control. Until the law was amended in 1954, private ownership of fissionable materials, of facilities for their production, and of patents covering the productive processes was forbidden. The production, exportation, and importation of such materials were made government monopolies. The Commission is empowered to issue licenses to govern the sale and delivery of the original ores, the manufacture of facilities for the production of fissionables, and the manufacture of equipment for their use. It is authorized to lend or lease fissionables, in safe quantities, with or without charge, for research or medical therapy or, under license, for industrial use. In the latter case, it must notify the Congress and wait ninety days before its license takes effect. The Commission retains title to such materials and controls their transfer. It may also distribute non-fissionable radioactive by-products for use in research, medicine, and industry. Persons engaging in regulated activities without its permission are subject to heavy penalties.

The Manhattan Engineer District did not itself conduct the researches, construct the facilities, or carry on the operations through which the materials for the atomic weapon were produced. Instead, it accomplished its purpose by entering into agreements with private contractors. Continuance of this procedure is authorized by the Act of 1946. The Atomic Energy Commission may itself engage in research, construction, and production, or it may employ private contractors. Its contractors must submit reports, permit inspection, and obey its regulations respecting safety and security. But the terms of its contracts, in the main, are within its own discretion. Competitive bidding is not required.

Under the law, all information concerning the manufacture or utilization of atomic weapons, the production of fissionable materials, and the use of such materials in the production of power is classified as restricted. The Commission is authorized to declassify such data as it determines may be published without endangering national security. Disclosure of restricted information is punishable by fines up to $20,000 and by imprisonment up to twenty years. Disclosure with intent to injure the United States is punishable by death or by imprisonment for life.

The Act of 1946 was without precedent. It sought to provide in advance for the development and control of a new source of power. It established a public monopoly in a new and growing industry. It made a sweeping delegation of authority to a governmental agency. And it required this body to carry on its operations in strictest secrecy. This policy was hazardous, but it was felt to be essential to national security.

Atomic Energy Act of 1954

Between 1946 and 1954 there were significant changes affecting atomic policy. The Communist powers came to present a serious threat to the security of the United States and other nations of the West. The Soviet Union succeeded in developing atomic weapons of its own. The western powers joined in organizations dedicated to their mutual defense. Canada, Great Britain, and others among these nations embarked upon atomic programs. The people of many countries looked upon the armament race between the great powers with growing fear. Those of the underdeveloped countries, in particular, complained that the new source of energy was being put to destructive rather than constructive use. The powers of the East and those of the West came to compete for the friendship of neutral states. In the meantime the United States had accumulated a huge store of weapons. It had demonstrated the feasibility of employing atomic energy to produce industrial power. And it had the capacity to devote a part of its resources to this activity. Given this situation, President Eisenhower proposed, in February, 1954, that Congress amend the atomic energy law.

The changes recommended by the President were three. (1) The secrecy required under the Act of 1946 was to be relaxed to permit the government to share with its military allies a limited amount of information concerning atomic weapons that were to be used for mutual defense. (2) It was to be relaxed, too, to allow the exchange of knowledge with friendly nations concerning the peaceful uses of atomic energy, thus opening the way to the constructive use of such energy in other parts of the world. (3) The limitations on private possession of fissionable materials, atomic facilities, and patents relating to atomic technology were to be relaxed to permit and encourage private enterprise to undertake the generation of industrial power from atomic fuel.

The first two of these recommendations gave rise to little controversy, and the powers requested by the President were written into the law. The proposals relating to employment of the atom by private enterprise, however, evoked a long debate. Private ownership of patents was opposed on the ground that it would give the first companies permitted to enter the field an unfair advantage over those that might seek to enter later on. The issue of public versus private power was thrown into the debate. The proponents of public power sought to confer on the Atomic Energy Commission itself the right to generate and sell electricity, to give other public agencies, such as the TVA, the same opportunity that was given private enterprise to employ atomic energy for this purpose, and to maintain the principle that municipal and co-operative distributors be given preference in buying publicly generated power.

As the law was finally passed, in August, 1954, it permits the private construction, ownership, and operation of atomic power plants, the private possession and use of nuclear fuel, and the private sale of by-product material, all under license by the AEC. It permits the private ownership of patents, but requires that licenses be freely granted for the first five years, at royalties to be determined by the AEC. The law forbids the Commission to go into the commercial power business, but allows it to sell the power that it may generate at experimental installations. It grants public agencies an equal right with private utilities to apply to the AEC for licenses. And it maintains the principle of preference for municipal and co-operative distributors.

The Atomic Energy Commission

The first members of the Atomic Energy Commission were appointed by President Truman, with David E. Lilienthal of the Tennessee Valley Authority as Chairman. They were confirmed by the Senate in November, 1946, after protracted hearings. The Commission took over the assets of the Manhattan District on January 1, 1947. It acquired establishments with a capital investment of $1,400,000,000, including a weapons research laboratory and a town of 9,000 at Los Alamos, New Mexico, production plants, a research laboratory, and a town of 36,000 at Oak Ridge, Tennessee, and another plant and town of 17,000 at Hanford, Washington. It inherited a contract system with 5,000 government employees and 50,000 contractor employees. It was entrusted with the knowledge required to produce fissionable materials and atomic bombs. It was given custody of the nation's stock of bombs.

The Commission's responsibilities are many and heavy. (1) It must provide for the production and storage of such kinds and quantities of weapons as the President decides may be required. (2) It must promote the discovery, mining, and initial processing of uranium and thorium, license their production and shipment, purchase and import them, and provide for their handling and storage. (3) If larger supplies of fissionable materials are required, it must decide what processes to use in producing them, what plants to build, and where to locate them. It must build the plants itself or select private builders, make contracts with them, and supervise their work. It must license the manufacturers of the equipment it installs. (4) It must operate the plants producing fissionables or select private operators, enter into contracts, and check on performance to insure compliance with their terms. (5) It must store fissionables, allocate supplies not required for military purposes among claimants for research, medicine, and industry, and regulate such uses by issuing licenses. It must also handle the distribution of radioactive by-products, by gift or sale. (6) It must pass on applications from private firms or from other public agencies to build and operate atomic power plants. (7) It must provide such operators with nuclear fuel. (8) It must control their sale of by-product material. (9) It must administer the patent provisions of the law, described below. (10) It must so regulate the production and use of all atomic materials as to protect the health and safety of workers and surrounding communities. (11) It must stimulate and support research in nuclear physics and in the possible applications of atomic energy, conducting such research itself or entering into contracts with private laboratories. And here, again, its contractors must be supervised. (12) It must examine the information in its possession to determine what is to be kept secret and what may be disclosed. (13) It must take elaborate precautions to insure security, subjecting its employees and those of its contractors to extensive investigation by the Civil Service Commission and the FBI. In addition to these responsibilities, the Commission must manage the towns it inherited from the Manhattan District, providing for housing, common facilities, and public services. In later installations, it has left this function to private enterprise.

By 1954 the investment controlled by the AEC passed $6 billion—more than that of U.S. Steel, General Motors, or Standard Oil of New Jersey. By the end of 1955 it was expected to reach $9 billion, making the enterprise one of the largest on earth. The Commission has installations in 22 states. To supplement the plants at Oak Ridge and Hanford, new plants for the production of fissionables are being built at Portsmouth, Ohio, at Paducah, Kentucky, and on the Savannah River in South Carolina. The last of these is said to involve the greatest construction project in history. There is a center at Fernald, Ohio, for processing feed materials, and a pilot plant is being built at Grand Junction, Colorado, to test new methods of extracting uranium from ores. There are plants to manufacture weapons at Los Alamos and Sandia, New Mexico, and testing ranges for weapons at Frenchman's Flat in Nevada and at Eniwetok in the Pacific. In addition to the laboratories at Oak Ridge and Los Alamos, there are research facilities in seven states. There are land-based prototypes of atomic power plants for naval vessels at Arco, Idaho, and at Schenectady, New York. One large commercial power plant is being built and others have been planned. A great new industry has come into being, its birth and growth directed by the government.

The Contract System

Of the total amount spent on the atomic energy program in 1953, less than 5 per cent went to support the AEC; more than 95 per cent went to its contractors. The Commission itself had only 7,000 employees, its contractors 200,000. Research was carried on, plants were constructed, ores were processed, fissionable materials were produced, components of weapons were manufactured, and public services were provided in government towns—all by contractors. The research work was being done, largely, by universities, by independent agencies, and by industrial laboratories. The plants at Oak Ridge were being operated by the Carbide and Carbon Chemicals Corporation, that at Hanford by General Electric. The plant at Paducah was also to be run by Carbide and Carbon, that at Portsmouth by Goodyear Tire and Rubber, and that on the Savannah River by du Pont.

A minor part of the Commission's contracts (around 15 per cent by value) have been let by publishing specifications and inviting competitive bids. This method, resulting in awards at prices fixed in advance, has been used in constructing such facilities as roads, office buildings, and warehouses, and in buying standard equipment and supplies. For most expenditures, competitive bidding has been ruled out by the urgency of the projects, by their novelty and complexity, by the need for flexibility, and by the overriding requirement of secrecy. Contractors have therefore been selected on the basis of a number of administrative criteria—their ability to handle operations on a large scale, their willingness to assign to this work well-qualified managerial and technical personnel, their past experience and reputation, and their enthusiasm for the job—and the terms of their contracts have been settled by negotiation. In the case of research, the contracts have usually called for reimbursement of costs. In the case of construction and operation of productive facilities, they have called for cost plus a fixed fee. (Cost plus a percentage of cost was forbidden by the Act of 1946.) The nature of the fixed fee has varied from contract to contract. In some, it has been set at one dollar; in others, at an agreed share of home office expenses; in still others, at an amount running between 3 and 7 per cent of the estimated value of the contract. This payment has been regarded, in every case, as compensation for management, not as a reward for taking risks, since all the risks are shouldered by the government.

The Commission's relation to its contractors is somewhat similar to that of a parent company to its subsidiaries. It gives general guidance, sets goals for output and costs, and requires reports. It seeks to insure prudence in the use of public funds. It advances money to its contractors and audits their accounts. It supervises their operations to enforce compliance with the terms of their contracts and with the provisions of the law. It must protect workers and the public against hazards to health and safety. And it must preserve national security by checking on contractor personnel and keeping strict account of all atomic materials. The Commission has sought to decentralize its supervisory activities, maintaining a small staff at every site where work is done. Local officials are authorized to make decisions in minor matters on the spot, freeing Washington to concentrate on major issues of policy.

The contract system was necessary at the outset. Adopted by the Manhattan District, it enabled the government to call on the organization, personnel, and know-how of private industry, and thus to get into production more quickly than it otherwise could have done. Continued by the AEC, it kept a going enterprise in operation, avoiding the disruption that would have been occasioned by substituting public managements. The system still has its advantages. The Commission is relieved of the burden of administrative detail. The contractors are not handicapped by bureaucratic rules. Operating outside the governmental salary scale, they are able to attract and hold managerial and technical personnel of superior ability. Moreover, by enabling private enterprise to obtain experience in handling atomic materials, the contract system facilitates the eventual termination of the government's monopoly of the industry.

But the system also has its disadvantages. The cost-plus contract affords no incentive for efficiency, promising no penalty when costs are high and no reward when costs are low. Costs may be padded; a fixed-price contract that is frankly calculated to provide a profit may well be cheaper in the end. The need for supervision creates a serious dilemma. If control is lax, the public interest in safety and economy may suffer. If it is strict, the advantage of managerial flexibility may be lost. When it was shown, at one time, that General Electric had 8,000 employees at Hanford and the Commission only 340, a Senator asked how it could control so many with so few. He might have asked, with equal justice, how the GE management could function with so many people at its elbow, checking on its every move. Between the dangers of too little supervision and too much, the AEC must follow an uncertain course. And finally, the system makes for oligopoly rather than competition in the future of the industry. The contracts go, of necessity, to a few large firms. It is easier for the Commission to negotiate with those already possessing technical ability and large productive capacity than to educate and finance their smaller rivals. It is easier to supervise a handful of market leaders than to police an entire industry. But this means that the favored few are given a head start over their competitors in obtaining knowledge and experience in a whole new field of industrial technology. And this is a fact that cannot fail to affect the future structure of the industry.

Patent Policy

The patent system is intended to promote the disclosure of inventions; the production and use of atomic materials have been shrouded in secrecy. Patents are supposed to encourage the investment of private funds in research and development; investment in the atom was financed exclusively by government. Patent policy in this area has, therefore, differed from that in other industries.

All inventions financed by the AEC belong to the government, and private rights in other inventions are strictly limited. With respect to the production and military use of fissionable materials, no such rights can be granted under new patents, and any rights granted under old patents were revoked by the Act of 1946. With respect to all nonmilitary applications of atomic energy until 1954, the Commission was required to declare all patents to be affected with a public interest. Licensing at reasonable royalties was then required. As amended in 1954, the law permits private patents on new inventions in this area, but provides for compulsory licensing during the first five years. The amounts to be paid for patents taken by the government or for licenses under patents left in private hands are determined by a patent compensation board established by the AEC. The decisions of this body may be appealed to the courts.

Technical Progress

There can be no question that, in the case of atomic energy, a monopoly (and, what is more, a government monopoly) has made rapid strides in the advancement of technology. There has been striking progress, first of all, in the development of atomic weapons. The bomb that devastated Hiroshima had an explosive force equivalent to 15,000–20,000 tons of TNT. The atomic bombs being produced in 1953 were twenty-five times as powerful. And the destructive power of hydrogen bombs is measured in megatons, each equivalent to 1,000,000 tons of TNT. One such bomb, exploded in the Pacific on March 1, 1954, was said to have the force of 20 megatons. It was estimated that a bomb of this strength, exploded over a city at an altitude of 2,000 feet, could destroy everything within an area of 50 square miles, cause destruction by blast or fire within 2,000 square miles and produce a lethal radioactive fall-out over 7,000 square miles.[1] Atomic explosives have also been adapted to other types of weap-

[1] *New York Times*, April 1, 1954, February 16, 1955.

ons, such as guided missiles and artillery shells, for use not only by the Air Force but also by the Army and the Navy. Disclosure of the exact size of the stockpile of atomic weapons, or the current rate of output, is forbidden by law, under penalty of death. But President Eisenhower stated that the stockpile, at the end of 1953, exceeded by many times the destructive equivalent of all the bombs and shells exploded by all the belligerents during World War II. And an informed guess[2] put the probable figure for the end of 1954 at an explosive power equivalent to a billion tons of TNT.

Progress has also been made in the employment of the atom as a source of power. Experimental reactors have been built and operated with success. An atomic power plant has been installed in a submarine. Work has been started on a plant that can be flown to isolated bases, a plant for an aircraft carrier, and an atomic engine for military planes. Ground was broken in 1954 for an experimental plant for the large-scale production of industrial power, and plans had been made for other plants using different techniques.

A notable contribution has been made to research and medicine through the production and distribution of radioactive isotopes. When small amounts of such isotopes are introduced into large quantities of an element, the progress of the element through biological or industrial processes can be traced by using Geiger counters or similar devices. Such methods have been used in studying the way in which plants use fertilizers and other materials contained in soils. They have been used in industry to study engine wear through friction, the effectiveness of detergents and preservatives, and the combustion of fuels. They have been used, too, in measuring the thickness of materials, in detecting flaws in castings, in tracing flows of liquids and spotting leaks in pipelines, and in revealing the presence of poisonous fumes. Their most extensive use has been in medicine, where they have been employed as a substitute for radium in the treatment of disease. More than 50,000 shipments had been made to more than 2,000 users of isotopes by the middle of 1954. Though regarded as only incidental to the manufacture of fissionable materials, the provision of radioactive by-products has come to have great value in itself.

Secrecy

The AEC is forced to carry on its operations, in the main, in secrecy. Disclosure of restricted information is forbidden, under extreme penalties, in the mistaken belief that the nation's security is to be assured by keeping to itself "the secret" of the bomb. The Commission, in exercising its power to declassify information, is likely to lean over backward to avoid political attacks. And, as a result, information is withheld from the American people even though it may be known to their potential enemies.

Far from serving the national interest, secrecy may be positively harm-

[2] By Ralph E. Lapp in *The Reporter,* May 11, 1954, p. 10.

ful. Confidence in the power of the atomic stockpile may beget a false sense of security. Ignorance as to the nation's vulnerability to atomic attack may lead to inadequate expenditure on measures of defense. The conditions imposed in the name of secrecy may prevent the program from attracting and holding the ablest scientists and engineers. The erection of barriers to the interchange of knowledge may well retard the progress of technology, since it is by sharing ideas and experience that technology normally has grown. Secrecy may also deny the government many contributions that could be made by private industry to the construction and operation of atomic facilities; it is not to be assumed that the Commission's contractors possess a monopoly of useful skills. Secrecy, finally, prevents an adequate check on extravagance, inefficiency, and even corruption. It facilitates concealment of mistakes. It confuses the need for security with mere distaste for criticism of administrative policy.

The Atomic Energy Commission is under the nominal supervision of the Joint Committee on Atomic Energy, composed of nine members of the Senate and nine of the House of Representatives. The Committee is informed of major policy decisions and receives reports on subsequent performance. But it has no adequate basis for appraising policy or performance and no effective means of exercising control. The information given it is incomplete. It does not know the size of the atomic stockpile, the current rate of output, or the unit cost of production. It keeps hands off the selection of contractors and the determination of their fees. It does not pass on the Commission's budget, this function being left to appropriations committees that must act almost entirely in the dark.

The tenuous character of Congressional control, in this area, was revealed by the Joint Committee's investigation of the Commission in 1949 in response to a political charge of "incredible mismanagement." In six weeks of hearings, the testimony given related to peripheral matters—the wisdom of providing a pipeline to obtain gas, the cost of constructing certain buildings, the administration of government towns, the exportation of isotopes, and one or two alleged breaches of security—and not to the essential core of the Commission's work. The charge was not proven, the Commission being commended by the Democratic majority of the Committee and condemned by the Republican minority, on the basis, it said, of information it could not disclose.[3]

The Commission's freedom from supervision is not complete. It doubtless responds to suggestions made by the Joint Committee and by its advisory groups. It is influenced by the Bureau of the Budget, by the Department of Defense, and, on important matters, by the President. But it is not subjected to the discipline of an informed public opinion. Important steps, affecting the welfare of the whole population, are taken with scarcely a word of criticism or debate. Knowledge is hidden; skilled ob-

[3] 81st Cong. 1st Sess. Senate Report 1169, *Investigation into the U.S. Atomic Energy Commission,* 1949.

servers and interpreters are lacking; real questioning appears to be taboo. Policy is thus made in a vacuum; decisions of the greatest moment are entrusted to a very few. There is no evidence that power has been abused. But the situation, until corrected, will always carry with it the danger of abuse.

Politics in the AEC

In its early years, the Atomic Energy Commission was free of politics. Its members were appointed solely on the basis of ability. Their differences were not thrown into the arena of partisan debate. The prestige of the body was high. With the Eisenhower administration, the Commission underwent a change. The new chairman, Admiral Lewis L. Strauss, was also appointed adviser to the President. A provision inserted in the atomic energy bill, then in Congress, would have made the chairman the Commission's "principal officer." Other members complained that they were not told what was going on. They objected to further concentration of power in the chairman's hands. The provision was not enacted into law. One of the Commission's first steps under Chairman Strauss was to dismiss J. Robert Oppenheimer, the distinguished physicist who had directed the research that produced the atomic bomb, from his post as an adviser on the ground that his access to atomic information imperiled the nation's security.[4] This was followed by popular attacks on the competence, if not the loyalty, of other scientists. Whatever the merits of the action, its consequence was to involve the agency in violent controversy. Then President Eisenhower directed the AEC to enter into the Dixon-Yates contract, described in Chapter 26, as a means of checking the expansion of the TVA. And with this, the Commission was thrown into the thick of the fight over public power policy. Its freedom from political pressure was at an end.

ATOMIC POWER FOR INDUSTRY

Atomic energy may come, in time, to be harnessed for peaceful uses in ways that are as yet unknown. But atomic power plants, as now envisaged, embody the familiar methods of turning heat into steam and steam into electricity. They therefore employ equipment of conventional design: boilers, turbines, generators, transformers, and transmission lines. The only change is the substitution of the atomic reactor for the coal-burning furnace as a source of heat and of fissionable material for coal as a fuel. There is no question that such a substitution is possible. Experimental reactors have been operated with success and atomic engines have been designed for naval installations where their use is not prevented by their cost. The question about atomic power, in other uses, is whether it can be produced at a figure that will make it pay.

[4] See Joseph and Stewart Alsop, "We Accuse," *Harper's*, October, 1954, pp. 25–45.

Economic Feasibility

Prospective plants for the production of atomic power are of two types: the dual-purpose reactor and the single-purpose reactor. The dual-purpose plant would not only produce heat with which to generate electricity. In the process, it would also act as a breeder, changing non-fissionable uranium into fissionable plutonium, and thus producing as much (or more) fissionable material as it consumed. If this material could then be sold to the government for use in making weapons, or to other plants for use as a fuel, a large part of the cost of the project could thus be met. The production of heat for power could be regarded as a by-product. And, on this basis, power could be supplied at a cost that would compare favorably with that of coal-burning and hydroelectric plants. The feasibility of such an undertaking, however, turns upon the availability of an ample market for plutonium. No such market is assured. There would be a private demand for fuel only while the industry was increasing its capacity. The demand would disappear as it came to produce as much as it consumed. The government has made it clear that it can satisfy its own plutonium requirements. It will not commit itself to purchase the additional quantities that the private power industry might produce. The feasibility of atomic power depends, therefore, upon the economics of the single-purpose plant.

A single-purpose reactor will concentrate on the production of heat for power, producing no plutonium for sale. The cost of the related facilities for generating and distributing electricity will be the same as that incurred in a conventional plant. The cost of the reactor itself will be many times as great as that of a coal-burning furnace. A spacious site will be required for safety. Enormous shields of lead and concrete will have to be installed. Special provision will have to be made for the disposal of waste materials. All of this will make for a large investment and thus for high annual charges for capital. These charges may be offset, however, by savings in the cost of fuel. Atomic fuel, potentially, is cheap. A single pound of U-235 can produce as much heat as 1,300 tons of coal. Money can thus be saved in the costs of transportation, handling, and storage as well as in the price of the fuel itself. In accordance with the breeder principle, moreover, fuel can be recycled with further saving in its cost. Power from single-purpose plants has not yet been found to be competitive with that generated by conventional means. But it will become so if the cost of fuel can be made low enough to compensate for the high cost of capital.

Methods of Development

The development of an atomic power industry might be left to private enterprise alone. It might be promoted by various forms of government aid to private enterprise. Or it might be undertaken by government itself. In the present circumstances, it is likely that government will have to play the major part.

If Congress were merely to enact enabling laws and to wait for private enterprise to take the initiative, the development of the industry would be slow. The risks of the venture are great and its success uncertain. The sums required to finance it are larger than any private concern is now prepared to invest. When the AEC invited eight corporations, in four teams of two each, to study the problem and submit proposals, each of the groups presented a plan that called for some form of federal aid.

Under one plan, the corporations would have financed the construction of a dual-purpose plant, but the government would have been expected, in effect, to underwrite the enterprise by agreeing to purchase the output of plutonium. Under a second, the government would have built a dual-purpose reactor, producing plutonium for its own use, and the companies would have used the heat, themselves financing the generating and transmission facilities. Both of these plans were ruled out by the fact that the government had no need for growing supplies of plutonium. Under a third plan, the government would have built a small pilot plant and, if it proved to be successful, the companies would have considered reproducing it on a large scale. Under a fourth, the government would have built a plant at some remote location where demand for power was low and the cost of power from alternative sources was high. If such a plant could be operated successfully, private concerns might then reproduce it in areas where the markets were more promising.

The policy finally adopted by the Commission was that of contracting for the experimental construction and operation of a number of single-purpose commercial plants embodying different techniques. In January 1955 it invited proposals from private industry and announced that it was prepared to extend assistance in three principal ways: (1) by providing free use of nuclear fuel, (2) by providing, without charge, the research and development work done in its own laboratories, and (3) by making payments for the technical and economic data provided by private companies. At that time, a number of experimental power projects were in various stages of construction and several more were being planned. A large commercial power plant, capable of producing 60,000 kilowatts of electricity, was being constructed for the Duquesne Light Company of Pittsburgh. In 1955, too, it was announced that other utility companies were planning to build still larger plants near New York City and Detroit.

Methods of Control

The eventual pattern of the atomic power industry is unknown. The government, having financed the original development, might continue its monopoly, owning the power facilities and operating them itself. It might retain title to these facilities, providing for their operation, under contract, by private companies. Or it might open the way to ownership as well as operation by such concerns.

The first of these alternatives could lead to a great expansion of public enterprise. In quantity, in cost, and in flexibility, the atom has potential advantages as a source of power. If the atomic power plants as well as the major hydroelectric systems were to be publicly owned and operated, the government might well come, in time, to dominate the entire industry. Unless opinion changes, however, operation is to be placed in private hands.

Under the contract system, private operation would be possible. But government would still be required to provide the capital needed by the industry. Under private ownership, the industry would finance itself. It was to make this possible that the law was amended in 1954. Private companies may now be licensed to build, own, and operate power reactors, may be permitted to possess the fissionable material required for fuel, and may hold patents on inventions developed through their own researches in the field. Power from the Duquesne Light plant, when sold in 1958, will be produced with the aid of a substantial subsidy. It is reported, however, that Consolidated Edison will finance the plant it proposes to build near New York City, asking no assistance from the government.

If the industry were to be completely private, it would have to be given the right to produce its own fuel or to purchase it from commercial sources of supply. To this end, the government would have to relinquish its control over the sale of the original ores and its monopoly of the manufacture of fissionable materials. No such move is likely to be made. The production of fissionables so intimately affects the nation's security that it will not be transferred to private hands. The cost of the facilities required is so great that it cannot be privately financed. The government will not sell its plants. Private companies will not be permitted—and will not wish—to build plants of their own. The atomic power industry, therefore, will depend upon the government for its supplies of fuel.

The industry, if private, will necessarily operate under tight controls. A company that wishes to enter the field will have to obtain a separate license from the AEC for every step it takes: (1) a license to engage in the research and development required to design a plant, unless it adopts a design already approved by the AEC, (2) a license to build the plant, (3) a license to operate the plant, once it is built, (4) licenses to use the technology covered by patents held by the AEC, (5) a license to possess and transport nuclear fuel, and (6) a license to dispose of its by-product of radioactive materials. A company will have to grant licenses to others, for five years, under its own patents, at royalties fixed by the AEC. To protect workers and the public against extraordinary hazards, it will have to conform to detailed health and safety regulations prescribed and enforced by the AEC. If the company is ever to introduce changes in technology, or to employ its facilities and its materials for new purposes, it will have to obtain permission from the AEC. And under state and federal laws, as is the case with power produced in any other way, the industry will be subject to regulation, by state utility commissions and by the Federal Power Commission, of the services it renders and the rates at which it sells.

PROPOSALS FOR INTERNATIONAL CONTROL

The awful destructiveness of atomic weapons, the appalling prospect of an atomic arms race, the fear that civilization could not survive atomic warfare—all this, in contrast to the beneficent potentialities of atomic energy, has led to proposals for international control. The initiative in advancing such proposals has been taken by the United States. In the fall of 1945 this country proposed the establishment of a United Nations Atomic Energy Commission (UNAEC) to study the problems involved and prepare a plan for control. In January, 1946, such a commission was set up by the General Assembly of the United Nations without a dissenting vote. At the same time, the United States embarked upon the preparation of a plan to recommend. This undertaking was entrusted, first, to a committee appointed by the Secretary of State under the chairmanship of Dean Acheson, then Undersecretary, with the aid of a board of consultants headed by David E. Lilienthal, then chairman of the TVA. The report of this committee, made in March, 1946, became the basis of the proposal presented to the UN Commission by Bernard Baruch, as representative of the United States, in June, 1946. And this proposal, in its essentials, with the approval of all the nations belonging to the Commission except the Soviet Union and its satellites, was recommended to the United Nations in December, 1946.

The Acheson-Lilienthal Plan

The plan developed by the Acheson-Lilienthal Committee was based upon the fact that atomic energy may be used either for peaceful or for warlike purposes, and that the processes involved in producing atomic materials for either purpose, up to their later stages, are the same. The plan called for the establishment, by international agreement, of a United Nations Atomic Development Authority, to perform the sort of functions—eventually—that the AEC now performs in the United States. With respect to uses not found to be dangerous—research into peaceful applications, employment in medicine, and the production of power—the Authority was to license undertakings by governments and by private enterprises and agencies. With respect to dangerous activities, it was to retain complete control. No nation was to be permitted to mine, process, or own the ores of uranium or thorium, to produce or build up stores of fissionable materials, or to manufacture or possess atomic weapons. The mining and processing of ores, the production and storage of fissionables, and all research into atomic explosives were to be carried on exclusively by the Authority. The plants and stockpiles owned by the Authority were to be so distributed around the world that no nation, by seizing those within its borders, could obtain a preponderance of force. And the Authority was to be given powers of inspection to prevent any nation from engaging in secret mining, production, or stockpiling activities. The plan was to take effect in stages, starting with mining, proceeding next to the processing of ores, then to the production of fissionables, and finally to the control of atomic weapons and eventual disarmament. In this way, the United States was to preserve its own security while testing the good faith of others as the structure of international co-operation was being built.

Before it was presented to the UNAEC, this plan was altered in an important respect. As prepared by the Acheson-Lilienthal committee, it had provided no sanctions against violation, relying upon inspection and notification—that a nation was mining atomic ores, building atomic plants, or stockpiling atomic materials—to enable other nations to take action to protect themselves. As presented by Baruch, the plan called for abrogation of the veto—a right given by the United Nations Charter to the great powers on the Security Council which enabled any one of them to prevent collective action against a nation found to be guilty of aggression.[5] Such a step would have made it possible for a majority of the Council to invoke sanctions, including military sanctions, against a violator of the atomic treaty.

The plan, in this form, was not acceptable to the Soviet Union. With the veto removed, it would have opened the way to collective action against the Soviets. It would have disclosed information held secret by Russia at an early stage, holding America's secrets for disclosure later on. It would have pierced the Iron Curtain, bringing the Russian people into contact with the West. It offered little in the way of immediate advantage: the promised benefits from peaceful uses of the atom were remote. Whatever its reasons, the Soviet Union rejected the proposal, advancing a counterproposal of its own.

The Russian plan offered no real prospect of effective control. It called for the conclusion of an international agreement banning the use of atomic weapons. But it provided no means of enforcement. It would have permitted nations to mine and store atomic ores, to build and operate atomic factories, and to build up stocks of fissionable materials. It provided for the creation of a Control Commission. But the Commission's powers were limited to "periodic" inspection of "declared" facilities, and to the presentation of recommendations which were subject to veto by the Soviets.

This proposal, affording no safeguard against Russian aggression, was

[5] The action taken in Korea in 1950 was voted at meetings which the Soviet Union refused to attend.

unacceptable to the nations of the West. Between the two positions, negotiations stood at stalemate for the next seven years. During this period, it came to be known that the Soviet Union had developed and tested atomic weapons of its own. Then, on December 8, 1953, President Eisenhower, speaking before the General Assembly of the United Nations, advanced another proposal on behalf of the United States.

The Eisenhower Proposal

The new proposal was a modest one. It did not touch upon the mining of ores, the production of fissionable materials, or the manufacture of weapons. It did not call for powers of inspection. It thus avoided the issues that had evoked the Soviets' opposition to the plan presented by Baruch. What it asked was that the governments possessing atomic ores and fissionable materials begin and continue to make contributions from their stockpiles to a common pool to be administered, under the United Nations, by an International Atomic Energy Agency. This Agency would store the materials and protect them against seizure. It would employ scientists to experiment with the development of peaceful uses. And it would devise means of allocating the materials, for such uses, among the countries that do not produce them. In this way, it was hoped, international tension might be eased, a small part of the world's atomic resources turned to constructive uses, and a beginning made toward understandings that might, in time, serve to halt the race for atomic arms.

Negotiation between the United States and the Soviet Union on this proposal came to naught when the latter insisted on prior atomic disarmament as a condition for its participation in the plan. Thereupon, the United States agreed with Canada, Great Britain, France, and others to go ahead alone. In the fall of 1954 it announced a program of international education involving: the establishment of a reactor training school where fifty foreign scientists and engineers would be invited to study during 1955; the inauguration of courses for some 250 students in radiation safety, medicine, biology, and the like; and the provision of instruction in radioisotope tracer techniques. At the same time it renewed its proposal that an international agency be created by the United Nations to promote the peaceful uses of atomic energy. In its amended form the proposal dropped the idea of an atomic pool. As now envisaged, the new agency would serve as an information center and as a clearing house where requests for atomic materials would be received from countries lacking them and transmitted to countries possessing them. The actual transfer of such materials and agreement on conditions governing their use would be bilateral. A resolution endorsing this proposal was adopted unanimously by the General Assembly of the United Nations on December 4, 1954. The Soviet Union voted for the plan in principle. But Russian participation in the program remained in doubt. The United States had proposed that the new agency be set up independently. The Soviet Union insisted that it be made subordinate to the Security Council where the Soviet veto could be exercised. This difference was still to be resolved.

The Acheson-Lilienthal plan called for the inauguration of international public enterprise in the production of atomic ores and fissionable materials. The new plan does not. The former would have given an international agency the power, through licensing, to control the uses of atomic energy throughout the world. The latter does not. But the agreements effected under the new plan will have to regulate the use, in non-producing countries, of the materials that are provided them. And every country producing or using such materials will presumably do so under regulations of its own. The very nature of the atom demands the exercise of public control.

SUGGESTIONS FOR FURTHER READING

The best book for the layman on the American atomic program is Gordon Dean, *Report on the Atom* (New York: Alfred A. Knopf, 1953). An excellent series of articles on various phases of the program is contained in "The Impact of Atomic Energy," Vol. 290 of *The Annals of the American Academy of Political and Social Science*, November, 1953. The story of the Atomic Energy Act of 1946 is told in James R. Newman and Byron S. Miller, *The Control of Atomic Energy* (New York: McGraw-Hill Book Co., 1949). The issue raised by the conflict between secrecy and accountability is well presented by Robert Dahl and Ralph Brown, Jr. in *Domestic Control of Atomic Energy* (New York: Social Science Research Council, 1951). Three government reports worth looking into are: Atomic Energy Commission, *AEC Contract Policy and Operations* (Washington: Government Printing Office, 1951), Joint Committee on Atomic Energy, *Atomic Power and Private Enterprise* (82d Cong., 2d Sess., Joint Committee Print, 1952), and *Investigation into the U.S. Atomic Energy Commission* (81st Cong., 1st Sess., Senate Report No. 1169, 1949). For a criticism of the Atomic Energy Act of 1954, see Walter Adams, "Atomic Energy: the Congressional Abandonment of Competition," *Columbia Law Review*, LV (1955), 158–79. For current developments, see *The Bulletin of the Atomic Scientists.*

Chapter 29 PROBLEMS OF PUBLIC ENTERPRISE

The method employed in the development of atomic energy, described in the previous chapter, has been that of government ownership and private operation under government contracts. This experience is not unique. Production by private contractors, using their own facilities, has been the method commonly employed in handling the construction of public works and in procuring equipment and supplies in time of war. Productive facilities have also been provided by government, in certain fields, for use by private firms. This was the case, in World War II, with synthetic rubber and with a number of other goods whose output was required. But public enterprise, more frequently, has involved operation as well as ownership by government.

It is with the problems raised by public operation that the present chapter is concerned. How—without the reward of profit or the penalty of bankruptcy—are efficiency and progress to be obtained? How—when there is a monopoly, even though it be a government monopoly—are the interests of the consumer to be protected? And how—given the inconsistency of productive efficiency and public accountability—is the inevitable conflict between efficiency and accountability to be resolved?

EFFICIENCY AND PROGRESS

In the writings of socialists, in the past, much was said concerning the shortcomings of private enterprise, but little or nothing concerning those of public enterprise. In the writings of socialism's critics, on the other hand, the inevitable failures of public enterprise were asserted, but little was offered in the way of proof. Discussion of the merits and demerits of public enterprise thus had an air of unreality. But with the spread of nationalization, in recent years, the difficulties inherent in government operation of industry have come increasingly to be recognized. Evidence is accumulating on problems of organization and management, on factors affecting efficiency and costs, and on the influence that public operation exerts on the morale of labor and on the advancement of technology. In

England, particularly, and also in the United States, the issues raised by public enterprise are being brought into a clearer light.

Comparisons of Efficiency

Comparisons have sometimes been made of similar industries administered by private and by public managements. It is possible, for instance, to compare the railroad, airline, telephone and telegraph, and radio and television services provided privately in the United States with those provided publicly abroad. It is possible, too, to compare private transit, water, gas, and electric utility services in some American cities with similar public undertakings in others. But so many variables are involved, in every case, that sweeping generalizations concerning relative efficiency cannot be justified.

When quality of service is compared, the judgments made are largely subjective. It would be possible, of course, to measure the speed and frequency of trains, planes, and transit vehicles, their adherence to schedules, and their records of accidents, the time required to make a telephone connection or to deliver a telegram, the pressure and purity of water, the heating value of gas, the constancy of electric current, the number of stations providing broadcasts, the number of hours they are on the air, and the frequency and duration of interruptions to all these services. But such comparisons are seldom made. And with respect to other matters, such as comfort and cleanliness of transport equipment, the convenience of all types of public services, and the courtesy of service personnel, methods of measurement are not available. In the case of broadcasting, in particular, objective standards are lacking. One listener may prefer the singing commercials of American radio, another the heavy intellectual fare of the Third Program on the BBC. The difference cannot be measured; it is a matter of taste.

Rates can be compared, but such comparisons may be misleading. Where the quality of service differs, there is no comparable unit to which the rates can be applied. Rate structures are complicated; charges vary with customer classes, with types of service, and with quantities consumed. It is therefore difficult to find, in different schedules, particular rates that are properly to be compared. And even though services and rates were standardized, comparisons might not be meaningful. A high rate might cover costs and yield a profit; a low rate might be subsidized. Subsidization may have been necessitated by failures of management; it may have been adopted as a deliberate policy. In either case, with one enterprise expected to pay its own way and another supported, in part, by taxes, their rates cannot be taken as an index of their relative efficiency.

So, too, with comparisons of cost. The conditions under which private and public enterprises provide their services may differ in many respects, and these differences will be reflected in differences in costs. Transportation costs, for instance, will be influenced by the density of traffic and the character of the terrain, telephone costs by the size of the exchanges, water costs by the accessibility of adequate supplies. Electric costs will vary with differences in the method of generation, the scale of operation, and the degree of physical integration. In the case of multipurpose projects, as was seen in Chapter 26, they will depend upon the principle that may be used in allocating some part of the joint costs to the business of producing power. Costs will be affected, too, by differences in the burden of taxes, in the charges for capital, and in the policies adopted in depreciating assets and retiring debts. As a consequence, where the costs of private and public enterprises differ, it is difficult to determine how much of the difference is properly to be attributed to factors such as these, how much to differences in the efficiency of managements.

There is no basis, in the evidence available, for asserting that greater efficiency is always to be attained by private or by public enterprise. Examples can be adduced to support a case for either side of the argument. But no conclusion is justified. It is possible, however to recognize some of the factors that influence efficiency and costs.

Factors Affecting Costs

Public enterprise has certain advantages that may make for lower costs. For one thing, it can effect economies by unifying and co-ordinating competitive services. When the government operated the railroads, during World War I, it eliminated competing trains and circuitous routes, pooled locomotives and cars, and required the common use of terminals and shops. If the government were to operate all types of carriers, it could doubtless establish common terminals, dovetail transportation by water, air, road, and rail, and employ shorter hauls by busses and trucks to supplement longer hauls by trains. In the same way, if a city were to undertake the distribution of milk, it could realize substantial savings by eliminating parallel delivery routes. In all such cases, moreover, costs could be cut by eliminating competition in advertising and in other methods of promoting sales. All this, however, is less an argument for public enterprise than for monopoly. The savings promised could also be realized by private enterprise under public control. But, in either case, there might be offsetting losses. For the regulatory force of competition would be gone.

A second advantage of public enterprise is its ability to obtain capital at a lower cost. The credit of government is supported by its ability to tax. Bonds issued by agencies of government therefore bear little risk. As a consequence, they can be sold at a low interest rate. The annual charge for borrowed money, accordingly, is lower for public than for private enterprise. This advantage is offset, of course, to the extent that government pays excessive sums in acquiring private properties or adopts extravagant standards in constructing new facilities. Also, since public enterprises, unlike private companies, are usually required to pay off their debts, their charges for capital may be higher during the years when this is being done. But once the debts are paid, these charges—compared with those of private firms—will be low indeed. Another fact, however, must be noted. The capitalization of a private enterprise is likely to be partly in bonds that bear a fixed return and partly in preferred and common stocks whose owners need not be given dividends in years when profits are not earned. The capitalization of a public enterprise will be exclusively in bonds. As a result, its payments to its creditors must be as large in bad years as in good. Its capital cost, though low, will be inflexible. Its legal obligation, during a depression, may be heavier than that of a private firm.

Another advantage sometimes claimed for public enterprise is the abandonment of regulation and the saving of its costs. With complete authority in public hands, it is said, there will no longer be need for detailed supervision with the virtual duplication of managements that it has sometimes involved. But monopoly, though public, will still have to be supervised to insure efficiency and progress, to prevent dishonesty and undue discrimination, and to protect consumers against poor service and excessive rates. And such supervision will entail substantial costs.

Along with the factors that may tend to make the costs of public undertakings low, there are others that operate to make them high. There is danger, first, that public industries will spend too much on capital improvements. Such improvements afford a ready means of promoting recovery from depressions, and they may well be initiated for this purpose regardless of their influence on costs. There are likely to be regional pressures, too, for shares from the barrel of political pork. Most cities and towns in the United States have already been provided with post office buildings. But if the railways, for instance, were nationalized, Congressmen could run for re-election by promising handsome new terminals. And the process of logrolling would insure that many of them would be built.

There is danger, second, that public agencies will pay too much for their supplies. These agencies may call for competitive bids. They may buy on cost-plus contracts. But they will usually pay top prices. Sellers may discriminate in favor of large private buyers. They will seldom discriminate in favor of the government. Public bodies, moreover, have frequently been forced by state or federal law to purchase certain goods or to make their purchases from certain sellers despite the fact that they are high in price. Under the "Buy American" Act of 1933, as it has been administered, federal agencies are required to buy domestic goods unless their prices exceed those of imported goods by more than a specified percentage after the tariffs on imports have been paid. No private buyer suffers such a handicap.

Third, it is likely that public enterprises will spend too much for labor. They may be compelled to take on workers as a means of relieving unemployment. They may be required to retain more workers than they need. They may be forced, by the demands of political patronage, to discharge people who are competent and well trained in order to make room for those who are incompetent and untrained. They must meet the costs involved in civil service processes and security investigations. From all of this, private concerns are free. Top salaries are lower in public than in private employment. But the number of salaried workers is likely to be larger. And the wages of other workers, if not higher, are as high. Labor is organized to exert political as well as economic pressure. And such pressure may add to costs by raising wages, cutting hours, and providing a variety of special benefits.

Fourth, and finally, public enterprise may be prevented from taking action that would reduce its costs. Removal from uneconomic locations or abandonment of unprofitable services are likely to be forestalled by pressure politics. Unification of facilities, reorganization of operations, and modification of the methods of production may well be forbidden if they would threaten propertied interests or reduce the volume of employment in a trade. Public enterprise, being public, may often be governed by policies that do not make for economy.

When these disadvantages have been noted, it must be said that the difference between private and public enterprise is often not as great as the discussion would suggest. Private industries, too, are subject to political pressures that inflate their costs. With the railroads, for instance, labor has been accorded special benefits by law. And economies that would have lessened employment were forbidden by the Transportation Act of 1933. In these respects, the nationalization of railways would involve but little change.

Forms of Organization

Three major forms of organization have been used for the administration of public enterprise: the government department, the public corporation, and the mixed corporation. Of these, the first has had the longest history and the widest use. Departmental administration has typically been employed in the management of state and local enterprise in the United States. It is used by the federal government in the management of the Post Office, the social insurance system, and the public lands. Under this form of organization, departments are divided into bureaus, bureaus into branches, branches into sections, and so on. But the layers and lines of authority are well defined. There is a single administrator: the department head. He may be advised by a staff of specialists. But he alone is held responsible for the execution of legislative policies. Departmental management thus makes for strict accountability. But it is subject to political pressures and handicapped by bureaucratic controls. Its advantages and disadvantages will be considered, at some length, later on.

The public corporation is established as a separate legal entity. It functions like a private business, entering into contracts, acquiring and holding property, bringing suits and being sued. Its creditors can enforce their rights without obtaining the government's permission to sue or proceeding through the Court of Claims. The corporation's stock is usually held by the Treasury. The members of its board are appointed by the government, usually for long and overlapping terms, to afford assurance of continuity. Its management is appointed by the board and is made responsible to the board. The corporation is granted a considerable measure of autonomy with respect to its financial operations, its purchases, its personnel, and the general conduct of its business. It thus has the advantage of being insulated, to some extent, from political pressures and being freed, in part, from bureaucratic controls. But it may also escape accountability. This problem, too, will be considered later on.

The public corporation has been extensively employed in Europe for many years. It is the device adopted for the administration of all of the industries nationalized by Great Britain and many of those nationalized by France since World War II. Its history in this country, beginning with the Bank of North America in 1781 and the United States Bank in 1791, includes the acquisition of the Panama Railroad Company in 1904, the creation of several emergency corporations during World War I, and the establishment of the Port of New York Authority in 1921. Such corporations multiplied during the Great Depression and World War II, conspicuous among them being the RFC and the TVA. The Hoover Commission, in 1949, recommended the incorporation of a number of other federal activities. The corporate form has thus come to be widely regarded as most desirable for the administration of public enterprise.

In the mixed corporation, stock is owned both by private investors and by the government, and the board of directors includes representatives of both private and public interests. Where a majority of the stock is publicly owned, this form of organization may differ little, in operation, from the preceding one. Where a minority of the ownership is public, the government's power is limited, but its participation will enable it to exert some influence on policy. Mixed ownership has seldom been adopted, on its merits, as a permanent form of organization. It has usually resulted from the acquisition of partial shareholdings or the extension of public aid to depressed industries. In certain cases, as with the federal home loan banks and the intermediate credit banks, it has been used, during a period of transition, to promote the development of new forms of private enterprise. The device has been widely employed in Europe, characterizing much of the nationalization effected in France and most of that in Italy. It has been little used in Great Britain or the United States.

Administrative Boards

In some cases a public corporation is located within a government department and its directorate is composed, in whole or in part, of officials of the department. This is true, for instance, of the Panama Canal Company and the Commodity Credit Corporation. In such cases, there is departmental control of policy and the corporate device is employed simply as a means of delegating the management of operations. Elsewhere, however, corporations are independent of the departmental structure.

The boards of public corporations may be small or large, their members serving full-time or part-time, with or without compensation. In France board membership is part-time and unpaid. In Great Britain and the United States it is usually full-time and salaried. In Great Britain the boards are small, when compared with those of private companies. In the United States they are even smaller, numbering typically from three to five. The number of directors of the TVA, for instance, is three.

The large, part-time, unpaid board can deal only with matters of policy. But when a board is small, full-time, and salaried, its members may become deeply involved in administrative details. Such a development is undesirable, since administration is handled better by a single official than by a board. And there is another function which the board itself must perform: that of planning developments and programs and making determinations of policy. The typical board, like that of the TVA, has avoided this pitfall, delegating administration to a general manager and confining itself to planning and policy.

In France the boards of the newly nationalized industries are designed to be representative of different interest groups, members being appointed by the various ministries to speak for workers, consumers, and the government. This arrangement, based on the traditional syndicalist philosophy of the French trade unions, is not conducive to good administration. The members of an administrative board should have a common purpose, owing allegiance only to the enterprise they serve. The members of tripartite boards are loyal, not to their corporations, but to their outside interests. The boards are thus divided, devoting themselves to bargaining and negotiation instead of directing their efforts toward the adoption of common policies. Where unity is achieved, it is because labor, possessing the greatest political strength, has controlled the appointment of members who supposedly represent consumers and the government. And here there is danger that the demands of labor, whatever their merits, will always be satisfied, with consumers and taxpayers left to foot the bill.

In practice, the French boards have not played the part they were expected to play. Their part-time, unpaid members have lacked the knowledge and time required for administration, and the motivation and opportunity to learn. As a result, responsibility has devolved upon the government. Decisions as to policy are made by ministers. The public members on the boards are civil servants who take no action unless it is approved by ministers. The other members serve, in effect, in an advisory capacity. On paper, the boards run the nationalized industries; actually, they do not. The independence of the public corporations, in France, is therefore more nominal than real.

In Great Britain there have been two complaints concerning the corporate boards. According to one, the boards have been filled with businessmen, the nationalized industries being run by the same people who ran them before they were taken over by the government. According to the other, appointments have been made as a reward for political services, the boards being staffed with members who are lacking in competence. There are doubtless individual appointees who answer to the latter description. But the emphasis has clearly been on business experience. The question raised by objective observers is not whether board members, in general, are competent, but whether they possess sufficient breadth of view. The boards, it is felt, should not be composed of technical specialists, but of persons of diverse abilities whose interests are in broad issues of public policy.

It has been the experience in the United States that public agencies, when first established, attract administrators of high ability. As time goes by, however, public attention shifts to other activities, and men of superior talents are attracted by newer agencies. The older undertakings offer less of a challenge; they are handicapped in hiring and holding men of ability by the limits placed on government salaries. As a result, they fail to maintain the quality of their administrative personnel. And even though honesty be preserved, imagination and vigor are lost. This process of deterioration has been observed, over the years, in many public agencies. It offers a persisting threat to the efficiency of public enterprise.

Overcentralization

A common characteristic of undertakings of great size is a tendency toward excessive centralization in management. This tendency is widely regarded, in American business, as one of the disadvantages of operating on a large scale. Decentralization of administration is therefore a usual objective of business policy. But in government, overcentralization persists. In the United States, as we have seen, the Post Office is a case in point. In Great Britain, instead of nationalizing different companies separately, Parliament organized each industry as a whole. But it left the internal structure of the industries to be determined by their boards. Administration, thus, could legally have been decentralized. But the boards believed in bigness as a means of insuring efficiency. Regional and local units were established for the performance of certain administrative functions. But there was little delegation of real authority. So, in Britain, it is said that "everything is run from Whitehall" just as it is said, in this country, that "everything is run from Washington."

Centralized administration undoubtedly has its advantages during a period when the principal tasks to be accomplished are those of reorganizing an industry, modernizing its methods, and effecting over-all changes in policy. But, once established, it is likely to endure. And it is certain, in many ways, to be prejudicial to efficiency. Overcentralization makes for inflexibility, preventing adjustments which a local situation may require.

It forestalls the exercise of individual initiative, subjecting subordinates to remote, impersonal controls. It involves protracted delays, provoking a feeling of frustration and impairing morale. There are some functions, to be sure, that must be centralized. But there are many more that can and should be delegated to officials down the line. The usual failure of large-scale public enterprise to make such delegations is one of its principal shortcomings.

Labor Relations

A major argument advanced in support of proposals for the nationalization of industry has been the contribution it is supposed to make to productive efficiency by improving labor morale. A nationalized industry, it is said, does not belong to the employer but to the people as a whole. Its employees are engaged, not in producing profits for investors, but in promoting the welfare of the entire community. Workers, no longer governed autocratically, are invited to participate in management. Suspicion and hostility give way to willing co-operation. And, as a result, there is a rise in productivity. So runs the argument. It has not been borne out by the experience of nationalized industries in Great Britain or in France.

In both countries, the wages paid by public corporations are determined by collective bargaining. In Great Britain, nation-wide agreements are effected by bargaining between the unions and the boards. In France, the unions do not negotiate with the boards, since they are represented on the boards and would therefore be dealing with themselves. They bargain, instead, with the officials of the corporations, under the supervision of their respective ministries. In both cases, the agreements are concluded, in effect, between organized labor and the state. As a purchaser of labor, the state may be less inclined to resist the demands of the unions than private employers would have been. But the negotiators appear as adversaries, just as they do in bargaining with private industries.

In France the interest of workers in matters such as health, safety, education, and welfare is presumably protected by their representation on the boards. In Great Britain the public corporations are required to establish machinery for joint consultation in these fields. Such consultation could lead, through close co-operation, to determinations which would limit the independence of unions and of managements. In practice, it has been approached with the psychology of bargaining. In some cases, it has been resisted by administrators as a threat to their authority. In others, delays resulting from centralization of the power to make decisions have given consultation an appearance of futility. The program, in the eyes of most observers, has failed to give the workers any feeling of participation in the government of industry.

Nationalization, in operation, has made little difference in the relations between employers and employees. It has not affected the position of the worker at the mine or in the factory. It has not changed the attitude of labor. It has not removed suspicion or hostility. It has not improved morale. It has not produced a marked increase in productivity.

Advancement of Technology

When government takes over an established private industry, it inherits the industry's achievements in the development of technology. When it creates a new industry, it is inspired to develop methods of its own. But when an enterprise has long been operated by government, there is no assurance that continued improvements will be made. There is no profit incentive to encourage innovation. There may not even be investment in research. Rules laid down to govern operations are likely to harden into a rigid mold. Adherence to routine will be made certain. But there may be no stimulus to change.

Atomic energy, as a government monopoly, has made great strides in the advancement of technology. The TVA, too, has made progress through research. But progress, in both cases, has been stimulated by competition—in the case of atomic energy, by the threat of more rapid development by a potential enemy; in the case of the TVA, by the hostility of the private power industry. Where government is secure in a monopoly, on the other hand, progress is less likely to occur. With the Post Office, for instance, little has been invested in research, obsolete equipment has been retained in service, and newer methods of handling materials have barely been explored. Such backwardness has also been found in private industries: in coal, for instance, and in the railway, Pullman, and telegraph services. But, by and large, it would be generally agreed that public is less progressive than private enterprise.

PUBLIC ENTERPRISE AND THE CONSUMER

It is not to be assumed that the interests of consumers in the performance of an enterprise will be adequately safeguarded by virtue of the fact that it is owned and operated by the government. If there is competition, consumers will be afforded protection by the availability of alternatives. But if there is not, they may suffer the consequences of monopoly. The quality of service may be low. The level of prices may be high. The structure of prices may be unduly discriminatory. Nor are consumers fully protected by their right to vote. The ballot lacks precision as a method of control. And votes are also cast by members of producer and consumer groups whose interests differ from those of consumers as a whole. If consumers are really to have protection, some other method will be required.

The Price Level

As a matter of policy, a public enterprise may be operated at a loss, its rates being set to cover but a portion of its costs and its deficit being met from other sources of public revenue. Or it may be operated at a profit, its rates being kept high and its earnings used to defray the costs of other public activities. Or it may be required merely to pay its own way, its rates being designed to cover all its costs, but to yield no surplus for other purposes.

Operation at a loss may be adopted as a method of providing consumers with goods or services for which they cannot pay; low-rent housing is thus provided for families in the lower-income groups. It may be used as a means of subsidizing an industry; newspapers and magazines are thus delivered at less than cost. Operation at a profit, on the other hand, may be designed to check consumption; state liquor stores have kept their prices high. It may be employed as a means of providing public revenue; some cities with municipal electric plants have cut their taxes, financing their normal functions by charging high electric rates. Such policies, of course, produce a different allocation of resources than would have resulted from free consumer choice. More is spent, for instance, on housing and on newspapers and magazines; less on liquor and electricity. In some cases, such a change may be socially desirable; in others, it may not. But even where desirable, it might better be effected by some other means. If consumption is to be encouraged or discouraged by government, this should be done, in general, not by manipulating the rates of public enterprises, but by frankly paying subsidies in the one case and imposing taxes in the other.

Alteration of public prices might also be employed as a means of stabilizing the economy. During a recession, such prices could be cut in order to stimulate sales and maintain employment. During a boom, they could be raised to discourage sales and check overexpansion. Public enterprises, like the rest of the government, might be expected to balance their budgets over the cycle. In the one period, they would be operated at a deficit. In the other, they would pay off their debts. Such a policy might have its merits. For stabilization, unquestionably, is to be desired. But here, again, it is preferable that the end be sought by other means.

If there is to be an adequate basis for judging the economy and efficiency with which a public enterprise is conducted, it should be required to pay its own way. Its prices should be set at a level that is calculated to yield sufficient revenue to enable it to meet its costs. It should provide for depreciation and replacement. It might also amortize past debts and make some provision for future expansion. But its goal should be that of showing neither a profit nor a loss. Its budget, moreover, should be an annual one. For if it is the policy that public enterprises are to be self-supporting, this requirement must be continually enforced.

Costs may be covered by selling a smaller quantity at a higher price or a larger quantity at a lower one. A private enterprise may content itself with the smaller volume, hesitating to cut prices because it fears to take a chance on the elasticity of demand. A public enterprise will be more likely to run the risk. If demand proves to be inelastic, it will not go bankrupt.

Its loss will be made up by appropriations from other public revenues. If demand proves to be elastic, however, it will expand its service and continue to cover its costs.

But there is no assurance, under public enterprise, that rates will be lowered by reducing costs. Indeed, there is danger that they will steadily be raised to cover steadily increasing costs. Labor is organized, economically and politically, to demand higher wages and other benefits. A private enterprise, if faced by competition, would be constrained to resist such demands by the threat of bankruptcy. A public monopoly encounters no such threat. And there may be little or no resistance to passing repeated wage increases on to the consumer in higher rates.

A public enterprise, moreover, may not be permitted to cover its costs. Politicians may seek to curry favor by keeping rates so low that a service must be provided at a loss. This has been the case, for instance, with the postal service and with transit systems operated by municipalities. It might well be the case with railroads, if they were taken over by the government. Where workers and consumers are both exerting pressure, wages may be pushed up, rates held down, and an increasing burden loaded on the taxpayer.

The Price Structure

A public enterprise is no more likely than a private enterprise to charge the same amount for every unit sold. A public power plant will not make a flat charge per kilowatt-hour. A public railroad will not make a flat charge per ton-mile. For one thing, the costs involved in selling different units will differ, and prices will be adjusted to cover differences in cost. For another, the demands of different customers will differ in elasticity, and prices will make allowance for such differences. Overhead costs will not be spread evenly, but will be allocated in accordance with what the traffic will bear. Where consumers lack alternatives, rates will be high. Where they possess them, rates will be low. The use of the service will thus be maximized and costs and prices, in general, kept lower than they otherwise would be. Even though the enterprise be public, it will find it advantageous to follow the familiar principle of discriminating monopoly. The structure of its rates will be complex.

Both public and private enterprises will discriminate for economic reasons. But a public enterprise may also discriminate to serve political purposes. Such purposes may be commendable. School children are transported without charge by city transit systems. Books and records for the blind are delivered for nothing by the Post Office. The principle could be extended. Electricity could be supplied at a high price to gambling dens, at a low price to churches and hospitals. The railroads could charge high rates for hauling slot machines, low rates for hauling hymnals and medicines. The government could thus discourage activities that were considered bad, encourage those that were considered good. But here, too, its purpose might better be accomplished in another way. Taxes and subsidies should be made visible, not hidden in the structure of rates. Worthy causes should be supported by the taxpayers, not by the users of public services. In the interest of economy and efficiency, public enterprises should be permitted to base their rates on business principles alone.

Such enterprises may discriminate in favor of worthy causes. There is greater danger that they will be required to discriminate in favor of powerful pressure groups. The prices charged by public enterprises need not be fixed by legislation. But postal rates have always been so fixed, and others—such as railroad rates—might also be. The structure of freight rates, if thrown to Congress for determination, would afford even greater opportunities for political manipulation than did the tariff in the past. The railroads might well be required to favor particular communities and commodities, the lowest rates going to those with the greatest political power. The farmers, it may be presumed, would get such rates on everything they bought and sold. And other users of the service would be taxed, in higher rates, to finance the subsidy.

Consumer Protection

Under private enterprise, the consumer is protected against poor service, high prices, and undue discrimination in two different ways: by competition and by regulation. Under public enterprise, such protection is also possible. A nationalized industry could be organized as a number of competing units. Or separate organizations could be established for competing services, such as gas and electricity, communication by mail, telephone, telegraph, and radio, and transportation by rail, road, water, and air. Or, failing this, such industries could be organized as monopolies and independent tribunals authorized to regulate their services and rates. In most cases of nationalization, however, the consumer has been given protection in neither way.

In Great Britain, for instance, the emphasis has been on unification and co-ordination. The purpose has been efficiency; a consequence has been monopoly. Within each of the national industries, the organization is highly centralized. Gas and electricity are separate. But the Transport Commission, at the outset, controlled haulage by railway, highway, and waterway. Shippers were permitted to select their mode of transport. But their freedom of choice was more nominal than real. For the government decided what services were to be provided and what rates were to be charged. And its interest was in physical integration, not in the allocation of traffic in accordance with comparative costs.

So, too, with regulation. In Great Britain the rates charged by the Transport Commission are reviewed by the Transport Tribunal as were those charged, before nationalization, by the railroad companies. With other public industries, however, the prices fixed by managements are final, no formal provision being made for their control. In this country the rates of municipal utilities are subject to commission regulation in some states but not in others. Those of the Bonneville Power Administration and certain other projects must be approved by the Federal Power Commission. But this requirement is designed to assure the taxpayer—and the private power industry—that rates will not be set too low, not to assure the consumer that they will not be set too high. In general, the prices fixed by public enterprises are not reviewed by other agencies. The consumer is afforded less of an opportunity to protect himself against public monopoly than against private monopoly.

In Britain the government has sought to give consumers a voice by setting up a consumers' council or a system of national and regional or local councils in each of the nationalized industries. The councils are part-time bodies, holding meetings monthly or quarterly. Their membership, appointed by the respective ministries, is designed to be broadly representative. It is their function to receive, investigate, and settle consumer complaints. They may merely call the complaints to the attention of managements or they may make recommendations to managements or attempt to work out settlements themselves. They may also give advice on questions submitted to them by managements, raise questions of their own, and make recommendations to the ministries. In practice, the councils have been ineffective. They have been little known or used, receiving few complaints. They have been wanting in vigor, meeting infrequently and being poorly staffed. They have not been independent, relying on the public enterprises for their quarters, information, and facilities. They have had no means of enforcing their recommendations, lacking the support of an organized pressure group. Having sought, in many cases, to explain the policies of national industries to the public, they have come to be regarded as mouthpieces of managements.

EFFICIENCY versus ACCOUNTABILITY

A public enterprise should be administered efficiently. It should be held, in the fulfillment of its function, to strict accountability. But these two purposes are not consistent. For the rules established in the name of accountability are often prejudicial to efficiency. And the independence required for efficiency may carry with it freedom from accountability. This is the dilemma on which attention has been centered in the debate on the administration of public enterprises both in Great Britain and in the United States.

The Government Department

There is danger that the managers of public enterprises will be irresponsible, taking actions not authorized by law, or that they will be dishonest, enriching themselves through favoritism and fraud. There is danger, too, that political parties will seek to gain and hold office by firing government workers, however efficient, and giving their jobs to party followers. To guard against these dangers, certain controls have been imposed upon the budgets, accounts, and personnel practices of government agencies. Such controls apply to the departmental administration of public enterprise in the United States.

A department of the federal government must prepare its annual budget well in advance, itemizing its proposed expenditures. This budget is presented to the Budget Bureau to be analyzed, modified, and approved. It goes next to the appropriations committees of the House of Representatives and the Senate where it is further modified. From there it goes to the House, subsequently to the Senate, then to a conference committee, and finally back to the House and the Senate to be enacted in amended form. The department is thus given authority to spend particular funds for particular purposes within a fiscal year. It cannot borrow on its own responsibility to obtain new equipment or to expand its working capital. It cannot transfer unexpended sums from one appropriation item to another. It must draw all its funds from the Treasury and return all its earnings to the Treasury. While it is carrying on its operations in one year, it must be going through this process to obtain appropriations for the year ahead.

All expenditures made by a department are audited, at a later date, by the General Accounting Office. This agency, under a Controller General, is responsible to the Congress. It is its function to make sure that no expenditures are made without authority of law. The Office interprets the laws and issues rulings to which departments must conform. It prescribes the manner in which departments keep their accounts.

In hiring, promoting, transferring, and firing personnel, the departments are subject to control by the Civil Service Commission. Not all jobs are under Civil Service, but, for those that are, job descriptions must be prepared and job classifications obtained. And they must then be filled by persons whose qualifications the Commission has approved. Unless an agency is being abolished or reduced in size, employees cannot be discharged without observing prescribed procedures. And even when there is a reduction in force, discharges must be made in accordance with the priorities established on the Commission's retention register.

The Civil Service regulations may make a public enterprise less vulnerable to political pressure. The budgetary controls may make it more so. For these controls can be applied by Congress for purposes other than that of insuring honesty, economy, and efficiency in administration. They can be used—and have been used—to force an enterprise to favor powerful pressure groups. The administrator who resists such pressures, in the public interest, may have his appropriation cut. He may be denied the right to make expenditures for certain purposes. Nor are the personnel of a public agency immune from political attack. Persons appointed or reappointed to positions requiring Senatorial approval may be denied confirmation. And all public employees, including civil servants, may find themselves accused of incompetence, dishonesty, immorality, and disloyalty, subjected to inquisitions by ambitious politicians, their reputations blackened, under cover of Congressional immunity, in an effort to profit from personal publicity. These handicaps are not experienced by private enterprise.

The Costs of Bureaucracy

In operation, the controls established to insure accountability are clumsy and sluggish. In controlling budgets, the committees on appropriations and the houses of Congress lack the knowledge and the time required for adequate review. In the committee hearings and in the Congressional debates, the questions asked and the issues raised are likely to be irrelevant, petty, or partisan. If a budget is reduced, a flat percentage cut may be applied across the board, because the legislators are unable to distinguish between activities that are important and those that are not. Where distinctions are made, an integral part of a program may be denied support because an administrator has offended politicians who are thus enabled to obtain revenge. The process of making appropriations, far from being informed and precise, is usually arbitrary and even capricious. And it is always slow.

The rules governing public expenditures, issued by the General Accounting Office, are voluminous and meticulous. The audit of such expenditures, made by the Office, is designed to give assurance that every penny has been spent with strict legality. Sums spent in good faith may subsequently be disallowed. An official who has paid for a taxi on a business trip, for instance, may be denied a refund, months later, on the ground that he could have ridden on a bus. The GAO has frequently been criticized for failing to require business-like methods of accounting. The Office has been more interested in observance of legal restrictions than in economy or efficiency.

To the public administrator, the regulations of the Civil Service Commission appear to be designed to make it impossible for him to obtain or to retain competent personnel. He cannot employ a man, however able, until the Commission gives its consent. And the processes of investigation, examination, clearance, and approval may go on for months. Instead of the man he wants, the administrator may be forced to take another, whose talents are inferior, but whose paper qualifications come closer to satisfying the Commission's rules. When budgets are cut, the man last hired, though the best man in the office, will be the first to go. Some chairwarmer, dating from an earlier administration will have superior retention rights. If a man is attacked politically, he can be dropped. But if he is merely incompetent, the Commission will come to his defense. Discharge is made so difficult that the administrator may abandon the attempt, finding it simpler to move the undesirable employee to an empty room without a function, a title, a secretary, or a phone. The Commission, by withholding jobs from political patronage, may protect the public enterprise from a fate that would be worse. But to the administrator, attempting to carry out a program, the fate it leaves him with is bad enough.

In general, these controls obstruct good management. First, they carry the constant threat of reversal of policy. It is difficult or impossible to go on with projects, already initiated, when appropriations are curtailed or funds denied. It is difficult, too, to plan for the future when there is no assurance of continuity. Second, the controls involve delays. Where responsibility is centralized, decisions are taken to the top, and months may elapse before they come back down. In the meantime, the enterprise is unable to adjust to change. Action is suspended while papers move, deliberately, from desk to desk until the final signature has been obtained. Third, the controls provide no means for judging efficiency. The system of accounting used does not require that revenues shall cover costs. Nor does it analyze the costs themselves. An enterprise, thus controlled, may go on indefinitely operating at a loss, its costs far higher than they need to be. Fourth, and finally, the controls circumscribe the discretion and curb the initiative of managements. And so they discourage imagination, repress enthusiasm, and smother innovation. Strict accountability is assured by binding an enterprise with red tape. But another thing assured is immobility.

The Public Corporation

The public corporation was once envisaged as an entity that would be independent of the established departments of government and would be freed from hampering controls. Its autonomy was to be assured by entrusting its administration to a separate board, with members appointed for long and overlapping terms. Its freedom was to involve exemption from the procedures usually governing budgets and appropriations, from supervision by the General Accounting Office, and from Civil Service regulations as to personnel. The corporation was to obtain its initial capital from the Treasury and was to seek Congressional approval for expansion of its facilities. But otherwise it was to be self-supporting, paying its bills with the proceeds of its sales. It was not to be required to obtain its current revenues through Congressional appropriations or to turn its income over to the Treasury. In command of its own resources, it was to determine its own expenditures. Freed from the General Accounting Office, the corporation was to make its purchases and sales in accordance with its judgment of market opportunities. Freed from Civil Service, it was to make its own decisions in handling its employees.

This independence was expected to carry with it a number of advantages. It would protect an enterprise from partisan interference and enable it better to resist the demands of pressure groups. It would make for continuity of policy. It would permit quicker action and greater flexibility. It would promote the adoption of business-like methods of accounting, making it possible to apply commercial standards in judging economy and efficiency. It would encourage initiative and open the way to innovation. In short, it would enable the administrators of a public enterprise to run it as a private business would be run.

This is still the way the public corporation is regarded in Great Britain. But the freedom of such bodies has been steadily whittled down in the United States. Many of them have lost their independent status, being subordinated to government departments. All of them have been required by law, first, to submit their administrative expenses—a small but crucial part of their total expenditures—to the Bureau of the Budget for approval and, subsequently, to have them appropriated by Congress. All but the TVA and the Federal Deposit Insurance Corporation have been brought under Civil Service. And under the Government Corporation Control Act of 1945, all corporations belonging to the federal government must submit business-type budgets each year for approval by Congress. And their accounts are subjected to a business-type audit by the General Accounting Office. These requirements have clearly limited the freedom of the public corporation. Whether they have destroyed its advantages as an agency of administration is still a matter of dispute.

The Problem of Accountability

In Great Britain the public corporation retains more freedom than it does in the United States. But there, too, it is recognized that the independence that makes for efficiency may also make for irresponsibility. And the major issue debated, under nationalization, is how a balance can be struck between the two objectives of business-like management and political accountability.

Each of the public corporations, in Britain, is under a minister. He appoints the members of its board. He may prescribe the form of its record keeping, accounting, and reports. He may inspect its establishments to make sure that certain regulations, such as those relating to health and safety are observed. The corporation must submit reports to the minister. And some of its actions, including plans for reorganization, expansion, and borrowing, must be submitted for his approval. But the minister typically refrains from interfering in the day-to-day management of the business. He has the legal power to issue directives to the corporation. But its board would doubtless feel that such a move reflected on its competence. And, as a result, the power is seldom used.

Control by ministers may be lax. Control by Parliament is even more so. Departments of government have long been held accountable, under the Parliamentary system, by the device of raising questions about their operations to be answered by ministers during the question period in the House of Commons. This procedure, indeed, is taken so seriously that a member's threat to raise a question may induce an official to modify his policies. But with the public corporations, Labor and Conservative ministers alike have refused to answer questions concerning administrative details. The annual reports of the corporations can be debated in Parliament; their daily operations cannot.

It is charged in Britain that this situation, in effect, hands the corporate board a blank check, to be filled out, for better or for worse, at its pleasure. It is argued, moreover, that Parliament lacks the knowledge and the time properly to appraise the operations of all the national industries. Their submission to questioning, therefore, is not proposed. A number of other remedies have been considered: a standing committee of the House of Commons to review the activities of public corporations, a full-scale Parliamentary investigation of each corporation to be made periodically—say once in every seven years—or *ad hoc* investigations to be made as the need may arise, or an efficiency audit to be made periodically by an independent agency. Whatever the solution, it is widely felt that the public corporation cannot be given unlimited freedom, but must somehow be policed.

A fundamental difficulty remains. Even though mechanisms for controlling the performance of public enterprises may be provided, standards of appraisal may not. With nationalization, the yardstick of competition is abandoned and the market rendered ineffective as an arbiter of cost and price. There are no agreed criteria by which to judge success or failure, no way to tell how well an enterprise has done or how much better it might have done. Accountability may be enforced, but accountability for what? Parliament may exercise its right to act, but it will still be acting in the dark.

NATIONALIZATION AND DENATIONALIZATION

Some enterprises have been public from the beginning: the post office in all countries, the telegraph and telephone systems in Western Europe, atomic energy in the United States. Others, once private, have been taken over by governments. In some cases, governments have come to participate in business by extending aid to private companies that were heading into bankruptcy. In others, they have seized the properties of foreigners or traitors. In still others, they have seized all private properties. But aside from confiscation and revolution, nationalization has usually involved the payment of compensation for enterprises purchased by governments at forced or voluntary sales. The issues raised by the process have had to do with the amount to be paid and the form in which the payment was to be made.

In Great Britain the sale of the industries was forced, the procedure being to vest ownership in the government as of a certain day. In some cases—coal, transport, gas, and electricity—the government acquired an industry's assets, the former companies being left to enter another business, to continue as investment agencies, or to liquidate their holdings, as they chose. In others, such as iron and steel, it acquired the shares of corporations, superseding the former owners in control. Usually, the amount of compensation paid was fixed by Parliament. Matters of detail could be submitted to arbitration, but the level of payments could not be challenged in the courts. In general, the payments were designed to leave the former owners with securities of the same value or with earnings of the same size as they had before. The new securities, however, were bonds bearing a fixed rate of interest rather than stocks yielding a variable return, the risks of the enterprises being transferred to the taxpayer. The methods employed in effecting nationalization gave rise to little or no litigation and to little public criticism or debate.

In the United States, if the owners of a private enterprise were forced to sell it to a government, they would have the right, under state and federal constitutions, to appeal the amount of their compensation to the courts. In practice, most public enterprises have been initiated by governments. And where private assets have been acquired, it has been through voluntary sale. Here, the price has been arrived at through negotiation. And the government, instead of paying too little, is as likely to have paid too much.

In the event of denationalization, a frequent procedure has been to set up a liquidation agency and charge it with responsibility for selling the government properties. This has been done, for instance, in the case of the iron and steel mills and the trucking industry in Great Britain and in that of the synthetic rubber plants in the United States. In such cases, the seller is usually under pressure to make a sale, while the buyer is under no compulsion to buy. As a result, the price is likely to be low. The government loses money on the deal and the companies that buy its properties are subsidized. In Britain, where £30 million of the £80 million paid the trucking companies for their trucks went for "good will," it was clear that no such sum could be collected in selling them back. In the United States, the sale of the synthetic rubber plants was an exception, 24 of the 27 plants offered for sale being sold in 1955 at prices that covered 99 per cent of their replacement cost.[1]

The way in which public assets are sold will affect the future structure of an industry. If all the sales are made to a single company, the government may get a better price, but the industry may be monopolized. If sales can be made to many buyers, even though at a comparative loss, the industry may become competitive. This is a consideration which influenced the government of the United States in disposing of war assets, such as its aluminum plants. The British government, in denationalizing road haulage, offered trucks in lots of four or less to small operators before it gave the larger concerns an opportunity to bid. It abandoned the program of integrating all the modes of transport in favor of restoring competition between the roads and rails.

[1] *Business Week*, January 29, 1955, p. 96.

The success of denationalization may be imperiled by the threat of an opposition party, if returned to power, to renationalize. Such a threat has been made by the Labor Party in Britain, for instance, with respect to iron and steel. This makes it more difficult for the government to find buyers. And if the industry, once sold, were to be renationalized, it may be doubted that it could ever be denationalized again. Whatever the respective advantages and disadvantages of public and private enterprise, it is certain that either one is preferable to perpetual uncertainty.

SUGGESTIONS FOR FURTHER READING

The use of the public corporation as an administrative device is well discussed by V. O. Key in chap. xi of *Elements of Public Administration*, Fritz M. Marx (ed.) (New York: Prentice-Hall, 1946). Experience with such corporations in the United States is considered at greater length by Marshall E. Dimock in "Government Corporations: A Focus of Policy and Administration," *American Political Science Review*, XLIII (1949), 899–921, 1145–64. The argument for corporate rather than departmental management is presented by David E. Lilienthal and R. H. Marquis in "The Conduct of Business Enterprises by the Federal Government," *Harvard Law Review*, LIV (1941), 545–601. A criticism of the limitations placed on public corporations is contained in C. H. Pritchett, "Government Corporation Control Act of 1945," *American Political Science Review*, XL (1946), 495–510. A defense of such limitations is given by Harold Seidman in "The Theory of the Autonomous Corporation," *Public Administration Review*, XII (1952) 89–96.

British experience with public enterprise since the war is appraised in an excellent symposium on *Problems of Nationalized Industry*, William A. Robson (ed.) (2d ed.; New York: Oxford University Press, 1952), and in an equally able series of papers on *Nationalized Industry* published from time to time by the Acton Society Trust of London. Overcentralization in the administration of nationalized industries is attacked by H. A. Clegg and T. E. Chester in *The Future of Nationalization* (Oxford: Basil Blackwell, 1953). The position of the consumer is considered in Eldon L. Johnson, "Consumer 'Control' in British Nationalized Industries," *Journal of Politics*, XV (1953), 88–113. For current developments, the student should follow *The Economist*.

Experience in France is described by Mario Einaudi in "Nationalization of Industry in Western Europe," *American Political Science Review*, XLIV (1950), 177–91, by Henry P. De Vries and B. H. Hoeniger in "Post-Liberation Nationalizations in France," *Columbia Law Review*, L (1950), 629–56, and by Adolph Sturmthal in "The Structure of Nationalized Enterprises in France," *Political Science Quarterly*, LXII (1952), 357–77, and in "Nationalization and Worker's Control in Britain and France," *Journal of Political Economy*, LXI (1953), 43–79.

PART VII

Alternatives of Policy

Chapter 30 WHICH CONTROLS?

In the preceding parts of this book we have examined, in some detail, the principal policies adopted by government in dealing with business: maintaining competition, supplementing competition, moderating competition, substituting regulation for competition, and substituting public for private enterprise. It remains for us to compare these policies, assessing their relative merits and setting forth the factors that should be considered in choosing among them where such a choice can be made.

A decision as to policy may relate to the economy in general: shall resources be allocated through the market or by agencies of government? In time of war there is little opportunity for choice; allocation must be directed by the state. In peacetime, however, choice is possible. Allocation can be left to the market, and policy can deal with the implementation of market processes and with the prevention of harmful results.

Choices are also made in particular cases. Is one industry, characterized by monopoly, to be broken into competing parts, to be regulated by a public agency, or to be taken over by the government? Is another, where producers have suffered from competition, to be sheltered from its full effects? No policy can be applied across the board. Competition cannot be enforced in industries where unification of the service rendered necessitates monopoly or maintained without modification in cases where this would result in widespread hardship and distress. Private enterprise cannot always be preserved in areas where health and safety are endangered and where national security is at stake. Services and rates cannot readily be regulated or public operation undertaken in fields where firms are small and numerous and competition normally intense. Each of the controls available is likely to have some use.

The choice as to policy in general is one of relative emphasis: which of the controls are to be regarded as exceptions and which as the general rule? In the United States, as we have seen, the moderation of competition, the regulation of services and rates, and the substitution of public enterprise are the exceptions. The maintenance of competition, together with measures designed to set the plane of competition is the general rule. Has this policy been wise or unwise? Has it succeeded or has it failed?

MAINTAINING COMPETITION AS A GENERAL POLICY

The policy of maintaining competition has evoked extensive criticism from economists, lawyers, and businessmen. The policy is shown to be a failure, it is said, by evidence of the decline of competition and the increasing concentration of economic power. Some of the critics believe that failure was inevitable, holding the policy to have been mistaken from the start. They assert that the economies of large-scale production are to be realized only by establishments so large that their owners will dominate the markets where they sell. They contend that the research and development required for economic progress are to be expected only of firms possessing monopolistic powers. And they argue that action breaking large firms into smaller ones is futile, since the result is merely oligopoly, and oligopolists behave not like competitors but like monopolists. Other critics hold the policy of maintaining competition to be wise and attribute its failure to the fact that it has not been given a thorough trial. Public policy has been inconsistent. The antitrust laws have been vague. Provision for their enforcement has been inadequate. The enforcement effort has been spasmodic. It has been obstructed by adverse decisions of the courts. The penalties imposed have been too light. The remedies afforded have been ineffective. Save for these circumstances, competition might have been maintained. Such are the positions taken by the critics. Each of them will now be examined in its turn.

"The Decline of Competition" and "The Concentration of Economic Power"

It is often asserted and widely believed that economic power, in the United States, is concentrated in the hands of a few corporate giants, that such concentration has been increasing over the years, and that, as a result, competition has virtually disappeared from the American economy. If this were indeed the case, it might well be said that antitrust had failed. But the situation, upon examination, is far less serious than has often been supposed. There is evidence, to be sure, that corporate wealth is concentrated in the hands of larger firms, but there is none to demonstrate that concentration has been increasing, and none to justify the assertion that competition has declined.

A number of statistical studies, published during the past twenty years, have revealed the existence of substantial concentration, in the hands of a few large firms, of employment, assets, output, sales, or income (1) among all non-banking corporations, (2) for manufacturing as a whole, and (3) within particular manufacturing industries, and similar concentration (4) in the output, product by product, of manufactured goods.[1]

[1] See Adolf A. Berle, Jr. and Gardiner C. Means, *The Modern Corporation and Private Property* (New York: Macmillan Co., 1933); *Big Business: Its Growth and*

A few samples of the findings presented in these studies will suffice:

> In 1947 the 200 largest employers in the United States accounted for nearly one fifth of all employment in private nonagricultural establishments, and the 200 largest corporations held two fifths of all corporate assets and between one fifth and one fourth of all income-yielding wealth.
>
> Among manufacturers, in the same year, 163 concerns with more than 10,000 employees accounted for 30 per cent of the employment, and 133 concerns with assets of more than $100 million held 40 per cent of all the assets.[2]
>
> Among 275 manufacturing industries, in 1935, 8 firms hired more than half of the workers in each of 131, and 4 firms hired more than half of the workers in each of 75. Among 452 such industries, in 1947, the 4 largest firms accounted for more than half of the output in 150 and for more than three fourths of the output in 46.[3]
>
> Among 1,807 products reported for the Census of Manufacturers in 1937, the 4 largest producers accounted for more than 85 per cent of the output in one fourth of the cases, for more than 70 per cent in nearly half of the cases, and for more than 50 per cent in three fourths.[4]

This is the type of evidence that is usually cited in support of generalizations concerning the decline of competition. On the surface, it is impressive. But, upon analysis, it is less conclusive than it seems:

> The concentration figures for all non-banking corporations apply to a heterogeneous group that includes railroad and public utility companies whose monopolistic powers are subject to regulation by public authorities (such concerns accounting for half of the assets held by the 200 largest corporations), along with several companies, like Sears Roebuck, Macy's, and the A&P, that operate in highly competitive fields, and a number of other concerns that may or may not control the markets where they buy and sell. The figures throw no light upon the incidence of unregulated monopoly.
>
> The figures for manufacturing as a whole, apply likewise to an undifferentiated group, ranging all the way from industries that are highly competitive to those that are virtually monopolized. Two thirds of the concentrated assets in this group are found in only 4 among more than 450 manufacturing

Its Place (New York: Twentieth Century Fund, 1937); National Resources Committee, *The Structure of the American Economy* (Washington: Government Printing Office, 1939); Willard L. Thorp and Walter F. Crowder, *The Structure of Industry*, T.N.E.C. Monograph No. 27 (Washington: Government Printing Office, 1941); Federal Trade Commission, *Report on the Concentration of Productive Facilities, 1947* (Washington: Government Printing Office, 1949); Charles Sawyer, letter to Emanuel Celler, in Hearings before the Subcommittee on Study of Monopoly Power, Committee on the Judiciary, House of Representatives, 81st Cong. 1st Sess., Serial No. 14, Part 2 B, pp. 1436–56; M. A. Adelman, "The Measurement of Industrial Concentration," *Review of Economics and Statistics*, XXXIII (1951), 269–96.

[2] Adelman, *loc. cit.*, pp. 275–77.

[3] National Resources Committee, *op. cit.*, pp. 240–58; Sawyer, *op. cit.*, p. 1446.

[4] Thorp and Crowder, *op. cit.*, Part III.

> industries. The figures tell us little or nothing about the occurrence of competition and monopoly.
>
> The concentration ratios for particular industries are based upon a classification, employed by the Census of Manufactures, in which industries are defined, in part, according to the materials they use and the processes they employ. In some cases, firms manufacturing many different products are lumped together in a single category. In others, products that are closely competitive are listed as coming from different industries. Data on concentration within such categories afford little insight into the structure of markets for particular goods.
>
> The ratios for particular goods are based, similarly, upon a classification that defines products, in part, according to the materials from which they are made, the processes employed in their fabrication, and the degree of integration obtaining in the establishments where production is carried on. As a result, there may be many listings for a single commodity. In some cases, the degree of concentration is understated because the output figures are nationwide and markets are regional, or because dissimilar goods are lumped together in a common category. In others, the degree of concentration is seriously overstated because the figures are confined to domestic output and the competition afforded by imports is ignored, and because products that may be readily substituted for one another are listed in unrelated categories. These figures cannot afford an accurate index of concentrated power.[5]

The apparent degree of concentration revealed by such studies varies with the base that is used (whether all business, all corporations, all but financial corporations, all industrials, all manufactures, particular industries, or particular products, and how industries and products are defined), with the unit of measurement (whether a single plant or a firm, and whether a single-product or multiple-product firm), and with the index of concentration (whether employment, assets, output, sales, or income). The significance of the resulting ratios is obscured, too, by the fact that they pertain only to the largest three, four, six, or eight units, and do not reveal whether the members of such groups are dominated by a single firm, or approach equality of power. It should be noted, finally, that the indexes of concentration are not indexes of monopoly. They may reveal the consequences of monopolistic restriction and exclusion or those of competitive innovation, market development, and reductions in cost and price. They may conceal the influence of potential competition, and the presence—on the other side of the market—of countervailing power. The studies of concentration are suggestive, but they fall far short of proving the monopoly that they are often said to prove.

[5] For a more detailed criticism of these studies, see G. Warren Nutter, *The Extent of Enterprise Monopoly in the United States* (Chicago: University of Chicago Press, 1951), pp. 11–19; and Clair Wilcox, "On the Alleged Ubiquity of Oligopoly," *American Economic Review*, XL, No. 2 (1950), 67–73.

The Extent of Monopoly and Competition

There is reason to believe that monopoly made rapid headway in the United States during the latter part of the nineteenth century. But there is nothing to support the view that it has continued to do so during the twentieth. Indeed, all the evidence that is available appears to point the other way. Warren Nutter, in a pioneering study of the subject, compares the extent of monopoly obtaining in 1899 and 1939, identifying as monopolistic all industries in which the four largest firms produced half or more of the output, and measuring the relative extent of monopoly by estimating the share of national income originating in these industries. On this basis, he finds that the relative importance of monopoly increased only in the case of financial enterprises, remained the same in agriculture, services, trade, contract construction, and public utilities, and declined in manufacturing, mining, transportation, and communications.[6] M. A. Adelman, building on the foundation laid by Nutter, compares the concentration of output found in manufacturing industries in 1947 with that existing around 1901 and comes to the conclusion that "The odds are better than even that there has actually been some decline in concentration. It is a good bet that there has at least been no actual increase; and the odds do seem high against any substantial increase."[7] For the economy as a whole, Adelman finds that "The extent of concentration shows no tendency to grow, and it may possibly be declining. Any tendency either way, if it does exist, must be at the pace of glacial drift."[8] A. D. H. Kaplan points out that the number of business enterprises per thousand of population in the United States has been increasing—according to Dun and Bradstreet from 15.4 in 1900 to around 17 in 1950; according to the Department of Commerce from 25 in 1929 to 26 in 1949.[9] Kaplan finds that the growth of big business has been matched by the growth of the economy as a whole with no material alteration of its relative position over the past quarter century.[10] He compares the 100 largest industrial corporations in 1948 with the 100 largest in 1909 and finds that the share of this group in the assets of all such corporations has increased but slightly while their share in income has declined perceptibly.[11] More significantly, he contrasts the composition of the group in the 2 years, noting that only 36 of those among the 100 largest in 1909 were still on the list of the 100 largest in 1948, while most of those on the list had attained their position

[6] Nutter, *op. cit.*, pp. 35–43.

[7] Adelman, *op cit.*, pp. 292–93.

[8] *Ibid.*, p. 295.

[9] A. D. H. Kaplan, *Big Enterprise in a Competitive System* (Washington: Brookings Institution, 1954), p. 71.

[10] *Ibid.*, p. 73.

[11] *Ibid.*, chap. vi.

within the last twenty years.[12] Though concentration persists, the individual firm is not entrenched. The situation, rather, is a fluid one, with new leaders emerging as old ones are losing ground. Kaplan therefore concludes that "we are not justified in identifying increase of financial resources of large-scale enterprise with net decline in the scope and vigor of competition."[13]

These studies may not serve completely to demolish the decline-of-competition school of economics, but they have placed upon it a heavy burden of proof. Indeed, there are signs that our economy is becoming more rather than less competitive. The boundaries of products are constantly being pushed outward as industrial research provides us with an increasing variety of ready substitutes. Frozen foods compete with canned foods and synthetic fibers with cotton, silk, and wool. In the case of durable goods, moreover, new products must meet the competition of products sold at second hand. New cars compete with used cars and virgin metal competes with scrap. The boundaries of markets, too, are being steadily extended by the growth of transportation and communication. Refrigeration brings the fruits of California into competition with those of Florida. Hard roads bring the downtown merchant into competition with the suburban shopping center, the local merchant into competition with those in other towns. The jurisdictional lines in distribution are repeatedly breaking down. The supermarket competes with the drug store; the discount house with the specialty shop and the department store. These signs are present in abundance for all who have the eyes to see.

To what extent, today, is the American economy monopolized, to what extent is it competitive? Two estimates are available, both for 1939. According to George Stigler, one third of the income produced in that year came from industries controlled by individual monopolists or compulsory cartels and two thirds from industries that were competitive. According to Nutter, one fourth of nongovernmental production originated in monopolistic industries, including the public utilities, and three fourths in competitive or nonprofit industries.[14] Such estimates, of necessity, are little more than well-informed guesses. They are as likely to overstate as to understate the magnitude of the problem of monopoly.

The fields in which concentration presents a serious problem to antitrust are limited. Transportation and public utility enterprises are regulated by other agencies. Agriculture, forestry, fisheries, mining, building construction, wholesale and retail distribution, and the service trades are,

[12] *Ibid.*, chap. vii.

[13] *Ibid.*, p. 144.

[14] George Stigler, *Five Lectures on Economic Problems* (London: Longmans, Green & Co., 1949), p. 50; Nutter, *op cit.*, p. 20. Nutter identified as monopolistic all the industries that were so characterized in T.N.E.C. Monograph No. 21, plus all other industries where four firms produced half or more of the output in 1935, plus all other products where four firms accounted for three fourths or more of the output in 1937.

in general, actively competitive. Unregulated monopoly is confined almost entirely to manufacturing. And even here, there are many industries in which producers are numerous and the concentration of output is very low: including, for example, textiles and apparel, foods and beverages, furniture and furnishings, household appliances, small metal products, leather goods, pottery and porcelain wares, and printing and publishing. The industries in which a high degree of concentration, instead of being the exception, is the general rule, are those producing such basic materials as the primary metals, petroleum, chemicals, rubber, newsprint paper, glass, cement, and heavy machinery and equipment, certain durable consumers' goods, such as automobiles, refrigerators, radios, typewriters, vacuum cleaners, and sewing and washing machines, and a few lighter products such as tin cans, light bulbs, matches, soap, and cigarettes. In all of these fields, production is carried on by a small number of large firms. Here, the problem confronting antitrust is not monopoly but oligopoly.

Economies of Size in the Plant

Are the economies of large-scale production to be realized only through operation on a scale so great that competition cannot be maintained? In answering this question, it is necessary to distinguish between the advantages that pertain to size in an individual plant and those that pertain to size in a firm that may operate a number of plants. The economies of scale in a single plant will be considered first.

The large plant is generally assumed to possess certain marked advantages. It can effect a minute division of labor on the job. It can mechanize operations that would have been performed, on a smaller scale, by hand. It can install big, expensive, and highly specialized machines, provide them in great numbers, and arrange them in the proportions and in the sequences that are most conducive to continuous processes. It can utilize by-products and reclaim waste materials. It can employ skilled technicians, specializing in research and development and in the various branches of management.

It cannot be doubted that such economies exist. But empirical studies of the subject are fragmentary and inconclusive. A few investigators have attempted to measure the unit costs of output, or the physical input required for output, in plants of various sizes in particular industries. But such inquiries encounter serious difficulties. The effect of size cannot be measured with precision unless all other things are equal, and they seldom are. The composition of the product or the technology of production may differ from plant to plant. A product is rarely the only one turned out by all of the plants concerned. Its share in the product-mix may be large for one plant and small for another. Its apparent cost will be strongly influenced by the methods employed in allocating overhead. Cases simple enough to permit the measurement of the effect of size alone are rare indeed. In a number of instances, investigators have found higher costs in the largest plants and lower costs in plants of medium size.[15] But findings of this sort are scarcely to be generalized.

There are other indications that increasing size is not always advantageous. Big business typically expands, not by enlarging old plants but by building new ones, and the newer plants are not built on an ever larger scale. In half of our major industries, according to Kaplan, the plants are small in size. For industry in general, he finds no trend toward greater size.[16] In certain fields, indeed, recent developments in technology are making for operation on a smaller scale. Transportation by truck and the use of electric power permit decentralization. Newer materials, such as the light metals, alloys, plastics, and plywood, and newer processes, such as welding, stamping, and die casting, require less heavy installations and smaller investments of capital.[17] In the steel industry, today,

> . . . an integrated plant (with coke-fueled blast furnaces each producing 1,500 tons of pig iron per day, with a battery of open-hearth furnaces each producing up to 500 tons of steel, and with a continuous rolling mill) could not be built for much less than 250 million dollars. A significant consequence of recent advances in technology may conceivably be the emergence of enterprises conducting operations on a much smaller scale. The utilization of local deposits of ore in the direct reduction of iron or in the production of pig iron in the electric furnace or in the low-shaft blast furnace, the utilization of local supplies of iron and local surpluses of scrap in the production of steel in the electric furnace or in the turbo-hearth, the continuous casting of semi-finished steel, and the finishing of steel in small mills—all of these operations are feasible and all of them can be undertaken with an investment much smaller than that required for production on a larger scale.[18]

The growth of technology, in the past, has made for greater size. But there is no reason to suppose that it must always do so. In many cases, it may work the other way.

Even though lower costs can be obtained by a larger plant than by a smaller one, it does not follow that markets must be monopolized. Control over markets is usually achieved, not through the growth of a single plant, but by uniting several plants under common ownership. The size of plant required for efficiency and the scope of ownership required for monopoly are not to be confused. The advantages of size in the plant do not necessitate the attainment of greater size by the firm. They explain why Chevrolet can produce automobiles more cheaply than could the corner garage.

[15] See Federal Trade Commission, *Relative Efficiency of Large, Medium-Sized, and Small Business*, T.N.E.C. Monograph No. 13 (Washington: Government Printing Office, 1941), and John M. Blair, "The Relation between Size and Efficiency of Business," *Review of Economics and Statistics*, XXIV (1942), 125–36.

[16] Kaplan, *op. cit.*, p. 79.

[17] See John M. Blair, "Technology and Size," *American Economic Review*, XXXVIII, No. 2 (1948), 121–53.

[18] President's Materials Policy Commission, *Resources for Freedom* (Washington: Government Printing Office, 1952), Vol. II, p. 17.

They do not justify control by General Motors of Chevrolet, Pontiac, Oldsmobile, Buick, and Cadillac.

Joe S. Bain, in a significant study of this problem, took a representative sample of twenty industries and obtained engineering estimates on the plant size that had to be reached to obtain the lowest unit costs. Then he compared the output of such a plant with the total output of the industry. In nine of the industries, he found that the low-cost plant would account for less than 2½ per cent of the output, in fifteen for less than 7½ per cent, and in only one (typewriters) for more than 15 per cent. Recognizing that the sales of some plants are limited to regional markets, he also compared the output of the low-cost plant with the total sales in its market. Here, he found that such a plant would supply less than 5 per cent of the market in nine industries, less than 7½ per cent in fourteen, and less than 15 per cent in nineteen.[19] This demonstration leaves little ground for the view that the economies of size in the plant necessitate monopoly in the market.

Economies of Size in the Firm

A firm with several plants may be a horizontal combination of plants performing similar functions, a vertical combination of plants performing successive functions, a conglomeration of plants performing unrelated functions, or some combination of the three. In each of these cases, there are said to be advantages in size. Horizontal combination may enable management to standardize products and procedures, give wider scope to know-how, and lift the poorer units in a chain up to the level of the best. It may permit specialization among plants and more intensive specialization in administration. Where plants are scattered, it may cut the costs of transportation by eliminating cross freights. By making possible the use of a common selling organization, it may reduce the unit cost of sales. Vertical integration may improve control of quality and promise steadier operation by insuring regular delivery of materials and continued access to markets. Even a conglomerate combination may cut costs by employing common facilities for research and marketing. Its principal purpose, however, would appear to be that of diversifying investment risks. In all of these cases, moreover, size may enable its possessor to obtain capital and credit more easily, to buy materials in larger quantities, and to spend more money on research.

But there are also disadvantages in size. Combination, in any form, requires more effort in co-ordination and necessitates larger expenditures on administrative overhead. A business may grow so cumbersome that no man can hope to manage it efficiently. It may be so vast, so scattered, and so diversified that no one can really know what is going on. Under

[19] Joe S. Bain, "Economies of Scale, Concentration, and the Condition of Entry in Twenty Manufacturing Industries," *American Economic Review*, XLIV (1954), 15–38.

these circumstances, the manager loses contact with actual operations and is forced, instead, to obtain his information from accounts and statistics, to issue orders from a distance, and to rely upon paper controls. He may be bogged down with memoranda, reports, and routine. He may hesitate to make decisions and waste time in interminable delays. His subordinates may dissipate their energies in duplicated effort. They may be entangled in red tape. They may shift responsibility to others, failing to act decisively because they fear to be reversed. A whole organization may be beset with nepotism, political maneuvering, factional warfare, and petty jealousies. So efficiency may be sacrificed to size, and management may grow lax or take refuge in inflexibility, resisting adjustment to changing conditions and refusing opportunity to new ideas.

A number of studies have been made of the relation between company size and profits, productivity, or unit costs,[20] but the results have not been such that any firm conclusion would be justified. Some studies indicate that profits have fallen after mergers, others that multiplant companies have earned no more or even less than single plant concerns. Others suggest that profits have increased with size; still others that the larger firms have done less well than somewhat smaller ones. Profits, however, are not a perfect index, being influenced by many factors other than size. But there are studies, too, which show that output per man-hour has not been increased by mergers, and that the largest firms, in a number of industries, do not have the lowest unit costs. When Bain sought to obtain estimates with respect to the economies of multiplant operation in his sample of twenty industries, he found that such economies were held to be perceptible but small in six, to be negligible or absent in six, and he was unable to get any estimates for the other eight. Such evidence does not support the view that the economies of size in the firm lead inevitably to monopoly.

A business may be too small to realize the economies that are implicit in modern technology; it may be too large to be administered with competence. Between these extremes there may be a size of optimum efficiency. But this size will differ from industry to industry. It may change, almost overnight, with the development of new methods of production and new techniques of management. And no one can locate the optimum in any industry at any time with any certainty. It may even be that any one of several sizes will display the same efficiency. There is no

[20] See Arthur S. Dewing, "A Statistical Test of the Success of Consolidations," *Quarterly Journal of Economics,* XXXVI (1921), 84; *Mergers in Industry* (New York: National Industrial Conference Board, 1929); William L. Crum, *Corporate Size and Earning Power* (Cambridge: Harvard University Press, 1939); Federal Trade Commission, *op. cit.;* John M. Blair, *op. cit.;* Committee on Price Determination, Conference on Price Research, *Cost Behavior and Price Policy* (New York: National Bureau of *Economic Research,* 1943), pp. 219–63; Joseph Steindl, *Small and Big Business* (Oxford: Basil Blackwell, 1945); P. Sargant Florence, *Investment, Location, and Size of Plant* (Cambridge: Cambridge University Press, 1948): Joe S. Bain, *op. cit.*

basis for supposing that the largest unit in an industry will necessarily have the lowest costs.

Even where a corporate giant is highly successful, its success may reveal the possession of acquisitive rather than productive advantages. It may have forced sellers to discriminate in its favor and buyers to pay a monopoly price. If integrated, it may have put the squeeze on independents. If diversified, it may have subsidized the losses of one activity with the earnings of another until it drove its rivals from the field. Its higher profits may reflect the banking connections that give it a preferred position as a borrower, and the financial resources that strengthen its hand in litigation, in advertising, and in relations with agencies of government. They may show that its size is advantageous to its stockholders but not to the rest of the community.

Size and Innovation

It is a matter of common knowledge that many, if not most, of the more important technical developments of recent years have come from industries where production is concentrated in the hands of large firms. In some cases—among them railroad transportation, sleeping-car operation, telegraph service, and the production of anthracite coal—such industries have been notoriously unprogressive. But in others—notably chemicals, electrical manufacturing, and machinery—they have set the pace for change. New markets, new products, and new methods of production have been developed through industrial research. In the case of du Pont, for instance, three fifths of the products sold in 1948 did not exist in 1928. Here, as elsewhere, competition has been intensified through the development of substitutes. This "perennial gale of creative destruction" was hailed by Joseph Schumpeter as the source of economic progress.[21] It has led J. K. Galbraith to the happy conclusion that "a benign providence who, so far, has loved us for our worries, has made the modern industry of a few large firms an almost perfect instrument for inducing technical change."[22]

Two considerations support this view. First, innovation depends upon the capacity of a firm to finance research and development. Research is costly. The commercial exploitation of new inventions may require the prior investment of even larger sums. Du Pont is said to have spent twelve years and $27 million before it sold its first pound of nylon in 1940.[23] A firm must be large to spend on such a scale. Second, progress depends upon the motivation that leads voluntarily to innovation and the compulsion that induces innovation. Where there are important rivals in the field, both of these forces will be felt. A company's management is concerned

[21] Joseph Schumpeter, *Capitalism, Socialism, and Democracy*, (2d ed.; New York: Harper & Bros., 1947), chap. vii.

[22] J. K. Galbraith, *American Capitalism* (Boston: Houghton Mifflin, 1952), p. 91.

[23] Speech by Clifford H. Greenewalt, National Press Club, September 29, 1949.

with its prestige, with the full employment of its resources and the expansion of its markets, and with its reputation for progressiveness. The management is also impelled to push research and development by the fear that other firms will beat it to the Patent Office and the market. There are rewards for those who get there first. There may be penalties for those who lag.

W. Rupert Maclaurin of the Massachusetts Institute of Technology, who has conducted studies of technological progress in thirteen American industries, has found in general that progressiveness is low where firms are small and numerous, and high where they are large and few.[24] But there are significant exceptions to the general rule. On the one hand, in the highly competitive paper industry, a firm like Scott Paper has had a long record of research, product innovation, and market development. On the other, in the oligopolistic steel industry, there is the case of U.S. Steel. Here, according to the editors of *Fortune*, "the chief energies of the men who guided the corporation were directed to preventing deterioration in the investment value of the enormous properties confided to their care. To achieve this, they consistently tried to freeze the industry at present, or better yet, past levels."[25] In the opinion of a firm of industrial engineers that analyzed its operations, the Corporation was slow in introducing improvements in technology. Specifically, says George W. Stocking, in his summary of their report,

> . . . it was slow in introducing the continuous rolling mill; slow in getting into production of cold-rolled steel products; slow in recognizing the potentials of the wire business; slow to adopt the heat-treating process for the production of sheets; slow in getting into stainless steel products; slow in producing cold-rolled sheets; slow in tin-plate developments; slow in utilizing waste gases; slow in utilizing low-cost water transportation because of its consideration of the railroads; in short, slow to grasp the remarkable business opportunities that a dynamic America offered.[26]

But even if size in itself were invariably conducive to innovation, it would not follow that monopoly had a similar effect. The limited monopolies granted under the patent system may make for progress. Research is risky. The projects that do not pay off must be financed by those that do. Business might not take the chances involved if it were forced to bear the costs of failure but promptly deprived by competition of the offsetting profits of success. In this sense, innovation is fostered by monopoly. In a larger sense, it is not. The monopolist, if large in size, may possess the capacity to make improvements. But he has less incentive than the oligopolist to do so. Indeed, his interest may run the other way. With

[24] W. Rupert Maclaurin, "Technological Progress in Some American Industries," *American Economic Review*, XLIV, No. 2 (1954), 178–90.

[25] *Fortune*, March, 1936, p. 170.

[26] Hearings before the Subcommittee on Study of Monopoly Power, Committee on the Judiciary, 81st Cong., 2d Sess., H.R., Serial 14, Part 4-A, p. 967.

money already sunk in investments embodying an earlier technology, he may undertake to recover it before he makes a change. The monopolist is under no compulsion to innovate. And he is likely to employ his power to obstruct the introduction of improvements by potential competitors. In short, size in a firm is favorable to progress; monopoly in a market is not.

The Case of Oligopoly

Efficiency and progress, as we have seen, depend to some extent on size. And size, though it seldom requires monopoly, does make for oligopoly. The policy of maintaining competition, say its critics, is thus unrealistic and futile. For oligopolists cannot be expected to compete.

In a field where sellers are few in number, each of them exerts a significant influence on supply and each of them must consider how the others may react to any initiative that he may take. Each seller is likely to assume that any reduction in his price will promptly be matched by all of the others. He can therefore expect such action to increase his profits, not by expanding his share of the market, but only by enlarging the total volume of sales. If he believes that the industry as a whole will profit, he may make a cut. Otherwise, he will not. In short, he will behave as if he were a monopolist. Oligopoly thus precludes active competition in price.

So runs the theory. And, on the basis of this logic, it is argued that there is nothing to be gained from antitrust. Industries cannot be atomized without sacrificing efficiency and progress. But firms left big enough to be efficient and progressive will not compete. Agreements may be enjoined and combinations dissolved. There may be no evidence of conspiracy, no monopoly, no apparent violation of the law—and still, no competition. So antitrust stands helpless in the face of oligopoly.

The situation, however, is not as bad as it seems. The oligopolist, instead of selling at a price that is fixed for him by the market, is able to name his price himself. And the price, instead of fluctuating from day to day, is likely to remain at the same level over considerable periods of time. But when he states his price, the oligopolist is simply expressing his judgment as to what the market will take. He cannot ignore the forces of demand and supply. He must attempt to find a figure that will prove acceptable to buyers. And he must assess the possible response of potential as well as actual competitors. His apparent independence is illusory. The market still has the final word.

Under these circumstances, an antitrust decree that increases the number of sellers in an industry may have marked advantages. Such a decree is unlikely to establish the conditions required for perfect competition. But it can lessen the prospect of uniformity in policy and afford to buyers a larger number of alternatives. The desirability of breaking up large combinations, even though oligopoly may persist, was stressed by the Committee on Cartels and Monopoly of the Twentieth Century Fund:

The circumstances of individual sellers will seldom be the same. There will be differences in the temperaments, attitudes, and judgments of business managers; in cash position and financial needs; in location, techniques of production, efficiency, and methods of computing costs. The more sellers, the more likelihood of differences in opinion on market prospects and elasticity of demand, and resulting differences in price and production policies. It requires only one seller to introduce an innovation in product, quality, or price. The larger the number of sellers, the better is the chance that one or more of them will take an independent line. As a practical matter, therefore, oligopoly is generally to be preferred to monopoly and even as few as six or eight large sellers in a market to only three or four.[27]

The rivalry of a few great firms, as was shown in the preceding section, is highly conducive to innovation—more so than monopoly, and more so than competition among many small concerns. A differential advantage achieved through innovation, unlike one resulting from a cut in prices, may be retained. Rivalry, under oligopoly, is therefore most likely to manifest itself in new technology. But the compulsion to exercise initiative will vary with the number in the field. By keeping the number as large as possible, antitrust can increase the likelihood that innovation will occur.

The power of oligopoly is not only tempered by rivalry on the sellers' side of the market, but is also frequently offset by the existence, on the buyers' side of the market, of similar aggregations of power. In the case of producers' goods, for instance, a few salesmen representing oligopolists may deal, quite typically, with a few skilled purchasing agents representing oligopsonists. Iron ore is sold to the steel mills, steel mill products to the manufacturers of locomotives, railway cars, automobiles, and machinery, locomotives and railway cars to the railroads, machinery to factories and public utilities, chemicals to industrial users, tire fabrics to the rubber companies, and tires and plate glass to the automobile companies. So, too, with the wholesale markets for consumers' goods. Here, giant corporations, operating mail order houses and chain stores, act as purchasing agents for the consumer, using their mass buying power, in his behalf, to force down the prices that highly concentrated producers might otherwise be disposed to charge. In all such cases, however, the power exerted by large buyers will vary directly with the numbers of the sellers with whom they deal. The more numerous the sellers, the better is the chance that one can be played off against another and a better price obtained. Here, again, there is a task for antitrust. By preventing sellers from combining, and by breaking up combinations where they have occurred, it can contribute to the successful exercise of countervailing power.[28]

[27] George W. Stocking and Myron W. Watkins, *Monopoly and Free Enterprise* (New York: Twentieth Century Fund, 1951), pp. 550–51. On this subject, see also William Fellner, *Competition Among the Few* (New York: Alfred A. Knopf, 1949), pp. 292–311; and Kaplan, *op. cit.*, chaps. viii and ix.

[28] For a fuller discussion of the point, see Galbraith, *op. cit.*, chap. ix.

The Alleged Failure of Antitrust

Insofar as antitrust has failed, its failure has been explained, as we noted above, in two quite different ways. According to one view, the policy was doomed from the start, since machine technology leads inevitably to monopoly. We have now examined this position at length and found it to be fallacious. The other view, while holding the policy to be sound, attributes the failures of antitrust to lack of vigor in enforcement, to lack of sympathy and understanding in interpretation, and to lack of courage in the provision of remedies.

There is some basis for these criticisms. But even here, the record is better than the critics realize. Enforcement was sporadic and halfhearted until 1935. But no one can deny that antitrust has been given a fair trial during the past two decades. The courts refused to apply the law to monopolization from 1920 to 1945. But they have always applied it to conspiracy. And they have applied it with equal vigor to monopolization since 1945. The courts have not hesitated to cancel collusive arrangements among separate firms or to enjoin the restrictive practices of monopolists. They have been sparing, however, in their use of the remedy of dissolution, rarely breaking up a business enterprise. Their reluctance to take such action is to be explained by their uncertainty concerning the possible results. They have feared, first, that a reduction in size would impair efficiency and increase costs and, second, that it would restrain the progress of technology. In this, they may have been mistaken. But lacking definite assurance, they have chosen not to take a chance.

This is the point on which the critics fasten their attention when they say that antitrust is ineffective. But this is not the whole story. What the courts have actually done, in case after case, is to deprive the monopolist of devices that he has used to obstruct the entry and growth of rival firms. Patents have been opened to licensing with and without royalties. Access to know-how has been assured. The sale as well as the lease of machinery has been required. Tying and exclusive contracts have been invalidated. The employment of integration to handicap non-integrated competitors has been ended by divorcement. Artificial obstacles to enterprise have thus been cleared away and the door thrown open to competition. And this is no mean achievement in itself.

Observers differ in their appraisal of the effectiveness of antitrust. In one view, held by a minority, the program has been an utter failure. It has not maintained competition. It has not prevented increasing concentration of economic power. It has permitted markets, in general, to come under the control of cartels, monopolies, and oligopolies.[29] This view finds scant support, as we have seen, in any evidence that is at hand. No one contends that antitrust has been a complete success. But most observers would agree

[29] See, for instance, Arthur R. Burns, *The Decline of Competition* (New York: McGraw-Hill Book Co., 1936), pp. 17–21, 523–26.

that it is far from having been a complete failure.[30] It has done much to break up restrictive agreements and to correct monopolistic practices, where they have been found to exist. It may have done even more to prevent them from coming into existence. Corwin Edwards concludes that the antitrust laws "made it necessary for monopolistic and collusive restraints of trade to be nominally secret. They prevented any general endorsement of such arrangements by public authorities or responsible business organizations and forestalled most efforts to make participation in private restrictions compulsory. . . . They thus prevented the appearance in the United States of a formally organized and state supported cartel system."[31] Edward S. Mason finds that "the consideration of whether a particular course of business action may or may not be in violation of the antitrust acts is a persistent factor affecting business judgment."[32] And J. K. Galbraith, agreeing that antitrust has exerted a significant influence on corporate price policy, warns against underestimating its importance "in bringing business practice into accord with basic concepts of decency and equity or in preventing those with economic power from using it to combat innovation."[33] In the judgment of the Committee on Cartels and Monopoly:

> The more flagrant abuses of the nineteenth century have disappeared. Restraint of trade, where it occurs, generally is less ruthless and more circumspect. It is certain, moreover, that the situation in the United States is very different from that in countries whose policy has permitted or encouraged cartelization and the concentration of control. American industry is more vigorous, more resilient, more dynamic; it is more hospitable to new blood and new ideas. In most other countries, little or no effort has been made to enact or to enforce laws designed to insure the maintenance of competition. And in such countries, by contrast, industrial progress has been retarded by timidity and lethargy. It may well be that the greater vitality of American industry is attributable, in large part, to the survival of a wider area of competition in the American economy. And it may well be, in turn, that the wider area of competition is attributable, in large part, to . . . antitrust.[34]

ALTERNATIVES TO COMPETITION

It is unrealistic to pass judgment on the policy of maintaining competition, as its critics often do, without also considering the nature of the possible alternatives. What are they? In practice, *laissez faire* is not among

[30] See "The Antitrust Laws: A Symposium," *American Economic Review*, XXXIX (1949), 689–724.

[31] Corwin D. Edwards, *Maintaining Competition*, (New York: McGraw-Hill Book Co., 1949), p. 294.

[32] *American Economic Review*, XXXIX (1949), 713.

[33] Howard S. Ellis (ed.), *A Survey of Contemporary Economics* (Philadelphia: Blakiston Co., 1948), p. 119.

[34] Stocking and Watkins, *op. cit.*, p. 547.

them. If monopoly cannot be prevented or eliminated, it will ultimately be subjected in one way or another to public control. In general, the choice lies between public enterprise and public regulation of private enterprise. There are particular cases, of course, in which these policies are unavoidable and even desirable. The question is not whether they should be used at all, but whether they are to be preferred, as a general solution, to antitrust. This question will be considered in the pages that follow. Thereafter, attention will be directed to the problem of selecting the fields appropriate to public enterprise or regulation and to the problem of making a choice between the two.

Public Enterprise

No sweeping generalization concerning public enterprise would be justified. Sometimes it has been efficient and progressive; sometimes it has not. It has one clear advantage: it can borrow money more cheaply than can private firms. But it also has its problems. And these, as we saw in Chapter 29, are fully as numerous and as serious as those of antitrust. Public enterprise has all of the disadvantages of size: overcentralization, delay, impersonality, rigidity. It has the disadvantages of monopoly. How is the consumer to be protected against poor quality, high prices, and discrimination? How is progress in technology to be assured? Public enterprise, moreover, has the added disadvantages of politics. Group pressures may inflate costs, keeping the payments made for facilities, supplies, and labor high. They may depress revenues, keeping the general level of charges for service low. They may lead to unfair discrimination. They may obstruct the adoption of improvements in those cases where improvements are proposed. Public enterprise, finally, is faced with the dilemma of efficiency versus accountability. For efficiency, it must be free to exercise initiative. For accountability, it must be bound with red tape.

In the United States there is little support for the expansion of public enterprise. Indeed, the trend is the other way. The policy that is usually proposed as an alternative to antitrust is not public enterprise but the public regulation of private enterprise.

Commission Regulation

The task of regulating an industry, when undertaken in this country, is usually assigned to a specialized agency in the form of an independent commission whose three to seven members represent both major parties and serve for overlapping terms. This arrangement is supposed to possess the advantages of expertness, group judgment, impartiality, and continuity of policy. In practice, however, these advantages seldom come close to being realized.

The regulatory commission, all too often, is inadequately financed and seriously understaffed, hedged about with limitations, and granted powers that fall far short of its responsibilities. Its members are rarely equipped with special competence. Its personnel is exposed to political attack, its salaries are low, and its rate of turnover is high. Its internal organization is likely to be poorly designed, its administrative methods inefficient, and its procedures cumbersome. The commission typically takes little or no initiative, acting only in response to the complaints brought before it by consumers and the requests made by the regulated industry. It operates from day to day and from case to case, adopting no policies and planning no programs in advance, developing no standards, and promulgating no general rules. It acts only after prolonged delay. And it often fails to enforce the decisions that it makes. Its behavior in these regards is to be explained, in part, by the limitations and requirements imposed by law and by the inadequacy of the resources provided to fulfill the duties assigned. But this behavior is also to be attributed, in large measure, to the attitudes of the commissioners. Characteristic of these officials are a lack of imagination, an excess of caution, a distaste for forceful action, an inclination to temporize, to play it safe, to let well enough alone.

When a commission is first established, it may be able to act with vigor. It then has popular support. It is likely to be staffed with men of vision, courage, and skill. If it moves with speed, it may effect significant reforms. In time, however, the agency matures. The force that gave it impetus is spent. The quality of its personnel declines. Its policies are encrusted with tradition. Its procedures harden into routine. It comes to be institutionalized, embodying vested interests and seeming to have values in itself. Its members come to be more concerned with preserving its existence than with forwarding its purposes.

A commission is certain to be subjected to pressure by the industries it is supposed to regulate. The privileges that it can grant or withhold are worth millions to them. Its decisions affect their earnings and the value of their properties. They will wish to prevent unfavorable action, to delay it, modify it, or reverse it. And to this end, they will seek to win the commission's favor or to bring it under their control.

The independence of such an agency is more nominal than real. It may be able to withstand political pressures if it has the backing of a strong executive. Or it may do so if it can count on the loyalty of an offsetting pressure group, or if it can succeed in selling its program to the country as a whole. But failing such support, it is vulnerable to attack. The legislative bodies, at the behest of the regulated industries, can investigate its personnel and operations, refuse to confirm its members for reappointment, cut its appropriations, and withdraw its powers. In such a situation, the regulatory agency must come to terms with those it is supposed to regulate. It may attempt to persuade them that it is in their long-run interest to comply with the provisions of the law. It may invite them to participate in its administration. To insure its own survival, it may enlist their support by acquiescing in their views on policy. Even though the agency does not consciously surrender to the regulatees, it may come to share their views. Through constant association with their managements and continuous exposure to their problems, it is likely to become industry-minded, losing the perspective of the public interest. Impartiality in regulation cannot be assured.

This problem is not to be solved by according greater independence to the regulatory agency. Here, as in the case of public enterprise, public bodies must be held accountable. With greater independence, power might be abused. To prevent abuse, the agency must be subject to political control. And with political control, it is inescapably exposed to the pressures of special interests.

A few years ago, David Sarnoff, president of the Radio Corporation of America, predicted that man will eventually be able to control the weather. "We may yet have rain or sunshine by pressing radio buttons," he said. "When that day comes, we shall need a World Weather Bureau, in which . . . control will have to be vested." The editor of the *New Yorker* pondered this prediction. The prospect, he concluded, was one that left him cold:

> A World Weather Bureau suggests a Civil Service outfit. Who in it would decide whether a day was to be sunny, rainy, overcast, adorned with occasional showers, enriched by a stimulating blizzard? It would be some befuddled functionary, probably, bedevilled by the raincoat and galoshes interests, wined and dined by the makers of winter underwear, summer underwear, slacks for beach wear, and sunburn lotion, threatened by resort owners and farmers, tempted by the makers of sailboats, butterfly nets, parasols, and windshield wipers. Suppose the election of a President were engineered by a pressure group from California and he came into office committed to fifty-two sunny weeks a year. How could anyone, under such circumstances, save for a rainy day? Where would fishermen find angleworms? Conflicting interests are conflicting enough now, without giving them a great big bone like the weather to snarl over. Let the weather just go on happening, we beg, and that goes for storms, which Mr. Sarnoff is apparently against. "Man . . . may discover how to neutralize a storm or detour it from its course," he said, his inflection that of a bearer of good news. Detour it where? Out to sea, to hit some ship with no influence in Washington?[35]

Experience with Regulation

Our judgment of commission regulation need not be based on a priori reasoning alone. Experience with this device in the United States is an extensive one. In the case of public utilities, it stretches over half a century; in the case of transportation, over two thirds of a century. In the first case, the problem has been the relatively simple one of regulating firms possessing complete monopolies of essential services in local markets. In the second, it has been the more difficult one of regulating a competitive industry. In neither case has the undertaking been attended by conspicuous success.

[35] *The New Yorker,* October 12, 1946, p. 23.

The utility commissions, in the states, have taken little or no initiative in developing standards to govern the quality of service. In acting on the general level of rates, they have exercised no real control over operating costs. They have prescribed methods of accounting but have not regularly audited company accounts. In determining the rate base, they were handicapped for a quarter of a century by litigation. In fixing the rate of return, they have developed no clear principles. In general, they have set price levels on a cost-plus basis, establishing no connection between earnings and efficiency. They have centered their attention on the task of allowing a return that is fair to past investors and setting rates at a level that does not exploit consumers. But they have permitted earnings well in excess of those required to market new securities. And they have made no effort to promote consumption by reducing rates to the lowest level at which a fair return could be obtained. Expansion of use has been prompted, in recent years, less by the processes of regulation than by the demonstration, through the policies adopted by public power projects, that wider sales and higher profits are to be realized at lower rates. The commissions, finally, have left to the utilities all initiative with respect to the structure of rates. Large users have been favored, small users burdened, and discrimination justified through the sophistry of cost accounts. State regulation, in general, has afforded scant protection to the consumer of utility services.

The record of federal regulation in this field is somewhat better. The Securities and Exchange Commission, given extraordinary powers, and striking while the iron still glowed with the heat of public indignation, did succeed in effecting a thorough reorganization of the electrical utility industry. The Federal Power Commission and the Federal Communications Commission have provided leadership in the improvement of accounting practices. The FPC, at one stage, also displayed some courage in fixing the price of gas, and the FCC effected important reforms in the practices of the telephone industry and in the relation between the radio networks and the broadcasting companies. But the FPC retreated, under pressure, from its stand on gas. The FCC still lacks authority to control relations between A.T.&T. and the associated telephone companies, and its approach to the fulfillment of its responsibilities with respect to radio and television is characterized by extreme timidity.

In the case of transportation, in addition to difficulties such as those discussed above, there are others arising from competition between the different media and between individual carriers. It is national policy, enunciated by the Congress, that regulation is to be impartial and traffic allocated among the different media in accordance with their inherent advantages. But there is no co-ordination of promotion and regulation, of the several promotional programs, or of the regulation of surface carriers and air carriers. The allocation of traffic is distorted by differential subsidization. And this is then offset, in part, by discrimination in the structure of rates. An effort is made, moreover, to aid the railroads by restricting entry into trucking and by raising the truckers' rates. The Interstate Commerce Commission, in charge of this program, is notoriously railroad-minded. But in dealing with the railroads, it may have harmed as much as it has helped.

The Commission is required, in setting rates, to consider their probable effect upon the volume of traffic. In doing so, it may substitute its own judgment for that of railway managements. And here, if earnings fall, there is no one whom the owners of the roads can hold responsible. The managements are deprived of power; the Commission has power but lacks responsibility. And even if managements are not reversed, decisions are often so delayed that substantial losses are sustained. The railroads have been regulated for decades, intensively and sympathetically. Their state, in comparison with that of other industries, is not a happy one.

More Regulation?

Regulation, at best, is a pallid substitute for competition. It cannot prescribe quality, force efficiency, or require innovation, because such action would invade the sphere of management. But when it leaves these matters to the discretion of industry, it denies consumers the protection that competition would afford. Regulation cannot set prices below an industry's costs however excessive they may be. Competition does so, and the high-cost company is compelled to discover means whereby its costs can be reduced. Regulation does not enlarge consumption by setting prices at the lowest level consistent with a fair return. Competition has this effect. Regulation fails to encourage performance in the public interest by offering rewards and penalties. Competition offers both.

Should the effort to maintain competition be abandoned and regulation undertaken in all those fields where production is concentrated in the hands of larger firms? Should separate agencies be set up to govern steel, copper, aluminum, cement, automobiles, farm machinery, electrical equipment, chemicals, oil refining, meat packing, tin cans, cigarettes, soap, and a score of other industries? The task of regulation, in such cases, would present problems of even greater difficulty than in the fields already brought under control. It would be necessary to deal with numerous enterprises differing in size, in corporate structure, in degree of integration, in number and location of establishments, in number and proportionate output of different products, and in technology, efficiency, and costs. The regulatory agency, in each case, would be called upon to strike a balance between the interests of consumers and those of investors. In doing so, it would be compelled to control the efficiency of industry and to govern the rate of change. It would have to decide whether to set prices at levels that would only cover the costs of low-cost firms, promoting efficiency but inflicting losses on investors in high-cost firms, or to set them at levels that would cover the higher costs, protecting investors but denying consumers the benefits of efficiency; whether to permit the prompt introduction of new products and new technology, serving consumers but harming investors in outmoded products and obsolete technology, or to retard innovation, protecting investors but denying consumers the benefits of progress.[36] These are decisions that must be accepted when made by the market, but would lead to endless controversy, prolonged delay, and dubious results if subjected to the requirements of due process and submitted to the pressures of politics. If control were to be effective, finally, it would have to be extended to every aspect of business policy: to investment, to the quantity and quality of output, to the level and structure of prices, and to the size and distribution of earnings. Regulation might begin more modestly, but its final stage, if the history of the railroads is a guide, would be the virtual duplication of managements. American experience with regulation, in the past, has not been so happy as to encourage such an undertaking in any case where another solution can be found.

Market Economy or Planned Economy?

Where the share of publicly owned or regulated industry in the economy is small, the over-all direction of economic activity can be left to the market. But if the share of production brought under regulation or ownership were large, the many interrelationships of the industries concerned would necessitate co-ordination of the controls. Resources would have to be allocated among rival claimants, the output of one industry dovetailed with the requirements of another, and the prices established for different industries and different markets brought into some sort of harmony. The policy of socialization or regulation, if consistently pursued, could end only in comprehensive economic planning and the authoritative direction of economic activity. The question that is ultimately posed by any proposal to abandon the maintenance of competition as a general policy is that of making a choice between the market economy and the planned economy.

The issues involved in such a choice are too numerous and too complex to be debated here. But it is possible, by listing some of them, to indicate how serious they are. (1) Would resources, in a planned economy, be allocated in accordance with the wishes of consumers, with those of a majority of voters, with those of the bureaucracy, or with those of pressure groups? (2) Could a high level of output be attained, or would the performance of the economy be impaired by overcentralization of decisions, by the complexity of central planning, by the isolation and ignorance of the planners, by conflict, compromise, confusion, and delay, by the clumsiness and the rigidity of the controls, by the costs of bureaucratic overhead, and by the lack of tests by which success or failure could be judged? (3) Could progress be assured, or would it be restrained by

[36] Arthur R. Burns, who argues that competition is unattainable and regulation inevitable, seizes this nettle firmly in his hand. See Burns, *op. cit.*, chap. xi.

the absence of incentives, by the need for agreement, by the opposition of vested interests, and by reluctance to assume responsibility for taking risks? (4) Could stability be maintained, or would changes in administration (with policy uncertain for months before elections) and changes in plans by existing administration (with new plans hatched in secrecy and sprung without warning) make for greater instability? (5) Could trade with other nations be expanded and economic differences adjusted peaceably, or would the desire to protect the domestic plan from the disrupting effects of change abroad lead to isolation, and would the conversion of differences arising between private traders into differences between governments lead to irritation and ill will? (6) Could public morality be maintained, or would the larger number of permissions required and regulations imposed result in more bribery, black marketeering, bootlegging, and disrespect for law? (7) Could group conflict be prevented, or would the fact that each group's share in income was determined by the state intensify such conflict and reduce the nation's strength by threatening its unity? And finally, and most important, (8) could individual freedom be preserved, or would the centralization of power facilitate coercion of conformity?

Experience with public enterprise and public regulation and doubts concerning the outcome of comprehensive economic planning both lead to the same conclusion: these controls should be limited to exceptional circumstances where their use is unavoidable or their desirability so clear as to sustain a heavy burden of proof. The maintenance of competition should be the general rule.

Where Regulate; Where Own and Operate?

There are certain fields in which public enterprise is inevitable: those like atomic energy where public ownership is essential to national defense, and those like urban transit, in some cities, where the private operation of an essential service has broken down. There are other fields in which the desirability of public enterprise has never been questioned: among them, the provision of roads, waterways, airways, and postal services. There are still other fields in which the desirability of public enterprise, once disputed, is now taken for granted: education and recreation, for instance, and insurance against unemployment, dependent old age, and survivorship, the promotion of private enterprises by rediscounting or insuring loans, the ownership of national parks and forests, and the construction of works for irrigation, navigation, flood control, and the incidental generation of hydroelectric power. There are but few fields in which the propriety of public enterprise is at issue at the present time: production, such as the navy's manufacture of paint or rope, that is incidental to the operation of governmental agencies and is said to deprive private business of money-making opportunities; low-rent urban housing, health insurance, and the large-scale generation, transmission, and distribution of electricity. The pros and cons of these controversies are too detailed to be considered here. It can only be noted that judgment should turn, in each instance, on the merits of the particular case.

There are certain fields in which the nature of the service rendered is such as to necessitate unified control. This is true of the utility services: water, gas, electricity, transit, and telephone. Here, the consumer cannot be protected by competition. But he cannot be left without protection, since the services are essential and he would be at the mercy of monopolists. The only choice that can be made, therefore, is between public enterprise and regulation. In transportation, there is competition on some hauls, but there is none on others. The consumer would be the victim of undue discrimination in the absence of controls. Here, too, the choice lies between public enterprise and regulation.

There is no clear rule that can be laid down to govern such a choice. Public enterprise and regulation both have their advantages and disadvantages. It cannot be said that one would always work better than the other. It may even be impossible to predict, with any confidence, which would be better in a particular case. One point, however, can be made. It is desirable to have the two controls in operation side by side, so that each may be stimulated by the example of the other, and both judged by comparing their performance. In this way, competition may operate to serve the public interest.

Comprehensive direct controls over stabilization and allocation are unavoidable in time of war. But they are properly regarded as a necessary evil. There is little or no support, in the United States, for continuing their use in time of peace.

SUGGESTIONS FOR FURTHER READING

The most recent and the most authoritative studies of industrial concentration are: G. Warren Nutter, *The Extent of Enterprise Monopoly in the United States* (Chicago: University of Chicago Press, 1951); M. A. Adelman, "The Measurement of Industrial Concentration," *Review of Economics and Statistics*, XXXIII (1951), 269–96; and A. D. H. Kaplan, *Big Enterprise in a Competitive System* (Washington: Brookings Institution, 1954), chaps. iv, v, and vi. With regard to big business, the case pro is presented in Joseph Schumpeter, *Capitalism, Socialism, and Democracy* (New York: Harper & Bros., 1942), chaps. vi, vii, and viii; in J. K. Galbraith, *American Capitalism* (Boston: Houghton Mifflin Co., 1952); and in David Lilienthal, *Big Business: A New Era* (New York: Harper & Bros., 1953). The case con is presented in George J. Stigler, "The Case against Big Business," *Fortune*, May, 1952, pp. 123 ff.; in Morris L. Ernst, *Too Big* (Boston: Little, Brown & Co., 1940); and in T. K. Quinn, *Giant Business: Threat to Democracy* (New York: Exposition Press, 1953).

Excellent discussions of the economies of size are contained in John M. Blair, "Technology and Size," *American Economic Review*, XXXVIII, No. 2 (1948), 121–53; in Richard B. Heflebower, "The Economies of Size," *Journal of Business of the University of Chicago*, XXIV (1951), 253–68; and in Joe S.

Bain, "Economies of Scale . . . ," *American Economic Review*, XLIV (1954), 15–38. The best available analysis of the relation between monopoly and innovation is that by P. Hennipman, "Monopoly: Impediment or Stimulus to Economic Progress?"; in Edward H. Chamberlin (ed.) *Monopoly and Competition and Their Regulation* (London: Macmillan Co., 1954), pp. 421–56. The vitality of competition among oligopolists is examined in William Fellner, *Competition among the Few* (New York: Alfred A. Knopf, 1949), chap. xi; and in Kaplan's chaps. viii and ix. The opinions of lawyers and economists on the success or failure of antitrust are set forth in "The Antitrust Laws: A Symposium," *American Economic Review*, XXXIX (1949), 689–724.

The difficulties that would be encountered in adopting regulation as a general policy are considered in Arthur R. Burns, *The Decline of Competition* (New York: McGraw-Hill Book Co., 1936), chap. xi. Experience with regulatory agencies is discussed by James W. Fesler in Fritz M. Marx (ed.) *Elements of Public Administration* (New York: Prentice-Hall, Inc., 1946), chap. x; and by Leonard D. White in his *Introduction to the Study of Public Administration* (3d ed.; New York: Macmillan Co., 1948), chap. viii. The problems of regulation are examined at greater length in a number of other volumes by political scientists. Among the earlier studies are E. Pendleton Herring, *Public Administration and the Public Interest* (New York: McGraw-Hill Book Co., 1936); James M. Landis, *The Administrative Process* (New Haven: Yale University Press, 1938); F. F. Blachly and M. E. Oatman, *Federal Regulatory Action and Control* (Washington: Brookings Institution, 1940); Robert E. Cushman, *The Independent Regulatory Commissions* (New York: Oxford University Press, 1941); and Avery Leiserson, *Administrative Regulation* (Chicago: University of Chicago Press, 1942). The more recent works include Charles S. Hyneman, *Bureaucracy in a Democracy* (New York: Harper & Bros., 1950), David Truman, *The Governmental Process* (New York: Alfred A. Knopf, 1951); and Emmette S. Redford, *Administration of National Economic Control* (New York: Macmillan Co., 1952).

Chapter 31

HOW MUCH COMPETITION?

Though the maintenance of competition is the general policy in the United States, it is not applied consistently throughout the economy. Aside from business, every major group is granted some sort of exemption. Indeed, it might be said that restriction of competition, condemned as restraint of trade when practiced by business in general, is approved as collective bargaining for labor, as parity for agriculture, and as fair trade for the independent retailer. Wherever competition really hurts, steps are taken to moderate its force.

Where the policy of maintaining competition applies, there are complaints concerning the way in which it is enforced. The law is said to be too vague, failing to draw a clear line between the organizations and practices that are permitted and those that are prohibited. It is said to be too explicit, condemning organizations and practices according to their form when it ought to judge them by their results. Remedies are proposed for both of these shortcomings. In the one case, it is suggested that informal processes be substituted increasingly for litigation, and that offenses be made specific and other activities held not to violate the law. In the other, it is urged that a rule of reason be employed and monopolistic agreements and combinations judged by their performance in the public interest. In both cases, it is possible that the reforms proposed would operate to excuse monopoly that is now held to be illegal.

What are the prospects for competition? How serious are the exceptions to the antitrust laws? How desirable are the proposed reforms? What can be done to reinforce and strengthen antitrust? These are the questions with which the present—and final—chapter is concerned.

MODERATING COMPETITION

Competition, though generally beneficial to consumers, may sometimes be harsh in its impact on producers. Where the competitors are small in size and dependent on the continued sale, at adequate prices, of certain goods or services for their well-being and even for their very livelihood, its incidence in human hardship and social unrest may make its moderation seem desirable. Considerations other than those of economy and efficiency may be involved. People may be willing to accept a smaller social product, if this is the price that they must pay for greater equality in the distribution of income and for greater assurance of security. They may deem it wise, even at some cost in output, to afford the worker a measure of control over wages and working conditions and a sense of citizenship in industry. They may wish to preserve the independent merchant and the family farm as bulwarks of individualism and democracy, though making no effort to preserve the independent family factory. They may choose to relieve the small producer of some of the burden of change by retarding the speed of adjustment and socializing its cost. Policies such as these may be defended on social and political if not on economic grounds.

Whether they are defensible or not, such policies are bound to be adopted. Laborers, farmers, and merchants are numerous, and they have the right to vote. It would be unrealistic to suppose that they would not employ this right to serve what they conceive to be their interests. The question is not whether action to moderate competition will be taken in their behalf, but how. The efforts of other citizens should be directed, not toward preventing all such action, but toward assuring that it takes a form that is consistent with the general interest.

The measures protecting small producers are frequently inconsistent with the logic of competition, but it would be easy to exaggerate their harmful effects. The purpose may be open to criticism, but the underlying competitive forces are often so strong that the purpose is but partly realized. Certainly, it cannot be said that the consequences of these measures are so serious that competition has ceased to be the general rule.

The Case of Labor

While businessmen are forbidden, under the Sherman Act, to set up a common agency to sell their goods or services, workers are permitted to do so. It is generally believed that employers and employees should have equal power in fixing the terms of the wage bargain. It is obvious that employers cannot be so completely atomized that their power will not exceed that of employees. It follows, therefore, that power can be equalized only by permitting combination among employees. And this has long been national policy.

There are dangers in such a policy. Unions may reduce the supply of labor in two ways: by cutting the size of the labor force and by cutting the hours of labor. They may reduce output per man-hour by enforcing make-work rules, and by curbing the disciplinary authority of the employer. They may check investment by converting surplus earnings into higher wages, and by impairing the incentive to invest. In all these ways, they may reduce the size of the national product in the process of obtaining a larger share of this product for themselves. This outcome, however, is by no means certain. For organization may increase the worker's productivity by giving him a sense of status and security and thus contributing to his morale. And pressure for higher wages may stimulate the employer to find new means of increasing his efficiency. The net effect of these influences cannot be ascertained. It may be noted, however, that the growth of labor organization, over the past twenty years, has coincided with a marked expansion in investment and in the output of industry.

Where a union establishes a common wage for all the firms in a trade, it prevents them from competing with one another on the basis of differences in labor cost. It may contribute to concentration by raising this wage and thus making it impossible for the weaker firms to survive. And it may encourage employers to meet the common wage by maintaining a common price, either by restricting entry to the field, curtailing output, and sharing markets, or by fixing the price itself. There is some question, however, as to how far unions can go in raising wages. It is true that the general level of wages has risen since the thirties. But it has risen for unorganized as well as for organized labor. The higher level is to be attributed, apparently, less to unionism than to continued prosperity and strong demand. Labor, moreover, is not immune to competition. The United Mine Workers may fix a common hourly wage for all the coal mines. But its power to raise wages without losing employment is limited by the ability of the consumer to turn to gas or oil.

The results of abandoning competition in the sale of labor are unlikely to be disastrous. But the alternative policy of supporting countervailing power raises problems of its own. When the bargaining position of workers and employers is determined by public action and when disputes between them are settled by public agencies, each of them will seek to influence the state. And government, instead of maintaining its impartiality, is likely to respond to pressure, shifting its weight to whichever side controls the largest number of votes. The conflict in power is transferred from the arena of economics to that of politics. And there is no assurance, in such a situation, that the public interest will be served.

The Case of Agriculture

The farmers, like the workers, are permitted to sell through common agencies, in the form of co-operatives. More than this, the government undertakes, through loans and purchases, to support the prices of their crops. It permits them to join in voluntary cartels and subjects minorities to the requirements of compulsory cartels. It restricts the quantities that can be sold, assigns quotas, and controls acreage. In short, it abandons the market in favor of a planned economy.

There is much that can be said in criticism of agricultural policy. Mandatory supports at high percentages of base-period parity give the farmer a hidden subsidy and keep him producing things that are wanted less instead of those that are wanted more. Surpluses are accumulated to be dumped on foreign markets, diverted to inferior uses, or allowed to go to waste. Losses are incurred at the expense of the taxpayer and prices boosted at the expense of the consumer to transfer income, less to the little farmer who is needy, than to the big farmer who is well-to-do. All this is true, yet it must be admitted that the program has not prevented substantial gains in agricultural productivity, or a marked shift of labor from agriculture to industry, and that its cost is one which the American economy is easily able to bear.

Even if the present program were rejected, it would not follow that the farmer should be left to the mercy of the market. He cannot depend on last year's prices as guides for this year's plantings. His prices and his income are subject to violent fluctuations. They may be seriously depressed by a cyclical decline in demand, by a bumper crop that increases total supply, or by natural hazards that reduce his own supply. All of these matters are beyond the farmer's control. All of them point to needs for social action. To make price dependable as a guide to future production, supports might be announced from season to season on the basis, not of past parity, but of prospective demand and supply. To make income more stable, fluctuations in demand might be offset by collecting taxes in prosperity and distributing benefits in depression; fluctuations in supply might be offset by buying for storage in years of surplus and selling from stores in years of shortage, not raising the long-run level of prices but only narrowing their spread; losses due to natural hazards might be offset by crop insurance. To lessen rural poverty, the rehabilitation of low-income farmers might be undertaken on a larger scale.

Such measures would require extensive intervention in the market. They would mitigate the rigors of competition. They would be difficult to administer. But they would be more consistent with the principles of a market economy than is the present program.

The Case of Small Business

Despite the general profession of belief in freedom of enterprise and competition, the legislative bodies of local, state, and national governments have acted repeatedly to limit entry into sheltered occupations and local markets, to increase the costs of strong competitors by imposing discriminatory taxes, to prevent them from obtaining concessions in the prices paid for their supplies, to put a floor under the prices at which retailers can resell, and to permit complete elimination of competition in the resale prices of branded goods. Such action has been taken in the name of small business, but it has been confined, in the main, to the field of distribution and the service trades. It is clearly inconsistent with the maintenance of competition, but its influence on the character of the economy in general has been minimal.

The competitive forces in distribution have proved too powerful for the legislation to control. The chain store taxes were a failure. The effect of limits on discounts have been avoided, in many cases, by vertical integration, by the purchase of a factory's entire output, and by the development of private brands. The minimum markup laws, in operation, have not perceptibly affected the level of prices. Resale price maintenance, though fairly effective for drugs and toiletries, has proved to be unenforceable in the case of household appliances. The years since these measures were adopted have seen the rise of the supermarket and the discount house. There is small likelihood, in such a situation, that competition can be driven from the field.

A case can be made, on other than economic grounds, for preserving the independent merchant. When he is displaced by an agency or an outlet controlled or owned by the manufacturer, as Justice Douglas remarked in the Standard Oil of California case, ". . . entrepreneurs become employees of absentee owners. Then there is a serious loss in citizenship. Local leadership is diluted. He who was a leader in the village becomes dependent on outsiders for his action and policy. Clerks responsible to a superior in a distant place take the place of resident proprietors beholden to no one."[1] Perhaps this view should be dismissed as mere nostalgia for a vanished past. But if it is accepted, there should be no confusion as to the goal of policy. The preservation of competitors may have some value in itself. But it is not the preservation of competition and should not be defended as such.

Attention should be directed, too, to the selection of means that are both consistent with the public interest and appropriate to the end in view. It might be desirable, as Justice Douglas held, to permit full-requirements contracts as an alternative to manufacturers' agencies and branch stores. It would be possible to prevent discrimination in favor of the mass distributor without going as far as the Robinson-Patman Act has gone to require discrimination against him. It would be preferable, if loss-leader selling is to be checked, to establish stop-loss markups instead of permitting the maintenance of resale prices. Rather than restricting entry to trades and markets and attempting to freeze the channels of distribution, government might promote the interests of small business by breaking down existing barriers and opening up new opportunities. This is what was done by the consent decree worked out by the Antitrust Division and Eastman Kodak, ending the tying arrangement in the sale and processing of color film, and making Eastman's patents and know-how available to independent processors. There are doubtless other cases where this method could be used.

The Sick Industry

Another case where it is usually held that the policy of antitrust is inappropriate is that of the sick industry. Here there may be a long-run decline in demand, increasing competition from substitutes, from new locations and new technology, an unhappy history of unemployment and

[1] *Standard Oil Co. of California* v. *U.S.*, 337 U.S. 293, 319.

repeated bankruptcy. The industry may be concentrated geographically, its prosperity determining the welfare of whole communities. Its productive facilities may not be readily convertible to other uses; its labor force not easily relocated or trained for other jobs. Adjustment to change, in such a case, is ultimately inevitable and even desirable. But it can be effected, immediately, only at the cost of serious inconvenience or actual distress.

The remedy usually proposed and often adopted, in such a situation, is that of fixing minimum prices or restricting output and assigning market shares. For a time, such action may lend support to incomes. But in the long run, it can only serve to intensify the crisis, cutting the industry's sales and increasing those of its competitors. A better remedy might be found by investing in research to develop new uses for a product, improve its acceptability, and reduce its cost. In the case of bituminous coal, the classic example of a sick industry, the problems of unemployment and bankruptcy are to be solved, not by raising prices, but by improving technology.

Where a local industry is obviously dying, there is much to be said for public action to ease the process of adjustment and share the cost of change. The duration of unemployment benefits might be extended and workers aided in moving to new locations and in acquiring new skills. Companies might be assisted in finding new opportunities and granted loans to cover the cost of converting their facilities. Such a policy would cushion the impact of change on the individual while preserving the benefits of change for the economy as a whole.

PROPOSALS TO MODIFY ANTITRUST

The criticism of the antitrust laws most often voiced by lawyers and businessmen is not that the policy they embody is wrong but that its application is unfair. There are two principal complaints. First, it is said that voluntary compliance with the laws is inhibited by the vagueness of their requirements and the ambiguity of their interpretation by the courts. It is argued further that managements, when considering a change in organization or method, have no way to determine whether it would be legal or not. The imposition of penalties for such offenses is therefore held to be unjust. Second, it is objected that the courts are holding too many forms of organization and too many business practices to be illegal per se when these should be judged, instead, by their effects. The two complaints are obviously inconsistent. If uncertainty is to be eliminated, offenses must be made explicit. If flexibility is to be preserved, precision must be sacrificed. The critics of antitrust should take one position or the other. They cannot logically occupy them both.

The complaint that antitrust is vague is partly disingenuous and partly justified. It is disingenuous when made regarding practices whose illegality is all too clear. But it has some force where the lawfulness of the issues presented by proposed arrangements has never been adjudicated, and where the meaning of the decisions rendered is ambiguous. This will be less true in cases involving restrictive agreements and coercive practices, more so in those involving combination, monopolization, and business size. The complaint that business organization and behavior should be judged, not by their form, but by their results is not without its merits. But it raises far more problems than it solves.

Three types of remedies are proposed. Under the first, the number of formal actions leading to the imposition of penalties would be sharply reduced and reliance placed, to a larger extent, upon informal processes. Under the second, the text of the laws would be reworded so explicitly that their meaning could not be misunderstood. Under the third, an amplified rule of reason would be applied in passing judgment on business organization and practices, and decisions as to their legality would turn on evidence of their performance in the public interest. Each of these proposals appears to be reasonable. But each of them, on closer examination, will be found to be dangerous.

Informal Processes

A number of suggested reforms call for greater reliance upon informal processes. It has often been proposed that business be permitted to lay its plans before the Antitrust Division prior to their adoption and granted immunity from prosecution where they are not disapproved. In 1952 the Business Advisory Council of the Department of Commerce recommended that a board consisting of businessmen, engineers, economists, and lawyers be set up within the Division, that pending antitrust actions be submitted to it for review, and that no legal proceedings be initiated until its opinion had been obtained. The Council also urged that cases be settled in conference, instead of being carried to court, expressing the view that nine tenths of the Division's work load could be handled in this way.[2]

On the face of it, the case for prior administrative clearance of business arrangements is a persuasive one. The procedure could be inexpensive, expeditious, and flexible. It would look toward prevention rather than punishment. If the arrangements threatened to be harmful, they could be disapproved. If they were harmless, business would be permitted to go ahead without running the risk of prosecution. But the procedure would be open to abuse. In applications for clearance, something less than the whole truth might be told. A plan that looked innocent enough on paper might prove, in operation, to be less innocent that it had seemed. The scope of the immunity that was granted might be interpreted more broadly by business than by government. To guard against such abuses, the right to carry cases to the courts must be retained. For many years,

[2] *Effective Competition* (Washington: Department of Commerce, 1952), pp. 18–20.

plans proposed by business have been submitted to the Antitrust Division and advisory opinions given with respect to their probable legality. Where no objection to such proposals is perceived, those who submit them are assured that they will not be made defendants in a criminal suit. But the right to bring a civil suit against them is reserved. In this way, business is afforded an opportunity, when acting in good faith, to avoid the imposition of criminal penalties, but the community is protected, at the same time, against the possibility of later violation of the law.

The review board proposed by the Business Advisory Council might bring to bear on business problems a considerable body of knowledge and experience. It should prevent the initiation of ill-considered prosecutions. But it would act, in effect, as a court, without the responsibilities of a court. Supported by business opinion, it might well come to exercise a veto power, seriously obstructing the enforcement of the law. The settlement of cases in conference, likewise, would save time and money and might often prove effective in eliciting compliance. But it would be carried on in secret. And agreements might not be forthcoming when the threat of prosecution was not in view. Consent decrees negotiated in advance of formal action and submitted to the court the day the case is filed, as was the decree regarding Kodak color film, have all of the advantages of settlement in conference, and they are more effective. They can be obtained as quickly and as cheaply, they become a matter of public record, and they have the force of law.

Making the Law Specific

If the statutes and decisions are vague and administrative discretion dangerous, why not rewrite the prohibitions of antitrust in words made so precise that their intention would be plain? This solution, too, would be more difficult than it may seem. However numerous the restrictive practices described, precision of wording would limit the scope of the law, since any practices that differed in detail would then escape control. New forms of restraint could scarcely be foreseen; failure to anticipate and prohibit them would put a premium on their discovery. Many devices must be judged, moreover, not by their form but by their effects; the words defining their legality will therefore have to be indefinite. When Congress attempted, in 1914, to forbid a number of specific practices, it made them unlawful only "where the effect may be . . . to substantially lessen competition," but it did not define "may" or "substantially" or "competition." In such cases, revision of the statutes would be likely to alter the standards of legality. And where it did, every new phrase and word and punctuation mark would have to be interpreted. Such certainty as judicial construction has given to the law, over the years, would be discarded. Instead of being clarified, the meaning of antitrust would be shrouded, for decades, in new obscurity.

Proposals that the law be made more explicit have been advanced with respect to business organization as well as business practices. And it is here, as we have seen, that the greatest uncertainty remains. Some combinations have been found innocent and others guilty, some of the guilty broken up and others allowed to stand; the outcome of a dissolution suit, now as always, is beyond predictability. It is sometimes suggested, therefore, that a definite limit be placed on the permissible size of any firm in terms of its total assets, employment, output, or sales, or its share in those of an industry, or those related to a particular commodity.[3] It would then be perfectly clear that size in excess of the specified limit was illegal, and there would be no excuse for the government to fail to prosecute and no alternative for the courts but to dissolve. But here, again, the problem has been oversimplified.

Ceilings on Size

It would not be easy to establish a workable limit for size. If such a limit were set in absolute terms—so many millions in assets or so many thousands of employees—its significance would vary from industry to industry. If set low enough to maintain competition in fields where the volume of sales and the scale of production were small, it would be lower than needed to maintain competition and might be too low to permit efficient operation in fields where they were large. If set high enough to preserve efficiency in the second case, it would afford no protection against monopoly in the first. If set at some intermediate point, it might check efficiency in the larger industry without checking monopoly in the smaller one. If a limit on size is not to be arbitrary, it must be relative rather than absolute in character.

If the limit set is to be relative, other difficulties will arise. What share of what—and where and when—shall be regarded as enough? What percentage shall be taken: 15, 20, 25, or 33? How shall the choice of any one of them be justified? Shall the figure be the same for every industry? If not, what principle of differentiation shall be used? What shall be measured: value of assets, volume of employment, value added by production, or volume or value of output or sales? What shall be used as a base: an industry or a product? If an industry, how shall it be defined? How shall comparable figures be obtained from Census data that classify industries, variously, as comprising firms that make unlike products from like materials (woolen and worsted goods) or like processes (printing) or like products from unlike materials and processes (footwear) or unlike products from unlike materials and processes (sporting and athletic goods)? If the base is a product, where shall the line be drawn along the range of possible substitutes? Are butter and oleo, are cotton, wool, silk, rayon, and nylon, are aluminum, magnesium, stainless steel, laminated wood, and plastics the same products or different ones? What is the market within which the share to be measured is significant? Is it local, regional, national,

[3] See, for instance, Fred I. Raymond, *The Limitist* (New York: W. W. Norton & Co., 1947).

or international in scope? How are its boundaries to be ascertained? What is the period for which the measures are to be applied: the situation on a given day, experience over a year, or over several years? The answers given to these questions will determine whether a particular firm appears to be large or small. Whatever the answers, a ceiling established on this basis would be unfair in operation, since it would apply unequally to different companies.

A limit on size, in relation to the market, would check concentration; it would be a crude weapon with which to attack monopoly. A concentration ratio reveals one fact about the situation in a market, but it does not tell everything that may be relevant. The manufacturer who makes the bulk of a product may be a hardened monopolist, or he may be a vigorous pioneer in a field that is shortly to become competitive. Entry for rivals may be obstructed or open; the threat of potential competition may be weak or strong. On the other side of the market, the oligopolistic seller may deal with actively competing buyers; he may also be faced by oligopsonists. A concentration ratio may wisely be employed to identify the fields that should be examined for further evidences of monopoly. It cannot be taken, in itself, as an index of monopoly power.[4]

Even if these difficulties could be overcome, the wisdom of applying a rigid limit to size would be open to question. There may be advantages in size that such a limit would destroy. It may often be the case that lower costs and more rapid progress are to be attained by a larger firm than by a smaller one. Where the characteristics of an industry, in relation to the size of its market, are such that a firm could reach its optimum size without exceeding the statutory limit, these advantages could be retained. But where this is not the case, they would be sacrificed. As a firm approached the limit, moreover, its incentive to improve its product or reduce its costs and prices, thereby increasing its sales, would disappear. The law would thus induce stagnation and impose a rigid pattern of market sharing on the industry.

[4] Economists have not succeeded in devising a direct and practically useful index of monopoly. They have proposed, variously, that it be measured by the extent to which a firm's prices exceed its marginal costs, by the extent to which its freedom of action is limited by cross elasticities of demand, by the extent to which the demand for one firm's product is influenced by the reactions of other firms or by the extent to which one firm can penetrate the markets served by others but is insulated against penetration by them. These measures, whatever their validity in theory, cannot be applied in practice. It has also been suggested that monopoly be measured by employing data relating to the rate of a firm's profits. But such data, while practically available, do not distinguish the profits of monopoly from those that may result from other influences. See A. P. Lerner, "The Concept of Monopoly and the Measurement of Monopoly Power," *The Review of Economic Studies,* I (1933–34), 157–75; Joe S. Bain, "The Profit Rate as a Measure of Monopoly Power," *Quarterly Journal of Economics,* LV (1941), 271–93; K. W. Rothschild, "The Degree of Monopoly," *Economica,* N.S., IX (1942), 24–29; A. G. Papandreou, "Market Structure and Monopoly Power," *American Economic Review,* XXXIX (1949), 883–97; and Fritz Machlup, *The Political Economy of Monopoly* (Baltimore: Johns Hopkins Press, 1952), chap. xii.

Workable Competition and the Rule of Reason

A third proposal remains to be considered. The rule of reason, it is said, should be recast in terms of the workability of competition and applied more broadly in determining legality. Judgment should be based, not on mere form, but on actual results. If the performance of business is in the public interest, this is all that needs to be required. For the attainment of such results fulfills the purpose of the law.

Some of those who hold this view propose that the rule of reason be applied not only to combination and monopoly but also to collusive agreements and restrictive practices. Such a step would permit continuance of agreements to curtail output, assign quotas, and fix prices if it could be shown that their results had not been harmful. It would permit formation of new agreements of this sort if a court could be convinced that their terms were not unreasonable. This proposal would cancel the decision handed down by the Supreme Court in the Trenton Potteries case in 1927 and reverse the established interpretation of the law. For the American tradition of insisting on competition, it would substitute the European tolerance of the reasonable cartel.

Not all of the proponents of a new rule of reason go this far. Most of them, probably, would confine its use to cases of combination and monopoly. And here, the proposal stands on firmer ground. As a practical matter, the employment of a rule of reason in such cases is inescapable: it would scarcely be wise to break up "every" combination, as the Sherman Act requires. Such a rule has been continually employed, in fact, since 1911. It is true that Judge Hand, in the Aluminum case in 1945, did hold monopoly to be illegal per se. But his definition of monopoly was a narrow one, and the Aluminum Company was not dissolved. And Judge Wyzanski, in the United Shoe Machinery case of 1953, based his finding of illegality, not on the form of the company's organization and practices, but on their effect in excluding others from the field. The rule of reason persists, but its content is still unclear. It is known that combinations are allowed to stand when the courts think them reasonable and broken up when they do not. But no man can say whether a particular combination will be adjudged reasonable or unreasonable—or why. If the law is not always to remain uncertain, the line of reasonableness must be drawn, as time goes on, with a greater approach toward clarity.

The legality of the position occupied by a large-scale enterprise, under the new rule of reason, would be judged by its performance in the public interest. This approach was urged, in 1951, by the Committee on Cartels and Monopoly of the Twentieth Century Fund:

> The agencies of enforcement should attempt a painstaking formulation of criteria of the public interest and a thorough development of tests of industrial performance. These criteria should be applied and the results of these tests set forth in briefs presented by the government and their validity submitted to the

determination of the courts. It should be possible, through this approach, gradually to develop a body of law that would give explicit content to the rule of reason. The process would be a slow one, but it should serve, in time, to bring the decisions of the courts closer to the realities of economic life.

To obtain the evidence required for applying tests of performance, the Committee suggested this procedural device:

The Sherman Act might be amended to establish a rebuttable presumption that concentration exceeding a specified percentage of the market for any product, or related group of products, was prejudicial to the public interest. Enterprises seeking to retain or attain a size in excess of the limit specified would then be forced to bear the burden of proof. If they could demonstrate to the satisfaction of the courts in antitrust proceedings that greater concentration was in the public interest, they might be permitted to retain or expand their area of control. Otherwise, existing combinations might be dissolved and the right to enter into future ones denied. This device would make it necessary for defendants in dissolution proceedings to prepare and present their own briefs in terms of evidence of performance in the public interest. If industrial concentration is to be permitted to stand, it is not unreasonable to require that it be justified.[5]

The practicability of this proposal turns on the possibility of developing acceptable criteria of the public interest and clear tests of performance in the public interest and obtaining agreement on their use. Such an undertaking would encounter many difficulties.

Market Performance or Market Structure?

Among the many questions to be raised in judging the performance of a large-scale enterprise, there might well be the following:

1. Is it using scarce resources economically? Is it wasting natural resources? Has it tied up more resources in productive facilities than its market is likely to require? Has it diverted resources, in excessive quantities, to the promotion of sales?
2. Is it producing efficiently? Are its plants of optimum size? Within the limits set by fixed equipment, is it employing the best available techniques? Are its costs, per unit of output, as low as they could be?
3. Does it operate steadily over time, at a high percentage of capacity, providing regular employment and a dependable flow of goods and services?
4. Is it contributing to economic progress? Is it investing substantial sums in research and development? Is it improving the quality of old products, introducing new products, and adopting new processes? Is it constantly reducing unit costs?
5. Are lower costs passed on in lower prices? Is output large and steadily expanding? Are profits sought through high margins on low volume or through low margins on high volume? Have profits for years been well above the aver-

[5] George W. Stocking and Myron W. Watkins, *Monopoly and Free Enterprise* (New York: Twentieth Century Fund, 1951), pp. 552–53.

age for industry in general, or have they yielded no more than an average return?

To questions of this nature might be added many others, dealing with matters such as the treatment of labor, the promotion of friendly relations with other countries, and contributions to national defense.

It will be seen at once that most of these tests are qualitative in character, not lending themselves to measurement, but depending for their answers on individual judgment. In many cases, too, the evidence obtainable would be ambiguous. Predatory price cutting is not readily to be distinguished from vigorous competition, monopolistic overcapacity from prudent anticipation of demand, deliberate suppression of technology from a wise decision to reject an inferior process, an unpromising product, or an improvement whose immediate adoption would be premature. The tests, moreover, differ in character and importance. In a given case, it is likely that some of the answers would be favorable and some adverse. It would be difficult to balance one against the other, or even to weigh them on a common scale. The summation, again, would require an exercise of judgment. It would not be possible, in the circumstances, to foretell the final verdict. Uncertainty would thus persist.

The proposal that large firms be judged by their performance is also open to criticism on other grounds. For one thing, it is designed to operate only as an escape. The suggestion is not that firms whose performance is poor be required to improve it, but only that those whose performance is good be exempt from the penalties of antitrust. And there are doubtless many cases in which tests such as those of efficiency, progressiveness, and contribution to national defense could be used to condone monopoly. This approach, moreover, would impose on government a heavy burden of responsibility. It would involve the enforcement agencies in the enterprise of offering advice and guidance to businessmen. It would necessitate repeated reappraisals of performance and would thus require continued supervision of business activity. If adopted, it would move away from the automatic safeguards of competition and toward administrative regulation as the method of control.

The proposal is flatly rejected by many economists. Government, they say, should not be concerned with the results of business activity, but should confine itself to providing assurance of a fair field with no favors, leaving the results to take care of themselves. A firm should be judged, not by the social consequences of its operations, but by the power conferred by its position, not by market performance, but by market structure. A combination should be held to be unreasonable whenever it has the power to exclude outsiders from the market, to coerce competitors, or to exploit suppliers or customers. And this should be true even though its power had never been abused or had been used affirmatively in the public interest. A company's contributions to the general welfare, however laudable, should not preserve it if they were not compelled by competition but were granted, instead, as a voluntary dispensation to the rest of the community. The power to do good implies the power to do evil. So the possession of power, in itself, should be the test of legality.

But market structure, too, has its shortcomings as a basis for judgment. The rigid application of any limit on occupancy of the market would encounter all of the difficulties considered above in discussing ceilings on size. It is by no means easy to obtain proper definitions and accurate measurements of the industries or products and the markets to which such a limit would apply. Concentration ratios can be computed, but their significance is dubious. It cannot be assumed that a high ratio reveals a situation that does not compel performance in the public interest, while a low ratio reveals one that does. The best that can be done is to make a shrewd guess, all things considered, as to whether there are enough sellers, enough substitutes, and enough independence and rivalry in the market to afford the consumer real alternatives among which he may choose.

The legality of combination and monopolization cannot, in practice, be determined by a single standard. In arriving at final judgments, every sort of evidence that is available must be brought to bear. Evidence of market structure, if properly interpreted, throws light on the extent of market power. Evidence of actual behavior shows how this power has been employed. Has a firm erected barriers to entry to the market? Has it imposed unfair handicaps on the growth of its competitors? In some cases, evidence of intent may be irrelevant; in others, relevant. There are certain forms of power and certain types of behavior that should be held to be illegal in themselves. In other cases, however, evidence of intent may serve to illuminate the character of overt acts. What was the firm really doing? Was it merely engaging in vigorous competition, or was it inducing unfair discrimination in buying, and practicing dscriminatory sharp-shooting in selling, picking off its smaller competitors one by one? Evidence of performance, finally, reveals the results of structure and behavior and helps to interpret their significance.

Decisions as to legality must be made, inevitably, under a rule of reason, with each of these factors given such weight as seems to be wise. They will depend on human judgment, not always impartial, always fallible, varying from judge to judge and from case to case. Complete predictability, in the area of combination and monopolization, is not to be obtained. Uncertainty is inherent in the very nature of the problem with which the law must seek to deal. Greater clarity should certainly be sought. But it will be found, not by moving from black to white, but from the darker to the lighter shades of gray.

REINFORCING THE MAINTENANCE OF COMPETITION

If the maintenance of competition is to continue to be the general policy in the United States, with departures treated only as exceptions, there is much that could be done to add to its effectiveness. Some of the measures that are inconsistent with the purpose of the antitrust laws might be brought into closer harmony, and some of the exceptions to the provisions of these laws might be repealed or modified. Steps could be taken to strengthen the organization, administration, and enforcement of antitrust itself. More could be done to raise the general plane of competition, protecting the interests of consumers, investors, and workers, and those of present and future generations where the exploitation of natural resources is concerned. A greater effort could be made to support competition, not only by taking negative action to prevent restraints, but also by acting affirmatively to promote the establishment of new enterprises and the growth of small business.

Consistency of Policy

The burden of maintaining competition cannot be borne by antitrust alone. The competitiveness of the economy is affected by many other measures adopted by the federal government: by tariffs that exclude foreign goods, by patents that confer monopolies that are broader in scope and longer in duration than would be needed to promote research and development, by quirks in the tax laws that check the entry, growth, and survival of new and small concerns, by subsidies that favor one competitor over another, and by policies that favor larger firms in awarding government contracts, procuring materials, and disposing of surpluses. It is affected, too, by the exemption of certain industries and activities from the requirements of antitrust. In most cases where exemption is granted, some sort of regulation is imposed. But even here, there is reason for concern. The jurisdiction and power of the regulatory authority may not be as broad as the scope of the exemption, the regulatory program may not provide an effective substitute for the safeguards of competition, and regulated industries producing services that can be substituted for one another may not be required to compete. Competition is affected, too, by the policies of state and local governments: by the laws that relate to incorporation, and by those that exclude outsiders from local markets and from sheltered trades.

Given this situation, an effort should be made by the federal government to stop dealing with its various policies and programs in isolation and to consider the problem of maintaining competition as a whole. To this end, all matters affecting the competitiveness of the economy should be co-ordinated through an interagency committee whose members should represent all of the bodies operating in the field and whose chairman should have a voice at the highest levels of the administration. Issues of executive policy should be discussed by this committee and positions prepared for approval and promulgation by the President. Proposals for legislation should be made by the committee and prospective legislation submitted to it for advice. An attempt should be made, moreover, to check restraint of competition by the states. In some cases, as with resale price maintenance, this could be done simply by withdrawing federal support. In others, it would take affirmative action. The provisions of state corporation laws that facilitate corporate combination and concentration of control could be overcome, as President Taft once recommended, by requiring corporations doing business in interstate commerce to obtain federal charters or licenses. Through this device, too, other conditions safeguarding competition could be imposed. In the case of many state and local restraints, however, action to re-establish competition is not within the power of Congress but must be taken by state legislatures or city councils.

Not all of the policies that are inconsistent with antitrust can be brought into harmony. Acceptance of collective bargaining for labor is inescapable, as is public intervention, on some basis, in the markets for agricultural commodities. There are many exceptions to antitrust, however, whose repeal or modification would be favored by most economists. This is true, for instance, of the compulsory carelization of oil, of sugar, and of milk, and the voluntary cartelization of other products under the Agricultural Marketing Agreements Act. Export associations set up under the Webb-Pomerene Act would be permitted where they are used by small firms for the actual handling of foreign sales, but forbidden where they are used by large firms as a cover for participation in international cartels. The provisions of the Robinson-Patman Act that check discrimination in favor of larger buyers would be retained; those that require discrimination against them would be dropped. On one other point, economic opinion would be virtually unanimous: the fair trade laws should be repealed.

Strengthening Antitrust

Antitrust itself could be strengthened in many ways. The information on which action is taken could be broadened by increasing the powers and the facilities of the Federal Trade Commission for making studies and issuing reports, and by enabling the Antitrust Division to rely on comprehensive economic investigations rather than voluntary complaints as its normal basis for initiating suits. The handling of cases could be speeded by adopting various improvements in procedure and by providing staffs large enough to carry the load of work. The penalties in criminal cases could be made stiffer by raising the fines that can be imposed, relating them to the size and earnings of the defendants or to the magnitude and the duration of their crimes. The government, as well as private plaintiffs, could be empowered to sue for damages. The remedies provided in civil cases might be improved by bringing expert knowledge on business organization and practices to bear, more widely, in the formulation of decrees. The competitiveness of the economy might be increased by more frequent resort to the remedy of dissolution in suits involving monopolists and oligopolists. The effectiveness of Federal Trade Commission orders and antitrust decrees might be enhanced, moreover, by systematically policing the observance of their terms. All of this depends, of course, upon the willingness of Congress to provide adequate appropriations and upon the determination of the executive and the judicial branches of the government to enforce the law.

If these reforms should prove incapable of maintaining competition, more drastic measures are available. Concentration of control through the holding company device could be checked by revising state corporation laws, by requiring federal charters, and by reorganizing holding company structures in other industries as was done in the case of gas and electric utilities. The further growth of industrial giants through reinvestment of earnings could be retarded by taxing undistributed profits. The barriers that are raised to the entry and growth of new and small firms, in many fields, by heavy expenditures on advertising could be lowered by imposing limits on such expenditures or by taxing them at a progressive rate. Domestic monopolies could be exposed to foreign competition by removing protective tariffs. The monopolistic powers of private enterprises could be curbed by promoting competition by co-operative associations and by providing yardstick competition by public enterprise. Most of these proposals have their disadvantages. Few of them would now command political support. But they serve to illustrate the point that the policy of maintaining competition, if taken seriously, need not be impotent.

The Plane of Competition

The laws that serve to raise the plane of competition are quite consistent with the purposes of antitrust. Much progress has been made, as we have seen, in protecting consumers, investors, and workers, and in conserving natural resources. But there is more that could be done. More adequate provision should be made for the enforcement of existing legislation. In certain cases, moreover, further measures are to be desired. The Food and Drug Administration should be given authority to control the use of chemicals in foods and cosmetics. The FTC should be given more ample powers to cope with abuses in advertising. The consumer should be afforded impartial information concerning the qualities of goods. Such action was recommended by the Committee on Cartels and Monopoly:

> One of the major prerequisites of market freedom is the availability to buyers as well as sellers of complete and accurate information concerning the goods in which they deal. Such information may be provided for, depending upon the particular commodity, by instituting systems of grading and inspection, by forbidding deception and misrepresentation, by compelling the disclosure of significant facts, and by requiring truthful and informative labelling. Many such measures have long since been written into the laws of the United States. The principle they embody is capable of further extension. To require that sellers tell the truth, the whole truth, and nothing but the truth is not to

hamper private enterprise; it is to strengthen private enterprise by insuring its integrity.[6]

Further protection might be afforded, not only to consumers but also to investors, by more effective regulation of savings institutions and by the reformation of corporation laws. The social security program might well be extended, on behalf of labor, to cover the risks of sickness and disability as well as those of unemployment, old age, and survivorship. The conservation laws might be so strengthened and administered as to put less emphasis on conserving the rights of property owners and more on conserving natural resources. Reform, in all of these cases, is bound to come in time, but only when the need for it is strongly felt.

Promoting Competition

Government can contribute to the maintenance of competition not only by acting negatively to prohibit artificial restraints but also by acting affirmatively to promote the creation and growth of new and small enterprise. Such enterprise must surmount a number of handicaps. First, though it has ready access to short-term credit, it has great difficulty in obtaining equity capital. The investment banking machinery is not adapted to the flotation of small issues of securities, and the large investment institutions are not interested in the shares of unknown firms. Second, the enterprise is kept from attaining rapid growth through the reinvestment of earnings by the heavy burden of the corporate income tax. Third, it is less able than larger firms to obtain government contracts. And fourth, it lacks facilities for research, access to management guidance, and advice on market analysis, product development, and merchandising techniques.

Government has already done something and might do still more to reduce these handicaps. First, it could increase the availability of capital in a number of ways: by making loans directly, as was done by the Reconstruction Finance Corporation, by insuring loans made by banks or other private lenders, or by setting up a new system of investment institutions under private ownership to buy the stocks and bonds of small companies, guaranteeing their safety by requiring them to diversify their holdings and by reinsuring their loans. Second, it might exempt new concerns, for a limited period, from the corporate income tax, and fix a higher minimum exemption for small companies. Third, it might provide detailed assistance to small business in obtaining government contracts, as was done by the Smaller War Plants Corporation during World War II and by the Small Defense Plants Administration during the Korean war. And fourth, it might encourage the provision, on a commercial or co-operative basis, of research services and management and marketing advice, or it might provide such services itself. Government has long performed this function for the farmer. There seems to be no reason, in principle, why it should not perform it for the small businessman. There is danger, of course, that gov-

[6] *Ibid.*, p. 568.

ernmental action in this field would result in losses to the taxpayer and in the subsidization of inefficiency. But given the possible advantages, the risk is one it might be wise to take.

POLICIES IN PERSPECTIVE

In their total effect, in the perspective of history, the policies of government toward business in the United States appear to have been sound. Comprehensive planning and control of economic activity have been confined to time of war. The essential characteristics of a market economy have been preserved. Public enterprise has been limited, in general, to fields where it was really needed, and in some of them it has done well. Public regulation has been restricted, in the main, to fields where it was unavoidable. The plane of competition has been raised by a growing body of laws protecting consumers, investors, and workers, and conserving natural resources. The force of competition has been moderated in the cases of labor, agriculture, and the distribution trades. But this has been done without great social cost and without destroying the fundamentally competitive character of the economy. The antitrust laws have been influential in preserving market freedom. The courts have been consistent in their condemnation of restrictive agreements and monopolistic practices. They have been effective in striking down barriers to competitive enterprise. They have displayed discretion and common sense in dealing with combination and monopoly.

The American economy—whether because of these policies or despite them—is vigorous, productive, and progressive. It has achieved the longest span of life, the best standard of health, the greatest amount of leisure, the widest spread of education, and the highest level of living ever found, in combination, on earth. It has been moving, at the same time, toward greater stability in production, greater security for the individual, and greater equality in the distribution of income and opportunity. The policies that have promoted—or permitted—these developments cannot have been far wrong.

SUGGESTIONS FOR FURTHER READING

Proposals for the modification of the antitrust laws are presented in Clare E. Griffin, *An Economic Approach to Antitrust Laws* (New York: American Enterprise Assn., 1951), in S. Chesterfield Oppenheim, "Federal Antitrust Legislation: Guideposts to a Revised National Antitrust Policy," *Michigan Law Review*, L (1952), 1139, and in the Business Advisory Council's report on *Effective Competition* (Washington: Department of Commerce, 1952). These proposals are criticized in Joel B. Dirlam and Alfred E. Kahn, *Fair Competition: the Law and Economics of Antitrust Policy* (Ithaca, N.Y.: Cornell University Press, 1954), chaps. i, ii, and ix, and in Walter Adams, "The 'Rule of Reason': Workable Competition or Workable Monopoly?" *Yale Law Journal*,

LXIII (1954), 348. Methods of strengthening and reinforcing antitrust are considered in Corwin D. Edwards, *Maintaining Competition* (New York: McGraw-Hill Book Co., 1949), chaps. vii and viii; and in George W. Stocking and Myron W. Watkins, *Monopoly and Free Enterprise* (New York: Twentieth Century Fund, 1951), chaps. xv and xvi. The special problems of small business are discussed in Alfred R. Oxenfeldt, *New Firms and Free Enterprise* (Washington: American Council on Public Affairs, 1943); in A. D. H. Kaplan, *Small Business: Its Place and Problems* (New York: McGraw-Hill Book Co., 1948); in *Problems of Small Business*, T.N.E.C. Monograph No. 17 (Washington: Government Printing Office, 1941); and in *Review of Small Business*, Final Report of the Select Committee on Small Business, House of Representatives, 82d Cong., 2d Sess., House Report No. 2513 (1952). On the issues raised in this chapter, see also the *Report of the Attorney General's Committee to Study the Antitrust Laws* (Washington: Government Printing Office, 1955).

Indexes

INDEX OF CASES

INDEX OF NAMES

INDEX OF SUBJECTS

This book has been set on the Linotype in 10 and 9 point Janson leaded 2 points. Chapter numbers and chapter titles are in 18 point Spartan Medium. The size of the type page is 27 by 47 picas.